Selected Works

of

William Shakespeare

Selected Works

of

William

Shakespeare

MUNDUS
MEDIA™

"... she is mine own;
And I as rich in having such a jewel
As twenty seas, if all their sand were pearl,
The water nectar, and the rock pure gold"

Two Gentlemen of Verona
Act I, Scene IV
William Shakespeare

Published by Mundus Media™
A Registered Trademark of Ann Arbor Media Group, LLC
by special arrangement with State Street Press,
a division of Borders Group, Inc.

Ann Arbor Media Group, LLC
2500 S. State Street, Ann Arbor, MI 48104

Printed and bound in the United States of America
by Edwards Brothers, Inc.

ISBN 1-58726-017-4

10 9 8 7 6 5 4 3 2 1

Contents

THE TEMPEST

DRAMATIS PERSONÆ

ALONSO, *King of Naples.*
SEBASTIAN, *his brother.*
PROSPERO, *the rightful Duke of Milan.*
ANTONIO, *his brother, the usurping Duke of Milan.*
FERDINAND, *son to the King of Naples.*
GONZALO, *an honest old Counsellor of Naples.*
ADRIAN, } *Lords.*
FRANCISCO, }
CALIBAN, *a savage and deformed Slave.*
TRINCULO, *a Jester.*

STEPHANO, *a drunken Butler.*
Master of a Ship, Boatswain, and Mariners.
MIRANDA, *daughter to* PROSPERO.
ARIEL, *an airy Spirit.*
IRIS,
CERES,
JUNO, } *Spirits.*
Nymphs,
Reapers,

Other Spirits attending on PROSPERO.

SCENE,—*The Sea, with a Ship: afterwards an uninhabited Island.*

ACT I.

SCENE I.—*On a Ship at Sea.—A Storm, with Thunder and Lightning.*

Enter a Shipmaster *and a* Boatswain.

Master. Boatswain,—
Boats. Here, master: what cheer?
Master. Good: Speak to the mariners: fall to 't yarely, or we run ourselves aground; bestir, bestir. [*Exit.*

Enter Mariners.

Boats. Heigh, my hearts; cheerly, cheerly, my hearts; yare, yare: take in the top-sail; 'Tend to the master's whistle.—Blow till thou burst thy wind, if room enough!

Enter ALONSO, SEBASTIAN, ANTONIO, FERDINAND, GONZALO, *and others.*

Alon. Good Boatswain, have care. Where's the master? Play the men.
Boats. I pray now, keep below.
Ant. Where is the master, Boatswain?
Boats. Do you not hear him? You mar our labour; keep your cabins: you do assist the storm.
Gon. Nay, good, be patient.
Boats. When the sea is. Hence! What care these roarers for the name of king? To cabin: silence: trouble us not.
Gon. Good; yet remember whom thou hast aboard.
Boats. None that I more love than myself. You are a counsellor: if you can command these elements to silence, and work the peace of the present, we will not hand a rope more; use your authority. If you cannot, give thanks you have lived so long, and make yourself ready in your cabin for the mischance of the hour, if it so hap.—Cheerly, good hearts.— Out of our way, I say. [*Exit.*

Gon. I have great comfort from this fellow: methinks he hath no drowning mark upon him; his complexion is perfect gallows. Stand fast, good fate, to his hanging! make the rope of his destiny our cable, for our own doth little advantage! If he be not born to be hanged, our case is miserable. [*Exeunt.*

Re-enter Boatswain.

Boats. Down with the top-mast; yare; lower, lower; bring her to try with main-course. *A cry within.*] A plague upon this howling! They are louder than the weather, or our office.—

Re-enter SEBASTIAN, ANTONIO, *and* GONZALO.
Yet again? what do you here? Shall we give o'er, and drown? Have you a mind to sink?
Seb. A pox o' your throat! you bawling, blasphemous, incharitable dog!
Boats. Work you, then.
Ant. Hang, cur, hang! you whoreson, insolent noise-maker, we are less afraid to be drowned than thou art.
Gon. I'll warrant him from drowning; though the ship were no stronger than a nut-shell, and as leaky as an unstanch'd wench.
Boats. Lay her a-hold, a-hold: set her two courses; off to sea again, lay her off.

Enter Mariners, *wet.*

Mar. All lost! to prayers, to prayers! all lost! [*Exeunt.*
Boats. What, must our mouths be cold?
Gon. The king and prince at prayers! let us assist them,
For our case is as theirs.
Seb. I am out of patience.
Ant. We are merely cheated of our lives by drunkards.—
This wide - chapp'd rascal; — Would thou mightst lie drowning,

The washing of ten tides!
Gon. He'll be hanged yet;
Though every drop of water swear against it,
And gape at wid'st to glut him.
[*A confused noise within.*]—Mercy on us! We
split, we split!—Farewell, my wife and children!
Farewell, brother!—We split, we split, we
split!—
Ant. Let's all sink with the king.   [*Exit.*
Seb. Let's take leave of him.   [*Exit.*
Gon. Now would I give a thousand furlongs of
sea for an acre of barren ground; long heath,
brown furze, any thing: The wills above be
done! but I would fain die a dry death. [*Exit.*

SCENE II.—*The Island; before the Cell of*
PROSPERO.

Enter PROSPERO *and* MIRANDA.

Mira. If by your art, my dearest father, you
          have
Put the wild waters in this roar, allay them:
The sky, it seems, would pour down stinking
          pitch,
But that the sea, mounting to the welkin's
          cheek,
Dashes the fire out. O, I have suffer'd
With those that I saw suffer! a brave vessel,
Who had, no doubt, some noble creatures in her,
Dash'd all to pieces. O, the cry did knock
Against my very heart! poor souls! they
          perish'd.
Had I been any god of power, I would
Have sunk the sea within the earth, or e'er
It should the good ship so have swallowed, and
The freighting souls within her.
Pro.   Be collected;
No more amazement; tell your piteous heart,
There's no harm done.
Mira.   O, woe the day!
Pro.   No harm.
I have done nothing but in care of thee,
(Of thee, my dear one! thee, my daughter!) who
Art ignorant of what thou art, nought knowing
Of whence I am; nor that I am more better
Than Prospero, master of a full poor cell,
And thy no greater father.
Mira.   More to know
Did never meddle with my thoughts.
Pro.   'Tis time
I should inform thee further. Lend thy hand,
And pluck my magic garment from me.—So;
                    [*Lays down his mantle.*
Lie there my art.—Wipe thou thine eyes; have
          comfort.
The direful spectacle of the wreck, which touch'd
The very virtue of compassion in thee,
I have with such provision in mine art
So safely order'd, that there is no soul—
No, not so much perdition as an hair,
Betid to any creature in the vessel
Which thou heard'st cry, which thou saw'st
          sink. Sit down;
For thou must now know further.

Mira.   You have often
Begun to tell me what I am; but stopp'd,
And left me to a bootless inquisition;
Concluding, *Stay, not yet.*—
Pro.   The hour's now come;
The very minute bids thee ope thine ear;
Obey, and be attentive. Canst thou remember
A time before we came unto this cell?   [not
I do not think thou canst; for then thou wast
Out three years old.
Mira.   Certainly, sir, I can.
Pro. By what? by any other house, or person?
Of any thing the image tell me, that
Hath kept with thy remembrance.
Mira.   'Tis far off;
And rather like a dream than an assurance
That my remembrance warrants: Had I not
Four or five women once, that tended me?
Pro. Thou hadst, and more, Miranda: But how
          is it,   [else
That this lives in thy mind? What seest thou
In the dark backward and abysm of time?
If thou remember'st aught, ere thou cam'st here,
How thou cam'st here, thou mayst.
Mira.   But that I do not.
Pro. Twelve years since, Miranda, twelve years
          since,
Thy father was the Duke of Milan, and
A prince of power.
Mira.   Sir, are not you my father?
Pro. Thy mother was a piece of virtue, and
She said—thou wast my daughter; and thy
          father
Was Duke of Milan; and his only heir
A princess; no worse issued.
Mira.   O, the heavens!
What foul play had we that we came from thence;
Or blessed was't, we did?
Pro.   Both, both, my girl;
By foul play as thou say'st, were we heaved
          thence;
But blessedly holp hither.
Mira.   O, my heart bleeds
To think o' the teen that I have turn'd you to,
Which is from my remembrance! Please, you,
          further.
Pro. My brother, and thy uncle, call'd An-
          tonio—
I pray thee, mark me,—that a brother should
Be so perfidious!—he whom, next thyself,
Of all the world I loved, and to him put
The manage of my state; as, at that time,
Through all the signiories it was the first,
And Prospero the prime duke; being so reputed
In dignity, and, for the liberal arts,
Without a parallel: those being all my study,
The government I cast upon my brother,
And to my state grew stranger, being transported
And rapt in secret studies. Thy false uncle—
Dost thou attend me?
Mira.   Sir, most heedfully.
Pro. Being once perfected how to grant suits,
How to deny them; whom to advance, and
          whom

To trash for over-topping; new created
The creatures that were mine; I say, or chang'd
    them,
Or else new form'd them; having both the key
Of officer and office, set all hearts
To what tune pleased his ear; that now he was
The ivy, which had hid my princely trunk,
And suck'd my verdure out on 't.—Thou
    attend'st not;
I pray thee, mark me.
Mira.   O good sir, I do.
Pro. I thus neglecting worldly ends, all dedicate
To closeness, and the bettering of my mind
With that, which, but by being so retired,
O'er-prized all popular rate, in my false brother
Awaked an evil nature: and my trust,
Like a good parent, did beget of him
A falsehood, in its contrary as great
As my trust was; which had, indeed, no limit,
A confidence sans bound. He being thus lorded,
Not only with what my revenue yielded,
But what my power might else exact,—like one,
Who having, unto truth, by telling of it,
Made such a sinner of his memory,
To credit his own lie,—he did believe
He was the duke; out of the substitution,
And executing the outward face of royalty,
With all prerogative:—Hence his ambition
Growing,—Dost hear?
Mira. Your tale, sir, would cure deafness.
Pro. To have no screen between this part he
    play'd
And him he play'd it for, he needs will be
Absolute Milan: Me, poor man!—my library
Was dukedom large enough; of temporal
    royalties
He thinks me now incapable: confederates
(So dry he was for sway) with the king of Naples,
To give him annual tribute, do him homage;
Subject his coronet to his crown, and bend
The dukedom, yet unbowed, (alas, poor Milan!)
To most ignoble stooping.
Mira.   O the heavens!
Pro. Mark his condition, and the event; then
If this might be a brother.   [tell me,
Mira.   I should sin
To think but nobly of my grandmother:
Good wombs have borne bad sons.
Pro.   Now the condition.
This king of Naples being an enemy
To me inveterate, hearkens my brother's suit;
Which was that he in lieu o' the premises,—
Of homage, and I know not how much tribute,—
Should presently extirpate me and mine
Out of the dukedom; and confer fair Milan,
With all the honours, on my brother: Whereon,
A treacherous army levied, one midnight
Fated to the purpose, did Antonio open
The gates of Milan; and i' the dead of darkness,
The ministers for the purpose hurried thence
Me, and thy crying self.
Mira.   Alack, for pity!
I, not rememb'ring how I cried out then,
Will cry it o'er again: it is a hint,

That wrings mine eyes to 't.
Pro.   Hear a little further,
And then I'll bring thee to the present business
Which now's upon us; without the which, this
Were most impertinent.   [story
Mira.   Wherefore did they not,
That hour, destroy us?
Pro.   Well demanded, wench;
My tale provokes that question. Dear, they
    durst not;
(So dear the love my people bore me) nor set
A mark so bloody on the business; but
With colours fairer painted their foul ends.
In few, they hurried us aboard a bark;
Bore us some leagues to sea; where they prepar'd
A rotten carcass of a boat, not rigg'd,
Nor tackle, sail, nor mast; the very rats
Instinctively had quit it: there they hoist us,
To cry to the sea that roar'd to us; to sigh
To the winds, whose pity, sighing back again,
Did us but loving wrong.
Mira.   Alack! what trouble
Was I then to you!
Pro.   O! a cherubim
Thou wast, that did preserve me! Thou didst
    smile,
Infused with a fortitude from heaven,
When I have deck'd the sea with drops full salt;
Under my burden groan'd; which raised in me
An undergoing stomach, to bear up
Against what should ensue.
Mira.   How came we ashore?
Pro. By Providence divine.
Some food we had, and some fresh water, that
A noble Neapolitan, Gonzalo,
Out of his charity, (who being then appointed
Master of this design,) did give us; with
Rich garments, linens, stuffs, and necessaries,
Which since have steaded much; so, of his
    gentleness,
Knowing I loved my books, he furnish'd me,
From my own library, with volumes that
I prize above my dukedom.
Mira.   Would I might
But ever see that man!
Pro.   Now I arise:—
Sit still, and hear the last of our sea-sorrow.
Here in this island we arrived; and here
Have I, thy schoolmaster, made thee more profit
Than other princes can, that have more time
For vainer hours, and tutors not so careful.
Mira. Heavens thank you for 't! And now, I
    pray you, sir,
(For still 'tis beating in my mind,) your reason
For raising this sea-storm?
Pro.   Know thus far forth.—
By accident most strange, bountiful Fortune,
Now my dear lady, hath mine enemies
Brought to this shore: and by my prescience
I find my zenith doth depend upon
A most auspicious star; whose influence
If now I court not, but omit, my fortunes
Will ever after droop.—Here cease more ques-
    tions,

Thou art inclin'd to sleep; 'tis a good dulness,
And give it way;—I know thou canst not choose.
         [MIRANDA *sleeps*.
Come away, servant, come: I am ready now;
Approach, my Ariel; come.

    Enter ARIEL.

Ari. All hail, great master! grave sir, hail! I
   come
To answer thy best pleasure; be 't to fly,
To swim, to dive into the fire, to ride
On the curl'd clouds; to thy strong bidding, task
Ariel, and all his quality.
Pro.   Hast thou, spirit,
Perform'd to point the tempest that I bade thee?
Ari. To every article.
I boarded the king's ship; now on the beak,
Now in the waist, the deck, in every cabin,
I flamed amazement: Sometimes, I'd divide,
And burn in many places; on the top-mast,
The yards, and bowsprit, would I flame dis-
   tinctly,
Then meet and join: Jove's lightnings, the
   precursors
O' the dreadful thunder-claps, more momentary
And sight-out-running were not: The fire, and
   cracks
Of sulphurous roaring, the most mighty Neptune
Seem'd to besiege, and make his bold waves
Yea, his dread trident shake. [tremble,
Pro.   My brave spirit!
Who was so firm, so constant, that this coil
Would not infect his reason?
Ari.   Not a soul,
But felt a fever of the mad, and play'd
Some tricks of desperation: All, but mariners,
Plung'd in the foaming brine, and quit the vessel,
Then all afire with me: the king's son, Ferdinand,
With hair up-staring (then like reeds, not hair),
Was the first man that leap'd; cried, *Hell is*
And all the devils are here!   [empty,
Pro.   Why, that's my spirit!
But was not this nigh shore?
Ari.   Close by, my master.
Pro. But are they, Ariel, safe?
Ari.   Not a hair perish'd;
On their sustaining garments not a blemish,
But fresher than before: and, as thou bad'st me,
In troops I have dispersed them 'bout the isle;
The king's son have I landed by himself;
Whom I left cooling of the air with sighs,
In an odd angle of the isle, and sitting,
His arms in this sad knot.
Pro.   Of the king's ship,
The mariners, say, how thou hast disposed,
And all the rest o' the fleet?
Ari.   Safely in harbour
Is the king's ship; in the deep nook, where once
Thou call'dst me up at midnight to fetch dew
From the still-vex'd Bermoothes, there she's hid:
The mariners all under hatches stow'd;
Whom, with a charm join'd to their suffer'd
   labour,
I have left asleep: and for the rest o' the fleet,

Which I dispersed, they all have met again;
And are upon the Mediterranean flote,
Bound sadly home for Naples;
Supposing that they saw the king's ship wreck'd,
And his great person perish.
Pro.   Ariel, thy charge
Exactly is performed; but there's more work:
What is the time o' the day?
Ari.   Past the mid season.
Pro. At least two glasses: The time 'twixt six
   and now
Must by us both be spent most preciously.
Ari. Is there more toil? Since thou dost give
   me pains.
Let me remember thee what thou hast promis'd,
Which is not yet perform'd me.
Pro.   How now? moody?
What is't thou canst demand?
Ari.   My liberty.
Pro. Before the time be out? No more!
Ari.   I pray thee
Remember, I have done thee worthy service;
Told thee no lies, made no mistakings, serv'd
Without or grudge or grumblings: thou didst
   promise
To bate me a full year.
Pro.   Dost thou forget
From what a torment I did free thee?
Ari.   No.
Pro. Thou dost; and think'st
It much to tread the ooze of the salt deep;
To run upon the sharp wind of the north;
To do me business in the veins o' the earth,
When it is bak'd with frost.
Ari.   I do not, sir.
Pro. Thou liest, malignant thing! Hast thou
   forgot   [envy,
The foul witch, Sycorax, who, with age and
Was grown into a hoop? hast thou forgot her?
Ari. No, sir.
Pro.   Thou hast: Where was she born?
   speak; tell me.
Ari. Sir, in Argier.
Pro.   Oh, was she so? I must,
Once in a month, recount what thou has been.
Which thou forget'st. This damn'd witch,
   Sycorax,
For mischiefs manifold, and sorceries terrible
To enter human hearing, from Argier,
Thou know'st, was banished; for one thing she
   did,
They would not take her life: Is not this true?
Ari. Ay, sir.
Pro. This blear-eyed hag was hither brought
   with child,   [slave,
And here was left by the sailors: Thou, my
As thou report'st thyself, wast then her servant:
And, for thou wast a spirit too delicate
To act her earthy and abhorr'd commands,
Refusing her grand 'hests, she did confine thee,
By help of her more potent ministers,
And in her most unmitigable rage,
Into a cloven pine; within which rift
Imprison'd, thou didst painfully remain

A dozen years; within which space she died,
And left thee there: where thou didst vent thy
    groans,
As fast as mill-wheels strike: Then was this
    island,
(Save for the son that she did litter here,
A freckled whelp, hag-born,) not honour'd with
A human shape.
Ari.   Yes: Caliban her son.
Pro. Dull thing, I say so; he, that Caliban,
Whom now I keep in service. Thou best know'st
What torment I did find thee in: thy groans
Did make wolves howl, and penetrate the breasts
Of ever-angry bears; it was a torment
To lay upon the damn'd, which Sycorax
Could not again undo; it was mine art,
When I arriv'd, and heard thee that made gape
The pine, and let thee out.
Ari.   I thank thee, master.
Pro. If thou more murmur'st I will rend an
And peg thee in his knotty entrails, till [oak,
Thou hast howl'd away twelve winters.
Ari.   Pardon, master:
I will be correspondent to command,
And do my spriting gently.
Pro.   Do so; and after two days
I will discharge thee.
Ari.   That's my noble master!
What shall I do? say what? what shall I do?
Pro. Go, make thyself like to a nymph o' the
    sea;
Be subject to no sight but mine; invisible
To every eye-ball else. Go, take this shape
And hither come in 't: hence, with diligence.
                      [*Exit* ARIEL.
Awake, dear heart, awake! thou hast slept well;
Awake!
Mira. The strangeness of your story put
Heaviness in me.
Pro.   Shake it off; Come on;
We'll visit Caliban, my slave, who never
Yields us kind answer.
Mira.   'Tis a villain, sir,
I do not love to look on.
Pro.   But, as 'tis,
We cannot miss him: he does make our fire,
Fetch in our wood; and serves in offices
That profit us. What ho! slave! Caliban!
Thou earth, thou! speak.
Cal. [*Within*] There's wood enough within.
Pro. Come forth, I say; there's other business
    for thee:
Come forth, thou tortoise! when?

      Re-enter ARIEL, *like a water-nymph.*

Fine apparition! My quaint Ariel,
Hark in thine ear.
Ari.   My lord, it shall be done. [*Exit.*
Pro. Thou poisonous slave, got by the devil
    himself
Upon thy wicked dam, come forth!

        Enter CALIBAN.
Cal. As wicked dew as e'er my mother brush'd

With raven's feather from unwholesome fen,
Drop on you both! a south-west blow on ye,
And blister you all o'er.
Pro. For this, be sure, to-night thou shalt have
    cramps,
Side-stitches that shall pen thy breath up;
    urchins
Shall, for that vast of night that they may work,
All exercise on thee; thou shalt be pinch'd
As thick as honey-combs, each pinch more
    stinging
Than bees that made them.
Cal.   I must eat my dinner.
This island's mine, by Sycorax my mother,
Which thou tak'st from me. When thou camest
    first,
Thou strok'dst me, and mad'st much of me;
    wouldst give me
Water with berries in 't; and teach me how
To name the bigger light, and how the less,
That burn by day and night: and then I lov'd
    thee,
And shew'd thee all the qualities o' the isle,
The fresh springs, brine pits, barren place, and
    fertile;
Cursed be I that did so!—All the charms
Of Sycorax, toads, beetles, bats, light on you!
For I am all the subjects that you have,
Which first was mine own king; and here you
    sty me
In this hard rock, whiles you do keep from me
The rest of the island.
Pro.   Thou most lying slave,
Whom stripes may move, not kindness: I have
    used thee,   [thee
Filth as thou art, with human care; and lodged
In mine own cell, till thou didst seek to violate
The honour of my child.
Cal. O ho, O ho!—would it had been done!
Thou didst prevent me; I had peopled else
This isle with Calibans.
Pro.   Abhorred slave;
Which any print of goodness will not take,
Being capable of all ill! I pitied thee,
Took pains to make thee speak, taught thee
    each hour   [savage,
One thing or other: when thou didst not,
Know thine own meaning, but wouldst gabble
    like
A thing most brutish, I endow'd thy purposes
With words that made them known: But thy
    vile race,   [good natures
Though thou didst learn, had that in't which
Could not abide to be with: therefore wast thou
Deservedly confined into this rock,
Who hadst deserved more than a prison
Cal You taught me language; and my profit
    on 't
Is, I know how to curse; the red plague rid you,
For learning me your language!
Pro.   Hag-seed, hence!
Fetch us in fuel; and be quick, thou wert best,
To answer other business. Shrug'st thou,
    malice?

If thou neglect'st, or dost unwillingly
What I command, I'll rack thee with old cramps;
Fill all thy bones with aches; make thee roar,
That beasts shall tremble at thy din.
Cal. No, pray thee!—
I must obey: his art is of such power, [*Aside.*
It would control my dam's god, Setebos,
And make a vassal of him.
Pro. So, slave; hence!
[*Exit* CALIBAN.

Re-enter ARIEL *invisible, playing and singing;*
FERDINAND *following him.*

ARIEL'S SONG.

Come unto these yellow sands.
    And then take hands:
Court'sied when you have, and kiss'd.
    (The wild waves whist,)
Foot it featly here and there;
And sweet sprites, the burden bear.
    Hark, hark!
Bur, *Bowgh, wowgh,*   *Dispersedly.*
    The watch-dogs bark:
Bur, *Bowgh, wowgh.*   *Dispersedly.*
    Hark, hark! I hear
The strain of strutting chanticlere
Cry, Cock-a-doodle-doo.

Fer. Where should this music be? i' the air,
    or the earth?
It sounds no more:—and sure it waits upon
Some god of the island Sitting on a bank
Weeping again the king my father's wreck,
This music crept by me upon the waters;
Allaying both their fury, and my passion,
With its sweet air: thence I have follow'd it,
Or it hath drawn me rather:—But 'tis gone.
No, it begins again.

ARIEL *sings.*

Full fathom five thy father lies;
    Of his bones are coral made;
Those are pearls that were his eyes:
    Nothing of him that doth fade,
But doth suffer a sea-change
Into something rich and strange.
Sea-nymphs hourly ring his knell:
            Burden, *ding-dong.*
Hark! now I hear them,—ding-dong bell.

Fer. The ditty does remember my drown'd
    father:—
This is no mortal business, nor no sound
That the earth owes:—I hear it now above me.
Pro. The fringed curtains of thine eye advance,
And say, what thou seest yond'.
Mira. What is 't? a spirit?
Lord, how it looks about Believe me, sir,
It carries a brave form:—But 'tis a spirit.
Pro. No, wench; it eats and sleeps, and hath
    such senses   [seest,
As we have, such: This gallant, which thou
Was in the wreck: and but he's something
    stain'd   [call him
With grief, that's beauty's canker, thou might'st
A goodly person: he hath lost his fellows,
And strays about to find them.
Mira. I might call him

A thing divine; for nothing natural
I ever saw so noble.
Pro. It goes on,   [*Aside.*
As my soul prompts it:—Spirit, fine spirit I'll
    free thee
Within two days for this.
Fer. Most sure the goddess
On whom these airs attend!—Vouchsafe, my
    prayer
May know, if you remain upon this island;
And that you will some good instruction give,
How I may bear me here: My prime request,
Which I do last pronounce, is, O you wonder!
If you be maid or no?
Mira. No wonder, sir;
But certainly a maid.
Fer. My language! heavens!—
I am the best of them that speak this speech,
Were I but where 'tis spoken.
Pro. How! the best?
What wert thou, if the king of Naples heard thee?
Fer. A single thing, as I am now, that wonders
To hear thee speak of Naples: He does hear me;
And, that he does, I weep: myself am Naples;
Who with mine eyes, ne'er since at ebb, beheld
The king my father wreck'd.
Mira. Alack, for mercy!
Fer. Yes, faith, and all his lords: the Duke of
And his brave son, being twain.   [Milan,
Pro. The Duke of Milan,
And his more braver daughter, could control
    thee,   [*Aside.*
If now 'twere fit to do't:—At the first sight
They have changed eyes:—Delicate Ariel,
I'll set thee free for this!—A word, good sir;
I fear you have done yourself some wrong: a
    word.
Mira. Why speaks my father so ungently?
    This
Is the third man that e'er I saw; the first
That e'er I sigh'd for: pity, move my father
To be inclined my way!
Fer. O, if a virgin,
And your affection not gone forth, I'll make you
The queen of Naples.
Pro. Soft, sir; one word more.—
They are both in either's powers; but this swift
    business
I must uneasy make, lest too light winning [*Aside.*
Make the prize light.—One word more; I charge
    thee,
That thou attend me: thou dost here usurp
The name thou ow'st not; and hast put thyself
Upon this island, as a spy, to win it
From me, the lord on 't.
Fer. No, as I am a man.
Mira. There's nothing ill can dwell in such a
If the ill spirit have so fair an house, [temple:
Good things will strive to dwell with 't.
Pro. Follow me.—
            [*To* FERD.
Speak not you for him; he's a traitor.—Come.
I'll manacle thy neck and feet together:
Sea-water shalt thou drink; thy food shall be

The fresh-brook muscles, wither'd roots, and
    husks
Wherein the acorn cradled: Follow.
Fer.   No;
I will resist such entertainment, till
Mine enemy has more power.   [*He draws.*
Mira.   O dear father,
Make not too rash a trial of him, for
He's gentle, and not fearful.
Pro.   What, I say,
My foot my tutor! Put thy sword up, traitor;
Who makest a show, but darest not strike, thy
    conscience
Is so possess'd with guilt: come from thy ward;
For I can here disarm thee with this stick,
And make thy weapon drop.
Mira.   Beseech you, father!
Pro. Hence; hang not on my garments.
Mira.   Sir, have pity;
I'll be his surety.
Pro.   Silence! one word more
Shall make me chide thee, if not hate thee.
    What!
An advocate for an impostor? hush!
Thou think'st there are no more such shapes
    as he,   [wench!
Having seen but him and Caliban: Foolish
To the most of men this is a Caliban,
And they to him are angels.
Mira.   My affections
Are then most humble; I have no ambition
To see a goodlier man.
Pro.   Come on; obey: [*To* FERD.
Thy nerves are in their infancy again,
And have no vigour in them.
Fer.   So they are:
My spirits, as in a dream, are all bound up.
My father's loss, the weakness which I feel,
The wreck of all my friends, or this man's
    threats,
To whom I am subdued, are but light to me,
Might I but through my prison once a day
Behold this maid: all corners else o' the earth
Let liberty make use of; space enough
Have I, in such a prison.
Pro.   It works:—Come on.—
Thou hast done well fine Ariel!—Follow me.—
    [*To* FERD. *and* MIR.
Hark, what thou else shalt do me. [*To* ARIEL.
Mira.   Be of comfort;
My father's of a better nature, sir,
Than he appears by speech; this is unwonted,
Which now came from him.
Pro.   Thou shalt be as free
As mountain winds: but then exactly do
All points of my command.
Ari.   To the syllable.
Pro. Come, follow: speak not for him. [*Exeunt.*

ACT II.

SCENE 1.—*Another part of the Island.*

Enter ALONSO, SEBASTIAN, ANTONIO,
GONZALO, ADRIAN, FRANCISCO, *and others.*

Gon. Beseech you, sir, be merry: you have
(So have we all) of joy; for our escape   [cause
Is much beyond our loss: Our hint of woe
Is common: every day, some sailor's wife,
The masters of some merchant, and the mer-
    chant,
Have just our theme of woe: but for the miracle,
I mean our preservation, few in millions
Can speak like us: then wisely, good sir, weigh
Our sorrow with our comfort.
Alon.   Pr'ythee, peace.
Seb. He receives comfort like cold porridge.
Ant. The visitor will not give him o'er so.
Seb. Look, he's winding up the watch of his
By and by it will strike.   [wit;
Gon. Sir,—
Seb. One:—Tell.   [offer'd
Gon. When every grief is entertain'd, that's
Comes to the entertainer—
Seb. A dollar.
Gon. Dolour comes to him, indeed; you have
spoken truer than you purposed.
Seb. You have taken it wiselier than I meant
you should.
Gon. Therefore, my lord,—
Ant. Fye, what a spendthrift is he of his tongue!
Alon. I pr'ythee spare.
Gon. Well, I have done: But yet—
Seb. He will be talking.
Ant. Which of them, he, or Adrian, for a good
wager, first begins to crow?
Seb. The old cock.
Ant. The cockrel.
Seb. Done: the wager?
Ant. A laughter.
Seb. A match.
Adr. Though this island seem to be desert,—
Seb. Ha, ha, ha!
Ant. So, you've paid.
Adr. Uninhabitable, and almost inaccessible,—
Seb. Yet,—
Adr. Yet,—
Ant. He could not miss it.
Adr. It must needs be of subtle, tender, and
delicate temperance.
Ant. Temperance was a delicate wench
Seb. Ay, and a subtle; as he most
learnedly delivered.   [sweetly.
Adr. The air breathes upon us here most
Seb. As if it had lungs, and rotten ones.
Ant. Or, as 'twere perfumed by a fen.
Gon. Here is everything advantageous to life.
Ant. True; save means to live.
Seb. Of that there's none, or little.   [green!
Gon. How lush and lusty the grass looks! how
Ant. The ground, indeed, is tawny.
Seb. With an eye of green in 't.
Ant. He misses not much.
Seb. No; he doth but mistake the truth totally.
Gon. But the rarity of it is (which is indeed
almost beyond credit)—
Seb. As many vouch'd rarities are.
Gon. That our garments, being, as they were,
drenched in the sea, hold, notwithstanding.

their freshness and glosses; being rather new dyed, than stained with salt water.

Ant. If but one of his pockets could speak, would it not say, he lies?

Seb. Ay, or very falsely pocket up his report.

Gon. Methinks, our garments are now as .resh as when we put them on first in Africk, at the marriage of the king's fair daughter Claribel to the king of Tunis.

Seb. 'Twas a sweet marriage, and we prosper well in our return.

Adr. Tunis was never graced before with such a paragon to their queen.

Gon. Not since widow Dido's time.

Ant. Widow? a pox o' that! How came that widow in? Widow Dido!

Seb. What if he had said, widower Æneas too? good lord, how you take it!

Adr. Widow Dido, said you? you make me study of that: She was of Carthage, not of Tunis.

Gon. This Tunis, sir, was Carthage.

Adr. Carthage?

Gon. I assure you, Carthage.

Ant. His word is more than the miraculous harp.

Seb. He hath raised the wall, and houses too.

Ant. What impossible matter will he make easy next?

Seb. I think he will carry this island home in his pocket, and give it his son for an apple.

Ant. And, sowing the kernels of it in the sea, bring forth more islands.

Gon. Ay?

Ant. Why, in good time.

Gon. Sir, we were talking, that our garments seem now as fresh as when we were at Tunis at the marriage of your daughter, who is now queen.

Ant. And the rarest that e'er came there.

Seb. 'Bate, I beseech you, widow Dido.

Ant. O, widow Dido; ay, widow Dido.

Gon. Is not, sir, my doublet as fresh as the first day I wore it? I mean, in a sort.

Ant. That sort was well fish'd for.

Gon. When I wore it at your daughter's marriage?

Alon. You cram these words into mine ears, against
The stomach of my sense: Would I had never
Married my daughter there! for, coming thence,
My son is lost; and, in my rate, she too,
Who is so far from Italy removed,
I ne'er again shall see her. O thou mine heir
Of Naples and of Milan, what strange fish
Hath made his meal on thee!

Fran.   Sir, he may live;
I saw him beat the surges under him,
And ride upon their backs; he trod the water,
Whose enmity he flung aside, and breasted
The surge most swoln that met him; his bold head
'Bove the contentious waves he kept, and oar'd
Himself with his good arms in lusty stroke
To the shore, that o'er his wave-worn basis bow'd,
As stooping to relieve him; I not doubt

He came alive to land.

Alon.   No, no, he's gone.

Seb. Sir, you may thank yourself for this great loss;   [daughter,
That would not bless our Europe with your
But rather lose her to an African;
Where she, at least, is banish'd from your eye,
Who hath cause to wet the grief on 't.

Alon.   Pr'ythee, peace.

Seb. You were kneel'd to, and importun'd otherwise.
By all of us; and the fair soul herself
Weigh'd, between lothness and obedience, at
Which end o' the beam she'd bow. We have lost your son,
I fear, for ever: Milan and Naples have
More widows in them of this business' making,
Than we bring men to comfort them: the fault's
Your own.

Alon. So is the dearest of the loss.

Gon.   My lord Sebastian,
The truth you speak doth lack some gentleness,
And time to speak it in; you rub the sore,
When you should bring the plaster.

Seb.   Very well.

Ant. And most chirurgeonly.

Gon. It is foul weather in us all, good sir,
When you are cloudy.

Seb.   Foul weather?

Ant.   Very foul.

Gon. Had I a plantation of this isle, my lord,—

Ant. He'd sow it with nettle-seed.

Seb.   Or docks, or mallows.

Gon. And were the king of it, what would I do?

Seb. 'Scape being drunk, for want of wine.

Gon. I' the commonwealth, I would by contraries
Execute all things: for no kind of traffic
Would I admit; no name of magistrate;
Letters should not be known; no use of service,
Of riches, or of poverty; no contracts,
Successions; bound of land, tilth, vineyard, none:
No use of metal, corn, or wine, or oil:
No occupation; all men idle, all;
And women too; but innocent and pure:
No sovereignty:—

Seb.   And yet he would be king on 't.

Ant. The latter end of his commonwealth forgets the beginning.   [duce

Gon. All things in common nature should produce
Without sweat or endeavour: treason, felony,
Sword, pike, knife, gun, or need of any engine,
Would I not have; but nature should bring forth,
Of its own kind, all foison, all abundance,
To feed my innocent people.

Seb. No marrying 'mong his subjects?

Ant. None, man; all idle; whores and knaves.

Gon. I would with such perfection govern, sir,
To excel the golden age.

Seb.   Save his majesty!

Ant. Long live Gonzalo!

Gon.   And, do you mark me, sir?—

Alon. Pr'ythee, no more: thou dost talk nothing to me.

Gon. I do well believe your highness; and did it to minister occasion to these gentlemen, who are of such sensible and nimble lungs, that they always use to laugh at nothing.

Ant. 'Twas you we laugh'd at.

Gon. Who, in this kind of merry fooling, am nothing to you: so you may continue, and laugh at nothing still.

Ant. What a blow was there given!

Seb. An it had not fallen flat-long.

Gon. You are gentlemen of brave mettle; you would lift the moon out of her sphere, if she would continue in it five weeks without changing.

Enter ARIEL *invisible, playing solemn music.*

Seb. We would so, and then go a bat-fowling.

Ant. Nay, good my lord, be not angry.

Gon. No, I warrant you; I will not adventure my discretion so weakly. Will you laugh me asleep, for I am very heavy?

Ant. Go sleep, and hear us.

    [*All sleep but* ALON. SEB. *and* ANT.

Alon. What, all so soon asleep! I wish mine eyes   [I find
Would, with themselves, shut up my thoughts:
They are inclined to do so.

Seb.   Please you, sir,
Do not omit the heavy offer of it:
It seldom visits sorrow; when it doth,
It is a comforter.

Ant.   We two, my lord,
Will guard your person, while you take your
And watch your safety.   [rest,

Alon.   Thank you: wondrous heavy.—
    [ALONSO *sleeps. Exit* ARIEL.

Seb. What a strange drowsiness possesses them?

Ant. It is the quality o' the climate.

Seb.`   Why
Doth it not then our eyelids sink! I find not
Myself disposed to sleep.

Ant.   Nor I; my spirits are nimble
They fell together all, as by consent;
They dropp'd, as by a thunder-stroke. What might,   [more:—
Worthy Sebastian?—O, what might?—No
And yet, methinks, I see it in thy face,
What thou shouldst be: the occasion speaks thee; and
My strong imagination sees a crown
Dropping upon thy head.

Seb.   What, art thou waking?

Ant.. Do you not hear me speak?

Seb.   I do; and, surely,
It is a sleepy language; and thou speak'st
Out of thy sleep: What is it thou didst say?
This is a strange repose, to be asleep   [ing,
With eyes wide open, standing, speaking, mov-
And yet so fast asleep.

Ant.   Noble Sebastian,   [wink'st
Thou lett'st thy fortune sleep—die rather;
Whiles thou art waking.

Seb.   Thou dost snore distinctly;
There's meaning in thy snores.

Ant. I am more serious than my custom: you
Must be so too, if heed me; which to do
Trebles thee o'er.

Seb.   Well, I am standing water.

Ant. I'll teach you how to flow.

Seb.   Do so: to ebb,
Hereditary sloth instructs me.

Ant.   O,
If you but knew, how you the purpose cherish,
Whiles thus you mock it! how, in stripping it,
You more invest it! Ebbing men, indeed,
Most often do so near the bottom run,
By their own fear, or sloth.

Seb.   Pr'ythee, say on:
The setting of thine eye, and cheek, proclaim
A matter from thee; and a birth, indeed,
Which throes thee much to yield.

Ant.   Thus, sir:
Although this lord of weak remembrance, this,
Who shall be of as little memory
When he is earth'd, hath here almost persuaded
(For he's a spirit of persuasion only)
The king, his son's alive: 'tis as impossible
That he's undrown'd as he that sleeps here

Seb. I have no hope   [swims.
That he's undrown'd.

Ant.   O, out of that no hope,
What great hope have you! no hope, that way, is
Another way so high an hope, that even
Ambition cannot pierce a wink beyond,
But doubts discovery there. Will you grant, with me,
That Ferdinand is drown'd?

Seb.   He's gone.

Ant.   Then, tell me,
Who's the next heir of Naples?

Seb.   Claribel.

Ant. She that is queen of Tunis: she that dwells
Ten leagues beyond man's life; she that from Naples
Can have no note, unless the sun were post
(The man i' the moon's too slow,) till new-born
Be rough and razorable; she, from whom [chins
We were all sea-swallow'd, though some cast again;
And, by that, destined to perform an act,
Whereof what's past is prologue; what to come,
In yours and my discharge.

Seb.   What stuff is this?—How say you?
'Tis true, my brother's daughter's queen of Tunis:
So is she heir of Naples; 'twixt which regions
There is some space.

Ant.   A space whose every cubit
Seems to cry out, *How shall that Claribel*
Measure us back to Naples?—Keep in Tunis,
And let Sebastian wake!—Say, this were death
That now hath seized them; why, they were no worse
Than now they are: There be, that can rule Naples,
As well as he that sleeps; lords, that can prate
As amply and unnecessarily
As this Gonzalo; I myself could make
A chough of as deep chat. O, that you bore

The mind that I do! what a sleep were this
For your advancement! Do you understand me?
Seb. Methinks, I do.
Ant.   And how does your content
Tender your own good fortune?
Seb.   I remember,
You did supplant your brother Prospero.
Ant.   True:
And, look, how well my garments sit upon me;
Much feater than before: My brother's servants
Were then my fellows, now they are my men.
Seb. But, for your conscience—
Ant. Ay, sir; where lies that? if it were a kybe,
'Twould put me to my slipper: But I feel not
This deity in my bosom; twenty consciences,
That stand 'twixt me and Milan, candied be
                              they,   [brother,
And melt, ere they molest! Here lies your
No better than the earth he lies upon,
If he were that which now he's like: whom I,
With this obedient steel, three inches of it,
Can lay to bed for ever: whiles you, doing thus
To the perpetual wink for aye might put
This ancient morsel, this Sir Prudence, who
Should not upbraid our course. For all the rest,
They'll take suggestion, as a cat laps milk;
They'll tell the clock to any business that
We say befits the hour.
Seb.   Thy case, dear friend,
Shall be my precedent; as thou gott'st Milan,
I'll come by Naples. Draw thy sword: one
                    stroke   [pay'st;
Shall free thee from the tribute which thou
And I the king shall love thee.
Ant.   Draw together:
And when I rear my hand, do you the like,
To fall it on Gonzalo.
Seb.   O, but one word.
                    [*They converse apart.*

Music. Re-enter ARIEL, *invisible.*

Ari. My master through his art foresees the
                    danger   [forth,—
That these his friends, are in; and sends me
For else his project dies,—to keep the living.
                    [*Sings in* GONZALO's *ear.*

> While you here do snoring lie,
> Open-eyed conspiracy
>   His time doth take:
> If of life you keep a care,
> Shake off slumber, and beware:
>   Awake! Awake!

Ant. Then let us both be sudden.
Gon. Now, good angels, preserve the king!
                    [*They awake.*
Alon. Why, how now, ho! awake! Why are
                    you drawn?
Wherefore this ghastly looking?
Gon.   What's the matter?
Seb. Whiles we stood here securing your repose,
                    repose,
Even now, we heard a hollow burst of bellowing

Like bulls, or rather lions; did it not wake you?
It struck mine ear most terribly.
Alon.   I heard nothing.
Ant. O, 'twas a din to fright a monster's ear;
To make an earthquake! sure it was the roar
Of a whole herd of lions.
Alon.   Heard you this, Gonzalo?
Gon. Upon mine honour, sir, I heard a hum-
                    ming.   [me:
And that a strange one too, which did awake
I shaked you, sir, and cried; as mine eyes open'd,
I saw their weapons drawn:—there was a noise,
That's verity: 'Best stand upon our guard:
Or that we quit this place: let's draw our
                    weapons.   '[further search
Alon. Lead off this ground; and let's make
For my poor son.
Gon. Heavens keep him from these beasts!
For he is, sure, i' the island.
Alon.   Lead away.
Ari. Prospero my lord shall know what I have
                    done: [*Aside.*
So, king, go safely on to seek thy son. [*Exeunt.*

SCENE II.—*Another part of the Island.*

Enter CALIBAN, *with a burden of wood.*
A noise of thunder heard.

Cal. All the infections that the sun sucks up
From bogs, fens, flats, on Prosper fall, and
                    make him
By inch-meal a disease! His spirits hear me,
And yet I needs must curse. But they'll nor
                    pinch,   [mire,
Fright me with urchin-shows, pitch me i' the
Nor lead me, like a firebrand, in the dark
Out of my way, unless he bid them; but
For every trifle they are set upon me:
Sometime like apes, that moe and chatter at me,
And after, bite me; then like hedge-hogs, which
Lie tumbling in my bare-foot way, and mount
Their pricks at my foot-fall; sometime am I
All wound with adders, who, with cloven
                    tongues,
Do hiss me into madness:—Lo! now! lo!

Enter TRINCULO.

Here comes a spirit of his; and to torment me,
For bringing wood in slowly: I'll fall flat;
Perchance he will not mind me.
Trin. Here's neither bush nor shrub, to bear
off any weather at all, and another storm brew-
ing; I hear it sing i' the wind; yond same black
cloud, yond huge one, looks like a foul bumbard
that would shed his liquor. If it should thunder,
as it did before, I know not where to hide my
head: yond same cloud cannot choose but fall
by pailfuls.—What have we here? a man or a
fish? dead or alive? A fish: he smells like a fish:
a very ancient and fish-like smell; a kind of,
not of the newest, Poor-John. A strange fish!
Were I in England now (as once I was), and
had but this fish painted, not a holiday fool
there but would give a piece of silver: there

would this monster make a man; any strange beast there makes a man: when they will not give a doit to relieve a lame beggar, they will lay out ten to see a dead Indian. Legg'd like a man! and his fins like arms! Warm, o' my troth! I do now let loose my opinion, hold it no longer; this is no fish, but an islander, that hath lately suffered by a thunder-bolt. [*Thunder*] Alas! the storm is come again: my best way is to creep under his gaberdine; there is no other shelter hereabout: Misery acquaints a man with strange bedfellows. I will here shroud. till the dregs of the storm be past.

Enter STEPHANO *singing, a bottle in his hand.*

Ste.   I shall no more to sea, to sea,
     Here shall I die ashore;—

This is a very scurvy tune to sing at a man's funeral: Well, here's my comfort.   [*Drinks.*

The master, the swabber, the boatswain, and I,
    The gunner, and his mate,
Lov'd Mall, Meg, and Marian, and Margery,
    But none of us car'd for Kate:
    For she had a tongue with a tang,
    Would cry to a sailor, *Go, hang;*
She lov'd not the savour of tar nor of pitch,
Yet a tailor might scratch her where'er she did itch:
    Then to sea, boys, and let her go hang.

This is a scurvy tune too: But here's my comfort.
Cal. Do not torment me: Oh!   [*Drinks.*
Ste. What's the matter? Have we devils here? Do you put tricks upon us with savages, and men of Inde? Ha! I have not 'scaped drowning, to be afeard now of your four legs; for it hath been said, As proper a man as ever went on four legs cannot make him give ground: and it shall be said so again, while Stephano breathes at nostrils.
Cal. The spirit torments me: Oh!
Ste. This is some monster of the isle, with four legs: who hath got, as I take it, an ague: Where the devil should he learn our language? I will give him some relief, if it be but for that: If I can recover him, and keep him tame, and get to Naples with him, he's a present for any emperor that ever trod on neat's leather.
Cal. Do not torment me, pr'ythee;
I'll bring my wood home faster.
Ste. He's in his fit now; and does not talk after the wisest. He shall taste of my bottle: if he have never drunk wine afore, it will go near to remove his fit. If I can recover him, and keep him tame, I will not take too much for him: he shall pay for him that hath him, and that soundly.   [wilt
Cal. Thou dost me yet but little hurt; thou Anon; I know it by thy trembling;
Now Prosper works upon thee.
Ste. Come on your ways; open your mouth: here is that which will give language to you, cat; open your mouth: this will shake your shaking, I can tell you, and that soundly: you cannot

tell who's your friend: open your chaps again.
Trin. I should know that voice: It should be—But he is drowned; and these are devils: Oh! defend me!—
Ste. Four legs and two voices; a most delicate monster! His forward voice now is to speak well of his friend; his backward voice is to utter foul speeches, and to detract. If all the wine in my bottle will recover him, I will help his ague: Come—Amen! I will pour some in thy other mouth.
Trin. Stephano,—
Ste. Doth thy other mouth call me? Mercy, mercy! This is a devil, and no monster: I will leave him; I have no long spoon.
Trin. Stephano!—if thou beest Stephano, touch me, and speak to me; for I am Trinculo; —be not afeard,—thy good friend Trinculo.
Ste. If thou beest Trinculo, come forth; I'll pull thee by the lesser legs: if any be Trinculo's legs, these are they. Thou art very Trinculo indeed. How cam'st thou to be the siege of this moon-calf? Can he vent Trinculos?
Trin. I took him to be killed with a thunder-stroke:—But art thou not drowned, Stephano? I hope, now, thou art not drowned. Is the storm over-blown? I hid me under the dead moon-calf's gaberdine for fear of the storm. And art thou living, Stephano? O Stephano, two Neapolitans 'scaped!
Ste. Pr'ythee, do not turn me about; my stomach is not constant.   [sprites,
Cal. These be fine things, and if they be not That's a brave god, and bears celestial liquor: I will kneel to him
Ste. How didst thou 'scape? how cam'st thou hither? swear by this bottle, how thou cam'st hither I escaped upon a butt of sack, which the sailors heaved overboard, by this bottle! which I made of the bark of a tree, with mine own hands, since I was cast ashore.
Cal. I'll swear, upon that bottle, to be thy True subject; for the liquor is not earthly.
Ste. Here: swear then how thou escap'dst.
Trin. Swam ashore, man, like a duck; I can swim like a duck, I'll be sworn.
Ste. Here, kiss the book: Though thou canst swim like a duck, thou art made like a goose.
Trin. O Stephano, hast any more of this?
Ste. The whole butt, man; my cellar is in a rock by the sea-side, where my wine is hid. How now, moon-calf? how does thine ague?
Cal. Hast thou not dropped from heaven?
Ste. Out o' the moon, I do assure thee: I was the man i' the moon, when time was.
Cal. I have seen thee in her, and I do adore thee;
My mistress showed me thee, and thy dog and bush.
Ste. Come, swear to that; kiss the book: I will furnish it anon with new contents: swear.
Trin. By this good light, this is a very shallow monster:—I afeard of him? a very weak monster;—The man i' the moon!—a most poor

credulous monster: Well drawn, monster, in good sooth

Cal. I'll show thee every fertile inch o' the island;
And kiss thy foot: I pr'ythee, be my god.

Trin By this light, a most perfidious and drunken monster; when his god's asleep, he'll rob his bottle.

Cal. I'll kiss thy foot: I'll swear myself thy subject.

Ste. Come on, then; down, and swear.

Trin. I shall laugh myself to death at this puppy-headed monster: a most scurvy monster! I could find in my heart to beat him,—

Ste. Come, kiss.

Trin. —but that the poor monster's in drink; An abominable monster!

Cal. I'll show thee the best springs; I'll pluck thee berries;
I'll fish for thee, and get thee wood enough.
A plague upon the tyrant that I serve!
I'll bear him no more sticks, but follow thee,
Thou wondrous man.

Trin. A most ridiculous monster! to make a wonder of a poor drunkard.

Cal. I pr'ythee, let me bring thee where crabs grow;
And I with my long nails will dig thee pig-nuts;
Show thee a jay's nest, and instruct thee how
To snare the nimble marmozet; I'll bring thee
To clust'ring filberts, and sometimes I'll get thee
Young sea-mells from the rock: Wilt thou go with me?

Ste. I pr'ythee now lead the way, without any more talking.—Trinculo, the king and all our company else being drowned, we will inherit here.—Here; [*To* CAL.] bear my bottle. Fellow Trinculo, we'll fill him by and by again.

Cal. Farewell, master: farewell, farewell.
                                   [*Sings drunkenly.*

Trin. A howling monster; a drunken monster.

Cal. No more dams I'll make for fish;
    Nor fetch in firing
      At requiring,
    Nor scrape trencher, nor wash dish;
      'Ban 'Ban, Ca—Caliban,
      Has a new master—Get a new man.

Freedom, hey-day hey-day, freedom! freedom, hey-day, freedom!

Ste. O brave monster! lead the way. [*Exeunt.*

ACT III.

SCENE I.—*Before* PROSPERO'S *Cell.*

Enter FERDINAND, *bearing a log.*

Fer. There be some sports are painful, and their labour
Delight in them sets off: some kinds of baseness
Are nobly undergone; and most poor matters
Point to rich ends. This my mean task would be
As heavy to me, as 'tis odious; but
The mistress which I serve quickens what's dead
And makes my labours pleasures: Oh, she is

Ten times more gentle than her father's crabbed;
And he's composed of harshness. I must remove
Some thousands of these logs, and pile them up,
Upon a sore injunction: My sweet mistress
Weeps when she sees me work; and says such baseness
Had never like executor. I forget: [labours;
But these sweet thoughts do even refresh my
Most busy, least when I do it.

Enter MIRANDA, *and* PROSPERO *at a distance.*

Mira.   Alas, now! pray you,
Work not so hard: I would the lightning had
Burnt up those logs that you are enjoin'd to pile!
Pray, set it down, and rest you: when this burns,
'Twill weep for having wearied you. My father
Is hard at study; pray, now, rest yourself;
He's safe for these three hours.

Fer.   O most dear mistress
The sun will set before I shall discharge
What I must strive to do.

Mira.   If you'll sit down,
I'll bear your logs the while: pray, give me that;
I'll carry it to the pile.

Fer.   No, precious creature:
I had rather crack my sinews, break my back,
Than you should such dishonour undergo,
While I sit lazy by.

Mira.   It would become me
As well as it does you: and I should do it
With much more ease; for my good will is to it,
And yours against.

Pro. [*Aside.*] Poor worm! thou art infected;
This visitation shows it.

Mira.   You look wearily.

Fer. No, noble mistress; 'tis fresh morning with me
When you are by at night. I do beseech you,
Chiefly that I might set it in my prayers,
What is your name?

Mira.   Miranda:—O my father,
I have broke your 'hest to say so!

Fer.   Admir'd Miranda!
Indeed the top of admiration; worth
What's dearest to the world! Full many a lady
I have eyed with best regard; and many a time
The harmony of their tongues hath into bondage
Brought my too diligent ear: for several virtues
Have I lik'd several women: never any
With so full soul, but some defect in her
Did quarrel with the noblest grace she owed;
And put it to the foil: but you, O you,
So perfect and so peerless, are created
Of every creature's best.

Mira.   I do not know
One of my sex! no woman's face remember,
Save, from my glass, mine own; nor have I seen
More that I may call men, than you, good friend,
And my dear father: how features are abroad,
I am skill-less of; but, by my modesty,—
The jewel in my dower,—I would not wish
Any companion in the world but you;
Nor can imagination form a shape,
Besides yourself, to like of. But I prattle

Something too wildly, and my father's precepts
Therein forget.
Fer.　　　　　I am, in my condition,
A prince, Miranda; I do think, a king,—
I would, not so!—and would no more endure
This wooden slavery than I would suffer
The flesh-fly blow my mouth. Hear my soul
　　　　speak:
The very instant that I saw you, did
My heart fly to your service; there resides,
To make me slave to it; and for your sake
Am I this patient log-man.
Mira.　　　　　　　Do you love me?
Fer. O heaven, O earth, bear witness to this
　　　　sound,
And crown what I profess with kind event,
If I speak true! if hollowly, invert
What best is boded me to mischief! I,
Beyond all limit of what else i' the world,
Do love, prize, honour you.
Mira.　　　　　　　I am a fool
To weep at what I am glad of.
Pro. [*Aside.*]　　　　　Fair encounter
Of two most rare affections! Heavens rain grace
On that which breeds between them!
Fer.　　　　　　Wherefore weep you?
Mira. At mine unworthiness, that dare not offer
What I desire to give; and much less take
What I shall die to want. But this is trifling;
And all the more it seeks to hide itself,
The bigger bulk it shows. Hence, bashful cun-
　　　　ning;
And prompt me, plain and holy innocence!
I am your wife, if you will marry me;
If not, I'll die your maid: to be your fellow
You may deny me; but I'll be your servant
Whether you will or no.
Fer.　　　　　My mistress, dearest,
And I thus humble ever.
Mir.　　　　　　My husband, then?
Fer. Ay, with a heart as willing
As bondage e'er of freedom: here's my hand.
Mira. And mine, with my heart in 't: and now
　　　　farewell
Till half an hour hence.
Fer.　　　　　A thousand! thousand!
　　　　　　　[*Exeunt* FERD. *and* MIRA.
Pro. So glad of this as they I cannot be,
Who are surprised withal; but my rejoicing
At nothing can be more. I'll to my book;
For yet, ere supper time, must I perform
Much business appertaining.　　　　[*Exit.*

SCENE II.—*Another part of the Island.*

Enter STEPHANO *and* TRINCULO; CALIBAN
following with a bottle.

Ste. Tell not me;—when the butt is out, we
will drink water; not **a** drop before: therefore
bear up, and board 'em: Servant-monster,
drink to me.
Trin. Servant-monster the folly of this island!
They say there's but five upon this isle: we

are three of them; if the other two be brained
like us, the state totters.
Ste. Drink, servant-monster, when I bid thee:
thy eyes are almost set in thy head.
Trin. Where should they be set else? he were
a brave monster indeed, if they were set in
his tail.
Ste. My man-monster hath drowned his
tongue in sack: for my part, the sea cannot
drown me: I swam, ere I could recover the
shore, five-and-thirty leagues, off and on, by
this light.—Thou shalt be my lieutenant, monster, or my standard.　　　　　　[standard.
Trin. Your lieutenant, if you list; he's no
Ste. We'll not run, monsieur-monster.
Trin. Nor go neither: but you'll lie, like dogs;
and yet say nothing neither.
Ste. Moon-calf, speak once in thy life, if thou
beest a good moon-calf.
Cal. How does thy honour? Let me lick thy
　　　　shoe.
I'll not serve him; he is not valiant.
Trin. Thou liest, most ignorant monster: I
am in case to justle a constable. Why, thou
deboshed fish thou, was there ever a man a
coward that hath drunk so much sack as I to-
day? Wilt thou tell a monstrous lie, being but
half a fish and half a monster?
Cal. Lo, how he mocks me! wilt thou let him,
my lord?
Trin. Lord, quoth he!—that a monster should
be such a natural!
Cal. Lo, lo again! bite him to death, I pr'ythee.
Ste. Trinculo, keep a good tongue in your
head: if you prove a mutineer, the next tree.—
The poor monster's my subject, and he shall
not suffer indignity.
Cal. I thank my noble lord. Wilt thou be
pleased to hearken once again to the suit I
made thee?
Ste. Marry will I: kneel and repeat it; I will
stand, and so shall Trinculo.

Enter ARIEL, *invisible.*

Cal. As I told thee before, I am subject to a
tyrant; a sorcerer, that by his cunning hath
cheated me of this island.
Ari.　　　　　　Thou liest.
Cal. Thou liest, thou jesting monkey, thou;
I would my valiant master would destroy thee!
I do not lie.
Ste. Trinculo, if you trouble him any more
in his tale, by this hand, I will supplant some
of your teeth.
Trin. Why, I said nothing.
Ste. Mum, then, and no more.—[*To* CALIBAN.]
Proceed.
Cal. I say, by sorcery he got this isle;
From me he got it. If thy greatness will
Revenge it on him—for I know thou dar'st,
But this thing dare not.
Ste.　　　　　　That's most certain.
Cal. Thou shalt be lord of it, and I'll serve thee.

Ste. How now shall this be compassed? Canst thou bring me to the party?   [*asleep*,

Cal. Yea, yea my lord; I'll yield him thee Where thou mayst knock a nail into his head.

Ari. Thou liest; thou canst not.

Cal. What a pied ninny's this? Thou scurvy patch!—
I do beseech thy greatness, give him blows,
And take his bottle from him: when that's gone
He shall drink nought but brine; for I'll not show him
Where the quick freshes are.

Ste. Trinculo, run into no further danger; interrupt the monster one word further, and by this hand, I'll turn my mercy out of doors, and make a stock-fish of thee.

Trin. Why, what did I? I did nothing. I'll go further off.

Ste. Didst thou not say, he lied?

Ari. Thou liest.

Ste. Do I so? take thou that. [*Strikes him.*] As you like this, give me the lie another time.

Trin. I did not give the lie.—Out o' your wits and hearing too?——A pox o' your bottle this can sack and drinking do.—A murrain on your monster, and the devil take your fingers!

Cal. Ha, ha, ha!

Ste. Now, forward with your tale. Pr'ythee, stand further off.

Cal. Beat him enough: after a little time I'll beat him too.

Ste. Stand further.—Come, proceed.

Cal. Why, as I told thee, 'tis a custom with him I' the afternoon to sleep: there thou mayst brain him,
Having first seized his books; or with a log
Batter his skull, or paunch him with a stake,
Or cut his wezand with thy knife. Remember,
First to possess his books; for without them
He's but a sot, as I am, nor hath not
One spirit to command: they all do hate him
As rootedly as I. Burn but his books.
He has brave utensils,—for so he calls them,—
Which, when he has a house, he'll deck withal.
And that most deeply to consider is
The beauty of his daughter; he himself
Calls her a nonpareil; I never saw woman,
But only Sycorax my dam and she;
But she as far surpasseth Sycorax,
As great'st does least.

Ste.   Is it so brave a lass?

Cal. Ay, lord; she will become thy bed, I warrant,
And bring thee forth brave brood.

Ste. Monster, I will kill this man: his daughter and I will be king and queen;—save our graces!—and Trinculo and thyself shall be viceroys.—Dost thou like the plot, Trinculo?

Trin. Excellent.

Ste. Give me thy hand; I am sorry I beat thee: but while thou livest, keep a good tongue in thy head.

Cal. Within this half hour will he be asleep; Wilt thou destroy him then?

Ste.   Ay, on mine honour.

Ari. This will I tell my master.

Cal. Thou mak'st me merry: I am full of pleasure;
Let us be jocund: will you troll the catch
You taught me but while-ere?

Ste. At thy request, monster, I will do reason, any reason. Come on, Trinculo, let us sing.
                [*Sings.*

Flout 'em, and scout 'em; and scout 'em and flout 'em;
    Thought is free.

Cal. That's not the tune.
        [ARIEL *plays the tune on a tabor and pipe.*

Ste. What is this same?

Trin. This is the tune of our catch, played by the picture of Nobody.

Ste. If thou beest a man, show thyself in thy likeness: if thou beest a devil, tak't as thou list.

Trin. O, forgive me my sins!

Ste. He that dies, pays all debts: I defy thee:—Mercy upon us!

Cal. Art thou afeard?

Ste. No, monster, not I.

Cal. Be not afeard; the isle is full of noises,
Sounds, and sweet airs, that give delight and hurt not.
Sometimes a thousand twangling instruments
Will hum about mine ears; and sometimes voices,
That, if I then had waked after long sleep,
Will make me sleep again; and then, in dreaming,   [*riches*
The clouds, methought, would open and show
Ready to drop upon me: that, when I waked,
I cried to dream again.

Ste. This will prove a brave kingdom to me, where I shall have my music for nothing.

Cal. When Prospero is destroyed.

Ste. That shall be by and by: I remember the story.

Trin. The sound is going away: let's follow it, and after, do our work.

Ste. Lead, monster, we'll follow.—I would I could see this taborer: he lays it on.

Trin. Wilt come? I'll follow, Stephano. [*Exeunt.*

SCENE III.—*Another part of the Island.*

Enter ALONSO, SEBASTIAN, ANTONIO, GONZALO, ADRIAN, FRANCISCO, *and others.*

Gon. By'r lakin, I can go no further, sir;
My old bones ache: here's a maze trod, indeed,
Through forth-rights and meanders! by your
I needs must rest me.   [*patience.*

Alon.   Old lord, I cannot blame thee,
Who am myself attach'd with weariness,
To the dulling of my spirits: sit down, and rest.
Even here I will put off my hope, and keep it
No longer for my flatterer: he is drown'd
Whom thus we stray to find: and the sea mocks
Our frustrate search on land. Well, let him go.

Ant. I am right glad that he's so out of hope.
                [*Aside to* SEB.

Do not, for one repulse, forego the purpose
That you resolved to effect.
Seb.   The next advantage
Will we take thoroughly.   [*Aside to* ANT.
Ant. [*Aside to* SEB.] Let it be to-night;
For, now they are oppress'd with travel, they
Will not, nor cannot, use such vigilance,
As when they are fresh.
Seb. [*Aside to* ANT.] I say to-night; no more.

Solemn and strange music; and PROSPERO *above,
    invisible. Enter several strange* Shapes, *bring-
    ing in a banquet; they dance about it with
    gentle actions of salutation, and inviting the
    King, &c., to eat, they depart.*

Alon. What harmony is this? My good friends
                hark!
Gon.   Marvellous sweet music!
Alon. Give us kind keepers, heavens! What
                were these?
Seb. A living drollery: now I will believe,
That there are unicorns; that, in Arabia
There is one tree, the phœnix' throne; one
At this hour reigning there.   [phœnix
Ant.   I'll believe both;
And what does else want credit, come to me,
And I'll be sworn 'tis true: travellers ne'er did lie,
Though fools at home condemn them.
Gon.   If in Naples
I should report this now, would they believe me?
If I should say, I saw such islanders,—
For, certes, these are people of the island,—
Who, though they are of monstrous shape, yet,
                note,
Their manners are more gentle-kind than of
Our human generation you shall find
Many, nay, almost any.
Pro.   Honest lord,
Thou hast said well; for some of you there
                present
Are worse than devils.   [*Aside.*
Alon.   I cannot too much muse,
Such shapes, such gesture, and such sound,
                expressing,—
Although they want the use of tongue,—a kind
Of excellent dumb discourse.
Pro.   Praise in departing. [*Aside.*
Fran. They vanish'd strangely.
Seb.   No matter, since
They have left their viands behind; for we have
                stomachs,—
Will 't please you taste of what is here?
Alon.   Not I.
Gon. Faith, sir, you need not fear. When we
                were boys,   [eers,
Who would believe that there were mountain-
Dew-lapp'd like bulls, whose throats had hang-
                ing at them
Wallets of flesh? or that there were such men,
Whose heads stood in their breasts? which now
                we find,
Each putter-out of one for five, will bring us
Good warrant of.
Alon.   I will stand to, and feed,

Although my last: no matter, since I feel,
The best is past:—Brother, my lord the duke,
Stand to, and do as we.

Thunder and lightning. Enter ARIEL *like a
    harpy; claps his wings upon the table, and
    with a quaint device the banquet vanishes.*

Ari. You are three men of sin, whom destiny,
That hath to instrument this lower world,
And what is in 't,—the never-surfeited sea
Hath caused to belch up; and on this island
Where man doth not inhabit; you 'mongst men
Being most unfit to live. I have made you mad;
And even with such like valour, men hang and
Their proper selves.   [drown
        [ALON., SEB. &c., *draw their swords.*
                You fools! I and my fellows
Are ministers of fate; the elements,
Of whom your swords are temper'd, may as well
Wound the loud winds, or with bemock'd-at stabs
Kill the still-closing waters, as diminish
One dowle that's in my plume; my fellow-
                ministers
Are like invulnerable; if you could hurt,
Your swords are now too massy for your strengths,
And will not be uplifted. But, remember,—
For that's my business to you,—that you three
From Milan did supplant good Prospero;
Expos'd unto the sea, which hath requit it.
Him, and his innocent child: for which foul deed
The powers, delaying, not forgetting have
Incensed the seas and shores, yea, all the
                creatures.
Against your peace: Thee, of thy son, Alonso,
They have bereft; and do pronounce by me,
Ling'ring perdition,—worse than any death
Can be at once,—shall step by step attend
You and your ways; whose wraths to guard
                you from,—
Which here, in this most desolate isle; else falls
Upon your heads,—is nothing but heart's sorrow,
And a clear life ensuing.

*He vanishes in thunder: then, to soft music, enter
    the* Shapes *again, and dance with mops and
    mows, and carry out the table.*

Pro. [*Aside.*] Bravely the figure of this harpy
                hast thou
Perform'd, my Ariel; a grace it had devouring:
Of my instruction hast thou nothing 'bated,
In what thou hadst to say: so, with good life,
And observation strange, my meaner ministers
Their several kinds have done: my high charms
And these, mine enemies, are all knit up [work,
In their distractions: they now are in my power;
And in these fits I leave them, whilst I visit
Young Ferdinand,—who they suppose is
And his and my loved darling.   [drown'd,—
                [*Exit* PROSPERO *from above.*
Gon. I' the name of something holy, sir, why
In this strange stare?   [stand you
Alon.   O, it is monstrous! monstrous!
Methought the billows spoke, and told me of it;
The winds did sing it to me; and the thunder,

That deep and dreadful organ-pipe, pronounced
The name of Prosper; it did bass my trespass.
Therefore my son i' the ooze is bedded; and
I'll seek him deeper than e'er plummet sounded
And with him there lie mudded.   [*Exit*.
Seb.   But one fiend at a time,
I'll fight their legions o'er.
Ant.   I'll be thy second.
            [*Exeunt* SEB. *and* ANT.
Gon. All three of them are desperate; their
        great guilt,
Like poison given to work a great time after,
Now 'gins to bite the spirits:—I do beseech you
That are of suppler joints, follow them swiftly,
And hinder them from what this ecstacy
May now provoke them to.
Adr.   Follow, I pray you. [*Exeunt*.

ACT IV.

SCENE I.—*Before* PROSPERO'S *Cell*.

Enter PROSPERO, FERDINAND, *and* MIRANDA.

Pro. If I have too austerly punished you,
Your compensation makes amends; for I
Have given you here a thread of mine own life,
Or that for which I live; who once again
I tender to thy hand: all thy vexations
Were but my trials of thy love, and thou
Hast strangely stood the test: here, afore Heaven,
I ratify this my rich gift. O Ferdinand,
Do not smile at me, that I boast her off,
For thou shalt find she will outstrip all praise,
And make it halt behind her.
Fer.   I do believe it,
Against an oracle.
Pro. Then, as my gift, and thine own acqui-
        sition
Worthily purchas'd, take my daughter: But
If thou dost break her virgin knot before
All sanctimonious ceremonies may
With full and holy rite be minister'd,
No sweet aspersion shall the heavens let fall
To make this contract grow: but barren hate,
Sour-eyed disdain, and discord, shall bestrew
The union of your bed with weeds so loathly,
That you shall hate it both: therefore, take
As Hymen's lamps shall light you.   [heed,
Fer.   As I hope
For quiet days, fair issue, and long life,
With such love as 'tis now; the murkiest den,
The most oppórtune place, the strong'st sugges-
Our worser Genius can, shall never melt [tion
Mine honour into lust; to take away
The edge of that day's celebration, [founder'd,
When I shall think, or Phœbus' steeds are
Or night kept chain'd below.
Pro.   Fairly spoke:
Sit, then, and talk with her, she is thine own.—
What, Ariel; my industrious servant, Ariel!

Enter ARIEL.

Ari. What would my potent master? here I
        am.   [service
Pro. Thou and thy meaner fellows your last

Did worthily perform; and I must use you
In such another trick: go, bring the rabble,
O'er whom I give thee power, here, to this place:
Incite them to quick motion; for I must
Bestow upon the eyes of this young couple
Some vanity of mine art; it is my promise,
And they expect it from me.
Ari.   Presently?
Pro. Ay, with a twink.
Ari. Before you can say, *Come* and *go*,
And breathe twice; and cry, *so, so;*
Each one, tripping on his toè,
Will be here with mop and mow:
Do you love me, master? no?   [proach
Pro. Dearly, my delicate Ariel. Do not ap-
Till thou dost hear me call.
Ari.   Well I conceive. [*Exit*.
Pro. Look thou be true: do not give dalliance
Too much the rein: the strongest oaths are straw
To the fire i' the blood: be more abstemious,
Or else, good night your vow!
Fer.   I warrant you, sir.
The white cold virgin snow upon my heart
Abates the ardour of my liver.
Pro.   Well.—
Now come, my Ariel: bring a corollary,
Rather than want a spirit: appear, and pertly.—
No tongue; all eyes; be silent.   [*Soft music*.

A Masque. Enter IRIS.

Iris. Ceres, most bounteous lady, thy rich leas
Of wheat, rye, barley, vetches, oats, and pease;
Thy turfy mountains, where live nibbling sheep,
And flat meads thatch'd with stover, them to
Thy banks with peonied and lilied brims, [keep;
Which spongy April at thy 'hest betrims,
To make cold nymphs chaste crowns; and thy
        broom groves,
Whose shadow the dismissed bachelor loves,
Being lass-lorn; thy pole-clipt vineyard;
And thy sea-marge, sterile and rocky-hard,
Where thou thyself dost air: The queen o' the sky
Whose watery arch, and messenger, am I,
Bids thee leave these; and with her sovereign
        grace,
Here on this grass-plot, in this very place,
To come and sport: her peacocks fly amain;
Approach, rich Ceres, her to entertain.

Enter CERES.

Cer. Hail, many-colour'd messenger, that ne'er
Dost disobey the wife of Jupiter;
Who, with thy saffron wings, upon my flowers
Diffusest honey drops, refreshing showers;
And with each end of thy blue bow dost crown
My bosky acres, and my unshrubb'd down,
Rich scarf to my proud earth;—why hath thy
        queen
Summon'd me hither, to this short-grass'd green?
Iris. A contract of true love to celebrate;
And some donation freely to estate
On the bless'd lovers.
Cer.   Tell me, heavenly bow,
If Venus, or her son, as thou dost know,

Do now attend the queen? since they did plot
The means, that dusky Dis my daughter got,
Her and her blind boy's scandal'd company
I have forsworn.
Iris.   Of her society
Be not afraid. I met her deity
Cutting the clouds towards Paphos; and her son
Dove-drawn with her: here thought they to
                                      have done
Some wanton charm upon this man and maid,
Whose vows are that no bed-rite shall be paid
Till Hymen's torch be lighted; but in vain;
Mars' hot minion is return'd again;
Her waspish-headed son has broke his arrows,
Swears he will shoot no more, but play with
And be a boy right out.   [sparrows,
Cer.   Highest queen of state,
Great Juno comes; I know her by her gait.

Enter JUNO.

Jun. How does my bounteous sister? Go with
                                      me,
To bless this twain, that they may prosperous be,
And honour'd in their issue.

SONG.

Jun.—Honour, riches, marriage-blessing,
          Long continuance, and increasing,
          Hourly joys be still upon you!
          Juno sings her blessings on you.

Cer.—Earth's increase, and foison plenty,
          Barns and garners never empty;
          Vines, with clust'ring bunches growing;
          Plants, with goodly burden bowing;
          Spring come to you, at the farthest,
          In the very end of harvest!
          Scarcity and want shall shun you
          Ceres' blessing so is on you.

Fer. This is a most majestic vision, and
Harmonious charmingly: May I be bold
To think these spirits?
Pro.   Spirits, which by mine art
I have from their confines called to enact
My present fancies.
Fer.   Let me live here ever;
So rare a wonder'd father, and a wise,
Makes this place Paradise.
          [JUNO *and* CERES *whisper, and*
                send IRIS *on employment.*
Pro.   Sweet now, silence;
Juno and Ceres whisper seriously;
There's something else to do; hush, and be mute,
Or else our spell is marr'd.
Iris. You nymphs, call'd Naiads, of the
          wind'ring brooks,   [looks,
With your sedged crowns, and ever harmless
Leave your crisp channels, and on this green land
Answer your summons: Juno does command.
Come, temperate nymphs, and help to celebrate
A contract of true love; be not too late.

Enter certain Nymphs.

You sun-burn'd sicklemen, of August weary,
Come hither from the furrow, and be merry;

Make holiday: your rye-straw hats put on,
And these fresh nymphs encounter every one
In country footing.

Enter certain Reapers, *properly habited; they
join with the* Nymphs *in a graceful dance;
towards the end whereof* PROSPERO *starts suddenly, and speaks; after which, to a strange,
hollow, and confused noise, they heavily vanish.*

Pro. [*Aside.*] I had forgot that foul conspiracy
Of the beast Caliban and his confederates
Against my life; the minute of their plot
Is almost come.—[*To the Spirits.*] Well done;
          —avoid;—no more.   passion
Fer. This is strange: your father's in some
That works him strongly.
Mira.   Never till this day,
Saw I him touch'd with anger so distemper'd.
Pro. You do look, my son, in a moved sort,
As if you were dismay'd: be cheerful, sir:
Our revels now are ended: these our actors,
As I foretold you, were all spirits, and
Are melted into air, into thin air:
And, like the baseless fabric of this vision
The cloud-capp'd towers, the gorgeous palaces,
The solemn temples, the great globe itself,
Yea, all which it inherit, shall dissolve,
And, like this insubstantial pageant faded,
Leave not a rack behind: We are such stuff
As dreams are made of, and our little life
Is rounded with a sleep.—Sir, I am vex'd;
Bear with my weakness; my old brain is troubled,
Be not disturb'd with my infirmity;
If you be pleased, retire into my cell,
And there repose; a turn or two I'll walk,
To still my beating mind.
Fer. Mira.   We wish your peace.
                                      [*Exeunt.*
Pro. Come, with a thought:—I thank you;
          —Ariel, come.

Enter ARIEL.

Ari. Thy thoughts I cleave to: What's thy
          pleasure?
Pro.   Spirit,
We must prepare to meet with Caliban.
Ari. Ay, my commander; when I presented
          Ceres,
I thought to have told thee of it; but I fear'd
Lest I might anger thee.   [varlets?
Pro. Say again, where didst thou leave these
Ari. I told you, sir, they were red-hot with
          drinking:
So full of valour that they smote the air
For breathing in their faces; beat the ground
For kissing of their feet; yet always bending
Towards their project: Then I beat my tabor,
At which, like unback'd colts, they prick'd
          their ears,
Advanced their eyelids, lifted up their noses
As they smelt music; so I charm'd their ears,
That, calf-like, they my lowing follow'd through
Tooth'd briers, sharp furzes, pricking goss, and
          thorns.

Which enter'd their frail shins: at last I left them
I' the filthy mantled pool beyond your cell,
There dancing up to the chins, that the foul lake
O'erstunk their feet.
Pro.　　　　This was well done, my bird;
Thy shape invisible retain thou still:
The trumpery in my house, go, bring it hither,
For stale to catch these thieves.
Ari.　　　　　　　　I go, I go. [*Exit.*
Pro. A devil, a born devil, on whose nature
Nurture can never stick; on whom my pains,
Humanely taken, all, all lost, quite lost:
And as, with age, his body uglier grows,
So his mind cankers: I will plague them all,

Re-enter ARIEL, *loaden with glistering
apparel, &c.*

Even to roaring:—Come, hang them on this line.

PROSPERO *and* ARIEL *remain invisible. Enter*
CALIBAN, STEPHANO, *and* TRINCULO, *all wet.*
Cal. Pray you, tread softly, that the blind
　　　　mole may not
Hear a footfall: we now are near his cell.
Ste. Monster, your fairy, which you say is a
harmless fairy, has done little better than
played the Jack with us.
Trin. Monster, I do smell all horse-piss; at
which my nose is in great indignation.
Ste. So is mine. Do you hear, monster? If I
should take a displeasure against you; look you,—
Trin. Thou wert but a lost monster.
Cal. Good, my lord, give my thy favour still:
Be patient, for the prize I'll bring thee to
Shall hood-wink this mischance: therefore speak
All's hush'd as midnight yet.　　　[*softly,*
Trin. Ay, but to lose our bottles in the pool—
Ste. There is not only disgrace and dishonour
in that, monster, but an infinite loss.
Trin. That's more to me than my wetting:
yet this is your harmless fairy monster.
Ste. I will fetch off my bottle, though I be
o'er ears for my labour.　　　　　[*here,*
Cal. Pr'ythee, my king, be quiet: Seest thou
This is the mouth o' the cell: no noise, and enter.
Do that good mischief, which may make this
　　　　island
Thine own for ever, and I, thy Caliban,
For aye thy foot-licker.
Ste. Give me thy hand: I do begin to have
bloody thoughts.
Trin. O king Stephano! O peer! O worthy
Stephano! look, what a wardrobe here is for thee.
Cal. Let it alone, thou fool; it is but trash.
Trin. O, ho, monster; we know what belongs
to a frippery.—O king Stephano!
Ste. Put off that gown, Trinculo; by this hand,
I'll have that gown.
Trin. Thy grace shall have it.　　　[*mean,*
Cal. The dropsy drown this fool! what do you
To dote thus on such luggage? Let's along,
And do the murder first: if he awake,
From toe to crown he'll fill our skins with
　　　　pinches;
Make us strange stuff.

Ste. Be you quiet, monster.—Mistress line, is
not this my jerkin? Now is the jerkin under
the line: now, jerkin, you are like to lose your
hair, and prove a bald jerkin.
Trin. Do, do: We steal by line and level, ain't
like your grace.
Ste. I thank thee for that jest: here's a garment for't: wit shall not go unrewarded while
I am king of this country: *Steal by line and
level,* is an excellent pass of pate; there's another garment for't.
Trin. Monster, come, put some lime upon
your fingers, and away with the rest.　　[*time,*
Cal. I will have none on't: we shall lose our
And all be turned to barnacles, or to apes
With foreheads villanous low.
Ste. Monster, lay to your fingers; help to bear
this away where my hogshead of wine is, or I'll
turn you out of my kingdom: go to, carry this.
Trin. And this.
Ste. Ay, and this.

A noise of hunters heard. Enter divers Spirits,
in shape of hounds, and hunt them about.
PROSPERO *and* ARIEL *setting them on.*

Pro. Hey, *Mountain,* hey!
Ari. Silver! there it goes, *Silver!*　　　[*hark!*
Pro. Fury, Fury! there, *Tyrant,* there! hark,
　　　[CAL., STE., *and* TRIN. *are driven out.*
Go, charge my goblins that they grind their joints
With dry convulsions; shorten up their sinews
With aged cramps; and more pinch-spotted make
Than pard or cat o' mountain.　　　　[*them,*
Ari.　　　　　　　　Hark, they roar.
Pro. Let them be hunted soundly: At this hour
Lie at my mercy all mine enemies:
Shortly shall all my labours end, and thou
Shalt have the air at freedom: for a little
Follow, and do me service.　　　　[*Exeunt.*

ACT V.

SCENE I.—*Before the Cell of* PROSPERO.

Enter PROSPERO *in his magic robes; and* ARIEL.

Pro. Now does my project gather to a head:
My charms crack not; my spirits obey; and time
Goes upright with his carriage. How's the day?
Ari. On the sixth hour; at which time, my
You said our work should cease.　　　[*lord,*
Pro.　　　　　　　　I did say so,
When first I raised the tempest. Say, my spirit,
How fares the king and 's followers?
Ari.　　　　　　　Confin'd together
In the same fashion as you gave in charge;
Just as you left them, sir; all prisoners
In the lime-grove which weather-fends your cell;
They cannot budge till your release. The king,
His brother, and yours, abide all three distracted;
And the remainder mourning over them,
Brimful of sorrow and dismay; but chiefly
Him you termed, sir, *The good old lord Gonzalo;*
His tears run down his beard, like winter's drops
From eaves of reeds: your charm so strongly
　　　　works them,

That if you now beheld them, your affections
Would become tender.
Pro.   Dost thou think so, spirit?
Ari. Mine would, sir, were I human.
Pro.   And mine shall.
Hast thou, which art but air, a touch, a feeling
Of their afflictions? and shall not myself
One of their kind, that relish all as sharply
Passion as they, be kindlier moved than thou art?
Though with their high wrongs I am struck to
                  the quick,
Yet, with my nobler reason, 'gainst my fury
Do I take part: the rarer action is
In virtue than in vengeance: they being pentient,
The sole drift of my purpose doth extend
Not a frown further. Go, release them, Ariel;
My charms I'll break, their senses I'll restore,
And they shall be themselves.
Ari.   I'll fetch them, sir. [*Exit.*
Pro. Ye elves of hills, brooks, standing lakes,
                  and groves;
And ye that on the sands with printless foot
Do chase the ebbing Neptune, and do fly him
When he comes back; you demi-puppets that
By moonshine do the green sour ringlets make,
Whereof the ewe not bites; and you whose pastime
Is to make midnight mushrooms, that rejoice
To hear the solemn curfew; by whose aid,—
Weak masters though ye be,—I have bedimm'd
The noontide sun, call'd forth the mutinous
                  winds,
And 'twixt the green sea and the azured vault
Set roaring war: to the dread rattling thunder
Have I given fire, and rifted Jove's stout oak
With his own bolt: the strong-based promontory
Have I made shake: and by the spurs pluck'd up
The pine and cedar: graves, at my command,
Have waked their sleepers, oped, and let them
                  forth
By my so potent art. But this rough magic
I here abjure: and, when I have required
Some heavenly music,—which even now I do,—
To work mine end upon their senses, that
This airy charm is for, I'll break my staff,
Bury it certain fathoms in the earth,
And deeper than did ever plummet sound
I'll drown my book.   [*Solemn music.*

Re-enter ARIEL: *after him* ALONSO, *with a frantic
     gesture, attended by* GONZALO; SEBASTIAN *and*
     ANTONIO *in like manner, attended by* ADRIAN
     and FRANCISCO: *they all enter the circle which*
     PROSPERO *had made, and there stand charmed;
     which* PROSPERO *observing, speaks.*

A solemn air, and the best comforter
To an unsettled fancy, cure thy brains, [stand,
Now useless, boil'd within thy skull! There
For you are spell-stopp'd.—
Holy Gonzalo, honourable man,
Mine eyes, even sociable to the show of thine,
Fall fellowly drops.—The charm dissolves apace;
And as the morning steals upon the night,
Melting the darkness, so their rising senses
Begin to chase the ignorant fumes that mantle

Their clearer reason.—O good Gonzalo,
My true preserver, and a loyal sir
To him thou follow'st; I will pay thy graces
Home, both in word and deed.—Most cruelly
Didst thou, Alonso, use me and my daughter:
Thy brother was a furtherer in the act;—
Thou 'rt pinch'd for't now, Sebastian, flesh and
                  blood.—
You brother mine, that entertain ambition,
Expell'd remorse and nature; who, with Sebas-
                  tian,—   [strong,—
Whose inward pinches therefore are most
Would here have kill'd your king; I do forgive
                  thee,   [standing
Unnatural though thou art.—Their under-
Begins to swell; and the approaching tide
Will shortly fill the reasonable shore
That now lies foul and muddy. Not one of them
That yet looks on me, or would know me.—Ariel,
Fetch me the hat and rapier in my cell;
                  [*Exit* ARIEL.
I will discase me, and myself present
As I was sometime Milan: quickly, spirit;
Thou shalt ere long be free.

*ARIEL re-enters, singing, and helps to attire
     PROSPERO.*

Ari. Where the bee sucks, there suck I;
     In the cowslip's bell I lie:
     There I couch when owls do cry.
     On the bat's back I do fly
     After summer merrily:
     Merrily, merrily shall I live now,
     Under the blossom that hangs on the bough.

Pro. Why, that's my dainty Ariel: I shall miss
                  thee;
But yet thou shalt have freedom: so, so, so.—
To the king's ship, invisible as thou art:
There shalt thou find the mariners asleep
Under the hatches; the master and the boatswain
Being awake, enforce them to this place;
And presently, I pr'ythee.
Ari. I drink the air before me, and return
Or e'er your pulse twice beat.   [*Exit* ARIEL.
Gon. All torment, trouble, wonder, and amaze-
                  ment
Inhabits here. Some heavenly power guide us
Out of this fearful country!
Pro.   Behold, sir king,
The wronged Duke of Milan, Prospero:
For more assurance that a living prince
Does now speak to thee, I embrace thy body;
And to thee and thy company I bid
A hearty welcome.
Alon.   Whether thou beest he or no,
Or some enchanted trifle to abuse me,
As late I have been, I not know: thy pulse
Beats, as of flesh and blood; and, since I saw
                  thee,
The affliction of my mind amends, with which,
I fear, a madness held me: this must crave,—
An if this be at all,—a most strange story.
Thy dukedom I resign; and do entreat
Thou pardon me my wrongs.—But how should
                  Prospero

Be living and be here?
Pro.   First, noble friend,
Let me embrace thine age, whose honour cannot
Be measured or confined.
Gon.   Whether this be
Or be not, I'll not swear.
Pro.   You do yet taste
Some subtilties o' the isle, that will not let you
Believe things certain.—Welcome, my friends,
         all:—   [*Aside to* SEB. *and* ANT.
But you, my brace of lords, were I so minded,
I here could pluck his highness' frown upon you,
And justify you traitors; at this time
I'll tell no tales.
Seb. The devil speaks in him.   [*Aside.*
Pro.   No:——
For you, most wicked sir, whom to call brother
Would even infect my mouth, I do forgive
Thy rankest fault,—all of them; and require
My dukedom of thee, which, perforce, I know
Thou must restore.
Alon.   If thou beest Prospero,
Give us particulars of thy preservation:
How thou hast met us here, who three hours since
Were wreck'd upon this shore; where I have
         lost—
How sharp the point of this remembrance is!—
My dear son Ferdinand.
Pro.   I am woe for 't, sir.
Alon. Irreparable is the loss; and patience
Says it is past her cure.
Pro.   I rather think
You have not sought her help; of whose soft grace
For the like loss I have her sovereign aid,
And rest myself content.
Alon.   You the like loss?
Pro. As great to me as late; and, supportable
To make the dear loss, have I means much weaker
Than you may call to confort you; for I
Have lost my daughter.
Alon.   A daughter!
O heavens, that they were living both in Naples,
The king and queen there! that they were, I wish
Myself were mudded in that oozy bed
Where my son lies. When did you lose your
         daughter?   [lords
Pro. In this last tempest. I perceive these
At this encounter do so much admire
That they devour their reason, and scarce think
Their eyes do offices of truth, their words
Are natural breath: but, howsoe'er you have
Been justled from your senses, know for certain
That I am Prospero, and that very duke
Which was thrust forth of Milan; who most
         strangely   [landed,
Upon this shore, where you were wreck'd, was
To be the lord on 't. No more yet of this;
For 'tis a chronicle of day by day,
Not a relation for a breakfast, nor
Befitting this first meeting. Welcome, sir;
This cell's my court: here have I few attendants,
And subjects none abroad: pray you, look in.
My dukedom since you have given me again,
I will requite you with as good a thing:

At least bring forth a wonder, to content ye
As much as me my dukedom.

The entrance of the Cell opens, and discovers
    FERDINAND *and* MIRANDA *playing at chess.*
Mira. Sweet lord, you play me false.
Fer.   No, my dearest love,
I would not for the world.
Mira. Yes, for a score of kingdoms you should
         wrangle,
And I would call it fair play.
Alon.   If this prove
A vision of the island, one dear son
Shall I twice lose.
Seb.   A most high miracle!
Fer. Though the seas threaten, they are merci-
         ful:
I have cursed them without cause.
                        [FERD. *kneels to* ALON.
Alon.   Now all the blessings
Of a glad father compass thee about!
Arise and say how thou cam'st here.
Mira.   O, wonder!
How many goodly creatures are there here!
How beauteous mankind is! O brave new world
That hath such people in 't!
Pro.   'Tis new to thee.
Alon. What is this maid, with whom thou wast
         at play?
Your eld'st acquaintance cannot be three hours:
Is she the goddess that hath sever'd us,
And brought us thus together?
Fer.   Sir, she's mortal;
But by immortal providence she's mine;
I chose her when I could not ask my father
For his advice, nor thought I had one: she
Is daughter to this famous Duke of Milan,
Of whom so often I have heard renown
But never saw before; of whom I have
Received a second life; and second father
This lady makes him to me.
Alon.   I am hers:
But O, how oddly will it sound that I
Must ask my child forgiveness!
Pro.   There, sir, stop;
Let us not burden our remembrances
With a heaviness that's gone.
Gon.   I have inly wept,
Or should have spoke ere this. Look down, you
         gods,
And on this couple drop a blessed crown;
For it is you that have chalk'd forth the way
Which brought us hither!
Alon.   I say, Amen, Gonzalo!
Gon. Was Milan thrust from Milan, that his
         issue,
Should become kings of Naples? O, rejoice
Beyond a common joy; and set it down
With gold on lasting pillars: in one voyage
Did Claribel her husband find at Tunis;
And Ferdinand, her brother, found a wife
Where he himself was lost; Prospero his duke-
In a poor isle; and all of us ourselves   [dom
When no man was his own.

Alon.   Give me your hands:
                                    [*To* FERD. *and* MIR.
Let grief and sorrow still embrace his heart
That doth not wish you joy!
Gon.   Be 't so! Amen!

Re-enter ARIEL, *with the* Master *and* Boatswain *amazedly following.*

O look, sir, look, sir; here are more of us!
I prophesied, if a gallows were on land,
This fellow could not drown. Now, blasphemy,
That swear'st grace o'erboard, not an oath on
        shore?
Hast thou no mouth by land? What is the news?
Boats. The best news is, that we have safely
        found
Our king and company: the next, our ship,—
Which, but three glasses since, we gave out split,
Is tight, and yare, and bravely rigg'd, as when
We first put out to sea.
Ari.   Sir, all this service ⎫
Have I done since I went.   ⎬ *Aside.*
Pro.   My tricksy spirit! ⎭
Alon. These are not natural events; they
        strengthen   [hither?
From strange to stranger:—Say, how came you
Boats. If I did think, sir, I were well awake,
I'd strive to tell you. We were dead of sleep,
And,—how, we know not,—all clapp'd under
        hatches,   [noises
Where, but even now, with strange and several
Of roaring, shrieking, howling, jingling chains,
And more diversity of sounds, all horrible,
We were awaked; straightway, at liberty:
Where we, in all her trim, freshly beheld
Our royal, good, and gallant ship; our master
Capering to eye her: on a trice, so please you,
Even in a dream, were we divided from them,
And were brought moping hither.
Ari.   Was 't well done? ⎫
Pro. Bravely, my diligence. Thou shalt ⎬ *Aside.*
        be free.   ⎭
Alon. This is as strange a maze as e'er men trod:
And there is in this business more than nature
Was ever conduct of: some oracle
Must rectify our knowledge.
Pro.   Sir, my liege,
Do not infest your mind with beating on
The strangeness of this business: at pick'd leisure,
Which shall be shortly, single I'll resolve you,—
Which to you shall seem probable,—of every
These happen'd accidents: till when, be cheerful,
And think of each thing well.—Come hither,
        spirit;   [*Aside.*
Set Caliban and his companions free.
Untie the spell. [*Exit* ARIEL.] How fares my
        gracious sir?
There are yet missing of your company
Some few odd lads that you remember not.

Re-enter ARIEL, *driving in* CALIBAN, STEPHANO,
and TRINCULO, *in their stolen apparel.*

Ste. Every man shift for all the rest, and let

no man take care for himself; for all is but for-
tune:—Coragio, bully-monster, coragio!
Trin. If these be true spies which I wear in
my head, here's a goodly sight.
Cal. O Setebos, these be brave spirits indeed!
How fine my master is! I am afraid
He will chastise me.
Seb.   Ha, ha;-
What things are these, my lord Antonio|
Will money buy them?
Ant. Very like; one of them
Is a plain fish, and, no doubt, marketable.
Pro. Mark but the badges of these men, my
        lords,   [knave,——
Then say if they be true.—This mis-shapen
His mother was a witch; and one so strong
That could control the moon, make flows and
        ebbs,
And deal in her command, without her power:
These three have robb'd me: and this demi-
        devil,—
For he's a bastard one,—had plotted with them
To take my life: two of these fellows you
Must know and own; this thing of darkness I
Acknowledge mine.
Cal.   I shall be pinch'd to death.
Alon. Is not this Stephano, my drunken butler?
Seb. He is drunk now: where had he wine?
Alon. And Trinculo is reeling ripe: where
        should they
Find this grand liquor that hath gilded them?—
How cam'st thou in this pickle?
Trin. I have been in such a pickle since I saw
you last that, I fear me, will never out of my
bones: I shall not fear fly-blowing.
Seb. Why, how now, Stephano?
Ste. O, touch me not; I am not Stephano, but
        a cramp.
Pro. You'd be king of the isle, sirrah!
Ste. I should have been a sore one then.
Alon. This is as strange a thing as e'er I
        look'd on.   [*Pointing to* CALIBAN.
Pro. He is as disproportioned in his manners
As in his shape.—Go, sirrah, to my cell;
Take with you your companions; as you look
To have my pardon, trim it handsomely.
Cal. Ay, that I will; and I'll be wise hereafter,
And seek for grace. What a thrice-double ass
Was I to take this drunkard for a god,
And worship this dull fool!
Pro.   Go to; away!
Alon. Hence, and bestow your luggage where
        you found it.
Seb. Or stole it, rather.
                    [*Exeunt* CAL., STE., *and* TRIN.
Pro. Sir, I invite your highness and your train
To my poor cell: where you shall take your rest
For this one night; which (part of it) I'll waste
With such discourse as, I not doubt, shall
        make it
Go quick away,—the story of my life,
And the particular accidents gone by
Since I came to this isle: and in the morn
I'll bring you to your ship, and so to Naples,

Where I have hope to see the nuptial
Of these our dear-belovèd solemniz'd;
And thence retire me to my Milan, where
Every third thought shall be my grave.
Alon.   I long
To hear the story of your life, which must
Take the ear strangely.
Pro.   I'll deliver all;
And promise you calm seas, auspicious gales,
And sail so expeditious, that shall catch
Your royal fleet afar off.—My Ariel,—chick,—
That is thy charge: then to the elements
Be free, and fare thou well!—[*Aside.*] Please
   you, draw near.   [*Exeunt.*

EPILOGUE.

SPOKEN BY PROSPERO.

Now my charms are all o'erthrown,
And what strength I have's mine own,—
Which is most faint: now 'tis true,
I must be here confined by you,
Or sent to Naples. Let me not,
Since I have my dukedom got,
And pardon'd the deceiver, dwell
In this bare island by your spell;
But release me from my bands
With the help of your good hands.
Gentle breath of yours my sails
Must fill, or else my project fails,
Which was to please. Now I want
Spirits to enforce, art to enchant;
And my ending is despair
Unless I be relieved by prayer;
Which pierces so, that it assaults
Mercy itself, and frees all faults.
As you from crimes would pardon'd be,
Let your indulgence set me free.

TWO GENTLEMEN OF VERONA

DRAMATIS PERSONÆ

DUKE OF MILAN, *Father to* SILVIA.
VALENTINE, } *Gentlemen of Verona.*
PROTEUS,
ANTONIO, *Father to* PROTEUS.
THURIO, *a foolish Rival to* VALENTINE.
EGLAMOUR, *Agent for* SILVIA *in her escape.*
SPEED, *a clownish Servant to* VALENTINE.
LAUNCE, *Servant to* PROTEUS.
PANTHINO, *Servant to* ANTONIO.

Host, *where* JULIA *lodges in Milan.*
Outlaws.

JULIA, *a lady of Verona, beloved by* PROTEUS.
SILVIA, *the Duke's daughter, beloved by* VALENTINE.
LUCETTA, *Waiting-woman to* JULIA.

Servants. Musicians.

SCENE.—*Sometimes in* VERONA; *sometimes in* MILAN; *and on the frontiers of* MANTUA.

ACT I.

SCENE I.—*An open place in* VERONA.

Enter VALENTINE *and* PROTEUS.

Val. Cease to persuade, my loving Proteus;
Home-keeping youth have ever homely wits;
Wer't not affection chains thy tender days
To the sweet glances of thy honour'd love,
I rather would entreat thy company
To see the wonders of the world abroad,
Than, living dully sluggardiz'd at home,
Wear out thy youth with shapeless idleness.
But since thou lov'st, love still, and thrive therein,
Even as I would, when I to love begin. [adieu!
Pro. Wilt thou be gone? Sweet Valentine,
Think on thy Proteus, when thou haply seest
Some rare noteworthy object in thy travel:
Wish me partaker in thy happiness
When thou dost meet good hap: and in thy
      danger,
If ever danger do environ thee,
Commend thy grievance to my holy prayers,
For I will be thy beadsman, Valentine.
Val. And on a love-book pray for my success.
Pro. Upon some book I love I'll pray for thee.
Val. That's on some shallow story of deep love,
How young Leander cross'd the Hellespont.
Pro. That's a deep story of a deeper love;
For he was more than over shoes in love.
Val. 'Tis true; for you are over boots in love,
And yet you never swam the Hellespont.
Pro. Over the boots! nay, give me not the
      boots.
Val. No, I will not, for it boots thee not.
Pro.   What?
Val. To be in love, where scorn is bought with
      groans;
Coy looks with heart-sore sighs; one fading
      moment's mirth
With twenty watchful, weary, tedious nights:
If haply won, perhaps a hapless gain;
If lost, why then a grievous labour won;
However, but a folly bought with wit,

Or else a wit by folly vanquishèd.   [fool.
Pro. So, by your circumstance, you call me
Val. So, by your circumstance, I fear you'll
      prove.
Pro. 'Tis love you cavil at; I am not Love.
Val. Love is your master, for he masters you:
And he that is so yokèd by a fool,
Methinks should not be chronicled for wise.
Pro. Yet writers say, As in the sweetest bud
The eating canker dwells, so eating love
Inhabits in the finest wits of all.
Val. And writers say, As the most forward bud
Is eaten by the canker ere it blow,
Even so by love the young and tender wit
Is turn'd to folly; blasting in the bud,
Losing his verdure even in the prime,
And all the fair effects of future hopes.
But wherefore waste I time to counsel thee
That art a votary to fond desire?
Once more adieu: my father at the road
Expects my coming, there to see me shipp'd.
Pro. And thither will I bring thee, Valentine.
Val. Sweet Proteus, no; now let us take our
      leave.
At Milan let me hear from thee by letters
Of thy success in love, and what news else
Betideth here in absence of thy friend;
And I likewise will visit thee with mine.
Pro. All happiness bechance to thee in Milan!
Val. As much to you at home! and so farewell.
                              [*Exit* VALENTINE.
Pro. He after honour hunts, I after love:
He leaves his friends to dignify them more;
I leave myself, my friends, and all for love.
Thou, Julia, thou hast metamorphos'd me;
Made me neglect my studies, lose my time,
War with good counsel, set the world at nought:
Made wit with musing weak, heart sick with
      thought.

Enter SPEED.

Speed. Sir Proteus, save you. Saw you my
      master?

Pro. But now he parted hence, to embark for
    Milan.
Speed. Twenty to one, then, he is shipp'd
    already;
And I have play'd the sheep in losing him.
Pro. Indeed a sheep doth very often stray
An if the shepherd be awhile away.
Speed. You conclude that my master is a
    shepherd, then, and I a sheep?
Pro. I do.
Speed. Why, then, my horns are his horns
    whether I wake or sleep.
Pro. A silly answer, and fitting well a sheep.
Speed. This proves me still a sheep.
Pro. True; and thy master a shepherd.
Speed. Nay; that I can deny by a circumstance.
Pro. It shall go hard but I'll prove it by another.
Speed. The shepherd seeks the sheep, and not
the sheep the shepherd; but I seek my master,
and my master seeks not me: therefore, I am
no sheep.
Pro. The sheep for fodder follow the shepherd,
the shepherd for food follows not the sheep;
thou for wages followest thy master, thy master for wages follows not thee: therefore, thou
art a sheep.
Speed. Such another proof will make me cry
baa.
Pro. But dost thou hear? gav'st thou my letter
to Julia?
Speed. Ay, sir; I, a lost mutton, gave your
letter to her, a laced mutton; and she, a laced
mutton, gave me, a lost mutton, nothing for
my labour!
Pro. Here's too small a pasture for such a store
of muttons.
Speed. If the ground be overcharged you were
best stick her?
Pro. Nay; in that you are astray: 'twere best
pound you.
Speed. Nay, sir; less than a pound shall serve
me for carrying your letter.
Pro. You mistake; I mean the pound, a pinfold.
Speed. From a pound to a pin? fold it over
    and over.   [your lover.
'Tis threefold too little for carrying a letter to
Pro. But what said she? did she nod?
Speed. [*Nodding.*] Ay.
Pro. Nod—Ay—why, that's noddy.
Speed. You mistook, sir; I say she did nod:
and you ask me if she did nod; and I say, Ay.
Pro. And that set together is—noddy.
Speed. Now you have taken the pains to set it
together, take it for your pains.
Pro. No, no; you shall have it for bearing the
letter.
Speed. Well, I perceive I must be fain to bear
with you.
Pro. Why, sir, how do you bear with me?
Speed. Marry, sir, the letter very orderly: hav-
ing nothing but the word noddy for my pains.
Pro. Beshrew me, but you have a quick wit.
Speed. And yet it cannot overtake your slow
purse.

Pro. Come, come; open the matter in brief:
what said she?
Speed. Open your purse, that the money and
the matter may be both at once delivered.
Pro. Well, sir, here is for your pains: what said
she?
Speed. Truly, sir, I think you'll hardly win her.
Pro. Why, couldst thou perceive so much from
her?
Speed. Sir, I could perceive nothing at all from
her; no, not so much as a ducat for delivering
your letter: and being so hard to me that
brought your mind, I fear she'll prove as hard
to you in telling her mind. Give her no token
but stones; for she's as hard as steel.
Pro. What! said she nothing?
Speed. No, not so much as—*Take this for thy
pains.* To testify your bounty, I thank you,
you have testern'd me; in requital whereof,
henceforth carry your letters yourself: and, sir,
I'll commend you to my master.   [wreck,
Pro. Go, go; begone, to save your ship from
Which cannot perish, having thee aboard,
Being destined to a drier death on shore.
I must go send some better messenger:
I fear my Julia would not deign my lines,
Receiving them from such a worthless post.
                      [*Exeunt.*

SCENE II.—*The same. Garden of* JULIA'S
             House.

Enter JULIA *and* LUCETTA.

Jul. But say, Lucetta, now we are alone,
Wouldst thou then counsel me to fall in love?
Luc. Ay, madam; so you stumble not unheed-
    fully.
Jul. Of all the fair resort of gentlemen
That every day with parle encounter me,
In thy opinion which is worthiest love?
Luc. Please you, repeat their names; I'll show
    my mind
According to my shallow simple skill.
Jul. What think'st thou of the fair Sir Egla-
    mour?
Luc. As of a knight well-spoken, neat, and fine;
But, were I you, he never should be mine.
Jul. What think'st thou of the rich Mercatio?
Luc. Well of his wealth; but of himself, so so.
Jul. What think'st thou of the gentle Proteus?
Luc. Lord, Lord! to see what folly reigns in us!
Jul. How now! what means this passion at his
    name?
Luc. Pardon, dear madam; 'tis a passing shame
That I, unworthy body as I am,
Should censure thus on lovely gentlemen.
Jul. Why not on Proteus, as of all the rest?
Luc. Then thus: of many good I think him best.
Jul. Your reason?
Luc. I have no other but a woman's reason;
think him so, because I think him so.
Jul. And wouldst thou have me cast my love
    on him?   [away.
Luc. Ay, if you thought your love not cast

Jul. Why, he of all the rest hath never moved
    me.   [loves ye.
Luc. Yet he of all the rest, I think, best
Jul. His little speaking shows his love but
    small.
Luc. Fire that is closest kept burns most of all.
Jul. They do not love that do not show their
    love.   [love.
Luc. O, they love least that let men know their
Jul. I would I knew his mind.
Luc. Peruse this paper, madam. [*Gives a letter.*
Jul. [*reads*] 'To Julia,'—Say, from whom?
Luc. That the contents will show.
Jul. Say, say; who gave it thee?
Luc. Sir Valentine's page; and sent, I think
    'from Proteus: [the way,
He would have given it you; but I, being in
Did in your name receive it; pardon the fault,
    I pray.
Jul. Now, by my modesty, a goodly broker!
Dare you presume to harbour wanton lines?
To whisper and conspire against my youth?
Now, trust me, 'tis an office of great worth,
And you an officer fit for the place.
There, take the paper; see it be return'd;
Or else return no more into my sight.
Luc. To plead for love deserves more fee than
Jul. Will you be gone?   [hate.
Luc.   That you may ruminate. [*Exit.*
Jul. And yet, I would I had o'erlook'd the
It were a shame to call her back again, [letter.
And pray her to a fault for which I chid her.
What fool is she, that knows I am a maid,
And would not force the letter to my view?
Since maids, in modesty, say *No* to that
Which they would have the profferer construe Ay.
Fie, fie! how wayward is this foolish love,
That, like a testy babe, will scratch the nurse,
And presently, all humbled, kiss the rod!
How churlishly I chid Lucetta hence,
When willingly I would have had her here!
How angrily I taught my brow to frown,
When inward joy enforced my heart to smile!
My penance is to call Lucetta back,
And ask remission for my folly past:—
What, ho! Lucetta?

Re-enter LUCETTA.

Luc.   What would your ladyship?
Jul. Is it near dinner time?
Luc.   I would it were;
That you might kill your stomach on your
And not upon your maid.   [meat,
Jul.   What is 't you took up
So gingerly?
Luc.   Nothing.
Jul.   Why didst thou stoop then?
Luc. To take a paper up that I let fall.
Jul. And is that paper nothing?
Luc.   Nothing concerning me.
Jul. Then let it lie for those that it concerns.
Luc. Madam, it will not lie where it concerns,
Unless it have a false interpreter.

Jul. Some love of yours hath writ to you in
    rhyme.
Luc. That I might sing it, madam, to a tune:
Give me a note: your ladyship can set.
Jul. As little by such toys as may be possible;
Best sing it to the tune of *Light o' love.*
Luc. It is too heavy for so light a tune.
Jul. Heavy! belike it hath some burden, then.
Luc. Ay; and melodious were it, would you
    sing it.
Jul. And why not you?
Luc.   I cannot reach so high.
Jul. Let's see your song.—How now, minion?
Luc. Keep tune there still, so you will sing it out:
And yet methinks I do not like this tune.
Jul. You do not?
Luc. No, madam; it is too sharp.
Jul. You, minion, are too saucy.
Luc. Nay, now you are too flat,
And mar the concord with too harsh a descant;
There wanteth but a mean to fill your song.
Jul. The mean is drown'd with your unruly
    base.
Luc. Indeed, I bid the base for Proteus. [me.
Jul. This babble shall not henceforth trouble
Here is a coil with protestation!—
                [*Tears the letter.*
Go, get you gone; and let the papers lie:
You would be fingering them, to anger me.
Luc. She makes it strange; but she would be
    best pleased
To be so anger'd with another letter.   [*Exit.*
Jul. Nay, would I were so anger'd with the
    same!
O hateful hands, to tear such loving words!
Injurious wasps! to feed on such sweet honey,
And kill the bees that yield it, with your stings!
I'll kiss each several paper for amends.
And here is writ—*kind Julia;*—unkind Julia!
As in revenge of thy ingratitude,
I throw thy name against the bruising stones,
Trampling contemptuously on thy disdain.
Look, here is writ—*love-wounded Proteus:*—
Poor wounded name! my bosom, as a bed,
Shall lodge thee till thy wound be thoroughly
    heal'd;
And thus I search it with a sovereign kiss,
But twice or thrice was Proteus written down:
Be calm, good wind, blow not a word away
Till I have found each letter in the letter, [bear
Except mine own name; that some whirlwind
Unto a ragged, fearful, hanging rock,
And throw it thence into the raging sea!
Lo, here in one line is his name twice writ,—
Poor forlorn Proteus, passionate Proteus,
To the sweet Julia; that I'll tear away;
And yet I will not, sith so prettily
He couples it to his complaining names.
Thus will I fold them one upon another;
Now kiss, embrace, contend, do what you will.

Re-enter LUCETTA.

Luc. Madam, dinner's ready, and your father
Jul. Well, let us go.   [stays.

Luc. What! shall these papers lie like tell-tales
    here?
Jul. If you respect them, best to take them up.
Luc. Nay, I was taken up for laying them
    down;
Yet here they shall not lie for catching cold.
Jul. I see you have a month's mind to them.
Luc. Ay, madam, you may say what sights
    you see;
I see things too, although you judge I wink.
Jul. Come, come; wilt please you go? [*Exeunt.*

SCENE III.—*The same. A Room in*
ANTONIO'S *House.*

Enter ANTONIO *and* PANTHINO.

Ant. Tell me, Panthino, what sad talk was that
Wherewith my brother held you in the cloister?
Pan. 'Twas of his nephew Proteus, your son.
Ant. Why, what of him?
Pan.   He wonder'd that your lordship
Would suffer him to spend his youth at home,
While other men, of slender reputation,
Put forth their sons to seek preferment out:
Some to the wars, to try their fortune there;
Some to discover islands far away;
Some to the studious universities.
For any, or for all these exercises,
He said that Proteus, your son, was meet;
And did request me to impórtune you
To let him spend his time no more at home,
Which would be great impeachment to his age,
In having known no travel in his youth. [that
Ant. Nor need'st thou much impórtune me to
Whereon this month I have been hammering.
I have consider'd well his loss of time,
And how he cannot be a perfect man,
Not being tried and tutor'd in the world:
Experience is by industry achieved,
And perfected by the swift course of time:
Then tell me, whither were I best to send him?
Pan. I think your lordship is not ignorant
How his companion, youthful Valentine,
Attends the emperor in his royal court.
Ant. I know it well.   [him thither:
Pan. 'Twere good, I think, your lordship sent
There shall he practise tilts and tournaments,
Hear sweet discourse, converse with noblemen,
And be in eye of every exercise
Worthy his youth and nobleness of birth.
Ant. I like thy counsel; well hast thou advised:
And that thou may'st perceive how well I like
The execution of it shall make known;   [it,
Even with the speediest execution
I will dispatch him to the emperor's court.
Pan. To-morrow, may it please you, Don Al-
With other gentlemen of good esteem, [phonso,
Are journeying to salute the emperor,
And to commend their serviee to his will.
Ant. Good company; with them shall Proteus
    go.
And—in good time;—now will we break with
    him.

Enter PROTEUS.

Pro. Sweet love! sweet lines! sweet life!
Here is her hand, the agent of her heart;
Here is her oath for love, her honour's pawn:
O that our fathers would applaud our loves,
To seal our happiness with their consents!
O heavenly Julia!   [there?
Ant. How now? what letter are you reading
Pro. May 't please your lordship, 'tis a word or
Of commendation sent from Valentine,   [two
Deliver'd by a friend that came from him.
Ant. Lend me the letter; let me see what news.
Pro. There is no news, my lord; but that he
    writes.
How happily he lives, how well-beloved
And daily graced by the emperor;
Wishing me with him, partner of his fortune.
Ant. And how stand you affected to his wish?
Pro. As one relying on your lordship's will,
And not depending on his friendly wish.
Ant. My will is something sorted with his wish.
Muse not that I thus suddenly proceed;
For what I will, I will, and there an end.
I am resolved that thou shalt spend some time
With Valentinus in the emperor's court;
What maintenance he from his friends receives,
Like exhibition shalt thou have from me.
To-morrow be in readiness to go:
Excuse it not, for I am peremptory.
Pro. My lord, I cannot be so soon provided;
Please you, deliberate a day or two.   [thee:
Ant. Look, what thou want'st shall be sent after
No more of stay; to-morrow thou must go.—
Come on, Panthino; you shall be employ'd
To hasten on his expedition.
          [*Exeunt* ANT. *and* PAN.
Pro. Thus have I shunn'd the fire, for fear of
    burning,   [drown'd;
And drench'd me in the sea, where I am
I fear'd to show my father Julia's letter,
Lest he should take exceptions to my love;
And with the vantage of mine own excuse
Hath he excepted most against my love.
O, how this spring of love resembleth
The uncertain glory of an April day;
Which now shows all the beauty of the sun,
And by and by a cloud takes all away!

Re-enter PANTHINO.

Pan. Sir Proteus, your father calls for you;
He is in haste; therefore, I pray you, go.
Pro. Why, this it is! my heart accords thereto;
And yet a thousand times it answers no.
          [*Exeunt.*

ACT II.

SCENE I.—MILAN. *An apartment in the*
DUKE'S *Palace.*

Enter VALENTINE *and* SPEED.

Speed. [*Picking up a glove.*] Sir, your glove.
Val. Not mine; my gloves are on.
Speed. Why, then, this may be yours; for this
    is but one.

Val. Ha! let me see: ay, give it me; it's mine:—
Sweet ornament that decks a thing divine!
Ah, Silvia! Silvia!

Speed. [*Calling.*] Madam Silvia! Madam Silvia!

Val. How now, sirrah?

Speed. She is not within hearing, sir.

Val. Why, sir, who bade you call her?

Speed. Your worship, sir; or else I mistook.

Val. Well, you'll still be too forward.

Speed. And yet I was last chidden for being too
        slow.   [Silvia?

Val. Go to, sir; tell me; do you know Madam

Speed. She that your worship loves?

Val. Why, how know you that I am in love?

Speed. Marry, by these special marks: first you
have learned, like Sir Proteus, to wreath your
arms like a mal-content; to relish a love-song,
like a robin redbreast; to walk alone, like one
that had the pestilence; to sigh, like a school-
boy that had lost his A B C; to weep, like a
young wench that had buried her grandam; to
fast, like one that takes diet; to watch, like one
that fears robbing; to speak puling, like a beggar at Hallowmas. You were wont, when you
laughed, to crow like a cock; when you walked,
to walk like one of the lions; when you fasted,
it was presently after dinner; when you looked
sadly, it was for want of money: and now you
are metamorphosed with a mistress, that, when
I look on you, I can hardly think you my master.

Val. Are all these things perceived in me?

Speed. They are all perceived without you.

Val. Without me? they cannot.

Speed. Without you? nay, that's certain; for
without you were so simple, none else would:
but you are so without these follies, that these
follies are within you, and shine through you
like the water in a urinal; that not an eye that
sees you but is a physician to comment on your
malady.

Val. But tell me, dost thou know my lady
Silvia?

Speed. She that you gaze on so, as she sits at
supper?

Val. Hast thou observed that? even she I
        mean.

Speed. Why, sir, I know her not.

Val. Dost thou know her by my gazing on her,
and yet knowest her not?

Speed. Is she not hard favoured, sir?

Val. Not so fair, boy, as well favoured.

Speed. Sir, I know that well enough.

Val. What dost thou know?

Speed. That she is not so fair as (of you) well
favoured.

Val. I mean that her beauty is exquisite, but
her favour infinite.

Speed. That's because the one is painted and
the other out of all count.

Val. How painted? and how out of count?

Speed. Marry, sir, so painted, to make her fair,
that no man counts of her beauty.

Val. How esteemest thou me? I account of
her beauty.

Speed. You never saw her since she was deformed.

Val. How long hath she been deformed?

Speed. Ever since you loved her.

Val. I have loved her ever since I saw her;
and still I see her beautiful.

Speed. If you love her, you cannot see her.

Val. Why?

Speed. Because love is blind. O that you had
mine eyes; or your own eyes had the lights they
were wont to have when you chid at Sir Proteus for going ungartered!

Val. What should I see then?

Speed. Your own present folly and her passing
deformity; for he, being in love, could not see
to garter his hose; and you, being in love, can
not see to put on your hose.

Val. Belike, boy, then you are in love: for last
morning you could not see to wipe my shoes.

Speed. True, sir; I was in love with my bed;
I thank you, you swinged me for my love, which
makes me the bolder to chide you for yours.

Val. In conclusion, I stand affected to her.

Speed. I would you were set; so your affection
would cease.

Val. Last night she enjoined me to write some
lines to one she loves.

Speed. And have you?

Val. I have.

Speed. Are they not lamely writ?

Val. No, boy, but as well as I can do them;—
Peace; here she comes.

Speed. O excellent motion! O exceeding puppet!
now will he interpret to her.

Enter SILVIA.

Val. Madam and mistress, a thousand good-
morrows.

Speed. O, give you good even!—Here's a million of manners.   [*Aside.*

Sil. Sir Valentine and servant, to you two
thousand.

Speed. He should give her interest, and she
gives it him.   [*Aside.*

Val. As you enjoin'd me, I have writ your letter
Unto the secret nameless friend of yours;
Which I was much unwilling to proceed in
But for my duty to your ladyship.

Sil. I thank you, gentle servant; 'tis very
clerkly done.

Val. Now trust me, madam, it came hardly off;
For, being ignorant to whom it goes
I writ at random, very doubtfully.   [pains?

Sil. Perchance you think too much of so much

Val. No, madam; so it stead you, I will write,
Please you command, a thousand times as much:
And yet;—

Sil. A pretty period! Well, I guess the sequel;
And yet I will not name it:—and yet I care not;—
And yet take this again;—and yet I thank you;
Meaning henceforth to trouble you no more.

Speed. And yet you will; and yet another yet.
          [*Aside.*

Val. What means your ladyship? do you not like it?

Sil. Yes, yes; the lines are very quaintly writ: But since unwillingly, take them again; Nay, take them. [*Gives back the letter.*

Val. Madam, they are for you.

Sil. Ay, ay, you writ them, sir, at my request; But I will none of them; they are for you: I would have had them writ more movingly.

Val. Please you, I'll write your ladyship another. [*over;*

Sil. And when it's writ, for my sake read it And if it please you, so; if not, why, so.

Val. If it please me, madam! what then?

Sil. Why, if it please you, take it for your labour.

And so good morrow, servant. [*Exit* SILVIA.

Speed. O jest unseen, inscrutable, invisible, As a nose on a man's face, or a weather-cock on a steeple!

My master sues to her; and she hath taught her suitor,

He being her pupil, to become her tutor.

O excellent device! was there ever heard a better.

That my master, being scribe, to himself should write the letter?

Val. How now, sir? what are you reasoning with yourself?

Speed. Nay, I was rhyming: 'tis you that have the reason.

Val. To do what?

Speed. To be a spokesman from Madam Silvia.

Val. To whom?

Speed. To yourself: why, she woos you by a figure.

Val. What figure?

Speed. By a letter, I should say.

Val. Why, she hath not writ to me?

Speed. What need she when she hath made you write to yourself? Why, do you not perceive

Val. No, believe me. [*the jest?*

Speed. No believing you indeed, sir. But did you perceive her earnest?

Val. She gave me none except an angry word.

Speed. Why, she hath given you a letter.

Val. That's the letter I writ to her friend.

Speed. And that letter hath she deliver'd, and there an end.

Val. I would it were no worse.

Speed. I'll warrant you 'tis as well.

For often you have writ to her; and she, in modesty,

Or else for want of idle time, could not again reply;

Or fearing else some messenger that might her mind discover,

Herself hath taught her love himself to write unto her lover.—

All this I speak in print, for in print I found it.— Why muse you, sir? 'tis dinner time.

Val. I have dined.

Speed. Ay, but hearken, sir; though the cameleon Love can feed on the air, I am one that am nourished by my victuals, and would fain have meat; O, be not like your mistress; be moved, be moved. [*Exeunt.*

SCENE II.—VERONA. *A Room in* JULIA'S *House.*

Enter PROTEUS *and* JULIA.

Pro. Have patience, gentle Julia.

Jul. I must, where is no remedy.

Pro. When possibly I can I will return.

Jul. If you turn not you will return the sooner: Keep this remembrance for thy Julia's sake. [*Giving a ring.*

Pro. Why, then, we'll make exchange; here, take you this.

Jul. And seal the bargain with a holy kiss.

Pro. Here is my hand for my true constancy; And when that hour o'erslips me in the day Wherein I sigh not, Julia, for thy sake, The next ensuing hour some foul mischance Torment me for my love's forgetfulness! My father stays my coming; answer not: The tide is now: nay, not thy tide of tears; That tide will stay me longer than I should: [*Exit* JULIA.

Julia, farewell.—What! gone without a word? Ay; so true love should do: it cannot speak; For truth hath better deeds than words to grace it.

Enter PANTHIO.

Pan. Sir Proteus, you are stay'd for.

Pro. Go; I come, I come:— Alas! this parting strikes poor lovers dumb. [*Exeunt.*

SCENE III.—*The same. A Street.*

Enter LAUNCE *leading a dog.*

Laun. Nay, 'twill be this hour ere I have done weeping; all the kind of the Launces have this very fault: I have received my proportion, like the prodigious son, and am going with Sir Proteus to the Imperial's court. I think Crab my dog be the sourest-natured dog that lives: my mother weeping, my father wailing, my sister crying, our maid howling, our cat wringing her hands, and all our house in a great perplexity; yet did not this cruel-hearted cur shed one tear: he is a stone, a very pebble stone, and has no more pity in him than a dog: a Jew would have wept to have seen our parting; why, my grandam having no eyes, look you, wept herself blind at my parting. Nay, I'll show you the manner of it: this shoe is my father,—no, this left shoe is my father;—no, no, this left shoe is my mother; nay, that cannot be so neither; yes, it is so, it is so; it hath the worser sole. This shoe with the hole in it is my mother, and this my father. A vengeance on 't! there 'tis. Now, sir, this staff is my sister; for, look you, she is as white as a lily and as small as a wand; this hat is Nan our maid; I am the dog:—no, the dog is himself, and I am the dog,—O, the dog is me, and I am myself; ay, so, so. Now come I to my father; *Father, your blessing;*—now should not the shoe speak a word for weeping; now should I kiss my father; well, he weeps on:—now come I to my mother (O, that she could speak now!) like a wood woman;—well, I kiss her:—why there 'tis; here's my mother's breath up and down; now come I to my sister; mark the moan she makes: now the dog all this while sheds not a tear, nor speaks a word; but see how I lay the dust with my tears.

Enter PANTHINO.

Pan. Launce, away, away aboard; thy master is shipped, and thou art to post after with oars. What's the matter! why weep'st thou, man? Away, ass; you will lose the tide if you tarry any longer.

Laun. It is no matter if the tied were lost; for it is the unkindest tied that ever man tied.

Pan. What's the unkindest tide?   [dog.

Laun. Why, he that's tied here: Crab, my

Pan. Tut, man; I mean thou'lt lose the flood: and, in losing the flood, lose thy voyage; and, in losing thy voyage, lose thy master; and in losing thy master, lose thy service; and, in losing thy service,—Why dost thou stop my mouth?

Laun. For fear thou shouldst lose thy tongue.

Pan. Where should I lose my tongue?

Laun. In thy tale.

Pan. In thy tail?

Laun. Lose the tide, and the voyage, and the master, and the service? The tide! Why, man, if the river were dry, I am able to fill it with my tears; if the wind were down, I could drive the boat with my sighs.

Pan. Come, come away, man; I was sent to call thee.

Laun. Sir, call me what thou darest.

Pan. Wilt thou go?

Laun. Well, I will go.   [*Exeunt.*

SCENE IV.—MILAN. *An Apartment in the* DUKE'S *Palace.*

Enter VALENTINE, SILVIA, THURIO, *and* SPEED.

Sil. Servant—

Val. Mistress?

Speed. Master, Sir Thurio frowns on you.

Val. Ay, boy, it's for love.

Speed. Not of you.

Val. Of my mistress, then.

Speed. 'Twere good you knocked him.

Sil. Servant, you are sad.

Val. Indeed, madam, I seem so.

Thu. Seem you that you are not?

Val. Haply I do.

Thu. So do counterfeits.

Val. So do you.

Thu. What seem I that I am not?

Val. Wise.

Thu. What instance of the contrary?

Val. Your folly.

Thu. And how quote you my folly?

Val. I quote it in your jerkin.

Thu. My jerkin is a doublet.

Val. Well, then, I'll double your folly.

Thu. How?

Sil. What, angry, Sir Thurio? do you change colour?

Val. Give him leave, madam: he is a kind of cameleon.

Thu. That hath more mind to feed on your blood than live in your air.

Val. You have said, sir.

Thu. Ay, sir, and done too, for this time.

Val. I know it well, sir; you always end ere you begin.   [quickly shot off.

Sil. A fine volley of words, gentlemen, and

Val. 'Tis indeed, madam; we thank the giver.

Sil. Who is that, servant?

Val. Yourself, sweet lady; for you gave the fire. Sir Thurio borrows his wit from your ladyship's looks, and spends what he borrows kindly in your company.

Thu. Sir, if you spend word for word with me, I shall make your wit bankrupt.

Val. I know it well, sir; you have an exchequer of words, and, I think, no other treasure to give your followers; for it appears by their bare liveries that they live by your bare words.

Sil. No more, gentlemen, no more; here comes my father.

Enter DUKE.

Duke. Now, daughter Silvia, you are hard beset. Sir Valentine, your father's in good health: What say you to a letter from your friends Of much good news?

Val.   My lord, I will be thankful To any happy messenger from thence.

Duke. Know you Don Antonio, your country- man?

Val. Ay, my good lord; I know the gentleman To be of worth, and worthy estimation, And not without desert so well reputed.

Duke. Hath he not a son?

Val. Ay, my good lord; a son that well deserves The honour and regard of such a father.

Duke. You know him well?

Val. I know him as myself; for from our infancy We have conversed and spent our hours together: And though myself have been an idle truant, Omitting the sweet benefit of time To clothe mine age with angel-like perfection, Yet hath Sir Proteus—for that's his name— Made use and fair advantage of his days; His years but young, but his experience old; His head unmellow'd, but his judgment ripe; And, in a word,—for far behind his worth Come all the praises that I now bestow,— He is complete in feature and in mind, With all good grace to grace a gentleman.

Duke. Beshrew me, sir, but if he make this He is as worthy for an empress' love   [good, As meet to be an emperor's counsellor. Well, sir; this gentleman is come to me, With commendation from great potentates;

And here he means to spend his time awhile:
I think 'tis no unwelcome news to you.   [he.
Val. Should I have wished a thing it had been
Duke. Welcome him, then, according to his
      worth;
Silvia, I speak to you; and you, Sir Thurio:—
For Valentine, I need not 'cite him to it:
I'll send him hither to you presently.
                [*Exit* DUKE.
Val. This is the gentleman I told your ladyship
Had come along with me, but that his mistress
Did hold his eyes lock'd in her crystal looks.
Sil. Belike that now she hath enfranchised
Upon some other pawn for fealty.   [them
Val. Nay, sure, I think she holds them pris-
    oners still.   [blind,
Sil. Nay, then, he should be blind; and, being
How could he see his way to seek out you?
Val. Why, lady, love hath twenty pair of eyes.
Thu. They say that love hath not an eye at all.
Val. To see such lovers, Thurio, as yourself;
Upon a homely object love can wink.

Enter PROTEUS.

Sil. Have done, have done; here comes the
      gentleman.   [seech you
Val. Welcome, dear Proteus!—Mistress, I be-
Confirm his welcome with some special favour
Sil. His worth is warrant for his welcome
      hither,
If this be he you oft have wish'd to hear from.
Val. Mistress, it is: sweet lady, entertain him
To be my fellow-servant to your ladyship.
Sil. Too low a mistress for so high a servant.
Pro. Not so, sweet lady; but too mean a servant
To have a look of such a worthy mistress.
Val. Leave off discourse of disability:—
Sweet lady, entertain him for your servant.
Pro. My duty will I boast of, nothing else.
Sil. And duty never yet did want his meed.
Servant, you are welcome to a worthless mistress.
Pro. I'll die on him that says so but yourself.
Sil. That you are welcome?
Pro.   No; that you are worthless.

Enter Servant.

Ser. Madam, my lord your father would speak
      with you.
Sil. I'll wait upon his pleasure. [*Exit* Servant.
      Come, Sir Thurio,
Go with me.—Once more, new servant, welcome.
I'll leave you to confer of home affairs;
When you have done we look to hear from you.
Pro. We'll both attend upon your ladyship.
      [*Exeunt* SIL., THU., *and* SPEED.
Val. Now, tell me, how do all from whence
      you came?   [much commended.
Pro. Your friends are well, and have them
Val. And how do yours?
Pro.   I left them all in health.
Val. How does your lady? and how thrives
      your love?
Pro. My tales of love were wont to weary you;
I know you joy not in a love-discourse.

Val. Ay, Proteus; but that life is alter'd now:
I have done penance for contemning love;
Whose high imperious thoughts have punish'd
With bitter fasts, with penitential groans, [me
With nightly tears, and daily heart-sore sighs;
For, in revenge of my contempt of love,
Love hath chased sleep from my enthralled eyes,
And made them watchers of mine own heart's
      sorrow.
O, gentle Proteus, love's a mighty lord;
And hath so humbled me, as I confess,
There is no woe to his correction,
Nor, to his service, no such joy on earth!
Now no discourse, except it be of love;
Now can I break my fast, dine, sup, and sleep,
Upon the very naked name of love.
Pro. Enough; I read your fortune in your eye:
Was this the idol that you worship so?
Val. Even she; and is she not a heavenly saint?
Pro. No; but she is an earthly paragon.
Val. Call her divine.
Pro.   I will not flatter her.
Val. O, flatter me; for love delights in praises.
Pro. When I was sick you gave me bitter pills,
And I must minister the like to you.
Val. Then speak the truth by her; if not divine,
Yet let her be a principality,
Sovereign to all the creatures on the earth.
Pro. Except my mistress.
Val.   Sweet, except not any;
Except thou wilt except against my love.
Pro. Have I not reason to prefer mine own?
Val. And I will help thee to prefer her too:
She shall be dignified with this high honour—
To bear my lady's train, lest the base earth
Should from her vesture chance to steal a kiss,
And, of so great a favour growing proud,
Disdain to root the summer-swelling flower,
And make rough winter everlastingly.
Pro. Why, Valentine, what braggardism is this?
Val. Pardon me, Proteus: all I can is nothing
To her whose worth makes other worthies
She is alone.   [nothing;
Pro.   Then let her alone.   [own;
Val. Not for the world; why, man, she is mine
And I as rich in having such a jewel
As twenty seas, if all their sand were pearl,
The water nectar, and the rocks pure gold.
Forgive me that I do not dream on thee
Because thou seest me dote upon my love.
My foolish rival, that her father likes
Only for his possessions are so huge,
Is gone with her along; and I must after,
For love, thou know'st is full of jealousy.
Pro. But she loves you?
Val.   Ay, we are betroth'd:
Nay, more; our marriage hour,
With all the cunning manner of our flight,
Determined of: how I must climb her window,
The ladder made of cords; and all the means
Plotted and 'greed on for my happiness.
Good Proteus, go with me to my chamber,
In these affairs to aid me with thy counsel.
Pro. Go on before; I shall inquire you forth:

I must unto the road to disembark
Some necessaries that I needs must use;
And then I'll presently attend you.
Val. Will you make haste?
Pro. I will.— 　　　　　　　　　　[*Exit* VAL.
Even as one heat another heat expels,
Or as one nail by strength drives out another,
So the remembrance of my former love
Is by a newer object quite forgotten.
Is it mine eye, or Valentinus' praise,
Her true perfection, or my false transgression,
That makes me, reasonless, to reason thus?
She's fair; and so is Julia that I love,—
That I did love, for now my love is thaw'd;
Which like a waxen image 'gainst a fire
Bears no impression of the thing it was.
Methinks my zeal to Valentine is cold,
And that I love him not as I was wont:
O! but I love his lady too, too much;
And that's the reason I love him so little.
How shall I dote on her with more advice,
That thus without advice begin to love her?
'Tis but her picture I have yet beheld,
And that hath dazzled my reason's light;
But when I look on her perfections,
There is no reason but I shall be blind.
If I can check my erring love, I will:
If not, to compass her I'll use my skill.　[*Exit.*

SCENE V.—*The same. A Street.*

Enter SPEED *and* LAUNCE.

Speed. Launce! by mine honesty, welcome to Milan.
Laun. Forswear not thyself, sweet youth; for I am not welcome. I reckon this always—that a man is never undone till he be hanged; nor never welcome to a place till some certain shot be paid and the hostess say, welcome.
Speed. Come on, you madcap; I'll to the ale-house with you presently; where, for one shot of fivepence, thou shalt have five thousand welcomes. But, sirrah, how did thy master part with Madam Julia?
Laun. Marry, after they closed in earnest they parted very fairly in jest.
Speed. But shall she marry him?
Laun. No.
Speed. How, then? shall he marry her?
Laun. No; neither.
Speed. What! are they broken?
Laun. No; they are both as whole as a fish.
Speed. Why, then, how stands the matter with them?
Laun. Marry, thus; when it stands well with him it stands well with her.
Speed. What an ass art thou? I understand thee not.
Laun. What a block art thou, that thou canst not! My staff understands me.
Speed. What thou say'st?
Laun. Ay, and what I do, too; look thee, I'll but lean, and my staff understands me.

Speed. It stands under thee, indeed.　　[one.
Laun. Why, stand under and understand is all
Speed. But tell me true, will't be a match?
Laun. Ask my dog: if he say ay, it will; if he say no, it will; if he shake his tail and say nothing, it will.
Speed. The conclusion is, then, that it will.
Laun. Thou shalt never get such a secret from me but by a parable.
Speed. 'Tis well that I get it so. But, Launce, how say'st thou—that my master is become a notable lover?
Laun. I never knew him otherwise.
Speed. Than how?
Laun. A notable lubber as thou reportest him to be.
Speed. Why, thou whoreson ass, thou mistakest me.
Laun. Why, fool, I meant not thee, I meant thy master.
Speed. I tell thee, my master is become a hot lover.
Laun. Why, I tell thee I care not though he burn himself in love. If thou wilt go with me to the ale-house, so; if not, thou art an Hebrew, a Jew, and not worth the name of a Christian.
Speed. Why?
Laun. Because thou hast not so much charity in thee as to go to the ale with a Christian. Wilt thou go?
Speed. At thy service.　　　　　　[*Exeunt*

SCENE VI.—*The same. An Apartment in the Palace.*

Enter PROTEUS.

Pro. To leave my Julia, shall I be forsworn;
To love fair Silvia shall I be forsworn;
To wrong my friend, I shall be much forsworn;
And even that power which gave me first my oath
Provokes me to this threefold perjury.
Love bade me swear, and love bids me forswear:
O sweet-suggesting love, if thou hast sinn'd,
Teach me, thy tempted subject, to excuse it.
At first I did adore a twinkling star,
But now I worship a celestial sun.
Unheedful vows may heedfully be broken;
And he wants wit that wants resolved will
To learn his wit to exchange the bad for better.—
Fie, fie, unreverend tongue! to call her bad,
Whose sovereignty so oft thou hast preferr'd
With twenty thousand soul-confirming oaths.
I cannot leave to love, and yet I do;
But there I leave to love where I should love.
Julia I lose, and Valentine I lose:
If I keep them, I needs must lose myself;
If I lose them, thus find I by their loss,
For Valentine, myself; for Julia, Silvia.
I to myself am dearer than a friend:
For love is still more precious in itself: [fair!—
And Silvia—witness heaven, that made her
Shows Julia but a swarthy Ethiope.
I will forget that Julia is alive,
Rememb'ring that my love to her is dead;

And Valentine I'll hold an enemy,
Aiming at Silvia 'as a sweeter friend.
I cannot now prove constant to myself
Without some treachery used to Valentine:—
This night he meaneth with a corded ladder
To climb celestial Silvia's chamber-window—
Myself in counsel, his competitor:
Now presently I'il give her father notice
Of their disguising and pretended flight;
Who, all enraged, will banish Valentine;
For Thurio, he intends, shall wed his daughter:
But, Valentine being gone, I'll quickly cross,
By some sly trick, blunt Thurio's dull proceeding.
Love, lend me wings to make my purpose swift,
As thou has lent me wit to plot this drift! [*Exit*

Scene VII.—Verona. *A Room in Julia's House.*

Enter Julia *and* Lucetta.

Jul. Counsel, Lucetta! gentle girl, assist me!
And, even in kind love, I do conjure thee,—
Who art the table wherein all my thoughts
Are visibly character'd and engraved,—
To lesson me; and tell me some good mean,
How, with my honour, I may undertake
A journey to my loving Proteus.
Luc. Alas! the way is wearisome and long.
Jul. A true-devoted pilgrim is not weary
To measure kingdoms with his feeble steps;
Much less shall she that hath love's wings to fly,
And when the flight is made to one so dear,
Of such divine perfection, as Sir Proteus.
Luc. Better forbear till Proteus make return.
Jul. O, know'st thou not his looks are my
          soul's food?
Pity the dearth that I have pined in
By longing for that food so long a time.
Didst thou but know the inly touch of love,
Thou wouldst as soon go kindle fire with snow
As seek to quench the fire of love with words.
Luc. I do not seek to quench your love's hot
But qualify the fire's extreme rage,   [fire;
Lest it should burn above the bounds of reason.
Jul. The more thou damm'st it up, the more
          it burns;
The current that with gentle murmur glides,
Thou know'st, being stopp'd, impatiently doth
          rage;
But when his fair course is not hindered,
He makes sweet music with the enamell'd stones,
Giving a gentle kiss to every sedge
He overtaketh in his pilgrimage;
And so by many winding nooks he strays,
With willing sport, to the wild ocean.
Then let me go, and hinder not my course:
I'll be as patient as a gentle stream,
And make a pastime of each weary step,
Till the last step have brought me to my love;
And there I'll rest as, after much turmoil,
A blessed soul doth in Elysium.
Luc. But in what habit will you go along?
Jul. Not like a woman; for I would prevent
The loose encounters of lascivious men;

Gentle Lucetta, fit me with such weeds
As may beseem some well-reputed page   [hair.
Luc. Why, then, your ladyship must cut your
Jul. No, girl; I'll knit it up in silken strings,
With twenty odd-conceited true-love knots:
To be fantastic may become a youth
Of greater time than I shall show to be.
Luc. What fashion, madam, shall I make your
          breeches?   [lord,
Jul. That fits as well as—"Tell me, good my
What compass will you wear your farthingale?"
Why. even that fashion thou best lik'st, Lucetta.
Luc. You must needs have them with a cod-
          piece, madam.
Jul. Out, out, Lucetta! that will be ill-favour'd.
Luc. A round hose, madam, now's not worth
          a. pin,
Unless you have a cod-piece to stick pins on.
Jul. Lucetta, as thou lov'st me, let me have
What thou think'st meet, and is most mannerly:
But tell me, wench, how will the world repute me
For undertaking so unstaid a journey?   [me
I fear me it will make me scandaliz'd.   [not.
Luc. If you think so, then stay at home, and go
Jul. Nay, that I will not.
Luc. Then never dream on infamy, but go.
If Proteus like your journey when you come,
No matter who's displeas'd when you are gone:
I fear me he will scarce be pleased withal.
Jul. That is the least, Lucetta, of my fear:
A thousand oaths, an ocean of his tears,
And instances as infinite of love,
Warrant me welcome to my Proteus.
Luc. All these are servants to deceitful men.
Jul. Base men, that use them to so base effect!
But truer stars did govern Proteus' birth:
His words are bonds, his oaths are oracles;
His love sincere, his thoughts immaculate;
His tears pure messengers sent from his heart;
His heart as far from fraud as heaven from earth.
Luc. Pray heaven he prove so when you come
          to him!   [wrong,
Jul. Now, as thou lov'st me, do him not that
To bear a hard opinion ot his truth;
Only deserve my love by loving him,
And presently go with me to my chamber,
To take a note of what I stand in need of
To furnish me upon my longing journey.
All that is mine I leave at thy dispose,
My goods, my lands, my reputation;
Only, in lieu thereof, dispatch me hence:
Come, answer not, but to it presently:
I am impatient of my tarriance.   [*Exeunt.*

ACT III.

Scene I.—Milan. *An Ante-room in the Duke's Palace.*

Enter Duke, Thurio, *and* Proteus.

Duke. Sir Thurio, give us leave, I pray, awhile;
We have some secrets to confer about.
                              [*Exit* Thurio.
Now, tell me, Proteus, what's your will with
          me?

Pro. My gracious lord, that which I would dis-
　　　cover,
The law of friendship bids me to conceal;
But, when I call to mind your gracious favours
Done to me, undeserving as I am,
My duty pricks me on to utter that　　　[me.
Which else no worldly good should draw from
Know, worthy prince, Sir Valentine, my friend,
This night intends to steal away your daughter;
Myself am one made privy to the plot.
I know you have determined to bestow her
On Thurio, whom your gentle daughter hates;
And should she thus be stolen away from you,
It would be much vexation to your age.
Thus, for my duty's sake, I rather chose
To cross my friend in his intended drift,
Than, by concealing it, heap on your head
A pack of sorrows, which would press you down,
Being unprevented, to your timeless grave.
Duke. Proteus, I thank thee for thine honest
　　　care;
Which to requite, command me while I live.
This love of theirs myself have often seen,
Haply when they have judged me fast asleep;
And oftentimes have purposed to forbid
Sir Valentine her company and my court:
But, fearing lest my jealous aim might err,
And so, unworthily, disgrace the man,—
A rashness that I ever yet have shunn'd,—
I gave him gentle looks; thereby to find
That which thyself hast now disclos'd to me.
And, that thou may'st perceive my fear of this,
Knowing that tender youth is soon suggested,
I nightly lodge her in an upper tower,
The key whereof myself have ever kept;
And thence she cannot be conveyed away.
Pro. Know, noble lord, they have devised a
　　　mean
How he her chamber-window will ascend,
And with a corded ladder fetch her down;
For which the youthful lover now is gone,
And this way comes he with it presently;
Where, if it please you, you may intercept him.
But, good my lord, do it so cunningly,
That my discovery be not aimed at;
For love of you, not hate unto my friend,
Hath made me publisher of this pretence.
Duke. Upon mine honour, he shall never know
That I had any light from thee of this.
Pro. Adieu, my lord; Sir Valentine is coming.
　　　　　　　　　　　　　　　　[*Exit.*

Enter VALENTINE.

Duke. Sir Valentine, whither away so fast?
Val. Please it your grace, there is a messenger
That stays to bear my letters to my friends,
And I am going to deliver them.
Duke. Be they of much import?
Val. The tenor of them doth but signify
My health and happy being at your court.
Duke. Nay, then, no matter; stay with me
　　　awhile;
I am to break with thee of some affairs
That touch me near, wherein thou must be secret.

'Tis not unknown to thee that I have sought
To match my friend, Sir Thurio, to my daughter.
Val. I know it well, my lord; and, sure, the
　　　match　　　　　　　　　　　　[man
Were rich and honourable; besides, the gentle-
Is full of virtue, bounty, worth, and qualities
Beseeming such a wife as your fair daughter:
Cannot your grace win her to fancy him?
Duke. No, trust me; she is peevish, sullen, fro-
　　　ward,
Proud, disobedient, stubborn, lacking duty;
Neither regarding that she is my child
Nor fearing me as if I were her father:
And, may I say to thee, this pride of hers,
Upon advice, hath drawn my love from her;
And, where I thought the remnant of mine age
Should have been cherished by her child-like
　　　duty,
I am now full resolved to take a wife,
And turn her out to who will take her in:
Then let her beauty be her wedding-dower;
For me and my possession she esteems not.
Val. What would your grace have me to do in
　　　this?
Duke. There is a lady, sir, in Milan, here,
Whom I affect; but she is nice, and coy,
And nought esteems my aged eloquence:
Now, therefore, would I have thee to my tutor,—
For long agone I have forgot to court:
Besides, the fashion of the time is chang'd;—
How and which way I may bestow myself
To be regarded in her sun-bright eye.
Val. Win her with gifts, if she respect not words;
Dumb jewels often, in their silent kind,
More than quick words do move a woman's mind.
Duke. But she did scorn a present that I sent
　　　her.　　　　　　　　　　　　　[tents her:
Val. A woman sometimes scorns what best con-
Send her another; never give her o'er;
For scorn at first makes after-love the more.
If she do frown, 'tis not in hate of you,
But rather to beget more love in you:
If she do chide, 'tis not to have you gone;
For why, the fools are mad if left alone.
Take no repulse whatever she doth say:
For, *get you gone,* she doth not mean *away:*
Flatter and praise, commend, extol their graces;
Though ne'er so black, say they have angels'
　　　faces.
That man that hath a tongue, I say, is no man,
If with his tongue he cannot win a woman.
Duke. But she I mean is promised by her friends
Unto a youthful gentleman of worth;
And kept severely from resort of men,
That no man hath access by day to her.
Val. Why, then, I would resort to her by night.
Duke. Ay, but the doors be lock'd, and keys
　　　kept safe,
That no man hath recourse to her by night.
Val. What lets but one may enter at her win-
　　　dow?　　　　　　　　　　　　[ground;
Duke. Her chamber is aloft, far from the
And built so shelving, that one cannot climb it
Without apparent hazard of his life.

Val. Why, then, a ladder, quaintly made of cords,
To cast up with a pair of anchoring hooks
Would serve to scale another Hero's tower,
So bold Leander would adventure it.
Duke. Now, as thou art a gentleman of blood,
Advise me where I may have such a ladder.
Val. When would you use it? pray, sir, tell me that.
Duke. This very night; for love is like a child,
That longs for everything that he can come by.
Val. By seven o'clock I'll get you such a ladder.
Duke. But, hark thee; I will go to her alone;
How shall I best convey the ladder thither?
Val. It will be light, my lord, that you may bear it.
Under a cloak that is of any length.   [turn.
Duke. A cloak as long as thine will serve the
Val. Ay, my good lord.
Duke. Then let me see thy cloak:
I'll get me one of such another length.   [lord.
Val. Why, any cloak will serve the turn, my
Duke. How shall I fashion me to wear a cloak?—
I pray thee, let me feel thy cloak upon me.—
What letter is this same? What's here?—*To Silvia?*
And here an engine fit for my proceeding!
I'll be so bold to break the seal for once. [*Reads.*
My thoughts do harbour with my Silvia nightly;
  And slaves they are to me, that send them flying.
O, could their master come and go as lightly,
  Himself would lodge where senseless they are lying.
My herald thoughts in thy pure bosom rest them,
  While I, their king, that thither them importune,
Do curse the grace that with such grace hath bless'd them,
  Because myself do want my servants' fortune:
I curse myself, for they are sent by me,
That they should harbour where their lord should be.
What's here?
Silvia, this night I will enfranchise thee:
'Tis so; and here's the ladder for the purpose.
Why, Phaeton,—for thou art Merops' son,—
Wilt thou aspire to guide the heavenly car,
And with thy daring folly burn the world?
Wilt thou reach stars because they shine on thee?
Go, base intruder! over-weening slave!
Bestow thy fawning smiles on equal mates;
And think my patience, more than thy desert,
Is privilege for thy departure hence:
Thank me for this, more than for all the favours
Which, all too much, I have bestow'd on thee.
But if thou linger in my territories
Longer than swiftest expedition
Will give thee time to leave our royal court,
By heaven, my wrath shall far exceed the love
I ever bore my daughter or thyself.
Begone, I will not hear thy vain excuse,
But, as thou lov'st thy life, make speed from hence.   [*Exit* DUKE.

Val. And why not death, rather than living torment?
To die is to be banish'd from myself;
And Silvia is myself: banish'd from her
Is self from self: a deadly banishment!
What light is light if Silvia be not seen?
What joy is joy if Silvia be not by?
Unless it be to think that she is by,
And feed upon the shadow of perfection.
Except I be by Silvia in the night
There is no music in the nightingale;
Unless I look on Silvia in the day
There is no day for me to look upon:
She is my essence; and I leave to be,
If I be not by her fair influence
Foster'd, illumined, cherish'd, kept alive.
I fly not death to fly his deadly doom:
Tarry I here I but attend on death;
But fly I hence I fly away from life.

Enter PROTEUS *and* LAUNCE.

Pro. Run, boy, run, run, and seek him out.
Laun. So-ho! so-ho!
Pro. What seest thou?
Laun. Him we go to find: there's not a hair on's head but 'tis a Valentine.
Pro. Valentine?
Val. No.
Pro. Who then? his spirit?
Val. Neither.
Pro. What then?
Val. Nothing.
Laun. Can nothing speak? master, shall I strike?
Pro. Whom wouldst thou strike?
Laun. Nothing.
Pro. Villain, forbear.   [you,—
Laun. Why, sir, I'll strike nothing: I pray
Pro. Sirrah, I say, forbear: Friend Valentine, a word.   [good news
Val. My ears are stopp'd, and cannot hear
So much of bad already hath possess'd them.
Pro. Then in dumb silence will I bury mine,
For they are harsh, untuneable, and bad.
Val. Is Silvia dead?
Pro. No, Valentine.
Val. No Valentine, indeed, for sacred Silvia!—
Hath she forsworn me?
Pro. No, Valentine.   [me!—
Val. No Valentine, if Silvia have forsworn
What is your news?
Laun. Sir, there's a proclamation that you are vanish'd.   [news;
Pro. That thou art banished; O, that's the
From hence, from Silvia, and from me thy friend.
Val. O, I have fed upon this woe already,
And now excess of it will make me surfeit.
Doth Silvia know that I am banished?
Pro. Ay, ay; and she hath offer'd to the doom,—
Which unreversed, stands in effectual force,—
A sea of melting pearl, which some call tears:
Those at her father's churlish feet she tender'd,
With them, upon her knees, her humble self;
Wringing her hands, whose whiteness so became them,

As if but now they waxed pale for woe:
But neither bended knees, pure hands held up,
Sad sighs, deep groans, nor silver-shedding tears,
Could penetrate her uncompassionate sire;
But Valentine, if he be ta'en, must die.
Besides, her intercession chafed him so,
When she for thy repeal was suppliant,
That to close prison he commanded her,
With many bitter threats of 'biding there.
Val. No more; unless the next word that thou speak'st
Have some malignant power upon my life:
If so, I pray thee, breathe it in mine ear,
As ending anthem of my endless dolour. [help,
Pro. Cease to lament for that thou canst not
And study help for that which thou lament'st.
Time is the nurse and breeder of all good.
Here if thou stay thou canst not see thy love;
Besides, thy staying will abridge thy life.
Hope is a lover's staff; walk hence with that,
And manage it against despairing thoughts.
Thy letters may be here though thou art hence:
Which, being writ to me, shall be deliver'd
Even in the milk-white bosom of thy love.
The time now serves not to expostulate:
Come, I'll convey thee through the city gate;
And, ere I part with thee, confer at large
Of all that may concern thy love affairs:
As thou lov'st Silvia, though not for thyself,
Regard thy danger, and along with me.
Val. I pray thee, Launce, an if thou seest my boy,   [gate.
Bid him make haste and meet me at the north
Pro. Go, sirrah, find him out. Come, Valentine.
Val. O my dear Silvia, hapless Valentine!
                          [*Exeunt* VAL. *and* PRO.
Laun. I am but a fool, look you; and yet I
have the wit to think my master is a kind of
knave: but that's all one if he be but one knave.
He lives not now that knows me to be in love:
yet I am in love; but a team of horse shall not
pluck that from me; nor who 'tis I love, and
yet 'tis a woman: but what woman I will not
tell myself; and yet 'tis a milkmaid; yet 'tis
not a maid, for she hath had gossips: yet 'tis a
maid, for she is her master's maid, and serves
for wages. She hath more qualities than a
water-spaniel,—which is much in a bare Christian. Here is the cat-log [*Pulling out a paper*]
of her conditions. Imprimis, *She can fetch and
carry.* Why, a horse can do no more: nay, a
horse cannot fetch, but only carry; therefore is
she better than a jade. Item, *She can milk;*
look you, a sweet virtue in a maid with clean
hands.

Enter SPEED.

Speed. How now, Signior Launce? what news
with your mastership?
Laun. With my master's ship? why, it is at sea.
Speed. Well, your old vice still; mistake the word.
What news, then, in your paper?   [heard'st.
Laun. The blackest news that ever thou

Speed. Why, man, how black?
Laun. Why, as black as ink.
Speed. Let me read them.   [read.
Laun. Fie on thee, jolthead; thou canst not
Speed. Thou liest, I can.
Laun. I will try thee: Tell me this: Who begot thee?
Speed. Marry, the son of my grandfather.
Laun. O illiterate loiterer! it was the son of
thy grandmother: this proves that thou canst
not read.
Speed. Come, fool, come: try me in thy paper.
Laun. There; and St. Nicholas be thy speed!
Speed. Imprimis, *She can milk.*
Laun. Ay, that she can.
Speed. Item, *She brews good ale.*
Laun. And thereof comes the proverb,—Bless-
ing of your heart, you brew good ale.
Speed. Item, *She can sew.*
Laun. That's as much as to say, can she so?
Speed. Item, *She can knit.*
Laun. What need a man care for a stock with
a wench, when she can knit him a stock.
Speed. Item, *She can wash and scour.*
Laun. A special virtue; for then she need not
be washed and scoured.
Speed. Item, *She can spin.*
Laun. Then may I set the world on wheels,
when she can spin for her living.
Speed. Item, *She hath many nameless virtues.*
Laun. That's as much as to say, bastard vir-
tues; that, indeed, know not their fathers, and
therefore have no names.
Speed. Here follow her vices.
Laun. Close at the heels of her virtues.
Speed. Item, *She is not to be kissed fasting, in
respect of her breath.*
Laun. Well, that fault may be mended with a
breakfast. Read on.
Speed. Item, *She hath a sweet mouth.*
Laun. That makes amends for her sour breath.
Speed. Item, *She doth talk in her sleep.*
Laun. It's no matter for that, so she sleep not
in her talk.
Speed. Item, *She is slow in words.*
Laun. O villain, that set this down among her
vices! To be slow in words is a woman's only
virtue: I pray thee, out with't; and place it
for her chief virtue.
Speed. Item, *She is proud.*
Laun. Out with that too; it was Eve's legacy,
and cannot be ta'en from her.
Speed. Item, *She hath no teeth.*
Laun. I care not for that neither, because I
love crusts.
Speed. Item, *She is curst.*
Laun. Well; the best is, she hath no teeth to
bite.
Speed. Item, *She will often praise her liquor.*
Laun. If her liquor be good, she shall: if she
will not, I will; for good things should be praised.
Speed. Item, *She is too liberal.*
Laun. Of her tongue she cannot; for that's
writ down she is slow of: of her purse she shall

not; for that I'll keep shut: now of another
thing she may; and that I cannot help. Well,
proceed.
Speed. Item, *She hath more hair than wit, and
more faults than hairs, and more wealth than
faults.*
Laun. Stop there; I'll have her: she was mine,
and not mine, twice or thrice in that last article. Rehearse that once more.
Speed. Item, *She hath more hair than wit,—*
Laun. More hair than wit,—it may be; I'll
prove it: The cover of the salt hides the salt,
and therefore it is more than the salt; the hair
that covers the wit is more than the wit; for
the greater hides the less. What's next?
Speed.—And more faults than hairs,—
Laun. That's monstrous: O, that that were out!
Speed.—And more wealth than faults.
Laun. Why, that word makes the faults gra-
cious. Well, I'll have her: and if it be a match,
as nothing is impossible.
Speed. What then?
Laun. Why, then will I tell thee,—that thy
master stays for thee at the north gate.
Speed. For me?
Laun. For thee? ay: who art thou? he hath
stay'd for a better man than thee.
Speed. And must I go to him?
Laun. Thou must run to him, for thou hast
stay'd so long that going will scarce serve the turn.
Speed. Why didst not tell me sooner? 'pox of
your love-letters!   [*Exit.*
Laun. Now will he be swinged for reading my
letter. An unmannerly slave that will thrust
himself into secrets!—I'll after, to rejoice in the
boy's correction.   [*Exit.*

SCENE II.—*The same. A Room in the
Duke's Palace.*

Enter Duke *and* Thurio; Proteus *behind.*

Duke. Sir Thurio, fear not but that she will
　　love you
Now Valentine is banish'd from her sight.
Thu. Since his exile she hath despised me most,
Forsworn my company and rail'd at me,
That I am desperate of obtaining her.
Duke. This weak impress of love is as a figure
Trenched in ice; which with an hour's heat
Dissolves to water and doth lose his form.
A little time will melt her frozen thoughts,
And worthless Valentine shall be forgot.—
How now, Sir Proteus? Is your countryman,
According to our proclamation, gone?
Pro. Gone, my good lord.
Duke. My daughter takes his going grievously.
Pro. A little time, my lord, will kill that grief.
Duke. So I believe; but Thurio thinks not so.—
Proteus, the good conceit I hold of thee,—
For thou hast shown some sign of good desert,—
Makes me the better to confer with thee.
Pro. Longer than I prove loyal to your grace,
Let me not live to look upon your grace.
Duke. Thou know'st, how willingly I would effect

The match between Sir Thurio and my daughter.
Pro. I do, my lord.
Duke. And also I think, thou art not ignorant
How she opposes her against my will.
Pro. She did, my lord, when Valentine was
　　here.
Duke. Ay, and perversely she persévers so.
What might we do to make the girl forget
The love of Valentine and love Sir Thurio?
Pro. The best way is to slander Valentine
With falsehood, cowardice, and poor descent;
Three things that women highly hold in hate.
Duke. Ay, but she'll think that it is spoke in
　　hate.
Pro. Ay, if his enemy deliver it:
Therefore it must, with circumstance, be spoken
by one whom she esteemeth as his friend. [him.
Duke. Then you must undertake to slander
Pro. And that, my lord, I shall be loth to do:
'Tis an ill office for a gentleman;
Especially against his very friend.   [tage him
Duke. Where your good word cannot advan-
Your slander never can endamage him;
Therefore, the office is indifferent,
Being entreated to it by your friend.   [it
Pro. You have prevail'd, my lord: if I can do it
By aught that I can speak in his dispraise,
She shall not long continue love to him.
But say this weed her love from Valentine,
It follows not that she will love Sir Thurio.
Thu. Therefore, as you unwind her love from
　　him,
Lest it should ravel, and be good to none,
You must provide to bottom it on me:
Which must be done by praising me as much
As you in worth dispraise Sir Valentine.
Duke. And, Proteus, we dare trust you in this
　　kind;
Because we know, on Valentine's report,
You are already love's firm votary,
And cannot soon revolt and change your mind.
Upon this warrant shall you have access
Where you with Silvia may confer at large;
For she is lumpish, heavy, melancholy,
And, for your friend's sake, will be glad of you;
Where you may temper her by your persuasion
To hate young Valentine and love my friend.
Pro. As much as I can do I will effect:—
But you, Sir Thurio, are not sharp enough;
You must lay lime to tangle her desires
By wailful sonnets, whose composed rhymes
Should be full fraught with serviceable vows.
Duke. Ay, much the force of heaven-bred poesy.
Pro. Say that upon the altar of her beauty
You sacrifice your tears, your sighs, your heart;
Write till your ink be dry; and with your tears
Moist it again; and frame some feeling line
That may discover such integrity:
For Orpheus' lute was strung with poets' sinews;
Whose golden touch could soften steel and
　　stones,
Make tigers tame and huge leviathans
Forsake unsounded deeps to dance on sands.
After your dire lamenting elegies,

Visit by night your lady's chamber-window
With some sweet concert: to their instruments
Tune a deploring dump; the night's dead silence
Will well become such sweet complaining griev-
    ance.
This, or else nothing, will inherit her.
Duke. This discipline shows thou hast been in
    love.   [tice:
Thu. And thy advice this night I'll put in prac-
Therefore, sweet Proteus, my direction-giver,
Let us into the city presently
To sort some gentlemen well skill'd in music:
I have a sonnet that will serve the turn
To give the onset to thy good advice.
Duke. About it, gentlemen.   [per;
Pro. We'll wait upon your grace till after sup-
And afterward determine our proceedings.
Duke. Even now about it; I will pardon you.
                                      [*Exeunt.*

ACT IV.

Scene I.—*A Forest near* Mantua.

Enter certain Outlaws.

1 Out. Fellows, stand fast; I see a passenger.
2 Out. If there be ten, shrink not, but down
    with 'em.

Enter Valentine *and* Speed.

3 Out. Stand, sir, and throw us that you have
    about you;
If not, we'll make you sit, and rifle you.
Speed. Sir, we are undone! these are the villains
That all the travellers do fear so much.
Val. My friends,—
1 Out. That's not so, sir; we are your enemies.
2 Out. Peace; we'll hear him.
3 Out. Ay, by my beard, will we;
For he's a proper man.   [lose;
Val. Then know that I have little wealth to
A man I am crossed with adversity;
My riches are these poor habiliments,
Of which if you should here disfurnish me,
You take the sum and substance that I have.
2 Out. Whither travel you?
Val. To Verona.
1 Out. Whence came you?
Val. From Milan.
3 Out. Have you long sojourn'd there?
Val. Some sixteen months; and longer might
    have stay'd
If crooked fortune had not thwarted me.
1 Out. What! were you banish'd thence?
Val. I was.
2 Out. For what offence?   [hearse;
Val. For that which now torments me to re-
I kill'd a man, whose death I much repent;
But yet I slew him manfully in fight,
Without false vantage or base treachery.
1 Out. Why, ne'er repent it, if it were done so.
But were you banish'd for so small a fault?
Val. I was, and held me glad of such a doom.
2 Out. Have you the tongues?   [happy;
Val. My youthful travel therein made me

Or else I often had been miserable.   [friar,
3 Out. By the bare scalp of Robin Hood's fat
This fellow were a king for our wild faction.
1 Out. We'll have him; sirs, a word.
Speed.   Master, be one of them;
It is an honourable kind of thievery.
Val. Peace, villain!   [to?
2 Out. Tell us this. Have you anything to take
Val. Nothing but my fortune.   [men;
3 Out. Know, then, that some of us are gentle-
Such as the fury of ungovern'd youth
Thrust from the company of lawful men:
Myself was from Verona banish'd
For practising to steal away a lady,
An heir, and near allied unto the duke.
2 Out. And I from Mantua, for a gentleman,
Whom, in my mood, I stabb'd unto the heart.
1 Out. And I for such like petty crimes as these.
But to the purpose,—for we cite our faults
That they may hold excused our lawless lives,—
And, partly, seeing you are beautified
With goodly shape, and by your own report
A linguist, and a man of such perfection
As we do in our quality much want;—
2 Out. Indeed, because you are a banish'd man,
Therefore, above the rest, we parley to you.
Are you content to be our general?
To make a virtue of necessity,
And live, as we do, in this wilderness?
3 Out. What say'st thou? wilt thou be of our
    consórt?
Say ay, and be the captain of us all:
We'll do thee homage, and be ruled by thee,
Love thee as our commander and our king.
1 Out. But if thou scorn our courtesy thou
    diest.   [offer'd.
2 Out. Thou shalt not live to brag what we have
Val. I take your offer, and will live with you,
Provided that you do no outrages
On silly women or poor passengers.
3 Out. No; we detest such vile base practices.
Come, go with us, we'll bring thee to our crews,
And show thee all the treasure we have got;
Which, with ourselves, all rest at thy dispose.
                                      [*Exeunt.*

Scene II.—Milan. *Court of the Palace.*

Enter Proteus.

Pro. Already have I been false to Valentine,
And now I must be as unjust to Thurio.
Under the colour of commending him
I have access my own love to prefer;
But Silvia is too fair, too true, too holy,
To be corrupted with my worthless gifts.
When I protest true loyalty to her
She twits me with my falsehood to my friend:
When to her beauty I commend my vows
She bids me think how I have been forsworn
In breaking faith with Julia whom I loved:
And, notwithstanding all her sudden quips,
The least whereof would quell a lover's hope,
Yet, spaniel-like, the more she spurns my love
The more it grows, and fawneth on her still.

But here comes Thurio: now must we to her
    window,
And give some evening music to her ear.

Enter THURIO *and Musicians.*

Thu. How now, Sir Proteus? are you crept be-
    fore us?
Pro. Ay, gentle Thurio; for you know that love
Will creep in service where it cannot go. [here.
Thu. Ay, but I hope, sir, that you love not
Pro. Sir, but I do; or else I would be hence.
Thu. Whom? Silvia?
Pro. Ay, Silvia—for your sake. [men,
Thu. I thank you for your own. Now, gentle-
Let's tune, and to it lustily awhile.

Enter HOST, *at a distance; and* JULIA, *in
boy's clothes.*

Host. Now, my young guest! methinks you're
allycholly; I pray you, why is it?
Jul. Marry, mine host, because I cannot be
    merry.
Host. Come, we'll have you merry: I'll bring
you where you shall hear music, and see the
gentleman that you ask'd for.
Jul. But shall I hear him speak?
Host. Ay, that you shall.
Jul. That will be music. [*Music plays.*
Host. Hark! Hark!
Jul. Is he among these?
Host. Ay; but peace, let's hear 'em.

SONG.

Who is Silvia? what is she,
    That all our swains commend her?
Holy, fair, and wise is she,
    The heavens such grace did lend her,
That she might admired be.

Is she kind as she is fair?
    For beauty lives with kindness:
Love doth to her eyes repair,
    To help him of his blindness;
And, being help'd, inhabits there.

Then to Silvia, let us sing,
    That Silvia is excelling;
She excels each mortal thing
    Upon the dull earth dwelling.
To her let us garlands bring.

Host. How now? are you sadder than you were
    before?
How do you, man! the music likes you not.
Jul. You mistake; the musician likes me not.
Host. Why, my pretty youth?
Jul. He plays false, father.
Host. How! out of tune on the strings?
Jul. Not so; but yet so false that he grieves
my very heart-strings.
Host. You have a quick ear.
Jul. Ay, I would I were deaf! it makes me
have a slow heart.
Host. I perceive you delight not in music.
Jul. Not a whit, when it jars so.
Host. Hark, what fine change is in the music.

Jul. Ay; that change is the spite.
Host. You would have them always play but
one thing? [thing.
Jul. I would always have one play but one
But, host, doth this Sir Proteus, that we talk
on, often resort unto this gentlewoman?
Host. I'll tell you what, Launce, his man, told
me he loved her out of all nick.
Jul. Where is Launce?
Host. Gone to seek his dog; which, tomorrow,
by his master's command, he must carry for a
present to his lady.
Jul. Peace! stand aside! the company parts.
Pro. Sir Thurio, fear not you! I will so plead
That you shall say my cunning drift excels.
Thu. Where meet we?
Pro. At Saint Gregory's well.
Thu. Farewell.

[*Exeunt* THURIO *and Musicians.*

SILVIA *appears above, at her window.*

Pro. Madam, good even to your ladyship.
Sil. I thank you for your music, gentlemen:
Who is that that spake? [truth,
Pro. One, lady, if you knew his pure heart's
You'd quickly learn to know him by his voice.
Sil. Sir Proteus, as I take it. [vant.
Pro. Sir Proteus, gentle lady, and your ser-
Sil. What is your will?
Pro.   That I may compass yours.
Sil. You have your wish; my will is even this,—
That presently you hie you home to bed,
Thou subtle, perjured, false, disloyal man!
Think'st thou I am so shallow, so conceitless,
To be seducèd by thy flattery,
That hast deceived so many with thy vows?
Return, return, and make thy love amends.
For me,—by this pale queen of night I swear
I am so far from granting thy request
That I despise thee for thy wrongful suit,
And by and by intend to chide myself
Even for this time I spend in talking to thee.
Pro. I grant, sweet love, that I did love a lady;
But she is dead.
Jul. 'Twere false if I should speak it;
For I am sure she is not buried. [*Aside.*
Sil. Say that she be; yet Valentine, thy friend,
Survives; to whom, thyself art witness,
I am betrothed. And art thou not ashamed
To wrong him with thy importúnacy?
Pro. I likewise hear that Valentine is dead.
Sil. And so suppose am I; for in his grave
Assure thyself my love is buried.
Pro. Sweet lady, let me rake it from the earth.
Sil. Go to thy lady's grave, and call hers thence;
Or, at the least, in hers sepulchre thine.
Jul. He heard not that. [*Aside.*
Pro. Madam, if your heart be so obdúrate,
Vouchsafe me yet your picture for my love;
The picture that is hanging in your chamber;
To that I'll speak, to that I'll sigh and weep:
For, since the substance of your perfect self
Is else devoted, I am but a shadow:
And to your shadow I will make true love.

Jul. If 'twere a substance, you would, sure, de-
    ceive it,
And make it but a shadow, as I am.   [*Aside.*
Sil. I am very loth to be your idol, sir;
But, since your falsehood shall become you well
To worship shadows and adore false shapes,
Send to me in the morning, and I'll send it:
And so, good rest.
Pro.   As wretches have o'er-night,
That wait for execution in the morn.
     [*Exeunt* PRO.; *and* SIL., *from above.*
Jul. Host, will you go?
Host. By my hallidom, I was fast asleep.
Jul. Pray you, where lies Sir Proteus?
Host. Marry, at my house. Trust me, I think
'tis almost day.
Jul. Not so; but it hath been the longest night
That e'er I watch'd, and the most heaviest.
                     [*Exeunt.*

SCENE III.—*The same.*

Enter EGLAMOUR.

Egl. This is the hour that Madam Silvia
Entreated me to call and know her mind;
There's some great matter she'd employ me
Madam, madam!   [*in.—*

SILVIA *appears above, at her window.*

Sil. Who calls?
Egl.   Your servant and your friend;
One that attends your ladyship's command.
Sil. Sir Eglamour, a thousand times good mor-
    row.
Egl. As many, worthy lady, to yourself.
According to your ladyship's impose,
I am thus early come to know what service
It is your pleasure to command me in.
Sil. O Eglamour, thou art a gentleman,—
Think not I flatter, for I swear I do not,—
Valiant, wise, remorseful, well accomplish'd.
Thou art not ignorant what dear good will
I bear unto the banish'd Valentine;
Nor how my father would enforce me marry
Vain Thurio, whom my very soul abhorr'd.
Thyself hast loved; and I have heard thee say
No grief did ever come so near thy heart
As when thy lady and thy true love died,
Upon whose grave thou vow'dst pure chastity.
Sir Eglamour, I would to Valentine,
To Mantua, where, I hear, he makes abode;
And, for the ways are dangerous to pass,
I do desire thy worthy company,
Upon whose faith and honour I repose.
Urge not my father's anger, Eglamour,
But think upon my grief, a lady's grief;
And on the justice of my flying hence.
To keep me from a most unholy match,
Which heaven and fortune still reward with
I do desire thee, even from a heart   [plagues.
As full of sorrows as the sea of sands,
To bear me company, and go with me:
If not, to hide what I have said to thee,
That I may venture to depart alone.
Egl. Madam, I pity much your grievances;

Which, since I know they virtuously are placed,
I give consent to go along with you;
Recking as little what betideth me
As much I wish all good befortune you.
When will you go?
Sil.   This evening coming.
Egl. Where shall I meet you?
Sil.   At Friar Patrick's cell,
Where I intend holy confession.
Egl. I will not fail your ladyship:
Good morrow, gentle lady.
Sil. Good morrow, kind Sir Eglamour.
                     [*Exeunt.*

SCENE IV.—*The same.*

Enter LAUNCE, *with his dog.*

Laun. When a man's servant shall play the
cur with him, look you, it goes hard: one that
I brought up of a puppy: one that I saved from
drowning, when three or four of his blind
brothers and sisters went to it! I have taught
him—even as one would say precisely, Thus I
would teach a dog. I was sent to deliver him
as a present to Mistress Silvia from my master;
and I came no sooner into the dining-chamber
but he steps me to her trencher and steals her
capon's leg. O, 'tis a foul thing when a cur
cannot keep himself in all companies! I would
have, as one should say, one that takes upon
him to be a dog indeed, to be, as it were, a dog
at all things. If I had not had more wit than
he, to take a fault upon me that he did, I think
verily he had been hang'd for 't; sure as I live
he had suffer'd for 't; you shall judge. He
thrusts me himself into the company of three
or four gentleman-like dogs under the duke's
table: he had not been there—bless the mark—
a pissing while, but all the chamber smelt him.
Out with the dog, says one; *What cur is that?*
says another; *Whip him out,* says a third;
Hang him up, says the duke. I, having been
acquainted with the smell before, knew it was
Crab; and goes me to the fellow that whips
the dogs: *Friend,* quoth I, *you mean to whip
the dog? Ay, marry do I,* quoth he. *You do him
the more wrong,* quoth I; *'twas I did the thing
you wot of.* He makes me no more ado, but
whips me out of the chamber. How many masters would do this for their servant? Nay, I'll
be sworn, I have sat in the stocks for puddings
he hath stolen, otherwise he had been executed: I have stood on the pillory for geese he
hath killed, otherwise he had suffer'd for 't:
thou thinkest not of this now!—Nay, I remember the trick you served me when I took my
leave of Madam Silvia; did not I bid thee still
mark me and do as I do? When didst thou see
me heave up my leg and make water against
a gentlewomen's farthingale? didst thou ever
see me do such a trick?

Enter PROTEUS *and* JULIA.

Pro. Sebastian is thy name? I like thee well,
And will employ thee in some service presently.

Jul. In what you please;—I will do what I can.
Pro. I hope thou wilt.—How now, you whore-
   son peasant?   [*To* LAUNCE.
Where have you been these two days loitering?
Laun. Marry, sir, I carried Mistress Silvia the
dog you bade me.
Pro. And what says she to my little jewel?
Laun. Marry, she says your dog was a cur;
and tells you currish thanks is good enough for
such a present.
Pro. But she received my dog?
Laun. No, indeed, she did not; here have I
brought him back again.
Pro. What! didst thou offer her this from me?
Laun. Ay, sir; the other squirrel was stolen
from me by the hangman's boys in the market-
place: and then I offer'd her mine own; who
is a dog as big as ten of yours, and therefore
the gift the greater.
Pro. Go, get thee hence and find my dog **again**,
Or ne'er return again into my sight.
Away, I say. Stay'st thou to vex me here?
A slave, that still an end turns me to shame.
        [*Exit* LAUNCE.
Sebastian, I have entertain'd thee,
Partly that I have need of such a youth
That can with some discretion do my business,
For 'tis no trusting to yond foolish lout;
But, chiefly, for thy face and thy behaviour,
Which—if my augury deceive me not—
Witness good bringing up, fortune, and truth:
Therefore, know thou, for this I entertain thee.
Go presently, and take this ring with thee,
Deliver it to Madam Silvia:
She loved me well deliver'd it to me.
Jul. It seems you loved not her, to leave her
   token:
She's dead, belike.
Pro.   Not so: I think she lives.
Jul. Alas!
Pro. Why dost thou cry, Alas!
Jul. I cannot choose but pity her.
Pro. Wherefore shouldst thou pity her?
Jul. Because, methinks, that she loved you as
   well
As you do love your lady Silvia:
She dreams on him that has forgot her love;
You dote on her that cares not for your love.
'Tis pity love should be so contrary;
And thinking on it makes me cry, Alas!
Pro. Well, give her that ring, and therewithal
This letter;—that's her chamber.—Tell my lady
I claim the promise for her heavenly picture.
Your message done, hie home unto my chamber,
Where thou shalt find me sad and solitary.
        [*Exit* PROTEUS.
Jul. How many women would do such a mes-
   sage?
Alas, poor Proteus! thou hast entertain'd
A fox to be the shepherd of thy lambs;
Alas, poor fool! why do I pity him
That with his very heart despiseth me?
Because he loves her, he despiseth me;
Because I love him, I must pity him.

This ring I gave him, when he parted from me,
To bind him to remember my good will:
And now am I—unhappy messenger—
To plead for that which I would not obtain;
To carry that which I would have refused;
To praise his faith, which I would have dispraised.
I am my master's true confirmèd love,
But cannot be true servant to my master
Unless I prove false traitor to myself.
Yet will I woo for him; but yet so coldly
As, heaven it knows, I would not have him speed.

Enter SILVIA, *attended*

Gentlewoman, good day! I pray you, be my mean
To bring me where to speak with Madam Silvia.
Sil. What would you with her if that I be she?
Jul. If you be she I do entreat your patience
To hear me speak the message I am sent on.
Sil. From whom?
Jul. From my master, Sir Proteus, madam.
Sil. Oh!—he sends you for a picture?
Jul. Ay, madam.
Sil. Ursula, bring my picture there.
       [*Picture brought.*
Go, give your master this: tell him from me,
One Julia, that his changing thoughts forget,
Would better fit his chamber than this shadow.
Jul. Madam, please you peruse this letter.
Pardon me, madam; I have unadvised
Delivered you a paper that I should not.
This is the letter to your ladyship.
Sil. I pray thee, let me look on that again.
Jul. It may not be; good madam, pardon me.
Sil. There, hold.
I will not look upon your master's lines:
I know they are stuff'd with protestations,
And full of new-found oaths; which he will break
As easily as I do tear his paper.
Jul. Madam, he sends your ladyship this ring.
Sil. The more shame for him that he sends it
   me;
For I have heard him say a thousand times
His Julia gave it him at his departure:
Though his false finger have profaned the ring,
Mine shall not do his Julia so much wrong.
Jul. She thanks you.
Sil. What say'st thou?
Jul. I thank you, madam, that you tender her:
Poor gentlewoman! my master wrongs her much.
Sil. Dost thou know her?
Jul. Almost as well as I do know myself:
To think upon her woes, I do protest,
That I have wept an hundred several times.
Sil. Belike she thinks that Proteus hath for-
   sook her.   [sorrow.
Jul. I think she doth, and that's her cause of
Sil. Is she not passing fair?
Jul. She hath been fairer, madam, than she is:
When she did think my master loved her well,
She, in my judgment, was as fair as you;
But since she did neglect her looking-glass,
And threw her sun-expelling mask away,
The air hath starv'd the roses in her cheeks,
And pinch'd the lily-tincture of her face,

That now she is become as black as I.
Sil. How tall was she?
Jul. About my stature: for at Pentecost,
When all our pageants of delight were play'd,
Our youth got me to play the woman's part,
And I was trimm'd in Madam Julia's gown;
Which serv'd me as fit, by all men's judgment,
As if the garment had been made for me:
Therefore, I know she is about my height.
And at that time I made her weep a-good,
For I did play a lamentable part;
Madam, 'twas Ariadne, passioning
For Theseus' perjury and unjust flight;
Which I so lively acted with my tears
That my poor mistress, moved therewithal,
W~pt bitterly; and would I might be dead
It I in thought felt not her very sorrow!
Sil. She is beholden to thee, gentle youth!—
Alas, poor lady! desolate and left!—
I weep myself, to think upon thy words.
Here, youth, there is my purse: I give thee this
For thy sweet mistress' sake, because thou
　　　　lov'st her.
Farewell.　　　　　　　[*Exit* SILVIA.
Jul. And she shall thank you for't if e'er you
　　　　know her.
A virtuous gentlewoman, mild and beautiful.
I hope my master's suit will be but cold,
Since she respects my mistress' love so much.
Alas, how love can trifle with itself!
Here is her picture. Let me see; I think,
If I had such a tire, this face of mine
Were full as lovely as is this of hers:
And yet the painter flatter'd her a little,
Unless I flatter with myself too much.
Her hair is auburn, mine is perfect yellow:
It that be all the difference in his love,
I'll get me such a colour'd periwig.
Her eyes are grey as glass; and so are mine:
Ay, but her forehead's low, and mine's as high.
What should it be that he respects in her
But I can make respective in myself,
If this fond love were not a blinded god?
Come, shadow, come, and take this shadow up,
For 'tis thy rival. O thou senseless form,
Thou shalt be worshipp'd, kiss'd, lov'd, and
　　　　ador'd;
And were there sense in his idolatry
My substance should be statue in thy stead.
I'll use thee kindly for thy mistress' sake,
That used me so; or else, by Jove I vow,
I should have scratch'd out your unseeing eyes,
To make my master out of love with thee.
　　　　　　　　　　　　　　　[*Exit.*

ACT V.

SCENE I.—*The same. An Abbey.*

Enter EGLAMOUR.

Egl. The sun begins to gild the western sky:
And now it is about the very hour
That Silvia at Patrick's cell should meet me.
She will not fail; for lovers break not hours,

Unless it be to come before their time;
So much they spur their expedition.

Enter SILVIA.

See where she comes: Lady, a happy evening!
Sil. Amen, amen! gc on, good Eglamour!
Out at the postern by the abbey wall;
I fear I am attended by some spies.
Egl. Fear not: the forest is not three leagues off!
If we recover that, we are sure enough.
　　　　　　　　　　　　　　　[*Exeunt.*

SCENE II.—*The same. An Apartment in the*
DUKE'S *Palace.*

Enter THURIO, PROTEUS, *and* JULIA.

Thu. Sir Proteus, what says Silvia to my suit?
Pro. O, sir, I find her milder than she was;
And yet she takes exceptions at your person.
Thu. What! that my leg is too long?
Pro. No; that it is too little.　　　　[rounder.
Thu. I'll wear a boot to make it somewhat
Pro. But love will not be spurr'd to what it
　　　　loaths.
Thu. What says she to my face?
Pro. She says it is a fair one.　　　　[black.
Thu. Nay, then, the wanton lies; my face is
Pro. But pearls are fair; and the old saying is,
Black men are pearls in beauteous ladies' eyes.
Jul. 'Tis true, such pearls as put out ladies'
　　　　eyes;
For I had rather wink than look on them.
　　　　　　　　　　　　　　　[*Aside.*
Thu. How likes she my discourse?
Pro. Ill when you talk of war.　　　　[peace?
Thu. But well when I discourse of love and
Jul. But better, indeed, when you hold your
　　　　peace.　　　　　　　　　[*Aside.*
Thu. What says she to my valour?
Pro. O, sir, she makes no doubt of that.
Jul. She needs not, when she knows it cow-
　　　　ardice.　　　　　　　　　[*Aside.*
Thu. What says she to my birth?
Pro. That you are well derived.
Jul. True; from a gentleman to a fool. [*Aside.*
Thu. Considers she my possessions?
Pro. O, ay, and pities them.
Thu. Wherefore?
Jul. That such an ass should owe them. [*Aside.*
Pro. That they are out by lease.
Jul. Here comes the Duke.

Enter DUKE.

Duke. How now, Sir Proteus? how now, Thurio?
Which of you saw Sir Eglamour of late?
Thu. Not I.
Pro.　　　　Nor I.
Duke.　　　　　　　Saw you my daughter?
Pro.　　　　　　　　　　　　Neither.
Duke. Why, then she's fled unto that peasant
　　　　Valentine;
And Eglamour is in her company.
'Tis true; for Friar Lawrence met them both
As he in penance wander'd through the forest:

Him he knew well, and guess'd that it was she;
But, being mask'd, he was not sure of it:
Besides, she did intend confession
At Patrick's cell this even; and there she was not:
These likelihoods confirm her flight from hence:
Therefore, I pray you, stand not to discourse,
But mount you presently; and meet with me
Upon the rising of the mountain-foot   [fled.
That leads towards Mantua, whither they are
Dispatch, sweet gentlemen, and follow me. [*Exit.*
Thu. Why, this it is to be a peevish girl,
That flies her fortune when it follows her:
I'll after; more to be revenged on Eglamour
Than for the love of reckless Silvia.   [*Exit.*
Pro. And I will follow, more for Silvia's love
Than hate of Eglamour that goes with her. [*Exit.*
Jul. And I will follow, more to cross that love
Than hate for Silvia, that is gone for love. [*Exit.*

SCENE III.—*Frontiers of* MANTUA. *The Forest.*

Enter SILVIA, *and* Outlaws.

1 *Out.* Come, come;
Be patient; we must bring you to our captain.
Sil. A thousand more mischances than this one
Have learn'd me how to brook this patiently.
2 *Out.* Come, bring her away.
1 *Out.* Where is the gentleman that was with
        her?
2 *Out.* Being nimble-footed, he hath outrun us,
But Moyses and Valerius follow him.
Go thou with her to the west end of the wood;
There is our captain: we'll follow him that's
The thicket is beset; he cannot 'scape.   [fled.
1 *Out.* Come, I must bring you to our captain's
        cave;
Fear not; he bears an honourable mind,
And will not use a woman lawlessly.
Sil. O Valentine, this I endure for thee.
                                        [*Exeunt.*

SCENE IV.—*Another part of the Forest.*

Enter VALENTINE.

Val. How use doth breed a habit in a man!
This shadowy desert, unfrequented woods,
I better brook than flourishing peopled towns:
Here can I sit alone, unseen of any,
And to the nightingale's complaining notes
Tune my distresses and record my woes.
O thou that dost inhabit in my breast,
Leave not the mansion so long tenantless,
Lest, growing ruinous, the building fall,
And leave no memory of what it was!
Repair me with thy presence, Silvia;
Thou gentle nymph, cherish thy forlorn swain!—
What halloing and what stir is this to-day!
These are my mates, that make their wills their
Have some unhappy passenger in chase: [law,
They love me well; yet I have much to do
To keep them from uncivil outrages.
Withdraw thee, Valentine; who's this comes
        here?   [*Steps aside.*

Enter PROTEUS, SILVIA, *and* JULIA.

Pro. Madam, this service I have done for
        you,—   [doth,—
Though you respect not aught your servant
To hazard life, and rescue you from him [love.
That would have forced your honour and your
Vouchsafe me, for my meed, but one fair look;
A smaller boon than this I cannot beg,
And less than this, I am sure, you cannot give.
Val. How like a dream is this I see and hear!
Love, lend me patience to forbear awhile.
                                        [*Aside.*
Sil. O miserable, unhappy that I am!
Pro. Unhappy were you, madam, ere I came;
But, by my coming, I have made you happy.
Sil. By thy approach thou makest me most
        unhappy.
Jul. And me, when he approacheth to your
        presence.   [*Aside.*
Sil. Had I been seized by a hungry lion,
I would have been a breakfast to the beast,
Rather than have false Proteus rescue me.
O, heaven be judge how I love Valentine,
Whose life's as tender to me as my soul;
And full as much,—for more there cannot be,—
I do detest false, perjured Proteus:
Therefore begone: solicit me no more.
Pro. What dangerous action, stood it next to
        death,
Would I not undergo for one calm look?
O, 'tis the curse in love, and still approved,
When women cannot love where they're be-
        loved.   [loved.
Sil. When Proteus cannot love where he's be-
Read over Julia's heart, thy first best love,
For whose dear sake thou didst then rend thy faith
Into a thousand oaths; and all those oaths
Descended into perjury, to love me.   [two,
Thou hast no faith left now, unless thou hadst
And that's far worse than none; better have none
Than plural faith, which is too much by one:
Thou counterfeit to thy true friend!
Pro.   In love,
Who respects friends?
Sil.   All men but Proteus.
Pro. Nay, if the gentle spirit of moving words
Can no way change you to a milder form,
I'll woo you like a soldier, at arms' end; [you.
And love you 'gainst the nature of love—force
Sil. O heaven!
Pro.   I'll force thee yield to my desire.
Val. Ruffian, let go that rude uncivil touch;
Thou friend of an ill fashion!
Pro.   Valentine!
Val. Thou common friend, that's without faith
        or love,—
For such is a friend now;—treacherous man!
Thou hast beguil'd my hopes; nought but mine
        eye
Could have persuaded me. Now I dare not say
I have one friend alive; thou wouldst disprove
        me.   [hand
Who should be trusted now, when one's right

Is perjured to the bosom? Proteus,
I am sorry I must never trust thee more,
But count the world a stranger for thy sake.
The private wound is deepest : O time, most curst!
'Mongst all foes, that a friend should be the worst.
Pro. My shame and guilt confound me.—
Forgive me, Valentine: if hearty sorrow
Be a sufficient ransom for offence,
I tender it here; I do as truly suffer
As e'er I did commit.
Val.   Then I am paid;
And once again I do receive thee honest.—
Who by repentance is not satisfied
Is nor of heaven nor earth; for these are pleased;
By penitence the Eternal's wrath's appeas'd:—
And, that my love may appear plain and free,
All that was mine in Silvia I give thee.
Jul. O, me, unhappy!   [*Faints.*
Pro. Look to the boy.   [the matter?
Val. Why, boy! why, wag! how now? what is
Look up; speak.
Jul.   O good sir, my master charged me
To deliver a ring to Madam Silvia;
Which, out of my neglect, was never done.
Pro. Where is that ring, boy?
Jul.   Here 'tis: this is it.
                                    [*Gives a ring.*
Pro. How! let me see:
Why, this is the ring I gave to Julia.
Jul. O, cry you mercy, sir I have mistook;
This is the ring you sent to Silvia.
                              [*Shows another ring.*
Pro. But how camest thou by this ring? at my
        depart
I gave this unto Julia.
Jul. And Julia herself did give it me;
And Julia herself hath brought it hither.
Pro. How! Julia!
Jul. Behold her that gave aim to all thy oaths,
And entertain'd them deeply in her heart:
How oft hast thou with perjury cleft the root?
O Proteus, let this habit make thee blush!
Be thou asham'd that I have took upon me
Such an immodest raiment; if shame live
In a disguise of love:
It is the lesser blot, modesty finds,   [minds.
Women to change their shapes, than men their
Pro. Than men their minds! 'tis true; O heaven!
        were man
But constant, he were perfect: that one error
Fills him with faults; makes him run through
        all th' sins:
Inconstancy falls off ere it begins:
What is in Silvia's face but I may spy
More fresh in Julia's with a constant eye?
Val. Come, come, a hand from either:
Let me be blest to make this happy close:
'Twere pity two such friends should be long foes.
Pro. Bear witness, Heaven, I have my wish
        for ever.
Jul. And I have mine.

Enter Outlaws, *with* DUKE *and* THURIO.
Out.   A prize, a prize, a prize!
Val. Forbear. I say; it is my lord the duke.
Your grace is welcome to a man disgrac'd,
Banished Valentine.
Duke.   Sir Valentine!
Thu. Yonder is Silvia; and Silvia's mine.
Val. Thurio, give back, or else embrace thy
        death;
Come not within the measure of my wrath:
Do not name Silvia thine; if once again,
Milan shall not behold thee. Here she stands,
Take but possession of her with a touch;—
I dare thee but to breathe upon my love.—
Thu. Sir Valentine, I care not for her, I;
I hold him but a fool that will endanger
His body for a girl that loves him not:
I claim her not, and therefore she is thine.
Duke. The more degenerate and base art thou,
To make such means for her as thou hast done,
And leave her on such slight conditions.—
Now, by the honour of my ancestry,
I do applaud thy spirit, Valentine,
And think thee worthy of an empress' love.
Know then, I here forget all former griefs,
Cancel all grudge, repeal thee home again.—
Plead a new state in thy unrivall'd merit,
To which I thus subscribe,—Sir Valentine,
Thou art a gentleman, and well derived;
Take thou thy Silvia, for thou hast deserv'd her.
Val. I thank your grace: the gift hath made
        me happy.
I now beseech you, for your daughter's sake,
To grant one boon that I shall ask of you.
Duke. I grant it for thine own, whate'er it be.
Val. These banish'd men, that I have kept
        withal,
Are men endued with worthy qualities;
Forgive them what they have committed here,
And let them be recall'd from their exile:
They are reform'd, civil, full of good,
And fit for great employment, worthy lord.
Duke. Thou hast prevail'd; I pardon them, and
        thee;
Dispose of them as thou know'st their deserts.
Come, let us go; we will include all jars
With triumphs, mirth, and rare solemnity.
Val. And, as we walk along, I dare be bold
With our discourse to make your grace to smile:
What think you of this page, my lord?
Duke. I think the boy hath grace in him; he
        blushes.   [boy.
Val. I warrant you, my lord; more grace than
Duke. What mean you by that saying?
Val. Please you, I'll tell you, as we pass along,
That you will wonder what hath fortuned.—
Come, Proteus: 'tis your penance, but to hear
The story of your loves discovered:
That done, our day of marriage shall be yours;
One feast, one house, one mutual happiness.
                                    [*Exeunt.*

MERRY WIVES OF WINDSOR

DRAMATIS PERSONÆ

SIR JOHN FALSTAFF.
FENTON.
SHALLOW, *a Country Justice.*
SLENDER, *Cousin to* SHALLOW.
MR. FORD, } *two Gentlemen dwelling at*
MR. PAGE, } *Windsor.*
WILLIAM PAGE, *a boy, Son to* MR. PAGE.
SIR HUGH EVANS, *a Welsh Parson.*
DR. CAIUS, *a French Physician.*
Host of the Garter Inn.
BARDOLPH, }
PISTOL, } *Followers of* FALSTAFF.
NYM, }

ROBIN, *Page to* FALSTAFF.
SIMPLE, *Servant to* SLENDER.
RUGBY, *Servant to* DR. CAIUS.

MRS. FORD.
MRS. PAGE.
MRS. ANNE PAGE, *her Daughter, in love with*
FENTON.
MRS. QUICKLY, *Servant to* DR. CAIUS.

Servants to PAGE, FORD, *&c.*

SCENE—WINDSOR; *and the parts adjacent.*

ACT I.

SCENE I.—WINDSOR. *Before* PAGE'S *House.*

Enter Justice SHALLOW, SLENDER, *and Sir*
HUGH EVANS.

Shal. Sir Hugh, persuade me not; I will make a Star-chamber matter of it; if he were twenty Sir John Falstaffs he shall not abuse Robert Shallow, esquire.

Slen. In the county of Gloser, justice of peace, and *coram.*

Shal. Ay, cousin Slender, and *Custalorum.*

Slen. Ay, and *Ratolorum* too; and a gentleman born, master parson; who writes himself *Armigero;* in any bill, warrant, quittance, or obligation,—*Armigero!*

Shal. Ay, that we do; and have done any time these three hundred years.

Slen. All his successors, gone before him, have don't; and all his ancestors, that come after him, may: they may give the dozen white luces in their coat.

Shal. It is an old coat.

Eva. The dozen white louses do become an old coat well; it agrees well, passant: it is a familiar beast to man, and signifies—love.

Shal. The luce is the fresh fish; the salt fish is an old coat.

Slen. I may quarter, coz?

Shal. You may, by marrying.

Eva. It is marrying indeed, if he quarter it.

Shal. Not a whit.

Eva. Yes, py'r lady; if he has a quarter of your coat, there is but three skirts for yourself, in my simple conjectures: but this is all one. If Sir John Falstaff have committed disparagements unto you, I am of the church, and will be glad to do my benevolence to make atonements and compromises between you.

Shal. The Council shall hear it; it is a riot.

Eva. It is not meet the Council hear a riot; there is no fear of Got in a riot; the Council, look you, shall desire to hear the fear of Got, and not to hear a riot; take your vizaments in that.

Shal. Ha! o' my life, if I were young again, the sword should end it.

Eva. It is petter that friends is the sword, and end it: and there is also another device in my prain, which, peradventure, prings goot discretions with it. There is Anne Page, which is daughter to Master George Page, which is pretty virginity.

Slen. Mistress Anne Page? She has brown hair, and speaks small like a woman.

Eva. It is that fery person for all the 'orld, as just as you will desire; and seven hundred pounds of monies, and gold, and silver, is her grandsire, upon his death's bed, (Got deliver to a joyful resurrection!) give, when she is able to overtake seventeen years old: it were a goot motion if we leave our pribbles and prabbles and desire a marriage between Master Abraham and Mistress Anne Page.

Shal. Did her grandsire leave her seven hundred pound? [*penny.*

Eva. Ay, and her father is make her a petter

Shal. I know the young gentlewoman; she has good gifts.

Eva. Seven hundred pounds, and possibilities, is goot gifts.

Shal. Well, let us see honest Master Page. Is Falstaff there?

Eva. Shall I tell you a lie? I do despise a liar as I do despise one that is false; or, as I despise one that is not true. The knight, Sir John, is there; and, I beseech you, be ruled by your well-willers. I will peat the door [*knocks*] for

[45]

Master Page. What, hoa! Got pless your house here!

Enter PAGE.

Page. Who's there?

Eva. Here is Got's plessing, and your friend, and Justice Shallow: and here young Master Slender; that, peradventures, shall tell you another tale, if matters grow to your likings.

Page. I am glad to see your worships well: I thank you for my venison, Master Shallow.

Shal. Master Page, I am glad to see you; much good do it your good heart! I wished your venison better; it was ill killed:—How doth good Mistress Page?—and I love you always with my heart, la; with my heart.

Page. Sir, I thank you.

Shal. Sir, I thank you; by yea and no, I do.

Page. I am glad to see you, good Master Slender.

Slen. How does your fallow greyhound, sir? I heard say he was outrun on Cotsale.

Page. It could not be judged, sir.

Slen. You'll not confess; you'll not confess.

Shal. That he will not;—'tis your fault; 'tis your fault:—'Tis a good dog.

Page. A cur, sir.

Shal. Sir, he's a good dog, and a fair dog. Can there be more said? he is good, and fair. Is Sir John Falstaff here?

Page. Sir, he is within; and I would I could do a good office between you.

Eva. It is spoke as a Christians ought to speak.

Shal. He hath wronged me, Master Page.

Page. Sir, he doth in some sort confess it.

Shal. If it be confessed, it is not redressed; is not that so, Master Page? He hath wronged me; indeed he hath;—at a word he hath;—believe me; Robert Shallow, esquire, saith he is wronged.

Page. Here comes Sir John.

Enter Sir JOHN FALSTAFF, BARDOLPH, NYM, *and* PISTOL.

Fal. Now, Master Shallow; you'll complain of me to the king?

Shal. Knight, you have beaten my men, killed my deer, and broke open my lodge.

Fal. But not kissed your keeper's daughter?

Shal. Tut, a pin! this shall be answered.

Fal. I will answer it straight;—I have done all this:—That is now answered.

Shal. The Council shall know this.

Fal. 'Twere better for you if it were known in counsel: you'll be laughed at.

Eva. Pauca verba, Sir John, goot worts.

Fal. Good worts! good cabbage.—Slender, I broke your head; what matter have you against me?

Slen. Marry, sir, I have matter in my head against you; and against your coney-catching rascals, Bardolph, Nym, and Pistol. They carried me to the tavern, and made me drunk, and afterwards picked my pocket.

Bard. You Banbury cheese!

Slen. Ay, it is no matter.

Pist. How now, Mephostophilus?

Slen. Ay, it is no matter.

Nym. Slice, I say! *pauca, pauca;* slice! that's my humour.   [cousin?

Slen. Where's Simple, my man?—can you tell,

Eva. Peace: I pray you! Now let us understand. There is three umpires in this matter as I understand: that is—Master Page, *fidelicit,* Master Page; and there is myself, *fidelicit,* myself; and the three party is, lastly and finally, mine host of the Garter.   [them.

Page. We three to hear it, and end it between

Eva. Fery goot. I will make a prief of it in my note-book; and we will afterwards 'ork upon the cause, with as great discreetly as we can.

Fal. Pistol,—

Pist. He hears with ears.

Eva. The tevil and his tam! what phrase is this, *He hears with ear?* Why, it is affectations.

Fal. Pistol, did you pick Master Slender's purse?

Slen. Ay, by these gloves, did he, (or I would I might never come in mine own great chamber again else,) of seven groats in mill-sixpences, and two Edward shovel-boards, that cost me two shilling and two pence a-piece of Yead Miller, by these gloves.

Fal. Is this true, Pistol?

Eva. No; it is false, if it is a pick-purse.

Pist. Ha, thou mountain-foreigner!—Sir John, and master mine,
I combat challenge of this latten bilbo:
Word of denial in thy labras here;
Word of denial: froth and scum, thou liest.

Slen. By these gloves, then, 'twas he.

Nym. Be advised, sir, and pass good humours: I will say, *marry trap,* with you, if you run the nuthook's humour on me: that is the very note of it.

Slen. By this hat, then, he in the red face had it: for though I cannot remember what I did when you made me drunk, yet I am not altogether an ass.

Fal. What say you, Scarlet and John?

Bard. Why, sir, for my part, I say the gentleman had drunk himself out of his five sentences.

Eva. It is his five senses; fie, what the ignorance is!

Bard. And being fap, sir, was, as they say, cashiered; and so conclusions passed the careires.

Slen. Ay, you spake in Latin then too; but 'tis no matter: I'll ne'er be drunk whilst I live again, but in honest, civil, godly company, for this trick. If I be drunk, I'll be drunk with those that have the fear of God, and not with drunken knaves.

Eva. So Got 'udge me, that is a virtuous mind.

Fal. You hear all these matters denied, gentlemen; you hear it.

Enter Mrs. ANNE PAGE *with wine; Mrs.*
FORD *and Mrs.* PAGE *following.*

Page. Nay, daughter, carry the wine in; we'll drink within.   [*Exit* ANNE PAGE.

Slen. O heaven! this is Mistress Anne Page.
Page. How now, Mistress Ford?
Fal. Mistress Ford, by my troth, you are very well met: by your leave, good mistress.
                    [*Kissing her.*
Page. Wife, bid these gentlemen welcome:—Come, we have a hot venison pasty to dinner; come, gentlemen, I hope we shall drink down all unkindness.
          [*Exeunt all but* SHAL., SLEN.,
                    and EVANS.
Slen. I had rather than forty shillings I had my Book of Songs and Sonnets here.—

Enter SIMPLE.

How now, Simple! Where have you been? I must wait on myself, must I? You have not *The Book of Riddles* about you, have you?
Sim. *Book of Riddles!* why, did you not lend it to Alice Shortcake upon All-hallowmas last, a fortnight afore Michaelmas?
Shal. Come, coz; come, coz; we stay for you. A word with you, coz; marry this, coz; there is, as 'twere, a tender, a kind of tender, made afar off by Sir Hugh here.—Do you understand me?
Slen. Ay, sir, you shall find me reasonable; if it be so, I shall do that that is reason.
Shal. Nay, but understand me.
Slen. So I do, sir.
Eva. Give ear to his motions, Master Slender: I will description the matter to you, if you be capacity of it.
Slen. Nay, I will do as my cousin Shallow says: I pray you, pardon me; he's a justice of peace in his country, simple though I stand here.
Eva. But this is not the question; the question is concerning your marriage.
Shal. Ay, there's the point, sir.
Eva. Marry is it; the very point of it; to Mistress Anne Page.
Slen. Why, if it be so, I will marry her upon any reasonable demands.
Eva. But can you affection the 'oman? Let us command to know that of your mouth, or of your lips; for divers philosophers hold that the lips is parcel of the mouth.—Therefore, precisely, can you carry your good will to the maid?
Shal. Cousin Abraham Slender, can you love her?
Slen. I hope, sir,—I will do as it shall become one that would do reason.
Eva. Nay, Got's lords and his ladies, you must speak possitable if you can carry her your desires towards her.
Shal. That you must. Will you, upon good dowry, marry her?
Slen. I will do a greater thing than that upon your request, cousin, in any reason.
Shal. Nay, conceive me, conceive me, sweet coz; what I do is to pleasure you, coz. Can you love the maid?
Slen. I will marry her, sir, at your request; but if there be no great love in the beginning, yet Heaven may decrease it upon better acquaint-ance, when we are married, and have more occasion to know one another. I hope, upon familiarity will grow more contempt: but if you say, *marry her,* I will marry her, that I am freely dissolved, and dissolutely.
Eva. It is a fery discretion answer; save, the faul' is in the 'ort dissolutely: the 'ort is, according to our meaning, resolutely;—his meaning is good.
Shal. Ay, I think my cousin meant well.
Slen. Ay, or else I would I might be hanged, la.

Re-enter ANNE PAGE.

Shal. Here comes fair Mistress Anne.—Would I were young for your sake, Mistress Anne!
Anne. The dinner is on the table; my father desires your worships' company.
Shal. I will wait on him, fair Mistress Anne.
Eva. Od's plessed will! I will not be absence at the grace.
                    [*Exeunt* SHAL. *and Sir* H. EVANS.
Anne. Will't please your worship to come in, sir?   [very well.
Slen. No, I thank you, forsooth, heartily; I am
Anne. The dinner attends you, sir.
Slen. I am not a-hungry, I thank you, forsooth. Go, sirrah, for all you are my man, go wait upon my cousin Shallow [*Exit* SIMPLE.] A justice of peace sometime may be beholden to his friend for a man.—I keep but three men and a boy yet, till my mother be dead: but what though? yet I live like a poor gentleman born.
Anne. I may not go in without your worship; they will not sit till you come.
Slen. I' faith, I'll eat nothing; I thank you as much as though I did.
Anne. I pray you, sir, walk in.
Slen. I had rather walk here, I thank you; I bruised my shin the other day with playing at sword and dagger with a master of fence, three veneys for a dish of stewed prunes; and, by my troth, I cannot abide the smell of hot meat since. Why do your dogs bark so? be there bears i' the town?   [talked of.
Anne. I think there are, sir; I heard them
Slen. I love the sport well; but I shall as soon quarrel at it as any man in England:—You are afraid, if you see the bear loose, are you not?
Anne. Ay, indeed, sir.
Slen. That's meat and drink to me now. I have seen Sackerson loose twenty times; and have taken him by the chain: but, I warrant you, the women have so cried and shrieked at it that it passed:—but women, indeed, cannot abide 'em; they are very ill-favoured rough things.

Re-enter PAGE.

Page. Come, gentle Master Slender, come; we stay for you.
Slen. I'll eat nothing, I thank you, sir.
Page. By cock and pye, you shall not choose, sir: come, come.
Slen. Nay, pray you, lead the way.
Page. Come on, sir.

Slen. Mistress Anne, yourself shall go first.

Anne. Not I, sir; pray you, keep on.

Slen. Truly, I will not go first; truly, la: I will not do you that wrong.

Anne. I pray you, sir.

Slen. I'll rather be unmannerly than troublesome: you do yourself wrong indeed, la.

[*Exeunt.*

SCENE II.—*The same.*

Enter Sir HUGH EVANS *and* SIMPLE.

Eva. Go your ways, and ask of Doctor Caius' house which is the way: and there dwells one Mistress Quickly, which is in the manner of his nurse, or his dry nurse, or his cook, or his laundry, his washer, and his wringer.

Simp. Well, sir.

Eva. Nay, it is petter yet:—give her this letter; for it is a 'oman that altogether's acquaintance with Mistress Anne Page: and the letter is, to desire and require her to solicit your master's desires to Mistress Anne Page: I pray you, be-gone; I will make an end of my dinner; there's pippins and cheese to come.

[*Exeunt.*

SCENE III.—*A Room in the* GARTER INN.

Enter FALSTAFF, HOST, BARDOLPH, NYM, PISTOL, *and* ROBIN.

Fal. Mine host of the Garter,—

Host. What says my bully-rook? Speak scholarly and wisely.

Fal. Truly, mine host, I must turn away some of my followers.

Host. Discard, bully Hercules; cashier: let them wag; trot, trot.

Fal. I sit at ten pounds a-week.

Host. Thou'rt an emperor, Cæsar, Keisar, and Pheezar. I will entertain Bardolph; he shall draw, he shall tap: said I well, bully Hector?

Fal. Do so, good mine host.

Host. I have spoke; let him follow. Let me see thee froth and lime: I am at a word: follow.

[*Exit* HOST.

Fal. Bardolph, follow him: a tapster is a good trade: an old cloak makes a new jerkin; a with-ered servingman a fresh tapster. Go; adieu.

Bard. It is a life that I have desired; I will thrive.

[*Exit* BARDOLPH.

Pist. O base Gongarian wight! wilt thou the spigot wield?

Nym. He was gotten in drink: is not the humour conceited? His mind is not heroic, and there's the humour of it.

Fal. I am glad I am so acquit of this tinder-box; his thefts were too open; his filching was like an unskilful singer; he kept not time.

Nym. The good humour is, to steal at a min-ute's rest.

Pist. Convey, the wise it call: Steal! foh; a fico for the phrase!

Fal. Well, sirs, I am almost out at heels.

Pist. Why, then, let kibes ensue.

Fal. There is no remedy; I must coney-catch; I must shift.

Pist. Young ravens must have food.

Fal. Which of you know Ford of this town?

Pist. I ken the wight; he is of substance good.

Fal. My honest lads, I will tell you what I am about.

Pist. Two yards, and more.

Fal. No quips now, Pistol. Indeed I am in the waist two yards about: but I am now about no waste; I am about thrift. Briefly, I do mean to make love to Ford's wife; I spy entertainment in her; she discourses, she carves, she gives the leer of invitation: I can construe the action of her familiar style; and the hardest voice of her behaviour, to be English'd rightly, is, *I am Sir John Falstaff's.*

Pist. He hath studied her well, and translated her well; out of honesty into English. [pass?

Nym. The anchor is deep: will that humour

Fal. Now, the report goes, she has all the rule of her husband's purse; she hath legions of angels.

Pist. As many devils entertain; and, *To her, boy,* say I.

Nym. The humour rises; it is good: humour me the angels.

Fal. I have writ me here a letter to her: and here another to Page's wife; who even now gave me good eyes too, examined my parts with most judicious eyliads: sometimes the beam of her view gilded my foot, sometimes my portly belly.

Pist. Then did the sun on dunghill shine.

Nym. I thank thee for that humour.

Fal. O, she did so course o'er my exteriors with such a greedy intention, that the appetite of her eye did seem to scorch me up like a burn-ing-glass! Here's another letter to her: she bears the purse too; she is a region in Guiana, all gold and bounty. I will be cheater to them both, and they shall be exchequers to me; they shall be my East and West Indies, and I will trade to them both. Go, bear thou this letter to Mistress Page; and thou this to Mistress Ford; we will thrive, lads, we will thrive.

Pist. Shall I Sir Pandarus of Troy become, And by my side wear steel? then, Lucifer take all!

Nym. I will run no base humour: here, take the humour letter; I will keep the 'haviour of reputation.

Fal. Hold, sirrah, [*to* ROB.,] bear you these let-ters tightly;

Sail like my pinnace to these golden shores.—

Rogues, hence, avaunt! vanish like hailstones, go; [pack!

Trudge, plod, away, o' the hoof; seek shelter, Falstaff will learn the humour of this age,

French thrift, you rogues; myself, and skirted page. [*Exeunt* FAL. *and* ROB.

Pist. Let vultures gripe thy guts! for gourd and fullam holds,

And high and low beguile the rich and poor;

Tester I'll have in pouch when thou shalt lack, Base Phrygian Turk!

Nym. I have operations in my head, which be humours of revenge.

Pist. Wilt thou revenge?

Nym. By welkin, and her star!
Pist. With wit or steel?
Nym. With both the humours, I:
I will discuss the humour of this love to Page.
Pist. And I to Ford shall eke unfold,
　　How Falstaff, varlet vile.
　　　His dove will prove, his gold will hold,
　　　And his soft couch defile.
Nym. My humour shall not cool: I will incense
Page to deal with poison; I will possess him
with yellowness, for the revolt of mien is dan-
gerous: that is my true humour.
Pist. Thou art the Mars of malcontents: I sec-
ond thee; troop on.　　　　　　　　　[*Exeunt.*

SCENE IV.—*A Room in Dr.* CAIUS'S *House.*

Enter Mrs. QUICKLY, SIMPLE, *and* RUGBY.

Quick. What: John Rugby!—I pray thee go to
the casement and see if you can see my master,
Master Doctor Caius, coming: if he do, i' faith,
and find anybody in the house, here will be an
old abusing of God's patience and the king's
English.
Rug. I'll go watch.　　　　　　　[*Exit* RUGBY.
Quick. Go; and we'll have a posset for't soon
at night, in faith, at the latter end of a sea-coal
fire. An honest, willing, kind fellow, as ever
servant shall come in house withal; and I warrant you, no tell-tale, nor no breed-bate: his
worst fault is that he is given to prayer; he is
something peevish that way; but nobody but
has his fault;—but let that pass. Peter Simple,
you say your name is?
Sim. Ay, for fault of a better.
Quick. And Master Slender's your master?
Sim. Ay, forsooth.
Quick. Does he not wear a great round beard,
like a glover's paring-knife?
Sim. No, forsooth: he hath but a little wee face,
with a little yellow beard; a Cain-coloured beard.
Quick. A softly-sprighted man, is he not?
Sim. Ay, forsooth: but he is as tall a man of
his hands as any is between this and his head:
he hath fought with a warrener.
Quick. How say you?—O, I should remember
him. Does he not hold up his head, as it were?
and strut in his gait?
Sim. Yes, indeed does he.
Quick. Well, heaven send Anne Page no worse
fortune! Tell Master Parson Evans, I will do
what I can for your master: Anne is a good
girl, and I wish—

Re-enter RUGBY.

Rug. Out, alas! here comes my master.
Quick. We shall all be shent. Run in here, good
young man; go into his closet. [*Shuts* SIMPLE
in the closet.] He will not stay long.—What,
John Rugby! John, what John, I say!—Go,
John, go inquire for my master; I doubt he be
not well that he comes not home:—*and down,
down, adown-a,* &c.　　　　　　　[*Sings.*

Enter Dr. CAIUS.

Caius. Vat is you sing? I do not like dese toys.
Pray you, go and vetch me in my closet *un
boitier verd;* a box, a green-a box. Do intend
vat I speak? a green-a box.
Quick. Ay, forsooth, I'll fetch it you. I am glad
he went not in himself: if he had found the young
man, he would have been horn-mad.　[*Aside.*
Caius. Fe, fe, fe, fe! ma foi, il fait fort chaud.
Je m'en vais a la Cour,—la grande affaire.
Quick. Is it this, sir?
Caius. Ouy; mette le au mon pocket: *depeche,*
quickly:—Vere is dat knave, Rugby?
Quick. What, John Rugby! John?
Rug. Here, sir.
Caius. You are John Rugby, and you are Jack
Rugby. Come, take-a your rapier, and come
after my heel to de court.
Rug. 'Tis ready, sir, here in the porch.
Caius. By my trot, I tarry too long:—Od's me!
Qu'ay j' oublié? dere is some simples in my closet
dat I vill not for the varld I shall leave behind.
Quick. Ah me! he'll find the young man there,
and be mad!
Caius. O diable, diable! vat is in my closet?—
Villany! larron! [*Pulling* SIMPLE *out.*] Rugby,
my rapier.
Quick. Good master, be content.
Caius. Verefore shall I be content-a!
Quick. The young man is an honest man.
Caius. Vat shall de honest man do in my closet?
dere is no honest man dat shall come in my closet.
Quick. I beseech you, be not so phlegmatic:
hear the truth of it. He came of an errand to
me from Parson Hugh.
Caius. Vell?
Sim. Ay, forsooth, to desire her to—
Quick. Peace, I pray you.　　　　　　[tale.
Caius. Peace-a your tongue:—Speak-a your
Sim. To desire this honest gentlewoman, your
maid, to speak a good word to Mistress Anne
Page for my master, in the way of marriage.
Quick. This is all, indeed, la; but I'll ne'er put
my finger in the fire, and need not.
Caius. Sir Hugh send-a you?—Rugby, *baille*
me some paper. Tarry you a little-a while.
　　　　　　　　　　　　　　[*Writes.*
Quick. I am glad he is so quiet: if he had been
thoroughly moved, you should have heard him
so loud, and so melancholy;—but not with-
standing, man, I'll do your master what good I
can: and the very yea and the no is, the French
doctor, my master,—I may call him my master, look you, for I keep his house: and I wash,
wring, brew, bake, scour, dress meat and drink,
make the beds, and do all myself:—
Sim. 'Tis a great charge to come under one
body's hand.
Quick. Are you avised o' that? you shall find
it a great charge: and to be up early and down
late;—but notwithstanding,—to tell you in
your ear; I would have no words of it,—my
master himself is in love with Mistress Anne

Page: but notwithstanding that,—I know Anne's mind,—that's neither here nor there.
Caius. You jack'nape; give-a dis letter to Sir Hugh; by gar, it is a shallenge; I will cut his troat in de park; and I vill teach a scurvy jack-a-nape priest to meddle or make:—you may be gone; it is not good you tarry here:—by gar, I vill cut all his two stones; by gar, he shall not have a stone to trow at his dog.

                     [*Exit* SIMPLE.

Quick. Alas, he speaks but for his friend.
Caius. It is no matter-a for dat:—do not you tell-a me dat I shall have Anne Page for my-self?—by gar, I will kill de Jack priest; and I have appointed mine host of *de Jar terre* to measure our weapon:—by gar, I vill myself have Anne Page.
Quick. Sir, the maid loves you, and all shall be well: we must give folks leave to prate. What, the good-jer!
Caius. Rugby, come to de court vit me.—By gar, if I have not Anne Page, I shall turn your head out of my door:—follow my heels, Rugby.

           [*Exeunt* CAIUS *and* RUGBY.

Quick. You shall have An fool's-head of your own. No, I know Anne's mind for that: never a woman in Windsor knows more of Anne's mind than I do; nor can do more than I do with her, I thank heaven.
Fent. [*Within.*] Who's within there? ho!
Quick. Who's there, I trow? Come near the house, I pray you.

Enter FENTON.

Fent. How now, good woman; how dost thou?
Quick. The better that it pleases your good worship to ask.   [Anne?
Fent. What news? How does pretty Mistress
Quick. In truth, sir, and she is pretty, and honest, and gentle; and one that is your friend, I can tell you that by the way; I praise heaven for it.   [Shall I not lose my suit?
Fent. Shall I do any good, think'st thou?
Quick. Troth, sir, all is in his hands above: but notwithstanding, Master Fenton, I'll be sworn on a book she loves you:—Have not your worship a wart above your eye?
Fent. Yes, marry, have I; what of that?
Quick. Well, thereby hangs a tale; good faith, it is such another Nan;—but, I detest, an honest maid as ever broke bread. We had an hour's talk of that wart:—I shall never laugh but in that maid's company! But, indeed, she is given too much to allicholly and musing: But for you—Well, go to.
Fent. Well, I shall see her to-day. Hold, there's money for thee; let me have thy voice in my behalf: if thou seest her before me, commend me—
Quick. Will I? i' faith, that we will; and I will tell your worship more of the wart the next time we have confidence; and of other wooers.
Fent. Well, farewell; I am in great haste now.

                          [*Exit.*

Quick. Farewell to your worship.—Truly, an honest gentleman; but Anne loves him not; for I know Anne's mind as well as another does:—Out upon't! what have I forgot?   [*Exit.*

ACT II.

SCENE I.—*Before* PAGE'S *House.*

Enter Mrs. PAGE, *with a letter.*

Mrs. Page. What! have I 'scaped love-letters in the holiday time of my beauty, and am I now a subject for them? Let me see: [*Reads.*

Ask me no reason why I love you: for though love use reason for his precisian, he admits him not for his counsellor. You are not young; no more am I: go to then, there's sympathy: you are merry; so am I. Ha! ha! then there's more sympathy; you love sack, and so do I. Would you desire better sympathy? Let it suffice thee, Mistress Page, (at the least, if the love of a soldier can suffice), that I love thee. I will not say, pity me: 'tis not a soldier-like phrase; but I say, love me. By me,

> Thine own true knight,
> By day or night,
> Or any kind of light,
> With all his might,
> For thee to fight,   JOHN FALSTAFF.

What a Herod of Jewry is this?—O wicked, wicked world!—one that is well-nigh worn to pieces with age to show himself a young gallant! What an unweighed behaviour hath this Flemish drunkard picked (with the devil's name) out of my conversation, that he dares in this manner assay me? Why, he hath not been thrice in my company!—What should I say to him?—I was then frugal of my mirth:—heaven forgive me!—Why, I'll exhibit a bill in the parliament for the putting down of men. How shall I be revenged on him? for revenged I will be, as sure as his guts are made of puddings.

Enter Mrs. FORD.

Mrs. Ford. Mistress Page! trust me, I was going to your house!
Mrs. Page. And, trust me, I was coming to you. You look very ill.
Mrs. Ford. Nay, I'll ne'er believe that; I have to show to the contrary.
Mrs. Page. 'Faith, but you do, in my mind.
Mrs. Ford. Well, I do, then; yet, I say, I could show you to the contrary. O, Mistress Page, give me some counsel!
Mrs. Page. What's the matter, woman?
Mrs. Ford. O woman, if it were not for one trifling respect, I could come to such honour!
Mrs. Page. Hang the trifle, woman; take the honour. What is it?——dispense with trifles;—what is it?
Mrs. Ford. If I would but go to hell for an eternal moment, or so, I could be knighted.
Mrs. Page. What? thou liest!—Sir Alice Ford!—These knights will hack; and so thou shouldst not alter the article of thy gentry.

Mrs. Ford. We burn day-light:—here, read, read;—perceive how I might be knighted.—I shall think the worse of fat men as long as I have an eye to make difference of men's liking. And yet he would not swear; praised women's modesty; and gave such orderly and well-behaved reproof to all uncomeliness, that I would have sworn his disposition would have gone to the truth of his words; but they do no more adhere and keep place together than the hundredth psalm to the tune of *Green sleeves* What tempest, I trow, threw this whale, with so many tuns of oil in his belly, ashore at Windsor? How shall I be revenged on him? I think the best way were to entertain him with hope till the wicked fire of lust have melted him in his own grease.—Did you ever hear the like?

Mrs. Page. Letter for letter; but that the name of Page and Ford differs!—To thy great comfort in this mystery of ill opinions, here's the twin-brother of thy letter: but let thine inherit first; for, I protest, mine never shall. I warrant he hath a thousand of these letters, writ with blank space for different names, (sure more,) and these are of the second edition. He will print them out of doubt; for he cares not what he puts into the press when he would put us two. I had rather be a giantess, and lie under Mount Pelion. Well, I will find you twenty lascivious turtles ere one chaste man.

Mrs. Ford. Why, this is the very same; the very hand, the very words. What doth he think of us?

Mrs. Page. Nay, I know not; it makes me almost ready to wrangle with mine own honesty. I'll entertain myself like one that I am not acquainted withal; for, sure, unless he know some strain in me that I know not myself, he would never have boarded me in this fury.

Mrs. Ford. Boarding, call you it? I'll be sure to keep him above deck.

Mrs. Page. So will I; if he come under my hatches, I'll never to sea again. Let's be revenged on him: let's appoint him a meeting; give him a show of comfort in his suit; and lead him on with a fine baited delay, till he hath pawned his horses to mine host of the Garter.

Mrs. Ford. Nay, I will consent to act any villany against him that may not sully the chariness of our honesty. O, that my husband saw this letter! it would give eternal food to his jealousy.

Mrs. Page. Why, look where he comes; and my good man too; he's as far from jealousy as I am from giving him cause; and that, I hope, is an unmeasurable distance.

Mrs. Ford. You are the happier woman.

Mrs. Page. Let's consult together against this greasy knight: Come hither. [*They retire.*

Enter FORD, PISTOL, PAGE, *and* NYM.

Ford. Well, I hope it be not so.

Pist. Hope is a curtail dog in some affairs: Sir John affects thy wife.

Ford. Why, sir, my wife is not young.

Pist. He woos both high and low, both rich
    and poor,
Both young and old, one with another, Ford;
He loves thy gally-mawfry; Ford, perpend.

Ford. Love my wife? [thou,

Pist. With liver burning hot. Prevent, or go
Like Sir Actæon he, with Ring-wood at thy
O, odious is the name. [heels:—

Ford. What name, sir?

Pist. The horn, I say. Farewell.
Take heed; have open eye; for thieves do foot
    by night: [do sing.—
Take heed, ere summer comes, or cuckoo birds
Away, Sir Corporal Nym.—
Believe it, Page; he speaks sense.
        [*Exit* PISTOL.

Ford. I will be patient; I will find out this.

Nym. And this is true [*to* PAGE]. I like not the humour of lying. He hath wronged me in some humours; I should have borne the humoured letter to her; but I have a sword, and it shall bite upon my necessity. He loves your wife; there's the short and the long. My name is Corporal Nym; I speak, and I avouch. 'Tis true:—my name is Nym, and Falstaff loves your wife.—Adieu! I love not the humour of bread and cheese; and there's the humour of it. Adieu. [*Exit* NYM.

Page. The humour of it, quotha! here's a fellow frights humour out of his wits.

Ford. I will seek out Falstaff.

Page. I never heard such a drawling, affecting rogue.

Ford. If I do find it, well.

Page. I will not believe such a Cataian though the priest of the town commended him for a true man.

Ford. 'Twas a good sensible fellow. Well.

Page. How now, Meg?

Mrs. Page. Whither go you, George?—Hark you.

Mrs. Ford. How now, sweet Frank? why art thou melancholy?

Ford. I melancholy! I am not melancholy.—Get you home; go.

Mrs. Ford. 'Faith, thou hast some crotchets in thy head now.—Will you go, Mistress Page?

Mrs. Page. Have with you.—You'll come to dinner, George? Look, who comes yonder: she shall be our messenger to this paltry knight.
        [*Aside to Mrs.* FORD.

Enter Mrs. QUICKLY.

Mrs. Ford. Trust me, I thought on her: she'll fit it.

Mrs. Page. You are come to see my daughter Anne?

Quick. Ay, forsooth; and, I pray, how does good Mistress Anne?

Mrs. Page. Go in with us and see; we have an hour's talk with you.
      [*Exeunt Mrs.* PAGE, *Mrs.* FORD,
        and Mrs. QUICKLY.

Page. How now, Master Ford?

Ford. You heard what this knave told me; did you not?

Page. Yes; and you heard what the other told me?

Ford. Do you think there is truth in them?

Page. Hang 'em slaves; I do not think the knight would offer it: but these that accuse him in his intent towards our wives are a yoke of his discarded men: very rogues, now they be out of service.

Ford. Were they his men?

Page. Marry, were they.

Ford. I like it never the better for that.—Does he lie at the Garter?

Page. Ay, marry, does he. If he should intend this voyage towards my wife, I would turn her loose to him; and what he gets of her more than sharp words, let it lie on my head.

Ford. I do not misdoubt my wife; but I would be loth to turn them together. A man may be too confident: I would have nothing lie on my head: I cannot be thus satisfied.

Page. Look where my ranting host of the Garter comes: there is either liquor in his pate or money in his purse when he looks so merrily.—How now, mine host?

Enter HOST and SHALLOW.

Host. How now, bully-rook! thou'rt a gentleman: cavalero-justice, I say.

Shal. I follow, mine host, I follow.—Good even, and twenty, good Master Page! Master Page, will you go with us? we have sport in hand.

Host. Tell him, cavalero-justice; tell him, bully-rook.

Shal. Sir, there is a fray to be fought between Sir Hugh the Welsh priest and Caius the French doctor.

Ford. Good mine host o' the Garter, a word with you.

Host. What say'st thou, bully-rook?

[*They go aside.*

Shal. Will you [*to* PAGE] go with us to behold it? My merry host hath had the measuring of their weapons; and, I think, he hath appointed them contrary places: for, believe me, I hear the parson is no jester. Hark, I will tell you what our sport shall be.

Host. Hast thou no suit against my knight, my guest-cavalier.

Ford. None, I protest: but I'll give you a pottle of burnt sack to give me recourse to him, and tell him my name is Brook; only for a jest.

Host. My hand, bully: thou shalt have egress and regress; said I well? and thy name shall be Brook: it is a merry knight.—Will you go on, hearts?

Shal. Have with you, mine host.

Page. I have heard the Frenchman hath good skill in his rapier.

Shal. Tut, sir, I could have told you more. In these times you stand on distance, your passes, stoccadoes, and I know not what: 'tis the heart, Master Page; 'tis here, 'tis here. I have seen the time with my long sword I would have made you four tall fellows skip like rats.

Host. Here, boys, here, here! shall we wag?

Page. Have with you:—I had rather hear them scold than fight.

[*Exeunt* HOST, SHAL., *and* PAGE.

Ford. Though Page be a secure fool, and stands so firmly on his wife's frailty, yet I cannot put off my opinion so easily. She was in his company at Page's house; and what they made there I know not. Well, I will look further into't: and I have a disguise to sound Falstaff: if I find her honest, I lose not my labour; if she be otherwise, 'tis labour well bestowed. [*Exit.*

SCENE II.—*A Room in the Garter Inn.*

Enter FALSTAFF *and* PISTOL.

Fal. I will not lend thee a penny.

Pist. Why, then the world's mine oyster,
Which I with sword will open.—
I will retort the sum in equipage.

Fal. Not a penny. I have been content, sir, you should lay my countenance to pawn; I have grated upon my good friends for three reprieves for you and your coach fellow, Nym; or else you had looked through the grate, like a geminy of baboons. I am damned in hell for swearing to gentlemen my friends you were good soldiers and tall fellows: and when Mistress Bridget lost the handle of her fan, I took't upon mine honour thou hadst it not.

Pist. Didst thou not share? hadst thou not fifteen pence?

Fal. Reason, you rogue, reason. Think'st thou I'll endanger my soul *gratis?* At a word, hang no more about me, I am no gibbet for you;—go.—A short knife and a throng;—to your manor of Pickthatch, go.—You'll not bear a letter for me, you rogue!—you stand upon your honour!—Why, thou unconfinable baseness, it is as much as I can do to keep the terms of my honour precise. I, I, I myself sometimes, leaving the fear of heaven on the left hand, and hiding mine honour in my necessity, am fain to shuffle, to hedge, and to lurch; and yet you, rogue, will ensconce your rags, your cat-a-mountain looks, your red lattice phrases, and your bold-beating oaths, under the shelter of your honour! You will not do it, you? [man?

Pist. I do relent. What wouldst thou more of

Enter ROBIN.

Rob. Sir, here's a woman would speak with you.

Fal. Let her approach.

Enter Mrs. QUICKLY.

Quick. Give your worship good-morrow.

Fal. Good-morrow, good wife.

Quick. Not so, an't please your worship.

Fal. Good maid, then.

Quick. I'll be sworn; as my mother was, the first hour I was born.

Fal. I do believe the swearer. What with me?

Quick. Shall I vouchsafe your worship a word or two?

Fal. Two thousand, fair woman: and I'll vouchsafe thee the hearing.

Quick. There is one, Mistress Ford, sir:—I pray, come a little nearer this ways:—I myself dwell with Master Doctor Caius.

Fal. Well, on: Mistress Ford, you say,——

Quick. Your worship says very true: I pray your worship come a little nearer this ways.

Fal. I warrant thee nobody hears;—mine own people, mine own people.

Quick. Are they so? Heaven bless them, and make them his servants!

Fal. Well: Mistress Ford;—what of her?

Quick. Why, sir, she's a good creature. Lord, lord! your worship's a wanton. Well, heaven forgive you, and all of us, I pray!

Fal. Mistress Ford;—come, Mistress Ford,—

Quick. Marry, this is the short and the long of it; you have brought her into such a canaries as 'tis wonderful. The best courtier of them all, when the court lay at Windsor, could never have brought her to such a canary. Yet there has been knights, and lords, and gentlemen, with their coaches; I warrant you, coach after coach, letter after letter, gift after gift; smelling so sweetly, (all musk) and so rushling, I warrant you, in silk and gold; and in such alligant terms; and in such wine and sugar of the best, and the fairest, that would have won any woman's heart; and, I warrant you, they could never get an eye-wink of her.—I had myself twenty angels given me this morning; but I defy all angels, (in any such sort, as they say,) but in the way of honesty:—and, I warrant you, they could never get her so much as sip on a cup with the proudest of them all: and yet there has been earls, nay, which is more, pensioners; but, I warrant you, all is one with her.

Fal. But what says she to me? be brief, my good she Mercury.

Quick. Marry, she hath received your letter; for the which she thanks you a thousand times; and she gives you to notify that her husband will be absence from his house between ten and eleven.

Fal. Ten and eleven?

Quick. Ay, forsooth; and then you may come and see the picture, she says, that you wot of;—Master Ford, her husband, will be from home. Alas! the sweet woman leads an ill life with him: he's a very jealousy man: she leads a very frampold life with him, good heart.

Fal. Ten and eleven. Woman, commend me to her; I will not fail her.

Quick. Why, you say well: but I have another messenger to your worship. Mistress Page hath her hearty commendations to you too;—and let me tell you in your ear, she's as fartuous a civil, modest wife, and one (I tell you) that will not miss you morning nor evening prayer, as any is in Windsor, whoe'er be the other: and she bade me tell your worship that her husband is seldom from home; but she hopes there will come a time. I never knew a woman so dote upon a man; surely I think you have charms, la; yes, in truth.

Fal. Not I, I assure thee; setting the attraction of my good parts aside, I have no other charms.

Quick. Blessing on your heart for't!

Fal. But, I pray thee, tell me this: has Ford's wife and Page's wife acquainted each other how they love me?

Quick. That were a jest indeed!—they have not so little grace, I hope:—that were a trick indeed! But Mistress Page would desire you to send her your little page, of all loves: her husband has a marvellous infection to the little page: and, truly, Master Page is an honest man. Never a wife in Windsor leads a better life than she does; do what she will, say what she will, take all, pay all, go to bed when she list, rise when she list, all is as she will; and truly, she deserves it: for if there be a kind woman in Windsor, she is one. You must send her your

Fal. Why, I will.   [page; no remedy.

Quick. Nay, but do so then: and, look you, he may come and go between you both; and in any case have a nay-word that you may know one another's mind, and the boy never need to understand any thing: for 'tis not good that children should know any wickedness: old folks, you know, have discretion, as they say, and know the world.

Fal. Fare thee well: commend me to them both: there's my purse; I am yet thy debtor.—Boy, go along with this woman.——This news distracts me!

[*Exeunt* QUICKLY *and* ROBIN.

Pist. This punk is one of Cupid's carriers:—Clap on more sails; pursue; up with your fights; give fire; she is my prize, or ocean whelm them all!   [*Exit* PISTOL.

Fal. Say'st thou so, old Jack! go thy ways; I'll make more of thy old body than I have done. Will they yet look after thee? Wilt thou, after the expense of so much money, be now a gainer? Good body, I thank thee. Let them say 'tis grossly done; so it be fairly done, no matter.

Enter BARDOLPH.

Bard. Sir John, there's one Master Brook below would fain speak with you, and be acquainted with you; and hath sent your worship a morning's draught of sack.

Fal. Brook is his name?

Bard. Ay, sir.

Fal. Call him in; [*Exit* BARDOLPH.] Such Brooks are welcome to me that o'erflow such liquor. Ah! ha! Mistress Ford and Mistress Page, have I encompassed you? go to; *via!*

Re-enter BARDOLPH, *with* FORD *disguised.*

Ford. Bless you, sir.

Fal. And you, sir. Would you speak with me?

Ford. I make bold to press with so little preparation upon you.

Fal. You're welcome; what's your will? Give us leave, drawer. [*Exit* BARDOLPH.

Ford. Sir, I am a gentleman that have spent much; my name is Brook.

Fal. Good Master Brook, I desire more acquaintance of you.

Ford. Good Sir John, I sue for yours: not to charge you; for I must let you understand I think myself in better plight for a lender than you are: the which has something emboldened me to this unseasoned intrusion: for they say if money go before, all ways do lie open.

Fal. Money is a good soldier, sir, and will on.

Ford. Troth, and I have a bag of money here troubles me; if you will help me to bear it, Sir John, take all or half for easing me of the carriage.

Fal. Sir, I know not how I may deserve to be your porter.

Ford. I will tell you, sir, if you will give me the hearing.

Fal. Speak, good Master Brook; I shall be glad to be your servant.

Ford. Sir, I hear you are a scholar,—I will be brief with you,———and you have been a man long known to me, though I had never so good means as desire to make myself acquainted with you. I shall discover a thing to you, wherein I must very much lay open mine own imperfection: but, good Sir John, as you have one eye upon my follies, as you hear them unfolded, turn another into the register of your own; that I may pass with a reproof the easier, sith you yourself know how easy it is to be such an

Fal. Very well, sir; proceed.   [offender.

Ford. There is a gentlewoman in this town, her husband's name is Ford.

Fal. Well, sir.

Ford. I have long loved her, and I protest to you bestowed much on her; followed her with a doting observance; engrossed opportunities to meet her; fee'd every slight occasion that could but niggardly give me sight of her; not only bought many presents to give her, but have given largely to many to know what she would have given: briefly, I have pursued her as love hath pursued me; which hath been on the wing of all occasions. But whatsoever I have merited, either in my mind or in my means, meed, I am sure, I have received none; unless experience be a jewel; that I have purchased at an infinite rate; and that hath taught me to say this:

Love like a shadow flies, when substance love
        pursues;
Pursuing that that flies, and flying what pursues.

Fal. Have you received no promise of satisfaction at her hands?

Ford. Never.   [pose?

Fal. Have you importuned her to such a pur-

Ford. Never.

Fal. Of what quality was your love, then?

Ford. Like a fair house built upon another man's ground; so that I have lost my edifice by mistaking the place where I erected it.

Fal. To what purpose have you unfolded this to me?

Ford. When I have told you that, I have told you all. Some say that though she appear honest to me, yet in other places she enlargeth her mirth so far that there is shrewd construction made of her. Now, Sir John, here is the heart of my purpose. You are a gentleman of excellent breeding, admirable discourse, of great admittance, authentic in your place and person, generally allowed for your many war-like, court-like, and learned preparations.

Fal. O, sir!

Ford. Believe it, for you know it:—There is money; spend it, spend it; spend more; spend all I have; only give me so much of your time in exchange of it as to lay an amiable siege to the honesty of this Ford's wife; use your art of wooing, win her to consent to you; if any man may, you may as soon as any.

Fal. Would it apply well to the vehemency of your affection, that I should win what you would enjoy? Methinks you prescribe to yourself very preposterously.

Ford. O, understand my drift! She dwells so securely on the excellency of her honour that the folly of my soul dares not present itself; she is too bright to be looked against. Now, could I come to her with any detection in my hand, my desires had instance and argument to commend themselves; I could drive her then from the ward of her purity, her reputation, her marriage vow, and a thousand other her defences, which now are too strongly embattled against me. What say you to't, Sir John?

Fal. Master Brook, I will first make bold with your money; next, give me your hand: and last, as I am a gentleman, you shall, if you will, enjoy Ford's wife.

Ford. O good sir!

Fal. Master Brook, I say you shall.

Ford. Want no money, Sir John, you shall want none.

Fal. Want no Mistress Ford, Master Brook, you shall want none. I shall be with her (I may tell you) by her own appointment: even as you came in to me her assistant, or go-between, parted from me: I say, I shall be with her between ten and eleven; for at that time the jealous rascally knave, her husband, will be forth. Come you to me at night; you shall know how I speed.

Ford. I am blest in your acquaintance. Do you know Ford, sir?

Fal. Hang him, poor cuckoldly knave! I know him not:—yet I wrong him to call him poor; they say the jealous wittolly knave hath masses of money; for the which his wife seems to me well-favoured. I will use her as the key of the cuckoldly rogue's coffer; and there's my harvest-home.

Ford. I would you knew Ford, **sir**; that you might avoid him if you saw him.

Fal. Hang him, mechanical salt-butter rogue! I will stare him out of his wits; I will awe him with my cudgel: it shall hang like a meteor o'er the cuckold's horns: Master Brook, thou shalt know, I will predominate o'er the peasant, and thou shalt lie with his wife.—Come to me soon at night:—Ford's a knave, and I will aggravate his stile; thou, Master Brook, shalt know him for a knave and cuckold:—come to me soon at night. *[Exit.*

Ford. What a damned Epicurean rascal is this! —My heart is ready to crack with impatience.— Who says this is improvident jealousy? My wife hath sent to him, the hour is fixed, the match is made. Would any man have thought this?—See the hell of having a false woman! my bed shall be abused, my coffers ransacked, my reputation gnawn at; and I shall not only receive this villanous wrong, but stand under the adoption of abominable terms, and by him that does me this wrong. Terms! names!—— Amaimon sounds well; Lucifer, well; Barbason, well; yet they are devils' additions, the names of fiends: but cuckold! wittol-cuckold! the devil himself hath not such a name. Page is an ass, a secure ass! he will trust his wife; he will not be jealous! I will rather trust a Fleming with my butter, Parson Hugh the Welshman with my cheese, an Irishman with my aqua-vitæ bottle, or a thief to walk my ambling gelding, than my wife with herself: then she plots, then she ruminates, then she devises: and what they think in their hearts they may effect, they will break their hearts but they will effect. Heaven be praised for my jealousy!—Eleven o'clock the hour:—I will prevent this, detect my wife, be revenged on Falstaff, and laugh at Page. I will about it; better three hours too soon than a minute too late. Fie, fie, fie! cuckold! cuckold! cuckold! *[Exit.*

SCENE III.—*Windsor Park.*

Enter CAIUS *and* RUGBY.

Caius. Jack Rugby!

Rug. Sir?

Caius. Vat is de clock, Jack?

Rug. 'Tis past the hour, sir, that Sir Hugh promised to meet.

Caius. By gar, he has saved his soul, dat he is no come; he has pray his Pible vell, dat he is no come: by gar, Jack Rugby, he is dead already, if he be come.

Rug. He is wise, sir; he knew your worship would kill him if he came.

Caius. By gar, de herring is no dead, so as I vill kill him. Take your rapier, Jack; I vill tell you how I vill kill him.

Rug. Alas, sir, I cannot fence.

Caius. Villany, take your rapier.

Rug. Forbear: here's company.

Enter HOST, SHALLOW, SLENDER, *and* PAGE.

Host. Bless thee, bully doctor.

Shal. Save you, Master Doctor Caius.

Page. Now, good master doctor!

Slen. Give you good morrow, sir.

Caius. Vat be all you, one, two, tree, four, come for?

Host. To see thee fight, to see thee foin, to see thee traverse, to see thee here, to see thee there; to see thee pass thy punto, thy stock, thy reverse, thy distance, thy montánt. Is he dead, my Ethiopian? is he dead, my Francisco? ha, bully! What says my Æsculapius? my Galen? my heart of elder? ha! is he dead, bully Stale? is he dead?

Caius. By gar, he is de coward Jack priest of the vorld; he is not show his face.

Host. Thou art a Castilian King Urinal! Hector of Greece, my boy!

Caius. I pray you, bear vitness that me have stay six, or seven, two, tree hours for him, and he is no come.

Shal. He is the wiser man, master doctor: he is a curer of souls, and you a curer of bodies; if you should fight, you go against the hair of your professions; is it not true, Master Page?

Page. Master Shallow, you have yourself been a great fighter, though now a man of peace.

Shal. Bodikins, Master Page, though I now be old, and of the peace, if I see a sword out my finger itches to make one: though we are justices, and doctors, and churchmen, Master Page, we have some salt of our youth in us; we are the sons of women, Master Page.

Page. 'Tis true, Master Shallow.

Shal. It will be found so, Master Page. Master Doctor Caius, I am come to fetch you home. I am sworn of the peace; you have showed yourself a wise physician, and Sir Hugh hath shown himself a wise and patient churchman: you must go with me, master doctor.

Host. Pardon, guest justice:—A word, Monsieur Muck-water.

Caius. Muck-vater! vat is dat?

Host. Muck-water, in our English tongue, is valour, bully.

Caius. By gar, then I have as much muck-vater as de Englishman:——Scurvy jack-dog priest! by gar, me vill cut his ears.

Host. He will clapper-claw thee tightly, bully.

Caius. Clapper-de-claw! vat is dat?

Host. That is, he will make thee amends.

Caius. By gar, me do look he shall clapper-de-claw me; for, by gar, me vill have it.

Host. And I will provoke him to't, or let him wag.

Caius. Me tank you for dat.

Host. And, moreover, bully,—But first, master guest, and Master Page, and eke Cavalero Slender, go you through the town to Frogmore. *[Aside to them.*

Page. Sir Hugh is there, is he?

Host. He is there: see what humour he is in;

and I will bring the doctor about by the fields. Will it do well?

Shal. We will do it.

Page, Shal., and Slen. Adieu, good master doctor. [*Exeunt* PAGE, SHAL., *and* SLEN.

Caius. By gar, me vill kill de priest: for he speak for a jack-an-ape to Anne Page.

Host. Let him die; but first sheathe thy impatience; throw cold water on thy choler; go about the fields with me through Frogmore; I will bring thee where Mistress Anne Page is, at a farm-house, a-feasting; and thou shalt woo her. Cryed game, said I well?

Caius. By gar, me tank you for dat: by gar, I love you; and I shall procure-a you de good guest, de earl, de knight, de lords, de gentlemen, my patients.

Host. For the which I will be thy adversary towards Anne Page; said I well?

Caius. By gar, 'tis good: vell said.

Host. Let us wag, then.

Caius. Come at my heels, Jack Rugby. [*Exeunt.*

ACT III.

SCENE I.—*A Field near Frogmore.*

Enter Sir HUGH EVANS *and* SIMPLE.

Eva. I pray you now, good Master Slender's serving-man, and friend Simple by your name, which way have you looked for Master Caius, that calls himself *Doctor of Physick?*

Sim. Marry, sir, the city-ward, the park-wd,ra every way; old Windsor way, and every way but the town way. [also look that way.

Eva. I most fehemently desire you, you will

Sim. I will, sir.

Eva. 'Pless my soul! how full of cholers I am, and trempling of mind!—I shall be glad if he have deceived me:—how melancholies I am!— I will knog his urinals about his knave's costard when I have good opportunities for the 'ork—'pless my soul! [*Sings.*

> To shallow rivers, to whose falls
> Melodious birds sing madrigals;
> There will we make our peds of roses,
> And a thousand fragrant posies.
>   To shallow——

Mercy on me! I have a great dispositions to cry.

> Melodious birds sing madrigals—
> When as I sat in Pabylon——
> And a thousand vagram posies.
>   To shallow——

Sim. Yonder he is, coming this way, Sir Hugh.

Eva. He's welcome:

> To shallow rivers, to whose falls——

Heaven prosper the right!—What weapons is he?

Sim. No weapons, sir. There comes my master, Master Shallow, and another gentleman, from Frogmore, over the stile, this way.

Eva. Pray you, give me my gown; or else keep it in your arms.

Enter PAGE, SHALLOW, *and* SLENDER.

Shal. How now, master parson? Good-morrow, good Sir Hugh. Keep a gamester from the dice, and a good student from his book, and it is wonderful.

Slen. Ah, sweet Anne Page!

Page. Save you, good Sir Hugh!

Eva. 'Pless you from his mercy sake, all of you!

Shall. What! the sword and the word! Do you study them both, master parson?

Page. And youthful still, in your doublet and hose, this raw rheumatic day?

Eva. There is reasons and causes for it.

Page. We are come to you to do a good office, master parson.

Eva. Fery well: what is it?

Page. Yonder is a most reverend gentleman, who, belike having received wrong by some person, is at most odds with his own gravity and patience that ever you saw.

Shal. I have lived fourscore years and upward; I never heard a man of his place, gravity, and learning, so wide of his own respect.

Eva. What is he?

Page. I think you know him; Master Doctor Caius, the renowned French physician.

Eva. Got's will, and his passion of my heart! I had as lief you would tell me of a mess of porridge.

Page. Why?

Eva. He has no more knowledge in Hibocrates and Galen,—and he is a knave besides; a cowardly knave, as you would desires to be acquainted withal.

Page. I warrant you he's the man should fight with him.

Slen. O, sweet Anne Page!

Shal. It appears so, by his weapons.—Keep them asunder;—here comes Doctor Caius.

Enter HOST, CAIUS, *and* RUGBY.

Page. Nay, good master parson, keep in your weapon.

Shal. So do you, good master doctor.

Host. Disarm them, and let them question; let them keep their limbs whole and hack our English.

Caius. I pray you, let-a me speak a word vit your ear. Verefore vill you not meet-a me?

Eva. Pray you use your patience: in good time.

Caius. By gar, you are de coward, de Jack dog, John ape.

Eva. Pray you, let us not be laughing-stogs to other men's humours; I desire you in friendship, and I will one way or another make you amends:—I will knog your urinals about your knave's cogscomb, for missing your meetings and appointments.

Caius. Diable!—Jack Rugby,—mine *Host de Jarterre*, have I not stay for him to kill him, have I not, at de place I did appoint?

Eva. As I am a Christians soul, now, look you, this is the place appointed. I'll be judgment by mine host of the Garter.

Host. Peace, I say, Gallia and Gaul, French and Welsh; soul-curer and body-curer.

Caius. Ay, dat is very good! excellent!

Host. Peace, I say; hear mine host of the Garter. Am I politic? am I subtle? am I a Machiavel? Shall I lose my doctor? no; he gives me the potions and the motions. Shall I lose my parson? my priest? my Sir Hugh? no; he gives me the proverbs and the no-verbs. Give me thy hand, terrestrial; so:—Give me thy hand, celestial, so.—Boys of art, I have deceived you both; I have directed you, to wrong places; your hearts are mighty, your skins are whole, and let burnt sack be the issue.—Come, lay their swords to pawn:—Follow me, lad of peace; follow, follow, follow.

Shal. Trust me, a mad host:—Follow, gentlemen, follow.

Slen. O, sweet Anne Page!

[*Exeunt* SHAL., SLEN., PAGE, *and* HOST.

Caius. Ha! do I perceive dat? have you make-a de sot of us? ha, ha!

Eva. This is well; he has made us his vlouting-stog,—I desire you that we may be friends; and let us knog our prains together, to be revenge on this same scall, scurvy, cogging companion, the host of the Garter.

Caius. By gar, vit all my heart; he promise to bring me vere is Anne Page; by gar, he deceive me too.

Eva. Well, I will smite his noddles:—Pray you, follow.   [*Exeunt.*

SCENE II.—*The Street in Windsor.*

Enter Mrs. PAGE *and* ROBIN.

Mrs. Page. Nay, keep your way, little gallant; you were wont to be a follower, but now you are a leader. Whether had you rather lead mine eyes or eye your master's heels?

Rob. I had rather, forsooth, go before you like a man than follow him like a dwarf.

Mrs. Page. O you are a flattering boy; now, I see, you'll be a courtier.

Enter FORD.

Ford. Well met, Mistress Page. Whither go you?

Mrs. Page. Truly, sir, to see your wife. Is she at home?

Ford. Ay; and as idle as she may hang together, for want of company; I think, if your husbands were dead, you two would marry.

Mrs. Page. Be sure of that,—two other husbands.   [cock?

Ford. Where had you this pretty weather-

Mrs. Page. I cannot tell what the dickens his name is my husband had him off: What do you call your knight's name, sirrah!

Rob. Sir John Falstaff.

Ford. Sir John Falstaff!

Mrs. Page. He, he; I can never hit on's name. There is such a league between my good man and he!—Is your wife at home indeed?

Ford. Indeed she is.

Mrs. Page. By your leave, sir;—I am sick till I see her.   [*Exeunt Mrs.* PAGE *and* ROBIN.

Ford. Has Page any brains? hath he any eyes? hath he any thinking? Sure, they sleep; he hath no use of them. Why, this boy will carry a letter twenty miles as easy as a cannon will shoot point-blank twelve score. He pieces out his wife's inclination; he gives her folly motion and advantage: and now she's going to my wife, and Falstaff's boy with her. A man may hear this shower sing in the wind!—and Falstaff's boy with her!—Good plots!—they are laid; and our revolted wives share damnation together. Well; I will take him, then torture my wife, pluck the borrowed veil of modesty from the so seeming Mistress Page, divulge Page himself for a secure and wilful Actæon; and to these violent proceedings all my neighbours shall cry aim. [*Clock strikes.*] The clock gives me my cue, and my assurance bids me search; there I shall find Falstaff: I shall be rather praised for this than mocked; for it is as positive as the earth is firm that Falstaff is there. I will go.

Enter PAGE, SHALLOW, SLENDER, HOST, *Sir* HUGH EVANS, CAIUS, *and* RUGBY.

Shal., Page, &c. Well met, Master Ford.

Ford. Trust me, a good knot: I have good cheer at home; and, I pray you, all go with me.

Shal. I must excuse myself, Master Ford.

Slen. And so must I, sir; we have appointed to dine with Mistress Anne, and I would not break with her for more money than I'll speak of.

Shal. We have lingered about a match between Anne Page and my cousin Slender, and this day we shall have our answer.

Slen. I hope I have your good will, father Page.

Page. You have, Master Slender; I stand wholly for you:—but my wife, master doctor, is for you altogether.

Caius. Ay, by gar; and de maid is love a-me; my nursh-a Quickly tell me so mush.

Host. What say you to young Master Fenton? he capers, he dances, he has eyes of youth, he writes verses, he speaks holiday, he smells April and May; he will carry't, he will carry't; 'tis in his buttons; he will carry't.

Page. Not by my consent, I promise you. The gentleman is of no having: he kept company with the wild Prince and Poins; he is of too high a region, he knows too much. No; he shall not knit a knot in his fortunes with the finger of my substance: if he take her, let him take her simply; the wealth I have waits on my consent, and my consent goes not that way.

Ford. I beseech you, heartily, some of you go home with me to dinner: besides your cheer, you shall have sport; I will show you a monster.—Master doctor, you shall go;—so shall you, Master Page;—and you, Sir Hugh.

Shal. Well, fare you well:—we shall have the freer wooing at Master Page's.
[*Exeunt* SHAL. and SLEN.
Caius. Go home, John Rugby; I come anon.
[*Exit* RUGBY.
Host. Farewell, my hearts, I will to my honest knight Falstaff, and drink canary with him.
[*Exit* HOST.
Ford. [*Aside.*] I think I shall drink in pipe-wine first with him; I'll make him dance. Will you go, gentles?
All. Have with you, to see this monster.
[*Exeunt.*

SCENE III.—*A Room in* FORD'S *House.*

Enter Mrs. FORD *and Mrs.* PAGE.

Mrs. Ford. What, John! what, Robert!
Mrs. Page. Quickly, quickly: Is the buck-basket—
Mrs. Ford. I warrant:—What, Robin, I say.

Enter Servants, *with a basket.*

Mrs. Page. Come, come, come.
Mrs. Ford. Here, set it down.
Mrs. Page. Give your men the charge; we must be brief.
Mrs. Ford. Marry, as I told you before, John, and Robert, be ready here hard by in the brew-house; and when I suddenly call you, come forth, and, without any pause or staggering, take this basket on your shoulders: that done, trudge with it in all haste, and carry it among the whitsters in Datchet mead, and there empty it in the muddy ditch, close by the Thames
Mrs. Page. You will do it?   [side.
Mrs. Ford. I have told them over and over; they lack no direction. Begone, and come when you are called.   [*Exeunt* Servants.
Mrs. Page. Here comes little Robin.

Enter ROBIN.

Mrs. Ford. How now, my eyas-musket? what news with you?
Rob. My master, Sir John, is come in at your back-door, Mistress Ford, and requests your company.   [been true to us?
Mrs. Page. You little Jack-a-lent, have you
Rob. Ay, I'll be sworn. My master knows not of your being here; and hath threatened to put me into everlasting liberty. if I tell you of it; for he swears he'll turn me away.
Mrs. Page. Thou'rt a good boy; this secrecy of thine shall be a tailor to thee, and shall make thee a new doublet and hose.—I'll go hide me.
Mrs. Ford. Do so.—Go tell thy master I am alone. Mrs. Page, remember you your cue.
[*Exit* ROBIN.
Mrs. Page. I warrant thee; if I do not act it, hiss me.   [*Exit Mrs.* PAGE.
Mrs. Ford. Go to then; we'll use this unwhole-some humidity, this gross watery pumpion;—we'll teach him to know turtles from jays.

Enter FALSTAFF.

Fal. Have I caught thee, *my heavenly jewel?* Why, now let me die, for I have lived long enough; this is the period of my ambition: O this blessed hour!
Mrs. Ford. O sweet Sir John!
Fal. Mistress Ford, I cannot cog, I cannot prate, Mrs. Ford. Now shall I sin in my wish. I would thy husband were dead; I'll speak it before the best lord, I would make thee my lady.
Mrs. Ford. I your lady, Sir John! alas, I should be a pitiful lady.
Fal. Let the court of France show me such another; I see how thine eye would emulate the diamond: thou hast the right arched bent of the brow, that becomes the ship-tire, the tire-val-iant, or any tire of Venetian admittance.
Mrs. Ford. A plain kerchief, Sir John: my brows become nothing else; nor that well neither.
Fal. Thou art a traitor to say so: thou wouldst make an absolute courtier; and the firm fixture of thy foot would give an excellent motion to thy gait, in a semi-circled farthingale. I see what thou wert, if fortune thy foe were not; na-ture is thy friend. Come, thou canst not hide it.
Mrs. Ford. Believe me, there's no such thing in me.
Fal. What made me love thee? let that per-suade thee, there's something extraordinary in thee. Come, I cannot cog, and say thou art this and that, like a many of these lisping hawthorn buds that come like women in men's apparel, and smell like Buckler's-bury in simple-time; I cannot: but I love thee; none but thee; and thou deservest it.
Mrs. Ford. Do not betray me, sir; I fear you love Mrs. Page.
Fal. Thou mightst as well say I love to walk by the counter-gate; which is as hateful to me as the reek of a lime-kiln.
Mrs. Ford. Well, heaven knows how I love you; and you shall one day find it.
Fal. Keep in that mind; I'll deserve it.
Mrs. Ford. Nay, I must tell you, so you do, or else I could not be in that mind.
Rob. [*Within.*] Mistress Ford, Mistress Ford! here's Mrs. Page at the door, sweating, and blowing, and looking wildly, and would needs speak with you presently.
Fal. She shall not see me; I will ensconce me behind the arras.
Mrs. Ford. Pray you, do so: she's a very tat-tling woman.—   [FALSTAFF *hides himself.*

Enter Mrs. PAGE *and* ROBIN.

What's the matter? how now?
Mrs. Page. O Mistress Ford, what have you done? You're shamed, you are overthrown, you are undone for ever.
Mrs. Ford. What's the matter, good Mistress Page?
Mrs. Page. O well-a-day, Mistress Ford! hav-ing an honest man to your husband, to give him such cause of suspicion!

Mrs. Ford. What cause of suspicion?

Mrs. Page. What cause of suspicion!—out upon you! how am I mistook in you?

Mrs. Ford. Why, alas! what's the matter?

Mrs. Page. Your husband's coming hither, woman, with all the officers in Windsor, to search for a gentleman that, he says, is here now in the house, by your consent, to take an ill advantage of his absence: you are undone.

Mrs. Ford. Speak louder.—[*Aside.*]—'Tis not so, I hope.

Mrs. Page. Pray heaven it be not so, that you have such a man here; but 'tis more certain your husband's coming with half Windsor at his heels, to search for such a one. I come before to tell you: if you know yourself clear, why, I am glad of it; but if you have a friend here, convey, convey him out. Be not amazed; call all your senses to you; defend your reputation, or bid farewell to your good life for ever.

Mrs. Ford. What shall I do?—There is a gentleman, my dear friend; and I fear not mine own shame so much as his peril: I had rather than a thousand pounds he were out of the house.

Mrs. Page. For shame, never stand *you had rather*, and *you had rather*; your husband's here at hand, bethink you of some conveyance: in the house you cannot hide him.—O, how have you deceived me!—Look, here is a basket; if he be of any reasonable stature, he may creep in here; and throw foul linen upon him, as if it were going to bucking: or, it is whiting-time, send him by your two men to Datchet mead.

Mrs. Ford. He's too big to go in there. What shall I do?

Re-enter FALSTAFF.

Fal. Let me see't, let me see't! O let me see't! I'll in, I'll in; follow your friend's counsel:—I'll in.

Mrs. Page. What! Sir John Falstaff! Are these your letters, knight?

Fal. I love thee, and none but thee; help me away: let me creep in here; I'll never—

[*He goes into the basket; they cover him with foul linen.*

Mrs. Page. Help to cover your master, boy. Call your men, Mistress Ford:—You dissembling knight!

Mrs. Ford. What, John! Robert! John! [*Exit* ROBIN. *Re-enter* Servants.] Go take up these clothes here, quickly; where's the cowl-staff? look, how you drumble: carry them to the laundress in Datchet mead; quickly, come.

Enter FORD, PAGE, CAIUS, *and Sir* HUGH EVANS.

Ford. Pray you, come near: if I suspect without cause, why, then make sport at me, then let me be your jest; I deserve it.—How now? whither bear you this?

Serv. To the laundress, forsooth.

Mrs. Ford. Why, what have you to do whither they bear it? You were best meddle with buck-washing.

Ford. Buck? I would I could wash myself of the buck! Buck, buck, buck? Ay, buck; I warrant you, buck; and of the season too; It shall appear. [*Exeunt* Servants *with the basket.*] Gentlemen, I have dreamed to-night; I'll tell you my dream. Here, here, here be my keys: ascend my chambers, search, seek, find out: I'll warrant we'll unkennel the fox:—Let me stop this way first:—so, now uncape.

Page. Good Master Ford, be contented: you wrong yourself too much.

Ford. True, Master Page.—Up, gentlemen; you shall see sport anon: follow me, gentlemen.   [*Exit.*

Eva. This is fery fantastical humours and jealousies.

Caius. By gar, 'tis no de fashion of France: it is not jealous in France.

Page. Nay, follow him, gentlemen; see the issue of his search.

[*Exeunt* EVANS, PAGE, *and* CAIUS.

Mrs. Page. Is there not a double excellency in this?

Mrs. Ford. I know not which pleases me better, that my husband is deceived, or Sir John

Mrs. Page. What a taking was he in when your husband asked who was in the basket!

Mrs. Ford. I am half afraid he will have need of washing; so throwing him into the water will do him a benefit.

Mrs. Page. Hang him, dishonest rascal! I would all of the same strain were in the same distress.

Mrs. Ford. I think my husband hath some special suspicion of Falstaff's being here; for I never saw him so gross in his jealousy till now.

Mrs. Page. I will lay a plot to try that: and we will yet have more tricks with Falstaff: his dissolute disease will scarce obey this medicine.

Mrs. Ford. Shall we send that foolish carrion, Mrs. Quickly, to him, and excuse his throwing into the water; and give him another hope, to betray him to another punishment?

Mrs. Page. We'll do it; let him be sent for to-morrow eight o'clock, to have amends.

Re-enter FORD, PAGE, CAIUS, *and Sir* HUGH EVANS.

Ford. I cannot find him: maybe the knave bragged of that he could not compass.

Mrs. Page. Heard you that?

Mrs. Ford. Ay, ay, peace:—You use me well, Master Ford, do you?

Ford. Ay, I do so.   [thoughts!

Mrs. Ford. Heaven make you better than your

Ford. Amen.   [Master Ford.

Mrs. Page. You do yourself mighty wrong,

Ford. Ay, ay; I must bear it.

Eva. If there be any pody in the house, and in the chambers, and in the coffers, and in the presses, heaven forgive my sins at the day of judgment!

Caius. By gar, nor I too; dere is no—bodies.

Page. Fie, fie, Master Ford! are you not ashamed? What spirit, what devil suggests this imagination? I would not have your distemper in this kind for the wealth of Windsor Castle.
Ford. 'Tis my fault, Master Page: I suffer for it.
Eva. You suffer for a pad conscience: your wive is as honest a 'omans as I will desires among five thousand, and five hundred too.
Caius. By gar, I see 'tis an honest woman.
Ford. Well;—I promised you a dinner:—Come, come, walk in the park: I pray you, pardon me; I will hereafter make known to you why I have done this.—Come, wife;—come, Mistress Page; I pray you, pardon me; pray heartily, pardon me.
Page. Let's go in, gentlemen; but, trust me, we'll mock him. I do invite you to-morrow morning to my house to breakfast; after, we'll a-birding together; I have a fine hawk for the bush. Shall it be so?
Ford. Any thing.   [company.
Eva. If there is one, I shall make two in the
Caius. If there be one or two, I shall make-a de turd.
Eva. In your teeth: for shame.
Ford. Pray you go, Master Page.
Eva. I pray you now, remembrance to-morrow on the lousy knave, mine host.
Caius. Dat is good; by gar, vit all my heart.
Eva. A lousy knave; to have his gibes and his mockeries.   [*Exeunt.*

SCENE IV.—*A Room in* PAGE'S *House.*

Enter FENTON *and Mrs.* ANNE PAGE.

Fent. I see, I cannot get thy father's love;
Therefore, no more turn me to him, sweet Nan.
Anne. Alas! how then?
Fent.   Why, thou must be thyself.
He doth object I am too great of birth;
And that, my state being gall'd with my expense,
I seek to heal it only by his wealth.
Besides these, other bars he lays before me,——
My riots past, my wild societies;
And tells me 'tis a thing impossible.
I should love thee but as a property.
Anne. Maybe he tells you true?
Fent. No; heaven so speed me in my time to
                    come!
Albeit, I will confess, thy father's wealth
Was the first motive that I woo'd thee, Anne:
Yet, wooing thee, I found thee of more value
Than stamps in gold, or sums in sealed bags;
And 'tis the very riches of thyself
That now I aim at.
Anne.   Gentle Master Fenton,
Yet seek my father's love; still seek it, sir:
If opportunity and humblest suit
Cannot attain it, why then.—Hark you hither.
                    [*They converse apart.*

Enter SHALLOW, SLENDER, *and Mrs.* QUICKLY.

Shal. Break their talk, Mistress Quickly; my kinsman shall speak for himself.
Slen. I'll make a shaft or a bolt on't; 'slid, 'tis but venturing.

Shal. Be not dismayed.
Slen. No; she shall not dismay me. I care not for that,—but that I am afeard.
Quick. Hark ye: Master Slender would speak a word with you.   [choice.
Anne. I come to him.—This is my father's
O, what a world of vile ill-favour'd faults.
Looks handsome in three hundred pounds a-
                    year!   [*Aside.*
Quick. And how does good Master Fenton? Pray you, a word with you.
Shal. She's coming; to her, coz. O boy, thou hadst a father!
Slen. I had a father, Mistress Anne—my uncle can tell you good jests of him:—Pray you, uncle, tell Mistress Anne the jest, how my father stole two geese out of a pen, good uncle.
Shal. Mistress Anne, my cousin loves you.
Slen. Ay, that I do; as well as I love any woman in Gloucestershire.
Shal. He will maintain you like a gentlewoman.
Slen. Ay, that I will, come cut and long-tail, under the degree of a 'squire.
Shal. He will make you a hundred and fifty pounds jointure.   [himself.
Anne. Good Master Shallow, let him woo for
Shal. Marry, I thank you for it; I thank you for that good comfort. She calls you, coz; I'll leave you.
Anne. Now, Master Slender.
Slen. Now, good Mistress Anne.
Anne. What is your will?
Slen. My will? 'od's heartlings, that's a pretty jest indeed! I ne'er made my will yet, I thank heaven; I am not such a sickly creature, I give heaven praise.   [with me?
Anne. I mean, Master Slender, what would you
Slen. Truly, for mine own part I would little or nothing with you. Your father and my uncle have made motions: if it be my luck, so: if not, happy man be his dole! They can tell you how things go better than I can. You may ask your father; here he comes.

Enter PAGE *and Mrs.* PAGE.

Page. Now, Master Slender:—Love him, daughter Anne.—
Why, how now! what does Master Fenton here? You wrong me, sir, thus still to haunt my house: I told you, sir, my daughter is disposed of.
Fent. Nay, Master Page, be not impatient.
Mrs. Page. Good Master Fenton, come not to my child.
Page. She is no match for you.
Fent. Sir, will you hear me?
Page.   No, good Master Fenton.
Come, Master Shallow; come, son Slender, in:—   [Fenton.
Knowing my mind, you wrong me, Master
                    [*Exeunt* PAGE, SHAL., *and* SLEN.
Quick. Speak to Mrs. Page.
Fent. Good Mistress Page, for that I love your daughter

In such a righteous fashion as I do, [ners,
Perforce, against all checks, rebukes, and man-
I must advance the colours of my.love,
And not retire. Let me have your good will.
Anne. Good mother, do not marry me to yond
fool.
Mrs. Page. I mean it not; I seek you a better
husband.
Quick. That's my master, master doctor.
Anne. Alas! I had rather be set quick i' the
earth.
And bowled to death with turnips.
Mrs. Page. Come, trouble not yourself, Good
Master Fenton.
I will not be your friend, nor enemy:
My daughter will I question how she loves you,
And as I find her, so am I affected;
Till then, farewell, sir:—She must needs go in;
Her father will be angry.
        [*Exeunt Mrs.* PAGE *and* ANNE.
Fent. Farewell, gentle mistress; farewell, Nan.
Quick. This is my doing, now:—Nay, said I,
will you cast away your child on a fool, and
a physician? Look on Master Fenton:—this is
my doing.
Fent. I thank thee; and I pray thee, once to-
night
Give my sweet Nan this ring. There's for thy
        pains.   [*Exit.*
Quick. Now heaven send thee good fortune!
A kind heart he hath: a woman would run
through fire and water for such a kind heart.
But yet I would my master had Mistress Anne:
or I would Master Slender had her: or, in sooth,
I would Master Fenton had her: I will do what
I can for them all three; for so I have promised,
and I'll be as good as my word; but speciously
for Master Fenton. Well, I must of another
errand to Sir John Falstaff from my two mistresses. What a beast am I to slack it! [*Exit.*

SCENE V.—*A Room in the Garter Inn.*

Enter FALSTAFF *and* BARDOLPH.

Fal. Bardolph, I say,—
Bard. Here, sir.
Fal. Go fetch me a quart of sack; put a toast
in't. [*Exit* BARD.] Have I lived to be carried
in a basket, like a barrow of butcher's offal;
and to be thrown into the Thames? Well, if I
be served such another trick, I'll have my
brains ta'en out and butter'd, and give them
to a dog for a new year's gift. The rogues
slighted me into the river with as little remorse
as they would have drowned a bitch's blind
puppies, fifteen i' the litter: and you may know
by my size that I have a kind of alacrity in
sinking; if the bottom were as deep as hell I
should down. I had been drowned but that the
shore was shelvy and shallow: a death that I
abhor; for the water swells a man; and what a
thing should I have been when I had been
swelled! I should have been a mountain of
mummy.

Re-enter BARDOLPH, *with the wine.*

Bard. Here's Mistress Quickly, sir, to speak
with you.
Fal. Come, let me pour in some sack to the
Thames water; for my belly's as cold as if I had
swallowed snow-balls for pills to cool the reins.
Call her in.
Bard. Come in, woman.

Enter Mrs. QUICKLY.

Quick. By your leave; I cry you mercy. Give
your worship good-morrow
Fal. Take away these chalices. Go, brew me
a bottle of sack finely.
Bard. With eggs, sir?
Fal. Simple of itself; I'll no pullet-sperm in
my brewage —[*Exit* BARD.]—How now?
Quick. Marry, sir, I come to your worship
from Mistress Ford.
Fal. Mistress Ford! I have had ford enough:
I was thrown into the ford: I have my belly
full of ford.
Quick. Alas the day! good heart, that was not
her fault: she does so take on with her men;
they mistook their erection.
Fal. So did I mine, to build upon a foolish
woman's promise.
Quick. Well, she laments, sir, for it, that it
would yearn your heart to see it. Her husband
goes this morning a-birding; she desires you
once more to come to her between eight and
nine; I must carry her word quickly: she'll
make you amends, I warrant you.
Fal. Well, I will visit her. Tell her so; and bid
her think what a man is: let her consider his
frailty, and then judge of my merit.
Quick. I will tell her.
Fal. Do so. Between nine and ten, say'st thou?
Quick. Eight and nine, sir.
Fal. Well, begone: I will not miss her.
Quick. Peace be with you, sir.   [*Exit.*
Fal. I marvel I hear not of Master Brook; he
sent me word to stay within: I like his money
well. O, here he comes.

Enter FORD.

Ford. Bless you, sir!
Fal. Now, Master Brook? you come to know
what hath passed between me and Ford's wife.
Ford. That, indeed, Sir John, is my business.
Fal. Master Brook, I will not lie to you; I
was at her house the hour she appointed me.
Ford. And how sped you, sir?
Fal. Very ill-favouredly, Master Brook.
Ford. How so, sir? Did she change her determination?
Fal. No, Master Brook; but the peaking cor-
nuto her husband, Master Brook, dwelling in a
continual 'larum of jealousy, comes me in the
instant of our encounter, after we had embraced,
kissed, protested, and, as it were, spoke the prologue of our comedy; and at his heels a rabble
of his companions, thither provoked and insti-

gated by his distemper, and forsooth, to search his house for his wife's love.

Ford. What! while you were there?

Fal. While I was there. [find you?

Ford. And did he search for you and could not

Fal. You shall hear. As good luck would have it, comes in one Mistress Page; gives intelligence of Ford's approach; and, by her invention and Ford's wife's distraction, they conveyed me into a buck-basket.

Ford. A buck-basket!

Fal. By the Lord, a buck-basket: rammed me in with foul shirts and smocks, socks, foul stockings, and greasy napkins; that, Master Brook, there was the rankest compound of villanous smell that ever offended nostril.

Ford. And how long lay you there?

Fal. Nay, you shall hear, Master Brook, what I have suffered to bring this woman to evil for your good. Being thus crammed in the basket, a couple of Ford's knaves, his hinds, were called forth by their mistress to carry me in the name of foul clothes to Datchet-lane: they took me on their shoulders; met the jealous knave their master in the door; who asked them once or twice what they had in their basket: I quaked for fear lest the lunatic knave would have searched it; but fate, ordaining he should be a cuckold, held his hand. Well: on went he for a search, and away went I for foul clothes. But mark the sequel, Master Brook; I suffered the pangs of three several deaths: first, an intolerable fright to be detected with a jealous rotten bell-wether: next, to be compassed, like a good bilbo, in the circumference of a peck, hilt to point, heel to head: and then, to be stopped in, like a strong distillation, with stinking clothes that fretted in their own grease: think of that, —a man of my kidney,—think of that: that am as subject to heat as butter; a man of continual dissolution and thaw; it was a miracle to 'scape suffocation. And in the height of this bath, when I was more than half-stewed in grease, like a Dutch dish, to be thrown into the Thames, and cooled, glowing hot, in that surge, like a horse-shoe; think of that,—hissing hot,—think of that, Master Brook.

Ford. In good sadness, sir, I am sorry that for my sake you have suffered all this. My suit, then, is desperate; you'll undertake her no more.

Fal. Master Brook, I will be thrown into Etna, as I have been into Thames, ere I will leave her thus. Her husband is this morning gone a-birding: I have received from her another embassy of meeting; 'twixt eight and nine is the hour, Master Brook.

Ford. 'Tis past eight already, sir.

Fal. Is it? I will then address me to my appointment. Come to me at your convenient leisure, and you shall know how I speed; and the conclusion shall be crowned with your enjoying her. Adieu. You shall have her, Master Brook; Master Brook, you shall cuckold Ford. [*Exit.*

Ford. Hum! ha! is this a vision? is this a dream? do I sleep? Master Ford, awake; awake, Master Ford; there's a hole made in your best coat, Master Ford. This 'tis to be married! this 'tis to have linen and buck-baskets!—Well, I will proclaim myself what I am: I will now take the lecher; he is at my house: he cannot 'scape me; 'tis impossible he should; he cannot creep into a halfpenny purse nor into a pepper box; but, lest the devil that guides him should aid him, I will search impossible places. Though what I am I cannot avoid, yet to be what I would not shall not make me tame; if I have horns to make one mad, let the proverb go with me, I'll be horn mad. [*Exit.*

ACT IV.

SCENE I.—*The Street.*

Enter Mrs. PAGE, *Mrs.* QUICKLY, *and* WILLIAM.

Mrs. Page. Is he at Master Ford's already, think'st thou?

Quick. Sure he is by this; or will be presently: but truly he is very courageous mad about his throwing into the water. Mistress Ford desires you to come suddenly.

Mrs. Page. I'll be with her by and by; I'll but bring my young man here to school. Look, where his master comes; 'tis a playing day, I see.

Enter Sir HUGH EVANS.

How now, Sir Hugh? no school to-day?

Eva. No; Master Slender is let the boys leave to play.

Quick. Blessing of his heart!

Mrs. Page. Sir Hugh, my husband says my son profits nothing in the world at his book; I pray you ask him some questions in his accidence.

Eva. Come hither, William; hold up your head; come.

Mrs. Page. Come on, sirrah: hold up your head; answer your master; be not afraid.

Eva. William, how many numbers is in nouns?

Will. Two.

Quick. Truly, I thought there had been one number more; because they say od's nouns.

Eva. Peace your tattlings. What is *fair*, William?

Will. Pulcher.

Quick. Polecats! there are fairer things than polecats, sure.

Eva. You are a very simplicity, 'oman; I pray you, peace. What is *lapis*, William?

Will. A stone.

Eva. And what is a stone, William?

Will. A pebble.

Eva. No, it is *lapis:* I pray you remember in your prain.

Will. Lapis.

Eva. That is good, William. What is he, William, that does lend articles?

Will. Articles are borrowed of the pronoun;

and be thus declined, *Singulariter, nominativo, hic, hæc, hoc.*

Eva. Nominativo, *hig, hag, hog:*—pray you, mark: *genitivo, hujus.* Well, what is your *accusative case?*

Will. Accusativo, *hinc.*

Eva. I pray you, have your remembrance, child. *Accusativo, hing, hang, hog.* [you.

Quick. Hang hog is Latin for bacon, I warrant

Eva. Leave your prabbles, 'oman. What is the focative case, William?

Will. O—*vocativo,* O.

Eva. Remember, William, focative is *caret.*

Quick. And that's a good root.

Eva. 'Oman, forbear.

Mrs. Page. Peace.

Eva. What is your *genitive case plural,* William?

Will. Genitive case?

Eva. Ay.

Will. Genitive,—*horum, harum, horum.*

Quick. 'Vengeance of *Jenny's* case! fie on her! —never name her, child, if she be a whore.

Eva. For shame, 'oman.

Quick. You do ill to teach the child such words: he teaches him to hick and to hack, which they'll do fast enough of themselves, and to call horum: fie upon you!

Eva. 'Oman, art thou lunatics? hast thou no understandings for thy cases, and the numbers of the genders? Thou art as foolish Christian creatures as I would desires.

Mrs. Page. Pr'ythee, hold thy peace.

Eva. Show me now, William, some declensions of your pronouns.

Will. Forsooth, I have forgot.

Eva. It is *ki, kæ, cod;* if you forget your *kies,* your *kæs,* and your *cods,* you must be preeches. Go your ways and play, go.

Mrs. Page. He is a better scholar than I thought he was.

Eva. He is a good sprag memory. Farewell, Mistress Page.

Mrs. Page. Adieu, good Sir Hugh. [*Exit Sir Hugh.*] Get you home, boy.—Come, we stay too long. [*Exeunt.*

SCENE II.—*A Room in* FORD'S *House.*

Enter FALSTAFF *and Mrs.* FORD.

Fal. Mistress Ford, your sorrow hath eaten up my sufferance: I see you are obsequious in your love, and I profess requital to a hair's breadth; not only, Mistress Ford, in the simple office of love, but in all the accoutrement, complement, and ceremony of it. But are you sure of your husband now?

Mrs. Ford. He is a-birding, sweet Sir John.

Mrs. Page. [*Within.*] What hoa, gossip Ford, what hoa!

Mrs. Ford. Step into the chamber, Sir John. [*Exit* FALSTAFF.

Enter Mrs. PAGE.

Mrs. Page. How now, sweetheart? who's at home beside yourself?

Mrs. Ford. Why, none but mine own people.

Mrs. Page. Indeed?

Mrs. Ford. No, certainly;—Speak louder.
[*Aside.*

Mrs. Page. Truly I am so glad you have nobody here.

Mrs. Ford. Why?

Mrs. Page. Why, woman, your husband is in his old lunes again: he so takes on yonder with my husband; so rails against all married mankind: so curses all Eve's daughters, of what complexion soever; and so buffets himself on the forehead, crying *Peer-out, peer-out!* that any madness I ever yet beheld seemed but tameness, civility, and patience, to this his distemper he is in now: I am glad the fat knight is not here.

Mrs. Ford. Why? does he talk of him?

Mrs. Page. Of none but him; and swears he was carried out, the last time he searched for him, in a basket: protests to my husband he is now here; and hath drawn him and the rest of their company from their sport to make another experiment of his suspicion; but I am glad the knight is not here; now he shall see his own foolery.

Mrs. Ford. How near is he, Mistress Page?

Mrs. Page. Hard by; at street end; he will be here anon.

Mrs. Ford. I am undone!—The knight is here.

Mrs. Page. Why, then, you are utterly ashamed, and he's but a dead man. What a woman are you!—Away with him, away with him; better shame than murder.

Mrs. Ford. Which way should he go? How should I bestow him? Shall I put him into the basket again?

Re-enter FALSTAFF.

Fal. No, I'll come no more i' the basket. May I not go out ere he come?

Mrs. Page. Alas! three of Master Ford's brothers watch the door with pistols, that none shall issue out: otherwise you might slip away ere he came. But what make you here?

Fal. What shall I do?—I'll creep up into the chimney.

Mrs. Ford. There they always used to discharge their birding pieces. Creep into the kiln-hole.

Fal. Where is it?

Mrs. Ford. He will seek there, on my word. Neither press, coffer, chest, trunk, well, vault, but he hath an abstract for the remembrance of such places, and goes to them by his note. There is no hiding you in the house.

Fal. I'll go out then.

Mrs. Page. If you go out in your own semblance, you die, Sir John. Unless you go out disguised,—

Mrs. Ford. How might we disguise him?

Mrs. Page. Alas the day, I know not. There is no woman's gown big enough for him; otherwise he might put on a hat, a muffler, and a kerchief, and so escape.

Fal. Good hearts, devise something: any extremity rather than a mischief.

Mrs. Ford. My maid's aunt, the fat woman of Brentford, has a gown above.

Mrs. Page. On my word, it will serve him; she's as big as he is: and there's her thrummed hat, and her muffle too. Run up, Sir John.

Mrs. Ford. Go, go, sweet Sir John. Mistress Page and I will look some linen for your head.

Mrs. Page. Quick, quick; we'll come dress you straight: put on the gown the while.

               [*Exit* FALSTAFF.

Mrs. Ford. I would my husband would meet him in this shape: he cannot abide the old woman of Brentford; he swears she's a witch, forbade her my house, and hath threatened to beat her.

Mrs. Page. Heaven guide him to thy husband's cudgel; and the devil guide his cudgel afterwards!

Mrs. Ford. But is my husband coming?

Mrs. Page. Ay, in good sadness is he; and he talks of the basket too, howsoever he hath had intelligence.

Mrs. Ford. We'll try that; for I'll appoint my men to carry the basket again to meet him at the door with it as they did last time.

Mrs. Page. Nay, but he'll be here presently: let's go dress him like the witch of Brentford.

Mrs. Ford. I'll first direct my men what they shall do with the basket. Go up, I'll bring linen for him straight.   [*Exit.*

Mrs. Page. Hang him, dishonest varlet! we cannot misuse him enough.

> We'll leave a proof, by that which we will do,
> Wives may be merry and yet honest too:
> We do not act that often jest and laugh;
> 'Tis old but true, *Still swine eat all the draff.*

                     [*Exit.*

Re-enter Mrs. FORD, *with two* Servants.

Mrs. Ford. Go, sirs, take the basket again on your shoulders: your master is hard at door; if he bid you set it down, obey him: quickly, despatch.   [*Exit.*

1 Serv. Come, come, take it up.

2 Serv. Pray heaven it be not full of the knight again.   [lead.

1 Serv. I hope not; I had as lief bear so much

Enter FORD, PAGE, SHALLOW, CAIUS, *and Sir* HUGH EVANS.

Ford. Ay, but if it prove true, Master Page, have you any way then to unfool me again?—Set down the basket, villain:—Somebody call my wife.—You, youth in a basket, come out here!—O, you panderly rascals! there's a knot, a gin, a pack, a conspiracy against me. Now shall the devil be shamed. What! wife, I say! come, come forth; behold what honest clothes you send forth to bleaching.

Page. Why, this passes! Master Ford, you are not to go loose any longer; you must be pinioned.

Eva. Why, this is lunatics! this is mad as a mad dog!

Shal. Indeed, Master Ford, this is not well: indeed.

Enter Mrs. FORD.

Ford. So say I too, sir.—Come hither, Mistress Ford; Mistress Ford, the honest woman, the modest wife, the virtuous creature, that hath the jealous fool to her husband!—I suspect without cause, mistress, do I?

Mrs. Ford. Heaven be my witness, you do, if you suspect me in any dishonesty.

Ford. Well said, brazen-face; hold it out.—Come forth, sirrah.

         [*Pulls the clothes out of the basket.*

Page. This passes!   [clothes alone.

Mrs. Ford. Are you not ashamed? Let the

Ford. I shall find you anon.

Eva. 'Tis unreasonable! Will you take up your wife's clothes? Come away.

Ford. Empty the basket, I say.

Mrs. Ford. Why, man, why,—

Ford. Master Page, as I am a man, there was one conveyed out of my house yesterday in this basket. Why may not he be there again? In my house I am sure he is: my intelligence is true: my jealousy is reasonable. Pluck me out all the linen.

Mrs. Ford. If you find a man there he shall die a flea's death.

Page. Here's no man.

Shal. By my fidelity, this is not well, Master Ford; this wrongs you.

Eva. Master Ford, you must pray, and not follow the imaginations of your own heart: this is jealousies.

Ford. Well, he's not here I seek for.

Page. No, nor no where else but in your brain.

Ford. Help to search my house this one time: if I find not what I seek, show no colour for my extremity; let me for ever be your table sport; let them say of me, As jealous as Ford, that searched a hollow walnut for his wife's leman. Satisfy me once more; once more search with me.

Mrs. Ford. What, hoa, Mistress Page! come you and the old woman down; my husband will come into the chamber.

Ford. Old woman! What old woman's that?

Mrs. Ford. Why, it is my maid's aunt of Brentford.

Ford. A witch, a quean, an old cozening quean! Have I not forbid her my house? She comes of errands, does she? We are simple men; we do not know what's brought to pass under the profession of fortune telling. She works by charms, by spells, by the figure, and such daubery as this is; beyond our element: we know nothing. ——Come down, you witch, you hag you; come down, I say.

Mrs. Ford. Nay, good, sweet husband;—good gentlemen, let him not strike the old woman.

Enter FALSTAFF *in women's clothes, led by Mrs.* PAGE.

Mrs. Page. Come, Mother Prat, come; give me your hand.

Ford. I'll *prat* her:———Out of my door, you witch, [*beats him*] you rag, you baggage, you polecat, you ronyon! out! out! I'll conjure you, I'll fortune-tell you.　　　　　[*Exit* FALSTAFF.

Mrs. Page. Are you not ashamed? I think you have killed the poor woman.

Mrs. Ford. Nay, he will do it:—'Tis a goodly credit for you.

Ford. Hang her, witch!

Eva. By yea and no, I think the 'oman is a witch indeed: I like not when a 'oman has a great peard; I spy a great peard under her muffler.

Ford. Will you follow, gentlemen? I beseech you follow; see but the issue of my jealousy: if I cry out thus upon no trail, never trust me when I open again.

Page. Let's obey his humour a little farther. Come, gentlemen.
　　　　[*Exeunt* PAGE, FORD, SHAL., *and* EVANS.

Mrs. Page. Trust me, he beat him most pitifully.

Mrs. Ford. Nay, by the mass, that he did not; he beat him most unpitifully methought.

Mrs. Page. I'll have the cudgel hallowed and hung o'er the altar; it hath done meritorious service.

Mrs. Ford. What think you? May we, with the warrant of womanhood and the witness of a good conscience, pursue him with any further revenge?

Mrs. Page. The spirit of wantonness is, sure, scared out of him; if the devil have him not in fee-simple, with fine and recovery, he will never, I think, in the way of waste, attempt us again.

Mrs. Ford. Shall we tell our husbands how we have served him?

Mrs. Page. Yes, by all means; if it be but to scrape the figures out of your husband's brains. If they can find in their hearts the poor unvirtuous fat knight shall be any further afflicted, we two will still be the ministers.

Mrs. Ford. I'll warrant they'll have him publicly shamed: and methinks there would be no period to the jest should he not be publicly shamed.

Mrs. Page. Come, to the forge with it then, shape it: I would not have things cool. [*Exeunt.*

SCENE III.—*A Room in the Garter Inn.*

Enter HOST *and* BARDOLPH.

Bard. Sir, the Germans desire to have three of your horses: the duke himself will be to-morrow at court, and they are going to meet him.

Host. What duke should that be comes so secretly? I hear not of him in the court. Let me speak with the gentlemen; they speak English.

Bard. Ay, sir; I'll call them to you.

Host. They shall have my horses; but I'll make them pay; I'll sauce them: they have had my houses a week at command; I have turned away my other guests: they must come off; I'll sauce them. Come.　　　　　　[*Exeunt.*

SCENE IV.—*A Room in* FORD's *House.*

Enter PAGE, FORD, *Mrs.* PAGE, *Mrs.* FORD, *and Sir* HUGH EVANS

Eva. 'Tis one of the pest discretions of a 'oman as ever I did look upon.

Page. And did he send you both these letters at an instant?

Mrs. Page. Within a quarter of an hour.

Ford. Pardon me, wife. Henceforth, do what thou wilt;
I rather will suspect the sun with cold
Than thee with wantonness: now doth thy honour stand,
In him that was of late an heretic,
As firm as faith.

Page.　　　　　'Tis well, 'tis well; no more.
Be not as éxtreme in submission
As in offence;
But let our plot go forward: let our wives
Yet once again, to make us public sport,
Appoint a meeting with this old fat fellow,
Where we may take him and disgrace him for it.

Ford. There is no better way than that they spoke of.

Page. How! to send him word they'll meet him in the park at midnight; fie, fie; he'll never come.

Eva. You say he has been thrown into the rivers; and has been grievously peaten as an old 'oman; methinks there should be terrors in him that he should not come; methinks his flesh is punished, he shall have no desires.

Page. So think I too.　　　　　[he comes,

Mrs. Ford. Devise but how you'll use him when
And let us two devise to bring him thither.

Mrs. Page. There is an old tale goes, that Herne the hunter,
Sometime a keeper here in Windsor forest,
Doth all the winter time, at still midnight,
Walk round about an oak, with great ragg'd horns;
And there he blasts the tree, and takes the cattle,
And makes milch-kine yield blood, and shakes a chain
In a most hideous and dreadful manner: [know
You have heard of such a spirit; and well you
The supersitious idle-headed eld
Received, and did deliver to our age,
This tale of Herne the hunter for a truth. [fear

Page. Why, yet there want not many that do
In deep of night to walk by this Herne's oak:
But what of this?

Mrs. Ford.　　　　　Marry, this is our device;
That Falstaff at that oak shall meet with us,
Disguised, like Herne, with huge horns on his head.　　　　　　[come,

Page. Well, let it not be doubted but he'll
And in this shape. When you have brought him thither,
What shall be done with him? what is your plot?

Mrs. Page. That likewise have we thought upon, and thus:
Nan Page my daughter, and my little son,

And three or four more of their growth, we'll
     dress   [white,
Like urchins, ouphes, and fairies, green and
With rounds of waxen tapers on their heads,
And rattles in their hands; upon a sudden,
As Falstaff, she, and I, are newly met,
Let them from forth a saw-pit rush at once
With some diffused song; upon their sight
We two in great amazedness will fly:
Then let them all encircle him about,
And fairy-like, to pinch the unclean knight;
And ask him why that hour of fairy revel
In their so sacred paths he dares to tread
In shape profane.
Mrs. Ford.   And till he tell the truth,
Let the supposed fairies pinch him sound,
And burn him with their tapers.
Mrs. Page.   The truth being known,
We'll all present ourselves, dis-horn the spirit,
And mock him home to Windsor.
Ford.   The children must
Be practised well to this or they'll ne'er do't.
Eva. I will teach the children their behaviours;
and I will be like a jack-an-apes also, to burn
the knight with my taber.
Ford. That will be excellent. I'll go buy them
vizards.   [the fairies,
Mrs. Page. My Nan shall be the queen of all
Finely attired in a robe of white.   [time.
Page. That silk will I go buy;—and in that
Shall Master Slender steal my Nan away. [*Aside.*
And marry her at Eton.——Go, send to Fal-
     staff straight.
Ford. Nay, I'll to him again, in name of Brook;
He'll tell me all his purpose. Sure, he'll come.
Mrs. Page. Fear not you that. Go, get us
     properties,
And tricking for our fairies.
Eva. Let us about it. It is admirable pleasures,
and fery honest knaveries.
     [*Exeunt* PAGE, FORD, *and* EVANS.
Mrs. Page. Go, Mistress Ford,
Send quickly to Sir John to know his mind.
     [*Exit Mrs.* FORD.
I'll to the doctor; he hath my good-will,
And none but he, to marry with Nan Page.
That Slender, though well landed, is an idiot;
And he my husband best of all affects:
The doctor is well money'd, and his friends
Potent at court; he, none but he, shall have her.
Though twenty thousand worthier come to
     crave her.   [*Exit.*

SCENE V.—*A Room in the Garter Inn.*

Enter HOST *and* SIMPLE.

Host. What wouldst thou have, boor? what,
thick-skin? speak, breathe, discuss; brief, short,
quick, snap.
Sim. Marry, sir, I come to speak with Sir John
Falstaff from Master Slender.
Host. There's his chamber, his house, his castle,
his standing-bed and truckle-bed; 'tis painted
about with the story of the Prodigal, fresh and

new. Go, knock and call; he'll speak like an
Anthropophaginian unto thee. Knock, I say.
Sim. There's an old woman, a fat woman, gone
up into his chamber; I'll be so bold as stay, sir,
till she come down; I come to speak with her,
indeed.
Host. Ha! a fat woman! the knight may be
robbed: I'll call.—Bully knight! Bully Sir
John! speak from thy lungs military. Art thou
there? it is thine host, thine Ephesian, calls.
Fal. [*Above.*] How now, mine host?
Host. Here's a Bohemian-Tartar tarries the
coming down of thy fat woman. Let her descend, bully, let her descend; my chambers are
honourable. Fie! privacy? fie!

Enter FALSTAFF.

Fal. There was, mine host, an old fat woman
even now with me; but she's gone.
Sim. Pray you, sir, was't not the wise woman
of Brentford?
Fal. Ay, marry was it, muscle-shell. What
would you with her?
Sim. My master, sir, my Master Slender, sent
to her, seeing her go thorough the streets, to
know, sir, whether one Nym, sir, that beguiled
him of a chain had the chain or no.
Fal. I spake with the old woman about it.
Sim. And what says she, I pray, sir?
Fal. Marry, she says that the very same man
that beguiled Master Slender of his chain coz-
ened him of it.
Sim. I would I could have spoken with the
woman herself; I had other things to have
spoken with her too, from him.
Fal. What are they? let us know.
Host. Ay, come; quick.
Sim. I may not conceal them, sir.
Fal. Conceal them, or thou diest.
Sim. Why, sir, they were nothing but about
Mistress Anne Page; to know if it were my
master's fortune to have her or no.
Fal. 'Tis, 'tis his fortune.
Sim. What, sir?
Fal. To have her,—or no. Go; say the woman
told me so.
Sim. May I be so bold to say so, sir?
Fal. Ay, Sir Tike; who more bold?
Sim. I thank your worship: I shall make my
master glad with these tidings. [*Exit* SIMPLE.
Host. Thou art clerkly, thou art clerkly, Sir
John. Was there a wise woman with thee?
Fal. Ay, that there was, mine host; one that
hath taught me more wit than ever I learned
before in my life: and I paid nothing for it
neither, but was paid for my learning.

Enter BARDOLPH.

Bard. Out, alas, sir! cozenage! mere cozenage!
Host. Where be my horses? speak well of them,
varletto.
Bard. Run away with the cozeners: for so soon
as I came beyond Eton they threw me off from
behind one of them in a slough of mire; and

set spurs and away, like three German devils, three Doctor Faustuses.

Host. They are gone but to meet the duke, villain: do not say they be fled; Germans are honest men.

Enter Sir HUGH EVANS.

Eva. Where is mine host?

Host. What is the matter, sir?

Eva. Have a care of your entertainments: there is a friend of mine come to town tells me there is three couzin germans that has cozened all the hosts of Readings, of Maidenhead, of Colebrook, of horses and money. I tell you for good-will, look you: you are wise, and full of gibes and vlouting-stogs; and 'tis not convenient you should be cozened: fare you well.   [*Exit.*

Enter Dr. CAIUS.

Caius. Vere is mine *Host de Jarterre?*

Host. Here, master doctor, in perplexity and doubtful dilemma.

Caius. I cannot tell vat is dat: but it is tell-a me dat you make grand preparation for a duke *de Jarmany:* by my trot dere is no duke dat de court is know to come; I tell you for good-vill: adieu.   [*Exit.*

Host. Hue and cry, villain, go:—assist me, knight; I am undone: fly, run, hue and cry, villain! I am undone!

                [*Exeunt* HOST *and* BARD.

Fal. I would all the world might be cozened; for I have been cozened and beaten too. If it should come to the ear of the court how I have been transformed, and how my transformation hath been washed and cudgelled, they would melt me out of my fat, drop by drop, and liquor fishermen's boots with me; I warrant they would whip me with their fine wits till I were as crest-fallen as a dried pear. I never prospered since I foreswore myself at *primero.* Well, if my wind were but long enough to say my prayers, I would repent.—

Enter Mrs. QUICKLY.

Now! whence come you?

Quick. From the two parties, forsooth.

Fal. The devil take one party and his dam the other, and so they shall be both bestowed! I have suffered more for their sakes, more than the villanous inconstancy of man's disposition is able to bear.

Quick. And have not they suffered? Yes, I warrant; speciously one of them; Mistress Ford, good heart, is beaten black and blue, that you cannot see a white spot about her.

Fal. What tell'st thou me of black and blue? I was beaten myself into all the colours of the rainbow; and I was like to be apprehended for the witch of Brentford; but that my admirable dexterity of wit, my counterfeiting the action of an old woman, delivered me, the knave constable had set me i' the stocks, i' the common stocks, for a witch.

Quick. Sir, let me speak with you in your chamber: you shall hear how things go; and, I warrant, to your content. Here is a letter will say somewhat. Good hearts, what ado here is to bring you together! Sure, one of you does not serve heaven well, that you are so crossed.

Fal. Come up into my chamber.   [*Exeunt.*

SCENE VI.—*Another Room in the Garter Inn.*

Enter FENTON and HOST.

Host. Master Fenton, talk not to me; my mind is heavy, I will give over all.   [pose,

Fent. Yet hear me speak. Assist me in my pur-
And, as I am a gentleman, I'll give thee
A hundred pound in gold, more than your loss.

Host. I will hear you, Master Fenton; and I will, at the least, keep your counsel.

Fent. From time to time I have acquainted you
With the dear love I bear to fair Anne Page;
Who, mutually, hath answer'd my affection,—
So far forth as herself might be her chooser,—
Even to my wish: I have a letter from her
Of such contents as you will wonder at;
The mirth whereof so larded with my matter
That neither, singly, can be manifested
Without the show of both;—wherein fat Falstaff
Hath a great scene: the image of the jest
                [*Showing the letter*
I'll show you here at large. Hark, good mine
          host,   [one,
To-night at Herne's oak, just 'twixt twelve and
Must my sweet Nan present the fairy queen·
The purpose why is here; in which disguise,
While other jests are something rank on foot,
Her father hath commanded her to slip
Away with Slender, and with him at Eton
Immediately to marry: she hath consented:
Now, sir,
Her mother, ever strong against that match,
And firm for Doctor Caius, hath appointed
That he shall likewise shuffle her away
While other sports are tasking of their minds,
And at the deanery, where a priest attends,
Straight marry her: to this her mother's plot
She, seemingly obedient, likewise hath
Made promise to the doctor:—Now thus it rests;
Her father means she shall be all in white;
And in that habit, when Slender sees his time
To take her by the hand and bid her go,
She shall go with him: her mother hath intended,
The better to denote her to the doctor,—
For they must all be mask'd and vizarded,—
That, quaint in green, she shall be loose enrobed,
With ribands pendant, flaring 'bout her head;
And when the doctor spies his vantage ripe,
To pinch her by the hand, and, on that token,
The maid hath given consent to go with him.

Host. Which means she to deceive? father or
          mother?

Fent. Both, my good host, to go along with me:
And here it rests,—that you'll procure the vicar
To stay for me at church, 'twixt twelve and one,
And, in the lawful name of marrying,

To give our hearts united ceremony.   [vicar:
Host. Well, husband your device; I'll to the
Bring you the maid, you shall not lack a priest.
Fent. So shall I evermore be bound to thee;
Besides, I'll make a present recompense.
                                        [*Exeunt.*

ACT V.

SCENE I.—*A Room in the Garter Inn.*

Enter FALSTAFF *and* Mrs. QUICKLY.

Fal. Pr'ythee, no more prattling:—go.——I'll
hold. This is the third time; I hope good luck
lies in odd numbers. Away, go; they say there
is divinity in odd numbers, either in nativity,
chance, or death.—Away.
Quick. I'll provide you a chain: and I'll do
what I can to get you a pair of horns.
Fal. Away, I say; time wears: hold up your
head, and mince.   [*Exit Mrs.* QUICKLY.

Enter FORD.

How now, Master Brook? Master Brook, the
matter will be known to-night or never. Be
you in the Park about midnight, at Herne's
oak, and you shall see wonders.
Ford. Went you not to her yesterday, sir, as
you told me you had appointed.
Fal. I went to her, Master Brook, as you see,
like a poor old man; but I came from her,
Master Brook, like a poor old woman. That
same knave, Ford her husband, hath the finest
mad devil of jealousy in him, Master Brook,
that ever governed frenzy. I will tell you.—
He beat me grievously, in the shape of a
woman; for in the shape of man, Master Brook,
I fear not Goliath with a weaver's beam; because I know also life is a shuttle. I am in
haste; go along with me; I'll tell you all, Master
Brook. Since I plucked geese, played truant,
and whipped top, I knew not what it was to
be beaten till lately. Follow me: I'll tell you
strange things of this knave Ford, on whom
to-night I will be revenged, and I will deliver
his wife into your hand.—Follow. Strange
things in hand, Master Brook! follow. [*Exeunt*

SCENE II.—*Windsor Park.*

Enter PAGE, SHALLOW, *and* SLENDER.

Page. Come, come; we'll couch i' the castle-
ditch till we see the light of our fairies.—
Remember, son Slender, my daughter.
Slen. Ay, forsooth; I have spoke with her, and
we have a nay-word how to know one another;
I come to her in white and cry *mum;* she cries
budget; and by that we know one another.
Shal. That's good too: but what needs either
your *mum* or her *budget?* the white will decipher
her well enough.—It hath struck ten o'clock.
Page. The night is dark; light and spirits will
become it well. Heaven prosper our sport! No
man means evil but the devil, and we shall
know him by his horns. Let's away; follow
me.   [*Exeunt.*

SCENE III.—*The Street in Windsor.*

Enter Mrs. PAGE, Mrs. FORD, *and Dr.* CAIUS.

Mrs. Page. Master doctor, my daughter is in
green: when you see your time, take her by
the hand, away with her to the deanery, and
dispatch it quickly. Go before into the park;
we two must go together.
Caius. I know vat I have to do; adieu.
Mrs. Page. Fare you well, sir.   [*Exit*
CAIUS.] My husband will not rejoice so much
at the abuse of Falstaff as he will chafe at the
doctor's marrying my daughter: but 'tis no
matter; better a little chiding than a great deal
of heart-break.
Mrs. Ford. Where is Nan now, and her troop
of fairies? and the Welsh devil, Hugh?
Mrs. Page. They are all couched in a pit hard
by Herne's oak, with obscured lights; which,
at the very instant of Falstaff's and our meeting, they will at once display to the night.
Mrs. Ford. That cannot choose but amaze him.
Mrs. Page. If he be not amazed he will be
mocked; if he be amazed he will every way be
mocked.
Mrs. Ford. We'll betray him finely.
Mrs. Page. Against such lewdsters and their
                    lechery,
Those that betray them do no treachery.
Mrs. Ford. The hour draws on. To the oak,
to the oak!   [*Exeunt.*

SCENE IV.—*Windsor Park.*

Enter Sir HUGH EVANS, *and* Fairies.

Eva. Trib, trib, fairies; come; and remember
your parts: be pold, I pray you; follow me into
the pit; and when I give the watch-'ords, do as
I pid vou. Come, come; trib, trib.   [*Exeunt.*

SCENE V.—*Another part of the Park.*

Enter FALSTAFF *disguised, with a buck's head on.*

Fal. The Windsor bell hath struck twelve; the
minute draws on. Now the hot-blooded gods
assist me:—Remember, Jove, thou wast a bull
for thy Europa; love set on thy horns.—O powerful love! that in some respects makes a beast
a man; in some other a man a beast.—You
were also, Jupiter, a swan, for the love of Leda:
—O omnipotent love! how near the god drew
to the complexion of a goose?—A fault done
first in the form of a beast:—O Jove, a beastly
fault! and then another fault in the semblance
of a fowl; think on't, Jove; a foul fault.—When
gods have hot backs what shall poor men do?
For me, I am here a Windsor stag; and the
fattest, I think, i' the forest. Send me a cool
rut-time, Jove, or who can blame me to piss
my tallow? Who comes here? my doe?

Enter Mrs. FORD *and* Mrs. PAGE.

Mrs. Ford. Sir John? art thou there, my deer?
my male deer?

Fal. My doe with the black scut?—Let the sky rain potatoes; let it thunder to the tune of *Green Sleeves;* hail kissing-comfits, and snow eringoes; let there come a tempest of provocation, I will shelter me here.   [*Embracing her.*
Mrs. Ford. Mistress Page is come with me, sweetheart.
Fal. Divide me like a bribe-buck, each a haunch: I will keep my sides to myself, my shoulders for the fellow of this walk, and my horns I bequeath your husbands. Am I a woodman? ha! Speak I like Herne the hunter?—Why, now is Cupid a child of conscience; he makes restitution. As I am a true spirit, welcome!   [*Noise within.*
Mrs. Page. Alas! what noise?
Mrs. Ford. Heaven forgive our sins!
Fal. What should this be?
Mrs. Ford. } Away, away.   [*They run off.*
Mrs. Page. }
Fal. I think the devil will not have me damned lest the oil that is in me should set hell on fire; he would never else cross me thus.

Enter Sir HUGH EVANS, *like a satyr; Mrs.* QUICKLY *and* PISTOL; ANNE PAGE, *as the Fairy Queen, attended by her brother and others, dressed like fairies, with waxen tapers on their heads.*

Quick. Fairies, black, gray, green, and white,
You moonshine revellers and shades of night,
You orphan-heirs of fixed destiny,
Attend your office and your quality.
Crier Hobgoblin, make the fairy o-yes.
Pist. Elves, list your names; silence, you airy toys.
Cricket, to Windsor chimneys shalt thou leap:
Where fires thou find'st unrak'd, and hearths unswept,
There pinch the maids as blue as bilberry:
Our radiant queen hates sluts and sluttery.
Fal. They are fairies; he that speaks to them shall die: [eye.
I'll wink and couch: no man their works must
    [*Lies down upon his face.*
Eva. Where's *Pede?*—Go you, and where you find a maid
That, ere she sleep, has thrice her prayers said,
Raise up the organs of her fantasy,
Sleep she as sound as careless infancy;
But those as sleep and think not on their sins,
Pinch them, arms, legs, backs, shoulders, sides, and shins.
Quick. About, about;
Search Windsor castle, elves, within and out:
Strew good luck, ouphes, on every sacred room;
That it may stand till the perpetual doom,
In state as wholesome as in state 'tis fit,
Worthy the owner and the owner it.
The several chairs of order look you scour
With juice of balm and every precious flower;
Each fair instalment, coat, and several crest,
With loyal blazon evermore be blest!
And nightly, meadow-fairies, look you sing,

Like to the Garter's compass, in a ring:
The expressure that it bears, green let it be,
More fertile-fresh than all the field to see;
And, *Hony soit qui mal y pense* write,
In emerald tufts, flowers purple, blue and white:
Like sapphire, pearl, and rich embroidery,
Buckled below fair knighthood's bending knee:
Fairies use flowers for their charáctery.
Away; disperse: but, 'tis one o'clock,
Our dance of custom, round about the oak
Of Herne the hunter, let us not forget.
Eva. Pray you, lock hand in hand; yourselves in order set:
And twenty glow-worms shall our lanterns be,
To guide our measure round about the tree.
But, stay: I smell a man of middle earth.
Fal. Heavens defend me from that Welsh fairy! lest he transform me to a piece of cheese!
Pist. Vile worm, thou wast o'erlook'd even in thy birth.
Quick. With trial-fire touch me his finger end:
If he be chaste, the flame will back descend
And turn him to no pain; but if he start,
It is the flesh of a corrupted heart.
Pist. A trial, come.
Eva.   Come, will this wood take fire?
    [*They burn him with their tapers.*
Fal. Oh, oh, oh!
Quick. Corrupt, corrupt, and tainted in desire!
About him, fairies; sing a scornful rhyme;
And, as you trip, still pinch him to your time.
Eva. It is right; indeed he is full of lecheries and iniquity.

SONG.
    Fye on sinful fantasy!
    Fye on lust and luxury!
    Lust is but a bloody fire,
    Kindled with unchaste desire,
    Fed in heart; whose flames aspire,
    As thoughts do blow them, higher and higher,
    Pinch him, fairies, mutually;
    Pinch him for his villany;
Pinch him, and burn him, and turn him about,
Till candles, and star-light, and moonshine be out.

During this song the fairies pinch FALSTAFF. *Doctor* CAIUS *comes one way, and steals away a fairy in green;* SLENDER *another way, and takes off a fairy in white; and* FENTON *comes, and steals away Mrs.* ANNE PAGE. *A noise of hunting is made within. All the fairies run away.* FALSTAFF *pulls off his buck's head and rises.*

Enter PAGE, FORD, *Mrs.* PAGE, *and Mrs.* FORD. *They lay hold on him.*

Page. Nay, do not fly; I think we have watch'd you now:
Will none but Herne the hunter serve your turn?
Mrs. Page. I pray you come; hold up the jest no higher:—
Now, good Sir John, how like you Windsor wives?
See you these, husband? do not these fair yokes
Become the forest better than the town?
Ford. Now, sir, who's a cuckold now?—Master Brook, Falstaff's a knave, a cuckoldly knave; here are his horns, Master Brook: and,

Master Brook, he hath enjoyed nothing of Ford's but his buck-basket, his cudgel, and twenty pounds of money; which must be paid to Master Brook; his horses are arrested for it, Master Brook.

Mrs. Ford. Sir John, we have had ill luck; we could never meet. I will never take you for my love again, but I will always count you my deer.

Fal. I do begin to perceive that I am made an ass.

Ford. Ay, and an ox too; both the proofs are extant.

Fal. And these are not fairies? I was three or four times in the thought they were not fairies: and yet the guiltiness of my mind, the sudden surprise of my powers, drove the grossness of the foppery into a received belief, in despite of the teeth of all rhyme and reason, that they were fairies. See now how wit may be made a Jack-a-lent when 'tis upon ill employment.

Eva. Sir John Falstaff, serve Got and leave your desires, and fairies will not pinse you.

Ford. Well said, fairy Hugh.

Eva. And leave you your jealousies too, I pray you.

Ford. I will never mistrust my wife again, till thou art able to woo her in good English.

Fal. Have I laid my brain in the sun, and dried it, that it wants matter to prevent so gross o'er-reaching as this? Am I ridden with a Welsh goat too? Shall I have a coxcomb of frize? 'Tis time I were choked with a piece of toasted cheese.

Eva. Seese is not good to give putter; your pelly is all putter.

Fal. Seese and putter! have I lived to stand at the taunt of one that makes fritters of English? This is enough to be the decay of lust and late-walking through the realm.

Mrs. Page. Why, Sir John, do you think, though we would have thrust virtue out of our hearts by the head and shoulders, and have given ourselves without scruple to hell, that ever the devil could have made you our delight?

Ford. What! a hodge-pudding? a bag of flax?

Mrs. Page. A puffed man?

Page. Old, cold, withered, and of intolerable entrails?

Ford. And one that is as slanderous as Satan?

Page. And as poor as Job?

Ford. And as wicked as his wife?

Eva. And given to fornications, and to taverns, and sack, and wine, and metheglins, and to drinkings, and swearings, and starings, pribbles, and prabbles?

Fal. Well, I am your theme: you have the start of me; I am dejected; I am not able to answer the Welsh flannel: ignorance itself is a plummet o'er me; use me as you will.

Ford. Marry, sir, we'll bring you to Windsor, to one Master Brook, that you have cozened of money, to whom you should have been a pander: over and above that you have suffered, I think, to repay that money will be a biting affliction.

Mrs. Ford. Nay, husband, let that go to make amends:

Forgive that sum, and so we'll all be friends.

Ford. Well, here's my hand; all's forgiven at last.

Page. Yet be cheerful, knight: thou shalt eat a posset to-night at my house; where I will desire thee to laugh at my wife, that now laughs at thee. Tell her Master Slender hath married her daughter.

Mrs. Page. Doctors doubt that: if Anne Page be my daughter, she is by this Doctor Caius' wife. [*Aside.*

Enter SLENDER.

Slen. Who—ho! ho! father Page!

Page. Son! how now? how now, son? have you dispatched?

Slen. Dispatched!—I'll make the best in Gloucestershire know on't; would I were hanged, la, else.

Page. Of what, son?

Slen. I came yonder at Eton to marry Mistress Anne Page, and she's a great lubberly boy. If it had not been i' the church I would have swinged him, or he should have swinged me. If I did not think it had been Anne Page, would I might never stir, and 'tis a post-master's boy.

Page. Upon my life then you took the wrong.

Slen. What need you tell me that? I think so, when I took a boy for a girl. If I had been married to him, for all he was in woman's apparel, I would not have had him.

Page. Why, this is your own folly. Did not I tell you how you should know my daughter by her garments?

Slen. I went to her in white and cried *mum*, and she cried *budget*, as Anne and I had appointed; and yet it was not Anne, but a post-master's boy.

Eva. Jeshu! Master Slender, cannot you see but marry boys?

Page. Oh, I am vexed at heart: what shall I do?

Mrs. Page. Good George, be not angry: I knew of your purpose; turned my daughter into green; and, indeed, she is now with the doctor at the deanery, and there married.

Enter CAIUS.

Caius. Vere is Mistress Page? By gar, I am cozened; I ha' married *un garçon*, a boy; *un paisan*, by gar, a boy; it is not Anne Page: by gar, I am cozened.

Mrs. Page. Why, did you take her in green?

Caius. Ay, by gar, and 'tis a boy: by gar, I'll raise all Windsor. [*Exit* CAIUS.

Ford. This is strange. Who hath got the right Anne?

Page. My heart misgives me:—here comes Master Fenton.

Enter FENTON and ANNE PAGE.

How now, Master Fenton?

Anne. Pardon, good father! good my mother,
    pardon!
Page. Now, Mistress, how chance you went
not with Master Slender?
Mrs. Page. Why went you not with master
    doctor, maid?
Fent. You do amaze her: Hear the truth of it.
You would have married her most shamefully,
Where there was no proportión held in love.
The truth is, she and I, long since contracted,
Are now so sure that nothing can dissolve us.
The offence is holy that she hath committed:
And this deceit loses the name of craft,
Of disobedience, or unduteous title;
Since therein she doth evitate and shun
A thousand irreligious cursed hours,
Which forced marriage would have brought upon
    her.
Ford. Stand not amazed: here is no remedy:—
In love, the heavens themselves do guide the
    state;

Money buys lands, and wives are sold by fate.
Fal. I am glad, though you have ta'en a spe-
cial stand to strike at me, that your arrow hath
glanced.
Page. Well, what remedy? Fenton, heaven give
    thee joy!
What cannot be eschewed must be embraced.
Fal. When night-dogs run all sorts of deer are
    chased.
Eva. I will dance and eat plums at your
    wedding.
Mrs. Page. Well, I will muse no further:—
    Master Fenton,
Heaven give you many, many merry days!—
Good husband, let us every one go home,
And laugh this sport o'er by a country fire;
Sir John and all.
Ford. Let it be so:—Sir John,
To Master Brook you yet shall hold your word;
For he, to-night, shall lie with Mistress Ford.
                      [*Exeunt.*

TWELFTH NIGHT; OR, WHAT YOU WILL

DRAMATIS PERSONÆ

ORSINO, *Duke of Illyria.*
SEBASTIAN, *a young Gentleman, brother to* VIOLA.
ANTONIO, *a Sea Captain, friend to* SEBASTIAN.
A SEA CAPTAIN, *friend to* VIOLA.
VALENTINE, } *Gentlemen attending on the*
CURIO, } *Duke.*
SIR TOBY BELCH, *Uncle of* OLIVIA.
SIR ANDREW AGUE-CHEEK.

MALVOLIO, *Steward to* OLIVIA.
FABIAN, } *Servants to* OLIVIA.
CLOWN, }

OLIVIA, *a rich Countess.*
VIOLA, *in love with the Duke.*
MARIA, OLIVIA's *Woman.*

Lords, Priests, Sailors, Officers, Musicians, *and other* Attendants.

SCENE.—*A City in* ILLYRIA; *and the Sea-coast near it.*

ACT I.

SCENE I.—*An Apartment in the* DUKE'S *Palace.*

Enter DUKE, CURIO, Lords; Musicians *attending.*

Duke. If music be the food of love, play on,
Give me excess of it; that, surfeiting,
The appetite may sicken and so die.—
That strain again;—it had a dying fall;
O, it came o'er my ear like the sweet south,
That breathes upon a bank of violets,
Stealing, and giving odour.—Enough; no more;
'Tis not so sweet now as it was before.
O spirit of love, how quick and fresh art thou!
That, notwithstanding thy capacity
Receiveth as the sea, nought enters there,
Of what validity and pitch soever,
But falls into abatement and low price
Even in a minute! so full of shapes is fancy,
That it alone is high-fantastical.
Cur. Will you go hunt, my lord?
Duke.   What, Curio?
Cur.   The hart.
Duke. Why, so I do, the noblest that I have:
O, when mine eyes did see Olivia first,
Methought she purg'd the air of pestilence;
That instant was I turn'd into a hart;
And my desires, like fell and cruel hounds,
E'er since pursue me.—How now? what news from her?

Enter VALENTINE.

Val. So please my lord, I might not be admitted,
But from her handmaid do return this answer:
The element itself, till seven years' heat,
Shall not behold her face at ample view;
But, like a cloistress, she will veiled walk,
And water once a-day her chamber round
With eye-offending brine: all this to season
A brother's dead love, which she would keep fresh

And lasting in her sad remembrance.   [frame,
Duke. O, she that hath a heart of that fine
To pay this debt of love but to a brother,
How will she love when the rich golden shaft
Hath kill'd the flock of all affections else
That live in her! when liver, brain, and heart,
These sov'reign thrones, are all supplied and fill'd,—
Her sweet perfections,—with one self king!—
Away before me to sweet beds of flowers;
Love-thoughts lie rich when canopied with bowers.   [*Exeunt.*

SCENE II.—*The Sea-coast.*

Enter VIOLA, Captain, *and* Sailors.

Vio. What country, friends, is this?
Cap.   Illyria, lady.
Vio. And what should I do in Illyria?
My brother he is in Elysium.
Perchance he is not drown'd:—What think you, sailors?   [sav'd.
Cap. It is perchance that you yourself were
Vio. O my poor brother! and so perchance, may he be.   [chance,
Cap. True, madam; and, to comfort you with
Assure yourself, after our ship did split,
When you, and that poor number sav'd with you,
Hung on our driving boat, I saw your brother,
Most provident in peril, bind himself,—
Courage and hope both teaching him the practice,—
To a strong mast that liv'd upon the sea;
Where, like Arion on the dolphin's back,
I saw him hold acquaintance with the waves
So long as I could see.
Vio.   For saying so, there's gold:
Mine own escape unfoldeth to my hope,
Whereto thy speech serves for authority,
The like of him. Know'st thou this country?
Cap. Ay, madam, well; for I was bred and born
Not three hours' travel from this very place.
Vio. Who governs here?

Cap.   A noble duke, in nature
As in his name.
Vio.   What is his name?
Cap.   Orsino.
Vio. Orsino! I have heard my father name him.
He was a bachelor then.
Cap.   And so is now,
Or was so very late: for but a month
Ago I went from hence; and then 'twas fresh
In murmur,—as you know, what great ones do,
The less will prattle of,—that he did seek
The love of fair Olivia.
Vio.   What's she?
Cap. A virtuous maid, the daughter of a count
That died some twelvemonth since; then leav-
         ing her
In the protection of his son, her brother,
Who shortly also died: for whose dear love,
They say, she hath abjured the company
And sight of men.
Vio.   O that I served that lady!
And might not be delivered to the world,
Till I had made mine own occasion mellow
What my estate is.
Cap.   That were hard to compass:
Because she will admit no kind of suit,
No, not the duke's.
Vio. There is a fair behaviour in thee, captain;
And though that nature with a beauteous wall
Doth oft close in pollution, yet of thee
I will believe thou hast a mind that suits
With this thy fair and outward character.
I pray thee, and I'll pay thee bounteously,
Conceal me what I am; and be my aid
For such disguise as, haply, shall become
The form of my intent. I'll serve this duke;
Thou shalt present me as an eunuch to him;
It may be worth thy pains; for I can sing,
And speak to him in many sorts of music
That will allow me very worth his service.
What else may hap to time I will commit;
Only shape thou thy silence to my wit.
Cap. Be you his eunuch and your mute I'll be;
When my tongue blabs, then let mine eyes not see!
Vio. I thank thee. Lead me on.   [*Exeunt.*

SCENE III.—*A Room in* OLIVIA'S *House.*

Enter Sir TOBY BELCH *and* MARIA.

Sir To. What a plague means my niece, to take the death of her brother thus? I am sure care's an enemy to life.

Mar. By my troth, Sir Toby, you must come in earlier o' nights; your cousin, my lady, takes great exceptions to your ill hours.

Sir To. Why, let her except, before excepted.

Mar. Ay, but you must confine yourself within the modest limits of order.

Sir To. Confine? I'll confine myself no finer than I am: these clothes are good enough to drink in, and so be these boots too; an they be not, let them hang themselves in their own straps.

Mar. That quaffing and drinking will undo you: I heard my lady talk of it yesterday; and

of a foolish knight that you brought in one night here to be her wooer.

Sir To. Who? Sir Andrew Ague-cheek?

Mar. Ay, he.

Sir To. He's as tall a man as any's in Illyria.

Mar. What's that to the purpose?

Sir To. Why, he has three thousand ducats a-year.

Mar. Ay, but he'll have but a year in all these ducats; he's a very fool, and a prodigal.

Sir To. Fye, that you'll say so! he plays o' the viol-de-gambo, and speaks three or four languages word for word without book, and hath all the good gifts of nature.

Mar. He hath, indeed,—almost natural: for, besides that he's a fool, he's a great quarreler; and, but that he hath the gift of a coward to allay the gust he hath in quarrelling, 'tis thought among the prudent he would quickly have the gift of a grave.

Sir To. By this hand, they are scoundrels and substractors that say so of him. Who are they?

Mar. They that add, moreover, he's drunk nightly in your company.

Sir To. With drinking healths to my niece; I'll drink to her as long as there is a passage in my throat and drink in Illyria. He's a coward and a coystril that will not drink to my niece till his brains turn o' the toe like a parish-top. What, wench? Castiliano-vulgo! for here comes Sir Andrew Ague-face.

Enter Sir ANDREW AGUE-CHEEK.

Sir And. Sir Toby Belch! how now, Sir Toby Belch?

Sir To. Sweet Sir Andrew?

Sir And. Bless you, fair shrew.

Mar. And you too, sir.

Sir To. Accost, Sir Andrew, accost.

Sir And. What's that?

Sir To. My niece's chamber-maid.

Sir And. Good Mistress Accost, I desire better acquaintance.

Mar. My name is Mary, sir.

Sir And. Good Mistress Mary Accost,—

Sir To. You mistake, knight: accost is, front her, board her, woo her, assail her.

Sir And. By my troth, I would not undertake her in this company. Is that the meaning of accost?

Mar. Fare you well, gentlemen.

Sir To. An thou let part so, Sir Andrew, would thou mightst never draw sword again.

Sir And. An you part so, mistress, I would I might never draw sword again. Fair lady, do you think you have fools in hand?

Mar. Sir, I have not you by the hand.

Sir And. Marry, but you shall have; and here's my hand.

Mar. Now, sir, thought is free. I pray you, bring your hand to the buttery-bar and let it drink.

Sir And. Wherefore, sweetheart? what's your metaphor?

Mar. It's dry, sir.

Sir And. Why, I think so; I am not such an ass but I can keep my hand dry. But what's your jest?

Mar. A dry jest, sir.

Sir And. Are you full of them?

Mar. Ay, sir; I have them at my fingers' ends: marry, now I let go your hand I am barren.

[*Exit* MARIA.

Sir To. O knight, thou lack'st a cup of canary: When did I see thee so put down?

Sir And. Never in your life, I think; unless you see canary put me down. Methinks sometimes I have no more wit than a Christian or an ordinary man has; but I am a great eater of beef, and, I believe, that does harm to my wit.

Sir To. No question.

Sir And. An I thought that, I'd forswear it. I'll ride home to-morrow, Sir Toby.

Sir To. Pourquoy, my dear knight?

Sir And. What is *pourquoy?* do or not do? I would I had bestowed that time in the tongues that I have in fencing, dancing, and bear-baiting. O, had I but followed the arts!

Sir To. Then hadst thou had an excellent head of hair.

Sir And. Why, would that have mended my hair?

Sir To. Past question; for thou seest it will not curl by nature.

Sir And. But it becomes me well enough, does't not?

Sir To. Excellent; it hangs like flax on a distaff; and I hope to see a housewife take thee between her legs and spin it off.

Sir And. Faith, I'll home to-morrow, Sir Toby; your niece will not be seen; or, if she be, it's four to one she'll none of me; the count himself here hard by woos her.

Sir To. She'll none o' the count; she'll not match above her degree, neither in estate, years, nor wit; I have heard her swear it. Tut, there's life in't, man.

Sir And. I'll stay a month longer. I am a fellow o' the strangest mind i' the world; I delight in masques and revels sometimes altogether.

Sir To. Art thou good at these kick-shaws, knight?

Sir And. As any man in Illyria, whatsoever he be, under the degree of my betters; and yet I will not compare with an old man.

Sir To. What is thy excellence in a galliard, knight?

Sir And. Faith, I can cut a caper.

Sir To. And I can cut the mutton to't.

Sir And. And, I think, I have the back-trick simply as strong as any man in Illyria.

Sir To. Wherefore are these things hid? wherefore have these gifts a curtain before them? are they like to take dust, like Mistress Mall's picture? why dost thou not go to church in a galliard and come home in a coranto? My very walk should be a jig; I would not so much as make water but in a sink-a-pace. What dost thou mean? is it a world to hide virtues in? I did think, by the excellent constitution of thy leg, it was formed under the star of a galliard.

Sir And. Ay, 'tis strong, and it does indifferent well in a flame-coloured stock. Shall we set about some revels?

Sir To. What shall we do else? were we not born under Taurus?

Sir And. Taurus? that's sides and heart.

Sir To. No, sir; it is legs and thighs. Let me see thee caper: ha! higher: ha, ha!—excellent!

[*Exeunt.*

SCENE IV.—*A Room in the* DUKE'S *Palace.*

Enter VALENTINE, *and* VIOLA *in man's attire.*

Val. If the duke continue these favours towards you, Cesario, you are like to be much advanced; he hath known you but three days, and already you are no stranger.

Vio. You either fear his humour or my negligence, that you call in question the continuance of his life. Is he inconstant, sir, in his favours?

Val. No, believe me.

Enter DUKE, CURIO, *and* Attendants.

Vio. I thank you. Here comes the count.

Duke. Who saw Cesario, ho?

Vio. On your attendance, my lord; here.

Duke. Stand you awhile aloof.—Cesario,
Thou know'st no less but all; I have unclasp'd
To thee the book even of my secret soul:
Therefore, good youth, address thy gait unto her;
Be not denied access, stand at her doors,
And tell them there thy fixed foot shall grow
Till thou have audience.

Vio. Sure, my noble lord,
If she be so abandon'd to her sorrow
As it is spoke, she never will admit me.

Duke. Be clamorous, and leap all civil bounds
Rather than make unprofited return.

Vio. Say I do speak with her, my lord. What
then?

Duke. O, then unfold the passion of my love,
Surprise her with discourse of my dear faith:
It shall become thee well to act my woes;
She will attend it better in thy youth
Than in a nuncio of more grave aspect.

Vio. I think not so, my lord.

Duke. Dear lad, believe it,
For they shall yet belie thy happy years
That say thou art a man: Diana's lip
Is not more smooth and rubious; thy small pipe
Is as the maiden's organ, shrill and sound,
And all is semblative a woman's part.
I know thy constellation is right-apt
For this affair:—Some four or five attend him:
All, if you will; for I myself am best
When least in company:—Prosper well in this
And thou shalt live as freely as thy lord,
To call his fortunes thine.

Vio. I'll do my best

To woo your lady: yet, [*aside*] a barful strife!
Whoe'er I woo, myself would be his wife.

SCENE V.—*A Room in* OLIVIA'S *House.*

Enter MARIA *and* CLOWN.

Mar. Nay; either tell me where thou hast been,
or I will not open my lips so wide as a bristle
may enter in way of thy excuse: my lady will
hang thee for thy absence.

Clo. Let her hang me: he that is well hanged
in this world needs to fear no colours.

Mar. Make that good.

Clo. He shall see none to fear.

Mar. A good lenten answer: I can tell thee
where that saying was born, of, I fear no colours.

Clo. Where, good Mistress Mary?

Mar. In the wars; and that may you be bold
to say in your foolery.

Clo. Well, God give them wisdom that have
it; and those that are fools, let them use their
talents.

Mar. Yet you will be hanged for being so long
absent: or, to be turned away; is not that as
good as a hanging to you?

Clo. Many a good hanging prevents a bad
marriage; and for turning away, let summer
bear it out.

Mar. You are resolute, then?

Clo. Not so neither: but I am resolved on two
points.

Mar. That, if one break, the other will hold;
or, if both break, your gaskins fall.

Clo. Apt, in good faith; very apt! Well, go
thy way; if Sir Toby would leave drinking,
thou wert as witty a piece of Eve's flesh as any
in Illyria.

Mar. Peace, you rogue; no more o' that; here
comes my lady: make your excuse wisely; you
were best.   [*Exit.*

Enter OLIVIA *and* MALVOLIO.

Clo. Wit, and 't be thy will, put me into good
fooling! Those wits that think they have thee,
do very oft prove fools; and I, that am sure I
lack thee, may pass for a wise man. For what
says Quinapalus? Better a witty fool than a
foolish wit.——God bless thee, lady!

Oli. Take the fool away.   [lady.

Clo. Do you not hear, fellows? Take away the

Oli. Go to, you're a dry fool; I'll no more of
you: besides, you grow dishonest.

Clo. Two faults, madonna, that drink and
good counsel will amend: for give the dry fool
drink, then is the fool not dry; bid the dishonest man mend himself: if he mend, he is no
longer dishonest; if he cannot, let the botcher
mend him. Anything that's mended is but
patched; virtue that transgresses is but patched
with sin; and sin that amends is but patched
with virtue. If that this simple syllogism will
serve, so; if it will not, what remedy? As there
is no true cuckold but calamity, so beauty's

a flower:—the lady bade take away the fool;
therefore, I say again, take her away.

Oli. Sir, I bade them take away you.

Clo. Misprision in the highest degree!—Lady,
Cucullus non facit monachum; that's as much
as to say, I wear not motley in my brain. Good
madonna, give me leave to prove you a fool.

Oli. Can you do it?

Clo. Dexterously, good madonna.

Oli. Make your proof.

Clo. I must catechise you for it, madonna.
Good my mouse of virtue, answer me.

Oli. Well, sir, for want of other idleness, I'll
'bide your proof.

Clo. Good madonna, why mourn'st thou?

Oli. Good fool, for my brother's death.

Clo. I think his soul is in hell, madonna.

Oli. I know his soul is in heaven, fool.

Clo. The more fool you, madonna, to mourn
for your brother's soul being in heaven.—Take
away the fool, gentlemen.

Oli. What think you of this fool, Malvolio?
doth he not mend?

Mal. Yes; and shall do, till the pangs of death
shake him. Infirmity, that decays the wise,
doth ever make the better fool.

Clo. God send you, sir, a speedy infirmity, for
the better increasing your folly! Sir Toby will
be sworn that I am no fox; but he will not pass
his word for twopence that you are no fool.

Oli. How say you to that, Malvolio?

Mal. I marvel your ladyship takes delight in
such a barren rascal; I saw him put down the
other day with an ordinary fool that has no
more brain than a stone. Look you now, he's
out of his guard already; unless you laugh and
minister occasion to him, he is gagged. I protest, I take these wise men, that crow so at
these set kind of fools, no better than the fools'
zanies.

Oli. O, you are sick of self-love, Malvolio, and
taste with a distempered appetite. To be generous, guiltless, and of free disposition, is to
take those things for bird-bolts that you deem
cannon-bullets. There is no slander in an allowed fool, though he do nothing but rail; nor
no railing in a known discreet man, though he
do nothing but reprove.

Clo. Now Mercury endue thee with leasing, for
thou speakest well of fools!

Re-enter MARIA.

Mar. Madam, there is at the gate a young
gentleman much desires to speak with you.

Oli. From the Count Orsino, is it?

Mar. I know not, madam; 'tis a fair young
man, and well attended.

Oli. Who of my people hold him in delay?

Mar. Sir Toby, madam, your kinsman.

Oli. Fetch him off, I pray you; he speaks nothing but madman. Fie on him! [*Exit* MARIA.]
Go you, Malvolio; if it be a suit from the
count, I am sick, or not at home; what you will
to dismiss it. [*Exit* MALVOLIO.] Now you see,

sir, how your fooling grows old, and people dislike it.

Clo. Thou hast spoke for us, madonna, as if thy eldest son should be a fool: whose skull Jove cram with brains, for here he comes, one of thy kin, has a most weak *pia mater.*

Enter Sir TOBY BELCH.

Oli. By mine honour, half drunk.—What is he at the gate, cousin?

Sir To. A gentleman.

Oli. A gentleman? What gentleman?

Sir To. 'Tis a gentleman here—A plague o' these pickle-herrings!—How now, sot?

Clo. Good Sir Toby,——

Oli. Cousin, cousin, how have you come so early by this lethargy?

Sir To. Lechery! I defy lechery. There's one at the gate.

Oli. Ay, marry; what is he?

Sir To. Let him be the devil an he will, I care not: give me faith, say I. Well, it's all one. [*Exit.*

Oli. What's a drunken man like, fool?

Clo. Like a drowned man, a fool, and a madman: one draught above heat makes him a fool; the second mads him; and a third drowns him.

Oli. Go thou and seek the coroner, and let him sit o' my coz; for he is in the third degree of drink; he's drowned: go, look after him.

Clo. He is but mad yet, madonna; and the fool shall look to the madman. [*Exit* CLOWN.

Re-enter MALVOLIO.

Mal. Madam, yond young fellow swears he will speak with you. I told him you were sick; he takes on him to understand so much, and therefore comes to speak with you; I told him you were asleep; he seems to have a foreknowledge of that too, and therefore comes to speak with you. What is to be said to him, lady? he's fortified against any denial.

Oli. Tell him, he shall not speak with me.

Mal. He has been told so; and he says he'll stand at your door like a sheriff's post, and be the supporter of a bench, but he'll speak with you.

Oli. What kind of man is he?

Mal. Why, of mankind.

Oli. What manner of man?

Mal. Of very ill manner; he'll speak with you, will you or no.

Oli. Of what personage and years is he?

Mal. Not yet old enough for a man, nor young enough for a boy; as a squash is before 'tis a peascod, or a codling, when 'tis almost an apple: 'tis with him e'en standing water, between boy and man. He is very well-favoured, and he speaks very shrewishly; one would think his mother's milk were scarce out of him.

Oli. Let him approach. Call in my gentlewoman.

Mal. Gentlewoman, my lady calls. [*Exit.*

Re-enter MARIA.

Oli. Give me my veil: come, throw it o'er my face;
We'll once more hear Orsino's embassy.

Enter VIOLA.

Vio. The honourable lady of the house, which is she?

Oli. Speak to me, I shall answer for her. Your will?

Vio. Most radiant, exquisite, and unmatchable beauty,—I pray you, tell me if this be the lady of the house, for I never saw her: I would be loath to cast away my speech; for, besides that it is excellently well penned, I have taken great pains to con it. Good beauties, let me sustain no scorn; I am very comptible, even to the least sinister usage.

Oli. Whence came you, sir?

Vio. I can say little more than I have studied, and that question's out of my part. Good gentle one, give me modest assurance, if you be the lady of the house, that I may proceed in my speech.

Oli. Are you a comedian?

Vio. No, my profound heart; and yet, by the very fangs of malice, I swear I am not that I play. Are you the lady of the house?

Oli. If I do not usurp myself, I am.

Vio. Most certain, if you are she, you do usurp yourself; for what is yours to bestow is not yours to reserve. But this is from my commission: I will on with my speech in your praise, and then show you the heart of my message.

Oli. Come to what is important in't: I forgive you the praise.

Vio. Alas, I took great pains to study it, and 'tis poetical.

Oli. It is the more like to be feigned; I pray you keep it in. I heard you were saucy at my gates; and allowed your approach, rather to wonder at you than to hear you. If you be not mad, be gone; if you have reason, be brief: 'tis not that time of moon with me to make one in so skipping a dialogue. [way.

Mar. Will you hoist sail, sir? here lies your

Vio. No, good swabber; I am to hull here a little longer.—Some mollification for your giant, sweet lady.

Oli. Tell me your mind.

Vio. I am a messenger.

Oli. Sure, you have some hideous matter to deliver, when the courtesy of it is so fearful. Speak your office.

Vio. It alone concerns your ear. I bring no overture of war, no taxation of homage; I hold the olive in my hand: my words are as full of peace as matter.

Oli. Yet you began rudely. What are you? what would you?

Vio. The rudeness that hath appeared in me have I learned from my entertainment. What I am and what I would are as sacred as maidenhead: to your ears, divinity; to any other's, profanation.

Oli. Give us the place alone: we will hear this divinity. [*Exit* MARIA.] Now, sir, what is your text?

Vio. Most sweet lady,——

Oli. A comfortable doctrine, and much may be said of it. Where lies your text?

Vio. In Orsino's bosom.

Oli. In his bosom? In what chapter of his bosom?

Vio. To answer by the method, in the first of his heart.

Oli. O, I have read it; it is heresy. Have you no more to say?

Vio. Good madam, let me see your face.

Oli. Have you any commission from your lord to negotiate with my face? you are now out of your text: but we will draw the curtain and show you the picture. Look you, sir, such a one as I was this present. Is't not well done? [*Unveiling.*

Vio. Excellently done, if God did all.

Oli. 'Tis in grain, sir; 'twill endure wind and weather. [white

Vio. 'Tis beauty truly blent, whose red and Nature's own sweet and cunning hand laid on: Lady, you are the cruel'st she alive, If you will lead these graces to the grave, And leave the world no copy.

Oli. O, sir, I will not be so hard-hearted; I will give out divers schedules of my beauty. It shall be inventoried; and every particle and utensil labelled to my will: as, item, two lips indifferent red; item, two gray eyes with lids to them; item, one neck, one chin, and so forth. Were you sent hither to praise me? [proud;

Vio. I see you what you are: you are too But if you were the devil, you are fair. My lord and master loves you. O, such love Could be but recompens'd though you were crown'd The nonpareil of beauty!

Oli. How does he love me?

Vio. With adorations, with fertile tears, With groans that thunder love, with sighs of fire.

Oli. Your lord does know my mind, I cannot love him: Yet I suppose him virtuous, know him noble, Of great estate, of fresh and stainless youth; In voices well divulged, free, learn'd and valiant, And, in dimension and the shape of nature, A gracious person: but yet I cannot love him; He might have took his answer long ago.

Vio. If I did love you in my master's flame, With such a suffering, such a deadly life, In your denial I would find no sense, I would not understand it.

Oli. Why, what would you?

Vio. Make me a willow cabin at your gate, And call upon my soul within the house; Write loyal cantons of contemned love, And sing them loud, even in the dead of night; Holla your name to the reverberate hills, And make the babbling gossip of the air Cry out Olivia! O, you should not rest

Between the elements of air and earth, But you should pity me. [entage?

Oli. You might do much. What is your par-

Vio. Above my fortunes, yet my state is well: I am a gentleman.

Oli. Get you to your lord; I cannot love him: let him send no more; Unless, perchance, you come to me again, To tell me how he takes it. Fare you well: I thank you for your pains: spend this for me.

Vio. I am no fee'd post, lady; keep your purse; My master, not myself, lacks recompense. Love make his heart of flint that you shall love; And let your fervour, like my master's, be Placed in contempt! Farewell, fair cruelty. [*Exit.*

Oli. What is your parentage? *Above my fortunes, yet my state is well: I am a gentleman.*——I'll be sworn thou art; Thy tongue, thy face, thy limbs, actions, and spirit, [soft! soft! Do give thee fivefold blazon. Not too fast:— Unless the master were the man.—How now? Even so quickly may one catch the plague? Methinks I feel this youth's perfections With an invisible and subtle stealth To creep in at mine eyes. Well, let it be.— What, ho, Malvolio!—

Re-enter MALVOLIO.

Mal. Here, madam, at your service.

Oli. Run after that same peevish messenger, The county's man: he left this ring behind him, Would I, or not; tell him I'll none of it. Desire him not to flatter with his lord, Nor hold him up with hopes; I am not for him: If that the youth will come this way to-morrow, I'll give him reasons for't. Hie thee, Malvolio

Mal. Madam, I will. [*Exit.*

Oli. I do I know not what: and fear to find Mine eye too great a flatterer for my mind. Fate, show thy force. Ourselves we do not owe: What is decreed must be; and be this so! [*Exit.*

ACT II.

SCENE I.—*The Sea-coast.*

Enter ANTONIO *and* SEBASTIAN.

Ant. Will you stay no longer? nor will you not that I go with you?

Seb. By your patience, no: my stars shine darkly over me; the malignancy of my fate might, perhaps, distemper yours; therefore I shall crave of you your leave that I may bear my evils alone. It were a bad recompense for your love, to lay any of them on you.

Ant. Let me yet know of you whither you are bound.

Seb. No, 'sooth, sir; my determinate voyage is mere extravagancy. But I perceive in you so excellent a touch of modesty, that you will not extort from me what I am willing to keep in; therefore it charges me in manners the rather to express myself. You must know of me then, Antonio, my name is Sebastian, which I called Rodorigo; my father was that Sebastian of Messaline whom I know you have heard of: he left behind him myself and a sister, both born in an hour. If the heavens had been pleased, would we had so ended! but you, sir, altered that; for some hours before you took me from the breach of the sea was my sister drowned.

Ant. Alas the day!

Seb. A lady, sir, though it was said she much resembled me, was yet of many accounted beautiful: but though I could not, with such estimable wonder, overfar believe that, yet thus far I will boldly publish her,—she bore a mind that envy could not but call fair. She is drowned already, sir, with salt water, though I seem to drown her remembrance again with more.

Ant. Pardon me, sir, your bad entertainment.

Seb. O, good Antonio, forgive me your trouble.

Ant. If you will not murder me for my love, let me be your servant.

Seb. If you will not undo what you have done —that is, kill him whom you have recovered— desire it not. Fare ye well at once; my bosom is full of kindness; and I am yet so near the manners of my mother that, upon the least occasion more, mine eyes will tell tales of me. I am bound to the Count Orsino's court: farewell.   [*Exit.*

Ant. The gentleness of all the gods go with thee!
I have many enemies in Orsino's court,
Else would I very shortly see thee there:
But come what may, I do adore thee so
That danger shall seem sport, and I will go.
                                        [*Exit.*

SCENE II.—*A Street.*

Enter VIOLA; MALVOLIO *following.*

Mal. Were not you even now with the Countess Olivia?

Vio. Even now, sir; on a moderate pace I have since arrived but hither.

Mal. She returns this ring to you, sir; you might have saved me my pains, to have taken it away yourself. She adds moreover, that you should put your lord into a desperate assurance she will none of him: and one thing more; that you be never so hardy to come again in his affairs, unless it be to report your lord's taking of this. Receive it so.

Vio. She took the ring of me: I'll none of it.

Mal. Come, sir, you peevishly threw it to her; and her will is, it should be so returned. If it be worth stooping for, there it lies in your eye; if not, be it his that finds it.   [*Exit.*

Vio. I left no ring with her. What means this lady?
Fortune forbid my outside have not charm'd her!
She made good view of me; indeed, so much,
That, sure, methought her eyes had lost her tongue,
For she did speak in starts distractedly

She loves me, sure; the cunning of her passion
Invites me in this churlish messenger.
None of my lord's ring! why, he sent her none.
I am the man;—if it be so,—as 'tis,—
Poor lady, she were better love a dream.
Disguise, I see, thou art a wickedness
Wherein the pregnant enemy does much.
How easy is it for the proper-false
In women's waxen hearts to set their forms!
Alas, our frailty is the cause, not we;
For, such as we are made of, such we be.
How will this fadge? My master loves her dearly;
And I, poor monster, fond as much on him;
And she, mistaken, seems to dote on me.
What will become of this? As I am man,
My state is desperate for my master's love;
As I am woman, now alas the day!
What thriftless sighs shall poor Olivia breathe?
O time, thou must untangle this, not I;
It is too hard a knot for me to untie.   [*Exit.*

SCENE III.—*A Room in* OLIVIA'S *House.*

Enter Sir TOBY BELCH *and Sir* ANDREW AGUE-CHEEK.

Sir To. Approach, Sir Andrew: not to be a-bed after midnight is to be up betimes; and *diluculo surgere*, thou know'st.

Sir And. Nay; by my troth, I know not: but I know to be up late is to be up late.

Sir To. A false conclusion; I hate it as an unfilled can. To be up after midnight, and to go to bed then is early: so that to go to bed after midnight is to go to bed betimes. Do not our lives consist of the four elements?

Sir And. Faith, so they say; but I think it rather consists of eating and drinking.

Sir To. Thou art a scholar; let us therefore eat and drink.—Marian, I say!——a stoop of wine.

Enter CLOWN.

Sir And. Here comes the fool, i' faith.

Clo. How now, my hearts? Did you never see the picture of we three?

Sir To. Welcome, ass. Now let's have a catch.

Sir And. By my troth, the fool has an excellent breast. I had rather than forty shillings I had such a leg; and so sweet a breath to sing as the fool has. In sooth, thou wast in very gracious fooling last night when thou spokest of Pigrogromitus, of the Vapians passing the equinoctial of Queubus; 'twas very good, i' faith. I sent thee sixpence for thy leman. Hadst it?

Clo. I did impeticos thy gratillity; for Malvolio's nose is no whipstock. My lady has a white hand, and the Myrmidons are no bottle-ale houses.

Sir And. Excellent! Why, this is the best fooling, when all is done. Now, a song.

Sir To. Come on; there is sixpence for you: let's have a song.

Sir And. There's a testril of me too: if one knight give a——

Clo. Would you have a love-song, or a song of good life?
Sir To. A love-song, a love-song.
Sir And. Ay, ay; I care not for good life.

SONG.

Clo.   O, mistress mine, where are you roaming?
    O stay and hear; your true love's coming,
      That can sing both high and low:
    Trip no further, pretty sweeting;
    Journeys end in lovers' meeting,
      Every wise man's son doth know.

Sir And. Excellent good, i' faith.
Sir To. Good, good.

Clo.   What is love? 'tis not hereafter;
    Present mirth hath present laughter;
      What's to come is still unsure:
    In delay there lies no plenty;
    Then come kiss me, sweet and twenty,
      Youth's a stuff will not endure.

Sir And. A mellifluous voice, as I am true knight.
Sir To. A contagious breath.
Sir And. Very sweet and contagious, i' faith.
Sir To. To hear by the nose, it is dulcet in contagion. But shall we make the welkin dance indeed? Shall we rouse the night-owl in a catch that will draw three souls out of one weaver? shall we do that?
Sir And. An you love me, let's do 't: I am dog at a catch.
Clo. By'r lady, sir, and some dogs will catch well.
Sir And. Most certain: let our catch be, *Thou knave.*
Clo. Hold thy peace, thou knave, knight? I shall be constrained in 't to call thee knave, knight.
Sir And. 'Tis not the first time I have constrained one to call me knave. Begin, fool; it begins *Hold thy peace.*
Clo. I shall never begin if I hold my peace.
Sir And. Good, i' faith! Come begin.
                              [*They sing a catch.*

Enter MARIA.

Mar. What a caterwauling do you keep here! If my lady have not called up her steward, Malvolio, and bid him turn you out of doors, never trust me.
Sir To. My lady's a Cataian, we are politicians; Malvolio's a Peg-a-Ramsay, and *Three merry men be we.* Am not I consanguineous? am I not of her blood? Tilly-valley, lady! *There dwelt a man in Babylon, lady, lady.*   [*Singing.*
Clo. Beshrew me, the knight's in admirable fooling.
Sir And. Ay, he does well enough if he be disposed, and so do I too; he does it with a better grace, but I do it more natural.
Sir To. O, *the twelfth day of December,*—
                              [*Singing.*
Mar. For the love o' God, peace.

Enter MALVOLIO.

Mal. My masters, are you mad? or what are you? Have you no wit, manners, nor honesty, but to gabble like tinkers at this time of night? Do ye make an ale-house of my lady's house, that ye squeak out your coziers' catches without any mitigation or remorse of voice? Is there no respect of place, persons, nor time, in you?
Sir To. We did keep time, sir, in our catches. Sneck up!
Mal. Sir Toby, I must be round with you. My lady bade me tell you that though she harbours you as her kinsman she's nothing allied to your disorders. If you can separate yourself and your misdemeanours, you are welcome to the house; if not, an it would please you to take leave of her, she is very willing to bid you farewell.
Sir To. Farewell, dear heart, since I must needs be gone.
Mar. Nay, good Sir Toby.
Clo. His eyes do show his days are almost done.
Mal. Is 't even so?
Sir To. But I will never die.
Clo. Sir Toby, there you lie.
Mal. This is much credit to you.
Sir To. Shall I bid him go?   [*Singing.*
Clo. What an if you do?
Sir To. Shall I bid him go and spare not?
Clo. O no, no, no, no, you dare not.
Sir To. Out o' tune? sir, ye lie.—Art any more than a steward? Dost thou think, because thou art virtuous, there shall be no more cakes and ale?
Clo. Yes, by Saint Anne; and ginger shall be hot i' the mouth too.
Sir To. Thou'rt i' the right.—Go, sir, rub your chain with crumbs:—A stoop of wine, Maria!
Mal. Mistress Mary, if you prized my lady's favour at anything more than contempt, you would not give means for this uncivil rule; she shall know of it, by this hand.   [*Exit.*
Mar. Go shake your ears.
Sir And. 'Twere as good a deed as to drink when a man's a-hungry, to challenge him to the field, and then to break promise with him and make a fool of him.
Sir To. Do 't, knight; I'll write thee a challenge; or I'll deliver thy indignation to him by word of mouth.
Mar. Sweet Sir Toby, be patient for to-night; since the youth of the count's was to-day with my lady she is much out of quiet. For Monsieur Malvolio, let me alone with him: if I do not gull him into a nayword, and make him a common recreation, do not think I have wit enough to lie straight in my bed. I know I can do it.
Sir To. Possess us, possess us; tell us something of him.
Mar. Marry, sir, sometimes he is a kind of Puritan.
Sir And. O, if I thought that, I'd beat him like a dog.

Sir To. What, for being a Puritan? thy exquisite reason, dear knight?

Sir And. I have no exquisite reason for 't, but I have reason good enough.

Mar. The devil a Puritan that he is, or anything constantly but a time pleaser: an affection'd ass that cons state without book and utters it by great swarths; the best persuaded of himself, so crammed, as he thinks, with excellences, that it is his ground of faith that all that look on him love him; and on that vice in him will my revenge find notable cause to work.

Sir To. What wilt thou do?

Mar. I will drop in his way some obscure epistles of love; wherein, by the colour of his beard, the shape of his leg, the manner of his gait, the expressure of his eye, forehead, and complexion, he shall find himself most feelingly personated. I can write very like my lady, your niece; on a forgotten matter we can hardly make distinction of our hands.

Sir To. Excellent! I smell a device.

Sir And. I have 't in my nose too.

Sir To. He shall think, by the letters that thou wilt drop, that they come from my niece, and that she is in love with him.   [*colour.*

Mar. My purpose is, indeed, a horse of that

Sir And. And your horse now would make him an ass.

Mar. Ass, I doubt not.

Sir And. O 'twill be admirable.

Mar. Sport royal, I warrant you. I know my physic will work with him. I will plant you two, and let the fool make a third, where he shall find the letter; observe his construction of it. For this night, to bed, and dream on the event. Farewell.   [*Exit.*

Sir To. Good-night, Penthesilea.

Sir And. Before me, she's a good wench.

Sir To. She's a beagle, true bred, and one that adores me. What o' that?

Sir And. I was adored once too.

Sir To. Let's to bed, knight.—Thou hadst need send for more money.

Sir And. If I cannot recover your niece I am a foul way out.

Sir To. Send for money, knight; if thou hast her not i' the end, call me Cut.

Sir And. If I do not, never trust me; take it how you will.

Sir To. Come, come; I'll go burn some sack; 'tis too late to go to bed now: come, knight; come, knight.   [*Exeunt.*

SCENE IV.—*A Room in the* DUKE'S *Palace.*

Enter DUKE, VIOLA, CURIO, *and others.*

Duke. Give me some music:—Now, good morrow, friends:—
Now, good Cesario, but that piece of song,
That old and antique song we heard last night;
Methought it did relieve my passion much;
More than light airs and recollected terms

Of these most brisk and giddy-paced times:——
Come, but one verse.

Cur. He is not here, so please your lordship.
that should sing it.

Duke. Who was it?

Cur. Feste, the jester, my lord; a fool that the Lady Olivia's father took much delight in: he is about the house.

Duke. Seek him out, and play the tune the while.   [*Exit* CURIO.—*Music.*
Come hither, boy. If ever thou shalt love,
In the sweet pangs of it remember me:
For, such as I am, all true lovers are;
Unstaid and skittish in all motions else,
Save in the constant image of the creature
That is belov'd.—How dost thou like this tune?

Vio. It gives a very echo to the seat
Where Love is throned.

Duke. Thou dost speak masterly:
My life upon 't, young though thou art, thine eye
Hath stayed upon some favour that it loves;
Hath it not, boy?

Vio.   A little, by your favour.

Duke. What kind of woman is 't?

Vio.   Of your complexion.

Duke. She is not worth thee, then. What years, i' faith?

Vio. About your years, my lord.

Duke. Too old, by heaven. Let still the woman take
An elder than herself; so wears she to him,
So sways she level in her husband's heart.
For, boy, however we do praise ourselves,
Our fancies are more giddy and unfirm,
More longing, wavering, sooner lost and worn
Than women's are.

Vio.   I think it well, my lord.

Duke. Then let thy love be younger than thyself,
Or thy affection cannot hold the bent:
For women are as roses, whose fair flower,
Being once display'd, doth fall that very hour.

Vio. And so they are: alas, that they are so;
To die even when they to perfection grow!

Re-enter CURIO *and* CLOWN.

Duke. O fellow, come, the song we had last night:—
Mark it, Cesario; it is old and plain:
The spinsters and the knitters in the sun,
And the free maids that weave their thread with bones,
Do use to chant it: it is silly sooth,
And dallies with the innocence of love
Like the old age.

Clo. Are you ready, sir?

Duke. Ay; pr'ythee, sing.   [*Music.*

SONG.

Clo.   Come away, come away, death,
     And in sad cypress let me be laid;
       Fly away, fly away, breath;
     I am slain by a fair cruel maid.
     My shroud of white, stuck all with yew,
       O prepare it:

My part of death no one so true
Did share it.

Not a flower, not a flower sweet,
On my black coffin let there be strown:
Not a friend, not a friend greet
My poor corpse where my bones shall be
thrown:
A thousand thousand sighs to save,
Lay me, O, where
Sad true lover never find my grave,
To weep there.

Duke. There's for thy pains. [sir.
Clo. No pains, sir; I take pleasure in singing,
Duke. I'll pay thy pleasure, then.
Clo. Truly, sir, and pleasure will be paid one
time or another.
Duke. Give me now leave to leave thee.
Clo. Now, the melancholy god protect thee;
and the tailor make thy doublet of changeable
taffata, for thy mind is a very opal!—I would
have men of such constancy put to sea, that
their business might be everything, and their
intent everywhere; for that's it that always
makes a good voyage of nothing.—Farewell.
[*Exit* CLOWN.
Duke. Let all the rest give place.——
[*Exeunt* CURIO *and* Attendants.
Once more, Cesario,
Get thee to yon same sovereign cruelty:
Tell her my love, more noble than the world,
Prizes not quantity of dirty lands;
The parts that fortune hath bestow'd upon her,
Tell her, I hold as giddily as fortune;
But 'tis that miracle and queen of gems
That Nature pranks her in attracts my soul.
Vio. But if she cannot love you, sir?
Duke. I cannot be so answer'd.
Vio.   'Sooth, but you must.
Say that some lady, as perhaps there is,
Hath for your love as great a pang of heart
As you have for Olivia: you cannot love her;
You tell her so. Must she not then be answer'd?
Duke. There is no woman's sides
Can bide the beating of so strong a passion
As love doth give my heart: no woman's heart
So big to hold so much; they lack retention.
Alas, their love may be called appetite,—
No motion of the liver, but the palate,—
That suffer surfeit, cloyment, and revolt;
But mine is all as hungry as the sea,
And can digest as much: make no compare
Between that love a woman can bear me
And that I owe Olivia.
Vio.   Ay, but I know,—
Duke. What dost thou know?
Vio. Too well what love women to men may
owe.
In faith, they are as true of heart as we.
My father had a daughter loved a man,
As it might be, perhaps, were I a woman,
I should your lordship.
Duke.   And what's her history?
Vio. A blank, my lord. She never told her love,
But let concealment, like a worm i' the bud,

Feed on her damask cheek: she pined in thought;
And, with a green and yellow melancholy,
She sat like patience on a monument,
Smiling at grief. Was not this love, indeed?
We men may say more, swear more; but, indeed,
Our shows are more than will; for still we prove
Much in our vows, but little in our love.
Duke. But died thy sister of her love, my boy?
Vio. I am all the daughters of my father's
house,
And all the brothers too;—and yet I know not.—
Sir, shall I to this lady?
Duke.   Ay, that's the theme.
To her in haste: give her this jewel; say
My love can give no place, bide no denay.
[*Exeunt.*

SCENE V.—OLIVIA'S *Garden.*

Enter Sir TOBY BELCH, *Sir* ANDREW AGUE-
CHEEK, *and* FABIAN.

Sir To. Come thy ways, Signior Fabian.
Fab. Nay, I'll come; if I lose a scruple of this
sport let me be boiled to death with melancholy.
Sir To. Wouldst thou not be glad to have the
niggardly rascally sheep-biter come by some
notable shame?
Fab. I would exult, man: you know he brought
me out o' favour with my lady about a bear-
baiting here.
Sir To. To anger him we'll have the bear again;
and we will fool him black and blue:—Shall we
not, Sir Andrew?
Sir And. An we do not, it is pity of our lives.

Enter MARIA.

Sir To. Here comes the little villain:—How
now, my nettle of India?
Mar. Get ye all three into the box-tree: Malvolio's coming down this walk; he has been
yonder i' the sun, practising behaviour to his
own shadow this half-hour: observe him, for
the love of mockery; for I know this letter will
make a contemplative idiot of him. Close, in
the name of jesting! [*The men hide themselves.*]
Lie thou there; [*throws down a letter*] for here
comes the trout that must be caught with
tickling. [*Exit* MARIA.

Enter MALVOLIO.

Mal. 'Tis but fortune; all is fortune. Maria
once told me she did affect me: and I have heard
herself come thus near, that, should she fancy, it
should be one of my complexion. Besides, she
uses me with a more exalted respect than anyone
else that follows her. What should I think on 't?
Sir To. Here's an overweening rogue!
Fab. O, peace! Contemplation makes a rare
turkey-cock of him; how he jets under his advanced plumes!
Sir And. 'Slight, I could so beat the rogue:—
Sir To. Peace, I say,
Mal. To be Count Malvolio;—

Sir To. Ah, rogue!

Sir And. Pistol him, pistol him.

Sir To. Peace, peace.

Mal. There is example for 't; the lady of the Strachy married the yeoman of the wardrobe.

Sir And. Fie on him, Jezebel!

Fab. O, peace! now he's deeply in; look how imagination blows him.

Mal. Having been three months married to her, sitting in my state,—

Sir To. O for a stone-bow to hit him in the eye!

Mal. Calling my officers about me in my branched velvet gown; having come from a day-bed, where I have left Olivia sleeping.

Sir To. Fire and brimstone!

Fab. O, peace, peace.

Mal. And then to have the humour of state: and after a demure travel of regard,—telling them I know my place as I would they should do theirs,—to ask for my kinsman Toby.

Sir To. Bolts and shackles!

Fab. O, peace, peace, peace! now, now.

Mal. Seven of my people, with an obedient start, make out for him: I frown the while; and perchance, wind up my watch, or play with some rich jewel. Toby approaches; court'sies there to me:

Sir To. Shall this fellow live?

Fab. Though our silence be drawn from us with cars, yet peace.

Mal. I extend my hand to him thus, quenching my familiar smile with an austere regard of control:

Sir To. And does not Toby take you a blow o' the lips then?

Mal. Saying, *Cousin Toby, my fortunes having cast me on your niece, give me this prerogative of speech:—*

Sir To. What, what?

Mal. *You must amend your drunkenness.*

Sir To. Out, scab!   [our plot.

Fab. Nay, patience, or we break the sinews of

Mal. *Besides, you waste the treasure of your time with a foolish knight;*

Sir And. That's me, I warrant you.

Mal. *One Sir Andrew:*

Sir And. I knew 'twas I; for many do call me fool.

Mal. What employment have we here?

                   [*Taking up the letter.*

Fab. Now is the woodcock near the gin.

Sir To. O, peace! and the spirit of humours intimate reading aloud to him!

Mal. By my life, this is my lady's hand: these be her very *C*'s, her *U*'s, and her *T*'s; and thus makes she her great *P*'s. It is in contempt of question, her hand.

Sir And. Her *C*'s, her *U*'s, and her *T*'s. Why that?

Mal. [*reads.*] *To the unknown beloved, this, and my good wishes:* her very phrases!—By your leave, wax.—Soft!—and the impressure her Lucrece, with which she uses to seal: 'tis my lady. To whom should this be?

Fab. This wins him, liver and all.

Mal. [*reads.*]

> *Jove knows I love:*
> > *But who?*
> *Lips do not move,*
> *No man must know.*

No man must know.—What follows? the numbers altered!—*No man must know:*—If this should be thee, Malvolio?

Sir To. Marry, hang thee, brock!

Mal.   *I may command where I adore:*
> *But silence, like a Lucrece knife,*
> *With bloodiest stroke my heart doth gore;*
>   *M, O, A, I, doth sway my life.*

Fab. A fustian riddle!

Sir To. Excellent wench, say I.

Mal. M, O, A, I, *doth sway my life.*—Nay, but first let me see,—let me see,—let me see.

Fab. What a dish of poison hath she dressed him!

Sir To. And with what wing the stannyel checks at it!

Mal. *I may command where I adore.* Why, she may command me: I serve her, she is my lady. Why, this is evident to any formal capacity. There is no obstruction in this;—And the end, —What should that alphabetical position portend? If I could make that resemble something in me,—Softly!—*M, O, A, I.*—

Sir To. O, ay! make up that:—he is now at a cold scent.

Fab. Sowter will cry upon 't for all this, though it be as rank as a fox.

Mal. *M,*—Malvolio;—*M,*—why, that begins my name.

Fab. Did not I say he would work it out? the cur is excellent at faults.

Mal. *M,*—But then there is no consonancy in the sequel; that suffers under probation: *A* should follow, but *O* does.

Fab. And *O* shall end, I hope.   [cry *O.*

Sir To. Ay, or I'll cudgel him, and make him

Mal. And then *I* comes behind.

Fab. Ay, an you had any eye behind you, you might see more detraction at your heels than fortunes before you.

Mal. *M, O, A, I;*—This simulation is not as the former:—and yet, to crush this a little, it would bow to me, for every one of these letters are in my name. Soft; here follows prose.— *If this fall into thy hand, revolve. In my stars I am above thee; but be not afraid of greatness. Some are born great, some achieve greatness, and some have greatness thrust upon them. Thy fates open their hands; let thy blood and spirit embrace them. And, to inure thyself to what thou art like to be, cast thy humble slough and appear fresh. Be opposite with a kinsman, surly with servants: let thy tongue tang arguments of state; put thyself into the trick of singularity: She thus advises thee that sighs for thee. Remember who commended thy yellow stockings, and wished to see thee ever cross-gartered. I say, remember. Go to; thou art made, if thou desirest to be so; if not, let me see thee a steward still, the fellow of servants, and not worthy to touch fortune's fingers. Farewell. She that would alter services with thee,*

> *The fortunate unhappy.*

Daylight and champian discovers not more: this is open. I will be proud, I will read politic authors, I will baffle Sir Toby, I will wash off gross acquaintance, I will be point-device, the very man. I do not now fool myself to let imagination jade me; for every reason excites to this, that my lady loves me. She did commend my yellow stockings of late, she did praise my leg being cross-gartered; and in this she manifests herself to my love, and, with a kind of injunction, drives me to these habits of her liking. I thank my stars I am happy. I will be strange, stout, in yellow stockings, and cross-gartered, even with the swiftness of putting on. Jove and my stars be praised!—Here is yet a postscript. *Thou canst not choose but know who I am. If thou entertainest my love, let it appear in thy smiling; thy smiles become thee well: therefore in my presence still smile, dear my sweet, I pr'ythee.* Jove, I thank thee.—I will smile: I will do everything that thou wilt have me. [*Exit.*

Fab. I will not give my part of this sport for a pension of thousands to be paid from the Sophy.
Sir To. I could marry this wench for this device:
Sir And. So could I too.
Sir To. And ask no other dowry with her but such another jest.

Enter MARIA.

Sir And. Nor I neither.
Fab. Here comes my noble gull-catcher.
Sir To. Wilt thou set thy foot o' my neck?
Sir And. Or o' mine either?
Sir To. Shall I play my freedom at tray-trip, and become thy bond-slave?
Sir And. I' faith, or I either.
Sir To. Why, thou hast put him in such a dream, that, when the image of it leaves him, he must run mad.
Mar. Nay, but say true; does it work upon him?
Sir To. Like aqua-vitæ with a midwife.
Mar. If you will then see the fruits of the sport, mark his first approach before my lady: he will come to her in yellow stockings, and 'tis a colour she abhors; and cross-gartered, a fashion she detests; and he will smile upon her, which will now be so unsuitable to her disposition, being addicted to a melancholy as she is, that it cannot but turn him into a notable contempt: if you will see it, follow me.
Sir To. To the gates of Tartar, thou most excellent devil of wit!
Sir And. I'll make one too. [*Exeunt.*

ACT III.

SCENE I.—OLIVIA's *Garden.*

Enter VIOLA, *and* CLOWN *with a tabor.*

Vio. Save thee, friend, and thy music. Dost thou live by thy tabor?
Clo. No, sir, I live by the church.
Vio. Art thou a churchman?
Clo. No such matter, sir; I do live by the church; for I do live at my house, and my house doth stand by the church.
Vio. So thou mayst say, the king lies by a beggar, if a beggar dwell near him; or the church stands by thy tabor, if thy tabor stand by the church.
Clo. You have said, sir.—To see this age!—A sentence is but a cheveril glove to a good wit. How quickly the wrong side may be turned outward!
Vio. Nay, that's certain; they that dally nicely with words may quickly make them wanton.
Clo. I would, therefore, my sister had had no name, sir.
Vio. Why, man?
Clo. Why, sir, her name's a word; and to dally with that word might make my sister wanton. But indeed, words are very rascals, since bonds disgraced them.
Vio. Thy reason, man?
Clo. Troth, sir, I can yield you none without words; and words are grown so false, I am loath to prove reason with them.
Vio. I warrant, thou art a merry fellow, and carest for nothing.
Clo. Not so, sir, I do care for something: but in my conscience, sir, I do not care for you; if that be to care for nothing, sir, I would it would make you invisible.
Vio. Art not thou the Lady Olivia's fool?
Clo. No, indeed, sir; the Lady Olivia has no folly: she will keep no fool, sir, till she be married; and fools are as like husbands as pilchards are to herrings, the husband's the bigger; I am, indeed, not her fool, but her corrupter of words.
Vio. I saw thee late at the Count Orsino's.
Clo. Foolery, sir, does walk about the orb like the sun; it shines everywhere. I would be sorry, sir, but the fool should be as oft with your master as with my mistress: I think I saw your wisdom there.
Vio. Nay, an thou pass upon me, I'll no more with thee. Hold, there's expenses for thee.
Clo. Now Jove, in his next commodity of hair, send thee a beard!
Vio. By my troth, I'll tell thee, I am almost sick for one; though I would not have it grow on my chin. Is thy lady within?
Clo. Would not a pair of these have bred, sir?
Vio. Yes, being kept together and put to use.
Clo. I would play Lord Pandarus of Phrygia, sir, to bring a Cressida to this Troilus.
Vio. I understand you, sir; 'tis well begged.
Clo. The matter, I hope, is not great, sir, beg-

ging but a beggar: Cressida was a beggar. My lady is within, sir. I will construe to them whence you come; who you are and what you would are out of my welkin: I might say element; but the word is overworn. [*Exit.*

Vio. This fellow's wise enough to play the fool;
And, to do that well, craves a kind of wit:
He must observe their mood on whom he jests,
The quality of persons, and the time;
And, like the haggard, check at every feather
That comes before his eye. This is a practice
As full of labour as a wise man's art:
For folly, that he wisely shows, is fit;
But wise men, folly-fallen, quite taint their wit.

Enter Sir TOBY BELCH, *and Sir* ANDREW
AGUE-CHEEK.

Sir To. Save you, gentleman.
Vio. And you, sir.
Sir And. Dieu vous garde, monsieur.
Vio. Et vous aussi: votre serviteur.
Sir And. I hope, sir, you are; and I am yours.
Sir To. Will you encounter the house? my niece is desirous you should enter, if your trade be to her.
Vio. I am bound to your niece, sir: I mean, she is the list of my voyage.
Sir To. Taste your legs, sir; put them to motion.
Vio. My legs do better understand me, sir, than I understand what you mean by bidding me taste my legs.
Sir To. I mean to go, sir, to enter.
Vio. I will answer you with gait and entrance: but we are prevented.

Enter OLIVIA *and* MARIA.

Most excellent accomplished lady, the heavens rains odours on you.
Sir And. That youth's a rare courtier! *Rain odours!* well.
Vio. My matter hath no voice, lady, but to your own most pregnant and vouchsafed ear.
Sir And. Odours, pregnant, and *vouchsafed:—*
I'll get 'em all three ready.
Oli. Let the garden door be shut, and leave me to my hearing.
[*Exeunt Sir* To., *Sir* AND., *and* MAR.
Give me your hand, sir. [service.
Vio. My duty, madam, and most humble
Oli. What is your name? [princess.
Vio. Cesario is your servant's name, fair
Oli. My servant, sir! 'Twas never merry world,
Since lowly feigning was call'd compliment:
You are servant to the Count Orsino, youth.
Vio. And he is yours, and his must needs be yours;
Your servant's servant is your servant, madam.
Oli. For him, I think not on him: for his thoughts, [me!
Would they were blanks rather than fill'd with
Vio. Madam, I come to whet your gentle thoughts
On his behalf:—

Oli. O, by your leave, I pray you;
I bade you never speak again of him:
But, would you undertake another suit,
I had rather hear you to solicit that
Than music from the spheres.
Vio. Dear lady,——
Oli. Give me leave, I beseech you: I did send,
After the last enchantment you did here,
A ring in chase of you; so did I abuse
Myself, my servant, and, I fear me, you:
Under your hard construction must I sit;
To force that on you, in a shameful cunning,
Which you knew none of yours. What might you think?
Have you not set mine honour at the stake,
And baited it with all the unmuzzl'd thoughts
That tyrannous heart can think? To one of your receiving
Enough is shown; a cyprus, not a bosom,
Hides my poor heart: so let me hear you speak.
Vio. I pity you.
Oli. That's a degree to love.
Vio. No, not a grise; for 'tis a vulgar proof
That very oft we pity enemies. [again:
Oli. Why, then, methinks 'tis time to smile
O world, how apt the poor are to be proud!
If one should be a prey, how much the better
To fall before the lion than the wolf!
[*Clock strikes.*
The clock upbraids me with the waste of time.—
Be not afraid, good youth, I will not have you:
And yet, when wit and youth is come to harvest,
Your wife is like to reap a proper man.
There lies your way due-west.
Vio. Then westward-ho:
Grace and good disposition 'tend your ladyship!
You'll nothing, madam, to my lord by me?
Oli. Stay:
I pr'ythee tell me what thou think'st of me.
Vio. That you do think you are not what you are.
Oli. If I think so, I think the same of you.
Vio. Then think you right; I am not what I am.
Oli. I would you were as I would have you be!
Vio. Would it be better, madam, that I am,
I wish it might; for now I am your fool.
Oli. O what a deal of scorn looks beautiful
In the contempt and anger of his lip!
A murd'rous guilt shows not itself more soon
Than love that would seem hid: love's night is noon.
Cesario, by the roses of the spring,
By maidhood, honour, truth, and everything,
I love thee so that, maugre all thy pride,
Nor wit, nor reason, can my passion hide:
Do not extort thy reasons from this cause,
For, that I woo, thou therefore hast no cause:
But, rather, reason thus with reason fetter:
Love sought is good, but given unsought is better.
Vio. By innocence I swear, and by my youth,
I have one heart, one bosom, and one truth,
And that no woman has; nor never none

Shall mistress be of it, save I alone.
And so adieu, good madam; never more
Will I my master's tears to you deplore.
Oli. Yet come again: for thou, perhaps, mayst
    move
That heart, which now abhors, to like his love.
    [*Exeunt.*

SCENE II.—*A Room in* OLIVIA's *House.*

Enter Sir TOBY BELCH, *Sir* ANDREW AGUE-
CHEEK, *and* FABIAN.

Sir And. No, faith, I'll not stay a jot longer.
Sir To. Thy reason, dear venom: give thy
reason.
Fab. You must needs yield your reason, Sir
Andrew.
Sir And. Marry, I saw your niece do more
favours to the count's serving man than ever
she bestowed upon me; I saw 't i' the orchard.
Sir To. Did she see thee the while, old boy?
tell me that.
Sir And. As plain as I see you now.
Fab. This was a great argument of love in her
toward you.
Sir And. 'Slight! will you make an ass o' me?
Fab. I will prove it legitimate, sir, upon the
oaths of judgment and reason.
Sir To. And they have been grand jurymen
since before Noah was a sailor.
Fab. She did show favour to the youth in your
sight only to exasperate you, to awake your
dormouse valour, to put fire in your heart and
brimstone in your liver. You should then have
accosted her; and with some excellent jests,
fire-new from the mint, you should have banged
the youth into dumbness. This was looked for
at your hand, and this was baulked: the double
gilt of this opportunity you let time wash off,
and you are now sailed into the north of my
lady's opinion; where you will hang like an
icicle on a Dutchman's beard, unless you do
redeem it by some laudable attempt, either of
valour or policy.
Sir And. And 't be any way, it must be with
valour: for policy I hate; I had as lief be a
Brownist as a politician.
Sir To. Why, then, build me thy fortunes upon
the basis of valour. Challenge me the count's
youth to fight with him; hurt him in eleven
places; my niece shall take note of it: and
assure thyself there is no love-broker in the
world can more prevail in man's commendation with woman than report of valour.
Fab. There is no way but this, Sir Andrew.
Sir And. Will either of you bear me a challenge
to him?
Sir To. Go, write it in a martial hand; be curst
and brief; it is no matter how witty, so it be
eloquent and full of invention; taunt him with
the licence of ink: if thou *thou's* him some
thrice, it shall not be amiss; and as many lies
as will lie in thy sheet of paper, although the
sheet were big enough for the bed of Ware in

England, set 'em down; go about it. Let there
be gall enough in thy ink; though thou write
with a goose-pen, no matter. About it.
Sir And. Where shall I find you?
Sir To. We'll call thee at the *cubiculo.* Go.
    [*Exit Sir* ANDREW.
Fab. This is a dear manikin to you, Sir Toby.
Sir To. I have been dear to him, lad; some
two thousand strong, or so.
Fab. We shall have a rare letter from him:
but you'll not deliver it.
Sir To. Never trust me then; and by all means
stir on the youth to an answer. I think oxen
and wainropes cannot hale them together. For
Andrew, if he were opened, and you find so
much blood in his liver as will clog the foot of
a flea, I'll eat the rest of the anatomy.
Fab. And his opposite, the youth, bears in his
visage no great presage of cruelty.

Enter MARIA.

Sir To. Look where the youngest wren of nine
comes.
Mar. If you desire the spleen, and will laugh
yourselves into stitches, follow me: yon gull,
Malvolio, is turned heathen, a very renegado;
for there is no Christian, that means to be
saved by believing rightly, can ever believe
such impossible passages of grossness. He's in
yellow stockings.
Sir To. And cross-gartered?
Mar. Most villanously; like a pedant that
keeps a school i' the church.—I have dogged
him like his murderer. He does obey every
point of the letter that I dropped to betray
him. He does smile his face into more lines
than are in the new map, with the augmenta-
tion of the Indies: you have not seen such a
thing as 'tis; I can hardly forbear hurling things
at him. I know my lady will strike him; if she
do, he'll smile, and tak 't for a great favour.
Sir To. Come, bring us, bring us where he is.
    [*Exeunt.*

SCENE III.—*A Street.*

Enter ANTONIO *and* SEBASTIAN.

Seb. I would not by my will have troubled you;
But, since you make your pleasure of your pains,
I will no further chide you.
Ant. I could not stay behind you; my desire,
More sharp than filed steel, did spur me forth;
And not all love to see you,—though so much,
As might have drawn one to a longer voyage,—
But jealousy what might befall your travel,
Being skilless in these parts; which to a stranger,
Unguided and unfriended, often prove
Rough and unhospitable. My willing love,
The rather by these arguments of fear,
Set forth in your pursuit.
Seb.   My kind Antonio,
I can no other answer make but thanks,
And thanks, and ever thanks. Often good turns
Are shuffled off with such uncurrent pay;

But were my worth, as is my conscience, firm,
You should find better dealing. What's to do?
Shall we go see the reliques of this town?
Ant. To-morrow, sir; best, first, go see your
    lodging.
Seb. I am not weary, and 'tis long to night;
I pray you, let us satisfy our eyes
With the memorials and the things of fame
That do renown this city.
Ant.   Would you'd pardon me:
I do not without danger walk these streets:
Once, in a sea-fight, 'gainst the count, his
    galleys,
I did some service; of such note, indeed,
That were I ta'en here, it would scarce be
        answered.   [people.
Seb. Belike you slew great number of his
Ant. The offence is not of such a bloody
    nature;
Albeit the quality of the time and quarrel
Might well have given us bloody argument.
It might have since been answered in repaying
What we took from them; which, for traffic's
    sake,
Most of our city did: only myself stood out:
For which, if I be lapsed in this place,
I shall pay dear.
Seb.   Do not then walk too open.
Ant. It doth not fit me. Hold, sir, here's my
    purse.
In the south suburbs, at the Elephant,
Is best to lodge: I will bespeak our diet
Whiles you beguile the time and feed your
    knowledge
With viewing of the town; there shall you have
    me.
Seb. Why I your purse?
Ant. Haply your eye shall light upon some toy
You have desire to purchase; and your store,
I think, is not for idle markets, sir.
Seb. I'll be your purse-bearer, and leave you
for an hour.
Ant. To the Elephant.—
Seb.   I do remember.
                             [*Exeunt.*

SCENE IV.—OLIVIA'S *Garden.*

Enter OLIVIA *and* MARIA.

Oli. I have sent after him. He says he'll come;
How shall I feast him? what bestow on him?
For youth is bought more oft than begged or
    borrowed.
I speak too loud.——
Where is Malvolio?—he is sad and civil,
And suits well for a servant with my fortunes;—
Where is Malvolio?
Mar.   He's coming, madam:
But in strange manner. He is sure possessed.
Oli. Why, what's the matter? does he rave?
Mar.   No, madam,
He does nothing but smile: your ladyship
Were best have guard about you if he come;
For, sure, the man is tainted in his wits.

Oli. Go call him hither.—I'm as mad as he,
If sad and merry madness equal be.—

Enter MALVOLIO.

How now, Malvolio?
Mal. Sweet lady, ho, ho.
                    [*Smiles fantastically.*
Oli. Smil'st thou?
I sent for thee upon a sad occasion.
Mal. Sad, lady? I could be sad: this does make
some obstruction in the blood, this cross-gar-
tering. But what of that; if it please the eye
of one, it is with me as the very true sonnet is:
Please one and please all.
Oli. Why, how dost thou, man? what is the
matter with thee?
Mal. Not black in my mind, though yellow in
my legs. It did come to his hands, and com-
mands shall be executed. I think we do know
the sweet Roman hand.
Oli. Wilt thou go to bed, Malvolio?
Mal. To bed? ay, sweetheart; and I'll come to
thee.
Oli. God comfort thee! Why dost thou smile
on, and kiss thy hand so oft?
Mar. How do you, Malvolio?
Mal. At your request? Yes; nightingales an-
swer daws.
Mar. Why appear you with this ridiculous
boldness before my lady?
Mal. Be not afraid of greatness:—'twas well
writ.
Oli. What meanest thou by that, Malvolio?
Mal. Some are born great,—
Oli. Ha?
Mal. Some achieve greatness,—
Oli. What say'st thou?
Mal. And some have greatness thrust upon them.
Oli. Heaven restore thee!
*Mal. Remember who commended thy yellow
stockings;*—
Oli. Thy yellow stockings?
Mal. And wished to see thee cross-gartered.
Oli. Cross-gartered?
*Mal. Go to: thou art made, if thou desirest to be
so:*—
Oli. Am I made?
Mal. If not, let me see thee a servant still.
Oli. Why, this is very midsummer madness.

Enter Servant.

Ser. Madam, the young gentleman of the
Count Orsino's is returned; I could hardly
entreat him back; he attends your ladyship's
pleasure.
Oli. I'll come to him. [*Exit* Servant.] Good
Maria, let this fellow be looked to. Where's
my cousin Toby? Let some of my people have
a special care of him; I would not have him
miscarry for the half of my dowry.
              [*Exeunt* OLIVIA *and* MARIA.
Mal. Oh, ho! do you come near me now? no
worse man than Sir Toby to look to me? This
concurs directly with the letter: she sends him

on purpose that I may appear stubborn to him; for she incites me to that in the letter. *Cast thy humble slough*, says she;—*be opposite with a kinsman, surly with servants,—let thy tongue tang with arguments of state,—put thyself into the trick of singularity;——and*, consequently, sets down the manner how; as, a sad face, a reverend carriage, a slow tongue, in the habit of some sir of note, and so forth. I have limed her; but it is Jove's doing, and Jove make me thankful! And, when she went away now, *Let this fellow be looked to:* Fellow! not Malvolio, nor after my degree, but fellow. Why, everything adheres together; that no dram of a scruple, no scruple of a scruple, no obstacle, no incredulous or unsafe circumstance,—What can be said? Nothing, that can be, can come between me and the full prospect of my hopes. Well, Jove, not I, is the doer of this, and he is to be thanked.

Re-enter MARIA, *with Sir* TOBY BELCH *and* FABIAN.

Sir To. Which way is he, in the name of sanctity? If all the devils of hell be drawn in little, and Legion himself possessed him, yet I'll speak to him.

Fab. Here he is, here he is:—How is 't with you, sir? how is 't with you, man?

Mal. Go off; I discard you; let me enjoy my private; go off.

Mar. Lo, how hollow the fiend speaks within him! did not I tell you?—Sir Toby, my lady prays you to have a care of him.

Mal. Ah, ah! does she so?

Sir To. Go to, go to; peace, peace, we must deal gently with him; let me alone. How do you, Malvolio? how is 't with you? What, man! defy the devil: consider, he's an enemy to mankind.

Mal. Do you know what you say?

Mar. La you, an you speak ill of the devil, how he takes it at heart! Pray God he be not bewitched.

Fab. Carry his water to the wise woman.

Mar. Marry, and it shall be done to-morrow morning, if I live. My lady would not lose him for more than I'll say.

Mal. How now, mistress?

Mar. O lord!

Sir To. Pr'ythee, hold thy peace; this is not the way. Do you not see you move him? let me alone with him.

Fab. No way but gentleness; gently, gently: the fiend is rough, and will not be roughly used.

Sir To. Why, how now, my bawcock? how dost thou, chuck.

Mal. Sir?

Sir To. Ay, Biddy, come with me. What, man! 'tis not for gravity to play at cherry-pit with Satan. Hang him, foul collier!

Mar. Get him to say his prayers; good Sir Toby, get him to pray.

Mal. My prayers, minx?

Mar. No, I warrant you, he will not hear of godliness.

Mal. Go, hang yourselves all! you are idle shallow things: I am not of your element; you shall know more hereafter. [*Exit.*

Sir To. Is 't possible?

Fab. If this were played upon the stage now, I could condemn it as an improbable fiction.

Sir To. His very genius hath taken the infection of the device, man.

Mar. Nay, pursue him now; lest the device take air and taint.

Fab. Why, we shall make him mad indeed.

Mar. The house will be the quieter.

Sir To. Come, we'll have him in a dark room and bound. My niece is already in the belief that he is mad; we may carry it thus, for our pleasure and his penance, till our very pastime, tired out of breath, prompt us to have mercy on him: at which time we will bring the device to the bar, and crown thee for a finder of madmen. But see, but see.

Enter Sir ANDREW AGUE-CHEEK.

Fab. More matter for a May morning.

Sir And. Here's the challenge, read it; I warrant there's vinegar and pepper in 't.

Fab. Is 't so saucy?

Sir And. Ay is it, I warrant him; do but read.

Sir To. Give me. [*Reads.*] *Youth, whatsoever thou art, thou art but a scurvy fellow.*

Fab. Good and valiant.

Sir To. Wonder not, nor admire not in thy mind, why I do call thee so, for I will show thee no reason for 't.

Fab. A good note: that keeps you from the blow of the law.

Sir To. Thou comest to the Lady Olivia, and in my sight she uses thee kindly: but thou liest in thy throat; that is not the matter I challenge thee for.

Fab. Very brief, and exceeding good senseless.

Sir To. I will waylay thee going home; where if it be thy chance to kill me,——

Fab. Good.

Sir To. Thou killest me like a rogue and a villain.

Fab. Still you keep o' the windy side of the law. Good.

Sir To. Fare thee well; and God have mercy upon one of our souls! He may have mercy upon mine; but my hope is better, and so look to thyself. Thy friend, as thou usest him, and thy sworn enemy, ANDREW AGUE-CHEEK.

Sir To. If this letter move him not, his legs cannot: I'll give 't him.

Mar. You may have very fit occasion for 't; he is now in some commerce with my lady, and will by and by depart.

Sir To. Go, Sir Andrew; scout me for him at the corner of the orchard, like a bum-bailiff; so soon as ever thou seest him, draw; and, as thou drawest, swear horrible; for it comes to pass oft that a terrible oath, with a swaggering accent sharply twanged off, gives manhood more approbation than ever proof itself would have earned him. Away.

Sir And. Nay, let me alone for swearing. [*Exit.*

Sir To. Now will not I deliver his letter; for the behaviour of the young gentleman gives him out to be of good capacity and breeding; his employment between his lord and my niece confirms no less; therefore this letter, being so excellently ignorant, will breed no terror in the youth: he will find it comes from a clodpole. But, sir, I will deliver his challenge by word of mouth, set upon Ague-cheek a notable report of valour, and drive the gentleman,—as I know his youth will aptly receive it,—into a most hideous opinion of his rage, skill, fury, and impetuosity. This will so fright them both that they will kill one another by the look, like cockatrices.

Enter OLIVIA and VIOLA.

Fab. Here he comes with your niece; give them way till he take leave, and presently after him.

Sir To. I will meditate the while upon some horrid message for a challenge.

[*Exeunt Sir* To., FAB., *and* MAR.

Oli. I have said too much unto a heart of stone, And laid mine honour too unchary on it: There's something in me that reproves my fault; But such a headstrong potent fault it is That it but mocks reproof. [bears

Vio. With the same 'haviour that your passion Go on my master's griefs. [ture;

Oli. Here, wear this jewel for me, 'tis my pic- Refuse it not, it hath no tongue to vex you: And, I beseech you, come again to-morrow. What shall you ask of me that I'll deny, That, honour saved, may upon asking give?

Vio. Nothing but this, your true love for my master. [that

Oli. How with mine honour may I give him Which I have given to you?

Vio. I will acquit you.

Oli. Well, come again to-morrow. Fare thee well; A fiend like thee might bear my soul to hell. [*Exit.*

Re-enter Sir TOBY BELCH and FABIAN.

Sir To. Gentleman, God save thee.

Vio. And you, sir.

Sir To. That defence thou hast, betake thee to 't. Of what nature the wrongs are thou hast done him, I know not; but thy intercepter, full of despight, bloody as the hunter, attends thee at the orchard end: dismount thy tuck, be yare in thy preparation, for thy assailant is quick, skilful, and deadly.

Vio. You mistake, sir; I am sure no man hath any quarrel to me; my remembrance is very free and clear from any image of offence done to any man.

Sir To. You'll find it otherwise, I assure you: therefore, if you hold your life at any price, betake you to your guard; for your opposite hath in him what youth, strength, skill, and wrath can furnish man withal.

Vio. I pray you, sir, what is he?

Sir To. He is a knight, dubbed with unhacked rapier, and on carpet consideration; but he is a devil in private brawl; souls and bodies hath he divorced three; and his incensement at this moment is so implacable that satisfaction can be none but by pangs of death and sepulchre: hob, nob, is his word; give 't or take 't.

Vio. I will return again into the house and desire some conduct of the lady. I am no fighter. I have heard of some kind of men that put quarrels purposely on others to taste their valour: belike this is a man of that quirk.

Sir To. Sir, no; his indignation derives itself out of a very competent injury; therefore, get you on, and give him his desire. Back you shall not to the house, unless you undertake that with me which with as much safety you might answer him: therefore on, or strip your sword stark naked; for meddle you must, that's certain, or forswear to wear iron about you.

Vio. This is as uncivil as strange. I beseech you, do me this courteous office as to know of the knight what my offence to him is, it is something of my negligence, nothing of my purpose.

Sir To. I will do so. Signior Fabian, stay you by this gentleman till my return.

[*Exit Sir* TOBY.

Vio. Pray you, sir, do you know of this matter?

Fab. I know the knight is incensed against you, even to a mortal arbitrement; but nothing of the circumstance more.

Vio. I beseech you, what manner of man is he?

Fab. Nothing of that wonderful promise, to read him by his form, as you are like to find him in the proof of his valour. He is indeed, sir, the most skilful, bloody, and fatal opposite that you could possibly have found in any part of Illyria. Will you walk towards him? I will make your peace with him if I can.

Vio. I shall be much bound to you for 't. I am one that would rather go with sir priest than sir knight: I care not who knows so much of my mettle. [*Exeunt.*

Re-enter Sir TOBY with Sir ANDREW.

Sir To. Why, man, he's a very devil; I have not seen such a virago. I had a pass with him, rapier, scabbard, and all, and he gives me the stuck-in with such a mortal motion that it is inevitable; and on the answer, he pays you as surely as your feet hit the ground they step on. They say he has been fencer to the Sophy.

Sir And. Pox on 't, I'll not meddle with him.

Sir To. Ay, but he will not now be pacified: Fabian can scarce hold him yonder.

Sir And. Plague on 't; an I thought he had been valiant, and so cunning in fence, I'd have seen him damned ere I'd have challenged him. Let him let the matter slip and I'll give him my horse, gray Capilet.

Sir To. I'll make the motion. Stand here, make a good show on t; this shall end without the perdition of souls. Marry, I'll ride your horse as well as I ride you.   [*Aside.*

Re-enter FABIAN *and* VIOLA.

I have his horse [*to* FAB.] to take up the quarrel; I have persuaded him the youth's a devil.

Fab. He is as horribly conceited of him; and pants and looks pale, as if a bear were at his heels.

Sir To. There's no remedy, sir; he will fight with you for his oath sake: marry, he hath better bethought him of his quarrel, and he finds that now scarce to be worth talking of: therefore draw, for the supportance of his vow; he protests he will not hurt you.

Vio. Pray God defend me! A little thing would make me tell them how much I lack of a man.
                    [*Aside.*

Fab. Give ground if you see him furious.

Sir To. Come, Sir Andrew, there's no remedy; the gentleman will, for his honour's sake, have one bout with you: he cannot by the duello avoid it; but he has promised me, as he is a gentleman and a soldier, he will not hurt you. Come on: to 't.

Sir And. Pray God, he kept his oath. [*Draws.*

Enter ANTONIO.

Vio. I do assure you 'tis against my will.
                    [*Draws.*

Ant. Put up your sword:—If this young gentleman
Have done offence, I take the fault on me;
If you offend him I for him defy you.
                    [*Drawing.*

Sir To. You, sir? why, what are you?

Ant. One, sir, that for his love dares yet do more
Than you have heard him brag to you he will.

Sir To. Nay, if you be an undertaker I am for you.   [*Draws.*

Enter two Officers.

Fab. O good Sir Toby, hold; here come the officers.

Sir To. I'll be with you anon.   [*To* ANTONIO.

Vio. Pray, sir, put up your sword, if you please.   [*To Sir* ANDREW.

Sir And. Marry, will I, sir; and, for that I promised you, I'll be as good as my word. He will bear you easily and reins well.

1 *Off.* This is the man; do thy office.

2 *Off.* Antonio, I arrest thee at the suit
Of Count Orsino.

Ant.   You do mistake me, sir.

1 *Off.* No, sir, no jot; I know your favour well,
Though now you have no sea-cap on your
                    head.—
Take him away; he knows I know him well.

Ant. I must obey.—This comes from seeking
                    you;
But there's no remedy; I shall answer it.

What will you do? Now my necessity   [me
Makes me to ask you for my purse. It grieves
Much more for what I cannot do for you
Than what befalls myself. You stand amazed;
But be of comfort.

2 *Off.* Come, sir, away.

Ant. I must entreat of you some of that money.

Vio. What money, sir?

For the fair kindness you have showed me here,
And part being prompted by your present
                    trouble,
Out of my lean and low ability
I'll lend you something; my having is not much;
I'll make division of my present with you:.
Hold, there is half my coffer.

Ant.   Will you deny me now?
I'st possible that my deserts to you
Can lack persuasion? Do not tempt my misery
Lest that it make me so unsound a man
As to upbraid you with those kindnesses
That I have done for you.

Vio.   I know of none,
Nor know I you by voice or any feature:
I hate ingratitude more in a man
Than lying, vainness, babbling, drunkenness,
Or any taint of vice whose strong corruption
Inhabits our frail blood.

Ant.   O heavens themselves!

2 *Off.* Come, sir, I pray you go.

Ant. Let me speak a little. This youth that
                    you see here
I snatched one half out of the jaws of death,
Relieved him with such sanctity of love,——
And to his image, which methought did promise
Most venerable worth, did I devotion.

1 *Off.* What's that to us? The time goes by;
                    away.

Ant. But O how vile an idol proves this god!
Thou hast, Sebastian, done good feature shame.
In nature there's no blemish but the mind;
None can be call'd deform'd but the unkind:
Virtue is beauty; but the beauteous-evil
Are empty trunks o'erflourish'd by the devil.

1 *Off.* The man grows mad; away with him.
Come, come, sir.

Ant. Lead me on.
                    [*Exeunt* Officers *with* ANTONIO.

Vio. Methinks his words do from such passion
                    fly
That he believes himself; so do not I.
Prove true, imagination; O prove true,
That I, dear brother, be now ta'en for you!

Sir To. Come hither, knight; come hither,
Fabian; we'll whisper o'er a couple or two of
most sage saws.

Vio. He named Sebastian; I my brother know
Yet living in my glass; even such and so
In favour was my brother; and he went
Still in this fashion, colour, ornament,
For him I imitate. O, if it prove,
Tempests are kind, and salt waves fresh in
love!   [*Exit.*

Sir To. A very dishonest paltry boy, and more
a coward than a hare: his dishonesty appears

in leaving his friend here in necessity, and de-
nying him; and for his cowardship, ask Fabian.
Fab. A coward, a most devout coward, reli-
gious in it. [him.
Sir And. 'Slid, I'll after him again and beat
Sir To. Do, cuff him soundly, but never draw
thy sword.
Sir And. An' I do not,— [*Exit.*
Fab. Come, let's see the event.
Sir To. I dare lay any money 'twill be nothing
yet. [*Exeunt.*

ACT IV.

SCENE I.—*The Street before* OLIVIA'S *House.*

Enter SEBASTIAN *and* CLOWN.

Clo. Will you make me believe that I am not
sent for you?
Seb. Go to, go to, thou art a foolish fellow;
Let me be clear of thee.
Clo. Well held out, i' faith! No, I do not know
you; nor I am not sent to you by my lady, to
bid you come speak with her; nor your name
is not Master Cesario; nor this is not my nose
neither.—Nothing that is so is so.
Seb. I pr'ythee, vent thy folly somewhere else.
Thou knowst not me.
Clo. Vent my folly! he has heard that word of
some great man, and now applies it to a fool.
Vent my folly! I am afraid this great lubber,
the world, will prove a cockney.—I pr'ythee
now, ungird thy strangeness, and tell me what
I shall vent to my lady. Shall I vent to her
that thou art coming?
Seb. I pr'ythee, foolish Greek, depart from me;
There's money for thee; if you tarry longer
I shall give worse paymant.
Clo. By my troth, thou hast an open hand:—
These wise men that give fools money get
themselves a good report after fourteen years'
purchase.

Enter Sir ANDREW, *Sir* TOBY, *and* FABIAN.

Sir And. Now, sir, have I met you again?
there's for you. [*Striking* SEBASTIAN.
Seb. Why, there's for thee, and there, and
there.
Are all the people mad?
[*Beating Sir* ANDREW.
Sir To. Hold, sir, or I'll throw your dagger
o'er the house.
Clo. This will I tell my lady straight I would
not be in some of your coats for twopence.
[*Exit* CLOWN.
Sir To. Come on, sir; hold.
[*Holding* SEBASTIAN.
Sir And. Nay, let him alone; I'll go another
way to work with him; I'll have an action of
battery against him, if there be any law in
Illyria: though I struck him first, yet it's no
matter for that.
Seb. Let go thy hand.
Sir To. Come, sir, I will not let you go. Come,

my young soldier, put up your iron: you are
well fleshed; come on.
Seb. I will be free from thee. What wouldst
thou now?
If thou dar'st tempt me further, draw thy
sword. [*Draws.*
Sir To. What, what? Nay, then I must have
an ounce or two of this malapert blood from
you. [*Draws.*

Enter OLIVIA.

Oli. Hold, Toby; on thy life, I charge thee,
hold.
Sir To. Madam?
Oli. Will it be ever thus? Ungracious wretch,
Fit for the mountains and the barbarous caves,
Where manners ne'er were preach'd! Out of
my sight!
Be not offended, dear Cesario!——
Rudesby, be gone!—I pr'ythee, gentle friend,
[*Exeunt Sir* TO., *Sir* AND., *and* FAB.
Let thy fair wisdom, not thy passion, sway
In this uncivil and unjust extent
Against thy peace. Go with me to my house,
And hear thou there how many fruitless pranks
This ruffian hath botch'd up, that thou thereby
Mayst smile at this: thou shalt not choose but go;
Do not deny. Beshrew his soul for me,
He started one poor heart of mine in thee.
Seb. What relish is in this? how runs the stream?
Or am I mad? or else this is a dream:—
Let fancy still my sense in Lethe steep;
If it be thus to dream, still let me sleep!
Oli. Nay, come, I pr'ythee. Would thou'dst
be ruled by me!
Seb. Madam, I will.
Oli. O, say so, and so be!
[*Exeunt.*

SCENE II.—*A Room in* OLIVIA'S *House.*

Enter MARIA *and* CLOWN.

Mar. Nay, I pr'ythee, put on this gown and
this beard; make him believe thou art Sir
Topas the curate; do it quickly: I'll call Sir
Toby the whilst. [*Exit* MARIA.
Clo. Well, I'll put it on, and I will dissemble
myself in 't; and I would I were the first that
ever dissembled in such a gown. I am not fat
enough to become the function well: nor lean
enough to be thought a good student: but to be
said, an honest man and a good housekeeper,
goes as fairly as to say, a careful man and a
great scholar. The competitors enter.

Enter Sir TOBY BELCH *and* MARIA.

Sir To. Jove bless thee, master parson.
Clo. Bonos dies, Sir Toby: for as the old hermit of Prague, that never saw pen and ink,
very wittily said to a niece of King Gorboduc,
That that is, is: so I, being master parson, am
master parson: for what is that but that? and
is but is?
Sir To To him, Sir Topas.

Clo. What, hoa, I say,—Peace in this prison!

Sir To. The knave counterfeits well; a good knave.

Mal. [*In an inner chamber.*] Who calls there?

Clo. Sir Topas the curate, who comes to visit Malvolio the lunatic.

Mal. Sir Topas, Sir Topas, good Sir Topas, go to my lady.

Clo. Out, hyperbolical fiend! how vexest thou this man? talkest thou nothing but of ladies?

Sir To. Well said, master parson.

Mal. Sir Topas, never was man thus wronged: good Sir Topas, do not think I am mad; they have laid me here in hideous darkness.

Clo. Fie, thou dishonest Sathan! I call thee by the most modest terms; for I am one of those gentle ones that will use the devil himself with courtesy. Say'st thou that house is dark?

Mal. As hell, Sir Topas.

Clo. Why, it hath bay-windows, transparent as barricadoes, and the clear storeys towards the south-north are as lustrous as ebony; and yet complainest thou of obstruction?

Mal. I am not mad, Sir Topas; I say to you this house is dark.

Clo. Madman, thou errest. I say there is no darkness but ignorance; in which thou art more puzzled than the Egyptians in their fog.

Mal. I say this house is as dark as ignorance, though ignorance were as dark as hell; and I say there was never man thus abused. I am no more mad than you are; make the trial of it in any constant question.

Clo. What is the opinion of Pythagoras concerning wild-fowl?

Mal. That the soul of our grandam might haply inhabit a bird.

Clo. What thinkest thou of his opinion?

Mal. I think nobly of the soul, and no way approve of his opinion.

Clo. Fare thee well. Remain thou still in darkness: thou shalt hold the opinion of Pythagoras ere I will allow of thy wits; and fear to kill a woodcock lest thou dispossess the soul of thy grandam. Fare thee well.

Mal. Sir Topas, Sir Topas!

Sir To. My most exquisite Sir Topas!

Clo. Nay, I am for all waters.

Mar. Thou mightst have done this without thy beard and gown; he sees thee not.

Sir To. To him in thine own voice, and bring me word how thou findest him: I would we were well rid of this knavery. If he may be conveniently delivered, I would he were; for I am now so far in offence with my niece that I cannot pursue with any safety this sport to the upshot. Come by and by to my chamber.

[*Exeunt Sir* To. *and* MAR.

Clo.   Hey, Robin, jolly Robin,
            Tell me how thy lady does.   [*Singing.*

Mal. Fool,—

Clo. My lady is unkind, perdy.

Mal. Fool,—

Clo. Alas, why is she so?

Mal. Fool, I say;—

Clo. She loves another—Who calls, ha?

Mal. Good fool, as ever thou wilt deserve well at my hand, help me to a candle, and pen, ink, and paper; as I am a gentleman, I will live to be thankful to thee for 't.

Clo. Master Malvolio!

Mal. Ay, good fool.

Clo. Alas, sir, how fell you besides your five wits?

Mal. Fool, there was never man so notoriously abused; I am as well in my wits, fool, as thou art.

Clo. But as well? then you are mad indeed, if you be no better in your wits than a fool.

Mal. They have here propertied me; keep me in darkness, send ministers to me, asses, and do all they can to face me out of my wits.

Clo. Advise you what you say; the minister is here.—Malvolio, Malvolio, thy wits the heavens restore! endeavour thyself to sleep, and leave thy vain bibble-babble.

Mal. Sir Topas,——

Clo. Maintain no words with him, good fellow. Who, I, sir? not I, sir. God b' wi' you, good Sir Topas.—Marry, amen.—I will, sir, I will.

Mal. Fool, fool, fool, I say,—

Clo. Alas, sir, be patient. What say you, sir? I am shent for speaking to you.

Mal. Good fool, help me to some light and some paper; I tell thee I am as well in my wits as any man in Illyria.

Clo. Well-a-day,—that you were, sir!

Mal. By this hand, I am: Good fool, some ink, paper, and light, and convey what I will set down to my lady; it shall advantage thee more than ever the bearing of letter did.

Clo. I will help you to 't. But tell me true, are you not mad indeed? or do you but counterfeit?

Mal. Believe me, I am not; I tell thee true.

Clo. Nay, I'll ne'er believe a madman till I see his brains. I will fetch you light, and paper, and ink.

Mal. Fool, I'll requite it in the highest degree: I pr'ythee, be gone.

Clo.   I am gone, sir,
                    And anon, sir,
                I'll be with you again,
                    In a trice,
                    Like to the old vice,
                Your need to sustain;
                Who with dagger of lath,
                In his rage and his wrath,
                    Cries ah, ha! to the devil:
                Like a mad lad,
                Pare thy nails, dad,
                    Adieu, goodman drivel.   [*Exit.*

SCENE III.—OLIVIA'S *Garden.*

Enter SEBASTIAN.

Seb. This is the air; that is the glorious sun;
This pearl she gave me, I do feel 't, and see 't:
And though 'tis wonder that enwraps me thus,

Yet 'tis not madness. Where's Antonio, then?
I could not find him at the Elephant;
Yet there he was; and there I found this credit,
That he did range the town to seek me out.
His counsel now might do me golden service:
For though my soul disputes well with my sense,
That this may be some error, but no madness,
Yet doth this accident and flood of fortune
So far exceed all instance, all discourse,
That I am ready to distrust mine eyes
And wrangle with my reason, that persuades me
To any other trust but that I am mad,
Or else the lady's mad; yet if 'twere so,
She could not sway her house, command her
   followers,
Take and give back affairs and their despatch
With such a smooth, discreet, and stable bearing
As I perceive she does: there's something in 't
That is deceivable. But here comes the lady.

Enter OLIVIA *and a* Priest.

Oli. Blame not this haste of mine. If you mean
   well,
Now go with me and with this holy man
Into the chantry by: there, before him
And underneath that consecrated roof,
Plight me the full assurance of your faith,
That my most jealous and too doubtful soul
May live at peace. He shall conceal it
Whiles you are willing it shall come to note;
What time we will our celebration keep
According to my birth.—What do you say?
Seb. I'll follow this good man, and go with you;
And, having sworn truth, ever will be true.
Oli. Then lead the way, good father;——And
   heavens so shine
That they may fairly note this act of mine!
         [*Exeunt.*

ACT V.

SCENE I.—*The Street before* OLIVIA'S *House.*

Enter CLOWN *and* FABIAN.

Fab. Now, as thou lovest me, let me see his
letter.
Clo. Good Master Fabian, grant me another
request.
Fab. Anything.
Clo. Do not desire to see this letter.
Fab. That is to give a dog; and in recompense,
desire my dog again.

Enter DUKE, VIOLA, *and* Attendants.

Duke. Belong you to the Lady Olivia, friends?
Clo. Ay, sir; we are some of her trappings.
Duke. I know thee well. How dost thou, my
good fellow?
Clo. Truly sir, the better for my foes and the
worse for my friends.   [friends.
Duke. Just the contrary; the better for thy
Clo. No, sir, the worse.
Duke. How can that be?
Clo. Marry, sir, they praise me, and make an

ass of me; now my foes tell me plainly I am
an ass: so that by my foes, sir, I profit in the
knowledge of myself, and by my friends I am
abused: so that, conclusions to be as kisses, if
your four negatives make your two affirma-
tives, why then, the worse for my friends and
the better for my foes.
Duke. Why, this is excellent.
Clo. By my troth, sir, no; though it please you
to be one of my friends.
Duke. Thou shalt not be the worse for me;
there's gold.
Clo. But that it would be double-dealing, sir,
I would you could make it another.
Duke. O, you give me ill counsel.
Clo. Put your grace in your pocket, sir, for
this once, and let your flesh and blood obey it.
Duke. Well, I will be so much a sinner to be a
double-dealer: there's another.
Clo. *Primo, secundo, tertio,* is a good play; and
the old saying is, the third pays for all; the
triplex, sir, is a good tripping measure; or the
bells of St. Bennet, sir, may put you in mind;
One, two, three.
Duke. You can fool no more money out of me
at this throw: if you will let your lady know I
am here to speak with her, and bring her along
with you, it may awake my bounty further.
Clo. Marry, sir, lullaby to your bounty till I
come again. I go, sir; but I would not have
you to think that my desire of having is the sin
of covetousness: but, as you say, sir, let your
bounty take a nap, I will awake it anon.
         [*Exit* CLOWN.

Enter ANTONIO *and* Officers.

Vio. Here comes the man, sir, that did rescue
me.
Duke. That face of his I do remember well:
Yet, when I saw it last, it was besmeared
As black as Vulcan in the smoke of war:
A bawbling vessel was he captain of,
For shallow draught and bulk unprizable;
With which such scathful grapple did he make
With the most noble bottom of our fleet,
That very envy and the tongue of loss
Cried fame and honour on him.—What's the
   matter?
1 *Off.* Orsino, this is that Antonio [Candy:
That took the Phœnix and her fraught from
And this is he that did the Tiger board
When your young nephew Titus lost his leg:
Here in the streets, desperate of shame and state,
In private brabble did we apprehend him.
Vio. He did me kindness, sir; drew on my side;
But, in conclusion, put strange speech upon me,
I know not what 'twas, but distraction.
Duke. Notable pirate! thou salt-water thief!
What foolish boldness brought thee to their
   mercies,
Whom thou, in terms so bloody and so dear,
Hast made thine enemies?
Ant.   Orsino, noble sir,

Be pleased that I shake off these names you
    give me;
Antonio never yet was thief or pirate,
Though, I confess, on base and ground enough,
Orsino's enemy. A witchcraft drew me hither:
That most ingrateful boy there, by your side,
From the rude sea's enraged and foamy mouth
Did I redeem; a wreck past hope he was:
His life I gave him, and did thereto add
My love, without retention or restraint,
All his in dedication: for his sake,
Did I expose myself, pure for his love,
Into the danger of this adverse town;
Drew to defend him when he was beset:
Where being apprehended, his false cunning,—
Not meaning to partake with me in danger,—
Taught him to face me out of his acquaintance,
And grew a twenty-years-removed thing
While one would wink; denied me mine own
    purse,
Which I had recommended to his use
Not half an hour before.
Vio.   How can this be?
Duke. When came he to this town?
Ant. To-day, my lord; and for three months
    before,—
No interim, not a minute's vacancy,—
Both day and night did we keep company.

Enter OLIVIA and Attendants.

Duke. Here comes the countess; now heaven
    walks on earth.——
But for thee, fellow, fellow, thy words are
    madness:
Three months this youth hath tended upon me;
But more of that anon.——Take him aside.
Oli. What would my lord, but that he may not
    have,
Wherein Olivia may seem serviceable!—
Cesario, you do not keep promise with me.
Vio. Madam?
Duke. Gracious Olivia,——
Oli. What do you say, Cesario?——Good my
    lord,——
Vio. My lord would speak, my duth hushes me.
Oli. If it be aught to the old tune, my lord,
It is as fat and fulsome to mine ear
As howling after music.
Duke.   Still so cruel?
Oli. Still so constant, lord.
Duke. What! to perverseness? you uncivil lady,
To whose ingrate and unauspicious altars
My soul the faithfull'st offerings hath breathed
    out
That e'er devotion tender'd! What shall I do?
Oli. Even what it please my lord, that shall
    become him.   [do it.
Duke. Why should I not, had I the heart to
Like to the Egyptian thief, at point of death,
Kill what I love; a savage jealousy   [this:
That sometime savours nobly?—But hear me
Since you to non-regardance cast my faith,
And that I partly know the instrument

That screws me from my true place in your
    favour,
Live you the marble-breasted tyrant still;
But this your minion, whom I know you love,
And whom by heaven I swear, I tender dearly,
Him will I tear out of that cruel eye
Where he sits crowned in his master's sprite.—
Come, boy, with me; my thoughts are ripe in
    mischief:
I'll sacrifice the lamb that I do love,
To spite a raven's heart within a dove.
                        [*Going.*
Vio. And I, most jocund, apt, and willingly,
To do you rest, a thousand deaths would die.
                     [*Following.*
Oli. Where goes Cesario?
Vio.   After him I love
More than I love these eyes, more than my life,
More, by all mores, than e'er I shall love wife;
If I do feign, you witnesses above
Punish my life for tainting of my love!
Oli. Ah me, detested! how am I beguiled?
Vio. Who does beguile you? who does do you
    wrong?
Oli. Hast thou forgot thyself? Is it so long?
Call forth the holy father.
               [*Exit an* Attendant.
Duke.   Come away. [*To* VIOLA.
Oli. Whither, my lord? Cesario, husband, stay.
Duke. Husband?
Oli.   Ay, husband, can he that deny?
Duke. Her husband, sirrah?
Vio.   No, my lord, not I
Oli. Alas, it is the baseness of thy fear
That makes thee strangle thy propriety:
Fear not, Cesario, take thy fortunes up;
Be that thou know'st thou art, and then thou
    art   [father!
As great as that thou fear'st—O, welcome,

Re-enter Attendant and Priest.

Father, I charge thee, by thy reverence,
Here to unfold—though lately we intended
To keep in darkness what occasion now
Reveals before 'tis ripe,—what thou dost know
Hath newly past between this youth and me.
Priest. A contract of eternal bond of love,
Confirmed by mutual joinder of your hands,
Attested by the holy close of lips,
Strengthen'd by interchangement of your rings;
And all the ceremony of this compact
Sealed in my function, by my testimony:
Since when, my watch hath told me, toward
    my grave
I have travelled but two hours.   [be,
Duke. O thou dissembling cub! what wilt thou
When time hath sowed a grizzle on thy case?
Or will not else thy craft so quickly grow
That thine own trip shall be thine overthrow?
Farewell, and take her; but direct thy feet
Where thou and I henceforth may never meet.
Vio. My lord, I do protest,—
Oli.   O, do not swear;
Hold little faith, though thou hast too much fear.

Enter Sir ANDREW AGUE-CHEEK, *with his head broke.*

Sir And. For the love of God, a surgeon; send one presently to Sir Toby.

Oli. What's the matter?

Sir And. He has broke my head across, and has given Sir Toby a bloody coxcomb too: for the love of God, your help: I had rather than forty pound I were at home.

Oli. Who has done this, Sir Andrew?

Sir And. The count's gentleman, one Cesario: we took him for a coward, but he's the very devil incardinate.

Duke. My gentleman, Cesario?

Sir And. Od's lifelings, here he is:—You broke my head for nothing; and that that I did I was set on to do't by Sir Toby.   [you:

Vio. Why do you speak to me? I never hurt You drew your sword upon me without cause; But I bespake you fair and hurt you not.

Sir And. If a bloody coxcomb be a hurt, you have hurt me; I think you set nothing by a bloody coxcomb.

Enter Sir TOBY BELCH *drunk, led by the* CLOWN.

Here comes Sir Toby halting; you shall hear more: but if he had not been in drink he would have tickled you othergates than he did.

Duke. How now, gentleman? how is't with you?

Sir To. That's all one; he has hurt me, and there's the end on't.—Sot, didst see Dick surgeon, sot?

Clo. O he's drunk, Sir Toby, an hour agone; his eyes were set at eight i' the morning.

Sir To. Then he's a rogue. After a passy-measure, or a pavin, I hate a drunken rogue.

Oli. Away with him. Who hath made this havoc with them?

Sir And. I'll help you, Sir Toby, because we'll be dressed together.

Sir To. Will you help an ass-head, and a coxcomb, and a knave? a thin-faced knave, a gull?

Oli. Get him to bed, and let his hurt be looked to.   [*Exeunt* CLOWN, *Sir* TO., *and Sir* AND.

Enter SEBASTIAN.

Seb. I am sorry, madam, I have hurt your kinsman;
But, had it been the brother of my blood,
I must have done no less, with wit and safety.
You throw a strange regard upon me, and
By that I do perceive it hath offended you;
Pardon me, sweet one, even for the vows
We made each other but so late ago.

Duke. One face, one voice, one habit, and two persons;
A natural perspective, that is, and is not.

Seb. Antonio, O my dear Antonio!
How have the hours rack'd and tortur'd me
Since I have lost thee.

Ant. Sebastian are you?

Seb.   Fear'st thou that, Antonio?

Ant. How have you made division of yourself?—
An apple, cleft in two, is not more twin
Than these two creatures. Which is Sebastian?

Oli. Most wonderful!

Seb. Do I stand there? I never had a brother:
Nor can there be that deity in my nature
Of here and everywhere. I had a sister
Whom the blind waves and surges have devoured:—
Of charity, what kin are you to me? [*To* VIOLA.
Whatcountryman?whatname?whatparentage?

Vio. Of Messaline: Sebastian was my father;
Such a Sebastian was my brother too;
So went he suited to his watery tomb:
If spirits can assume both form and suit,
You come to fright us.

Seb.   A spirit I am indeed:
But am in that dimension grossly clad,
Which from the womb I did participate.
Were you a woman, as the rest goes even,
I should my tears let fall upon your cheek,
And say—Thrice welcome, drowned Viola!

Vio. My father had a mole upon his brow.

Seb. And so had mine.

Vio. And died that day when Viola from her birth
Had numbered thirteen years.

Seb. O, that record is lively in my soul!
He finished, indeed, his mortal act
That day that made my sister thirteen years.

Vio. If nothing lets to make us happy both
But this my masculine usurp'd attire,
Do not embrace me till each circumstance
Of place, time, fortune, do cohere, and jump,
That I am Viola: which to confirm,
I'll bring you to a captain in this town, [help
Where lie my maiden's weeds; by whose gentle
I was preserv'd to serve this noble count;
All the occurrence of my fortune since
Hath been between this lady and this lord.

Seb. So comes it, lady, you have been mistook:
But nature to her bias drew in that. [*To* OLIVIA.
You would have been contracted to a maid;
Nor are you therein, by my life, deceived;
You are betroth'd both to a maid and man.

Duke. Be not amazed; right noble is his blood.—
If this be so, as yet the glass seems true,
I shall have share in this most happy wreck:
Boy, thou hast said to me a thousand times,
          [*To* VIOLA.
Thou never shouldst love woman like to me.

Vio. And all those sayings will I over-swear;
And all those swearings keep as true in soul
As doth that orbed continent the fire
That severs day from night.

Duke.   Give me thy hand;
And let me see thee in thy woman's weeds.

Vio. The captain that did bring me first on shore   [action,
Hath my maid's garments: he, upon some
Is now in durance, at Malvolio's suit;
A gentleman and follower of my lady's.

Oli. He shall enlarge him:—Fetch Malvolio
     hither:—
And yet, alas, now I remember me,
They say, poor gentleman, he's much distract.

       Re-enter CLOWN, *with a letter*.

A most extracting frenzy of mine own
From my remembrance clearly banished his.—
How does he, sirrah?
Clo. Truly, madam, he holds Beelzebub at the
stave's end as well as a man in his case may do:
he has here writ a letter to you; I should have
given it you to-day morning; but as a madman's epistles are no gospels, so it skills not
much when they are delivered.
Oli. Open it, and read it.
Clo. Look then to be well edified when the fool
delivers the madman:—*By the Lord, madam,*—
Oli. How now! art thou mad?
Clo. No, madam, I do but read madness: an
your ladyship will have it as it ought to be, you
must allow *vox*.
Oli. Pr'ythee, read i' thy right wits.
Clo. So I do, madonna; but to read his right
wits to read thus: therefore perpend, my princess, and give ear.
Oli. Read it you, sirrah.   [*To* FABIAN.
Fab. [reads.] *By the Lord, madam, you wrong
me, and the world shall know it: though you have
put me into darkness and given your drunken
cousin rule over me, yet have I the benefit of my
senses as well as your ladyship. I have your own
letter that induced me to the semblance I put on;
with the which I doubt not but to do myself much
right or you much shame. Think of me as you
please. I leave my duty a little unthought of, and
speak out of my injury.*
       The madly used MALVOLIO.
Oli. Did he write this?
Clo. Ay, madam.
Duke. This savours not much of distraction.
Oli. See him delivered, Fabian: bring him
     hither.   [*Exit* FABIAN.
My lord, so please you, these things further
     thought on,
To think me as well a sister as a wife,
One day shall crown the alliance on't, so please
     you,
Here at my house, and at my proper cost.
Duke. Madam, I am most apt to embrace your
     offer.—   [service done him,
Your master quits you; [*to* VIOLA] and, for your
So much against the metal of your sex,
So far beneath your soft and tender breeding,
And since you called me master for so long,
Here is my hand; you shall from this time be
Your master's mistress.
Oli.   A sister?—you are she.

       Re-enter FABIAN *with* MALVOLIO.

Duke. Is this the madman?
Oli.   Ay, my lord, this same;
How now, Malvolio?

Mal.   Madam, you have done me wrong,
Notorious wrong.
Oli.   Have I, Malvolio? no.
Mal. Lady, you have. Pray you, peruse that
     letter:
You must not now deny it is your hand,
Write from it, if you can, in hand or phrase;
Or say, 'tis not your seal, nor your invention:
You can say none of this. Well, grant it then,
And tell me, in the modesty of honour,
Why you have given me such clear lights of
     favour;
Bade me come smiling and cross-garter'd to you;
To put on yellow stockings, and to frown
Upon Sir Toby and the lighter people:
And, acting this in an obedient hope,
Why have you suffer'd me to be imprison'd,
Kept in a dark house, visited by the priest,
And made the most notorious geck and gull
That e'er invention play'd on? tell me why.
Oli. Alas, Malvolio, this is not my writing,
Though, I confess, much like the character:
But, out of question, 'tis Maria's hand.
And now I do bethink me, it was she
First told me thou wast mad; then cam'st in
     smiling,
And in such forms which here were presuppos'd
Upon thee in the letter. Pr'ythee, be content:
This practice has most shrewdly pass'd upon
     thee:
But, when we know the grounds and authors
     of it,
Thou shalt be both the plaintiff and the judge
Of thine own cause.
Fab.   Good madam, hear me speak;
And let no quarrel, nor no brawl to come,
Taint the condition of this present hour,
Which I have wonder'd at. In hope it shall not,
Most freely I confess, myself and Toby
Set this device against Malvolio here,
Upon some stubborn and uncourteous parts
We had conceiv'd against him. Maria writ
The letter, at Sir Toby's great importance;
In recompense whereof he hath married her.
How with a sportful malice it was follow'd
May rather pluck on laughter than revenge,
If that the injuries be justly weigh'd
That have on both sides past.
Oli. Alas, poor fool! how have they baffled thee!
Clo. Why, *some are born great, some achieve
greatness, and some have greatness thrown upon
them. I* was one, sir, in this interlude; one Sir
Topas, sir; but that's all one:—*By the Lord,
fool, I am not mad;*—But do you remember?
*Madam, why laugh you at such a barren rascal?
an you smile not, he's gagged*. And thus the
whirligig of time brings in his revenges.
Mal. I'll be revenged on the whole pack of you.
       [*Exit*.
Oli He hath been most notoriously abus'd.
Duke. Pursue him, and entreat him to a peace:—
He hath not told us of the captain yet;
When that is known, and golden time convents,
A solemn combination shall be made

Of our dear souls.—Meantime, sweet sister,
we will not part from hence.—Cesario, come:
For so you shall be while you are a man;
But, when in other habits you are seen,
Orsino's mistress, and his fancy's queen.
                                        [*Exeunt.*

SONG

Clo. When that I was and a little tiny boy,
    With hey, ho, the wind and the rain,
A foolish thing was but a toy,
    For the rain it raineth every day.

But when I came to man's estate,
    With hey, ho, the wind and the rain,
'Gainst knave and thief men shut their gate,
    For the rain it raineth every day.

But when I came, alas! to wive,
    With hey, ho, the wind and the rain,
By swaggering could I never thrive,
    For the rain it raineth every day.

But when I came unto my bed,
    With hey, ho, the wind and the rain,
With toss-pots still had drunken head,
    For the rain it raineth every day.

A great while ago the world began,
    With hey, ho, the wind and the rain,
But that's all one, our play is done,
    And we'll strive to please you every day.
                                        [*Exit.*

MEASURE FOR MEASURE

DRAMATIS PERSONÆ

VICENTIO, *Duke of Vienna.*
ANGELO, *Lord Deputy in the Duke's absence.*
ESCALUS, *an ancient Lord, joined with An-*
    GELO *in the Deputation.*
CLAUDIO, *a young Gentleman.*
LUCIO, *a Fantastic.*
TWO OTHER LIKE GENTLEMEN.
VARRIUS, *a Gentleman, Servant to the Duke.*
PROVOST.
THOMAS, } *two Friars.*
PETER, }
A JUSTICE.
ELBOW, *a simple Constable.*

FROTH, *a foolish Gentleman.*
CLOWN, *Servant to* MRS. OVERDONE.
ABHORSON, *an Executioner.*
BARNARDINE, *a dissolute Prisoner.*

ISABELLA, *Sister to* CLAUDIO.
MARIANA, *betrothed to* ANGELO.
JULIET, *beloved by* CLAUDIO.
FRANCISCA, *a Nun.*
MISTRESS OVERDONE, *a Bawd.*

Lords, Gentlemen, Guards, Officers, *and*
    other Attendants.

SCENE,—VIENNA.

ACT I.

SCENE I.—*An Apartment in the* DUKE'S *Palace.*

En er DUKE, ESCALUS, Lords, *and* Attendants.

Duke. Escalus,—
Escal. My lord.
Duke. Of government the properties to unfold,
Would seem in me to affect speech and discourse;
Since I am put to know that your own science
Exceeds, in that, the lists of all advice
My strength can give you: then no more remains
But that to your sufficiency, as your worth is able,
And let them work. The nature of our people,
Our city's institutions, and the terms
For common justice, you are as pregnant in
As art and practice hath enriched any
That we remember. There is our commission,
From which we would not have you warp.—
    Call hither,
I say, bid come before us Angelo.—
                [*Exit an* Attendant.
What figure of us think you he will bear?
For you must know we have with special soul
Elected him our absence to supply;
Lent him our terror, drest him with our love,
And given his deputation all the organs
Of our own power: what think you of it?
Escal. If any in Vienna be of worth
To undergo such ample grace and honour,
It is Lord Angelo.

Enter ANGELO.

Duke. Look where he comes.
Ang. Always obedient to your grace's will,
I come to know your pleasure.
Duke.   Angelo,
There is a kind of character in thy life,
That to the observer doth thy history

Fully unfold. Thyself and thy belongings
Are not thine own so proper as to waste
Thyself upon thy virtues, they on thee.
Heaven doth with us as we with torches do,
Not light them for themselves: for if our virtues
Did not go forth of us, 'twere all alike
As if we had them not. Spirits are not finely
    touch'd
But to fine issues: nor nature never lends
The smallest scruple of her excellence
But, like a thrifty goddess, she determines
Herself the glory of a creditor,
Both thanks and use. But I do bend my speech
To one that can my part in him advertise;
Hold, therefore, Angelo;
In our remove be thou at full ourself:
Mortality and mercy in Vienna
Live in thy tongue and heart! Old Escalus,
Though first in question, is thy secondary:
Take thy commission.
Ang.   Now, good my lord,
Let there be some more test made of my metal,
Before so noble and so great a figure
Be stamped upon it.
Duke.   No more evasion:
We have with a leaven'd and prepared choice
Proceeded to you; therefore take your honours.
Our haste from hence is of so quick condition
That it prefers itself, and leaves unquestion'd
Matters of needful value. We shall write to you
As time and our concernings shall impórtune
How it goes with us; and do look to know
What doth befall you here. So, fare you well:
To the hopeful execution do I leave you
Of your commissions.
Ang.   Yet, give leave, my lord,
That we may bring you something on the way.
Duke. My haste may not admit it;
Nor need you, on mine honour, have to do
With any scruple: your scope is as mine own:

So to enforce or qualify the laws
As to your soul seems good. Give me your hand;
I'll privily away: I love the people,
But do not like to stage me to their eyes:
Though it do well, I do not relish well
Their loud applause and *aves* vehement:
Nor do I think the man of safe discretion
That does affect it. Once more, fare you well.
Ang. The heavens give safety to your purposes!
Escal. Lead forth and bring you back in hap-
      piness.
Duke. I thank you. Fare you well.   [*Exit.*
Escal. I shall desire you, sir, to give me leave
To have free speech with you; and it concerns me
To look into the bottom of my place:
A power I have, but of what strength and nature
I am not yet instructed.   [gether,
Ang. 'Tis so with me.—Let us withdraw to-
And we may soon our satisfaction have
Touching that point.
Escal.   I'll wait upon your honour.
                   [*Exeunt.*

SCENE II.—*A Street.*

Enter LUCIO *and two* GENTLEMEN.

Lucio. If the duke, with the other dukes, come not to composition with the King of Hungary, why, then, all the dukes fall upon the king.

1 Gent. Heaven grant us its peace, but not the

2 Gent. Amen.   [king of Hungary's!

Lucio. Thou concludest like the sanctimonious pirate that went to sea with the ten commandments, but scraped one out of the table.

2 Gent. Thou shalt not steal?

Lucio. Ay, that he razed.

1 Gent. Why, 'twas a commandment to command the captain and all the rest from their functions; they put forth to steal. There's not a soldier of us all that, in the thanksgiving before meat, doth relish the petition well that prays for peace.

2 Gent. I never heard any soldier dislike it.

Lucio. I believe thee; for I think thou never wast where grace was said.

2 Gent. No? a dozen times at least.

1 Gent. What? in metre?

Lucio. In any proportion or in any language.

1 Gent. I think, or in any religion.

Lucio. Ay! why not? Grace is grace, despite of all controversy. As for example;—thou thyself art a wicked villain, despite of all grace.

1 Gent. Well, there went but a pair of shears between us.

Lucio. I grant; as there may between the lists and the velvet. Thou art the list.

1 Gent. And thou the velvet: thou art good velvet; thou art a three-piled piece, I warrant thee: I had as lief be a list of an English kersey as be piled, as thou art piled, for a French velvet. Do I speak feelingly now?

Lucio. I think thou dost; and, indeed, with most painful feeling of thy speech. I will, out of thine own confession, learn to begin thy

health; but, whilst I live, forget to drink after thee.

1 Gent. I think I have done myself wrong; have I not?

2 Gent. Yes, that thou hast; whether thou art tainted or free.

Lucio. Behold, behold, where Madam Mitigation comes! I have purchased as many diseases under her roof as come to—

2 Gent. To what, I pray?

1 Gent. Judge.

2 Gent. To three thousand dollars a-year.

1 Gent. Ay, and more.

Lucio. A French crown more.

1 Gent. Thou art always figuring diseases in me, but thou art full of error; I am sound.

Lucio. Nay, not as one would say, healthy; but so sound as things that are hollow: thy bones are hollow; impiety has made a feast of thee.

Enter BAWD.

1 Gent. How now! which of your hips has the most profound sciatica?

Bawd. Well, well; there's one yonder arrested and carried to prison was worth five thousand of you all.

1 Gent. Who's that, I pray thee?

Bawd. Marry, sir, that's Claudio, Signior Claudio.

1 Gent. Claudio to prison! 'tis not so.

Bawd. Nay, but I know 'tis so: I saw him arrested; saw him carried away; and, which is more, within these three days his head's to be chopped off.

Lucio. But, after all his fooling, I would not have it so. Art thou sure of this?

Bawd. I am too sure of it: and it is for getting Madam Julietta with child.

Lucio. Believe me, this may be: he promised to meet me two hours since; and he was ever precise in promise-keeping.

2 Gent. Besides, you know, it draws something near to the speech we had to such a purpose.

1 Gent. But most of all agreeing with the proclamation.

Lucio. Away; let's go learn the truth of it.
    [*Exeunt* LUCIO *and* GENTLEMEN.

Bawd. Thus, what with the war, what with the sweat, what with the gallows, and what with poverty, I am custom-shrunk. How now! what's the news with you?

Enter CLOWN.

Clo. Yonder man is carried to prison.

Bawd. Well: what has he done?

Clo. A woman.

Bawd. But what's his offence?

Clo. Groping for trouts in a peculiar river.

Bawd. What! is there a maid with child by him?

Clo. No; but there's a woman with maid by him. You have not heard of the proclamation, have you?

Bawd. What proclamation, man?

Clo. All houses in the suburbs of Vienna must be plucked down.   [city?

Bawd. And what shall become of those in the

Clo. They shall stand for seed: they had gone down too, but that a wise burgher put in for them.

Bawd. But shall all our houses of resort in the suburbs be pulled down?

Clo. To the ground, mistress.

Bawd. Why, here's a change indeed in the commonwealth! What shall become of me?

Clo. Come; fear not you: good counsellors lack no clients: though you change your place you need not change your trade; I'll be your tapster still. Courage; there will be pity taken on you: you that have worn your eyes almost out in the service, you will be considered.

Bawd. What's to do here, Thomas Tapster? Let's withdraw.

Clo. Here comes Signior Claudio, led by the provost to prison: and there's Madam Juliet.
                                        [*Exeunt.*

SCENE III.—*The same.*

Enter PROVOST, CLAUDIO, JULIET, *and* Officers; LUCIO *and two* GENTLEMEN.

Claud. Fellow, why dost thou show me thus to
          the world?
Bear me to prison, where I am committed.

Prov. I do it not in evil disposition,
But from Lord Angelo by special charge.

Claud. Thus can the demi-god Authority
Make us pay down for our offence by weight.—
The words of heaven;—on whom it will, it will;
On whom it will not, so; yet still 'tis just.

Lucio. Why, how now, Claudio? whence comes
this restraint?   [erty:

Claud. From too much liberty, my Lucio, lib-
As surfeit is the father of much fast,
So every scope by the immoderate use
Turns to restraint. Our natures do pursue,—
Like rats that ravin down their proper bane,—
A thirsty evil; and when we drink we die.

Lucio. If I could speak so wisely under an arrest, I would send for certain of my creditors;
and yet, to say the truth, I had as lief have the
foppery of freedom as the morality of imprisonment.—What's thy offence, Claudio?

Claud. What but to speak of would offend
          again.

Lucio. What, is it murder?

Claud. No.

Lucio. Lechery?

Claud. Call it so.

Prov. Away, sir; you must go.

Claud. One word, good friend:—Lucio, a word
          with you.   [*Takes him aside.*

Lucio. A hundred, if they'll do you any good.
Is lechery so looked after?

Claud. Thus it stands with me:—Upon a true
          contráct
I got possession of Julietta's bed:
You know the lady; she is fast my wife,
Save that we do the denunciation lack

Of outward order: this we came not to
Only for propagation of a dower
Remaining in the coffer of her friends;
From whom we thought it meet to hide our love
Till time had made them for us. But it chances
The stealth of our most mutual entertainment,
With character too gross, is writ on Juliet.

Lucio. With child, perhaps?

Claud. Unhappily, even so.
And the new deputy now for the duke,—
Whether it be the fault and glimpse of newness,
Or whether that the body public be
A horse whereon the governor doth ride,
Who, newly in the seat, that it may know
He can command, lets it straight feel the spur:
Whether the tyranny be in his place,
Or in his eminence that fills it up,
I stagger in.—But this new governor
Awakes me all the enrolled penalties
Which have, like unscour'd armour, hung by
          the wall
So long that nineteen zodiacs have gone round
And none of them been worn; and, for a name,
Now puts the drowsy and neglected act
Freshly on me;—'tis surely for a name.

Lucio. I warrant it is: and thy head stands so
tickle on thy shoulders that a milkmaid, if she
be in love, may sigh it off. Send after the duke,
and appeal to him.

Claud. I have done so, but he's not to be found.
I pr'ythee, Lucio, do me this kind service:
This day my sister should the cloister enter,
And there receive her approbation:
Acquaint her with the danger of my state;
Implore her, in my voice, that she make friends
To the strict deputy; bid herself assay him;
I have great hope in that: for in her youth
There is a prone and speechless dialect
Such as moves men; beside, she hath prosper
          ous art
When she will play with reason and discourse,
And well she can persuade.

Lucio. I pray she may; as well for the encour-
agement of the like, which else would stand
under grievous imposition, as for the enjoying
of thy life, who I would be sorry should be thus
foolishly lost at a game of tick-tack. I'll to her.

Claud. I thank you, good friend Lucio.

Lucio. Within two hours,——

Claud. Come, officer, away.   [*Exeunt.*

SCENE IV.—*A Monastery.*

Enter DUKE *and Friar* THOMAS.

Duke. No; holy father; throw away that thought;
Believe not that the dribbling dart of love
Can pierce a complete bosom: why I desire thee
To give me secret harbour hath a purpose
More grave and wrinkled than the aims and ends
Or burning youth.

Fri.   May your grace speak of it?

Duke. My holy sir, none better knows than you
How I have ever lov'd the life remov'd,
And held in idle price to haunt assemblies

Where youth, and cost, and witless bravery
   keeps.
I have deliver'd to Lord Angelo,—
A man of stricture and firm abstinence,—
My absolute power and place here in Vienna
And he supposes me travell'd to Poland;
For so I have strew'd it in the common ear,
And so it is received. Now, pious sir,
You will demand of me why I do this?
Fri. Gladly, my lord.
Duke. We have strict statutes and most biting
   laws,—
The needful bits and curbs for headstrong
   steeds,—
Which for these fourteen years we have let sleep,
Even like an o'ergrown lion in a cave,
That goes not out to prey. Now, as fond fathers,
Having bound up the threat'ning twigs of birch,
Only to stick it in their children's sight
For terror, not to use, in time the rod
Becomes more mock'd than fear'd: so our
   decrees,
Dead to infliction, to themselves are dead;
And liberty plucks justice by the nose;
The baby beats the nurse, and quite athwart
Goes all decorum.
Fri.   It rested in your grace
To unloose this tied-up justice when you
   pleas'd:
And it in you more dreadful would have seem'd
Than in Lord Angelo.
Duke.   I do fear, too dreadful:
Sith 'twas my fault to give the people scope,
'Twould be my tyranny to strike and gall them
For what I bid them do: for we bid this be done
When evil deeds have their permissive pass
And not the punishment. Therefore, indeed,
   my father,
I have on Angelo impos'd the office;
Who may, in the ambush of my name, strike
   home,
And yet my nature never in the fight,
To do it slander. And to behold his sway,
I will, as 'twere a brother of your order,
Visit both prince and people: therefore, I
   pr'ythee,
Supply me with the habit, and instruct me
How I may formally in person bear me
Like a true friar. More reasons for this action
At our more leisure shall I render you;
Only, this one:—Lord Angelo is precise;
Stands at a guard with envy; scarce confesses
That his blood flows, or that his appetite
Is more to bread than stone: hence shall we see,
If power change purpose, what our seemers
   be.
                       [Exeunt.

Scene V.—*A Nunnery.*

Enter Isabella *and* Francisca.

Isab. And have you nuns no further privileges?
Fran. Are not these large enough?
Isab. Yes, truly: I speak not as desiring more,
But rather wishing a more strict restraint
Upon the sisterhood, the votaries of St. Clare.
Lucio. Ho! Peace be in this place!   *[Within.*
Isab.   Who's that which calls?
Fran. It is a man's voice. Gentle Isabella,
Turn you the key, and know his business of him;
You may, I may not; you are yet unsworn:
When you have vow'd, you must not speak
   with men
But in the presence of the prioress;   [face.
Then, if you speak, you must not show your
Or, if you show your face, you must not speak.
He calls again; I pray you answer him.
                    [Exit Francisca.
Isab. Peace and prosperity! Who is 't that calls?

Enter Lucio.

Lucio. Hail, virgin, if you be; as those cheek-
   roses
Proclaim you are no less! Can you so stead me
As bring me to the sight of Isabella,
A novice of this place, and the fair sister
To her unhappy brother Claudio?
Isab. Why her unhappy brother? let me ask;
The rather, for I know must make you know
I am that Isabella, and his sister.
Lucio. Gentle and fair, your brother kindly
   greets you:
Not to be weary with you, he's in prison.
Isab. Woe me! For what?
Lucio. For that which, if myself might be his
   judge,
He should receive his punishment in thanks:
He hath got his friend with child.
Isab. Sir, make me not your story.
Lucio.   It is true.
I would not—though 'tis my familiar sin
With maids to seem the lapwing, and to jest
Tongue far from heart—play with all virgins so:
I hold you as a thing ensky'd and sainted;
By your renouncement an immortal spirit;
And to be talk'd with in sincerity,
As with a saint.   [me.
Isab. You do blaspheme the good in mocking
Lucio. Do not believe it. Fewness and truth,
   'tis thus:
Your brother and his lover have embraced:
As those that feed grow full: as blossoming time,
That from the seedness the bare fallow brings
To teeming foison; even so her plenteous womb
Expresseth his full tilth and husbandry.
Isab. Some one with child by him?—My cousin
   Juliet?
Lucio. Is she your cousin?
Isab. Adoptedly; as schoolmaids change their
   names
By vain though apt affection.
Lucio.   She it is.
Isab. O, let him marry her!
Lucio.   This is the point.
The duke is very strangely gone from hence;
Bore many gentlemen, myself being one.
In hand, and hope of action: but we do learn
By those that know the very nerves of state,

His givings out were of an infinite distance
From his true-meant design. Upon his place,
And with full line of his authority,
Governs Lord Angelo: a man whose blood
Is very snow-broth; one who never feels
The wanton stings and motions of the sense,
But doth rebate and blunt his natural edge
With profits of the mind, study, and fast.
He,—to give fear to use and liberty,
Which have for long run by the hideous law,
As mice by lions,—hath pick'd out an act,
Under whose heavy sense your brother's life
Falls into forfeit: he arrests him on it;
And follows close the rigour of the statute
To make him an example; all hope is gone,
Unless you have the grace by your fair prayer
To soften Angelo: and that's my pith
Of business 'twixt you and your poor brother.
Isab. Doth he so seek his life?
Lucio.   Has censur'd him
Already; and, as I hear, the provost hath
A warrant for his execution.
Isab. Alas! what poor ability's in me
To do him good.
Lucio.   Assay the power you have.
Isab. My power! alas, I doubt,—
Lucio.   Our doubts are traitors,
And make us lose the good we oft might win
By fearing to attempt. Go to Lord Angelo,
And let him learn to know, when maidens sue,
Men give like gods; but when they weep and
          kneel,
All their petitions are as freely theirs
As they themselves would owe them.
Isab. I'll see what I can do.
Lucio.   But speedily.
Isab. I will about it straight;
No longer staying but to give the mother
Notice of my affair. I humbly thank you:
Commend me to my brother: soon at night
I'll send him certain word of my success.
Lucio. I take my leave of you.
Isab.   Good sir, adieu.
                                    [*Exeunt.*

ACT II.

SCENE I—*A Hall in* ANGELO'S *House*

Enter ANGELO, ESCALUS, *a* JUSTICE, PROVOST,
      Officers, *and other* Attendants.

Ang. We must not make a scarecrow of the law,
Setting it up to fear the birds of prey,
And let it keep one shape till custom make it
Their perch, and not their terror.
Escal.   Ay, but yet
Let us be keen, and rather cut a little
Than fall and bruise to death. Alas! this gen-
          tleman,
Whom I would save, had a most noble father.
Let but your honour know,—
Whom I believe to be most strait in virtue,—
That, in the working of your own affections,
Had time coher'd with place, or place with
          wishing,

Or that the resolute acting of your blood
Could have attain'd the effect of your own
          purpose,
Whether you had not sometime in your life
Err'd in this point which now you censure him,
And pull'd the law upon you.
Ang. 'Tis one thing to be tempted, Escalus,
Another thing to fall. I not deny,
The jury, passing on the prisoner's life,
May, in the sworn twelve, have a thief or two
Guiltier than him they try. What's open made
          to justice,
That justice seizes. What know the laws
That thieves do pass on thieves? 'Tis very
          pregnant,
The jewel that we find, we stoop and take it,
Because we see it; but what we do not see
We tread upon, and never think of it.
You may not so extenuate his offence
For I have had such faults; but rather tell me,
When I, that censure him, do so offend,
Let mine own judgment pattern out my death,
And nothing come in partial. Sir, he must die.
Escal. Be it as your wisdom will.
Ang.   Where is the provost?
Prov. Here, if it like your honour.
Ang.   See that Claudio
Be executed by nine to-morrow morning:
Bring him his confessor; let him be prepared;
For that's the utmost of his pilgrimage.
                              [*Exit* PROVOST.
Escal. Well, heaven forgive him! and forgive
          us all!
Some rise by sin and some by virtue fall:
Some run from brakes of vice, and answer none;
And some condemnéd for a fault alone.

Enter ELBOW, FROTH, CLOWN, Officers, &c.

Elb. Come, bring them away: if these be good
people in a commonweal that do nothing but
use their abuses in common houses, I know no
law; bring them away.
Ang. How now, sir! What's your name? and
what's the matter?
Elb. If it please your honour, I am the poor
duke's constable, and my name is Elbow; I do
lean upon justice, sir, and do bring in here before your good honour two notorious benefactors.
Ang. Benefactors! Well; what benefactors are
they? are they not malefactors?
Elb. If it please your honour, I know not well
what they are: but precise villains they are,
that I am sure of; and void of all profanation in
the world that good Christians ought to have.
Escal. This comes off well; here's a wise officer.
Ang. Go to;—what quality are they of? Elbow
is your name? Why dost thou not speak,
Elbow?
Clo. He cannot, sir; he's out at elbow.
Ang. What are you, sir?
Elb. He, sir? a tapster, sir; parcel-bawd; one
that serves a bad woman; whose house, sir,
was, as they say, plucked down in the suburbs;

and now she professes a hot-house, which, I think, is a very ill house too.

Escal. How know you that?

Elb. My wife, sir, whom I detest before heaven and your honour,—

Escal. How! thy wife!

Elb. Ay, sir; who, I thank heaven, is an honest woman,—

Escal. Dost thou detest her therefore?

Elb. I say, sir, I will detest myself also, as well as she, that this house, if it be not a bawd's house, it is pity of her life, for it is a naughty house.

Escal. How dost thou know that, constable?

Elb. Marry, sir, by my wife; who, if she had been a woman cardinally given, might have been accused in fornication, adultery, and all uncleanliness there.

Escal. By the woman's means?

Elb. Ay, sir, by Mistress Overdone's means: but as she spit in his face, so she defied him.

Clo. Sir, if it please your honour, this is not so.

Elb. Prove it before these varlets here, thou honourable man, prove it.

Escal. Do you hear how he misplaces?

           [*To* ANGELO.

Clo. Sir, she came in great with child; and longing—saving your honour's reverence—for stewed prunes, sir; we had but two in the house, which at that very distant time stood as it were, in a fruit-dish, a dish of some three-pence; your honours have seen such dishes; they are not China dishes, but very good dishes.

Escal. Go to, go to; no matter for the dish, sir.

Clo. No, indeed, sir, not of a pin; you are therein in the right: but to the point. As I say, this Mistress Elbow, being, as I say, with child, and being great-bellied, and longing, as I said, for prunes; and having but two in the dish, as I said, Master Froth here, this very man, having eaten the rest, as I said, and, as I say, paying for them very honestly;—for, as you know, Master Froth, I could not give you threepence again,—

Froth. No, indeed.

Clo. Very well: you being then, if you be remembered, cracking the stones of the aforesaid prunes,—

Froth. Ay, so I did, indeed.

Clo. Why, very well: I telling you then, if you be remembered, that such a one and such a one were past cure of the thing you wot of, unless they kept very good diet, as I told you,—

Froth. All this is true.

Clo. Why, very well then.

Escal. Come, you are a tedious fool: to the purpose.—What was done to Elbow's wife that he hath cause to complain of? Come me to what was done to her.

Clo. Sir, your honour cannot come to that yet.

Escal. No, sir, nor I mean it not.

Clo. Sir, but you shall come to it, by your honour's leave. And I beseech you, look into Master Froth here, sir; a man of fourscore

pound a-year; whose father died at Hallow-mas:—was't not at Hallowmas, Master Froth?

Froth. All-hallond eve.

Clo. Why, very well; I hope here be truths: He, sir, sitting, as I say, in a lower chair, sir; —'twas in the *Bunch of Grapes*, where, indeed, you have a delight to sit, have you not?—

Froth. I have so; because it is an open room, and good for winter.   [truths.

Clo. Why, very well then;—I hope here be

Ang. This will last out a night in Russia, When nights are longest there: I'll take my leave, And leave you to the hearing of the cause; Hoping you'll find good cause to whip them all.

Escal. I think no less. Good morrow to your   lordship.   [*Exit* ANGELO. Now, sir, come on: what was done to Elbow's wife, once more?   [once.

Clo. Once, sir? there was nothing done to her

Elb. I beseech you, sir, ask him what this man did to my wife.

Clo. I beseech your honour, ask me.

Escal. Well, sir: what did this gentleman to her?

Clo. I beseech you, sir, look in this gentleman's face.—Good Master Froth, look upon his honour; 'tis for a good purpose.—Doth your honour mark his face?

Escal. Ay, sir, very well.

Clo. Nay, I beseech you, mark it well.

Escal. Well, I do so.

Clo. Doth your honour see any harm in his face?

Escal. Why, no.

Clo. I'll be supposed upon a book, his face is the worst thing about him. Good then; if his face be the worst thing about him, how could Master Froth do the constable's wife any harm? I would know that of your honour.

Escal. He's in the right.—Constable, what say you to it?

Elb. First, an it like you, the house is a respected house; next, this is a respected fellow; and his mistress is a respected woman.

Clo. By this hand, sir, his wife is a more respected person than any of us all.

Elb. Varlet, thou liest; thou liest, wicked varlet: the time is yet to come that she was ever respected with man, woman, or child.

Clo. Sir, she was respected with him before he married with her.

Escal. Which is the wiser here? Justice or Iniquity?—Is this true?

Elb. O thou caitiff! O thou varlet! O thou wicked Hannibal! I respected with her before I was married to her? If ever I was respected with her, or she with me, let not your worship think me the poor duke's officer.—Prove this, thou wicked Hannibal, or I'll have mine action of battery on thee.

Escal. If he took you a box o' th' ear, you might have your action of slander too.

Elb. Marry, I thank your good worship for it. What is't your worship's pleasure I should do with this wicked caitiff?

Escal. Truly, officer, because he hath some offences in him that thou wouldst discover if thou couldst, let him continue in his courses till thou knowest what they are.

Elb. Marry, I thank your worship for it.—Thou seest, thou wicked varlet, now, what's come upon thee; thou art to continue now, thou varlet; thou art to continue.

Escal. Where were you born, friend?

[*To* FROTH.

Froth. Here in Vienna, sir.

Escal. Are you of fourscore pounds a-year?

Froth. Yes, an't please you, sir.

Escal. So.—What trade are you of, sir?

[*To the* CLOWN.

Clo. A tapster; a poor widow's tapster.

Escal. Your mistress's name?

Clo. Mistress Overdone.

Escal. Hath she had any more than one husband?

Clo. Nine, sir; Overdone by the last.

Escal. Nine!—Come hither to me, Master Froth. Master Froth, I would not have you acquainted with tapsters: they will draw you, Master Froth, and you will hang them. Get you gone, and let me hear no more of you.

Froth. I thank your worship. For mine own part, I never come into any room in a tap-house but I am drawn in.

Escal. Well; no more of it, Master Froth: farewell. [*Exit* FROTH.]—Come you hither to me, master tapster; what's your name, master tapster?

Clo. Pompey.

Escal. What else?

Clo. Bum, sir.

Escal. 'Troth, and your bum is the greatest thing about you; so that, in the beastliest sense, you are Pompey the great. Pompey, you are partly a bawd, Pompey, howsoever you colour it in being a tapster. Are you not? come, tell me true; it shall be the better for you.

Clo. Truly, sir, I am a poor fellow that would live.

Escal. How would you live, Pompey? by being a bawd? What do you think of the trade, Pompey? is it a lawful trade?

Clo. If the law would allow it, sir.

Escal. But the law will not allow it, Pompey: nor it shall not be allowed in Vienna.

Clo. Does your worship mean to geld and splay all the youth in the city?

Escal. No, Pompey.

Clo. Truly, sir, in my poor opinion, they will to't then. If your worship will take order for the drabs and the knaves, you need not to fear the bawds.

Escal. There are pretty orders beginning, I can tell you. It is but heading and hanging.

Clo. If you head and hang all that offend that way but for ten year together, you'll be glad to give out a commission for more heads. If this law hold in Vienna ten year, I'll rent the fairest house in it, after threepence a bay. If

you live to see this come to pass, say Pompey told you so.

Escal. Thank you, good Pompey: and, in requital of your prophecy, hark you,—I advise you, let me not find you before me again upon any complaint whatsoever, no, not for dwelling where you do; if I do, Pompey, I shall beat you to your tent, and prove a shrewd Cæsar to you; in plain dealing, Pompey, I shall have you whipt: so for this time, Pompey, fare you well.

Clo. I thank your worship for your good counsel; but I shall follow it as the flesh and fortune shall better determine.

Whip me? No, no; let carman whip his jade;
The valiant heart's not whipt out of his trade.

[*Exit.*

Escal. Come hither to me, Master Elbow; come hither, Master Constable. How long have you been in this place of constable?

Elb. Seven year and a half, sir.

Escal. I thought, by your readiness in the office, you had continued in it some time. You say seven years together?

Elb. And a half, sir.

Escal. Alas! it hath been great pains to you!—They do you wrong to put you so oft upon't. Are there not men in your ward sufficient to serve it?

Elb. Faith, sir, few of any wit in such matters: as they are chosen, they are glad to choose me for them; I do it for some piece of money, and go through with all.

Escal. Look you, bring me in the names of some six or seven, the most sufficient of your parish.

Elb. To your worship's house, sir?

Escal. To my house. Fare you well. [*Exit.* ELBOW.] What's o'clock, think you?

Just. Eleven, sir.

Escal. I pray you home to dinner with me.

Just. I humbly thank you.

Escal. It grieves me for the death of Claudio; But there's no remedy.

Just. Lord Angelo is severe.

Escal.   It is but needful:
Mercy is not itself, that oft looks so;
Pardon is still the nurse of second woe:
But yet,—Poor Claudio!—There's no remedy.
Come, sir.   [*Exeunt.*

SCENE III.—*Another Room in the same.*

Enter PROVOST *and a* Servant.

Serv. He's hearing of a cause; he will come
                straight.
I'll tell him of you.

Prov. Pray you do. [*Exit* Servant.] I'll know
His pleasure; may be he will relent. Alas,
He hath but as offended in a dream!
All sects, all ages, smack of this vice; and he
To die for it!

Enter ANGELO.

Ang.   Now, what's the matter, provost?

Prov. Is it your will Claudio shall die to-
                morrow?

Ang. Did I not tell thee yea? hadst thou not
    order?
Why dost thou ask again?
Prov.   Lest I might be too rash:
Under your good correction, I have seen
When, after execution, judgment hath
Repented o'er his doom.
Ang.   Go to; let that be mine:
Do you your office, or give up your place,
And you shall well be spared.
Prov.   I crave your honour's pardon:
What shall be done, sir, with the groaning Juliet?
She's very near her hour.
Ang.   Dispose of her
To some more fitter place; and that with speed.

Re-enter Servant.

Serv. Here is the sister of the man condemned
Desires access to you.
Ang.   Hath he a sister?
Prov. Ay, my good lord; a very virtuous maid,
And to be shortly of a sisterhood,
If not already.
Ang.   Well, let her be admitted.
                [*Exit* Servant.
See you the fornicatress be remov'd;
Let her have needful but not lavish means;
There shall be order for it.

Enter LUCIO *and* ISABELLA.

Prov. Save your honour!   [*Offering to retire.*
Ang. Stay a little while.—[*To* ISAB.] You are
    welcome. What's your will?
Isab. I am a woeful suitor to your honour,
Please but your honour hear me.
Ang.   Well; what's your suit?
Isab. There is a vice that most I do abhor,
And most desire should meet the blow of justice;
For which I would not plead, but that I must;
For which I must not plead, but that I am
At war 'twixt will and will not.
Ang.   Well; the matter?
Isab. I have a brother is condemn'd to die;
I do beseech you, let it be his fault,
And not my brother.
Prov.   Heaven give thee moving graces.
Ang. Condemn the fault and not the actor of it!
Why, every fault's condemn'd ere it be done;
Mine were the very cipher of a function,
To find the fault whose fine stands in record,
And let go by the actor.
Isab.   O just but severe law!
I had a brother, then.—Heaven keep your
    honour!   [*Retiring.*
Lucio. [*To* ISAB.] Giv't not o'er so: to him
    again, entreat him;
Kneel down before him, hang upon his gown;
You are too cold; if you should need a pin,
You could not with more tame a tongue desire it:
To him, I say.
Isab. Must he needs die?
Ang.   Maiden, no remedy.
Isab. Yes; I do think that you might pardon
    him,

And neither heaven nor man grieve at the mercy.
Ang. I will not do't.
Isab.   But can you, if you would?
Ang. Look, what I will not, that I cannot do.
Isab. But might you do't, and do the world
    no wrong,
If so your heart were touch'd with that remorse
As mine is to him.
Ang.   He's sentenc'd; 'tis too late.
Lucio. You are too cold.   [*To* ISABELLA.
Isab. Too late? why, no; I, that do speak a
    word,
May call it back again. Well, believe this,
No ceremony that to great ones 'longs,
Not the king's crown nor the deputed sword,
The marshal's truncheon nor the judge's robe,
Become them with one half so good a grace
As mercy does. If he had been as you,
And you as he, you would have slipp'd like him;
But he, like you, would not have been so stern.
Ang. Pray you, be gone.
Isab. I would to heaven I had your potency.
And you were Isabel! should it then be thus?
No; I would tell what 'twere to be a judge
And what a prisoner.
Lucio. Ay, touch him; there's the vein. [*Aside.*
Ang. Your brother is a forfeit of the law,
And you but waste your words.
Isab.   Alas! alas!
Why, all the souls that were were forfeit once;
And He that might the vantage best have took
Found out the remedy. How would you be
If He, which is the top of judgment, should
But judge you as you are? O, think on that;
And mercy then will breathe within your lips,
Like man new made.
Ang.   Be you content, fair maid;
It is the law, not I, condemns your brother:
Were he my kinsman, brother, or my son,
It should be thus with him;—he must die to-
    morrow.   [spare him!
Isab. To-morrow! O that's sudden! Spare him,
He's not prepared for death. Even for our
    kitchens
We kill the fowl of season: shall we serve heaven
With less respect than we do minister   [you;
To our gross selves? Good, good my lord, bethink
Who is it that hath died for this offence?
There's many have committed it.
Lucio.   Ay, well said.
Ang. The law hath not been dead, though it
    hath slept:
Those many had not dared to do that evil
If the first man that did the edict infringe
Had answer'd for his deed: now 'tis awake;
Takes note of what is done; and, like a prophet,
Looks in a glass that shows what future evils,—
Either now, or by remissness new-conceiv'd,
And so in progress to be hatch'd and born,—
Are now to have no successive degrees,
But, where they live, to end.
Isab.   Yet show some pity.
Ang. I show it most of all when I show justice;
For then I pity those I do not know,

Which a dismiss'd offence would after gall,
And do him right that, answering one foul wrong,
Lives not to act another. Be satisfied;
Your brother dies to-morrow: be content.
Isab. So you must be the first that gives this
        sentence;
And he that suffers. O, it is excellent
To have a giant's strength; but it is tyrannous
To use it like a giant.
Lucio.   That's well said.
Isab. Could great men thunder
As Jove himself does, Jove would ne'er be quiet,
For every pelting petty officer
Would use his heaven for thunder: nothing but
        thunder.——
Merciful heaven!
Thou rather, with thy sharp and sulphurous bolt,
Splitt'st the unwedgeable and gnarled oak
Than the soft myrtle;—but man, proud man!
Dress'd in a little brief authority,—
Most ignorant of what he's most assured,
His glassy essence,—like an angry ape,
Plays such fantastic tricks before high heaven
As make the angels weep; who, with our spleens,
Would all themselves laugh mortal.
Lucio. O, to him, to him, wench: he will relent;
He's coming; I perceive 't.
Prov.   Pray heaven she win him!
Isab. We cannot weigh our brother with our-
        self:
Great men may jest with saints: 'tis wit in them;
But, in the less, foul profanation.
Lucio. Thou 'rt in the right, girl; more o' that.
Isab. That in the captain's but a choleric word
Which in the soldier is flat blasphemy.
Lucio. Art advised o' that? more on 't.
Ang. Why do you put these sayings upon me?
Isab. Because authority, though it err like
        others,
Hath yet a kind of medicine in itself
That skins the vice o' the top. Go to your bosom;
Knock there; and ask your heart what it doth
        know
That's like my brother's fault; if it confess
A natural guiltiness such as is his,
Let it not sound a thought upon your tongue
Against my brother's life.
Ang.   She speaks, and 'tis
Such sense that my sense breeds with it.——
        Fare you well.
Isab. Gentle, my lord, turn back.
Ang. I will bethink me:—Come again to-
        morrow.
Isab. Hark how I'll bribe you. Good, my lord,
        turn back.
Ang. How! bribe me?
Isab. Ay, with such gifts that heaven shall
        share with you.
Lucio. You had marr'd all else.
Isab. Not with fond shekels of the tested gold,
Or stones, whose rates are either rich or poor
As fancy values them: but with true prayers,
That shall be up at heaven, and enter there,
Ere sunrise: prayers from preserved souls,

From fasting maids, whose minds are dedicate
To nothing temporal.
Ang.   Well; come to me
To-morrow.
Lucio. Go to; it is well; away.
                    [*Aside to* ISABELLA.
Isab. Heaven keep your honour safe!
Ang.   Amen: for I
Am that way going to temptation,   [*Aside.*
Where prayers cross.
Isab.   At what hour to-morrow
Shall I attend your lordship?
Ang.   At any time 'fore noon.
Isab. Save your honour!
                    [*Exeunt* LUCIO, ISAB., *and* PROV.
Ang.   From thee; even from thy virtue!—
What's this? what's this? Is this her fault or
        mine?   [Ha!
The tempter or the tempted, who sins most?
Not she; nor doth she tempt; but it is I
That, lying by the violet, in the sun
Do, as the carrion does, not as the flower,
Corrupt with virtuous season. Can it be
That modesty may more betray our sense
Than woman's lightness? Having waste ground
        enough,
Shall we desire to raze the sanctuary
And pitch our evils there? O, fie, fie, fie!
What dost thou? or what art thou, Angelo?
Dost thou desire her foully for those things
That make her good? O, let her brother live;
Thieves for their robbery have authority
When judges steal themselves. What! do I love
        her,
That I desire to hear her speak again
And feast upon her eyes? What is 't I dream on?
O cunning enemy, that, to catch a saint,
With saints dost bait thy look! Most dangerous
Is that temptation that doth goad us on
To sin in loving virtue: never could the strumpet,
With all her double vigour, art, and nature,
Once stir my temper; but this virtuous maid
Subdues me quite.—Ever till now,
When men were fond, I smil'd and wonder'd
        how.   [*Exit.*

SCENE III.—*A Room in a Prison.*

Enter DUKE, *habited like a Friar, and* PROVOST.

Duke. Hail to you, provost! so I think you are.
Prov. I am the provost. What's your will, good
        friar?
Duke. Bound by my charity and my bless'd
        order,
I come to visit the afflicted spirits
Here in the prison: do me the common right
To let me see them, and to make me know
The nature of their crimes, that I may minister
To them accordingly.   [needful.
Prov. I would do more than that, if more were

Enter JULIET.

Look, here comes one; a gentlewoman of mine,
Who, falling in the flames of her own youth,

Hath blister'd her report. She is with child;
And he that got it, sentenç'd: a young man;
More fit to do another such offence
Than die for this.
Duke.   When must he die?
Prov. As I do think, to-morrow,—
I have provided for you; stay awhile
                                        [*To* Juliet.
And you shall be conducted.
Duke. Repent you, fair one, of the sin you carry?
Juliet. I do; and bear the shame most patiently.
Duke. I'll teach you how you shall arraign
                    your conscience,
And try your penitence, if it be sound
Or hollowly put on.
Juliet.   I'll gladly learn.
Duke. Love you the man that wrong'd you?
Juliet. Yes, as I love the woman that wrong'd
                    him.   [act
Duke. So then, it seems, your most offenceful
Was mutually committed?
Juliet.   Mutually.   [his.
Duke. Then was your sin of heavier kind than
Juliet. I do confess it, and repent it, father.
Duke. 'Tis meet so, daughter: but lest you do
                    repent   [shame,—
As that the sin hath brought you to this
Which sorrow is always toward ourselves, not
                    heaven,   [love it,
Showing we would not spare heaven as we
But as we stand in fear,—
Juliet. I do repent me as it is an evil,
And take the shame with joy.
Duke.   There rest.
Your partner, as I hear, must die to-morrow,
And I am going with instruction to him.—
Juliet. Grace go with you!
Duke. Benedicite!   [*Exit.*
Juliet. Must die to-morrow! O, injurious law,
That respites me a life whose very comfort
Is still a dying horror!
Prov.   'Tis pity of him! [*Exeunt.*

Scene IV.—*A Room in* Angelo's *House.*
                    Enter Angelo.

Ang. When I would pray and think, I think
                    and pray   [words;
To several subjects. Heaven hath my empty
Whilst my invention, hearing not my tongue,
Anchors on Isabel: Heaven in my mouth,
As if I did but only chew his name;
And in my heart the strong and swelling evil
Of my conception. The state whereon I studied
Is like a good thing, being often read,
Grown sear'd and tedious; yea, my gravity,
Wherein—let no man hear me—I take pride,
Could I with boot change for an idle plume,
Which the air beats for vain. O place! O form!
How often dost thou with thy case, thy habit,
Wrench awe from fools, and tie the wiser souls
To thy false seeming? Blood, thou still art
                    blood:
Let's write good angel on the devil's horn,
'Tis not the devil's crest.

Enter Servant.

How now, who's there?
Serv.   One Isabel, a sister,
Desires access to you.
Ang.   Teach her the way. [*Exit* Serv.
O heavens!
Why does my blood thus muster to my heart,
Making both it unable for itself
And dispossessing all the other parts
Of necessary fitness?   [swoons;
So play the foolish throngs with one that
Come all to help him, and so stop the air
By which he should revive: and even so
The general, subject to a well-wished king,
Quit their own part, and in obsequious fondness
Crowd to his presence, where their untaught love
Must needs appear offence.

Enter Isabella.

How now, fair maid?
Isab.   I am come to know your pleasure.
Ang. That you might know it, would much
                    better please me   [live.
Than to demand what 'tis. Your brother cannot
Isab. Even so?—Heaven keep your honour!
                                        [*Retiring.*
Ang. Yet may he live awhile: and, it may be,
As long as you or I: yet he must die.
Isab. Under your sentence?
Ang. Yea.   [prieve,
Isab. When, I beseech you? that in his re-
Longer or shorter, he may be so fitted
That his soul sicken not.   [good
Ang. Ha! Fie, these filthy vices! It were as
To pardon him that hath from nature stolen
A man already made, as to remit   [image
Their saucy sweetness that do coin heaven's
In stamps that are forbid; 'tis all as easy
Falsely to take away a life true made
As to put metal in restrained means
To make a false one.   [earth.
Isab. 'Tis set down so in heaven, but not in
Ang. Say you so? then I shall poze you quickly.
Which had you rather,—that the most just law
Now took your brother's life; or, to redeem him
Give up your body to such sweet uncleanness
As she that he hath stain'd?
Isab.   Sir, believe this,
I had rather give my body than my soul.
Ang. I talk not of your soul; our compell'd sins
Stand more for number than accompt.
Isab.   How say you?
Ang. Nay, I'll not warrant that; for I can speak
Against the thing I say. Answer to this;—
I, now the voice of the recorded law,
Pronounce a sentence on your brother's life:
Might there not be a charity in sin,
To save this brother's life?
Isab.   Please you to do't,
I'll take it as a peril to my soul
It is no sin at all, but charity.
Ang. Pleas'd you to do't at peril of your soul,
Were equal poise of sin and charity.

Isab. That I do beg his life, if it be sin,
Heaven let me bear it! you granting of my suit,
If that be sin, I'll make it my morn prayer
To have it added to the faults of mine,
And nothing of your answer.
Ang.　　　　　　　　Nay, but hear me:
Your sense pursues not mine: either you are
　　　　ignorant
Or seem so, craftily; and that's not good.
Isab. Let me be ignorant, and in nothing good
But graciously to know I am no better.
Ang. Thus wisdom wishes to appear most
　　　　bright
When it doth tax itself: as these black masks
Proclaim an enshield beauty ten times louder
Than beauty could, displayed.—But mark me;
To be received plain, I'll speak more gross:
Your brother is to die.
Isab. So.
Ang. And his offence is so, as it appears
Accountant to the law upon that pain.
Isab. True.
Ang. Admit no other way to save his life,—
As I subscribe not that, nor any other,
But in the loss of question,—that you, his sister,
Finding yourself desir'd of such a person,
Whose credit with the judge, or own great place,
Could fetch your brother from the manacles
Of the all-binding law; and that there were
No earthly mean to save him but that either
You must lay down the treasures of your body
To this suppos'd, or else let him suffer;
What would you do?
Isab. As much for my poor brother as myself:
That is, were I under the terms of death,
The impression of keen whips I'd wear as rubies,
And strip myself to death, as to a bed
That longing I have been sick for, ere I'd yield
My body up to shame.
Ang.　　　　　　Then must your brother die.
Isab. And 'twere the cheaper way:
Better it were a brother died at once
Than that a sister, by redeeming him,
Should die for ever.　　　　　　　　[tence
Ang. Were not you, then, as cruel as the sen-
That you have slandered so?
Isab. Ignominy in ransom and free pardon
Are of two houses; lawful mercy is
Nothing akin to foul redemption.　　　[tyrant;
Ang. You seem'd of late to make the law a
And rather prov'd the sliding of your brother
A merriment than a vice.
Isab. O, pardon me, my lord; it oft falls out,
To have what we would have, we speak not
　　　　what we mean:
I something do excuse the thing I hate,
For his advantage that I dearly love.
Ang. We are all frail.
Isab.　　　　　　Else let my brother die,
If not a feodary, but only he,
Owe, and succeed by weakness.
Ang.　　　　　　Nay, women are frail too.
Isab. Ay, as the glasses where they view them-
　　　　selves;

Which are as easy broke as they make forms.
Women!—Help heaven! men their creation mar
In profiting by them. Nay, call us ten times
　　　　frail;
For we are soft as our complexions are,
And credulous to false prints.
Ang.　　　　　　　I think it well
And from this testimony of your own sex,—
Since, I suppose, we are made to be no stronger
Than faults may shake our frames,—let me be
　　　　bold;—
I do arrest your words. Be that you are,
That is, a woman; if you be more, you're none;
If you be one,—as you are well express'd
By all external warrants,—show it now
By putting on the destin'd livery.
Isab. I have no tongue but one: gentle, my lord,
Let me intreat you, speak the former language.
Ang. Plainly conceive, I love you.
Isab. My brother did love Juliet; and you tell
　　　　me
That he shall die for it.
Ang. He shall not, Isabel, if you give me love.
Isab. I know your virtue hath a license in't,
Which seems a little fouler than it is,
To pluck on others.
Ang.　　　　　　Believe me, on mine honour,
My words express my purpose.
Isab. Ha! little honour to be much believed,
And most pernicious purpose!—Seeming, seem-
　　　　ing!—
I will proclaim thee, Angelo; look for't:
Sign me a a present pardon for my brother
Or, with an outstretch'd throat, I'll tell the world
Aloud what man thou art.
Ang.　　　　　Who will believe thee, Isabel?
My unsoil'd name, the austereness of my life,
My vouch against you, and my place i' the state
Will so your accusation overweigh
That you shall stifle in your own report,
And smell of calumny. I have begun;
And now I give my sensual race the rein:
Fit thy consent to my sharp appetite;
Lay by all nicety and prolixious blushes
That banish what they sue for: redeem thy
　　　　brother
By yielding up thy body to my will;
Or else he must not only die the death,
But thy unkindness shall his death draw out
To lingering sufferance: answer me to-morrow,
Or, by the affection that now guides me most,
I'll prove a tyrant to him. As for you,
Say what you can, my false o'erweighs your
　　　　true.　　　　　　　　　　[*Exit.*
Isab. To whom shall I complain? Did I tell
　　　　this,
Who would believe me? O perilous mouths,
That bear in them one and the self-same tongue
Either of condemnation or approof!
Bidding the law make court'sy to their will;
Hooking both right and wrong to the appetite,
To follow as it draws! I'll to my brother:
Though he hath fallen by prompture of the
　　　　blood,

Yet hath he in him such a mind of honour
That, had he twenty heads to tender down
On twenty bloody blocks, he'd yield them up
Before his sister should her body stoop
To such abhorr'd pollution
Then, Isabel, live chaste, and, brother, die:
More than our brother is our chastity.
I'll tell him yet of Angelo's request,
And fit his mind to death for his soul's rest.
                                        [*Exit.*

ACT III.

SCENE I.—*A Room in the Prison.*

Enter DUKE, CLAUDIO, *and* PROVOST.

Duke. So, then you hope of pardon from Lord
                Angelo?
Claud. The miserable have no other medicine
But only hope:
I have hope to live, and am prepar'd to die.
Duke. Be absolute for death; either death or
        life   [with life,—
Shall thereby be the sweeter. Reason thus
If I do lose thee, I do lose a thing   [art
That none but fools would keep: a breath thou
Servile to all the skiey influences
That dost this habitation, where thou keep'st,
Hourly afflict; merely, thou art death's fool;
For him thou labour'st by thy flight to shun,
And yet runn'st toward him still. Thou art not
                noble;
For all the accommodations that thou bear'st
Are nurs'd by baseness. Thou art by no means
                valiant;
For thou dost fear the soft and tender fork
Of a poor worm. Thy best of rest is sleep,
And that thou oft provok'st; yet grossly fear'st
Thy death, which is no more. Thou art not
                thyself:
For thou exist'st on many a thousand grains
That issue out of dust. Happy thou art not;
For what thou hast not, still thou striv'st to get;
And what thou hast, forgett'st. Thou art not
                certain;
For thy complexion shifts to strange effects,
After the moon. If thou art rich, thou art poor;
For, like an ass whose back with ingots bows,
Thou bear'st thy heavy riches but a journey,
And death unloads thee. Friend hast thou none;
For thine own bowels, which do call thee sire,
The mere effusion of thy proper loins,
Do curse the gout, serpigo, and the rheum,
For ending thee no sooner. Thou hast nor
                youth nor age,
But, as it were, an after-dinner's sleep,
Dreaming on both: for all thy blessed youth
Becomes as aged, and doth beg the alms
Of palsied eld; and when thou art old and rich
Thou hast neither heat, affection, limb, nor
                beauty.   [this
To make thy riches pleasant. What's yet in
That bears the name of life? Yet in this life
Lie hid more thousand deaths: yet death we
                fear,

That makes these odds all even.
Claud.   I humbly thank you.
To sue to live, I find I seek to die;
And, seeking death, find life. Let it come on.
Isab. [*Within.*] What, ho! Peace here; grace
                and good company!
Prov. Who's there? come in: the wish deserves
                a welcome.
Duke. Dear sir, ere long I'll visit you again.
Claud. Most holy sir, I thank you.

Enter ISABELLA.

Isab. My business is a word or two with
                Claudio.   [your sister.
Prov. And very welcome. Look, signior, here's
Duke. Provost, a word with you.
Prov.   As many as you please.
Duke. Bring me to hear them speak where I
                may be conceal'd.
                [*Exeunt* DUKE *and* PROVOST.
Claud.   Now, sister, what's the comfort?
Isab. Why, as all comforts are; most good in
                deed:
Lord Angelo, having affairs to heaven,
Intends you for his swift embassador,
Where you shall be an everlasting lieger.
Therefore, your best appointment make with
                speed;
To-morrow you set on.
Claud.   Is there no remedy?
Isab. None, but such remedy as, to save a head,
To cleave a heart in twain.
Claud.   But is there any?
Isab. Yes, brother, you may live:
There is a devilish mercy in the judge,
If you'll implore it, that will free your life,
But fetter you till death.
Claud.   Perpetual durance?
Isab. Ay, just perpetual durance; a restraint,
Though all the world's vastidity you had,
To a determin'd scope.
Claud.   But in what nature?
Isab. In such a one as, you consenting to't,
Would bark your honour from that trunk you
                bear,
And leave you naked.
Claud.   Let me know the point.
Isab. O, I do fear thee, Claudio; and I quake,
Lest thou a feverous life shouldst entertain,
And six or seven winters more respect
Than a perpetual honour. Dar'st thou die?
The sense of death is most in apprehension;
And the poor beetle that we tread upon,
In corporal sufferance finds a pang as great
As when a giant dies.
Claud.   Why give you me this shame?
Think you I can a resolution fetch
From flowery tenderness? If I must die
I will encounter darkness as a bride,
And hug it in mine arms.   [father's grave
Isab. There spake my brother; there my
Did utter forth a voice! Yes, thou must die:
Thou art too noble to conserve a life

In base appliances. This outward-sainted de-
                puty,—
Whose settled visage and deliberate word
Nips youth i' the head, and follies doth emmew
As falcon doth the fowl,—is yet a devil;
His filth within being cast, he would appear
A pond as deep as hell.
Claud.   The princely Angelo?
Isab. O, 'tis the cunning livery of hell,
The damned'st body to invest and cover
In princely guards! Dost thou think, Claudio,
If I would yield him my virginity
Thou mightst be freed?
Claud.   O heavens! it cannot be.
Isab. Yes, he would give it thee, from this
                rank offence
So to offend him still. This night's the time
That I should do what I abhor to name,
Or else thou diest to-morrow.
Claud.   Thou shalt not do't.
Isab. O, were it but my life,
I'd throw it down for your deliverance
As frankly as a pin.
Claud.   Thanks, dear Isabel.
Isab. Be ready, Claudio, for your death to-
                morrow.
Claud. Yes.—Has he affections in him
That thus can make him bite the law by the nose
When he would force it? Sure it is no sin;
Or of the deadly seven it is the least.
Isab. Which is the least?
Claud. If it were damnable, he, being so wise,
Why would he for the momentary trick
Be perdurably fined?—O Isabel!
Isab. What says my brother?
Claud.   Death is a fearful thing.
Isab. And shamed life a hateful.
Claud. Ay, but to die, and go we know not
                where;
To lie in cold obstruction, and to rot;
This sensible warm motion to become
A kneaded clod; and the delighted spirit
To bathe in fiery floods or to reside
In thrilling regions of thick-ribbed ice;
To be imprison'd in the viewless winds,
And blown with restless violence round about
The pendent world; or to be worse than worst
Of those that lawless and incertain thoughts
Imagine howling!—'tis too horrible!
The weariest and most loathed worldly life
That age, ache, penury, and imprisonment
Can lay on nature is a paradise
To what we fear of death.
Isab. Alas! alas!
Claud.   Sweet sister, let me live:
What sin you do to save a brother's life
Nature dispenses with the deed so far
That it becomes a virtue.
Isab.   O you beast!
O faithless coward! O dishonest wretch!
Wilt thou be made a man out of my vice?
Is't not a kind of incest to take life   [think?
From thine own sister's shame. What should I
Heaven shield my mother play'd my father fair!

For such a warped slip of wilderness
Ne'er issued from his blood. Take my defiance:
Die; perish! might but my bending down
Reprieve thee from thy fate, it should proceed:
I'll pray a thousand prayers for thy death,—
No word to save the.
Claud. Nay, hear me, Isabel.
Isab.   O fie, fie, fie!
Thy sin's not accidental, but a trade:
Mercy to thee would prove itself a bawd:
'Tis best that thou diest quickly.   [*Going.*
Claud.   O hear me, Isabella.

Re-enter DUKE.

Duke. Vouchsafe a word, young sister, but one
word.
Isab. What is your will?
Duke. Might you dispense with your leisure
I would by and by have some speech with you:
the satisfaction I would require is likewise your
own benefit.
Isab. I have no superfluous leisure; my stay
must be stolen out of other affairs; but I will
attend you awhile.
Duke. [*To* CLAUDIO *aside.*] Son, I have overheard what hath passed between you and your
sister. Angelo had never the purpose to corrupt
her; only he hath made an essay of her virtue
to practise his judgment with the disposition
of natures; she, having the truth of honour in
her, hath made him that gracious denial which
he is most glad to receive: I am confessor to
Angelo, and I know this to be true; therefore
prepare yourself to death. Do not satisfy your
resolution with hopes that are fallible: to-
morrow you must die; go to your knees and
make ready.
Claud. Let me ask my sister pardon. I am so
out of love with life that I will sue to be rid of it.
Duke. Hold you there. Farewell.
                              [*Exit* CLAUDIO.

Re-enter PROVOST.

Provost, a word with you.
Prov. What's your will, father?
Duke. That, now you are come, you will be
gone. Leave me a while with the maid; my
mind promises with my habit no loss shall
touch her by my company.
Prov. In good time.   [*Exit* PROVOST.
Duke. The hand that hath made you fair hath
made you good: the goodness that is cheap in
beauty makes beauty brief in goodness: but
grace, being the soul of your complexion, should
keep the body of it ever fair. The assault that
Angelo hath made to you, fortune hath conveyed to my understanding; and, but that
frailty hath examples for his falling, I should
wonder at Angelo. How will you do to content
this substitute, and to save your brother?
Isab. I am now going to resolve him; I had
rather my brother die by the law than my son
should be unlawfully born. But O, how much
is the good duke deceived in Angelo! If ever

he return, and I can speak to him, I will open my lips in vain, or discover his government.

Duke. That shall not be much amiss: yet, as the matter now stands, he will avoid your accusation; he made trial of you only.—Therefore fasten your ear on my advisings; to the love I have in doing good a remedy presents itself. I do make myself believe that you may most uprighteously do a poor wronged lady a merited benefit; redeem your brother from the angry law; do no stain to your own gracious person; and much please the absent duke if, peradventure, he shall ever return to have hearing of this business.

Isab. Let me hear you speak further; I have spirit to do anything that appears not foul in the truth of my spirit.

Duke. Virtue is bold, and goodness never fearful. Have you not heard speak of Mariana, the sister of Frederick the great soldier who miscarried at sea?

Isab. I have heard of the lady, and good words went with her name.

Duke. Her should this Angelo have married; was affianced to her by oath, and the nuptial appointed: between which time of the contract and limit of the solemnity her brother Frederick was wrecked at sea, having in that perished vessel the dowry of his sister. But mark how heavily this befell to the poor gentlewoman: there she lost a noble and renowned brother, in his love toward her ever most kind and natural; with him the portion and sinew of her fortune, her marriage-dowry; with both, her combinate husband, this well-seeming Angelo.

Isab. Can this be so? Did Angelo so leave her?

Duke. Left her in her tears, and dried not one of them with his comfort; swallowed his vows whole, pretending, in her, discoveries of dishonour; in few, bestowed her on her own lamentation, which she yet wears for his sake; and he, a marble to her tears, is washed with them, but relents not.

Isab. What a merit were it in death to take this poor maid from the world! What corruption in this life that it will let this man live!—But how out of this can she avail?

Duke. It is a rupture that you may easily heal; and the cure of it not only saves your brother, but keeps you from dishonour in doing it.

Isab. Show me how, good father.

Duke. This forenamed maid hath yet in her the continuance of her first affection; his unjust unkindness, that in all reason should have quenched her love, hath, like an impediment in the current, made it more violent and unruly. Go you to Angelo; answer his requiring with a plausible obedience; agree with his demands to the point: only refer yourself to this advantage,—first, that your stay with him may not be long; that the time may have all shadow and silence in it; and the place answer to convenience: this being granted in course, now follows all. We shall advise this wronged maid to stead up your appointment, go in your place; if the encounter acknowledge itself hereafter, it may compel him to her recompense: and here, by this, is your brother saved, your honour untainted, the poor Mariana advantaged, and the corrupt deputy scaled. The maid will I frame and make fit for his attempt. If you think well to carry this as you may, the doubleness of the benefit defends the deceit from reproof. What think you of it?

Isab. The image of it gives me content already; and I trust it will grow to a most prosperous perfection.

Duke. It lies much in your holding up. Haste you speedily to Angelo: if for this night he entreat you to his bed, give him promise of satisfaction. I will presently to St. Luke's; there, at the moated grange, resides this dejected Mariana. At that place call upon me; and despatch with Angelo, that it may be quickly.

Isab. I thank you for this comfort. Fare you well, good father.   [*Exeunt severally.*

SCENE II.—*The Street before the Prison.*

Enter DUKE, *as a Friar; to him* ELBOW, CLOWN, *and* Officers.

Elb. Nay, if there be no remedy for it, but that you will needs buy and sell men and women like beasts, we shall have all the world drink brown and white bastard.

Duke. O heavens! what stuff is here?

Clo. 'Twas never merry world since, of two usuries, the merriest was put down, and the worser allowed by order of law a furred gown to keep him warm; and furred with fox and lamb-skins, too, to signify that craft, being richer than innocency, stands for the facing.

Elb. Come your way, sir.—Bless you, good father friar.

Duke. And you, good brother father. What offence hath this man made you, sir?

Elb. Marry, sir, he hath offended the law; and sir, we take him to be a thief too, sir; for we have found upon him, sir, a strange picklock, which we have sent to the deputy.

Duke. Fie, sirrah; a bawd, a wicked bawd!
The evil that thou causest to be done,
That is thy means to live. Do thou but think
What 'tis to cram a maw or clothe a back
From such a filthy vice: say to thyself,
From their abominable and beastly touches
I drink, I eat, array myself, and live.
Canst thou believe thy living is a life,
So stinkingly depending? Go mend, go mend.

Clo. Indeed, it does stink in some sort, sir; but yet, sir, I would prove——

Duke. Nay, if the devil have given thee proof for sin,
Thou wilt prove his. Take him to prison, officer;
Correction and instruction must both work
Ere this rude beast will profit.

Elb. He must before the deputy, sir; he has

given him warning: the deputy cannot abide a whoremaster: if he be a whoremonger, and comes before him, he were as good go a mile on his errand.

Duke. That we were all, as some would seem to be,
Free from our faults, as faults from seeming free!

Elb. His neck will come to your waist, a cord, sir.

Clo. I spy comfort; I cry bail! Here's a gentleman, and a friend of mine.

Enter LUCIO.

Lucio. How now, noble Pompey? What, at the heels of Cæsar! Art thou led in triumph? What, is there none of Pygmalion's images, newly made woman, to be had now, for putting the hand in the pocket and extracting it clutched? What reply, ha? What say'st thou to this tune, matter, and method? Is't not drowned i' the last rain, ha? What say'st thou to't? Is the world as it was, man? Which is the way? Is it sad, and few words? or how? The trick of it?

Duke. Still thus, and thus! still worse!

Lucio. How doth my dear morsel, thy mistress? Procures she still, ha?

Clo. Troth, sir, she hath eaten up all her beef, and she is herself in the tub.

Lucio. Why, 'tis good: it is the right of it: it must be so: ever your fresh whore and your powdered bawd: an unshunned consequence; it must be so. Art going to prison, Pompey?

Clo. Yes, faith, sir.

Lucio. Why, 'tis not amiss, Pompey. Farewell; go, say I sent thee thither. For debt, Pompey? or how?

Elb. For being a bawd, for being a bawd.

Lucio. Well, then, imprison him: if imprisonment be the due of a bawd, why, 'tis his right; bawd is he doubtless, and of antiquity, too: bawd-born. Farewell, good Pompey. Commend me to the prison, Pompey. You will turn good husband now, Pompey; you will keep the house.

Clo. I hope, sir, your good worship will be my bail.

Lucio. No, indeed, will I not, Pompey; it is not the wear. I will pray, Pompey, to increase your bondage: if you take it not patiently, why, your mettle is the more. Adieu, trusty Pompey.—Bless you, friar.

Duke. And you.

Lucio. Does Bridget paint still, Pompey, ha?

Elb. Come your ways, sir; come.

Clo. You will not bail me then, sir?

Lucio. Then, Pompey, nor now.—What news abroad, friar? what news?

Elb. Come your ways, sir; come.

Lucio. Go,—to kennel, Pompey, go:
        [*Exeunt* ELBOW, CLOWN, *and* Officers.
What news, friar, of the duke?

Duke. I know none. Can you tell me of any?

Lucio. Some say he is with the Emperor of Russia; other some, he is in Rome: but where is he, think you?

Duke. I know not where; but wheresoever, I wish him well.

Lucio. It was a mad fantastical trick of him to steal from the state and usurp the beggary he was never born to. Lord Angelo dukes it well in his absence; he puts transgression to't.

Duke. He does well in't.

Lucio. A little more lenity to lechery would do no harm in him: something too crabbed that way, friar.

Duke. It is too general a vice, and severity must cure it.

Lucio. Yes, in good sooth, the vice is of a great kindred; it is well allied: but it is impossible to extirp it quite, friar, till eating and drinking be put down. They say this Angelo was not made by man and woman after the downright way of creation: is it true, think you?

Duke. How should he be made, then?

Lucio. Some report a sea-maid spawned him; some, that he was begot between two stock-fishes.—But it is certain that, when he makes water, his urine is congealed ice; that I know to be true: and he is a motion ungenerative; that's infallible.

Duke. You are pleasant, sir, and speak apace.

Lucio. Why, what a ruthless thing is this in him, for the rebellion of a cod-piece to take away the life of a man? Would the duke that is absent have done this? Ere he would have hanged a man for the getting a hundred bastards, he would have paid for the nursing a thousand. He had some feeling of the sport; he knew the service, and that instructed him to mercy.

Duke. I never heard the absent duke much detected for women; he was not inclined that way.

Lucio. O, sir, you are deceived.

Duke. 'Tis not possible.

Lucio. Who, not the duke? yes, your beggar of fifty;—and his use was to put a ducat in her clack-dish: the duke had crotchets in him. He would be drunk too: that let me inform you.

Duke. You do him wrong, surely.

Lucio. Sir, I was an inward of his. A shy fellow was the duke: and I believe I know the cause of his withdrawing.

Duke. What, I pr'ythee, might be the cause?

Lucio. No,—pardon;—'tis a secret must be locked within the teeth and the lips: but this I can let you understand,—the greater file of the subject held the duke to be wise.

Duke. Wise? why, no question but he was.

Lucio. A very superficial, ignorant, unweighing fellow.

Duke. Either this is envy in you, folly, or mistaking; the very stream of his life, and the business he hath helmed, must, upon a warranted need, give him a better proclamation. Let him be but testimonied in his own bringings forth, and he shall appear to the envious a scholar, a statesman, and a soldier. Therefore you speak unskilfully; or, if your knowledge be more, it is much darkened in your malice.

Lucio. Sir, I know him, and I love him.

Duke. Love talks with better knowledge, and knowledge with dearer love.

Lucio. Come, sir, I know what I know.

Duke. I can hardly believe that, since you know not what you speak. But, if ever the duke return,—as our prayers are he may,—let me desire you to make your answer before him. If it be honest you have spoke, you have courage to maintain it: I am bound to call upon you; and, I pray you, your name?

Lucio. Sir, my name is Lucio; well known to the duke.

Duke. He shall know you better, sir, if I may live to report you.

Lucio. I fear you not.

Duke. O, you hope 'the duke will return no more; or you imagine me too unhurtful an opposite. But, indeed, I can do you little harm: you'll forswear this again.

Lucio. I'll be hanged first! thou art deceived in me, friar. But no more of this. Canst thou tell if Claudio die to-morrow or no?

Duke. Why should he die, sir?

Lucio. Why, for filling a bottle with a tundish. I would the duke we talk of were returned again: this ungenitured agent will unpeople the province with continency; sparrows must not build in his house-eaves because they are lecherous. The duke yet would have dark deeds darkly answered; he would never bring them to light: would he were returned! Marry, this Claudio is condemned for untrussing. Farewell, good friar: I pry'thee, pray for me. The duke, I say to thee again, would eat mutton on Fridays. He's now past it; yet, and I say to thee, he would mouth with a beggar though she smelt brown bread and garlic: say that I said so.—Farewell.   [*Exit.*

Duke. No might nor greatness in morality Can censure 'scape; back-wounding calumny The whitest virtue strikes. What king so strong Can tie the gall up in the slanderous tongue? But who comes here?

Enter ESCALUS, PROVOST, BAWD, *and* Officers.

Escal. Go, away with her to prison.

Bawd. Good my lord, be good to me; your honour is accounted a merciful man; good my lord.

Escal. Double and treble admonition, and still forfeit in the same kind? This would make mercy swear and play the tyrant.

Prov. A bawd of eleven years' continuance, may it please your honour.

Bawd. My lord, this is one Lucio's information against me: Mistress Kate Keepdown was with child by him in the duke's time; he promised her marriage; his child is a year and a quarter old come Philip and Jacob: I have kept it myself; and see how he goes about to abuse me.

Escal. That fellow is a fellow of much licence: —let him be called before us.—Away with her to prison. Go to; no more words. [*Exeunt* BAWD *and* Officers.] Provost, my brother Angelo will not be altered, Claudio must die to-morrow: let him be furnished with divines, and have all charitable preparation: if my brother wrought by my pity it should not be so with him.

Prov. So please you, this friar hath been with him, and advised him for the entertainment of death.

Escal. Good even, good father.

Duke. Bliss and goodness on you!

Escal. Of whence are you?   [now

Duke. Not of this country, though my chance is To use it for my time: I am a brother Of gracious order, late come from the see In special business from his holiness.

Escal. What news abroad i' the world?

Duke. None, but that there is so great a fever on goodness, that the dissolution of it must cure it: novelty is only in request; and it is as dangerous to be aged in any kind of course as it is virtuous to be constant in any undertaking. There is scarce truth enough alive to make societies secure; but security enough to make fellowships accursed: much upon this riddle runs the wisdom of the world. This news is old enough, yet it is every day's news. I pray you, sir, of what disposition was the duke?

Escal. One that, above all other strifes, contended especially to know himself.

Duke. What pleasure was he give to?

Escal. Rather rejoicing to see another merry, than merry at anything which professed to make him rejoice: a gentleman of all temperance. But leave we him to his events, with a prayer they may prove prosperous; and let me desire to know how you find Claudio prepared. I am made to understand that you have lent him visitation.

Duke. He professes to have received no sinister measure from his judge, but most willingly humbles himself to the determination of justice: yet had he framed to himself, by the instruction of his frailty, many deceiving promises of life; which I, by my good leisure, have discredited to him, and how is he resolved to die.

Escal. You have paid the heavens your function and the prisoner the very debt of your calling. I have laboured for the poor gentleman to the extremest shore of my modesty; but my brother justice have I found so severe that he hath forced me to tell him he is indeed—justice.

Duke. If his own life answer the straitness of his proceeding, it shall become him well; wherein if he chance to fail, he hath sentenced himself.

Escal. I am going to visit the prisoner. Fare you well.

Duke. Peace be with you!

     [*Exeunt* ESCAL. *and* PROV.

He who the sword of heaven will bear Should be as holy as severe;

Pattern in himself to know,
Grace to stand, and virtue go;
More nor less to others paying
Than by self-offences weighing.
Shame to him whose cruel striking
Kills for faults of his own liking!
Twice treble shame on Angelo,
To weed my vice and let his grow!
O, what man man within him hide,
Though angel on the outward side!
How may likeness, made in crimes,
Making practice on the times,
Draw with idle spiders' strings
Most pond'rous and substantial things!
Craft against vice I must apply;
With Angelo to-night shall lie
His old betrothed but despis'd;
So disguise shall, by the disguis'd,
Pay with falsehood false exacting,
And perform an old contracting.   [*Exit.*

ACT IV.

SCENE I.—*A Room in* MARIANA'S *House.*

MARIANA *discovered sitting: a* Boy *singing.*

SONG.

Take, O take those lips away,
  That so sweetly were forsworn;
And those eyes, the break of day,
  Lights that do mislead the morn:
But my kisses bring again,
                Bring again;
Seals of love, but seal'd in vain,
                Sealed in vain.

Mari. Break off thy song, and haste thee quick
            away;
Here comes a man of comfort, whose advice
Hath often still'd my brawling discontent.—
                        [*Exit* Boy.

Enter DUKE.

I cry you mercy, sir; and well could wish
You had not found me here so musical:
Let me excuse me, and believe me so,   [woe.
My mirth it much displeas'd, but pleas'd my
Duke. 'Tis good: though music oft hath such
            a charm
To make bad good and good provoke to harm.
I pray you, tell me, hath anybody inquired for
me here to-day? much upon this time have I
promised here to meet.
Mari. You have not been inquired after: I
have sat here all day.

Enter ISABELLA.

Duke. I do constantly believe you.—The time
is come even now. I shall crave your forbear-
ance a little: may be I will call upon you anon,
for some advantage to yourself.
Mari. I am always bound to you.   [*Exit.*
Duke. Very well met, and welcome.
What is the news from this good deputy?
Isab. He hath a garden circummur'd with brick,

Whose western side is with a vineyard back'd;
And to that vineyard is a planched gate
That makes his opening with this bigger key:
This other doth command a little door
Which from the vineyard to the garden leads;
There have I made my promise to call on him
Upon the heavy middle of the night.
Duke. But shall you on your knowledge find
            this way?
Isab. I have ta'en a due and wary note upon't;
With whispering and most guilty diligence,
In action all of precept, he did show me
The way twice o'er.
Duke.   Are there no other tokens
Between you 'greed concerning her observance?
Isab. No, none, but only a repair i' the dark;
And that I have possess'd him my most stay
Can be but brief: for I have made him know
I have a servant comes with me along,
That stays upon me; whose persuasion is
I come about my brother.
Duke.   'Tis well borne up.
I have not yet made known to Mariana.
A word of this.—What, ho! within! come forth.

Re-enter MARIANA.

I pray you be acquainted with this maid;
She comes to do you good.
Isab.   I do desire the like.
Duke. Do you persuade yourself that I respect
            you?
Mari. Good friar, I know you do, and I have
            found it.   [hand,
Duke. Take, then, this your companion by the
Who hath a story ready for your ear:
I shall attend your leisure; but make haste;
The vaporous night approaches.
Mari.   Will't please you walk aside?
                [*Exeunt* MARI. *and* ISAB.
Duke. O place and greatness, millions of false
            eyes
Are stuck upon thee! volumes of report
Run with these false and most contrarious quests
Upon thy doings! thousand 'scapes of wit
Make thee the father of their idle dream,
And rack thee in their fancies!—Welcome!
            How agreed?

Re-enter MARIANA *and* ISABELLA.

Isab. She'll take the enterprise upon her, father
If you advise it.
Duke.   It is not my consent,
But my entreaty too.
Isab.   Little have you to say,
When you depart from him, but, soft and low,
Remember now my brother.
Mari.   Fear me not.
Duke. Nor, gentle daughter, fear you not at all:
He is your husband on a pre-contract:
To bring you thus together 'tis no sin,
Sith that the justice of your title to him
Doth flourish the deceit. Come, let us go;
Our corn's to reap, for yet our tilth's to sow.
                        [*Exeunt.*

SCENE II.—*A Room in the Prison.*

Enter PROVOST *and* CLOWN.

Prov. Come hither, sirrah. Can you cut off a man's head?

Clo. If the man be a bachelor, sir, I can: but if he be a married man, he is his wife's head, and I can never cut off a woman's head.

Prov. Come, sir, leave me your snatches and yield me a direct answer. To-morrow morning are to die Claudio and Barnardine. Here is in our prison a common executioner who in his office lacks a helper; if you will take it on you to assist him, it shall redeem you from your gyves; if not, you shall have your full time of imprisonment, and your deliverance with an unpitied whipping; for you have been a notorious bawd.

Clo. Sir, I have been an unlawful bawd time out of mind; but yet I will be content to be a lawful hangman. I would be glad to receive some instruction from my fellow-partner.

Prov. What ho, Abhorson! Where's Abhorson, there?

Enter ABHORSON.

Abhor. Do you call, sir?

Prov. Sirrah, here's a fellow will help you to-morrow in your execution. If you think it meet, compound with him by the year, and let him abide here with you; if not, use him for the present, and dismiss him. He cannot plead his estimation with you; he hath been a bawd.

Abhor. A bawd, sir? Fie upon him; he will discredit our mystery.

Prov. Go to, sir; you weigh equally; a feather will turn the scale.　　　　　　　　　[*Exit.*

Clo. Pray, sir, by your good favour,—for, surely, sir, a good favour you have, but that you have a hanging look,—do you call, sir, your occupation a mystery?

Abhor. Ay, sir; a mystery.

Clo. Painting, sir, I have heard say, is a mystery; and your whores, sir, being members of my occupation, using painting, do prove my occupation a mystery: but what mystery there should be in hanging, if I should be hanged, I cannot imagine.

Abhor. Sir, it is a mystery.

Clo. Proof.

Abhor. Every true man's apparel fits your thief: if it be too little for your thief, your true man thinks it big enough; if it be too big for your thief, your thief thinks it little enough: so every true man's apparel fits your thief.

Re-enter PROVOST.

Prov. Are you agreed?

Clo. Sir, I will serve him; for I do find your hangman is a more penitent trade than your bawd; he doth oftener ask forgiveness.

Prov. You, sirrah, provide your block and your axe to-morrow four o'clock.

Abhor. Come on, bawd; I will instruct thee in my trade; follow.

Clo. I do desire to learn, sir; and I hope, if you have occasion to use me for your own turn, you shall find me yare: for, truly sir, for your kindness I owe you a good turn.

Prov. Call hither Barnardine and Claudio.

　　　　　　　　　[*Exeunt* CLO. *and* ABHOR.

One has my pity; not a jot the other,
Being a murderer, though he were my brother.

Enter CLAUDIO.

Look, here's the warrant, Claudio, for thy death:
'Tis now dead midnight, and by eight to-morrow
Thou must be made immortal. Where's Bar-
　　　　　nardine?　　　　　　　　　[labour

Claud. As fast lock'd up in sleep as guiltless
When it lies starkly in the traveller's bones:
He will not wake.

Prov.　　　　　　Who can do good on him?
Well, go, prepare yourself. But, hark! what
　　　　　noise?　　　　　　[*Knocking within.*
Heaven give your spirits comfort!
　　　　　　　　　　　　[*Exit* CLAUDIO.
　　　　By and by!—
I hope it is some pardon or reprieve
For the most gentle Claudio.—Welcome, father.

Enter DUKE.

Duke. The best and wholesomest spirits of the
　　　　　night　　　　　　　　　[of late?
Envelop you, good provost! Who call'd here

Prov. None, since the curfew rung.

Duke.　　　　　　　　　　　Not Isabel?

Prov. No.

Duke.　　　They will, then, ere't be long.

Prov. What comfort is for Claudio?

Duke.　　　　　　　There's some in hope.

Prov. It is a bitter deputy.

Duke. Not so, not so; his life is parallel'd
Even with the stroke and line of his great justice;
He doth with holy abstinence subdue
That in himself which he spurs on his power
To qualify in others: were he meal'd
With that which he corrects, then were he
　　　　　tyrannous;
But this being so, he's just.—Now are they come.
　　　[*Knocking within.*—PROVOST *goes out.*
This is a gentle provost: seldom when
The steeled gaoler is the friend of men.—
How now? what noise? That spirit's possess'd
　　　　　with haste　　　　　　　[strokes.
That wounds the unsisting postern with these

PROVOST *returns, speaking to one at the door.*

Prov. There he must stay until the officer
Arise to let him in; he is call'd up.　　　[yet,

Duke. Have you no countermand for Claudio
But he must die to-morrow?

Prov.　　　　　　　None, sir, none.

Duke. As near the dawning, Provost, as it is,
You shall hear more ere morning.

Prov.　　　　　　　　　　Happily
You something know; yet I believe there comes

No countermand; no such example have we:
Besides, upon the very siege of justice,
Lord Angelo hath to the public ear
Profess'd the contrary.

Enter a Messenger.

Duke. This is his lordship's man.
Prov. And here comes Claudio's pardon.
Mess. My lord hath sent you this note; and
by me this further charge, that you swerve not
from the smallest article of it, neither in time,
matter, or other circumstance. Good-morrow;
for as I take it, it is almost day.
Prov. I shall obey him.   [*Exit* Messenger.
Duke. This is his pardon purchas'd by such
    sin,   [*Aside.*
For which the pardoner himself is in:
Hence hath offence his quick celerity
When it is borne in high authority:
When vice makes mercy, mercy's so extended
That for the fault's love is the offender friend-
    ed.—
Now, sir, what news?
Prov. I told you: Lord Angelo, belike thinking
me remiss in mine office, awakens me with this
unwonted putting on; methinks strangely, for
he hath not used it before.
Duke. Pray you, let's hear.
Prov. [Reads.] *Whatsoever you may hear to the
contrary, let Claudio be executed by four of the
clock; and, in the afternoon, Barnardine: for my
better satisfaction, let me have Claudio's head sent
me by five. Let this be duly performed; with a
thought that more depends on it than we must yet
deliver. Thus fail not to do your office, as you
will answer it at your peril.*
What say you to this, sir?
Duke. What is that Barnardine who is to be
executed in the afternoon?
Prov. A Bohemian born; but here nursed up
and bred: one that is a prisoner nine years old.
Duke. How came it that the absent duke had
not either delivered him to his liberty or executed him? I have heard it was ever his manner to do so.
Prov. His friends still wrought reprieves for
him: and, indeed, his fact, till now in the government of Lord Angelo, came not to an un-
doubtful proof.
Duke. Is it now apparent?
Prov. Most manifest, and not denied by himself.
Duke. Hath he borne himself penitently in
prison? How seems he to be touched?
Prov. A man that apprehends death no more
dreadfully but as a drunken sleep; careless,
reckless, and fearless of what's past, present,
or to come; insensible of mortality and desperately mortal.
Duke. He wants advice.
Prov. He will hear none; he hath evermore had
the liberty of the prison; give him leave to
escape hence, he would not: drunk many times
a-day, if not many days entirely drunk. We
have very often awaked him, as if to carry him
to execution, and showed him a seeming warrant for it: it hath not moved him at all.
Duke. More of him anon. There is written in
your brow, Provost, honesty and constancy:
if I read it not truly, my ancient skill beguiles
me; but in the boldness of my cunning I will
lay myself in hazard. Claudio, whom here you
have a warrant to execute, is no greater forfeit
to the law than Angelo who hath sentenced
him. To make you understand this in a manifested effect, I crave but four days' respite; for
the which you are to do me both a present and
a dangerous courtesy.
Prov. Pray, sir, in what?
Duke. In the delaying death.
Prov. Alack! how may I do it? having the
hour limited; and an express command, under
penalty, to deliver his head in the view of
Angelo? I may make my case as Claudio's, to
cross this in the smallest.
Duke. By the vow of mine order, I warrant
you, if my instructions may be your guide.
Let this Barnardine be this morning executed,
and his head borne to Angelo.
Prov. Angelo hath seen them both, and will
discover the favour.
Duke. O, death's a great disguiser: and you
may add to it. Shave the head and tie the
beard; and say it was the desire of the penitent
to be so bared before his death. You know the
course is common. If anything fall to you upon
this, more than thanks and good fortune, by
the saint whom I profess, I will plead against
it with my life.
Prov. Pardon me, good father; it is against
my oath.
Duke. Were you sworn to the duke, or to the
deputy?
Prov. To him and to his substitutes.
Duke. You will think you have made no offence
if the duke avouch the justice of your dealing?
Prov. But what likelihood is in that?
Duke. Not a resemblance, but a certainty. Yet
since I see you fearful that neither my coat,
integrity, nor my persuasion can with ease attempt you, I will go further than I meant, to
pluck all fears out of you. Look you, sir, here
is the hand and seal of the duke. You know
the character, I doubt not; and the signet is
not strange to you.
Prov. I know them both.
Duke. The contents of this is the return of
the duke; you shall anon over-read it at your
pleasure; where you shall find, within these
two days he will be here. This is a thing that
Angelo knows not: for he this very day receives
letters of strange tenor: perchance of the duke's
death; perchance entering into some monastery; but, by chance, nothing of what is writ.
Look, the unfolding star calls up the shepherd.
Put not yourself into amazement how these
things should be: all difficulties are but easy
when they are known. Call your executioner,

and off with Barnardine's head: I will give him a present shift, and advise him for a better place. Yet you are amazed: but this shall absolutely resolve you. Come away; it is almost clear dawn. *[Exeunt.*

SCENE III.—*Another Room in the same.*

Enter CLOWN.

Clo. I am as well acquainted here as I was in our house of profession: one would think it were Mistress Overdone's own house, for here be many of her old customers. First, here's young Master Rash; he's in for a commodity of brown paper and old ginger, ninescore and seventeen pounds; of which he made five marks, ready money: marry, then, ginger was not much in request, for the old women were all dead. Then is there here one Master Caper, at the suit of Master Threepile the mercer, for some four suits of peach-coloured satin, which now peaches him a beggar. Then have we here young Dizy, and young Master Deepvow, and Master Copperspur, and Master Starvelackey the rapier and dagger-man, and young Dropheir that killed lusty Pudding, and Master Forthright the tilter, and brave Master Shoetie the great traveller, and wild Halfcan that stabbed Pots, and, I think, forty more; all great doers in our trade, and are now "for the Lord's sake."

Enter ABHORSON.

Abhor. Sirrah, bring Barnardine hither.
Clo. Master Barnardine! you must rise and be hanged, Master Barnardine!
Abhor. What, ho, Barnardine!
Barnar. [*Within.*] A pox o' your throats! Who makes that noise there? What are you?
Clo. Your friend, sir; the hangman. You must be so good, sir, to rise and be put to death.
Barnar. [*Within.*] Away, you rogue, away; I am sleepy.
Abhor. Tell him he must awake, and that quickly too.
Clo. Pray, Master Barnardine, awake till you are executed, and sleep afterwards.
Abhor. Go in to him, and fetch him out.
Clo. He is coming, sir, he is coming; I hear his straw rustle.

Enter BARNARDINE.

Abhor. Is the axe upon the block, sirrah?
Clo. Very ready, sir.
Barnar. How now, Abhorson? what's the news with you?
Abhor. Truly, sir, I would desire you to clap into your prayers; for, look you, the warrant's come.
Barnar. You rogue, I have been drinking all night; I am not fitted for't.
Clo. O, the better, sir; for he that drinks all night and is hanged betimes in the morning may sleep the sounder all the next day.

Enter DUKE.

Abhor. Look you, sir, here comes your ghostly father. Do we jest now, think you?
Duke. Sir, induced by my charity, and hearing how hastily you are to depart, I am come to advise you, comfort you, and pray with you.
Barnar. Friar, not I; I have been drinking hard all night, and I will have more time to prepare me, or they shall beat out my brains with billets: I will not consent to die this day, that's certain.
Duke. O, sir, you must; and therefore, I beseech you,
Look forward on the journey you shall go.
Barnar. I swear I will not die to-day for any man's persuasion.
Duke. But hear you,——
Barnar. Not a word; if you have anything to say to me, come to my ward; for thence will not I to-day. *[Exit.*
Duke. Unfit to live or die. O gravel heart!—
After him, fellows; bring him to the block.
[Exeunt ABHOR. *and* CLOWN.

Enter PROVOST.

Prov. Now, sir, how do you find the prisoner?
Duke. A creature unprepar'd, unmeet for death;
And to transport him in the mind he is
Were damnable.
Prov.　　　　　　Here in the prison, father,
There died this morning of a cruel fever
One Ragozine, a most notorious pirate,
A man of Claudio's years; his beard and head
Just of his colour. What if we do omit
This reprobate till he were well inclined;
And satisfy the deputy with the visage
Of Ragozine, more like to Claudio?
Duke. O, 'tis an accident that Heaven provides!
Despatch it presently; the hour draws on
Prefix'd by Angelo: see this be done,
And sent according to command; whiles I
Persuade this rude wretch willingly to die.
Prov. This shall be done, good father, presently.
But Barnardine must die this afternoon:
And how shall we continue Claudio,
To save me from the danger that might come
If he were known alive?
Duke.　　　　　　　　Let this be done;—
Put them in secret holds; both Barnardine and
　　　　　　Claudio. 　　　　　　[ing
Ere twice the sun hath made his journal greet-
To the under generation, you shall find
Your safety manifested.
Prov. I am your free dependent.
Duke.　　　　　　　　Quick, despatch,
And send the head to Angelo.
　　　　　　　　　　　　[*Exit* PROVOST.
Now will I write letters to Angelo,—　　[tents
The provost, he shall bear them,—whose con-
Shall witness to him I am near at home,
And that, by great injunctions, I am bound
To enter publicly: him I'll desire
To meet me at the consecrated fount,

A league below the city; and from thence,
By cold gradation and weal-balanced form,
We shall proceed with Angelo.

Re-enter PROVOST.

Prov. Here is the head; I'll carry it myself.
Duke. Convenient is it. Make a swift return;
For I would commune with you of such things
That want no ear but yours.
Prov. I'll make all speed. [*Exit.*
Isab. [*Within.*] Peace, ho, be here!
Duke. The tongue of Isabel.—She's come to
    know
If yet her brother's pardon be come hither:
But I will keep her ignorant of her good,
To make her heavenly comforts of despair
When it is least expected.

Enter ISABELLA

Isab. Ho, by your leave!
Duke. Good morning to you, fair and gracious
    daughter.
Isab. The better, given me by so holy a man.
Hath yet the deputy sent my brother's pardon?
Duke. He hath released him, Isabel, from the
    world:
His head is off and sent to Angelo.
Isab. Nay, but it is not so.
Duke. It is no other:
Show your wisdom, daughter, in your close
    patience.
Isab. O, I will to him and pluck out his eyes.
Duke. You shall not be admitted to his sight.
Isab. Unhappy Claudio! Wretched Isabel! In-
jurious world! Most damned Angelo!
Duke. This nor hurts him nor profits you a jot:
Forbear it, therefore; give your cause to Heaven.
Mark what I say; which you shall find
By every syllable a faithful verity:
The duke comes home to-morrow;—nay, dry
    your eyes;
One of our convent, and his confessor,
Gives me this instance. Already he hath carried
Notice to Escalus and Angelo,
Who do prepare to meet him at the gates,
There to give up their power. If you can, pace
    your wisdom
In that good path that I would wish it go,
And you shall have your bosom on this wretch,
Grace of the duke, revenges to your heart,
And general honour.
Isab. I am directed by you.
Duke. This letter, then, to Friar Peter give;
'Tis that he sent me of the duke's return:
Say, by this token, I desire his company
At Mariana's house to-night. Her cause and
    yours
I'll perfect him withal; and he shall bring you
Before the duke; and to the head of Angelo
Accuse him home, and home. For my poor self,
I am combined by a sacred vow,
And shall be absent. Wend you with this letter:
Command these fretting waters from your eyes

With a light heart; trust not my holy order
If I pervert your course.—Who's here?

Enter LUCIO.

Lucio. Good even,
Friar; where is the provost?
Duke. Not within, sir.
Lucio. O, pretty Isabella, I am pale at mine
heart to see thine eyes so red: thou must be
patient: I am fain to dine and sup with water
and bran; I dare not for my head fill my belly;
one fruitful meal would set me to 't. But they
say the duke will be here to-morrow. By my
troth, Isabel, I loved thy brother. If the old
fantastical duke of dark corners had been at
home, he had lived. [*Exit* ISABELLA.
Duke. Sir, the duke is marvellous little beholding to your reports; but the best is, he lives
not in them.
Lucio. Friar, thou knowest not the duke so
well as I do: he's a better woodman than thou
takest him for. [ye well.
Duke. Well, you'll answer this one day. Fare
Lucio. Nay, tarry; I'll go along with thee; I
can tell thee pretty tales of the duke.
Duke. You have told me too many of him already, sir, if they be true: if not true, none
were enough.
Lucio. I was once before him for getting a
wench with child.
Duke. Did you such a thing?
Lucio. Yes, marry, did I: but was fain to forswear it; they would else have married me to
the rotten medlar.
Duke. Sir, your company is fairer than honest.
Rest you well.
Lucio. By my trot, I'll go with thee to the
lane's end. If bawdy talk offend you, we'll
have very little of it. Nay, friar, I am a kind
of burr; I shall stick. [*Exeunt.*

SCENE IV.—*A Room in* ANGELO'S *House.*

Enter ANGELO *and* ESCALUS.

Escal. Every letter he hath writ hath dis-
vouched other.
Ang. In most uneven and distracted manner.
His actions show much like to madness; pray
heaven his wisdom be not tainted! And why
meet him at the gates, and re-deliver our au-
thorities there?
Escal. I guess not.
Ang. And why should we proclaim it in an
hour before his entering, that if any crave redress of injustice, they should exhibit their petitions in the streets?
Escal. He shows his reason for that: to have a
despatch of complaints; and to deliver us from
devices hereafter, which shall then have no
power to stand against us.
Ang. Well, I beseech you, let it be proclaimed:
Betimes i' the morn I'll call you at your house:
Give notice to such men of sort and suit
As are to meet him.
Escal. I shall, sir: fare you well. [*Exit.*

Ang. Good night.—   [pregnant,
This deed unshapes me quite, makes me un-
And dull to all proceedings. A deflower'd maid!
And by an eminent body that enforced
The law against it!—But that her tender shame
Will not proclaim against her maiden loss,
How might she tongue me? Yet reason dares
          her—no:
For my authority bears a credent bulk,
That no particular scandal once can touch
But it confounds the breather. He should have
          liv'd,   [sense,
Save that his riotous youth, with dangerous
Might in the times to come have ta'en revenge,
By so receiving a dishonour'd life
With ransom of such shame. Would yet he
          had liv'd!
Alack, when once our grace we have forgot,
Nothing goes right; we would, and we would
          not.   [*Exit.*

SCENE V.—*Fields without the Town.*

Enter DUKE *in his own habit, and Friar* PETER.

Duke. These letters at fit time deliver me.
                              [*Giving letters.*
The provost knows our purpose and our plot.
The matter being afoot, keep your instruction
And hold you ever to our special drift;
Though sometimes you do blench from this to
          that   [house,
As cause doth minister. Go, call at Flavius'
And tell him where I stay: give the like notice
To Valentinus, Rowland, and to Crassus,
And bid them bring the trumpets to the gate;
But send me Flavius first.
F. Peter.   It shall be speeded well.
                              [*Exit* FRIAR.

Enter VARRIUS.

Duke. I thank thee, Varrius; thou hast made
          good haste: [friends
Come, we will walk. There's other of our
Will greet us here anon, my gentle Varrius.
                              [*Exeunt.*

SCENE VI.—*Street near the City Gate.*
Enter ISABELLA *and* MARIANA.

Isab. To speak so indirectly I am loath;
I would say the truth; but to accuse him so,
That is your part: yet I'm advis'd to do it;
He says, to 'vailfull purpose.
Mari.   Be ruled by him.
Isab. Besides, he tells me that, if peradventure
He speak against me on the adverse side,
I should not think it strange; for 'tis a physic
That's bitter to sweet end.
Mari. I would friar Peter.—
Isab.   O, peace; the friar is come.

Enter Friar PETER.

F. Peter. Come, I have found you out a stand
          most fit,
Where you may have such vantage on the duke

He shall not pass you. Twice have the trum-
          pets sounded;
The generous and gravest citizens
Have hent the gates, and very near upon
The duke is entering; therefore, hence, away.
                              [*Exeunt.*

ACT V.

SCENE I.—*A public Place near the City Gate.*

MARIANNA (*veiled*), ISABELLA, *and* PETER, *at
    a distance. Enter at opposite doors* DUKE,
    VARRIUS, Lords; ANGELO, ESCALUS, LUCIO,
    PROVOST, Officers, *and* Citizens.

Duke. My very worthy cousin, fairly met;—
Our old and faithful friend, we are glad to see
          you.   [grace!
Ang. and Escal. Happy return be to your royal
Duke. Many and hearty thankings to you both.
We have made inquiry of you; and we hear
Such goodness of your justice that our soul
Cannot but yield you forth to public thanks,
Forerunning more requital.
Ang.   You make my bonds still greater.
Duke. O, your desert speaks loud; and I should
          wrong it
To lock it in the wards of covert bosom,
When it deserves, with characters of brass,
A forted residence 'gainst the tooth of time
And rasure of oblivion. Give me your hand,
And let the subject see, to make them know
That outward courtesies would fain proclaim
Favours that keep within.—Come, Escalus;
You must walk by us on our other hand:
And good supporters are you.

PETER *and* ISABELLA *come forward.*

F. Peter. Now is your time; speak loud, and
          kneel before him.
Isab. Justice, O royal duke! Vail your regard
Upon a wrong'd, I'd fain have said, a maid!
O worthy prince, dishonour not your eye
By throwing it on any other object
Till you have heard me in my true complaint,
And give me justice, justice, justice, justice!
Duke. Relate your wrongs. In what? By whom?
          Be brief:
Here is Lord Angelo shall give you justice.
Reveal yourself to him.
Isab.   O, worthy duke,
You bid me seek redemption of the devil:
Hear me yourself; for that which I must speak
Must either punish me, not being believ'd,
Or wring redress from you; hear me, O, hear
          me here.
Ang. My lord, her wits, I fear me, are not firm:
She hath been a suitor to me for her brother,
Cut off by course of justice.
Isab.   By course of justice!
Ang. And she will speak most bitterly and
          strange.   [I speak:
Isab. Most strange, but yet most truly, will
That Angelo's forsworn, is it not strange?
That Angelo's a murderer, is't not strange?

That Angelo is an adulterous thief,
An hypocrite, a virgin-violator,
Is it not strange and strange?
Duke.   Nay, it is ten times strange.
Isab. It is not truer he is Angelo.
Than this is all as true as it is strange:
Nay, it is ten times true; for truth is truth
To the end of reckoning.
Duke.   Away with her!—Poor soul,
She speaks this in the infirmity of sense.
Isab. O prince, I cónjure thee, as thou believ'st
There is another comfort than this world,
That thou neglect me not with that opinion
That I am touch'd with madness: make not
          impossible   [sible
That which but seems unlike; 'tis not impos-
But one, the wicked'st caitiff on the ground,
May seem as shy, as grave, as just, as absolute
As Angelo; even so may Angelo,
In all his dressings, characts, titles, forms,
Be an arch-villain; believe it, royal prince,
If he be less, he's nothing; but he's more,
Had I more name for badness.
Duke.   By mine honesty,
If she be mad, as I believe no other,
Her madness hath the oddest frame of sense,
Such a dependency of thing on thing,
As e'er I heard in madness.
Isab.   O gracious duke,
Harp not on that: nor do not banish reason
For inequality; but let your reason serve
To make the truth appear where it seems hid
And hide the false seems true.
Duke.   Many that are not mad
Have, sure, more lack of reason.—What would
          you say?
Isab. I am the sister of one Claudio,
Condemn'd upon the act of fornication
To lose his head; condemn'd by Angelo:
I, in probation of a sisterhood,
Was sent to by my brother: one Lucio
As then the messenger;—
Lucio.   That's I, an't like your grace:
I came to her from Claudio, and desir'd her
To try her gracious fortune with Lord Angelo
For her poor brother's pardon.
Isab.   That's he, indeed.
Duke. You were not bid to speak.
Lucio.   No, my good lord:
Nor wish'd to hold my peace.
Duke.   I wish you now, then;
Pray you, take note of it: and when you have
A business for yourself, pray Heaven you then
Be perfect.
Lucio. I warrant your honour,   [it.
Duke. The warrant's for yourself; take heed to
Isab. This gentleman told somewhat of my tale.
Lucio. Right.
Duke. It may be right; but you are in the wrong
To speak before your time.—Proceed.
Isab.   I went
To this pernicious caitiff deputy.
Duke. That's somewhat madly spoken.
Isab.   Pardon it;

The phrase is to the matter.
Duke. Mended again. The matter;—proceed.
Isab. In brief,—to set the needless process by,
How I persuaded, how I pray'd, and kneel'd,
How he refell'd me, and how I replied,—
For this was of much length,—the vile con-
          clusion
I now begin with grief and shame to utter:
He would not, but by gift of my chaste body
To his concupiscible intemperate lust,   [ment,
Release my brother; and, after much debate-
My sisterly remorse confutes mine honour,
And I did yield to him. But the next morn
          betimes,
His purpose surfeiting, he sends a warrant
For my poor brother's head.
Duke.   This is most likely.
Isab. O, that it were as like as it is true!
Duke. By heaven, fond wretch, thou know'st
          not what thou speak'st,
Or else thou art suborn'd against his honour
In hateful practice. First, his integrity
Stands without blemish:—next, it imports no
          reason
That with such vehemency he should pursue
Faults proper to himself: if he had so offended,
He would have weigh'd thy brother by himself,
And not have cut him off. Some one hath set
          you on;
Confess the truth, and say by whose advice
Thou cam'st here to complain.
Isab.   And is this all?
Then, O you blessed ministers above,
Keep me in patience; and, with ripen'd time,
Unfold the evil which is here wrapt up
In countenance!—Heaven shield your grace
          from woe,
As I, thus wrong'd, hence unbelieved go!
Duke. I know you'd fain be gone.—An officer!
To prison with her!—Shall we thus permit
A blasting and a scandalous breath to fall
On him so near us? This needs must be a
          practice.
Who knew of your intent and coming hither?
Isab. One that I would were here, friar Lodo-
          wick.
Duke. A ghostly father, belike. Who knows
          that Lodowick?
Lucio. My lord, I know him; 'tis a meddling
          friar.   [lord,
I do not like the man: had he been lay, my
For certain words he spake against your grace
In your retirement, I had swing'd him soundly.
Duke. Words against me? This a good friar,
          belike!
And to set on this wretched woman here
Against our substitute!—Let this friar be found.
Lucio. But yesternight, my lord, she and that
          friar
I saw them at the prison: a saucy friar,
A very scurvy fellow.
F. Peter.   Bless'd be your royal grace!
I have stood by, my lord, and I have heard
Your royal ear abus'd. First, hath this woman

Most wrongfully accus'd your substitute;
Who is as free from touch or soil with her
As she from one ungot.
Duke. We did believe no less.
Know you that friar Lodowick that she speaks
    of? [holy;
F. Peter. I know him for a man divine and
Not scurvy, nor a temporary meddler,
As he's reported by this gentleman;
And, on my trust, a man that never yet
Did, as he vouches, misreport your grace.
Lucio. My lord, most villanously; believe it.
F. Peter. Well, he in time may come to clear
    himself;
But at this instant he is sick, my lord,
Of a strange fever. Upon his mere request,—
Being come to knowledge that there was com-
    plaint
Intended 'gainst Lord Angelo,—came I hither
To speak, as from his mouth, what he doth know
Is true and false; and what he, with his oath
And all probation, will make up full clear,
Whensoever he's convented. First, for this
    woman—
To justify this worthy nobleman,
So vulgarly and personally accus'd,—
Her shall you hear disproved to her eyes,
Till she herself confess it.
Duke. Good friar, let's hear it.
    [ISABELLA *is carried off, guarded; and*
      MARIANA *comes forward.*
Do you not smile at this, Lord Angelo?—
O heaven! the vanity of wretched fools!
Give us some seats.—Come, cousin Angelo;
In this I'll be impartial; be you judge
Of your own cause.—Is this the witness, friar?
First, let her show her face, and after speak.
Mari. Pardon, my lord; I will not show my
    face
Until my husband bid me.
Duke. What! are you married?
Mari. No, my lord.
Duke. Are you a maid?
Mari. No, my lord.
Duke. A widow, then?
Mari. Neither, my lord.
Duke. Why, you
Are nothing then:—neither maid, widow, nor
    wife?
Lucio. My lord, she may be a punk; for many
of them are neither maid, widow, nor wife.
Duke. Silence that fellow: I would he had some
    cause
To prattle for himself.
Lucio. Well, my lord. [ried;
Mari. My lord, I do confess I ne'er was mar-
And I confess, besides, I am no maid:
I have known my husband; yet my husband
    knows not
That ever he knew me.
Lucio. He was drunk, then, my lord; it can be
no better.
Duke. For the benefit of silence, would thou
wert so too.

Lucio. Well, my lord.
Duke. This is no witness for Lord Angelo.
Mari. Now I come to 't, my lord:
She that accuses him of fornication.
In self-same manner doth accuse my husband;
And charges him, my lord, with such a time
When I'll depose I had him in mine arms,
With all the effect of love.
Ang. Charges she more than me?
Mari. Not that I know.
Duke. No? you say, your husband.
Mari. Why, just, my lord, and that is Angelo,
Who thinks he knows that he ne'er knew my
    body,
But knows he thinks that he knows Isabel's.
Ang. This is a strange abuse.—Let's see thy
    face. [mask..
Mari. My husband bids me; now I will un-
    [*Unveiling.*
This is that face, thou cruel Angelo, [on:
Which once thou swor'st was worth the looking
This is the hand which, with a vow'd contráct,
Was fast belock'd in thine: this is the body
That took away the match from Isabel,
And did supply thee at thy garden-house
In her imagin'd person.
Duke. Know you this woman?
Lucio. Carnally, she says.
Duke. Sirrah, no more.
Lucio. Enough, my lord.
Ang. My lord, I must confess I know this
    woman;
And five years since there was some speech of
    marriage
Betwixt myself and her; which was broke off.
Partly for that her promis'd proportions
Came short of composition; but in chief
For that her reputation was disvalued
In levity: since which time of five years [her,
I never spake with her, saw her, nor heard from
Upon my faith and honour.
Mari. Noble prince,
As there comes light from heaven and words
    from breath,
As there is sense in truth and truth in virtue,
I am affianc'd this man's wife as strongly
As words could make up vows: and, my good
    lord, [house,
But Tuesday night last gone, in his garden-
He knew me as a wife. As this is true,
Let me in safety raise me from my knees,
Or else for ever be confixed here,
A marble monument!
Ang. I did but smile till now:
Now, good my lord, give me the scope of
    justice;
My patience here is touch'd. I do perceive
These poor informal women are no more
But instruments of some more mightier member
That sets them on. Let me have way, my lord,
To find this practice out.
Duke. Ay, with my heart;
And punish them unto your height of pleasure.—
Thou foolish friar, and thou pernicious woman,

Compáct with her that's gone, thinkst thou thy
          oaths,   [saint,
Though they would swear down each particular
Were testimonies against his worth and credit,
That's seal'd in approbation?—You, Lord
          Escalus,
Sit with my cousin; lend him your kind pains
To find out this abuse, whence 'tis deriv'd.—
There is another friar that set them on;
Let him be sent for.   [indeed
F. Peter. Would he were here, my lord; for he
Hath set the women on this complaint:
Your provost knows the place where he abides,
And he may fetch him.
Duke. Go, do it instantly.—[*Exit* PROVOST.
And you, my noble and well-warranted cousin,
Whom it concerns to hear this matter forth,
Do with your injuries as seems you best
In any chastisement. I for awhile   [well
Will leave you: but stir not you till you have
Determined upon these slanderers.
Escal. My lord, we'll do it thoroughly. [*Exit*
DUKE.]—Signior Lucio, did not you say you
knew that friar Lodowick to be a dishonest
person?
Lucio. Cucullus non facit monachum: honest
in nothing but in his clothes; and one that hath
spoke most villanous speeches of the duke.
Escal. We shall entreat you to abide here till
he come, and enforce them against him: we
shall find this friar a notable fellow.
Lucio. As any in Vienna, on my word.
Escal. Call that same Isabel here once again
[*to an* Attendant]; I would speak with her.
Pray you, my lord, give me leave to question;
you shall see how I handle her.
Lucio. Not better than he, by her own report.
Escal. Say you?
Lucio. Marry, sir, I think if you handled her
privately she would sooner confess: perchance,
publicly, she'll be ashamed.

Re-enter Officers, *with* ISABELLA.

Escal. I will go darkly to work with her.
Lucio. That's the way; for women are light at
midnight.
Escal. Come on, mistress [*to* ISABELLA]: here's
a gentlewoman denies all that you have said.

Re-enter the DUKE, *in the Friar's habit,
and* PROVOST.

Lucio. My lord, here comes the rascal I spoke
of; here with the provost.
Escal. In very good time:—speak not you to
him till we call upon you.
Lucio. Mum.
Escal. Come, sir: did you set these women on
to slander Lord Angelo? they have confessed
you did.
Duke. 'Tis false.
Escal. How! know you where you are?
Duke. Respect to your great place! and let the
          devil

Be sometime honour'd for his burning throne!—
Where is the duke? 'tis he should hear me speak.
Escal. The duke's in us; and we will hear you
          speak:
Look you speak justly.
Duke. Boldly, at least. But, O, poor souls,
Come you to seek the lamb here of the fox,
Good night to your redress! Is the duke gone!
Then is your cause gone too. The duke's unjust
Thus to retort your manifest appeal,
And put your trial in the villain's mouth
Which here you come to accuse.
Lucio. This is the rascal; this is he I spoke of.
Escal. Why, thou unreverend and unhallow'd
          friar!
Is't not enough thou hast suborn'd these women
To accuse this worthy man, but, in foul mouth,
And in the witness of his proper ear,
To call him villain?
And then to glance from him to the duke him-
          self,
To tax him with injustice? Take him hence;
To the rack with him.—We'll touze you joint
          by joint,
But we will know this purpose.—What! unjust?
Duke. Be not so hot; the duke
Dare no more stretch this finger of mine than he
Dare rack his own; his subject am I not,
Nor here provincial. My business in this state
Made me a looker-on here in Vienna,
Where I have seen corruption boil and bubble
Till it o'errun the stew: laws for all faults,
But faults so countenanc'd that the strong
          statutes
Stand like the forfeits in a barber's shop,
As much in mock as mark.
Escal. Slander to the state! Away with him to
          prison!
Ang. What can you vouch against him, Signior
          Lucio?
Is this the man that you did tell us of?
Lucio. 'Tis he, my lord. Come hither, good-
man bald-pate. Do you know me?
Duke. I remember you, sir, by the sound of
your voice. I met you at the prison, in the ab-
sence of the duke.
Lucio. O did you so? And do you remember
what you said of the duke?
Duke. Most notedly, sir.
Lucio. Do you so, sir? And was the duke a
fleshmonger, a fool, and a coward, as you then
reported him to be?
Duke. You must, sir, change persons with me
ere you make that my report: you, indeed,
spoke so of him; and much more, much worse.
Lucio. O thou damnable fellow! Did not I
pluck thee by the nose for thy speeches?
Duke. I protest I love the duke as I love myself.
Ang. Hark how the villain would gloze now,
after his treasonable abuses!
Escal. Such a fellow is not to be talked withal.
Away with him to prison!—Where is the provost?—Away with him to prison! lay bolts
enough upon him: let him speak no more.—

Away with those giglots too, and with the
other confederate companion!
    [*The* PROVOST *lays hands on the* DUKE.
Duke. Stay, sir; stay awhile.
Ang. What! resists he?—Help him, Lucio.
Lucio. Come, sir; come, sir! come, sir; foh, sir.
Why, you bald-pated, lying rascal! you must
be hooded, must you? Show your knave's vis-
age, with a pox to you! show your sheep-biting
face, and be hanged an hour! Will't not off?
    [*Pulls off the Friar's hood, and discovers
        the* DUKE.
Duke. Thou art the first knave that e'er made
    a duke.——
First, Provost, let me bail these gentle three:——
Sneak not away, sir [*to* LUCIO]; for the friar
    and you
Must have a word anon:—Lay hold on him.
Lucio. This may prove worse than hanging.
Duke. What you have spoke I pardon; sit you
    down.——   [*To* ESCALUS.
We'll borrow place of him.—Sir, by your leave:
                [*To* ANGELO.
Hast thou or word, or wit, or impudence
That yet can do thee office? If thou hast,
Rely upon it till my tale be heard,
And hold no longer out.
Ang.   O my dread lord,
I should be guiltier than my guiltiness,
To think I can be undiscernible,
When I perceive your grace, like power divine,
Hath look'd upon my passes. Then, good prince,
No longer session hold upon my shame,
But let my trial be mine own confession:
Immediate sentence then, and sequent death
Is all the grace I beg.
Duke.   Come hither, Mariana:—
Say, wast thou e'er contracted to this woman?
Ang. I was, my lord.
Duke. Go, take her hence and marry her in-
    stantly.
Do you the office, friar; which consummate,
Return him here again.—Go with him, Provost.
    [*Exeunt* ANG., MARI., PET., *and* PROV.
Escal. My lord, I am more amazed at his dis-
    honour
Than at the strangeness of it.
Duke.   Come hither, Isabel:
Your friar is now your prince. As I was then
Advértising and holy to your business,
Not changing heart with habit, I am still
Attorney'd at your service.
Isab.   O give me pardon,
That I, your vassal, have employ'd and pain'd
Your unknown sovereignty.
Duke.   You are pardon'd, Isabel.
And now, dear maid, be you as free to us.
Your brother's death, I know, sits at your heart;
And you may marvel why I obscur'd myself,
Labouring to save his life, and would not rather
Make rash remonstrance of my hidden power
Than let him so be lost. O most kind maid,
It was the swift celerity of his death,
Which I did think with slower foot came on,

That brain'd my purpose. But peace be with
    him!
That life is better life, past fearing death,
Than that which lives to fear: make it your
    comfort,
So happy is your brother.
Isab.   I do, my lord.

Re-enter ANGELO, MARIANA, PETER, *and*
    PROVOST.

Duke. For this new-married man approaching
    here,
Whose salt imagination yet hath wrong'd
Your well-defended honour, you must pardon
For Mariana's sake: but as he adjudg'd your
    brother,—
Being criminal, in double violation
Of sacred chastity and of promise-breach
Thereon dependent, for your brother's life,—
The very mercy of the law cries out
Most audible, even from his proper tongue,
An Angelo for Claudio, death for death.
Haste still pays haste, and leisure answers
    leisure;
Like doth quit like, and measure still for
    measure.
Then, Angelo, thy fault thus manifested,—
Which though thou wouldst deny, denies thee
    vantage,—
We do condemn thee to the very block
Where Claudio stoop'd to death, and with like
    haste.—
Away with him.
Mari.   O my most gracious lord,
I hope you will not mock me with a husband!
Duke. It is your husband mock'd you with a
    husband.
Consenting to the safeguard of your honour,
I thought your marriage fit; else imputation,
For that he knew you, might reproach your life,
And choke your good to come: for his posses-
    sions,
Although by confiscation they are ours,
We do instate and widow you withal,
To buy you a better husband.
Mari.   O my dear lord,
I crave no other, nor no better man.
Duke. Never crave him; we are definitive.
Mari. Gentle, my liege,—   [*Kneeling.*
Duke.   You do but lose your labour.—
Away with him to death.—Now, sir [*to* LUCIO],
    to you.   [*part;*
Mari. O my good lord!—Sweet Isabel, take my
Lend me your knees, and all my life to come
I'll lend you all my life to do you service.
Duke. Against all sense you do impórtune her:
Should she kneel down, in mercy of this fact,
Her brother's ghost his pavèd bed would break,
And take her hence in horror.
Mari.   Isabel,
Sweet Isabel, do yet but kneel by me;
Hold up your hands, say nothing,—I'll speak all.
They say, best men are moulded out of faults:

And, for the most, become much more the better
For being a little bad: so may my husband.
O Isabel, will you not lend a knee?
Duke. He dies for Claudio's death.
Isab.　　　　　　　Most bounteous sir, [*Kneeling.*
Look, if it please you, on this man condemn'd,
As if my brother liv'd: I partly think
A due sincerity govern'd his deeds
Till he did look on me; since it is so,
Let him not die. My brother had but justice,
In that he did the thing for which he died:
For Angelo,
His act did not o'ertake his bad intent,
And must be buried but as an intent　[jects;
That perish'd by the way: thoughts are no sub-
Intents but merely thoughts.
Mari.　　　　　　　　　Merely, my lord.
Duke. Your suit's unprofitable; stand up, I
　　say.—
I have bethought of another fault.—
Provost, how came it Claudio was beheaded
At an unusual hour?
Prov.　　　　　　　It was commanded so.
Duke. Had you a special warrant for the deed?
Prov. No, my good lord; it was by private
　　message.
Duke. For which I do discharge you of your
　　office:
Give up your keys.
Prov.　　　　　　Pardon me, noble lord:
I thought it was a fault, but knew it not;
Yet did repent me, after more advice:
For testimony whereof, one in the prison,
That should by private order else have died,
I have reserved alive.
Duke.　　　　　　What's he?
Prov.　　　　　　His name is Barnardine.
Duke. I would thou hadst done so by Claudio.—
Go fetch him hither; let me look upon him.
　　　　　　　　　　　　[*Exit* PROVOST.
Escal. I am sorry one so learned and so wise
As you, Lord Angelo, have still appear'd,
Should slip so grossly, both in the heat of blood
And lack of temper'd judgment afterward.
Ang. I am sorry that such sorrow I procure:
And so deep sticks it in my penitent heart
That I crave death more willingly than mercy;
Tis my deserving, and I do entreat it.

　　Re-enter PROVOST, *with* BARNARDINE,

　　CLAUDIO (*muffled*), *and* JULIET.

Duke. Which is that Barnardine?
Prov.　　　　　　　　This, my lord.
Duke. There was a friar told me of this man:—
Sirrah, thou art said to have a stubborn soul,
That apprehends no further than this world,
And squar'st thy life according. Thou 'rt con-
　　demn'd;
But, for those earthly faults, I quit them all,
And pray thee take this mercy to provide
For better times to come:——Friar, advise him;
I leave him to your hand.—What muffled fel-
　　low's that?

Prov. This is another prisoner that I sav'd,
Who should have died when Claudio lost his
　　head;
As like almost to Claudio as himself.
　　　　　　　　　　　[*Unmuffles* CLAUDIO.
Duke. If he be like your brother, [*to* ISABELLA],
　　for his sake
Is he pardon'd; and, for your lovely sake,
Give me your hand, and say you will be mine;
He is my brother too: but fitter time for that.
By this Lord Angelo perceives he's safe;
Methinks I see a quick'ning in his eye.—
Well, Angelo, your evil quits you well:
Look that you love your wife; her worth worth
　　yours.—
I find an apt remission in myself;
And yet here's one in place I cannot pardon.—
You, sirrah [*to* LUCIO], that knew me for a
　　fool, a coward,
One all of luxury, an ass, a madman;
Wherein have I so deserved of you
That you extol me thus?
Lucio. 'Faith, my lord, I spoke it but accord-
ing to the trick. If you will hang me for it, you
may; but I had rather it would please you I
might be whipped.
Duke. Whipp'd first, sir, and hang'd after.—
Proclaim it, Provost, round about the city,
If any woman's wrong'd by this lewd fellow,—
As I have heard him swear himself there's one
Whom he begot with child,—let her appear,
And he shall marry her: the nuptial finish'd,
Let him be whipp'd and hang'd.
Lucio. I beseech your highness, do not marry
me to a whore! Your highness said even now I
made you a duke; good my lord, do not recom-
pense me in making me a cuckold.
Duke. Upon mine honour, thou shalt marry her.
Thy slanders I forgive; and therewithal
Remit thy other forfeits.—Take him to prison;
And see our pleasure herein executed.
Lucio. Marrying a punk, my lord, is pressing
to death, whipping, and hanging.
Duke. Slandering a prince deserves it.—
　　　　　　　　　[*Exeunt Officers with* LUCIO.
She, Claudio, that you wrong'd, look you re-
　　store.—
Joy to you, Mariana!—Love her, Angelo;
I have confess'd her, and I know her virtue.—
Thanks, good friend Escalus, for thy much
　　goodness
There's more behind that is more gratulate.
Thanks, Provost, for thy care and secrecy;
We shall employ thee in a worthier place.—
Forgive him, Angelo, that brought you home
The head of Ragozine for Claudio's:
The offence pardons itself.—Dear Isabel,
I have a motion much imports your good;
Whereto if you'll a willing ear incline,
What's mine is yours, and what is yours is
　　mine:—
So, bring us to our palace; where we'll show
What's yet behind that's meet you all should
　　know.　　　　　　　　　　[*Exeunt.*

MUCH ADO ABOUT NOTHING

DRAMATIS PERSONÆ

DON PEDRO, *Prince of Arragon.*
DON JOHN, *his bastard Brother.*
CLAUDIO, *a young Lord of Florence, favourite to* DON PEDRO.
BENEDICK, *a young Lord of Padua, favourite likewise of* DON PEDRO.
LEONATO, *Governor of Messina.*
ANTONIO, *his Brother.*
BALTHAZAR, *Servant to* DON PEDRO.
BORACHIO, ⎱ *Followers of* DON JOHN.
CONRADE, ⎰

DOGBERRY, ⎱ *two foolish Officers.*
VERGES, ⎰
A SEXTON.
A FRIAR.
A BOY.

HERO, *Daughter to* LEONATO.
BEATRICE, *Niece to* LEONATO.
MARGARET, ⎱ *Gentlewomen attending on*
URSULA, ⎰ HERO.

Messengers,.Watch, *and* Attendants.

SCENE,—MESSINA

ACT I.

SCENE I.—*Before* LEONATO'S *House.*

Enter LEONATO, HERO, BEATRICE, *and others, with a* Messenger.

Leon. I learn in this letter that Don Pedro of Arragon comes this night to Messina.

Mess. He is very near by this; he was not three leagues off when I left him.

Leon. How many gentlemen have you lost in this action?

Mess. But few of any sort, and none of name.

Leon. A victory is twice itself when the achiever brings home full numbers. I find here that Don Pedro hath bestowed much honour on a young Florentine called Claudio.

Mess. Much deserved on his part, and equally remembered by Don Pedro. He hath borne himself beyond the promise of his age; doing, in the figure of a lamb, the feats of a lion: he hath, indeed, better bettered expectation than you must expect of me to tell you how.

Leon. He hath an uncle here in Messina will be very much glad of it.

Mess. I have already delivered him letters, and there appears much joy in him; even so much that joy could not show itself modest enough without a badge of bitterness.

Leon. Did he break out into tears?

Mess. In great measure.

Leon. A kind overflow of kindness. There are no faces truer than those that are so washed. How much better is it to weep at joy than to joy at weeping?

Beat. I pray you, is Signior Montanto returned from the wars or no?

Mess. I know none of that name, lady; there was none such in the army of any sort.

Leon. What is he that you ask for, niece?

Hero. My cousin means Signior Benedick of Padua.

Mess. O, he is returned, and as pleasant as ever he was.

Beat. He set up his bills here in Messina, and challenged Cupid at the flight: and my uncle's fool, reading the challenge, subscribed for Cupid, and challenged him at the bird-bolt.— I pray you, how many hath he killed and eaten in these wars? But how many hath he killed? for, indeed, I promised to eat all of his killing.

Leon. Faith, niece, you tax Signior Benedick too much; but he'll be meet with you, I doubt it not.

Mess. He hath done good service, lady, in these wars.

Beat. You had musty victual, and he hath holp to eat it: he is a very valiant trencherman; he hath an excellent stomach.

Mess. And a good soldier too, lady.

Beat. And a good soldier to a lady: but what is he to a lord?

Mess. A lord to a lord, a man to a man; stuffed with all honourable virtues.

Beat It is so, indeed: he is no less than a stuffed man: but for the stuffing,—well, we are all mortal.

Leon. You must not, sir, mistake my niece: there is a kind of merry war betwixt Signior Benedick and her: they never meet but there is a skirmish of wit between them.

Beat. Alas, he gets nothing by that. In our last conflict four of his five wits went halting off, and now is the old man governed with one: so that if he have wit enough to keep himself warm, let him bear it for a difference between himself and his horse; for it is all the wealth that he hath left, to be known a reasonable creature.—Who is his companion now? He hath every month a new sworn brother.

Mess. Is it possible?

Beat. Very easily possible: he wears his faith but as the fashion of his hat; it ever changes with the next block.

Mess. I see, lady, the gentleman is not in your books.

Beat. No: an he were I would burn my study. But, I pray you, who is his companion? Is there no young squarer, now, that will make a voyage with him to the devil?

Mess. He is most in the company of the right noble Claudio.

Beat. O Lord! he will hang upon him like a disease: he is sooner caught than the pestilence, and the taker runs presently mad. God help the noble Claudio! if he have caught the Benedick, it will cost him a thousand pound ere he be cured.

Mess. I will hold friends with you, lady.

Beat. Do, good friend.

Leon. You will never run mad, niece.

Beat. No, not till a hot January.

Mess. Don Pedro is approached.

Enter DON PEDRO, *attended by* BALTHAZAR *and others,* DON JOHN, CLAUDIO, *and* BENEDICK.

D. Pedro. Good Signior Leonato, you are come to meet your trouble: the fashion of the world is to avoid cost, and you encounter it.

Leon. Never came trouble to my house in the likeness of your grace; for trouble being gone, comfort should remain; but when you depart from me, sorrow abides, and happiness takes his leave.

D. Pedro. You embrace your charge too willingly.—I think this is your daughter.

Leon. Her mother hath many times told me so.

Bene. Were you in doubt, sir, that you asked her?   [a child.

Leon. Signior Benedick, no; for then were you

D. Pedro. You have it full, Benedick: we may guess by this what you are, being a man. Truly, the lady fathers herself.—Be happy, lady! for you are like an honourable father.

Bene. If Signior Leonato be her father, she would not have his head on her shoulders for all Messina, as like him as she is.

Beat. I wonder that you will still be talking, Signior Benedick; nobody marks you.

Bene. What, my dear lady Disdain! are you yet living?

Beat. Is it possible disdain should die while she hath such meet food to feed it as Signior Benedick? Courtesy itself must convert to disdain if you come in her presence.

Bene. Then is courtesy a turn-coat.—But it is certain I am loved of all ladies, only you excepted: and I would I could find in my heart that I had not a hard heart; for, truly, I love none.

Beat. A dear happiness to women; they would else have been troubled with a pernicious suitor. I thank God, and my cold blood, I am of your humour for that: I had rather hear my dog bark at a crow than a man swear he loves me.

Bene. God keep your ladyship still in that mind! so some gentleman or other shall 'scape a predestinate scratched face.

Beat. Scratching could not make it worse an 'twere such a face as yours were.

Bene. Well, you are a rare parrot-teacher.

Beat. A bird of my tongue is better than a beast of yours.

Bene. I would my horse had the speed of your tongue, and so good a continuer. But keep your way o' God's name; I have done.

Beat. You always end with a jade's trick; I know you of old.

D. Pedro. This is the sum of all: Leonato,—Signior Claudio, and Signior Benedick,—my dear friend Leonato hath invited you all. I tell him we shall stay here at the least a month; and he heartily prays some occasion may detain us longer: I dare swear he is no hypocrite, but prays from his heart.

Leon. If you swear, my lord, you shall not be forsworn.—Let me bid you welcome, my lord: being reconciled to the prince your brother, I owe you all duty.

D. John. I thank you: I am not of many words, but I thank you.

Leon. Please it your grace lead on?

D. Pedro. Your hand, Leonato; we will go together.   [*Exeunt all but* BENE., *and* CLAUD.

Claud. Benedick, didst thou note the daughter of Signior Leonato?

Bene. I noted her not, but I looked on her.

Claud. Is she not a modest young lady?

Bene. Do you question me, as an honest man should do, for my simple true judgment; or would you have me speak after my custom, as being a professed tyrant to their sex?

Claud. No, I pray thee, speak in sober judgment.

Bene. Why, i' faith, methinks she is too low for a high praise, too brown for a fair praise, and too little for a great praise: only this commendation I can afford her; that were she other than she is, she were unhandsome; and being no other but as she is, I do not like her.

Claud. Thou thinkest I am in sport: I pray thee, tell me truly how thou likest her.

Bene. Would you buy her, that you inquire after her?

Claud. Can the world buy such a jewel?

Bene. Yea, and a case to put it into. But speak you this with a sad brow? or do you play the floating Jack, to tell us Cupid is a good harefinder, and Vulcan a rare carpenter? Come, in what key shall a man take you to go in the song?

Claud. In mine eye, she is the sweetest lady that ever I looked on.

Bene. I can see yet without spectacles, and I see no such matter: there's her cousin, an she were not possessed with a fury, exceeds her as much in beauty as the first of May doth the last of December. But I hope you have no intent to turn husband, have you?

Claud. I would scarce trust myself, though I had sworn the contrary, if Hero would be my wife.

Bene. Is it come to this, i' faith? Hath not the world one man but he will wear his cap with suspicion? Shall I never see a bachelor of three-score again? Go to, i' faith; an thou wilt needs thrust thy neck into a yoke, wear the print of it, and sigh away Sundays. Look, Don Pedro is returned to seek you.

Re-enter DON PEDRO.

D. Pedro. What secret hath held you here, that you followed not to Leonato's?
Bene. I would your grace would constrain me to tell.
D. Pedro. I charge thee on thy allegiance.
Bene. You hear, Count Claudio: I can be secret as a dumb man,—I would have you think so; but on my allegiance,—mark you this,—on my allegiance:—He is in love. With who?—Now that is your grace's part.—Mark how short his answer is:—With Hero, Leonato's short daughter.
Claud. If this were so, so were it uttered.
Bene. Like the old tale, my lord: "It is not so, nor 'twas not so; but, indeed, God forbid it should be so."
Claud. If my passion change not shortly, God forbid it should be otherwise.
D. Pedro. Amen, if you love her; for the lady is very well worthy.
Claud. You speak this to fetch me in, my lord?
D. Pedro. By my troth, I speak my thought.
Claud. And, in faith, my lord, I spoke mine.
Bene. And, by my two faiths and troths, my lord, I spoke mine.
Claud. That I love her, I feel.
D. Pedro. That she is worthy, I know.
Bene. That I neither feel how she should be loved, nor know how she should be worthy, is the opinion that fire cannot melt out of me: I will die in it at the stake.
D. Pedro. Thou wast ever an obstinate heretic in the despite of beauty.
Claud. And never could maintain his part but in the force of his will.
Bene. That a woman conceived me, I thank her; that she brought me up, I likewise give her most humble thanks; but that I will have a recheat winded in my forehead, or hang my bugle in an invisible baldrick, all women shall pardon me. Because I will not do them the wrong to mistrust any, I will do myself the right to trust none; and the fine is,—for the which I may go the finer,—I will live a bachelor.
D. Pedro. I shall see thee, ere I die, look pale with love.
Bene. With anger, with sickness, or with hunger, my lord; not with love: prove that ever I lose more blood with love than I will get again with drinking, pick out mine eyes with a ballad-maker's pen, and hang me up at the door of a brothel-house, for the sign of blind Cupid.
D. Pedro. Well, if ever thou dost fall from this faith, thou wilt prove a notable argument.

Bene. If I do, hang me in a bottle like a cat, and shoot at me; and he that hits me, let him be clapped on the shoulder and called Adam.
D. Pedro. Well, as time shall try:
In time the savage bull doth bear the yoke.
Bene. The savage bull may; but if ever the sensible Benedick bear it, pluck off the bull's horns and set them in my forehead: and let me be vilely painted; and in such great letters as they write *Here is good horse to hire*, let them signify under my sign,—*Here you may see Benedick the married man.*
Claud. If this should ever happen, thou wouldst be horn-mad.
D. Pedro. Nay, if Cupid have not spent all his quiver in Venice, thou wilt quake for this shortly.
Bene. I look for an earthquake too, then.
D. Pedro. Well, you will temporise with the hours. In the meantime, good Signior Benedick, repair to Leonato's; commend me to him, and tell him I will not fail him at supper; for, indeed, he hath made great preparation.
Bene. I have almost matter enough in me for such an embassage; and so I commit you—
Claud. To the tuition of God: From my house, —if I had it—
D. Pedro. The sixth of July. Your loving friend, Benedick.
Bene. Nay, mock not, mock not. The body of your discourse is sometime guarded with fragments, and the guards are but slightly basted on neither: ere you flout old ends any further, examine your conscience; and so I leave you.
                                        [*Exit* BENEDICK.
Claud. My liege, your highness now may do me good.
D. Pedro. My love is thine to teach; teach it but how,
And thou shalt see how apt it is to learn
Any hard lesson that may do thee good.
Claud. Hath Leonato any son, my lord?
D. Pedro. No child but Hero, she's his only heir:
Dost thou affect her, Claudio?
Claud.   O my lord,
When you went onward on this ended action,
I looked upon her with a soldier's eye,
That liked, but had a rougher task in hand
Than to drive liking to the name of love:
But now I am return'd, and that war-thoughts
Have left their places vacant, in their rooms
Come thronging soft and delicate desires,
All prompting me how fair young Hero is,
Saying, I liked her ere I went to wars.
D. Pedro. Thou wilt be like a lover presently,
And tire the hearer with a book of words:
If thou dost love fair Hero, cherish it;
And I will break with her, and with her father,
And thou shalt have her. Was't not to this end
That thou began'st to twist so fine a story?
Claud. How sweetly do you minister to love,
That know love's grief by his complexion!
But lest my liking might too sudden seem,
I would have slav'd it with a longer treatise.

D. Pedro. What need the bridge much broader
    than the flood!
The fairest grant is the necessity.
Look, what will serve is fit: 'tis once, thou lov'st;
And I will fit thee with the remedy.
I know we shall have revelling to-night;
I will assume thy part in some disguise,
And tell fair Hero I am Claudio;
And in her bosom I'll unclasp my heart,
And take her hearing prisoner with the force
And strong encounter of my amorous tale:
Then, after, to her father will I break;
And the conclusion is, she shall be thine:
In practice let us put it presently.   [*Exeunt.*

SCENE II.--*A Room in* LEONATO'S *House.*

Enter, severally, LEONATO *and* ANTONIO.

Leon. How now, brother! Where is my cousin,
your son? Hath he provided this music?
Ant. He is very busy about it. But, brother, I
can tell you strange news that you yet dreamed
not of.
Leon. Are they good?
Ant. As the event stamps them; but they have
a good cover; they show well outward. The
prince and Count Claudio, walking in a thick-
pleached alley in my orchard, were thus much
overheard by a man of mine: the prince discovered to Claudio that he loved my niece your
daughter, and meant to acknowledge it this
night in a dance; and, if he found her accord-
ant, he meant to take the present time by the
top, and instantly break with you of it.
Leon. Hath the fellow any wit that told you
this?
Ant. A good sharp fellow; I will send for him,
and question him yourself.
Leon. No, no; we will hold it as a dream, till
it appear itself:—but I will acquaint my daughter withal, that she may be the better prepared
for an answer, if peradventure this be true.
Go you and tell her of it. [*Several persons cross
the stage.*] Cousins, you know what you have to
do.—O, I cry you mercy, friend: you go with
me, and I will use your skill.—Good cousin,
have a care this busy time.   [*Exeunt.*

SCENE III.—*Another Room in* LEONATO'S
House.

Enter DON JOHN *and* CONRADE.

Con. What the good-year, my lord! why are
you thus out of measure sad?
D. John. There is no measure in the occasion
that breeds it; therefore the sadness is without
limit.
Con. You should hear reason.
D. John. And when I have heard it, what
blessing bringeth it?   [sufferance.
Con. If not a present remedy, yet a patient
D. John. I wonder that thou, being—as thou
say'st thou art—born under Saturn, goest about
to apply a moral medicine to a mortifying mischief. I cannot hide what I am: I must be sad
when I have cause, and smile at no man's jests;

eat when I have stomach, and wait for no man's
leisure; sleep when I am drowsy, and 'tend to
no man's business; laugh when I am merry, and
claw no man in his humour.
Con. Yea, but you must not make the full
show of this till you may do it without controlment. You have of late stood out against your
brother, and he hath ta'en you newly into his
grace; where it is impossible you should take
true root but by the fair weather that you make
yourself: it is needful that you frame the season for your own harvest.
D. John. I had rather be a canker in a hedge
than a rose in his grace; and it better fits my
blood to be disdained of all than to fashion a
carriage to rob love from any: in this, though
I cannot be said to be a flattering honest man,
it must be not be denied that I am a plain-dealing
villain. I am trusted with a muzzle and enfranchised with a clog: therefore I have decreed not
to sing in my cage. If I had my mouth I would
bite; If I had my liberty I would do my liking:
in the meantime let me be that I am, and seek
not to alter me.
Con. Can you make no use of your discontent?
D. John. I make all use of it, for I use it only.
Who comes here? What news, Borachio?

Enter BORACHIO.

Bora. I came yonder from a great supper: the
prince, your brother, is royally entertained by
Leonato; and I can give you intelligence of an
intended marriage.
D. John. Will it serve for any model to build
mischief on? What is he for a fool that betroths
himself to unquietness?
Bora. Marry, it is your brother's right hand.
D. John. Who! the most exquisite Claudio?
Bora. Even he.
D. John. A proper squire! And who, and who?
which way looks he?
Bora. Marry, on Hero, the daughter and heir
of Leonato.
D. John. A very forward March-chick! How
came you to this?
Bora. Being entertained for a perfumer, as I
was smoking a musty room, comes me the
prince and Claudio hand in hand, in sad conference. I whipt me behind the arras, and there
heard it agreed upon that the prince should
woo Hero for himself, and, having obtained
her, give her to Count Claudio.
D. John. Come, come, let us thither; this may
prove food to my displeasure: that young start-
up hath all the glory of my overthrow. If I
can cross him any way, I bless myself every
way. You are both sure, and will assist me?
Con. To the death, my lord.
D. John. Let us to the great supper: their
cheer is the greater that I am subdued. Would
the cook were of my mind!—Shall we go prove
what's to be done?
Bora. We'll wait upon your lordship. [*Exeunt.*

ACT II.

SCENE I.—*A Hall in* LEONATO'S *House.*

Enter LEONATO, ANTONIO, HERO, BEATRICE,
and others.

Leon. Was not Count John here at supper?
Ant. I saw him not.
Beat. How tartly that gentleman looks! I never can see him but I am heart-burned an hour after.
Hero. He is of a very melancholy disposition.
Beat. He were an excellent man that were made just in the mid-way between him and Benedick: the one is too like an image, and says nothing; and the other too like my lady's eldest son, evermore tattling.
Leon. Then half Signior Benedick's tongue in Count John's mouth, and half Count John's melancholy in Signior Benedick's face,—
Beat. With a good leg and a good foot, uncle, and money enough in his purse, such a man would win any woman in the world,—if he could get her good-will.
Leon. By my troth, niece, thou wilt never get thee a husband if thou be so shrewd of thy tongue.
Ant. In faith, she is too curst.
Beat. Too curst is more than curst. I shall lessen God's sending that way: for it is said, *God sends a curst cow short horns;* but to a cow too curst he sends none.
Leon. So, by being too curst, God will send you no horns.
Beat. Just if he send me no husband; for the which blessing I am at him upon my knees every morning and evening. Lord! I could not endure a husband with a beard on his face: I had rather lie in the woollen.
Leon. You may light upon a husband that hath no beard.
Beat. What should I do with him? dress him in my apparel, and make him my waiting gentlewoman? He that hath a beard is more than a youth; and he that hath no beard is less than a man: and he that is more than a youth is not for me; and he that is less than a man I am not for him: therefore I will even take sixpence in earnest of the bear-ward, and lead his apes into hell.
Leon. Well then, go you into hell?
Beat. No; but to the gate; and there will the devil meet me, like an old cuckold, with horns on his head, and say, *Get you to heaven, Beatrice; get you to heaven: here's no place for you maids:* so deliver I up my apes and away to Saint Peter for the heavens; he shows me where the bachelors sit, and there live we as merry as the day is long.
Ant. Well, niece [*to* HERO], I trust you will be ruled by your father.
Beat. Yes, faith; it's my cousin's duty to make courtesy, and say, *Father, as it please you:*—but yet for all that, cousin, let him be a handsome fellow, or else make another courtesy, and say, *Bather, as it please me.*
Leon. Well, niece, I hope to see you one day fitted with a husband.
Feat. Not till God make men of some other metal than earth. Would it not grieve a woman to be over-mastered with a piece of valiant dust! to make an account of her life to a clod of wayward marl? No, uncle, I'll none: Adam's sons are my brethren; and, truly, I hold it a sin to match in my kindred.
Leon. Daughter, remember what I told you: if the prince do solicit you in that kind, you know your answer.
Beat. The fault will be in the music, cousin, if you be not wooed in good time: if the prince be too important, tell him there is measure in everything, and so dance out the answer. For, hear me, Hero, wooing, wedding, and repenting is as a Scotch jig, a measure, and a cinque-pace: the first suit is hot and hasty, like a Scotch jig, and full as fantastical; the wedding, mannerly modest as a measure, full of state and ancientry; and then comes repentance, and, with his bad legs, falls into the cinque-pace faster and faster, till he sink into his grave.
Leon. Cousin, you apprehend passing shrewdly.
Beat. I have a good eye, uncle; I can see a church by daylight.
Leon. The revellers are entering, brother; make good room.

Enter DON PEDRO, CLAUDIO, BENEDICK, BALTHAZAR; DON JOHN, BORACHIO, MARGARET, URSULA, *and others, masked.*

D. Pedro. Lady, will you walk about with your friend?
Hero. So you walk softly, and look sweetly, and say nothing, I am yours for the walk; and, especially, when I walk away.
D. Pedro. With me in your company?
Hero. I may say so, when I please.
D. Pedro. And when please you to say so?
Hero. When I like your favour; for God defend the lute should be like the case!
D. Pedro. My visor is Philemon's roof; within the house is Jove.
Hero. Why, then, your visor should be thatched.
D. Pedro. Speak low, if you speak love.
                                    [*Takes her aside.*
Balth. Well, I would you did like me.
Marg. So would not I, for your own sake; for I have many ill qualities.
Balth. Which is one?
Marg. I say my prayers aloud.
Balth. I love you the better; the hearers may cry Amen.
Marg. God match me with a good dancer!
Balth. Amen.
Marg. And God keep him out of my sight when the dance is done!—Answer, clerk.
Balth. No more words; the clerk is answered.
Urs. I know you well enough; you are Signior Antonio.

Ant. At a word, I am not.

Urs. I know you by the waggling of your head.

Ant. To tell you true, I counterfeit him.

Urs. You could never do him so ill-well unless you were the very man. Here's his dry hand up and down: you are he; you are he.

Ant. At a word, I am not.

Urs. Come, come; do you think I do not know you by your excellent wit? Can virtue hide itself? Go to; mum; you are he: graces will appear, and there's an end.

Beat. Will you not tell me who told you so?

Bene. No, you shall pardon me.

Beat. Nor will you not tell me who you are?

Bene. Not now.

Beat. That I was disdainful!—and that I had my good wit out of the *Hundred Merry Tales!*— Well, this was Signior Benedick that said so.

Bene. What's he?

Beat. I am sure you know him well enough.

Bene. Not I, believe me.

Beat. Did he never make you laugh?

Bene. I pray you, what is he?

Beat. Why, he is the prince's jester: a very dull fool; only his gift is in devising impossible slanders: none but libertines delight in him; and the commendation is not in his wit but in his villany; for he both pleaseth men and angers them, and then they laugh at him and beat him. I am sure he is in the fleet: I would he had boarded me.

Bene. When I know the gentleman I'll tell him what you say.

Beat. Do, do: he'll but break a comparison or two on me; which, peradventure, not marked, or not laughed at, strikes him into melancholy; and then there's a partridge wing saved, for the fool will eat no supper that night. [*Music within.*] We must follow the leaders.

Bene. In every good thing.

Beat. Nay, if they lead to any ill, I will leave them at the next turning.

[*Dance. Then exeunt all but* DON JOHN, BORACHIO, *and* CLAUDIO.

D. John. Sure, my brother is amorous on Hero, and hath withdrawn her father to break with him about it. The ladies follow her, and but one visor remains.   [bearing.

Bora. And that is Claudio. I know him by his

D. John. Are not you Signior Benedick?

Claud. You know me well; I am he.

D. John. Signior, you are very near my brother in his love: he is enamoured on Hero; I pray you dissuade him from her; she is no equal for his birth: you may do the part of an honest man in it.

Claud. How know you he loves her?

D. John. I heard him swear his affection.

Bora. So did I too; and he swore he would marry her to-night.

D. John. Come, let us to the banquet.

[*Exeunt* DON JOHN *and* BORACHIO.

Claud. Thus answer I in name of Benedick, But hear these ill news with the ears of Claudio.

'Tis certain so;—the prince woos for himself. Friendship is constant in all other things Save in the office and affairs of love: Therefore, all hearts in love use their own tongues: Let every eye negotiate for itself, And trust no agent: for beauty is a witch, Against whose charms faith melteth into blood. This is an accident of hourly proof,   [Hero! Which I mistrusted not: farewell, therefore,

Re-enter BENEDICK.

Bene. Count Claudio?

Claud. Yea, the same.

Bene. Come, will you go with me?

Claud. Whither?

Bene. Even to the next willow, about your own business, count. What fashion will you wear the garland of? About your neck, like an usurer's chain? or under your arm like a lieutenant's scarf? You must wear it one way, for the prince hath got your Hero.

Claud. I wish him joy of her.

Bene. Why, that's spoken like an honest drover; so they sell bullocks. But did you think the prince would have served you thus?

Claud. I pray you, leave me.

Bene. Ho! now you strike like the blind man; 'twas the boy that stole your meat, and you'll beat the post.

Claud. If it will not be, I'll leave you. [*Exit.*

Bene. Alas, poor hurt fowl! Now will he creep into sedges.——But, that my Lady Beatrice should know me, and not know me! The prince's fool!—Ha, it may be I go under that title because I am merry.—Yea, but so I am apt to do myself wrong; I am not so reputed: it is the base, the bitter disposition of Beatrice that puts the world into her person, and so gives me out. Well, I'll be revenged as I may.

Re-enter DON PEDRO.

D. Pedro. Now, signior, where's the count? Did you see him?

Bene. Troth, my lord, I have played the part of Lady Fame. I found him here as melancholy as a lodge in a warren; I told him, and I think I told him true, that your grace had got the good-will of this young lady; and I offered him my company to a willow tree, either to make him a garland, as being forsaken, or to bind him up a rod, as being worthy to be whipped.

D. Pedro. To be whipped! What's his fault?

Bene. The flat transgression of a school-boy, who, being overjoyed with finding a bird's nest, shows it his companion, and he steals it.

D. Pedro. Wilt thou make a trust a transgression? The transgression is in the stealer.

Bene. Yet it had not been amiss the rod had been made, and the garland too; for the garland he might have worn himself; and the rod he might have bestowed on you, who, as I take it, have stolen his bird's nest.

D. Pedro. I will but teach them to sing, and restore them to the owner.

Bene. If their singing answer your saying, by my faith, you say honestly.

D. Pedro. The Lady Beatrice hath a quarrel to you; the gentleman that danced with her told her she is much wronged by you.

Bene. O, she misused me past the endurance of a block; an oak but with one green leaf on it would have answered her; my very visor began to assume life and scold with her: she told me,—not thinking I had been myself,—that I was the prince's jester; that I was duller than a great thaw; huddling jest upon jest with such impossible conveyance upon me, that I stood like a man at a mark, with a whole army shooting at me. She speaks poniards, and every word stabs: if her breath were as terrible as her terminations, there were no living near her; she would infect to the north star. I would not marry her though she were endowed with all that Adam had left him before he transgressed: she would have made Hercules have turned spit; yea, and have cleft his club to make the fire too. Come, talk not of her: you shall find her the infernal Até in good apparel. I would to God some scholar would conjure her; for certainly, while she is here, a man may live as quiet in hell as in a sanctuary; and people sin upon purpose, because they would go thither; so, indeed, all disquiet, horror, and perturbation follows her.

D. Pedro. Look, here she comes.

Re-enter CLAUDIO *and* BEATRICE, LEONATO *and* HERO.

Bene. Will your grace command me any service to the world's end? I will go on the slightest errand now to the antipodes that you can devise to send me on; I will fetch you a toothpicker now from the farthest inch of Asia; bring you the length of Prester John's foot; fetch you a hair off the great Cham's beard; do you any embassage to the Pigmies;—rather than hold three words' conference with this harpy. You have no employment for me?

D. Pedro. None, but to desire your good company.

Bene. O God, sir, here's a dish I love not; I cannot endure my Lady Tongue.   [*Exit.*

D. Pedro. Come, lady, come; you have lost the heart of Signior Benedick.

Beat. Indeed, my lord, he lent it me awhile; and I gave him use for it,—a double heart for his single one: marry, once before he won it of me with false dice, therefore your grace may well say I have lost it.

D. Pedro. You have put him down, lady, you have put him down.

Beat. So I would not he should do me, my lord, lest I should prove the mother of fools. I have brought Count Claudio, whom you sent me to seek.   [are you sad?

D. Pedro. Why, how now, count! wherefore

Claud. Not sad, my lord.

D. Pedro. How then? Sick?

Claud. Neither, my lord.

Beat. The count is neither sad, nor sick, nor merry, nor well: but civil, count; civil as an orange, and something of that jealous complexion.

D. Pedro. I' faith, lady, I think your blazon to be true; though I'll be sworn, if he be so, his conceit is false. Here, Claudio, I have wooed in thy name, and fair Hero is won. I have broke with her father, and his good-will obtained: name the day of marriage, and God give thee joy!

Leon. Count, take of me my daughter, and with her my fortunes; his grace hath made the match, and all grace say Amen to it!

Beat. Speak, count, 'tis your cue.

Claud. Silence is the perfectest herald of joy: I were but little happy if I could say how much.—Lady, as you are mine, I am yours: I give away myself for you, and dote upon the exchange.

Beat. Speak, cousin; or, if you cannot, stop his mouth with a kiss, and let not him speak neither.   [heart.

D. Pedro. In faith, lady, you have a merry

Beat. Yea, my lord; I thank it, poor fool, it keeps on the windy side of care.—My cousin tells him in his ear that he is in her heart.

Claud. And so she doth, cousin.

Beat. Good lord, for alliance!—Thus goes every one to the world but I, and I am sunburnt; I may sit in a corner and cry heigh-ho! for a husband.

D. Pedro. Lady Beatrice, I will get you one.

Beat. I would rather have one of your father's getting. Hath your grace ne'er a brother like you? Your father got excellent husbands, if a maid could come by them.

D. Pedro. Will you have me, lady?

Beat. No, my lord, unless I might have another for working-days; your grace is too costly to wear every day. But, I beseech your grace, pardon me; I was born to speak all mirth and no matter.

D. Pedro. Your silence most offends me, and to be merry best becomes you; for, out of question, you were born in a merry hour.

Beat. No, sure, my lord, my mother cried; but then there was a star danced, and under that was I born. Cousins, God give you joy!

Leon. Niece, will you look to those things I told you of?

Beat. I cry you mercy, uncle.—By your grace's pardon.   [*Exit* BEATRICE.

D. Pedro. By my troth, a pleasant-spirited lady.

Leon. There's little of the melancholy element in her, my lord: she is never sad but when she sleeps; and not ever sad then; for I have heard my daughter say she hath often dreamed of unhappiness, and waked herself with laughing.

D. Pedro. She cannot endure to hear tell of a husband.

Leon. O, by no means; she mocks all her wooers out of suit.   [dick.

D. Pedro. She were an excellent wife for Bene-

Leon. O Lord, my lord, if they were but a week married, they would talk themselves mad.

D. Pedro. Count Claudio, when mean you to go to church?

Claud. To-morrow, my lord. Time goes on crutches till love have all his rites.

Leon. Not till Monday, my dear son, which is hence a just seven-night; and a time too brief too, to have all things answer my mind.

D. Pedro. Come, you shake the head at so long a breathing; but I warrant thee, Claudio, the time shall not go dully by us. I will in the interim undertake one of Hercules' labours; which is, to bring Signior Benedick and the Lady Beatrice into a mountain of affection the one with the other. I would fain have it a match; and I doubt not but to fashion it if you three will but minister such assistance as I shall give you direction.

Leon. My lord, I am for you, though it cost me ten nights' watchings.

Claud. And I, my lord.

D. Pedro. And you too, gentle Hero?

Hero. I will do any modest office, my lord, to help my cousin to a good husband.

D. Pedro. And Benedick is not the unhope-fullest husband that I know: thus far can I praise him; he is of a noble strain, of approved valour, and confirmed honesty. I will teach you how to humour your cousin that she shall fall in love with Benedick:—and I, with your two helps, will so practise on Benedick, that, in despite of his quick wit and his queasy stomach, he shall fall in love with Beatrice. If we can do this, Cupid is no longer an archer; his glory shall be ours, for we are the only love-gods. Go in with me, and I will tell you my drift.   [*Exeunt.*

SCENE II.—*Another Room in* LEONATO'S *House.*

Enter DON JOHN *and* BORACHIO.

D. John. It is so: the Count Claudio shall marry the daughter of Leonato.

Bora. Yea, my lord, but I can cross it.

D. John. Any bar, any cross, any impediment will be medicinal to me; I am sick in displeasure to him; and whatsoever comes athwart his affection ranges evenly with mine. How canst thou cross this marriage?

Bora. Not honestly, my lord; but so covertly that no dishonesty shall appear in me.

D. John. Show me briefly how.

Bora. I think I told your lordship a year since how much I am in the favour of Margaret, the waiting-gentlewoman to Hero.

D. John. I remember.

Bora. I can at any unseasonable instant of the night appoint her to look out at her lady's chamber-window.

D. John. What life is in that, to be the death of this marriage?

Bora. The poison of that lies in you to temper. Go you to the prince your brother; spare not to tell him that he hath wronged his honour in marrying the renownèd Claudio—whose estimation do you mightily hold up—to a contaminated stale, such a one as Hero.

D. John. What proof shall I make of that?

Bora. Proof enough to misuse the prince, to vex Claudio, to undo Hero, and kill Leonato. Look you for any other issue?

D. John. Only to despite them I will endeavour anything.

Bora. Go, then; find me a meet hour to draw Don Pedro and the Count Claudio alone: tell them that you know that Hero loves me; intend a kind of zeal both to the prince and Claudio, as,—in love of your brother's honour, who hath made this match, and his friend's reputation, who is thus like to be cozened with the semblance of a maid,—that you have discovered thus. They will scarcely believe this without trial: offer them instances; which shall bear no less likelihood than to see me at her chamber-window; hear me call Margaret Hero; hear Margaret term me Borachio; and bring them to see this the very night before the intended wedding: for, in the meantime I will so fashion the matter that Hero shall be absent; and there shall appear such seeming truth of Hero's disloyalty that jealousy shall be called assurance, and all the preparation overthrown.

D. John. Grow this to what adverse issue it can, I will put it in practice. Be cunning in the working this, and thy fee is a thousand ducats.

Bora. Be you constant in the accusation, and my cunning shall not shame me.

D. John. I will presently go learn their day of marriage.   [*Exeunt.*

SCENE III.—LEONATO'S *Garden.*

Enter BENEDICK *and a* Boy.

Bene. Boy,—

Boy. Signior.

Bene. In my chamber-window lies a book; bring it hither to me in the orchard.

Boy. I am here already, sir.

Bene. I know that; but I would have thee hence and here again. [*Exit* Boy.] I do much wonder that one man, seeing how much another man is a fool when he dedicates his behaviours to love, will, after he hath laughed at such shallow follies in others, become the argument of his own scorn by falling in love. And such a man is Claudio. I have known when there was no music with him but the drum and fife; and now had he rather hear the tabor and the pipe: I have known when he would have walked ten mile afoot to see a good armour; and now will he lie ten nights awake carving the fashion of a new doublet. He was wont to speak plain and to the purpose, like an honest

man and a soldier; and now is he turned or-
thographer; his words are a very fantastical
banquet, just so many strange dishes. May I
be so converted, and see with these eyes? I
cannot tell; I think not: I will not be sworn
but Love may transform me to an oyster; but
I'll take my oath on it, till he have made an
oyster of me he shall never make me such a
fool. One woman is fair; yet I am well: another
is wise; yet I am well: another virtuous; yet I
am well: but till all graces be in one woman,
one woman shall not come in my grace. Rich
she shall be, that's certain; wise, or I'll none;
virtuous, or I'll never cheapen her; fair, or I'll
never look on her; mild, or come not near me;
noble, or not I for an angel; of good discourse,
an excellent musician, and her hair shall be of
what colour it please God. Ha! the prince and
Monsieur Love! I will hide me in the arbour.
[*Withdraws.*

Enter DON PEDRO, LEONATO, *and* CLAUDIO.

D. Pedro. Come, shall we hear this music?
Claud. Yea, my good lord.—How still the eve-
ning is,
As hushed on purpose to grace harmóny!
D. Pedro. See you where Benedick hath hid
himself?
Claud. O, very well, my lord: the music ended,
We'll fit the kid-fox with a pennyworth.

Enter BALTHAZAR, *with Music.*

D. Pedro. Come, Balthazar, we'll hear that
song again.
Balth. O, good my lord, tax not so bad a voice
To slander music any more than once.
D. Pedro. It is the witness still of excellency
To put a strange face on his own perfection:—
I pray thee, sing, and let me woo no more.
Balth. Because you talk of wooing, I will sing:
Since many a wooer doth commence his suit
To her he thinks not worthy; yet he woos;
Yet will he swear he loves.
D. Pedro.   Nay, pray thee, come:
Or, if thou wilt hold longer argument,
Do it in notes.
Balth.   Note this before my notes,
There's not a note of mine that's worth the
noting.   [*he speaks;*
D. Pedro. Why, these are very crotchets that
Note notes, forsooth, and noting!   [*Music.*
Bene. Now, divine air! now is his soul ravished!
Is it not strange that sheeps' guts should hale
souls out of men's bodies?—Well, a horn for
my money, when all's done.

BALTHAZAR *sings.*

I.

Sigh no more, ladies, sigh no more;
    Men were deceivers ever;
One foot in sea and one on shore,
    To one thing constant never;
        Then sigh not so,
        But let them go,

And be you blithe and bonny;
Converting all your sounds of woe
Into. Hey nonny, nonny.

II.

Sing no more ditties, sing no mo
    Of dumps so dull and heavy;
The fraud of men was ever so
    Since summer first was leavy.
        Then sigh not so, &c.

D. Pedro. By my troth, a good song.
Balth. And an ill singer, my lord.
Claud. Ha, no; no, faith; thou singest well
enough for a shift.
Bene. [*Aside.*] An he had been a dog that
should have howled thus they would have
hanged him: and I pray God his bad voice
bode no mischief! I had as lief have heard the
night-raven, come what plague could have
come after it.
D. Pedro. Yea, marry [*to* CLAUDIO].—Dost
thou hear, Balthazar! I pray thee get us some
excellent music; for to-morrow night we would
have it at the lady Hero's chamber-window.
Balth. The best I can, my lord.
D. Pedro. Do so: farewell. [*Exeunt* BALTHAZAR
and Music.] Come hither, Leonato. What was
it you told me of to-day,—that your niece
Beatrice was in love with Signior Benedick?
Claud. O ay:—stalk on, stalk on: the fowl sits
[*aside to* PEDRO]. I did never think that lady
would have loved any man.
Leon. No, nor I neither; but most wonderful
that she should so dote on Signior Benedick,
whom she hath in all outward behaviours
seemed ever to abhor.
Bene. Is't possible? Sits the wind in that
corner?   [*Aside.*
Leon. By my troth, my lord, I cannot tell
what to think of it; but that she loves him with
an enraged affection,—it is past the infinite of
thought.
D. Pedro. May be she doth but counterfeit.
Claud. 'Faith, like enough.
Leon. O Good! counterfeit! There was never
counterfeit of passion came so near the life of
passion as she discovers it.
D. Pedro. Why, what effects of passion shows
she?
Claud. Bait the hook well; this fish will bite.
                           [*Aside.*
Leon. What effects, my lord! She will sit you,
—You heard my daughter tell you how.
Claud. She did, indeed.
D. Pedro. How, how, I pray you? You amaze
me: I would have thought her spirit had been
invincible against all assaults of affection.
Leon. I would have sworn it had, my lord; es-
pecially against Benedick.
Bene. [*Aside.*] I should think this a gull, but
that the white bearded fellow speaks it: knav-
ery cannot, sure, hide itself in such reverence.
Claud. He hath ta'en the infection; hold it up.
                           [*Aside.*

D. Pedro. Hath she made her affection known to Benedick.

Leon. No; and swears she never will: that's her torment.

Claud. 'Tis true, indeed; so your daughter says: *Shall I,* says she, *that have so oft encountered him with scorn, write to him that I love him?*

Leon. This says she now, when she is beginning to write to him: for she'll be up twenty times a night: and there will she sit in her smock till she have writ a sheet of paper:—my daughter tells us all.

Claud. Now you talk of a sheet of paper, I remember a pretty jest your daughter told us of.

Leon. O!—When she had writ it, and was reading it over, she found Benedick and Beatrice between the sheet?—

Claud. That.

Leon. O! she tore the letter into a thousand halfpence; railed at herself that she should be so immodest to write to one that she knew would flout her. *I measure him,* says she, *by my own spirit; for I should flout him if he writ to me; yea, though I love him, I should.*

Claud. Then down upon her knees she falls, weeps, sobs, beats her heart, tears her hair, prays, curses;—*O sweet Benedick! God give me patience!*

Leon. She doth indeed; my daughter says so; and the ecstasy hath so much overborne her that my daughter is sometime afraid she will do a desperate outrage to herself. It is very true.

D. Pedro. It were good that Benedick knew of it by some other, if she will not discover it.

Claud. To what end? He would but make a sport of it, and torment the poor lady worse.

D. Pedro. An he should, it were an alms to hang him. She's an excellent sweet lady; and, out of all suspicion, she is virtuous.

Claud. And she is exceeding wise.

D. Pedro. In everything but in loving Benedick.

Leon. O my lord, wisdom and blood combating in so tender a body, we have ten proofs to one that blood hath the victory. I am sorry for her, as I have just cause, being her uncle and her guardian.

D. Pedro. I would she had bestowed this dotage on me: I would have daffed all other respects and made her half myself. I pray you, tell Benedick of it, and hear what he will say.

Leon. Were it good, think you?

Claud. Hero thinks surely she will die; for she says she will die if he love her not; and she will die ere she makes her love known: and she will die if he woo her, rather than she will 'bate one breath of her accustomed crossness.

D. Pedro. She doth well; if she should make tender of her love, 'tis very possible he'll scorn it: for the man, as you know all, hath a contemptible spirit.

Claud. He is a very proper man.

D. Pedro. He hath, indeed, a good outward happiness.

Claud. 'Fore God, and in my mind, very wise.

D. Pedro. He doth, indeed, show some sparks that are like wit.

Leon. And I take him to be valiant.

D. Pedro. As Hector, I assure you: and in the managing of quarrels you may say he is wise; for either he avoids them with great discretion, or undertakes them with a most Christian-like fear.

Leon. If he do fear God, he must necessarily keep peace; if he break the peace, he ought to enter into a quarrel with fear and trembling.

D. Pedro. And so will he do; for the man doth fear God, howsoever it seems not in him by some large jests he will make. Well, I am sorry for your niece. Shall we go see Benedick, and tell him of her love?

Claud. Never tell him, my lord; let her wear it out with good counsel.

Leon. Nay, that's impossible; she may wear her heart out first.

D. Pedro. Well, we'll hear further of it by your daughter: let it cool the while. I love Benedick well: and I could wish he would modestly examine himself, to see how much he is unworthy to have so good a lady.

Leon. My lord, will you walk? dinner is ready.

Claud. If he do not dote on her upon this, I will never trust my expectation. [*Aside.*

D. Pedro. Let there be the same net spread for her: and that must your daughter and her gentlewoman carry. The sport will be when they hold one an opinion of another's dotage, and no such matter; that's the scene that I would see, which will be merely a dumb show. Let us send her to call him in to dinner. [*Aside.*
[*Exeunt* DON PEDRO, CLAUDIO, *and* LEONATO.

BENEDICK *advances from the arbour.*

Bene. This can be no trick. The conference was sadly borne.—They have the truth of this from Hero. They seem to pity the lady; it seems her affections have their full bent. Love me! why, it must be requited. I hear how I am censured: they say I will bear myself proudly if I perceive the love come from her; they say, too, that she will rather die than give any sign of affection.—I did never think to marry—I must not seem proud.—Happy are they that hear their detractions and can put them to mending. They say the lady is fair; 'tis a truth, I can bear them witness: and virtuous—'tis so, I cannot reprove it; and wise, but for loving me.—By my troth, it is no addition to her wit;—nor no great argument of her folly, for I will be horribly in love with her.—I may chance have some odd quirks and remnants of wit broken on me because I have railed so long against marriage; but doth not the appetite alter? A man loves the meat in his youth that he cannot endure in his age. Shall quips, and sentences, and these paper bullets of the brain awe a man from the career of his humour? No: the world must be peopled. When I said I would die a bachelor I did not think I should

live till I were married.—Here comes Beatrice.
By this day, she's a fair lady: I do spy some
marks of love in her.

Enter BEATRICE.

Beat. Against my will I am sent to bid you
come in to dinner.   [pains.
Bene. Fair Beatrice, I thank you for your
Beat. I took no more pains for those thanks
than you take pains to thank me; if it had
been painful I would not have come.
Bene. You take pleasure, then, in the message?
Beat. Yea, just so much as you may take upon
a knife's point, and choke a daw withal.—You
have no stomach, signior; fare you well. [*Exit.*
Bene. Ha! *Against my will I am sent to bid you
come to dinner*—there's a double meaning in
that. *I took no more pains for those thanks than
you took pains to thank me*—that's as much as
to say, Any pains that I take for you is as easy
as thanks.—If I do not take pity of her, I am
a villain; if I do not love her, I am a Jew: I
will go get her picture.   [*Exit.*

ACT III.

SCENE I.—LEONATO'S *Garden.*

Enter HERO, MARGARET, *and* URSULA.

Hero. Good Margaret, run thee into the parlour;
There shalt thou find my cousin Beatrice
Proposing with the prince and Claudio:
Whisper her ear, and tell her I and Ursula
Walk in the orchard, and our whole discourse
Is all of her; say that thou overheard'st us;
And bid her steal into the pleached bower,
Where honeysuckles, ripen'd by the sun,
Forbid the sun to enter;—like favourites,
Made proud by princes, that advance their pride
Against that power that bred it:—there will
          she hide her,
To listen our propose. This is thy office,
Bear thee well in it, and leave us alone.
Marg. I'll make her come, I warrant you,
presently.   [*Exit.*
Hero. Now, Ursula, when Beatrice doth come
As we do trace this alley up and down,
Our talk must only be of Benedick:
When I do name him, let it be thy part
To praise him more than ever man did merit:
My talk to thee must be how Benedick
Is sick in love with Beatrice. Of this matter
Is little Cupid's crafty arrow made,
That only wounds by hearsay. Now begin;

Enter BEATRICE, *behind.*

For look where Beatrice, like a lapwing, runs
Close by the ground, to hear our conference.
Urs. The pleasant'st angling is to see the fish
Cut with her golden oars the silver stream,
And greedily devour the treacherous bait:
So angle we for Beatrice; who even now
Is couched in the woodbine coverture:
Fear you not my part of the dialogue.

Hero. Then go we near her, that her ear lose
          nothing.
Of the false sweet bait that we lay for it.—
                    [*They advance to the bower.*
No, truly, Ursula, she is too disdainful;
I know her spirits are as coy and wild
As haggards of the rock.
Urs.   But are you sure
That Benedick loves Beatrice so entirely?
Hero. So says the prince and my new-trothed
lord.   [madam?
Urs. And did they bid you tell her of it,
Hero. They did entreat me to acquaint her
          of it;
But I persuaded them, if they lov'd Benedick,
To wish him wrestle with affection,
And never to let Beatrice know of it.   [man
Urs. Why did you so? Doth not the gentle-
Deserve as full, as fortunate a bed
As ever Beatrice shall couch upon?
Hero. O God of love! I know he doth deserve
As much as may be yielded to a man:
But nature never framed a woman's heart
Of prouder stuff than that of Beatrice:
Disdain and scorn ride sparkling in her eyes,
Misprizing what they look on; and her wit
Values itself so highly, that to her
All matter else seems weak: she cannot love,
Nor take no shape nor project of affection,
She is so self-endeared.
Urs.   Sure, I think so;
And therefore, certainly, it were not good
She knew his love, lest she make sport at it.
Hero. Why, you speak truth: I never yet saw
          man,   [tured,
How wise, how noble, young, how rarely fea-
But she would spell him backward: if fair-faced,
She'd swear the gentleman should be her sister;
If black, why, Nature, drawing of an antic,
Made a foul blot; if tall, a lance ill-headed;
If low, an agate very vilely cut:
If speaking, why, a vane blown with all winds;
If silent, why, a block moved with none.
So turns she every man the wrong side out;
And never gives to truth and virtue that
Which simpleness and merit purchaseth.
Urs. Sure, sure, such carping is not commend-
          able.   [ions
Hero. No: not to be so odd and from all fash-
As Beatrice is, cannot be commendable:
But who dare tell her so? If I should speak,
She'd mock me into air; O, she would laugh me
Out of myself, press me to death with wit.
Therefore let Benedick, like covered fire,
Consume away in sighs, waste inwardly:
It were a better death than die with mocks;
Which is as bad as die with tickling.
Urs. Yet tell her of it; hear what she will say.
Hero. No; rather I will go to Benedick
And counsel him to fight against his passion:
And truly, I'll devise some honest slanders
To stain my cousin with. One doth not know
How much an ill word may empoison liking.
Urs. O, do not do your cousin such a wrong.

She cannot be so much without true judgment,—
Having so swift and excellent a wit
As she is priz'd to have,—as to refuse
So rare a gentleman as Signior Benedick.
Hero. He is the only man of Italy,
Always excepted my dear Claudio.
Urs. I pray you be not angry with me, madam,
Speaking my fancy; Signior Benedick,
For shape, for bearing, argument, and valour,
Goes foremost in report through Italy.
Hero. Indeed, he hath an excellent good name.
Urs. His excellence did earn it ere he had it.—
When are you married, madam?   [go in;
Hero. Why, every day;—to-morrow. Come,
I'll show thee some attires, and have thy counsel
Which is the best to furnish me to-morrow.
Urs. [*Aside.*] She's lim'd, I warrant you; we
          have caught her, madam.
Hero. If it prove so, then loving goes by haps:
Some Cupid kills with arrows, some with traps.
          [*Exeunt* HERO *and* URSULA.

BEATRICE *advances.*

Beat. What fire is in mine ears? Can this be
          true?   [much?
     Stand I condemn'd for pride, and scorn so
Contempt, farewell! and maiden pride, adieu!
     No glory lives behind the back of such.
And, Benedick, love on; I will requite thee;
     Taming my wild heart to thy loving hand:
If thou dost love, my kindness shall incite thee
     To bind our loves up in a holy band:
For others say thou dost deserve, and I
Believe it better than reportingly.   [*Exit.*

SCENE II.—*A Room in* LEONATO'S *House.*

Enter DON PEDRO, CLAUDIO, BENEDICK, *and*
          LEONATO.

D. Pedro. I do but stay till your marriage be
consummate, and then I go toward Arragon.
Claud. I'll bring you thither, my lord, if you'll
vouchsafe me.
D. Pedro. Nay, that would be as great a soil
in the new gloss of your marriage as to show a
child his new coat, and forbid him to wear it.
I will only be bold with Benedick for his company; for, from the crown of his head to the
sole of his foot, he is all mirth; he hath twice
or thrice cut Cupid's bow-string, and the little
hangman dare not shoot at him: he hath a heart
as sound as a bell, and his tongue is the clapper;
for what his heart thinks his tongue speaks.
Bene. Gallans, I am not as I have been.
Leon. So say I; methinks you are sadder.
Claud. I hope he be in love.
D. Pedro. Hang him, truant; there's no true
drop of blood in him to be truly touched with
love: if he be sad he wants money.
Bene. I have the toothache.
D. Pedro. Draw it.
Bene. Hang it!
Claud. You must hang it first and draw it
afterwards.
D. Pedro. What, sigh for the toothache!

Leon. Where is but a humour or a worm!
Bene. Well, every one can master a grief but
he that has it.
Claud. Yet, say I, he is in love.
D. Pedro. There is no appearance of fancy in
him, unless it be a fancy that he hath to strange
disguises; as, to be a Dutchman to-day, a
Frenchman to-morrow, or in the shape of two
countries at once, as a German from the waist
downward, all slops, and a Spaniard from the
hip upward, no doublet. Unless he have a fancy
to this foolery, as it appears he hath, he is no
fool for fancy, as you would have it appear he is.
Claud. If he be not in love with some woman
there is no believing old signs: he brushes his
hat o'mornings: what should that bode?
D. Pedro. Hath any man seen him at the
barber's?
Claud. No, but the barber's man hath been
seen with him; and the old ornament of his
cheek hath already stuffed tennis-balls.
Leon. Indeed, he looks younger than he did,
by the loss of a beard.
D. Pedro. Nay, he rubs himself with civet.
Can you smell him out by that?
Claud. That's as much as to say the sweet
youth's in love.
D. Pedro. The greatest note of it is his mel-
ancholy.
Claud. And when was he wont to wash his face?
D. Pedro. Yea, or to paint himself? for the
which I hear what they say of him.
Claud. Nay, but his jesting spirit; which is
now crept into a lute-string, and now governed
by stops.
D. Pedro. Indeed, that tells a heavy tale for
him: conclude, conclude, he is in love.
Claud. Nay, but I know who loves him.
D. Pedro. That would I know too; I warrant
one that knows him not.
Claud. Yes, and his ill conditions; and, in de-
spite of all, dies for him.
D. Pedro. She shall be buried with her face
upwards.
Bene. Yet is this no charm for the toothache.
—Old signior, walk aside with me; I have
studied eight or nine wise words to speak to
you, which these hobby-horses must not hear.
          [*Exeunt* BENEDICK *and* LEONATO.
D. Pedro. For my life, to break with him about
Beatrice.
Claud. 'Tis even so: Hero and Margaret have
by this played their parts with Beatrice; and
then the two bears will not bite one another
when they meet.

Enter DON JOHN.

D. John. My lord and brother, God save you.
D. Pedro. Good den, brother.
D. John. If your leisure served, I would speak
with you.
D. Pedro. In private?
D. John. If it please you;—yet Count Claudio

may hear; for what I would speak of concerns him.

D. Pedro. What's the matter?

D. John. Means your lordship to be married to-morrow?   [*To* CLAUDIO.

D. Pedro. You know he does.

D. John. I know not that, when he knows what I know.

Claud. If there be any impediment, I pray you discover it.

D. John. You may think I love you not; let that appear hereafter, and aim better at me by that I now will manifest. For my brother, I think he holds you well, and in dearness of heart hath holp to effect your ensuing marriage; surely suit ill spent, and labour ill bestowed!

D. Pedro. Why, what's the matter?

D. John. I came hither to tell you: and, circumstances shortened,—for she hath been too long a-talking of,—the lady is disloyal.

Claud. Who? Hero?

D. John. Even she; Leonato's Hero, your Hero, every man's Hero.

Claud. Disloyal?

D. John. The word is too good to paint out her wickedness; I could say she were worse: think you of a worse title and I will fit her to it. Wonder not till further warrant: go but with me to-night, you shall see her chamber-window entered, even the night before her wedding-day: if you love her then, to-morrow wed her; but it would better fit your honour to change your mind.

Claud. May this be so?

D. Pedro. I will not think it.

D. John. If you dare not trust that you see, confess not that you know: if you will follow me I will show you enough; and when you have seen more, and heard more, proceed accordingly.

Claud. If I see anything to-night why I should not marry her to-morrow, in the congregation where I should wed, there will I shame her.

D. Pedro. And, as I wooed for thee to obtain her, I will join with thee to disgrace her.

D. John. I will disparage her no farther till you are my witnesses: bear it coldly but till midnight, and let the issue show itself.

D. Pedro. O day untowardly turned!

Claud. O mischief strangely thwarting!

D. John. O plague right well prevented! So will you say when you have seen the sequel.
                                        [*Exeunt.*

SCENE III.—*A Street.*

Enter DOGBERRY *and* VERGES, *with the* Watch.

Dogb. Are you good men and true?

Verg. Yea, or else it were pity but they should suffer salvation, body and soul.

Dogb. Nay, that were a punishment too good for them, if they should have any allegiance in them, being chosen for the prince's watch.

Verg. Well, give them their charge, neighbour Dogberry.

Dogb. First, who think you the most desertless man to be constable?

1 Watch. Hugh Oatcake, sir, or George Seacoal; for they can write and read.

Dogb. Come hither, neighbour Seacoal: God hath blessed you with a good name: to be a well-favoured man is the gift of fortune: but to write and read comes by nature.

2 Watch. Both which, master constable,——

Dogb. You have; I knew it would be your answer. Well, for your favour, sir, why, give God thanks, and make no boast of it; and for your writing and reading, let that appear when there is no need of such vanity. You are thought here to be the most senseless and fit man for the constable of the watch; therefore bear you the lantern. This is your charge;—you shall comprehend all vagrom men; you are to bid any man stand, in the prince's name.

2 Watch. How if'a will not stand?

Dogb. Why, then, take no note of him, but let him go; and presently call the rest of the watch together, and thank God you are rid of a knave.

Verg. If he will not stand when he is bidden, he is none of the prince's subjects.

Dogb. True, and they are to meddle with none but the prince's subjects.—You shall also make no noise in the streets; for for the watch to babble and talk is most tolerable and not to be endured.

2 Watch. We will rather sleep than talk; we know what belongs to a watch.

Dogb. Why, you speak like an ancient and most quiet watchman; for I cannot see how sleeping should offend: only, have a care that your bills be not stolen.—Well, you are to call at all the ale-houses, and bid them that are drunk get them to bed.

2 Watch. How if they will not?

Dogb. Why, then, let them alone till they are sober; if they make you not then the better answer, you may say they are not the men you took them for.

2 Watch. Well, sir.

Dogb. If you meet a thief, you may suspect him, by virtue of your office, to be no true man: and, for such kind of men, the less you meddle or make with them, why, the more is for your honesty.

2 Watch. If we know him to be a thief, shall we not lay hands on him?

Dogb. Truly, by your office you may; but I think they that touch pitch will be defiled: the most peaceable way for you, if you do take a thief, is to let him show himself what he is, and steal out of your company.

Verg. You have been always called a merciful man, partner.

Dogb. Truly, I would not hang a dog by my will; much more a man who hath any honesty in him.

Verg. If you hear a child cry in the night you must call to the nurse and bid her still it.

2 Watch. How if the nurse be asleep and will not hear us?

Dogb. Why, then, depart in peace, and let the child .wake her with crying: for the ewe that will not hear her lamb when it baas will never answer a calf when he bleats.

Verg. 'Tis very true.

Dogb. This is the end of the charge. You, constable, are to present the prince's own person; if you meet the prince in the night you may stay him.

Verg. Nay, by'r lady, that I think'a cannot.

Dogb. Five shillings to one on 't, with any man that knows the statues, he may stay him: marry, not without the prince be willing: for, indeed, the watch ought to offend no man; and it is an offence to stay a man against his will.

Verg. By'r lady, I think it be so.

Dogb. Ha, ha, ha! Well, masters, good night: an there be any matter of weight chances, call up me: keep your fellows' counsels and your own, and good night.—Come, neighbour.

2 Watch. Well, masters, we hear our charge: let us go sit here upon the church-bench till two, and then all to bed.

Dogb. One word more, honest neighbours: I pray you, watch about Signior Leonato's door; for the wedding being there to-morrow, there is a great coil to-night. Adieu, be vigilant, I beseech you. [*Exeunt* DOGBERRY *and* VERGES.

Enter BORACHIO *and* CONRADE.

Bora. What, Conrade!—

Watch. Peace, stir not.　　　　　　[*Aside.*

Bora. Conrade, I say!

Con. Here, man, I am at thy elbow.

Bora. Mass, and my elbow itched; I thought there would a scab follow.

Con. I will owe thee an answer for that; and now forward with thy tale.

Bora. Stand thee close then under this penthouse, for it drizzles rain; and I will, like a true drunkard, utter all to thee.

Watch. [*Aside.*] Some treason, masters; yet stand close.

Bora. Therefore know, I have earned of Don John a thousand ducats.　　　　　[so dear?

Con. Is it possible that any villany should be

Bora. Thou shouldst rather ask if it were possible any villany should be so rich; for when rich villains have need of poor ones, poor ones may make what price they will.

Con. I wonder at it.

Bora. That shows thou art unconfirmed. Thou knowest that the fashion of a doublet, or a hat, or a cloak is nothing to a man.

Con. Yes, it is apparel.

Bora. I mean the fashion.

Con. Yes, the fashion is the fashion.

Bora. Tush! I may as well say the fool's the fool. But seest thou not what a deformed thief this fashion is?

Watch. I know that Deformed; 'a has been a

vile thief this seven year; 'a goes up and down like a gentleman: I remember his name.

Bora. Didst thou not hear somebody?

Con. No; 'twas the vane on the house.

Bora. Seest thou not, I say, what a deformed thief this fashion is? how giddily he turns about all the hot bloods between fourteen and five-and-thirty? sometimes fashioning them like Pharaoh's soldiers in the reechy painting; sometimes like god Bel's priests in the old church window; sometimes like the shaven Hercules in the smirched worm-eaten tapestry, where his cod-piece seems as massy as his club?

Con. All this I see; and see that the fashion wears out more apparel than the man. But art not thou thyself giddy with the fashion too, that thou hast shifted out of thy tale into telling me of the fashion?

Bora. Not so neither; but know that I have to-night wooed Margaret, the Lady Hero's gentlewoman, by the name of Hero; she leans me out at her mistress's chamber-window, bids me a thousand times good night,—I tell this tale vilely:—I should first tell thee, how the prince, Claudio, and my master, planted and placed and possessed by my master Don John, saw afar off in the orchard this amiable encounter.

Con. And thought they Margaret was Hero?

Bora. Two of them did, the prince and Claudio; but the devil my master knew she was Margaret; and partly by his oaths, which first possessed them, partly by the dark night, which did deceive them, but chiefly by my villany, which did confirm any slander that Don John had made, away went Claudio enraged; swore he would meet her, as he was appointed, next morning at the temple, and there, before the whole congregation, shame her with what he saw over-night, and send her home again without a husband.

1 Watch. We charge you in the prince's name, stand.

2 Watch. Call up the right master constable: we have here recovered the most dangerous piece of lechery that ever was known in the commonwealth.

1 Watch. And one Deformed is one of them; I know him, 'a wears a lock.

Con. Masters, masters!

2 Watch. You'll be made bring Deformed forth, I warrant you.

Con. Masters,—

1 Watch. Never speak; we charge you, let us obey you to go with us.

Bora. We are like to prove a goodly commodity, being taken up of these men's bills.

Con. A commodity in question, I warrant you. Come, we'll obey you.　　　　　　[*Exeunt.*

SCENE IV.—*A Room in* LEONATO'S *House.*

Enter HERO, MARGARET, *and* URSULA.

Hero. Good Ursula, wake my cousin Beatrice, and desire her to rise.

Urs. I will, lady.
Hero. And bid her come hither.
Urs. Well.   [*Exit* URSULA.
Marg. Troth, I think your other rabato were better.
Hero. No, pray thee, good Meg, I'll wear this.
Marg. By my troth, it's not so good; and I warrant your cousin will say so.
Hero. My cousin's a fool, and thou art another; I'll wear none but this.
Marg. I like the new tire within excellently, if the hair were a thought browner: and your gown's a most rare fashion, i' faith. I saw the Duchess of Milan's gown that they praise so.
Hero. O, that exceeds, they say.
Marg. By my troth, it's but a night-gown in respect of yours. Cloth of gold, and cuts, and laced with silver; set with pearls, down-sleeves, side-sleeves, and skirts round, underborne with a blueish tinsel: but for a fine, quaint, graceful, and excellent fashion, yours is worth ten on't.
Hero. God give me joy to wear it, for my heart is exceeding heavy!
Marg. 'Twill be heavier soon, by the weight of a man.
Hero. Fie upon thee! art not ashamed?
Marg. Of what, lady? of speaking honourably? Is not marriage honourable in a beggar? Is not your lord honourable without marriage? I think, you would have me say, saving your reverence,—*a husband:* an bad thinking do not wrest true speaking I'll offend nobody. Is there any harm in—*the heavier for a husband?* None, I think, an it be the right husband and the right wife; otherwise 'tis light, and not heavy. Ask my Lady Beatrice else,—here she comes.

Enter BEATRICE.

Hero. Good morrow, coz.
Beat. Good morrow, sweet Hero.
Hero. Why, how now! do you speak in the sick tune?
Beat. I am out of all other tune, methinks.
Marg. Clap's into *Light o' love;* that goes without a burden: do you sing it and I'll dance it.
Beat. Yea, *Light o' love,* with your heels!— then if your husband have stables enough you'll see he shall lack no barns.
Marg. O illegitimate construction! I scorn that with my heels.
Beat. 'Tis almost five o'clock, cousin; 'tis time you were ready. By my troth, I am exceeding ill:—hey-ho!
Marg. For a hawk, a horse, or a husband?
Beat. For the letter that begins them all, H.
Marg. Well, an you be not turned Turk, there's no more sailing by the star.
Beat. What means the fool, trow?
Marg. Nothing I; but God send every one their heart's desire!
Hero. These gloves the count sent me; they are an excellent perfume.
Beat. I am stuffed, cousin, I cannot smell.

Marg. A maid and stuffed; there's goodly catching of cold.
Beat. O, God help me! God help me! how long have you professed apprehension?
Marg. Ever since you left it:—doth not my wit become me rarely?
Beat. It is not seen enough; you should wear it in your cap.—By my troth, I am sick.
Marg. Get you some of this distilled Carduus Benedictus and lay it to your heart; it is the only thing for a qualm.
Hero. There thou prick'st her with a thistle.
Beat. Benedictus! why Benedictus? you have some moral in this Benedictus.
Marg. Moral? no, by my troth, I have no moral meaning; I meant plain holy-thistle. You may think, perchance, that I think you are in love: nay, by'r lady, I am not such a fool to think what I list; nor I list not to think what I can; nor, indeed, I cannot think, if I would think my heart out of thinking, that you are in love, or that you will be in love, or that you can be in love: yet Benedick was such another, and now is he become a man: he swore he would never marry; and yet now, in despite of his heart, he eats his meat without grudging: and how you may be converted I know not; but methinks you look with your eyes as other women do.
Beat. What pace is this that thy tongue keeps?
Marg. Not a false gallop.

Re-enter URSULA.

Urs. Madam, withdraw; the prince, the count, Signior Benedick, Don John, and all the gallants of the town are come to fetch you to church.
Hero. Help to dress me, good coz, good Meg, good Ursula.   [*Exeunt.*

SCENE V.—*Another Room in* LEONATO'S *House.*

Enter LEONATO, *with* DOGBERRY *and* VERGES.

Leon. What would you with me, honest neighbour?
Dogb. Marry, sir, I would have some confidence with you that decerns you nearly.
Leon. Brief, I pray you; for you see 'tis a busy time with me.
Dogb. Marry, this it is, sir.
Verg. Yes, in truth it is, sir.
Leon. What is it, my good friends?
Dogb. Goodman Verges, sir, speaks a little off the matter: an old man, sir, and his wits are not so blunt as, God help, I would desire they were; but, in faith, honest as the skin between his brows.
Verg. Yes, I thank God I am as honest as any man living that is an old man and no honester than I.
Dogb. Comparisons are odorous: *palabras,* neighbour Verges.
Leon. Neighbours, you are tedious.
Dogb. It pleases your worship to say so, but

we are the poor duke's officers: but, truly, for mine own part, if I were as tedious as a king, I could find in my heart to bestow it all of your worship.

Leon. All thy tediousness on me! ha!

Dogb. Yea, and 'twere a thousand t imes more than 'tis: for I hear as good exclamation on your worship as of any man in the city; and though I be put a poor man, I am glad to hear it.

Verg. And so am I.

Leon. I would fain know what you have to say.

Verg. Marry, sir, our watch to-night, excepting your worship's presence, have ta'en a couple of as arrant knaves as any in Messina.

Dogb. A good old man, sir; he will be talking; as they say, When the age is in the wit is out; God help us! it is a world to see!—Well said, i' faith, neighbour Verges:—well, God's a good man; an two men ride of a horse, one must ride behind.—An honest soul, i' faith, sir; by my troth he is, as ever broke bread: but God is to be worshipped. All men are not alike,—alas, good neighbour! [you.

Leon. Indeed, neighbour, he comes too short of

Dogb. Gifts that God gives.

Leon. I must leave you.

Dogb. One word, sir: our watch, sir, have indeed comprehended two auspicious persons, and we would have them this morning examined before your worship.

Leon. Take their examination yourself, and bring it me; I am now in great haste, as it may appear unto you.

Dogb. It shall be suffigance. [well.

Leon. Drink some wine ere you go: fare you

Enter a Messenger.

Mess. My lord, they stay for you to give your daughter to her husband.

Leon. I will wait upon them; I am ready.

[*Exeunt* LEON. *and* Messenger.

Dogb. Go, good partner, go, get you to Francis Seacoal; bid him bring his pen and inkhorn to the gaol: we are now to examination these men.

Verg. And we must do it wisely.

Dogb. We will spare for no wit, I warrant you; here's that [*touching his forehead*] shall drive some of them to a *non com:* only get the learned writer to set down our excommunication, and meet me at the gaol. [*Exeunt.*

ACT IV.

SCENE I.—*The inside of a Church.*

Enter DON PEDRO, DON JOHN, LEONATO, FRIAR, CLAUDIO, BENEDICK, HERO, *and* BEATRICE, *&c.*

Leon. Come, Friar Francis, be brief; only to the plain form of marriage, and you shall recount their particular duties afterwards.

Friar. You come hither, my lord, to marry this lady?

Claud. No. [marry her.

Leon. To be married to her, friar; you come to

Friar. Lady, you come hither to be married to this count?

Hero. I do.

Friar. If either of you know any inward impediment why you should not be conjoined I charge you, on your souls, to utter it.

Claud. Know you any, Hero?

Hero. None, my lord.

Friar. Know you any, count?

Leon. I dare make his answer, none.

Claud. O, what men dare do! what men may do! what men daily do! not knowing what they do!

Bene. How now! Interjections? Why, then, some be of laughing, as, ha! ha! he!

Claud. Stand thee by, friar:—Father, by your leave;

Will you with free and unconstrained soul
Give me this maid, your daughter?

Leon. As freely, son, as God did give her me.

Claud. And what have I to give you back, whose worth
May counterpoise this rich and precious gift?

D. Pedro. Nothing, unless you render her again.

Claud. Sweet prince, you learn me noble thankfulness.—
There, Leonato, take her back again;
Give not this rotten orange to your friend;
She's but the sign and semblance of her honour.—
Behold, how like a maid she blushes here!
O, what authority and show of truth
Can cunning sin cover itself withal!
Comes not that blood as modest evidence
To witness simple virtue? Would you not swear,
All you that see her, that she were a maid,
By these exterior shows? But she is none:
She knows the heat of a luxurious bed:
Her blush is guiltiness, not modesty.

Leon. What do you mean, my lord?

Claud. Not to be married,
Not to knit my soul to an approved wanton.

Leon. Dear, my lord, if you, in your own proof,
Have vanquish'd the resistance of her youth,
And made defeat of her virginity,——

Claud. I know what you would say: if I have known her,
You'll say, she did embrace me as a husband,
And so extenuate the 'forehand sin:
No, Leonato,
I never tempted her with word too large;
But, as a brother to his sister, show'd
Bashful sincerity and comely love.

Hero. And seem'd I ever otherwise to you?

Claud. Out on thy seeming! I will write against it:
You seem to me as Dian in her orb;
As chaste as is the bud ere it be blown;
But you are more intemperate in your blood
Than Venus, or those pamper'd animals
That rage in savage sensuality. [wide?

Hero. Is my lord well, that he doth speak so

Claud. Sweet prince, why speak not you?

D. Pedro. What should I speak?

I stand dishonour'd, that have gone about
To link my dear friend to a common stale.
Leon. Are these things spoken? or do I but
    dream?
D. John. Sir, they are spoken, and these things
    are true.
Bene. This looks not like a nuptial.
Hero.   True!—O God!
Claud. Leonato, stand I here?
Is this the prince? Is this the prince's brother?
Is this face Hero's? Are our eyes our own?
Leon. All this is so; but what of this, my lord?
Claud. Let me but move one question to your
    daughter;
And, by that fatherly and kindly power
That you have in her, bid her answer truly.
Leon. I charge thee do so, as thou art my child.
Hero. O God defend me! how am I beset!—
What kind of catechising call you this?
Claud. To make you answer truly to your
    name.
Hero. Is it not Hero? Who can blot that name
With any just reproach?
Claud.   Marry, that can Hero;
Hero itself can blot out Hero's virtue.
What man was he talk'd with you yesternight
Out at your window, betwixt twelve and one?
Now, if you are a maid, answer to this.
Hero. I talk'd with no man at that hour, my
    lord.   [Leonato,
D. Pedro. Why, then are you no maiden.—
I am sorry you must hear: upon mine honour,
Myself, my brother, and this grieved count,
Did see her, hear her, at that hour last night,
Talk with a ruffian at her chamber-window;
Who hath, indeed, most like a liberal villain,
Confess'd the vile encounters they have had
A thousand times in secret.
D. John.   Fie, fie! they are
Not to be named, my lord, not to be spoke of;
There is not chastity enough in language,
Without offence, to utter them. Thus, pretty
    lady,
I am sorry for thy much misgovernment.
Claud. O Hero! what a Hero hadst thou been
If half thy outward graces had been placed
About thy thoughts and counsels of thy heart!
But fare thee well, most foul, most fair! fare-
    well,
Thou pure impiety and impious purity!
For thee I'll lock up all the gates of love,
And on my eyelids shall conjecture hang,
To turn all beauty into thoughts of harm,
And never shall it more be gracious.
Leon. Hath no man's dagger here a point for
    me?   [Hero *swoons.*
Beat. Why, how now, cousin? wherefore sink
    you down?
D. John. Come, let us go: these things, come
    thus to light,
Smother her spirits up.
    [*Exeunt* D. Pedro, D. John, *and* Claud.
Bene. How doth the lady?
Beat.   Dead, I think;—help, uncle;—

Hero! why, Hero!—Uncle!—Signior Benedick!
    —friar!
Leon. O fate, take not away thy heavy hand!
Death is the fairest cover for her shame
That may be wish'd for.
Beat.   How now, cousin Hero?
Friar. Have comfort, lady.
Leon.   Dost thou look up?
Friar. Yea; wherefore should she not?
Leon. Wherefore! Why, doth not every earthly
    thing
Cry shame upon her? Could she here deny
The story that is printed in her blood?—
Do not live, Hero; do not ope thine eyes:
For did I think thou wouldst not quickly die,
Thought I thy spirits were stronger than thy
    shames,
Myself would, on the rearward of reproaches,
Strike at thy life. Griev'd I I had but one?
Chid I for that at frugal nature's frame?
O, one too much by thee! Why had I one?
Why ever wast thou lovely in my eyes?
Why had I not, with charitable hand,
Took up a beggar's issue at my gates;
Who, smirched thus and mir'd with infamy,
I might have said, *No part of it is mine;*
This shame derives itself from unknown loins?
But mine, and mine I lov'd, and mine I prais'd,
And mine that I was proud on; mine so much
That I myself was to myself not mine,
Valuing of her; why, she—O, she is fallen
Into a pit of ink, that the wide sea
Hath drops too few to wash her clean again,
And salt too little, which may season give
To her foul tainted flesh!
Bene.   Sir, sir, be patient:
For my part, I am so attir'd in wonder
I know not what to say.
Beat. O, on my soul, my cousin is belied!
Bene. Lady, were you her bedfellow last night?
Beat. No, truly not: although, until last night
I have this twelvemonth been her bedfellow.
Leon. Confirm'd, confirm'd! O, that is stronger
    made
Which was before barr'd up with ribs of iron!
Would the two princes lie? and Claudio lie,
Who lov'd her so that, speaking of her foulness,
Wash'd it with tears? Hence from her! let her
    die.
Friar. Hear me a little;
For I have only been silent so long,
And given way unto this course of fortune,
By nothing of the lady: I have mark'd
A thousand blushing apparitions start
Into her face; a thousand innocent shames
In angel whiteness bear away those blushes;
And in her eye there hath appear'd a fire
To burn the errors that these princes hold
Against her maiden truth. Call me a fool;
Trust not my reading, nor my observation,
Which with experimental seal doth warrant
The tenor of my book; trust not my age,
My reverence, calling, nor divinity,
If this sweet lady lie not guiltless here

Under some biting error.
Leon.   Friar, it cannot be:
Thou seest that all the grace that she hath left
Is that she will not add to her damnation
A sin of perjury; she not denies it:
Why seek'st thou then to cover with excuse
That which appears in proper nakedness?
Friar. Lady, what man is he you are accused of?
Hero. They know that do accuse me; I know
     none:
If I know more of any man alive
Than that which maiden modesty doth warrant,
Let all my sins lack mercy!—O my father,
Prove you that any man with me convers'd
At hours unmeet, or that I yesternight
Maintained the change of words with any
     creature,
Refuse me, hate me, torture me to death!
Friar. There is some strange misprison in the
        princes.   [our;
Bene. Two of them have the very bent of hon-
And if their wisdoms be misled in this,
The practice of it lives in John the bastard,
Whose spirits toil in frame of villanies.
Leon. I know not. If they speak but truth of
        her,   [honour,
These hands shall tear her; if they wrong her
The proudest of them shall well hear of it.
Time hath not yet so dried this blood of mine,
Nor age so eat up my invention,
Nor fortune made such havoc of my means,
Nor my bad life reft me so much of friends,
But they shall find, awak'd in such a kind,
Both strength of limb and policy of mind,
Ability in means and choice of friends,
To quit me of them throughly.
Friar.   Pause awhile,
And let my counsel sway you in this case.
Your daughter here the princes left for dead;
Let her awhile be secretly kept in,
And publish it that she is dead indeed:
Maintain a mourning ostentation,
And on your family's old monument
Hang mournful epitaphs, and do all rites
That appertain unto a burial.
Leon. What shall become of this? What will
       this do?   [behalf
Friar. Marry, this, well carried, shall on her
Change slander to remorse; that is some good;
But not for that dream I on this strange course,
But on this travail look for greater birth.
She dying, as it must be so maintain'd,
Upon the instant that she was accus'd,
Shall be lamented, pitied, and excus'd
Of every hearer: for it so falls out
That what we have we prize not to the worth
Whiles we enjoy it; but being lack'd and lost,
Why, then we rack the value; then we find
The virtue that possession would not show us
Whiles it was ours. So will it fare with Claudio:
When he shall hear she died upon his words,
The idea of her life shall sweetly creep
Into his study of imagination;
And every lovely organ of her life

Shall come apparell'd in more precious habit,
More moving delicate, and full of life,
Into the eye and prospect of his soul,
Than when she liv'd indeed:—then shall he
     mourn,—
If ever love had interest in his liver,—
And wish he had not so accused her;
No, though he thought his accusation true.
Let this be so, and doubt not but success
Will fashion the event in better shape
Than I can lay it down in likelihood.
But if all aim but this be levell'd false,
The supposition of the lady's death
Will quench the wonder of her infamy:
And, if it sort not well, you may conceal her,—
As best befits her wounded reputation,—
In some reclusive and religious life,
Out of all eyes, tongues, minds, and injuries.
Bene. Signior Leonato, let the friar advise you;
And though you know my inwardness and love
Is very much unto the prince and Claudio,
Yet, by mine honour, I will deal in this
As secretly and justly as your soul
Should with your body.
Leon.   Being that I flow in grief
The smallest twine may lead me.
Friar. 'Tis well consented; presently away;
    For to strange sores strangely they strain the
       cure.—
Come, lady, die to live: this wedding-day
    Perhaps is but prolonged; have patience, and
       endure.
         [*Exeunt* FRIAR, HERO, *and* LEON.
Bene. Lady Beatrice, have you wept all this
while?
Beat. Yea, and I will weep a while longer.
Bene. I will not desire that.
Beat. You have no reason; I do it freely.
Bene. Surely, I do believe your fair cousin is
wrong'd.
Beat. Ah, how much might the man deserve of
me that would right her!
Bene. Is there any way to show such friendship?
Beat. A very even way, but no such friend.
Bene. May a man do it?
Beat. It is a man's office, but not yours.
Bene. I do love nothing in the world so well as
you. Is not that strange?
Beat. As strange as the thing I know not. It
were as possible for me to say I loved nothing
so well as you: but believe me not; and yet I
lie not; I confess nothing, nor I deny nothing —
I am sorry for my cousin.
Bene. By my sword, Beatrice, thou lovest me.
Beat. Do not swear by it and eat it.
Bene. I will swear by it that you love me; and
I will make him eat it that says I love not you.
Beat. Will you not eat your word?
Bene. With no sauce that can be devised to it:
I protest I love thee.
Beat. Why, then, God forgive me!
Bene. What offence, sweet Beatrice?
Beat. You have stayed me in a happy hour: I
was about to protest I loved you.

Bene. And do it with all thy heart?
Beat. I love you with so much of my heart that none is left to protest.
Bene. Come, bid me do anything for thee.
Beat. Kill Claudio.
Bene. Ha! not for the wide world.
Beat. You kill me to deny it. Farewell.
Bene. Tarry, sweet Beatrice.
Beat. I am gone though I am here;—there is no love in you:—nay, I pray you, let me go.
Bene. Beatrice,—
Beat. In faith, I will go
Bene. We'll be friends first.
Beat. You dare easier be friends with me than fight with mine enemy.
Bene. Is Claudio thine enemy?
Beat. Is he not approved in the height a villain that hath slandered, scorned, dishonoured my kinswoman?—O that I were a man!—What! bear her in hand until they come to take hands, and then with public accusation, uncovered slander, unmitigated rancour,—O God, that I were a man! I would eat his heart in the market-place!
Bene. Hear me, Beatrice;—
Beat. Talk with a man out at a window!—a proper saying!
Bene. Nay but, Beatrice;—
Beat. Sweet Hero!—she is wronged, she is slandered, she is undone.
Bene. Beat—
Beat. Princes and counties! Surely, a princely testimony, a goodly count-confect; a sweet gallant, surely! O that I were a man for his sake! or that I had any friend would be a man for my sake! But manhood is melted into courtesies, valour into compliment, and men are only turned into tongue, and trim ones too: he is now as valiant as Hercules that only tells a lie and swears it.—I cannot be a man with wishing, therefore I will die a woman with grieving.   [love thee.
Bene. Tarry, good Beatrice. By this hand, I
Beat. Use it for my love some other way than swearing by it.
Bene. Think you in your soul the Count Claudio hath wronged Hero?   [soul.
Beat. Yea, as sure as I have a thought or a
Bene. Enough, I am engaged; I will challenge him; I will kiss your hand and so leave you. By this hand, Claudio shall render me a dear account. As you hear of me, so think of me. Go, comfort your cousin; I must say she is dead; and so, farewell.   [*Exeunt.*

Scene II.—*A Prison.*

Enter DOGBERRY, VERGES, *and* SEXTON, *in gowns; and the* Watch, *with* CONRADE *and* BORACHIO.

Dogb. Is our whole dissembly appeared?
Verg. O, a stool and a cushion for the sexton!
Sexton. Which be the malefactors?
Dogb. Marry, that am I and my partner.

Verg. Nay, that's certain; we have the exhibition to examine.
Sexton. But which are the offenders that are to be examined? let them come before master constable.
Dogb. Yea, marry, let them come before me.—What is your name, friend?
Bora. Borachio.
Dogb. Pray write down—Borachio.——Yours, sirrah?   [Conrade.
Con. I am a gentleman, sir, and my name is
Dogb. Write down—master gentleman Conrade.—Masters, do you serve God?
Con. }
Bora. } Yea, sir, we hope.
Dogb. Write down—that they hope they serve God:—and write God first; for God defend but God should go before such villains!—Masters, it is proved already that you are little better than false knaves; and it will go near to be thought so shortly. How answer you for yourselves?
Con. Marry, sir, we say we are none.
Dogb. A marvellous witty fellow, I assure you; but I will go about with him.—Come you hither, sirrah: a word in your ear, sir; I say to you, it is thought you are false knaves.
Bora. Sir, I say to you, we are none.
Dogb. Well, stand aside.—'Fore God, they are both in a tale. Have you writ down—that they are none?
Sexton. Master constable, you go not the way to examine; you must call forth the Watch that are their accusers.
Dogb. Yea, marry, that's the eftest way.—Let the Watch come forth.—Masters, I charge you in the prince's name, accuse these men.
1 *Watch.* This man said, sir, that Don John, the prince's brother, was a villain.
Dogb. Write down—Prince John a villain.—Why, this is flat perjury, to call a prince's brother villain.
Bora. Master constable,—
Dogb. Pray thee, fellow, peace; I do not like thy look, I promise thee.
Sexton. What heard you him say else?
2 *Watch.* Marry, that he had received a thousand ducats off Don John for accusing the Lady Hero wrongfully.
Dogb. Flat burglary as ever was committed.
Verg. Yea, by the mass, that it is.
Sexton. What else, fellow?
1 *Watch.* And that Count Claudio did mean, upon his words, to disgrace Hero before the whole assembly, and not marry her.
Dogb. O villain! thou wilt be condemned into everlasting redemption for this.
Sexton. What else?
2 *Watch.* This is all.
Sexton. And this is more, masters, than you can deny. Prince John is this morning secretly stolen away; Hero was in this manner accused, in this very manner refused, and upon the grief of this suddenly died.—Master constable, let

these men be bound and brought to Leonato's;
I will go before and show him their examina-
tion.   [*Exit.*
Dogb. Come, let them be opinioned.
Verg. Let them be in band.
Con. Off, coxcomb!
Dogb. God's my life! where's the sexton? let
him write down—the prince's officer, coxcomb.
—Come, bind them.——Thou naughty varlet!
Con. Away! you are an ass, you are an ass.
Dogb. Dost thou not suspect my place? Dost
thou not·suspect my years?—O that he were
here to write me down an ass! but, masters,
remember, that I am an ass; though it be not
written down, yet forget not that I am an ass.
—No, thou villain, thou art full of piety, as
shall be proved upon thee by good witness, I
am a wise fellow; and, which is more, an officer;
and, which is more, a householder; and, which
is more, as pretty a piece of flesh as any is in
Messina: and one that knows the law, go to;
and a rich fellow enough, go to; and a fellow
that hath had losses; and one that hath two
gowns, and everything handsome about him.—
Bring him away. O that I had been writ down
an ass!   [*Exeunt.*

ACT V.

SCENE I.—*Before* LEONATO'S *House.*

Enter LEONATO *and* ANTONIO.

Ant. If you go on thus you will kill yourself;
And 'tis not wisdom thus to second grief
Against yourself.
Leon.   I pray thee, cease thy counsel,
Which falls into mine ears as profitless
As water in a sieve: give not me counsel;
Nor let no comforter delight mine ear
But such a one whose wrongs do suit with mine.
Bring me a father that so lov'd his child,
Whose joy of her is overwhelm'd like mine,
And bid him speak of patience;   [mine,
Measure his woe the length and breadth· of
And let it answer every strain for strain;
As thus for thus, and such a grief for such,
In every lineament, branch, shape, and form:
If such a one will smile, and stroke his beard,
Cry—sorrow, wag! and hem when he should
              groan,   [drunk
Patch grief with proverbs, make misfortune
With candle-wasters,—bring him yet to me,
And I of him will gather patience.
But there is no such man: for, brother, men
Can counsel and speak comfort to that grief
Which they themselves not feel; but, tasting it,
Their counsel turns to passion, which before
Would give preceptial medicine to rage,
Fetter strong madness in a silken thread,
Charm ache with air and agony with words:
No, no; 'tis all men's office to speak patience
To those that wring under the load of sorrow;
But no man's virtue nor sufficiency
To be so moral when he shall endure
The like himself: therefore, give me no counsel:

My griefs cry louder than advertisement.
Ant. Therein do men from children nothing
              differ.   [blood;
Leon. I pray thee, peace; I will be flesh and
For there was never yet philosopher
That could endure the toothache patiently,
However they have writ the style of gods,
And make a pish at chance and sufferance.
Ant. Yet bend not all the harm upon yourself;
Make those that do offend you suffer too.
Leon. There thou speak'st reason: nay, I will
              do so.
My soul doth tell me Hero is belied;
And that shall Claudio know; so shall the
              prince,
And all of them that thus dishonour her.
Ant. Here comes the prince and Claudio hastily

Enter DON PEDRO *and* CLAUDIO.

D. Pedro. Good den, good den.
Claud.   Good day to both of you.
Leon. Hear you, my lords,—
D. Pedro.   We have some haste, Leonato.
Leon. Some haste, my lord!—well, fare you
              well, my lord:—
Are you so hasty now?—well, all is one.
D. Pedro. Nay, do not quarrel with us, good
              old man.
Ant. If he could right himself with quarrelling,
Some of us would lie low.
Claud.   Who wrongs him?
Leon. Marry, thou dost wrong me: thou dis-
              sembler, thou:—
Nay, never lay thy hand upon thy sword—
I fear thee not.
Claud.   Marry, beshrew my hand
If it should give your age such cause of fear:
In faith, my hand meant nothing to my sword.
Leon. Tush, tush, man; never fleer and jest at
              me;
I speak not like a dotard nor a fool;
As, under privilege of age, to brag   [do
What I have done being young, or what would
Were I not old. Know, Claudio, to thy head,
Thou hast so wrong'd mine innocent child and
              me
That I am forc'd to lay my reverence by,
And with gray hairs and bruise of many days,
Do challenge thee to trial of a man.
I say thou hast belied mine innocent child;
Thy slander hath gone through and through
              her heart,
And she lies buried with her ancestors,—
O! in a tomb where never scandal slept,
Save this of hers, fram'd by thy villany.
Claud. My villany!
Leon.   Thine, Claudio; thine, I say.
D. Pedro. You say not right, old man.
Leon.   My lord, my lord,
I'll prove it on his body if he dare,
Despite his nice fence and his active practice,
His May of youth and bloom of lustihood.
Claud. Away! I will not have to do with you.

Leon. Canst thou so daff me? Thou hast kill'd
    my child;
If thou kill'st me, boy, thou shalt kill a man.
Ant. He shall kill two of us, and men indeed;
But that's no matter; let him kill one first;—
Win me and wear me,—let him answer me.—
Come, follow me, boy; come, boy, follow me:
Sir boy, I'll whip you from your foining fence;
Nay, as I am a gentleman, I will.
Leon. Brother,—   [niece;
Ant. Content yourself. God knows I lov'd my
And she is dead, slander'd to death by villains,
That dare as well answer a man, indeed,
As I dare take a serpent by the tongue:
Boys, apes, braggarts, Jacks, milksops!—
Leon.   Brother Anthony,—
Ant. Hold you content. What, man! I know
    them, yea,   [scruple,—
And what they weigh, even to the utmost
Scambling, out-facing, fashion-mong'ring boys,
That lie, and cog, and flout, deprave and slander,
Go anticly, and show outward hideousness,
And speak off half a dozen dangerous words,
How they might hurt their enemies, if they
    durst;
And this is all.
Leon. But, brother Anthony,—
Ant.   Come, 'tis no matter;
Do not you meddle, let me deal in this.
D. Pedro. Gentlemen both, we will not wake
    your patience.
My heart is sorry for your daughter's death;
But, on my honour, she was charg'd with nothing
But what was true, and very full of proof.
Leon. My lord, my lord,—
D. Pedro.   I will not hear you.
Leon.   No?
Come, brother, away.—I will be heard;—
Ant.   And shall,
Or some of us will smart for it.
                [*Exeunt* LEON. *and* ANT.
D. Pedro. See, see; here comes the man we
went to seek.

Enter BENEDICK.

Claud. Now, signior! what news?
Bene. Good day, my lord.
D. Pedro. Welcome, signior: you are almost
come to part almost a fray.
Claud. We had like to have had our two noses
snapped off with two old men without teeth.
D. Pedro. Leonato and his brother. What
think'st thou? Had we fought, I doubt we
should have been too young for them.
Bene. In a false quarrel there is no true valour.
I came to seek you both.
Claud. We have been up and down to seek
thee; for we are high proof melancholy, and
would fain have it beaten away. Wilt thou use
thy wit?
Bene. It is in my scabbard: shall I draw it?
D. Pedro. Dost thou wear thy wit by thy side?
Claud. Never any did so, though very many
have been beside their wit.—I will bid thee

draw, as we do the minstrels; draw, to pleasure us.
D. Pedro. As I am an honest man, he looks
pale.—Art thou sick or angry?
Claud. What! courage, man! What though care
killed a cat, thou hast mettle enough in thee
to kill care.
Bene. Sir, I shall meet your wit in the career,
an you charge it against me.—I pray you,
choose another subject.
Claud. Nay, then, give him another staff; this
last was broke cross.
D. Pedro. By this light, he changes more and
more; I think he be angry indeed.
Claud. If he be, he knows how to turn his girdle.
Bene. Shall I speak a word in your ear?
Claud. God bless me from a challenge!
Bene. You are a villain;—I jest not:—I will
make it good how you dare, with what you
dare, and when you dare.—Do me right, or I
will protest your cowardice. You have killed a
sweet lady, and her death shall fall heavy on
you. Let me hear from you.
Claud. Well, I will meet you, so I may have
good cheer.
D. Pedro. What, a feast? a feast?
Claud. I' faith, I thank him; he hath bid me to
a calf's head and a capon, the which if I do not
carve most curiously, say my knife's naught.—
Shall I not find a woodcock too?
Bene. Sir, your wit ambles well; it goes easily.
D. Pedro. I'll tell thee how Beatrice praised
thy wit the other day: I said thou hadst a fine
wit; *True,* says she, *a fine little one. No,* said I,
a great wit; Right, says she, *a great gross one.
Nay,* said I, *a good wit. Just,* said she, *it hurts
nobody. Nay,* said I, *the gentleman is wise. Certain,* said she, *a wise gentleman. Nay,* said I,
he hath the tongues. That I believe, said she,
*for he swore a thing to me on Monday night
which he foreswore on Tuesday morning; there's
a double tongue; there's two tongues.* Thus did
she, an hour together, trans-shape thy particular virtues; yet, at last, she concluded, with
a sigh, thou wast the properest man in Italy.
Claud. For the which she wept heartily, and
said she cared not.
D. Pedro. Yea, that she did; but yet, for all
that, an if she did not hate him deadly, she
would love him dearly: the old man's daughter
told us all.
Claud. All, all; and, moreover, *God saw him
when he was hid in the garden.*
D. Pedro. But when shall we set the savage
bull's horns on the sensible Benedick's head?
Claud. Yea, and text underneath, *Here dwells
Benedick the married man?*
Bene. Fare you well, boy; you know my mind.
I will leave you now to your gossip-like humour: you break jests as braggarts do their
blades, which, God be thanked, hurt not.—
My lord, for your many courtesies I thank
you: I must discontinue your company: your
brother the bastard is fled from Messina: you

have among you killed a sweet and innocent lady. For my Lord Lackbeard there, he and I shall meet; and till then, peace be with him.

                    [*Exit* BENEDICK.

D. Pedro. He is in earnest.

Claud. In most profound earnest; and I'll warrant you for the love of Beatrice.

D. Pedro. And hath challenged thee?

Claud. Most sincerely.

D. Pedro. What a pretty thing man is when he goes in his doublet and hose, and leaves off his wit!

Claud. He is then a giant to an ape: but then is an ape a doctor to such a man.

D. Pedro. But, soft, you, let be; pluck up, my heart, and be sad! Did he not say my brother was fled?

Enter DOGBERRY, VERGES, *and the* Watch, *with* CONRADE *and* BORACHIO.

Dogb. Come, you, sir; if justice cannot tame you, she shall ne'er weigh more reasons in her balance; nay, an you be a cursing hypocrite once, you must be looked to.

D. Pedro. How now! two of my brother's men bound! Borachio one!

Claud. Hearken after their offence, my lord.

D. Pedro. Officers, what offence hath these men done?

Dogb. Marry, sir, they have committed false report; moreover, they have spoken untruths; secondarily, they are slanders; sixth and lastly, they have belied a lady; thirdly, they have verified unjust things: and, to conclude, they are lying knaves.

D. Pedro. First, I ask thee what they have done; thirdly, I ask thee what's their offence; sixth and lastly, why they are committed; and, to conclude, what you lay to their charge?

Claud. Rightly reasoned, and in his own division; and, by my troth, there's one meaning well suited.

D. Pedro. Whom have you offended, masters, that you are thus bound to your answer? this learned constable is too cunning to be understood. What's your offence?

Bora. Sweet prince, let me go no further to mine answer; do you hear me, and let this count kill me. I have deceived even your very eyes: what your wisdoms could not discover these shallow fools have brought to light; who, in the night, overheard me confessing to this man how Don John your brother incensed me to slander the Lady Hero; how you were brought into the orchard, and saw me court Margaret in Hero's garments; how you disgraced her, when you should marry her: my villany they have upon record; which I had rather seal with my death than repeat over to my shame. The lady is dead upon mine and my master's false accusation; and, briefly, I desire nothing but the reward of a villain.

D. Pedro. Runs not this speech like iron through your blood?

Claud. I have drunk poison whiles he uttered it.

D. Pedro. But did my brother set thee on to this?

Bora. Yea, and paid me richly for the practice of it.   [ery:

D. Pedro. He is compos'd and fram'd of treach-
And fled he is upon this villany.   [pear

Claud. Sweet Hero! now thy image doth ap-
In the rare semblance that I lov'd it first.

Dogb. Come, bring away the plaintiffs; by this time our sexton hath reformed Signior Leonato of the matter: and, masters, do not forget to specify, when time and place shall serve, that I am an ass.

Verg. Here, here comes master Signior Leonato and the sexton too.

Re-enter LEONATO *and* ANTONIO, *with the* SEXTON.

Leon. Which is the villain? let me see his eyes,
That when I note another man like him
I may avoid him: which of these is he?

Bora. If you would know your wronger, look on me.

Leon. Art thou the slave that with thy breath hast kill'd
Mine innocent child?

Bora.   Yea, even I alone.

Leon. No, not so, villain; thou bely'st thyself:
Here stand a pair of honourable men—
A third is fled—that had a hand in it.—
I thank you, princes, for my daughter's death;
Record it with your high and worthy deeds:
'Twas bravely none, if you bethink you of it.

Claud. I know not how to pray your patience,
Yet I must speak. Choose your revenge yourself;
Impose me to what penance your invention
Can lay upon my sin: yet sinned I not
But in mistaking.

D. Pedro.   By my soul, nor I;
And yet, to satisfy this good old man,
I would bend under any heavy weight
That he'll enjoin me to.

Leon. I cannot bid you bid my daughter live—
That were impossible; but, I pray you both,
Possess the people in Messina here
How innocent she died: and, if your love
Can labour aught in sad invention,
Hang her an epitaph upon her tomb,
And sing it to her bones; sing it to-night:—
To-morrow morning come you to my house;
And since you could not be my son-in-law,
Be yet my nephew: my brother hath a daughter,
Almost the copy of my child that's dead.
And she alone is heir to both of us;
Give her the right you should have given her cousin,
And so dies my revenge.

Claud.   O, noble sir,
Your overkindness doth wring tears from me!
I do embrace your offer; and dispose
For henceforth of poor Claudio.

Leon. To-morrow, then, I will expect your
    coming;
To-night I take my leave.—This naughty man
Shall face to face be brought to Margaret,
Who, I believe, was pack'd in all this wrong,
Hir'd to it by your brother.
Bora.   No, by my soul, she was not;
Nor knew not what she did when she spoke to
    me;
But always hath been just and virtuous
In anything that I do know by her.
Dogb. Moreover, sir,—which, indeed, is not
under white and black,—this plaintiff here, the
offender, did call me ass: I beseech you, let it
be remembered in this punishment. And also,
the Watch heard them talk of one Deformed:
they say he wears a key in his ear and a lock
hanging by it, and borrows money in God's
name; the which he hath used so long, and
never paid, that now men grow hard-hearted,
and will lend nothing for God's sake: pray you,
examine him upon that point.
Leon. I thank thee for thy care and honest
pains.
Dogb. Your worship speaks like a most thankful
and reverend youth, and I praise God for you.
Leon. There's for thy pains.
Dogb. God save the foundation!
Leon. Go; I discharge thee of thy prisoner, and
I thank thee.
Dogb. I leave an arrant knave with your worship; which I beseech your worship to correct
yourself, for the example of others. God keep
your worship; I wish your worship well; God
restore you to health; I humbly give you leave
to depart; and if a merry meeting may be
wished, God prohibit it.—Come, neighbour.
        [*Exeunt* DOGB., VERG., *and* Watch.
Leon. Until to-morrow morning, lords, farewell.
Ant. Farewell, my lords; we look for you to-
morrow.
D. Pedro. We will not fail.
Claud. To-night I'll mourn with Hero.
        [*Exeunt* DON PEDRO *and* CLAUD.
Leon. Bring you these fellows on: we'll talk
    with Margaret
How her acquaintance grew with this lewd
    fellow.   [*Exeunt.*

SCENE II.—LEONATO'S *Garden.*

Enter BENEDICK *and* MARGARET, *meeting.*

Bene. Pray thee, sweet Mistress Margaret, deserve well at my hands by helping me to the
speech of Beatrice.
Marg. Will you then write me a sonnet in
praise of my beauty?
Bene. In so high a style, Margaret, that no
man living shall come over it; for, in most
comely truth, thou deservest it.
Marg. To have no man come over me? why,
shall I always keep below stairs?
Bene. Thy wit is as quick as the greyhound's
mouth; it catches.

Marg. And yours as blunt as the fencer's foils,
which hit, but hurt not.
Bene. A most manly wit, Margaret; it will not
hurt a woman; and so, I pray thee, call Beatrice: I give thee the bucklers.
Marg. Give us the swords; we have bucklers
of our own.
Bene. If you use them, Margaret, you must
put in the pikes with a vice; and they are dangerous weapons for maids.
Marg. Well, I will call Beatrice to you, who I
think, hath legs.   [*Exit* MARGARET.
Bene. And therefore will come.   [*Singing.*

    The god of love,
    That sits above,
And knows me, and knows me,
    How pitiful I deserve,——

I mean in singing; but in loving—Leander the
good swimmer, Troilus the first employer of
panders, and a whole book full of these quondam carpet-mongers, whose names yet run
smoothly in the even road of a blank verse,
why, they were never so truly turned over and
over as my poor self in love. Marry, I cannot
show it in rhyme; I have tried; I can find out
no rhyme to *lady* but *baby*—an innocent rhyme;
for *scorn, horn*—a hard rhyme; for *school, fool*
—a babbling rhyme; very ominous endings,
No, I was not born under a rhyming planet
nor I cannot woo in festival terms.

Enter BEATRICE.

Sweet Beatrice, wouldst thou come when I
called thee?
Beat. Yea, signior, and depart when you bid me
Bene. O, stay but till then!
Beat. Then is spoken; fare you well now:—
and yet, ere I go, let me go with that I came
for, which is, with knowing what hath passed
between you and Claudio.
Bene. Only foul words; and thereupon I will
kiss thee.
Beat. Foul words is but foul wind and foul
wind is but foul breath, and foul breath is
noisome; therefore I will depart unkissed.
Bene. Thou hast frighted the word out of his
right sense, so forcible is thy wit. But, I must
tell thee plainly, Claudio undergoes my chal
lenge; and either I must shortly hear from him
or I will subscribe him a coward. And, I pray
thee now, tell me, for which of my bad parts
didst thou first fall in love with me?
Beat. For them all together; which maintained
so politic a state of evil that they will not
admit any good part to intermingle with them.
But for which of my good parts did you first
suffer love for me?
Bene. Suffer love; a good epithet! I do suffer
love, indeed, for I love thee against my will.
Beat. In spite of your heart, I think; alas!
poor heart! If you spite it for my sake, I will
spite it for yours; for I will never love that
which my friend hates.

Bene. Thou and I are too wise to woo peaceably.
Beat. It appears not in this confession: there's not one wise man among twenty that will praise himself.
Bene. An old, an old instance, Beatrice, that lived in the time of good neighbours: if a man do not erect in this age his own tomb ere he dies, he shall live no longer in monument than the bell rings and the widow weeps.
Beat. And how long is that, think you?
Bene. Question:—why, an hour in clamour, and a quarter in rheum: therefore it is most expedient for the wise (if Don Worm, his conscience, find no impediment to the contrary) to be the trumpet of his own virtues, as I am to myself. So much for praising myself, who, I myself will bear witness, is praiseworthy, and now tell me, how doth your cousin?
Beat. Very ill.
Bene. And how do you?
Beat. Very ill too.
Bene. Serve God, love me, and mend: there will I leave you too, for here comes one in haste.

Enter URSULA.

Urs. Madam, you must come to your uncle. Yonder's old coil at home: it is proved my Lady Hero hath been falsely accused, the prince and Claudio mightily abused; and Don John is the author of all, who is fled and gone. Will you come presently?
Beat. Will you go hear this news, signior?
Bene. I will live in thy heart, die in thy lap, and be buried in thy eyes; and, moreover, I will go with thee to thy uncle's.   [*Exeunt.*

SCENE III.—*The inside of a Church.*

Enter DON PEDRO, CLAUDIO, *and* Attendants, *with music and tapers.*

Claud. Is this the monument of Leonato?
Atten. It is, my lord.
Claud. reads from a scroll.]

Done to death by slanderous tongues
    Was the Hero that here lies:
Death in guerdon of her wrongs,
    Gives her fame which never dies:
So the life, that died with shame,
Lives in death with glorious fame.
Hang thou there upon the tomb,   [*affixing it.*
Praising her when I am dumb.—

Now, music, sound, and sing your solemn hymn.

SONG.

Pardon, Goddess of the night,
Those that slew thy virgin knight;
For the which, with songs of woe,
Round about her tomb they go.
    Midnight, assist our moan!
    Help us to sigh and groan,
        Heavily, heavily;
    Graves, yawn, and yield your dead,
    Till death be uttered,
        Heavily, heavily.

Claud. Now unto thy bones good night:
    Yearly will I do this rite.
D. Pedro. Good morrow, masters; put your torches out:
The wolves have prey'd; and look, the gentle day,
Before the wheels of Phœbus, round about
    Dapples the drowsy east with spots of gray.
Thanks to you all, and leave us: fare you well.
Claud. Good morrow, masters; each his several way.   [weeds;
D. Pedro. Come, let us hence, and put on other
And then to Leonato's we will go.
Claud. And Hymen now with luckier issue speeds
Than this, for whom we render'd up this woe!
        [*Exeunt.*

SCENE IV.—*A Room in* LEONATO'S *House.*

Enter LEONATO, ANTONIO, BENEDICK, BEATRICE, MARGARET, URSULA, FRIAR, *and* HERO.

Friar. Did I not tell you she was innocent?
Leon. So are the prince and Claudio, who accus'd her
Upon the error that you heard debated:
But Margaret was in some fault for this,
Although against her will, as it appears
In the true course of all the question.
Ant. Well, I am glad that all things sort so well.
Bene. And so am I, being else by faith enforc'd
To call young Claudio to a reckoning for it.
Leon. Well, daughter, and you gentlewomen all,
Withdraw into a chamber by yourselves;
And when I send for you, come hither mask'd:
The prince and Claudio promis'd by this hour
To visit me.—You know your office, brother;
You must be father to your brother's daughter,
And give her to young Claudio.
        [*Exeunt* Ladies.
Ant. Which I will do with confirm'd countenance.
Bene. Friar, I must entreat your pains, I think.
Friar. To do what, signior?
Bene. To bind me, or undo me, one of them.—
Signior Leonato, truth it is, good signior,
Your niece regards me with an eye of favour.
Leon. That eye my daughter lent her. 'Tis most true.
Bene. And I do with an eye of love requite her.
Leon. The sight whereof, I think, you had from me,
From Claudio, and the prince. But what's your will?
Bene. Your answer, sir, is enigmatical:
But, for my will, my will is your good-will
May stand with ours, this day to be conjoin'd
In the estate of honourable marriage;—
In which, good friar, I shall desire your help.
Leon. My heart is with your liking.
Friar   And my help.—
Here come the prince and Claudio.

Enter DON PEDRO *and* CLAUDIO, *with* Attendants.

D. Pedro. Good morrow to this fair assembly.

Leon. Good morrow, prince; good morrow,
    Claudio;
We here attend you. Are you yet determin'd
To-day to marry with my brother's daughter?
Claud. I'll hold my mind where she an Ethiope.
Leon. Call her forth, brother; here's the friar
    ready.   [*Exit* ANTONIO.
D. Pedro. Good morrow, Benedick. Why,
    what's the matter,
That you have such a February face,
So full of frost, of storm, and cloudiness?
Claud. I think he thinks upon the savage bull.—
Tush, fear not, man; we'll tip thy horns with
    gold,
And all Europa shall rejoice at thee,
As once Europa did at lusty Jove,
When he would play the noble beast in love.
Bene. Bull Jove, sir, had an amiable low;
And some such strange bull leap'd your father's
    cow,
And got a calf in that same noble feat
Much like to you, for you have just his bleat.

Re-enter ANTONIO, *with the* Ladies *masked*.

Claud. For this I owe you: here come other
    reckonings.
Which is the lady I must seize upon?
Ant. This same is she, and I do give you her.
Claud. Why, then, she's mine. Sweet, let me
    see your face.   [hand
Leon. No, that you shall not, till you take her
Before this friar, and swear to marry her.
Claud. Give me your hand before this holy
    friar;
I am your husband if you like of me.
Hero. And when I lived I was your other wife:
                [*Unmasking*.
And when you lov'd you were my other husband.
Claud. Another Hero?
Hero.   Nothing certainer:
One Hero died defil'd; but I do live,
And, surely as I live, I am a maid.
D. Pedro. The former Hero! Hero that is dead!
Leon. She died, my lord, but whiles her slan-
    der liv'd.
Friar. All this amazement can I qualify;
When, after that the holy rites are ended,
I'll tell you largely of fair Hero's death:
Meantime let wonder seem familiar,
And to the chapel let us presently.
Bene. Soft and fair, friar.—Which is Beatrice?
Beat. I answer to that name;   [*Unmasking*.
What is your will?
Bene. Do not you love me?
Beat.   No, no more than reason.
Bene. Why, then your uncle, and the prince,
    and Claudio
Have been deceived; for they swore you did.
Beat. Do not you love me?
Bene.   No, no more than reason.
Beat. Why, then my cousin, Margaret, and
    Ursula,
Are much deceived; for they did swear you did.

Bene. They swore that you were almost sick
    for me.   [for me.
Beat. They swore that you were well-nigh dead
Bene. 'Tis no such matter.—Then you do not
    love me?
Beat. No, truly, but in friendly recompense.
Leon. Come, cousin, I am sure you love the,
    gentleman.
Claud. And I'll be sworn upon 't that he loves
    her;
For here's a paper written in his hand—
A halting sonnet of his own pure brain,
Fashion'd to Beatrice.
Hero.   And here's another,
Writ in my cousin's hand, stolen from her
    pocket,
Containing her affection unto Benedick.
Bene. A miracle!—here's our own hands against
our hearts!—Come, I will have thee; but, by
this light, I take thee for pity.
Beat. I would not deny you;—but, by this
good day, I yield upon great persuasion; and
partly to save your life, for I was told you were
in a consumption.
Bene. Peace; I will stop your mouth.
                [*Kissing her*.
D. Pedro. How dost thou, Benedick the mar-
    ried man?
Bene. I'll tell thee what, prince; a college of
wit-crackers cannot flout me out of my humour. Dost thou think I care for a satire, or
an epigram? No: if a man will be beaten with
brains, he shall wear nothing handsome about
him. In brief, since I do purpose to marry, I
will think nothing to any purpose that the
world can say against it; and therefore never
flout at me for what I have said against it; for
man is a giddy thing, and this is my conclusion.—For thy part, Claudio, I did think to
have beaten thee; but in that thou art like to
be my kinsman, live unbruised, and love my
cousin.
Claud. I had well hoped thou wouldst have
denied Beatrice, that I might have cudgelled
thee out of thy single life, to make thee a
double dealer; which, out of question thou
wilt be if my cousin do not look exceeding
narrowly to thee.
Bene. Come, come, we are friends:—let's have
a dance ere we are married, that we may lighten
our own hearts and our wives' heels.
Leon. We'll have dancing afterwards.
Bene. First, o' my word; therefore, play, music.
—Prince, thou art sad; get thee a wife, get thee
a wife: there is no staff more reverend than one
tipped with horn.

Enter a Messenger.

Mess. My lord, your brother John is ta'en in
    flight,
And brought with arm'd men back to Messina.
Bene. Think not on him till to-morrow: I'll devise thee brave punishments for him.—Strike
up, pipers.   [*Dance. Exeunt*

A MIDSUMMER NIGHT'S DREAM

DRAMATIS PERSONÆ

THESEUS, *Duke of Athens.*
EGEUS, *Father to* HERMIA.
LYSANDER, ⎫ *in love with* HERMIA.
DEMETRIUS, ⎭
PHILOSTRATE, *Master of the Revels to* THE-
　　SEUS.
QUINCE, *the Carpenter.*
SNUG, *the Joiner.*
BOTTOM, *the Weaver.*
FLUTE, *the Bellows-mender.*
SNOUT, *the Tinker.*
STARVELING, *the Tailor.*

HIPPOLYTA, *Queen of the Amazons, betrothed
　　to* THESEUS.
HERMIA, *Daughter to* EGEUS, *in love with*
　　LYSANDER.
HELENA, *in love with* DEMETRIUS.

OBERON, *King of the Fairies.*
TITANIA, *Queen of the Fairies.*
PUCK, *or* ROBIN GOODFELLOW, *a Fairy.*

PEASBLOSSOM, ⎫
COBWEB, ⎪ *Fairies.*
MOTH, ⎬
MUSTARDSEED, ⎭

PYRAMUS, ⎫
THISBE, ⎪ *Characters in the Interlude
WALL,* ⎬ *performed by the Clowns.*
MOONSHINE, ⎪
LION, ⎭

Other Fairies *attending their* King *and* Queen.

Attendants *on* THESEUS *and* HIPPOLYTA.

SCENE,—ATHENS, *and a Wood not far from it.*

ACT I.

SCENE I.—ATHENS. *A Room in the Palace
of* THESEUS.

Enter THESEUS, HIPPOLYTA, PHILOSTRATE,
and Attendants.

The. Now, fair Hippolyta, our nuptial hour
Draws on apace; four happy days bring in
Another moon: but, oh, methinks, how slow
This old moon wanes! she lingers my desires,
Like to a step-dame or a dowager,
Long withering out a young man's revenue.
Hip. Four days will quickly steep themselves
　　　　in nights;
Four nights will quickly dream away the time;
And then the moon, like to a silver bow
New bent in heaven, shall behold the night
Of our solemnities.
The.　　　　　Go, Philostrate,
Stir up the Athenian youth to merriments;
Awake the pert and nimble spirit of mirth;
Turn melancholy forth to funerals—
The pale companion is not for our pomp.—
　　　　　　　　[*Exit* PHILOSTRATE.
Hippolyta, I woo'd thee with my sword,
And won thy love doing thee injuries;
But I will wed thee in another key,
With pomp, with triumph, and with revelling.

Enter EGEUS, HERMIA, LYSANDER, *and*
DEMETRIUS.

Ege. Happy be Theseus, our renowned duke!
The. Thanks, good Egeus: what's the news
　　with thee?

Ege. Full of vexation come I, with complaint
Against my child, my daughter Hermia.—
Stand forth, Demetrius.—My noble lord,
This man hath my consent to marry her:—
Stand forth, Lysander;—and, my gracious duke,
This hath bewitch'd the bosom of my child.
Thou, thou, Lysander, thou hast given her
　　　　rhymes,
And interchang'd love-tokens with my child:
Thou hast by moonlight at her window sung,
With feigning voice, verses of feigning love;
And stol'n the impression of her fantasy
With bracelets of thy hair, rings, gawds, con-
　　　　ceits,　　　　　　　　　　[sengers,
Knacks, trifles, nosegays, sweatmeats,—mes-
Of strong prevailment in unharden'd youth;—
With cunning hast thou filch'd my daughter's
　　　　heart;
Turned her obedience, which is due to me,
To stubborn harshness.—And, my gracious
　　　　duke,
Be it so she will not here before your grace
Consent to marry with Demetrius,
I beg the ancient privilege of Athens,—
As she is mine I may dispose of her:
Which shall be either to this gentleman
Or to her death; according to our law
Immediately provided in that case.
The. What say you, Hermia? be advis'd, fair
　　　　maid:
To you your father should be as a god;
One that compos'd your beauties; yea, and one
To whom you are but as a form in wax,
By him imprinted, and within his power
To leave the figure, or disfigure it.

Demetrius is a worthy gentleman.
Her. So is Lysander.
The.   In himself he is:
But, in this kind, wanting your father's voice,
The other must be held the worthier.   [eyes.
Her. I would my father look'd but with my
The. Rather your eyes must with his judgment
    look.
Her. I do entreat your grace to pardon me.
I know not by what power I am made bold,
Nor how it may concern my modesty
In such a presence here to plead my thoughts:
But I beseech your grace that I may know
The worst that may befall me in this case
If I refuse to wed Demetrius.
The. Either to die the death, or to abjure
For ever the society of men.
Therefore, fair Hermia, question your desires,
Know of your youth, examine well your blood,
Whether, if you yield not to your father's choice,
You can endure the livery of a nun;
For aye to be in shady cloister mew'd,
To live a barren sister all your life,
Chanting faint hymns to the cold, fruitless moon.
Thrice blessed they that master so their blood
To undergo such maiden pilgrimage:
But earthlier happy is the rose distill'd,
Than that which, withering on the virgin thorn,
Grows, lives, and dies in single blessedness.
Her. So will I grow, so live, so die, my lord,
Ere I will yield my virgin patent up
Unto his lordship, whose unwished yoke
My soul consents not to give sovereignty.
The. Take time to pause; and by the next new
    moon,—
The sealing-day betwixt my love and me,
For everlasting bond of fellowship,—
Upon that day either prepare to die
For disobedience to your father's will;
Or else to wed Demetrius, as he would;
Or on Diana's altar to protest
For aye austerity and single life.
Dem. Relent, sweet Hermia;—and, Lysander,
    yield
Thy crazed title to my certain right.
Lys. You have her father's love, Demetrius;
Let me have Hermia's: do you marry him.
Ege. Scornful Lysander! true, he hath my love;
And what is mine my love shall render him;
And she is mine; and all my right of her
I do estate unto Demetrius.
Lys. I am, my lord, as well deriv'd as he,
As well possess'd; my love is more than his;
My fortunes every way as fairly rank'd,
If not with vantage, as Demetrius's;
And, which is more than all these boasts can be,
I am belov'd of beauteous Hermia:
Why should not I then prosecute my right?
Demetrius, I'll avouch it to his head,
Made love to Nedar's daughter, Helena,
And won her soul; and she, sweet lady, dotes,
Devoutly dotes, dotes in idolatry,
Upon this spotted and inconstant man.
The. I must confess that I have heard so much,

And with Demetrius thought to have spoke
    thereof;
But, being over-full of self-affairs,
My mind did lose it.—But, Demetrius, come;
And come, Egeus; you shall go with me;
I have some private schooling for you both.—
For you, fair Hermia, look you arm yourself
To fit your fancies to your father's will,
Or else the law of Athens yields you up,—
Which by no means we may extenuate,—
To death, or to a vow of single life.—
Come, my Hippolyta: what cheer, my love?
Demetrius, and Egeus, go along:
I must employ you in some business
Against our nuptial, and confer with you
Of something nearly that concerns yourselves.
Ege. With duty and desire we follow you.
[*Exeunt* THES., HIP., EGE., DEM., *and* TRAIN.
Lys. How now, my love! why is your cheek so
    pale?
How chance the roses there do fade so fast?
Her. Belike for want of rain, which I could well
Beteem them from the tempest of mine eyes.
Lys. Ah me! for aught that ever I could read,
Could ever hear by tale or history,
The course of true love never did run smooth:
But either it was different in blood,——
Her. O cross! too high to be enthrall'd to low!
Lys. Or else misgraffed in respect of years;—
Her. O spite! too old to be engag'd to young!
Lys. Or else it stood upon the choice of friends:
Her. O hell! to choose love by another's eye!
Lys. Or, if there were a sympathy in choice!
War, death, or sickness, did lay siege to it,
Making it momentary as a sound,
Swift as a shadow, short as any dream;
Brief as the lightning in the collied night
That, in a spleen, unfolds both heaven and
    earth,
And ere a man hath power to say, Behold!
The jaws of darkness do devour it up:
So quick bright things come to confusion.
Her. If, then, true lovers have been ever cross'd,
It stands as an edict in destiny:
Then let us teach our trial patience,
Because it is a customary cross;
As due to love as thoughts, and dreams, and sighs,
Wishes, and tears, poor fancy's followers.
Lys. A good persuasion; therefore, hear me,
    Hermia.
I have a widow aunt, a dowager
Of great revenue, and she hath no child:
From Athens is her house remote seven leagues;
And she respects me as her only son.
There, gentle Hermia, may I marry thee;
And to that place the sharp Athenian law
Cannot pursue us. If thou lov'st me, then,
Steal forth thy father's house to-morrow night;
And in the wood a league without the town,
Where I did meet thee once with Helena,
To do observance to a morn of May,
There will I stay for thee.
Her.   My good Lysander!
I swear to thee by Cupid's strongest bow,

By his best arrow with the golden head,
By the simplicity of Venus' doves,
By that which knitteth souls and prospers loves,
And by that fire which burn'd the Carthage
      queen,
When the false Trojan under sail was seen,—
By all the vows that ever men have broke,
In number more than ever woman spoke,—
In that same place thou hast appointed me,
To-morrow truly will I meet with thee.
Lys. Keep promise, love. Look, here comes
      Helena.

Enter HELENA.

Her. God speed fair Helena! Whither away?
Hel. Call you me fair? that fair again unsay.
Demetrius loves your fair. O happy fair!
Your eyes are lode-stars; and your tongue's
      sweet air
More tuneable than lark to shepherd's ear,
When wheat is green, when hawthorn buds
      appear.
Sickness is catching: O, were favour so,
Yours would I catch, fair Hermia, ere I go;
My ear should catch your voice, my eye your
      eye,   [*melody.*
My tongue should catch your tongue's sweet
Were the world mine, Demetrius being bated,
The rest I'll give to be to you translated.
O, teach me how you look; and with what art
You sway the motion of Demetrius' heart.
Her. I frown upon him, yet he loves me still.
Hel. O that your frowns would teach my smiles
      such skill!
Her. I give him curses, yet he gives me love.
Hel. O that my prayers could such affection
      move!
Her. The more I hate, the more he follows me.
Hel. The more I love, the more he hateth me.
Her. His folly, Helena, is no fault of mine.
Hel. None, but your beauty: would that fault
      were mine!   [*face;*
Her. Take comfort; he no more shall see my
Lysander and myself will fly this place.—
Before the time I did Lysander see,
Seem'd Athens like a paradise to me:
O then, what graces in my love do dwell,
That he hath turn'd a heaven unto hell!
Lys. Helen, to you our minds we will unfold:
To-morrow night, when Phœbe doth behold
Her silver visage in the watery glass,
Decking with liquid pearl the bladed grass,—
A time that lovers' flights doth still conceal,—
Through Athens' gates have we devis'd to steal.
Her. And in the wood where often you and I
Upon faint primrose beds were wont to lie,
Emptying our bosoms of their counsel sweet,
There my Lysander and myself shall meet:
And thence from Athens turn away our eyes,
To seek new friends and stranger companies.
Farewell, sweet playfellow: pray thou for us,
And good luck grant thee thy Demetrius!—
Keep word, Lysander: we must starve our sight
From lovers' food, till morrow deep midnight.

Lys. I will, my Hermia.   [*Exit* HERMIA.
         Helena adieu:
As you on him, Demetrius dote on you!
                              [*Exit* LYS.
Hel. How happy some o'er other some can be!
Through Athens I am thought as fair as she.
But what of that? Demetrius thinks not so;
He will not know what all but he do know.
And as he errs, doting on Hermia's eyes,
So I, admiring of his qualities.
Things base and vile, holding no quantity,
Love can transpose to form and dignity.
Love looks not with the eyes, but with the mind;
And therefore is wing'd Cupid painted blind.
Nor hath love's mind of any judgment taste;
Wings and no eyes figure unheedy haste:
And therefore is love said to be a child,
Because in choice he is so oft beguil'd.
As waggish boys in game themselves forswear,
So the boy Love is perjur'd everywhere:
For ere Demetrius look'd on Hermia's eyne,
He hail'd down oaths that he was only mine;
And when this hail some heat from Hermia felt,
So he dissolv'd, and showers of oaths did melt.
I will go tell him of fair Hermia's flight;
Then to the wood will he to-morrow night
Pursue her; and for this intelligence
If I have thanks, it is a dear expense:
But herein mean I to enrich my pain,
To have his sight thither and back again. [*Exit.*

SCENE II.—*The same. A Room in a Cottage.*

Enter SNUG, BOTTOM, FLUTE, SNOUT, QUINCE, *and* STARVELING.

Quin. Is all our company here?
Bot. You were best to call them generally, man
by man, according to the scrip.
Quin. Here is the scroll of every man's name,
which is thought fit, through all Athens, to play
in our interlude before the duke and duchess
on his wedding-day at night.
Bot. First, good Peter Quince, say what the
play treats on; then read the names of the
actors; and so grow to a point.
Quin. Marry, our play is—The most lamentable comedy, and most cruel death of Pyramus
and Thisby.
Bot. A very good piece of work, I assure you,
and a merry.—Now, good Peter Quince, call
forth your actors by the scroll.—Masters,
spread yourselves.   [*weaver.*
Quin. Answer, as I call you.—Nick Bottom, the
Bot. Ready. Name what part I am for, and
proceed.   [*Pyramus.*
Quin. You, Nick Bottom, are set down for
Bot. What is Pyramus? a lover, or a tyrant?
Quin. A lover, that kills himself most gallantly
for love.
Bot. That will ask some tears in the true per-
forming of it. If I do it, let the audience look
to their eyes; I will move storms; I will con-
dole in some measure. To the rest:—yet my
chief humour is for a tyrant: I could play Ercles

rarely, or a part to tear a cat in, to make all split.

> The raging rocks, And Phibbus' car
> With shivering shocks, Shall shine from far,
> Shall break the locks And make and mar
> Of prison gates: The foolish Fates.

This was lofty!—Now, name the rest of the players.—This is Ercles' vein, a tyrant's vein; —a lover is more condoling.

Quin. Francis Flute, the bellows-mender.

Flu. Here, Peter Quince.

Quin. You must take Thisby on you.

Flu. What is Thisby? a wandering knight?

Quin. It is the lady that Pyramus must love.

Flu. Nay, faith, let me not play a woman; I have a beard coming.

Quin. That's all one; you shall play it in a mask, and you may speak as small as you will.

Bot. An I may hide my face, let me play Thisby too: I'll speak in a monstrous little voice;—*Thisne, Thisne.—Ah, Pyramus, my lover dear; thy Thisby dear! and lady dear!*

Quin. No, no, you must play Pyramus; and, Flute, you Thisby.

Bot. Well, proceed.

Quin. Robin Starveling, the tailor.

Star. Here, Peter Quince.

Quin. Robin Starveling, you must play Thisby's mother.—Tom Snout, the tinker.

Snout. Here, Peter Quince.

Quin. You, Pyramus's father; myself, Thisby's father;—Snug, the joiner, you, the lion's part; —and, I hope, here is a play fitted.

Snug. Have you the lion's part written? pray you, if it be, give it me, for I am slow of study.

Quin. You may do it extempore, for it is nothing but roaring.

Bot. Let me play the lion too: I will roar, that I will do any man's heart good to hear me; I will roar, that I will make the duke say, *Let him roar again, let him roar again.*

Quin. An you should do it too terribly you would fright the duchess and the ladies, that they would shriek; and that were enough to hang us all.

All. That would hang us every mother's son.

Bot. I grant you, friends, if that you whould fright the ladies out of their wits, they would have no more discretion but to hang us: but I will aggravate my voice so that I will roar you as gently as any sucking dove; I will roar you an 'twere any nightingale.

Quin. You can play no part but Pyramus, for Pyramus is a sweet-faced man; a proper man, as one shall see on a summer's day; a most lovely, gentleman-like man; therefore you must needs play Pyramus.

Bot. Well, I will undertake it. What beard were I best to play it in?

Quin. Why, what you will.

Bot. I will discharge it in either your straw-coloured beard, your orange-tawny beard, your purple-in-grain beard, or your French-crown-colour beard, your perfect yellow.

Quin. Some of your French crowns have no hair at all, and then you will play barefaced.— But, masters, here are your parts: and I am to entreat you, request you, and desire you, to con them by to-morrow night; and meet me in the palace wood, a mile without the town, by moonlight; there will we rehearse: for if we meet in the city, we shall be dogg'd with company, and our devices known. In the meantime I will draw a bill of properties, such as our play wants. I pray you, fail me not.

Bot. We will meet; and there we may rehearse more obscenely and courageously. Take pains: be perfect; adieu.

Quin. At the duke's oak we meet.

Bot. Enough; hold, or cut bow-strings.

[*Exeunt.*

ACT II.

Scene I.—*A Wood near Athens.*

Enter a Fairy *at one door, and* Puck *at another.*

Puck. How now, spirit! whither wander you?

Fai. Over hill, over dale,
>   Thorough bush, thorough brier,
> Over park, over pale,
>   Thorough flood, thorough fire,
> I do wander everywhere,
> Swifter than the moon's sphere;
> And I serve the fairy queen,
> To dew her orbs upon the green.
> The cowslips tall her pensioners be:
> In their gold coats spots you see;
> Those be rubies, fairy favours,
> In those freckles live their savours:
I must go seek some dew-drops here,
And hang a pearl in every cowslip's ear.
Farewell, thou lob of spirits; I'll be gone:
Our queen and all our elves come here anon.

Puck. The king doth keep his revels here to-
>   night;
Take heed the queen come not within his sight.
For Oberon is passing fell and wrath,
Because that she, as her attendant, hath
A lovely boy, stol'n from an Indian king;
She never had so sweet a changeling:
And jealous Oberon would have the child
Knight of his train, to trace the forests wild:
But she perforce withholds the loved boy,
Crowns him with flowers, and makes him all
>   her joy:
And now they never meet in grove or green,
By fountain clear or spangled starlight sheen,
But they do square; that all their elves, for fear,
Creep into acorn cups, and hide them there.

Fai. Either I mistake your shape and making
>   quite,
Or else you are that shrewd and knavish sprite
Call'd Robin Goodfellow: are you not he
That frights the maidens of the villagery;
Skim milk, and sometimes labour in the quern,

And bootless make the breathless housewife
    churn;
And sometime make the drink to bear no barm;
Mislead night-wanderers, laughing at their
    harm?
Those that Hobgoblin call you, and sweet Puck,
You do their work, and they shall have good luck:
Are not you he?
Puck.   Thou speak'st aright;
I am that merry wanderer of the night.
I jest to Oberon, and make him smile,
When I a fat and bean-fed horse beguile,
Neighing in likeness of a filly foal:
And sometime lurk I in a gossip's bowl,
In very likeness of a roasted crab;
And, when she drinks, against her lips I bob,
And on her wither'd dew-lap pour the ale.
The wisest aunt, telling the saddest tale,
Sometime for three-foot stool mistaketh me;
Then slip I from her bum, down topples she,
And *tailor* cries, and falls into a cough;
And then the whole quire hold their hips and
    loffe,
And waxen in their mirth, and neeze, and swear
A merrier hour was never wasted there.—
But room, fairy, here comes Oberon.
Fai. And here my mistress.—Would that he
    were gone!

SCENE II.

Enter OBERON *at one door, with his* Train,
and TITANIA, *at another, with hers.*

Obe. Ill met by moonlight, proud Titania.
Tita. What, jealous Oberon! Fairies, skip hence;
I have forsworn his bed and company.
Obe. Tarry, rash wanton: am not I thy lord?
Tita. Then I must be thy lady: but I know
When thou hast stol'n away from fairy-land,
And in the shape of Corin sat all day,
Playing on pipes of corn, and versing love
To amorous Phillida. Why art thou here,
Come from the farthest steep of India?
But that, forsooth, the bouncing Amazon,
Your buskin'd mistress and your warrior love,
To Theseus must be wedded; and you come
To give their bed joy and prosperity.
Obe. How can'st thou thus, for shame, Titania,
Glance at my credit with Hippolyta,
Knowing I know thy love to Theseus?
Didst thou not lead him through the glimmer-
    ing night
From Perigenia, whom he ravish'd?
And make him with fair Æglé break his faith,
With Ariadne and Antiopa?
Tita. These are the forgeries of jealousy:
And never, since the middle summer's spring,
Met we on hill, in dale, forest, or mead,
By paved fountain, or by rushy brook,
Or on the beached margent of the sea,
To dance our ringlets to the whistling wind,
But with thy brawls thou hast disturb'd our
    sport.
Therefore the winds, piping to us in vain,
As in revenge, have suck'd up from the sea

Contagious fogs; which, falling in the land,
Have every pelting river made so proud
That they have overborne their continents:
The ox hath therefore stretch'd his yoke in vain,
The ploughman lost his sweat; and the green
    corn
Hath rotted ere his youth attain'd a beard:
The fold stands empty in the drowned field,
And crows are fatted with the murrain flock;
The nine men's morris is fill'd up with mud;
And the quaint mazes in the wanton green,
For lack of tread, are undistinguishable:
The human mortals want their winter here;
No night is now with hymn or carol blest:—
Therefore the moon, the governess of floods,
Pale in her anger, washes all the air,
That rheumatic diseases do abound:
And thorough this distemperature we see
The seasons alter: hoary-headed frosts
Fall in the fresh lap of the crimson rose;
And on old Hyem's chin and icy crown
An odorous chaplet of sweet summer buds
Is, as in mockery, set: the spring, the summer,
The childing autumn, angry winter, change
Their wonted liveries; and the maz'd world,
By their increase, now knows not which is
    which:
And this same progeny of evils comes
From our debate, from our dissension:
We are their parents and original.
Obe. Do you amend it, then: it lies in you:
Why should Titania cross her Oberon?
I do but beg a little changeling boy
To be my henchman.
Tita.   Set your heart at rest;
The fairy-land buys not the child of me.
His mother was a vot'ress of my order:
And, in the spiced Indian air, by night,
Full often hath she gossip'd by my side;
And sat with me on Neptune's yellow sands,
Marking the embarked traders on the flood;
When we have laugh'd to see the sails conceive,
And grow big-bellied with the wanton wind:
Which she, with pretty and with swimming gait,
Following,—her womb then rich with my young
    squire,—
Would imitate; and sail upon the land,
To fetch me trifles, and return again,
As from a voyage, rich with merchandise.
But she, being mortal, of that boy did die;
And for her sake I do rear up her boy:
And for her sake I will not part with him.
Obe. How long within this wood intend you
    stay?   [day.
Tita. Perchance till after Theseus' wedding-
If you will patiently dance in our round,
And see our moonlight revels, go with us;
If not, shun me, and I will spare your haunts.
Obe. Give me that boy and I will go with thee.
Tita. Not for thy fairy kingdom. Fairies, away:
We shall chide downright if I longer stay.
            [*Exit* TITANIA *and her* Train.
Obe. Well, go thy way: thou shalt not from
    this grove

Till I torment thee for this injury —
My gentle Puck, come hither: thou remember'st
Since once I sat upon a promontory,
And heard a mermaid, on a dolphin's back,
Uttering such dulcet and harmonious breath,
That the rude sea grew civil at her song,
And certain stars shot madly from their spheres
To hear the sea-maid's music.
Puck.   I remember.
Obe. That very time I saw,—but thou couldst
    not,—
Flying between the cold moon and the earth,
Cupid all arm'd: a certain aim he took
At a fair vestal, throned by the west;
And loos'd his love-shaft smartly from his bow,
As it should pierce a hundred thousand hearts:
But I might see young Cupid's fiery shaft
Quench'd in the chaste beams of the watery
    moon;
And the imperial votaress passèd on,
In maiden meditation, fancy-free.
Yet mark'd I where the bolt of Cupid fell:
It fell upon a little western flower,—
Before milk-white, now purple with love's
    wound,—
And maidens call it love-in-idleness.
Fetch me that flower; the herb I show'd thee
    once:
The juice of it on sleeping eyelids laid
Will make or man or woman madly dote
Upon the next live creature that it sees.
Fetch me this herb: and be thou here again
Ere the leviathan can swim a league.
Puck. I'll put a girdle round about the earth
In forty minutes.   [*Exit* PUCK.
Obe.   Having once this juice,
I'll watch Titania when she is asleep,
And drop the liquor of it in her eyes:
The next thing then she waking looks upon,—
Be it on lion, bear, or wolf, or bull,
On meddling monkey, or on busy ape,—
She shall pursue it with the soul of love.
And ere I take this charm off from her sight,—
As I can take it with another herb,
I'll make her render up her page to me.
But who comes here? I am invisible;
And I will overhear their conference.

Enter DEMETRIUS, HELENA *following him.*

Dem. I love thee not, therefore pursue me not.
Where is Lysander and fair Hermia?
The one I'll slay, the other slayeth me.
Thou told'st me they were stol'n into this wood,
And here am I, and wood within this wood,
Because I cannot meet with Hermia.
Hence, get thee gone, and follow me no more.
Hel. You draw me, you hard-hearted adamant;
But yet you draw not iron, for my heart
Is true as steel. Leave you your power to draw,
And I shall have no power to follow you.
Dem. Do I entice you? Do I speak you fair?
Or, rather, do I not in plainest truth
Tell you I do not, nor I cannot love you?
Hel. And even for that do I love you the more.

I am your spaniel; and, Demetrius,
The more you beat me, I will fawn on you:
Use me but as your spaniel, spurn me, strike me,
Neglect me, lose me; only give me leave,
Unworthy as I am, to follow you.
What worser place can I beg in your love,
And yet a place of high respect with me,—
Than to be used as you use your dog?
Dem. Tempt not too much the hatred of my
    spirit;
For I am sick when I do look on thee.
Hel. And I am sick when I look not on you.
Dem. You do impeach your modesty too much,
To leave the city, and commit yourself
Into the hands of one that loves you not;
To trust the opportunity of night,
And the ill counsel of a desert place,
With the rich worth of your virginity.
Hel. Your virtue is my privilege for that.
It is not night when I do see your face,
Therefore I think I am not in the night:
Nor doth this wood lack worlds of company;
For you, in my respect, are all the world:
Then how can it be said I am alone
When all the world is here to look on me?
Dem. I'll run from thee, and hide me in the
    brakes,
And leave thee to the mercy of wild beasts.
Hel. The wildest hath not such a heart as you.
Run when you will, the story shall be chang'd;
Apollo flies, and Daphne holds the chase;
The dove pursues the griffin; the mild hind
Makes speed to catch the tiger,—bootless speed,
When cowardice pursues and valour flies.
Dem. I will not stay thy question; let me go:
Or, if thou follow me, do not believe
But I shall do thee mischief in the wood.
Hel. Ay, in the temple, in the town, the field,
You do me mischief. Fie, Demetrius!
Your wrongs do set a scandal on my sex:
We cannot fight for love as men may do:
We should be woo'd, and were not made to woo.
I'll follow thee, and make a heaven of hell,
To die upon the hand I love so well.
              [*Exeunt* DEM. *and* HEL.
Obe. Fare thee well, nymph: ere he do leave
    this grove,
Thou shalt fly him, and he shall seek thy love.—

Re-enter PUCK.

Hast thou the flower there? Welcome, wanderer.
Puck. Ay, there it is.
Obe.   I pray thee, give it me.
I know a bank whereon the wild thyme blows,
Where ox-lips and the nodding violet grows;
Quite over-canopied with lush woodbine,
With sweet musk roses, and with eglantine:
There sleeps Titania sometime of the night,
Lulled in these flowers with dances and delight;
And there the snake throws her enamell'd skin,
Weed wide enough to wrap a fairy in:
And with the juice of this I'll streak her eyes,
And make her full of hateful fantasies.

Take thou some of it, and seek through this
    grove:
A sweet Athenian lady is in love
With a disdainful youth: anoint his eyes;
But do it when the next thing he espies
May be the lady: thou shalt know the man
By the Athenian garments he hath on.
Effect it with some care, that he may prove
More fond on her than she upon her love:
And look thou meet me ere the first cock crow.
Puck. Fear not, my lord, your servant shall do
    so.   [*Exeunt.*

SCENE III.—*Another part of the Wood.*

Enter TITANIA, *with her* Train.

Tita. Come, now a roundel and a fairy song;
Then, for the third part of a minute, hence;
Some to kill cankers in the musk-rose buds;
Some war with rere-mice for their leathern
    wings,
To make my small elves coats; and some keep
    back   [wonders
The clamorous owl, that nightly hoots and
At our quaint spirits. Sing me now asleep;
Then to your offices, and let me rest.

SONG.

I.

1 *Fai.* You spotted snakes, with double tongue,
    Thorny hedgehogs, be not seen;
    Newts and blind-worms do no wrong;
    Come not near our fairy queen:

CHORUS.

Philomel, with melody,
    Sing in our sweet lullaby:
Lulla, lulla, lullaby; lulla, lulla, lullaby:
    Never harm, nor spell, nor charm,
    Come our lovely lady nigh;
So, good-night, with lullaby:

II.

2 *Fai.* Weaving spiders, come not here;
    Hence, you long-legg'd spinners, hence,
    Beetles black, approach not near;
    Worm nor snail do no offence.

CHORUS.

Philomel, with melody, &c.

1 *Fai.* Hence, away; now all is well:
One, aloof, stand sentinel.
        [*Exeunt* Fairies. TITANIA *sleeps.*

Enter OBERON.

Obe. What thou seest, when thou dost wake,
    [*Squeezes the flower on* TITANIA'S *eyelids.*
Do it for thy true-love take;
Love and languish for his sake;
Be it ounce, or cat, or bear,
Pard, or boar with bristled hair,
In thy eye that shall appear
When thou wak'st, it is thy dear;
Wake when some vile thing is near.   [*Exit.*

Enter LYSANDER *and* HERMIA.

Lys. Fair love, you faint with wandering in
    the wood;
   And, to speak troth, I have forgot our way;
We'll rest us Hermia, if you think it good,
   And tarry for the comfort of the day.
Her. Be it so, Lysander: find you out a bed,
For I upon this bank will rest my head.
Lys. One turf shall serve as pillow for us both;
One heart, one bed, two bosoms, and one troth.
Her. Nay, good Lysander; for my sake, my
    dear,
Lie farther off yet, do not lie so near.
Lys. O, take the sense, sweet, of my innocence;
Love takes the meaning in love's conference.
I mean, that my heart unto yours is knit;
So that but one heart we can make of it:
Two bosoms interchained with an oath;
So then two bosoms and a single troth.
Then by your side no bed-room me deny;
For lying so, Hermia, I do not lie.
Her. Lysander riddles very prettily:—
Now much beshrew my manners and my pride
If Hermia meant to say Lysander lied.
But, gentle friend, for love and courtesy
Lie farther off; in human modesty,
Such separation as may well be said
Becomes a virtuous bachelor and a maid:
So far be distant; and, good night, sweet friend:
Thy love ne'er alter till thy sweet life end!
Lys. Amen, amen, to that fair prayer, say I;
And then end life when I end loyalty!
Here is my bed: Sleep give thee all his rest!
Her. With half that wish the wisher's eyes be
    pressed!   [*They sleep.*

Enter PUCK.

Puck. Through the forest have I gone,
    But Athenian found I none,
    On whose eyes I might approve
    This flower's force in stirring love.
    Night and silence! who is here?
    Weeds of Athens he doth wear:
    This is he, my master said,
    Despised the Athenian maid;
    And here the maiden, sleeping sound,
    On the dank and dirty ground.
    Pretty soul! she durst not lie
    Near this lack-love, this kill-courtesy.
    Churl, upon thy eyes I throw
    All the power this charm doth owe;
    When thou wak'st let love forbid
    Sleep his seat on thy eyelid:
    So awake when I am gone;
    For I must now to Oberon.   [*Exit.*

Enter DEMETRIUS *and* HELENA, *running.*

Hel. Stay, though thou kill me, sweet Deme-
    trius.
Dem. I charge thee, hence, and do not haunt
    me thus.
Hel. O, wilt thou darkling leave me? do not so.
Dem. Stay on thy peril; I alone will go.
                [*Exit* DEMETRIUS.

Hel. O, I am out of breath in this fond chase!
The more my prayer the lesser is my grace.
Happy is Hermia, wheresoe'er she lies,
For she hath blessed and attractive eyes. [*tears:*
How came her eyes so bright? Not with salt
If so, my eyes are oftener wash'd than hers.
No, no, I am as ugly as a bear;
For beasts that meet me run away for fear:
Therefore no marvel though Demetrius
Do, as a monster, fly my presence thus.
What wicked and dissembling glass of mine
Made me compare with Hermia's sphery eyne?—
But who is here?—Lysander! on the ground!
Dead? or asleep? I see no blood, no wound.
Lysander, if you live, good sir, awake.

Lys. And run through fire I will for thy sweet
        sake.   [*Waking.*
Transparent Helena! Nature here shows art,
That through thy bosom makes me see thy heart.
Where is Demetrius? O, how fit a word
Is that vile name to perish on my sword!

Hel. Do not say so, Lysander; say not so:
What though he love your Hermia? Lord, what
        though?
Yet Hermia still loves you: then be content.

Lys. Content with Hermia? No: I do repent
The tedious minutes I with her have spent.
Not Hermia but Helena I love:
Who will not change a raven for a dove?
The will of man is by his reason sway'd;
And reason says you are the worthier maid.
Things growing are not ripe until their season;
So I, being young, till now ripe not to reason;
And touching now the point of human skill,
Reason becomes the marshal to my will,
And leads me to your eyes, where I o'erlook
Love's stories, written in love's richest book.

Hel. Wherefore was I to this keen mockery
        born?
When at your hands did I deserve this scorn?
Is't not enough, is't not enough, young man,
That I did never, no, nor never can
Deserve a sweet look from Demetrius' eye,
But you must flout my insufficiency?
Good troth, you do me wrong,—good sooth,
        you do—
In such disdainful manner me to woo.
But fare you well: perforce I must confess,
I thought you lord of more true gentleness.
O, that a lady of one man refus'd,
Should of another therefore be abus'd!   [*Exit.*

Lys. She sees not Hermia:—Hermia, sleep thou
        there;
And never mayst thou come Lysander near!
For, as a surfeit of the sweetest things
The deepest loathing to the stomach brings;
Or, as the heresies that men do leave
Are hated most of those they did deceive;
So thou, my surfeit and my heresy,
Of all be hated, but the most of me!
And, all my powers, address your love and might
To honour Helen, and to be her knight! [*Exit.*

Her. [*Starting.*] Help me, Lysander, help me!
        do thy best

To pluck this crawling serpent from my breast!
Ah me, for pity!—what a dream was here!
Lysander, look how I do quake with fear!
Methought a serpent eat my heart away,
And you sat smiling at his cruel prey.—
Lysander! what, removed? Lysander! lord!
What, out of hearing? gone? no sound, no word?
Alack, where are you? speak, an if you hear;
Speak, of all loves! I swoon almost with fear.
No?—then I well perceive you are not nigh:
Either death or you I'll find immediately.
                                    [*Exit.*

ACT III.

SCENE I.—*The Wood. The* Queen of Fairies
        lying asleep.

Enter QUINCE, SNUG, BOTTOM, FLUTE,
        SNOUT, *and* STARVELING.

Bot. Are we all met?

Quin. Pat, pat; and here is a marvellous convenient place for our rehearsal. This green plot
shall be our stage, this hawthorn brake our
tiring-house; and we will do it in action, as we
will do it before the duke.

Bot. Peter Quince,—

Quin. What say'st thou, bully Bottom?

Bot. There are things in this comedy of *Pyramus and Thisby* that will never please. First,
Pyramus must draw a sword to kill himself;
which the ladies cannot abide. How answer
you that?

Snout. By'r lakin, a parlous fear.

Star. I believe you must leave the killing out,
when all is done.

Bot. Not a whit: I have a device to make all
well. Write me a prologue; and let the prologue
seem to say, we will do no harm with our
swords, and that Pyramus is not killed indeed:
and for the more better assurance, tell them
that I Pyramus am not Pyramus, but Bottom
the weaver: this will put them out of fear.

Quin. Well, we will have such a prologue; and
it shall be written in eight and six.

Bot. No, make it two more; let it be written
in eight and eight.

Snout. Will not the ladies be afeard of the lion?

Star. I fear it, I promise you.

Bot. Masters, you ought to consider with yourselves: to bring in, God shield us! a lion among
ladies is a most dreadful thing: for there is not
a more fearful wild-fowl than your lion living;
and we ought to look to it.

Snout. Therefore another prologue must tell
he is not a lion.

Bot. Nay, you must name his name, and half
his face must be seen through the lion's neck;
and he himself must speak through, saying
thus, or to the same defect,—"Ladies," or
"Fair Ladies! I would wish you, or, I would
request you, or, I would entreat you, not to
fear, not to tremble: my life for yours. If you
think I come hither as a lion, it were pity of
my life. No, I am no such thing; I am a man

as other men are:"—and there, indeed, let him name his name, and tell them plainly he is Snug the joiner.

Quin. Well, it shall be so. But there is two hard things; that is, to bring the moonlight into a chamber: for, you know, Pyramus and Thisby meet by moonlight.

Snug. Doth the moon shine that night we play our play?

Bot. A calendar, a calendar! look in the almanack; find out moonshine, find out moonshine.

Quin. Yes, it doth shine that night.

Bot. Why, then you may leave a casement of the great chamber-window, where we play, open; and the moon may shine in at the casement.

Quin. Ay; or else one must come in with a bush of thorns and a lantern, and say he comes to disfigure or to present the person of moonshine. Then there is another thing: we must have a wall in the great chamber; for Pyramus and Thisby, says the story, did talk through the chink of a wall.

Snug. You never can bring in a wall.—What say you, Bottom?

Bot. Some man or other must present wall: and let him have some plaster, or some loam, or some rough-cast about him, to signify wall; or let him hold his fingers thus, and through that cranny shall Pyramus and Thisby whisper.

Quin. If that may be, then all is well. Come, sit down, every mother's son, and rehearse your parts. Pyramus, you begin: when you have spoken your speech, enter into that brake; and so every one according to his cue.

Enter PUCK *behind.*

Puck. What hempen homespuns have we swaggering here,
So near the cradle of the fairy queen?
What, a play toward! I'll be an auditor;
An actor too, perhaps, if I see cause.

Quin. Speak, Pyramus.—Thisby, stand forth.

Pyr. Thisby, the flowers of odious savours sweet,

Quin. Odours, odours.

Pyr. ——*odours savours sweet:*
    So doth they breath, my dearest Thisby dear.—
But hark, a voice! stay thou but here awhile,
    And by and by I will to thee appear.   [*Exit.*

Puck. A stranger Pyramus than e'er played here!   [*Aside.—Exit.*

This. Must I speak now?

Quin. Ay, marry, must you: for you must understand he goes but to see a noise that he heard, and is to come again.

This. Most radiant Pyramus, most lily white of hue,
    Of colour like the red rose on triumphant brier,
Most brisky juvenal, and eke most lovely Jew,
    As true as truest horse, that yet would never tire,
I'll meet thee, Pyramus, at Ninny's tomb.

Quin. Ninus' tomb, man: why, you must not speak that yet: that you answer to Pyramus. You speak all your part at once, cues and all.—

Pyramus enter: your cue is past; it is, *never tire.*

Re-enter PUCK, *and* BOTTOM *with an ass's head.*

This. O,—As true as truest horse, that yet would never tire.

Pyr. If I were fair, Thisby, I were only thine:—

Quin. O monstrous! O strange! we are haunted. Pray, masters! fly, masters!—Help!

    [*Exeunt* Clowns.

Puck. I'll follow you; I'll lead you about a round,   [through brier;
    Through bog, through bush, through brake,
Sometime a horse I'll be, sometime a hound,
    A hog, a headless bear, sometime a fire;
And neigh, and bark, and grunt, and roar, and burn,
Like horse, hound, hog, bear, fire, at every turn.

    [*Exit.*

Bot. Why do they run away? this is a knavery of them to make me afeard.

Re-enter SNOUT.

Snout. O Bottom, thou art changed! what do I see on thee?

Bot. What do you see? you see an ass-head of your own, do you?

Re-enter QUINCE.

Quin. Bless thee, Bottom! bless thee! thou art translated.   [*Exit.*

Bot. I see their knavery; this is to make an ass of me; to fright me, if they could. But I will not stir from this place, do what they can: I will walk up and down here, and I will sing, that they shall hear I am not afraid.   [*Sings.*

    The ousel-cock, so black of hue,
        With orange-tawny bill,
    The throstle with his note so true,
        The wren with little quill.

Tita. What angel wakes me from my flowery bed?   [*Waking.*

Bot.   The finch, the sparrow, and the lark,
        The plain-song cuckoo gray,
    Whose note full many a man doth mark,
        And dares not answer nay;—

for, indeed, who would set his wit to so foolish a bird? who would give a bird the lie, though he cry *cuckoo* never so?

Tita. I pray thee, gentle mortal, sing again: Mine ear is much enamour'd of thy note. So is mine eye enthralled to thy shape;   [me, And thy fair virtue's force perforce doth move On the first view, to say, to swear, I love thee.

Bot. Methinks, mistress, you should have little reason for that: and yet, to say the truth, reason and love keep little company together now-a-days: the more the pity that some honest neighbours will not make them friends. Nay, I can gleek upon occasion.

Tita. Thou art as wise as thou are beautiful.

Bot. Not so, neither: but if I had wit enough

to get out of this wood, I have enough to serve mine own turn.

Tita. Out of this wood do not desire to go;
Thou shalt remain here whether thou wilt or no.
I am a spirit of no common rate,—
The summer still doth tend upon my state;
And I do love thee: therefore, go with me,
I'll give thee fairies to attend on thee;
And they shall fetch thee jewels from the deep,
And sing, while thou on pressed flowers dost
    sleep:
And I will purge thy mortal grossness so
That thou shalt like an airy spirit go.—
Peasblossom! Cobweb! Moth! and Mustard-
    seed!

Enter Four Fairies.

1 *Fai.* Ready.
2 *Fai.*   And I.
3 *Fai.*   And I.
4 *Fai.*   Where shall we go?
Tita. Be kind and courteous to this gentleman;
Hop in his walks and gambol in his eyes;
Feed him with apricocks and dewberries,
With purple grapes, green figs, and mulberries;
The honey bags steal from the humble-bees,
And, for night-tapers, crop their waxen thighs,
And light them at the fiery glow-worm's eyes,
To have my love to bed and to arise;
And pluck the wings from painted butterflies,
To fan the moonbeams from his sleeping eyes:
Nod to him, elves, and do him courtesies.
1 *Fai.* Hail, mortal!
2 *Fai.* Hail!
3 *Fai.* Hail!
4 *Fai.* Hail!
Bot. I cry your worship's mercy heartily.—I beseech your worship's name.
Cob. Cobweb.
Bot. I shall desire you of more acquaintance, good Master Cobweb. If I cut my finger I shall make bold with you.—Your name, honest gentleman?
Peas. Peasblossom.
Bot. I pray you, commend me to Mistress Squash, your mother, and to Master Peascod, your father. Good Master Peasblossom, I shall desire you of more acquaintance too.—Your name, I beseech you, sir?
Mus. Mustardseed.
Bot. Good Master Mustardseed, I know your patience well: that same cowardly giant-like ox-beef hath devoured many a gentleman of your house: I promise you, your kindred hath made my eyes water ere now. I desire you more acquaintance, good Master Mustardseed.
Tita. Come, wait upon him; lead him to my
    bower.
  The moon, methinks, looks with a watery eye;
And when she weeps, weeps every little flower,
  Lamenting some enforced chastity.
  Tie up my love's tongue, bring him silently.
                    [Exeunt.

SCENE II:—*Another part of the Wood.*
Enter OBERON.

Obe. I wonder if Titania be awak'd;
Then what it was that next came in her eye,
Which she must dote on in extremity.

Enter PUCK.

Here comes my messenger.—How now, mad
    spirit?
What night-rule now about this haunted grove?
Puck. My mistress with a monster is in love.
Near to her close and consecrated bower,
While she was in her dull and sleeping hour,
A crew of patches, rude mechanicals,
That work for bread upon Athenian stalls,
Were met together to rehearse a play
Intended for great Theseus' nuptial day.
The shallowest thickskin of that barren sort
Who Pyramus presented in their sport,
Forsook his scene and enter'd in a brake;
When I did him at his advantage take,
An ass's nowl I fixed on his head;
Anon, his Thisbe must be answered,   [spy,
And forth my mimic comes. When they him
As wild geese that the creeping fowler eye,
Or russet-pated choughs, many in sort,
Rising and cawing at the gun's report,
Sever themselves, and madly sweep the sky,
So at his sight away his fellows fly:
And at our stamp here o'er and o'er one falls;
He murder cries, and help from Athens calls.
Their sense, thus weak, lost with their fears,
    thus strong,
Made senseless things begin to do them wrong:
For briers and thorns at their apparel snatch;
Some sleeves, some hats: from yielders all
    things catch.
I led them on in this distracted fear,
And left sweet Pyramus translated there:
When in that moment,—so it came to pass,—
Titania wak'd, and straightway lov'd an ass.
Obe. This falls out better than I could devise.
But hast thou yet latch'd the Athenian's eyes
With the love-juice, as I did bid thee do?
Puck. I took him sleeping,—that is finish'd
    too,—
And the Athenian woman by his side;
That, when he wak'd, of force she must be ey'd.

Enter DEMETRIUS *and* HERMIA.

Obe. Stand close; this is the same Athenian.
Puck. This is the woman, but not this the man.
Dem. O, why rebuke you him that loves you so?
Lay breath so bitter on your bitter foe.
Her. Now I but chide, but I should use thee
    worse;
For thou, I fear, hast given me cause to curse.
If thou hast slain Lysander in his sleep,
Being o'er shoes in blood, plunge in the deep,
And kill me too.
The sun was not so true unto the day
As he to me: would he have stol'n away

From sleeping Hermia? I'll believe as soon
This whole earth may be bor'd; and that the moon
May through the centre creep, and so displease
Her brother's noontide with the antipodes.
It cannot be but thou hast murder'd him;
So should a murderer look; so dead, so grim.
Dem. So should the murder'd look; and so should I,
Pierc'd through the heart with your stern cruelty:
Yet you, the murderer, look as bright, as clear,
As yonder Venus in her glimmering sphere.
Her. What's this to my Lysander? where is he?
Ah, good Demetrius, wilt thou give him me?
Dem. I had rather give his carcass to my hounds.
Her. Out, dog! out, cur! thou driv'st me past the bounds   [then?
Of maiden's patience. Hast thou slain him,
Henceforth be never number'd among men!
Oh! once tell true, tell true, even for my sake;
Durst thou have look'd upon him, being awake,
And hast thou kill'd him sleeping? O brave touch!
Could not a worm, an adder, do so much?
An adder did it; for with doubler tongue
Than thine, thou serpent, never adder stung.
Dem. You spend your passion on a mispris'd mood:
I am not guilty of Lysander's blood;
Nor is he dead, for aught that I can tell.
Her. I pray thee, tell me, then, that he is well.
Dem. An if I could, what should I get therefore?
Her. A privilege never to see me more.—
And from thy hated presence part I so:
See me no more whether he be dead or no.
                                          [*Exit.*
Dem. There is no following her in this fierce vein:
Here, therefore, for awhile I will remain.
So sorrow's heaviness doth heavier grow
For debt that bankrupt sleep doth sorrow owe;
Which now in some light measure it will pay,
If for his tender here I make some stay.
                                       [*Lies down.*
Obe. What hast thou done? thou hast mistaken quite,   [sight:
And laid the love-juice on some true-love's
Of thy misprision must perforce ensue
Some true-love turn'd, and not a false turn'd true.   [ing troth,
Puck. Then fate o'er-rules, that, one man hold-
A million fail, confounding oath on oath.
Obe. About the wood go, swifter than the wind,
And Helena of Athens look thou find:
All fancy-sick she is, and pale of cheer,
With sighs of love, that cost the fresh blood dear.
By some illusion see thou bring her here;
I'll charm his eyes against she do appear.
Puck. I go, I go; look how I go,—
Swifter than arrow from the Tartar's bow.
                                          [*Exit.*

Obe. Flower of this purple dye,
Hit with Cupid's archery,
Sink in apple of his eye!
When his love he doth espy,
Let her shine as gloriously
As the Venus of the sky.—
When thou wak'st, if she be by,
Beg of her for remedy.

Re-enter PUCK.

Puck. Captain of our fairy band,
Helena is here at hand,
And the youth mistook by me
Pleading for a lover's fee;
Shall we their fond pageant see?
Lord, what fools these mortals be!
Obe. Stand aside: the noise they make
Will cause Demetrius to awake.
Puck. Then will two at once woo one,—
That must needs be sport alone;
And those things do best please me
That befall preposterously.

Enter LYSANDER *and* HELENA.

Lys. Why should you think that I should woo in scorn?
   Scorn and derision never come in tears.
Look, when I vow, I weep; and vows so born,
   In their nativity all truth appears.
How can these things in me seem scorn to you,
Bearing the badge of faith, to prove them true?
Hel. You do advance your cunning more and more.
   When truth kills truth, O devilish-holy fray!
These vows are Hermia's: will you give her o'er?
   Weigh oath with oath and you will nothing weigh:
Your vows to her and me, put in two scales,
Will even weigh; and both as light as tales.
Lys. I had no judgment when to her I swore.
Hel. Nor none, in my mind, now you give her o'er.   [you.
Lys. Demetrius loves her, and he loves not
Dem. [*Awaking.*] O Helen, goddess, nymph, perfect, divine!
To what, my love, shall I compare thine eyne?
Crystal is muddy. O, how ripe in show
Thy lips, those kissing cherries, tempting grow!
That pure congealed white, high Taurus' snow,
Fann'd with the eastern wind, turns to a crow
When thou hold'st up thy hand: O let me kiss
This princess of pure white, this seal of bliss!
Hel. O spite! O hell! I see you all are bent
To set against me for your merriment.
If you were civil, and knew courtesy,
You would not do me thus much injury.
Can you not hate me, as I know you do,
But you must join in souls to mock me too?
If you were men, as men you are in show,
You would not use a gentle lady so;
To vow, and swear, and superpraise my parts,
When I am sure you hate me with your hearts.
You both are rivals, and love Hermia;
And now both rivals, to mock Helena:

A trim exploit, a manly enterprise,
To conjure tears up in a poor maid's eyes
With your derision! None of noble sort
Would so offend a virgin, and extort
A poor soul's patience, all to make you sport.
Lys. You are unkind, Demetrius; be not so;
For you love Hermia: this you know I know:
And here, with all good will, with all my heart,
In Hermia's love I yield you up my part;
And yours of Helena to me bequeath,
Whom I do love, and will do to my death.
Hel. Never did mockers waste more idle breath.
Dem. Lysander keep thy Hermia; I will none:
If e'er I lov'd her, all that love is gone.
My heart with her but as guest-wise sojourn'd;
And now to Helen is it home return'd,
There to remain.
Lys.   Helen, it is not so.
Dem. Disparage not the faith thou dost not
        know,
Lest, to thy peril, thou aby it dear.—
Look where thy love comes; yonder is thy dear.

Enter HERMIA.

Her. Dark night, that from the eye his func-
        tion takes,
The ear more quick of apprehension makes;
Wherein it doth impair the seeing sense,
It pays the hearing double recompense:—
Thou art not by mine eye, Lysander, found;
Mine ear, I thank it, brought me to thy sound.
But why unkindly didst thou leave me so?
Lys. Why should he stay whom love doth press
        to go?
Her. What love could press Lysander from my
        side?   [bide,—
Lys. Lysander's love, that would not let him
Fair Helena,—who more engilds the night
Than all yon fiery oes and eyes of light.
Why seek'st thou me? could not this make
        thee know
The hate I bare thee made me leave thee so?
Her. You speak not as you think; it cannot be.
Hel. Lo, she is one of this confederacy!
Now I perceive they have conjoin'd all three
To fashion this false sport in spite of me,
Injurious Hermia! most ungrateful maid!
Have you conspir'd, have you with these con-
        triv'd
To bait me with this foul derision?
Is all the counsel that we two have shar'd,
The sisters' vows, the hours that we have spent,
When we have chid the hasty-footed time
For parting us,—O, is all forgot?   [cence?
All school-days' friendship, childhood inno-
We, Hermia, like two artificial gods,
Have with our needls created both one flower,
Both on one sampler, sitting on one cushion,
Both warbling of one song, both in one key;
As if our hands, our sides, voices, and minds
Had been incorporate. So we grew together,
Like to a double cherry, seeming parted;
But yet a union in partition,
Two lovely berries moulded on one stem:

So, with two seeming bodies, but one heart,
Two of the first, like coats in heraldry,
Due but to one, and crowned with one crest.
And will you rent our ancient love asunder,
To join with men in scorning your poor friend?
It is not friendly, 'tis not maidenly:
Our sex, as well as I, may chide you for it,
Though I alone do feel the injury.
Her. I am amazed at your passionate words:
I scorn you not; it seems that you scorn me.
Hel. Have you not sent Lysander, as in scorn,
To follow me, and praise my eyes and face?
And made your other love, Demetrius,—
Who even but now did spurn me with his foot,—
To call me goddess, nymph, divine, and rare,
Precious, celestial? Wherefore speaks he this
To her he hates? and wherefore doth Lysander
Deny your love, so rich within his soul,
And tender me, forsooth, affection,
But by your setting on, by your consent?
What though I be not so in grace as you,
So hung upon with love, so fortunate;
But miserable most, to love unlov'd?
This you should pity, rather than despise.
Her. I understand not what you mean by this.
Hel. Ay, do perséver, counterfeit sad looks,
Make mows upon me when I turn my back;
Wink at each other; hold the sweet jest up:
This sport, well carried, shall be chronicled.
If you have any pity, grace, or manners,
You would not make me such an argument.
But, fare ye well: 'tis partly mine own fault;
Which death, or absence, soon shall remedy.
Lys. Stay, gentle Helena; hear my excuse;
My love, my life, my soul, fair Helena!
Hel. O excellent!
Her.   Sweet, do not scorn her so.
Dem. If she cannot entreat, I can compel.
Lys. Thou canst compel no more than she en-
        treat;
Thy threats have no more strength than her
        weak prayers.—
Helen, I love thee; by my life I do;
I swear by that which I will lose for thee
To prove him false that says I love thee not.
Dem. I say I love thee more than he can do.
Lys. If thou say so, withdraw, and prove it too.
Dem. Quick, come,—
Her.   Lysander, whereto tends all this?
Lys. Away, you Ethiope!
Dem.   No, no, sir:—he will
Seem to break loose; take on as you would
        follow:
But yet come not. You are a tame man; go!
Lys. Hang off, thou cat, thou burr: vile thing,
        let loose,
Or I will shake thee from me like a serpent.
Her. Why are you grown so rude? what change
        is this,
Sweet love?
Lys.   Thy love? out, tawny Tartar, out!
Out, loath'd medicine! hated potion, hence!
Her. Do you not jest?
Hel.   Yes, 'sooth; and so do you.

Lys. Demetrius, I will keep my word with thee.
Dem. I would I had your bond; for I perceive
A weak bond holds you; I'll not trust your
    word.   [her dead?
Lys. What! should I hurt her, strike her, kill
Although I hate her I'll not harm her so.
Her. What! can you do me greater harm than
    hate?   [love?
Hate me! wherefore? O me! what news, my
Am not I Hermia? Are not you Lysander?
I am as fair now as I was erewhile.   [left me:
Since night you lov'd me; yet since night you
Why, then, you left me,—O, the gods forbid!—
In earnest, shall I say?
Lys.   Ay, by my life;
And never did desire to see thee more.
Therefore be out of hope, of question, doubt,
Be certain, nothing truer; 'tis no jest
That I do hate thee and love Helena.
Her. O me! you juggler! you canker-blossom!
You thief of love! What! have you come by
    night,
And stol'n my love's heart from him?
Hel.   Fine, i' faith!
Have you no modesty, no maiden shame,
No touch of bashfulness? What! will you tear
Impatient answers from my gentle tongue?
Fie, fie! you counterfeit, you puppet, you!
Her. Puppet! why so? Ay, that way goes the
    game.
    Now I perceive that she hath made compare
Between our statures; she hath urg'd her height;
And with her personage, her tall personage,
Her height, forsooth, she hath prevail'd with
    him.—
And are you grown so high in his esteem
Because I am so dwarfish and so low?
How low am I, thou painted maypole? speak;
How low am I? I am not yet so low
But that my nails can reach unto thine eyes.
Hel. I pray you, though you mock me, gentle-
    men,
Let her not hurt me. I was never curst;
I have no gift at all in shrewishness;
I am a right maid for my cowardice;
Let her not strike me. You perhaps may think
Because she's something lower than myself,
That I can match her.
Her.   Lower! hark, again.
Hel. Good Hermia, do not be so bitter with me.
I evermore did love you, Hermia;   [you;
Did ever keep your counsels; never wrong'd
Save that, in love unto Demetrius,
I told him of your stealth unto this wood:
He follow'd you; for love I follow'd him;
But he hath chid me hence, and threaten'd me
To strike me, spurn me, nay, to kill me too:
And now, so you will let me quiet go,
To Athens will I bear my folly back,
And follow you no farther. Let me go:
You see how simple and how fond I am.
Her. Why, get you gone: who is 't that hinders
    you?
Hel. A foolish heart that I leave here behind.

Her. What! with Lysander?
Hel.   With Demetrius.
Lys. Be not afraid: she shall not harm thee,
    Helena.
Dem. No sir, she shall not, though you take
    her part.
Hel. O, when she's angry, she is keen and
    shrewd:
She was a vixen when she went to school;
And, though she be but little, she is fierce.
Her. Little again! nothing but low and little!
Why will you suffer her to flout me thus?
Let me come to her.
Lys.   Get you gone, you dwarf;
You minimus, of hind'ring knot-grass made;
You bead, you acorn.
Dem.   You are too officious
In her behalf that scorns your services.
Let her alone; speak not of Helena;
Take not her part; for if thou dost intend
Never so little show of love to her,
Thou shalt aby it.
Lys.   Now she holds me not;
Now follow, if thou dar'st, to try whose right,
Or thine or mine, is most in Helena.
Dem. Follow! nay, I'll go with thee, cheek by
    jole.   [*Exeunt* Lys. *and* Dem.
Her. You, mistress, all this coil is 'long of you:
Nay, go not back.
Hel.   I will not trust you, I;
Nor longer stay in your curst company.
Your hands than mine are quicker for a fray;
My legs are longer though, to run away.
                         [*Exit.*
Her. I am amaz'd, and know not what to say.
           [*Exit, pursuing* Helena.
Obe. This is thy negligence: still thou mistak'st,
Or else commit'st thy knaveries wilfully.
Puck. Believe me, king of shadows, I mistook.
Did not you tell me I should know the man
By the Athenian garments he had on?
And so far blameless proves my enterprise,
That I have 'nointed an Athenian's eyes:
And so far am I glad it so did sort,
As this their jangling I esteem a sport.
Obe. Thou seest these lovers seek a place to
    fight:
Hie therefore, Robin, overcast the night;
The starry welkin cover thou anon
With drooping fog, as black as Acheron;
And lead these testy rivals so astray,
As one come not within another's way.
Like to Lysander sometime frame thy tongue,
Then stir Demetrius up with bitter wrong;
And sometime rail thou like Demetrius;
And from each other look thou lead them thus,
Till o'er their brows death-counterfeiting sleep
With leaden legs and batty wings doth creep:
Then crush this herb into Lysander's eye;
Whose liquor hath this virtuous property,
To take from thence all error with his might,
And make his eyeballs roll with wonted sight.
When they next wake, all this derision
Shall seem a dream and fruitless vision;

And back to Athens shall the lovers wend,
With league whose date till death shall never end
Whiles I in this affair do thee employ,
I'll to my queen, and beg her Indian boy;
And then I will her charmed eye release
From monster's view, and all things shall be
    peace.
Puck. My fairy lord, this must be done with
    haste,
For night's swift dragons cut the clouds full fast;
And yonder shines Aurora's harbinger,
At whose approach ghosts, wandering here and
    there,
Troop home to churchyards: damned spirits all,
That in cross-ways and floods have burial,
Already to their wormy beds are gone;
For fear lest day should look their shames upon
They wilfully exile themselves from light,
And must for aye consort with black-brow'd
    night.
Obe. But we are spirits of another sort:
I with the morning's love have oft made sport;
And, like a forester, the groves may tread
Even till the eastern gate, all fiery-red,
Opening on Neptune with fair blessed beams,
Turns into yellow gold his salt-green streams.
But, notwithstanding, haste; make no delay:
We may effect this business yet ere day.
                    [*Exit* OBE.

Puck. Up and down, up and down;
I will lead them up and down:
I am fear'd in field and town:
Goblin, lead them up and down.
Here comes one.

Enter LYSANDER.

Lys. Where art thou, proud Demetrius? speak
    thou now.   [art thou?
Puck. Here, villain; drawn and ready. Where
Lys. I will be with thee straight.
Puck.   Follow me, then,
To plainer ground.
           [*Exit* LYS. *as following the voice.*

Enter DEMETRIUS.

Dem.   Lysander! speak again.
Thou runaway, thou coward, art thou fled?
Speak. In some bush? where dost thou hide,
    thy head?   [stars
Puck. Thou coward, art thou bragging to the
Telling the bushes that thou look'st for wars,
And wilt not come? Come, recreant; come,
    thou child;
I'll whip thee with a rod: he is defiled
That draws a sword on thee.
Dem.   Yea, art thou there?
Puck. Follow my voice; we'll try no manhood
    here.   [*Exeunt.*

Re-enter LYSANDER.

Lys. He goes before me, and still dares me on;
When I come where he calls, then he is gone.
The villain is much lighter heeled than I:
I follow'd fast, but faster he did fly;

That fallen am I in dark uneven way,
And here will rest me. Come, thou gentle day!
                [*Lies down.*
For if but once thou show me thy gray light,
I'll find Demetrius, and revenge this spite.
                [*Sleeps*

Re-enter PUCK *and* DEMETRIUS.

Puck. Ho, ho! ho, ho! Coward, why com'st
    thou not?
Dem. Abide me if thou dar'st; for well I wot
Thou runn'st before me, shifting every place;
And dar'st not stand, nor look me in the face.
Where art thou?
Puck.   Come hither; I am here.
Dem. Nay, then, thou mock'st me. Thou shalt
    buy this dear,
If ever I thy face by daylight see:
Now, go thy way. Faintness constraineth me
To measure out my length on this cold bed.—
By day's approach look to be visited.
             [*Lies down and sleeps.*

Enter HELENA.

Hel. O weary night, O long and tedious night,
Abate thy hours! Shine comforts from the east,
That I may back to Athens by daylight,
From these that my poor company detest:—
And sleep, that sometimes shuts up sorrow's eye,
Steal me awhile from mine own company.
              [*Sleeps.*

Puck. Yet but three? Come one more;
    Two of both kinds makes up four.
    Here she comes, curst and sad:—
    Cupid is a knavish lad,
    Thus to make poor females mad.

Enter HERMIA.

Her. Never so weary, never so in woe,
    Bedabbled with the dew, and torn with briers;
I can no farther crawl, no farther go;
    My legs can keep no pace with my desires.
Here will I rest me till the break of day.
Heaven shield Lysander, if they mean a fray!
             [*Lies down.*

Puck. On the ground
    Sleep sound:
    I'll apply
    To your eye,
Gentle lover, remedy.
    [*Squeezing the juice on* LYSANDER'S *eye.*
    When thou wak'st,
    Thou tak'st
    True delight
    In the sight
Of thy former lady's eye:
And the country proverb known,
That every man should take his own,
In your waking shall be shown:
    Jack shall have Jill;
    Nought shall go ill;   [be well.
The man shall have his mare again, and all shall
    [*Exit* PUCK.—DEM., HEL., &*c, sleep.*

ACT IV.

SCENE I.—*The Wood.*

Enter TITANIA *and* BOTTOM, Fairies *attending;* OBERON *behind, unseen.*

Tita. Come, sit thee down upon this flowery bed,
　　While I thy amiable cheeks do coy,
And stick musk-roses in thy sleek smooth head,
　　And kiss thy fair large ears, my gentle joy.
Bot. Where's Peasblossom?
Peas. Ready.
Bot. Scratch my head, Peasblossom.—Where's
　　Monsieur Cobweb?
Cob. Ready.
Bot. Monsieur Cobweb; good monsieur, get your weapons in your hand and kill me a red-hipped humble-bee on the top of a thistle; and, good monsieur, bring me the honey-bag. Do not fret yourself too much in the action, monsieur; and, good monsieur, have a care the honey-bag break not; I would be loath to have you over-flown with a honey-bag, signior.—Where's Monsieur Mustardseed?
Must. Ready.　　　　　　　　　　　[seed.
Bot. Give me your neif, Monsieur Mustard-Pray you, leave your courtesy, good monsieur.
Must. What's your will?
Bot. Nothing, good monsieur, but to help Cavalero Cobweb to scratch. I must to the barber's, monsieur; for methinks I am marvellous hairy about the face: and I am such a tender ass, if my hair do but tickle me I must scratch.
Tita. What, wilt thou hear some music, my
　　sweet love?
Bot. I have a reasonable good ear in music; let us have the tongs and the bones.　　　[eat.
Tita. Or say, sweet love, what thou desir'st to
Bot. Truly, a peck of provender; I could munch your good dry oats. Methinks I have a great desire to a bottle of hay: good hay, sweet hay, hath no fellow.
Tita. I have a venturous fairy that shall seek The squirrel's hoard, and fetch thee new nuts.
Bot. I had rather have a handful or two of dried peas. But, I pray you, let none of your people stir me; I have an exposition of sleep come upon me.　　　　　　　　　　　[arms.
Tita. Sleep thou, and I will wind thee in my Fairies, be gone, and be all ways away.
So doth the woodbine the sweet honeysuckle Gently entwist,—the female ivy so
Enrings the barky fingers of the elm.
O, how I love thee! how I dote on thee!
　　　　　　　　　　　　　　[They sleep.

OBERON *advances. Enter* PUCK.

Obe. Welcome, good Robin. Seest thou this
　　sweet sight?
Her dotage now I do begin to pity.
For, meeting her of late behind the wood,
Seeking sweet savours for this hateful fool,
I did upbraid her, and fall out with her:
For she his hairy temples then had rounded
With coronet of fresh and fragrant flowers;
And that same dew, which sometime on the buds
Was wont to swell like round and orient pearls,
Stood now within the pretty flow'rets' eyes,
Like tears that did their own disgrace bewail.
When I had, at my pleasure, taunted her,
And she, in mild terms, begg'd my patience,
I then did ask of her her changeling child;
Which straight she gave me, and her fairy sent
To bear him to my bower in fairy-land.
And now I have the boy, I will undo
This hateful imperfection of her eyes.
And, gentle Puck, take this transformed scalp
From off the head of this Athenian swain;
That he awaking when the other do,
May all to Athens back again repair,
And think no more of this night's accidents
But as the fierce vexation of a dream.
But first I will release the fairy queen.
　　Be as thou wast wont to be;
　　　　　[*Touching her eyes with an herb.*
　　See as thou wast wont to see:
　　Dian's bud o'er Cupid's flower
　　Hath such force and blessed power.
Now, my Titania; wake you, my sweet queen.
Tita. My Oberon! what visions have I seen!
Methought I was enamour'd of an ass.
Obe. There lies your love.
Tita.　　　　How came these things to pass?
O, how mine eyes do loathe his visage now!
Obe. Silence awhile.—Robin, take off this head.
Titania, music call; and strike more dead
Than common sleep, of all these five, the sense.
Tita. Music, ho! music; such as charmeth sleep.
Puck. Now, when thou wak'st, with thine own
　　fool's eyes peep.
Obe. sound, music. [*Still music.*] Come, my
　　queen, take hands with me,
And rock the ground whereon these sleepers be.
Now thou and I are new in amity,
And will to-morrow midnight solemnly
Dance in Duke Theseus' house triumphantly,
And bless it to all fair posterity:
There shall the pairs of faithful lovers be
Wedded, with Theseus, all in jollity.
Puck. Fairy king, attend and mark;
I do hear the morning lark.
Obe. Then, my queen, in silence sad,
Trip we after the night's shade:
We the globe can compass soon,
Swifter than the wand'ring moon.
Tita. Come, my lord; and in our flight,
Tell me how it came this night
That I sleeping here was found,
With these mortals on the ground.
　　　　　　　　　　　　　　[*Exeunt.*
　　　　　　　　　　　　　　[*Horns sound within.*

Enter THESEUS, HIPPOLYTA, EGEUS, *and* Train.

The. Go, one of you, find out the forester;—
For now our observation is perform'd;
And since we have the vaward of the day,
My love shall hear the music of my hounds.

Uncouple in the western valley; go:—
Despatch, I say, and find the forester.—
We will, fair queen, up to the mountain's top,
And mark the musical confusion
Of hounds and echo in conjunction.
Hip. I was with Hercules and Cadmus once,
When in a wood of Crete they bay'd the bear
With hounds of Sparta: never did I hear
Such gallant chiding; for, besides the groves,
The skies, the fountains, every region near
Seem'd all one mutual cry: I never heard
So musical a discord, such sweet thunder.
The. My hounds are bred out of the Spartan
        kind,
So flew'd, so sanded; and their heads are hung
With ears that sweep away the morning dew;
Crook-kneed and dew-lap'd like Thessalian
        bulls;
Slow in pursuit, but match'd in mouth like bells,
Each under each. A cry more tuneable
Was never holla'd to, nor cheer'd with horn,
In Crete, in Sparta, nor in Thessaly:
Judge when you hear.—But, soft, what nymphs
        are these?
Ege. My lord, this is my daughter here asleep;
And this Lysander; this Demetrius is;
This Helena, old Nedar's Helena:
I wonder of their being here together.
The. No doubt, they rose up early to observe
The rite of May; and, hearing our intent,
Came here in grace of our solemnity.—
But speak, Egeus; is not this the day
That Hermia should give answer of her choice?
Ege. It is, my lord.
The. Go, bid the huntsmen wake them with
        their horns.
        [*Horns, and shout within.* DEM., LYS.,
            HER., *and* HEL., *awake and start up.*
The. Good-morrow, friends. Saint Valentine is
        past;
Begin these wood-birds but to couple now?
Lys. Pardon, my lord.
        [*He and the rest kneel to* THESEUS.
The.   I pray you all, stand up.
I know you two are rival enemies;
How comes this gentle concord in the world,
That hatred is so far from jealousy
To sleep by hate, and fear no enmity?
Lys. My lord, I shall reply amazedly,
Half 'sleep, half waking: but as yet, I swear,
I cannot truly say how I came here:
But, as I think,—for truly would I speak—
And now I do bethink me, so it is,—
I came with Hermia hither: our intent   [be
Was to be gone from Athens, where we might
Without the peril of the Athenian law.
Ege. Enough, enough, my lord; you have
        enough;
I beg the law, the law upon his head.—
They would have stol'n away, they would,
        Demetrius,
Thereby to have defeated you and me:
You of your wife, and me of my consent,—
Of my consent that she should be your wife.

Dem. My lord, fair Helen told me of their stealth,
Of this their purpose hither to this wood;
And I in fury hither follow'd them,
Fair Helena in fancy following me.
But, my good lord, I wot not by what power,—
But by some power it is,—my love to Hermia
Melted as doth the snow—seems to me now
As the remembrance of an idle gawd
Which in my childhood I did dote upon:
And all the faith, the virtue of my heart,
The object and the pleasure of mine eye,
Is only Helena. To her, my lord,
Was I betroth'd ere I saw Hermia:
But, like in sickness, did I loathe this food;
But, as in health, come to my natural taste,
Now do I wish it, love it, long for it,
And will for evermore be true to it.
The. Fair lovers, you are fortunately met:
Of this discourse we more will hear anon.—
Egeus, I will overbear your will;
For in the temple, by and by with us,
These couples shall eternally be knit.
And, for the morning now is something worn,
Our purpos'd hunting shall be set aside.—
Away with us to Athens three and three,
We'll hold a feast in great solemnity.—
Come, Hippolyta.
        [*Exeunt* THE., HIP., EGE., *and* Train.
Dem. These things seem small and undistin-
        guishable,
Like far-off mountains turned into clouds.
Her. Methinks I see these things with parted
        eye,
When everything seems double.
Hel.   So methinks:
And I have found Demetrius like a jewel.
Mine own, and not mine own.
Dem.   If seems to me
That we yet sleep, we dream.—Do you not
        think
The duke was here, and bid us follow him?
Her. Yea, and my father.
Hel.   And Hippolyta.
Lys. And he did bid us follow to the temple.
Dem. Why, then, we are awake: let's follow him;
And by the way let us recount our dreams.
        [*Exeunt.*

As they go out, BOTTOM *awakes.*

Bot. When my cue comes, call me, and I will
answer:—my next is, *Most fair Pyramus.*——
Heigh-ho!—Peter Quince! Flute, the bellows-
mender! Snout, the tinker! Starveling! God's
my life, stolen hence, and left me asleep! I
have had a most rare vision. I have had a
dream—past the wit of man to say what dream
it was.—Man is but an ass if he go about to expound this dream. Methought I was—there is
no man can tell what. Methought I was, and
methought I had,—But man is but a patched
fool, if he will offer to say what methought I
had. The eye of man hath not heard, the ear of
man hath not seen; man's hand is not able to
taste, his tongue to conceive, nor his heart to

report what my dream was. I will get Peter Quince to write a ballad of this dream: it shall be called Bottom's Dream, because it hath no bottom; and I will sing it in the latter end of a play, before the duke: peradventure, to make it the more gracious, I shall sing it at her death. [*Exit.*

SCENE II.—ATHENS. *A Room in* QUINCE'S *House.*

Enter QUINCE, FLUTE, SNOUT, *and* STARVELING.

Quin. Have you sent to Bottom's house? is he come home yet?

Star. He cannot be heard of. Out of doubt, he is transported.

Flu. If he come not, then the play is marred; it goes not forward, doth it?

Quin. It is not possible: you have not a man in all Athens able to discharge Pyramus but he.

Flu. No; he hath simply the best wit of any handicraft man in Athens.

Quin. Yea, and the best person too: and he is a very paramour for a sweet voice.

Flu. You must say paragon: a paramour is, God bless us, a thing of naught.

Enter SNUG.

Snug. Masters, the duke is coming from the temple; and there is two or three lords and ladies more married: if our sport had gone forward we had all been made men.

Flu. O sweet bully Bottom! Thus hath he lost sixpence a-day during his life; he could not have 'scaped sixpence a-day: an the duke had not given him sixpence a-day for playing Pyramus, I'll be hanged; he would have deserved it: sixpence a-day in Pyramus, or nothing.

Enter BOTTOM.

Bot. Where are these lads? where are these hearts?

Quin. Bottom!—O most courageous day! O most happy hour!

Bot. Masters, I am to discourse wonders: but ask me not what; for if I tell you, I am no true Athenian. I will tell you everything, right as it fell out.

Quin. Let us hear, sweet Bottom.

Bot. Not a word of me. All that I will tell you is, that the duke hath dined. Get your apparel together; good strings to your beards, new ribbons to your pumps; meet presently at the palace; every man look over his part; for, the short and the long is, our play is preferred. In any case, let Thisby have clean linen; and let not him that plays the lion pare his nails, for they shall hang out for the lion's claws. And, most dear actors, eat no onions nor garlick; for we are to utter sweet breath; and I do not doubt but to hear them say it is a sweet comedy. No more words: away! go; away! [*Exeunt.*

ACT V.

SCENE I.—ATHENS. *An Apartment in the Palace of* THESEUS.

Enter THESEUS, HIPPOLYTA, PHILOSTRATE, Lords *and* Attendants.

Hip. 'Tis strange, my Theseus, that these lovers speak of.

The. More strange than true. I never may believe
These antique fables, nor these fairy toys.
Lovers and madmen have such seething brains,
Such shaping fantasies, that apprehend
More than cool reason ever comprehends.
The lunatic, the lover, and the poet
Are of imagination all compact:
One sees more devils than vast hell can hold;
That is the madman: the lover, all as frantic,
Sees Helen's beauty in a brow of Egypt:
The poet's eye, in a fine frenzy rolling,
Doth glance from heaven to earth, from earth to heaven,
And, as imagination bodies forth
The forms of things unknown, the poet's pen
Turns them to shapes, and gives to airy nothing
A local habitation and a name.
Such tricks hath strong imagination,
That, if it would but apprehend some joy,
It comprehends some bringer of that joy;
Or in the night, imagining some fear,
How easy is a bush supposed a bear?

Hip. But all the story of the night told over,
And all their minds transfigur'd so together,
More witnesseth than fancy's images,
And grows to something of great constancy;
But, howsoever, strange and admirable.

Enter LYSANDER, DEMETRIUS, HERMIA, *and* HELENA.

The. Here come the lovers, full of joy and mirth.—
Joy, gentle friends! joy and fresh days of love
Accompany your hearts!

Lys.   More than to us
Wait on your royal walks, your board, your bed!

The. Come now; what masques, what dances shall we have,
To wear away this long age of three hours
Between our after-supper and bed-time?
Where is our usual manager of mirth?
What revels are in hand? Is there no play,
To ease the anguish of a torturing hour?
Call Philostrate.

Philost.   Here, mighty Theseus.

The. Say, what abridgment have you for this evening?
What masque? what music? How shall we beguile
The lazy time, if not with some delight?

Philost. There is a brief how many sports are ripe;
Make choice of which your highness will see first.   [*Giving a paper.*

The. [*reads.*] *The battle with the Centaurs, to be*
   sung
   By an Athenian eunuch to the harp.
We'll none of that: that I have told my love,
In glory of my kinsman Hercules.
   The riot of the tipsy Bacchanals,
   Tearing the Thracian singer in their rage.
That is an old device, and it was play'd
When I from Thebes came last a conqueror.
   The thrice-three Muses mourning for the death
   Of learning, late deceas'd in beggary.
That is some satire, keen and critical,
Not sorting with a nuptial ceremony.
   A tedious brief scene of young Pyramus,
   And his love Thisbe; very tragical mirth.
Merry and tragical! tedious and brief!
That is, hot ice and wondrous strange snow.
How shall we find the concord of this discord?
Philost. A play there is, my lord, some ten
   words long,
Which is as brief as I have known a play;
But by ten words, my lord, it is too long,
Which makes it tedious: for in all the play
There is not one word apt, one player fitted:
And tragical, my noble lord, it is;
For Pyramus therein doth kill himself:
Which when I saw rehears'd, I must confess,
Made mine eyes water; but more merry tears
The passion of loud laughter never shed.
The. What are they that do play it?
Philost. Hard-handed men that work in Athens
   here,
Which never labour'd in their minds till now;
And now have toil'd their unbreath'd memories
With this same play against your nuptial.
The. And we will hear it.
Philost.   No, my noble lord,
It is not for you: I have heard it over,
And it is nothing, nothing in the world;
Unless you can find sport in their intents,
Extremely stretch'd, and conn'd with cruel pain,
To do you service.
The.   I will hear that play;
For never anything can be amiss
When simpleness and duty tender it.
Go, bring them in: and take your places, ladies.
                [*Exit* PHILOSTRATE.
Hip. I love not to see wretchedness o'er-
   charged,
And duty in his service perishing.   [thing.
The. Why, gentle sweet, you shall see no such
Hip. He says they can do nothing in this kind.
The. The kinder we, to give them thanks for
   nothing.
Our sport shall be to take what they mistake:
And what poor duty cannot do,
Noble respect takes it in might, not merit.
Where I have come, great clerks have purposed
To greet me with premeditated welcomes;
Where I have seen them shiver and look pale,
Make periods in the midst of sentences,
Throttle their practis'd accent in their fears,
And, in conclusion, dumbly have broke off,
Not paying me a welcome. Trust me, sweet,

Out of this silence yet I pick'd a welcome
And in the modesty of fearful duty
I read as much as from the rattling tongue
Of saucy and audacious eloquence.
Love, therefore, and tongue-tied simplicity
In least speak most to my capacity.

Enter PHILOSTRATE.

Philost. So please your grace, the prologue is
   address'd.
The. Let him approach.
                [*Flourish of Trumpets.*

Enter Prologue.

Prol. If we offend, it is with our good will.
   That you should think we come not to offend
But with good will. To show our simple skill,
   That is the true beginning of our end.
Consider, then, we come but in despite.
   We do not come as minding to content you.
Our true intent is. All for your delight
   We are not here. That you should here repent
      you.
The actors are at hand: and, by their show,
You shall know all that you are like to know.

The. This fellow doth not stand upon points.
Lys. He hath rid his prologue like a rough
colt; he knows not the stop. A good moral,
my lord: it is not enough to speak, but to
speak true.
Hip. Indeed he hath played on this prologue
like a child on a recorder; a sound, but not in
government.
The. His speech was like a tangled chain;
nothing impaired, but all disordered. Who is
next?

Enter PYRAMUS *and* THISBE, WALL, MOON-
   SHINE, *and* LION, *as in dumb show.*

Prol. Gentles, perchance you wonder at this
   show;   [plain.
   But wonder on, till truth make all things
This man is Pyramus, if you would know;
   This beauteous lady Thisby is, certáin.
This man, with lime and rough-cast, doth per-
   sent   [sunder:
Wall, that vile Wall which did these lovers
And through Wall's chink, poor souls, they are
   content
   To whisper, at the which let no man wonder.
This man, with lantern, dog, and bush of thorn,
   Presenteth Moonshine: for, if you will know,
By moonshine did these lovers think no scorn
   To meet at Ninus' tomb, there, there to woo.
This grisly beast, which by name Lion hight,
The trusty Thisby, coming first by night,
Did scare away, or rather did affright:
And as she fled, her mantle she did fall;
   Which Lion vile with bloody mouth did stain:
Anon comes Pyramus, sweet youth, and tall,
   And finds his trusty Thisby's mantle slain;
Whereat with blade, with bloody blameful blade,
   He bravely broach'd his boiling bloody breast;

And Thisby, tarrying in mulberry shade,
His dagger drew, and died. For all the rest,
Let Lion, Moonshine, Wall, and lovers twain
At large discourse while here they do remain.
[*Exeunt* Prol., This., Lion, *and* Moon.
The. I wonder if the lion be to speak.
Dem. No wonder, my lord: one lion may, when many asses do.
Wall. In this same interlude it doth befall
That I, one Snout by name, present a wall:
And such a wall as I would have you think
That had in it a crannied hole or chink,
Through which the lovers, Pyramus and Thisby,
Did whisper often very secretly.   [show
This loam, this rough-cast, and this stone doth
That I am that same wall; the truth is so:
And this the cranny is, right and sinister,
Through which the fearful lovers are to whisper.
The. Would you desire lime and hair to speak better?
Dem. It is the wittiest partition that ever I heard discourse, my lord.
The. Pyramus draws near the wall: silence!

Enter PYRAMUS.

Pyr. O grim-look'd night! O night with hue so black!
    O night, which ever art when day is not!
O night, O night, alack, alack, alack,
    I fear my Thisby's promise is forgot!—
And thou, O wall, O sweet, O lovely wall,
    That stand'st between her father's ground and mine;
Thou wall, O wall, O sweet and lovely wall,
    Show me thy chink, to blink through with mine eyne.
                [WALL *holds up his fingers.*
Thanks, courteous wall: Jove shield thee well for this!
    But what see I? No Thisby do I see.
O wicked wall, through whom I see no bliss;
    Curst be thy stones for thus deceiving me!
The. The wall, methinks, being sensible, should curse again.
Pyr. No, in truth, sir, he should not. *Deceiving me* is Thisby's cue: she is to enter now, and I am to spy her through the wall. You shall see it will fall pat as I told you.—Yonder she comes.

Enter THISBE.

This. O wall, full often hast thou heard my moans,
For parting my fair Pyramus and me:
My cherry lips have often kiss'd thy stones:
    Thy stones with lime and hair knit up in thee.
Pyr. I see a voice; now will I to the chink,
    To spy an I can hear my Thisby's face.
Thisby!
This. My love! thou art my love, I think.
Pyr. Think what thou wilt, I am thy lover's grace:
And like Limander am I trusty still.
This. And I like Helen, till the fates me kill.
Pyr. Not Shafalus to Procrus was so true.

This. As Shafalus to Procrus, I to you.
Pyr. O, kiss me through the hole of this vile wall.
This. I kiss the wall's hole, not your lips at all.
Pyr. Wilt thou at Ninny's tomb meet me straightway?
This. 'Tide life, 'tide death, I come without delay.
Wall. Thus have I, wall, my part discharged so;
And, being done, thus wall away doth go.
                [*Exeunt* WALL, PYR., *and* THIS.
The. Now is the mural down between the two neighbours.
Dem. No remedy, my lord, when walls are so wilful to hear without warning.
Hip. This is the silliest stuff that ever I heard.
The. The best in this kind are but shadows; and the worst are no worse, if imagination amend them.   [not theirs.
Hip. It must be your imagination then, and
The. If we imagine no worse of them than they of themselves, they may pass for excellent men. Here come two noble beasts in, a moon and a lion.

Enter LION *and* MOONSHINE.

Lion. You, ladies, you, whose gentle hearts do fear   [on floor,
    The smallest monstrous mouse that creeps
May now, perchance, both quake and tremble here,
    When lion rough in wildest rage doth roar.
Then know that I, one Snug, the joiner, am
A lion fell, nor else no lion's dam:
For if I should as lion come in strife
Into this place, 'twere pity of my life.
The. A very gentle beast, and of a good conscience.   [e'er I saw.
Dem. The very best at a beast, my lord, that
Lys. This lion is a very fox for his valour.
The. True; and a goose for his discretion.
Dem. Not so, my lord; for his valour cannot carry his discretion; and the fox carries the goose.
The. His discretion, I am sure, cannot carry his valour; for the goose carries not the fox. It is well: leave it to his discretion, and let us listen to the moon.
Moon. This lantern doth the horned moon present: [head.
Dem. He should have worn the horns on his
The. He is no crescent, and his horns are invisible within the circumference.
Moon. This lantern doth the horned moon present;
Myself the man i' the moon do seem to be.
The. This is the greatest error of all the rest: the man should be put into the lantern. How is it else the man i' the moon?
Dem. He dares not come there for the candle: for, you see, it is already in snuff.
Hip. I am weary of this moon: would he would change!
The. It appears, by his small light of discre-

tion, that he is in the wane: but yet, in courtesy, in all reason, we must stay the time,

Lys. Proceed, moon.

Moon. All that I have to say, is to tell you that the lantern is the moon; I, the man in the moon; this thorn-bush, my thorn-bush; and this dog, my dog.

Dem. Why, all these should be in the lantern; for all these are in the moon. But, silence; here comes Thisbe.

Enter THISBE.

This. This is old Ninny's tomb. Where is my love?

Lion. Oh!

    [*The LION roars.—THISBE runs off.*

Dem. Well roared, lion.

The. Well run, Thisbe.

Hip. Well shone, moon.—Truly, the moon shines with a good grace.

The. Well moused, lion

    [*The LION tears THISBE's mantle and exit.*

Dem. And so comes Pyramus.

Lys. And then the lion vanishes.

Enter PYRAMUS.

Pyr. Sweet moon, I thank thee for thy sunny
  beams;   [bright:
I thank thee, moon, for shining now so
For, by thy gracious, golden, glittering streams,
 I trust to taste of truest Thisby's sight.
    But stay;—O spite!
    But mark,—poor knight,
 What dreadful dole is here!
    Eyes, do you see?
    How can it be?
 O dainty duck! O dear!
    Thy mantle good,
    What! stained with blood?
 Approach, ye furies fell!
    O fates! come, come;
    Cut thread and thrum;
    Quail, rush, conclude, and quell!

The. This passion, and the death of a dear friend, would go near to make a man look sad.

Hip. Beshrew my heart, but I pity the man.

Pyr. O wherefore, nature, didst thou lions
  frame?
 Since lion vile hath here deflower'd my dear:
Which is—no, no—which was the fairest dame
 That liv'd, that lov'd, that lik'd, that look'd
  with cheer.
    Come, tears, confound;
    Out, sword, and wound
 The pap of Pyramus:
    Ay, that left pap,
    Where heart doth hop:—
 Thus die I, thus, thus, thus.
    Now am I dead,
    Now am I fled;
 My soul is in the sky:
    Tongue, lose thy light!
    Moon, take thy flight!

  Now die, die, die, die, die.

    [*Dies.—Exit MOONSHINE.*

Dem. No die, but an ace, for him; for he is but one.   [is nothing.

Lys. Less than an ace, man; for he is dead; he

The. With the help of a surgeon he might yet recover and prove an ass.

Hip. How chance moonshine is gone before Thisbe comes back and finds her lover?

The. She will find him by starlight.—Here she comes; and her passion ends the play.

Enter THISBE.

Hip. Methinks she should not use a long one for such a Pyramus: I hope she will be brief.

Dem. A mote will turn the balance, which Pyramus, which Thisbe, is the better.

Lys. She hath spied him already with those sweet eyes.

Dem. And thus she moans, *videlicet.*——

This.   Asleep, my love?
    What, dead, my dove?
  O Pyramus, arise,
    Speak, speak. Quite dumb?
    Dead, dead? A tomb
  Must cover thy sweet eyes.
    These lily brows,
    This cherry nose,
  These yellow cowslip cheeks,
    Are gone, are gone:
    Lovers, make moan!
  His eyes were green as leeks
    O Sisters Three,
    Come, come to me,
  With hands as pale as milk;
    Lay them in gore,
    Since you have shore
  With shears his thread of silk.
    Tongue, not a word:—
    Come, trusty sword;
  Come, blade, my breast imbrue:
    And farewell, friends:—
    Thus Thisby ends:
  Adieu, adieu, adieu.   [*Dies.*

The. Moonshine and lion are left to bury the dead.

Dem. Ay, and wall too.

Bot. No, I assure you; the wall is down that parted their fathers. Will it please you to see the epilogue, or to hear a Bergomask dance between two of our company.

The. No epilogue, I pray you; for your play needs no excuse. Never excuse; for when the players are all dead there need none to be blamed. Marry, if he that writ it had played Pyramus, and hanged himself in Thisbe's garter, it would have been a fine tragedy: and so it is, truly; and very notably discharged. But come, your Bergomask: let your epilogue alone.

    [*Here a dance of CLOWNS.*

The iron tongue of midnight hath told twelve:—
Lovers, to bed; 'tis almost fairy time.
I fear we shall out-sleep the coming morn,
As much as we this night have overwatch'd.

This palpable-gross play hath well beguil'd
The heavy gait of night.—Sweet friends, to
        bed.—
A fortnight hold we this solemnity,
In nightly revels and new jollity.   [*Exeunt.*

SCENE II.

Enter PUCK.

Puck. Now the hungry lion roars,
        And the wolf behowls the moon;
    Whilst the heavy ploughman snores,
        All with weary task fordone.
    Now the wasted brands do glow,
        Whilst the scritch-owl, scritching loud,
    Puts the wretch that lies in woe
        In remembrance of a shroud.
    Now it is the time of night
        That the graves, all gaping wide
    Every one lets forth its sprite,
        In the church-way paths to glide:
    And we fairies, that do run
        By the triple Hecate's team,
    From the presence of the sun
        Following darkness like a dream,
    Now are frolic; not a mouse
        Shall disturb this hallow'd house:
    I am sent with broom before,
        To sweep the dust behind the door.

Enter OBERON *and* TITANIA, *with their* Train.

Obe. Through this house give glimmering light,
        By the dead and drowsy fire:
    Every elf and fairy sprite
        Hop as light as bird from brier:
    And this ditty, after me,
    Sing and dance it trippingly.
Tita. First, rehearse your song by rote,
        To each word a warbling note,
    Hand in hand, with fairy grace,
    Will we sing, and bless this place.

SONG AND DANCE.

Obe. Now, until the break of day,
        Through this house each fairy stray,
    To the best bride-bed will we,
        Which by us shall blessed be;
    And the issue there create
    Ever shall be fortunate.
    So shall all the couples three
    Ever true in loving be;
    And the blots of Nature's hand
    Shall not in their issue stand:
    Never mole, hare-lip, nor scar,
    Nor mark prodigious, such as are
    Despised in nativity,
    Shall upon their children be.—
    With this field-dew consecrate,
    Every fairy take his gate;
    And each several chamber bless,
    Through this palace, with sweet peace;
    E'er shall it in safety rest,
    And the owner of it blest.
        Trip away:
        Make no stay:
    Meet me all by break of day.
            [*Exeunt* OBE., TITA., *and* Train.
Puck. If we shadows have offended,
        Think but this—and all is mended—
    That you have but slumber'd here
    While these visions did appear.
    And this weak and idle theme,
    No more yielding but a dream,
    Gentles, do not reprehend;
    If you pardon, we will mend.
    And, as I'm an honest Puck,
    If we have unearned luck
    Now to 'scape the serpent's tongue,
    We will make amends ere long;
    Else the Puck a liar call:
    So, good night unto you all.
    Give me your hands, if we be friends,
    And Robin shall restore amends. [*Exit.*

LOVE'S LABOUR'S LOST

DRAMATIS PERSONÆ

FERDINAND, *King of Navarre.*
BIRON, ⎫
LONGAVILLE, ⎬ *Lords attending on the* KING.
DUMAIN, ⎭
BOYET, ⎫ *Lords attending on the* PRIN-
MERCADE, ⎭ CESS OF FRANCE.
DON ADRIANO DE ARMADO, *a Fantastical Spaniard.*
SIR NATHANIEL, *a Curate.*
HOLOFERNES, *a Schoolmaster.*
DULL, *a Constable.*
COSTARD, *a Clown.*

MOTH, *Page to* ARMADO.
A Forester.

PRINCESS OF FRANCE.
ROSALINE, ⎫
MARIA, ⎬ *Ladies attending on the*
KATHARINE, ⎭ PRINCESS.
JAQUENETTA, *a Country Wench.*

Officers *and* Others, *Attendants on the* KING *and* PRINCESS.

SCENE,—NAVARRE.

ACT I.

SCENE I.—NAVARRE. *A Park, with a Palace in it.*

Enter the KING, BIRON, LONGAVILLE, *and* DUMAIN.

King. Let fame, that all hunt after in their lives,
Live register'd upon our brazen tombs,
And then grace us in the disgrace of death;
When, spite of cormorant devouring time,
The endeavour of this present breath may buy
That honour which shall bate his scythe's keen edge,
And make us heirs of all eternity.
Therefore, brave conquerors,—for so you are,
That war against your own affections,
And the huge army of the world's desires,—
Our late edict shall strongly stand in force:
Navarre shall be the wonder of the world·
Our court shall be a little Academe,
Still and contemplative in living art.
You three, Birón, Dumain, and Longaville,
Have sworn for three years' term to live with me
My fellow-scholars, and to keep those statutes
That are recorded in this schedule here:
Your oaths are pass'd; and now subscribe your names,
That his own hand may strike his honour down
That violates the smallest branch herein:
If you are arm'd to do as sworn to do,
Subscribe to your deep oaths, and keep it too.
Long. I am resolv'd; 'tis but a three years' fast:
The mind shall banquet though the body pine
Fat paunches have lean pates; and dainty bits.
Make rich the ribs, but bankrupt quite the wits:
Dum. My loving lord, Dumain, is mortified:
The grosser manner of these world's delights
He throws upon the gross world's baser slaves:

To love, to wealth, to pomp, I pine and die;
With all these living in philosophy.
Biron. I can but say their protestation over;
So much, dear liege, I have already sworn,
That is, to live and study here three years.
But there are other strict observances:
As, not to see a woman in that term;
Which I hope well is not enrolled there:
And one day in a week to touch no food,
And but one meal on every day beside;
The which I hope is not enrolled there:
And then, to sleep but three hours in the night,
And not be seen to wink of all the day,—
When I was wont to think no harm all night,
And make a dark night too of half the day,—
Which I hope well is not enrolled there:
O, these are barren tasks too hard to keep;
Not to see ladies—study—fast—not sleep.
King. Your oath is pass'd to pass away from these. [please;
Biron. Let me say no, my liege, and if you
I only swore to study with your grace,
And stay here in your court for three years' space.
Long. You swore to that, Birón, and to the rest.
Biron. By yea and nay, sir, then I swore in jest.—
What is the end of study? let me know.
King. Why, that to know which else we should not know.
Biron. Things hid and barr'd, you mean, from common sense?
King. Ay, that is study's god-like recompense.
Biron. Come on, then, I will swear to study so,
To know the thing I am forbid to know:
As thus,—to study where I well may dine,
 When I to feast expressly am forbid;
Or study where to meet some mistress fine,
 When mistresses from common sense are hid:
Or, having sworn too-hard-a-keeping oath,
Study to break it, and not break my troth.

175

If study's gain be thus, and this be so,
Study knows that which yet it doth not know:
Swear me to this, and I will ne'er say no.
King. These be the stops that hinder study
    quite,
And train our intellects to vain delight.
Biron. Why, all delights are vain; but that
    most vain
Which, with pain purchas'd, doth inherit pain:
As painfully to pore upon a book
    To seek the light of truth; while truth the
    while
Doth falsely blind the eyesight of his look:
    Light, seeking light, doth light of light beguile.
So, ere you find where light in darkness lies,
Your light grows dark by losing of your eyes.
Study me how to please the eye indeed,
    By fixing it upon a fairer eye;
Who dazzling so, that eye shall be his heed,
    And give him light that it was blinded by.
Study is like the heaven's glorious sun,
    That will not be deep-search'd with saucy
    looks;
Small have continual plodders ever won,
    Save base authority from others' books,
These earthly godfathers of heaven's lights,
    That give a name to every fixed star,
Have no more profit of their shining nights
    Than those that walk and wot not what they
    are.
Too much to know is to know naught but fame;
And every godfather can give a name.
King. How well he's read, to reason against
    reading!
Dum. Proceeded well, to stop all good pro-
    ceeding!
Long. He weeds the corn, and still lets grow
    the weeding.
Biron. The spring is near, when green geese are
    a-breeding.
Dum. How follows that?
Biron.   Fit in his place and time.
Dum. In reason nothing.
Biron.   Something then in rhyme.
Long. Birón is like an envious sneaping frost,
That bites the first-born infants of the spring.
Biron. Well, say I am; why should proud sum-
    mer boast
Before the birds have any cause to sing?
Why should I joy in an abortive birth?
At Christmas I no more desire a rose
Than wish a snow in May's new-fangled shows;
But like of each thing that in season grows.
So you, to study now it is too late,
Climb o'er the house to unlock the little gate.
King. Well, sit you out: go home, Birón: adieu.
Biron. No, my good lord; I have sworn to stay
    with you:
And though I have for barbarism spoke more
    Than for that angel knowledge you can say,
Yet confident I'll keep what I have swore,
    And bide the penance of each three years' day.
Give me the paper, let me read the same;
And to the strict'st decrees I'll write my name.

King. How well this yielding rescues thee from
    shame!
Biron. [*reads.*] Item, *That no woman shall come
within a mile of my court.*—
And hath this been proclaim'd?
Long.   Four days ago.
Biron. Let's see the penalty.
[*Reads.*]—*On pain of losing her tongue.*
                Who devis'd this?
Long. Marry, that did I.
Biron. Sweet lord, and why?   [penalty.
Long. To fright them hence with that dread
Biron. A dangerous law against gentility.
[*Reads.*] Item, *If any man be seen to talk with
a woman within the term of three years, he shall
endure such public shame as the rest of the court
can possibly devise.*—
This article, my liege, yourself must break;
    For well you know here comes in embassy
The French king's daughter, with yourself to
    speak,—
    A maid of grace and cómplete majesty,—
About surrender-up of Aquitain
    To her decrepit, sick, and bed-rid father:
Therefore this article is made in vain.
    Or vainly comes the admired princess hither.
King. What say you, lords? why, this was quite
    forgot.
Biron. So study evermore is over-shot;
While it doth study to have what it would,
It doth forget to do the thing it should:
And when it hath the thing it hunteth most,
'Tis won as towns with fire,—so won, so lost.
King. We must, of force, dispense with this
    decree;
She must lie here on mere necessity.
Biron. Necessity will make us all forsworn
    Three thousand times within this three years'
    space:
For every man with his affects is born;
    Not by might master'd, but by special grace:
If I break faith, this word shall speak for me,
I am forsworn on mere necessity.—
So to the laws at large I write my name:
                 [*Subscribes.*
And he that breaks them in the least degree
Stands in attainder of eternal shame.
    Suggestions are to others as to me;
But I believe, although I seem so loath;
I am the last that will last keep his oath.
But is there no quick recreation granted?
King. Ah, that there is: our court, you know,
    is haunted
With a refined traveller of Spain;
A man in all the world's new fashion planted,
    That hath a mint of phrases in his brain:
One whom the music of his own vain tongue
    Doth ravish, like enchanting harmony;
A man of complements, whom right and wrong
    Have chose as umpire of their mutiny:
This child of fancy, that Armado hight,
    For interim to our studies, shall relate,
In high-born words, the worth of many a knight
    From tawny Spain, lost in the world's debate.

How you delight, my lords, I know not, I;
But, I protest, I love to hear him lie,
And I will use him for my minstrelsy.
Biron. Armado is a most illustrious wight,
A man of fire-new words, fashion's own knight.
Long. Costard, the swain, and he shall be our
　　　sport;
And so to study—three years is but short.

Enter DULL *with a letter, and* COSTARD.

Dull. Which is the duke's own person?
Biron. This, fellow; what wouldst?
Dull. I myself reprehend his own person, for I am his grace's tharborough: but I would see his own person in flesh and blood.
Biron. This is he.
Dull. Signior Arme—Arme—commends you. There's villany abroad: this letter will tell you more.
Cost. Sir, the contempts thereof are as touching me.
King. A letter from the magnificent Armado.
Biron. How low soever the matter, I hope in God for high words.
Long. A high hope for a low heaven: God grant us patience!
Biron. To hear? or forbear laughing?
Long. To hear meekly, sir, and to laugh moderately; or to forbear both.
Biron. Well, sir, be it as the style shall give us cause to climb in the merriness.
Cost. The matter is to me, sir, as concerning Jaquenetta. The manner of it is, I was taken with the manner.
Biron. In what manner?
Cost. In manner and form following, sir, all those three: I was seen with her in the manor house, sitting with her upon the form, and taken following her into the park; which, put together, is in manner and form following. Now, sir, for the manner,—it is the manner of a man to speak to a woman: for the form,—in some form.
Biron. For the following, sir?
Cost. As it shall follow in my correction: and God defend the right!
King. Will you hear this letter with attention?
Biron. As we would hear an oracle.
Cost. Such is the simplicity of man to hearken after the flesh.
King. [*reads.*] Great deputy, the welkin's vicegerent and sole dominator of Navarre, my soul's earth's God and body's fostering patron,—
Cost. Not a word of Costard yet.
King. [*reads.*] So it is,—
Cost. It may be so: but if he say it is so, he is in telling true, but so so.
King. Peace!
Cost. —be to me, and every man that dares not fight!
King. No words!
Cost. —of other men's secrets, I beseech you.
King. [*reads.*] So it is, besieged with sable-coloured melancholy, I did commend the black-oppressing humour to the most wholesome

physic of thy health-giving air; and, as I am a gentleman, betook myself to walk. The time when? About the sixth hour; when beasts most graze, birds best peck, and men sit down to that nourishment which is called supper: so much for the time when. Now for the ground which; which, I mean, I walked upon: it is ycleped thy park. Then for the place where; where, I mean, I did encounter that obscene and most preposterous event that draweth from my snow-white pen the ebon-coloured ink, which here thou viewest, beholdest, surveyest, or seest: but to the place where,—it standeth north-north-east and by-east from the west corner of thy curious-knotted garden. There did I see that low-spirited swain, that base minnow of thy mirth,—
Cost. Me.
King. —that unlettered small-knowing soul,—
Cost. Me.
King. —that shallow vassal,—
Cost. Still me.
King. —which, as I remember, hight Costard,—
Cost. O, me.
King. —sorted and consorted, contrary to thy established proclaimed edict and continent canon, with—with,—O, with—but with this I passion to say wherewith,—
Cost. With a wench.
King. —with a child of our grandmother Eve, a female; or, for thy more sweet understanding, a woman. Him,—I as my ever esteemed duty pricks me on,—have sent to thee, to receive the meed of punishment, by thy sweet grace's officer, Antony Dull, a man of good repute, carriage, bearing, and estimation.
Dull. Me, an 't shall please you; I am Antony Dull.
King. [*reads.*] For Jaquenetta,—so is the weaker vessel called, which I apprehended with the aforesaid swain,—I keep her as a vessel of thy law's fury; and shall, at the least of thy sweet notice, bring her to trial. Thine, in all compliments of devoted and heart-burning heat of duty,　　DON ADRIANO DE ARMADO.
Biron. This is not so well as I looked for, but the best that ever I heard.
King. Ay, the best for the worst. But, sirrah, what say you to this?
Cost. Sir, I confess the wench.
King. Did you hear the proclamation?
Cost. I do confess much of the hearing it, but little of the marking of it.
King. It was proclaimed a year's imprisonment, to be taken with a wench.
Cost. I was taken with none, sir, I was taken with a damosel.
King. Well, it was proclaimed damosel.
Cost. This was no damosel neither, sir; she was a virgin.　　　　　　　　　　　　　　　[virgin.
King. It is so varied too; for it was proclaimed
Cost. If it were, I deny her virginity; I was taken with a maid.
King. This maid will not serve your turn, sir.

Cost. This maid will serve my turn, sir.

King. Sir, I will pronounce your sentence: you shall fast a week with bran and water.

Cost. I had rather pray a month with mutton and porridge.

King. And Don Armado shall be your keeper.— My Lord Birón, see him delivered over.— And go we, lords, to put in practice that Which each to other hath so strongly sworn.—

[*Exeunt* KING, LONG. *and* DUM.

Biron. I'll lay my head to any good man's hat, These oaths and laws will prove an idle scorn.— Sirrah, come on.

Cost. I suffer for the truth, sir: for true it is, I was taken with Jaquenetta, and Jaquenetta is a true girl; and therefore, Welcome the sour cup of prosperity! Affliction may one day smile again, and till then, Sit thee down, sorrow!

[*Exeunt.*

SCENE II.—*Another part of the Park.*

Enter ARMADO *and* MOTH.

Arm. Boy, what sign is it when a man of great spirit grows melancholy?

Moth. A great sign, sir, that he will look sad.

Arm. Why, sadness is one and the self-same thing, dear imp.

Moth. No, no; O lord, sir, no.

Arm. How canst thou part sadness and melancholy, my tender juvenal?

Moth. By a familiar demonstration of the working, my tough senior.

Arm. Why tough senior? why tough senior?

Moth. Why tender juvenal? why tender juvenal?

Arm. I spoke it, tender juvenal, as a congruent epitheton appertaining to thy young days, which we may nominate tender.

Moth. And I, tough senior, as an appertinent title to your old time, which we may name tough.

Arm. Pretty, and apt.

Moth. How mean you, sir; I pretty, and my saying apt? or I apt, and my saying pretty?

Arm. Thou pretty, because little.

Moth. Little pretty, because little. Wherefore apt?

Arm. And therefore apt, because quick.

Moth. Speak you this in my praise, master?

Arm. In thy condign praise.

Moth. I will praise an eel with the same praise.

Arm. What, that an eel is ingenious?

Moth. That an eel is quick.

Arm. I do say thou art quick in answers: thou heatest my blood.

Moth. I am answered, sir.

Arm. I love not to be crossed.

Moth. He speaks the mere contrary; crosses love not him.   [*Aside.*

Arm. I have promised to study three years with the duke.

Moth. You may do it in an hour, sir.

Arm. Impossible.

Moth. How many is one thrice told?

Arm. I am ill at reckoning; it fitteth the spirit of a tapster.

Moth. You are a gentleman and a gamester, sir.

Arm. I confess both,—they are both the varnish of a complete man.

Moth. Then, I am sure, you know how much the gross sum of deuce-ace amounts to.

Arm. It doth amount to one more than two.

Moth. Which the base vulgar do call three.

Arm. True.

Moth. Why, sir, is this such a piece of study? Now here is three studied ere you'll thrice wink: and how easy it is to put years to the word three, and study three years in two words, the dancing horse will tell you.

Arm. A most fine figure!

Moth. To prove you a cipher.   [*Aside.*

Arm. I will hereupon confess I am in love: and, as it is base for a soldier to love, so am I in love with a base wench. If drawing my sword against the humour of affection would deliver me from the reprobate thought of it, I would take desire prisoner, and ransom him to any French courtier for a new devised courtesy. I think scorn to sigh; methinks, I should outswear Cupid. Comfort me, boy: what great men have been in love?

Moth. Hercules, master.

Arm. Most sweet Hercules!—More authority, dear boy, name more; and, sweet my child, let them be men of good repute and carriage.

Moth. Samson, master; he was a man of good carriage, great carriage,—for he carried the town-gates on his back like a porter: and he was in love.

Arm. O well-knit Samson! strong-jointed Samson! I do excel thee in my rapier as much as thou didst me in carrying gates. I am in love too:—who was Samson's love, my dear Moth?

Moth. A woman, master.

Arm. Of what complexion?

Moth. Of all the four, or the three, or the two; or one of the four.

Arm. Tell me precisely of what complexion.

Moth. Of the sea-water green, sir.

Arm. Is that one of the four complexions?

Moth. As I have read, sir: and the best of them too.

Arm. Green, indeed, is the colour of lovers; but to have a love of that colour, methinks Samson had small reason for it. He surely affected her for her wit.

Moth. It was so, sir; for she had a green wit.

Arm. My love is most immaculate white and red.

Moth. Most maculate thoughts, master, are masked under such colours.

Arm. Define, define, well-educated infant.

Moth. My father's wit and my mother's tongue, assist me!

Arm. Sweet invocation of a child; most pretty, and pathetical!

Moth. If she be made of white and red,
   Her faults will ne'er be known;
For blushing cheeks by faults are bred,

And fears by pale white shown:
Then if she fear, or be to blame,
  By this you shall not know;
For still her cheeks possess the same
  Which native she doth owe.
A dangerous rhyme, master, against the reason
of white and red.
Arm. Is there not a ballad, boy, of the King
and the Beggar.
Moth. The world was very guilty of such a
ballad some three ages since: but, I think, now
'tis not to be found; or, if it were, it would
neither serve for the writing nor the tune.
Arm. I will have the subject newly writ o'er,
that I may example my digression by some
mighty precedent. Boy, I do love that country
girl that I took in the park with the rational
hind Costard: she deserves well.
Moth. To be whipped: and yet a better love
than my master.   [*Aside.*
Arm. Sing, boy; my spirit grows heavy in love.
Moth. And that's great marvel, loving a light
           wench.
Arm. I say, sing.
Moth. Forbear till this company be past.

Enter DULL, COSTARD, *and* JAQUENETTA.

Dull. Sir, the duke's pleasure is, that you
keep Costard safe: and you must let him take
no delight nor no penance; but 'a must fast
three days a-week. For this damsel, I must
keep her at the park: she is allowed for the
day-woman. Fare you well.   [*Maid.*
Arm. I do betray myself with blushing.—
Jaq. Man.
Arm. I will visit thee at the lodge.
Jaq. That's here by.
Arm. I know where it is situate.
Jaq. Lord, how wise you are!
Arm. I will tell thee wonders.
Jaq. With that face?
Arm. I love thee.
Jaq. So I heard you say.
Arm. And so farewell.
Jaq. Fair weather after you!
Dull. Come, Jaquenetta, away.
              [*Exeunt* DULL *and* JAQUENETTA.
Arm. Villain, thou shalt fast for thy offences
ere thou be pardoned.
Cost. Well, sir, I hope, when I do it I shall do
it on a full stomach.
Arm. Thou shalt be heavily punished.
Cost. I am more bound to you than your fel-
lows, for they are but lightly rewarded.
Arm. Take away this villain; shut him up.
Moth. Come, you transgressing slave: away.
Cost. Let me not be pent up, sir; I will fast,
being loose.
Moth. No, sir; that were fast and loose: thou
shalt to prison.
Cost. Well, if ever I do see the merry days of
desolation that I have seen, some shall see—
Moth. What shall some see?
Cost. Nay, nothing, Master Moth, but what

they look upon. It is not for prisoners to be too
silent in their words; and therefore I will say
nothing: I thank God I have as little patience
as another man; and therefore I can be quiet.
              [*Exeunt* MOTH *and* COSTARD.
Arm. I do affect the very ground, which is
base, where her shoe, which is baser, guided by
her foot, which is basest, doth tread. I shall be
forsworn,—which is a great argument of falsehood,—if I love. And how can that be true love
which is falsely attempted? Love is a familiar;
love is a devil; there is no evil angel but love.
Yet Samson was so tempted,—and he had an
excellent strength: yet was Solomon so seduced,
—and he had a very good wit. Cupid's butt-
shaft is too hard for Hercules's club, and therefore too much odds for a Spaniard's rapier.
The first and second cause will not serve my
turn; the passado he respects not, the duello
he regards not: his disgrace is to be called boy;
but his glory is to subdue men. Adieu, valour!
rust, rapier! be still, drum! for your manager
is in love; yea, he loveth. Assist me, some ex-
temporal god of rhyme, for I am sure I shall
turn sonneteer. Devise, wit; write, pen; for I
am for whole volumes in folio.   [*Exit.*

ACT II.

SCENE I.—*Another part of the Park. A Pavilion and Tents at a distance.*

Enter the PRINCESS OF FRANCE, ROSALINE,
MARIA, KATHARINE, BOYET, Lords, *and
other* Attendants.

Boyet. Now, madam, summon up your dearest
           spirits:
Consider who the king your father sends;
To whom he sends; and what's his embassy:
Yourself, held precious in the world's esteem,
To parley with the sole inheritor
Of all perfections that a man may owe,
Matchless Navarre; the plea of no less weight
Than Aquitain,—a dowry for a queen.
Be now as prodigal of all dear grace
As nature was in making graces dear
When she did starve the general world beside,
And prodigally gave them all to you.
Prin. Good Lord Boyet, my beauty, though
           but mean,
Needs not be painted flourish of your praise;
Beauty is bought by judgment of the eye,
Not utter'd by base sale of chapmen's tongues:
I am less proud to hear you tell my worth
Than you much willing to be counted wise
In spending your wit in the praise of mine.
But now to task the tasker:—good Boyet,
You are not ignorant, all-telling fame
Doth noise abroad Navarre hath made a vow,
Till painful study shall out-wear three years
No woman may approach his silent court:
Therefore to us seemeth it a needful course,
Before we enter his forbidden gates,
To know his pleasure; and in that behalf,
Bold of your worthiness, we single you

As our best-moving fair solicitor.
Tell him the daughter of the King of France,
On serious business, craving quick despatch,
Importunes personal conference with his grace.
Haste, signify so much; while we attend,
Like humbly-visag'd suitors, his high will.
Boyet. Proud of employment, willingly I go.
Prin. All pride is willing pride, and yours is
  so.—   [*Exit* BOYET.
Who are the votaries, my loving lords,
That are vow-fellows with this virtuous duke?
1 *Lord.* Longaville is one.
Prin.   Know you the man?
Mar. I know him, madam; at a marriage feast,
Between Lord Perigort and the beauteous heir
Of Jaques Falconbridge, solémnized
In Normandy, saw I this Longaville:
A man of sovereign parts he is esteem'd;
Well fitted in the arts, glorious in arms:
Nothing becomes him ill that he would well.
The only soil of his fair virtue's gloss,—
If virtue's gloss will stain with any soil,—
Is a sharp wit matched with too blunt a will;
Whose edge hath power to cut, whose will still
  wills
It should none spare that come within his power.
Prin. Some merry mocking lord, belike; is't so?
Mar. They say so most that most his humours
  know.
Prin. Such short-liv'd wits do wither as they
  grow.
Who are the rest?   [youth
Kath. The young Dumain, a well-accomplish'd
Of all that virtue love for virtue lov'd:
Most power to do most harm, least knowing ill;
For he hath wit to make an ill shape good,
And shape to win grace though he had no wit.
I saw him at the Duke Alençon's once;
And much too little of that good I saw
Is my report to his great worthiness.
Ros. Another of these students at that time
Was there with him; if I have heard a truth,
Biron they call him; but a merrier man,
Within the limit of becoming mirth,
I never spent an hour's talk withal:
His eye begets occasion for his wit:
For every object that the one doth catch,
The other turns to a mirth-moving jest;
Which his fair tongue—conceit's expositor—
Delivers in such apt and gracious words
That aged ears play truant at his tales,
And younger hearings are quite ravished;
So sweet and voluble is his discourse.
Prin. God bless my ladies! are they all in love,
That every one her own hath garnished
With such bedecking ornaments of praise?
Mar. Here comes Boyet.

Re-enter BOYET.

Prin.   Now, what admittance, lord?
Boyet. Navarre had notice of your fair ap-
  proach;
And he and his competitors in oath
Were all address'd to meet you, gentle lady,

Before I came. Marry, thus much I have
  learnt,—
He rather means to lodge you in the field,
Like one that comes here to besiege his court,
Than seek a dispensation for his oath,
To let you enter his unpeopled house.
Here comes Navarre.   [*The* Ladies *mask.*

Enter KING, LONGAVILLE, DUMAIN, BIRON,
  and Attendants.

King. Fair princess, welcome to the court of
  Navarre.
Prin. Fair, I give you back again; and *welcome*
I have not yet: the roof of this court is too
high to be yours; and welcome to the wide fields
too base to be mine.   [court.
King. You shall be welcome, madam, to my
Prin. I will be welcome then; conduct me
  thither.   [oath.
King. Hear me, dear lady,—I have sworn an
Prin. Our lady help my lord! he'll be forsworn.
King. Not for the world, fair madam, by my
  will.   [ing else.
Prin. Why, will shall break it; will, and noth-
King. Your ladyship is ignorant what it is.
Prin. Were my lord so, his ignorance were wise,
Where now his knowledge must prove ignorance.
I hear your grace hath sworn-out housekeeping:
'Tis deadly sin to keep that oath, my lord,
And sin to break it:
But pardon me, I am too sudden bold;
To teach a teacher ill beseemeth me.
Vouchsafe to read the purpose of my coming,
And suddenly resolve me in my suit.
      [*Gives a paper*
King. Madam, I will, if suddenly I may.
Prin. You will the sooner that I were away;
For you'll prove perjur'd if you make me stay.
Biron. Did not I dance with you in Brabant
  once?
Ros. Did not I dance with you in Brabant once?
Biron. I know you did.
Ros.   How needless was it then
To ask the question!
Biron.   You must not be so quick.
Ros. 'Tis 'long of you, that spur me with such
  questions.
Biron. Your wit's too hot, it speeds too fast,
  'twill tire.
Ros. Not till it leave the rider in the mire.
Biron. What time o' day?
Ros. The hour that fools should ask.
Biron. Now fair befall your mask!
Ros. Fair fall the face it covers!
Biron. And send you many lovers!
Ros. Amen, so you be none.
Biron. Nay, then will I be gone.
King. Madam, your father here doth intimate
The payment of a hundred thousand crowns;
Being but the one-half of an entire sum
Disbursed by my father in his wars.
But say that he or we,—as neither have,—
Receiv'd that sum, yet there remains unpaid

A hundred thousand more; in surety of the
　　　　which,
One part of Aquitain is bound to us,
Although not valued to the money's worth.
If, then, the king your father will restore
But that one-half which is unsatisfied,
We will give up our right in Aquitain,
And hold fair friendship with his majesty.
But that, it seems, he little purposeth,
For here he doth demand to have repaid
An hundred thousand crowns; and not demands,
On payment of a hundred thousand crowns,
To have his title live in Aquitain;
Which we much rather had depart withal,
And have the money by our father lent,
Than Aquitain so gelded as it is.
Dear princess, were not his requests so far
From reason's yielding, your fair self should
　　　　make
A yielding, 'gainst some reason, in my breast,
And go well satisfied to France again.
Prin. You do the king my father too much
　　　　wrong,
And wrong the reputation of your name,
In so unseeming to confess receipt
Of that which hath so faithfully been paid.
King. I do protest I never heard of it;
And if you prove it, I'll repay it back,
Or yield up Aquitain.
Prin.　　　　　We arrest your word:—
Boyet, you can produce acquittances
For such a sum from special officers
Of Charles his father.
King.　　　　Satisfy me so.　　[come,
Boyet. So please your grace, the packet is not
Where that and other specialties are bound;
To-morrow you shall have a sight of them.
King. It shall suffice me; at which interview
All liberal reason I will yield unto.
Meantime receive such welcome at my hand
As honour, without breach of honour, may
Make tender of to thy true worthiness:
You may not come, fair princess, in my gates;
But here without you shall be so receiv'd
As you shall deem yourself lodg'd in my heart,
Though so denied fair harbour in my house.
Your own good thoughts excuse me, and farewell:
To-morrow shall we visit you again.
Prin. Sweet health and fair desires consort
　　　　your grace!
King. Thy own wish wish I thee in every place!
　　　　[Exeunt KING *and his* Train.
Biron. Lady, I will commend you to my own
　　　　heart.
Ros. Pray you, do my commendations; I would
be glad to see it.
Biron. I would you heard it groan.
Ros. Is the fool sick?
Biron. Sick at heart.
Ros. Alack, let it blood.
Biron. Would that do it good?
Ros. My physic says ay.
Biron. Will you prick 't with your eye?
Ros. No poynt, with my knife.

Biron. Now, God save thy life!
Ros. And yours from long living!
Biron. I cannot stay thanksgiving.　　*[Retiring.*
Dum. Sir, I pray you, a word! what lady is
　　　　that same?
Boyet. The heir of Alençon, Katharine her
　　　　name.
Dum. A gallant lady! Monsieur, fare you well.
　　　　　　　　　　　　　　[Exit.
Long. I beseech you a word: what is she in the
　　　　white?　　　　　　　*[the light.*
Boyet. A woman sometimes, an you saw her in
Long. Perchance, light in the light. I desire her
　　　　name.
Boyet. She hath but one for herself; to desire
　　　　that were a shame.
Long. Pray you, sir, whose daughter?
Boyet. Her mother's, I have heard.
Long. God's blessing on your beard!
Boyet. Good sir, be not offended:
She is an heir of Falconbridge.
Long. Nay, my choler is ended.
She is a most sweet lady.
Boyet. Not unlike, sir: that may be.
　　　　　　　　　　　　[Exit LONG.
Biron. What's her name in the cap?
Boyet. Rosaline, by good hap.
Biron. Is she wedded or no?
Boyet. To her will, sir, or so.
Biron. You are welcome, sir: adieu!
Boyet. Farewell to me, sir, and welcome to you.
　　　　　[Exit BIRON.—Ladies *unmask.*
Mar. That last is Biron, the merry mad-cap
　　　　lord;
Not a word with him but a jest.
Boyet.　　　　　And every jest but a word.
Prin. It was well done of you to take him at
　　　　his word.
Boyet. I was as willing to grapple as he was to
　　　　board.
Mar. Two hot sheeps, marry!
Boyet.　　　　　And wherefore not ships?
No sheep, sweet lamb, unless we feed on your
　　　　lips.　　　　　　　　*[ish the jest?*
Mar. You sheep and I pasture: shall that fin-
Boyet. So you grant pasture for me.
　　　　　　　　　　Offering to kiss her.
Mar.　　　　　Not so, gentle beast;
My lips are no common, though several they be.
Boyet. Belonging to whom?
Mar.　　　　　To my fortunes and me.
Prin. Good wits will be jangling: but, gentles,
　　　　agree:
The civil war of wits were much better used
On Navarre and his book-men; for here 'tis
　　　　abus'd.　　　　　　　*[lies,—*
Boyet. If my observation,—which very seldom
By the heart's still rhetoric disclos'd with eyes,
Deceive me not now, Navarre is infected.
Prin. With what?　　　　　　*[fected.*
Boyet. With that which we lovers entitle af-
Prin. Your reason?　　　　　*[retire*
Boyet. Why, all his behaviours did make their
To the court of his eye, peeping thorough desire:

His heart, like an agate, with your print im-
　　press'd,
Proud with his form, in his eye pride express'd:
His tongue, all impatient to speak and not see,
Did stumble with haste in his eye-sight to be;
All senses to that sense did make their repair,
To feel only looking on fairest of fair:
Methought all his senses were lock'd in his eye,
As jewels in crystal for some prince to buy;
Who, tend'ring their own worth from where
　　they were glass'd,
Did point you to buy them, along as you pass'd
His face's own margent did quote such amazes
That all eyes saw his eyes enchanted with gazes:
I'll give you Aquitain, and all that is his,
An you give him for my sake but one loving kiss.
Prin. Come to our pavilion: Boyet is dispos'd—
Boyet. But to speak that in words which his
　　eye hath disclos'd:
I only have made a mouth of his eye,
By adding a tongue which I know will not lie.
Ros. Thou art an old love-monger, and speak'st
　　skilfully.　　　　　　　　　[news of him.
Mar. He is Cupid's grandfather, and learns
Ros. Then was Venus like her mother; for her
　　father is but grim.
Boyet. Do you hear, my mad wenches?
Mar.　　　　　　　　　　　　No.
Boyet.　　　　　　What, then; do you see?
Ros. Ay, our way to be gone.
Boyet.　　　　　　You are too hard for me.
　　　　　　　　　　　　　　　　[*Exeunt.*

ACT III.

SCENE I.—*A part of the Park.*

Enter ARMADO *and* MOTH.

Arm. Warble, child; make passionate my sense
　　of hearing.
Moth. Concolinel——　　　　　　　[*Singing.*
Arm. Sweet air!—Go, tenderness of years!
take this key, give enlargement to the swain,
bring him festinately hither; I must employ
him in a letter to my love.
Moth. Master, will you win your love with a
French brawl?
Arm. How mean'st thou? brawling in French?
Moth. No, my complete master: but to jig off
a tune at the tongue's end, canary to it with
your feet, humour it with turning up your eyelids; sigh a note and sing a note; sometime
through the throat, as if you swallowed love
with singing love; sometime through the nose,
as if you snuffed up love by smelling love; with
your hat penthouse-like, o'er the shop of your
eyes; with your arms crossed on your thin belly-
doublet, like a rabbit on a spit; or your hands
in your pocket, like a man after the old painting; and keep not too long in one tune, but a
snip and away. These are complements, these
are humours; these betray nice wenches—that
would be betrayed without those; and make
them men of note,—do you note me?—that
most are affected to these.

Arm. How hast thou purchased this experi-
ence?
Moth. By my penny of observation.
Arm. But O,—but O—
Moth. —the hobby-horse is forgot.
Arm. Callest thou my love hobby-horse?
Moth. No, master; the hobby-horse is but a
colt, and your love perhaps a hackney. But
have you forgot your love?
Arm. Almost I had.
Moth. Negligent student! learn her by heart.
Arm. By heart and in heart, boy.
Moth. And out of heart, master: all those three
I will prove.
Arm. What wilt thou prove?
Moth. A man, if I live; and this, by, in, and
without, upon the instant: by heart you love
her, because your heart cannot come by her; in
heart you love her, because your heart is in love
with her; and out of heart you love her, being
out of heart that you cannot enjoy her.
Arm. I am all these three.
Moth. And three times as much more, and yet
nothing at all.
Arm. Fetch hither the swain; he must carry
me a letter.
Moth. A message well sympathized; a horse to
be ambassador for an ass!
Arm. Ha, ha! what sayest thou?
Moth. Marry, sir, you must send the ass upon
the horse, for he is very slow-gaited. But I go.
Arm. The way is but short: away.
Moth. As swift as lead, sir.
Arm. Thy meaning, pretty ingenious?
Is not lead a metal heavy, dull, and slow?
Moth. Minimè, honest master; or rather, mas-
ter, no.
Arm. I say lead is slow.
Moth.　　　　　You are too swift, sir, to say so:
Is that lead slow which is fired from a gun?
Arm. Sweet smoke of rhetoric!　　　　[he:—
He reputes me a cannon; and the bullet, that's
I shoot thee at the swain.
Moth.　　　　　　Thump, then, and I flee.
　　　　　　　　　　　　　　　　[*Exit.*
Arm. A most acute juvenal; voluble and free
　　of grace!　　　　　　　　　　[face:
By thy favour, sweet welkin, I must sigh in thy
Most rude melancholy, valour gives thee place.
My herald is return'd.

Re-enter MOTH *with* COSTARD.

Moth. A wonder, master; here's a Costard
　　broken in a shin.
Arm. Some enigma, some riddle: come,—thy
　　l'envoy;—begin.
Cost. No egma, no riddle, no *l'envoy;*—no salve
in the mail, sir: O, sir, plantain, a plain plantain; no *l'envoy,* no *l'envoy,* no salve, sir, but a
plantain!
Arm. By virtue thou enforcest laughter; thy
silly thought, my spleen; the heaving of my
lungs provokes me to ridiculous smiling: O,
pardon me, my stars! Doth the inconsiderate

take salve for *l'envoy*, and the word *l'envoy* for
a salve?　　　　　　　　　　[*l'envoy* a salve?
Moth. Do the wise think them other? is not
Arm. No, page: it is an epilogue or discourse,
　　　to make plain　　　　　　[sain.
Some obscure precedence that hath tofore been
I will example it:
　　The fox, the ape, and the humble-bee
　　　Were still at odds, being but three.
There's the moral. Now the *l'envoy*.　　[again.
Moth. I will add the *l'envoy*. Say the moral
Arm. The fox, the ape, and the humble-bee
　　　Were still at odds, being but three:
Moth. Until the goose came out of door,
　　And stay'd the odds by adding four.
Now will I begin your moral, and do you follow
with my *l'envoy*.
　　The fox, the ape, and the humble-bee,
　　　Were still at odds, being but three:
Arm. Until the goose came out of door.
　　Staying the odds by adding four.
Moth. A good *l'envoy*, ending in the goose;
Would you desire more?
Cost. The boy hath sold him a bargain, a goose,
　　　that's flat:—　　　　　　[fat.—
Sir, your pennyworth is good, and your goose be
To sell a bargain well is as cunning as fast and
　　　loose:
Let me see a fat *l'envoy*; ay, that's a fat goose.
Arm. Come hither, come hither. How did this
　　　argument begin?
Moth. By saying that *a Costard* was broken in
　　a shin.
Then call'd you for the *l'envoy*.
Cost. True, and I for a plantain: thus came
　　　your argument in;　　　[bought;
Then the boy's fat *l'envoy*, the goose that you
And he ended the market.
Arm. But tell me; how was there a Costard
broken in a shin?
Moth. I will tell you sensibly.
Cost. Thou hast no feeling of it, Moth; I will
speak that *l'envoy*.
I, Costard, running out, that was safely within,
Fell over the threshold and broke my shin.
Arm. We will talk no more of this matter.
Cost. Till there be more matter in the shin.
Arm. Sirrah, Costard, I will enfranchise thee.
Cost. O, marry me to one Frances;—I smell
some *l'envoy*, some goose in this.
Arm. By my sweet soul, I mean setting thee
at liberty, enfreedoming thy person; thou wert
immured, restrained, captivated, bound.
Cost. True, true; and now you will be my pur-
gation, and let me loose.
Arm. I give thee thy liberty, set thee from
durance; and, in lieu thereof, impose on thee
nothing but this:—bear this significant to the
country maid Jaquenetta: there is remuneration [*giving him money*]; for the best ward of
mine honour is rewarding my dependents.
Moth, follow.　　　　　　　　　[*Exit*.
Moth. Like the sequel, I.—Signior Costard,
　　adieu.

Cost. My sweet ounce of man's flesh! my in-
　　cony Jew!　　　　　　　[*Exit* MOTH.
Now will I look to his remuneration. Remuneration! O, that's the Latin word for three
farthings: three farthings—remuneration.—
*What's the price of this inkle?—A penny.—
No, I'll give you a remuneration:* why, it carries
it.—Remuneration!—why, it is a fairer name
than French crown. I will never buy and sell
out of this word.

Enter BIRON.

Biron. O, my good knave Costard! exceedingly
well met.
Cost. Pray you, sir, how much carnation rib-
bon may a man buy for a remuneration?
Biron. What is a remuneration?
Cost. Marry, sir, halfpenny farthing.　　[silk.
Biron. O, why then, three-farthings-worth of
Cost. I thank your worship: God be with you!
Biron. O, stay, slave; I must employ thee:
As thou wilt win my favour good my knave,
Do one thing for me that I shall entreat.
Cost. When you would have it done, sir?
Biron. O, this afternoon.
Cost. Well, I will do it, sir: fare you well.
Biron. O, thou knowest not what it is.
Cost. I shall know, sir, when I have done it.
Biron. Why, villain, thou must know first.
Cost. I will come to your worship to-morrow
morning.
Biron. It must be done this afternoon.
Hark, slave, it is but this:—
The princess comes to hunt here in the park,
And in her train there is a gentle lady;
When tongues speak sweetly, then they name
　　　her name,
And Rosaline they call her: ask for her;
And to her white hand see thou do commend
This seal'd-up counsel. There's thy guerdon;
　　　go.　　　　　　　[*Gives him money*.
Cost. Gardon,—O sweet gardon! better than
remuneration; elevenpence farthing better:
most sweet gardon!—I will do it, sir, in print.
—Gardon—remuneration.　　　　[*Exit*.
Biron. O!—and I, forsooth, in love! I, that
　　have been love's whip;
A very beadle to a humourous sigh;
A critic; nay, a night-watch constable;
A domineering pedant o'er the boy,
Than whom no mortal so magnificent!
This wimpled, whining, purblind, wayward boy;
This senior-junior, giant-dwarf, Dan Cupid:
Regent of love-rhymes, lord of folded arms,
The anointed sovereign of sighs and groans,
Liege of all loiterers and malcontents,
Dread prince of plackets, king of codpieces,
Sole imperator, and great general
Of trotting paritors: O my little heart!—
And I to be a corporal of his field,
And wear his colours like a tumbler's hoop!
What! I! I love! I sue! I seek a wife!
A woman, that is like a German clock,
Still a-repairing: ever out of frame:

And never going aright, being a watch,
But being watch'd that it may still go right!
Nay, to be perjur'd, which is worst of all;
And, among three, to love the worst of all;
A whitely wanton with a velvet brow,
With two pitch balls stuck in her face for eyes;
Ay, and, by heaven, one that will do the deed,
Though Argus were her eunuch and her guard:
And I to sigh for her! to watch for her!
To pray for her! Go to; it is a plague
That Cupid will impose for my neglect
Of his almighty dreadful little might.
Well, I will love, write, sigh, pray, sue, watch,
    groan;
Some men must love my lady, and some Joan.
                  [*Exit.*

ACT IV.

Scene I.—*A part of the Park.*

Enter the Princess, Rosaline, Maria, Kath-
    arine, Boyet, Lords, Attendants, *and a*
    Forester.

Prin. Was that the king that spurr'd his horse
    so hard
Against the steep uprising of the hill?
Boyet. I know not; but I think it was not he.
Prin. Whoe'er he was, he show'd a mounting
    mind.
Well, lords, to-day we shall have our despatch;
On Saturday we will return to France.—
Then, forester, my friend, where is the bush
That we must stand and play the murderer in?
For. Here by, upon the edge of yonder coppice;
A stand where you may make the fairest shoot.
Prin. I thank my beauty, I am fair that shoot,
And thereupon thou speak'st the fairest shoot.
For. Pardon me, madam, for I meant not so.
Prin. What, what? first praise me, and again
    say no?
O short-liv'd pride! Not fair? alack for woe!
For. Yes, madam, fair.
Prin.   Nay, never paint me now;
Where fair is not, praise cannot mend the brow.
Here, good my glass, take this for telling true;
              [*Giving him money.*
Fair payment for foul words is more than due.
For. Nothing but fair is that which you inherit.
Prin. See, see, my beauty will be sav'd by merit.
O heresy in fair, fit for these days!   [praise.—
A giving hand, though foul, shall have fair
But come, the bow:—now mercy goes to kill,
And shooting well is then accounted ill.
Thus will I save my credit in the shoot:
Not wounding, pity would not let me do't;
If wounding, then it was to show my skill,
That more for praise than purpose meant to kill.
And, out of question, so it is sometimes,—
Glory grows guilty of detested crimes;   [part,
When, for fame's sake, for praise, an outward
We bend to that the working of the heart:
As I, for praise alone, now seek to spill   [ill.
The poor deer's blood, that my heart means no

Boyet. Do not curst wives hold that self-
    sovereignty
Only for praise' sake, when they strive to be
Lords o'er their lords?
Prin. Only for praise: and praise we may afford
To any lady that subdues a lord.
Here comes a member of the commonwealth.

Enter Costard.

Cost. God dig-you-den all! Pray you, which is
the head-lady?   [that have no heads.
Prin. Thou shalt know her, fellow, by the rest
Cost. Which is the greatest lady, the highest?
Prin. The thickest and the tallest.
Cost. The thickest and the tallest! it is so;
    truth is truth.   [wit,
An your waist, mistress, were as slender as my
One of these maids' girdles for your waist should
    be fit.   [est here.
Are not you the chief woman? you are the thick-
Prin. What's your will, sir? what's your will?
Cost. I have a letter from Monsieur Biron, to
    one Lady Rosaline.
Prin. O, thy letter, thy letter; he's a good
    friend of mine: [carve;
Stand aside, good bearer.—Boyet, you can
Break up this capon.
Boyet.   I am bound to serve.—
This letter is mistook, it importeth none here;
It is writ to Jaquenetta.
Prin.   We will read it, I swear:
Break the neck of the wax and every one give
    ear.
Boyet. [*reads.*] By heaven, that thou art fair is
most infallible; true that thou art beauteous;
truth itself that thou art lovely. More fairer
than fair, beautiful than beauteous, truer than
truth itself: have commiseration on thy hero-
ical vassal! The magnanimous and most illustrious king *Cophetua* set eye upon the pernicious
and indubitate beggar *Zenelophon;* and he it
was that might rightly say, *veni, vidi, vici;* which
to anatomize in the vulgar,—O base and obscure vulgar!—*videlicet,* he came, saw, and overcame: he came one; saw two; overcame three.
Who came? the king: why did he come? to see:
why did he see? to overcome: to whom came
he? to the beggar: what saw he? the beggar:
who overcame he? the beggar. The conclusion
is victory; on whose side? the king's: the captive is enriched; on whose side? the beggar's:
the catastrophe is a nuptial; on whose side? the
king's?—no on both in one, or one in both. I
am the king; for so stands the comparison: thou
the beggar; for so witnesseth thy lowliness.
Shall I command thy love? I may: shall I enforce thy love? I could: shall I entreat thy love?
I will. What shalt thou exchange for rags?
robes: for tittles? titles: for thyself? me. Thus,
expecting thy reply, I profane my lips on thy
foot, my eyes on thy picture, and my heart on
thy every part.
    Thine in the dearest design of industry,
        Don Adriano de Armado.

Thus dost thou hear the Nemean lion roar
　'Gainst thee, thou lamb, that standest as his
　　　　prey;
Submissive fall his princely feet before,
　And he from forage will incline to play:
But if thou strive, poor soul, what art thou
　　then?
Food for his rage, repasture for his den.

　Prin. What plume of feathers is he that in-
　　dited this letter?
What vane? what weather-cock? did you ever
　　hear better?
　Boyet. I am much deceiv'd but I remember
　　the style.
　Prin. Else your memory is bad, going o'er it
　　erewhile.
　Boyet. This Armado is a Spaniard, that keeps
　　here in court;　　　　　　　　　　　[sport
A phantasm, a Monarcho, and one that makes
To the prince and his book-mates.
　Prin.　　　　　　　　Thou fellow, a word:
Who gave thee this letter?
　Cost.　　　　　　　　I told you; my lord.
　Prin. To whom shouldst thou give it?
　Cost.　　　　　　From my lord to my lady.
　Prin. From which lord to which lady?
　Cost. From my Lord Biron, a good master of
　　mine,
To a lady of France that he call'd Rosaline.
　Prin. Thou hast mistaken this letter. Come,
　　lords, away.
Here, sweet, put up this; 'twill be thine another
　　day.　　　　[*Exeunt* PRINCESS *and* Train.
　Boyet. Who is the shooter? who is the shooter?
　Ros. Shall I teach you to know?
　Boyet. Ay, my continent of beauty.
　Ros.　　　　　　Why, she that bears the bow.
Finely put off!　　　　　　　　　[thou marry,
　Boyet. My lady goes to kill horns; but, if
Hang me by the neck if horns that year mis-
　　carry.
Finely put on!
　Ros. Well then, I am the shooter.
　Boyet.　　　　　　　And who is your deer?
　Ros. If we choose by the horns, yourself:
　　come near.
Finely put on indeed!—
　Mar. You still wrangle with her, Boyet, and
　　she strikes at the brow.　　　　　[her now?
　Boyet. But she herself is hit lower: have I hit
　Ros. Shall I come upon thee with an old say-
ing, that was a man when King Pepin of France
was a little boy, as touching the hit it?
　Boyet. So I may answer thee with one as old,
that was a woman when Queen Guinever of
Britain was a little wench, as touching the hit it.
　　　　　　　　　　　　　　　　[*Singing.*
　Ros. *Thou canst not hit it, hit it, hit it,*
　　　　Thou canst not hit it, my good man.
　Boyet. *An I cannot, cannot, cannot,*
　　　　An I cannot, another can.
　　　　　　　　　[*Exeunt* Ros. *and* KATH.
　Cost. By my troth, most pleasant! how both
　　did fit it!

　Mar. A mark marvellous well shot; for they
　　both did hit it.
　Boyet. A mark! O, mark but that mark! A
　　mark, says my lady!　　　　　　　[may be.
Let the mark have a prick in 't, to mete at, if it
　Mar. Wide o' the bow-hand! I' faith your
　　hand is out.
　Cost. Indeed, 'a must shoot nearer, or he'll
　　ne'er hit the clout.
　Boyet. And if my hand be out, then belike
　　your hand is in.　　　　　　　[ing the pin.
　Cost. Then will she get the upshot by cleav-
　Mar. Come, come, you talk greasily, your
　　lips grow foul.
　Cost. She's too hard for you at pricks, sir;
　　challenge her to bowl.
　Boyet. I fear too much rubbing; good-night,
　　my good owl.
　　　　　　　　　[*Exeunt* BOYET *and* MARIA.
　Cost. By my soul, a swain! a most simple
　　clown!　　　　　　　　　　　　[down!
Lord, lord! how the ladies and I have put him
O' my troth, most sweet jests! most incony
　　vulgar wit!
When it comes so smoothly off, so obscenely, as
　　it were, so fit.
Armador o' the one side,—O, a most dainty
　　man!　　　　　　　　　　　　　[fan!
To see him walk before a lady and to bear her
To see him kiss his hand! and how most sweetly
　　'a will swear!—
And his page o' t' other side, that handful of
　　wit!
Ah, heavens, it is a most pathetical nit!
Sola, sola!　　　　　　　　[*Shouting within.*
　　　　　　　　　[*Exit* COSTARD *running.*

SCENE II.—*Another part of the Park.*

Enter HOLOFERNES, *Sir* NATHANIEL, *and* DULL.

　Nath. Very reverend sport, truly; and done
in the testimony of a good conscience.
　Hol. The deer was, as you know, *sanguis,*—
in blood; ripe as a pomewater, who now hangeth like a jewel in the ear of *cælo,*—the sky, the
welkin, the heaven; and anon falleth like a crab
on the face of *terra,*—the soil, the land, the
earth.
　Nath. Truly, Master Holofernes, the epithets
are sweetly varied, like a scholar at the least:
but, sir, I assure ye it was a buck of the first
head.
　Hol. Sir Nathaniel, *haud credo.*
　Dull. 'Twas not a *haud credo;* 'twas a pricket.
　Hol. Most barbarous intimation! yet a kind
of insinuation, as it were, *in via,* in way, of
explication; *facere,* as it were, replication, or,
rather, *ostentare,* to show, as it were, his inclination,—after his undressed, unpolished, unedu-
cated, unpruned, untrained, or, rather, unlettered, or, ratherest, unconfirmed fashion,—to
insert again my *haud credo* for a deer.
　Dull. I said the deer was not a *haud credo;*
'twas a pricket.
　Hol. Twice sod simplicity, *bis coctus!*—

O thou monster Ignorance, how deformed dost
    thou look!

Nath. Sir, he hath never fed of the dainties
    that are bred in a book;
He hath not eat paper, as it were; he hath not
drunk ink; his intellect is not replenished; he
is only an animal only sensible in the duller
parts;
And such barren plants are set before us that
    we thankful should be,—
Which we of taste and feeling are,—for those
    parts that do fructify in us more than he.
For as it would ill become me to be vain, in-
    discreet, or a fool,
So, were there a patch set on learning, to see
    him in a school:
But, *omne, bene,* say I; being of an old father's
    mind,   [*wind.*
Many can brook the weather that love not the

Dull. You two are book-men: can you tell
    by your wit
What was a month old at Cain's birth that's
    not five weeks old as yet?

Hol. Dictynna, good man Dull; Dictynna,
good man Dull.

Dull. What is Dictynna?

Nath. A title to Phœbe, to Luna, to the
    moon.

Hol. The moon was a month old when Adam
    was no more,   [*five-score.*
And raught not to five weeks when he came to
The allusion holds in the exchange.

Dull. 'Tis true indeed; the collusion holds in
the exchange.

Hol. God comfort thy capacity! I say the
allusion holds in the exchange.

Dull. And I say the pollution holds in the
exchange; for the moon is never but a month
old: and I say beside, that 'twas a pricket that
the princess killed.

Hol. Sir Nathaniel, will you hear an extem-
poral epitaph on the death of the deer? and, to
humour the ignorant, I have called the deer the
princess killed a pricket.

Nath. Perge, good Master Holofernes, *perge;*
so it shall please you to abrogate scurrility.

Hol. I will something affect the letter; for it
argues facility.
The praiseful princess pierc'd and prick'd a
    pretty pleasing pricket;
    Some say a sore; but not a sore, till now
        made sore with shooting.
The dogs did yell; put l to sore, then sorel
    jumps from thicket;   [*a-hooting.*
    Or pricket, sore, or else sorel; the people fall
If sore be sore, then l to sore makes fifty sores;
    O sore l!   [*one more l.*
Of one sore I an hundred make by adding but

Nath. A rare talent!

Dull. If a talent be a claw, look how he
claws him with a talent.

Hol. This is a gift that I have, simple, simple; a foolish extravagant spirit, full of forms,
figures, shapes, objects, ideas, apprehensions,
motions, revolutions: these are begot in the
ventricle of memory, nourished in the womb of
pia mater, and delivered upon the mellowing
of occasion. But the gift is good in those in
whom it is acute, and I am thankful for it.

Nath. Sir, I praise the Lord for you; and so
may my parishioners; for their sons are well
tutored by you, and their daughters profit very
greatly under you: you are a good member of
the commonwealth.

Hol. Mehercle, if their sons be ingenious,
they shall want no instruction: if their daughters be capable, I will put it to them: but, *vir
sapit qui pauca loquitur:* a soul feminine salut-
eth us.

Enter JAQUENETTA *and* COSTARD.

Jaq. God give you good-morrow, master
person.

Hol. Master person,—*quasi* pers-on. And if
one should be pierced, which is the one?

Cost. Marry, master schoolmaster, he that is
likest to a hogshead.

Hol. Of piercing a hogshead! a good lustre
of conceit in a turf of earth; fire enough for a
flint, pearl enough for a swine; 'tis pretty; it is
well.

Jaq. Good master person, be so good as read
me this letter; it was given me by Costard, and
sent me from Don Armado: I beseech you,
read it.

*Hol. Fauste, precor gelidâ quando pecus omne
    sub umbrâ*   [*tuan!*
Ruminat,—and so forth. Ah, good old Man-
I may speak of thee as the traveller doth of
Venice:

    ——*Vinegia, Vinegia,*
    Chi non te vede, ei non te pregia.

Old Mantuan! old Mantuan! who understand-
eth thee not, loves thee not?—*Ut, re, sol, la, mi,
fa.*—Under pardon, sir, what are the contents?
or rather, as Horace says in his—What, my
soul, verses?

Nath. Ay, sir, and very learned.

Hol. Let me hear a staff, a stanza, a verse;
Lege, domine.

Nath. [*reads.*] If love make me forsworn,
    how shall I swear to love?   [*vow'd!*
    Ah, never faith could hold if not to beauty
Though to myself forsworn, to thee I'll faith-
    ful prove;
    Those thoughts to me were oaks, to thee
        like osiers bow'd.
Study his bias leaves, and makes his book
    thine eyes;
    Where all those pleasures live that art
        would comprehend:
If knowledge be the mark, to know thee shall
    suffice;   [*thee commend:*
    Well learned is that tongue that well can
All ignorant that soul that sees thee without
    wonder,—
    Which is to me some praise that I thy
        parts admire,—

Thy eye Jove's lightning bears, thy voice his
   dreadful thunder,
    Which, not to anger bent, is music and
      sweet fire.
Celestial as thou art, O pardon, love, this
   wrong.
That sings heaven's praise with such an
   earthly tongue.

Hol. You find not the apostrophes, and so
miss the accent: let me supervise the canzonet.
Here are only numbers ratified; but, for the
elegancy, facility, and golden cadence of poesy,
caret. Ovidius Naso was the man: and why,
indeed, Naso; but for smelling out the oderi-
ferous flowers of fancy, the jerks of invention?
Imitari is nothing: so doth the hound his master, the ape his keeper, the tired horse his rider.
But damosella virgin, was this directed to you?

Jaq. Ay, sir, from one Monsieur Biron, one
of the strange queen's lords.

Hol. I will overglance the superscript.

*To the snow-white hand of the most beauteous
Lady Rosaline.*
I will look again on the intellect of the letter,
for the nomination of the party writing to the
person written unto:

Your Ladyship's in all desired employment,
                BIRON.
Sir Nathaniel, this Biron is one of the votaries
with the king; and here he hath framed a letter
to a sequent of the stranger queen's, which accidentally, or by the way of progression, hath
miscarried.—Trip and go, my sweet; deliver
this paper into the royal hand of the king; it
may concern much. Stay not thy compliment;
I forgive thy duty: adieu.

Jaq. Good Costard, go with me.—Sir, God
save your life!

Cost. Have with thee, my girl.
               [Exeunt COST. *and* JAQ.

Nath. Sir, you have done this in the fear of
God, very religiously; and, as a certain father
saith——

Hol. Sir, tell not me of the father; I do fear
colourable colours. But to return to the verses:
did they please you, Sir Nathaniel?

Nath. Marvellous well for the pen.

Hol. I do dine to-day at the father's of a
certain pupil of mine; where if, before repast,
it shall please you to gratify the table with a
grace, I will, on my privilege I have with the
parents of the foresaid child or pupil, undertake your *ben venuto;* where I will prove those
verses to be very unlearned, neither savouring
of poetry, wit, nor invention: I beseech your
society.

Nath. And thank you too: for society, saith
the text, is the happiness of life.

Hol. And certes, the text most infallibly
concludes it.—Sir [*to* DULL], I do invite you
too; you shall not say me nay: *pauca verba.*
Away; the gentles are at their game, and we
will to our recreation.
                     [Exeunt.

SCENE III.—*Another part of the Park.*

Enter BIRON, *with a paper.*

Biron. The king he is hunting the deer; I am
coursing myself: they have pitched a toil; I am
toiling in a pitch,—pitch that defiles: defile! a
foul word. Well, sit thee down, sorrow! for so
they say the fool said, and so say I, and I the
fool. Well proved, wit! By the Lord, this love
is as mad as Ajax: it kills sheep; it kills me, I a
sheep: well proved again on my side! I will not
love: if I do, hang me; i' faith, I will not. O,
but her eye,—by this light, but for her eye I
would not love her; yes, for her two eyes. Well,
I do nothing in the world but lie, and lie in my
throat. By heaven, I do love: and it hath
taught me to rhyme, and to be melancholy;
and here is part of my rhyme, and here my
melancholy. Well, she hath one o' my sonnets
already; the clown bore it, the fool sent it, and
the lady hath it: sweet clown, sweeter fool,
sweetest lady! By the world, I would not care
a pin if the other three were in. Here comes one
with a paper; God give him grace to groan.
               [Gets up into a tree.

Enter the KING, *with a paper.*

King. Ah me!

Biron. [*aside.*] Shot, by heaven!—Proceed,
sweet Cupid; thou hast thumped him with thy
bird-bolt under the left pap;—I' faith, secrets.—

King. [*reads.*] So sweet a kiss the golden sun
   gives not
To those fresh morning drops upon the rose,
As thy eyebeams, when their fresh rays have
   smote   [*flows:*
The night of dew that on my cheeks down
Nor shines the silver moon one half so bright
   Through the transparent bosom of the deep,
As doth thy face through tears of mine give
   light:
Thou shin'st in every tear that I do weep;
No drop but as a coach doth carry thee;
So ridest thou triúmphing in my woe.
Do but behold the tears that swell in me,
   And they thy glory through my grief will
      show:
But do not love thyself; then thou wilt keep
My tears for glasses, and still make me weep.
O queen of queens, how far dost thou excel!
No thought can think nor tongue of mortal
   tell.—
How shall she know my griefs? I'll drop the
   paper;
Sweet leaves, shade folly. Who is he comes
   here?   *[Steps aside.*

Enter LONGAVILLE, *with a paper.*

What, Longaville; and reading! listen, ear.

Biron. Now, in thy likeness, one more fool,
   appear!   [*Aside.*

Long. Ah me! I am forsworn.

Biron. Why, he comes in like a perjure,
    wearing papers.   [*Aside.*
King. In love, I hope: sweet fellowship in
    shame!   [*Aside.*
Biron. One drunkard loves another of the
    name.   [*Aside.*
Long. Am I the first that have been perjur'd
    so?
Biron. [*aside.*] I could put thee in comfort;
    not by two that I know:
Thou mak'st the triumviry, the corner cap of
    society,
The shape of Love's Tyburn that hangs up
    simplicity.
Long. I fear these stubborn lines lack power
    to move:—
O sweet Maria, empress of my love!
These numbers will I tear and write in prose.
    Biron. [*aside.*] O, rhymes are guards on
        wanton Cupid's hose:
Disfigure not his slop.
    Long.   This same shall go.—
              [*He reads the sonnet.*
Did not the heavenly rhetoric of thine eye,—
    'Gainst whom the world cannot hold argu-
        ment,—
Persuade my heart to this false perjury?
    Vows for thee broke deserve not punishment.
A woman I forswore: I will prove,
    Thou being a goddess, I forswore not thee;
My vow was earthly, thou a heavenly love;
    Thy grace being gain'd cures all disgrace in me.
Vows are but breath, and breath a vapour is:
    Then thou, fair sun, which on my earth dost
        shine,
Exhal'st this vapour vow; in thee it is:
    If broken, then it is no fault of mine:
If by me broke, what fool is not so wise
To lose an oath to win a paradise?
    Biron. [*aside.*] This is the liver vein, which
        makes flesh a deity,
A green goose a goddess: pure, pure idolatry.
God amend us, God amend! we are much out
    o' the way.
    Long. By whom shall I send this?—Com-
        pany! stay.   [*Stepping aside.*
    Biron. [*aside.*] All hid, all hid, an old infant
        play.
Like a demi-god here sit I in the sky,
And wretched fools' secrets heedfully o'er-eye.
More sacks to the mill! O heavens, I have my
    wish!

Enter DUMAIN, *with a paper.*

Dumain transform'd: four woodcocks in a dish!
    Dum. O most divine Kate!
    Biron.   O most profane coxcomb!
              [*Aside.*
    Dum. By heaven, the wonder of a mortal eye!
    Biron. By earth, she is but corporal: there
        you lie.   [*Aside.*
    Dum. Her amber hairs for foul have amber
        quoted.

    Biron. An amber-colour'd raven was well
        noted.   [*Aside.*
    Dum. As upright as the cedar.
    Biron.   Stoop, I say;
Her shoulder is with child.   [*Aside.*
    Dum.   As fair as day.
    Biron. Ay, as some days; but then no sun
        must shine.   [*Aside.*
    Dum. O that I had my wish!
    Long.   And I had mine!
               [*Aside.*
    King. And I mine too, good Lord! ⸰
              [*Aside.*
    Biron. Amen, so I had mine: is not that a
        good word?   [*Aside.*
    Dum. I would forget her; but a fever she
Reigns in my blood, and will remember'd be.
    Biron. A fever in your blood? why, then
        incision
Would let her out in saucers: sweet misprison!
              [*Aside.*
    Dum. Once more I'll read the ode that I
        have writ.
    Biron. Once more I'll mark how love can
        vary wit.   [*Aside.*
    Dum. [*reads.*] On a day,—alack the day!
    Love, whose month is ever May,
    Spied a blossom passing fair
    Playing in the wanton air:
    Through the velvet leaves the wind
    All unseen, can passage find;
    That the lover, sick to death,
    Wish'd himself the heaven's breath.
    Air, quoth he, thy cheeks may blow:
    Air, would I might triumph so!
    But, alack, my hand is sworn
    Ne'er to pluck thee from thy thorn:
    Vow, alack, for youth unmeet;
    Youth so apt to pluck a sweet.
    Do not call it sin in me
    That I am forsworn for thee:
    Thou for whom even Jove would swear
    Juno but an Ethiope were;
    And deny himself for Jove,
    Turning mortal for thy love.—
This will I send; and something else more plain,
That shall express my true love's fasting pain.
O, would the King, Birón, and Longaville,
Were lovers too! Ill, to example ill,
Would from my forehead wipe a perjur'd note
For none offend where all alike do dote.
    Long. Dumain [*advancing*], thy love is far
        from charity,
That in love's grief desir'st society:
You may look pale, but I should blush, I know,
To be o'erheard and taken napping so.
    King. Come, sir [*advancing*], you blush; as
        his your case is such;
You chide at him, offending twice as much:
You do not love Maria; Longaville
Did never sonnet for her sake compile;
Nor never lay his wreathed arms athwart
His loving bosom, to keep down his heart.
I have been closely shrouded in this bush.

And mark'd you both, and for you both did
    blush.   [fashion;
I heard your guilty rhymes, observ'd your
Saw sighs reek from you, noted well your pas-
    sion:
Ah me! says one; O Jove! the other cries;
One her hairs were gold, crystal the other's
    eyes;
You would for paradise break faith and troth;
                       [*To* LONG.
And Jove for your love would infringe an oath.
                       [*To* DUMAIN.
What will Birón say when that he shall hear
A faith infring'd which such a zeal did swear?
How will he scorn! how will he spend his wit!
How will he triumph, leap, and laugh at it!
For all the wealth that ever I did see
I would not have him know so much by me.
   Biron. Now step I forth to whip hypocrisy.—
              [*Descends from the tree.*
Ah, good my liege, I pray thee pardon me.
Good heart, what grace hast thou, thus to re-
    prove
These worms for loving, that art most in love?
Your eyes do make no coaches; in your tears
There is no certain princess that appears:
You'll not be perjur'd 'tis a hateful thing;
Tush, none but minstrels like of sonneting.
But are you not asham'd? nay, are you not,
All three of you, to be thus much o'ershot?
You found his mote; the king your mote did see;
But I a beam do find in each of three.
O, what a scene of foolery I have seen,
Of sighs, of groans, of sorrow, and of teen!
O me, with what strict patience have I sat
To see a king transformed to a gnat!
To see great Hercules whipping a gig,
And profound Solomon tuning a jig,
And Nestor play at push-pin with the boys,
And critic Timon laugh at idle toys!
Where lies thy grief, O, tell me, good Dumain?
And, gentle Longaville, where lies thy pain?
And where my liege's? all about the breast:—
A caudle, ho!
   King.   Too bitter is thy jest.
Are we betray'd thus to thy over-view?
   Biron. Not you to me, but I betray'd by you:
I, that am honest; I, that hold it sin
To break the vow I am engaged in;
I am betray'd by keeping company
With moon-like men of strange inconstancy.
When shall you see me write a thing in rhyme?
Or groan for Joan? or spend a minute's time
In pruning me? When shall you hear that I
Will praise a hand, a foot, a face, an eye,
A gait, a state, a brow, a breast, a waist,
A leg, a limb?—
   King.   Soft! whither away so fast?
A true man or a thief that gallops so?
   Biron. I post from love; good lover, let me
    go.

     Enter JAQUENETTA *and* COSTARD.

   Jaq. God bless the king!

   King.   What present hast thou there?
   Cost. Some certain treason.
   King.   What makes treason here?
   Cost. Nay, it makes nothing, sir.
   King.   If it mar nothing neither,
The treason and you go in peace away together.
   Jaq. I beseech your grace, let this letter be
    read;
Our parson misdoubts it; 'twas treason he said.
   King. Birón, read it over.
             [*Giving him the letter.*
Where hadst thou it?
   Jaq. Of Costard.
   King. Where hadst thou it?
   Cost. Of Dun Adramadio, Dun Adramadio.
   King. How now! what is in you? why dost
    thou tear it?
   Biron. A toy, my liege, a toy: your grace
needs not fear it.
   Long. It did move him to passion, and there-
    fore let's hear it.
   Dum. It is Birón's writing, and here is his
    name.   [*Picks up the pieces.*
   Biron. Ah, you whoreson loggerhead [*to*
    COSTARD], you were born to do me
    shame.—
Guilty, my lord, guilty; I confess, I confess.
   King. What?
   Biron. That you three fools lack'd me fool
    to make up the mess;
He, he, and you, my liege, and I,
Are pick-purses in love, and we deserve to die.
O, dismiss this audience, and I shall tell you
    more.
   Dum. Now the number is even.
   Biron.   True, true; we are four:—
Will these turtles be gone?
   King.   Hence, sirs, away.
   Cost. Walk aside the true folk, and let the
    traitors stay.
          [*Exeunt* COST. *and* JAQ.
   Biron. Sweet lords, sweet lovers, O let us
    embrace!
As true we are as flesh and blood can be;
The sea will ebb and flow, heaven show his face;
Young blood will not obey an old decree:
We cannot cross the cause why we were born;
Therefore of all hands must we be forsworn.
   King. What! did these rent lines show some
    love of thine?
   Biron. Did they, quoth you? Who sees the
    heavenly Rosaline
That, like a rude and savage man of Inde
   At the first opening of the gorgeous east,
Bows not his vassal head; and, strucken blind,
   Kisses the base ground with obedient breast?
What peremptory eagle-sighted eye
Dares look upon the heaven of her brow,
That is not blinded by her majesty?
   King. What zeal, what fury hath inspir'd
    thee now?
My love, her mistress, is a gracious moon,
She an attending star, scarce seen a light.
   Biron. My eyes are then no eyes, nor I Birón:

O, but for my love, day would turn to night!
Of all complexions the cull'd sovereignty
　Do meet, as at a fair, in her fair cheek;
Where several worthies make one dignity;
　Where nothing wants that want itself doth
　　seek.
Lend me the flourish of all gentle tongues,—
　Fie, painted rhetoric! O, she needs it not;
To things of sale a seller's praise belongs;
　She passes praise: then praise too short doth
　　blot.
A wither'd hermit, five-score winters worn,
　Might shake off fifty, looking in her eye:
Beauty doth varnish age, as if new-born,
　And gives the crutch the cradle's infancy.
O, 'tis the sun, that maketh all things shine!
　King. By heaven, thy love is black as ebony.
　Biron. Is ebony like her? O wood divine!
A wife of such wood were felicity.
O, who can give an oath? where is a book?
　That I may swear beauty doth beauty lack
If that she learn not of her eye to look:
　No face is fair that is not full so black.
　King. O paradox! Black is the badge of hell,
　The hue of dungeons, and the scowl of night;
And beauty's crest becomes the heavens well.
　Biron. Devils soonest tempt, resembling
　　spirits of light.
O, if in black my lady's brows be deckt,
　It mourns that painting and usurping hair
Should ravish doters with a false aspéct;
　And therefore is she born to make black fair.
Her favour turns the fashion of the days;
　For native blood is counted painting now;
And therefore red, that would avoid dispraise,
　Paints itself black, to imitate her brow.
　Dum. To look like her are chimney-sweepers
　　black.　　　　　　　　　　　[bright.
　Long. And, since her time, are colliers counted
　King. And Ethiopes of their sweet complex-
　　ion crack.　　　　　　　　　　[is light.
　Dum. Dark needs no candles now, for dark
　Biron. Your mistresses dare never come in
　　rain,
For fear their colours should be washed away.
　King. 'Twere good yours did; for, sir, to tell
　　you plain,
I'll find a fairer face not wash'd to-day.
　Biron. I'll prove her fair, or talk till dooms-
　　day here.
　King. No devil will fright thee then so much
　　as she.　　　　　　　　　　　　[dear.
　Dum. I never knew man hold vile stuff so
　Long. Look, here's thy love: my foot and
　　her face see.　　　　　[*Showing his shoe.*
　Biron. O, if the streets were paved with
　　thine eyes
Her feet were much too dainty for such tread!
　Dum. O vile! then, as she goes, what up-
　　ward lies
The street should see as she walk'd over head.
　King. But what of this? are we not all in
　　love?　　　　　　　　　　[forsworn.
　Biron. O, nothing so sure; and thereby all

　King. Then leave this chat; and, good Birón,
　　now prove
Our loving lawful, and our faith not torn.
　Dum. Ay, marry, there;—some flattery for
　　this evil.
　Long. O, some authority how to proceed;
Some tricks, some quillets, how to cheat the
　　devil.
　Dum. Some salve for perjury.
　Biron.　　　　　O, 'tis more than need!—
Have at you, then, affection's men-at-arms:
Consider what you first did swear unto;—
To fast,—to study,—and to see no woman;—
Flat treason 'gainst the kingly state of youth.
Say, can you fast? your stomachs are too young,
And abstinence engenders maladies.
And where that you have vow'd to study, lords,
In that each of you hath forsworn his book,—
Can you still dream, and pore, and thereon
　　look?
Why, universal plodding prisons up
The nimble spirits in the arteries,
As motion and long-during action tires
The sinewy vigour of the traveller.
Now, for not looking on a woman's face,
You have in that forsworn the use of eyes,
And study, too, the causer of your vow:
For when would you, my liege, or you, or you,
In leaden contemplation, have found out
Such fiery numbers as the prompting eyes
Of beauteous tutors have enrich'd you with?
Other slow arts entirely keep the brain,
And therefore, finding barren practisers,
Scarce show a harvest of their heavy toil;
But love, first learned in a lady's eyes,
Lives not alone immured in the brain,
But, with the motion of all elements,
Courses as swift as thought in every power,
And gives to every power a double power
Above their functions and their offices.
It adds a precious seeing to the eye:
A lover's eyes will gaze an eagle blind;
A lover's ear will hear the lowest sound,
When the suspicious head of theft is stopp'd,
Love's feeling is more soft and sensible
Than are the tender horns of cockled snails;
Love's tongue proves dainty Bacchus gross in
　　taste:
For valour, is not love a Hercules,
Still climbing trees in the Hesperides?
Subtle as sphinx; as sweet and musical
As bright Apollo's lute, strung with his hair?
And when love speaks, the voice of all the gods
Makes heaven drowsy with the harmony.
Never durst poet touch a pen to write
Until his ink were temper'd with love's sighs:
O, then his lines would ravish savage ears,
And plant in tyrants mild humility.
From women's eyes this doctrine I derive:
They sparkle still the right Promethean fire;
They are the books, the arts, the academes,
That show, contain, and nourish all the world,
Else none at all in aught proves excellent.
Then fools you were these women to forswear;

Or, keeping what is sworn, you will prove fools.
For wisdom's sake—a word that all men love,
Or for love's sake—a word that loves all men,
Or for men's sake, the authors of these women,
Or women's sake, by whom we men are men,
Let us once lose our oaths to find ourselves,
Or else we lose ourselves to keep our oaths:
It is religion to be thus forsworn;
For charity itself fulfils the law,
And who can sever love from charity?
 King. Saint Cupid, then! and, soldiers, to
  the field!   [them, lords;
 Biron. Advance your standards, and upon
Pell-mell, down with them! but be first advis'd
In conflict that you get the sun of them.
 Long. Now to plain-dealing; lay these glozes
  by;
Shall we resolve to woo these girls of France?
 King. And win them too: therefore let us
  devise
Some entertainment for them in their tents.
 Biron. First, from the park let us conduct
  them thither;
Then homeward every man attach the hand
Of his fair mistress: in the afternoon
We will with some strange pastime solace them,
Such as the shortness of the time can shape;
For revels, dances, masks, and merry hours,
Forerun fair Love, strewing her way with
  flowers.
 King. Away, away! no time shall be omitted,
That will be time, and may by us be fitted.
 Biron. Allons! Allons!—Sow'd cockle reap'd
  no corn;
And justice always whirls in equal measure:
Light wenches may prove plagues to men for-
  sworn;
If so, our copper buys no better treasure.
           [*Exeunt.*

ACT V.

SCENE I.—*Another part of the Park.*

Enter HOLOFERNES, *Sir* NATHANIEL, *and*
DULL.

Hol. Satis quod sufficit.
 Nath. I praise God for you, sir: your reasons
at dinner have been sharp and sententious;
pleasant without scurrility, witty without affection, audacious without impudency, learned
without opinion, and strange without heresy.
I did converse this *quondam* day with a companion of the king's, who is intituled, nominated, or called, Don Adriano de Armado.
 Hol. Novi hominem tanquam te: his humour
is lofty, his discourse peremptory, his tongue
filed, his eye ambitious, his gait majestical, and
his general behaviour vain, ridiculous, and
thrasonical. He is too picked, too spruce, too
affected, too odd, as it were, too peregrinate,
as I may call it.
 Nath. A most singular and choice epithet.
       [*Takes out his table-book.*

 Hol. He draweth out the thread of his ver-
bosity finer than the staple of his argument. I
abhor such fanatical fantasms, such insociable
and point-devise companions; such rackers of
orthography, as to speak dout, fine, when he
should say doubt; det, when he should pronounce debt, d, e, b, t, not d, e, t: he clepeth
a calf, cauf; half, hauf; neighbour *vocatur*
nebour; neigh abbreviated ne. This is abho-
minable (which he would call abominable), it
insinuateth me of insanie: *Ne intelligis, domine?*
to make frantic, lunatic.
 Nath. Laus Deo, bone intelligo.
 Hol. Bone!——bone for *bene: Priscian* a little
scratched; 'twill serve.
 Nath. Videsne quis venit?
 Hol. Video, et gaudeo.

Enter ARMADO, MOTH, *and* COSTARD.

 Arm. Chirra!   [*To* MOTH.
 Hol. Quare Chirra, not sirrah?
 Arm. Men of peace, well encountered.
 Hol. Most military sir, salutation.
 Moth. They have been at a great feast of
languages and stolen the scraps.
      [*To* COSTARD, *aside.*
 Cost. O, they have lived long on the alms-
basket of words! I marvel thy master hath not
eaten thee for a word; for thou art not so long
by the head as *honorificabilitudinitatibus:* thou
art easier swallowed than a flap-dragon.
 Moth. Peace; the peal begins.   [tered?
 Arm. Monsieur [*to* HOL.], are you not let-
 Moth. Yes, yes; he teaches boys the horn-
book;—What is a, b, spelt backward with the
horn on his head.
 Hol. Ba, *pueritia,* with a horn added.
 Moth. Ba, most silly sheep, with a horn.—
You hear his learning.
 Hol. Quis, quis, thou consonant?
 Moth. The third of the five vowels, if you
repeat them; or the fifth, if I.
 Hol. I will repeat them, a, e, i.—
 Moth. The sheep; the other two concludes
it; o, u.
 Arm. Now, by the salt wave of the Mediter-
raneum, a sweet touch, a quick venew of wit:
snip, snap, quick and home; it rejoiceth my
intellect: true wit.   [which is wit-old.
 Moth. Offered by a child to an old man;
 Hol. What is the figure? what is the figure?
 Moth. Horns.   [thy gig.
 Hol. Thou disputest like an infant: go, whip
 Moth. Lend me your horn to make one, and
I will whip about your infamy *circum circâ;* a
gig of cuckold's horn!
 Cost. An I had but one penny in the world
thou shouldst have it to buy gingerbread: hold,
there is the very remuneration I had of thy
master, thou halfpenny purse of wit, thou
pigeon-egg of discretion. O, an the heavens
were so pleased that thou wert but my bastard,
what a joyful father wouldst thou make me!

Go to; thou hast it *ad dunghill*, at the fingers' ends, as they say.   [*unguem.*

Hol. O, I smell false Latin; *dunghill* for

Arm. Arts-man, *præambula;* we will be singled from the barbarous. Do you not educate youth at the charge-house on the top of the mountain?

Hol. Or *mons*, the hill.   [tain.

Arm. At your sweet pleasure, for the moun-

Hol. I do, *sans* question.

Arm. Sir, it is the king's most sweet pleasure and affection to congratulate the princess at her pavilion, in the posteriors of this day; which the rude multitude call the afternoon.

Hol. The posterior of the day, most generous sir, is liable, congruent, and measurable for the afternoon: the word is well culled, choice; sweet and apt, I do assure you, sir, I do assure.

Arm. Sir, the king is a noble gentleman, and my familiar, I do assure you, very good friend:—For what is inward between us, let it pass:—I do beseech thee, remember thy courtesy:—I beseech thee, apparel thy head;—and among other importunate and most serious designs,—and of great import indeed too;—but let that pass;—for I must tell thee, it will please his grace, by the world, sometime to lean upon my poor shoulder; and with his royal finger, thus, dally with my excrement, with my mustachio: but, sweet heart, let that pass. By the world, I recount no fable; some certain special honours it pleaseth his greatness to impart to Armado, a soldier, a man of travel, that hath seen the world: but let that pass.—The very all of all is,—but, sweetheart, I do implore secrecy,—that the king would have me present the princess, sweet chuck, with some delightful ostentation, or show, or pageant, or antic, or firework. Now, understanding that the curate and your sweet self are good at such eruptions and sudden breaking out of mirth, as it were, I have acquainted you withal, to the end to crave your assistance.

Hol. Sir, you shall present before her the nine worthies.—Sir Nathaniel, as concerning some entertainment of time, some show in the posterior of this day, to be rendered by our assistance,—the king's command, and this most gallant, illustrate, and learned gentleman,—before the princess, I say, none so fit as to present the nine worthies.

Nath. Where will you find men worthy enough to present them?

Hol. Joshua, yourself; myself, or this gallant gentleman, Judas Maccabæus; this swain, because of his great limb or joint, shall pass Pompey the Great; the page, Hercules.

Arm. Pardon, sir; error: he is not quantity enough for that worthy's thumb: he is not so big as the end of his club.

Hol. Shall I have audience? he shall present Hercules in minority; his *enter* and *exit* shall be strangling a snake; and I will have an apology for that purpose.

Moth. An excellent device! so, if any of the audience hiss, you may cry: *Well done, Hercules! now thou crushest the snake!* that is the way to make an offence gracious, though few have the grace to do it.

Arm. For the rest of the worthies?-

Hol. I will play three myself.

Moth. Thrice-worthy gentleman!

Arm. Shall I tell you a thing?

Hol. We attend.

Arm. We will have, if this fadge not, an antic. I beseech you, follow.

Hol. Via, goodman Dull! thou hast spoken no word all this while.

Dull. Nor understood none neither, sir.

Hol. Allons! we will employ thee.

Dull. I'll make one in a dance, or so; or I will play on the tabor to the worthies, and let them dance the hay.

Hol. Most dull, honest Dull!—to our sport, away.   [*Exeunt.*

SCENE II.—*Another part of the Park.*
Before the PRINCESS'S *Pavilion.*

Enter the PRINCESS, KATHARINE, ROSALIND,
and MARIA.

Prin. Sweet hearts, we shall be rich ere we depart,
If fairings come thus plentifully in:
A lady wall'd about with diamonds!
Look you what I have from the loving king.

Ros. Madam, came nothing else along with that?   [in rhyme

Prin. Nothing but this? yes, as much love
As would be cramm'd up in a sheet of paper,
Writ on both sides the leaf, margent and all;
That he was fain to seal on Cupid's name.

Ros. That was the way to make his godhead wax;
For he hath been five thousand years a boy.

Kath. Ay, and a shrewd unhappy gallows too.

Ros. You'll ne'er be friends with him; he kill'd your sister.   [heavy;

Kath. He made her melancholy, sad, and
And so she died: had she been light, like you,
Of such a merry, nimble, stirring spirit,
She might have been a grandam ere she died:
And so may you; for a light heart lives long.

Ros. What's your dark meaning, mouse, of this light word?

Kath. A light condition in a beauty dark.

Ros. We need more light to find your meaning out.   [snuff;

Kath. You'll mar the light by taking it in
Therefore, I'll darkly end the argument.

Ros. Look what you do, you do it still i' the dark.   [wench.

Kath. So do not you; for you are a light

Ros. Indeed, I weigh not you; and therefore light.

Kath. You weigh me not?—O, that's you care not for me.   [care.

Ros. Great reason; for, Past cure is still past

Prin. Well bandied both; a set of wit well
 play'd.
But, Rosaline, you have a favour too:
Who sent it? and what is it?
 Ros.   I would you knew!
An if my face were but as fair as yours,
My favour were as great; be witness this.
Nay, I have verses too, I thank Birón:
The numbers true; and, were the numb'ring too,
I were the fairest goddess on the ground:
I am compar'd to twenty thousand fairs.
O, he hath drawn my picture in his letter!
 Prin. Anything like?
 Ros. Much in the letters; nothing in the
  praise.
 Prin. Beauteous as ink; a good conclusion.
 Kath. Fair as a text B in a copy-book.
 Ros. 'Ware pencils, ho! let me not die your
  debtor.
My rod dominical, my golden letter:
O that your face were not so full of O's!
 Kath. A pox of that jest! and be shrew all
  shrows!   [from fair Dumain?
 Prin. But, Katharine, what was sent to you
 Kath. Madam, this glove.
 Prin.   Did he not send you twain?
 Kath. Yes, madam; and, moreover,
Some thousand verses of a faithful lover;
A huge translation of hypocrisy,
Vilely compil'd, profound simplicity.
 Mar. This, and these pearls, to me sent
  Longaville;
The letter is too long by half a mile. [heart
 Prin. I think no less. Dost thou not wish in
The chain were longer and the letter short?
 Mar. Ay, or I would these hands might
  never part.
 Prin. We are wise girls to mock our lovers so.
 Ros. They are worse fools to purchase mock-
  ing so.
That same Birón I'll torture ere I go.
O that I knew he were but in by the week!
How I would make him fawn, and beg, and
 seek,
And wait the season, and observe the times,
And spend his prodigal wits in bootless rhymes,
And shape his service wholly to my 'hests,
And make him proud to make me proud that
 jests!
So portent-like would I o'ersway his state
That he should be my fool and I his fate.
 Prin. None are so surely caught, when they
  are catch'd,
As wit turn'd fool: folly, in wisdom hatch'd,
Hath wisdom's warrant, and the help of school,
And wit's own grace to grace a learned fool.
 Ros. The blood of youth burns not with such
  excess
As gravity's revolt to wantonness.
 Mar. Folly in fools bears not so strong a note
As foolery in the wise, when wit doth dote,
Since all the power thereof it doth apply
To prove, by wit, worth in simplicity. [face.
 Prin. Here comes Boyet, and mirth is in his

Enter BOYET.

 Boyet. O, I am stabb'd with laughter
  Where's her grace?
 Prin. Thy news, Boyet?
 Boyet.   Prepare, madam, prepare!—
Arm, wenches, arm! encounters mounted are
Against your peace: Love doth approach dis-
  guis'd,
 Armed in arguments; you'll be surpris'd:
Muster your wits: stand in your own defence;
Or hide your heads like cowards, and fly hence.
 Prin. Saint Dennis to Saint Cupid! What
  are they   [say.
That charge their breath against us? say, scout,
 Boyet. Under the cool shade of a sycamore
I thought to close mine eyes some half an hour;
When, lo! to interrupt my purpos'd rest,
Toward that shade I might behold addrest
The king and his companions: warily
I stole into a neighbour thicket by,
And overheard what you shall overhear,
That, by and by, disguis'd they will be here.
Their herald is a pretty knavish page,
That well by heart hath conn'd his embassage:
Action and accent did they teach him there;
Thus must thou speak and thus thy body bear:
And ever and anon they made a doubt
Presence majestical would put him out;
For, quoth the king, *an angel shalt thou see,*
Yet fear not thou, but speak audaciously.
The boy reply'd, *An angel is not evil;*
I should have fear'd her had she been a devil.
With that all laugh'd, and clapp'd him on the
  shoulder,
Making the bold wag, by their praises bolder.
One rubb'd his elbow, thus, and fleer'd, and
  swore
A better speech was never spoke before:
Another with his finger and his thumb
Cried, *Via! we will do't, come what will come:*
The third he caper'd, and cried, *All goes well.*
The fourth turn'd on the toe, and down he fell,
With that they all did tumble on the ground,
With such a zealous laughter, so profound,
That in this spleen ridiculous appears,
To check their folly, passion's solemn tears.
 Prin. But what, but what, come they to
  visit us?   [thus,—
 Boyet. They do, they do; and are apparel'd
Like Muscovites, or Russians, as I guess;
Their purpose is to parle, to court, and dance;
And every one his love-suit will advance
Unto his several mistress; which they'll know
By favours several which they did bestow.
 Prin. And will they so? the gallants shall be
  task'd:—
For, ladies, we will every one be mask'd;
And not a man of them shall have the grace,
Despite of suit, to see a lady's face.—
Hold, Rosaline, this favour thou shalt wear;
And then the king will court thee for his dear;
Hold, take thou this, my sweet, and give me
  thine;

So shall Birón take me for Rosaline.—
And change your favours too; so shall your loves
Woo contrary, deceiv'd by these removes.

Ros. Come on, then; wear the favours most in sight.   [intent?

Kath. But, in this changing, what is your

Prin. The effect of my intent is to cross theirs:
They do it but in mocking merriment;
And mock for mock is only my intent.
Their several counsels they unbosom shall
To loves mistook; and so be mock'd withal
Upon the next occasion that we meet
With visages display'd to talk and greet.

Ros. But shall we dance if they desire us to't?

Prin. No; to the death we will not move a foot:
Nor to their penn'd speech render we no grace:
But while 'tis spoke, each turn away her face.

Boyet. Why, that contempt will kill the speaker's heart,
And quite divorce his memory from his part.

Prin. Therefore I do it; and I make no doubt
The rest will ne'er come in if he be out.
There's no such sport as sport by sport o'er-thrown;   [own:
To make theirs ours, and ours none but our own:
So shall we stay, mocking intended game;
And they, well mock'd, depart away with shame.   [*Trumpets sound within.*

Boyet. The trumpet sounds; be mask'd; the maskers come.   [*The* Ladies *mask.*

Enter the KING, BIRON, LONGAVILLE, *and* DUMAIN, *in Russian habits and masked;* MOTH, Musicians, *and* Attendants.

Moth. All hail the richest beauties on the earth!

Boyet. Beauties no richer than rich taffeta.

Moth. A holy parcel of the fairest dames!
        [*The* Ladies *turn their backs to him.*
That ever turn'd their—backs—to mortal views!

Biron. Their eyes, villain, *their* eyes.

Moth. That ever turn'd their eyes to mortal views!

Out—

Boyet. True; *out* indeed.   [vouchsafe

Moth. Out of your favours, heavenly spirits
Not to behold—

Biron. Once to behold, rogue.

Moth. Once to behold with your sun-beamed eyes,——with your sun-beamed eyes—

Boyet. They will not answer to that epithet;
You were best call it daughter-beamed eyes.

Moth. They do not mark me, and that brings me out.

Biron. Is this your perfectness? be gone, you rogue.   [*Exit* MOTH.

Ros. What would these strangers? Know their minds, Boyet:
If they do speak our language, 'tis our will
That some plain man recount our purposes:
Know what they would.

Boyet. What would you with the princess?

Biron. Nothing but peace and gentle visita-tion.

Ros. What would they, say they?   [tion.

Boyet. Nothing but peace and gentle visita-

Ros. Why, that they have; and bid them so be gone.   [gone.

Boyet. She says you have it, and you may be

King. Say to her we have measured many miles
To tread a measure with her on this grass.

Boyet. They say that they have measured many a mile
To tread a measure with you on this grass.

Ros. It is not so. Ask them how many inches
Is in one mile: if they have measur'd many,
The measure, then, of one is easily told.

Boyet. If to come hither you have measur'd miles,
And many miles, the princess bids you tell
How many inches do fill up one mile.   [steps.

Biron. Tell her we measure them by weary

Boyet. She hears herself.

Ros.   How many weary steps,
Of many weary miles you have o'ergone,
Are number'd in the travel of one mile?

Biron. We number nothing that we spend for you;
Our duty is so rich, so infinite,
That we may do it still without accompt.
Vouchsafe to show the sunshine of your face,
That we, like savages, may worship it.

Ros. My face is but a moon, and clouded too.

King. Blessed are clouds, to do as such clouds do!   [shine,—
Vouchsafe, bright moon, and these thy stars, to shine,
Those clouds removed,—upon our wat'ry eyne.

Ros. O vain petitioner! beg a greater matter;
Thou now request'st but moonshine in the water.

King. Then, in our measure do but vouch-safe one change;
Thou bid'st me beg; this begging is not strange.

Ros. Play music, then: nay, you must do it soon.   [*Music plays.*
Not yet;—no dance:—thus change I like the moon.

King. Will you not dance? How come you thus estrang'd?

Ros. You took the moon at full; but now she's chang'd.   [man.

King. Yet still she is the moon and I the man.
The music plays; vouchsafe some motion to it.

Ros. Our ears vouchsafe it.

King.   But your legs should do it.

Ros. Since you are strangers, and come here by chance,   [dance.
We'll not be nice; take hands;—we will not dance.

King. Why take we hands, then?

Ros.   Only to part friends;—
Court'sy, sweet hearts; and so the measure ends.   [nice.

King. More measure of this measure; be not nice.

Ros. We can afford no more at such a price.

King. Prize you yourselves: what buys your company?

Ros. Your absence only.

King. That can never be.

Ros. Then cannot we be bought: and so adieu;

Twice to your visor and half once to you!

King. If you deny to dance, let's hold more chat.

Ros. In private then.

King. I am best pleas'd with that.
[*They converse apart*

Biron. White-handed mistress, one sweet word with thee. [three.

Prin. Honey, and milk, and sugar; there is

Biron. Nay, then, two treys,—an if you grow so nice,—

Metheglin, wort, and malmsey;—well run, dice!

There's half a dozen sweets.

Prin. Seventh sweet, adieu!

Since you can cog, I'll play no more with you.

Biron. One word in secret.

Prin. Let it not be sweet.

Biron. Thou griev'st my gall.

Prin. Gall? bitter.

Biron. Therefore meet.
[*They converse apart.*

Dum. Will you vouchsafe with me to change a word?

Mar. Name it.

Dum. Fair lady,—

Mar. Say you so? Fair lord,—

Take that for your fair lady.

Dum. Please it you,

As much in private, and I'll bid adieu.
[*They converse apart.*

Kath. What, was your visard made without a tongue?

Long. I know the reason, lady, why you ask.

Kath. O for your reason! quickly, sir; I long.

Long. You have a double tongue within your mask,

And would afford my speechless visard half.

Kath. Veal, quoth the Dutchman;—is not veal a calf?

Long. A calf, fair lady!

Kath. No, a fair lord calf.

Long. Let's part the word.

Kath. No, I'll not be your half:

Take all, and wean it; it may prove an ox.

Long. Look how you butt yourself in these sharp mocks!

Will you give horns, chaste lady? do not so.

Kath. Then die a calf, before your horns do grow.

Long. One word in private with you ere I die.

Kath. Bleat softly, then; the butcher hears you cry. [*They converse apart.*

Boyet. The tongues of mocking wenches are as keen

As is the razor's edge invisible,

Cutting a smaller hair than may be seen;

Above the sense of sense; so sensible

Seemeth their conference; their conceits have wings, [swifter things

Fleeter than arrows, bullets, wind, thought,

Ros. Not one word more, my maids; break of, break off. [scoff!

Biron. By heaven, all dry-beaten with pure

King. Farewell, mad wenches; you have simple wits.

[*Exeunt* KING, LORDS, *Music, and* Attendants.

Prin. Twenty adieus, my frozen Muscovites.—

Are these the breed of wits so wonder'd at?

Boyet. Tapers they are, with your sweet breaths puffed out.

Ros. Well-liking wits they have; gross, gross; fat, fat.

Prin. O poverty in wit, kingly-poor flout!

Will they not, think you, hang themselves to-night?

Or ever, but in visards, show their faces?

This pert Birón was out of countenance quite.

Ros. O, they were all in lamentable cases!

The king was weeping-ripe for a good word.

Prin. Birón did swear himself out of all suit.

Mar. Dumain was at my service, and his sword: [mute.

No *point*, quoth I; my servant straight was

Kath. Lord Longaville said I came o'er his heart;

And trow you what he called me?

Prin. Qualm, perhaps.

Kath. Yes, in good faith.

Prin. Go, sickness as thou art!

Ros. Well, better wits have worn plain statue-caps.

But will you hear? the king is my love sworn.

Prin. And quick Birón hath plighted faith to me. [born.

Kath. And Longaville was for my service

Mar. Dumain is mine, as sure as bark on tree. [ear:

Boyet. Madam, and pretty mistresses, give

Immediately they will again be here

In their own shapes; for it can never be

They will digest this harsh indignity.

Prin. Will they return?

Boyet. They will, they will, God knows,

And leap for joy, though they are lame with blows; [repair,

Therefore, change favours; and, when they

Blow like sweet roses in this summer air.

Prin. How blow? how blow? speak to be understood. [bud:

Boyet. Fair ladies mask'd are roses in their

Dismask'd, their damask sweet commixture shown,

Are angels vailing clouds, or roses blown.

Prin. Avaunt, perplexity! What shall we do

If they return in their own shapes to woo?

Ros. Good madam, if by me you'll be advis'd,

Let's mock them still, as well known as disguis'd:

Let us complain to them what fools were here,

Disguis'd like Muscovites, in shapeless gear;

And wonder what they were, and to what end
Their shallow shows and prologue vilely penn'd,
And their rough carries so ridiculous,
Should be presented at our tent to us.   [hand.
Boyet. Ladies, withdraw; the gallants are at
Prin. Whip to our tents, as roes run over
   land.
          [*Exeunt* PRIN., ROS., KATH., *and* MAR.

Re-enter the KING, BIRON, LONGAVILLE, *and*
     DUMAIN, *in their proper habits*.

King. Fair sir, God save you! Where is the
     princess?   [majesty
Boyet. Gone to her tent. Please it your
Command me any service to her thither?
King. That she vouchsafe me audience for
     one word.
Boyet. I will; and so will she, I know, my
     lord.   [*Exit*.
Birob. This fellow pecks up wit as pigeons
     peas,
And utters it again when God doth please:
He is wit's pedlar, and retails his wares
At wakes, and wassels, meetings, markets, fairs;
And we that sell by gross, the Lord doth know,
Have not the grace to grace it with such show.
This gallant pins the wenches on his sleeve,—
Had he been Adam, he had tempted Eve:
He can carve too, and lisp: why this is he
That kiss'd away his hand in courtesy:
This is the ape of form, monsieur the nice,
That, when he plays at tables, chides the dice
In honourable terms; nay, he can sing
A mean most meanly; and in ushering,
Mend him who can: the ladies call him sweet;
The stairs, as he treads on them, kiss his feet:
This is the flower that smiles on every one,
To show his teeth as white as whalé's bone:
And consciences that will not die in debt
Pay him the due of honey-tongu'd Boyet.
King. A blister on his sweet tongue, with my
     heart,
That put Armado's page out of his part!
Biron. See where it comes!—Behaviour,
     what wert thou   [now?
Till this man show'd thee? and what art thou

Re-enter the PRINCESS, *ushered by* BOYET;
     ROSALINE, MARIA, KATHARINE, *and* At-
     tendants.

King. All hail, sweet madam, and fair time
     of day!
Prin. Fair, in all hail, is foul, as I conceive.
King. Construe my speeches better, if you
     may.
Prin. Then wish me better, I will give you
     leave.
King. We came to visit you; and purpose now
To lead you to our court: vouchsafe it then.
Prin. This field shall hold me; and so hold
     your vow:
Nor God, nor I, delight in perjur'd men.
King. Rebuke me not for that which you
     provoke;

The virtue of your eye must break my oath.
Prin. You nickname virtue: vice you should
     have spoke:
For virtue's office never breaks men's troth.
Now, by my maiden honour, yet as pure
     As the unsullied lily; I protest.
A world of torments though I should endure,
     I would not yield to be your house's guest:
So much I hate a breaking cause to be
Of heavenly oaths, vow'd with integrity.
King. O, you have liv'd in desolation here,
Unseen, unvisited, much to our shame.
Prin. Not so, my lord; it is not so, I swear;
We have had pastime here, and pleasant
     game;
A mess of Russians left us but of late.
King. How, madam! Russians!
Prin.   Ay, in truth, my lord;
Trim gallants, full of courtship and of state.
Ros. Madam, speak true.—It is not so, my
     lord;
My lady,—to the manner of the days,—
In courtesy, gives undeserving praise.
We four, indeed, confronted here with four
In Russian habit; here they stay'd an hour
And talk'd apace; and in that hour, my lord,
They did not bless us with one happy word.
I dare not call them fools; but this I think,
When they are thirsty, fools would fain have
     drink.   [sweet,
Biron. This jest is dry to me.—Fair, gentle
Your wit makes wise things foolish; when we
     greet
With eyes best seeing heaven's fiery eye,
By light we lose light: your capacity
Is of that nature, that to your huge store
Wise things seem foolish and rich things but
     poor.   [my eye,—
Ros. This proves you wise and rich, for in
Biron. I am a fool, and full of poverty.
Ros. But that you take what doth to you
     belong,
It were a fault to snatch words from my tongue.
Biron. O, I am yours, and all that I possess.
Ros. All the fool mine?
Biron.   I cannot give you less.
Ross. Which of the visards was it that you
     wore?
Biron. Where? when? what visard? why de-
     mand you this?   [ous case
Ros. There, then, that visard; that superflu-
That hid the worse and show'd the better face.
King. We are descried: they'll mock us now
     downright.
Dum. Let us confess, and turn it to a jest.
Prin. Amaz'd, my lord? why looks your
     highness sad?
Ros. Help, hold his brows! he'll swoon! Why
     look you pale?—
Sea-sick, I think, coming from Muscovy.
Biron. Thus pour the stars down plagues for
     perjury.
Can any face of brass hold longer out?—
Here stand I, lady: dart thy skill at me;

Bruise me with scorn, confound me with a
   flout;
Thrust thy sharp wit quite through my ignor-
   ance;
   Cut me to pieces with thy keen conceit;
And I will wish thee never more to dance,
   Nor never more in Russian habit wait.
O, never will I trust to speeches penn'd,
   Nor to the motion of a school-boy's tongue;
Nor never come in visard to my friend;
   Nor woo in rhyme, like a blind harper's song:
Taffeta phrases, silken terms precise,
   Three-pil'd hyperboles, spruce affectation,
Figures pedantical; these summer-flies
   Have blown me full of maggot ostentation;
I do forswear them: and I here protest,
   By this white glove,—how white the hand,
     God knows!—
Henceforth my wooing mind shall be express'd
   In russet yeas, and honest kersey noes:
And, to begin, wench,—so God help me, la!—
My love to thee is sound, sans crack or flaw.
   Ros. Sans sans, I pray you.
   Biron.   Yet I have a trick
Of the old rage:—bear with me, I am sick;
I'll leave it by degrees. Soft, let us see;—
Write, *Lord have mercy on us*, on those three;
They are infected; in their hearts it lies:
They have the plague, and caught it of your
   eyes:
These lords are visited; you are not free,
For the Lord's tokens on you do I see.
   Prin. No, they are free that gave these tok-
     ens to us.   [undo us.
   Biron. Our states are forfeit: seek not to
   Ros. It is not so; for how can this be true,
That you stand forfeit, being those that sue?
   Biron. Peace; for I will not have to do with
     you.
   Ros. Nor shall not, if I do as I intend.
   Biron. Speak for yourselves; my wit is at an
     end.   [transgression
   King. Teach us, sweet madam, for our rude
Some fair excuse.
   Prin.   The fairest is confession.
Were you not here but even now, disguis'd?
   King. Madam, I was.
   Prin.   And were you well advis'd?
   King. I was, fair madam.
   Prin.   When you then were here,
What did you whisper in your lady's ear?
   King. That more than all the world I did re-
     spect her.
   Prin. When she shall challenge this you will
     reject her.
   King. Upon mine honour, no.
   Prin.   Peace, peace, forbear;
Your oath once broke, you force not to for-
   swear.
   King. Despise me when I break this oath of
   mine.
   Prin. I will: and therefore keep it:—Rosa-
     line,
What did the Russian whisper in your ear?

   Ros. Madam, he swore that he did hold me
     dear
As precious eyesight; and did value me
Above this world: adding thereto, moreover,
That he would wed me, or else die my lover.
   Prin. God give thee joy of him! the noble
     lord
Most honourably doth uphold his word.
   King. What mean you, madam? by my life,
     my troth,
I never swore this lady such an oath.   [plain;
   Ros. By heaven you did; and, to confirm it
You gave me this: but take it, sir, again.
   King. My faith and this the princess I did
     give;
I knew her by this jewel on her sleeve.
   Prin. Pardon me, sir; this jewel she did wear;
And Lord Birón, I thank him, is my dear:—
What; will you have me, or your pearl again?
   Biron.   Neither of either; I remit both
     twain.—
I see the trick on 't;—here was a consent,
Knowing aforehand of our merriment,
To dash it like a Christmas comedy: [zany,
Some carry-tale, some please-man, some slight
Some mumble-news, some trencher-knight,
   some Dick,—   [trick
That smiles his cheek in years, and knows the
To make my lady laugh when she's dispos'd,—
Told our intents before: which once disclos'd,
The ladies did change favours; and then we,
Following the signs, woo'd but the sign of she.
Now, to our perjury to add more terror,
We are again forsworn,—in will and error.
Much upon this it is:—and might not you
              [*To* BOYET.
Forestal our sport, to make us thus untrue?
Do not you know my lady's foot by the squire,
   And laugh upon the apple of her eye?
And stand between her back, sir, and the fire,
   Holding a trencher, jesting merrily?
You put our page out: go, you are allow'd;
Die when you will, a smock shall be your
   shroud.
You leer upon me, do you? there's an eye
Wounds like a leaden sword.
   Boyet.   Full merrily
Hath this brave manage, this career, been run.
   Biron. Lo, he is tilting straight! Peace; I
     have done.

Enter COSTARD.

Welcome, pure wit! thou partest a fair fray.
   Cost. O Lord, sir, they would know
Whether the three worthies shall come in or no.
   Biron. What, are there but three?
   Cost.   No, sir; but it is vara fine,
For every one pursents three.
   Biron.   And three times thrice is nine.
   Cost. Not so, sir; under correction, sir; I
     hope it is not so:
You cannot beg us, sir, I can assure you, sir:
     we know what we know;
I hope, sir, three times thrice, sir,—

Biron. Is not nine.

Cost. Under correction, sir, we know where- [for nine.
until it doth amount.

Biron. By Jove, I always took three threes

Cost. O Lord, sir, it were pity you should
get your living by reckoning, sir.

Biron. How much is it?

Cost. O Lord, sir, the parties themselves,
the actors, sir, will show whereuntil it doth
amount; for my own part, I am, as they say,
but to parfect one man in one poor man;
Pompion the Great, sir.

Biron. Art thou one of the worthies?

Cost. It pleased them to think me worthy of
Pompion the Great: for mine own part, I know
not the degree of the worthy; but I am to stand
for him.

Biron. Go, bid them prepare.

Cost. We will turn it finely off, sir; we will
take some care. [*Exit* COSTARD.

King. Birón, they will shame us; let them
not approach.

Biron. We are shame-proof, my lord: and
'tis some policy
To have one show worse than the king's and
his company.

King. I say they shall not come. [now:

Prin. Nay, my good lord, let me o'errule you
That sport best pleases that doth least know
how;
Where zeal strives to content, and the contents
Die in the zeal of them which it presents,
Their form confounded makes most form in
mirth,
When great things labouring perish in their
birth.

Biron. A right description of our sport, my
lord.

Enter ARMADO.

Arm. Anointed, I implore so much expense
of thy royal sweet breath as will utter a brace
of words. [ARMADO *converses with the* KING,
and delivers him a paper.

Prin. Doth this man serve God?

Biron. Why ask you? [making.

Prin. He speaks not like a man of God's

Arm. That's all one, my fair, sweet, honey
monarch: for, I protest, the schoolmaster is exceeding fantastical; too, too vain; too, too vain:
but we will put it, as they say, to *fortuna della
guerra.* I wish you the peace of mind, most
royal couplement! [*Exit* ARMADO.

King. Here is like to be a good presence of
worthies. He presents Hector of Troy; the
swain, Pompey the Great; the parish curate,
Alexander; Armado's page, Hercules; the
pedant, Judas Maccabæus.
And if these four worthies in their first show
thrive, [other five.
These four will change habits and present the

Biron. There is five in the first show.

King. You are deceived, 'tis not so.

Biron. The pedant, the braggart, the hedge-
priest, the fool, and the boy;— [again
Abate throw at novum; and the whole world
Cannot prick out five such, take each one in his
vein. [comes amain.

King. The ship is under sail, and here she
[*Seats brought for the* KING, PRIN., &c.

Pageant of the Nine Worthies.

Enter COSTARD, *armed, for* Pompey.

Cost. I Pompey am——

Boyet. You lie, you are not he.

Cost. I Pompey am——

Boyet. With libbard's head on knee.

Biron. Well said, old mocker; I must needs
be friends with thee. [*Big,*——

Cost. I *Pompey am, Pompey surnamed the
Dum.* The Great.

Cost. It is *Great,* sir;—*Pompey surnamed the
Great,*
*That oft in field, with targe and shield, did make
my foe to sweat;* [chance,
*And travelling along this coast, I here am come by
And lay my arms before the legs of this sweet lass
of France.* [had done.
If your ladyship would say, *Thanks, Pompey,* I

Prin. Great thanks, great Pompey.

Cost. 'Tis not so much worth; but I hope I
was parfect: I made a little fault in *Great.*

Biron. My hat to a halfpenny, Pompey
proves the best worthy.

Enter Sir NATHANIEL, *armed, for* Alexander.

*Nath. When in the world I liv'd, I was the
world's commander;*
*By east, west, north, and south I spread my con-
quering might:*
My 'scutcheon plain declares that I am Alisander.

Boyet. Your nose says, no, you are not; for
it stands too right.

Biron. Your nose smells no in this, most
tender-smelling knight.

Prin. The conqueror is dismay'd.—Proceed,
good Alexander.

*Nath. When in the world I liv'd, I was the
world's commander:—* [sander.

Boyet. Most true, 'tis right; you were so, Ali-

Biron. Pompey the Great,—

Cost. Your servant, and Costard.

Biron. Take away the conqueror, take away
Alisander.

Cost. O, sir [*to* NATH.], you have overthrown
Alisander the conqueror! You will be scraped
out of the painted cloth for this: your lion, that
holds his poll-ax sitting on a close stool, will be
given to Ajax: he will be the ninth worthy. A
conqueror and afeard to speak! run away for
shame, Alisander. [*Sir* NATH. *retires.*] There,
an't shall please you; á foolish mild man; an
honest man, look you, and soon dashed! he is a
marvellous good neighbour, insooth; and a very
good bowler: but, for Alisander,—alas, you see,
how 'tis,—a little o'erparted.—But there are

worthies a-coming will speak their mind in some other sort.

Prin. Stand aside, good Pompey.

Enter HOLOFERNES, *armed, for* Judas; *and* MOTH, *armed, for* Hercules.

Hol. Great Hercules is presented by this imp,
Whose club kill'd Cerberus, that three-headed canus;
And when he was a babe, a child, a shrimp,
Thus did he strangle serpents in his manus:
Quoniam *he seemeth in minority,*
Ergo *I come with this apology.—*
Keep some state in thy *exit,* and vanish.

[MOTH *retires.*

Judas I am,—
Dum. A Judas!
Hol. Not Iscariot, sir,—
Judas I am, ycleped Maccabæus.
Dum. Judas Maccabæus clipt is plain Judas.
Biron. A kissing traitor. How art thou proved Judas?
Hol. Judas I am,—
Dum. The more shame for you, Judas.
Hol. What mean you, sir?
Boyet. To make Judas hang himself.
Hol. Begin, sir; you are my elder.
Biron. Well followed: Judas was hanged on an elder.
Hol. I will not be put out of countenance.
Biron. Because thou hast no face.
Hol. What is this?
Boyet. A cittern head.
Dum. The head of a bodkin.
Biron. A death's face in a ring.   [seen.
Long. The face of an old Roman coin, scarce
Boyet. The pummel of Cæsar's faulchion.
Dum. The carv'd-bone face on a flask.
Biron. St. George's half-cheek in a brooch.
Dum. Ay, and in a brooch of lead.
Biron. Ay, and worn in the cap of a tooth-drawer;
And now, forward; for we have put thee in countenance.
Hol. You have put me out of countenance.
Biron. False: we have given thee faces.
Hol. But you have outfaced them all.
Biron. An thou wert a lion we would do so.
Boyet. Therefore, as he is an ass, let him go.
And so adieu, sweet Jude! nay, why dost thou stay?
Dum. For the latter end of his name.
Biron. For the ass to the Jude; give it him:—Jud-as, away.
Hol. This is not generous, not gentle, not humble.
Boyet. A light for Monsieur Judas! it grows dark, he may stumble.   [been baited!
Prin. Alas, poor Maccabæus, how hath he

Enter ARMADO, *armed, for* Hector.

Biron. Hide thy head, Achilles: here comes Hector in arms.

Dum. Though my mocks come home by me, I will now be merry.   [this.
King. Hector was but a Trojan in respect of
Boyet. But is this Hector?
Dum. I think Hector was not so clean-timbered.
Long. His leg is too big for Hector.
Dum. More calf, certain.
Boyet. No; he is best indued in the small.
Biron. This cannot be Hector.   [faces.
Dum. He's a god or a painter, for he makes
Arm. The armipotent Mars, of lances the al-mighty,
Gave Hector a gift,—
Dum. A gilt nutmeg.
Biron. A lemon.
Long. Stuck with cloves.
Dum. No, cloven.
Arm. Peace!
The armipotent Mars, of lances the almighty,
Gave Hector a gift, the heir of Ilion;   [yea,
A man so breath'd, that certain he would fight,
From morn till night, out of his pavilion.
I am that flower,—
Dum.   That mint.
Long.   That columbine.
Arm. Sweet Lord Longaville, rein thy tongue.
Long. I must rather give it the rein, for it runs against Hector.
Dum. Ay, and Hector's a greyhound.
Arm. The sweet war-man is dead and rotten; sweet chucks, beat not the bones of the buried: when he breathed, he was a man.—But I will forward with my device. Sweet royalty [*to the* PRINCESS], bestow on me the sense of hearing.

[BIRON *whispers* COSTARD.

Prin. Speak, brave Hector: we are much delighted.
Arm. I do adore thy sweet grace's slipper.
Boyet. Loves her by the foot.
Dum. He may not by the yard.   [bal,—
Arm. This Hector far surmounted Hanni-
Cost. The party is gone, fellow Hector; she is gone: she is two months on her way.
Arm. What meanest thou?
Cost. Faith, unless you play the honest Trojan, the poor wench is cast away: she's quick; the child brags in her belly already; 'tis yours.
Arm. Dost thou infamonize me among potentates? thou shalt die.
Cost. Then shall Hector be whipped for Jaquenetta that is quick by him, and hanged for Pompey that is dead by him.
Dum. Most rare Pompey!
Boyet. Renowned Pompey!
Biron. Greater than great, great, great, great Pompey! Pompey the Huge!
Dum. Hector trembles.
Biron. Pompey is mov'd.—More Ates, more Ates! stir them on! stir them on!
Dum. Hector will challenge him.
Biron. Ay, if he have no more man's blood in 's belly than will sup a flea.
Arm. By the north pole, I do challenge thee.

Cost. I will not fight with a pole, like a northern man: I'll slash; I'll do it by the sword.—I pray you, let me borrow my arms again.

Dum. Room for the incensed worthies.

Cost. I'll do it in my shirt.

Dum. Most resolute Pompey!

Moth. Master, let me take you a button-hole lower. Do you not see Pompey is uncasing for the combat? What mean you? you will lose your reputation.

Arm. Gentlemen and soldiers, pardon me; I will not combat in my shirt.

Dum. You may not deny it: Pompey hath made the challenge.

Arm. Sweet bloods, I both may and will.

Biron. What reason have you for 't?

Arm. The naked truth of it is, I have no shirt; I go woolward for penance.

Boyet. True, and it was enjoined him in Rome for want of linen; since when, I'll be sworn, he wore none but a dish-clout of Jaquenetta's; and that'a wears next his heart for a favour.

Enter NERCADE.

Mer. God save you, madam!

Prin. Welcome, Mercade;
But that thou interrupt'st our merriment.

Mer. I am sorry, madam; for the news I bring
Is heavy in my tongue. The king your father,—

Prin. Dead, for my life!

Mer. Even so; my tale is told.   [cloud.

Biron. Worthies, away; the scene begins to

Arm. For mine own part, I breathe free breath: I have seen the day of wrong through the little hole of discretion, and I will right myself like a soldier.   [*Exeunt* Worthies.

King. How fares your Majesty?

Prin. Boyet, prepare; I will away to-night.

King. Madam, not so; I do beseech you, stay.   [lords,

Prin. Prepare, I say.—I thank you, gracious
For all your fair endeavours; and entreat
Out of a new-sad soul, that you vouchsafe,
In your rich wisdom, to excuse or hide
The liberal opposition of our spirits;
If over-boldly we have borne ourselves
In the converse of breath, your gentleness
Was guilty of it.—Farewell, worthy lord;
A heavy heart bears not a nimble tongue:
Excuse me so, coming so short of thanks
For my great suit so easily obtain'd.   [form

King. The extreme parts of time extremely
All causes to the purpose of his speed;
And often, at his very loose, decides
That which long process could not arbitrate:
And though the mourning brow of progeny
Forbid the smiling courtesy of love
The holy suit which fain it would convince,
Yet, since love's argument was first on foot,
Let not the cloud of sorrow justle it
From what it purpos'd: since to wail friends lost
Is not by much so wholesome-profitable

As to rejoice at friends but newly found.

Prin. I understand you not: my griefs are
dull.   [ear of grief;—

Biron. Honest plain words best pierce the
And by these badges understand the king.
For your fair sakes have we neglected time,
Play'd foul play with our oaths; your beauty,
ladies,
Hath much deform'd us, fashioning our humours
Even to the opposed end of our intents:
And what in us hath seem'd ridiculous,—
As love is full of unbefitting strains,—
All wanton as a child, skipping, and vain;
Form'd by the eye, and therefore, like the eye,
Full of strange shapes, of habits, and of forms,
Varying in subjects as the eye doth roll
To every varied object in his glance:
Which party-coated presence of loose love
Put on by us, if in your heavenly eyes
Have misbecom'd our oaths and gravities,
Those heavenly eyes that look into these faults
Suggested us to make. Therefore, ladies,
Our love being yours, the error that love makes
Is likewise yours: we to ourselves prove false,
By being once false, for ever to be true
To those that make us both—fair ladies, you:
And even that falsehood, in itself a sin,
Thus purifies itself and turns to grace.   [love;

Prin. We have receiv'd your letters, full of
Your favours, the ambassadors of love;
And, in our maiden council, rated them
At courtship, pleasant jest, and courtesy,
As bombast, and as lining to the time:
But more devout than this in our respects
Have we not been; and therefore met your loves
In their own fashion, like a merriment.

Dum. Our letters, madam, show'd much
more than jest.

Long. So did our looks.

Ros.   We did not quote them so.

King. Now, at the latest minute of the hour,
Grant us your loves.

Prin.   A time, methinks, too short
To make a world-without-end bargain in.
No, no, my lord, your grace is perjur'd much,
Full of dear guiltiness; and therefore this,—
If for my love—as there is no such cause—
You will do aught, this shall you do for me:
Your oath I will not trust; but go with speed
To some forlorn and naked hermitage,
Remote from all the pleasures of the world;
There stay until the twelve celestial signs
Have brought about their annual reckoning.
If this austere insociable life
Change not your offer, made in heat of blood;
If frosts and fasts, hard lodging and thin weeds,
Nip not the gaudy blossoms of your love,
But that it bear this trial, and last love,
Then, at the expiration of the year,
Come, challenge, challenge me by these deserts,
And, by this virgin palm now kissing thine,
I will be thine; and, till that instant, shut
My woeful self up in a mournful house,
Raining the tears of lamentation

For the remembrance of my father's death.
If this thou do deny, let our hands part,
Neither intitled in the other's heart.
　　King. If this, or more than this, I would deny,
　　To flatter up these powers of mine with rest,
The sudden hand of death close up mine eye!
　　Hence ever, then, my heart is in thy breast.
　　Biron. And what to me, my love? and what
　　　to me?　　　　　　　　　　　　[rank;
　　Ros. You must be purged too; your sins are
You are attaint with faults and perjury;
Therefore, if you my favour mean to get,
A twelvemonth shall you spend, and never rest,
But seek the weary beds of people sick.
　　Dum. But what to me, my love? but what
　　　to me?
　　Kath. A wife!—A beard, fair health, and
　　　honesty;
With threefold love I wish you all these three.
　　Dum. O, shall I say I thank you, gentle
　　　wife?
　　Kath. Not so, my lord;—a twelvemonth and
　　　a day　　　　　　　　　　　　[say:
I'll mark no words that smooth-fac'd wooers
Come when the king doth to my lady come,
Then, if I have much love I'll give you some.
　　Dum. I'll serve thee true and faithfully till
　　　then.
　　Kath. Yet swear not, lest you be forsworn
　　　again.
　　Long. What says Maria?
　　Mar.　　　　　　　At the twelvemonth's end
I'll change my black gown for a faithful friend.
　　Long. I'll stay with patience; but the time
　　　is long.
　　Mar. The liker you; few taller are so young.
　　Biron. Studies my lady? mistress, look on
　　　me;
Behold the window of my heart, mine eye,
What humble suit attends thy answer there!
Impose some service on me for thy love.
　　Ros. Oft have I heard of you, my Lord
　　　Birón,
Before I saw you: and the world's large tongue
Proclaims you for a man replete with mocks,
Full of comparisons and wounding flouts,
Which you on all estates will execute
That lie within the mercy of your wit.
To weed this wormwood from your fruitful
　　　brain,
And therewithal to win me, if you please,—
Without the which I am not to be won,—
You shall this twelvemonth term from day to
　　　day
Visit the speechless sick, and still converse
With groaning wretches; and your task shall be,
With all the fierce endeavour of your wit
To enforce the pained impotent to smile.
　　Biron. To move wild laughter in the throat
　　　of death!
It cannot be; it is impossible:
Mirth cannot move a soul in agony.
　　Ros. Why, that's the way to choke a gibing
　　　spirit,

Whose influence is begot of that loose grace
Which shallow laughing hearers give to fools:
A jest's prosperity lies in the ear
Of him that hears it, never in the tongue
Of him that makes it: then, if sickly ears,
Deaf'd with the clamours of their own dear
　　　groans,
Will hear your idle scorns, continue them,
And I will have you and that fault withal;
But if they will not, throw away that spirit,
And I shall find you empty of that fault,
Right joyful of your reformation.
　　Biron. A twelvemonth! well, befall what
　　　will befall,
I'll jest a twelvemonth in an hospital.
　　Prin. Ay, sweet my lord; and so I take my
　　　leave.　　　　　　　　　　[*To the* KING.
　　King. No, madam: we will bring you on
　　　your way.　　　　　　　　　　[play;
　　Biron. Our wooing doth not end like an old
Jack hath not Jill: these ladies' courtesy
Might well have made our sport a comedy.
　　King. Come, sir, it wants a twelvemonth
　　　and a day,
And then 'twill end.
　　Biron.　　　　　　That's too long for a play.

Enter ARMADO.

　　Arm. Sweet majesty, vouchsafe me,—
　　Prin. Was not that Hector?
　　Dum. The worthy knight of Troy.
　　Arm. I will kiss thy royal finger, and take
leave: I am a votary; I have vowed to Jaquenetta to hold the plough for her sweet love three
years. But, most esteemed greatness, will you
hear the dialogue that the two learned men
have compiled in praise of the owl and the
cuckoo? it should have followed in the end of
our show.
　　King. Call them forth quickly, we will do so.
　　Arm. Holla! approach.

Enter HOLOFERNES, NATHANIEL, MOTH,
　　COSTARD, *and others.*

This side is Hiems, Winter—this Ver, the
Spring; the one maintained by the owl, the
other by the cuckoo. Ver, begin.

SONG.

I.

Spring. When daisies pied, and violets blue,
　　　And lady-smocks all silver-white,
　　And cuckoo-buds of yellow hue,
　　　Do paint the meadows with delight,
　　The cuckoo then, on every tree,
　　Mocks married men, for thus sings he—
　　　　　Cuckoo;
　　Cuckoo, cuckoo,—O word of fear,
　　Unpleasing to a married ear!

II.

When shepherds pipe on oaten straws,
　　　And merry larks are ploughmen's clocks,
When turtles tread, and rooks and daws,
　　　And maidens bleach their summer smocks,

The cuckoo then, on every tree,
Mocks married men, for thus sings he—
      Cuckoo;
Cuckoo, cuckoo,—O word of fear,
Unpleasing to a married ear!

III.

Winter. When icicles hang by the wall,
    And *Dick* the shepherd blows his nail,
And *Tom* bears logs into the hall,
    And milk comes frozen home in pail,
When blood is nipp'd and ways be foul,
Then nightly sings the staring owl—
      To-who;
To-whit, to-who, a merry note,
While greasy *Joan* doth keel the pot.

IV.

When all aloud the wind doth blow,
    And coughing drowns the parson's saw,
And birds sit brooding in the snow,
    And *Marion's* nose looks red and raw,
When roasted crabs hiss in the bowl,
Then nightly sings the staring owl—
      To-who;
Tu-whit, to-who, a merry note,
While greasy *Joan* doth keel the pot.

Arm. The words of Mercury are harsh after the songs of Apollo. You that way; we this way.   [*Exeunt.*

THE MERCHANT OF VENICE

DRAMATIS PERSONÆ

DUKE OF VENICE.
PRINCE OF MOROCCO, } *Suitors to* PORTIA.
PRINCE OF ARRAGON, }
ANTONIO, *the Merchant of Venice.*
BASSANIO, *his Friend.*
SOLANIO, }
SALARINO, } *Friends to* ANTONIO *and*
GRATIANO, } BASSANIO.
LORENZO, *in love with* JESSICA.
SHYLOCK, *a Jew.*
TUBAL, *a Jew, his Friend.*
LAUNCELOT GOBBO, *a Clown, Servant to* SHYLOCK.

OLD GOBBO, *Father to* LAUNCELOT.
SALERIO, *a Messenger from Venice.*
LEONARDO, *Servant to* BASSANIO.
BALTHAZAR, } *Servants to* PORTIA.
STEPHANO, }

PORTIA, *a rich Heiress.*
NERISSA, *her Waiting-maid.*
JESSICA, *Daughter to* SHYLOCK.

Magnificoes of Venice, Officers of the Court of Justice, Gaoler, Servants, *and other* Attendants.

SCENE,—*Partly at* VENICE, *and partly at* BELMONT, *the Seat of* PORTIA, *on the Continent.*

ACT I.

SCENE I.—VENICE. *A Street.*

Enter ANTONIO, SALARINO, *and* SOLANIO.

Ant. In sooth, I know not why I am so sad:
It wearies me; you say it wearies you;
But how I caught it, found it, or came by it,
What stuff 'tis made of, whereof it is born,
I am to learn;
And such a want-wit sadness makes of me
That I have much ado to know myself.

Salar. Your mind is tossing on the ocean;
There, where your argosies, with portly sail,—
Like signiors and rich burghers of the flood,
Or, as it were, the pageants of the sea,—
Do overpeer the petty traffickers
That curt'sy to them, do them reverence,
As they fly by them with their woven wings.

Solan. Believe me, sir, had I such venture forth,
The better part of my affections would
Be with my hopes abroad. I should be still
Plucking the grass, to know where sits the wind;
Peering in maps for ports, and piers, and roads;
And every object that might make me fear
Misfortune to my ventures, out of doubt
Would make me sad.

Salar. My wind, cooling my broth,
Would blow me to an ague when I thought
What harm a wind too great might do at sea.
I should not see the sandy hour-glass run
But I should think of shallows and of flats,
And see my wealthy Andrew dock'd in sand,
Vailing her high-top lower than her ribs,
To kiss her burial. Should I go to church,
And see the holy edifice of stone,
And not bethink me straight of dangerous rocks,
Which, touching but my gentle vessel's side,
Would scatter all her spices on the stream,
Enrobe the roaring waters with my silks,
And, in a word, but even now worth this,
And now worth nothing? Shall I have the thought
To think on this; and shall I lack the thought
That such a thing bechanc'd would make me sad?
But tell not me; I know Antonio
Is sad to think upon his merchandize.

Ant. Believe me, no: I thank my fortune for it,
My ventures are not in one bottom trusted,
Nor to one place; nor is my whole estate
Upon the fortune of this present year:
Therefore my merchandize makes me not sad.

Solan. Why, then you are in love.

Ant. Fie, fie!

Solan. Not in love neither? Then let's say you are sad
Because you are not merry: and 'twere as easy
For you to laugh, and leap, and say you are merry,
Because you are not sad. Now, by two-headed Janus,
Nature hath framed strange fellows in her time:
Some that will ever more peep through their eyes,
And laugh, like parrots, at a bag-piper:
And other of such vinegar aspéct,
That they'll not show their teeth in way of smile,
Though Nestor swear the jest be laughable.
Here comes Bassanio, your most noble kinsman,
Gratiano and Lorenzo. Fare ye well;
We leave you now with better company.

Salar. I would have stay'd till I had made you merry.
If worthier friends had not prevented me.

Ant. Your worth is very dear in my regard.
I take it your own business calls on you,
And you embrace the occasion to depart.

Enter BASSANIO, LORENZO, *and* GRATIANO.

Salar. Good-morrow, my good lords.

Bass. Good signiors both, when shall we
    laugh? say, when?
You grow exceeding strange: must it be so?

Salar. We'll make our leisures to attend on
    yours.   *[Exeunt* SALAR. *and* SOLAN.

Lor. My Lord Bassanio, since you have
    found Antonio,
We two will leave you; but at dinner-time,
I pray you, have in mind where we must meet.

Bass. I will not fail you.

Gra. You look not well, Signior Antonio;
You have too much respect upon the world:
They lose it that do buy it with much care.
Believe me, you are marvelously chang'd.

Ant. I hold the world but as the world,
    Gratiano—
A stage, where every man must play a part,
And mine a sad one.

Gra.   Let me play the fool:
With mirth and laughter let old wrinkles come;
And let my liver rather heat with wine
Than my heart cool with mortifying groans,
Why should a man, whose blood is warm within,
Sit like his grandsire cut in alabaster?
Sleep when he wakes? and creep into the
    jaundice
By being peevish? I tell thee what, Antonio,—
I love thee, and it is my love that speaks,—
There are a sort of men whose visages
Do cream and mantle like a standing pond,
And do a wilful stillness entertain,
With purpose to be dress'd in an opinion
Of wisdom, gravity, profound conceit;
As who should say, *I am Sir Oracle,*
And, when I ope my lips, let no dog bark!
O, my Antonio, I do know of these,
That therefore only are reputed wise
For saying nothing; who, I am very sure,
If they should speak, would almost damn those
    ears   [fools.
Which, hearing them, would call their brothers
I'll tell thee more of this another time:
But fish not, with this melancholy bait,
For this fool's gudgeon, this opinion.—
Come, good Lorenzo.—Fare ye well awhile;
I'll end my exhortation after dinner.   [time:

Lor. Well, we will leave you then till dinner-
I must be one of these same dumb wise men,
For Gratiano never lets me speak.   [moe,

Gra. Well, keep me company but two years
Thou shalt not know the sound of thine own
    tongue.

Ant. Farewell: I'll grow a talker for this
    gear.

Gra. Thanks, i' faith; for silence is only
    commendable   [dible.
In a neat's tongue dried and a maid not ven-
        [Exeunt GRA. *and* LOR.

Ant. Is that anything now?

Bass. Gratiano speaks an infinite deal of
nothing, more than any man in all Venice.

His reasons are as two grains of wheat hid in
two bushels of chaff: you shall seek all day ere
you find them; and, when you have them, they
are not worth the search.   [same

Ant. Well; tell me now, what lady is this
To whom you swore a secret pilgrimage,
That you to-day promis'd to tell me of?

Bass. 'Tis not unknown to you, Antonio,
How much I have disabled mine estate
By something showing a more swelling port
Than my faint means would grant continuance:
Nor do I now make moan to be abridg'd
From such a noble rate; but my chief care
Is to come fairly off from the great debts
Wherein my time, something too prodigal,
Hath left me gag'd. To you, Antonio,
I owe the most, in money and in love;
And from your love I have a warranty
To unburthen all my plots and purposes
How to get clear of all the debts I owe.   [it;

Ant. I pray you, good Bassanio, let me know
And if it stand, as you yourself still do,
Within the eye of honour, be assur'd
My purse, my person, my extremest means
Lie all unlock'd to your occasions.   [shaft,

Bass. In my school-days, when I had lost one
I shot his fellow of the self-same flight
The self-same way, with more advised watch,
To find the other forth; and by advent'ring
    both
I oft found both: I urge this childhood proof,
Because what follows is pure innocence.
I owe you much; and, like a wilful youth,
That which I owe is lost: but if you please
To shoot another arrow that self-way
Which you did shoot the first, I do not doubt,
As I will watch the aim, or to find both
Or bring your latter hazard back again,
And thankfully rest debtor for the first.   [time

Ant. You know me well, and herein spent but
To wind about my love with circumstance;
And out of doubt you do me now more wrong,
In making question of my uttermost,
Than if you had made waste of all I have.
Then do but say to me what I should do,
That in your knowledge may by me be done,
And I am press'd unto it: therefore, speak.

Bass. In Belmont is a lady richly left,
And she is fair, and fairer than that word,
Of wondrous virtues: sometimes from her eyes
I did receive fair speechless messages:
Her name is Portia; nothing undervalued
To Cato's daughter, Brutus' Portia.
Nor is the wide world ignorant of her worth;
For the four winds blow in from every coast
Renowned suitors: and her sunny locks
Hang on her temples like a golden fleece;
Which makes her seat of Belmont Colchos'
    strand,
And many Jasons come in quest of her.
O my Antonio, had I but the means
To hold a rival place with one of them,
I have a mind presages me such thrift
That I should questionless be fortunate.

Ant. Thou know'st that all my fortunes are
　　at sea;
Neither have I money nor commodity
To raise a present sum: therefore go forth;
Try what my credit can in Venice do:
That shall be rack'd, even to the uttermost,
To furnish thee to Belmont, to fair Portia
Go, presently inquire, and so will I,
Where money is; and I no question make
To have it of my trust or for my sake. [*Exeunt.*

SCENE II.—BELMONT. *A Room in* PORTIA'S
House.

Enter PORTIA *and* NERISSA.

Por. By my troth, Nerissa, my little body is
a-weary of this great world.

Ner. You would be, sweet madam, if your
miseries were in the same abundance as your
good fortunes are: and yet for aught I see, they
are as sick that surfeit with too much as they
that starve with nothing. It is no mean happiness, therefore, to be seated in the mean: super-
fluity comes sooner by white hairs, but com-
petency lives longer.

Por. Good sentences, and well pronounced.

Ner. They would be better if well followed.

Por. If to do were as easy as to know what
were good to do, chapels had been churches,
and poor men's cottages princes' palaces. It is
a good divine that follows his own instructions:
I can easier teach twenty what were good to be
done, than be one of the twenty to follow mine
own teaching. The brain may devise laws for
the blood, but a hot temper leaps over a cold
decree; such a hare is madness, the youth to
skip o'er the meshes of good council, the cripple.
But this reasoning is not in the fashion to choose
me a husband.—O me, the word choose! I
may neither choose whom I would nor refuse
whom I dislike; so is the will of a living
daughter curbed by the will of a dead father.—
Is it not hard, Nerissa, that I cannot choose
one, nor refuse none?

Ner. Your father was ever virtuous; and
holy men, at their death, have good inspira-
tions; therefore, the lottery that he hath devised in these three chests, of gold, silver, and
lead,—whereof who chooses his meaning chooses
you,—will, no doubt, never be chosen by any.
rightly, but one who you shall rightly love.
But what warmth is there in your affection
towards any of these princely suitors that are
already come?

Por. I pray thee, over-name them; and as
thou namest them, I will describe them; and
according to my description, level at my affection.

Ner. First, there is the Neapolitan prince.

Por. Ay, that's a colt indeed, for he doth
nothing but talk of his horse; and he makes it
a great appropriation to his own good parts
that he can shoe him himself: I am much afraid
my lady his mother played false with a smith.

Ner. Then is there the County Palatine.

Por. He doth nothing but frown; as who
should say, *An if you will not have me, choose:*
he hears merry tales and smiles not: I fear he
will prove the weeping philosopher when he
grows old, being so full of unmannerly sadness
in his youth. I had rather be married to a
death's head with a bone in his mouth than to
either of these. God defend me from these two!

Ner. How say you by the French lord,
Monsieur Le Bon?

Por. God made him, and therefore let him
pass for a man. In truth, I know it is a sin to
be a mocker: but, he! why, he hath a horse
better than the Neapolitan's; a better bad
habit of frowning than the Count Palatine: he
is every man and no man: if a throstle sing he
falls straight a-capering; he will fence with his
own shadow: if I should marry him I should
marry twenty husbands. If he would despise
me I would forgive him; for if he love me to
madness I shall never requite him.

Ner. What say you then to Falconbridge,
the young baron of England?

Por. You know I say nothing to him; for he
understands not me, nor I him; he hath neither
Latin, French, nor Italian; and you will come
into the court and swear that I have a poor
pennyworth in the English. He is a proper
man's picture; but, alas! who can converse
with a dumb show? How oddly he is suited!
I think, he bought his doublet in Italy, his
round hose in France, his bonnet in Germany,
and his behaviour everywhere.

Ner. What think you of the Scottish lord,
his neighbour?

Por. That he hath a neighbourly charity in
him; for he borrowed a box of the ear of the
Englishman, and swore he would pay him again
when he was able: I think the Frenchman became his surety, and sealed under for another.

Ner. How like you the young German, the
Duke of Saxony's nephew?

Por. Very vilely in the morning when he is
sober; and most vilely in the afternoon when
he is drunk; when he is best he is a little worse
than a man; and when he is worst, he is little
better than a beast. An the worst fall that ever
fell, I hope I shall make shift to go without him.

Ner. If he should offer to choose, and choose
the right casket, you should refuse to perform
your father's will if you should refuse to accept
him.

Por. Therefore, for fear of the worst, I pray
thee set a deep glass of Rhenish wine on the
contrary casket: for, if the devil be within and
that temptation without, I know he will choose
it. I will do anything, Nerissa, ere I will be
married to a sponge.

Ner. You need not fear, lady, the having any
of these lords; they have acquainted me with
their determinations; which is indeed, to return
to their home, and to trouble you with no more
suit, unless you may be won by some other

sort than your father's imposition, depending on the caskets.

Por. If I live to be as old as Sibylla, I will die as chaste as Diana, unless I be obtained by the manner of my father's will. I am glad this parcel of wooers are so reasonable; for there is not one among them but I dote on his very absence, and I pray God grant them a fair departure.

Ner. Do you not remember, lady, in your father's time, a Venetian, a scholar and a soldier, that came hither in company of the Marquis of Montferrat?

Por. Yes, yes, it was Bassanio; as I think, so was he called.

Ner. True, madam; he, of all the men that ever my foolish eyes looked upon, was the best deserving a fair lady.

Por. I remember him well; and I remember him worthy of thy praise.—

Enter a Servant.

How now! what news?

Serv. The four strangers seek for you, madam, to take their leave; and there is a fore-runner come from a fifth, the prince of Morocco, who brings word, the prince his master will be here to-night.

Por. If I could bid the fifth welcome with so good heart as I can bid the other four farewell, I should be glad of his approach: if he have the condition of a saint and the complexion of a devil, I had rather he should shrive me than wive me.

Come, Nerissa.—Sirrah, go before.—

Whiles we shut the gate upon one wooer, another knocks at the door.   [*Exeunt.*

SCENE III.—VENICE. *A Public Place.*

Enter BASSANIO *and* SHYLOCK.

Shy. Three thousand ducats,—well.

Bass. Ay, sir, for three months.

Shy. For three months,—well.

Bass. For the which, as I told you, Antonio shall be bound.

Shy. Antonio shall become bound,—well.

Bass. May you stead me? Will you pleasure me? Shall I know your answer?

Shy. Three thousand ducats for three months, and Antonio bound.

Bass. Your answer to that.

Shy. Antonio is a good man.

Bass. Have you heard any imputation to the contrary?

Shy. Ho, no, no, no; no, no;—my meaning, in saying he is a good man, is to have you understand me that he is sufficient: yet his means are in supposition: he hath an argosy bound to Tripolis, another to the Indies; I understand, moreover, upon the Rialto, he hath a third at Mexico, a fourth for England,——and other ventures he hath, squandered abroad. But ships are but boards, sailors but men: there be land-rats and water-rats, water-thieves and land-thieves; I mean pirates; and then there is the peril of waters, winds, and rocks. The man is, notwithstanding, sufficient;—three thousand ducats:—I think I may take his bond.

Bass. Be assured you may.

Shy. I will be assured I may; and, that I may be assured, I will bethink me. May I speak with Antonio?

Bass. If it please you to dine with us.

Shy. Yes, to smell pork; to eat of the habitation which your prophet, the Nazarite, conjured the devil into; I will buy with you, sell with you, talk with you, walk with you, and so following; but I will not eat with you, drink with you, nor pray with you.—What news on the Rialto?—Who is he comes here?

Enter ANTONIO.

Bass. This is Signior Antonio.

Shy. [*Aside.*] How like a fawning publican he looks!
I hate him for he is a Christian;
But more for that, in low simplicity.
He lends out money gratis, and brings down
The rate of usance here with us in Venice.
If I can catch him once upon the hip,
I will feed fat the ancient grudge I bear him.
He hates our sacred nation; and he rails,
Even there where merchants most do congregate,
On me, my bargains, and my well-won thrift,
Which he calls interest. Cursed be my tribe
If I forgive him!

Bass.   Shylock, do you hear?

Shy. I am debating of my present store:
And, by the near guess of my memory,
I cannot instantly raise up the gross
Of full three thousand ducats. What of that?
Tubal, a wealthy Hebrew of my tribe,
Will furnish me. But soft! how many months
Do you desire?—Rest you fair, good signior:
        [*To* ANTONIO.
Your worship was the last man in our mouths.

Ant. Shylock, albeit I neither lend nor borrow,
By taking nor by giving of excess,
Yet, to supply the ripe wants of my friend,
I'll break a custom.—Is he yet possess'd
How much he would?

Shy.   Ay, ay, three thousand ducats.

Ant. And for three months.   [me so.

Shy. I had forgot,—three months; you told
Well then, your bond; and, let me see,——But hear you:
Methought you said you neither lend nor borrow
Upon advantage.

Ant.   I do never use it.

Shy. When Jacob graz'd his uncle Laban's sheep,—
This Jacob from our holy Abraham was—
As his wise mother wrought in his behalf—
The third possessor; ay, he was the third,—

Ant. And what of him? did he take interest?

Shy. No, not take interest; not, as you would
    say,
Directly interest: mark what Jacob did.
When Laban and himself were compromis'd
That all the eanlings which were streak'd and
    pied   [rank,
Should fall as Jacob's hire; the ewes, being
In end of autumn turned to the rams:
And when the work of generation was
Between these wooly breeders in the act,
The skilful shepherd peel'd me certain wands,
And, in the doing of the deed of kind,
He stuck them up before the fulsome ewes,
Who, then conceiving, did in eaning time
Fall party-colour'd lambs, and those were
    Jacob's.
This was a way to thrive, and he was blest;
And thrift is blessing if men steal it not.
    Ant. This was a venture, sir, that Jacob
    serv'd for;
A thing not in his power to bring to pass,
But sway'd and fashion'd by the hand of
    heaven.
Was this inserted to make interest good?
Or is your gold and silver ewes and rams?
    Shy. I cannot tell; I make it breed as fast:—
But note me, signior.
    Ant.   Mark you this, Bassanio,
The devil can cite scripture for his purpose.
An evil soul producing holy witness
Is like a villain with a smiling cheek—
A goodly apple rotten at the heart:
O, what a goodly outside falsehood hath!
    Shy. Three thousand ducats,—'tis a good
    round sum.   [rate.
Three months from twelve, then let me see the
    Ant. Well, Shylock, shall we be beholden to
    you?
    Shy. Signior Antonio, many a time and oft,
In the Rialto, you have rated me
About my moneys and my usances:
Still have I borne it with a patient shrug;
For sufferance is the badge of all our tribe:
You call me misbeliever, cut-throat dog,
And spit upon my Jewish gaberdine,
And all for use of that which is mine own.
Well, then, it now appears you need my help:
Go to, then; you come to me, and you say,
Shylock, we would have moneys:—you say so;
You, that did void your rheum upon my beard,
And foot me as you spurn a stranger cur
Over your threshold: moneys is your suit.
What should I say to you? Should I not say,
Hath a dog money? is it possible
A cur can lend three thousand ducats? or
Shall I bend low, and in a bondman's key,
With 'bated breath and whispering humbleness
Say this?—
Fair sir, you spit on me on Wednesday last.
You spurn'd me such a day; another time
You call'd me dog; and for these courtesies
I'll lend you thus much moneys.
    Ant. I am as like to call thee so again,
To spit on thee again, to spurn thee too.

If thou wilt lend this money, lend it not
As to thy friends (for when did friendship take
A breed for barren metal of his friend?)
But lend it rather to thine enemy,
Who if he break, thou mayst with better face
Exact the penalty.
    Shy.   Why, look you, how you storm!
I would be friends with you, and have your love,
Forget the shames that you have stain'd me
    with,
Supply your present wants, and take no doit
Of usance for my moneys, and you'll not hear
    me:
This is kind I offer.
    Bass. This were kindness.
    Shy.   This kindness will I show.—
Go with me to a notary, seal me there
Your single bond; and, in a merry sport,
If you repay me not on such a day,
In such a place, such sum or sums as are
Express'd in the condition, let the forfeit
Be nominated for an equal pound
Of your fair flesh, to be cut off and taken
In what part of your body pleaseth me. [bond,
    Ant. Content, in faith: I'll seal to such a
And say there is much kindness in the Jew.
    Bass. You shall not seal to such a bond for
    me:
I'll rather dwell in my necessity.   [it;
    Ant. Why fear not, man; I will not forfeit
Within these two months—that's a month be-
    fore
This bond expires—I do expect return
Of thrice three times the value of this bond.
    Shy. O father Abraham, what these Chris-
    tians are,
Whose own hard dealings teaches them suspect
The thoughts of others! Pray you, tell me this;
If he should break his day, what should I gain
By the exaction of the forfeiture?
A pound of man's flesh, taken from a man,
Is not so estimable, profitable neither,
As flesh of muttons, beefs, or goats. I say,
To buy his favour I extend this friendship;
If he will take it, so; if not, adieu;
And for my love, I pray you wrong me not.
    Ant. Yes, Shylock, I will seal unto this bond.
    Shy. Then meet me forthwith at the no-
    tary's;
Give him direction for this merry bond,
And I will go and purse the ducats straight,
See to my house, left in the fearful guard
Of an unthrifty knave, and presently
I will be with you.
    Ant.   Hie thee, gentle Jew:
                    [*Exit* SHYLOCK.
This Hebrew will turn Christian: he grows
    kind.
    Bass. I like not fair terms and a villain's
    mind.
    Ant. Come on; in this there can be no dis-
    may;
My ships come home a month before the day.
                        [*Exeunt.*

ACT II.

SCENE I.—BELMONT. *A Room in* PORTIA'S *House.*

Flourish of Cornets. Enter the PRINCE OF MOROCCO *and his* Train; PORTIA, NERISSA *and other of her* Attendants.

Mor. Mislike me not for my complexion,
The shadow'd livery of the burnish'd sun,
To whom I am a neighbour, and near bred.
Bring me the fairest creature northward born,
Where Phœbus' fire scarce thaws the icicles,
And let us make incision for your love,
To prove whose blood is reddest, his or mine.
I tell thee lady, this aspect of mine
Hath fear'd the valiant; by my love, I swear,
The best-regarded virgins of our clime
Have lov'd it too: I would not change this hue
Except to steal your thoughts, my gentle queen.
Por. In terms of choice I am not solely led
By nice direction of a maiden's eyes:
Besides, the lottery of my destiny
Bars me the right of voluntary choosing:
But, if my father had not scanted me,
And hedg'd me by his wit, to yield myself
His wife who wins me by that means I told you,
Yourself, renowned prince, then stood as fair
As any comer I have look'd on yet
For my affection.
Mor.   Even for that I thank you;
Therefore, I pray you, lead me to the caskets,
To try my fortune. By this scimitar,—
That slew the Sophy, and a Persian prince
That won three fields of Sultan Solyman,—
I would out-stare the sternest eyes that look,
Out-brave the heart most daring on the earth,
Pluck the young sucking cubs from the she-bear,
Yea, mock the lion when he roars for prey,
To win thee, lady. But, alas the while!
If Hercules and Lichas play at dice
Which is the better man, the greater throw
May turn by fortune from the weaker hand:
So is Alcides beaten by his page;
And so may I, blind fortune leading me,
Miss that which one unworthier may attain,
And die with grieving.
Por.   You must take your chance;
And either not attempt to choose at all,
Or swear before you choose, if you choose wrong,
Never to speak to lady afterward
In way of marriage; therefore be advis'd.
Mor. Nor will not; come, bring me unto my chance.
Por. First, forward to the temple: after dinner
Your hazard shall be made.
Mor.   Good fortune then!
To make me blest or cursed'st among men.
                    [*Cornets and exeunt.*

SCENE II.—VENICE. *A Street.*

Enter LAUNCELOT GOBBO.

Laun. Certainly my conscience will serve me to run from this Jew, my master. The fiend is at mine elbow, and tempts me, saying to me, *Gobbo, Launcelot Gobbo, good Launcelot,* or *good Gobbo,* or *good Launcelot Gobbo, use your legs, take the start, run away.* My conscience says,— *No; take heed, honest Launcelot; take heed, honest Gobbo:* or as aforesaid, *honest Launcelot Gobbo; do not run, scorn running with thy heels.* Well, the most courageous fiend bids me pack: *Via!* says the fiend; *away!* says the fiend, *for the heavens; rouse up a brave mind,* says the fiend, *and run.* Well, my conscience, hanging about the neck of my heart, says very wisely to me,— *My honest friend, Launcelot, being an honest man's son,* or rather an honest woman's son;— for indeed, my father did something smack, something grow to, he had a kind of taste;— well, my conscience says, *Launcelot, budge not.* *Budge,* says the fiend. *Budge not,* says my conscience. Conscience, say I, you counsel well; fiend, say I, you counsel well: to be ruled by my conscience, I should stay with the Jew, my master, who (God bless the mark!) is a kind of devil; and, to run away from the Jew, I should be ruled by the fiend, who, saving your reverence, is the devil himself. Certainly the Jew is the very devil incarnation: and, in my conscience, my conscience is but a kind of hard conscience, to offer to counsel me to stay with the Jew. The fiend gives the more friendly counsel: I will run, fiend; my heels are at your commandment; I will run.

Enter Old GOBBO, *with a basket.*

Gob. Master young man, you, I pray you, which is the way to master Jew's?
Laun. [*Aside.*] O heavens, this is my true begotten father! who, being more than sand-blind, high-gravel blind, knows me not:—I will try confusions with him.
Gob. Master young gentleman, I pray you, which is the way to Master Jew's?
Laun. Turn up on your right hand at the next turning, but, at the next turning of all, on your left; marry, at the very next turning, turn of no hand, but turn down indirectly to the Jew's house.
Gob. By God's sonties, 'twill be a hard way to hit. Can you tell me whether one Launcelot, that dwells with him, dwell with him or no?
Laun. Talk you of young Master Launcelot? —[*Aside.*] Mark me now; now will I raise the waters.—Talk you of young Master Launcelot?
Gob. No master, sir, but a poor man's son: his father, though I say it, is an honest exceeding poor man, and, God be thanked, well to live.
Laun. Well, let his father be what 'a will, we talk of young Master Launcelot.   [sir.
Gob. Your worship's friend, and Launcelot,
Laun. But I pray you, *ergo,* old man, *ergo,* I

beseech you, talk you of young Master Launcelot?

Gob. Of Launcelot, an 't please your mastership.

Laun. *Ergo*, Master Launcelot. Talk not of
Master Launcelot, father; for the young gentleman,—according to Fates and Destinies,
and such odd sayings, the Sisters Three, and
such branches of learning,—is indeed deceased;
or, as you would say in plain terms, gone to
heaven.

Gob. Marry, God forbid! the boy was the
very staff of my age, my very prop.

Laun. Do I look like a cudgel, or a hovel-
post, a staff or a prop?—Do you know me,
father?

Gob. Alack the day, I know you not, young
gentleman: but, I pray you, tell me, is my boy
(God rest his soul!) alive or dead?

Laun. Do you not know me, father?

Gob. Alack, sir, I am sand-blind, I know
you not.

Laun. Nay, indeed, if you had your eyes you
might fail of the knowing me: it is a wise father
that knows his own child. Well, old man, I will
tell you news of your son. Give me your blessing; truth will come to light; murder cannot
be hid long: a man's son may; but, in the end,
truth will out.

Gob. Pray you, sir, stand up; I am sure you
are not Launcelot, my boy.

Laun. Pray you, let's have no more fooling
about it, but give me your blessing; I am
Launcelot, your boy that was, your son that is,
your child that shall be.

Gob. I cannot think you are my son.

Laun. I know not what I shall think of that;
but I am Launcelot, the Jew's man; and I am
sure Margery your wife is my mother.

Gob. Her name is Margery, indeed: I'll be
sworn, if thou be Launcelot, thou art mine own
flesh and blood. Lord worshipped might he be!
what a beard hast thou got! thou hast got more
hair on thy chin than Dobbin my thill-horse
has on his tail.

Laun. It should seem, then, that Dobbin's
tail grows backward; I am sure he had more
hair of his tail than I have of my face when I
last saw him.

Gob. Lord, how thou art changed! How dost
thou and thy master agree? I have brought him
a present. How 'gree you now?

Laun. Well, well; but, for mine own part, as
I have set up my rest to run away, so I will not
rest till I have run some ground. My master's
a very Jew: give him a present! give him a
halter: I am famished in his service; you may
tell every finger I have with my ribs. Father, I
am glad you are come; give me your present to
one Master Bassanio, who indeed gives rare
new liveries: if I serve not him, I will run as far
as God has any ground.—O rare fortune! here
comes the man;—to him, father; for I am a
Jew if I serve the Jew any longer.

Enter BASSANIO, *with* LEONARDO, *and
other* Followers.

Bass. You may do so;—but let it be so
hasted that supper be ready at the farthest by
five of the clock. See these letters delivered; put
the liveries to making; and desire Gratiano to
come anon to my lodging.　[*Exit c* Servant.

Laun. To him, father.

Gob. God bless your worship!　[me?

Bass. Gramercy: wouldst thou aught with

Gob. Here's my son, sir, a poor boy,—

Laun. Not a poor boy, sir, but the rich
Jew's man, that would, sir, as my father shall
specify,—

Gob. He hath a great infection, sir, as one
would say, to serve,—

Laun. Indeed, the short and the long is, I
serve the Jew, and have a desire, as my father
shall specify,—

Gob. His master and he,—saving your worship's reverence,—are scarce cater-cousins,—

Laun. To be brief, the very truth is, that the
Jew having done me wrong, doth cause me, as
my father, being I hope an old man, shall
frutify unto you,—

Gob. I have here a dish of doves that I would
bestow upon your worship; and my suit is,—

Laun. In very brief, the suit is impertinent
to myself, as your worship shall know by this
honest old man; and, though I say it, though
old man, yet, poor man, my father.

Bass. One speak for both.—What would
you?

Laun. Serve you, sir.

Gob. That is the very defect of the matter,
sir.

Bass. I know thee well; thou hast obtain'd
　　thy suit:
Shylock, thy master, spoke with me this day,
And hath preferr'd thee—if it be preferment
To leave a rich Jew's service, to become
The follower of so poor a gentleman.

Laun. The old proverb is very well parted
between my master, Shylock, and you, sir; you
have the grace of God, sir, and he hath enough.

Bass. Thou speak'st it well. Go, father, with
　　thy son.—
Take leave of thy old master, and inquire
My lodging out.—Give him a livery
　　　　　[*To his* Followers.
More guarded than his fellows': see it done.

Laun. Father, in.—I cannot get a service,
no:—I have ne'er a tongue in my head.—
Well; [*looking on his palm*] if any man in Italy
have a fairer table which doth offer to swear
upon a book, I shall have good fortune!—Go
to, here's a simple line of life! here's a small
trifle of wives: alas, fifteen wives is nothing,
eleven widows and nine maids is a simple coming in for one man! and then to 'scape drowning thrice, and to be in peril of my life with
the edge of a feather-bed;—here are simple
'scapes. Well, if Fortune be a woman, she's a

good wench for this gear.—Father, come: I'll
take my leave of the Jew in the twinkling of
an eye.   [*Exeunt* LAUN. *and Old* GOB.

Bass. I pray thee, good Leonardo, think on
          this: [stow'd,
These things being bought and orderly be-
Return in haste, for I do feast to-night
My best esteem'd acquaintance: hie thee, go.
Leon. My best endeavours shall be done
          herein.

Enter GRATIANO.

Gra. Where is your master?
Leon.   Yonder, sir, he walks. [*Exit.*
Gra. Signior Bassanio,——
Bass. Gratiano!
Gra. I have a suit to you.
Bass.   You have obtain'd it.
Gra. You must not deny me: I must go with
          you to Belmont.   [Gratiano;
Bass. Why, then you must.—But hear thee,
Thou art too wild, too rude, and bold of voice;—
Parts that become thee happily enough,
And in such eyes as ours appear not faults;
But where thou art not known, why, there
          they show
Something too liberal. Pray thee, take pain
To allay with some cold drops of modesty
Thy skipping spirit; lest, through thy wild be-
          haviour,
I be misconstrued in the place I go to,
And lose my hopes.
Gra.   Signior Bassanio, hear me:
If I do not put on a sober habit,
Talk with respect, and swear but now and then,
Wear prayer-books in my pocket, look de-
          murely,
Nay more, while grace is saying, hood mine
          eyes
Thus with my hat, and sigh, and say amen,
Use all the observance of civility,
Like one well studied in a sad ostent
To please his grandam, never trust me more.
Bass. Well, we shall see your bearing.
Gra. Nay, but I bar to-night; you shall not
          gage me
By what we do to-night.
Bass.   No, that were pity;
I would entreat you rather to put on
Your boldest suit of mirth, for we have friends
That purpose merriment. But fare you well:
I have some business.
Gra. And I must to Lorenzo and the rest;
But we will visit you at supper-time.
          [*Exeunt.*

SCENE III.—*The same. A Room in* SHYLOCK'S
          House.

Enter JESSICA *and* LAUNCELOT.

Jes. I am sorry thou wilt leave my father so:
Our house is hell; and thou, a merry devil,
Didst rob it of some taste of tediousness.
But fare thee well; there is a ducat for thee:
And, Launcelot, soon at supper shalt thou see

Lorenzo, who is thy new master's guest:
Give him this letter; do it secretly;—
And so farewell: I would not have my father
See me in talk with thee.
Laun. Adieu!—tears exhibit my tongue.—
Most beautiful pagan, most sweet Jew! if a
Christian did not play the knave, and get thee,
I am much deceived. But adieu! these foolish
drops do somewhat drown my manly spirit;
adieu!   [*Exit.*
Jes. Farewell, good Launcelot.
Alack, what heinous sin is it in me
To be asham'd to be my father's child!
But though I am a daughter to his blood,
I am not to his manners. O Lorenzo,
If thou keep promise, I shall end this strife,
Become a Christian, and thy loving wife.
          [*Exit.*

SCENE IV.—*The same. A Street.*

Enter GRATIANO, LORENZO, SALARINO, *and* SOLANIO.

Lor. Nay, we will slink away in supper-time;
Disguise us at my lodging, and return
All in an hour.
Gra. We have not made good preparation.
Salar. We have not spoke us yet of torch-
          bearers.   [order'd;
Solan. 'Tis vile, unless it may be quaintly
And better, in my mind, not undertook.
Lor. 'Tis now but four o'clock; we have two
          hours
To furnish us;—

Enter LAUNCELOT, *with a letter.*

          Friend Launcelot, what's the news?
Laun. An it shall please you to break up
this, it shall seem to signify.
Lor. I know the hand: in faith, 'tis a fair
          hand;
And whiter than the paper it writ on
Is the fair hand that writ.
Gra.   Love-news, in faith.
Laun. By your leave, sir.
Lor. Whither goest thou?
Laun. Marry, sir, to bid my old master, the
Jew, to sup to-night with my new master, the
Christian.   [Jessica
Lor. Hold here, take this:—tell gentle
I will not fail her;—speak it privately; go.—
Gentlemen,   [*Exit* LAUNCELOT.
Will you prepare you for this masque to-night?
I am provided of a torch-bearer.
Salar. Ay, marry, I'll be gone about it
          straight.
Solan. And so will I.
Lor.   Meet me and Gratiano
At Gratiano's lodging some hour hence.
Salar. 'Tis good we do so.
          [*Exeunt* SALAR. *and* SOLAN.
Gra. Was not that letter from fair Jessica?
Lor. I must needs tell thee all. She hath
          directed
How I shall take her from her father's house;

What gold and jewels she is furnish'd with;
What page's suit she hath in readiness.
If e'er the Jew her father come to heaven,
It will be for his gentle daughter's sake:
And never dare misfortune cross her foot,
Unless she do it under this excuse,—
That she is issue to a faithless Jew.
Come, go with me; peruse this as thou goest:
Fair Jessica shall be my torch-bearer.

[*Exeunt.*

SCENE V.—*The same. Before* SHYLOCK's *House.*

Enter SHYLOCK *and* LAUNCELOT.

Shy. Well, thou shalt see; thy eyes shall be thy judge.
The difference of old Shylock and Bassanio:—
What, Jessica!—thou shalt not gormandize
As thou hast done with me;—What, Jessica!—
And sleep and snore, and rend apparel out;—
Why, Jessica, I say!
Laun.　　　Why, Jessica!　　[call.
Shy. Who bids thee call? I do not bid thee
Laun. Your worship was wont to tell me I
could do nothing without bidding.

Enter JESSICA.

Jes. Call you? what is your will?
Shy. I am bid forth to supper, Jessica:
There are my keys.—But wherefore should I go?
I am not bid for love; they flatter me:
But yet I'll go in hate, to feed upon
The prodigal Christian.—Jessica, my girl,
Look to my house.—I am right loath to go;
There is some ill a-brewing towards my rest,
For I did dream of money-bags to-night.
Laun. I beseech you, sir, go; my young master doth expect your reproach.
Shy. So do I his.
Laun. And they have conspired together,—
I will not say you shall see a masque; but if you do, then it was not for nothing that my nose fell a-bleeding on Black-Monday last at six o'clock i' the morning, falling out that year on Ash-Wednesday was four year in the afternoon.
Shy. What! are there masques? Hear you me, Jessica:
Lock up my doors; and when you hear the drum,
And the vile squeaking of the wry-neck'd fife,
Clamber not you up to the casements then,
Nor thrust your head into the public street
To gaze on Christian fools with varnish'd faces:
But stop my house's ears,—I mean my casements:
Let not the sound of shallow foppery enter
My sober house.—By Jacob's staff, I swear
I have no mind of feasting forth to-night:
But I will go.—Go you before me, sirrah;
Say I will come.
Laun.　　　I will go before, sir.—
Mistress, look out at window for all this;
There will come a Christian by
Will be worth a Jewess' eye.　　[*Exit.*

Shy. What says that fool of Hagar's off-spring, ha?　　│nothing else.
Jes. His words were, Farewell, mistress;
Shy. The patch is kind enough, but a huge feeder,
Snail-slow in profit, and he sleeps by day
More than the wild cat: drones hive not with me;
Therefore I part with him; and part with him
To one that I would have him help to waste
His borrow'd purse.—Well, Jessica, go in;
Perhaps I will return immediately:
Do as I bid you;
Shut doors after you: fast bind, fast find—
A proverb never stale in thrifty mind.　[*Exit.*
Jes. Farewell; and if my fortune be not cross'd,
I have a father, you a daughter, lost.　[*Exit.*

SCENE VI.—*The same.*

Enter GRATIANO *and* SALARINO, *masked.*

Gra. This is the pent-house under which Lorenzo
Desir'd us to make stand.
Salar.　　　His hour is almost past,
Gra. And it is marvel he out-dwells his hour,
For lovers ever run before the clock.
Salar. O, ten times faster Venus' pigeons fly
To seal love's bonds new made, than they are wont
To keep obliged faith unforfeited!　　[feast
Gra. That ever holds; who riseth from a
With that keen appetite that he sits down?
Where is the horse that doth untread again
His tedious measures with the unbated fire
That he did pace them first? All things that are,
Are with more spirit chased than enjoy'd.
How like a younker or a prodigal
The scarfed bark puts from her native bay,
Hugg'd and embraced by the strumpet wind!
How like the prodigal doth she return,
With over-weather'd ribs and ragged sails,
Lean, rent, and beggar'd by the strumpet wind!
Salar. Here comes Lorenzo;—more of this hereafter.

Enter LORENZO.

Lor. Sweet friends, your patience for my long abode;
Not I, but my affairs, have made you wait:
When you shall please to play the thieves for wives
I'll watch as long for you then.—Approach;
Here dwells my father Jew.—Ho! who's within?

Enter JESSICA, *above, in boy's clothes.*

Jes. Who are you? Tell me, for more certainty,
Albeit I'll swear that I do know your tongue.
Lor. Lorenzo, and thy love.
Jes. Lorenzo, certain; and my love indeed;
For who love I so much? and now who knows
But you, Lorenzo, whether I am yours?

Lor. Heaven and thy thoughts are witness
    that thou art.   [pains.
Jes. Here, catch this casket; it is worth the
I am glad 'tis night, you do not look on me,
For I am much asham'd of my exchange:
But love is blind, and lovers cannot see
The pretty follies that themselves commit;
For if they could, Cupid himself would blush
To see me thus transformed to a boy.
    Lor. Descend, for you must be my torch-
    bearer.   [shames?
    Jes. What! must I hold a candle to my
They in themselves, good sooth, are too, too
    light.
Why, 'tis an office of discovery, love;
And I should be obscur'd.
    Lor.   So are you, sweet,
Even in the lovely garnish of a boy.
But come at once;
For the close night doth play the runaway,
And we are stay'd for at Bassanio's feast.
    Jes. I will make fast the doors, and gild my-
    self
With some more ducats, and be with you
    straight.   [*Exit, above.*
    Gra. Now, by my hood, a Gentile, and no
    Jew.
    Lor. Beshrew me, but I love her heartily:
For she is wise, if I can judge of her;
And fair she is, if that mine eyes be true;
And true she is, as she hath prov'd herself;
And therefore, like herself, wise, fair, and true.
Shall she be placed in my constant soul.

Enter Jessica, *below.*

What, art thou come?—On, gentlemen, away;
Our masquing mates by this time for us stay.
    [*Exit, with* Jes. *and* Salar.

Enter Antonio.

    Ant. Who's there?
    Gra. Signior Antonio!
    Ant. Fie, fie, Gratiano! where are all the
    rest?
'Tis nine o'clock: our friends all stay for you:—
No mask to-night; the wind is come about;
Bassanio presently will go aboard:
I have sent twenty out to seek for you.
    Gra. I am glad on't; I desire no more delight
Than to be under sail. and gone to-night.
            [*Exeunt.*

Scene VII.—Belmont. *A Room in*
Portia's *House.*

Flourish of Cornets. Enter Portia, *with the*
Prince of Morocco, *and their* Trains.

    Por. Go draw aside the curtains, and dis-
    cover
The several caskets to this noble prince.—
Now make your choice.
    Mor. The first of gold, who this inscription
    bears;—   [*desire.*
Who chooseth me shall gain what many men
The second, silver, which this promise carries;—

Who chooseth me shall get as much as he deserves.
This third, dull lead, with warning all as
    blunt;—   [*hath.*
Who chooseth me must give and hazard all he
How shall I know if I do choose the right?
    Por. The one of them contains my picture,
    prince;
If you choose that, then I am yours withal.
    Mor. Some god direct my judgment! Let me
    see,
I will survey the inscriptions back again:
What says this leaden casket?—   [*hath.*
Who chooseth me must give and hazard all he
Must give—for what? for lead? hazard for
    lead?
This casket threatens: men that hazard all
Do it in hope of fair advantages:
A golden mind stoops not to shows of dross:
I'll then nor give nor hazard aught for lead.
What says the silver with her virgin hue?
Who chooseth me shall get as much as he deserves.
As much as he deserves!—Pause there, Mo-
    rocco,
And weigh thy value with an even hand;
If thou be'st rated by thy estimation,
Thou dost deserve enough; and yet enough
May not extend so far as to the lady;
And yet to be afeard of my deserving
Were but a weak disabling of myself.
As much as I deserve!—Why, that's the lady:
I do in birth deserve her, and in fortunes,
In graces, and in qualities of breeding;
But more than these, in love I do deserve.
What if I stray'd no further, but chose here?—
Let's see once more this saying grav'd in gold.
Who chooseth me shall gain what many men
    desire.
Why, that's the lady: all the world desires her:
From the four corners of the earth they come,
To kiss this shrine, this mortal breathing saint.
The Hyrcanian deserts and the vasty wilds
Of wide Arabia are as throughfares now
For princes to come view fair Portia:
The wat'ry kingdom, whose ambitious head
Spits in the face of heaven, is no bar
To stop the foreign spirits; but they come,
As o'er a brook, to see fair Portia.
One of these three contains her heavenly pic-
    ture.   [nation
Is't like that lead contains her? 'Twere dam-
To think so base a thought: it were too gross
To rid her cerecloth in the obscure grave.
Or shall I think in silver she's immur'd,
Being ten times undervalued to tried gold?
O sinful thought! Never so rich a gem   [land
Was set in worse than gold. They have in Eng-
A coin that bears the figure of an angel
Stamped in gold; but that's insculp'd upon;
But here an angel in a golden bed
Lies all within.—Deliver me the key;
Here do I choose, and thrive I as I may!
    Por. There, take it, prince; and if my form
    lie there,
Then I am yours.   [*He opens the golden casket.*

Mor. O hell! what have we here?
A carrion Death, within whose empty eye
There is a written scroll! I'll read the writing.

All that glisters is not gold,—
Often have you heard that told;
Many a man his life hath sold
But my outside to behold;
Gilded tombs do worms infold.
Had you been as wise as bold,
Young in limbs, in judgment old,
Your answer had not been inscroll'd
Fare you well; your suit is cold.

Cold indeed, and labour lost:
Then, farewell heat; and, welcome frost.—
Portia, adieu! I have too griev'd a heart
To take a tedious leave: thus losers part.
                              [Exit with his Train.
Por. A gentle riddance.—Draw the curtains, go.
Let all of his complexion choose me so.
                                     [Exeunt.

SCENE VIII.—VENICE. *A Street.*

Enter SALARINO *and* SOLANIO.

Salar. Why, man, I saw Bassanio under sail;
With him is Gratiano gone along;
And in their ship I am sure Lorenzo is not.
  Solan. The villain Jew with outcries rais'd the duke,
Who went with him to search Bassanio's ship.
  Salar. He came too late, the ship was under sail:
But there the duke was given to understand
That in a gondola were seen together
Lorenzo and his amorous Jessica:
Besides, Antonio certify'd the duke
They were not with Bassanio in his ship.
  Solan. I never heard a passion so confused,
So strange, outrageous, and so variable
As the dog Jew did utter in the streets:
My daughter!—O my ducats!—O my daughter!
Fled with a Christian!—O my Christian ducats!—
Justice! the law! my ducats and my daughter!
A sealed bag, two sealed bags of ducats,
Of double ducats, stolen from me by my daughter!
And jewels,—two stones, two rich and precious stones,
Stolen by my daughter!—Justice! find the girl!
She hath the stones upon her and the ducats!
  Salar. Why, all the boys in Venice follow him,
                                  [ducats.
Crying,—his stones, his daughter, and his
  Solan. Let good Antonio look he keep his day,
Or he shall pay for this.
  Salar.   Marry, well remember'd;
I reason'd with a Frenchman yesterday,
Who told me,—in the narrow seas that part
The French and English, there miscarrièd
A vessel of our country richly fraught:
I thought upon Antonio when he told me,
And wish'd in silence that it were not his.

Solan. You were best to tell Antonio what you hear;
Yet do not suddenly, for it may grieve him.
  Salar. A kinder gentleman treads not the earth.
I saw Bassanio and Antonio part:
Bassanio told him he would make some speed
Of his return; he answered—*Do not so;*
Slubber not business for my sake, Bassanio,
But stay the very riping of the time;
And for the Jew's bond which he hath of me,
Let it not enter in your mind of love:
Be merry; and employ your chiefest thoughts
To courtship, and such fair ostents of love
As shall conveniently become you there.
And even there, his eye being big with tears,
Turning his face, he put his hand behind him,
And with affection wondrous sensible
He wrung Bassanio's hand; and so they parted.
  Solan. I think he only loves the world for him.
I pray thee, let us go and find him out,
And quicken his embraced heaviness
With some delight or other.
  Salar.   Do we so.   *[Exeunt.*

SCENE IX.—BELMONT. *A Room in* PORTIA'S *House.*

Enter NERISSA, *with a* Servant.

Ner. Quick, quick, I pray thee; draw the curtain straight:
The Prince of Arragon hath ta'en his oath,
And comes to his election presently.

Flourish of Cornets. Enter the PRINCE OF ARRAGON, PORTIA, *and their* Trains.

  Por. Behold, there stands the caskets, noble prince.
If you choose that wherein I am contain'd.
Straight shall our nuptial rites be solemniz'd:
But if you fail, without more speech, my lord,
You must be gone from hence immediately.
  Ar. I am enjoin'd by oath to observe three things:
First, never to unfold to any one
Which casket 'twas I chose; next, if I fail
Of the right casket, never in my life
To woo a maid in way of marriage; lastly,
If I do fail in fortune of my choice,
Immediately to leave you and be gone.
  Por. To these injunctions every one doth swear
That comes to hazard for my worthless self.
  Ar. And so have I address'd me. Fortune now
                                  [lead.
To my heart's hope!—Gold, silver, and base
Who chooseth me must give and hazard all he hath:
You shall look fairer ere I give or hazard.
What says the golden chest? ha! let me see:—
Who chooseth me shall gain what many men desire.   [meant
What many men desire.—That many may be
By the fool multitude, that choose by show,

Not learning more than the fond eye doth
    teach;
Which pries not to the interior, but, like the
    martlet,
Builds in the weather on the outward wall,
Even in the force and road of casualty.
I will not choose what many men desire,
Because I will not jump with common spirits,
And rank me with the barbarous multitudes.
Why, then, to thee, thou silver treasure-house;
Tell me once more what title thou dost bear:
Who chooseth me shall get as much as he deserves:
And well said too; for who shall go about
To cozen fortune, and be honourable   [sume
Without the stamp of merit! Let none pre-
To wear an undeserved dignity.
O, that estates, degrees, and offices,
Were not deriv'd corruptly! and that clear
    honour
Were purchas'd by the merit of the wearer!
How many then should cover that stand bare!
How many be commanded that command!
How much low peasantry would then be
    glean'd   [honour
From the true seed of honour! and how much
Pick'd from the chaff and ruin of the times,
To be new varnish'd! Well, but to my choice.
Who chooseth me shall get as much as he deserves:
I will assume desert.—Give me a key for this,
And instantly unlock my fortunes here.

                    [He opens the silver casket.

Por. Too long a pause for that which you
    find there.   [idiot
Ar. What's here? the portrait of a blinking
Presenting me a schedule! I will read it.
How much unlike art thou to Portia!
How much unlike my hopes and my deservings!
Who chooseth me shall have as much as he de-
    serves.
Did I deserve no more than a fool's head?
Is that my prize? are my deserts no better?
Por. To offend and judge are distinct offices
And of opposed natures.
Ar.   What is here?

    The fire seven times tried this;
    Seven times tried that judgment is
    That did never choose amiss:
    Some there be that shadows kiss;
    Such have but a shadow's bliss:
    There be fools alive, I wis,
    Silver'd o'er; and so was this.
    Take what wife you will to bed,
    I will ever be your head:
    So be gone: you are sped.

Still more fool I shall appear
By the time I linger here:
With one fool's head I came to woo,
But I go away with two.—
Sweet, adieu! I'll keep my oath,
Patiently to bear my roth.
             [Exit with his Train.
Por. Thus hath the candle singed the moth.
O these deliberate fools! when they do choose,

They have the wisdom by their wit to lose.
  Ner. The ancient saying is no heresy,—
Hanging and wiving goes by destiny.
  Por. Come, draw the curtain, Nerissa.

        Enter a Servant.

Serv. Where is my lady?
Por.   Here; what would my lord?
Serv. Madam, there is alighted at your gate
A young Venetian, one that comes before
To signify the approaching of his lord:
From whom he bringeth sensible regreets;
To wit, besides commends and courteous
    breath,
Gifts of rich value. Yet I have not seen
So likely an ambassador of love:
A day in April never came so sweet,
To show how costly summer was at hand,
As this forespurrer comes before his lord.
  Por. No more, I pray thee; I am half afeard
Thou wilt say anon he is some kin to thee,
Thou spend'st such high-day wit in praising
    him.—
Come, come, Nerissa; for I long to see
Quick Cupid's post, that comes so mannerly.
  Ner. Bassanio, lord Love, if thy will it be!
                        [Exeunt.

ACT III.

Scene I.—Venice. *A Street.*

Enter Solanio *and* Salarino.

Solan. Now, what news on the Rialto?
Salar. Why, yet it lives there unchecked,
that Antonio hath a ship of rich lading wrecked
on the narrow seas; the Goodwins I think they
call the place; a very dangerous flat and fatal,
where the carcases of many a tall ship lie buried,
as they say, if my gossip report be an honest
woman of her word.
Solan. I would she were as lying a gossip in
that as ever knapped ginger or made her neighbours believe she wept for the death of a third
husband. But it is true,—without any slips of
prolixity of crossing the plain highway of talk,
—that the good Antonio, the honest Antonio,
—O that I had a title good enough to keep his
name company!—
Salar. Come, the full stop.
Solan. Ha,—what sayest thou?—Why the
end is, he hath lost a ship.
Salar. I would it might prove the end of his
losses!
Solan. Let me say amen betimes, lest the
devil cross my prayer; for here he comes in the
likeness of a Jew.

Enter Shylock.

How now, Shylock? what news among the merchants?
Shy. You knew, none so well, none so well as
you, of my daughter's flight.
Salar. That's certain: I, for my part, knew
the tailor that made the wings she flew withal.

Solan. And Shylock, for his own part, knew the bird was fledg'd; and then it is the complexion of them all to leave the dam.

Shy. She is damned for it.

Salar. That's certain, if the devil may be her judge.

Shy. My own flesh and blood to rebel!

Solan. Out upon it, old carrion! rebels it at these years?

Shy. I say my daughter is my flesh and blood.

Salar. There is more difference between thy flesh and hers than between jet and ivory; more between your bloods than there is between red wine and Rhenish.—But tell us, do you hear whether Antonio have had any loss at sea or no?

Shy. There I have another bad match: a bankrupt, a prodigal, who dare scarce show his head on the Rialto;—a beggar, that was used to come so smug upon the mart;—let him look to his bond! he was wont to call me usurer;—let him look to his bond! he was wont to lend money for a Christian courtesy;—let him look to his bond.

Salar. Why, I am sure if he forfeit thou wilt not take his flesh. What's that good for?

Shy. To bait fish withal: if it will feed nothing else it will feed my revenge. He hath disgraced me and hindered me of half a million; laughed at my losses, mocked at my gains, scorned my nation, thwarted my bargains, cooled my friends, heated mine enemies! and what's his reason? I am a Jew! Hath not a Jew eyes? hath not a Jew hands, organs, dimensions, senses, affections, passions? fed with the same food, hurt with the same weapons, subject to the same diseases, healed by the same means, warmed and cooled by the same winter and summer as a Christian is? If you prick us, do we not bleed? if you tickle us, do we not laugh? if you poison us, do we not die? and if you wrong us, shall we not revenge? If we are like you in the rest, we will resemble you in that.—If a Jew wrong a Christian, what is his humility? revenge. If a Christian wrong a Jew, what should his sufferance be by Christian example? why, revenge. The villany you teach me I will execute; and it shall go hard but I will better the instruction.

Enter a Servant.

Serv. Gentlemen, my master Antonio is at his house, and desires to speak with you both.

Salar. We have been up and down to seek him.

Solan. Here comes another of the tribe; a third cannot be matched unless the devil himself turn Jew.

[*Exeunt* SOLAN., SALAR.. *and* Serv.

Enter TUBAL.

Shy. How now, Tubal, what news from Genoa? hast thou found my daughter?

Tub. I often came where I did hear of her, but cannot find her.

Shy. Why there, there, there, there! a diamond gone, cost me two thousand ducats in Frankfort! The curse never fell upon our nation till now; I never felt it till now:—two thousand ducats in that; and other precious, precious jewels.—I would my daughter were dead at my foot, and the jewels in her ear! would she were hearsed at my foot, and the ducats in her coffin! No news of them?—Why, so:—and I know not what's spent in the search. Why, thou loss upon loss! the thief gone with so much, and so much to find the thief; and no satisfaction, no revenge: nor no ill luck stirring but what lights o' my shoulders; no sighs but o' my breathing; no tears but o' my shedding.

Tub. Yes, other men have ill luck too; Antonio, as I heard in Genoa,—

Shy. What, what, what? ill luck, ill luck?

Tub. —hath an argosy cast away coming from Tripolis.

Shy. I thank God, I thank God.—Is it true? is it true?

Tub. I spoke with some of the sailors that escaped the wreck.

Shy. I thank thee, good Tubal.—Good news, good news: ha! ha!—Where? in Genoa?

Tub. Your daughter spent in Genoa, as I heard, one night, fourscore ducats.

Shy. Thou stick'st a dagger in me:—I shall never see my gold again. Fourscore ducats at a sitting! fourscore ducats!

Tub. There came divers of Antonio's creditor's in my company to Venice that swear he cannot choose but break.

Shy. I am very glad of it: I'll plague him; I'll torture him: I am glad of it.

Tub. One of them showed me a ring that he had of your daughter for a monkey.

Shy. Out upon her! Thou torturest me, Tubal. It was my turquoise: I had it of Leah when I was a bachelor: I would not have given it for a wilderness of monkeys.

Tub. But Antonio is certainly undone.

Shy. Nay, that's true; that's very true. Go, Tubal, fee me an officer; bespeak him a fortnight before. I will have the heart of him if he forfeit; for, were he out of Venice, I can make what merchandize I will. Go, go, Tubal, and meet me at our synagogue: go, good Tubal; at our synagogue, Tubal. [*Exeunt.*

SCENE II.—BELMONT. *A Room in* PORTIA'S *House.*

Enter BASSANIO, PORTIA, GRATIANO, NERISSA, *and* Attendants.

Por. I pray you, tarry: pause a day or two
Before you hazard; for, in choosing wrong,
I lose your company; therefore forbear awhile:
There's something tells me,—but it is not love,—
I would not lose you: and you know yourself

Hate counsels not in such a quality:
But lest you should not understand me well,—
And yet a maiden hath no tongue but thought,—
I would detain you here some month or two
Before you venture for me. I could teach you
How to choose right, but then I am forsworn;
So will I never be; so may you miss me:
But if you do, you'll make me wish a sin,
That I had been forsworn. Beshrew your eyes,
They have o'erlook'd me and divided me;
One half of me is yours, the other half yours,—
Mine own, I would say; but if mine, then yours,
And so all yours. O! these naughty times
Put bars between the owners and their rights;
And so, though yours, not yours.—Prove it so,
Let fortune go to hell for it,—not I.
I speak too long; but 'tis to peise the time,
To eke it, and to draw it out in length,
To stay you from election.
   Bass.   Let me choose;
For, as I am, I live upon the rack.
   Por. Upon the rack, Bassanio? then confess
What treason there is mingled with your love.
   Bass. None but that ugly treason of mis-
     trust,
Which makes me fear the enjoying of my love:
There may as well be amity and life
'Tween snow and fire, as treason and my love.
   Por. Ay, but I fear you speak upon the rack,
Where men, enforced, do speak anything.
   Bass. Promise me life, and I'll confess the
     truth.
   Por. Well, then, confess and live.
   Bass.   Confess and love
Had been the very sum of my confession:
O happy torment, when my torturer
Doth teach me answers for deliverance!
But let me to my fortune and the caskets.
        [Curtain drawn from before the caskets.
   Por. Away, then. I am lock'd in one of them;
If you do love me you will find me out.—
Nerissa and the rest, stand all aloof.—
Let music sound while he doth make his choice;
Then, if he lose, he makes a swan-like end,
Fading in music: that the comparison
May stand more proper, my eye shall be the
     stream
And wat'ry death-bed for him. He may win,
And what is music then? then music is
Even as the flourish when true subjects bow
To a new-crowned monarch: such it is
As are those dulcet sounds in break of day
That creep into the dreaming bridegroom's ear
And summon him to marriage. Now he goes,
With no less presence but with much more love
Than young Alcides when he did redeem
The virgin tribute paid by howling Troy
To the sea-monster. I stand for sacrifice;
The rest aloof are the Dardanian wives,
With bleared visages, come forth to view
The issue of the exploit. Go, Hercules!
Live thou, I live.—With much, much more
     dismay
I view the fight than thou that mak'st the fray.

Music and the following Song whilst BASSANIO
comments on the caskets to himself.

     Tell me, where is fancy bred,
     Or in the heart, or in the head?
     How begot, how nourished?
         Reply, reply.
     It is engender'd in the eyes,
     With gazing fed; and fancy dies
     In the cradle where it lies:
       Let us all ring fancy's knell;
     I'll begin it,——Ding, dong, bell.
All.   Ding, dong, bell.

   Bass. So may the outward shows be least
     themselves;
The world is still deceiv'd with ornament.
In law, what plea so tainted and corrupt
But, being season'd with a gracious voice,
Obscures the show of evil? In religion,
What damned error but some sober brow
Will bless it, and approve it with a text,
Hiding the grossness with fair ornament?
There is no vice so simple but assumes
Some mark of virtue on his outward parts.
How many cowards, whose hearts are all as
     false
As stairs of sand, wear yet upon their chins
The beards of Hercules and frowning Mars;
Who, inward search'd, have livers white as
     milk!
And these assume but valour's excrement
To render them redoubted. Look on beauty
And you shall see 'tis purchas'd by the weight
Which therein works a miracle in nature,
Making them lightest that wear most of it:
So are those crisped snaky golden locks,
Which make such wanton gambols with the
     wind,
Upon supposed fairness, often known
To be the dowry of a second head—
The skull that bred them in the sepulchre.
Thus ornament is but the guiled shore
To a most dangerous sea; the beauteous scarf
Veiling an Indian beauty; in a word,
The seeming truth which cunning times put on
To entrap the wisest. Therefore, thou gaudy
     gold,
Hard food for Midas, I will none of thee:
Nor none of thee, thou pale and common
     drudge
'Tween man and man: but thou, thou meagre
     lead,   [aught,
Which rather threat'nest than dost promise
Thy plainness moves me more than eloquence,
And here choose I. Joy be the consequence!
   Por. How all the other passions fleet to air,
As doubtful thoughts, and rash-embrac'd de-
     spair,
And shudd'ring fear, and green-ey'd jealousy!
O love, be moderate, allay thy ecstacy,
In measure rain thy joy, scant this excess;
I feel too much thy blessing; make it less,
For fear I surfeit!
   Bass.   What find I here?
             [Opening the leaden casket.

Fair Portia's counterfeit? What demi-god
Hath come so near creation? Move these eyes?
Or whether, riding on the balls on mine,
Seem they in motion? Here are sever'd lips,
Parted with sugar breath; so sweet a bar [hairs
Should sunder such sweet friends. Here in her
The painter plays the spider, and hath woven
A golden mesh to entrap the hearts of men,
Faster than gnats in cobwebs. But her eyes!—
How could he see to do them? having made one,
Methinks it should have power to steal both
    his,
And leave itself unfurnish'd. Yet look how far
The substance of my praise doth wrong this
    shadow
In underprizing it, so far this shadow. [scroll,
Doth limp behind the substance.—Here's the
The continent and summary of my fortune.

> You that choose not by the view,
> Chance as fair and choose as true!
> Since this fortune falls to you,
> Be content and seek no new.
> If you be well pleased with this,
> And hold your fortune for your bliss,
> Turn you where your lady is,
> And claim her with a loving kiss.

A gentle scroll.—Fair lady, by your leave:
                                    [*Kissing her.*
I come by note, to give and to receive.
Like one of two contending in a prize,
That thinks he hath done well in people's eyes,
Hearing applause and universal shout,
Giddy in spirit, still gazing, in a doubt
Whether those peals of praise be his or no,
So, thrice fair lady, stand I even so;
As doubtful whether what I see be true,
Until confirm'd, sign'd, ratified by you.
  Por. You see me, Lord Bassanio, where I
    stand,
Such as I am: though for myself alone
I would not be ambitious in my wish
To wish myself much better; yet for you
I would be trebled twenty times myself;
A thousand times more fair, ten thousand times
More rich;
That only to stand high in your account
I might in virtues, beauties, livings, friends,
Exceed account: but the full sum of me
Is sum of something, which, to term in gross,
Is an unlesson'd girl, unschool'd, unpractis'd:
Happy in this, she is not yet so old
But she may learn; and happier than this,
She is not bred so dull but she can learn;
Happiest of all is, that her gentle spirit
Commits itself to yours to be directed,
As from her lord, her governor, her king.
Myself, and what is mine, to you and yours
Is now converted: but now I was the lord
Of this fair mansion, master of my servants,
Queen o'er myself; and even now, but now
This house, these servants, and this same my-
    self
Are yours, my lord; I give them with this ring,

Which when you part from, lose, or give away,
Let it presage the ruin of your love,
And be my vantage to exclaim on you.
  Bass. Madam, you have bereft me of all
    words;
Only my blood speaks to you in my veins:
And there is such confusion in my powers,
As, after some oration fairly spoke
By a beloved prince, there doth appear
Among the buzzing pleased multitude,
Where every something, being blent together,
Turns to a wild of nothing, save of joy.   [ring
Express'd, and not express'd. But when this
Parts from this finger, then parts life from
    hence;
O, then, be bold to say Bassanio's dead.
  Ner. My lord and lady, it is now our time
That have stood by and seen our wishes pros-
    per
To cry, good joy. Good joy, my lord and lady!
  Gra. My Lord Bassanio, and my gentle lady,
I wish you all the joy that you can wish;
For I am sure you can wish none from me:
And, when your honours mean to solemnize
The bargain of your faith, I do beseech you,
Even at that time I may be married too.
  Bass. With all my heart, so thou canst get a
    wife.
  Gra. I thank your lordship; you have got me
    one.
My eyes, my lord, can look as swift as yours:
You saw the mistress, I beheld the maid;
You lov'd, I lov'd; for intermission
No more pertains to me, my lord, than you,
Your fortune stood upon the caskets there,
And so did mine too, as the matter falls:
For wooing here until I sweat again,
And swearing till my very roof was dry
With oaths of love, at last,—if promise last,—
I got a promise of this fair one here,
To have her love provided that your fortune
Achiev'd her mistress.
  Por.   Is this true, Nerissa?
  Ner. Madam, it is, so you stand pleas'd
    withal.
  Bass. And do you, Gratiano, mean good
    faith?
  Gra. Yes, faith, my lord.
  Bass. Our feast shall be much honour'd in
    your marriage.
  Gra. We'll play with them, the first boy for a
thousand ducats.
  Ner. What, and stake down?
  Gra. No; we shall ne'er win at that sport,
    and stake down.—
But who comes here? Lorenzo and his infidel?
What, and my old Venetian friend, Solanio!

Enter LORENZO, JESSICA, *and* SOLANIO.

  Bass. Lorenzo and Solanio, welcome hither,
If that the youth of my new interest here
Have power to bid you welcome.—By your
    leave,
I bid my very friends and countrymen,

Sweet Portia, welcome.

Por.   So do I, my lord;
They are entirely welcome.   [lord,

Lor. I thank your honour.—For my part, my
My purpose was not to have seen you here;
But meeting with Solanio by the way,
He did entreat me past all saying nay,
To come with him along.

Solan.   I did, my lord,
And I have reason for it. Signior Antonio
Commends him to you.

                    [*Gives* BASSANIO *a letter*.

Bass.   Ere I ope his letter,
I pray you, tell me how my good friend doth.

Solan. Not sick, my lord, unless it be in
          mind;
Nor well, unless in mind: his letter there
Will show you his estate.

                    [BASS. *reads the letter*.

Gra. Nerissa, cheer yond stranger; bid her
          welcome.   [Venice?
Your hand, Solanio: what's the news from
How doth that royal merchant, good Antonio?
I know he will be glad of our success:
We are the Jasons; we have won the fleece.

Solan. Would you had won the fleece that he
          hath lost!   [same paper,

Por. There are some shrewd contents in yon
That steal the colour from Bassanio's cheek;
Some dear friend dead; else nothing in the world
Could turn so much the contrition [worse?—
Of any constant man. What, worse and
With leave, Bassanio; I am half yourself,
And I must freely have the half of anything
That this same paper brings you.

Bass.   O sweet Portia,
Here are a few of the unpleasant'st words
That ever blotted paper! Gentle lady,
When I did first impart my love to you
I freely told you all the wealth I had
Ran in my veins—I was a gentleman;
And then I told you true: and yet, dear lady,
Rating myself at nothing, you shall see
How much I was a braggart. When I told you
My state was nothing, I should then have told
          you
That I was worse than nothing; for, indeed,
I have engag'd myself to a dear friend,
Engag'd my friend to his mere enemy,
To feed my means. Here is a letter, lady,
The paper as the body of my friend,
And every word in it a gaping wound,
Issuing life-blood. But is it true, Solanio?
Have all his ventures fail'd? What! not one hit?
From Tripolis, from Mexico, and England;
From Lisbon, Barbary, and India?
And not one vessel 'scape the dreadful touch
Of merchant-marring rocks?

Solan.   Not one, my lord.
Besides, it should appear that if he had
The present money to discharge the Jew
He would not take it. Never did I know
A creature that did bear the shape of man
So keen and greedy to confound a man:

He plies the duke at morning and at night,
And doth impeach the freedom of the state
If they deny him justice: twenty merchants,
The duke himself, and the magnificoes
Of greatest port have all persuaded with him;
But none can drive him from the envious plea
Of forfeiture, of justice, and his bond.

Jes. When I was with him I have heard him
          swear
To Tubal and to Chus, his countrymen,
That he would rather have Antonio's flesh
Than twenty times the value of the sum
That he did owe him; and I know, my lord,
If law, authority, and power deny not,
It will go hard with poor Antonio.

Por. Is it your dear friend that is thus in
          trouble?

Bass. The dearest friend to me, the kindest
          man,
The best condition'd and unwearied spirit
In doing courtesies; and one in whom
The ancient Roman honour more appears
Than any that draws breath in Italy.

Por. What sum owes he the Jew?

Bass. For me, three thousand ducats.

Por.   What! no more?
Pay him six thousand, and deface the bond;
Double six thousand, and then treble that,
Before a friend of this description
Shall lose a hair through Bassanio's fault.
First, go with me to church, and call me wife,
And then away to Venice to your friend;
For never shall you lie by Portia's side
With an unquiet soul. You shall have gold
To pay the petty debt twenty times over;
When it is paid bring your true friend along:
My maid Nerissa and myself, meantime,
Will live as maids and widows. Come, away;
For you shall hence upon your wedding-day:
Bid your friends welcome, show a merry cheer:
Since you are dear bought, I will love you dear.
But let me hear the letter of your friend.

Bass. [*Reads.*] *Sweet Bassanio, my ships have
all miscarried, my creditors grow cruel, my estate
is very low, my bond to the Jew is forfeit; and
since, in paying it, it is impossible I should live,
all debts are cleared between you and I, if I might
but see you at my death: notwithstanding, use
your pleasure; if your love do not persuade you to
come, let not my letter.*

Por. O love, despatch all business, and be
          gone.

Bass. Since I have your good leave to go
          away,
I will make haste: but, till I come again,
No bed shall e'er be guilty of my stay,
No rest be interposer 'twixt us twain.

                              [*Exeunt.*

SCENE III.—VENICE. *A Street*.

Enter SHYLOCK, SALARINO, ANTONIO *and*
          Gaoler.

Shy. Gaoler, look to him. Tell not me of
          mercy;—

This is the fool that lent out money gratis.—
Gaoler, look to him.
   Ant.   Hear me yet, good Shylock.
   Shy. I'll have my bond: speak not against
      my bond.
I have sworn an oath that I will have my bond.
Thou call'dst me dog before thou hadst a cause:
But, since I am a dog, beware my fangs:
The duke shall grant me justice.—I do wonder,
Thou naughty gaoler, that thou art so fond
To come abroad with him at his request.
   Ant. I pray thee, hear me speak.
   Shy. I'll have my bond; I will not hear thee
      speak: [more.
I'll have my bond; and therefore speak no
I'll not be made a soft and dull-ey'd fool,
To shake the head, relent, and sigh, and yield
To Christian intercessors. Follow not;
I'll have no speaking: I will have my bond.
                          [Exit.
   Salar. It is the most impenetrable cur
That ever kept with men.
   Ant.   Let him alone;
I'll follow him no more with bootless prayers.
He seeks my life; his reason well I know:
I oft deliver'd from his forfeitures
Many that have at times made moan to me;
Therefore he hates me.
   Salar.   I am sure the duke
Will never grant this forfeiture to hold.
   Ant. The duke cannot deny the course of
      law;
For the commodity that strangers have
With us in Venice, if it be denied,
Will much impeach the justice of the state;
Since that the trade and profit of the city
Consisteth of all nations. Therefore, go:
These griefs and losses have so 'bated me
That I shall hardly spare a pound of flesh
To-morrow to my bloody creditor.——
Well, gaoler, on.—Pray God, Bassanio come
To see me pay his debt, and then I care not!
                      [Exeunt.

SCENE IV.—BELMONT. *A Room in* PORTIA'S
          House.

Enter PORTIA, NERISSA, LORENZO, JESSICA,
     and BALTHAZAR.

   Lor. Madam, although I speak it in your
      presence,
You have a noble and a true conceit
Of god-like amity, which appears most strongly
In bearing thus the absence of your lord.
But if you knew to whom you show this honour,
How true a gentleman you send relief,
How dear a lover of my lord your husband,
I know you would be prouder of the work
Than customary bounty can enforce you.
   Por. I never did repent for doing good,
Nor shall not now: for in companions
That do converse and waste the time together,
Whose souls do bear an equal yoke of love,
There must be needs a like proportion
Of lineaments, of manners, and of spirit,

Which makes me think that this Antonio,
Being the bosom lover of my lord,
Must needs be like my lord. If it be so,
How little is the cost I have bestow'd
In purchasing the semblance of my soul
From out the state of hellish cruelty!
This comes too near the praising of myself;
Therefore, no more of it: hear other things.—
Lorenzo, I commit into your hands
The husbandry and manage of my house
Until my lord's return: for mine own part,
I have toward heaven breath'd a secret vow
To live in prayer and contemplation,
Only attended by Nerissa here,
Until her husband and my lord's return:
There is a monastery two miles off,
And there we will abide. I do desire you
Not to deny this imposition,
The which my love and some necessity
Now lays upon you.
   Lor.   Madam, with all my heart
I shall obey you in all fair commands.
   Por. My people do already know my mind,
And will acknowledge you and Jessica
In place of Lord Bassanio and myself.
So fare you well till we shall meet again.
   Lor. Fair thoughts and happy hours attend
      on you!
   Jes. I wish your ladyship all heart's content.
   Por. I thank you for your wish, and am well
      pleas'd
To wish it back on you: fare you well, Jessica.—
      [Exeunt JESSICA *and* LORENZO.
Now Balthazar,
As I have ever found thee honest, true,
So let me find thee still. Take this same letter,
And use thou all the endeavour of a man
In speed to Padua; see thou render this
Into my cousin's hand, Doctor Bellario;
And, look, what notes and garments he doth
      give thee
Bring them, I pray thee, with imagin'd speed
Unto the tranect, to the common ferry [words,
Which trades to Venice:—waste no time in
But get thee gone; I shall be there before thee.
   Balth. Madam, I go with all convenient
      speed.   *[Exit.*
   Por. Come on, Nerissa; I have work in hand
That you yet know not of: we'll see our hus-
      bands
Before they think of us.
   Ner.   Shall they see us?
   Por. They shall, Nerissa; but in such a habit
That they shall think we are accomplished
With that we lack. I'll hold thee any wager,
When we are both accouter'd like young men,
I'll prove the prettier fellow of the two,
And wear my dagger with the braver grace;
And speak, between the change of man and
      boy,
With a reed voice; and turn two mincing steps
Into a manly stride; and speak of frays,
Like a fine bragging youth: and tell quaint lies,
How honourable ladies sought my love,

Which I denying, they fell sick and died;
I could not do withal: then I'll repent,
And wish, for all that, that I had not kill'd
    them:
And twenty of these puny lies I'll tell,
That men shall swear I have discontinued
    school
Above a twelvemonth.—I have within my mind
A thousand raw tricks of these bragging Jacks
Which I will practise.
    Ner.   Why, shall we turn to men?
    Por. Fie! what a question's that
If thou wert ne'er a lewd interpreter?
But come, I'll tell thee all my whole device
When I am in my coach, which stays for us
At the park-gate; and, therefore, haste away,
For we must measure twenty miles to-day.
                        [Exeunt.

SCENE V.—*The same. A Garden.*

Enter LAUNCELOT *and* JESSICA.

    Laun. Yes, truly;—for, look you, the sins of
the father are to be laid upon the children;
therefore, I promise you, I fear you. I was
always plain with you, and so now I speak my
agitation of the matter: therefore, be of good
cheer; for, truly, I think you are damned.
There is but one hope in it that can do you any
good; and that is but a kind of bastard hope
neither.
    Jes. And what hope is that, I pray thee?
    Laun. Marry, you may partly hope that
your father got you not,—that you are not the
Jew's daughter.
    Jes. That were a kind of bastard hope, in-
deed; so the sins of my mother should be visited
upon me.
    Laun. Truly then I fear you are damned
both by father and mother: thus when I shun
Scylla your father, I fall into Charybdis, your
mother; well, you are gone both ways.
    Jes. I shall be saved by my husband; he hath
made me a Christian.
    Laun. Truly, the more to blame he: we were
Christians enow before; e'en as many as could
well live, one by another. This making of
Christians will raise the price of hogs; if we
grow all to be pork eaters we shall not shortly
have a rasher on the coals for money.
    Jes. I'll tell my husband, Launcelot, what
you say; here he comes.

Enter LORENZO

    Lor. I shall grow jealous of you shortly,
Launcelot, if you thus get my wife into corners.
    Jes. Nay, you need not fear for us, Lorenzo;
Launcelot and I are out: he tells me flatly there
is no mercy for me in heaven, because I am a
Jew's daughter: and he says you are no good
member of the commonwealth; for, in converting Jews to Christians, you raise the price of
pork.

    Lor. I shall answer that better to the com-
monwealth than you can the getting up of the
negro's belly; the Moor is with child by you,
Launcelot.
    Laun. It is much that the Moor should be
more than reason: but if she be less than an
honest woman, she is indeed more than I took
her for.
    Lor. How every fool can play upon the word!
I think the best grace of wit will shortly turn
into silence, and discourse grow commendable
in none only but parrots.—Go in, sirrah; bid
them prepare for dinner.
    Laun. That is done, sir; they have all
stomachs.
    Lor. Goodly lord, what a wit-snapper are
you! then bid them prepare dinner.
    Laun. That is done too, sir: only. cover is
the word.
    Lor. Will you cover, then, sir?
    Laun. Not so, sir, neither; I know my duty.
    Lor. Yet more quarrelling with occasion!
Wilt thou show the whole wealth of thy wit in
an instant? I pray thee, understand a plain
man in his plain meaning: go to thy fellows;
bid them cover the table, serve in the meat, and
we will come in to dinner.
    Laun. For the table, sir, it shall be served
in; for the meat, sir, it shall be covered; for
your coming in to dinner, sir, why, let it be as
humours and conceits shall govern.   *[Exit.*
    Lor. O dear discretion, how his words are
        suited!
The fool hath planted in his memory
An army of good words; and I do know
A many fools that stand in better place,
Garnish'd like him, that for a tricksy word
Defy the matter. How cheer'st thou, Jessica?
And now, good sweet, say thy opinion,—
How dost thou like the Lord Bassanio's wife?
    Jes. Past all expressing. It is very meet
The Lord Bassanio live an upright life;
For, having such a blessing in his lady,
He finds the joys of heaven here on earth;
And, if on earth he do not mean it, then
In reason he should never come to heaven.
Why, if two gods should play some heavenly
        match,
And on the wager lay two earthly women,
And Portia one, there must be something else
Pawn'd with the other; for the poor rude world
Hath not her fellow.
    Lor.   Even such a husband
Hast thou of me as she is for a wife.
    Jes. Nay, but ask my opinion too of that.
    Lor. I will anon; first let us go to dinner
    Jes. Nay, let me praise you while I have a
        stomach.
    Lor. No, pray thee, let it serve for table-talk;
Then, howsoe'er thou speak'st, 'mong other
        things
I shall digest it.
    Jes.   Well, I'll set you forth.
                        [Exeunt.

ACT IV.

SCENE I.—VENICE. *A Court of Justice.*

Enter the DUKE, *the* Magnificoes: ANTONIO,
BASSANIO, GRATIANO, SALARINO, SOLANIO,
and others.

Duke. What, is Antonio here?
Ant. Ready, so please your grace.
Duke. I am sorry for thee; thou art come to
    answer
A stony adversary, an inhuman wretch
Uncapable of pity, void and empty
From any dram of mercy.
Ant.   I have heard
Your grace hath ta'en great pains to qualify
His rigorous course; but since he stands ob-
    durate,
And that no lawful means can carry me
Out of his envy's reach, I do oppose
My patience to his fury, and am arm'd
To suffer, with a quietness of spirit,
The very tyranny and rage of his.
Duke. Go one, and call the Jew into the
    court.   [my lord.
Solan. He's ready at the door: he comes,

Enter SHYLOCK.

Duke. Make room, and let him stand before
    our face.—
Shylock, the world thinks, and I think so too,
Thou thou but lead'st this fashion of thy malice
To the last hour of act; and then, 'tis thought,
Thou'lt show thy mercy and remorse, more
    strange
Than is thy strange apparent cruelty;
And where thou now exact'st the penalty,—
Which is a pound of this poor merchant's flesh,—
Thou wilt not only lose the forfeiture,
But, touch'd with human gentleness and love,
Forgive a moiety of the principal,
Glancing an eye of pity on his losses,
That have of late so huddled on his back;
Enough to press a royal merchant down,
And pluck commiseration of his state
From brassy bosoms and rough hearts of flint,
From stubborn Turks and Tartars, never train'd
To offices of tender courtesy.
We all expect a gentle answer, Jew.
Shy. I have possess'd your grace of what I
    purpose;
And by our holy Sabbath have I sworn
To have the due and forfeit of my bond.
If you deny it, let the danger light
Upon your charter and your city's freedom.
You'll ask me why I rather choose·to have
A weight of carrion flesh than to receive
Three thousand ducats: I'll not answer that:
But say, it is my humour. Is it answered?
What if my house be troubled with a rat,
And I be pleas'd to give ten thousand ducats
To have it baned? What, are you answer'd yet?
Some men there are love not a gaping pig;
Some that are mad if they behold a cat;

And others, when the bagpipe sings i' the nose,
Cannot contain their urine; for affection,
Master of passion, sways it to the mood
Of what it likes or loathes. Now, for your
    answer,
As there is no firm reason to be render'd
Why he cannot abide a gaping pig;
Why he, a harmless necessary cat;
Why he, a swollen bagpipe, but of force
Must yield to such inevitable shame
As to offend, himself being offended:
So can I give no reason, nor I will not,
More than a lodg'd hate and a certain loathing
I bear Antonio, that I follow thus
A losing suit against him. Are you answer'd?
Bass. This is no answer, thou unfeeling man,
To excuse the current of thy cruelty.
Shy. I am not bound to please thee with my
    answer.   [love?
Bass. Do all men kill the thing they do not
Shy. Hates any man the thing he would not
    kill?
Bass. Every offence is not a hate at first.
Shy. What! wouldst thou have a serpent
    sting thee twice?   [the Jew:
Ant. I pray you, think you question with
You may as well go stand upon the beach
And bid the main-flood bait his usual height;
You may as well use question with the wolf
Why he hath made the ewe bleat for the lamb;
You may as well forbid the mountain pines
To wag their high tops, and to make no noise,
When they are fretted with the gusts of heaven;
You may as well do anything most hard
As seek to soften that,—than which what's
    harder?—   [you,
His Jewish heart.—Therefore, I do beseech
Make no more offers, use no further means,
But, with all brief and plain conveniency,
Let me have judgment and the Jew his will.
Bass. For thy three thousand ducats here is
    six.
Shy. If every ducat in six thousand ducats
Were in six parts, and every part a ducat,
I would not draw them; I would have my bond.
Duke. How shalt thou hope for mercy,
    rend'ring none?   [no wrong?
Shy. What judgment shall I dread, doing
You have among you many a purchas'd slave,
Which, like your asses, and your dogs, and mules,
You use in abject and in slavish parts,
Because you bought them.—Shall I say to you,
Let them be free, marry them to your heirs?
Why sweat they under burdens? let their beds
Be made as soft as yours, and let their palates
Be season'd with such viands? You will answer,
The slaves are ours:—So do I answer you;
The pound of flesh which I demand of him
Is dearly bought, is mine, and I will have it:
If you deny me, fie upon your law!
There is no force in the decrees of Venice.—
I stand for judgment: answer: shall I have it?
Duke. Upon my power I may dismiss this
    court,

Unless Bellario, a learned doctor,
Whom I have sent for to determine this,.
Come here to-day.
Solan.   My lord, here stays without
A messenger with letters from the doctor,
New come from Padua.   [senger.
Duke. Bring us the letters;—call the mes-
Bass. Good cheer, Antonio! What, man,
            courage yet!   [and all,
The Jew shall have my flesh, blood, bones,
Ere thou shalt lose for me one drop of blood.
Ant. I am a tainted wether of the flock,
Meetest for death: the weakest kind of fruit
Drops earliest to the ground, and so let me:
You cannot better be employ'd, Bassanio,
Than to live still, and write mine epitaph.

Enter NERISSA, *dressed like a lawyer's clerk.*

Duke. Came you from Padua, from Bellario?
Ner. From both, my lord: Bellario greets
            your grace.   [*Presents a letter.*
Bass. Why dost thou whet thy knife so
            earnestly?   [rupt there.
Shy. To cut the forfeiture from that bank-
Gra. Not on thy sole, but on thy soul,
            harsh Jew,
Thou mak'st thy knife keen: but no metal can,
No, not the hangman's axe, bear half the keen-
            ness
Of thy sharp envy. Can no prayers pierce thee?
Shy. No; none that thou hast wit enough to
            make.
Gra. O, be thou damn'd, inexorable dog!
And for thy life let justice be accus'd.
Thou almost mak'st me waver in my faith,
To hold opinion with Pythàgoras,
That souls of animals infuse themselves
Into the trunks of men: thy currish spirit
Govern'd a wolf, who, hang'd for human
            slaughter,
Even from the gallows did his fell soul fleet,
And, whilst thou lay'st in thy unhallow'd dam,
Infus'd itself in thee; for thy desires
Are wolfish, bloody, starv'd, and ravenous.
Shy. Till thou canst rail the seal from off my
            bond
Thou but offend'st thy lungs to speak so loud:
Repair thy wit, good youth, or it will fall
To cureless ruin.—I stand here for law.
Duke. This letter from Bellario doth com-
            mend
A young and learned doctor to our court:—
Where is he?
Ner.   He attendeth here hard by,
To know your answer, whether you'll admit
            him.
Duke. With all my heart:—some three or
            four of you
Go give him courteous conduct to this place.—
Meantime, the court shall hear Bellario's letter.

[*Clerk reads.*] Your grace shall understand that, at
the receipt of your letter, I am very sick; but in the
instant that your messenger came, in loving visitation was with me a young doctor of Rome; his name
is Balthazar: I acquainted him with the cause in
controversy between the Jew and Antonio the
merchant; we turned o'er many books together: he
is furnish'd with my opinion; which, better'd with
his own learning (the greatness whereof I cannot
enough commend), comes with him, at my impor-
tunity to fill up your grace's request in my stead.
I beseech you, let his lack of years be no impediment to let him lack a reverend estimation; for I
never knew so young a body with so old a head.
I leave him to your gracious acceptance, whose trial
shall better publish his commendation.

Duke. You hear the learn'd Bellario, what he
            writes:
And here, I take it, is the doctor come.—

Enter PORTIA, *dressed like a doctor of laws.*

Give me your hand: came you from old Bellario?
Por. I did, my lord.   [place.
Duke.   You are welcome: take your
Are you acquainted with the difference
That holds this present question in the court?
Por. I am informed throughly of the cause.
Which is the merchant here, and which the
            Jew?   [forth.
Duke. Antonio and old Shylock, both stand
Por. Is your name Shylock?
Shy.   Shylock is my name.
Por. Of a strange nature is the suit you
            follow:
Yet in such rule, that the Venetian law
Cannot impugn you as you do proceed.—
You stand within his danger, do you not?
            [*To* ANTONIO.
Ant. Ay, so he says.
Por.   Do you confess the bond?
Ant. I do.
Por.   Then must the Jew be merciful.
Shy. On what compulsion must I? tell me
            that.
Por. The quality of mercy is not strain'd;
It droppeth as the gentle rain from heaven
Upon the place beneath: it is twice bless'd;
It blesseth him that gives and him that takes:
'Tis mightiest in the mightiest, it becomes
The throned monarch better than his crown,
His sceptre shows the force of temporal power,
The attribute to awe and majesty,
Wherein doth sit the dread and fear of kings;
But mercy is above this scepter'd sway,—
It is enthroned in the heart of kings,
It is an attribute to God himself;
And earthly power doth then show likest God's
When mercy seasons justice. Therefore, Jew,
Though justice be thy plea consider this—
That in the course of justice none of us
Should see salvation: we do pray for mercy;
And that same prayer doth teach us all to
            render
The deeds of mercy. I have spoke thus much
To mitigate the justice of thy plea;
Which if thou follow, this strict court of Venice
Must needs give sentence 'gainst the merchant
            there.

Shy. My deeds upon my head! I crave the law,
The penalty and forfeit of my bond.

Por. Is he not able to discharge the money?

Bass. Yes; here I tender it for him in the court;
Yea, twice the sum: if that will not suffice
I will be bound to pay it ten times o'er,
On forfeit of my hands, my head, my heart:
If this will not suffice, it must appear   [you
That malice bears down truth. And I beseech
Wrest once the law to your authority:
To do a great right do a little wrong,
And curb this cruel devil of his will.

Por. It must not be; there is no power in Venice
Can alter a decree established:
'Twill be recorded for a precedent,
And many an error, by the same example,
Will rush into the state: it cannot be.

Shy. A Daniel come to judgment! yea, a Daniel!
O wise young judge! how I do honour thee!

Por. I pray you, let me look upon the bond.

Shy. Here 'tis, most reverend doctor; here it is.

Por. Shylock, there's thrice thy money offered thee.

Shy. An oath, an oath; I have an oath in heaven:
Shall I lay perjury upon my soul?
No, not for Venice.

Por.   Why, this bond is forfeit;
And lawfully by this the Jew may claim
A pound of flesh, to be by him cut off
Nearest the merchant's heart.—Be merciful!
Take thrice thy money; bid me tear the bond.

Shy. When it is paid according to the tenor.—
It doth appear you are a worthy judge;
You know the law; your exposition
Hath been most sound: I charge you by the law,
Whereof you are a well-deserving pillar,
Proceed to judgment: by my soul I swear
There is no power in the tongue of man
To alter me.—I stay here on my bond.

Ant. Most heartily I do beseech the court
To give the judgment.

Por.   Why then, thus it is.
You must prepare your bosom for his knife:

Shy. O noble judge! O excellent young man!

Por. For the intent and purpose of the law
Hath full relation to the penalty,
Which here appeareth due upon the bond.

Shy. 'Tis very true: O wise and upright judge,
How much more elder art thou than thy looks!

Por. Therefore, lay bare your bosom.

Shy.   Ay, his breast:
So says the bond;—doth it not, noble judge?—
Nearest his heart: those are the very words.

Por. It is so. Are there balance here to weigh
The flesh?

Shy. I have them ready.

Por. Have by some surgeon, Shylock, on your charge,
To stop his wounds, lest he do bleed to death.

Shy. Is it so nominated in the bond?

Por. It is not so express'd; but what of that?
'Twere good you do so much for charity.

Shy. I cannot find it; 'tis not in the bond.

Por. Come, merchant, have you anything to say?

Ant. But little; I am arm'd and well prepar'd.—
Give me your hand, Bassanio; fare you well.
Grieve not that I am fallen to this for you;
For herein fortune shows herself more kind
Than is her custom: it is still her use
To let the wretched man out-live his wealth,
To view with hollow eye and wrinkled brow
An age of poverty; from which lingering penance
Of such misery doth she cut me off.
Commend me to your honourable wife:
Tell her the process of Antonio's end;
Say how I lov'd you; speak me fair in death;
And, when the tale is told, bid her be judge
Whether Bassanio had not once a love.
Repent not you that you shall lose your friend,
And he repents not that he pays your debt;
For, if the Jew do cut but deep enough,
I'll pay it instantly with all my heart.

Bass. Antonio, I am married to a wife
Which is as dear to me as life itself;
But life itself, my wife, and all the world
Are not with me esteem'd above thy life;
I would lose all, ay, sacrifice them all
Here to this devil, to deliver you.

Por. Your wife would give you little thanks for that,
If she were by to hear you make the offer.

Gra. I have a wife whom, I protest, I love;
I would she were in heaven, so she could
Entreat some power to change this currish Jew.

Ner. 'Tis well you offer it behind her back;
The wish would make else an unquiet house.

Shy. These be the Christian husbands: I have a daughter;
Would any of the stock of Barrabas
Had been her husband, rather than a Christian!
                                        [*Aside.*
We trifle time;—I pray thee, pursue sentence.

Por. A pound of that same merchant's flesh is thine;
The court awards it and the law doth give it.

Shy. Most rightful judge!   [his breast;

Por. And you must cut this flesh from off
The law allows it and the court awards it.

Shy. Most learned judge!—A sentence; come, prepare.   [else.—

Por. Tarry a little;—there is something
This bond doth give thee here no jot of blood;
The words expressly are a pound of flesh:
Take then thy bond, take thou thy pound of flesh;
But, in the cutting, if thou dost shed   [goods
One drop of Christian blood, thy lands and
Are, by the laws of Venice, confiscate

Unto the state of Venice. [learned judge!
Gra. O upright judge!—Mark, Jew;—O
Shy. Is that the law?
Por. Thyself shall see the act:
For, as thou urgest justice, be assur'd
Thou shalt have justice, more than thou desir'st.
Gra. O learned judge!—Mark, Jew;—a
learned judge! [thrice,
Shy. I take this offer then,—pay the bond
And let the Christian go.
Bass. Here is the money.
Por. Soft; [haste:—
The Jew shall have all justice:—soft;—no
He shall have nothing but the penalty.
Gra. O Jew! an upright judge, a learned
judge!
Por. Therefore, prepare thee to cut off the
flesh.
Shed thou no blood; nor cut thou less nor more
But just a pound of flesh: if thou tak'st more
Or less than a just pound,—be it but so much
As makes it light or heavy in the substance,
Or the division of the twentieth part
Of one poor scruple: nay, if the scale do turn
But in the estimation of a hair,—
Thou diest, and all thy goods are confiscate.
Gra. A second Daniel, a Daniel, Jew!
Now, infidel, I have thee on the hip.
Por. Why doth the Jew pause? take thy for-
feiture.
Shy. Give me my principal, and let me go.
Bass. I have it ready for thee; here it is.
Por. He hath refus'd it in the open court;
He shall have merely justice, and his bond.
Gra. A Daniel, still say I; a second Daniel!—
I thank thee, Jew, for teaching me that word.
Shy. Shall I not have barely my principal?
Por. Thou shalt have nothing but the for-
feiture
To be so taken at thy peril, Jew.
Shy. Why, then the devil give him good of it!
I'll stay no longer question.
Por. Tarry, Jew;
The law hath yet another hold on you.
It is enacted in the laws of Venice,—
If it be prov'd against an alien,
That by direct or indirect attempts
He seek the life of any citizen,
The party 'gainst the which he doth contrive
Shall seize one half his goods; the other half
Comes to the privy coffer of the state;
And the offender's life lies in the mercy
Of the duke only, 'gainst all other voice.
In which predicament, I say, thou stand'st;
For it appears by manifest proceeding,
That indirectly, and directly too,
Thou hast contriv'd against the very life
Of the defendant; and thou hast incurr'd
The danger formerly by me rehears'd.
Down, therefore, and beg mercy of the duke.
Gra. Beg that thou mayst have leave to hang
thyself:
And yet, thy wealth being forfeit to the state,
Thou hast not left the value of a cord;

Therefore, thou must be hang'd at the state's
charge. [spirit,
Duke. That thou shalt see the difference of our
I pardon thee thy life before thou ask it:
For half thy wealth, it is Antonio's:
The other half comes to the general state,
Which humbleness may drive unto a fine.
Por. Ay, for the state; not for Antonio.
Shy. Nay, take my life and all, pardon not
that:
You take my house when you do take the prop
That doth sustain my house; you take my life
When you do take the means whereby I live.
Por. What mercy can you render him,
Antonio? [sake.
Gra. A halter gratis; nothing else; for God's
Ant. So please my lord the duke, and all the
court,
To quit the fine for one half of his goods;
I am content, so he will let me have
The other half in use, to render it,
Upon his death, unto the gentleman
That lately stole his daughter:
Two things provided more,—that for this
favour,
He presently become a Christian;
The other, that he do record a gift,
Here in the court, of all he dies possess'd
Unto his son Lorenzo and his daughter.
Duke. He shall do this; or else I do recant
The pardon that I late pronounced here.
Por. Art thou contented, Jew? what dost
thou say?
Shy. I am content.
Por. Clerk, draw a deed of gift.
Shy. I pray you, give me leave to go from
hence:
I am not well; send the deed after me
And I will sign it.
Duke. Get thee gone, but do it.
Gra. In christening, thou shalt have two
godfathers:
Had I been judge, thou shouldst have had ten
more,
To bring thee to the gallows, not the font.
[*Exit* SHYLOCK.
Duke. Sir, I entreat you home with me to
dinner.
Por. I humbly do desire your grace of par-
don;
I must away this night toward Padua;
And it is meet I presently set forth.
Duke. I am sorry that your leisure serves
you not.
Antonio, gratify this gentleman;
For, in my mind, you are much bound to him.
[*Exeunt* DUKE, Magnificoes, *and* Train.
Bass. Most worthy gentleman, I and my
friend
Have by your wisdom been this day acquitted
Of grievous penalties; in lieu whereof,
Three thousand ducats, due unto the Jew,
We freely cope your courteous pains withal.
Ant. And stand indebted, over and above

In love and service to you evermore.
  Por. He is well paid that is·well satisfied,
And I, delivering you, am satisfied,
And therein do account myself well paid:
My mind was never yet more mercenary.
I pray you, know me when we meet again;
I wish you well, and so I take my leave.
  Bass. Dear sir, of force I must attempt you
      further;
Take some remembrance of us, as a tribute,
Not as a fee; grant me two things, I pray you,
Not to deny me, and to pardon me.
  Por. You press me far, and therefore I will
      yield.
Give me your gloves, I'll wear them for your
      sake;
And, for your love, I'll take this ring from
      you:—
Do not draw back your hand; I'll take no
      more;
And you in love shall not deny me this.
  Bass. This ring, good sir,—alas, it is a trifle;
I will not shame myself to give you this.
  Por. I will have nothing else but only this;
And now, methinks, I have a mind to it.
  Bass. There's more depends on this than on
      the value.
The dearest ring in Venice will I give you,
And find it out by proclamation;
Only for this, I pray you, pardon me.
  Por. I see, sir, you are liberal in offers:
You taught me first to beg, and now, methinks,
You teach me how a beggar should be answer'd.
  Bass. Good sir, this ring was given me by my
      wife,
And, when she put it on, she made me vow
That I should neither sell, nor give, nor lose
      it.
  Por. That 'scuse serves many men to save
      their gifts.
An if your wife be not a mad woman,
And know how well I have deserv'd this ring,
She would not hold out enemy for ever,
For giving it to me. Well, peace be with you!
          [*Exeunt* PORTIA *and* NERISSA.
  Ant. My Lord Bassanio, let him have the
      ring:
Let his deservings, and my love withal,
Be valued 'gainst your wife's commandment.
  Bass. Go, Gratiano, run and overtake him,
Give him the ring; and bring him, if thou canst,
Unto Antonio's house:—away, make haste.
          [*Exit* GRATIANO.
Come, you and I will thither presently;
And in the morning early will we both
Fly toward Belmont. Come, Antonio.
          [*Exeunt*.

SCENE II.—*The same. A Street.*

Enter PORTIA *and* NERISSA.

  Por. Inquire the Jew's house out, give him
      this deed,
And let him sign it; we'll away to-night,

And be a day before our husbands home.
This deed will be well welcome to Lorenzo.

Enter GRATIANO.

  Gra. Fair sir, you are well overta'en:
My Lord Bassanio, upon more advice,
Hath sent you here this ring; and doth entreat
Your company at dinner.
  Por.   That cannot be:
His ring I do accept most thankfully.
And so, I pray you, tell him. Furthermore,
I pray you, show my youth old Shylock's house.
  Gra. That will I do.
  Ner. Sir, I would speak with you:—
I'll see if I can get my husband's ring,
                    [*To* PORTIA.
Which I did make him swear to keep for ever.
  Por. Thou mayst, I warrant. We shall have
      old swearing
That they did give the rings away to men;
But we'll outface them and outswear them too.
Away, make haste; thou know'st where I will
      tarry.
  Ner. Come, good sir, will you show me to
      this house?   [*Exeunt*.

ACT V.

SCENE I.—BELMONT. *Pleasure grounds of* PORTIA'S *House.*

Enter LORENZO *and* JESSICA.

  Lor. The moon shines bright!—In such a
      night as this,
When the sweet wind did gently kiss the trees,
And they did make no noise; in such a night,
Troilus, methinks, mounted the Trojan walls,
And sigh'd his soul toward the Grecian tents,
Where Cressid lay that night.
  Jes.   In such a night
Did Thisbe fearfully o'ertrip the dew,
And saw the lion's shadow ere himself.
And ran dismay'd away.
  Lor.   In such a night
Stood Dido with a willow in her hand
Upon the wild sea-banks, and wav'd her love
To come again to Carthage.
  Jes.   In such a night
Medea gather'd the enchanted herbs
That did renew old Æson.
  Lor.   In such a night
Did Jessica steal from the wealthy Jew
And, with an unthrift love, did run from Venice
As far as Belmont.
  Jes.   In such a night
Did young Lorenzo swear he lov'd her well—
Stealing her soul with many vows of faith,
And ne'er a true one
  Lor   In such a night
Did pretty Jessica, like a little shrew,
Slander her love, and he forgave it her.
  Jes. I would out-night you, did nobody
      come:
But hark, I hear the footing of a man.

Enter STEPHANO.

Lor. Who comes so fast in silence of the
    night?
Steph. A friend.
Lor. A friend! what friend? your name, I
    pray you, friend?
Steph. Stepháno is my name; and I bring
    word
My mistress will before the break of day
Be here at Belmont; she doth stray about
By holy crosses, where she kneels and prays
For happy wedlock hours.
Lor.   Who comes with her?
Steph. None but a holy hermit and her maid.
I pray you, is my master yet return'd?
Lor. He is not, nor we have not heard from
    him.—
But go we in, I pray thee, Jessica,
And ceremoniously let us prepare
Some welcome for the mistress of the house.

Enter LAUNCELOT.

Laun. Sola, sola, wo ha, ho, sola, sola!
Lor. Who calls?
Laun. Sola! did you see Master Lorenzo and
Mistress Lorenzo? sola, sola!
Lor. Leave hollaing, man: here.
Laun. Sola! where? where?
Lor. Here.
Laun. Tell him there's a post come from my
master with his horn full of good news; my
master will be here ere morning.   [*Exit*.
Lor. Sweet soul, let's in, and there expect
    their coming.
And yet no matter;—why should we go in?
My friend Stepháno, signify, I pray you,
Within the house, your mistress is at hand:
And bring your music forth into the air.—
                          [*Exit* STEPHANO.
How sweet the moonlight sleeps upon this bank!
Here will we sit, and let the sounds of music
Creep in our ears; soft stillness and the night
Become the touches of sweet harmony.
Sit, Jessica. Look how the floor of heaven
Is thick inlaid with patines of bright gold;
There's not the smallest orb which thou be-
    hold'st
But in his motion like an angel sings,
Still quiring to the young-ey'd cherubims:
Such harmony is in immortal souls;
But, whilst this muddy vesture of decay
Doth grossly close it in, we cannot hear it.—

Enter Musicians.

Come, ho, and wake Diana with a hymn;
With sweetest touches pierce your mistress' ear,
And draw her home with music.   [*Music*.
Jes. I am never merry when I hear sweet
    music.
Lor. The reason is, your spirits are attentive:
For do but note a wild and wanton herd,
Or race of youthful and unhandled colts,

Fetching mad bounds, bellowing, and neighing
    loud,
Which is the hot condition of their blood—
If they but hear perchance a trumpet sound,
Or any air of music touch their ears,
You shall perceive them make a mutual stand,
Their savage eyes turn'd to a modest gaze
By the sweet power of music; therefore the poet
Did feign that Orpheus drew trees, stones, and
    floods;
Since naught so stockish, hard, and full of rage
But music for the time doth change his nature.
The man that hath no music in himself,
Nor is not mov'd with concord of sweet sounds,
Is fit for treasons, stratagems, and spoils;
The motions of his spirit are dull as night,
And his affections dark as Erebus:
Let no such man be trusted.—Mark the music.

Enter PORTIA *and* NERISSA, *at a distance*.

Por. That light we see is burning in my hall:
How far that little candle throws his beams!
So shines a good deed in a naughty world.
Ner. When the moon shone we did not see
    the candle.
Por. So doth the greater glory dim the less:
A substitute shines brightly as a king
Until a king be by; and then his state
Empties itself, as doth an inland brook
Into the main of waters. Music! hark!
Ner. It is your music, madam, of the house.
Por. Nothing is good, I see, without respect;
Methinks it sounds much sweeter than by day.
Ner. Silence bestows that virtue on it, madam.
Por. The crow doth sing as sweetly as the
    lark
When neither in attended; and, I think,
The nightingale, if she should sing by day,
When every goose is cackling, would be thought
No better a musician than the wren.
How many things by season season'd are
To their right praise and true perfection!—
Peace, ho! the moon sleeps with Endymion,
And would not be awaked!   [*Music ceases*.
Lor.   That is the voice,
Or I am much deceived, of Portia.
Por. He knows me, as the blind man knows
    the cuckoo,
By the bad voice.
Lor.   Dear lady, welcome home.
Por. We have been praying for our husbands'
    welfare,
Which speed, we hope, the better for our words.
Are they return'd?
Lor.   Madam, they are not yet;
But there is come a messenger before,
To signify their coming.
Por.   Go in, Nerissa,
Give order to my servants that they take
No note at all of our being absent hence;—
Nor you, Lorenzo;—Jessica, nor you.
                          [*A tucket sounds*.
Lor. Your husband is at hand, I hear his
    trumpet:

We are no tell-tales, madam; fear you not.
  Por. This night methinks is but the daylight
      sick—
It looks a little paler; 'tis a day
Such as the day is when the sun is hid.

Enter BASSANIO, ANTONIO, GRATIANO *and
      their followers.*

  Bass. We should hold day with the Antipodes
If you would walk in absence of the sun.
  Por. Let me give light, but let me not be
      light;
For a light wife doth make a heavy husband,
And never be Bassanio so for me;   [lord.
But God sort all!—you are welcome home, my
  Bass. I thank you, madam; give welcome to
      my friend.—
This is the man; this is Antonio,
To whom I am so infinitely bound.   [to him,
  Por. You should in all sense be much bound
For, as I hear, he was much bound for you.
  Ant. No more than I am well acquitted of.
  Por. Sir, you are very welcome to our house:
It must appear in other ways than words,
Therefore, I scant this breathing courtesy.
            [GRA. *and* NER. *seem to talk apart.*
  Gra. By yonder moon, I swear you do me
      wrong;
In faith, I gave it to the judge's clerk:
Would he were gelt that had it, for my part,
Since you do take it, love, so much at heart.
  Por. A quarrel, ho, already? what's the
      matter?
  Gra. About a hoop of gold, a paltry ring
That she did give me; whose posy was,
For all the world, like cutler's poetry
Upon a knife, *Love me, and leave me not.*
  Ner. What, talk you of the posy, or the
      value?
You swore to me, when I did give it you,
That you would wear it till your hour of death;
And that it should lie with you in your grave:
Though not for me, yet for your vehement
      oaths
You should have been respective, and have
      kept it.
Gave it a judge's clerk!—no, God's my judge,
The clerk will ne'er wear hair on's face that had
      it.
  Gra. He will, an if he live to be a man.
  Ner. Ay, if a woman live to be a man.
  Gra. Now, by this hand, I gave it to a
      youth,—
A kind of boy; a little scrubbed boy
No higher than thyself, the judge's clerk;
A prating boy that begg'd it as a fee;
I could not for my heart deny it him.
  Por. You were to blame, I must be plain
      with you,
To part so slightly with your wife's first gift;
A thing stuck on with oaths upon your finger,
And so riveted with faith unto your flesh.
I gave my love a ring, and made him swear
Never to part with it, and here he stands;

I dare be sworn for him, he would not leave it
Nor pluck it from his finger for the wealth
That the world masters. Now, in faith,
      Gratiano,
You gave your wife too unkind a cause of grief;
An 'twere to me, I should be mad at it.   [off,
  Bass. Why, I were best to cut my left hand
And swear I lost the ring defending it. [*Aside.*
  Gra. My Lord Bassanio gave his ring away
Unto the judge that begg'd it, and, indeed,
Deserv'd it too; and then the boy, his clerk,
That took some pains in writing, he begg'd
      mine:
And neither man nor master would take aught
But the two rings.
  Por.   What ring gave you, my lord?
Not that, I hope, which you receiv'd of me.
  Bass. If I could add a lie unto a fault
I would deny it; but you see my finger
Hath not the ring upon it; it is gone.
  Por. Even so void is your false heart of truth.
By heaven, I will ne'er come in your bed
Until I see the ring.
  Ner.   Nor I in yours
Till I again see mine.
  Bass.   Sweet Portia,
If you did know to whom I gave the ring,
If you did know for whom I gave the ring,
And would conceive for what I gave the ring,
And how unwillingly I left the ring,
When naught would be accepted but the ring,
You would abate the strength of your dis-
      pleasure.
  Por. If you had known the virtue of the ring,
Or half her worthiness that gave the ring,
Or your own honour to contain the ring,
You would not then have parted with the ring.
What man is there so much unreasonable,
If you had pleas'd to have defended it
With any terms of zeal, wanted the modesty
To urge the thing held as a ceremony?
Nerissa teaches me what to believe;
I'll die for't, but some woman had the ring.
  Bass. No, by mine honour, madam, by my
      soul,
No woman had it, but a civil doctor,
Which did refuse three thousand ducats of me,
And begg'd the ring; the which I did deny him,
And suffer'd him to go displeas'd away;
Even he that had held up the very life
Of my dear friend. What should I say, sweet
      lady?
I was enforc'd to send it after him;
I was beset with shame and courtesy:
My honour would not let ingratitude
So much besmear it. Pardon me, good lady;
For by these blessed candles of the night,
Had you been there, I think you would have
      begg'd
The ring of me to give the worthy doctor.
  Por. Let not that doctor e'er come near my
      house:
Since he hath got the jewel that I lov'd,
And that which you did swear to keep for me,

I will become as liberal as you;
I'll not deny him anything I have,
No, not my body, nor my husband's bed:
Know him I shall, I am well sure of it:
Lie not a night from home; watch me like
     Argus:
If you do not, if I be left alone,
Now, by mine honour, which is yet mine own,
I'll have that doctor for my bedfellow.

    Ner. And I his clerk; therefore be well ad-
     vis'd
How you do leave me to mine own protection.

    Gra. Well, do you so: let not me take him
     then;
For, if I do, I'll mar the young clerk's pen.

    Ant. I am the unhappy subject of these
     quarrels.   [notwithstanding.

    Por. Sir, grieve not you; you are welcome

    Bass. Portia, forgive me this enforced wrong;
And, in the hearing of these many friends,
I swear to thee, even by thine own fair eyes,
Wherein I see myself,——

    Por.   Mark you but that!
In both my eyes he doubly sees himself:
In each eye one:—swear by your double self,
And there's an oath of credit.

    Bass.   Nay, but hear me:
Pardon this fault, and by my soul I swear,
I never more will break an oath with thee.

    Ant. I once did lend my body for his wealth;
Which, but for him that had your husband's
     ring,
Had quite miscarried: I dare be bound again,
My soul upon the forfeit, that your lord
Will never more break faith advisedly.

    Por. Then you shall be his surety: give him
     this;
And bid him keep it better than the other.

    Ant. Here, Lord Bassanio; swear to keep
     this ring.

    Bass. By heaven, it is the same I gave the
     doctor!

    Por. I had it of him: pardon me, Bassanio;
For by this ring the doctor lay with me.

    Ner. And pardon me, my gentle Gratiano;
For that same scrubbed boy, the doctor's clerk,
In lieu of this, last night did lie with me.

    Gra. Why, this is like the mending of high-
     ways
In summer, where the ways are fair enough:
What! are we cuckolds ere we have deserved it?

    Por. Speak not so grossly.—You are all
     amaz'd:
Here is a letter, read it at your leisure;
It comes from Padua, from Bellario:
There you shall find that Portia was the doctor;
Nerissa there, her clerk: Lorenzo here
Shall witness I set forth as soon as you,
And but even now return'd; I have not yet
Enter'd my house.—Antonio, you are welcome;
And I have better news in store for you
Than you expect; unseal this letter soon;
There you shall find three of your argosies
Are richly come to harbour suddenly:
You shall not know by what strange accident
I chanced on this letter.

    Ant.   I am dumb.

    Bass. Were you the doctor; and I knew you
     not?   [cuckold?

    Gra. Were you the clerk that is to make me

    Ner. Ay, but the clerk that never means to
     do it,
Unless he live until he be a man.   [fellow;

    Bass. Sweet doctor, you shall be my bed-
When I am absent, then lie with my wife.

    Ant. Sweet lady, you have given me life and
     living;
For here I read for certain that my ships
Are safely come to road.

    Por.   How now, Lorenzo?
My clerk hath some good comforts too for you.

    Ner. Ay, and I'll give them him without a
     fee.—
There do I give to you and Jessica,
From the rich Jew, a special deed of gift,
After his death, of all he dies possess'd of.

    Lor. Fair ladies, you drop manna in the way
Of starved people.

    Por.   It is almost morning,
And yet, I am sure, you are not satisfied
Of these events at full. Let us go in;
And charge us there upon inter'gatories,
And we will answer all things faithfully.

    Gra. Let it be so:—the first inter'gatory
That my Nerissa shall be sworn on is,
Whether till the next night she had rather stay,
Or go to bed now, being two hours to day:
But were the day come, I should wish it dark,
That I were couching with the doctor's clerk.
Well, while I live, I'll fear no other thing
So sore as keeping safe Nerissa's ring.

                  [*Exeunt.*

AS YOU LIKE IT

DRAMATIS PERSONÆ

DUKE, *living in exile.*
FREDERICK, *Brother to the* DUKE, *and Usurper of his Dominions.*
AMIENS, } *Lords attending upon the* DUKE
JAQUES, } *in his Banishment.*
LE BEAU, *a Courtier attending upon* FREDERICK.
CHARLES, *his Wrestler.*
OLIVER,
JAQUES, } *Sons of* SIR ROWLAND DE BOIS.
ORLANDO,
ADAM,
DENNIS, } *Servants to* OLIVER.
TOUCHSTONE, *a Clown.*

SIR OLIVER MARTEXT, *a Vicar.*
CORIN, } *Shepherds.*
SILVIUS, }
WILLIAM, *a Country Fellow, in love with* AUDREY.
A Person representing HYMEN.

ROSALIND, *Daughter to the banished* DUKE.
CELIA, *Daughter to* FREDERICK.
PHEBE, *a Shepherdess.*
AUDREY, *a Country Wench.*

Lords *belonging to the two Dukes;* Pages, Foresters, *and other* Attendants.

The SCENE *lies first near* OLIVER'S *House; afterwards partly in the Usurper's Court and partly in the Forest of* ARDEN.

ACT I.

SCENE I.—*An Orchard near* OLIVER'S *House.*

Enter ORLANDO *and* ADAM.

Orl. As I remember, Adam, it was upon this fashion,—bequeathed me by will but poor a thousand crowns, and as thou say'st, charged my brother, on his blessing, to breed me well: and there begins my sadness. My brother Jaques he keeps at school, and report speaks goldenly of his profit: for my part, he keeps me rustically at home, or, to speak more properly, stays me here at home unkept: for call you that keeping for a gentleman of my birth that differs not from the stalling of an ox? His horses are bred better; for, besides that they are fair with their feeding, they are taught their manage, and to that end riders dearly hired: but I, his brother, gain nothing under him but growth; for the which his animals on his dunghills are as much bound to him as I. Besides this nothing that he so plentifully gives me, the something that nature gave me, his countenance seems to take from me: he lets me feed with his hinds, bars me the place of a brother, and as much as in him lies, mines my gentility with my education. This is it, Adam, that grieves me; and the spirit of my father, which I think is within me, begins to mutiny against this servitude: I will no longer endure it, though yet I know no wise remedy how to avoid it.

Adam. Yonder comes my master, your brother.

Orl. Go apart, Adam, and thou shalt hear how he will shake me up. [ADAM *retires.*

Enter OLIVER.

Oli. Now, sir! what make you here?

Orl. Nothing: I am not taught to make anything.

Oli. What mar you then, sir?

Orl. Marry, sir, I am helping you to mar that which God made, a poor unworthy brother of yours, with idleness.

Oli. Marry, sir, be better employed, and be naught awhile.

Orl. Shall I keep your hogs, and eat husks with them? What prodigal portion have I spent that I should come to such penury?

Oli. Know you where you are, sir?

Orl. O, sir, very well: here in your orchard.

Oli. Know you before whom, sir?

Orl. Ay, better than him I am before knows me. I know you are my eldest brother: and in the gentle condition of blood you should so know me. The courtesy of nations allows you my better, in that you are the first-born; but the same tradition takes not away my blood, were there twenty brothers betwixt us: I have as much of my father in me as you; albeit, I confess, your coming before me is nearer to his reverence.

Oli. What, boy!

Orl. Come, come, elder brother, you are too young in this.

Oli. Wilt thou lay hands on me, villain?

Orl. I am no villain: I am the youngest son of Sir Rowland de Bois: he was my father; and he is thrice a villain that says such a father begot villains. Wert thou not my brother I would not take this hand from thy throat till this other had pulled out thy tongue for saying so: thou hast railed on thyself.

Adam. [*Coming forward.*] Sweet masters, be patient; for your father's remembrance, be at accord.

Oli. Let me go, I say.

Orl. I will not, till I please: you shall hear me. My father charged you in his will to give me good education: you have trained me like a peasant, obscuring and hiding from me all gentleman-like qualities: the spirit of my father grows strong in me, and I will no longer endure it: therefore, allow me such exercises as may become a gentleman, or give me the poor allottery my father left me by testament: with that I will go buy my fortunes.

Oli. And what wilt thou do? beg, when that is spent? Well, sir, get you in: I will not long be troubled with you: you shall have some part of your will: I pray you, leave me.

Orl. I will no further offend you than becomes me for my good.

Oli. Get you with him, you old dog.

Adam. Is old dog my reward? Most true, I have lost my teeth in your service.—God be with my old master! he would not have spoke such a word.   [*Exeunt* ORLANDO *and* ADAM.

Oli. Is it even so? begin you to grow upon me? I will physic your rankness, and yet give no thousand crowns neither. Holla, Dennis!

Enter DENNIS.

Den. Calls your worship?

Oli. Was not Charles, the duke's wrestler, here to speak with me?

Den. So please you, he is here at the door, and importunes access to you.

Oli. Call him in. [*Exit* DENNIS.]—'Twill be a good way, and to-morrow the wrestling is.

Enter CHARLES.

Cha. Good morrow to your worship.

Oli. Good Monsieur Charles!—what's the new news at the new court?

Cha. There's no news at the court, sir, but the old news, that is, the old duke is banished by his younger brother the new duke; and three or four loving lords have put themselves into voluntary exile with him, whose lands and revenues enrich the new duke; therefore he gives them good leave to wander.

Oli. Can you tell if Rosalind, the duke's daughter, be banished with her father?

Cha. O no; for the duke's daughter, her cousin, so loves her,—being ever from their cradles bred together,—that she would have followed her exile, or have died to stay behind her. She is at the court, and no less beloved of her uncle than his own daughter; and never two ladies loved as they do.

Oli. Where will the old duke live?

Cha. They say he is already in the forest of Arden, and a many merry men with him; and there they live like the old Robin Hood of England: they say many young gentlemen flock to him every day, and fleet the time carelessly, as they did in the golden world.

Oli. What, you wrestle to-morrow before the new duke?

Cha. Marry, do I, sir; and I came to acquaint you with a matter. I am given, sir, secretly to understand that your younger brother, Orlando, hath a disposition to come in disguis'd against me to try a fall. To-morrow, sir, I wrestle for my credit; and he that escapes me without some broken limb shall acquit him well. Your brother is but young and tender; and, for your love, I would be loath to foil him, as I must for my own honour, if he come in: therefore, out of my love to you, I came hither to acquaint you withal; that either you might stay him from his intendment, or brook such disgrace well as he shall run into; in that it is a thing of his own search, and altogether against my will.

Oli. Charles, I thank thee for thy love to me, which thou shalt find I will most kindly requite. I had myself notice of my brother's purpose herein, and have by underhand means laboured to dissuade him from it; but he is resolute. I'll tell thee, Charles, it is the stubbornest young fellow of France; full of ambition, an envious emulator of every man's good parts, a secret and villanous contriver against me his natural brother; therefore use thy discretion: I had as lief thou didst break his neck as his finger. And thou wert best look to't; for if thou dost him any slight disgrace, or if he do not mightily grace himself on thee, he will practise against thee by poison, entrap thee by some treacherous device, and never leave thee till he hath ta'en thy life by some indirect means or other: for, I assure thee, and almost with tears I speak it, there is not one so young and so villanous this day living. I speak but brotherly of him; but should I anatomize him to thee as he is, I must blush and weep, and thou must look pale and wonder.

Cha. I am heartily glad I came hither to you. If he comes to-morrow I'll give him his payment. If ever he go alone again I'll never wrestle for prize more: and so, God keep your worship!   [*Exit.*

Oli. Farewell, good Charles.—Now will I stir this gamester: I hope I shall see an end of him; for my soul, yet I know not why, hates nothing more than he. Yet he's gentle; never schooled and yet learned; full of noble device of all sorts enchantingly beloved; and, indeed, so much in the heart of the world, and especially of my own people, who best know him, that I am altogether misprised: but it shall not be so long; this wrestler shall clear all: nothing remains but that I kindle the boy thither, which now I'll go about.   [*Exit.*

SCENE II.—*A Lawn before the* DUKE's *Palace*

Enter ROSALIND and CELIA.

Cel. I pray thee, Rosalind, sweet my coz, be merry.

Ros. Dear Celia, I show more mirth than I am mistress of; and would you yet I were merrier? Unless you could teach me to forget a banished father, you must not learn me how to remember any extraordinary pleasure.

Cel. Herein I see thou lovest me not with the full weight that I love thee; if my uncle, thy banished father, had banished thy uncle, the duke my father, so thou hadst been still with me, I could have taught my love to take thy father for mine; so wouldst thou, if the truth of thy love to me were so righteously tempered as mine is to thee.

Ros. Well, I will forget the condition of my estate, to rejoice in yours.

Cel. You know my father hath no child but I, nor none is like to have; and, truly, when he dies thou shalt be his heir: for what he hath taken away from thy father perforce, I will render thee again in affection: by mine honour, I will: and when I break that oath, let me turn monster; therefore, my sweet Rose, my dear Rose, be merry.

Ros. From henceforth I will, coz, and devise sports: let me see; what think you of falling in love?

Cel. Marry, I pr'ythee, do, to make sport withal: but love no man in good earnest; nor no further in sport neither than with safety of a pure blush thou mayst in honour come off again.

Ros. What shall be our sport, then?

Cel. Let us sit and mock the good housewife Fortune from her wheel, that her gifts may henceforth be bestowed equally.

Ros. I would we could do so; for her benefits are mightily misplaced; and the bountiful blind woman doth most mistake in her gifts to women.

Cel. 'Tis true: for those that she makes fair she scarce makes honest; and those that she makes honest she makes very ill-favouredly.

Ros. Nay; now thou goest from fortune's office to nature's: fortune reigns in gifts of the world, not in the lineaments of nature.

Cel. No; when nature hath made a fair creature may she not by fortune fall into the fire?—Though nature hath given us wit to flout at fortune, hath not fortune sent in this fool to cut off the argument?

Enter TOUCHSTONE.

Ros. Indeed, there is fortune too hard for nature, when fortune makes nature's natural the cutter off of nature's wit.

Cel. Peradventure this is not fortune's work neither, but nature's, who perceiveth our natural wits too dull to reason of such goddesses, and hath sent this natural for our whetstone: for always the dulness of the fool is the whetstone of the wits.—How now, wit? whither wander you?

Touch. Mistress, you must come away to your father.

Cel. Were you made the messenger?

Touch. No, by mine honour; but I was bid to come for you.

Ros. Where learned you that oath, fool?

Touch. Of a certain knight that swore by his honour they were good pancakes, and swore by his honour the mustard was naught; now, I'll stand to it, the pancakes were naught and the mustard was good: and yet was not the knight forsworn.

Cel. How prove you that, in the great heap of your knowledge?

Ros. Ay, marry; now unmuzzle your wisdom.

Touch. Stand you both forth now: stroke your chins, and swear by your beards that I am a knave.

Cel. By our beards, if we had them, thou art.

Touch. By my knavery, if I had it, then I were: but if you swear by that that is not, you are not forsworn: no more was this knight, swearing by his honour, for he never had any; or if he had, he had sworn it away before ever he saw those pancakes or that mustard.

Cel. Pr'ythee, who is't that thou mean'st?

Touch. One that old Frederick, your father, loves.

Cel. My father's love is enough to honour him enough: speak no more of him: you'll be whipp'd for taxation one of these days.

Touch. The more pity that fools may not speak wisely what wise men do foolishly.

Cel. By my troth, thou say'st true: for since the little wit that fools have was silenced, the little foolery that wise men have makes a great show. Here comes Monsieur Le Beau.

Ros. With his mouth full of news.

Cel. Which he will put on us as pigeons feed their young.

Ros. Then shall we be news-crammed.

Cel. All the better; we shall be the more marketable.

Enter LE BEAU.

Bon jour, Monsieur Le Beau. What's the news?

Le Beau. Fair princess, you have lost much good sport.

Cel. Sport! of what colour?

Le Beau. What colour, madam? How shall I answer you?

Ros. As wit and fortune will.

Touch. Or as the destinies decree.

Cel. Well said; that was laid on with a trowel.

Touch. Nay, if I keep not my rank,—

Ros. Thou loosest thy old smell.

Le Beau. You amaze me, ladies: I would have told you of good wrestling, which you have lost the sight of.

Ros. Yet tell us the manner of the wrestling.

Le Beau. I will tell you the beginning, and, if it please your ladyships, you may see the end; for the best is yet to do; and here, where you are, they are coming to perform it.

Cel. Well,—the beginning, that is dead and buried.

Le Beau. There comes an old man and his three sons,—

Cel. I could match this beginning with an old tale.

Le Beau. Three proper young men, of excellent growth and presence, with bills on their necks,—

Ros. Be it known unto all men by these presents,—

Le Beau. The eldest of the three wrestled with Charles, the duke's wrestler; which Charles in a moment threw him, and broke three of his ribs, that there is little hope of life in him: so he served the second, and so the third. Yonder they lie; the poor old man, their father, making such pitiful dole over them that all the beholders take his part with weeping.

Ros. Alas!

Touch. But what is the sport, monsieur, that the ladies have lost?

Le Beau. Why, this that I speak of.

Touch. Thus men may grow wiser every day! It is the first time that ever I heard breaking of ribs was sport for ladies.

Cel. Or I, I promise thee.

Ros. But is there any else longs to see this broken music in his sides? is there yet another dotes upon rib-breaking?—Shall we see this wrestling, cousin?

Le Beau. You must, if you stay here: for here is the place appointed for the wrestling, and they are ready to perform it.

Cel. Yonder, sure, they are coming: let us now stay and see it.

Flourish. Enter Duke Frederick, Lords, Orlando, Charles, *and* Attendants.

Duke F. Come on; since the youth will not be entreated, his own peril on his forwardness.

Ros. Is yonder the man?

Le Beau. Even he, madam.

Cel. Alas, he is too young: yet he looks successfully.

Duke F. How now, daughter, and cousin? are you crept hither to see the wrestling?

Ros. Ay, my liege: so please you give us leave.

Duke F. You will take little delight in it, I can tell you, there is such odds in the men. In pity of the challenger's youth I would fain dissuade him, but he will not be entreated. Speak to him, ladies; see if you can move him.

Cel. Call him hither, good Monsieur Le Beau.

Duke F. Do so; I'll not be by.

[Duke F. *goes apart.*

Le Beau. Monsieur the challenger, the princesses call for you.

Orl. I attend them with all respect and duty.

Ros. Young man, have you challenged Charles the wrestler?

Orl. No, fair princess; he is the general challenger: I come but in, as others do, to try with him the strength of my youth.

Cel. Young gentleman, your spirits are too bold for your years. You have seen cruel proof of this man's strength: if you saw yourself with your eyes, or knew yourself with your judgment, the fear of your adventure would counsel you to a more equal enterprise. We pray you, for your own sake, to embrace your own safety, and give over this attempt.

Ros. Do, young sir; your reputation shall not therefore be misprised: we will make it our suit to the duke that the wrestling might not go forward.

Orl. I beseech you, punish me not with your hard thoughts: wherein I confess me much guilty, to deny so fair and excellent ladies anything. But let your fair eyes and gentle wishes go with me to my trial: wherein if I be foiled, there is but one shamed that was never gracious; if killed, but one dead that is willing to be so: I shall do my friends no wrong, for I have none to lament me: the world no injury, for in it I have nothing; only in the world I fill up a place, which may be better supplied when I have made it empty.

Ros. The little strength that I have, I would it were with you.

Cel. And mine to eke out hers.

Ros. Fare you well. Pray heaven, I be deceived in you!

Cel. Your heart's desires be with you.

Cha. Come, where is this young gallant that is so desirous to lie with his mother earth?

Orl. Ready, sir; but his will hath in it a more modest working.

Duke F. You shall try but one fall.

Cha. No; I warrant your grace, you shall not entreat him to a second, that have so mightily persuaded him from a first.

Orl. You mean to mock me after; you should not have mocked me before: but come your ways.

Ros. Now, Hercules be thy speed, young man!

Cel. I would I were invisible, to catch the strong fellow by the leg.

[Charles *and* Orlando *wrestle.*

Ros. O excellent young man!

Cel. If I had a thunderbolt in mine eye, I can tell who should down.

[Charles *is thrown. Shout.*

Duke F. No more, no more.

Orl. Yes, I beseech your grace; I am not yet well breathed.

Duke F. How dost thou, Charles?

Le Beau. He cannot speak, my lord.

Duke F. Bear him away.

[Charles *is borne out.*

What is thy name, young man?

Orl. Orlando, my liege; the youngest son of Sir Rowland de Bois. [man else.

Duke F. I would thou hadst been son to some
The world esteem'd thy father honourable,
But I did find him still mine enemy: [deed
Thou shouldst have better pleas'd me with this
Hadst thou descended from another house.
But fare thee well; thou art a gallant youth;

I would thou hadst told me of another father.
  [*Exeunt* DUKE F., Train, *and* LE BEAU.
  Cel. Were I my father, coz, would I do this?
  Orl. I am more proud to be Sir Rowland's
          son,
His youngest son;—and would not change that
    calling
To be adopted heir to Frederick.
  Ros. My father loved Sir Rowland as his
          soul,
And all the world was of my father's mind:
Had I before known this young man his son,
I should have given him tears unto entreaties,
Ere he should thus have ventur'd.
  Cel.   Gentle cousin,
Let us go thank him, and encourage him:
My father's rough and envious disposition
Sticks me at heart.—Sir, you have well de-
    serv'd:
If you do keep your promises in love
But justly, as you have exceeded promise,
Your mistress shall be happy.
  Ros.   Gentleman,
    [*Giving him a chain from her neck.*
Wear this for me; one out of suits with fortune,
That could give more, but that her hand lacks
    means.—
Shall we go, coz?
  Cel.   Ay.—Fare you well, fair gentleman.
  Orl. Can I not say, I thank you? My better
          parts   [stands up
Are all thrown down; and that which here
Is but a quintain, a mere lifeless block.
  Ros. He calls us back: my pride fell with my
          fortunes:
I'll ask him what he would.—Did you call,
    sir?—
Sir, you have wrestled well, and overthrown
More than your enemies.
  Cel.   Will you go, coz?
  Ros. Have with you.—Fare you well.
          [*Exeunt* ROSALIND *and* CELIA.
  Orl. What passion hangs these weights upon
          my tongue?
I cannot speak to her, yet she urg'd conference.
O poor Orlando! thou art overthrown:
Or Charles, or something weaker, masters thee.

Re-enter LE BEAU.

Le Beau. Good sir, I do in friendship counsel
          you.
To leave this place. Albeit you have deserv'd
High commendation, true applause, and love,
Yet such is now the duke's condition,
That he misconstrues all that you have done.
The duke is humorous; what he is, indeed,
More suits you to conceive than I to speak of.
  Orl. I thank you, sir: and pray you, tell me
          this;
Which of the two was daughter of the duke
That here was at the wrestling?   [manners;
  Le Beau. Neither his daughter, if we judge by
But yet, indeed, the smaller is his daughter:

The other is daughter to the banish'd duke,
And here detain'd by her usurping uncle,
To keep his daughter company; whose loves
Are dearer than the natural bond of sisters.
But I can tell you that of late this duke
Hath ta'en displeasure 'gainst his gentle niece,
Grounded upon no other argument
But that the people praise her for her virtues
And pity her for her good father's sake;
And, on my life, his malice 'gainst the lady
Will suddenly break forth.—Sir, fare you well!
Hereafter, in a better world than this,
I shall desire more love and knowledge of you.
  Orl. I rest much bounden to you: fare you
          well!   [*Exit* LE BEAU.
Thus must I from the smoke into the smother;
From tyrant duke unto a tyrant brother:—
But heavenly Rosalind!   [*Exit.*

SCENE III.—*A Room in the Palace.*

Enter CELIA *and* ROSALIND.

  Cel. Why, cousin; why, Rosalind;—Cupid
have mercy!—Not a word?
  Ros. Not one to throw at a dog.
  Cel. No, thy words are too precious to be
cast away upon curs, throw some of them at
me; come, lame me with reasons.
  Ros. Then there were two cousins laid up;
when the one should be lamed with reasons and
the other mad without any.
  Cel. But is all this for your father?
  Ros. No, some of it is for my father's child.
O, how full of briers is this working-day world!
  Cel. They are but burs, cousin, thrown upon
thee in holiday foolery; if we walk not in the
trodden paths our very petticoats will catch
them.
  Ros. I could shake them off my coat: these
burs are in my heart.
  Cel. Hem them away.   [have him.
  Ros. I would try, if I could cry hem and
  Cel. Come, come, wrestle with thy affections.
  Ros. O, they take the part of a better
wrestler than myself.
  Cel. O, a good wish upon you! you will try
in time, in despite of a fall.—But, turning these
jests out of service, let us talk in good earnest:
is it possible, on such a sudden, you should fall
into so strong a liking with old Sir Rowland's
youngest son?
  Ros. The duke my father loved his father
dearly.
  Cel. Doth it therefore ensue that you should
love his son dearly? By this kind of chase I
should hate him, for my father hated his father
dearly; yet I hate not Orlando.
  Ros. No, 'faith, hate him not, for my sake.
  Cel. Why should I not? doth he not deserve
well?
  Ros. Let me love him for that; and do you
love him because I do.—Look, here comes the
duke.
  Cel. With his eyes full of anger.

Enter DUKE FREDERICK, *with* Lords.

Duke F. Mistress, despatch you with your safest haste,
And get you from our court.
    Ros.   Me, uncle?
    Duke F.   You, cousin:
Within these ten days if that thou be'st found
So near our public court as twenty miles,
Thou diest for it.
    Ros.   I do beseech your grace,   [me:
Let me the knowledge of my fault bear with
If with myself I hold intelligence,
Or have acquaintance with mine own desires;
If that I do not dream, or be not frantic,—
As I do trust I am not,—then, dear uncle,
Never so much as in a thought unborn
Did I offend your highness.
    Duke F.   Thus do all traitors;
If their purgation did consist in words,
They are as innocent as grace itself:—
Let it suffice thee that I trust thee not.
    Ros. Yet your mistrust cannot make me a
        traitor:
Tell me whereon the likelihood depends.
    Duke F. Thou art thy father's daughter;
        there's enough.   [dukedom;
    Ros. So was I when your highness took his
So was I when your highness banish'd him:
Treason is not inherited, my lord:
Or, if we did derive it from our friends,
What's that to me? my father was no traitor!
Then, good my liege, mistake me not so much
To think my poverty is treacherous.
    Cel. Dear sovereign, hear me speak.   [sake,
    Duke F. Ay, Celia: we stay'd her for your
Else had she with her father rang'd along.
    Cel. I did not then entreat to have her stay;
It was your pleasure, and your own remorse:
I was too young that time to value her;
But now I know her: if she be a traitor,
Why so am I: we still have slept together,
Rose at an instant, learn'd, play'd, eat together;
And wheresoe'er we went, like Juno's swans,
Still we went coupled and inseparable.
    Duke F. She is too subtle for thee; and her
        smoothness,
Her very silence, and her patience
Speak to the people, and they pity her.
Thou art a fool: she robs thee of thy name;
And thou wilt show more bright and seem more
        virtuous
When she is gone: then open not thy lips;
Firm and irrevocable is my doom
Which I have pass'd upon her;—she is banish'd.
    Cel. Pronounce that sentence, then, on me,
        my liege:
I cannot live out of her company.   [yourself:
    Duke F. You are a fool.—You, niece, provide
If you outstay the time, upon mine honour,
And in the greatness of my word, you die.
            [*Exeunt* DUKE F. *and* Lords.
    Cel. O my poor Rosalind! whither wilt thou
        go?

Wilt thou change fathers? I will give thee mine.
I charge thee, be not thou more griev'd than I
        am.
    Ros. I have more cause.
    Cel.   Thou hast not, cousin;
Pr'ythee, be cheerful: know'st thou not the
        duke
Hath banish'd me, his daughter?
    Ros.   That he hath not.
    Cel. No! hath not? Rosalind lacks, then, the
        love
Which teacheth thee that thou and I am one:
Shall we be sunder'd? shall we part, sweet girl?
No; let my father seek another heir.
Therefore devise with me how we may fly,
Whither to go, and what to bear with us:
And do not seek to take your change upon you,
To bear your griefs yourself, and leave me out;
For, by this heaven, now at our sorrows pale,
Say what thou canst, I'll go along with thee.
    Ros. Why, whither shall we go?
    Cel. To seek my uncle in the forest of Arden.
    Ros. Alas! what danger will it be to us,
Maids as we are, to travel forth so far?
Beauty provoketh thieves sooner than gold.
    Cel. I'll put myself in poor and mean attire,
And with a kind of umber smirch my face;
The like do you; so shall we pass along,
And never stir assailants.
    Ros.   Were it not better,
Because that I am more than common tall,
That I did suit me all points like a man?
A gallant curtle-axe upon my thigh,
A boar spear in my hand; and,—in my heart
Lie there what hidden woman's fear there will—
We'll have a swashing and a martial outside,
As many other mannish cowards have
That do outface it with their semblances.
    Cel. What shall I call thee when thou art a
        man?   [own page,
    Ros. I'll have no worse a name than Jove's
And, therefore, look you call me Ganymede.
But what will you be call'd?   [state:
    Cel. Something that hath a reference to my
No longer Celia, but Aliena.
    Ros. But, cousin, what if we assay'd to steal
The clownish fool out of your father's court?
Would he not be a comfort to our travel?
    Cel. He'll go along o'er the wide world with
        me;
Leave me alone to woo him. Let's away,
And get our jewels and our wealth together;
Devise the fittest time and safest way
To hide us from pursuit that will be made
After flight. Now go we in content
To liberty, and not to banishment.   [*Exeunt.*

ACT II.

SCENE I.—*The Forest of Arden.*

Enter DUKE *Senior,* AMIENS, *and other* Lords,
in the dress of Foresters.

    Duke S. Now, my co-mates and brothers in
        exile,

Hath not old custom made this life more sweet
Than that of painted pomp? Are not these woods
More free from peril than the envious court?
Here feel we but the penalty of Adam,—
The seasons' difference: as the icy fang
And churlish chiding of the winter's wind,
Which when it bites and blows upon my body,
Even till I shrink with cold, I smile and say,
This is no flattery: these are counsellors
That feelingly persuade me what I am.
Sweet are the uses of adversity;
Which, like the toad, ugly and venomous,
Wears yet a precious jewel in his head;
And this our life, exempt from public haunt,
Finds tongues in trees, books in the running brooks,
Sermons in stones, and good in everything.
I would not change it.
　　Ami. Happy is your grace,
That can translate the stubbornness of fortune
Into so quiet and so sweet a style.　　　[son?
　　Duke S. Come, shall we go and kill us veni-
And yet it irks me, the poor dappled fools,
Being native burghers of this desert city,
Should, in their own confines, with forked heads
Have their round haunches gor'd.
　　1 Lord.　　　　　　　　Indeed, my lord,
The melancholy Jaques grieves at that;
And, in that kind, swears you do more usurp
Than doth your brother that hath banish'd you.
To-day my lord of Amiens and myself
Did steal behind him as he lay along
Under an oak, whose antique root peeps out
Upon the brook that brawls along this wood:
To the which place a poor sequester'd stag,
That from the hunters' aim had ta'en a hurt,
Did come to languish; and, indeed, my lord,
The wretched animal heav'd forth such groans,
That their discharge did stretch his leathern coat
Almost to bursting; and the big round tears
Cours'd one another down his innocent nose
In piteous chase: and thus the hairy fool,
Much marked of the melancholy Jaques,
Stood on the extremest verge of the swift brook,
Augmenting it with tears.
　　Duke S.　　　　　　　But what said Jaques?
Did he not moralize the spectacle?
　　1 Lord. O, yes, into a thousand similies,
First, for his weeping into the needless stream;
Poor deer, quoth he, *thou mak'st a testament
As worldlings do, giving thy sum of more
To that which had too much:* then, being there alone,
Left and abandon'd of his velvet friends;
'Tis right, quoth he; *thus misery doth part
The flux of company:* anon, a careless herd,
Full of the pasture, jumps along by him,
And never stays to greet him; *Ay,* quoth Jaques,
Sweep on, you fat and greasy citizens;

*'Tis just the fashion; wherefore do you look
Upon that poor and broken bankrupt there?*
Thus most invectively he pierceth through
The body of the country, city, court,
Yea, and of this our life: swearing that we
Are mere usurpers, tyrants, and what's worse,
To fright the animals, and to kill them up
In their assign'd and native dwelling-place.
　　Duke S. And did you leave him in this con-
templation?　　　　　　　　　[menting
　　2 Lord. We did, my lord, weeping and com-
Upon the sobbing deer.
　　Duke S.　　　　　　Show me the place:
I love to cope him in these sullen fits,
For then he's full of matter.
　　2 Lord. I'll bring you to him straight.
　　　　　　　　　　　　　　　[*Exeunt.*

SCENE II.—*A Room in the Palace.*

Enter DUKE FREDERICK, Lords, *and* Attendants.

Duke F. Can it be possible that no man saw them?
It cannot be: some villains of my court
Are of consent and sufferance in this.
　　1 Lord. I cannot hear of any that did see her.
The ladies, her attendants of her chamber,
Saw her a-bed; and in the morning early
They found the bed untreasur'd of their mis-
tress.　　　　　　　　　　　　　[so oft
　　2 Lord. My lord, the roynish clown, at whom
Your grace was wont to laugh, is also missing.
Hesperia, the princess' gentlewoman,
Confesses that she secretly o'erheard
Your daughter and her cousin much commend
The parts and graces of the wrestler
That did but lately foil the sinewy Charles;
And she believes, wherever they are gone,
That youth is surely in their company.
　　Duke F. Send to his brother; fetch that gal-
lant hither:
If he be absent, bring his brother to me,
I'll make him find him: do this suddenly;
And let not search and inquisition quail
To bring again these foolish runaways.
　　　　　　　　　　　　　　　[*Exeunt.*

SCENE III.—*Before* OLIVER'S *House.*

Enter ORLANDO *and* ADAM, *meeting.*

　　Orl. Who's there?
　　Adam. What! my young master?—O, my gentle master!
O, my sweet master! O you memory
Of old Sir Rowland! why, what make you here?
Why are you virtuous? why do people love you?
And wherefore are you gentle, strong, and valiant?
Why would you be so fond to overcome
The bony prizer of the humorous duke?
Your praise is come too swiftly home before you.
Know you not, master, to some kind of men
Their graces serve them but as enemies?
No more do yours; your virtues, gentle master,

Are sanctified and holy traitors to you.
O, what a world is this, when what is comely
Envenoms him that bears it!
  Orl. Why, what's the matter?
  Adam.   O unhappy youth,
Come not within these doors; within this roof
The enemy of all your graces lives:
Your brother,—no, no brother; yet the son—
Yet not the son; I will not call him son—
Of him I was about to call his father,—
Hath heard your praises; and this night he
    means
To burn the lodging where you used to lie.
And you within it: if he fail of that,
He will have other means to cut you off;
I overheard him and his practices.
This is no place; this house is but a butchery:
Abhor it, fear it, do not enter it.   [me go?
  Orl. Why, whither, Adam, wouldst thou have
    Adam. No matter whither, so you come not
      here.
    Orl. What, wouldst thou have me go and beg
      my food?
Or with a base and boisterous sword enforce
A thievish living on the common road?
This I must do, or know not what to do:
Yet this I will not do, do how I can:
I rather will subject me to the malice
Of a diverted blood and bloody brother.
    Adam. But do not so. I have five hundred
      crowns,
The thrifty hire I sav'd under your father,
Which I did store to be my foster-nurse
When service should in my old limbs lie lame,
And unregarded age in corners thrown;
Take that: and He that doth the ravens feed,
Yea, providently caters for the sparrow,
Be comfort to my age! Here is the gold;
All this I give you. Let me be your servant;
Though I look old, yet I am strong and lusty:
For in my youth I never did apply
Hot and rebellious liquors in my blood;
Nor did not with unbashful forehead woo
The means of weakness and debility;
Therefore my age is as a lusty winter,
Frosty, but kindly: let me go with you;
I'll do the service of a younger man
In all your business and necessities.   [pears
  Orl. O good old man; how well in thee ap-
The constant service of the antique world,
When service sweat for duty, not for meed!
Thou art not for the fashion of these times,
Where none will sweat but for promotion;
And having that, do choke their service up
Even with the having: it is not so with thee.
But, poor old man, thou prun'st a rotten tree.
That cannot so much as a blossom yield
In lieu of all thy pains and husbandry:
But come thy ways, we'll go along together;
And ere we have thy youthful wages spent
We'll light upon some settled low content.
    Adam. Master, go on; and I will follow thee
To the last gasp, with truth and loyalty.—
From seventeen years till now almost fourscore

Here lived I, but now live here no more.
At seventeen years many their fortunes seek;
But at fourscore it is too late a week:
Yet fortune cannot recompense me better
Than to die well, and not my master's debtor.
                    [*Exeunt*.

SCENE IV.—*The Forest of Arden*.

Enter ROSALIND *in boy's clothes*, CELIA
dressed like a shepherdess, and TOUCHSTONE

  Ros. O Jupiter! how weary are my spirits!
  Touch. I care not for my spirits if my legs
were not weary.
  Ros. I could find in my heart to disgrace my
man's apparel, and to cry like a woman: but I
must comfort the weaker vessel, as doublet and
hose ought to show itself courageous to petticoat: therefore, courage, good Aliena.
  Cel. I pray you, bear with me; I can go no
farther.
  Touch. For my part, I had rather bear with
you than bear you: yet I should bear no cross if
I did bear you; for, I think, you have no money
in your purse.
  Ros. Well, this is the forest of Arden.
  Touch. Ay, now am I in Arden: the more
fool I; when I was at home I was in a better
place; but travellers must be content.
  Ros. Ay, be so, good Touchstone.—Look
you, who comes here? a young man and an old
in solemn talk.

Enter CORIN *and* SILVIUS.

  Cor. That is the way to make her scorn you
    still.   [love hcr!
  Sil. O Corin, that thou knew'st how I do
  Cor. I partly guess; for I have lov'd ere now.
  Sil. No, Corin, being old, thou canst not
    guess;
Though in thy youth thou wast as true a lover
As ever sigh'd upon a midnight pillow:
But if thy love were ever like to mine,—
As sure I think did never man love so,—
How many actions most ridiculous
Hast thou been drawn to by thy fantasy?
  Cor. Into a thousand that I have forgotten.
  Sil. O, thou didst then ne'er love so heartily:
If thou remember'st not the slightest folly
That ever love did make thee run into,
Thou hast not lov'd:
Or if thou hast not sat as I do now,
Wearying thy hearer in thy mistress' praise,
Thou hast not lov'd:
Or if thou hast not broke from company
Abruptly, as my passion now makes me,
Thou hast not lov'd: O Phebe, Phebe, Phebe!
                  [*Exit* SILVIUS.
  Ros. Alas, poor shepherd! searching of thy
    wound,
I have by hard adventure found mine own,
  Touch. And I mine. I remember, when I was
in love I broke my sword upon a stone, and bid
him take that for coming a-night to Jane Smile:

and I remember the kissing of her batlet, and the cow's dugs that her pretty chapp'd hands had milk'd: and I remember the wooing of a peascod instead of her; from whom I took two cods, and, giving her them again, said with weeping tears, *Wear these for my sake.* We that are true lovers run into strange capers; but as all is mortal in nature, so is all nature in love mortal in folly.

Ros. Thou speak'st wiser than thou art 'ware of.

Touch. Nay, I shall ne'er be 'ware of mine own wit till I break my shins against it.

Ros. Jove, Jove! this shepherd's passion Is much upon my fashion.

Touch. And mine: but it grows something stale with me.

Cel. I pray you, one of you question yond man If he for gold will give us any food: I faint almost to death.

Touch. Holla, you clown!

Ros.   Peace, fool; he's not thy kinsman.

Cor. Who calls?

Touch. Your betters, sir.

Cor. Else are they very wretched.

Ros.   Peace, I say.— Good even to you, friend.

Cor. And to you, gentle sir, and to you all.

Ros. I pr'ythee, shepherd, if that love or gold Can in this desert place buy entertainment, Bring us where we may rest ourselves and feed: Here's a young maid with travel much op-press'd, And faints for succour.

Cor.   Fair, sir, I pity her, And wish, for her sake more than for mine own, My fortunes were more able to relieve her: But I am shepherd to another man, And do not shear the fleeces that I graze: My master is of churlish disposition, And little recks to find the way to heaven By doing deeds of hospitality: Besides, his cote, his flocks, and bounds of feed Are now on sale; and at our sheepcote now, By reason of his absence, there is nothing That you will feed on; but what is, come see, And in my voice most welcome shall you be.

Ros. What is he that shall buy his flock and pasture?

Cor. That young swain that you saw here but erewhile, That little cares for buying anything.

Ros. I pray thee, if it stand with honesty, Buy thou the cottage, pasture, and the flock, And thou shalt have to pay for it of us.

Cel. And we will mend thy wages. I like this place, And willingly could waste my time in it.

Cor. Assuredly the thing is to be sold: Go with me: if you like, upon report, The soil, the profit, and this kind of life, I will your very faithful feeder be, And buy it with your gold right suddenly.

[*Exeunt.*

SCENE V.—*Another part of the Forest.*

Enter AMIENS, JAQUES, *and others.*

SONG.

Ami.   Under the greenwood tree,
            Who loves to lie with me,
            And tune his merry note
            Unto the sweet bird's throat,
      Come hither, come hither, come hither;
            Here shall he see
            No enemy.
      But winter and rough weather.

Jaq. More, more, I pr'ythee, more.

Ami. It will make you melancholy, Monsieur Jaques.

Jaq. I thank it. More, I pr'ythee, more. I can suck melancholy out of a song, as a weasel sucks eggs. More, I pr'ythee, more.

Ami. My voice is ragged; I know I cannot please you.

Jaq. I do not desire you to please me, I do desire you to sing. Come, more: another stanza: call you them stanzas?

Ami. What you will, Monsieur Jaques.

Jaq. Nay, I care not for their names; they owe me nothing. Will you sing?   [myself.

Ami. More at your request than to please

Jaq. Well then, if ever I thank any man, I'll thank you: but that they call compliment is like the encounter of two dog-apes; and when a man thanks me heartily, methinks I have given him a penny, and he renders me the beggarly thanks. Come, sing; and you that will not, hold your tongues.

Ami. Well, I'll end the song.—Sirs, cover the while: the duke will drink under this tree:—he hath been all this day to look you.

Jaq. And I have been all this day to avoid him. He is too disputable for my company: I think of as many matters as he; but I give heaven thanks, and make no boast of them. Come, warble, come.

SONG.

      Who doth ambition shun,   [*All together*
      And loves to live i' the sun,   *here.*
      Seeking the food he eats,
      And pleas'd with what he gets,
   Come hither, come hither, come hither;
      Here shall he see
      No enemy,
   But winter and rough weather.

Jaq. I'll give you a verse to this note, that I made yesterday in despite of my invention.

Ami. And I'll sing it.

Jaq. Thus it goes:

      If it do come to pass
      That any man turn ass,
      Leaving his wealth and ease
      A stubborn will to please,
   Ducdame, ducdame, ducdame;
      Here shall he see
      Gross fools as he,
   An if he will come to Ami.

Ami. What's that *ducdame?*

Jaq. 'Tis a Greek invocation, to call fools into a circle. I'll go sleep, if I can; if I cannot, I'll rail against all the first-born of Egypt.

Ami. And I'll go seek the duke; his banquet is prepared.   [*Exeunt severally.*

SCENE VI.—*Another part of the Forest.*

Enter ORLANDO *and* ADAM.

Adam. Dear master, I can go no farther: O, I die for food! Here lie I down, and measure out my grave. Farewell, kind master.

Orl. Why, how now, Adam! no greater heart in thee? Live a little; comfort a little; cheer thyself a little. If this uncouth forest yield anything savage, I will either be food for it or bring it for food to thee. Thy conceit is nearer death than thy powers. For my sake be comfortable: hold death awhile at the arm's end: I will here be with thee presently; and if I bring thee not something to eat, I'll give thee leave to die: but if thou diest before I come, thou art a mocker of my labour. Well said! thou look'st cheerily, and I'll be with thee quickly.—Yet thou liest in the bleak air: come, I will bear thee to some shelter; and thou shalt not die for lack of a dinner if there live anything in this desert. Cheerily, good Adam!   [*Exeunt.*

SCENE VII.—*Another part of the Forest.*
A Table set.

Enter DUKE *Senior,* AMIENS, *and others.*

Duke S. I think he be transform'd into a
    beast;
For I can nowhere find him like a man.

1 Lord. My lord, he is but even now gone
    hence;
Here was he merry, hearing of a song.

Duke S. If he, compact of jars, grow musi-
    cal,
We shall have shortly discord in the spheres.
Go, seek him; tell him I would speak with him.

1 Lord. He saves my labour by his own ap-
    proach.

Enter JAQUES.

Duke S. Why, how now, monsieur! what a
    life is this,
That your poor friends must woo your com-
    pany?
What! you look merrily.

Jaq. A fool, a fool!—I met a fool i' the forest,
A motley fool;—a miserable world!—
As I do live by food, I met a fool,
Who laid him down and bask'd him in the sun,
And rail'd on Lady Fortune in good terms,
In good set terms,—and yet a motley fool.
Good-morrow, fool, quoth I: *No, sir,* quoth he,
Call me not fool till heaven hath sent me fortune.
And then he drew a dial from his poke,
And, looking on it with lack-lustre eye,
Says very wisely, *It is ten o'clock:*
Thus may we see, quoth he, *how the world wags.*
'Tis but an hour ago since it was nine;

And after one hour more 'twill be eleven;
And so, from hour to hour, we ripe and ripe,
And then, from hour to hour, we rot and rot;
And thereby hangs a tale. When I did hear
The motley fool thus moral on the time,
My lungs began to crow like chanticleer,
That fools should be so deep contemplative;
And I did laugh, sans intermission,
An hour by his dial.—O noble fool!
A worthy fool!—Motley's the only wear.

Duke S. What fool is this?   [courtier,

Jaq. O worthy fool!—One that hath been a
And says, if ladies be but young and fair,
They have the gift to know it: and in his
    brain,—
Which is as dry as the remainder biscuit
After a voyage,—he hath strange places cramm'd
With observation, the which he vents
In mangled forms.—O that I were a fool!
I am ambitious for a motley coat.

Duke S. Thou shalt have one.

Jaq.   It is my only suit,
Provided that you weed your better judgments
Of all opinion that grows rank in them
That I am wise. I must have liberty
Withal, as large a charter as the wind,
To blow on whom I please; for so fools have:
And they that are most galled with my folly,
They most must laugh. And why, sir, must
    they so?
The *why* is plain as way to parish church:
He that a fool doth very wisely hit
Doth very foolishly, although he smart,
Not to seem senseless of the bob; if not,
The wise man's folly is anatomiz'd
Even by the squandering glances of the fool.
Invest me in my motley; give me leave
To speak my mind, and I will through and
    through
Cleanse the foul body of the infected world,
If they will patiently receive my medicine.

Duke S. Fie on thee! I can tell what thou
    wouldst do.

Jaq. What, for a counter, would I do but
    good?

Duke S. Most mischievous foul sin, in chid-
    ing sin:
For thou thyself hast been a libertine,
As sensual as the brutish sting itself;
And all the embossed sores and headed evils
That thou with license of free foot hast caught,
Wouldst thou disgorge into the general world.

Jaq. Why, who cries out on pride,
That can therein tax any private party?
Doth it not flow as hugely as the sea,
Till that the weary very means do ebb?
What woman in the city do I name
When that I say, The city-woman bears
The cost of princes on unworthy shoulders?
Who can come in and say that I mean her,
When such a one as she, such is her neighbour?
Or what is he of basest function,
That says his bravery is not on my cost,—
Thinking that I mean him,—but therein suits

His folly to the metal of my speech?
There then; how then? what then? Let me see
   wherein
My tongue hath wrong'd him: if it do him
   right,
Then he hath wrong'd himself; if he be free,
Why then, my taxing like a wild goose flies,
Unclaim'd of any man.—But who comes here?

Enter ORLANDO, *with his sword drawn.*

Orl. Forbear, and eat no more.
Jaq.   Why, I have eat none yet.
Orl. Nor shalt not, till necessity be serv'd.
Jaq. Of what kind should this cock come of?
Duke S. Art thou thus bolden'd, man, by
   thy distress:
Or else a rude despiser of good manners,
That in civility thou seem'st so empty? [*point*
Orl. You touch'd my vein at first: the thorny
Of bare distress hath ta'en from me the show
Of smooth civility: yet am I inland bred,
And know some nurture. But forbear, I say;
He dies that touches any of this fruit
Till I and my affairs are answered.
Jaq. An you will not be answered with
   reason,
I must die.
Duke S. What would you have? your gentle-
   ness shall force
More than your force move us to gentleness.
Orl. I almost die for food, and let me have it.
Duke S. Sit down and feed, and welcome to
   our table.   [*you:*
Orl. Speak you so gently? Pardon me, I pray
I thought that all things had been savage here;
And therefore put I on the countenance
Of stern commandment. But whate'er you are
That in this desert inaccessible,
Under the shade of melancholy boughs,
Lose and neglect the creeping hours of time;
If ever you have look'd on better days,
If ever been where bells have knoll'd to church,
If ever sat at any good man's feast,
If ever from your eyelids wip'd a tear,
And know what 'tis to pity and be pitied,
Let gentleness my strong enforcement be:
In the which hope I blush, and hide my sword.
Duke S. True is it that we have seen better
   days,
And have with holy bell been knoll'd to
   church,
And sat at good men's feasts, and wip'd our
   eyes
Of drops that sacred pity hath engender'd:
And therefore sit you down in gentleness,
And take upon command what help we have,
That to your wanting may be minister'd.
Orl. Then but forbear your food a little while
Whiles, like a doe, I go to find my fawn,
And give it food. There is an old poor man,
Who after me hath many a weary step
Limp'd in pure love: till he be first suffic'd,—
Oppress'd with two weak evils, age and hunger,—
I will not touch a bit.

Duke S.   Go find him out,
And we will nothing waste till you return.
Orl. I thank ye; and be bless'd for your good
   comfort!   [*Exit.*
Duke S. Thou seest we are not all alone un-
   happy;
This wide and universal theatre
Presents more woeful pageants than the scene
Wherein we play in.
Jaq.   All the world's a stage,
And all the men and women merely players;
They have their exits and their entrances;
And one man in his time plays many parts,
His acts being seven ages. At first the infant,
Mewling and puking in the nurse's arms;
When the whining school-boy, with his satchel
And shining morning face, creeping like snail
Unwillingly to school. And then the lover,
Sighing like furnace, with a woeful ballad
Made to his mistress' eyebrow. Then a soldier,
Full of strange oaths, and bearded like the
   pard,
Jealous in honour, sudden and quick in quarrel,
Seeking the bubble reputation
Even in the cannon's mouth. And then the
   justice,
In fair round belly with good capon lin'd,
With eyes severe and beard of formal cut,
Full of wise saws and modern instances;
And so he plays his part. The sixth age shifts
Into the lean and slipper'd pantaloon,
With spectacles on nose and pouch on side;
His youthful hose, well sav'd, a world too wide
For his shrunk shank; and his big manly voice,
Turning again toward childish treble, pipes
And whistles in his sound. Last scene of all,
That ends this strange eventful history,
Is second childishness and mere oblivion;
Sans teeth, sans eyes, sans taste, sans every-
   thing.

Re-enter ORLANDO *with* ADAM.

Duke S. Welcome. Set down your venerable
   burden,
And let him feed.
Orl.   I thank you most for him.
Adam. So had you need:
I scarce can speak to thank you for myself.
Duke S. Welcome, fall to: I will not trouble
   you
As yet, to question you about your fortunes.—
Give us some music; and, good cousin, sing.

AMIENS *sings.*

SONG.

I.

Blow, blow, thou winter wind,
   Thou art not so unkind
      As man's ingratitude;
   Thy tooth is not so keen,
   Because thou art not seen,
      Although thy breath be rude.
Heigh-ho! sing, heigh-ho! unto the green holly:

Most friendship is feigning, most loving mere folly:
          Then, heigh-ho, the holly!
     This life is most jolly.

II.

Freeze, freeze, thou bitter sky,
That dost not bite so nigh
     As benefits forgot:
Though thou the waters warp,
Thy sting is not so sharp
     As friend remember'd not.
Heigh-ho! sing, heigh-ho! &c.

Duke S. If that you were the good Sir Row-
          land's son,—
As you have whisper'd faithfully you were,
And as mine eye doth his effigies witness
Mot truly limn'd and living in your face,—
Be truly welcome hither: I am the duke
That lov'd your father. The residue of your
          fortune,
Go to my cave and tell me.—Good old man,
Thou art right welcome as thy master is;
Support him by the arm.—Give me your hand,
And let me all your fortunes understand.
                                   [*Exeunt*.

ACT III.

SCENE I.—*A Room in the Palace.*

Enter DUKE FREDERICK, OLIVER, Lords,
          and Attendants.

Duke F. Not see him since? Sir, sir, that
          cannot be:
But were I not the better part made mercy,
I should not seek an absent argument
Of my revenge, thou present. But look to it:
Find out thy brother wheresoe'er he is:
Seek him with candle; bring him dead or living
Within this twelvemonth, or turn thou no more
To seek a living in our territory.
Thy lands, and all things that thou dost call
          thine
Worth seizure, do we seize into our hands,
Till thou canst quit thee by thy brother's
          mouth
Of what we think against thee.
     Oli. O that your highness knew my heart in
          this!
I never lov'd my brother in my life.
     Duke F. More villain thou.—Well, push
          him out of doors,
And let my officers of such a nature
Make an extent upon his house and lands:
Do this expediently, and turn him going.
                                   [*Exeunt*.

SCENE II.—*The Forest of Arden.*

Enter ORLANDO, *with a paper.*

Orl. Hang there, my verse, in witness of my
          love,   [survey
And thou, thrice-crowned queen of night,
With thy chaste eye, from thy pale sphere
          above,   [sway.
Thy huntress' name, that my full life doth

O Rosalind! these trees shall be my books,
     And in their barks my thoughts I'll character,
That every eye which in this forest looks
     Shall see thy virtue witness'd everywhere.
Run, run, Orlando; carve on every tree,
The fair, the chaste, and unexpressive she.
                                   [*Exit*.

Enter CORIN *and* TOUCHSTONE.

Cor. And how like you this shepherd's life,
Master Touchstone?
     Touch. Truly, shepherd, in respect of itself,
it is a good life; but in respect that it is a shepherd's life, it is naught. In respect that it is
solitary, I like it very well; but in respect that
it is private, it is a very vile life. Now in respect it is in the fields, it pleaseth me well;
but in respect it is not in the court, it is tedious.
As it is a spare life, look you, it fits my humour
well; but as there is no more plenty in it, it goes
much against my stomach. Hast any philosophy in thee, shepherd?
     Cor. No more but that I know the more one
sickens the worse at ease he is; and that he that
wants money, means, and content, is without
three good friends; that the property of rain is
to wet, and fire to burn; that good pasture
makes fat sheep; and that a great cause of the
night is lack of the sun; that he that hath
learned no wit by nature nor art may complain
of good breeding, or comes of a very dull kindred.
     Touch. Such a one is a natural philosopher.
Wast ever in court, shepherd?
     Cor. No, truly.
     Touch. Then thou art damned.
     Cor. Nay, I hope,—
     Touch. Truly, thou art damned; like an ill-
roasted egg, all on one side.
     Cor. For not being at court? Your reason.
     Touch. Why, if thou never wast at court
thou never saw'st good manners; if thou never
saw'st good manners, then thy manners must
be wicked; and wickedness is sin, and sin is
damnation. Thou art in a parlous state, shepherd.
     Cor. Not a whit, Touchstone: those that are
good manners at the court are as ridiculous in
the country as the behaviour of the country is
most mockable at the court. You told me you
salute not at the court, but you kiss your
hands; that courtesy would be uncleanly if
courtiers were shepherds.
     Touch. Instance, briefly; come, instance.
     Cor. Why, we are still handling our ewes;
and their fells, you know, are greasy.
     Touch. Why, do not your courtier's hands
sweat? and is not the grease of a mutton as
wholesome as the sweat of a man? Shallow,
shallow: a better instance, I say; come.
     Cor. Besides, our hands are hard.
     Touch. Your lips will feel them the sooner.
Shallow again: a more sounder instance; come.
     Cor. And they are often tarred over with

the surgery of our sheep, and would you have us kiss tar? The courtier's hands are perfumed with civet.

Touch. Most shallow man! thou wormsmeat, in respect of a good piece of flesh, indeed!—Learn of the wise, and perpend: civet is of a baser birth than tar,—the very uncleanly flux of a cat. Mend the instance, shepherd.

Cor.   You have too courtly a wit for me: I'll rest.

Touch. Wilt thou rest damned? God help thee, shallow man! God make incision in thee! thou art raw.

Cor. Sir, I am a true labourer: I earn that I eat, get that I wear; owe no man hate, envy no man's happiness; glad of other men's good, content with my harm; and the greatest of my pride is, to see my ewes graze and my lambs suck.

Touch. That is another simple sin in you; to bring the ewes and the rams together, and to offer to get your living by the copulation of cattle: to be bawd to a bell-wether; and to betray a she-lamb of a twelvemonth to a crooked-pated, old, cuckoldly ram, out of all reasonable match. If thou be'st not damned for this, the devil himself will have no shepherds; I cannot see else how thou shouldst 'scape.

Cor. Here comes young Master Ganymede, my new mistress's brother.

Enter ROSALIND, *reading a paper.*

Ros.   From the east to western Ind,
No jewel is like Rosalind.
Her worth, being mounted on the wind,
Through all the world bears Rosalind.
All the pictures fairest lin'd
Are but black to Rosalind.
Let no face be kept in mind
But the fair of Rosalind.

Touch. I'll rhyme you so eight years together, dinners, and suppers, and sleeping hours excepted: It is the right butter-woman's rank to market.

Ros. Out, fool!

Touch. For a taste:—

If a hart do lack a hind,
Let him seek out Rosalind.
If the cat will after kind,
So, be sure, will Rosalind.
Winter garments must be lin'd,
So must slender Rosalind.
They that reap must sheaf and bind, —
Then to cart with Rosalind.
Sweetest nut hath sourest rind,
Such a nut is Rosalind.
He that sweetest rose will find
Must find love's prick, and Rosalind.

This is the very false gallop of verses: why do you infect yourself with them?

Ros. Peace, you dull fool! I found them on a tree.

Touch. Truly, the tree yields bad fruit.

Ros. I'll graff it with you, and then I shall graff it with a medlar: then it will be the earliest fruit in the country: for you'll be rotten ere you be half ripe, and that's the right virtue of the medlar.

Touch. You have said; but whether wisely or no, let the forest judge.

Enter CELIA, *reading a paper.*

Ros. Peace!
Here comes my sister, reading: stand aside!

Cel.   Why should this a desert be?
For it is unpeopled? No;
Tongues I'll hang on every tree,
That shall civil sayings show:
Some, how brief the life of man
Runs his erring pilgrimage,
That the stretching of a span
Buckles in his sum of age.
Some, of violated vows
'Twixt the souls of friend and friend;
But upon the fairest boughs,
Or at every sentence' end,
Will I Rosalinda write,
Teaching all that read to know
The quintessence of every sprite
Heaven would in little show.
Therefore heaven nature charg'd
That one body should be fill'd
With all graces wide enlarg'd:
Nature presently distill'd
Helen's cheek, but not her heart;
Cleopatra's majesty;
Atalanta's better part;
Sad Lucretia's modesty.
Thus Rosalind of many parts
By heavenly synod was devis'd,
Of many faces, eyes, and hearts,
To have the touches dearest priz'd.
Heaven would that she these gifts should have,
And I to live and die her slave.

Ros. O most gentle Jupiter!—what tedious homily of love have you wearied your parishioners withal, and never cried, *Have patience, Good people!*

Cel. How now! back, friends;—shepherd, go off a little:—go with him, sirrah.

Touch. Come, shepherd, let us make an honourable retreat; though not with bag and baggage, yet with scrip and scrippage.
[*Exeunt* CORIN *and* TOUCH.

Cel. Didst thou hear these verses?

Ros. O yes, I heard them all, and more too; for some of them had in them more feet than the verses would bear.

Cel. That's no matter; the feet might bear the verses.

Ros. Ay, but the feet were lame, and could not bear themselves without the verse, and therefore stood lamely in the verse.

Cel. But didst thou hear without wondering How thy name should be hanged and carved upon these trees?

Ros. I was seven of the nine days out of the wonder before you came; for look here what I found on a palm tree: I was never so berhymed since Pythagoras' time, that I was an Irish rat, which I can hardly remember.

Cel. Trow you who hath done this?

Ros. Is it a man?

Cel. And a chain, that you once wore, about his neck. Change you colour?

Ros. I pray thee, who?

Cel. O lord, lord! it is a hard matter for friends to meet; but mountains may be removed with earthquakes, and so encounter.

Ros. Nay, but who is it?

Cel. Is it possible?

Ros. Nay, I pr'ythee now, with most petitionary vehemence, tell me who it is.

Cel. O wonderful, wonderful, and most wonderful wonderful! and yet again wonderful, and after that, out of all whooping!

Ros. Good my complexion! dost thou think, though I am caparisoned like a man, I have a doublet and hose in my disposition? One inch of delay more is a South-sea of discovery. I pr'ythee, tell me, who is it? quickly, and speak apace. I would thou couldst stammer, that mightst pour this concealed man out of thy mouth, as wine comes out of a narrow-mouthed bottle; either too much at once or none at all. I pr'ythee take the cork out of thy mouth, that I may drink thy tidings.

Cel. So you may put a man in your belly.

Ros. Is he of God's making? What manner of man? Is his head worth a hat or his chin worth a beard?

Cel. Nay, he hath but a little beard.

Ros. Why, God will send more if the man will be thankful: let me stay the growth of his beard if thou delay me not the knowledge of his chin.

Cel. It is young Orlando, that tripped up the wrestler's heels and your heart both in an instant.

Ros. Nay, but the devil take mocking: speak sad brow and true maid.

Cel. I' faith, coz, 'tis he.

Ros. Orlando?

Cel. Orlando.

Ros. Alas the day! what shall I do with my doublet and hose?—What did he when thou saw'st him? What said he? How look'd he? Wherein went he? What makes he here? Did he ask for me? Where remains he? How parted he with thee? and when shalt thou see him again? Answer me in one word.

Cel. You must borrow me Gargantua's mouth first: 'tis a word too great for any mouth of this age's size. To say ay and no to these particulars is more than to answer in a catechism.

Ros. But doth he know that I am in this forest, and in man's apparel? Looks he as freshly as he did the day he wrestled?

Cel. It is as easy to count atomies as to resolve the propositions of a lover:—but take a taste of my finding him, and relish it with good observance. I found him under a tree, like a dropped acorn.

Ros. It may well be called Jove's tree, when it drops forth such fruit.

Cel. Give me audience, good madam.

Ros. Proceed.

Cel. There lay he, stretched along like a wounded knight.

Ros. Though it be pity to see such a sight, it well becomes the ground.

Cel. Cry, holla! to thy tongue, I pr'ythee; it curvets unseasonably. He was furnished like a hunter.

Ros. O, ominous! he comes to kill my heart.

Cel. I would sing my song without a burden: thou bring'st me out of tune.

Ros. Do you not know I am a woman? when I think, I must speak. Sweet, say on.

Cel. You bring me out.—Soft! comes he not here?

Ros. 'Tis he: slink by, and note him.

[CELIA *and* ROSALIND *retire.*

Enter ORLANDO *and* JAQUES.

Jaq. I thank you for your company; but, good faith, I had as lief have been myself alone.

Orl. And so had I; but yet, for fashion's sake, I thank you too for your society.   [as we can.

Jaq. God be with you: let's meet as little

Orl. I do desire we may be better strangers.

Jaq. I pray you, mar no more trees with writing love-songs in their barks.

Orl. I pray you, mar no more of my verses with reading them ill-favouredly.

Jaq. Rosalind is your love's name?

Orl. Yes, just.

Jaq. I do not like her name.

Orl. There was no thought of pleasing you when she was christened.

Jaq. What stature is she of?

Orl. Just as high as my heart.

Jaq. You are full of pretty answers. Have you not been acquainted with goldsmiths' wives, and conned them out of rings?

Orl. Not so; but I answer you right painted cloth, from whence you have studied your questions.

Jaq. You have a nimble wit: I think it was made of Atalanta's heels. Will you sit down with me? and we two will rail against our mistress the world, and all our misery.

Orl. I will chide no breather in the world but myself, against whom I know most faults.

Jaq. The worst fault you have is to be in love.

Orl. 'Tis a fault I will not change for your best virtue. I am weary of you.

Jaq. By my troth, I was seeking for a fool when I found you.

Orl. He is drowned in the brook; look but in, and you shall see him.

Jaq. There I shall see mine own figure.

Orl. Which I take to be either a fool or a cipher.

Jaq. I'll tarry no longer with you: farewell, good Signior Love.

Orl. I am glad of your departure: adieu, good Monsieur Melancholy.

[*Exit* JAQ.—CEL. *and* ROS. *come forward.*

Ros. I will speak to him like a saucy lacquey, and under that habit play the knave with him.—Do you hear, forester?

Orl. Very well. what would you?

Ros. I pray you, what is't o'clock?

Orl. You should ask me what time o' day; there's no clock in the forest.

Ros. Then there's no true lover in the forest, else sighing every minute and groaning every hour would detect the lazy foot of time as well as a clock.

Orl. And why not the swift foot of time? had not that been as proper?

Ros. By no means, sir. Time travels in divers paces with divers persons. I will tell you who time ambles withal, who time trots withal, who time gallops withal, and who he stands still withal.

Orl. I pr'ythee, who doth he trot withal?

Ros. Marry, he trots hard with a young maid between the contract of her marriage and the day it is solemnized; if the interim be but a se'nnight, time's pace is so hard that it seems the length of seven years.

Orl. Who ambles time withal?

Ros. With a priest that lacks Latin and a rich man that hath not the gout: for the one sleeps easily, because he cannot study; and the other lives merrily, because he feels no pain; the one lacking the burden of lean and wasteful learning; the other knowing no burden of heavy tedious penury. These time ambles withal.

Orl. Who doth he gallop withal?

Ros. With a thief to the gallows; for though he go as softly as foot can fall, he thinks himself too soon there.

Orl. Who stays it still withal?

Ros. With lawyers in the vacation; for they sleep between term and term, and then they perceive not how time moves.

Orl. Where dwell you, pretty youth?

Ros. With this shepherdess, my sister; here in the skirts of the forest, like fringe upon a petticoat.

Orl. Are you native of this place?

Ros. As the coney, that you see dwell where she is kindled.

Orl. Your accent is something finer than you could purchase in so removed a dwelling.

Ros. I have been told so of many: but indeed an old religious uncle of mine taught me to speak, who was in his youth an inland man; one that knew courtship too well, for there he fell in love. I have heard him read many lectures against it; and I thank God I am not a woman, to be touched with so many giddy offences as he hath generally taxed their whole sex withal.

Orl. Can you remember any of the principal evils that he laid to the charge of women?

Ros. There were none principal; they were all like one another as halfpence are; every one fault seeming monstrous till his fellow fault came to match it.

Orl. I pr'ythee, recount some of them.

Ros. No; I will not cast away my physic but on those that are sick. There is a man haunts the forest that abuses our young plants with carving Rosalind on their barks; hangs odes upon hawthorns, and elegies on brambles; all, forsooth, deifying the name of Rosalind. if I could meet that fancymonger I would give him some good counsel, for he seems to have the quotidian of love upon him.

Orl. I am he that is so love-shaked. I pray you, tell me your remedy.

Ros. There is none of my uncle's marks upon you: he taught me how to know a man in love; in which cage of rushes I am sure you are not prisoner.

Orl. What were his marks?

Ros. A lean cheek; which you have not: a blue eye and sunken; which you have not: an unquestionable spirit; which you have not: a beard neglected; which you have not: but I pardon you for that; for simply your having in beard is a younger brother's revenue:—then your hose should be ungartered, your bonnet unbanded, your sleeve unbuttoned, your shoe untied, and everything about you demonstrating a careless desolation. But you are no such man; you are rather point-device in your accoutrements; as loving yourself than seeming the lover of any other.

Orl. Fair youth, I would I could make thee believe I love.

Ros. Me believe it! you may as soon make her that you love believe it; which, I warrant, she is apter to do than to confess she does: that is one of the points in the which women still give the lie to their consciences. But, in good sooth, are you he that hangs the verses on the trees, wherein Rosalind is so admired?

Orl. I swear to thee, youth, by the white hand of Rosalind, I am that he, that unfortunate he.

Ros. But are you so much in love as your rhymes speak?

Orl. Neither rhyme nor reason can express how much.

Ros. Love is merely a madness; and, I tell you, deserves as well a dark house and a whip as madmen do: and the reason why they are not so punished and cured is, that the lunacy is so ordinary that the whippers are in love too. Yet I profess curing it by counsel.

Orl. Did you ever cure any so?

Ros. Yes, one; and in this manner. He was to imagine me his love, his mistress; and I set him every day to woo me: at which time would I, being but a moonish youth, grieve, be effeminate, changeable, longing, and liking; proud, fantastical, apish, shallow, inconstant, full of tears, full of smiles; for every passion something, and for no passion truly anything, as boys and women are for the most part cattle of this colour: would now like him, now loath him; then entertain him, then forswear him; now weep for him, then spit at him; that I drave my suitor from his mad humour of love to a loving humour of madness; which was, to forswear the full stream of the world, and to live in a nook nearly monastic. And thus I cured him; and this way will I take upon me to wash your liver as clean as a sound sheep's heart, that there shall not be one spot of love in 't.

Orl. I would not be cured, youth.

Ros. I would cure you if you would but call me Rosalind, and come every day to my cote and woo me.

Orl. Now, by the faith of my love, I will. tell me where it is.

Ros. Go with me to it, and I'll show it you: and, by the way, you shall tell me where in the forest you live. Will you go?

Orl. With all my heart, good youth.

Ros. Nay, you must call me Rosalind.— Come, sister, will you go?   [*Exeunt.*

SCENE III.—*Another part of the Forest.*

Enter TOUCHSTONE *and* AUDREY; JAQUES *at a distance observing them.*

Touch. Come apace, good Audrey; I will fetch up your goats, Audrey. And how, Audrey? am I the man yet? Doth my simple feature content you?

Aud. Your features! Lord warrant us! what features?

Touch. I am here with thee and thy goats, as the most capricious poet, honest Ovid, was among the Goths.

Jaq. O knowledge ill-inhabited! worse than Jove in a thatch'd house.   [*Aside.*

Touch. When a man's verses cannot be understood, nor a man's good wit seconded with the forward child understanding, it strikes a man more dead than a great reckoning in a little room.—Truly, I would the gods had made thee poetical.

Aud. I do not know what poetical is: is it honest in deed and word? is it a true thing?

Touch. No, truly: for the truest poetry is the most feigning; and lovers are given to poetry; and what they swear in poetry may be said, as lovers, they do feign.

Aud. Do you wish, then, that the gods had made me poetical?

Touch. I do, truly, for thou swear'st to me thou art honest; now, if thou wert a poet I might have some hope thou didst feign.

Aud. Would you not have me honest?

Touch. No, truly, unless thou wert hard-favoured; for honesty coupled to beauty is to have honey a sauce to sugar.

Jaq. A material fool!   [*Aside.*

Aud. Well, I am not fair; and therefore I pray the gods make me honest!

Touch. Truly, and to cast away honesty upon a foul slut were to put good meat into an unclean dish.

Aud. I am not a slut, though I thank the gods I am foul.

Touch. Well, praised be the gods for thy foulness! sluttishness may come hereafter. But be it as it may be, I will marry thee: and to that end I have been with Sir Oliver Martext, the vicar of the next village; who hath promised to meet me in this place of the forest, and to couple us.

Jaq. I would fain see this meeting. [*Aside.*

Aud. Well, the gods give us joy!

Touch. Amen. A man may, if he were of a fearful heart, stagger in this attempt; for here we have no temple but the wood, no assembly but horn-beasts. But what though? Courage! As horns are odious, they are necessary. It is said,—Many a man knows no end of his goods: right; many a man has good horns and knows no end of them. Well, that is the dowry of his wife; 'tis none of his own getting. Horns? Ever to poor men alone?——No, no; the noblest deer hath them as huge as the rascal. Is the single man therefore blessed? No: as a walled town is more worthier than a village, so is the forehead of a married man more honourable than the bare brow of a bachelor: and by how much defence is better than no skill, by so much is a horn more precious than to want. Here comes Sir Oliver.

Enter Sir OLIVER MARTEXT.

Sir Oliver Martext, you are well met. Will you despatch us here under this tree, or shall we go with you to your chapel?   [woman?

Sir Oli. Is there none here to give the

Touch. I will not take her on gift of any man.

Sir Oli. Truly, she must be given, or the marriage is not lawful.

Jaq. [*Discovering himself.*] Proceed proceed; I'll give her.

Touch. Good even, good Master *What-ye-call 't:* how do you, sir? You are very well met: God 'ild you for your last company: I am very glad to see you:—even a toy in hand here, sir:—nay; pray be covered.

Jaq. Will you be married, motley?

Touch. As the ox hath his bow, sir, the horse his curb, and the falcon her bells, so man hath his desires; and as pigeons bill, so wedlock would be nibbling.

Jaq. And will you, being a man of your breeding, be married under a bush, like a beggar? Get you to church and have a good priest that can tell you what marriage is: this fellow will but join you together as they join wainscot: then one of you will prove a shrunk panel, and like green timber, warp, warp.

Touch. I am not in the mind but I were better to be married of him than of another: for he is not like to marry me well; and not being well married, it will be a good excuse for me hereafter to leave my wife.   [*Aside.*

Jaq. Go thou with me and let me counsel thee.

Touch. Come, sweet Audrey;
We must be married or we must live in bawdry.
Farewell, good master Oliver!—Not,—

O sweet Oliver,
O brave Oliver,
Leave me not behind thee;

But,—

Wind away,——
Begone I say,
I will not to wedding with thee.

[*Exeunt* JAQ., TOUCH., *and* AUD.
Sir Oli. 'Tis no matter; ne'er a fantastical knave of them all shall flout me out of my calling.   [*Exit.*

SCENE IV.—*Another part of the Forest. Before a Cottage.*

Enter ROSALIND *and* CELIA.

Ros. Never talk to me; I will weep.
Cel. Do, I pr'ythee; but yet have the grace to consider that tears do not become a man.
Ros. But have I not cause to weep?
Cel. As good cause as one would desire; therefore weep.
Ros. His very hair is of the dissembling colour.
Cel. Something browner than Judas's: marry, his kisses are Judas's own children.
Ros. I' faith, his hair is of a good colour.
Cel. An excellent colour: your chestnut was ever the only colour.
Ros. And his kissing is as full of sanctity as the touch of holy bread.
Cel. He hath bought a pair of cast lips of Diana: a nun of winter's sisterhood kisses not more religiously; the very ice of chastity is in them.
Ros. But why did he swear he would come this morning, and comes not?
Cel. Nay, certainly, there is no truth in him.
Ros. Do you think so?
Cel. Yes; I think he is not a pickpurse nor a horse-stealer; but for his verity in love, I do think him as concave as a covered goblet or a worm-eaten nut.
Ros. Not true in love?   [in.
Cel. Yes, when he is in; but I think he is not
Ros. You have heard him swear downright he was.
Cel. *Was* is not *is:* besides, the oath of a lover is no stronger than the word of a tapster; they are both the confirmers of false reckonings. He attends here in the forest on the duke, your father.
Ros. I met the duke yesterday, and had much question with him. He asked me of what parentage I was; I told him, of as good as he; so he laughed and let me go. But what talk we of fathers when there is such a man as Orlando?
Cel. O, that's a brave man! he writes brave verses, speaks brave words, swears brave oaths and breaks them bravely, quite traverse,

athwart the heart of his lover; as a puny tilter, that spurs his horse but on one side, breaks his staff like a noble goose: but all's brave that youth mounts and folly guides.—Who comes here?

Enter CORIN.

Cor. Mistress and master, you have oft inquired
After the shepherd that complain'd of love,
Who you saw sitting by me on the turf,
Praising the proud disdainful shepherdess
That was his mistress.
Cel.   Well, and what of him?
Cor. If you will see a pageant truly play'd,
Between the pale complexion of true love
And the red glow of scorn and proud disdain,
Go hence a little, and I shall conduct you,
If you will mark it.
Ros.   O, come, let us remove:
The sight of lovers feedeth those in love.
Bring us unto this sight, and you shall say
I'll prove a busy actor in their play.   [*Exeunt.*

SCENE V.—*Another part of the Forest.*

Enter SILVIUS *and* PHEBE.

Sil. Sweet Phebe, do not scorn me do not Phebe:
Say that you love me not; but say not so
In bitterness. The common executioner,
Whose heart the accustom'd sight of death makes hard,
Falls not the axe upon the humbled neck
But first begs pardon. Will you sterner be
Than he that dies and lives by bloody drops?

Enter ROSALIND, CELIA, *and* CORIN, *at a distance.*

Phe. I would not be thy executioner:
I fly thee, for I would not injure thee.
Thou tell'st me there is murder in mine eye:
'Tis pretty, sure, and very probable,
That eyes,—that are the frail'st and softest things,
Who shut their coward gates on atomies,—
Should be called tyrants, butchers, murderers!
Now I do frown on thee with all my heart;
And if mine eyes can wound, now let them kill thee:
Now counterfeit to swoon; why, now fall down;
Or, if thou canst not, O, for shame, for shame,
Lie not, to say mine eyes are murderers.
Now show the wound mine eye hath made in thee:
Scratch thee but with a pin, and there remains
Some scar of it; lean but upon a rush,
The cicatrice and capable impressure   [eyes,
Thy palm some moment keeps, but now mine
Which I have darted at thee, hurt thee not;
Nor, I am sure, there is no force in eyes
That can do hurt.
Sil.   O dear Phebe,
If ever,—as that ever may be near,—

You meet in some fresh cheek the power of
    fancy,
Then shall you know the wounds invisible
That love's keen arrows make.
    Phe.   But till that time
Come not thou near me; and when that time
    comes
Afflict me with thy mocks, pity me not;
As till that time I shall not pity thee.
    Ros. [*Advancing.*] And why, I pray you?
    Who might be your mother,
That you insult, exult, and all at once,
Over the wretched? What though you have no
    beauty,—
As, by my faith, I see no more in you
Than without candle may go dark to bed,—
Must you be therefore proud and pitiless?
Why, what means this? Why do you look on
    me?
I see no more in you than in the ordinary
Of nature's sale-work:—Od's my little life,
I think she means to tangle my eyes too!—
No, faith, proud mistress, hope not after it;
'Tis not your inky brows, your black silk hair,
Your bugle eyeballs, nor your cheek of cream,
That can entame my spirits to your worship.—
You foolish shepherd, wherefore do you follow
    her,
Like foggy south, puffing with wind and rain?
You are a thousand times a properer man
Than she a woman. 'Tis such fools as you
That make the world full of ill-favour'd chil-
    dren:
'Tis not her glass, but you that flatters her;
And out of you she sees herself more proper
Than any of her lineaments can show her;—
But, mistress, know yourself; down on your
    knees,
And thank heaven, fasting, for a good man's
    love:
For I must tell you friendly in your ear,—
Sell when you can; you are not for all markets:
Cry the man mercy; love him; take his offer:
Foul is most foul, being foul to be a scoffer.
So take her to thee, shepherd;—fare you well.
    Phe. Sweet youth, I pray you chide a year
    together:
I had rather hear you chide than this man woo.
    Ros. He's fallen in love with her foulness,
and she'll fall in love with my anger. If it be so,
as fast as she answers thee with frowning looks,
I'll sauce her with bitter words.—Why look
you so upon me?
    Phe For no ill-will I bear you.
    Ros. I pray you, do not fall in love with me,
For I am falser than vows made in wine:
Besides, I like you not.—If you will know my
    house,
'Tis at the tuft of olives here hard by.—
Will you go, sister?—Shepherd, ply her hard.—
Come, sister.—Shepherdess, look on him better,
And be not proud; though all the world could
    see,
None could be so abus'd in sight as he.

Come to our flock.
               [*Exeunt* Ros., Cel., *and* Cor.
    Phe. Dead shepherd! now I find thy saw of
    might;
Who ever lov'd that lov'd not at first sight?
    Sil. Sweet Phebe,—
    Phe.   Ha! what say'st thou, Silvius?
    Sil. Sweet Phebe, pity me.
    Phe. Why, I am sorry for thee, gentle Silvius.
    Sil. Wherever sorrow is, relief would be:
If you do sorrow at my grief in love,
By giving love, your sorrow and my grief
Were both extermin'd.   [bourly?
    Phe. Thou hast my love: is not that neigh-
    Sil. I would have you.
    Phe.   Why, that were covetousness.
Silvius, the time was that I hated thee;
And yet it is not that I bear thee love:
But since that thou canst talk of love so well,
Thy company, which erst was irksome to me,
I will endure; and I'll employ thee too:
But do not look for further recompense
Than thine own gladness that thou art em-
    ploy'd.
    Sil. So holy and so perfect is my love,
And I in such a poverty of grace,
That I shall think it a most plenteous crop
To glean the broken ears after the man
That the main harvest reaps: lose now and then
A scatter'd smile, and that I'll live upon.
    Phe. Know'st thou the youth that spoke to
    me erewhile?
    Sil. Not very well; but I have met him oft;
And he hath bought the cottage and the bounds
That the old carlot once was master of. [him;
    Phe. Think not I love him, though I ask for
'Tis but a peevish boy:—yet he talks well;—
But what care I for words? yet words do well
When he that speaks them pleases those that
    hear.
It is a pretty youth:—not very pretty:—
But, sure, he's proud; and yet his pride be-
    comes him:
He'll make a proper man: the best thing in him
Is his complexion; and faster than his tongue
Did make offence, his eye did heal it up.
He is not tall; yet for his years he's tall;
His leg is but so-so; and yet 'tis well:
There was a pretty redness in his lip;
A little riper and more lusty red
Than that mix'd in his cheek; 'twas just the
    difference
Betwixt the constant red and mingled damask.
There be some women, Silvius, had they mark'd
    him
In parcels as I did, would have gone near
To fall in love with him: but, for my part,
I love him not, nor hate him not; and yet
I have more cause to hate him than to love
    him:
For what had he to do to chide at me?
He said mine eyes were black, and my hair
    black;
And, now I am remember'd, scorn'd at me:

I marvel why I answer'd not again
But that's all one; omittance is not quittance
I'll write to him a very taunting letter,
And thou shalt bear it; wilt thou, Silvius?

Sil. Phebe, with all my heart.

Phe.   I'll write it straight,
The matter's in my head and in my heart:
I will be bitter with him, and passing short:
Go with me, Silvius.   [*Exeunt.*

ACT IV.

Scene I.—*Forest of Arden.*

Enter Rosalind, Celia, *and* Jaques.

Jaq. I pr'ythee, pretty youth, let me be better acquainted with thee.

Ros. They say you are a melancholy fellow.

Jaq. I am so; I do love it better than laughing.

Ros. Those that are in extremity of either are abominable fellows, and betray themselves to every modern censure worse than drunkards.

Jaq. Why, 'tis good to be sad and say nothing.

Ros. Why, then, 'tis good to be a post.

Jaq. I have neither the scholar's melancholy, which is emulation; nor the musician's, which is fantastical; nor the courtier's, which is proud; nor the soldier's, which is ambitious; nor the lawyer's, which is politic; nor the lady's, which is nice; nor the lover's, which is all these: but it is a melancholy of mine own, compounded of many simples, extracted from many objects: and, indeed, the sundry contemplation of my travels, in which my often rumination wraps me in a most humorous sadness.

Ros. A traveller! By my faith, you have great reason to be sad: I fear you have sold your own land to see other men's; then, to have seen much, and to have nothing, is to have rich eyes and poor hands.

Jaq. Yes, I have gained my experience.

Ros. And your experience makes you sad: I had rather have a fool to make me merry than experience to make me sad; and to travel for it too.

Enter Orlando.

Orl. Good day, and happiness, dear Rosalind!

Jaq. Nay, then, God be wi' you, an you talk in blank verse.

Ros. Farewell, monsieur traveller: look you lisp and wear strange suits; disable all the benefits of your own country, be out of love with your nativity, and almost chide God for making you that countenance you are; or I will scarce think you have swam in a gondola. [*Exit* Jaques.] Why, how now, Orlando! where have you been all this while? You a lover!—An you serve me such another trick, never come in my sight more.

Orl. My fair Rosalind, I come within an hour of my promise.

Ros. Break an hour's promise in love! He that will divide a minute into a thousand parts, and break but a part of a thousandth part of a minute in the affairs of love, it may be said of him that Cupid hath clapped him o' the shoulder, but I warrant him heart-whole.

Orl. Pardon me, dear Rosalind.

Ros. Nay, an you be so tardy, come no more in my sight: I had as lief be woo'd of a snail.

Orl. Of a snail!

Ros. Ay, of a snail; for though he comes slowly, he carries his house on his head; a better jointure, I think, than you can make a woman: besides, he brings his destiny with him.

Orl. What's that?

Ros. Why, horns; which such as you are fain to be beholden to your wives for: but he comes armed in his fortune, and prevents the slander of his wife.

Orl. Virtue is no horn-maker; and my Rosalind is virtuous.

Ros. And I am your Rosalind.

Cel. It pleases him to call you so; but he hath a Rosalind of a better leer than you.

Ros. Come, woo me, woo me; for now I am in a holiday humour, and like enough to consent.—What would you say to me now, an I were your very very Rosalind?

Orl. I would kiss before I spoke.

Ros. Nay, you were better speak first; and when you were gravelled for lack of matter, you might take occasion to kiss. Very good orators, when they are out, they will spit; and for lovers lacking,—God warn us!—matter, the cleanliest shift is to kiss.

Orl. How if the kiss be denied?

Ros. Then she puts you to entreaty, and there begins new matter.

Orl. Who could be out, being before his beloved mistress?

Ros. Marry, that should you, if I were your mistress; or I should think my honesty ranker than my wit.

Orl. What, of my suit?

Ros. Not out of your apparel, and yet out of your suit. Am not I your Rosalind?

Orl. I take some joy to say you are, because I would be talking of her.   [have you.

Ros. Well, in her person, I say, I will not

Orl. Then, in mine own person, I die.

Ros. No, faith, die by attorney. The poor world is almost six thousand years old, and in all this time there was not any man died in his own person, *videlicet*, in a love-cause. Troilus had his brains dashed out with a Grecian club; yet he did what he could to die before; and he is one of the patterns of love. Leander, he would have lived many a fair year, though Hero had turned nun, if it had not been for a hot midsummer-night; for, good youth, he went but forth to wash him in the Hellespont, and, being taken with the cramp, was drawned; and the foolish chroniclers of that age found it was—Hero of Sestos. But these are all lies; men have died from time to time, and worms have eaten them, but not for love.

Orl. I would not have my right Rosalind of this mind, for, I protest, her frown might kill me.

Ros. By this hand, it will not kill a fly. But come, now I will be your Rosalind in a more coming-on disposition; and ask me what you will, I will grant it.

Orl. Then love me, Rosalind.

Ros. Yes, faith will I, Fridays and Saturdays, and all.

Orl. And wilt thou have me?

Ros. Ay, and twenty such.

Orl. What say'st thou?

Ros. Are you not good?

Orl. I hope so.

Ros. Why, then, can one desire too much of a good thing?—Come, sister, you shall be the priest, and marry us.—Give me your hand, Orlando:—What do you say, sister?

Orl. Pray thee, marry us.

Cel. I cannot say the words.   [lando,—

Ros. You must begin,——*Will you, Or-*

Cel. Go to:——Will you, Orlando, have to wife this Rosalind?

Orl. I will.

Ros. Ay, but when?

Orl. Why, now; as fast as she can marry us.

Ros. Then you must say,—*I take thee, Rosalind, for wife.*

Orl. I take thee, Rosalind, for wife.

Ros. I might ask you for your commission; but,—I do take thee, Orlando, for my husband:—there's a girl goes before the priest; and, certainly, a woman's thoughts run before her actions.

Orl. So do all thoughts; they are winged.

Ros. Now tell me how long you would have her, after you have possessed her.

Orl. For ever and a day.

Ros. Say a day, without the ever. No, no, Orlando; men are April when they woo, December when they wed: maids are May when they are maids, but the sky changes when they are wives. I will be more jealous of thee than a Barbary cock-pigeon over his hen; more clamorous than a parrot against rain; more new-fangled than an ape; more giddy in my desires than a monkey: I will weep for nothing, like Diana in the fountain, and I will do that when you are disposed to be merry; I will laugh like a hyen, and that when thou art inclined to sleep.

Orl. But will my Rosalind do so?

Ros. By my life, she will do as I do.

Orl. O, but she is wise.

Ros. Or else she could not have the wit to do this: the wiser, the waywarder: make the doors upon a woman's wit, and it will out at the casement; shut that, and it will out at the keyhole; stop that, 'twill fly with the smoke out at the chimney.

Orl. A man that had a wife with such a wit, he might say,—*Wit, whither wilt?*

Ros. Nay, you might keep that check for it, till you met your wife's wit going to your neighbour's bed.   [that?

Orl. And what wit could wit have to excuse

Ros. Marry, to say,—she came to seek you there. You shall never take her without her answer, unless you take her without her tongue. O, that woman that cannot make her fault her husband's occasion, let her never nurse her child herself, for she will breed it like a fool.

Orl. For these two hours, Rosalind, I will leave thee.   [hours!

Ros. Alas, dear love, I cannot lack thee two

Orl. I must attend the duke at dinner: by two o'clock I will be with thee again.

Ros. Ay, go your ways, go your ways; I knew what you would prove; my friends told me as much, and I thought no less:—that flattering tongue of yours won me:—'tis but one cast away, and so,—come, death!—Two o'clock is your hour?

Orl. Ay, sweet Rosalind.

Ros. By my troth, and in good earnest, and so God mend me, and by all pretty oaths that are not dangerous, if you break one jot of your promise, or come one minute behind your hour, I will think you the most pathetical break-promise, and the most hollow lover, and the most unworthy of her you call Rosalind, that may be chosen out of the gross band of the unfaithful: therefore beware my censure, and keep your promise.

Orl. With no less religion than if thou wert indeed my Rosalind: so, adieu!

Ros. Well, time is the old justice that examines all such offenders, and let time try: adieu!   [*Exit* ORLANDO.

Cel. You have simply misus'd our sex in your love-prate: we must have your doublet and hose plucked over your head, and show the world what the bird hath done to her own nest.

Ros. O coz, coz, coz, my pretty little coz, that thou didst know how many fathom deep I am in love! But it cannot be sounded: my affection hath an unknown bottom, like the bay of Portugal.

Cel. Or rather, bottomless; that as fast as you pour affection in, it runs out.

Ros. No; that same wicked bastard of Venus, that was begot of thought, conceived of spleen, and born of madness; that blind rascally boy, that abuses every one's eyes, because his own are out, let him be judge how deep I am in love:—I'll tell thee, Aliena, I cannot be out of the sight of Orlando: I'll go find a shadow, and sigh till he come.

Cel. And I'll sleep.   [*Exeunt*

SCENE II.—*Another part of the Forest.*

Enter JAQUES *and* Lords, *in the habit of Foresters.*

Jaq. Which is he that killed the deer?

1 *Lord.* Sir, it was I.

Jaq. Let's present him to the duke, like a Roman conqueror; and it would do well to set the deer's horns upon his head for a branch of victory.—Have you no song, forester, for this purpose?

2 Lord. Yes, sir.

Jaq. Sing it; 'tis no matter how it be in tune, so it make noise enough.

SONG.

1. What shall he have that kill'd the deer
2. His leather skin and horns to wear.
        1. Then sing him home:
                [The rest shall bear this burden.
Take thou no scorn to wear the horn;
It was a crest ere thou wast born.
        1. Thy father's father wore it;
        2. And thy father bore it:
All. The horn, the horn, the lusty horn,
Is not a thing to laugh to scorn.   [*Exeunt.*

SCENE III.—*Another part of the Forest.*

Enter ROSALIND *and* CELIA.

Ros. How say you now? Is it not past two o'clock? And here much Orlando!

Cel. I warrant you, with pure love and troubled brain, he hath ta'en his bow and arrows, and is gone forth—to sleep. Look, who comes here.

Enter SILVIUS.

Sil. My errand is to you, fair youth;—
My gentle Phebe bid me give you this:
                        [*Giving a letter.*
I know not the contents; but, as I guess
By the stern brow and waspish action
Which she did use as she was writing of it,
It bears an angry tenor: pardon me,
I am but as a guiltless messenger.   [letter,

Ros. Patience herself would startle at this
And play the swaggerer; bear this, bear all:
She says I am not fair; that I lack manners;
She calls me proud, and that she could not love me,
Were man as rare as Phœnix. Od's my will!
Her love is not the hare that I do hunt:
Why writes she so to me?—Well, shepherd, well,
This is a letter of your own device.

Sil. No, I protest, I know not the contents:
Phebe did write it.

Ros.   Come, come, you are a fool,
And turn'd into the extremity of love.
I saw her hand: she has a leathern hand,
A freestone-colour'd hand: I verily did think
That her old gloves were on, but 'twas her hands;
She has a huswife's hand: but that's no matter:
I say she never did invent this letter:
This is a man's invention, and his hand.

Sil. Sure, it is hers.

Ros. Why, 'tis a boisterous and a cruel style;
A style for challengers: why, she defies me,
Like Turk to Christian: woman's gentle brain
Could not drop forth such giant-rude invention,

Such Ethiop words, blacker in their effect
Than in their countenance.—Will you hear the letter?

Sil. So please you, for I never heard it yet;
Yet heard too much of Phebe's cruelty.

Ros. She Phebes me: mark how the tyrant writes. [*Reads.*]

        Art thou god to shepherd turn'd,
        That a maiden's heart hath burn'd?

Can a woman rail thus?

Sil. Call you this railing?

Ros. Why, thy godhead laid apart,
        Warr'st thou with a woman's heart?

Did you ever hear such railing?

        Whiles the eye of man did woo me,
        That could do no vengeance to me.—

Meaning me a beast.—

        If the scorn of your bright eyne
        Have power to raise such love in mind
        Alack, in me what strange effect
        Would they work in mild aspect
        Whiles you chid me I did love;
        How then might your prayers move
        He that brings this love to thee
        Little knows this love in me:
        And by him seal up thy mind;
        Whether that thy youth and kind
        Will the faithful offer take
        Of me, and all that I can make;
        Or else by him my love deny,
        And then I'll study how to die.

Sil. Call you this chiding?

Cel. Alas, poor shepherd!

Ros. Do you pity him? no, he deserves no pity.—Wilt thou love such a woman?—What, to make thee an instrument, and play false strains upon thee! Not to be endured!—Well, go your way to her,—for I see love hath made thee a tame snake,—and say this to her;—that if she love me, I charge her to love thee: if she will not, I will never have her, unless thou entreat for her.—If you be a true lover, hence, and not a word; for here comes more company.
                        [*Exit* SILVIUS.

Enter OLIVER.

Oli. Good-morrow, fair ones: pray you, if you know
Where in the purlieus of this forest stands
A sheep-cote fenc'd about with olive trees?

Cel. West of this place, down in the neighbour bottom:
The rank of osiers, by the murmuring stream,
Left on your right hand, brings you to the place.
But at this hour the house doth keep itself;
There's none within.

Oli. If that an eye may profit by a tongue,
Then should I know you by description;
Such garments, and such years. *The boy is fair,*

Of female favour, and bestows himself
Like a ripe sister: the woman low,
And browner than her brother. Are not you
The owner of the house I did inquire for?

 Cel. It is no boast, being ask'd, to say we are.

 Oli. Orlando doth commend him to you
  both;
And to that youth he calls his Rosalind
He sends this bloody napkin:—are you he?

 Ros. I am: what must we understand by
  this?   [me

 Oli. Some of my shame; if you will know of
What man I am, and how, and why, and where
This handkerchief was stain'd.

 Cel.   I pray you, tell it.

 Oli. When last the young Orlando parted
  from you,
He left a promise to return again
Within an hour; and, pacing through the forest,
Chewing the food of sweet and bitter fancy,
Lo, what befell! he threw his eye aside,
And, mark, what object did present itself!
Under an oak, whose boughs were moss'd with
  age,
And high top bald with dry antiquity,
A wretched ragged man, o'ergrown with hair,
Lay sleeping on his back: about his neck
A green and gilded snake had wreath'd itself,
Who, with her head, nimble in threats, ap-
  proach'd
The opening of his mouth; but suddenly,
Seeing Orlando, it unlink'd itself,
And with indented glides did slip away
Into a bush: under which bush's shade
A lioness, with udders all drawn dry,
Lay crouching, head on ground, with cat-like
  watch,   ['tis
When that the sleeping man should stir; for
The royal disposition of that beast
To prey on nothing that doth seem as dead:
This seen, Orlando did approach the man,
And found it was his brother, his elder brother.

 Cel. O, I have heard him speak of that same
  brother;
And he did render him the most unnatural
That liv'd 'mongst men.

 Oli.   And well he might so do,
For well I know he was unnatural. [there,

 Ros. But, to Orlando:—did he leave him
Food to the suck'd and hungry lioness?

 Oli. Twice did he turn his back, and pur-
  pos'd so;
But kindness, nobler ever than revenge,
And nature, stronger than his just occasion,
Made him give battle to the lioness,
Who quickly fell before him; in which hurtling
From miserable slumber I awak'd.

 Cel. Are you his brother?

 Ros.   Was it you he rescued?

 Cel. Was't you that did so oft contrive to
  kill him?

 Oli. 'Twas I; but 'tis not I: I do not shame
To tell you what I was, since my conversion
So sweetly tastes, being the thing I am.

 Ros. But, for the bloody napkin?—

 Oli.   By and by.
When from the first to last, betwixt us two,
Tears our recountments had most kindly bath'd,
As, how I came into that desert place;—
In brief, he led me to the gentle duke,
Who gave me fresh array and entertainment,
Committing me unto my brother's love,
Who led me instantly unto his cave,
There stripp'd himself, and here upon his arm
The lioness had torn some flesh away,
Which all this while had bled; and now he fainted,
And cried, in fainting, upon Rosalind.
Brief, I recover'd him, bound up his wound,
And, after some small space, being strong at
  heart,
He sent me hither, stranger as I am,
To tell this story, that you might excuse
His broken promise, and to give this napkin,
Dy'd in his blood, unto the shepherd-youth
That he in sport doth call his Rosalind.

 Cel. Why, how now, Ganymede! sweet
  Ganymede!   [ROSALIND *faints.*

 Oli. Many will swoon when they do look on
  blood.

 Cel. There is more in it:—Cousin—Ganymede!

 Oli. Look, he recovers.

 Ros.   I would I were at home.

 Cel. We'll lead you thither:—
I pray you, will you take him by the arm?

 Oli. Be of good cheer, youth:—you a man?—
You lack a man's heart.

 Ros. I do so, I confess it. Ah, sir, a body
'would think this was well counterfeited. I pray
you, tell your brother how well I counterfeited.
—Heigh-ho!—

 Oli. This was not counterfeit; there is too
great testimony in your complexion that it was
a passion of earnest.

 Ros. Counterfeit, I assure you.

 Oli. Well, then, take a good heart, and
counterfeit to be a man.

 Ros. So I do: but, i' faith, I should have been
a woman by right.

 Cel. Come, you look paler and paler: pray
you, draw homewards.—Good sir, go with us.

 Oli. That will I, for I must bear answer back
How you excuse my brother, Rosalind.

 Ros. I shall devise something: but, I pray
you, commend my counterfeiting to him.—Will
you go?   [*Exeunt.*

ACT V.

Scene I.—*The Forest of Arden.*

Enter TOUCHSTONE *and* AUDREY.

 Touch. We shall find a time, Audrey;
patience, gentle Audrey.

 Aud. Faith, the priest was good enough, for
all the old gentleman's saying.

 Touch. A most wicked Sir Oliver, Audrey, a
most vile Martext. But, Audrey, there is a
youth here in the forest lays claim to you.

Aud. Ay, I know who 'tis: he hath no interest in me in the world: here comes the man you mean.

Enter WILLIAM.

Touch. It is meat and drink to me to see a clown: By my troth, we that have good wits have much to answer for; we shall be flouting; we cannot hold.

Will. Good even, Audrey.

Aud. God ye good even, William.

Will. And good even to you, sir.

Touch. Good even, gentle friend. Cover thy head, cover thy head; nay, pr'ythee, be covered. How old are you, friend?

Will. Five-and-twenty, sir.

Touch. A ripe age. Is thy name William?

Will. William, sir.   [here?

Touch. A fair name. Wast born i' the forest

Will. Ay, sir, I thank God.   [rich?

Touch. Thank God;—a good answer. Art

Will. Faith, sir, so-so.

Touch. So-so is good, very good, very excellent good:—and yet it is not; it is but so-so. Art thou wise?

Will. Ay, sir, I have a pretty wit.

Touch. Why, thou say'st well. I do now remember a saying; *The fool doth think he is wise, but the wise man knows himself to be a fool.* The heathen philosopher, when he had a desire to eat a grape, would open his lips when he put it into his mouth; meaning thereby that grapes were made to eat and lips to open. You do love this maid?

Will. I do, sir.

Touch. Give me your hand. Art thou learned?

Will. No, sir.

Touch. Then learn this of me:—to have is to have; for it is a figure in rhetoric that drink, being poured out of a cup into a glass, by filling the one doth empty the other; for all your writers do consent that *ipse* is he; now, you are not *ipse*, for I am he.

Will. Which he, sir?

Touch. He, sir, that must marry this woman. Therefore, you clown, abandon,—which is in the vulgar, leave,—the society,—which in the boorish is company,—of this female,—which in the common is woman,—which together is abandon the society of this female; or, clown, thou perishest; or, to thy better understanding, diest; or, to wit, I kill thee, make thee away, translate thy life into death, thy liberty into bondage: I will deal in poison with thee, or in bastinado, or in steel; I will bandy with thee in faction; I will o'er-run thee with policy; I will kill thee a hundred and fifty ways; therefore tremble, and depart.

Aud. Do, good William.

Will. God rest you merry, sir.   [*Exit*

Enter CORIN.

Cor. Our master and mistress seek you; come away, away!

Touch. Trip, Audrey, trip, Audrey;—I attend, I attend.   [*Exeunt.*

SCENE II.—*Another part of the Forest.*

Enter ORLANDO *and* OLIVER.

Orl. Is't possible that, on so little acquaintance, you should like her? that, but seeing, you should love her? and, loving, woo? and, wooing, she should grant? and will you perséver to enjoy her?

Oli. Neither call the giddiness of it in question, the poverty of her, the small acquaintance, my sudden wooing, nor her sudden consenting; but say with me, I love Aliena; say, with her, that she loves me; consent with both, that we may enjoy each other: it shall be to your good; for my father's house, and all the revenue that was old Sir Rowland's, will I estate upon you, and here live and die a shepherd.

Orl. You have my consent. Let your wedding be to-morrow: thither will I invite the duke and all his contented followers. Go you and prepare Aliena; for, look you, here comes my Rosalind.

Enter ROSALIND.

Ros. God save you, brother.

Oli. And you, fair sister.   [*Exit.*

Ros. O, my dear Orlando, how it grieves me to see thee wear thy heart in a scarf.

Orl. It is my arm.

Ros. I thought thy heart had been wounded with the claws of a lion.

Orl. Wounded it is, but with the eyes of a lady.

Ros. Did your brother tell you how I counterfeited to swoon when he show'd me your handkercher.

Orl. Ay, and greater wonders than that.

Ros. O, I know where you are:—nay, 'tis true: there was never anything so sudden but the fight of two rams and Cæsar's thrasonical brag of—*I came, saw, and overcame:* for your brother and my sister no sooner met, but they looked; no sooner looked, but they loved; no sooner loved, but they sighed; no sooner sighed, but they asked one another the reason; no sooner knew the reason, but they sought the remedy: and in these degrees have they made a pair of stairs to marriage, which they will climb incontinent, or else be incontinent before marriage: they are in the very wrath of love, and they will together: clubs cannot part them.

Orl. They shall be married to-morrow; and I will bid the duke to the nuptial. But O, how bitter a thing it is to look into happiness through another man's eyes! By so much the more shall I to-morrow be at the height of heart-heaviness, by how much I shall think my brother happy in having what he wishes for.

Ros. Why, then, to-morrow I cannot serve your turn for Rosalind?

Orl. I can live no longer by thinking.

Ros. I will weary you, then, no longer with idle talking. Know of me, then,—for now I speak to some purpose,—that I know you are a gentleman of good conceit: I speak not this that you should bear a good opinion of my knowledge, insomuch I say I know you are; neither do I labour for a greater esteem than may in some little measure draw a belief from you, to do yourself good, and not to grace me. Believe, then, if you please, that I can do strange things: I have, since I was three year old, conversed with a magician, most profound in his art, and yet not damnable. If you do love Rosalind so near the heart as your gesture cries it out, when your brother marries Aliena, shall you marry her:—I know into what straits of fortune she is driven; and it is not impossible to me, if it appear not inconvenient to you, to set her before your eyes to-morrow, human as she is, and without any danger.

Orl. Speak'st thou in sober meanings?

Ros. By my life, I do; which I tender dearly, though I say I am a magician. Therefore, put you in your best array, bid your friends; for if you will be married to-morrow, you shall; and to Rosalind, if you will. Look, here comes a lover of mine, and a lover of hers.

Enter SILVIUS *and* PHEBE.

Phe. Youth, you have done me much un-
    gentleness,
To show the letter that I writ to you.

Ros. I care not, if I have: it is my study
To seem despiteful and ungentle to you:
You are there follow'd by a faithful shepherd;
Look upon him, love him; he worships you.

Phe. Good shepherd, tell this youth what
    'tis to love.

Sil. It is to be all made of sighs and tears;—
And so am I for Phebe.

Phe. And I for Ganymede.

Orl. And I for Rosalind.

Ros. And I for no woman.

Sil. It is to be all made of faith and ser-
    vice;—
And so am I for Phebe.

Phe. And I for Ganymede.

Orl. And I for Rosalind.

Ros. And I for no woman.

Sil. It is to be all made of fantasy,
All made of passion, and all made of wishes;
All adoration, duty, and obedience,
All humbleness, all patience, and impatience,
All purity, all trial, all observance;—
And so am I for Phebe.

Phe. And so am I for Ganymede.

Orl. And so am I for Rosalind.

Ros. And so am I for no woman.

Phe. If this be so, why blame you me to love
    you?   [*To* ROSALIND.

Sil. If this be so, why blame you me to love
    you?   [*To* PHEBE.

Orl. If this be so, why blame you me to love
    you?

Ros. Why do you speak too,—*Why blame
    you me to love you?*

Orl. To her that is not here, nor doth not hear.

Ros. Pray you, no more of this; 'tis like the howling of Irish wolves against the moon.—I will help you [*to* SILVIUS] if I can:—I would love you [*to* PHEBE] if I could.—To-morrow meet me all together.—I will marry you [*to* PHEBE] if ever I marry woman, and I'll be married to-morrow:—I will satisfy you [*to* ORLANDO] if ever I satisfied man, and you shall be married to-morrow:—I will content you [*to* SILVIUS] if what pleases you contents you, and you shall be married to-morrow.—As you [*to* ORLANDO] love Rosalind, meet;—as you [*to* SILVIUS] love Phebe, meet; and as I love no woman, I'll meet.—So, fare you well; I have left you commands.

Sil. I'll not fail, if I live.

Phe.   Nor I.

Orl.   Nor I.
                      [*Exeunt.*

SCENE III.—*Another part of the Forest.*

Enter TOUCHSTONE *and* AUDREY.

Touch. To-morrow is the joyful day, Audrey; to-morrow will we be married.

Aud. I do desire it with all my heart; and I hope it is no dishonest desire to desire to be a woman of the world. Here come two of the banished duke's pages.

Enter two Pages.

1 Page. Well met, honest gentleman.

Touch. By my troth, well met. Come sit, sit, and a song.

2 Page. We are for you: sit i' the middle.

1 Page. Shall we clap into 't roundly, without hawking, or spitting, or saying we are hoarse, which are the only prologues to a bad voice?

2 Page. I' faith, i' faith; and both in a tune, like two gipsies on a horse.

SONG.

I.

It was a lover and his lass,
    With a hey, and a ho, and a hey nonino,
That o'er the green corn-field did pass
    In the spring time, the only pretty ring time,
    When birds do sing, hey ding a ding, ding:
Sweet lovers love the spring.

II.

Between the acres of the rye,
    With a hey, and a ho, and a hey nonino,
These pretty country folks would lie,
    In the spring time, &c.

III.

This carol they began that hour,
    With a hey, and a ho, and a hey nonino,
How that a life was but a flower
    In the spring time, &c

IV.

And therefore take the present time,
   With a hey, and a ho, and a hey.nonino,
For love is crowned with the prime
   In the spring time, &c.

Touch. Truly, young gentlemen, though there was no great matter in the ditty, yet the note was very untimeable.

1 *Page.* You are deceived, sir; we kept time, we lost not our time.

Touch. By my troth, yes; I count it but time lost to hear such a foolish song. God be with you; and God mend your voices! Come, Audrey.
[*Exeunt.*

SCENE IV.—*Another part of the Forest.*

Enter DUKE *Senior,* AMIENS, JAQUES, OR-
LANDO, OLIVER, *and* CELIA.

Duke S. Dost thou believe, Orlando, that
   the boy
Can do all this that he hath promised?

Orl. I sometimes do believe and sometimes
   do not;   [fear.
As those that fear they hope, and know they

Enter ROSALIND, SILVIUS, *and* PHEBE.

Ros. Patience once more, whiles our com-
   pact is urg'd:—
You say, if I bring in your Rosalind,
             [*To the* DUKE.
You will bestow her on Orlando here?

Duke S. That would I, had I kingdoms to
   give with her.

Ros. And you say you will have her, when I
   bring her?   [*To* ORLANDO.

Orl. That would I, were I of all kingdoms
   king.

Ros. You say you'll marry me if I be willing?
            [*To* PHEBE.

Phe. That will I, should I die the hour after.

Ros. But if you do refuse to marry me,
You'll give yourself to this most faithful shepherd?

Phe. So is the bargain.

Ros. You say that you'll have Phebe, if she
   will?   [*To* SILVIUS.

Sil. Though to have her and death were
   both one thing.

Ros. I have promis'd to make all this matter
   even.
Keep you your word, O duke, to give your
   daughter;—
You yours, Orlando, to receive his daughter;—
Keep you your word, Phebe, that you'll marry
   me;
Or else, refusing me, to wed this shepherd:—
Keep your word, Silvius, that you'll marry her
If she refuse me:—and from hence I go,
To make these doubts all even.
       [*Exeunt* ROSALIND *and* CELIA.

Duke S. I do remember in this shepherd-boy
Some lively touches of my daughter's favour.

Orl. My lord, the first time that I ever saw
   him,
Methought he was a brother to your daughter:
But, my good lord, this boy is forest-born,
And hath been tutor'd in the rudiments
Of many desperate studies by his uncle,
Whom he reports to be a great magician,
Obscured in the circle of this forest.

Jaq. There is, sure, another flood toward, and these couples are coming to the ark. Here comes a pair of very strange beasts, which in all tongues are called fools.

Enter TOUCHSTONE *and* AUDREY.

Touch. Salutation and greeting to you all!

Jaq. Good my lord, bid him welcome. This is the motley-minded gentleman that I have so often met in the forest: he hath been a courtier, he swears.

Touch. If any man doubt that, let him put me to my purgation. I have trod a measure; I have flattered a lady; I have been politic with my friend, smooth with mine enemy; I have undone three tailors; I have had four quarrels, and like to have fought one.

Jaq. And how was that ta'en up?

Touch. Faith, we met, and found the quarrel was upon the seventh cause.

Jaq.. How seventh cause? Good my lord, like this fellow.

Duke S. I like him very well.

Touch. God 'ild you, sir; I desire you of the like. I press in here, sir, amongst the rest of the country copulatives, to swear and to for-swear; according as marriage binds and blood breaks:—A poor virgin, sir, an ill-favoured thing, sir, but mine own; a poor humour of mine, sir, to take that that no man else will: rich honesty dwells like a miser, sir, in a poor-house; as your pearl in your foul oyster.

Duke S. By my faith, he is very swift and sententious.

Touch. According to the fool's bolt, sir, and such dulcet diseases.

Jaq. But, for the seventh cause; how did you find the quarrel on the seventh cause?

Touch. Upon a lie seven times removed;— bear your body more seeming, Audrey:—as thus, sir, I did dislike the cut of a certain courtier's beard; he sent me word, if I said his beard was not cut well, he was in the mind it was: this is called the *Retort courteous.* If I sent him word again, it was not well cut, he would send me word he cut it to please himself: this is called the *Quip modest.* If again, it was not well cut, he disabled my judgment: this is called the *Reply churlish.* If again, it was not well cut, he would answer, I spake not true: this is called the *Reproof valiant.* If again, it was not well cut, he would say, I lie: this is called the *Countercheck quarrelsome:* and so, to the *Lie circumstantial,* and the *Lie direct.*

Jaq. And how oft did you say his beard was not well cut?

Touch. I durst go no farther than the *Lie circumstantial*, nor he durst not give me the *Lie direct;* and so we measured swords and parted.

Jaq. Can you nominate in order now the degrees of the lie?

Touch. O, sir, we quarrel in print by the book, as you have books for good manners: I will name you the degrees. The first, the Retort courteous; the second, the Quip modest; the third, the Reply churlish; the fourth, the Reproof valiant; the fifth, the Countercheck quarrelsome; the sixth, the Lie with circumstance; the seventh, the Lie direct. All these you may avoid but the lie direct; and you may avoid that too with an *If.* I knew when seven justices could not take up a quarrel; but when the parties were met themselves, one of them thought but of an *If,* as *If you said so, then I said so;* and they shook hands, and swore brothers. Your *If* is the only peace-maker:—much virtue in *If.*

Jaq. Is not this a rare fellow, my lord? he's as good at anything, and yet a fool.

Duke S. He uses his folly like a stalking-horse, and under the presentation of that he shoots his wit.

Enter HYMEN, *leading* ROSALIND *in woman's clothes: and* CELIA.

Still Music.

Hym. Then is there mirth in heaven,
 When earthly things made even
  Atone together.
 Good duke, receive thy daughter:
 Hymen from heaven brought her,
  Yea, brought her hither,
 That thou mightst join her hand with his,
 Whose heart within her bosom is.

Ros. To you I give myself, for I am yours.
        [*To* DUKE S.
To you I give myself, for I am yours.
        [*To* ORLANDO.
Duke S. If there be truth in sight, you are my daughter.
Orl. If there be truth in sight, you are my Rosalind.
Phe. If sight and shape be true,
Why, then, my love, adieu!
Ros. I'll have no father, if you be not he:—
        [*To* DUKE S.
I'll have no husband, if you be not he:—
        [*To* ORLANDO.
Nor e'er wed woman, if you be not she.
        [*To* PHEBE.
Hym. Peace Ho! I bar confusion:
 'Tis I must make conclusion
  Of these most strange events:
 Here's eight that must take hands,
 To join in Hymen's bands,
  If truth holds true contents.
You and you no cross shall part:
    [*To* ORLANDO *and* ROSALIND.

You and you are heart in heart:
    [*To* OLIVER *and* CELIA.
You to his love must accord, [*To* PHEBE.
Or have a woman to your lord:—
You and you are sure together,
    [*To* TOUCHSTONE *and* AUDREY.
As the winter to foul weather.
Whiles a wedlock-hymn we sing,
Feed yourselves with questioning,
That reason wonder may diminish,
How thus we met, and these things finish.

SONG.

Wedding is great Juno's crown;
 O blessed bond of board and bed!
'Tis Hymen peoples every town;
 High wedlock, then, be honoured;
Honour, high honour and renown,
To Hymen, god of every town!

Duke S. O my dear niece, welcome thou art to me!
Even daughter, welcome in no less degree.
Phe. I will not eat my word, now thou art mine;
Thy faith my fancy to thee doth combine.
       [*To* SILVIUS.

Enter JAQUES DE BOIS.

Jaq. de B. Let me have audience for a word or two;
I am the second son of old Sir Rowland,
That bring these tidings to this fair assembly:—
Duke Frederick, hearing how that every day
Men of great worth resorted to this forest,
Address'd a mighty power; which were on foot,
In his own conduct, purposely to take
His brother here, and put him to the sword:
And to the skirts of this wild wood he came;
Where, meeting with an old religious man,
After some question with him, was converted
Both from his enterprise and from the world;
His crown bequeathing to his banish'd brother,
And all their lands restored to them again
That were with him exil'd. This to be true
I do engage my life.
Duke S.   Welcome, young man:
Thou offer'st fairly to thy brother's wedding:
To one, his lands withheld; and to the other,
A land itself at large, a potent dukedom.
First, in this forest, let us do those ends
That here were well begun and well begot:
And after, every of this happy number,
That have endur'd shrewd days and nights with us,
Shall share the good of our returned fortune,
According to the measure of their states.
Meantime, forget this new-fall'n dignity,
And fall into our rustic revelry:—
Play, music!—and you, brides and bridegrooms all,
With measure heap'd in joy, to the measures fall.
Jaq. Sir, by your patience. If I heard you rightly,

The duke hath put on a religious life,
And thrown into neglect the pompous court?
   Jaq. de B. He hath.
   Jaq. To him will I: out of these convertites
There is much matter to be heard and learn'd.—
You to your former honour I bequeath;
                          [*To* DUKE S.
Your patience and your virtue well deserves
    it:—
You [*to* ORLANDO] to a love that your true faith
    doth merit:—
You [*to* OLIVER] to your land, and love, and
    great allies:—
You [*to* SILVIUS] to a long and well-deserved
    bed:—   [thy loving voyage
And you [*to* TOUCHSTONE] to wrangling; for
Is but for two months victual'd.—So to your
    pleasures;
I am for other than for dancing measures.
   Duke S. Stay, Jaques, stay.   [have
   Jaq. To see no pastime I: what you would
I'll stay to know at your abandon'd cave.
                            [*Exit*.
   Duke S. Proceed, proceed: we will begin
    these rites,
As we do trust they'll end, in true delights.
                          [*A dance*.

EPILOGUE.

   Ros. It is not the fashion to see the lady the epilogue; but it is no more unhandsome than to see the lord the prologue. If it be true that good wine needs no bush, 'tis true that a good play needs no epilogue. Yet to good wine they do use good bushes; and good plays prove the better by the help of good epilogues. What a case am I in, then, that am neither a good epilogue nor cannot insinuate with you in the behalf of a good play! I am not furnished like a beggar; therefore to beg will not become me: my way is to conjure you; and I'll begin with the women. I charge you, O women, for the love you bear to men, to like as much of this play as please you: and I charge you, O men, for the love you bear to women,—as I perceive by your simpering, none of you hates them,—that between you and the women the play may please. If I were a woman, I would kiss as many of you as had beards that pleased me, complexions that liked me, and breaths that I defied not: and, I am sure, as many as have good beards, or good faces, or sweet breaths, will, for my kind offer, when I make curtsy, bid me farewell.
                             [*Exeunt*.

ALL'S WELL THAT ENDS WELL

DRAMATIS PERSONÆ

KING OF FRANCE.
DUKE OF FLORENCE.
BERTRAM, *Count of Rousillon.*
LAFEU, *an old Lord.*
PAROLLES, *a Follower of* BERTRAM.
Several young French Lords, *that serve with*
BERTRAM *in the Florentine War.*
Steward, }
Clown, } *Servants to the* COUNTESS OF
A Page, } ROUSILLON.

COUNTESS OF ROUSILLON, *Mother to* BER-
TRAM.
HELENA, *a Gentlewoman protected by the*
COUNTESS.
An old Widow *of Florence.*
DIANA, *Daughter to the* Widow.
VIOLENTA, } *Neighbours and Friends to the*
MARIANA, } Widow.
Lords *attending on the* KING; Officers, Sol-
diers, &c., *French and Florentine.*

SCENE,—*Partly in* FRANCE, *and partly in* TUSCANY.

ACT I.

SCENE I.—ROUSILLON. *A Room in the* COUNTESS'S *Palace.*

Enter BERTRAM, *the* COUNTESS OF ROUSILLON, HELENA, *and* LAFEU, *in mourning.*

Count. In delivering my son from me, I bury a second husband.

Ber. And I, in going, madam, weep o'er my father's death anew: but I must attend his majesty's command, to whom I am now in ward, evermore in subjection.

Laf. You shall find of the king a husband, madam;—you, sir, a father: he that so generally is at all times good, must of necessity hold his virtue to you; whose worthiness would stir it up where it wanted, rather than lack it where there is such abundance.

Count. What hope is there of his majesty's amendment?

Laf. He hath abandoned his physicians, madam; under whose practices he hath persecuted time with hope; and finds no other advantage in the process but only the losing of hope by time.

Count. This young gentlewoman had a father—O, that *had!* how sad a passage 'tis!—whose skill was almost as great as his honesty; had it stretched so far, would have made nature immortal, and death should have play for lack of work. Would, for the king's sake, he were living! I think it would be the death of the king's disease.

Laf. How called you the man you speak of, madam?

Count. He was famous, sir, in his profession, and it was his great right to be so,—Gerard de Narbon.

Laf. He was excellent, indeed, madam: the king very lately spoke of him admiringly and mourningly: he was skilful enough to have lived still, if knowledge could be set up against mortality.

Ber. What is it, my good lord, the king languishes of?

Laf. A fistula, my lord.

Ber. I heard not of it before.

Laf. I would it were not notorious.—Was this gentlewoman the daughter of Gerard de Narbon?

Count. His sole child, my lord; and bequeathed to my overlooking. I have those hopes of her good that her education promises: her dispositions she inherits, which make fair gifts fairer; for where an unclean mind carries virtuous qualities, there commendations go with pity,—they are virtues and traitors too: in her they are the better for their simpleness; she derives her honesty, and achieves her goodness.

Laf. Your commendations, madam, get from her tears.

Count. 'Tis the best brine a maiden can season her praise in. The remembrance of her father never approaches her heart but the tyranny of her sorrows takes all livelihood from her cheek. No more of this, Helena,—go to, no more; lest it be rather thought you affect a sorrow than to have.

Hel. I do affect a sorrow indeed; but I have it too.

Laf. Moderate lamentation is the right of the dead; excessive grief the enemy to the living.

Count. If the living be enemy to the grief, the excess makes it soon mortal.

Ber. Madam, I desire your holy wishes.

Laf. How understand we that?

Count. Be thou blest, Bertram! and succeed thy father
In manners, as in shape! thy blood and virtue
Contend for empire in thee, and thy goodness
Share with thy birthright! Love all, trust a few,

Do wrong to none: be able for thine enemy
Rather in power than use; and keep thy friend
Under thy own life's key: be check'd for silence,
But never tax'd for speech. What heaven more
          will,
That thee may furnish and my prayers pluck
          down,
Fall on thy head! Farewell.—My lord,
'Tis an unseason'd courtier; good my lord,
Advise him.
     Laf.   He cannot want the best
That shall attend his love.
     Count. Heaven bless him!—Farewell, Ber-
          tram.   [*Exit* COUNTESS.
     Ber. The best wishes that can be forged in
your thoughts [*to* HELENA] be servants to you!
Be comfortable to my mother, your mistress,
and make much of her.
     Laf. Farewell, pretty lady: you must hold
the credit of your father.
                    [*Exeunt* BER. *and* LAF.
     Hel. O, were that all!—I think not on my
          father;   [more
And these great tears grace his remembrance
Than those I shed for him. What was he like?
I have forgot him; my imagination
Carries no favour in 't but Bertram's.
I am undone: there is no living, none,
If Bertram be away. It were all one
That I should love a bright particular star,
And think to wed it, he is so above me:
In his bright radiance and collateral light
Must I be comforted, not in his sphere.
The ambition in my love thus plagues itself:
The hind that would be mated by the lion
Must die for love. 'Twas pretty, though a
          plague,
To see him every hour; to sit and draw
His arched brows, his hawking eye, his curls,
In our heart's table,—heart too capable
Of every line and trick of his sweet favour:
But now he's gone, and my idolatrous fancy
Must sanctify his relics. Who comes here?
One that goes with him: I love him for his sake;
And yet I know him a notorious liar,
Think him a great way fool, solely a coward;
Yet these fix'd evils sit so fit in him
That they take place when virtue's steely bones
Look bleak i' the cold wind: withal, full oft we
          see
Cold wisdom waiting on superfluous folly.

Enter PAROLLES.

     Par. Save you, fair queen!
     Hel. And you, monarch!
     Par. No.
     Hel. And no.
     Par. Are you meditating on virginity?
     Hel. Ay. You have some stain of soldier in
you: let me ask you a question. Man is enemy
to virginity; how may we barricado it against
him?
     Par. Keep him out.

     Hel. But he assails; and our virginity, though
valiant in the defence, yet is weak: unfold to us
some warlike resistance.
     Par. There is none: man, sitting down before
you, will undermine you, and blow you up.
     Hel. Bless our poor virginity from under-
miners and blowers-up!—Is there no military
policy how virgins might blow up men?
     Par. Virginity being blown down, man will
quicklier be blown up: marry, in blowing him
down again, with the breach yourselves made,
you lose your city. It is not politic in the commonwealth of nature to preserve virginity. Loss
of virginity is rational increase; and there was
never virgin got till virginity was first lost.
That you were made of is metal to make virgins.
Virginity, by being once lost, may be ten times
found; by being ever kept, it is ever lost: 'tis
too cold a companion, away with it!
     Hel. I will stand for 't a little, though there-
fore I die a virgin.
     Par. There's little can be said in 't; 'tis
against the rule of nature. To speak on the part
of virginity is to accuse your mothers, which is
most infallible disobedience. He that hangs
himself is a virgin: virginity murders itself; and
should be buried in highways, out of all sanctified limit, as a desperate offendress against nature. Virginity breeds mites, much like a cheese;
consumes itself to the very paring, and so dies
with feeding his own stomach. Besides, virginity is peevish, proud, idle, made of self-love,
which is the most inhibited sin in the canon.
Keep it not, you cannot choose but lose by 't:
out with 't! within ten years it will make itself
ten, which is a goodly increase, and the principal itself not much the worse: away with it!
     Hel. How might one do, sir, to lose it to her
own liking?
     Par. Let me see: marry, ill, to like him that
ne'er it likes. 'Tis a commodity will lose the
gloss with lying; the longer kept, the less worth:
off with 't while 'tis vendible: answer the time
of request. Virginity, like an old courtier, wears
her cap out of fashion; richly suited, but unsuitable: just like the brooch and the toothpick which wear not now. Your date is better in
your pie and your porridge than in your cheek.
And your virginity, your old virginity, is like
one of our French withered pears; it looks ill, it
eats drily; marry, 'tis a withered pear; it was
formerly better; marry, yet 'tis a withered pear.
Will you anything with it?
     Hel. Not my virginity yet.
There shall your master have a thousand loves,
A mother, and a mistress, and a friend,
A phœnix, captain, and an enemy,
A guide, a goddess, and a sovereign,
A counsellor, a traitress, and a dear:
His humble ambition, proud humility,
His jarring concord, and his discord dulcet,
His faith, his sweet disaster; with a world
Of pretty, fond, adoptious christendoms,
That blinking Cupid gossips. Now shall he—

I know not what he shall:—God send him
    well!—
The court's a learning-place;—and he is one,—
  Par. What one, i' faith?
  Hel. That I wish well.—'Tis pity—
  Par. What's pity?
  Hel. That wishing well had not a body in 't
Which might be felt; that we, the poorer born,
Whose baser stars do shut us up in wishes,
Might with effects of them follow our friends,
And show what we alone must think; which
    never
Returns us thanks.

Enter a Page.

  Page. Monsieur Parolles, my lord calls for
you.   [*Exit* Page.
  Par. Little Helen, farewell: if I can remem-
ber thee, I will think of thee at court.
  Hel. Monsieur Parolles, you were born un-
der a charitable star.
  Par. Under Mars, I.
  Hel. I especially think, under Mars.
  Par. Why under Mars?
  Hel. The wars have so kept you under that
you must needs be born under Mars.
  Par. When he was predominant.
  Hel. When he was retrograde, I think, rather.
  Par. Why think you so?   [fight.
  Hel. You go so much backward when you
  Par. That's for advantage.
  Hel. So is running away, when fear proposes
the safety: but the composition that your valour and fear makes in you is a virtue of a good
wing, and I like the wear well.
  Par. I am so full of businesses I cannot answer thee acutely. I will return perfect courtier;
in the which my instruction shall serve to nat-
uralize thee, so thou wilt be capable of a courtier's counsel, and understand what advice shall
thrust upon thee; else thou diest in thine un-
thankfulness, and thine ignorance makes thee
away: farewell. When thou hast leisure, say thy
prayers; when thou hast none, remember thy
friends: get thee a good husband, and use him
as he uses thee: so, farewell.   [*Exit.*
  Hel. Our remedies oft in ourselves do lie,
Which we ascribe to heaven: the fated sky
Gives us free scope; only doth backward pull
Our slow designs when we ourselves are dull.
What power is it which mounts my love so
    high—
That makes me see, and cannot feed mine eye?
The mightiest space in fortune nature brings
To join like likes, and kiss like native things.
Impossible be strange attempts to those
That weigh their pains in sense, and do suppose
What hath been cannot be: who ever strove
To show her merit that did miss her love?
The king's disease,—my project may deceive
    me,
But my intents are fix'd, and will not leave me.
                       [*Exit.*

SCENE II.—PARIS. *A Room in the* KING'S
Palace.

Flourish of cornets. Enter the KING OF FRANCE,
with Letters; Lords *and others attending.*

  King. The Florentines and Senoys are by the
    ears;
Have fought with equal fortune, and continue
A braving war.
  1 Lord.   So 'tis reported, sir.
  King. Nay, 'tis most credible; we here re-
    ceive it
A certainty, vouch'd from our cousin Austria,
With caution that the Florentine will move us
For speedy aid; wherein our dearest friend
Prejudicates the business, and would seem
To have us make denial.
  1 Lord.   His love and wisdom,
Approv'd so to your majesty, may plead
For amplest credence.
  King.   He hath arm'd our answer,
And Florence is denied before he comes:
Yet, for our gentlemen that mean to see
The Tuscan service, freely have they leave
To stand on either part.
  2 Lord.   It well may serve
A nursery to our gentry, who are sick
For breathing and exploit.
  King.   What's he comes here?

Enter BERTRAM, LAFEU, *and* PAROLLES.

  1 Lord. It is the Count Rousillon, my good
    lord,
Young Bertram.
  King. Youth, thou bear'st thy father's face;
Frank nature, rather curious than in haste,
Hath well compos'd thee. Thy father's moral
    parts
Mayst thou inherit too! Welcome to Paris.
  Ber. My thanks and duty are your majesty's.
  King. I would I had that corporal soundness
    now,
As when thy father and myself in friendship
First tried our soldiership! He did look far
Into the service of the time, and was
Disciped of the bravest: he lasted long;
But on us both did haggish age steal on,
And wore us out of act. It much repairs me
To talk of your good father. In his youth
He had the wit which I can well observe
To-day in our young lords; but they may jest
Till their own scorn return to them unnoted,
Ere they can hide their levity in honour
So like a courtier: contempt nor bitterness
Were in his pride or sharpness; if they were,
His equal had awak'd them; and his honour,
Clock to itself, knew the true minute when
Exception bid him speak, and at this time
His tongue obey'd his hand: who were below
    him
He us'd as creatures of another place;
And bow'd his eminent top to their low ranks,
Making them proud of his humility,
In their poor praise he humbled. Such a man

Might be a copy to these younger times; [now
Which, follow'd well, would demonstrate them
But goers backward.

Ber.   His good remembrance, sir,
Lies richer in your thoughts than on his tomb;
So in approof lives not his epitaph
As in your royal speech.   [always say,—

King. Would I were with him! He would
Methinks I hear him now; his plausive words
He scatter'd not in ears, but grafted them,
To grow there, and to bear,—*Let me not live,*—
Thus his good melancholy oft began,
On the catastrophe and heel of pastime,
When it was out,—*Let me not live,* quoth he,
After my flame lacks oil, to be the snuff
Of younger spirits, whose apprehensive senses
All but new things disdain; whose judgments are
Mere fathers of their garments; whose constancies
Expire before their fashions:—This he wish'd.
I, after him, do after him wish too,
Since I nor wax nor honey can bring home,
I quickly were dissolv'd from my hive,
To give some labourers room.

2 Lord.   You are lov'd, sir.
They that least lend it you shall lack you first.

King. I fill a place, I know't.—How long
      is 't, count,
Since the physician at your father's died?
He was much fam'd.

Ber.   Some six months since, my lord.

King. If he were living I would try him yet;—
Lend me an arm;—the rest have worn me out
With several applications:—nature and sickness
Debate it at their leisure. Welcome, count;
My son's no dearer.

Ber.   Thank your majesty.
                   [*Exeunt. Flourish.*

SCENE III.—ROUSILLON. *A Room in the Palace.*

Enter COUNTESS, Steward, *and* Clown.

Count. I will now hear: what say you of this
gentlewoman?

Stew. Madam, the care I have had to even
your content, I wish might be found in the
calendar of my past endeavours; for then we
wound our modesty, and make foul the clear-
ness of our deservings, when of ourselves we
publish them.

Count. What does this knave here? Get you
gone, sirrah: the complaints I have heard of
you I do not at all believe; 'tis my slowness
that I do not; for I know you lack not folly to
commit them, and have ability enough to make
such knaveries yours.

Clo. 'Tis not unknown to you, madam, I am
a poor fellow.

Count. Well, sir.

Clo. No, madam, 'tis not so well that I am
poor; though many of the rich are damned: but
if I may have your ladyship's good will to go to
the world, Isbel the woman and I will do as we
may.

Count. Wilt thou needs be a beggar?

Clo I do beg your good will in this case.

Count. In what case?

Clo. In Isbel's case and mine own. Service is
no heritage: and I think I shall never have the
blessing of God till I have issue of my body; for
they say bairns are blessings.

Count. Tell me thy reason why thou wilt
marry.

Clo. My poor body, madam, requires it: I
am driven on by the flesh; and he must needs
go that the devil drives.

Count. Is this all your worship's reason?

Clo. Faith, madam, I have other holy reasons, such as they are.

Count. May the world know them?

Clo. I have been, madam, a wicked creature,
as you and all flesh and blood are; and, indeed,
I do marry that I may repent.

Count. Thy marriage, sooner than thy wick-
         edness.

Clo. I am out of friends, madam; and I hope
to have friends for my wife's sake.

Count. Such friends are thine enemies, knave.

Clo. You are shallow, madam, in great
friends: for the knaves come to do that for me
which I am a-weary of. He that ears my land
spares my team, and gives me leave to inn the
crop: if I be his cuckold, he's my drudge: he
that comforts my wife is the cherisher of my
flesh and blood; he that cherishes my flesh and
blood loves my flesh and blood; he that loves
my flesh and blood is my friend; *ergo,* he that
kisses my wife is my friend. If men could be
contented to be what they are, there were no
fear in marriage; for young Charbon the puritan and old Poysam the papist, how-some'er
their hearts are severed in religion, their heads
are both one; they may joll horns together like
any deer i' the herd.

Count. Wilt thou ever be a foul-mouthed and
calumnious knave?

Clo. A prophet I, madam; and I speak the
truth the next way:

     For I the ballad will repeat,
       Which men full true shall find;
     Your marriage comes by destiny,
       Your cuckoo sings by kind.

Count. Get you gone, sir; I'll talk with you
more anon.

Stew. May it please you, madam, that he bid
Helen come to you; of her I am to speak.

Count. Sirrah, tell my gentlewoman I would
speak with her; Helen I mean.

Clo. [*Singing.*] Was this fair face the cause, quoth
              she,
       Why the Grecians sacked Troy?
     Fond done, done fond,
       Was this King Priam's joy?
     With that she sighed as she stood,
     With that she sighed as she stood,
       And gave this sentence then:—
     Among nine bad if one be good,
     Among nine bad if one be good,
       There's yet one good in ten.

Count. What, one good in ten? you corrupt the song, sirrah.

Clo. One good woman in ten, madam, which is a purifying o' the song: would God would serve the world so all the year! we'd find no fault with the tithe-woman if I were the parson: one in ten, quoth a'! an we might have a good woman born but for every blazing star, or at an earthquake, 'twould mend the lottery well: a man may draw his heart out ere he pluck one.

Count. You'll be gone, sir knave, and do as I command you!

Clo. That man should be at woman's command, and yet no hurt done!—Though honesty be no puritan, yet it will do no hurt; it will wear the surplice of humility over the black gown of a big heart.—I am going, forsooth: the business is for Helen to come hither. [*Exit.*

Count. Well, now.

Stew. I know, madam, you love your gentle-woman entirely.

Count Faith, I do: her father bequeathed her to me; and she herself, without other advantage, may lawfully make title to as much love as she finds: there is more owing her than is paid; and more shall be paid her than she'll demand.

Stew. Madam, I was very late more near her than I think she wished me: alone she was, and did communicate to herself her own words to her own ears; she thought, I dare vow for her, they touched not any stranger sense. Her matter was, she loved your son: Fortune, she said, was no goddess, that had put such difference betwixt their two estates; Love no god, that would not extend his might only where qualities were level: Diana no queen of virgins, that would suffer her poor knight surprise, without rescue in the first assault, or ransom afterward. This she delivered in the most bitter touch of sorrow that e'er I heard virgin exclaim in: which I held my duty speedily to acquaint you withal; sithence, in the loss that may happen, it concerns you something to know it.

Count. You have discharged this honestly; keep it to yourself: many likelihoods informed me of this before, which hung so tottering in the balance that I could neither believe nor misdoubt. Pray you, leave me: stall this in your bosom; and I thank you for your honest care: I will speak with you further anon.

[*Exit* Steward.

Count. Even so it was with me when I was young:
If ever we are nature's, these are ours; this thorn
Doth to our rose of youth rightly belong;
Our blood to us, this to our blood is born:
It is the show and seal of nature's truth,
Where love's strong passion is impress'd in youth:
By our remembrances of days foregone,
Such were our faults:—or then we thought them none.

Enter HELENA.

Her eye is sick on't;—I observe her now.

Hel. What is your pleasure, madam?

Count.   You know, Helen,
I am a mother to you.

Hel. Mine honourable mistress.

Count.   Nay, a mother:
Why not a mother? When I said a mother,
Methought you saw a serpent: what's in mother,
That you start at it? I say I am your mother;
And put you in the catalogue of those
That were emwombed mine. 'Tis often seen
Adoption strives with nature; and choice breeds
A native slip to us from foreign seeds:
You ne'er oppress'd me with a mother's groan,
Yet I express to you a mother's care:—
God's mercy, maiden! does it curd thy blood
To say I am thy mother? What's the matter,
That this distemper'd messenger of wet,
The many-colour'd iris, rounds thine eye?
Why,—that you are my daughter?

Hel.   That I am not.

Count. I say, I am your mother.

Hel.   Pardon, madam;
The Count Rousillon cannot be my brother:
I am from humble, he from honour'd name;
No note upon my parents, his all noble;
My master, my dear lord he is; and I
His servant live, and will his vassal die:
He must not be my brother.

Count.   Nor I your mother?

Hel. You are my mother, madam; would you were,—
So that my lord your son were not my brother,—
Indeed my mother!—or were you both our mothers,
I care no more for than I do for heaven,
So I were not his sister. Can't no other,
But, I your daughter, he must be my brother?

Count. Yes, Helen, you might be my daugh-ter-in-law: [mother
God shield you mean it not! daughter and
So strive upon your pulse. What! pale again?
My fear hath catch'd your fondness: now I see
The mystery of your loneliness, and find
Your salt tears' head. Now to all sense 'tis gross
You love my son; invention is asham'd,
Against the proclamation of thy passion,
To say thou dost not: therefore tell me true;
But tell me then, 'tis so;—for, look, thy cheeks
Confess it, one to the other; and thine eyes
See it so grossly shown in thy behaviours,
That in their kind they speak it; only sin
And hellish obstinacy tie thy tongue,
That truth should be suspected Speak, is 't so?
If it be so, you have wound a goodly clue;
If it be not, forswear't: howe'er, I charge thee,
As heaven shall work in me for thine avail,
To tell me truly.

Hel.   Good madam, pardon me!

Count. Do you love my son?

Hel.   Your pardon, noble mistress!

Count. Love you my son?

Hel.   Do not you love him, madam?
Count. Go not about; my love hath in't a bond,   [close
Whereof the world takes note: come, come, dis-
The state of your affection; for your passions
Have to the full appeach'd.
Hel.   Then I confess,
Here on my knee, before high heaven and you,
That before you, and next unto high heaven,
I love your son:—
My friends were poor, but honest; so's my love:
Be not offended; for it hurts not him
That he is lov'd of me: I follow him not
By any token of presumptuous suit;
Nor would I have him till I do deserve him;
Yet never know how that desert should be.
I know I love in vain, strive against hope;
Yet in this captious and intenible sieve
I still pour in the waters of my love,
And lack not to lose still: thus, Indian-like,
Religious in mine error, I adore
The sun, that looks upon his worshipper,
But knows of him no more. My dearest madam,
Let not your hate encounter with my love,
For loving where you do; but, if yourself,
Whose aged honours cites a virtuous youth,
Did ever, in so true a frame of liking,
Wish chastely, and love dearly, that your Dian
Was both herself and love; O, then, give pity
To her whose state is such that cannot choose
But lend and give where she is sure to lose;
That seeks not to find that her search implies,
But, riddle-like, lives sweetly where she dies!
Count. Had you not lately an intent,—speak truly,—
To go to Paris?
Hel.   Madam, I had.
Count.   Wherefore? tell true.
Hel. I will tell truth; by grace itself I swear.
You know my father left me some prescriptions
Of rare and prov'd effects, such as his reading
And manifest experience had collected
For general sovereignty; and that he will'd me
In heedfulest reservation to bestow them,
As notes whose faculties inclusive were
More than they were in note: amongst the rest
There is a remedy, approv'd, set down,
To cure the desperate languishings whereof
The king is render'd lost.
Count.   This was your motive
For Paris, was it? speak.   [this;
Hel. My lord your son made me to think of
Else Paris, and the medicine, and the king,
Had from the conversation of my thoughts
Haply been absent then.
Count.   But think you, Helen,
If you should tender your supposed aid,
He would receive it? He and his physicians
Are of a mind; he, that they cannot help him,
They, that they cannot help: how shall they credit
A poor unlearned virgin, when the schools,
Embowell'd of their doctrine, have left off
The danger to itself?

Hel.   There's something in 't
More than my father's skill, which was the greatest
Of his profession, that his good receipt
Shall, for my legacy, be sanctified
By the luckiest stars in heaven: and, would your honour
But give me leave to try success, I'd venture
The well-lost life of mine on his grace's cure
By such a day and hour.
Count.   Dost thou believe 't?
Hel. Ay, madam, knowingly.
Count. Why, Helen, thou shalt have my leave, and love,
Means, and attendants, and my loving greetings
To those of mine in court: I'll stay at home,
And pray God's blessings into thy attempt:
Be gone to-morrow; and be sure of this,
What I can help thee to thou shalt not miss.
          [*Exeunt.*

ACT II.

SCENE I.—PARIS. *A Room in the* KING'S *Palace.*

Flourish. Enter KING, *with young* Lords *taking leave for the Florentine war;* BERTRAM, PA-ROLLES, *and* Attendants.

King. Farewell, young lord; these warlike principles   [farewell:—
Do not throw from you:—and you, my lord,
Share the advice betwixt you; if both gain all,
The gift doth stretch itself as 'tis received,
And is enough for both.
1 *Lord.*   It is our hope, sir,
After well-enter'd soldiers, to return
And find your grace in health.
King. No, no, it cannot be; and yet my heart
Will not confess he owes the malady   [lords;
That doth my life besiege. Farewell, young
Whether I live or die, be you the sons
Of worthy Frenchmen; let higher Italy,—
Those bated that inherit but the fall
Of the last monarchy,—see that you come
Not to woo honour, but to wed it; when
The bravest questant shrinks, find what you seek,
That fame may cry you loud: I say, farewell.
2 *Lord.* Health, at your bidding, serve your majesty!
King. Those girls of Italy, take heed of them:
They say our French lack language to deny,
If they demand: beware of being captives
Before you serve
Both.   Our hearts receive your warnings.
King. Farewell.—Come hither to me.
          [*The* KING *retires to a couch.*
1 *Lord.* O my sweet lord, that you will stay behind us!
Par. 'Tis not his fault; the spark——
2 *Lord.*   O, 'tis brave wars!
Par. Most admirable: I have seen those wars.   [with,
Ber. I am commanded here, and kept a coil
Too young, and *the next year,* and *'tis too early.*

Par. An thy mind stand to it, boy, steal
away bravely.   [smock,

Ber. I shall stay here the forehorse to a
Creaking my shoes on the plain masonry,
Till honour be bought up, and no sword worn
But one to dance with! By heaven, I'll steal
away.

1 Lord. There's honour in the theft.

Par.   Commit it, count.

2 Lord. I am your accessary, and so farewell.

Ber. I grow to you, and our parting is a tor-
tured body.

1 Lord. Farewell, captain.

2 Lord. Sweet Monsieur Parolles!

Par. Noble heroes, my sword and yours are
kin. Good sparks and lustrous, a word, good
metals.—You shall find in the regiment of the
Spinii one Captain Spurio, with his cicatrice, an
emblem of war, here on his sinister cheek, it
was this very sword entrenched it: say to him
I live, and observe his reports for me.

2 Lord. We shall, noble captain.

Par. Mars dote on you for his novices!
[*Exeunt* LORDS.] What will ye do?

Ber. Stay; the king——

Par. Use a more spacious ceremony to the
noble lords; you have restrained yourself within the list of too cold an adieu: be more expres-
sive to them; for they wear themselves in the
cap of the time; there do muster true gait, eat,
speak, and move under the influence of the
most received star; and though the devil lead
the measure, such are to be followed: after
them, and take a more dilated farewell.

Ber. And I will do so.

Par. Worthy fellows; and like to prove most
sinewy sword-men.

[*Exeunt* BERTRAM *and* PAROLLES

Enter LAFEU.

Laf. Pardon, my lord [*kneeling*], for me and
for my tidings.

King. I'll fee thee to stand up.

Laf. Then here's a man stands that has
bought his pardon.   [mercy;
I would you had kneel'd, my lord, to ask me
And that, at my bidding, you could so stand up.

King. I would I had; so I had broke thy
pate,
And ask'd thee mercy for't.

Laf.   Good faith, across;
But, my good lord, 'tis thus: Will you be cured
Of your infirmity?

King.   No.

Laf.   O, will you eat
No grapes, my royal fox? yes, but you will
My noble grapes, and if my royal fox
Could reach them: I have seen a medicine
That's able to breathe life into a stone,
Quicken a rock, and make you dance canary
With spritely fire and motion; whose simple
touch
Is powerful to araise King Pipin, nay,
To give great Charlemain a pen in his hand

And write to her a love-line.

King.   What *her* is that?

Laf. Why, doctor *she:* my lord, there's one
arriv'd,   [honour,
If you will see her,—now, by my faith and
If seriously I may convey my thoughts
In this my light deliverance, I have spoke
With one that in her sex, her years, profession,
Wisdom, and constancy hath amaz'd me more
Than I dare blame my weakness: will you see
her,—   [ness?
For that is her demand,—and know her busi-
That done, laugh well at me.

King.   Now, good Lafeu,
Bring in the admiration; that we with thee
May spend our wonder too, or take off thine
By wondering how thou took'st it.

Laf.   Nay, I'll fit you,
And not be all day neither.   [*Exit* LAFEU.

King. Thus he his special nothing ever prologues.

Re-enter LAFEU *with* HELENA.

Laf. Nay, come your ways.

King.   This haste hath wings indeed.

Laf. Nay, come your ways;
This is his majesty: say your mind to him:
A traitor you do look like; but such traitors
His majesty seldom fears: I am Cressid's uncle,
That dare leave two together: fare you well.
[*Exit.*

King. Now, fair one, does your business follow us?   [was

Hel. Ay, my good lord. Gerard de Narbon
My father; in what he did profess well found.

King. I knew him.

Hel. The rather will I spare my praises to-
wards him.
Knowing him is enough. On his bed of death
Many receipts he gave me; chiefly one,
Which, as the dearest issue of his practice,
And of his old experience the only darling,
He bade me store up as a triple eye,
Safer than mine own two, more dear: I have so
And, hearing your high majesty is touch'd
With that malignant cause wherein the honour
Of my dear father's gift stands chief in power,
I come to tender it, and my appliance,
With all bound humbleness.

King.   We thank you, maiden;
But may not be so credulous of cure,—
When our most learned doctors leave us, and
The congregated college have concluded
That labouring art can never ransom nature
From her inaidable estate,—I say we must not
So stain our judgment, or corrupt our hope,
To prostitute our past-cure malady
To empirics; or, to dissever so
Our great self and our credit, to esteem
A senseless help, when help past sense we deem.

Hel. My duty, then, shall pay me for my
pains:
I will no more enforce mine office on you;
Humbly entreating from your royal thoughts

A modest one to bear me back again.

King. I cannot give thee less, to be call'd
    grateful.   [I give
Thou thought'st to help me; and such thanks
As one near death to those that wish him live:
But what at full I know, thou know'st no part;
I knowing all my peril, thou no art.

Hel. What I can do can do no hurt to try,
Since you set up your rest 'gainst remedy.
He that of greatest works is finisher
Oft does them by the weakest minister:
So holy writ in babes hath judgment shown,
When judges have been babes. Great floods
    have flown
From simple sources; and great seas have dried
When miracles have by the greatest been denied.
Oft expectation fails, and most oft there
Where most it promises; and oft it hits
Where hope is coldest, and despair most fits.

King. I must not hear thee: fare thee well,
    kind maid;
Thy pains, not used, must by thyself be paid:
Proffers, not took, reap thanks for their reward.

Hel. Inspired merit so by breath is barred:
It is not so with Him that all things knows,
As 'tis with us that square our guess by shows:
But most it is presumption in us when
The help of heaven we count the act of men.
Dear sir, to my endeavours give consent:
Of heaven, not me, make an experiment.
I am not an impostor, that proclaim
Myself against the level of mine aim;
But know I think, and think I know most sure,
My art is not past power nor you past cure.

King. Art thou so confident? Within what
    space
Hop'st thou my cure?

Hel.   The greatest grace lending grace,
Ere twice the horses of the sun shall bring
Their fiery torcher his diurnal ring;
Ere twice in murk and occidental damp
Moist Hesperus hath quench'd his sleepy lamp;
Or four-and-twenty times the pilot's glass
Hath told the thievish minutes how they pass;
What is infirm from your sound parts shall fly,
Health shall live free, and sickness freely die.

King. Upon thy certainty and confidence,
What dars't thou venture?

Hel.   Tax of impudence,—
A strumpet's boldness, a divulged shame,—
Traduc'd by odious ballads; my maiden's name
Sear'd otherwise; ne worse of worst extended,
With vilest torture let my life be ended.

King. Methinks in thee some blessed spirit
    doth speak;
His powerful sound within an organ weak:
And what impossibility would slay.
In common sense, sense saves another way.
Thy life is dear; for all that life can rate
Worth name of life in thee hath estimate:
Youth, beauty, wisdom, courage, all
That happiness in prime can happy call;
Thou this to hazard needs must intimate
Skill infinite, or monstrous desperate.

Sweet practiser, thy physic I will try:
That ministers thine own death if I die.

Hel. If I break time, or flinch in property
Of what I spoke, unpitied let me die;
And well deserv'd. Not helping, death's my fee;
But, if I help, what do you promise me?

King. Make thy demand.

Hel.   But will you make it even?

King. Ay, by my sceptre and my hopes of
    heaven.   [ly hand,

Hel. Then shalt thou give me, with thy king-
What husband in thy power I will command:
Exempted be from me the arrogance
To choose from forth the royal blood of France,
My low and humble name to propagate
With any branch or image of thy state:
But such a one, thy vassal, whom I know
Is free for me to ask, thee to bestow.

King. Here is my hand; the premises ob-
    serv'd,
Thy will by my performance shall be serv'd;
So make the choice of thy own tie, for I,
Thy resolv'd patient, on thee still rely.
More should I question thee, and more I must,—
Though more to know could not be more to
    trust,—
From whence thou cam'st, how tended on.—
    But rest
Unquestion'd welcome and undoubted blest.—
Give me some help here, ho!—If thou proceed
As high as word, my deed shall match thy deed.
                      [*Flourish. Exeunt.*

SCENE II.—ROUSILLON. *A Room in the*
COUNTESS's *Palace.*

Enter COUNTESS *and* CLOWN.

Count. Come on, sir; I shall now put you to
the height of your breeding.

Clo. I will show myself highly fed and lowly
taught: I know my business is but to the court.

Count. To the court! why, what place make
you special, when you put off that with such
contempt? But to the court!

Clo. Truly, madam, if God have lent a man
any manners, he may easily put if off at court:
he that cannot make a leg, put off's cap, kiss his
hand, and say nothing, has neither leg, hands,
lip, nor cap; and, indeed, such a fellow, to say
precisely, were not for the court: but, for me, I
have an answer will serve all men.

Count. Marry, that's a bountiful answer that
fits all questions.

Clo. It is like a barber's chair, that fits all
buttocks,—the pin-buttock, the quatch-but-
tock, the brawn-buttock, or any buttock.

Count. Will your answer serve fit to all questions?

Clo. As fit as ten groats is for the hand of a
attorney, as your French crown for your taffeta
punk, as Tib's rush for Tom's forefinger, as a
pancake for Shrove-Tuesday, a morris for May-
day, as the nail to his hole, the cuckold to his
horn, as a scolding quean to a wrangling knave,

as the nun's lip to the friar's mouth; nay, as the pudding to his skin.

Count. Have you, I say, an answer of such fitness for all questions?

Clo. From below your duke to beneath your constable, it will fit any question.

Count. It must be an answer of most monstrous size that must fit all demands.

Clo. But a trifle neither, in good faith, if the learned should speak truth of it: here it is, and all that belongs to't. Ask me if I am a courtier: it shall do you no harm to learn.

Count. To be young again, if we could: I will be a fool in question, hoping to be the wiser by your answer. I pray you, sir, are you a courtier?

Clo. O Lord, sir!—There's a simple putting off;—more, more, a hundred of them.

Count. Sir, I am a poor friend of yours, that loves you.   [me.

Clo. O Lord, sir!—Thick, thick; spare not

Count. I think, sir, you can eat none of this homely meat.

Clo. O Lord, sir!—Nay, put me to't, I warrant you.

Count. You were lately whipped, sir, as I think.

Clo. O Lord, sir!—spare not me.

Count. Do you cry, *O Lord, sir!* at your whipping, and *spare not me?* Indeed, your *O Lord, sir!* is very sequent to your whipping: you would answer very well to a whipping, if you were but bound to't.

Clo. I ne'er had worse luck in my life in my —*O Lord, sir!* I see things may serve long, but not serve ever.

Count. I play the noble housewife with the time, to entertain it so merrily with a fool.

Clo. O Lord, sir!—Why, there't serves well again.

Count. An end, sir, to your business. Give Helen this,

And urge her to a present answer back:
Commend me to my kinsmen and my son:
This is not much.

Clo. Not much commendation to them.

Count. Not much employment for you: you understand me?

Clo. Most fruitfully: I am there before my legs.

Count. Haste you again.   [*Exeunt severally*.

SCENE III.—PARIS. *A Room in the* KING'S *Palace.*

Enter BERTRAM, LAFEU, *and* PAROLLES.

Laf. They say miracles are past; and we have our philosophical persons to make modern and familiar things supernatural and causeless. Hence is it that we make trifles of terrors, ensconcing ourselves into seeming knowledge when we should submit ourselves to an unknown fear.

Par. Why, 'tis the rarest argument of wonder that hath shot out in our latter times.

Ber. And so 'tis.

Laf. To be relinquished of the artists,—

Par. So I say; both of Galen and Paracelsus.

Laf. Of all the learned and authentic fellows,—

Par. Right; so I say.

Laf. That gave him out incurable,—

Par. Why, there 'tis; so say I too.

Laf. Not to be helped,—

Par. Right; as 'twere a man assured of a,—

Laf. Uncertain life and sure death.   [said.

Par. Just; you say well: so would I have

Laf. I may truly say, it is a novelty to the world.

Par. It is indeed: if you will have it in showing, you shall read it in,—What do you call there?—

Laf. A showing of a heavenly effect in an earthly actor.   [same.

Par. That's it I would have said; the very

Laf. Why, your dolphin is not lustier: 'fore me, I speak in respect,—

Par. Nay, 'tis strange, 'tis very strange; that is the brief and the tedious of it; and he is of a most facinorous spirit that will not acknowledge it to be the,—

Laf. Very hand of heaven.

Par. Ay; so I say.

Laf. In a most weak,—

Par. And debile minister, great power, great transcendence: which should, indeed, give us a further use to be made than alone the recovery of the king, as to be,—

Laf. Generally thankful.

Par. I would have said it; you say well. Here comes the king.

Enter KING, HELENA, *and* Attendants.

Laf. Lustic, as the Dutchman says: I'll like a maid the better, whilst I have a tooth in my head: why, he's able to lead her a coranto.

Par. *Mort du Vinaigre!* is not this Helen?

Laf. 'Fore God, I think so.

King. Go, call before me all the lords in court.—   [*Exit an* Attendant.
Sit, my preserver, by thy patient's side;
And with this healthful hand, whose banish'd sense
Thou hast repeal'd, a second time receive
The confirmation of my promis'd gift,
Which but attends thy naming.

Enter several Lords.

Fair maid, send forth thine eye: this youthful parcel
Of noble bachelors stand at my bestowing,
O'er whom both sovereign power and father's voice
I have to use: thy frank election make;
Thou hast power to choose, and they none to forsake.   [mistress

Hel. To each of you one fair and virtuous
Fall, when love please!—marry, to each, but one!

Laf. I'd give bay Curtal, and his furniture,

My mouth no more were broken than these
    boys',
And writ as little beard.
    King.   Peruse them well:
Not one of those but had a noble father.
    Hel. Gentlemen,
Heaven hath, through me, restor'd the king to
    health.   [you.
    All. We understand it, and thank heaven for
    Hel. I am a simple maid, and therein wealth-
    iest
That I protest I simply am a maid.—
Please it, your majesty, I have done already:
The blushes in my cheeks thus whisper me—
We blush that thou shouldst choose; but, be refus'd,
Let the white death sit on thy cheek for ever;
We'll ne'er come there again.
    King.   Make choice; and, see,
Who shuns thy love shuns all his love in me.
    Hel. Now, Dian, from thy altar do I fly,
And to imperial Love, that god most high,
Do my sighs stream.—Sir, will you hear my
    suit?
    1 *Lord.* And grant it.
    Hel.   Thanks, sir; all the rest is mute.
    Laf. I had rather be in this choice than
throw ames-ace for my life.   [eyes,
    Hel. The honour, sir, that flames in your fair
Before I speak, too threateningly replies:
Love make your fortunes twenty times above
Her that so wishes, and her humble love!
    2 *Lord.* No better, if you please.
    Hel.   My wish receive,
Which great Love grant! and so I take my
    leave.
    Laf. Do all they deny her? An they were
sons of mine I'd have them whipped; or I would
send them to the Turk to make eunuchs of.
    Hel. [*To third* Lord.] Be not afraid that I
    your hand should take;
I'll never do you wrong for your own sake:
Blessing upon your vows! and in your bed
Find fairer fortune, if you ever wed!
    Laf. These boys are boys of ice; they'll none
have her: sure, they are bastards to the English; the French ne'er got them.   [good
    Hel. You are too young, too happy, and too
To make yourself a son out of my blood.
    4 *Lord.* Fair one, I think not so.
    Laf. There's one grape yet,—I am sure thy
father drank wine.—But if thou beest not an
ass, I am a youth of fourteen; I have known
thee already.
    Hel. [*To* BERTRAM.] I dare not say I take
    you; but I give
Me and my service, ever whilst I live,
Into your guiding power.—This is the man.
    King. Why, then, young Bertram, take her;
    she's thy wife.   [highness,
    Ber. My wife, my liege! I shall beseech your
In such a business give me leave to use
The help of mine own eyes.
    King.   Know'st thou not, Bertram,
What she has done for me?

    Ber.   Yes, my good lord;
But never hope to know why I should marry
    her.   [my sickly bed.
    King. Thou know'st she has rais'd me from
    Ber. But follows it, my lord, to bring me
    down
Must answer for your raising? I know her well;
She had her breeding at my father's charge;
A poor physician's daughter my wife!—Disdain
Rather corrupt me ever!   [the which
    King. 'Tis only title thou disdain'st in her,
I can build up. Strange is it that our bloods,
Of colour, weight, and heat, pour'd all together,
Would quite confound distinction, yet stand off
In differences so mighty. If she be
All that is virtuous,—save what thou dislik'st,
A poor physician's daughter,—thou dislik'st
Of virtue for the name: but do not so:
From lowest place when virtuous things proceed,
The place is dignified by the doer's deed:
Where great additions swell 's, and virtue none,
It is a dropsied honour: good alone
Is good without a name, vileness is so:
The property by what it is should go,
Not by the title. She is young, wise, fair;
In these to nature she's immediate heir;
And these breed honour: that is honour's scorn
Which challenges itself as honour's born,
And is not like the sire: honours thrive,
When rather from our acts we them derive
Than our fore-goers: the mere word's a slave,
Debauch'd on every tomb; on every grave
A lying trophy; and as oft is dumb
Where dust and damn'd oblivion is the tomb
Of honour'd bones indeed. What should be
    said?
If thou canst like this creature as a maid,
I can create the rest: virtue and she
Is her own dower; honour and wealth from me.
    Ber. I cannot love her, nor will strive to do 't.
    King. Thou wrong'st thyself, if thou shouldst
    strive to choose.   [am glad:
    Hel. That you are well restor'd, my lord, I
Let the rest go.   [defeat,
    King. My honour's at the stake; which to
I must produce my power. Here, take her hand,
Proud scornful boy, unworthy this good gift;
That dost in vile misprision shackle up
My love and her desert; that canst not dream
We, poising us in her defective scale,
Shall weigh thee to the beam; that wilt not
    know
It is in us to plant thine honour where
We please to have it grow. Check thy con-
    tempt:
Obey our will, which travails in thy good:
Believe not thy disdain, but presently
Do thine own fortunes that obedient right
Which both thy duty owes and our power claims
Or I will throw thee from my care for ever,
Into the staggers and the careless lapse
Of youth and ignorance; both my revenge and
    hate
Loosing upon thee in the name of justice,

Without all terms of pity. Speak!—thine
    answer!

Ber. Pardon, my gracious lord; for I submit
My fancy to your eyes: when I consider
What great creation, and what dole of honour
Flies where you bid it, I find that she, which
    late
Was in my nobler thoughts most base, is now
The praised of the king; who, so ennobled,
Is as 'twere born so.

King.   Take her by the hand,
And tell her she is thine: to whom I promise
A counterpoise; if not to thy estate,
A balance more replete.

Ber.   I take her hand.

King. Good fortune and the favour of the king
Smile upon this contract; whose ceremony
Shall seem expedient on the new-born brief,
And be perform'd to-night: the solemn feast
Shall more attend upon the coming space,
Expecting absent friends. As thou lov'st her,
Thy love's to me religious; else, does err.

    [*Exeunt* KING, BER., HEL., Lords,
        and Attendants.

Laf. Do you hear, monsieur? a word with
you.

Par. Your pleasure, sir?

Laf. Your lord and master did well to make
his recantation.

Par. Recantation!—My lord! my master!

Laf. Ay; is it not a language I speak?

Par. A most harsh one, and not to be understood without bloody succeeding. My master!

Laf. Are you companion to the Count
Rousillon?   [is man.

Par. To any count; to all counts; to what

Laf. To what is count's man: count's master
is of another style.

Par. You are too old, sir; let it satisfy you,
you are too old.

Laf. I must tell thee, sirrah, I write man;
to which title age cannot bring thee.

Par. What I dare too well do, I dare not do.

Laf. I did think thee, for two ordinaries, to
be a pretty wise fellow; thou didst make tolerable vent of thy travel; it might pass: yet the
scarfs and the bannerets about thee did manifoldly dissuade me from believing thee a vessel
of two great a burden. I have now found thee,
when I lose thee again I care not: yet art thou
good for nothing but taking up; and that thou
art scarce worth.

Par. Hadst thou not the privilege of antiquity upon thee,—

Laf. Do not plunge thyself too far in anger,
lest thou hasten thy trial; which if—Lord have
mercy on thee for a hen! So, my good window
of lattice, fare thee well: thy casement I need
not open, for I look through thee. Give me thy
hand.   [indignity.

Par. My lord, you give me most egregious

Laf. Ay, with all my heart; and thou art
worthy of it.

Par. I have not, my lord, deserved it.

Laf. Yes, good faith, every dram of it: and
I will not bate thee a scruple.

Par. Well, I shall be wiser.

Laf. E'en as soon as thou canst, for thou hast
to pull at a smack o' the contrary. If ever thou
beest bound in thy scarf and beaten, thou shalt
find what it is to be proud of thy bondage. I
have a desire to hold my acquaintance with
thee, or rather my knowledge, that I may say,
in the default, he is a man I know.

Par. My lord, you do me most insupportable
vexation

Laf. I would it were hell-pains for thy sake,
and my poor doing eternal: for doing I am past;
as I will by thee, in what motion age will give
me leave.   [*Exit.*

Par. Well, thou hast a son shall take this
disgrace off me; scurvy, old, filthy, scurvy
lord!—Well, I must be patient; there is no fettering of authority. I'll beat him, by my life, if
I can meet him with any convenience, an he
were double and double a lord. I'll have no
more pity of his age than I would have of—I'll
beat him, an if I could but meet him again.

Re-enter LAFEU.

Laf. Sirrah, your lord and master's married;
there's news for you; you have a new mistress.

Par. I most unfeignedly beseech your lordship to make some reservation of your wrongs:
he is my good lord: whom I serve above is my
master.

Laf. Who? God?

Par. Ay, sir.

Laf. The devil it is that's thy master. Why
dost thou garter up thy arms o' this fashion?
dost make hose of thy sleeves? do other servants so? Thou wert best set thy lower part
where thy nose stands. By mine honour, if I
were but two hours younger I'd beat thee:
methink'st thou art a general offence, and
every man should beat thee. I think thou wast
created for men to breathe themselves upon
thee.

Par. This is hard and undeserved measure,
my lord.

Laf. Go to, sir; you were beaten in Italy for
picking a kernel out of a pomegranate; you are
a vagabond, and no true traveller: you are more
saucy with lords and honourable personages
than the heraldry of your birth and virtue gives
you commission. You are not worth another
word, else I'd call you knave. I leave you.

          [*Exit.*

Par. Good, very good; it is so then.—Good,
very good; let it be concealed awhile.

Enter BERTRAM.

Ber. Undone, and forfeited to cares for ever!

Par. What is the matter, sweet heart?

Ber. Although before the solemn priest I
    have sworn,
I will not bed her.

Par. What, what, sweet heart?

Ber. O my Parolles, they have married me!—
I'll to the Tuscan wars, and never bed her.

Par. France is a dog-hole, and it no more
　　merits
The tread of a man's foot:—to the wars!

Ber. There's letters from my mother: what
　　the import is
I know not yet.

Par. Ay, that would be known. To the wars,
　　my boy, to the wars!
He wears his honour in a box unseen
That hugs his kieksy-wieksy here at home,
Spending his manly marrow in her arms,
Which should sustain the bound and high curvet
Of Mars's fiery steed. To other regions!
France is a stable; we, that dwell in't, jades;
Therefore, to the war!　　　　　　[house,

Ber. It shall be so; I'll send her to my house,
Acquaint my mother with my hate to her,
And wherefore I am fled; write to the king
That which I durst not speak: his present gift
Shall furnish me to those Italian fields
Where noble fellows strike: war is no strife
To the dark house and the detested wife.

Par. Will this caprichio hold in thee, art
　　sure?　　　　　　　　　　　[me.

Ber. Go with me to my chamber and advise
I'll send her straight away: to-morrow
I'll to the wars, she to her single sorrow.

Par. Why, these balls bound; there's noise
　　in it. 'Tis hard;
A young man married is a man that's marr'd:
Therefore away, and leave her bravely; go:
The king has done you wrong: but, hush! 'tis
　　so.　　　　　　　　　　　[*Exeunt*

SCENE IV.—*The same. Another Room in the
same.*

Enter HELENA *and* Clown.

Hel. My mother greets me kindly: is she
well?

Clo. She is not well; but yet she has her
health: she's very merry; but yet she is not
well: but thanks be given, she's very well, and
wants nothing i' the world; but yet she is not
well.

Hel. If she be very well, what does she ail,
that she's not very well?

Clo. Truly, she's very well indeed, but for
two things.

Hel. What two things?

Clo. One, that she's not in heaven, whither
God send her quickly! the other, that she's in
earth, from whence God send her quickly!

Enter PAROLLES.

Par. Bless you, my fortunate lady!

Hel. I hope, sir, I have your good will to
have mine own good fortunes.

Par. You had my prayers to lead them on;
and to keep them on, have them still. O, my
knave,—how does my old lady?

Clo. So that you had her wrinkles and I her
money, I would she did as you say.

Par. Why, I say nothing.

Clo. Marry, you are the wiser man; for many
a man's tongue shakes out his master's undo-
ing: to say nothing, to do nothing, to know
nothing, and to have nothing, is to be a great
part of your title; which is within a very little
of nothing.

Par. Away! thou'rt a knave.

Clo. You should have said, sir, before a
knave thou art a knave; that is, before me thou
art a knave: this had been truth, sir.

Par. Go to, thou art a witty fool; I have
found thee.

Clo. Did you find me in yourself, sir? or
were you taught to find me? The search, sir,
was profitable; and much fool may you find in
you, even to the world's pleasure and the increase of laughter.

Par. A good knave, i' faith, and well fed.—
Madam, my lord will go away to-night:
A very serious business calls on him.
The great prerogative and right of love,
Which, as your due, time claims, he does ac-
　　knowledge;
But puts it off to a compell'd restraint;
Whose want and whose delay is strew'd with
　　sweets;
Which they distil now in the curbed time,
To make the coming hour o'erflow with joy,
And pleasure drown the brim.

Hel.　　　　　　　　What's his will else?

Par. That you will take your instant leave o'
　　the king,　　　　　　　　　[ing,
And make this haste as your own good proceed-
Strengthen'd with what apology you think
May make it probable need.

Hel.　　　　　What more commands he?

Par. That, having this obtain'd, you pre-
　　sently
Attend his further pleasure.

Hel. In everything I wait upon his will.

Par. I shall report it so.

Hel.　　　　　I pray you.—Come, sirrah.
　　　　　　　　　　　　　　[*Exeunt.*

SCENE V.—*Another Room in the same.*

Enter LAFEU *and* BERTRAM.

Laf. But I hope your lordship thinks not
him a soldier.

Ber. Yes, my lord, and of very valiant ap-
　proof.

Laf. You have it from his own deliverance.

Ber. And by other warranted testimony.

Laf. Then my dial goes not true: I took this
lark for a bunting.

Ber. I do assure you, my lord, he is very
great in knowledge, and accordingly valiant.

Laf. I have, then, sinned against his experience and transgressed against his valour; and
my state that way is dangerous, since I cannot
yet find in my heart to repent. Here he comes:
I pray you, make us friends; I will pursue the
amity.

Enter PAROLLES.

Par. These things shall be done, sir.
                                        [*To* BER.
Laf. Pray you, sir, who's his tailor?
Par. Sir!
Laf. O, I know him well, I, sir; he, sir, is a
good workman, a very good tailor.
Ber. Is she gone to the king? [*Aside to* PAR.
Par. She is.
Ber. Will she away to-night?
Par. As you'll have her.   [treasure,
Ber. I have writ my letters, casketed my
Given order for our horses; and to-night,
When I should take possession of the bride,
End ere I do begin.
Laf. A good traveller is something at the
latter end of a dinner; but one that lies three-
thirds and uses a known truth to pass a thou-
sand nothings with, should be once heard and
thrice beaten.—God save you, captain.
Ber. Is there any unkindness between my
lord and you, monsieur?
Par. I know not how I have deserved to run
into my lord's displeasure.
Laf. You have made shift to run into 't,
boots and spurs and all, like him that leaped
into the custard; and out of it you'll run again,
rather than suffer question for your residence.
Ber. It may be you have mistaken him, my
lord.
Laf. And shall do so ever, though I took him
at his prayers. Fare you well, my lord; and
believe this of me, there can be no kernel in
this light nut; the soul of this man is his clothes:
trust him not in matter of heavy consequence;
I have kept of them tame, and know their
natures.—Farewell, monsieur: I have spoken
better of you than you have or will deserve at
my hand; but we must do good against evil.
                                        [*Exit.*

Par. An idle lord, I swear.
Ber. I think so.
Par. Why, do you not know him?   [speech
Ber. Yes, I do know him well; and common
Gives him a worthy pass. Here comes my clog.

Enter HELENA.

Hel. I have, sir, as I was commanded from
        you,   [leave
Spoke with the king, and have procur'd his
For present parting; only, he desires
Some private speech with you.
Ber.   I shall obey his will.
You must not marvel, Helen, at my course,
Which holds not colour with the time, nor does
The ministration and required office
On my particular. Prepared I was not
For such a business; therefore am I found
So much unsettled: this drives me to entreat
        you
That presently you take your way for home,
And rather muse than ask why I entreat you:
For my respects are better than they seem;
And my appointments have in them a need

Greater than shows itself at the first view
To you that know them not. This to my
        mother: [*Giving a letter.*
'Twill be two days ere I shall see you; so
I leave you to your wisdom.
Hel.   Sir, I can nothing say
But that I am your most obedient servant.
Ber. Come, come, no more of that.
Hel.   And ever shall
With true obedience seek to eke out that
Wherein toward me my homely stars have
        fail'd
To equal my great fortune.
Ber.   Let that go:
My haste is very great. Farewell; hie home.
Hel. Pray, sir, your pardon.
Ber. Well, what would you say?
Hel. I am not worthy of the wealth I owe;
Nor dare I say 'tis mine, and yet it is;   [steal
But, like a timorous thief, most fain would
What law does vouch mine own.
Ber.   What would you have?
Hel. Something; and scarce so much:—no-
        thing, indeed.—   [faith, yes;—
I would not tell you what I would, my lord:—
Strangers and foes do sunder and not kiss.
Ber. I pray you, stay not, but in haste to
        horse.   [my lord.
Hel. I shall not break your bidding, good
Ber. Where are my other men, monsieur?—
        Farewell,   [*Exit* HELENA.
Go thou toward home, where I will never come
Whilst I can shake my sword or hear the
        drum:—
Away, and for our flight.
Par.   Bravely, coragio! [*Exeunt.*

ACT III.

SCENE I.—FLORENCE. *A Room in the*
        DUKE'S *Palace.*

Flourish. Enter the DUKE OF FLORENCE,
attended; two French Lords, *and* Soldiers.

Duke. So that, from point to point, now have
        you heard
The fundamental reasons of this war;
Whose great decision hath much blood let
        forth,
And more thirsts after.
1 Lord.   Holy seems the quarrel
Upon your grace's part; black and fearful
On the opposer.   [France
Duke. Therefore we marvel much our cousin
Would, in so just a business, shut his bosom
Against our borrowing prayers.
1 Lord.   Good my lord,
The reasons of our state I cannot yield,
But like a common and an outward man
That the great figure of a council frames
By self-unable motion: therefore dare not
Say what I think of it, since I have found
Myself in my uncertain grounds to fail
As often as I guess'd.
Duke.   Be it his pleasure.

2 Lord. But I am sure the younger of our
nature,
That surfeit on their ease, will day by day
Come here for physic.
Duke.   Welcome shall they be;
And all the honours that can fly from us
Shall on them settle. You know your places
well;
When better fall, for your avails they fell:
To-morrow to the field.   [*Flourish.   Exeunt.*

SCENE II.—ROUSILLON. *A Room in the*
COUNTESS'S *Palace.*

Enter COUNTESS *and* CLOWN.

Count. It hath happened all as I would have
had it, save that he comes not along with her.
Clo. By my troth, I take my young lord to
be a very melancholy man.
Count. By what observance, I pray you?
Clo. Why, he will look upon his boot and
sing; mend the ruff and sing; ask questions and
sing; pick his teeth and sing. I know a man that
had this trick of melancholy sold a goodly
manor for a song.
Count. Let me see what he writes, and when
he means to come.   [*Opening a letter.*
Clo. I have no mind to Isbel, since I was at
court: our old ling and our Isbels o' the country
are nothing like your old ling and your Isbels o'
the court: the brains of my Cupid's knocked
out; and I begin to love, as an old man loves
money, with no stomach.
Count. What have we here?
Clo. E'en that you have there.   [*Exit.*
Count. [*Reads.*] *I have sent you a daughter-in-*
law: she hath recovered the king and undone me. I
have wedded her, not bedded her; and sworn to
make the not eternal. You shall hear I am run
away: know it before the report come. If there
be breadth enough in the world I will hold a long
distance. My duty to you.
                    Your unfortunate son,
                              BERTRAM.

This is not well, rash and unbridled boy,
To fly the favours of so good a king;
To pluck his indignation on thy head
By the misprizing of a maid too virtuous
For the contempt of empire.

Re-enter Clown.

Clo. O madam, yonder is heavy news within,
between two soldiers and my young lady.
Count. What is the matter?
Clo. Nay, there is some comfort in the news,
some comfort; your son will not be killed so
soon as I thought he would.
Count. Why should he be killed?
Clo. So say I, madam, if he run away, as I
hear he does: the danger is in standing to't;
that's the loss of men, though it be the getting
of children. Here they come will tell you more:
for my part, I only hear your son was run away.
                                        [*Exit.*

Enter HELENA *and two* Gentlemen.

1 Gent. Save you, good madam.
Hel. Madam, my lord is gone, for ever gone.
2 Gent. Do not say so.   [gentlemen,—
Count. Think upon patience.—Pray you,
I have felt so many quirks of joy and grief
That the first face of neither, on the start,
Can woman me unto't.—Where is my son, I
pray you?   [of Florence:
2 Gent. Madam, he's gone to serve the duke
We met him thitherward; for thence we came,
And, after some despatch in hand at court,
Thither we bend again.   [passport.
Hel. Look on his letter, madam; here's my
[*Reads.*] *When thou canst get the ring upon my*
finger, which never shall come off, and show me
a child begotten of thy body that I am father to,
then call me husband; but in such a then I
write a never.
This is a dreadful sentence.
Count. Brought you this letter, gentlemen?
1 Gent.   Ay, madam;
And, for the contents' sake, are sorry for our
pains.
Count. I pr'ythee, lady, have a better cheer;
If thou engrossest all the griefs are thine,
Thou robb'st me of a moiety. He was my son:
But I do wash his name out of my blood,
And thou art all my child.—Towards Florence
is he?
2 Gent. Ay, madam.
Count. .   And to be a soldier?
2 Gent. Such is his noble purpose; and, be-
lieve't,
The duke will lay upon him all the honour
That good convenience claims.
Count.   Return you thither?
1 Gent. Ay, madam, with the swiftest wing
of speed.
Hel. [*Reads.*] *Till I have no wife, I have no-*
thing in France.
'Tis bitter.
Count. Find you that there?
Hel.   Ay, madam.
1 Gent. 'Tis but the boldness of his hand,
haply,
Which his heart was not consenting to.
Count. Nothing in France until he have no
wife!
There's nothing here that is too good for him
But only she; and she deserves a lord
That twenty such rude boys might tend upon,
And call her hourly mistress. Who was with
him?
1 Gent. A servant only, and a gentleman
Which I have sometime known.
Count.   Parolles, was't not?
1 Gent. Ay, my good lady, he.
Count. A very tainted fellow, and full of
wickedness.
My son corrupts a well-derived nature
With his inducement.
1 Gent.   Indeed, good lady,
The fellow has a deal of that too much,

Which holds him much to have.
 Count. You are welcome, gentlemen,
I will entreat you, when you see my son,
To tell him that his sword can never win
The honour that he loses: more I'll entreat you
Written to bear along.
 2 Gent.   We serve you, madam,
In that and all your worthiest affairs. [tesies.
 Count. Not so, but as we change our cour-
Will you draw near?
      [*Exeunt* COUNT. *and* Gentlemen.
 Hel. Till I have no wife, I have nothing in
  France.
Nothing in France until he has no wife!
Thou shalt have none, Rousillon, none in
  France;
Then hast thou all again. Poor lord! is't I
That chase thee from thy country, and expose
Those tender limbs of thine to the event
Of the none-sparing war? and is it I [thou
That drive thee from the sportive court, where
Wast shot at with fair eyes, to be the mark
Of smoky muskets? O you leaden messengers,
That ride upon the violent speed of fire,
Fly with false aim: move the still-peering air,
That sings with piercing; do not touch my lord!
Whoever shoots at him, I set him there;
Whoever charges on his forward breast,
I am the caitiff that do hold him to it;
And, though I kill him not, I am the cause
His death was so effected: better 'twere
I met the ravin lion when he roar'd
With sharp constraint of hunger; better 'twere
That all the miseries which nature owes
Were mine at once. No; come thou home,
  Rousillon,
Whence honour but of danger wins a scar,
As oft it loses all. I will be gone:
My being here it is that holds thee hence:
Shall I stay here to do't? no, no, although
The air of paradise did fan the house,
And angels offic'd all: I will be gone,
That pitiful rumour may report my flight,
To consolate thine ear. Come, night; end, day!
For with the dark, poor thief, I'll steal away.
         [*Exit.*

SCENE III.—FLORENCE. *Before the* DUKE's
  Palace.

Flourish. Enter the DUKE OF FLORENCE, BER-
TRAM, PAROLLES, Lords, Officers, Soldiers,
and others.

 Duke. The general of our horse thou art; and
  we,
Great in our hope, lay our best love and cre-
  dence
Upon thy promising fortune.
 Ber.   Sir, it is
A charge too heavy for my strength; but yet
We'll strive to bear it, for your worthy sake,
To the extreme edge of hazard.
 Duke.   Then go thou forth;

And fortune play upon thy prosperous helm,
As thy auspicious mistress!
 Ber.   This very day,
Great Mars, I put myself into thy file;
Make me but like my thoughts, and I shall
  prove
A lover of thy drum, hater of love. [*Exeunt.*

SCENE IV.—ROUSILLON. *A Room in the*
  COUNTESS'S *Palace.*

Enter COUNTESS *and* Steward.

 Count. Alas! and would you take the letter
  of her?   [done,
Might you not know she would do as she has
By sending me a letter? Read it again.
 Stew. [*Reads.*] *I am St. Jaques' pilgrim,*
  thither gone:
 Ambitious love hath so in me offended
That barefoot plod I the cold ground upon,
 With sainted vow my faults to have amended.
Write, write, that from the bloody course of war
 My dearest master, your dear son, may hie:
Bless him at home in peace, whilst I from far
 His name with zealous fervour sanctify:
His taken labours bid him me forgive;
 I, his despiteful Juno, sent him forth
From courtly friends, with camping foes to live,
 Where death and danger dog the heels of worth:
He is too good and fair for death and me;
Whom I myself embrace, to set him free.
 Count. Ah, what sharp stings are in her mild-
  est words!—
Rinaldo, you did never lack advice so much
As letting her pass so; had I spoke with her,
I could have well diverted her intents,
Which thus she hath prevented.
 Stew.   Pardon me, madam:
If I had given you this at over-night, [writes,
She might have been o'erta'en; and yet she
Pursuit would be but vain.
 Count.   What angel shall
Bless this unworthy husband? he cannot thrive,
Unless her prayers, whom heaven delights to
  hear,
And loves to grant, reprieve him from the
  wrath
Of greatest justice.—Write, write, Rinaldo,
To this unworthy husband of his wife:
Let every word weigh heavy of her worth,
That he does weigh too light: my greatest grief,
Though little he do feel it, set down sharply.
Despatch the most convenient messenger:—
When, haply, he shall hear that she is gone
He will return; and hope I may that she,
Hearing so much, will speed her foot again,
Led hither by pure love: which of them both
Is dearest to me I have no skill in sense
To make distinction:—provide this messen-
  ger:—
My heart is heavy, and mine age is weak;
Grief would have tears, and sorrow bids me
  speak.   [*Exeunt.*

SCENE V.—*Without the Walls of* FLORENCE.

Enter an old Widow *of Florence,* DIANA, VIO-
LENTA, MARIANA, *and other* Citizens.

Wid. Nay, come; for if they do approach the
city we shall lose all the sight.

Dia. They say the French count has done
most honourable service.

Wid. It is reported that he has taken their
greatest commander; and that with his own
hand he slew the duke's brother. [*A tucket afar
off.*] We have lost our labour; they are gone a
contrary way: hark! you may know by their
trumpets.

Mar. Come, let's return again, and suffice
ourselves with the report·of it. Well, Diana,
take heed of this French earl: the honour of a
maid is her name; and no legacy is so rich as
honesty.

Wid. I have told my neighbour how you
have been solicited by a gentleman his companion.

Mar. I know that knave; hang him! one
Parolles: a filthy officer he is in those suggestions for the young earl.—Beware of them,
Diana; their promises, enticements, oaths,
tokens, and all these engines of lust, are not the
things they go under: many a maid hath been
seduced by them; and the misery is, example,
that so terrible shows in the wreck of maiden-
hood, cannot for all that dissuade succession,
but that they are limed with the twigs that
threaten them. I hope I need not to advise you
further; but I hope your own grace will keep
you where you are, though there were no further danger known but the modesty which is so
lost.

Dia. You shall not need to fear me.

Wid. I hope so.—Look, here comes a pilgrim: I know she will lie at my house: thither
they send one another; I'll question her.—

Enter HELENA *in the dress of a pilgrim.*

God save you, pilgrim! Whither are you bound?

Hel. To Saint Jaques-le-Grand.

Where do the palmers lodge, I do beseech you?

Wid. At the Saint Francis here, beside the
port.

Hel. Is this the way?

Wid. Ay, marry, is it.—Hark you! They
come this way. [*A march afar off.*
If you will tarry, holy pilgrim,
But till the troops come by,
I will conduct you where you shall be lodg'd;
The rather for I think I know your hostess
As ample as myself.

Hel. Is it yourself?

Wid. If you shall please so, pilgrim.

Hel. I thank you, and will stay upon your
leisure.

Wid. You came, I think, from France?

Hel. I did so.

Wid. Here you shall see a countryman of
yours

That has done worthy service.

Hel. His name, I pray you.

Dia. The Count Rousillon: know you such a
one? [of him:

Hel. But by the ear, that hears most nobly
His face I know not.

Dia. Whatsoe'er he is,
He's bravely taken here. He stole from France,
As 'tis reported, for the king had married him
Against his liking: think you it is so?

Hel. Ay, surely, mere the truth; I know his
lady. [count

Dia. There is a gentleman that serves the
Reports but coarsely of her.

Hel. What's his name?

Dia. Monsieur Parolles.

Hel. O, I believe with him,
In argument of praise, or to the worth
Of the great count himself, she is too mean
To have her name repeated; all her deserving
Is a reserved honesty, and that
I have not heard examin'd.

Dia. Alas, poor lady!
'Tis a hard bondage to become the wife
Of a detesting lord.

Wid. Ay, right; good creature, wheresoe'er
she is
Her heart weighs sadly: this young maid might
do her
A shrewd turn if she pleas'd.

Hel. How do you mean?
May be, the amorous count solicits her
In the unlawful purpose.

Wid. He does, indeed;
And brokes with all that can in such a suit
Corrupt the tender honour of a maid;
But she is arm'd for him, and keeps her guard
In honestest defence.

Mar. The gods forbid else!

Wid. So, now they come:—

*Enter, with a drum and colours, a party of the
Florentine army,* BERTRAM, *and* PAROLLES.

That is Antonio, the duke's eldest son;
That, Escalus.

Hel. Which is the Frenchman?

Dia. He;
That with the plume: 'tis a most gallant fellow.
I would he lov'd his wife: if he were honester
He were much goodlier:—is't not a handsome
gentleman?

Hel. I like him well. [same knave

Dia. 'Tis pity he is not honest? yond's that
That leads him to these places; were I his lady
I'd poison that vile rascal.

Hel. Which is he?

Dia. The jack-an-apes with scarfs. Why is
he melancholy?

Hel. Perchance he's hurt i' the battle.

Par. Lose our drum! well.

Mar. He's shrewdly vexed at something:
look, he has spied us.

Wid. Marry, hang you!

Mar. And your courtesy, for a ring-carrier!
  [*Exeunt* BER., PAR., Officers, *and* Soldiers.
Wid. The troop is past. Come, pilgrim, I
  will bring you
Where you shall host: of enjoin'd penitents
There's four or five, to great Saint Jacques
  bound,
Already at my house.
Hel.   I humbly thank you:
Please it this matron and this gentle maid
To eat with us to-night; the charge and thank-
  ing
Shall be for me: and, to requite you further,
I will bestow some precepts on this virgin,
Worthy the note.
Both.   We'll take your offer kindly.
                                    [*Exeunt.*

SCENE VI.—*Camp before* FLORENCE.

Enter BERTRAM, *and the two* French Lords.

1 Lord. Nay, good my lord, put him to't; let
him have his way.

2 Lord. If your lordship find him not a hilding, hold me no more in your respect.

1 Lord. On my life, my lord, a bubble.

Ber. Do you think I am so far deceived in
him?

1 Lord. Believe it, my lord, in mine own direct knowledge, without any malice, but to
speak of him as my kinsman, he's a most notable coward, an infinite and endless liar, an
hourly promise-breaker, the owner of no one
good quality worthy your lordship's entertainment.

2 Lord. It were fit you knew him; lest, re-
posing too far in his virtue, which he hath not,
he might, at some great and trusty business, in
a main danger, fail you.

Ber. I would I knew in what particular
action to try him.

2 Lord. None better than to let him fetch off
his drum, which you hear him so confidently
undertake to do.

1 Lord. I, with a troop of Florentines, will
suddenly surprise him; such I will have, whom
I am sure he knows not from the enemy: we will
bind and hoodwink him so that he shall suppose
no other but that he is carried into the leaguer
of the adversaries when we bring him to our
tents. Be but your lordship present at his examination: if he do not, for the promise of his
life, and in the highest compulsion of base fear,
offer to betray you, and deliver all the intelligence in his power against you, and that with
the divine forfeit of his soul upon oath, never
trust my judgment in anything.

2 Lord. O, for the love of laughter, let him
fetch off his drum; he says he has a stratagem
for't: when your lordship sees the bottom of his
success in't, and to what metal this counterfeit
lump of ore will be melted, if you give him not
John Drum's entertainment, your inclining
cannot be removed. Here he comes.

1 Lord. O, for the love of laughter, hinder
not the humour of his design: let him fetch off
his drum in any hand.

Enter PAROLLES.

Ber. How now, monsieur? this drum sticks
sorely in your disposition.

2 Lord. A pox on't; let it go; 'tis but a drum.

Par. But a drum! Is't but a drum? A drum
so lost!—There was an excellent command! to
charge in with our horse upon our own wings,
and to rend our own soldiers.

2 Lord. That was not to be blamed in the
command of the service; it was a disaster of war
that Cæsar himself could not have prevented, if
he had been there to command.

Ber. Well, we cannot greatly condemn our
success; some dishonour we had in the loss of
that drum; but it is not to be recovered.

Par. It might have been recovered.

Ber. It might, but it is not now.

Par. It is to be recovered: but that the merit
of service is seldom attributed to the true and
exact performer, I would have that drum or another, or *hic jacet.*

Ber. Why, if you have a stomach to't, monsieur, if you think your mystery in stratagem
can bring this instrument of honour again into
his native quarter, be magnanimous in the enterprise, and go on; I will grace the attempt for
a worthy exploit; if you speed well in it the
duke shall both speak of it, and extend to you
what further becomes his greatness, even to the
utmost syllable of your worthiness.

Par. By the hand of a soldier, I will undertake it.

Ber. But you must not now slumber in it.

Par. I'll be about it this evening: and I will
presently pen down my dilemmas, encourage
myself in my certainty, put myself into my
mortal preparation, and, by midnight, look to
hear further from me.

Ber. May I be bold to acquaint his grace you
are gone about it?

Par. I know not what the success will be,
my lord, but the attempt I vow.

Ber. I know thou art valiant; and, to the
possibility of thy soldiership, will subscribe for
thee. Farewell.

Par. I love not many words.   [*Exit.*

1 Lord. No more than a fish loves water.—Is
not this a strange fellow, my lord? that so confidently seems to undertake this business, which
he knows is not to be done; damns himself to
do, and dares better be damned than to do't.

2 Lord. You do not know him, my lord, as
we do: certain it is that he will steal himself into a man's favour, and for a week escape a
great deal of discoveries; but when you find
him out, you have him ever after.

Ber. Why, do you think he will make no
deed at all of this, that so seriously he does
address himself unto?

1 Lord. None in the world; but return with
an invention, and clap upon you two or three

probable lies: but we have almost embossed him,—you shall see his fall to-night: for indeed he is not for your lordship's respect.

2 Lord. We'll make you some sport with the fox ere we case him. He was first smoked by the old Lord Lafeu: when his disguise and he is parted, tell me what a sprat you shall find him; which you shall see this very night.

1 Lord. I must go look my twigs; he shall be caught.

Ber. Your brother, he shall go along with me.

1 Lord. As't please your lordship: I'll leave you. [*Exit.*

Ber. Now will I lead you to the house, and show you
The lass I spoke of.

2 Lord. But you say she's honest.

Ber. That's all the fault: I spoke with her but once, [her,
And found her wondrous cold; but I sent to
By this same coxcomb that we have i' the wind,
Tokens and letters which she did re-send;
And this is all I have done. She's a fair creature;
Will you go see her?

2 Lord. With all my heart, my lord.
[*Exeunt.*

SCENE VII.—FLORENCE. *A Room in the* Widow's *House.*

Enter HELENA *and* Widow.

Hel. If you misdoubt me that I am not she,
I know not how I shall assure you further,
But I shall lose the grounds I work upon.

Wid. Though my estate be fallen, I was well born,
Nothing acquainted with these businesses;
And would not put my reputation now
In any staining act.

Hel. Nor would I wish you.
First give me trust, the count he is my husband,
And what to your sworn counsel I have spoken
Is so from word to word; and then you cannot,
By the good aid that I of you shall borrow,
Err in bestowing it.

Wid. I should believe you;
For you have show'd me that which well approves
You're great in fortune.

Hel. Take this purse of gold,
And let me buy your friendly help thus far,
Which I will over-pay, and pay again,
When I have found it. The count he wooes your daughter,
Lays down his wanton siege before her beauty,
Resolv'd to carry her: let her, in fine, consent,
As we'll direct her how 'tis best to bear it,
Now his important blood will naught deny
That she'll demand: a ring the county wears,
That downward hath succeeded in his house
From son to son, some four or five descents
Since the first father wore it: this ring he holds
In most rich choice; yet, in his idle fire,
To buy his will, it would not seem too dear,
Howe'er repented after.

Wid. Now I see
The bottom of your purpose.

Hel. You see it lawful then: it is no more
But that your daughter, ere she seems as won,
Desires this ring; appoints him an encounter;
In fine, delivers me to fill the time,
Herself most chastely absent; after this,
To marry her, I'll add three thousand crowns
To what is past already.

Wid. I have yielded:
Instruct my daughter how she shall perséver,
That time and place, with this deceit so lawful,
May prove coherent. Every night he comes
With musics of all sorts, and songs compos'd
To her unworthiness: it nothing steads us
To chide him from our eaves; for he persists,
As if his life lay on't.

Hel. Why, then, to-night
Let us assay our plot; which, if it speed,
Is wicked meaning in a lawful deed,
And lawful meaning in a lawful act;
Where both not sin, and yet a sinful fact:
But let's about it. [*Exeunt.*

ACT IV.

SCENE I.—*Without the* FLORENTINE *Camp.*

Enter first LORD, *with five or six* Soldiers *in ambush.*

1 Lord. He can come no other way but by this hedge-corner. When you sally upon him, speak what terrible language you will; though you understand it not yourselves, no matter; for we must not seem to understand him, unless some one among us, whom we must produce for an interpreter.

1 Sold. Good captain, let me be the interpreter.

1 Lord. Art not acquainted with him? knows he not thy voice?

1 Sold. No, sir, I warrant you.

1 Lord. But what linsey-woolsey hast thou to speak to us again?

1 Sold. Even such as you speak to me.

1 Lord. He must think us some band of strangers i' the adversary's entertainment. Now he hath a smack of all neighbouring languages; therefore we must every one be a man of his own fancy, not to know what we speak to one another; so we seem to know, is to know straight our purpose: chough's language, gabble enough, and good enough. As for you, interpreter, you must seem very politic. But couch, ho! here he comes; to beguile two hours in a sleep, and then to return and swear the lies he forges.

Enter PAROLLES.

Par. Ten o'clock: within these three hours 'twill be time enough to go home. What shall I say I have done? It must be a very plausive invention that carries it: they begin to smoke me: and disgraces have of late knocked too often at my door. I find my tongue is too foolhardy; but my heart hath the fear of Mars before it, and of his creatures, not daring the reports of my tongue.

1 Lord. This is the first truth that e'er thine own tongue was guilty of. [*Aside.*

Par. What the devil should move me to undertake the recovery of this drum; being not ignorant of the impossibility, and knowing I had no such purpose? I must give myself some hurts, and say I got them in exploit: yet slight ones will not carry it: they will say, Came you off with so little? and great ones I dare not give. Wherefore, what's the instance? Tongue, I must put you into a butter-woman's mouth, and buy myself another of Bajazet's mule, if you prattle me into these perils.

1 Lord. Is it possible he should know what he is, and be that he is? [*Aside.*

Par. I would the cutting of my garments would serve the turn, or the breaking of my Spanish sword.

1 Lord. We cannot afford you so. [*Aside.*

Par. Or the baring of my beard; and to say it was in stratagem.

1 Lord. 'Twould not do. [*Aside.*

Par. Or to drown my clothes, and say I was stripped.

1 Lord. Hardly serve. [*Aside.*

Par. Though I swore I leaped from the window of the citadel,—

1 Lord. How deep? [*Aside.*

Par. Thirty fathom.

1 Lord. Three great oaths would scarce make that be believed. [*Aside.*

Par. I would I had any drum of the enemy's; I would swear I recovered it.

1 Lord. You shall hear one anon. [*Aside.*

Par. A drum now of the enemy's!
[*Alarum within.*

1 Lord. Throca movousus, cargo, cargo, cargo.
All. Cargo, cargo, cargo, villianda par corbo, cargo.

Par. O! ransom, ransom:—Do not hide mine eyes. [*They seize and blindfold him.*

1 Sold. Boskos thromuldo boskos.

Par. I know you are the Musko's regiment, And I shall lose my life for want of language: If there be here German, or Dane, low Dutch, Italian, or French, let him speak to me; I will discover that which shall undo The Florentine.

2 Sold. Boskos vauvado:——
I understand thee, and can speak thy tongue:—
Kerelybonto:——Sir,
Betake thee to thy faith, for seventeen poniards
Are at thy bosom.

Par. Oh!

1 Sold. O, pray, pray, pray.——
Manka revania dulche.

1 Lord. Oscorbi dulchos volivorco.

1 Sold. The general is content to spare thee yet;

And, hoodwink'd as thou art, will lead thee on To gather from thee: haply thou mayst inform Something to save thy life.

Par. O, let me live, And all the secrets of our camp I'll show, Their force, their purposes: nay, I'll speak that Which you will wonder at.

1 Sold. But wilt thou faithfully?

Par. If I do not, damn me.

1 Sold. Acordo linta.——
Come on; thou art granted space.
[*Exit, with* PAROLLES *guarded.*

1 Lord. Go, tell the Count Rousillon and my brother
We have caught the woodcock, and will keep him muffled
Till we do hear from them.

2 Sold. Captain, I will.

1 Lord. He will betray us all unto ourselves;—
Inform 'em that.

2 Sold. So I will, sir.

1 Lord. Till then I'll keep him dark, and safely lock'd. [*Exeunt.*

SCENE II.—FLORENCE. *A Room in the Widow's House.*

Enter BERTRAM *and* DIANA.

Ber. They told me that your name was Fontibell.

Dia. No, my good lord, Diana.

Ber. Titled goddess;
And worth it, with addition! But, fair soul, In your fine frame hath love no quality? If the quick fire of youth light not your mind, You are no maiden, but a monument; When you are dead, you should be such a one As you are now, for you are cold and stern; And now you should be as your mother was When your sweet self was got.

Dia. She then was honest.

Ber. So should you be.

Dia. No:
My mother did but duty; such, my lord, As you owe to your wife.

Ber. No more of that!
I pr'ythee, do not strive against my vows: I was compell'd to her; but I love thee By love's own sweet constraint, and will for ever
Do thee all rights of service.

Dia. Ay, so you serve us
Till we serve you: but when you have our roses You barely leave our thorns to prick ourselves, And mock us with our bareness.

Ber. How. have I sworn?

Dia. 'Tis not the many oaths that make the truth,
But the plain single vow that is vow'd true. What is not holy, that we swear not by, But take the Highest to witness: then, pray you, tell me,

If I should swear by Jove's great attributes
I lov'd you dearly, would you believe my oaths,
When I did love you ill? this has no holding,
To swear by him whom I protest to love,
That I will work against him: therefore your
          oaths
Are words and poor conditions; but unseal'd,—
At least in my opinion.
    Ber.   Change it, change it;
Be not so holy-cruel: love is holy;
And my integrity ne'er knew the crafts
That you do charge men with. Stand no more
          off,
But give thyself unto my sick desires,
Who then recover: say thou art mine, and ever
My love as it begins shall so persévér.   [case,
    Dia. I see that men make hopes, in such a
That we'll forsake ourselves. Give me that ring.
    Ber. I'll lend it thee, my dear, but have no
          power
To give it from me.
    Dia.   Will you not, my lord?
    Ber. It is an honour 'longing to our house,
Bequeathed down from many ancestors;
Which were the greatest obloquy i' the world
In me to lose.
    Dia.   Mine honour's such a ring:
My chastity's the jewel of our house,
Bequeathed down from many ancestors;
Which were the greatest obloquy i' the world
In me to lose. Thus your own proper wisdom
Brings in the champion honour on my part,
Against your vain assault.
    Ber.   Here, take my ring:
My house, mine honour, yea, my life be thine,
And I'll be bid by thee.
    Dia. When midnight comes knock at my
          chamber-window;
I'll order take my mother shall not hear.
Now will I charge you in the band of truth,
When you have conquer'd my yet maiden-bed,
Remain there but an hour, nor speak to me:
My reasons are most strong; and you shall
          know them
When back again this ring shall be deliver'd;
And on your finger, in the night, I'll put
Another ring; that what in time proceeds
May token to the future our past deeds.
Adieu till then; then fail not. You have won
A wife of me, though there my hope be done.
    Ber. A heaven on earth I have won by woo-
          ing thee.   [*Exit.*
    Dia. For which live long to thank both
          heaven and me!
You may so in the end.——
My mother told me just how he would woo,
As if she sat in his heart; she says all men
Have the like oaths: he hath sworn to marry me
When his wife's dead; therefore I'll lie with him
When I am buried. Since Frenchmen are so
          braid,
Marry that will, I'll live and die a maid:
Only, in this disguise, I think't no sin
To cozen him that would unjustly win. [*Exit.*

SCENE III.—*The Florentine Camp.*

Enter the two French Lords, *and two or three*
          Soldiers.

    1 *Lord.* You have not given him his mother's
letter?
    2 *Lord.* I have delivered it an hour since:
there is something in't that stings his nature;
for, on the reading it, he changed almost into
another man.
    1 *Lord.* He has much worthy blame laid upon
him for shaking off so good a wife and so sweet
a lady.
    2 *Lord.* Especially he hath incurred the ever-
lasting displeasure of the king, who had even
tuned his bounty to sing happiness to him. I
will tell you a thing, but you shall let it dwell
darkly with you.
    1 *Lord.* When you have spoken it, 'tis dead,
and I am the grave of it.
    2 *Lord.* He hath perverted a young gentle-
woman here in Florence, of a most chaste renown; and this night he fleshes his will in the
spoil of her honour: he hath given her his
monumental ring, and thinks himself made in
the unchaste composition.
    1 *Lord.* Now, God delay our rebellion: as
we are ourselves, what things are we!
    2 *Lord.* Merely our own traitors. And as in
the common course of all treasons, we still see
them reveal themselves, till they attain to their
abhorred ends; so he that in this action con-
trives against his own nobility, in his proper
stream o'erflows himself.
    1 *Lord.* Is it not meant damnable in us to be
trumpeters of our unlawful intents? We shall
not then have his company to-night?
    2 *Lord.* Not till after midnight; for he is
dieted to his hour.
    2 *Lord.* That approaches apace: I would
gladly have him see his company anatomized,
that he might take a measure of his own judgments, wherein so curiously he had set this
counterfeit.
    2 *Lord.* We will not meddle with him till he
come; for his presence must be the whip of the
other.   [these wars?
    1 *Lord.* In the meantime, what hear you of
    2 *Lord.* I hear there is an overture of peace.
    1 *Lord.* Nay, I assure you, a peace con-
cluded.
    2 *Lord.* What will Count Rousillon do then?
will he travel higher, or return again into
France?
    1 *Lord.* I perceive, by this demand, you are
not altogether of his council.
    2 *Lord.* Let it be forbid, sir; so should I be a
great deal of his act.
    1 *Lord.* Sir, his wife, some two months since,
fled from his house: her pretence is a pilgrimage to St. Jacques-le-Grand; which holy undertaking, with most austere sanctimony, she accomplished; and, there residing, the tenderness
of her nature became as a prey to her grief; in

fine, made a groan of her last breath; and now she sings in heaven.

2 Lord. How is this justified?

1 Lord. The stronger part of it by her own letters, which make her story true even to the point of her death: her death itself, which could not be her office to say is come, was faithfully confirmed by the rector of the place.

2 Lord. Hath the count all this intelligence?

1 Lord. Ay, and the particular confirmations, point from point, to the full arming of the verity.

2 Lord. I am heartily sorry that he'll be glad of this.

1 Lord. How mightily, sometimes, we make us comforts of our losses!

2 Lord. And how mightily, some other times, we drown our gain in tears! The great dignity that his valour hath here acquired for him shall at home be encountered with a shame as ample.

1 Lord. The web of our life is of a mingled yarn, good and ill together: our virtues would be proud if our faults whipped them not; and our crimes would despair if they were not cherished by our virtues.—

Enter a Servant.

How now? where's your master?

Serv. He met the duke in the street, sir; of whom he hath taken a solemn leave: his lordship will next morning for France. The duke hath offered him letters of commendations to the king.

2 Lord. They shall be no more than needful there, if they were more than they can commend.

1 Lord. They cannot be too sweet for the king's tartness. Here's his lordship now.

Enter BERTRAM.

How now, my lord, is't not after midnight?

Ber. I have to-night despatched sixteen businesses, a month's length a-piece, by an abstract of success: I have conge'd with the duke, done my adieu with his nearest; buried a wife, mourned for her; writ to my lady-mother I am returning; entertained my convoy; and, between these main parcels of despatch, effected many nicer needs: the last was the greatest, but that I have not ended yet.

2 Lord. If the business be of any difficulty, and this morning your departure hence, it requires haste of your lordship.

Ber. I mean, the business is not ended, as fearing to hear of it hereafter. But shall we have this dialogue between the fool and the soldier?——Come, bring forth this counterfeit model: has deceived me like a double-meaning prophesier.

2 Lord. Bring him forth. [*Exeunt* Soldiers.] Has sat in the stocks all night, poor gallant knave.

Ber. No matter; his heels have deserved it,

in usurping his spurs so long. How does he carry himself?

1 Lord. I have told your lordship already; the stocks carry him. But to answer you as you would be understood; he weeps like a wench that had shed her milk: he hath confessed himself to Morgan, whom he supposes to be a friar, from the time of his remembrance to this very instant disaster of his setting i' the stocks: and what think you he hath confessed?

Ber. Nothing of me, has he?

2 Lord. His confession is taken, and it shall be read to his face: if your lordship be in't, as I believe you are, you must have the patience to hear it.

Re-enter Soldiers, *with* PAROLLES.

Ber. A plague upon him! muffled! he can say nothing of me; hush, hush!

1 Lord. Hoodman comes! *Porto tartarossa.*

1 Sold. He calls for the tortures: what will you say without 'em?

Par. I will confess what I know without constraint; if ye pinch me like a pasty I can say no more.

1 Sold. Bosko chimurco.

1 Lord. Boblibindo chicurmurco.

1 Sold. You are a merciful general:—Our general bids you answer to what I shall ask you out of a note.

Par. And truly, as I hope to live.

1 Sold. First demand of him how many horse the duke is strong. What say you to that?

Par. Five or six thousand; but very weak and unserviceable: the troops are all scattered, and the commanders very poor rogues, upon my reputation and credit, and as I hope to live.

1 Sold. Shall I set down your answer so?

Par. Do; I'll take the sacrament on't, how and which way you will.   [slave is this!

Ber. All's one to him. What a past-saving

1 Lord. You are deceived, my lord; this is Monsieur Parolles, the gallant militarist (that was his own phrase), that had the whole theoric of war in the knot of his scarf, and the practice in the chape of his dagger.

2 Lord. I will never trust a man again for keeping his sword clean; nor believe he can have everything in him by wearing his apparel neatly.

1 Sold. Well, that's set down.

Par. Five or six thousand horse, I said,—I will say true,—or thereabouts, set down,—for I'll speak truth.

1 Lord. He's very near the truth in this.

Ber. But I con him no thanks for't in the nature he delivers it.

Par. Poor rogues, I pray you say.

1 Sold. Well, that's set down.

Par. I humbly thank you, sir: a truth's a truth, the rogues are marvellous poor.

1 Sold. Demand of him of what strength they are a-foot. What say you to that?

Par. By my troth, sir, if I were to live this

present hour I will tell true. Let me see: Spurio a hundred and fifty, Sebastian so many, Corambus so many, Jacques so many; Guiltian, Cosmo, Lodowick, and Gratii, two hundred fifty each: mine own company, Chitopher, Vaumond, Bentii, two hundred fifty each: so that the muster-file, rotten and sound, upon my life, amounts not to fifteen thousand poll; half of the which dare not shake the snow from off their cassocks lest they shake themselves to pieces.

Ber. What shall be done to him?

1 *Lord.* Nothing, but let him have thanks. Demand of him my condition, and what credit I have with the duke.

1 *Sold.* Well, that's set down. *You shall demand of him whether one Captain Dumain be i' the camp, a Frenchman; what his reputation is with the duke, what his valour, honesty, expertness in wars; or whether he thinks it were not possible, with well-weighing sums of gold, to corrupt him to a revolt.* What say you to this? what do you know of it?

Par. I beseech you, let me answer to the particular of the inter'gatories: demand them singly.

1 *Sold.* Do you know this Captain Dumain?

Par. I know him: he was a botcher's 'prentice in Paris, from whence he was whipped for getting the shrieve's fool with child: a dumb innocent that could not say him nay.

[1 Lord *lifts up his hand in anger.*

Ber. Nay, by your leave, hold your hands; though I know his brains are forfeit to the next tile that falls.

1 *Sold.* Well, is this captain in the Duke of Florence's camp?

Par. Upon my knowledge, he is, and lousy.

1 *Lord.* Nay, look not so upon me; we shall hear of your lordship anon.

1 *Sold.* What is his reputation with the duke?

Par. The duke knows him for no other but a poor officer of mine; and writ to me this other day to turn him out o' the band: I think I have his letter in my pocket.

1 *Sold.* Marry, we'll search.

Par. In good sadness, I do not know; either it is there or it is upon a file, with the duke's other letters, in my tent.

1 *Sold.* Here 'tis; here's a paper. Shall I read it to you?

Par. I do not know if it be or no.

Ber. Our interpreter does it well.

1 *Lord.* Excellently.

1 *Sold.* [*Reads.*] *Dian, the Count's a fool, and full of gold,*—

Par. That is not the duke's letter, sir; that is an advertisement to a proper maid in Florence, one Diana, to take heed of the allurement of one Count Rousillon, a foolish, idle boy, but, for all that, very ruttish: I pray you, sir, put it up again.

1 *Sold.* Nay, I'll read it first, by your favour.

Par. My meaning in't, I protest, was very honest in the behalf of the maid; for I knew the young count to be a dangerous and lascivious boy, who is a whale to virginity, and devours up all the fry it finds.

Ber. Damnable! both sides rogue!

1 *Sold. Reads.* When he swears oaths, bid him drop gold, and take it:
After he scores, he never pays the score;
Half won is match well made; match, and well make it;
He ne'er pays after-debts, take it before;
And say a soldier, *Dian,* told thee this,
Men are to mell with, boys are not to kiss;
For count of this, the count 's a fool, I know it,
Who pays before, but not when he does owe it.
Thine, as he vow'd to thee in thine ear,
PAROLLES.

Ber. He shall be whipped through the army with this rhyme in his forehead.

2 *Lord.* This is your devoted friend, sir, the manifold linguist, and the armipotent soldier.

Ber. I could endure anything before but a cat, and now he's a cat to me.

1 *Sold.* I perceive, sir, by our general's looks we shall be fain to hang you.

Par. My life, sir, in any case: not that I am afraid to die, but that, my offences being many, I would repent out the remainder of nature: let me live, sir, in a dungeon, i' the stocks, or anywhere, so I may live.

1 *Sold.* We'll see what may be done, so you confess freely; therefore, once more to this Captain Dumain: you have answered to his reputation with the duke, and to his valour: what is his honesty?

Par. He will steal, sir, an egg out of a cloister; for rapes and ravishments he parallels Nessus. He professes not keeping of oaths; in breaking them he is stronger than Hercules. He will lie, sir, with such volubility that you would think truth were a fool: drunkenness is his best virtue, for he will be swine-drunk; and in his sleep he does little harm, save to his bed-clothes about him; but they know his conditions and lay him in straw. I have but little more to say, sir, of his honesty; he has everything that an honest man should not have; what an honest man should have he has nothing.

1 *Lord.* I begin to love him for this.

Ber. For this description of thine honesty? A pox upon him for me; he is more and more a cat.

1 *Sold.* What say you to his expertness in war?

Par. Faith, sir, has led the drum before the English tragedians,—to belie him I will not,—and more of his soldiership I know not, except in that country he had the honour to be the officer at a place there called Mile-end, to instruct for the doubling of files: I would do the man what honour I can, but of this I am not certain.

1 Lord. He hath out-villanied villany so far that the rarity redeems him.

Ber. A pox on him! he's a cat still.

1 Sold. His qualities being at this poor price, I need not ask you if gold will corrupt him to revolt.

Par. Sir, for a *quart d'ecu* he will sell the fee-simple of his salvation, the inheritance of it; and cut the entail from all remainders, and a perpetual succession for it perpetually.

1 Sold. What's his brother, the other Captain Dumain?

2 Lord. Why does he ask him of me?

1 Sold. What's he?

Par. E'en a crow of the same nest; not altogether so great as the first in goodness, but greater a great deal in evil. He excels his brother for a coward, yet his brother is reputed one of the best that is: in a retreat he outruns any lackey; marry, in coming on he has the cramp.

1 Sold. If your life be saved, will you undertake to betray the Florentine?

Par. Ay, and the captain of his horse, Count Rousillon.

1 Sold. I'll whisper with the general, and know his pleasure.

Par. I'll no more drumming; a plague of all drums! Only to seem to deserve well, and to beguile the supposition of that lascivious young boy, the count, have I run into this danger: yet who would have suspected an ambush where I was taken? [*Aside.*

1 Sold. There is no remedy, sir, but you must die: the general says, you that have so traitorously discovered the secrets of your army, and made such pestiferous reports of men very nobly held, can serve the world for no honest use; therefore you must die. Come, headsman, off with his head.

Par. O Lord! sir, let me live, or let me see my death.

1 Sold. That shall you, and take your leave of all your friends. [*Unmuffling him.* So look about you: know you any here?

Ber. Good morrow, noble captain.

2 Lord. Gold bless you, Captain Parolles.

1 Lord. God save you, noble captain.

2 Lord. Captain, what greeting will you to my Lord Lafeu? I am for France.

1 Lord. Good captain, will you give me a copy of the sonnet you writ to Diana in behalf of the Count Rousillon? an I were not a very coward I'd compel it of you; but fare you well.
[*Exeunt* BERTRAM, Lords, &c.

1 Sold. You are undone, captain: all but your scarf; that has a knot on't yet.

Par. Who cannot be crushed with a plot?

1 Sold. If you could find out a country where but women were that had received so much shame, you might begin an impudent nation. Fare you well, sir; I am for France too: we shall speak of you there. [*Exit.*

Par. Yet I am thankful: if my heart were great,
'Twould burst at this. Captain I'll be no more;
But I will eat and drink, and sleep as soft
As captain shall: simply the thing I am
Shall make me live. Who knows himself a braggart,
Let him fear this; for it will come to pass
That every braggart shall be found an ass.
Rust, sword! cool, blushes! and, Parolles, live
Safest in shame! being fool'd, by foolery thrive!
There's place and means for every man alive.
I'll after them. [*Exit.*

SCENE IV.—FLORENCE. *A Room in the* Widow's *House.*

Enter HELENA, Widow, *and* DIANA.

Hel. That you may well perceive I have not wrong'd you,
One of the greatest in the Christian world
Shall be my surety; 'for whose throne 'tis needful,
Ere I can perfect mine intents, to kneel:
Time was I did him a desired office,
Dear almost as his life; which gratitude
Through flinty Tartar's bosom would peep forth,
And answer, thanks: I duly am informed
His grace is at Marseilles; to which place
We have convenient convoy. You must know
I am supposed dead: the army breaking,
My husband hies him home; where, heaven aiding,
And by the leave of my good lord the king,
We'll be before our welcome.

Wid. Gentle madam,
You never had a servant to whose trust
Your business was more welcome.

Hel. Nor you, mistress,
Ever a friend whose thoughts more truly labour
To recompense your love: doubt not but heaven
Hath brought me up to be your daughter's dower,
As it hath fated her to be my motive
And helper to a husband. But, O strange men!
That can such sweet use make of what they hate,
When saucy trusting of the cozen'd thoughts
Defiles the pitchy night! so lust doth play
With what it loathes, for that which is away:
But more of this hereafter.—You, Diana,
Under my poor instructions yet must suffer
Something in my behalf.

Dia. Let death and honesty
Go with your impositions, I am yours
Upon your will to suffer.

Hel. Yet, I pray you:
But with the word the time will bring on summer,
When briars shall have leaves as well as thorns,
And be as sweet as sharp. We must away;
Our waggon is prepar'd, and time revives us:

All's well that ends well: still the fine's the
        crown:
Whate'er the course, the end is the renown.
                                                [*Exeunt.*

SCENE V.—ROUSILLON. *A Room in the*
        COUNTESS'S *Palace.*

Enter COUNTESS, LAFEU, *and* Clown.

Laf. No, no, no, your son was misled with
a snipt-taffeta fellow there, whose villanous
saffron would have made all the unbaked and
doughy youth of a nation in his colour: your
daughter-in-law had been alive at this hour,
and your son here at home, more advanced by
the king than by that red-tailed humble-bee I
speak of.

Count. I would I had not known him! it was
the death of the most virtuous gentlewoman
that ever nature had praise for creating: if she
had partaken of my flesh, and cost me the
dearest groans of a mother, I could not have
owed her a more rooted love.

Laf. 'Twas a good lady, 'twas a good lady:
we may pick a thousand salads ere we light on
such another herb.

Clo. Indeed, sir, she was the sweet marjoram of the salad, or rather, the herb of grace.

Laf. They are not salad-herbs, you knave;
they are nose-herbs.

Clo. I am no great Nebuchadnezzar, sir; I
have not much skill in grass.

Laf. Whether dost thou profess thyself,—a
knave or a fool?

Clo. A fool, sir, at a woman's service, and a
knave at a man's.

Laf. Your distinction?

Clo. I would cozen the man of his wife, and
do his service.   [deed.

Laf. So you were a knave at his service, in-

Clo. And I would give his wife my bauble,
sir, to do her service.

Laf. I will subscribe for thee; thou art both
knave and fool.

Clo. At your service.

Laf. No, no, no.

Clo. Why, sir, if I cannot serve you, I can
serve as great a prince as you are.

Laf. Who's that? a Frenchman?

Clo. Faith, sir, 'a has an English name; but
his phisnomy is more hotter in France than
there.

Laf. What prince is that?

Clo. The black prince, sir; *alias*, the prince
of darkness; *alias*, the devil.

Laf. Hold thee, there's my purse: I give thee
not this to suggest thee from thy master thou
talkest of; serve him still.

Clo. I am a woodland fellow, sir, that always
loved a great fire; and the master I speak of
ever keeps a good fire. But, sure, he is the
prince of the world; let his nobility remain in
his court. I am for the house with the narrow
gate, which I take to be too little for pomp to
enter: some that humble themselves may; but
the many will be too chill and tender; and
they'll be for the flow'ry way that leads to the
broad gate and the great fire.

Laf. Go thy ways, I begin to be a-weary of
thee; and I tell thee so before, because I would
not fall out with thee. Go thy ways; let my
horses be well looked to, without any tricks.

Clo. If I put any tricks upon 'em, sir, they
shall be jades' tricks; which are their own
right by the law of nature.   [*Exit.*

Laf. A shrewd knave, and an unhappy.

Count. So he is. My lord that's gone made
himself much sport out of him: by his authority
he remains here, which he thinks is a patent for
his sauciness; and, indeed, he has no pace, but
runs where he will.

Laf. I like him well; 'tis not amiss. And
I was about to tell you, since I heard of the
good lady's death, and that my lord your son
was upon his return home, I moved the king
my master to speak in the behalf of my daughter; which, in the minority of them both, his
majesty, out of a self-gracious remembrance,
did first propose: his highness hath promised
me to do it: and, to stop up the displeasure he
hath conceived against your son, there is no
fitter matter. How does your ladyship like it?

Count. With very much content, my lord;
and I wish it happily effected.

Laf. His highness comes post from Marseilles, of as able body as when he numbered
thirty; he will be here to-morrow, or I am deceived by him that in such intelligence hath
seldom failed.

Count. It rejoices me that I hope I shall see
him ere I die. I have letters that my son will
be here to-night: I shall beseech your lordship
to remain with me till they meet together.

Laf. Madam, I was thinking with what
manners I might safely be admitted.

Count. You need but plead your honourable
privilege.

Laf. Lady, of that I have made a bold charter; but, I thank my God, it holds yet.

Re-enter Clown.

Clo. O madam, yonder's my lord your son
with a patch of velvet on's face; whether there
be a scar under it or no, the velvet knows; but
'tis a goodly patch of velvet: his left cheek is a
cheek of two pile and a half, but his right cheek
is worn bare.

Laf. A scar nobly got, or a noble scar, is a
good livery of honour; so belike is that.

Clo. But it is your carbonadoed face.

Laf. Let us go see your son, I pray you; I
long to talk with the young noble soldier.

Clo. Faith, there's a dozen of 'em, with
delicate fine hats, and most courteous feathers,
which bow the head and nod at every man.
                                                [*Exeunt.*

ACT V.

SCENE I.—MARSEILLES. *A Street.*

Enter HELENA, Widow, *and* DIANA, *with*
two Attendants.

Hel. But this exceeding posting day and
night
Must wear your spirits low: we cannot help it:
But since you have made the days and nights
as one,
To wear you gentle limbs in my affairs,
Be bold you do so grow in my requital
As nothing can unroot you. In happy time;—

Enter a Gentleman.

This man may help me to his majesty's ear,
If he would spend his power.—God save you,
.sir.
Gent. And you.
Hel. Sir, I have seen you in the court of
France.
Gent. I have been sometimes there.
Hel. I do presume, sir, that you are not
fallen
From the report that goes upon your goodness;
And therefore, goaded with most sharp occa-
sions,
Which lay nice manners by, I put you to
The use of your own virtues, for the which
I shall continue thankful.
Gent.   What's your will?
Hel. That it will please you
To give this poor petition to the king;
And aid me with that store of power you have
To come into his presence.
Gent. The king's not here.
Hel.   Not here, sir?
Gent.   Not indeed:
He hence remov'd last night, and with more
haste
Than is his use.
Wid.   Lord, how we lose our pains!
Hel. All's well that ends well yet,
Though time seem so adverse and means
unfit?—
I do beseech you, whither is he gone?
Gent. Marry, as I take it, to Rousillon;
Whither I am going.
Hel.   I do beseech you, sir,
Since you are like to see the king before me,
Commend the paper to his gracious hand;
Which I presume shall render you no blame,
But rather make you thank your pains for it:
I will come after you, with what good speed
Our means will make us means.
Gent.   This I'll do for you.
Hel. And you shall find yourself to be well
thank'd,
Whate'er falls more.—We must to horse
again;—
Go, go, provide.   [*Exeunt.*

SCENE II.—ROUSILLON. *The inner Court of the* COUNTESS'S *Palace.*

Enter Clown *and* PAROLLES.

Par. Good Monsieur Lavatch, give my Lord
Lafeu this letter: I have ere now, sir, been
better known to you, when I have held familiarity with fresher clothes; but I am now, sir,
muddied in fortune's mood, and smell somewhat strong of her strong displeasure.
Clo. Truly, fortune's displeasure is but slut-
tish if it smell so strongly as thou speakest of:
I will henceforth eat no fish of fortune's butter-
ing. Pr'ythee, allow the wind.
Par. Nay, you need not to stop your nose,
sir; I spake but by a metaphor.
Clo. Indeed, sir, if your metaphor stink, I
will stop my nose; or against any man's metaphor. Pr'ythee, get thee further.
Par. Pray you, sir, deliver me this paper.
Clo. Foh, pr'ythee, stand away: a paper
from fortune's close-stool to give to a nobleman! Look, here he comes himself.

Enter LAFEU.

Here is a pur of fortune's, sir, or of fortune's
cat (but not a musk-cat), that has fallen into
the unclean fishpond of her displeasure, and, as
he says, is muddied withal: pray you, sir, use
the carp as you may; for he looks like a poor,
decayed, ingenious, foolish, rascally knave. I
do pity his distress in my smiles of comfort, and
leave him to your lordship.   [*Exit.*
Par. My lord, I am a man whom fortune
hath cruelly scratched.
Laf. And what would you have me to do?
'tis too late to pare her nails now. Wherein
have you played the knave with fortune, that
she should scratch you, who of herself is a good
lady, and would not have knaves thrive long
under her? There's a *quart d'ecu* for you: let the
justices make you and fortune friends; I am for
other business.
Par. I beseech your honour to hear me one
single word.
Laf. You beg a single penny more: come,
you shall ha't: save your word.
Par. My name, my good lord, is Parolles.
Laf. You beg more than one word then.—
Cox' my passion! give me your hand:—how
does your drum?
Par. O my good lord, you were the first that
found me.
Laf. Was I, in sooth? and I was the first that
lost thee.
Par. It lies in you, my lord, to bring me in
some grace, for you did bring me out.
Laf. Out upon thee, knave! dost thou put
upon me at once both the office of God and the
devil? one brings thee in grace, and the other
brings thee out.   [*Trumpets sound.*]
The king's coming; I know by his trumpets.
—Sirrah, inquire further after me; I had talk of

you last night: though you are a fool and a
knave, you shall eat: go to; follow.

Par. I praise God for you.   [*Exeunt.*

SCENE III.—*The same. A Room in the
COUNTESS's Palace.*

Flourish. Enter KING, COUNTESS, LAFEU,
Lords, Gentlemen, Guards, &c.

King. We lost a jewel of her; and our esteem
Was made much poorer by it: but your son,
As mad in folly, lack'd the sense to know
Her estimation home.

Count.   'Tis past, my liege:
And I beseech your majesty to make it
Natural rebellion, done i' the blaze of youth,
When oil and fire, too strong for reason's force,
O'erbears it, and burns on.

King.   My honour'd lady,
I have forgiven and forgotten all;
Though my revenges were high bent upon him,
And watch'd the time to shoot.

Laf.   This I must say,—
But first, I beg your pardon,—the young lord
Did to his majesty, his mother, and his lady,
Offence of mighty note; but to himself
The greatest wrong of all: he lost a wife
Whose beauty did astonish the survey
Of richest eyes; whose words all ears took cap-
          tive;
Whose dear perfection hearts that scorn'd to
          serve
Humbly call'd mistress.

King.   Praising what is lost
Makes the remembrance dear.—Well, call him
          hither;—
We are reconcil'd, and the first view shall kill
All repetition:—let him not ask our pardon;
The nature of his great offence is dead,
And deeper than oblivion do we bury
The incensing relics of it; let him approach,
A stranger, no offender; and inform him,
So 'tis our will he should.

Gent.   I shall, my liege.
                    [*Exit* Gentleman.

King. What says he to your daughter? have
          you spoke?

Laf. All that he is hath reference to your
          highness.

King. Then shall we have a match. I have
          letters sent me
That set him high in fame.

Enter BERTRAM.

Laf.   He looks well on't.

King. I am not a day of season,
For thou mayst see a sunshine and a hail
In me at once: but to the brightest beams
Distracted clouds give way; so stand thou
          forth,
The time is fair again.

Ber.   My high-repented blames,
Dear sovereign, pardon to me.

King.   All is whole;
Not one word more of the consumed time.

Let's take the instant by the forward top;
For we are old, and on our quick'st decrees
The inaudible and noiseless foot of time
Steals ere we can effect them. You remember
The daughter of this lord?

Ber. Admiringly, my liege: at first
I stuck my choice upon her, ere my heart
Durst make too bold a herald of my tongue:
Where the impression of mine eye infixing,
Contempt his scornful perspective did lend me,
Which warp'd the line of every other favour;
Scorned a fair colour, or express'd it stolen;
Extended or contracted all proportions
To a most hideous object: thence it came
That she whom all men prais'd, and whom my
          self,
Since I have lost, have lov'd, was in mine eye
The dust that did offend it.

King.   Well excus'd:
That thou didst love her, strikes some scores
          away
From the great compt: but love that comes too
          late,
Like a remorseful pardon slowly carried,
To the great sender turns a sour offence,
Crying, That's good that's gone. Our rash
          faults
Make trivial price of serious things we have,
Not knowing them until we know their grave:
Oft our displeasures, to ourselves unjust,
Destroy our friends, and after weep their dust:
Our own love waking cries to see what's done,
While shameful hate sleeps out the afternoon.
Be this sweet Helen's knell, and now forget her.
Send forth your amorous token for fair Maud-
          lin:
The main consents are had: and here we'll stay
To see our widower's second marriage-day.

Count. Which better than the first, O dear
          heaven, bless!
Or, ere they meet, in me, O nature, cesse!

Laf. Come on, my son, in whom my house's
          name
Must be digested, give a favour from you,
To sparkle in the spirits of my daughter,
That she may quickly come.—
          [BERTRAM *gives a ring to* LAFEU.
                              By my old beard,
And every hair that's on't, Helen, that's dead,
Was a sweet creature: such a ring as this,
The last that e'er I took her leave at court,
I saw upon her finger.

Ber.   Her's it was not.

King. Now, pray you, let me see it; for mine
          eye,
While I was speaking, oft was fasten'd to it.—
This ring was mine, and when I gave it Helen
I bade her, if her fortunes ever stood
Necessitated to help, that by this token
I would relieve her. Had you that craft to
          'reave her
Of what should stead her most?

Ber.   My gracious sovereign,
Howe'er it pleases you to take it so,

The ring was never hers.
 Count.   Son, on my life,
I have seen her wear it; and she reckon'd it
At her life's rate.
 Laf.   I'm sure I saw her wear it.
 Ber. You are deceiv'd, my lord; she never
    saw it:
In Florence was it from a casement thrown me,
Wrapp'd in a paper, which contain'd the name
Of her that threw it: noble she was, and
    thought
I stood engag'd: but when I had subscrib'd
To mine own fortune, and inform'd her fully
I could not answer in that course of honour
As she had made the overture, she ceas'd,
In heavy satisfaction, and would never
Receive the ring again.
 King.   Plutus himself,
That knows the tinct and multiplying medi-
    cine,
Hath not in nature's mystery more science
Than I have in this ring: 'twas mine, 'twas
    Helen's,
Whoever gave it you. Then, if you know
That you are well acquainted with yourself,
Confess 'twas hers, and by what rough en-
    forcement
You got it from her: she call'd the saints to
    surety
That she would never put it from her finger
Unless she gave it to yourself in bed,—
Where you have never come,—or sent it us
Upon her great disaster.
 Ber.   She never saw it.
 King. Thou speak'st it falsely, as I love
    mine honour;
And mak'st conjectural fears to come into me
Which I would fain shut out. If it should prove
That thou art so inhuman,—'twill not prove
    so:—
And yet I know not:—thou didst hate her
    deadly.
And she is dead; which nothing, but to close
Her eyes myself, could win me to believe
More than to see this ring.—Take him away.—
     [Guards *seize* BERTRAM.
My fore-past proofs, howe'er the matter fall,
Shall tax my fears of little vanity,
Having vainly fear'd too little.—Away with
    him;—
We'll sift this matter further.
 Ber.   If you shall prove
This ring was ever hers, you shall as easy
Prove that I husbanded her bed in Florence,
Where yet she never was.   [*Exit, guarded.*
 King. I am wrapp'd in dismal thinkings.

Enter a Gentleman.

 Gent.   Gracious sovereign,
Whether I have been to blame or no, I know
    not:
Here's a petition from a Florentine,
Who hath, for four or five removes, come short
To tender it herself. I undertook it,

Vanquish'd thereto by the fair grace and speech
Of the poor suppliant, who by this, I know,
Is here attending: her business looks in her
With an importing visage; and she told me,
In a sweet verbal brief, it did concern
Your highness with herself.
 King. [*Reads.*] *Upon his many protestations
to marry me, when his wife was dead, I blush to
say it, he won me. Now is the Count Rousillon a
widower; his vows are forfeited to me, and my
honour's paid to him. He stole from Florence,
taking no leave, and I follow him to his country
for justice: grant it me, O king; in you it best lies;
otherwise a seducer flourishes, and a poor maid is
undone.*   DIANA CAPULET.
 Laf. I will buy me a son-in-law in a fair, and
toll this: I'll none of him.
 King. The heaven's have thought well on
    thee, Lafeu,
To bring forth this discovery.—Seek these
    suitors:—
Go speedily, and bring again the count.
    [*Exeunt* Gentleman, *and some* Attendants.
I am afeard the life of Helen, lady,
Was foully snatch'd.
 Count.   Now, justice on the doers!

Enter BERTRAM, *guarded.*

 King. I wonder, sir, since wives are monsters
    to you,
And that you fly them as you swear them lord-
    ship,
Yet you desire to marry.—What woman's
    that?
Re-enter Gentleman, *with* Widow *and* DIANA.
 Dia. I am, my lord, a wretched Florentine,
Derived from the ancient Capulet;
My suit, as I do understand, you know,
And therefore know how far I may be pitied.
 Wid. I am her mother, sir, whose age and
    honour
Both suffer under this complaint we bring,
And both shall cease, without your remedy.
 King. Come hither, count; do you know
    these women?
 Ber. My lord, I neither can nor will deny
But that I know them: do they charge me
    further?
 Dia. Why do you look so strange upon your
    wife.
 Ber. She's none of mine, my lord.
 Dia.   If you shall marry,
You give away this hand, and that is mine;
You give away heaven's vows, and those are
    mine;
You give away myself, which is known mine;
For I by vow am so embodied yours·
That she which marries you must marry me,
Either both or none.
 Laf. [*To* BERTRAM.] Your reputation comes
too short for my daughter; you are no husband
for her.
 Ber. My lord, this is a fond and desperate
    creature

Whom sometimes I have laugh'd with: let your
          highness
Lay a more noble thought upon mine honour
Than for to think I would sink it here.
     King. Sir, for my thoughts, you have them
          ill to friend
Till your deeds gain them: fairer prove your
          honour
Than in my thought it lies!
     Dia.   Good, my lord,
Ask him upon his oath, if he does think
He had not my virginity.
     King. What say'st thou to her?
     Ber.   She's impudent, my lord;
And was a common gamester to the camp.
     Dia. He does me wrong, my lord; if I were so
He might have bought me at a common price:
Do not believe him. O, behold this ring,
Whose high respect and rich validity
Did lack a parallel; yet, for all that,
He gave it to a commoner o' the camp,
If I be one.
     Count. He blushes, and 'tis it:
Of six preceding ancestors, that gem,
Conferr'd by testament to the sequent issue,
Hath it been ow'd and worn. This is his wife;
That ring's a thousand proofs.
     King.   Methought you said
You saw one here in court could witness it.
     Dia. I did, my lord, but loath am to produce
So bad an instrument; his name's Parolles.
     Laf. I saw the man to-day, if man he be.
     King. Find him, and bring him hither.
                         [*Exit an* Attendant.
     Ber.   What of him?
He's quoted for a most perfidious slave,
With all the spots o' the world tax'd and de-
          bosh'd:
Whose nature sickens but to speak a truth:
Am I or that or this for what he'll utter,
That will speak anything?
     King.   She hath that ring of yours.
     Ber. I think she has: certain it is I lik'd her,
And boarded her i' the wanton way of youth:
She knew her distance, and did angle for me,
Madding my eagerness with her restraint,
As all impediments in fancy's course
Are motives of more fancy; and, in fine,
Her infinite coming with her modern grace,
Subdued me to her rate: she got the ring;
And I had that which any inferior might
At market-price have bought.
     Dia.   I must be patient:
You that have turn'd off a first so noble wife
May justly diet me. I pray you yet,—
Since you lack virtue, I will lose a husband,—
Send for your ring, I will return it home,
And give me mine again.
     Ber.   I have it not.
     King. What ring was yours, I pray you?
     Dia.   Sir, much like
The same upon your finger.
     King. Know you this ring? this ring was his
          of late.

Dia. And this was it I gave him, being a-bed.
     King. The story, then, goes false you threw
          it him
Out of a casement.
     Dia. I have spoke the truth.
     Ber. My lord, I do confess the ring was hers.
     King. You boggle shrewdly; every feather
          starts you.—

     Re-enter Attendant, *with* PAROLLES.
Is this the man you speak of?
     Dia.   Ay, my lord.
     King. Tell me, sirrah, but tell me true, I
          charge you,
Not fearing the displeasure of your master,—
Which, on your just proceeding, I'll keep off,—
By him and by this woman here what know
          you?
     Par. So please your majesty, my master hath
been an honourable gentleman; tricks he hath
had in him, which gentlemen have.
     King. Come, come, to the purpose: did he
love this woman?
     Par. Faith, sir, he did love her; but how?
     King. How, I pray you?
     Par. He did love her, sir, as a gentleman
loves a woman.
     King. How is that?
     Par. He loved her, sir, and loved her not.
     King. As thou art a knave and no knave.—
What an equivocal companion is this!
     Par. I am a poor man, and at your majesty's
command.
     Laf. He's a good drum, my lord, but a
naughty orator.
     Dia. Do you know he promised me marriage?
     Par. Faith, I know more than I'll speak.
     King. But wilt thou not speak all thou
know'st?
     Par. Yes, so please your majesty; I did go
between them, as I said; but more than that, he
loved her,—for, indeed, he was mad for her,
and talked of Satan, and of limbo, and of furies,
and I know not what: yet I was in that credit
with them at that time that I knew of their going to bed; and of other motions, as promising
her marriage, and things which would derive
me ill-will to speak of; therefore I will not
speak what I know.
     King. Thou hast spoken all already, unless
thou canst say they are married: but thou art
too fine in thy evidence; therefore stand aside.
—This ring, you say, was yours?
     Dia.   Ay, my good lord.
     King. Where did you buy it? or who gave it
          you?   [it.
     Dia. It was not given me, nor I did not buy
     King. Who lent it you?
     Dia.   It was not lent me neither.
     King. Where did you find it then?
     Dia.   I found it not.
     King. If it were yours by none of all these
          ways,
How could you give it him?

Dia.   I never gave it him.
Laf. This woman's an easy glove, my lord;
She goes off and on at pleasure.
  King. This ring was mine, I gave it his first
    wife.
  Dia. It might be yours or hers, for aught I
    know.
  King. Take her away, I do not like her now;
To prison with her: and away with him.—
Unless thou tell'st me where thou hadst this
    ring,
Thou diest within this hour.
  Dia.   I'll never tell you.
  King. Take her away.
  Dia.   I'll put in bail, my liege.
  King. I think thee now some common cus-
    tomer.
  Dia. By Jove, if ever I knew man, 'twas you.
  King. Wherefore hast thou accus'd him all
    this while?
  Dia. Because he's guilty, and he is not
    guilty:
He knows I am no maid, and he'll swear to't:
I'll swear I am a maid, and he knows not.
Great king, I am no strumpet, by my life;
I am either maid, or else this old man's wife.
                    [*Pointing to* LAFEU.
  King. She does abuse our ears; to prison
    with her.
  Dia. Good mother, fetch my bail.—Stay,
    royal sir;   [*Exit* Widow.
The jeweller that owes the ring is sent for,
And he shall surety me. But for this lord,
Who hath abus'd me, as he knows himself,
Though yet he never harm'd me, here I quit
    him:
He knows himself my bed he hath defil'd;
And at that time he got his wife with child.
Dead though she be, she feels her young one
    kick;
So there's my riddle—One that's dead is quick;
And now behold the meaning.

            Re-enter Widow *with* HELENA.

  King.   Is there no exorcist

Beguiles the truer office of mine eyes?
Is't real that I see?
  Hel.   No, my good lord;
'Tis but the shadow of a wife you see—
The name, and not the thing.
  Ber.   Both, both; O, pardon!
  Hel. O, my good lord, when I was like this
    maid;
I found you wondrous kind. There is your ring,
And, look you, here's your letter. This it says,
When from my finger you can get this ring,
And are by me with child, &c.—This is done:
Will you be mine, now you are doubly won?
  Ber. If she, my liege, can make me know
    this clearly,
I'll love her dearly, ever, ever dearly.
  Hel. If it appear not plain, and prove untrue,
Deadly divorce step between me and you!—
O, my dear mother, do I see you living?
  Laf. Mine eyes smell onions; I shall weep
anon:—Good Tom Drum [*to* PAROLLES], lend
me a handkercher: so, I thank thee; wait on
me home, I'll make sport with thee: let thy
courtesies alone, they are scurvy ones.
  King. Let us from point to point this story
    know,
To make the even truth in pleasure flow:—
If thou be'st yet a fresh uncropped flower,
                    [*To* DIANA.
Choose thou thy husband, and I'll pay thy
    dower;
For I can guess that, by thy honest aid,
Thou kep'st a wife herself, thyself a maid.—
Of that and all the progress, more and less,
Resolvedly more leisure shall express:
All yet seems well; and if it end so meet,
The bitter past, more welcome is the sweet.
                    [*Flourish.*
  The king's a beggar, now the play is done:
All is well-ended if this suit be won,
That you express content; which we will pay
With strife to please you, day exceeding day:
Ours be your patience then, and yours our
    parts;
Your gentle hands lend us, and take our hearts.
                    [*Exeunt.*

THE TAMING OF THE SHREW

DRAMATIS PERSONÆ

A Lord.
CHRISTOPHER SLY, *a drunken Tinker*
Hostess, Page, Players, Huntsmen, *and* Servants.
} *Persons in the Induction.*

BAPTISTA, *a rich Gentleman of Padua.*
VINCENTIO, *an old Gentleman of Pisa.*
LUCENTIO, *Son to* VINCENTIO, *in love with* BIANCA.
PETRUCHIO, *a Gentleman of Verona, a Suitor to* KATHARINA.
GREMIO,
HORTENSIO, } *Suitors to* BIANCA.

TRANIO,
BIONDELLO, } *Servants to* LUCENTIO.
GRUMIO,
CURTIS, } *Servants to* PETRUCHIO.
Pedant, *an old fellow set up to personate* VINCENTIO.

KATHARINA, *the Shrew,*
BIANCA, } *Daughters to* BAPTISTA.
Widow.

Tailor, Haberdasher, *and* Servants *attending on* BAPTISTA *and* PETRUCHIO.

SCENE,—*Sometimes in* PADUA, *and sometimes in* PETRUCHIO'S *House in the Country.*

INDUCTION.

SCENE I.—*Before an Alehouse on a Heath.*

Enter Hostess *and* SLY.

Sly. I'll pheeze you, in faith.

Host. A pair of stocks, you rogue!

Sly. Y'are a baggage: the Slys are no rogues; look in the chronicles; we came in with Richard Conqueror. Therefore, *paucas pallabris;* let the world slide: sessa!

Host. You will not pay for the glasses you have burst?

Sly. No, not a denier. Go by, Saint Jeronimy,—go to thy cold bed and warm thee.

Host. I know my remedy; I must go fetch the thirdborough. [*Exit.*

Sly. Third, or fourth, or fifth borough, I'll answer him by law: I'll not budge an inch, boy: let him come, and kindly.

[*Lies down on the ground and falls asleep.*

Horns winded. Enter a Lord *from hunting, with* Huntsmen *and* Servants.

Lord. Huntsman, I charge thee, tender well my hounds:
Brach Merriman,—the poor cur is emboss'd,
And couple Clowder with the deep-mouth'd brach.
Saw'st thou not, boy, how Silver made it good
At the hedge-corner, in the coldest fault?
I would not lose the dog for twenty pound.

1 Hun. Why, Belman is as good as he, my lord;
He cried upon it at the merest loss,
And twice to-day pick'd out the dullest scent:
Trust me, I take him for the better dog.

Lord. Thou art a fool: if Echo were as fleet,
I would esteem him worth a dozen such.
But sup them well, and look unto them all:

To-morrow I intend to hunt again.

1 Hun. I will, my lord.

Lord. What's here? one dead, or drunk? See, doth he breathe?

2 Hun. He breathes, my lord. Were he not warm'd with ale,
This were a bed but cold to sleep so soundly.

Lord. O monstrous beast! how like a swine he lies! [image!
Grim death, how foul and loathsome is thine
Sirs, I will practise on this drunken man.
What think you, if he were convey'd to bed,
Wrapp'd in sweet clothes, rings put upon his fingers,
A most delicious banquet by his bed,
And brave attendants near him when he wakes,
Would not the beggar then forget himself?

1 Hun. Believe me, lord, I think he cannot choose.

2 Hun. It would seem strange unto him when he wak'd. [less fancy.

Lord. Even as a flattering dream or worth-
Then take him up, and manage well the jest:—
Carry him gently to my fairest chamber.
And hang it round with all my wanton pictures:
Balm his foul head in warm distilled waters,
And burn sweet wood to make the lodging sweet:
Procure me music ready when he wakes,
To make a dulcet and a heavenly sound;
And if he chance to speak, be ready straight,
And, with a low, submissive reverence,
Say,—What is it your honour will command?
Let one attend him with a silver basin
Full of rose-water and bestrew'd with flowers;
Another bear the ewer, the third a diaper,
And say,—Will't please your lordship cool your hands?
Some one be ready with a costly suit,

And ask him what apparel he will wear;
Another tell him of his hounds and horse,
And that his lady mourns at his disease:
Persuade him that he hath been lunatic;
And, when he says he is, say that he dreams,
For he is nothing but a mighty lord.
This do, and do it kindly, gentle sirs:
It will be pastime passing excellent,
If it be husbanded with modesty. [our part,

1 Hun. My lord, I warrant you, we'll play
As he shall think, by our true diligence,
He is no less than what we say he is. [him;

Lord. Take him up gently, and to bed with
And each one to his office when he wakes.
[*Some bear out* SLY. *A trumpet sounds.*
Sirrah, go see what trumpet 'tis that sounds:—
[*Exit* Servant.
Belike, some noble gentleman, that means,
Travelling some journey, to repose him here.

Re-enter a Servant.

How now! who is it?
Serv. An it please your honour,
Players that offer service to your lordship.
Lord. Bid them come near.

Enter Players.

Now, fellows, you are welcome.
1 Play. We thank your honour.
Lord. Do you intend to stay with me to-
night?
2 Play. So please your lordship to accept our
duty. [member,
Lord. With all my heart.—This fellow I re-
Since once he play'd a farmer's eldest son:—
'Twas where you woo'd the gentlewoman so
well:
I have forgot your name; but, sure, that part
Was aptly fitted and naturally perform'd.
1 Play. I think 'twas Soto that your honour
means.
Lord. 'Tis very true: thou didst it excellent.—
Well, you are come to me in happy time;
The rather for I have some sport in hand,
Wherein your cunning can assist me much.
There is a lord will hear you play to-night:
But I am doubtful of your modesties;
Lest, over-eying of his odd behaviour,—
For yet his honour never heard a play,—
You break into some merry passion,
And so offend him; for I tell you, sirs,
If you should smile, he grows impatient.
1 Play. Fear not, my lord; we can contain
ourselves,
Were he the veriest antic in the world.
Lord. Go, sirrah, take them to the buttery,
And give them friendly welcome every one:
Let them want nothing that my house affords.
[*Exeunt* Servant *and* Players.
Sirrah, go you to Barthol'mew my page,
[*To a* Servant.
And see him dress'd in all suits like a lady:
That done, conduct him to the drunkard's
chamber;

And call him madam, do him obeisance.
Tell him from me,—as he will win my love,—
He bear himself with honourable action,
Such as he hath observ'd in noble ladies
Unto their lords, by them accomplished:
Such duty to the drunkard let him do,
With soft low tongue and lowly courtesy;
And say,—What is't your honour will com-
mand,
Wherein your lady and your humble wife
May show her duty and make known her love?
And then,—with kind embracements, tempting
kisses,
And with declining head into his bosom,—
Bid him shed tears, as being overjoy'd
To see her noble lord restor'd to health,
Who for this seven years hath esteemed him
No better than a poor and loathsome beggar:
And if the boy have not a woman's gift,
To rain a shower of commanded tears,
An onion will do well for such a shift;
Which in a napkin being close conveyed,
Shall in despite enforce a watery eye. [canst
See this despatch'd with all the haste thou
Anon I'll give thee more instructions.
[*Exit* Servant.
I know the boy will well usurp the grace,
Voice, gait, and action of a gentlewoman:
I long to hear him call the drunkard husband;
And how my men will stay themselves from
laughter
When they do homage to this simple peasant.
I'll to counsel them: haply my presence
May well abate the over-merry spleen,
Which otherwise would grow into extremes.
[*Exeunt.*

SCENE II.—*A Bedchamber in the* Lord's *House.*

SLY *is discovered in a rich nightgown, with*
Attendants; *some with apparel, others with
basin, ewer, and other appurtenances. Enter*
Lord, *dressed like a Servant.*

Sly. For God's sake, a pot of small ale.
1 Serv. Will't please your lordship drink a
cup of sack? [these conserves?
2 Serv. Will't please your honour taste of
3 Serv. What raiment will your honour wear
to-day?
Sly. I am Christophero Sly; call not me
honour nor lordship: I ne'er drank sack in my
life; and if you give me any conserves, give me
conserves of beef: ne'er ask me what raiment
I'll wear; for I have no more doublets than
backs, no more stockings than legs, nor no more
shoes than feet,—nay, sometime more feet than
shoes, or such shoes as my toes look through
the overleather. [honour!
Lord. Heaven cease this idle humour in your
O, that a mighty man, of such descent,
Of such possessions, and so high esteem,
Should be infused with so foul a spirit!
Sly. What, would you make me mad? Am
not I Christopher Sly, old Sly's son of Burton-
heath; by birth a pedler, by education a card-

maker, by transmutation a bear-herd, and now by present profession a tinker? Ask Marian Hacket, the fat ale-wife of Wincot, if she know me not: if she say I am not fourteen-pence on the score for sheer ale, score me up for the lyingest knave in Christendom. What! I am not bestraught: here's— [mourn!

1 Serv. O, this it is that makes your lady

2 Serv. O, this it is that makes your servants droop!

Lord. Hence comes it that your kindred shuns your house,
As beaten hence by your strange lunacy.
O noble lord, bethink thee of thy birth!
Call home thy ancient thoughts from banishment,
And banish hence these abject lowly dreams.
Look how thy servants do attend on thee,
Each in his office ready at thy beck.
Wilt thou have music? hark! Apollo plays,
[*Music.*
And twenty caged nightingales do sing:
Or wilt thou sleep? we'll have thee to a couch
Softer and sweeter than the lustful bed
On purpose trimm'd up for Semiramis.
Say thou wilt walk; we will bestrew the ground:
Or wilt thou ride? thy horses shall be trapp'd,
Their harness studded all with gold and pearl.
Dost thou love hawking? thou hast hawks will soar
Above the morning lark: or wilt thou hunt?
Thy hounds shall make the welkin answer them,
And fetch shrill echoes from the hollow earth.

1 Serv. Say thou wilt course; thy greyhounds are as swift
As breathed stags; ay, fleeter than the roe.

2 Serv. Dost thou love pictures? we will fetch thee straight
Adonis painted by a running brook,
And Cytherea all in sedges hid, [breath,
Which seem to move and wanton with her
Even as the waving sedges play with wind.

Lord. We'll show thee Io as she was a maid,
And how she was beguiled and surpris'd,
As lively painted as the deed was done.

3 Serv. Or Daphne roaming through a thorny wood, [bleeds;
Scratching her legs, that one shall swear she
And at that sight shall sad Apollo weep,
So workmanly the blood and tears are drawn.

Lord. Thou art a lord, and nothing but a lord:
Thou hast a lady far more beautiful
Than any woman in this waning age. [for thee,

1 Serv. And, till the tears that she hath shed
Like envious floods, o'er-run her lovely face,
She was the fairest creature in the world;
And yet she is inferior to none.

Sly. Am I a lord? and have I such a lady?
Or do I dream? or have I dream'd till now?
I do not sleep: I see, I hear, I speak;
I smell sweet savours, and I feel soft things:—
Upon my life, I am a lord indeed;

And not a tinker, nor Christophero Sly.—
Well, bring our lady hither to our sight;
And once again, a pot o' the smallest ale.

2 Serv. Will't please your mightiness to wash your hands?
[Servants *present a ewer, basin, and napkin.*
O, how we joy to see your wit restor'd!
O, that once more you knew but what you are!
These fifteen years you have been in a dream;
Or, when you wak'd, so wak'd as if you slept.

Sly. These fifteen years! by my fay, a goodly nap.
But did I never speak of all that time?

1 Serv. O yes, my lord; but very idle words:
For though you lay here in this goodly chamber,
Yet would you say, ye were beaten out of door;
And rail upon the hostess of the house;
And say, you would present her at the leet,
Because she brought stone jugs and no seal'd quarts:
Sometimes you would call out for Cicely Hacket.

Sly. Ay, the woman's maid of the house.

3 Serv. Why, sir, you know no house, nor no such maid;
Nor no such men as you have reckon'd up,—
As Stephen Sly, and old John Naps of Greece,
And Peter Turf, and Henry Pimpernell;
And twenty more such names and men as these,
Which never were nor no man ever saw.

Sly. Now, Lord be thanked for my good amends.

All. Amen.

Sly. I thank thee: thou shalt not lose by it.

Enter the Page *as a lady, with* Attendants.

Page. How fares my noble lord? [enough.

Sly. Marry, I fare well; for here is cheer
Where is my wife?

Page. Here, noble lord: what is thy will with her?

Sly. Are you my wife, and will not call me husband? [man.
My men should call me lord: I am your good-

Page. My husband and my lord, my lord and husband;
I am your wife in all obedience.

Sly. I know it well.—What must I call her?

Lord. Madam.

Sly. Al'ce madam, or Joan madam?

Lord. Madam, and nothing else: so lords call ladies. [dream'd,

Sly. Madam wife, they say that I have
And slept above some fifteen year or more.

Page. Ay, and the time seems thirty unto me,
Being all this time abandoned from your bed.

Sly. 'Tis much.—Servants, leave me and her alone.—
Madam, undress you, and come now to bed.

Page. Thrice noble lord, let me entreat of you
To pardon me yet for a night or two;
Or, if not so, until the sun be set:

For your physicians have expressly charg'd,
In peril to incur your former malady,
That I should yet absent me from your bed:
I hope this reason stands for my excuse.

Sly. Ay, it stands so, that I may hardly
tarry so long. But I would be loath to fall into
my dreams again: I will therefore tarry, in
despite of the flesh and the blood.

Enter a Servant.

Serv. Your honour's players, hearing your
    amendment,
Are come to play a pleasant comedy;
For so your doctors hold it very meet,
Seeing too much sadness hath congeal'd your
    blood,
And melancholy is the nurse of frenzy:
Therefore they thought it good you hear a play,
And frame your mind to mirth and merriment,
Which bars a thousand harms and lengthens
    life.

Sly. Marry, I will; let them play it. Is not a
commonty a Christmas gambol or a tumbling-
trick?   [stuff.

Page. No, my good lord; it is more pleasing

Sly. What, household stuff?

Page. It is a kind of history.

Sly. Well, we'll see't. Come, madam wife, sit
by my side, and let the world slip: we shall ne'er
be younger.   [*They sit down.*

ACT I.

Scene I.—Padua. *A public Place.*

Enter Lucentio *and* Tranio.

Luc. Tranio, since for the great desire I had
To see fair Padua, nursery of arts,
I am arriv'd for fruitful Lombardy,
The pleasant garden of great Italy;
And, by my father's love and leave, am arm'd
With his good-will and thy good company,
My trusty servant, well approv'd in all;
Here let us breathe, and haply institute
A course of learning and ingenious studies.
Pisa, renowned for grave citizens,
Gave me my being, and my father first,
A merchant of great traffic through the world,
Vincentio, come of the Bentivolii.
Vincentio's son, brought up in Florence,
It shall become, to serve all hopes conceiv'd,
To deck his fortune with his virtuous deeds:
And therefore, Tranio, for the time I study,
Virtue, and that part of philosophy
Will I apply that treats of happiness
By virtue specially to be achiev'd.
Tell me thy mind; for I have Pisa left,
And am to Padua come, as he that leaves
A shallow plash to plunge him in the deep,
And with satiety seeks to quench his thirst.

Tra. Mi perdonate, gentle master mine,
I am in all affected as yourself;
Glad that you thus continue your resolve
To suck the sweets of sweet philosophy.
Only, good master, while we do admire

This virtue and this moral discipline,
Let's be no stoics nor no stocks, I pray;
Or so devote to Aristotle's ethics
As Ovid be an outcast quite abjur'd:
Balk logic with acquaintance that you have,
And practise rhetoric in your common talk;
Music and poesy use to quicken you;
The mathematics and the metaphysics,
Fall to them as you find your stomach serves
    you;
No profit grows where is no pleasure ta'en:
In brief, sir, study what you most affect.

Luc. Gramercies, Tranio, well dost thou ad-
    vise.
If Biondello now were come ashore
We could at once put us in readiness,
And take a lodging fit to entertain
Such friends as time in Padua shall beget.
But stay awhile: what company is this?

Tra. Master, some show, to welcome us to
    town.

Enter Baptista, Katharina, Bianca, Gremio,
and Hortensio. Lucentio *and* Tranio
stand aside.

Bap. Gentlemen, impórtune me no further,
For how I firmly am resolv'd you know;
That is, not to bestow my youngest daughter
Before I have a husband for the elder·
If either of you both love Katharina,
Because I know you well, and love you well,
Leave shall you have to court her at your
    pleasure.

Gre. To cart her rather: she's too rough for
    me.—
There, there, Hortensio, will you any wife?

Kath. [*To* Bap.] I pray you, sir, is it your will
To make a stale of me amongst these mates?

Hor. Mates, maid! how mean you that? no
    mates for you,
Unless you were of gentler, milder mould.

Kath. I' faith, sir, you shall never need to
    fear;
I wis it is not half-way to her heart;
But if it were, doubt not her care should be
To comb your noddle with a three-legg'd stool,
And paint your face, and use you like a fool.

Hor. From all such devils, good Lord deliver
    us!

Gre. And me too, good Lord!

Tra. Hush master! here is some good pas-
    time toward;
That wench is stark mad or wonderful fro-
    ward.

Luc. But in the other's silence do I see
Maid's mild behaviour and sobriety.
Peace, Tranio!   [your fill.

Tra. Well said, master; mum! and gaze

Bap. Gentlemen, that I may soon make good
What I have said,—Bianca, get you in:
And let it not displease thee, good Bianca;
For I will love thee ne'er the less, my girl.

Kath. A pretty peat! it is best
Put finger in the eye,—an she knew why.

Bian. Sister, content you in my discontent.—
Sir, to your pleasure humbly I subscribe:
My books and instruments shall be my company,
On them to look, and practise by myself.

Luc. Hark, Tranio! thou mayst hear Minerva speak.   [*Aside.*

Hor. Signior Baptista, will you be so strange?
Sorry am I that our good-will effects
Bianca's grief.

Gre.   Why will you mew her up,
Signior Baptista, for this fiend of hell,
And make her bear the penance of her tongue?

Bap. Gentlemen, content ye; I am resolv'd:—
Go in, Bianca:—   [*Exit* BIANCA.
And for I know she taketh most delight
In music, instruments, and poetry,
Schoolmasters will I keep within my house,
Fit to instruct her youth.—If you, Hortensio,
Or, Signior Gremio, you,—know any such,
Prefer them hither; for to cunning men
I will be very kind, and liberal
To mine own children in good bringing-up:
And so, farewell. Katharina, you may stay;
For I have more to commune with Bianca.
[*Exit.*

Kath. Why, and I trust I may go too, may I
not?   [belike,
What! shall I be appointed hours; as though,
I knew not what to take and what to leave? Ha!
[*Exit.*

Gre. You may go to the devil's dam; your
gifts are so good here is none will hold you.
Their love is not so great, Hortensio, but we
may blow our nails together, and fast it fairly
out; our cake's dough on both sides. Farewell;
—yet, for the love I bear my sweet Bianca, if I
can by any means light on a fit man to teach
her that wherein she delights, I will wish him to
her father.

Hor. So will I, Signior Gremio; but a word, I
pray. Though the nature of our quarrel yet
never brooked parle, know now, upon advice,
it toucheth us both—that we may yet again
have access to our fair mistress, and be happy
rivals in Bianca's love—to labour and effect one
thing specially.

Gre. What's that, I pray?   [sister.

Hor. Marry, sir, to get a husband for her

Gre. A husband! a devil.

Hor. I say, a husband.

Gre. I say, a devil. Thinkest thou, Hortensio, though her father be very rich, any man
is so very a fool to be married to hell?

Hor. Tush, Gremio, though it pass your
patience and mine to endure her loud alarums,
why, man, there be good fellows in the world,
an a man could light on them, would take her
with all faults and money enough.

Gre. I cannot tell; but I had as lief take her
dowry with this condition,—to be whipped at
the high-cross every morning.

Hor. Faith, as you say, there's small choice
in rotten apples. But, come; since this bar in
law makes us friends, it shall be so far forth
friendly maintained, till, by helping Baptista's
eldest daughter to a husband, we set his
youngest free for a husband, and then have to't
afresh.—Sweet Bianca!—Happy man be his
dole! He that runs fastest gets the ring.
How say you, Signior Gremio?

Gre. I am agreed: and would I had given
him the best horse in Padua to begin his wooing, that would thoroughly woo her, wed her,
and bed her, and rid the house of her.   Come
on.   [*Exeunt* GRE. *and* HOR.

Tra. [*Advancing.*] I pray, sir, tell me,—
is it possible
That love should of a sudden take such hold?

Luc. O Tranio, till I found it to be true,
I never thought it possible or likely;
But see! while idly I stood looking on
I found the effect of love in idleness:
And now in plainness do confess to thee,—
That art to me as secret and as dear
As Anna to the Queen of Carthage was,—
Tranio, I burn, I pine, I perish, Tranio,
If I achieve not this young modest girl:
Counsel me, Tranio, for I know thou canst;
Assist me, Tranio, for I know thou wilt.

Tra. Master, it is no time to chide you now;
Affection is not rated from the heart; [so,—
If love have touch'd you, nought remains but
Redime te captum quam queas minimo.

Luc. Gramercies, lad; go forward; this contents:
The rest will comfort, for thy counsel's sound.

Tra. Master, you look'd so longly on the
maid,
Perhaps you mark'd not what's the pith of all.

Luc. O yes, I saw sweet beauty in her face,
Such as the daughter of Agenor had,   [hand,
That made great Jove to humble him to her
When with his knees he kiss'd the Cretan
strand.

Tra. Saw you no more? mark'd you not how
her sister
Began to scold, and raise up such a storm,
That mortal ears might hardly endure the din?

Luc. Tranio, I saw her coral lips to move,
And with her breath she did perfume the air;
Sacred and sweet was all I saw in her.

Tra. Nay, then, 'tis time to stir him from
his trance.
I pray, awake, sir. If you love the maid,
Bend thoughts and wits to achieve her. Thus
it stands:—
Her eldest sister is so curst and shrewd
That, till the father rid his hands of her,
Master, your love must live a maid at home;
And therefore has he closely mew'd her up,
Because she will not be annoy'd with suitors.

Luc. Ah, Tranio, what a cruel father's he!
But art thou not advis'd he took some care
To get her cunning schoolmasters to instruct
her?   [plotted.

Tra. Ay, marry, am I, sir: and now 'tis

Luc. I have it, Tranio
Tra.   Master, for my hand,
Both our inventions meet and jump in one.
  Luc. Tell me thine first.
  Tra.   You will be schoolmaster,
And undertake the teaching of the maid:
That's your device.
  Luc.   It is: may it be done?
  Tra. Not possible; for who shall bear your
        part,
And be in Padua here Vincentio's son;
Keep house, and ply his book; welcome his
        friends;
Visit his countrymen and banquet them?
  Luc. Basta; content thee; for I have it full.
We have not yet been seen in any house;
Nor can we be distinguished by our faces
For man or master: then it follows thus:—
Thou shalt be master, Tranio, in my stead,
Keep house, and port, and servants, as I should:
I will some other be; some Florentine,
Some Neapolitan, or meaner man of Pisa.
T'is hatch'd, and shall be so:—Tranio, at once
Uncase thee; take my colour'd hat and cloak:
When Biondello comes he waits on thee;
But I will charm him first to keep his tongue.
  Tra. So you had need.
                    [*They exchange habits.*
In brief, then, sir, sith it your pleasure is,
And I am tied to be obedient,—
For so your father charg'd me at our parting;
Be serviceable to my son, quoth he,
Although, I think, 'twas in another sense,—
I am content to be Lucentio,
Because so well I love Lucentio.
  Luc. Tranio, be so, because Lucentio loves:
And let me be a slave, to achieve that maid
Whose sudden sight hath thrall'd my wounded
        eye.
Here comes the rogue.

Enter BIONDELLO.

Sirrah, where have you been?
  Bion. Where have I been? Nay, how now!
        where are you?
Master, has my fellow Tranio stolen your
        clothes?
Or you stolen his? or both? pray, what's the
        news?
  Luc. Sirrah, come hither; 'tis no time to jest,
And therefore frame your manners to the time.
Your fellow Tranio here, to save my life,
Puts my apparel and my countenance on,
And I for my escape have put on his;
For in a quarrel, since I came ashore,
I kill'd a man, and fear I was descried.
Wait you on him, I charge you, as becomes,
While I make way from hence to save my life:
You understand me?
  Bion.   I, sir! ne'er a whit.
  Luc. And not a jot of Tranio in your mouth;
Tranio is chang'd into Lucentio.
  Bion. The better for him; would I were so
        too!

Tra. So could I, faith, boy, to have the next
        wish after,—   [daughter.
That Lucentio indeed had Baptista's youngest
But, sirrah,—not for my sake, but your mas-
        ter's, I advise   [companies:
You use your manners discreetly in all kind of
When I am alone, why, then I am Tranio;
But in all places else, your master Lucentio.
  Luc. Tranio, let's go:—
One thing more rests, that thyself execute,—
To make one among these wooers. If thou ask
        my why,—
Sufficeth, my reasons are both good and
        weighty.   [*Exeunt.*
  [1 *Serv.* My lord, you nod; you do not mind
        the play.
  Sly. Yes, by Saint Anne do I. A good matter,
surely; comes there any more of it?
  Page. My lord, 'tis but begun.
  Sly. 'Tis a very excellent piece of work,
madam lady; would 'twere done!]

SCENE II.—*The same. Before* HORTENSIO'S
        House.

Enter PETRUCHIO *and* GRUMIO.

  Pet. Verona, for awhile I take my leave,
To see my friends in Padua; but, of all,
My best beloved and approved friend,
Hortensio; and, I trow, this is his house:—
Here, sirrah Grumio; knock, I say.
  Gru. Knock, sir! whom should I knock? is
there any man has rebused your worship?
  Pet. Villain, I say, knock me here soundly.
  Gru. Knock you here, sir? why, sir, what am
I, sir, that I should knock you here, sir?
  Pet. Villain, I say, knock me at this gate,
And rap me well, or I'll knock your knave's
        pate.
  Gru. My master is grown quarrelsome: I
        should knock you first,
And then I know after who comes by the worst.
  Pet. Will it not be?
Faith, sirrah, an you'll not knock I'll wring it:
I'll try how you can *sol, fa*, and sing it.
                    [*He wrings* GRUMIO *by the ears.*
  Gru. Help, masters, help! my master is mad.
  Pet. Now, knock when I bid you; sirrah
        villain!

Enter HORTENSIO.

  Hor. How now! what's the matter?—My
old friend Grumio! and my good friend Petruchio!—How do you all at Verona?
  Pet. Signior Hortensio, come you to part the
fray? *Con tutto il core bene trovato*, may I say.
  Hor. *Alla nostra casa bene venuto, molto
honorato Signor mio Petruchio.*
Rise, Grumio, rise; we will compound this
        quarrel.
  Gru. Nay, 'tis no matter, sir, what he 'leges
in Latin.—If this be not a lawful cause for me
to leave his service,—look you, sir,—he bid me
knock him, and rap him soundly, sir: well, was
it fit for a servant to use his master so; being,

perhaps,—for ought I see,—two and thirty,—a
pip out?
Whom would to God I had well knock'd at first,
Then had not Grumio come by the worst.

Pet. A senseless villain!—Good Hortensio,
I bade the rascal knock upon your gate,
And could not get him for my heart to do it.

Gru. Knock at the gate!—O heavens!
Spake you not these words plain,—*Sirrah,
knock me here,
Rap me here, knock me well, and knock me
soundly?*
And come you now with—knocking at the
gate?

Pet. Sirrah, be gone, or talk not, I advise
you.   [pledge:

Hor. Petruchio, patience; I am Grumio's
Why, this' a heavy chance 'twixt him and you,
Your ancient, trusty, pleasant servant Grumio.
And tell me now, sweet friend, what happy gale
Blows you to Padua here from old Verona?

Pet. Such wind as scatters young men
through the world,
To seek their fortunes further than at home,
Where small experience grows. But, in a few,
Signior Hortensio, thus it stands with me:—
Antonio, my father, is deceas'd;
And I have thrust myself into this maze,
Haply to wive and thrive as best I may:
Crowns in my purse I have, and goods at home,
And so am come abroad to see the world.

Hor. Petruchio, shall I then come roundly to
thee,
And wish thee to a shrewd ill-favour'd wife?
Thou'dst thank me but a little for my counsel
And yet I'll promise thee she shall be rich,
And very rich:—but thou'rt too much my
friend,
And I'll not wish thee to her.   [we

Pet. Signior Hortensio, 'twixt such friends as
Few words suffice; and, therefore, if thou know
One rich enough to be Petruchio's wife,—
As wealth is burden of my wooing dance,—
Be she as foul as was Florentius' love,
As old as Sibyl, and as curst and shrewd
As Socrates' Xantippe, or a worse,
She moves me not, or not removes, at least,
Affection's edge in me—were she as rough
As are the swelling Adriatic seas:
I come to wive it wealthily in Padua;
If wealthily, then happily in Padua.

Gru. Nay, look you, sir, he tells you flatly
what his mind is: why, give him gold enough
and marry him to a puppet or an aglet-baby;
or an old trot with ne'er a tooth in her head,
though she have as many diseases as two and
fifty horses: why, nothing comes amiss, so
money comes withal.   [far in,

Hor. Petruchio, since we have stepp'd thus
I will continue that I broach'd in jest.
I can, Petruchio, help thee to a·wife
With wealth enough, and young and beauteous;
Brought up as best becomes a gentlewoman;
Her only fault,—and that is faults enough,—

Is—that she is intolerably curst,
And shrewd, and forward; so beyond all
measure,
That, were my state far worser than it is,
I would not wed her for a mine of gold.

Pet. Hortensio, peace! thou know'st not gold's
effect:—
Tell me her father's name, and 'tis enough;
For I will board her though she chide as loud
As thunder, when the clouds in autumn crack.

Hor. Her father is Baptista Minola,
An affable and courteous gentleman:
Her name is Katharina Minola,
Renown'd in Padua for her scolding tongue.

Pet. I know her father though I know not
her;
And he knew my deceased father well:
I will not sleep Hortensio, till I see her;
And therefore let me be thus bold with you,
To give you over at this first encounter,
Unless you will accompany me thither.

Gru. I pray you, sir, let him go while the
humour lasts. O' my word, an she knew him
as well as I do, she would think scolding would
do little good upon him. She may, perhaps,
call him half a score knaves, or so: why, that's
nothing; an he begin once, he'll rail in his rope-
tricks. I'll tell you what sir,—an she stand
him but a little, he will throw a figure in her
face, and so disfigure her with it that she shall
have no more eyes to see withal than a cat.
You know him not, sir.

Hor. Tarry, Petruchio, I must go with thee;
For in Baptista's keep my treasure is:
He hath the jewel of my life in hold,
His youngest daughter, beautiful Bianca;
And her withholds from me, and other more,
Suitors to her and rivals in my love:
Supposing it a thing impossible,—
For those defects I have before rehears'd,—
That ever Katharina will be woo'd,
Therefore this order hath Baptista ta'en;
That none shall have access unto Bianca
Till Katharine the curst have got a husband.

Gru. Katharine the curst!
A title for a maid, of all titles the worst.

Hor. Now shall my friend Petruchio do me
grace;
And offer me disguis'd in sober robes
To old Baptista as a schoolmaster
Well seen in music, to instruct Bianca;
That so I may, by this device, at least
Have leave and leisure to make love to her,
And, unsuspected, court her by herself.

Gro. [*Aside.*] Here's no knavery! See, to beguile the old folks, how the young folks lay
their heads together!

Enter GREMIO; *with him* LUCENTIO *disguised, with books under his arm.*

Master, master, look about you: who goes
there, ha?

Hor. Peace, Grumio! 'tis the rival of my love.
Petruchio, stand by awhile.

Gru. A proper stripling, and an amorous!
[*They retire.*

Gre. O, very well; I have perused the note.
Hark you, sir; I'll have them very fairly bound:
All books of love, see that at any hand;
And see you read no other lectures to her:
You understand me:—over and beside
Signior Baptista's liberality, [too,
I'll mend it with a largess:—take your papers
And let me have them very well perfum'd;
For she is sweeter than perfume itself, [her?
To whom they go to. What will you read to
Luc. Whate'er I read to her I'll plead for you
As for my patron,—stand you so assur'd,—
As firmly as yourself were still in place:
Yea, and perhaps with more successful words
Than you, unless you were a scholar, sir.
Gre. O this learning! what a thing it is!
Gru. O this woodcock! what an ass it is!
Pet. Peace, sirrah!
Hor. Grumio, mum!—[*Coming forward*].
God save you, Signior Gremio!
Gre. And you're well met, Signior Hortensio.
Trow you whither I am going?—To Baptista
Minola.
I promis'd to inquire carefully
About a schoolmaster for the fair Bianca:
And, by good fortune, I have lighted well
On this young man, for learning and behaviour
Fit for her turn; well read in poetry
And other books,—good ones, I warrant you.
Hor. 'Tis well; and I have met a gentleman
Hath promis'd me to help me to another,
A fine musician to instruct our mistress;
So shall I no whit be behind in duty
To fair Bianca, so belov'd of me. [prove.
Gra. Belov'd of me,—and that my deeds shall
Gru. And that his bags shall prove. [*Aside.*
Hor. Gremio, 'tis now no time to vent our
love:
Listen to me, and if you speak me fair
I'll tell you news indifferent good for either.
Here is a gentleman, whom by chance I met,
Upon agreement from us to his liking,
Will undertake to woo curst Katharine;
Yea, and to marry her, if her dowry please.
Gre. So said, so done, is well:—
Hortensio, have you told him all her faults?
Pet. I know she is an irksome brawling
scold;
If that be all, masters, I hear no harm.
Gre. No, say'st me so, friend? What country-
man?
Pet. Born in Verona, old Antonio's son:
My father dead, my fortune lives for me;
And I do hope good days and long to see.
Gre. O, sir, such a life, with such a wife, were
strange:
But if you have a stomach, to't o' God's name;
You shall have me assisting you in all.
But will you woo this wild-cat?
Pet. Will I live?
Gru. Will he woo her? ay, or I'll hang her.
Pet. Why came I hither but to that intent?

Think you a little din can daunt mine ears?
Have I not in my time heard lions roar?
Have I not heard the sea, puff'd up with winds,
Rage like an angry boar chafed with sweat?
Have I not heard great ordnance in the field,
And heaven's artillery thunder in the skies?
Have I not in a pitched battle heard [clang?
Loud 'larums, neighing steeds, and trumpets
And do you tell me of a woman's tongue;
That gives not half so great a blow to hear,
As will a chestnut in a farmer's fire?
Tush! tush! fear boys with bugs.
Gru. For he fears none.
Gre. Hortensio, hark:
This gentleman is happily arriv'd,
My mind presumes, for his own good and ours.
Hor. I promis'd we would be contributors,
And bear his charge of wooing, whatsoe'er.
Gre. And so we will—provided that he win
her.
Gru. I would I were as sure of a good dinner.

Enter TRANIO, *bravely apparelled, and*
BIONDELLO.

Tra. Gentlemen, God save you! If I may be
bold, [way
Tell me, I beseech you, which is the readiest
To the house of Signior Baptista Minola?
Bion. He that has the two fair daughters:—
is't [*aside to* TRANIO] he you mean?
Tra. Even he, Biondello!
Gre. Hark you, sir; you mean not her to,—
Tra. Perhaps, him and her, sir; what have
you to do? [pray.
Pet. Not her that chides, sir, at any hand, I
Tra. I love no chiders, sir; Biondello, let's
away.
Luc. Well begun, Tranio. [*Aside.*
Hor. Sir, a word ere you go;— [or no?
Are you a suitor to the maid you talk of, yea
Tra. An if I be, sir, is it any offence?
Gre. No; if without more words you will get
you hence. [free
Tra. Why, sir, I pray, are not the streets as
For me as for you?
Gre. But so is not she.
Tra. For what reason, I beseech you?
Gre. For this reason, if you'll know,—
That she's the choice love of Signior Gremio.
Hor. That she's the chosen of Signior Hor-
tensio.
Tra. Softly, my masters! if you be gentlemen
Do me this right,—hear me with patience.
Baptista is a noble gentleman,
To whom my father is not all unknown,
And, were his daughter fairer than she is,
She may more suitors have, and me for one.
Fair Leda's daughter had a thousand wooers;
Then well one more may fair Bianca have:
And so she shall; Lucentio shall make one,
Though Paris came in hope to speed alone.
Gre. What! this gentleman will out-talk us
all. [a jade.
Luc. Sir, give him head; I know he'll prove

Pet. Hortensio, to what end are all these
    words?

Hor. Sir, let me be so bold as ask you,
Did you yet ever see Baptista's daughter?

Tra. No, sir; but hear I do that he hath two;
The one as famous for a scolding tongue
As is the other for beauteous modesty.

Pet. Sir, sir, the first's for me; let her go by.

Gre. Yea, leave that labour to great Her-
    cules;
And let it be more than Alcides' twelve.

Pet. Sir, understand you this of me, in sooth:
The youngest daughter, whom you hearken for,
Her father keeps from all access of suitors,
And will not promise her to any man
Until the elder sister first be wed?
The younger then is free, and not before.

Tra. If it be so, sir, that you are the man ,
Must stead us all, and me amongst the rest;
And if you break the ice, and do this feat,—
Achieve the elder, set the younger free
For our access,—whose hap shall be to have her
Will not so graceless be to be ingrate.

Hor. Sir, you say well, and well you do con-
    ceive;
And since you do profess to be a suitor,
You must, as we do, gratify this gentleman,
To whom we all rest generally beholding.

Tra. Sir, I shall not be slack: in sign whereof
Please ye we may contrive this afternoon,
And quaff carouses to our mistress' health;
And do as adversaries do in law,—
Strive mightily, but eat and drink as friends.

Gru. Bion. O excellent motion! Fellows, let's
    be gone.   [so;—

Hor. The motion's good indeed, and be it
Petruchio, I shall be your *ben venuto*.
                                [*Exeunt.*

ACT II.

SCENE I.—*The same. A Room in BAP-
TISTA's House.*

Enter KATHARINA *and* BIANCA.

Bian. Good sister, wrong me not, nor wrong
    yourself,
To make a bondmaid and a slave of me;
That I disdain: but for these other gawds,
Unbind my hands, I'll pull them off myself,
Yea, all my raiment, to my petticoat;
Or what you will command me will I do,
So well I know my duty to my elders.

Kath. Of all thy suitors, here I charge thee,
    tell
Whom thou lov'st best: see thou dissemble not.

Bian. Believe me, sister, of all the men alive,
I never yet beheld that special face
Which I could fancy more than any other.

Kath. Minion, thou liest; is't not Hortensio?

Bian. If you affect him, sister, here I swear
I'll plead for you myself, but you shall have
    him.

Kath. O then, belike, you fancy riches more;
You will have Gremio to keep you fair.

Bian. Is it for him you do envy me so?
Nay, then you jest; and now I well perceive
You have but jested with me all this while:
I pr'ythee, sister Kate, untie my hands.

Kath. If that be jest, then all the rest was so.
                                [*Strikes her.*

Enter BAPTISTA.

Bap. Why, how now, dame! whence grows
    this insolence?—
Bianca, stand aside;—poor girl! she weeps:—
Go ply thy needle; meddle not with her.—
For shame, thou hilding of a devilish spirit,
Why dost thou wrong her that did ne'er wrong
    thee?
When did she cross thee with a bitter word?

Kath. Her silence flouts me and I'll be re-
    veng'd.   [*Flies after* BIANCA.

Bap. What, in my sight?—Bianca, get thee
    in.   [*Exit* BIANCA.

Kath. What, will you not suffer me? Nay,
    now I see
She is your treasure, she must have a husband;
I must dance bare-foot on her wedding-day,
And for your love to her lead apes in hell.
Talk not to me; I will go sit and weep,
Till I can find occasion of revenge.
                                [*Exit* KATHARINA.

Bap. Was ever gentleman thus griev'd as I?
But who comes here?

Enter GREMIO, *with* LUCENTIO *in the habit of a mean man;* PETRUCHIO, *with* HORTENSIO *as a musician; and* TRANIO, *with* BIONDELLO *bearing a lute and books.*

Gre. Good-morrow, neighbour Baptista.

Bap. Good-morrow, neighbour Gremio: God
save you, gentlemen!   [a daughter

Pet. And you, good sir! Pray, have you not
Call'd Katharina, fair and virtuous?

Bap. I have a daughter, sir, call'd Katharina.

Gre. You are too blunt: go to it orderly.

Pet. You wrong me, Signior Gremio: give me
    leave.—
I am a gentleman of Verona, sir,
That,—hearing of her beauty and her wit,
Her affability and bashful modesty,
Her wondrous qualities and mild behaviour,—
Am bold to show myself a forward guest
Within your house, to make mine eye the wit-
    ness
Of that report which I so oft have heard.
And, for an entrance to my entertainment,
I do present you with a man of mine,
                [*Presenting* HORTENSIO.
Cunning in music and the mathematics,
To instruct her fully in those sciences,
Whereof I know she is not ignorant:
Accept of him, or else you do me wrong:
His name is Licio, born in Mantua.

Bap. You're welcome, sir; and he for your
    good sake;
But for my daughter Katharine,—this I know,
She is not for your turn, the more my grief.

Pet. I see you do not mean to part with her;
Or else you like not of my company.
  Bap. Mistake me not, I speak but as I find.
Whence are you, sir? what may I call your
    name?
  Pet. Petruchio is my name; Antonio's son,
A man well known throughout all Italy.
  Bap. I know him well: you are welcome for
    his sake.
  Gre. Saving your tale, Petruchio, I pray,
Let us, that are poor petitioners, speak too:
Baccare! you are marvellous forward.
  Pet. O, pardon me, Signior Gremio: I would
    fain be doing.
  Gre. I doubt it not, sir; but you will curse
    your wooing.—
Neighbour, this is a gift very grateful, I am
sure of it. To express the like kindness myself,
that have been more kindly beholding to you
than any, I freely give unto you this young
scholar [*presenting* Lucentio], that hath been
long studying at Rheims; as cunning in Greek,
Latin, and other languages, as the other in
music and mathematics: his name is Cambio;
pray, accept his service.
  Bap. A thousand thanks, Signior Gremio:
welcome, good Cambio.—But, gentle sir [*to*
Tranio], methinks you walk like a stranger.
May I be so bold to know the cause of your
coming?   [own;
  Tra. Pardon me, sir, the boldness is mine
That, being a stranger in this city here,
Do make myself a suitor to your daughter,
Unto Bianco, fair and virtuous.
Nor is your firm resolve unknown to me,
In the preferment of the eldest sister.
This liberty is all that I request,—
That, upon knowledge of my parentage,
I may have welcome 'mongst the rest that woo,
And free access and favour as the rest.
And, toward the education of your daughters,
I here bestow a simple instrument,
And this small packet of Greek and Latin
    books;
If you accept them, then their worth is great.
  Bap. Lucentio is your name? of whence, I
    pray?
  Tra. Of Pisa, sir; son to Vincentio.
  Bap. A mighty man of Pisa: by report
I know him well: you are very welcome, sir.—
Take you [*to* Hor.] the lute, and you [*to* Luc.]
    the set of books;
You shall go see your pupils presently.
Holla, within!

Enter a Servant.

          Sirrah, lead these gentlemen
To my daughters; and tell them both,
These are their tutors; bid them use them well.
    [*Exit* Serv., *with* Hor., Luc., *and* Bion.
We will go walk a little in the orchard,
And then to dinner. You are passing welcome,
And so I pray you all to think yourselves.

  Pet. Signior Baptista, my business asketh
    haste,
And every day I cannot come to woo.
You knew my father well; and in him, me,
Left solely heir to all his lands and goods,
Which I have better'd rather than decreas'd:
Then tell me,—if I get your daughter's love,
What dowry shall I have with her to wife?
  Bap. After my death, the one half of my
    lands
And, in possession, twenty thousand crowns.
  Pet. And for that dowry, I'll assure her of
Her widowhood,—be it that she survive me,—
In all my lands and leases whatsoever:
Let specialties be therefore drawn between us,
That covenants may be kept on either hand.
  Bap. Ay, when the special thing is well ob-
    tain'd,
That is, her love; for that is all in all.
  Pet. Why, that is nothing; for I tell you,
    father,
I am as peremptory as she proud-minded;
And where two raging fires meet together,
They do consume the thing that feeds their
    fury:
Though little fire grows great with little wind,
Yet extreme gusts will blow out fire and all:
So I to her, and so she yields to me;
For I am rough, and woo not like a babe.
  Bap. Well mayst thou woo, and happy be
    thy speed!
But be thou arm'd for some unhappy words.
  Pet. Ay, to the proof; as mountains are for
    winds,
That shake not though they blow perpetually.

Re-enter Hortensio, *with his head broken.*

  Bap. How now, my friend! why dost thou
    look so pale?
  Hor. For fear, I promise you, if I look pale.
  Bap. What, will my daughter prove a good
    musician?
  Hor. I think she'll sooner prove a soldier:
Iron may hold with her, but never lutes.
  Bap. Why, then thou canst not break her to
    the lute?
  Hor. Why, no; for she hath broke the lute
    to me.
I did but tell her she mistook her frets,
And bow'd her hand to teach her fingering,
When, with a most impatient devilish spirit,
Frets, call you these? quoth she; *I'll fume with
    them:*
And, with that word, she struck me on the
    head,
And through the instrument my pate made
    way;
And there I stood amazed for awhile,
As on a pillory, looking through the lute,
While she did call me rascal fiddler
And twangling Jack, with twenty such vile
    terms,
As she had studied to misuse me so.

Pet. Now, by the world, it is a lusty wench;
I love her ten times more than e'er I did:
O, how I long to have some chat with her!
    Bap. Well, go with me, and be not so dis-
        comfited:
Proceed in practice with my younger daughter:
She's apt to learn, and thankful for good
        turns.—
Signior Petruchio, will you go with us,
Or shall I send my daughter Kate to you?
    Pet. I pray you do: I will attend her here,
        [*Exeunt,* BAP., GRE., TRA., *and* HOR.
And woo her with some spirit when she comes.
Say that she rail; why, then I'll tell her plain
She sings as sweetly as a nightingale:
Say that she frown; I'll say she looks as clear
As morning roses newly washed with dew:
Say she be mute, and will not speak a word;
Then I'll commend her volubility,
And say she uttereth piercing eloquence:
If she do bid me pack, I'll give her thanks,
As though she bid me stay by her a week:
If she deny to wed, I'll crave the day
When I shall ask the banns, and when be
        married.—
But here she comes; and now, Petruchio, speak.

Enter KATHARINA.

Good-morrow, Kate; for that's your name, I
        hear.
    Kath. Well have you heard, but something
        hard of hearing:
They call me Katharine that do talk of me.
    Pet. You lie, in faith; for you are call'd plain
        Kate,
And bonny Kate, and sometimes Kate the
        curst;
But, Kate, the prettiest Kate in Christendom,
Kate of Kate-Hall, my super-dainty Kate,
For dainties are all cates; and therefore, Kate,
Take this of me, Kate of my consolation;—
Hearing thy mildness prais'd in every town,
Thy virtues spoke of, and thy beauty sounded,—
Yet not so deeply as to thee belongs,—
Myself am mov'd to woo thee for my wife.
    Kath. Mov'd! in good time: let him that
        mov'd you hither
Remove you hence: I knew you at the first
You were a movable.
    Pet.   Why, what's a movable?
    Kath. A joint-stool.
    Pet.   Thou hast hit it: come, sit on me.
    Kath. Asses are made to bear, and so are you.
    Pet. Women are made to bear, and so are you.
    Kath. No such jade as bear you, if me you
        mean.
    Pet. Alas, good Kate, I will not burden thee!
For, knowing thee to be but young and light,—
    Kath. Too light for such a swain as you to
        catch;
And yet as heavy as my weight should be.
    Pet. Should be! should buzz.
    Kath.   Well ta'en, and like a buzzard.

Pet. O, slow-wing'd turtle! shall a buzzard
        take thee?
    Kath. Ay, for a turtle,—as he takes a buz-
        zard.
    Pet. Come, come, you wasp; i' faith, you are
        too angry.
    Kath. If I be waspish, best beware my sting.
    Pet. My remedy is then, to pluck it out.
    Kath. Ay, if the fool could find it where it
        lies.   [wear his sting?
    Pet. Who knows not where a wasp doth
In his tail.
    Kath.   In his tongue.
    Pet.   Whose tongue?
    Kath. Yours, if you talk of tails; and so
        farewell.   [come again,
    Pet. What, with my tongue in your tail? nay,
Good Kate; I am a gentleman.
    Kath.   That I'll try.
                                [*Striking him.*
    Pet. I swear I'll cuff you, if you strike again.
    Kath. So may you lose your arms:
If you strike me, you are no gentleman;
And if no gentleman, why then no arms.
    Pet. A herald, Kate? O, put me in thy books!
    Kath. What is your crest? a coxcomb?
    Pet. A combless cock, so Kate will be my hen.
    Kath. No cock of mine; you crow too like a
        craven.   [look so sour.
    Pet. Nay, come, Kate, come; you must not
    Kath. It is my fashion, when I see a crab.
    Pet. Why, here's no crab; and therefore look
        not sour.
    Kath. There is, there is.
    Pet. Then show it me.
    Kath.   Had I a glass I would.
    Pet. What, you mean my face?
    Kath.   Well aim'd of such a young one.
    Pet. Now, by Saint George, I am too young
        for you.
    Kath. Yet you are wither'd.
    Pet.   'Tis with cares.
    Kath.   I care not.
    Pet. Nay, hear you, Kate: in sooth, you
        'scape not so.
    Kath. I chafe you, if I tarry; let me go.
    Pet. No, not a whit: I find you passing
        gentle.
'Twas told me you were rough, and coy, and
        sullen,
And now I find report a very liar;   [teous;
For thou art pleasant, gamesome, passing cour-
But slow in speech, yet sweet as spring-time
        flowers:
Thou canst not frown, thou canst not look as-
        kance,
Nor bite the lip, as angry wenches will;
Nor hast thou pleasure to be cross in talk;
But thou with mildness entertain'st thy wooers
With gentle conference, soft and affable.
Why does the world report that Kate doth
        limp?
O slanderous world! Kate, like the hazel-twig,
Is straight and slender; and as brown in hue

As hazel-nuts, and sweeter than the kernels.
O, let me see thee walk: thou dost not halt.

Kath. Go, fool, and whom thou keep'st command.

Pet. Did ever Dian so become a grove
As Kate this chamber with her princely gait?
O, be thou Dian, and let her be Kate;
And then let Kate be chaste, and Dian sportful! [speech?

Kath. Where did you study all this goodly

Pet. It is extempore, from my mother-wit.

Kath. A witty mother! witless else her son.

Pet. Am I not wise?

Kath.   Yes, keep you warm.

Pet. Marry, so I mean, sweet Katharine, in thy bed:
And therefore, setting all this chat aside,
Thus in plain terms:—Your father hath consented [on;
That you shall be my wife; your dowry 'greed
And, will you, nill you, I will marry you.
Now, Kate, I am a husband for your turn;
For, by this light, whereby I see thy beauty,—
Thy beauty that doth make me like thee well—
Thou must be married to no man but me;
For I am he am born to tame you, Kate;
And bring you from a wild Kate to a Kate
Conformable, as other household Kates.
Here comes your father; never make denial;
I must and will have Katharine to my wife.

Re-enter BAPTISTA, GREMIO, *and* TRANIO.

Bap. Now, Signior Petruchio, how speed you
with my daughter?

Pet. How but well, sir? how but well?
It were impossible I should speed amiss.

Bap. Why, how now, daughter Katharine! in your dumps? [you

Kath. Call you me daughter? now, I promise
You have show'd a tender fatherly regard
To wish me wed to one half lunatic;
A mad-cap ruffian and a swearing Jack,
That thinks with oaths to face the matter out.

Pet. Father, 'tis thus:—yourself and all the world,
That talked of her, hath talk'd amiss of her;
If she be curst, it is for policy;
For she's not froward, but modest as the dove,
She is not hot, but temperate as the morn;
For patience she will prove a second Grissel,
And Roman Lucrece for her chastity:
And to conclude, we have 'greed so well together,
That upon Sunday is the wedding-day.

Kath. I'll see thee hang'd on Sunday first.

Gre. Hark, Petruchio; she says she'll see thee hang'd first.

Tra. Is this your speeding? nay, then, goodnight our part! [for myself;

Pet. Be patient, gentlemen; I choose her
If she and I be pleas'd, what's that to you?
'Tis bargain'd 'twixt us twain, being alone,
That she shall still be curst in company.
I tell you, 'tis incredible to believe

How much she loves me: O, the kindest Kate!—
She hung about my neck, and kiss on kiss
She vied so fast, protesting oath on oath,
That in a twink she won me to her love.
O, you are novices! 'tis a world to see,
How tame when men and women are alone,
A meacock wretch can make the curstest shrew.—
Give me thy hand, Kate: I will unto Venice,
To buy apparel 'gainst the wedding-day.—
Provide the feast, father, and bid the guests;
I will be sure my Katharine shall be fine.

Bap. I know not what to say: but give me your hands;
God send you joy, Petruchio! 'tis a match.

Gre. Tra. Amen, say we; we will be witnesses.

Pet. Father, and wife, and gentlemen, adieu;
I will to Venice; Sunday comes apace:—
We will have rings, and things, and fine array;
And, kiss me, Kate, we will be married o' Sunday.

[*Exeunt* PET. *and* KATH., *severally.*

Gre. Was ever match clapp'd up so suddenly?

Bap. Faith, gentlemen, now I play a merchant's part,
And venture madly on a desperate mart.

Tra. 'Twas a commodity lay fretting by you;
'Twill bring you gain, or perish on the seas.

Bap. The gain I seek is quiet in the match.

Gre. No doubt but he hath got a quiet catch.
But now, Baptista, to your younger daughter;—
Now is the day we long have looked for;
I am your neighbour, and was suitor first.

Tra. And I am one that love Bianca more
Than words can witness or your thoughts can guess. [as I.

Gre. Youngling! thou canst not love so dear

Tra. Graybeard! thy love doth freeze.

Gre.   But thine doth fry.
Skipper, stand back; 'tis age that nourisheth.

Tra. But youth in ladies' eyes that flourisheth. [this strife:

Bap. Content you, gentlemen; I'll compound
'Tis deeds must win the prize; and he, of both,
That can assure my daughter greatest dower
Shall have Bianca's love.—
Say, Signior Gremio, what can you assure her?

Gre. First, as you know, my house within the city
Is richly furnished with plate and gold;
Basins and ewers, to lave her dainty hands;
My hangings all of Tyrian tapestry:
In ivory coffers I have stuff'd my crowns;
In cypress chests my arras counterpoints,
Costly apparel, tents, and canopies,
Fine linen, Turkey cushions boss'd with pearl,
Valance of Venice gold in needle-work,
Pewter and brass, and all things that belong
To house or housekeeping: then, at my farm,
I have a hundred milch-kine to the pail,
Six score fat oxen standing in my stalls,
And all things answerable to this portion.
Myself am struck in years, I must confess;

And, if I die to-morrow this is hers:
If, whilst I live, she will be only mine. [me:
  Tra. That *only* came well in.—Sir, list to
I am my father's heir and only son:
If I may have your daughter to my wife,
I'll leave her houses three or four as good,
Within rich Pisa's walls, as any one
Old Signior Gremio has in Padua;
Besides two thousand ducats by the year
Of fruitful land, all which shall be her join-
      ture.—
What, have I pinch'd you Signior Gremio?
  Gre. Two thousand ducats by the year of
    land!
My land amounts not to so much in all:
That she shall have; besides an argosy,
That now is lying in Marseilles' road:—
What, have I chok'd you with an argosy?
  Tra. Gremio, 'tis known my father hath no
    less
Than three great argosies; besides two gal-
    liases,
And twelve tight galleys: these I will assure
    her,
And twice as much, whate'er thou offer'st next.
  Gre. Nay, I have offer'd all,—I have no
    more;
And she can have no more than all I have:—
If you like me, she shall have me and mine.
  Tra. Why, then the maid is mine from all
    the world,
By your firm promise: Gremio is out-vied.
  Bap. I must confess your offer is the best;
And, let your father make her the assurance,
She is your own; else, you must pardon me:
If you should die before him, where's her
    dower?
  Tra. That's but a cavil; he is old, I young.
  Gre. And may not young men die as well as
    old?
  Bap. Well, gentlemen,
I am thus resolv'd:—On Sunday next you know
My daughter Katharine is to be married:
Now, on the Sunday following shall Bianca
Be bride to you, if you make this assurance;
If not, to Signior Gremio:
And so I take my leave, and thank you both.
  Grè. Adieu, good neighbour.—
               [*Exit* BAPTISTA.
         Now I fear thee not:
Sirrah young gamester, your father were a fool
To give thee all, and in his waning age
Set foot under thy table. Tut! a toy!
An old Italian fox is not so kind, my boy.
                    [*Exit.*
  Tra. A vengeance on your crafty wither'd
    hide!
Yet I have faced it with a card of ten.
'Tis in my head to do my master good:—
I see no reason but suppos'd Lucentio
Must get a father, call'd—suppos'd Vincentio;
And that's a wonder: fathers commonly
Do get their children; but in this case of woo-
    ing,

A child shall get a sire, if I fail not of my
  cunning. [*Exit.*

ACT III.

SCENE I.—PADUA. *A Room in* BAPTISTA'S
         House.

Enter LUCENTIO, HORTENSIO, *and* BIANCA.

  Luc. Fiddler, forbear; you grow too forward,
    sir:
Have you so soon forgot the entertainment
Her sister Katharine welcom'd you withal?
  Hor. But, wrangling pedant, this is
The patroness of heavenly harmony:
Then give me leave to have prerogative;
And when in music we have spent an hour,
Your lecture shall have leisure for as much.
  Luc. Preposterous ass! that never read so far
To know the cause why music was ordain'd!
Was it not to refresh the mind of man
After his studies or his usual pain?
Then give me leave to read philosophy,
And while I pause serve in your harmony.
  Hor. Sirrah, I will not bear these braves of
    thine.
  Bian. Why, gentlemen, you do me double
    wrong,
To strive for that which resteth in my choice.
I am no breeching scholar in the schools:
I'll not be tied to hours nor 'pointed times,
But learn my lessons as I please myself.
And, to cut off all strife, here sit we down:—
Take you your instrument, play you the whiles;
His lecture will be done ere you have tun'd.
  Hor. You'll leave his lecture when I am in
    tune?
         [*To* BIANCA. HORTENSIO *retires.*
  Luc. That will be never:—tune your instru-
    ment.
  Bian. Where left we last?
  Luc. Here, madam:—
    Hac ibat Simois; hic est Sigeia tellus;
    Hic steterat Priami regia celsa senis.
  Bian. Construe them.
  Luc. Hac ibat, as I told you before,—*Simois,*
I am Lucentio,—*His est,* son unto Vincentio of
Pisa,—*Sigeia tellus,* disguised thus to get your
love;—*Hic steterat,* and that Lucentio that
comes a-wooing,—*Priami,* is my man Tranio,
—*regia,* bearing my port,—*celsa senis,* that we
might beguile the old pantaloon.
  Hor. [*Coming forward.*] Madam, my instru-
    ment's in tune.
  Bian. Let's hear.— [HORTENSIO *plays.*
O fie! the treble jars.
  Luc. Spit in the hole, man, and tune again.
  Bian. Now let me see if I can construe it:
—*Hac ibat Simois,* I know you not,—*hic est
Sigeia tellus,* I trust you not;—*Hic steterat
Priami,* take heed he hear us not,—*regia,* pre-
sume not,—*celsa senis,* despair not.
  Hor. Madam, 'tis now in tune.
  Luc.   All but the base.
  Hor. The base is right; 'tis the base knave
    that jars.

How fiery and forward our pedant is!
Now, for my life, the knave doth court my love:
Pedascule, I'll watch you better yet.   [*Aside.*
  Bian. In time I may believe, yet I mistrust.
  Luc. Mistrust it not; for, sure, Æacides
Was Ajax,—call'd so from his grandfather.
  Bian. I must believe my master; else, I
    promise you,
I should be arguing still upon that doubt:
But let it rest.—Now, Licio, to you:—
Good masters, take it not unkindly, pray,
That I have been thus pleasant with you both.
  Hor. You may go walk [*to* LUCENTIO], and
    give me leave awhile;
My lessons make no music in three parts.
  Luc. Are you so formal, sir? well, I must wait,
And watch withal; for, but I be deceiv'd,
Our fine musician groweth amorous.   [*Aside.*
  Hor. Madam, before you touch the instru-
    ment,
To learn the order of my fingering,
I must begin with rudiments of art;
To teach you gamut in a briefer sort,
More pleasant, pithy, and effectual,
Than hath been taught by any of my trade:
And there it is in writing, fairly drawn.
  Bian. Why, I am past my gamut long ago.
  Hor. Yet read the gamut of Hortensio.
  Bian. [*Reads.*] Gamut *I am, the ground of all
    accord,*
    A re, *to plead Hortensio's passion;*
B mi, *Bianca, take him for thy lord,*
    C fa ut, *that loves with all affection:*
D sol re, *one cliff, two notes have I;*
    E la mi, *show pity, or I die.*
Call you this gamut? tut, I like it not:
Old fashions please me best; I am not so nice,
To change true rules for odd inventions.

Enter a Servant.

  Serv. Mistress, your father prays you leave
    your books,
And help to dress your sister's chamber up:
You know to-morrow is the wedding-day.
  Bian. Farewell, sweet masters, both; I must
    be gone!
                [*Exeunt* BIANCA *and* Servant.
  Luc. Faith, mistress, then I have no cause to
    stay.   [*Exit.*
  Hor. But I have cause to pry into this
    pedant;
Methinks he looks as though he were in love:—
Yet if thy thoughts, Bianca, be so humble,
To cast thy wand'ring eyes on every stale,
Seize thee that list: if once I find thee ranging,
Hortensio will be quit with thee by changing.
                                      [*Exit.*

SCENE II.—*The same. Before* BAPTISTA'S *House.*

Enter BAPTISTA, GREMIO, TRANIO, KATHARINA,
BIANCA, LUCENTIO, *and* Attendants.

  Bap. Signior Lucentio [*to* TRANIO], this is the
    'pointed day

That Katharine and Petruchio should be
    married,
And yet we hear not of our son-in-law:
What will be said? what mockery will it be,
To want the bridegroom when the priest at-
    tends
To speak the ceremonial rites of marriage?
What says Lucentio to this shame of ours?
  Kath. No shame but mine: I must, forsooth,
    be forc'd
To give my hand, oppos'd against my heart,
Unto a mad-brain rudesby, full of spleen;
Who woo'd in haste, and means to wed at
    leisure.
I told you, I, he was a frantic fool,
Hiding his bitter jests in blunt behaviour:
And, to be noted for a merry man,
He'll woo a thousand, 'point the day of mar-
    riage,   [banns;
Make friends, invite them, and proclaim the
Yet never means to wed where he hath woo'd.
Now must the world point at poor Katharine,
And say, *Lo, there is mad Petruchio's wife,*
If it would please him come and marry her!
  Tra. Patience, good Katharine, and Bap-
    tista too.
Upon my life, Petruchio means but well!
Whatever fortune stays him from his word:
Though he be blunt, I know him passing wise;
Though he be merry, yet withal he's honest.
  Kath. Would Katharine had never seen him
    though!
[*Exit, weeping, followed by* BIANCA *and others.*
  Bap. Go, girl; I cannot blame thee now to
    weep;
For such an injury would vex a very saint,
Much more a shrew of thy impatient humour.

Enter BIONDELLO.

  Bion. Master, master! old news, and such
news as you never heard of!   [be?
  Bap. Is it new and old too? how may that
  Bion. Why, is it not news to hear of Petru-
chio's coming?
  Bap. Is he come?
  Bion. Why, no, sir.
  Bap. What then?
  Bion. He is coming.
  Bap. When will he be here?   [you there.
  Bion. When he stands where I am, and sees
  Tra. But, say, what to thine old news?
  Bion. Why, Petruchio is coming, in a new
hat and an old jerkin; a pair of old breeches
thrice turn'd; a pair of boots that have been
candle-cases, one buckled, another laced; an
old rusty sword ta'en out of the town armoury,
with a broken hilt, and chapeless; with two
broken points: his horse hipped with an old
mothy saddle, and stirrups of no kindred;
besides, possessed with the glanders, and like
to mose in the chine; troubled with the lam-
pass, infected with the fashions, fell of wind-
galls, sped with spavins, rayed with the yellows,
past cure of the fives, stark spoiled with the

staggers, begnawn with the bots, swayed in the back, and shoulder-shotten; ne'er legged before and with a half-checked bit; and a head-stall of sheep's leather, which, being restrained to keep him from stumbling, hath been often burst, and now repaired with knots; one girth six times pieced, and a woman's crupper of velure, which hath two letters for her name, fairly set down in studs, and here and there pieced with pack-thread.

Bap. Who comes with him?

Bion. O, sir, his lackey, for all the world caparisoned like the horse; with a linen stock on one leg and a kersey boot-hose on the other, gartered with a red and blue list; an old hat, and *The humour of forty fancies* pricked in 't for a feather: a monster, a very monster in apparel; and not like a Christian footboy or a gentleman's lackey.

Tra. 'Tis some odd humour pricks him to this fashion;
Yet oftentimes he goes but mean apparell'd.

Bap. I am glad he is come, howsoe'er he comes.

Bion. Why, sir, he comes not.

Bap. Didst thou not say he comes?

Bion. Who? that Petruchio came?

Bap. Ay, that Petruchio came.

Bion. No, sir; I say his horse comes with him on his back.

Bap. Why, that's all one.

Bion. Nay, by saint Jamy,
I hold you a penny,
A horse and a man
Is more than one,
And yet not many.

Enter PETRUCHIO *and* GRUMIO.

Pet. Come, where be these gallants? who's at home?

Bap. You are welcome, sir.

Pet.   And yet I come not well.

Bap. And yet you halt not.

Tra.   Not so well apparell'd
As I wish you were.

Pet. Were it better, I should rush in thus.
But where is Kate? where is my lovely bride?
How does my father?—Gentles, methinks you frown:
And wherefore gaze this goodly company,
As if they saw some wondrous monument,
Some comet or unusual prodigy?

Bap. Why, sir, you know this is your wedding-day:
First were we sad, fearing you would not come;
Now sadder, that you come so unprovided.
Fie, doff this habit, shame to your estate,
An eye-sore to our solemn festival!

Tra. And tell us, what occasion of import
Hath all so long detain'd you from your wife,
And sent you hither so unlike yourself?

Pet. Tedious it were to tell, and harsh to hear:
Sufficeth, I am come to keep my word,

Though in some part enforced to digress;
Which, at more leisure, I will so excuse
As you shall well be satisfied withal.
But where is Kate? I stay too long from her:
The morning wears, 'tis time we were at church.

Tra. See not your bride in these unreverent robes:
Go to my chamber, put on clothes of mine.

Pet. Not I, believe me: thus I'll visit her.

Bap. But thus, I trust, you will not marry her.

Pet. Good sooth, even thus; therefore ha' done with words;
To me she's married, not unto my clothes
Could I repair what she will wear in me,
As I can change these poor accoutrements,
'Twere well for Kate, and better for myself.
But what a fool am I to chat with you,
When I should bid good-morrow to my bride,
And seal the title with a lovely kiss!
                    [*Exeunt* PETRUCHIO *and* GRUMIO.

Tra. He hath some meaning in his mad attire.
We will persuade him, be it possible,
To put on better ere he go to church.

Bap. I'll after him, and see the event of this.
                    [*Exeunt* BAP., GREM., *and* BION.

Tra. But, sir, to her love concerneth us to add
Her father's liking: which to bring to pass,
As I before imparted to your worship,
I am to get a man,—whate'er he be,
It skills not much; we'll fit him to our turn,—
And he shall be Vincentio of Pisa;
And make assurance, here in Padua,
Of greater sums than I have promised.
So shall you quietly enjoy your hope,
And marry sweet Bianca with consent.

Luc. Were it not that my fellow-schoolmaster
Doth watch Bianca's steps so narrowly,
'Twere good, methinks, to steal our marriage;
Which once perform'd, let all the world say no,
I'll keep mine own, despite of all the world.

Tra. That by degrees we mean to look into,
And watch our vantage in this business:
We'll over-reach the graybeard, Gremio,
The narrow-prying father, Minola;
The quaint musician, amorous Licio;
All for my master's sake, Lucentio.

Re-enter GREMIO.

Signior Gremio,—came you from the church?

Gre. As willingly as e'er I came from school.

Tra. And is the bride and bridegroom coming home?

Gre. A bridegroom, say you? 'tis a groom indeed,
A grumbling groom, and that the girl shall find.

Tra. Curster than she? why, 'tis impossible.

Gre. Why, he's a devil, a devil, a very fiend,

Tra. Why, she's a devil, a devil, the devil's dam.

Gre. Tut, she's a lamb, a dove, a fool to him!
I'll tell you, Sir Lucentio: when the priest
Should ask, if Katharine should be his wife,
Ay, by gogs-wouns, quoth he; and swore so loud
That, all amaz'd, the priest let fall the book;
And, as he stoop'd again to take it up,
The mad-brain'd bridegroom took him such a
  cuff
That down fell priest and book, and book and
  priest:
Now take them up, quoth he, *if any list.*
 Tra. What said the wench, when he arose
  again?
 Gre. Trembled and shook; for why, he
  stamp'd and swore,
As if the vicar meant to cozen him.
But after many ceremonies done,
He calls for wine: *A health!* quoth he; as if
He had been aboard, carousing to his mates
After a storm: quaff'd off the muscadel,
And threw the sops all in the sexton's face;
Having no other reason
But that his beard grew thin and hungerly,
And seem'd to ask him sops as he was drinking.
This done, he took the bride about the neck,
And kiss'd her lips with such a clamorous
  smack
That, at the parting, all the church did echo.
I, seeing this, came thence for very shame;
And after me, I know, the rout is coming.
Such a mad marriage never was before:
Hark, Hark! I hear the minstrels play.
           [Music.

Enter PETRUCHIO, KATHARINA, BIANCA, BAP-
 TISTA, HORTENSIO, GRUMIO, *and* Train.

 Pet. Gentlemen and friends, I thank you for
  your pains:
I know you think to dine with me to-day,
And have prepar'd great store of wedding
  cheer;
But so it is, my haste doth call me hence,
And therefore here I mean to take my leave.
 Bap. Is't possible you will away to-night?
 Pet. I must away to-day, before night come:
Make it no wonder; if you knew my business,
You would entreat me rather go than stay.
And, honest company, I thank you all
That have beheld me give away myself
To this most patient, sweet, and virtuous wife:
Dine with my father, drink a health to me;
For I must hence; and farewell to you all.
 Tra. Let us entreat you stay till after dinner.
 Pet. It may not be.
 Gre.   Let me entreat you.
 Pet. It cannot be.
 Kath.   Let me entreat you.
 Pet. I am content.
 Kath.   Are you content to stay?
 Pet. I am content you shall entreat me stay;
But yet not stay, entreat me how you can.
 Kath. Now, if you love me, stay.
 Pet.   Grumio, my horse.

 Gru. Ay, sir, they be ready: the oats have
eaten the horses.
 Kath. Nay, then,
Do what thou canst, I will not go to-day;
No, nor to-morrow, nor till I please myself.
The door is open, sir; there lies your way;
You may be jogging whiles your boots are
  green;
For me, I'll not be gone till I please myself:
'Tis like you'll prove a jolly surly groom,
That take it on you at the first so roundly.
 Pet. O Kate, content thee; pr'ythee, be not
  angry.
 Kath. I will be angry; what hast thou to
  do?—
Father, be quiet: he shall stay my leisure.
 Gre. Ay, marry, sir, now it begins to work.
 Kath. Gentlemen, forward to the bridal
  dinner:
I see a woman may be made a fool
If she had not a spirit to resist.
 Pet. They shall go forward, Kate, at thy
  command.—
Obey the bride, you that attend on her;
Go to the feast, revel and domineer,
Carouse full measure to her maidenhead;
Be mad and merry,—or go hang yourselves:
But for my bonny Kate, she must with me.
Nay, look not big, nor stamp, nor stare, nor
  fret!
I will be master of what is mine own:
She is my goods, my chattels; she is my house,
My household stuff, my field, my barn,
My horse, my ox, my ass, my anything;
And here she stands, touch her whoever dare;
I'll bring mine action on the proudest he
That stops my way in Padua.—Grumio,
Draw forth thy weapon, we are beset with
  thieves;
Rescue thy mistress, if thou be a man.—
Fear not, sweet wench, they shall not touch
  thee, Kate;
I'll buckler thee against a million.
    [Exeunt PET., KATH., *and* GRU.
 Bap. Nay, let them go, a couple of quiet
  ones.
 Gre. Went they not quickly, I should die
  with laughing.
 Tra. Of all mad matches, never was the like!
 Luc. Mistress, what's your opinion of your
  sister?   [mated.
 Bian. That, being mad herself, she's madly
 Gre. I warrant him, Petruchio is Kated.
 Bap. Neighbours and friends, though bride
  and bridegroom wants,
For to supply the places at the table,
You know there wants no junkets at the feast.—
Lucentio, you shall supply the bridegroom's
  place;
And let Bianca take her sister's room.
 Tra. Shall sweet Bianca practise how to
  bride it?
 Bap. She shall, Lucentio.—Come, gentle-
  men, let's go.   *[Exeunt.*

ACT IV.

SCENE I.—*A Hall in* PETRUCHIO's *Country House.*

Enter GRUMIO.

Gru. Fie, fie on all tired jades, on all mad masters, and all foul ways! Was ever man so beaten? was ever man so rayed? was ever man so weary? I am sent before to make a fire, and they are coming after to warm them. Now, were not I a little pot, and soon hot, my very lips might freeze to my teeth, my tongue to the roof of my mouth, my heart in my belly, ere I should come by a fire to thaw me:—but I, with blowing the fire, shall warm myself; for, considering the weather, a taller man than I will take cold.—Holla, ho! Curtis!

Enter CURTIS.

Curt. Who is that calls so coldly?

Gru. A piece of ice: if thou doubt it, thou mayst slide from my shoulder to my heel with no greater a run but my head and my neck. A fire, good Curtis.

Curt. Is my master and his wife coming, Grumio?

Gru. O, ay, Curtis, ay: and therefore fire, fire; cast on no water.

Curt. Is she so hot a shrew as she's reported?

Gru. She was, good Curtis, before this frost; but, thou knowest, winter tames man, woman, and beast; for it hath tamed my old master, and my new mistress, and myself, fellow Curtis.

Curt. Away, you three-inch fool! I am no beast.

Gru. Am I but three inches? why, thy horn is a foot; and so long am I, at the least. But wilt thou make a fire, or shall I complain on thee to our mistress, whose hand,—she being now at hand,—thou shalt soon feel, to thy cold comfort, for being slow in thy hot office?

Curt. I pr'ythee, good Grumio, tell me, how goes the world?

Gru. A cold world, Curtis, in every office but thine; and, therefore, fire: do thy duty, and have thy duty; for my master and mistress are almost frozen to death.

Curt. There's fire ready; and, therefore, good Grumio, the news?

Gru. Why, *Jack boy! ho, boy!* and as much news as thou wilt. [ing!—

Curt. Come, you are so full of coney-catch-

Gru. Why, therefore, fire; for I have caught extreme cold. Where's the cook? is supper ready, the house trimmed, rushes strewed, cobwebs swept; the serving-men in their new fustian, their white stockings, and every officer his wedding-garment on? Be the jacks fair within, the jills fair without, the carpets laid, and everything in order? [news?

Curt. All ready; and, therefore, I pray thee,

Gru. First, know, my horse is tired; my master and mistress fallen out.

Curt. How?

Gru. Out of their saddles into the dirt; and thereby hangs a tale.

Curt. Let's ha't, good Grumio.

Gru. Lend thine ear.

Curt. Here.

Gru. There. [*Striking him.*

Curt. This is to feel a tale, not to hear a tale.

Gru. And therefore 'tis called a sensible tale: and this cuff was but to knock at your ear, and beseech listening. Now I begin: *Imprimis,* we came down a foul hill, my master riding behind my mistress:—

Curt. Both of one horse?

Gru. What's that to thee?

Curt. Why, a horse.

Gru. Tell thou the tale:—but hadst thou not crossed me, thou shouldst have heard how her horse fell, and she under her horse; thou shouldst have heard, in how miry a place; how she was bemoiled; how he left her with the horse upon her; how he beat me because her horse stumbled; how she waded through the dirt to pluck him off me; how he swore; how she prayed—that never pray'd before; how I cried; how the horses ran away; how her bridle was burst; how I lost my crupper; with many things of worthy memory; which now shall die in oblivion, and thou return unexperienced to thy grave.

Curt. By this reckoning, he is more shrew than she.

Gru. Ay; and that thou and the proudest of you all shall find when he comes home. But what talk I of this?—Call forth Nathaniel, Joseph, Nicholas, Philip, Walter, Sugarsop, and the rest: let their heads be sleekly combed, their blue coats brushed, and their garters of an indifferent knit: let them curtsy with their left legs; and not presume to touch a hair of my master's horse-tail till they kiss their hands. Are they all ready?

Curt. They are.

Gru. Call them forth.

Curt. Do you hear, ho? you must meet my master, to countenance my mistress.

Gru. Why, she hath a face of her own.

Curt. Who knows not that?

Gru. Thou, it seems, that callest for company to countenance her.

Curt. I call them forth to credit her.

Gru. Why, she comes to borrow nothing of them.

Enter several Servants.

Nath. Welcome home, Grumio!

Phil. How now, Grumio!

Jos. What, Grumio!

Nich. Fellow Grumio!

Nath. How now, old lad?

Gru. Welcome, you;—how now, you; what, you;—fellow, you;—and thus much for greeting. Now, my spruce companions, is all ready, and all things neat?

Nath. All things is ready. How near is our master?

Gru. E'en at hand, alighted by this;—and therefore be not,—Cock's passion, silence!—I hear my master.

Enter PETRUCHIO *and* KATHARINA.

Pet. Where be these knaves? What, no man at door
To hold my stirrup nor to take my horse!
Where is Nathaniel, Gregory, Philip?—

All Serv. Here, here, sir; here, sir.

Pet. Here, sir! here, sir! here, sir! here, sir!—
You logger-headed and unpolish'd grooms!
What, no attendance? no regard? no duty?—
Where is the foolish knave I sent before?

Gru. Here, sir; as foolish as I was before.

Pet. You peasant swain! you whoreson malt-horse drudge!
Did I not bid thee meet me in the park,
And bring along these rascal knaves with thee?

Gru. Nathaniel's coat, sir, was not fully made, [heel;
And Gabriel's pumps were all unpink'd i' the
There was no link to colour Peter's hat,
And Walter's dagger was not come from sheathing: [Gregory
There were none fine but Adam, Ralph, and
The rest were ragged, old, and beggarly;
Yet, as they are, here are they come to meet you. [in.—

Pet. Go, rascals, go, and fetch my supper
[*Exeunt some of the* Servants.

Where is the life that late I led— [*Sings*.
Where are those——Sit down, Kate, and welcome.
Soud, soud, soud, soud!

Re-enter Servants *with supper*.

Why, when, I say?—Nay, good sweet Kate, be merry. [when?
Off with my boots, you rogues! you villains,

It was the friar of orders gray;
As he forth walked on his way:— [*Sings*.

Out, you rogue! you pluck my foot awry:
Take that, and mend the plucking off the other.— [*Strikes him*.
Be merry, Kate.—Some water, here; what, ho!— [hence,
Where's my spaniel Troilus?—Sirrah, get you
And bid my cousin Ferdinand come hither:— [*Exit* Servant.
One, Kate, that you must kiss, and be acquainted with.— [water?
Where are my slippers?—Shall I have some
[*A bason is presented to him*.
Come, Kate, and wash, and welcome heartily.—
[Servant *lets the ewer fall*.
You whoreson villain! will you let it fall?
[*Strikes him*.

Kath. Patience, I pray you; 'twas a fault unwilling. [knave!

Pet. A whoreson, beetle-headed, flap-ear'd

Come, Kate, sit down; I know you have a stomach. [shall I?—
Will you give thanks, sweet Kate; or else
What's this? mutton?

1 Serv. Ay.

Pet. Who brought it?

1 Serv. I.

Pet. 'Tis burnt; and so is all the meat.
What dogs are these?—Where is the rascal cook? [dresser,
How durst you, villains, bring it from the
And serve it thus to me that love it not?
There, take it to you, trenchers, cups, and all:
[*Throws the meat, &c., about the stage*.
You heedless joltheads and unmanner'd slaves!
What, do you grumble? I'll be with you straight.

Kath. I pray you, husband, be not so disquiet;
The meat was well, if you were so contented.

Pet. I tell thee, Kate, 'twas burnt and dried away;
And I expressly am forbid to touch it,
For it engenders choler, planteth anger;
And better 'twere that both of us did fast,—
Since, of ourselves, ourselves are choleric,—
Then feed it with such over-roasted flesh.
Be patient; to-morrow 't shall be mended,
And, for this night, we'll fast for company:—
Come, I will bring thee to thy bridal chamber.
[*Exeunt* PET., KATH., *and* CURT.

Nath. Peter, didst ever see the like?

Peter. He kills her in her own humour.

Re-enter CURTIS.

Gru. Where is he?

Curt. In her chamber,
Making a sermon of continency to her, [soul,
And rails, and swears, and rates, that she, poor
Knows not which way to stand, to look, to speak,
And sits as one new-risen from a dream.
Away, away! for he is coming hither.
[*Exeunt*.

Re-enter PETRUCHIO.

Pet. Thus have I politicly begun my reign,
And 'tis my hope to end successfully.
My falcon now is sharp, and passing empty;
And, till she stoop, she must not be full-gorg'd,
For then she never looks upon her lure.
Another way I have to man my haggard,
To make her come, and know her keeper's call,
That is, to watch her, as we watch these kites
That bate, and beat, and will not be obedient.
She eat no meat to-day, nor none shall eat;
Last night she slept not, nor to-night she shall not;
As with the meat, some undeserved fault
I'll find about the making of the bed;
And here I'll fling the pillow, there the bolster,
This way the coverlet, another way the sheets:—
Ay, and amid this hurly, I intend
That all is done in reverend care of her;
And, in conclusion, she shall watch all night:

And, if she chance to nod, I'll rail and brawl,
And with the clamour keep her still awake.
This is a way to kill a wife with kindness:
And thus I'll curb her mad and headstrong
    humour.
He that knows better how to tame a shrew,
Now let him speak; 'tis charity to show.
                           [*Exit.*

SCENE II.—PADUA. *Before* BAPTISTA'S *House.*

Enter TRANIO *and* HORTENSIO.

Tra. Is't possible, friend Licio, that Bianca
Doth fancy any other but Lucentio?
I tell you, sir, she bears me fair in hand.
  Hor. Sir, to satisfy you in what I have said,
Stand by, and mark the manner of his teaching.
                       [*They stand aside.*

Enter BIANCA *and* LUCENTIO.

Luc. Now, mistress, profit you in what you
    read?
  Bian. What, master, read you? first resolve
    me that.
  Luc. I read that I profess, the Art to Love.
  Bian. And may you prove, sir, master of
    your art!
  Luc. While you, sweet dear, prove mistress
    of my heart.   [*They retire.*
  Hor. Quick proceeders, marry! Now, tell me,
    I pray,
You that durst swear that your Mistress Bianca
Lov'd none in the world so well as Lucentio.
  Tra. O despiteful love! unconstant woman-
    kind!—
I tell thee, Licio, this is wonderful.
  Hor. Mistake no more: I am not Licio,
Nor a musician, as I seem to be;
But one that scorn to live in this disguise,
For such a one as leaves a gentleman,
And makes a god of such a cullion:
Know, sir, that I am call'd Hortensio.
  Tra. Signior Hortensio, I have often heard
Of your entire affection to Bianca;
And since mine eyes are witness of her light-
    ness,
I will with you,—if you be so contented,—
Forswear Bianca and her love for ever.
  Hor. See, how they kiss and court!—Signior
    Lucentio,
Here is my hand, and here I firmly vow
Never to woo her more; but do forswear her,
As one unworthy all the former favours
That I have fondly flatter'd her withal.
  Tra. And here I take the like unfeigned oath,
Never to marry with her though she would en-
    treat: [him!
Fie on her! see, how beastly she doth court
  Hor. Would all the world but he had quite
    forsworn!
For me, that I may surely keep mine oath,
I will be married to a wealthy widow

Ere three days pass, which hath as long lov'd
    me
As I have lov'd this proud disdainful haggard:
And so farewell, Signior Lucentio.—
Kindness in women, not their beauteous looks,
Shall win my love: and so I take my leave,
In resolution as I swore before.
    [*Exit* HOR.—LUC. *and* BIAN. *advance.*
  Tra. Mistress Bianca, bless you with such
    grace
As 'longeth to a lover's blessed case!
Nay, I have ta'en you napping, gentle love;
And have forsworn you with Hortensio.
  Bian. Tranio, you jest; but have you both
    forsworn me?
  Tra. Mistress, we have.
  Luc.   Then we are rid of Licio.
  Tra. I' faith, he'll have a lusty widow now,
That shall be woo'd and wedded in a day.
  Bian. God give him joy!
  Tra. Ay, and he'll tame her.
  Bian.   He says so, Tranio.
  Tra. Faith, he is gone unto the taming-
    school.
  Bian. The taming-school! what, is there such
    a place?
  Tra. Ay, mistress, and Petruchio is the
    master;
That teacheth tricks eleven and twenty long,
To tame a shrew and charm her chattering
    tongue.

Enter BIONDELLO.

Bion. O master, master, I have watch'd so
    long
That I'm dog-weary; but at last I spied
An ancient angel coming down the hill,
Will serve the turn.
  Tra.   What is he, Biondello?
  Bion. Master, a mercatanté, or a pedant,
I know not what; but formal in apparel,
In gait and countenance surely like a father.
  Luc. And what of him, Tranio?
  Tra. If he be credulous, and trust my tale,
I'll make him glad to seem Vincentio,
And give assurance to Baptista Minola,
As if he were the right Vincentio.
Take in your love, and then let me alone.
    [*Exeunt* LUCENTIO *and* BIANCA.

Enter a Pedant.

Ped. God save you, sir!
  Tra.   And you, sir! you are welcome.
Travel you far on, or are you at the furthest?
  Ped. Sir, at the furthest for a week or two:
But then up further, and as far as Rome;
And so to Tripoli, if God lend me life.
  Tra. What countryman, I pray?
  Ped.   Of Mantua.
  Tra. Of Mantua, sir?—marry, God forbid!
And come to Padua, careless of your life? [hard.
  Ped. My life, sir! how, I pray? for that goes
  Tra. 'Tis death for any one in Mantua
To come to Padua. Know you not the cause?

Your ships are stayed at Venice; and the duke,—
For private quarrel 'twixt your duke and him,
Have publish'd and proclaim'd it openly:
'Tis marvel, but that you are but newly come,
You might have heard it else proclaim'd about.

Ped. Alas, sir, it is worse for me than so!
For I have bills for money by exchange
From Florence, and must here deliver them.

Tra. Well, sir, to do you courtesy,
This will I do, and this I will advise you:
First, tell me, have you ever been at Pisa?

Ped. Ay, sir, in Pisa have I often been:
Pisa, renowned for grave citizens.

Tra. Among them know you one Vincentio?

Ped. I know him not, but I have heard of
him;
A merchant of incomparable wealth.

Tra. He is my father, sir; and, sooth to say,
In countenance somewhat doth resemble you.

Bion. As much as an apple doth an oyster,
and all one. [*Aside.*

Tra. To save your life in this extremity,
This favour will I do you for his sake;
And think it not the worst of all your fortunes
That you are like to Sir Vincentio.
His name and credit shall you undertake,
And in my house you shall be friendly lodg'd:—
Look that you take upon you as you should;
You understand me, sir:—so shall you stay
Till you have done your business in the city:
If this be courtesy, sir, accept of it.

Ped. O, sir, I do; and will repute you ever
The patron of my life and liberty. [good.

Tra. Then go with me, to make the matter
This, by the way, I let you understand;—
My father is here look'd for every day,
To pass assurance of a dower in marriage
'Twixt me and one Baptista's daughter here:
In all these circumstances I'll instruct you:
Go with me, sir, to clothe you as becomes you.
[*Exeunt.*

SCENE III.—*A Room in* PETRUCHIO'S *House.*

Enter KATHARINA *and* GRUMIO.

Gru. No, no, forsooth; I dare not, for my life.

Kath. The more my wrong, the more his
spite appears:
What, did he marry me to famish me?
Beggars, that come unto my father's door,
Upon entreaty have a present alms;
If not, elsewhere they meet with charity:
But I,—who never knew how to entreat,
Nor never needed that I should entreat,—
Am starved for meat, giddy for lack of sleep;
With oaths kept waking, and with brawling
fed:
And that which spites me more than all these
wants,
He does it under the name of perfect love;
As who would say, if I should sleep or eat,
'Twere deadly sickness or else present death.—
I pr'ythee go, and get me some repast;
I care not what, so it be wholesome food.

Gru. What say you to a neat's foot?

Kath. 'Tis passing good; I pr'ythee let me
have it.

Gru. I fear it is too choleric a meat:
How say you to a fat tripe, finely broil'd?

Kath. I like it well: good Grumio, fetch it me.

Gru. I cannot tell; I fear 'tis choleric.
What say you to a piece of beef and mustard?

Kath. A dish that I do love to feed upon.

Gru. Ay, but the mustard is too hot a little.

Kath. Why, then the beef, and let the mustard rest. [the mustard,

Gru. Nay, then I will not; you shall have the
Or else you get no beef of Grumio.

Kath. Then both, or one, or anything thou
wilt.

Gru. Why, then the mustard without the
beef.

Kath. Go, get thee gone, thou false deluding
slave, [*Beats him.*
That feed'st me with the very name of meat:
Sorrow on thee, and all the pack of you,
That triumph thus upon my misery!
Go, get thee gone, I say.

Enter PETRUCHIO *with a dish of meat; and*
HORTENSIO.

Pet. How fares my Kate? What, sweeting,
all amort?

Hor. Mistress, what cheer?

Kath. Faith, as cold as can be.

Pet. Pluck up thy spirits, look cheerfully
upon me.
Here, love; thou see'st how diligent I am
To dress thy meat myself, and bring it thee:
[*Sets the dish upon a table.*
I am sure, sweet Kate, this kindness merits
thanks. [not;
What! not a word? Nay, then thou lov'st it
And all my pains is sorted to no proof.—
Here, take away this dish.

Kath. I pray you, let it stand.

Pet. The poorest service is repaid with
thanks;
And so shall mine, before you touch the meat.

Kath. I thank you, sir.

Hor. Signior Petruchio, fie! you are to blame!
Come, Mistress Kate, I'll bear you company.

Pet. Eat it up all, Hortensio, if thou lov'st
me.— [*Aside.*
Much good do it unto thy gentle heart!
Kate, eat apace:—and now, my honey-love,
Will we return unto thy father's house,
And revel it as bravely as the best,
With silken coats, and caps, and golden rings,
With ruffs and cuffs, and farthingales, and
things;
With scarfs, and fans, and double change of
bravery,
With amber bracelets, beads, and all this
knavery.
What, hast thou din'd? The tailor stays thy
leisure,
To deck thy body with his ruffling treasure.

Enter Tailor.

Come, tailor, let us see these ornaments;
Lay forth the gown.

Enter Haberdasher.

What news with you, sir?

Hab. Here is the cap your worship did bespeak.

Pet. Why, this was moulded on a porringer;
A velvet dish;—fie, fie! 'tis lewd and filthy;
Why, 'tis a cockle or a walnut-shell,
A knack, a toy, a trick, a baby's cap:
Away with it! come, let me have a bigger.

Kath. I'll have no bigger; this doth fit the
time,
And gentlewomen wear such caps as these.

Pet. When you are gentle, you shall have one
too,
And not till then.

Hor. That will not be in haste. [*Aside.*

Kath. Why, sir, I trust I may have leave to
speak;
And speak I will. I am no child, no babe:
Your betters have endur'd me say my mind;
And if you cannot, best you stop your ears.
My tongue will tell the anger of my heart;
Or else my heart concealing it, will break:
And rather than it shall, I will be free
Even to the uttermost, as I please, in words.

Pet. Why, thou say'st true; it is a paltry cap,
A custard-coffin, a bauble, a silken pie:
I love thee well, in that thou lik'st it not.

Kath. Love me or love me not, I like the cap;
And it I will have, or I will have none.

Pet. Thy gown? why, ay;—Come, tailor, let
us see't.
O mercy, God! what masquing stuff is here?
What's this? a sleeve? 'tis like a demi-cannon:
What, up and down, carv'd like an apple-tart?
Here's snip, and nip, and cut, and slish, and
slash,
Like to a censer in a barber's shop:— [this?
Why, what, o' devil's name, tailor, call'st thou

Hor. I see she's like to have neither cap nor
gown. [*Aside.*

Tai. You bid me make it orderly and well,
According to the fashion and the time. [ber'd,

Pet. Marry, and did; but if you be remem-
I did not bid you mar it to the time.
Go, hop me over every kennel home,
For you shall hop without my custom, sir:
I'll none of it: hence! make your best of it.

Kath. I never saw a better-fashion'd gown,
More quaint, more pleasing, nor more com-
mendable:
Belike you mean to make a puppet of me.

Pet. Why, true; he means to make a puppet
of thee. [a puppet of her.

Tai. She says your worship means to make

Pet. O monstrous arrogance! Thou liest,
thou thread,
Thou thimble, [nail,
Thou yard, three-quarters, half-yard, quarter,
Thou flea, thou nit, thou-winter-cricket thou!—

Brav'd in mine own house with a skein of
thread?
Away, thou rag, thou quantity, thou remnant;
Or I shall so be-mete thee with thy yard,
As thou shalt think on prating whilst thou
liv'st!
I tell thee, I, that thou hast marr'd her gown.

Tai. Your worship is deceiv'd; the gown is
made
Just as my master had direction:
Grumio gave order how it should be done.

Gru. I gave him no order; I gave him the
stuff. [made?

Tai. But how did you desire it should be

Gru. Marry, sir, with needle and thread.

Tai. But did you not request to have it cut?

Gru. Thou hast faced many things.

Tai. I have.

Gru. Face not me: thou hast braved many
men; brave not me; I will neither be faced nor
braved. I say unto thee, I bid thy master cut
out the gown; but I did not bid him cut it to
pieces: *ergo*, thou liest. [testify.

Tai. Why, here is the note of the fashion to

Pet. Read it. [said so.

Gru. The note lies in his throat, if he say I

Tai. *Imprimis, a loose-bodied gown:*

Gru. Master, if ever I said loose-bodied
gown, sew me in the skirts of it, and beat me to
death with a bottom of brown thread: I said a
gown.

Pet. Proceed.

Tai. *With a small compassed cape:*

Gru. I confess the cape.

Tai. *With a trunk sleeve:*

Gru. I confess two sleeves.

Tai. *The sleeves curiously cut.*

Pet. Ay, there's the villany.

Gru. Error i' the bill sir; error i' the bill. I
commanded the sleeves should be cut out, and
sewed up again; and that I'll prove upon thee,
though thy little finger be armed in a thimble.

Tai. This is true that I say: an I had thee in
place where, thou shouldst know it.

Gru. I am for thee straight: take thou the
bill, give me thy mete-yard, and spare not me.

Hor. God-a-mercy, Grumio! then he shall
have no odds.

Pet. Well, sir, in brief, the gown is not for me.

Gru. You are i' the right, sir; 'tis for my
mistress.

Pet. Go, take it up unto thy master's use.

Gru. Villain, not for thy life! Take up my
mistress' gown for thy master's use!

Pet. Why, sir, what's your conceit in that?

Gru. O, sir, the conceit is deeper than you
think for:
Take up my mistress' gown to his master's use!
O fie, fie, fie!

Pet. Hortensio, say thou wilt see the tailor
paid.— [*Aside.*
Go take it hence; be gone, and say no more.

Hor. Tailor, I'll pay thee for thy gown to-
morrow.

Take no unkindness of his hasty words:
Away, I say! commend me to thy master.
             [*Exeunt* Tailor *and* Haberdasher.
   Pet. Well, come, my Kate; we will unto your
     father's
Even in these honest mean habiliments:
Our purses shall be proud, our garments poor;
For 'tis the mind that makes the body rich;
And as the sun breaks through the darkest
     clouds,
So honour peereth in the meanest habit.
What, is the jay more precious than the lark,
Because his feathers are more beautiful?
Or is the adder better than the eel,
Because his painted skin contents the eye?
O no, good Kate; neither art thou the worse
For this poor furniture and mean array.
If thou account'st it shame, lay it on me;
And therefore frolic: we will hence forthwith,
To feast and sport us at thy father's house.—
Go, call my men, and let us straight to him;
And bring our horses unto Long-lane end;
There will we mount, and thither walk on
     foot.—
Let's see; I think 'tis now some seven o'clock,
And well we may come there by dinner-time.
   Kath. I dare assure you, sir, 'tis almost two;
And 'twill be supper-time ere you come there.
   Pet. It shall be seven ere I go to horse:
Look, what I speak, or do, or think to do,
You are still crossing it.—Sirs, let't alone:
I will not go to-day; and ere I do,
It shall be what o'clock I say it is.
   Hor. Why, so, this gallant will command the
     sun.   [*Exeunt.*

SCENE IV.—PADUA. *Before* BAPTISTA'S *House.*

Enter TRANIO, *and the* Pedant *dressed like*
VINCENTIO.

   Tra. Sir, this is the house: please it you that
     I call?
   Ped. Ay, what else? and, but I be deceived,
Signior Baptista may remember me,
Near twenty years ago, in Genoa, where
We were lodgers at the Pegasus.   [case,
   Tra. 'Tis well; and hold your own, in any
With such austerity as 'longeth to a father.
   Ped. I warrant you. But, sir, here comes
     your boy;
'Twere good he were school'd.

Enter BIONDELLO.

   Tra. Fear you not him.—Sirrah Biondello,
Now do your duty throughly, I advise you:
Imagine 'twere the right Vincentio.
   Bion. Tut! fear not me.   [tista?
   Tra. But hast thou done thy errand to Bap-
   Bion. I told him that your father was at
     Venice;
And that you look'd for him this day in Padua.
   Tra. Thou'rt a tall fellow: hold thee that to
     drink.   [sir.—
Here comes Baptista:—set your countenance,

Enter BAPTISTA *and* LUCENTIO.
Signior Baptista, you are happily met.—
Sir [*to the* Pedant], this is the gentleman I told
     you of:
I pray you, stand good father to me now,
Give me Bianca for my patrimony.
   Ped. Soft, son!—
Sir, by your leave, having come to Padua
To gather in some debts, my son Lucentio
Made me acquainted with a weighty cause
Of love between your daughter and himself:
And,—for the good report I hear of you;
And for the love he beareth to your daughter,
And she to him,—to stay him not too long,
I am content, in a good father's care,
To have him match'd; and,—if you please to
     like
No worse than I,—upon some agreement,
Me shall you find ready and willing
With one consent to have her so bestow'd;
For curious I cannot be with you,
Signior Baptista, of whom I hear so well.
   Bap. Sir, pardon me in what I have to say:
Your plainness and your shortness please me
     well.
Right true it is, your son Lucentio here
Doth love my daughter, and she loveth him,
Or both dissemble deeply their affections:
And therefore, if you say no more than this,
That like a father you will deal with him,
And pass my daughter a sufficient dower,
The match is made, and all is done:
Your son shall have my daughter with consent.
   Tra. I thank you, sir. Where, then, do you
     know best
We be affied, and such assurance ta'en
As shall with either part's agreement stand?
   Bap. Not in my house, Lucentio; for, you
     know,
Pitchers have ears, and I have many servants:
Besides, old Gremio is heark'ning still;
And, haply, we might be interrupted.
   Tra. Then at my lodging, an it like you:
There doth my father lie; and there, this night,
We'll pass the business privately and well:
Send for your daughter by your servant here;
My boy shall fetch the scrivener presently.
The worst is this,—that, at so slender warning,
You are like to have a thin and slender pittance.
   Bap. It likes me well.—Cambio, hie you
     home,
And bid Bianca make her ready straight;
And, if you will, tell what hath happened,—
Lucentio's father is arriv'd in Padua,
And now she's like to be Lucentio's wife.
   Luc. I pray the gods she may, with all my
     heart.   [gone.
   Tra. Dally not with the gods, but get thee
Signior Baptista, shall I lead the way?
Welcome! one mess is like to be your cheer:
Come, sir; we'll better it in Pisa.
   Bap. I follow you.
          [*Exeunt* TRA., Ped., *and* BAP.

Bion. Cambio.

Luc.   What sayest thou, Biondello?

Bion. You saw my master wink and laugh upon you?

Luc. Biondello, what of that?

Bion. Faith, nothing; but has left me here behind, to expound the meaning or moral of his signs and tokens.

Luc. I pray thee, moralize them.

Bion. Then thus. Baptista is safe, talking with the deceiving father of a deceitful son.

Luc. And what of him?

Bion. His daughter is to be brought by you to the supper.

Luc. And then?—

Bion. The old priest at Saint Luke's church is at your command at all hours.

Luc. And what of all this?

Bion. I cannot tell; expect they are busied about a counterfeit assurance. Take you assurance of her, *cum privilegio ad imprimendum solum:* to the church;—take the priest, clerk, and some sufficient honest witnesses:
If this be not that you look for, I have no more
          to say,
But bid Bianca farewell for ever and a day.
                                        [*Going.*

Luc. Hear'st thou, Biondello?

Bion. I cannot tarry: I knew a wench married in an afternoon as she went to the garden for parsley to stuff a rabbit; and so may you, sir; and so adieu, sir. My master hath appointed me to go to Saint Luke's, to bid the priest be ready to come against you come with your appendix.   [*Exit.*

Luc. I may, and will, if she be so contented:
She will be pleas'd; then wherefore should I
          doubt?
Hap what hap may, I'll roundly go about her;
It shall go hard if Cambio go without her.
                                        [*Exit.*

SCENE V.—*A Public Road.*

Enter PETRUCHIO, KATHARINA, *and*
HORTENSIO.

Pet. Come on, o' God's name; once more
          toward our father's.
Good Lord, how bright and goodly shines the
          moon!   [light now.
Kath. The moon! the sun: it is not moon-
Pet. I say it is the moon that shines so bright.
Kath. I know it is the sun that shines so
          bright.
Pet. Now, by my mother's son, and that's
          myself,
It shall be moon, or star, or what I list,
Or ere I journey to your father's house.—
Go one, and fetch our horses back again.—
Evermore cross'd and cross'd; nothing but
          cross'd!
Hor. Say as he says, or we shall never go.
Kath. Forward, I pray, since we have come
          so far,

And be it moon, or sun, or what you please:
And if you please to call it a rush-candle,
Henceforth I vow it shall be so for me.
Pet. I say it is the moon.
Kath.   I know it is the moon.
Pet. Nay, then you lie: it is the blessed sun.
Kath. Then, God be blessed, it is the
          blessed sun:
But sun it is not, when you say it is not;
And the moon changes even as your mind.
What you will have it nam'd, even that it is;
And so, it shall be so for Katherine.
Hor. Petruchio, go thy ways; the field is
          won.
Pet. Well, forward, forward! thus the bowl
          should run,
And not unluckily against the bias.—
But, soft! company is coming here.

Enter VINCENTIO, *in a travelling dress.*

Good-morrow, gentle mistress: where away?—
                              [*To* VINCENTIO.
Tell me, sweet Kate, and tell me truly too,
Hast thou beheld a fresher gentlewoman?
Such war of white and red within her cheeks!
What stars do spangle heaven with such beauty,
As those two eyes become that heavenly face?—
Fair lovely maid, once more good-day to thee:—
Sweet Kate, embrace her for her beauty's sake.
Hor. 'A will make the man mad, to make a
woman of him.
Kath. Young budding virgin, fair and fresh
          and sweet,
Whither away; or where is thy abode?
Happy the parents of so fair a child;
Happier the man whom favourable stars
Allot thee for his lovely bed-fellow!
Pet. Why, how now, Kate! I hope thou art
          not mad:
This is a man, old, wrinkled, faded, wither'd;
And not a maiden, as thou sayst he is.
Kath. Pardon, old father, my mistaking eyes,
That have been so bedazzled with the sun,
That everything I look on seemeth green:
Now I perceive thou art a reverend father;
Pardon, I pray thee, for my mad mistaking.
Pet. Do, good old grandsire; and withal
          make known
Which way thou travell'st: if along with us,
We shall be joyful of thy company.
Vin. Fair sir, and you my merry mistress,
That with your strange encounter much amaz'd
          me,
My name is call'd Vincentio; my dwelling Pisa;
And bound I am to Padua; there to visit
A son of mine, which long I have not seen.
Pet. What is his name?
Vin.   Lucentio, gentle sir.
Pet. Happily met; the happier for thy son.
And now by law, as well as reverend age,
I may entitle thee my loving father:
The sister to my wife, this gentlewoman,
Thy son by this hath married. Wonder not,
Nor be not griev'd: she is of good esteem

Her dowry wealthy, and of worthy birth;
Beside, so qualified as may beseem
The spouse of any noble gentleman.
Let me embrace with old Vincentio:
And wander we to see thy honest son,
Who will of thy arrival be full joyous.   [sure,
  Vin. But is this true? or is it else your plea-
Like pleasant travellers, to break a jest
Upon the company you overtake?
  Hor. I do assure thee, father, so it is.
  Pet. Come, go along, and see the truth here-
of:
For our first merriment hath made thee jealous.
          [*Exeunt* PET., KATH., *and* VIN.
  Hor. Well, Petruchio, this hath put me in
    heart.
Have to my widow; and if she be forward,
Then hast thou taught Hortensio to be un-
    toward.   [*Exit.*

ACT V.

SCENE I.—PADUA. *Before* LUCENTIO'S *House.*

Enter on one side BIONDELLO, LUCENTIO, *and*
BIANCA; GREMIO *walking on the other side.*

  Bion. Softly and swiftly, sir; for the priest is
ready.
  Luc. I fly, Biondello: but they may chance
to need thee at home, therefore leave us.
  Bion. Nay, faith, I'll see the church o' your
back; and then come back to my master as
soon as I can.
        [*Exeunt* LUC., BIAN., *and* BION.
  Gre. I marvel Cambio comes not all this
    while.

Enter PETRUCHIO, KATHARINA, VINCENTIO,
  GRUMIO, *and* Attendants.

  Pet. Sir, here's the door; this is Lucentio's
    house: [place;
My father's bears more toward the market-
Thither must I, and here I leave you, sir.
  Vin. You shall not choose but drink before
    you go:
I think I shall command your welcome here,
And, by all likelihood, some cheer is toward.
          [*Knocks.*
  Gre. They're busy within; you were best
knock louder.

Enter Pedant *above, at a window.*

  Ped. What's he that knocks as he would
beat down the gate?
  Vin. Is Signior Lucentio within, sir?
  Ped. He's within, sir, but not to be spoken
withal.
  Vin. What if a man bring him a hundred
pound or two, to make merry withal?
  Ped. Keep your hundred pounds to yourself:
he shall need none so long as I live.
  Pet. Nay, I told you your son was well beloved in Padua.—Do you hear, sir?—to leave
frivolous circumstances,—I pray you, tell Sig-

nior Lucentio that his father is come from Pisa,
and is here at the door to speak with him.
  Ped. Thou liest: his father is come from Pisa,
and here looking out at the window.
  Vin. Art thou his father?
  Ped. Ay, sir; so his mother says, if I may
believe her.
  Pet. Why, how now, gentleman! [*to* VINCEN.]
why, this is flat knavery, to take upon you
another man's name.
  Ped. Lay hands on the villain: I believe 'a
means to cozen somebody in this city under my
countenance.

Re-enter BIONDELLO.

  Bion. I have seen them in the church together: God send 'em good shipping!—But who
is here? mine old master, Vincentio! now we
are undone, and brought to nothing.
  Vin. Come hither, crack-hemp.
          [*Seeing* BIONDELLO.
  Bion. I hope I may choose, sir.
  Vin. Come hither, you rogue. What! have
you forgot me?
  Bion. Forgot you! no, sir: I could not forget
you, for I never saw you before in all my life.
  Vin. What, you notorious villain, didst thou
never see thy master's father, Vincentio?
  Bion. What, my old worshipful old master?
yes, marry, sir: see where he looks out of the
window.
  Vin. Is't so, indeed?   [*Beats* BIONDELLO.
  Bion. Help, help, help! here's a madman will
murder me.   [*Exit.*
  Ped. Help, son! help, Signior Baptista!
          [*Exit from the window.*
  Pet. Pr'ythee, Kate, let's stand aside, and
see the end of this controversy.   [*They retire.*

Re-enter Pedant *below; and* BAPTISTA,
  TRANIO, *and* Servants.

  Tra. Sir, what are you, that offer to beat my
servant?
  Vin. What am I, sir! nay, what are you, sir?
—O immortal gods! O fine villain! A silken
doublet! a velvet hose! a scarlet cloak! and a
copatain hat!—O, I am undone! I am undone!
while I play the good husband at home, my son
and my servant spend all at the university.
  Tra. How now! what's the matter?
  Bap. What, is the man lunatic?
  Tra. Sir, you seem a sober ancient gentleman
by your habit, but your words show you a madman. Why, sir, what concerns it you if I wear
pearl and gold? I thank my good father, I am
able to maintain it.
  Vin. Thy father! O villain! he is a sailmaker
in Bergamo.
  Bap. You mistake, sir; you mistake, sir.
Pray, what do you think is his name?
  Vin. His name! as if I knew not his name!
I have brought him up ever since he was three
years old, and his name is Tranio.
  Ped. Away, away, mad ass! his name is

Lucentio; and he is mine only son, and heir to
the lands of me, Signior Vincentio.

Vin. Lucentio! O, he hath murdered his
master!—Lay hold on him, I charge you, in the
duke's name.—O, my son, my son!—tell me,
thou villain, where is my son, Lucentio?

Tra. Call forth an officer.

Enter one with an Officer.

Carry this mad knave to the gaol.—Father
Baptista, I charge you see that he be forth-
coming.

Vin. Carry me to the gaol!

Gre. Stay, officer; he shall not go to prison.

Bap. Talk not, Signior Gremio; I say he
shall go to prison.

Gre. Take heed, Signior Baptista, lest you be
coney-catched in this business; I dare swear
this is the right Vincentio.

Ped. Swear, if thou darest.

Gre. Nay, I dare not swear it.   [Lucentio.

Tra. Then thou wert best say that I am not

Gre. Yes, I know thee to be Signior Lucentio.

Bap. Away with the dotard! to the gaol with
him!

Vin. Thus strangers may be haled and
abus'd.—O monstrous villain!

Re-enter BIONDELLO, *with* LUCENTIO *and*
BIANCA.

Bion. O, we are spoiled! and yonder he is:
deny him, forswear him, or else we are all undone.

Luc. Pardon, sweet father.   [*Kneeling.*

Vin.   Lives my sweet son?
           [BION., TRA., *and* Ped. *run out.*

Bian. Pardon, dear father.   [*Kneeling.*

Bap.   How hast thou offended?—
Where is Lucentio?

Luc.   Here's Lucentio,
Right son to the right Vincentio;
That hath by marriage made thy daughter
      mine,
While counterfeit supposes blear'd thine eyne.

Gre. Here's packing, with a witness, to deceive us all!

Vin. Where is that damned villain, Tranio,
That fac'd and brav'd me in this matter so?

Bap. Why, tell me, is not this my Cambio?

Bian. Cambio is chang'd into Lucentio.

Luc. Love wrought these miracles. Bianca's
      love
Made me exchange my state with Tranio,
While he did bear my countenance in the town;
And happily I have arrived at the last
Unto the wished-far haven of my bliss.
What Tranio did, myself enforc'd him to;
Then pardon him, sweet father, for my sake.

Vin. I'll slit the villain's nose, that would
have sent me to the gaol.

Bap. But do you hear, sir? [*to* LUCENTIO]
Have you married my daughter without asking
my good-will?   [go to:

Vin. Fear not, Baptista; we will content you,

But I will in, to be revenged for this villany!
                                    [*Exit.*

Bap. And I, to sound the depth of this knavery.   [*Exit.*

Luc. Look not pale, Bianca; thy father will
not frown.   [*Exeunt* LUC. *and* BIAN.

Gre. My cake is dough: but I'll in among the
rest;
Out of hope of all but my share of the feast.
                                    [*Exit.*

PETRUCHIO *and* KATHARINA *advance.*

Kath. Husband, let's follow, to see the end
of this ado.

Pet. First kiss me, Kate, and we will.

Kath. What, in the midst of the street?

Pet. What, art thou ashamed of me? [kiss.

Kath. No, sir; God forbid; but ashamed to

Pet. Why, then, let's home again.—Come,
sirrah let's away.

Kath. Nay, I will give thee a kiss, now, pray
thee, love, stay.

Pet. Is not this well?—Come, my sweet Kate;
Better once than never, for never too late.
                                  [*Exeunt.*

SCENE II.—*A Room in* LUCENTIO'S *House.*

A Banquet set out. Enter BAPTISTA, VINCENTIO,
GREMIO, *the* Pedant, LUCENTIO, BIANCA,
PETRUCHIO, KATHARINA, HORTENSIO, *and*
Widow. TRANIO, BIONDELLO, GRUMIO, *and
others, attending.*

Luc. At last, though long, our jarring notes
      agree:
And time it is, when raging war is done,
To smile at 'scapes and perils overblown.—
My fair Bianca, bid my father welcome,
While I with self-same kindness welcome
      thine.—
Brother Petruchio,—sister Katharina,—
And thou, Hortensio, with thy loving widow,—
Feast with the best, and welcome to my house:
My banquet is to close our stomachs up,
After our great good cheer. Pray you, sit down;
For now we sit to chat, as well as eat.
                      [*They sit at table.*

Pet. Nothing but sit and sit, and eat and
eat!

Bap. Padua affords this kindness, son Petruchio.

Pet. 'Padua affords nothing but what is kind.

Hor. For both our sakes I would that word
were true.

Pet. Now, for my life, Hortensio fears his
widow.

Wid. Then never trust me if I be afeard.

Pet. You are very sensible, and yet you miss
my sense:
I mean Hortensio is afeard of you.   [round.

Wid. He that is giddy thinks the world turns

Pet. Roundly replied.

Kath.   Mistress, how mean you that?

Wid. Thus I conceive by him.   [that?

Pet. Conceives by me!—How likes Hortensio

Hor. My widow says thus she conceives her tale.

Pet. Very well mended.—Kiss him for that, good widow.

Kath. He that is giddy thinks the world turns round:—
I pray you, tell me what you meant by that.

Wid. Your husband, being troubled with a shrew,
Measures my husband's sorrow by his woe:
And now you know my meaning.

Kath. A very mean meaning.

Wid. Right, I mean you.

Kath. And I am mean, indeed, respecting you.

Pet. To her, Kate!

Hor. To her, widow! [down.

Pet. A hundred marks, my Kate does put her

Hor. That's my office.

Pet. Spoke like an officer:—ha' to thee, lad.
[*Drinks to* HORTENSIO.

Bap. How likes Gremio these quick-witted folks?

Gre. Believe me, sir, they butt together well.

Bian. Head and butt! an hasty-witted body
Would say your head and butt were head and horn. [you?

Vin. Ay, mistress bride, hath that awaken'd

Bian. Ay, but not frighted me; therefore I'll sleep again.

Pet. Nay, that you shall not: since you have begun,
Have at you for a bitter jest or two. [bush,

Bian. Am I your bird? I mean to shift my
And then pursue me as you draw your bow.—
You are welcome all.
[*Exeunt* BIAN., KATH., *and* Wid.

Pet. She hath prevented me.—Here, Signior Tranio,
This bird you aim'd at, though you hit her not;
Therefore a health to all that shot and miss'd.

Tra. O, sir, Lucentio slipp'd me like his greyhound,
Which runs himself, and catches for his master.

Pet. A good swift simile, but something currish. [self;

Tra. 'Tis well, sir, that you hunted for your-
'Tis thought your deer does hold you at a bay.

Bap. O ho, Petruchio, Tranio hits you now.

Luc. I thank thee for that gird, good Tranio.

Hor. Confess, confess, hath he not hit you here?

Pet. 'A has a little gall'd me, I confess;
And, as the jest did glance away from me,
'Tis ten to one it maim'd you two outright.

Bap. Now, in good sadness, son Petruchio,
I think thou hast the veriest shrew of all.

Pet. Well, I say no: and therefore, for assurance,
Let's each one send unto his wife;
And he whose wife is most obedient
To come at first when he doth send for her,
Shall win the wager which we will propose.

Hor. Content. What is the wager?

Luc. Twenty crowns.

Pet. Twenty crowns!
I'll venture so much on my hawk or hound,
But twenty times so much upon my wife.

Luc. A hundred then.

Hor. Content.

Pet. A match! 'tis done.

Hor. Who shall begin?

Luc. That will I.—
Go, Biondello, bid your mistress come to me.

Bion. I go. [*Exit.*

Bap. Son, I will be your half, Bianca comes.

Luc. I'll have no halves; I'll bear it all myself.

Re-enter BIONDELLO.

How now! what news?

Bion. Sir, my mistress sends you word
That she is busy, and she cannot come.

Pet. How! she is busy, and she cannot come!
Is that an answer?

Gre. Ay, and a kind one too:
Pray God, sir, your wife send you not a worse.

Pet. I hope better.

Hor. Sirrah Biondello, go and entreat my wife
To come to me forthwith. [*Exit* BIONDELLO.

Pet. Oh, ho! entreat her!
Nay, then she must needs come.

Hor. I am afraid, sir,
Do what you can, yours will not be entreated.

Re-enter BIONDELLO.

Now, where's my wife?

Bion. She says you have some goodly jest in hand:
She will not come; she bids you come to her.

Pet. Worse and worse; she will not come! O vile,
Intolerable, not to be endur'd!—
Sirrah Grumio, go to your mistress;
Say I command her come to me.
[*Exit* GRUMIO.

Hor. I know her answer.

Pet. What?

Hor. She will not come.

Pet. The fouler fortune mine, and there an end.

Bap. Now, by my holidame, here comes Katharina!

Enter KATHARINA.

Kath. What is your will, sir, that you send for me? [wife?

Pet. Where is your sister, and Hortensio's

Kath. They sit conferring by the parlour fire.

Pet. Go, fetch them hither: if they deny to come,
Swinge me them soundly forth unto their husbands:
Away, I say, and bring them hither straight.
[*Exit* KATHARINA.

Luc. Here is a wonder, if you talk of a wonder.

Hor. And so it is: I wonder what it bodes.
Pet. Marry, peace it bodes, and love, and
  quiet life,
An awful rule, and right supremacy;   [happy.
And, to be short, what not, that's sweet and
Bap. Now fair befall thee, good Petruchio!
The wager thou hast won; and I will add
Unto their losses twenty thousand crowns;
Another dowry to another daughter,
For she is chang'd, as she had never been.
Pet. Nay, I will win my wager better yet;
And show more sign of her obedience,
Her new-built virtue and obedience.
See where she comes, and brings your froward
  wives
As prisoners to her womanly persuasion.—

Re-enter KATHARINA, *with* BIANCA *and* Widow.

Katharine, that cap of yours becomes you not:
Off with that bauble, throw it underfoot.
  [KATH. *pulls off her cap and throws it down.*
Wid. Lord, let me never have a cause to
  sigh,
Will I be brought to such a silly pass!
Bian. Fie! what a foolish duty call you this?
Luc. I would your duty were as foolish too:
The wisdom of your duty, fair Bianca,   [time.
Hath cost me an hundred crowns since supper-
Bian. The more fool you, for laying on my
  duty.
Pet. Katharine, I charge thee, tell these
  headstrong women
What duty they do owe their lords and hus-
  bands.
Wid. Come, come, you're mocking: we will
  have no telling.
Pet. Come on, I say; and first begin with her.
Wid. She shall not.
Pet. I say she shall;—and first begin with her.
Kath. Fie, fie! unknit that threat'ning un-
  kind brow;
And dart not scornful glances from those eyes,
To wound thy lord, thy king, thy governor:
It blots thy beauty, as frosts do bite the meads;
Confounds thy fame, as whirlwinds shake fair
  buds;
And in no sense is meet or amiable.
A woman mov'd is like a fountain troubled—
Muddy, ill-seeming, thick, bereft of beauty;
And while it is so, none so dry or thirsty
Will deign to sip or touch one drop of it.

Thy husband is thy lord, thy life, thy keeper,
Thy head, thy sovereign; one that cares for thee
And for thy maintenance; commits his body
To painful labour both by sea and land,
To watch the night in storms, the day in cold,
Whilst thou liest warm at home, secure and safe;
And craves no other tribute at thy hands
But love, fair looks, and true obedience,—
Too little payment for so great a debt!
Such duty as the subject owes the prince,
Even such a woman oweth to her husband;
And when she is froward, peevish, sullen, sour,
And not obedient to his honest will,
What is she but a foul contending rebel,
And graceless traitor to her loving lord?—
I am asham'd that women are so simple
To offer war where they should kneel for peace,
Or seek for rule, supremacy, and sway,
When they are bound to serve, love, and obey.
Why are our bodies soft and weak, and smooth,
Unapt to toil and trouble in the world,
But that our soft conditions and our hearts
Should well agree with our external parts?
Come, come, you froward and unable worms!
My mind hath been as big as one of yours,
My heart as great; my reason, haply, more,
To bandy word for word and frown for frown:
But now I see our lances are but straws;
Our strength as weak, our weakness past com-
  pare,—   [are.
That seeming to be most, which we indeed least
Then vail your stomachs, for it is no boot,
And place your hands below your husband's
  foot:
In token of which duty, if he please,
My hand is ready, may it do him ease.
 Pet. Why, there's a wench!—Come on, and
  kiss me, Kate.   [shalt ha't.
 Luc. Well, go thy ways, old lad; for thou
 Vin. 'Tis a good hearing when children are
  toward.   [froward.
 Luc. But a harsh hearing when women are
 Pet. Come, Kate, we'll to bed.—
We three are married, but you two are sped.
'Twas I won the wager, though you hit the
  white;   [*To* LUCENTIO.
And, being a winner, God give you good-night!
  [*Exeunt* PET. *and* KATH.
 Hor. Now go thy ways; thou hast tam'd a
  curst shrew.
 Luc. 'Tis a wonder, by your leave, she will
  be tam'd so.   [*Exeunt.*

THE WINTER'S TALE

DRAMATIS PERSONÆ

LEONTES, *King of Sicilia.*
MAMILLIUS, *his Son.*
CAMILLO,
ANTIGONUS,
CLEOMENES, } *Sicilian Lords.*
DION,
Other Sicilian Lords.
Sicilian Gentlemen.
Officers *of a Court of Judicature.*
POLIXENES, *King of Bohemia.*
FLORIZEL, *his Son.*
ARCHIDAMUS, *a Bohemian Lord.*
A Mariner.
Gaoler.
An Old Shepherd, *reputed father of* PERDITA.
Clown, *his Son.*

Servant *to the Old Shepherd.*
AUTOLYCUS, *a Rogue.*
Time, *as Chorus.*

HERMIONE, *Queen to* LEONTES.
PERDITA, *Daughter to* LEONTES *and* HERMIONE.
PAULINA, *Wife to* ANTIGONUS.
EMILIA, *a Lady,* } *attending the* QUEEN.
Other Ladies,
MOPSA, } *Shepherdesses.*
DORCAS,

Lords, Ladies, *and* Attendants; Satyrs *for a Dance;* Shepherds, Shepherdesses, Guards, &c.

SCENE,—*Sometimes in* SICILIA; *sometimes in* BOHEMIA.

ACT I.

SCENE I.—SICILIA. *An Antechamber in* LEONTES' *Palace.*

Enter CAMILLO *and* ARCHIDAMUS.

Arch. If you shall chance, Camillo, to visit Bohemia, on the like occasion whereon my services are now on foot, you shall see, as I have said, great difference betwixt our Bohemia and your Sicilia.

Cam. I think this coming summer the King of Sicilia means to pay Bohemia the visitation which he justly owes him.

Arch. Wherein our entertainment shall shame us we will be justified in our loves; for, indeed,—

Cam. Beseech you,—

Arch. Verily, I speak it in the freedom of my knowledge: we cannot with such magnificence —in so rare—I know not what to say.—We will give you sleepy drinks, that your senses, unintelligent of our insufficience, may, though they cannot praise us, as little accuse us.

Cam. You pay a great deal too dear for what's given freely.

Arch. Believe me, I speak as my understanding instructs me, and as mine honesty puts it to utterance.

Cam. Sicilia cannot show himself overkind to Bohemia. They were trained together in their childhoods; and there rooted betwixt them then such an affection which cannot choose but branch now. Since their more mature dignities and royal necessities made separation of their society, their encounters, though not personal, have been royally attor-

neyed, with interchange of gifts, letters, loving embassies; that they have seemed to be together, though absent; shook hands, as over a vast; and embraced, as it were, from the ends of opposed winds. The heavens continue their loves!

Arch. I think there is not in the world either malice or matter to alter it. You have an unspeakable comfort of your young Prince Mamillius: it is a gentleman of the greatest promise that ever came into my note.

Cam. I very well agree with you in the hopes of him. It is a gallant child; one that, indeed, physics the subject, makes old hearts fresh: they that went on crutches ere he was born desire yet their life to see him a man.

Arch. Would they else be content to die?

Cam. Yes; if there were no other excuse why they should desire to live.

Arch. If the king had no son they would desire to live on crutches till he had one.

[*Exeunt.*

SCENE II.—*The same. A Room of State in the Palace.*

Enter LEONTES, POLIXENES, HERMIONE, MAMILLIUS, CAMILLO, *and* Attendants.

Pol. Nine changes of the watery star have
    been   [throne
The shepherd's note since we have left our
Without a burden: time as long again
Would be fill'd up, my brother, with our thanks
And yet we should, for perpetuity,
Go hence in debt: and therefore, like a cipher,
Yet standing in rich place, I multiply

With one we-thank-you many thousands more
That go before it.

Leon.   Stay your thanks awhile,
And pay them when you part.

Pol.   Sir, that's to-morrow.
I am question'd by my fears, of what may
        chance
Or breed upon our absence; that may blow
No sneaping winds at home, to make us say,
This is put forth too truly. Besides, I have stay'd
To tire your royalty.

Leon.   We are tougher, brother,
Than you can put us to't.

Pol.   No longer stay.

Leon. One seven-night longer.

Pol.   Very sooth, to-morrow.

Leon. We'll part the time between's then:
        and in that
I'll no gainsaying.

Pol.   Press me not, beseech you, so.
There is no·tongue that moves, none, none i'
        the world   [now,
So soon as yours, could win me: so it should
Were there necessity in your request, although
'Twere needful I denied it. My affairs
Do even drag me homeward: which to hinder,
Were, in your love, a whip to me; my stay,
To you a charge and trouble: to save both,
Farewell, our brother.

Leon. Tongue-tied, our queen? Speak you.

Her. I had thought, sir, to have held my
        peace until
You had drawn oaths from him not to stay.
        You, sir,
Charge him too coldly. Tell him, you are sure
All in Bohemia's well: this satisfaction
The by-gone day proclaimed: say this to him,
He's beat from his best ward.

Leon.   Well said, Hermione.

Her. To tell he longs to see his son, were
        strong:
But let him say so then, and let him go;
But let him swear so, and he shall not stay,
We'll thwack him hence with distaffs.—
Yet of your royal presence [*to* POLIXENES] I'll
        adventure
The borrow of a week. When at Bohemia
You take my lord, I'll give him my commission
To let him there a month behind the gest
Prefix'd for his parting:—yet, good deed,
        Leontes,
I love thee not a jar of the clock behind
What lady she her lord.—You'll stay?

Pol.   No, madam.

Her. Nay, but you will?

Pol.   I may not, verily.

Her. Verily!
You put me off with limber vows; but I,
Though you would seek to unsphere the stars
        with oaths,
Should yet say, *Sir, no going.* Verily,
You shall not go; a lady's verily is
As potent as a lord's. Will you go yet?
Force me to keep you as a prisoner,

Not like a guest: so you shall pay your fees
When you depart, and save your thanks. How
        say you?
My prisoner or my guest? by your dread verily,
One of them you shall be.

Pol.   Your guest, then, madam:
To be your prisoner should import offending;
Which is for me less easy to commit
Than you to punish.

Her.   Not your gaoler, then,
But your kind hostess. Come, I'll question you
Of my lord's tricks and yours when you were
        boys:
You were pretty lordlings then.

Pol.   We were, fair queen,
Two lads that thought there were no more
        behind
But such a day to-morrow as to-day,
And to be boy eternal.   [two?

Her. Was not my lord the verier wag o' the

Pol. We were as twinn'd lambs that did
        frisk i' the sun
And bleat the one at the other. What we
        chang'd
Was innocence for innocence; we knew not
The doctrine of ill-doing, nor dream'd
That any did. Had we pursu'd that life,
And our weak spirits ne'er been higher rear'd
With stronger blood, we should have answer'd
        heaven
Boldly, *Not guilty;* the imposition clear'd
Hereditary ours.

Her.   By this we gather
You have tripp'd since.

Pol.   O my most sacred lady,
Temptations have since then been born to's! for
In those unfledg'd days was my wife a girl;
Your precious self had then not cross'd the eyes
Of my young play-fellow.

Her.   Grace to boot!
Of this make no conclusion, lest you say
Your queen and I are devils: yet, go on;
The offences we have made you do we'll an-
        swer;
If you first sinn'd with us, and that with us
You did continue fault, and that you slipp'd
        not
With any but with us.

Leon.   Is he won yet?

Her. He'll stay, my lord.

Leon.   At my request he would not.
Hermione, my dearest, thou never spok'st
To better purpose.

Her.   Never?

Leon.   Never but once.

Her. What! have I twice said well? when
        was't before?   [make's
I pr'ythee, tell me: cram's with praise, and
As fat as tame things: one good deed dying
        tongueless
Slaughters a thousand waiting upon that.
Our praises are our wages: you may ride's
With one soft kiss a thousand furlongs ere

With spur we heat an acre. But to the goal:—
My last good deed was to entreat his stay;
What was my first? it has an elder sister,
Or I mistake you: O, would her name were
　　　Grace!
But once before I spoke to the purpose: when?
Nay, let me have't; I long.
　　Leon.　　　　　　　　Why, that was when
Three crabbed months had sour'd themselves
　　　to death,
Ere I could make thee open thy white-hand,
And clap thyself my love; then didst thou
　　　utter
I am yours for ever.
　　Her.　　　　　　It is Grace indeed.—
Why, lo you now, I have spoke to the purpose
　　　twice;
The one for ever earn'd a royal husband;
The other for some while a friend.
　　　　　　　[*Giving her hand to* POLIXENES.
　　Leon.　　　　Too hot, too hot! [*Aside.*
To mingle friendship far is mingling bloods.
I have *tremor cordis* on me,—my heart dances;
But not for joy,—not joy.—This entertainment
May a free face put on; derive a liberty
From heartiness, from bounty, fertile bosom,
And well become the agent: 't may, I grant:
But to be paddling palms and pinching fingers,
As now they are; and making practis'd smiles,
As in a looking-glass; and then to sigh, as
　　　'twere
The mort o' the deer; O, that is entertainment
My bosom likes not, nor my brows,—Mamillius,
Art thou my boy?
　　Mam.　　　　　Ay, my good lord.
　　Leon.　　　　　　　　I' fecks!
Why, that's my bawcock. What! hast smutch'd
　　　thy nose?—
They say it's a copy out of mine. Come, cap-
　　　tain,
We must be neat;—not neat, but cleanly, cap-
　　　tain:
And yet the steer, the heifer, and the calf,
Are all call'd neat.—Still virginalling
　　　　　　　[*Observing* POL. *and* HER.
Upon his palm?—How now, you wanton calf!
Art thou my calf?
　　Mam.　　　　Yes, if you will, my lord.
　　Leon.　Thou want'st a rough pash, and the
　　　shoots that I have,
To be full like me:—yet they say we are
Almost as like as eggs; women say so,
That will say anything: but were they false
As o'erdyed blacks, as wind, as waters,—false
As dice are to be wish'd by one that fixes
No bourn 'twixt his and mine; yet were it true
To say this boy were like me.—Come, sir page,
Look on me with your welkin-eye: sweet vil-
　　　lain!　　　　　　　　　　[may't be?
Most dear'st! my collop!—Can thy dam?—
Affection! thy intention stabs the centre:
Thou dost make possible things not so held,
Communicat'st with dreams;—how can this
　　　be?—

With what's unreal thou co-active art,
And fellow'st nothing: then 'tis very credent
Thou mayst co-join with something; and thou
　　　dost,—
And that beyond commission; and I find it,—
And that to the infection of my brains
And hardening of my brows.
　　Pol.　　　　　　　What means Sicilia?
　　Her. He something seems unsettled.
　　Pol.　　　　　　　How! my lord!
What cheer! how is't with you, best brother?
　　Her.　　　　　　　　You look
As if you held a brow of much distraction:
Are you mov'd, my lord?
　　Leon.　　　　　No, in good earnest.—
How sometimes nature will betray its folly,
Its tenderness, and make itself a pastime
To harder bosoms! Looking on the lines
Of my boy's face, methoughts I did recoil
Twenty-three years; and saw myself unbreech'd,
In my green velvet coat; my dagger muzzled,
Lest it should bite its master, and so prove,
As ornaments oft do, too dangerous.
How like, methought, I then was to this kernel,
This quash, this gentleman.—Mine honest
　　　friend,
Will you take eggs for money?
　　Mam. No, my lord, I'll fight.
　　Leon. You will? Why, happy man be's dole!
　　—My brother,
Are you so fond of your young prince as we
Do seem to be of ours?
　　Pol.　　　　　　If at home, sir,
He's all my exercise, my mirth, my matter:
Now my sworn friend, and then mine enemy;
My parasite, my soldier, statesman, all:
He makes a July's day short as December;
And with his varying childness cures in me
Thoughts that would thick my blood.
　　Leon.　　　　　So stands this squire
Offic'd with me. We two will walk, my lord,
And leave you to your graver steps.—Her-
　　　mione,
How thou lov'st us show in our brother's wel-
　　　come;
Let what is dear in Sicily be cheap:
Next to thyself and my young rover, he's
Apparent to my heart.
　　Her.　　　　If you would seek us,
We are your's i' the garden: shall's attend you
　　　there?　　　　　　　　　　[be found,
　　Leon. To your own bents dispose you: you'll
Be you beneath the sky. [*Aside.*] I am angling
　　　now.
Though you perceive me not how I give line.
Go to, go to!　　　　[*Observing* POL. *and* HER.
How she holds up the neb, the bill to him!
And arms her with the boldness of a wife
To her allowing husband! Gone already!
　　　　　　　[*Exeunt* POL., HER., *and* Attendants.
Inch-thick, knee-deep, o'er head and ears a
　　　fork'd one!—
Go, play, boy, play:—thy mother plays, and I
Play too; but so disgrac'd a part, whose issue

Will hiss me to my grave: contempt and
    clamour   [have been,
Will be my knell.—Go, play, boy, play.—There
Or I am much deceiv'd, cuckolds ere now;
And many a man there is, even at this present,
Now while I speak this, holds his wife by the
    arm,   [absence,
That little thinks she has been sluic'd in his
And his pond fish'd by his next neighbour, by
Sir Smile, his neighbour: nay, there's comfort
    in't,   [open'd,
Whiles other men have gates, and those gates
As mine, against their will: should all despair
That have revolted wives, the tenth of mankind.
Would hang themselves. Physic for't there is
    none;
It is a bawdy planet, that will strike
Where 'tis predominant; and 'tis powerful,
    think it,
From east, west, north, and south: be it con-
    cluded,
No barricado for a belly; know't;
It will let in and out the enemy
With bag and baggage: many a thousand of us
Have the disease, and feel't not.—How now,
    boy!

  Mam. I am like you, they say.
  Leon.   Why, that's some comfort.—
What! Camillo there?
  Cam. Ay, my good lord.
  Leon. Go play, Mamillius; thou'rt an honest
    man.—   [*Exit* MAMILLIUS.
Camillo, this great sir will yet stay longer.
  Cam. You had much ado to make his anchor
    hold:
When you cast out, it still came home.
  Leon.   Didst note it?
  Cam. He would not stay at your petitions;
    made
His business more material.
  Leon.   Didst perceive it?—
They're here with me already; whispering,
    rounding,
Sicilia is a so-forth: 'tis far gone
When I shall gust it last.—How cam't, Camillo,
That he did stay?
  Cam.   At the good queen's entreaty.
  Leon. At the queen's be't: good should be
    pertinent;
But so it is, it is not. Was this taken
By any understanding pate but thine?
For thy conceit is soaking, will draw in
More than the common blocks:—not noted, is't,
But of the finer natures? by some severals
Of head-piece extraordinary? lower messes,
Perchance are to this business purblind? say.
  Cam. Business, my lord! I think most under-
    stand
Bohemia stays here longer.
  Leon.   Ha!
  Cam.   Stays here longer.
  Leon. Ay, but why?   [treaties
  Cam. To satisfy your highness, and the en-
Of our most gracious mistress.

  Leon.   Satisfy
The entreaties of your mistress!—satisfy!—
Let that suffice. I have trusted thee, Camillo,
With all the nearest things to my heart, as well
My chamber-councils, wherein, priest-like,
    thou
Hast cleans'd my bosom; I from thee departed
Thy penitent reform'd: but we have been
Deceiv'd in thy integrity, deceiv'd
In that which seems so.
  Cam.   Be it forbid, my lord!
  Leon. To bide upon't,—thou art not honest;
    or,
If thou inclin'st that way, thou art a coward,
Which hoxes honesty behind, restraining
From course requir'd; or else thou must be
    counted
A servant grafted in my serious trust,
And therein negligent; or else a fool,
That seest a game play'd home, the rich stake
    drawn,
And tak'st it all for jest.
  Cam.   My gracious lord,
I may be negligent, foolish, and fearful;
In every one of these no man is free,
But that his negligence, his folly, fear,
Amongst the infinite doings of the world,
Sometime puts forth: in your affairs, my lord,
If ever I were wilful-negligent,
It was my folly; if industriously
I play'd the fool, it was my negligence,
Not weighing well the end; if ever fearful
To do a thing, where I the issue doubted,
Whereof the execution did cry out
Against the non-performance, 'twas a fear
Which oft affects the wisest: these, my lord,
Are such allow'd infirmities that honesty
Is never free of. But, beseech your grace,
Be plainer with me; let me know my trespass
By its own visage: if I then deny it,
'Tis none of mine.
  Leon.   Have you not seen, Camillo,—
But that's past doubt: you have, or your eye-
    glass
Is thicker than a cuckold's horn,—or heard,—
For, to a vision so apparent, rumour
Cannot be mute,—or thought,—for cogitation
Resides not in that man that does not think
    it,—
My wife is slippery? If thou wilt confess,—
Or else be impudently negative,
To have nor eyes nor ears nor thought,—then
    say
My wife's a hobbyhorse; deserves a name
As rank as any flax-wench that puts to
Before her troth-plight: say't and justify't.
  Cam. I would not be a stander-by to hear
My sovereign mistress clouded so, without
My present vengeance taken: 'shrew my heart,
You never spoke what did become you less
Than this; which to reiterate were sin
As deep as that, though true.
  Leon.   Is whispering nothing?
Is leaning cheek to cheek? is meeting noses?

Kissing with inside lip? stopping the career
Of laughter with a sigh?—a note infallible
Of breaking honesty;—horsing foot on foot?
Skulking in corners? wishing clocks more swift?
Hours, minutes? noon, midnight? and all eyes
Blind with the pin and web, but theirs, theirs
    only,
That would unseen be wicked?—is this nothing?
Why, then the world and all that's in't is no-
    thing;
The covering sky is nothing; Bohemia nothing;
My wife is nothing; nor nothing have these no-
    things,
If this be nothing.
  Cam.   Good my lord, be cur'd
Of this diseas'd opinion, and betimes;
For 'tis most dangerous.
  Leon.   Say it be, 'tis true.
  Cam. No, no, my lord!
  Leon.   It is; you lie, you lie:
I say thou liest, Camillo, and I hate thee;
Pronounce thee a gross lout, a mindless slave;
Or else a hovering temporizer, that
Canst with thine eyes at once see good and evil.
Inclining to them both.—Were my wife's liver
Infected as her life, she would not live
The running of one glass.
  Cam.   Who does infect her?
  Leon. Why, he that wears her like her medal,
    hanging
About his neck, Bohemia: who—if I
Had servants true about me, that bare eyes
To see alike mine honour as their profits,
Their own particular thrifts,—they would do
    that
Which should undo more doing: ay, and thou,
His cupbearer,—whom I from meaner form
Have bench'd and rear'd to worship; who
    mayst see   [heaven,
Plainly, as heaven sees earth, and earth sees
How I am galled,—mightst bespice a cup,
To give mine enemy a lasting wink;
Which draught to me were cordial.
  Cam.   Sir, my lord,
I could do this; and that with no rash potion,
But with a ling'ring dram, that should not work
Maliciously like poison: but I cannot
Believe this crack to be in my dread mistress,
So sovereignly being honourable.
I have lov'd thee,—
  Leon. Make that thy question, and go rot!
Dost think I am so muddy, so unsettled,
To appoint myself in this vexation; sully
The purity and whiteness of my sheets,—
Which to preserve is sleep; which being spotted
Is goads, thorns, nettles, tails of wasps;
Give scandal to the blood o' the prince my son,—
Who I do think is mine, and love as mine,—
Without ripe moving to't?—Would I do this?
Could man so blench?
  Cam.   I must believe you, sir:
I do; and will fetch off Bohemia for't;   [ness
Provided that, when he's remov'd, your high-
Will take again your queen as yours at first,

Even for your son's sake; and thereby for seal-
    ing
The injury of tongues in courts and kingdoms
Known and allied to yours.
  Leon.   Thou dost advise me
Even so as I mine own course have set down:
I'll give no blemish to her honour, none.
  Cam. My lord,
Go then; and with a countenance as clear
As friendship wears at feasts, keep with Bohemia
And with your queen: I am his cupbearer.
If from me he have wholesome beverage
Account me not your servant.
  Leon.   This is all:
Do't and thou hast the one-half of my heart;
Do't not, thou splitt'st thine own.
  Cam.   I'll do't, my lord.
  Leon. I will seem friendly, as thou hast
    advis'd me.   [*Exit.*
  Cam. O miserable lady!—But, for me,
What case stand I in? I must be the poisoner
Of good Polixenes: and my ground to do't
Is the obedience to a master; one
Who, in rebellion with himself, will have
All that are his so too.—To do this deed,
Promotion follows: if I could find example
Of thousands that had struck anointed kings,
And flourish'd after, I'd not do't; but since
Nor brass, nor stone, nor parchment, bears not
    one,
Let villany itself forswear't. I must
Forsake the court: to do't, or no, is certain
To me a break-neck. Happy star, reign now!
Here comes Bohemia.

        Enter POLIXENES.

  Pol.   This is strange! methinks
My favour here begins to warp. Not speak?—
Good-day, Camillo.
  Cam.   Hail, most royal sir!
  Pol. What is the news i' the court?
  Cam.   None rare, my lord.
  Pol. The king hath on him such a counten-
    ance
As he had lost some province, and a region
Lov'd as he loves himself: even now I met him
With customary compliment; when he,
Wafting his eyes to the contrary, and falling
A lip of much contempt, speeds from me; and
So leaves me, to consider what is breeding
That changes thus his manners.
  Cam. I dare not know, my lord.
  Pol. How! dare not! do not. Do you know,
    and dare not
Be intelligent to me? 'Tis thereabouts;
For, to yourself, what you do know, you must,
And cannot say, you dare not. Good Camillo,
Your chang'd complexions are to me a mirror,
Which shows me mine chang'd too; for I must
    be
A party in this alteration, finding
Myself thus alter'd with it.
  Cam.   There is a sickness
Which puts some of us in distemper; but

I cannot name the disease; and it is caught
Of you that yet are well.
 Pol.   How! caught of me!
Make me not sighted like the basilisk:
I have look'd on thousands, who have sped the
  better
By my regard, but kill'd none so. Camillo,—
As you are certainly a gentleman; thereto
Clerk-like, experienc'd, which no less adorns
Our gentry than our parents' noble names,
In whose success we are gentle,—I beseech you,
If you know aught which does behove my
  knowledge
Thereof to be inform'd, imprison't not
In ignorant concealment.
 Cam.   I may not answer.
 Pol. A sickness caught of me, and yet I well!
I must be answer'd.—Dost thou hear, Camillo,
I cónjure thee, by all the parts of man,
Which honour does acknowledge,—whereof the
  least
Is not this suit of mine,—that thou declare
What incidency thou dost guess of harm
Is creeping toward me; how far off, how near;
Which way to be prevented, if to be;
If not, how best to bear it.
 Cam.   Sir, I will tell you;
Since I am charg'd in honour, and by him
That I think honourable: therefore mark my
  counsel,
Which must be even as swiftly follow'd as
I mean to utter it, or both yourself and me
Cry lost, and so good-night!
 Pol.   On, good Camillo.
 Cam. I am appointed him to murder you.
 Pol. By whom, Camillo?
 Cam.   By the king.
 Pol.   For what?
 Cam. He thinks, nay, with all confidence he
  swears,
As he had seen't or been an instrument
To vice you to't, that you have touch'd his queen
Forbiddingly.
 Pol. O, then my best blood turn
To an infected jelly, and my name
Be yok'd with his that did betray the best!
Turn then my freshest reputation to
A savour that may strike the dullest nostril
Where I arrive, and my approach be shunn'd,
Nay, hated too, worse than the great'st infection
That e'er was heard or read!
 Cam.   Swear his thought over
By each particular star in heaven and
By all their influences, you may as well
Forbid the sea for to obey the moon,
As, or by oath remove, or counsel shake
The fabric of his folly, whose foundation
Is pil'd upon his faith, and will continue
The standing of his body.
 Pol.   How should this grow?
 Cam. I know not: but I am sure 'tis safer to
Avoid what's grown than question how 'tis
  born.
If, therefore, you dare trust my honesty,—

That lies enclosed in this trunk, which you
Shall bear along impawn'd,—away to-night.
Your followers I will whisper to the business;
And will, by twos and threes, at several pos-
  terns,
Clear them o' the city: for myself, I'll put
My fortunes to your service, which are here
By this discovery lost. Be not uncertain;
For, by the honour of my parents, I
Have utter'd truth: which if you seek to prove,
I dare not stand by; nor shall you be safer
Than one condemn'd by the king's own mouth,
  thereon
His execution sworn.
 Pol.   I do believe thee;
I saw his heart in his face. Give me thy hand;
Be pilot to me, and thy places shall
Still neighbour mine. My ships are ready, and
My people did expect my hence departure
Two days ago.—This jealousy
Is for a precious creature: as she's rare,
Must it be great; and, as his person's mighty,
Must it be violent; and as he does conceive
He is dishonour'd by a man which ever
Profess'd to him, why, his revenges must
In that be made more bitter. Fear o'ershades
  me:
Good expedition be my friend, and comfort
The gracious queen, part of his theme, but no-
  thing
Of his ill ta'en suspicion! Come, Camillo;
I will respect thee as a father, if
Thou bear'st my life off hence: let us avoid.
 Cam. It is in mine authority to command
The keys of all the posterns: please your high-
  ness
To take the urgent hour: come, sir, away.
            [*Exeunt.*

ACT II.

SCENE I.—SICILIA. *A Room in the Palace.*

Enter HERMIONE, MAMILLIUS, *and* Ladies.

 Her. Take the boy to you: he so troubles me,
'Tis past enduring.
 1 *Lady.*   Come, my gracious lord,
Shall I be your playfellow?
 Mam.   No, I'll none of you.
 1 *Lady.* Why, my sweet lord?
 Mam. You'll kiss me hard, and speak to me
  as if
I were a baby still.—I love you better.
 2 *Lady.* And why so, my lord?
 Mam.   Not for because
Your brows are blacker; yet black brows, they
  say,
Become some women best; so that there be not
Too much hair there, but in a semicircle,
Or a half-moon made with a pen.
 2 *Lady.*   Who taught you this?
 Mam. I learn'd it out of women's faces.—
  Pray now,
What colour are your eyebrows?
 1 *Lady.*   Blue, my lord.

Mam. Nay, that's a mock: I have seen a
     lady's nose
That has been blue, but not her eyebrows.
   1 *Lady.*   Hark ye;
The queen your mother rounds apace: we shall
Present our services to a fine new prince
One of these days; and then you'd wanton
     with us,
If we would have you.
   2 *Lady.*   She is spread of late
Into a goodly bulk: good time encounter her!
   Her. What wisdom stirs amongst you?
     Come, sir, now
I am for you again: pray you, sit by us,
And tell's a tale.
   Mam.   Merry or sad shall't be?
   Her. As merry as you will.
   Mam.   A sad tale's best for winter:
I have one of sprites and goblins.
   Her. Let's have that, good sir.
Come on, sit down:—come on, and do your best
To fright me with your sprites: you're powerful
     at it.
   Mam. There was a man,—
   Her.   Nay, come, sit down: then on.
   Mam. Dwelt by a churchyard:—I will tell it
     softly;
Yond crickets shall not hear it.
   Her.   Come on, then,
And give't me in mine ear.

Enter LEONTES, ANTIGONUS, Lords *and* Guards.

   Leon. Was he met there? his train? Camillo
     with him?   [never
   1 *Lord.* Behind the tuft of pines I met them;
Saw I men scour so on their way: I ey'd them
Even to their ships.
   Leon.   How bless'd am I
In my just censure, in my true opinion!—
Alack, for lesser knowledge!—how accurs'd,
In being so blest!—There may be in the cup
A spider steep'd, and one may drink, depart,
And yet partake no venom; for his knowledge
Is not infected: but if one present
The abhorr'd ingredient to his eye, make
     known   [sides
How he hath drunk, he cracks his gorge, his
With violent hefts:—I have drunk, and seen
     the spider.
Camillo was his help in this, his pander:—
There is a plot against my life, my crown;
All's true that is mistrusted:—that false villain,
Whom I employ'd, was pre-employ'd by him:
He has discover'd my design, and I
Remain a pinch'd thing; yea, a very trick
For them to play at will.—How came the
     posterns
So easily open?
   1 *Lord.*   By his great authority;
Which often hath no less prevail'd than so,
On your command.
   Leon.   I know't too well.—
Give me the boy:—I am glad you did not
     nurse him:

Though he does bear some signs of me, yet you
Have too much blood in him.
   Her.   What is this? sport?
   Leon. Bear the boy hence; he shall not come
     about her;
Away with him!—and let her sport herself
     [*Exit* MAMILLIUS, *with some of the* Guards.
With that she's big with;—for 'tis Polixenes
Hath made thee swell thus.
   Her.   But I'd say he had not,
And I'll be sworn you would believe my saying,
Howe'er you learn the nayward.
   Leon.   You, my lords,
Look on her, mark her well; be but about
To say, *she is a goodly lady,* and
The justice of your hearts will thereto add,
'Tis pity she's not honest, honourable:
Praise her but for this her without-door form,—
Which, on my faith, deserves high speech,—
     and straight
The shrug, the hum, or ha,—these petty brands,
That calumny doth use:—O, I am out,
That mercy does; for calumny will sear
Virtue itself:—these shrugs, these hums, and
     ha's,
When you have said *she's goodly,* come between,
Ere you can say *she's honest:* but be it known,
From him that has most cause to grieve it
     should be,
She's an adultress!
   Her.   Should a villain say so,
The most replenish'd villain in the world,
He were as much more villain: you, my lord,
Do but mistake.
   Leon.   You have mistook, my lady,
Polixenes for Leontes: O thou thing,
Which I'll not call a creature of thy place,
Lest barbarism, making me the precedent,
Should a like language use to all degrees,
And mannerly distinguishment leave out
Betwixt the prince and beggar!—I have said,
She's an adultress; I have said with whom:
More, she's a traitor; and Camillo is
A federary with her; and one that knows
What she should shame to know herself
But with her most vile principal, that she's
A bed-swerver, even as bad as those
That vulgars give boldest titles; ay, and privy
To this their late escape.
   Her.   No, by my life,
Privy to none of this. How will this grieve you,
When you shall come to clearer knowledge, that
You thus have publish'd me! Gentle, my lord
You scarce can right me throughly then, to say
You did mistake.
   Leon.   No; if I mistake
In those foundations which I build upon,
The centre is not big enough to bear
A school-boy's top.—Away with her to
     prison!
He who shall speak for her is afar off guilty
But that he speaks.
   Her.   There's some ill planet reigns:
I must be patient till the heavens look

With an aspect more favourable.—Good my
   lords,
I am not prone to weeping, as our sex
Commonly are; the want of which vain dew
Perchance shall dry your pities; but I have
That honourable grief lodg'd here, which burns
Worse than tears drown: beseech you all, my
   lords,
With thoughts so qualified as your charities
Shall best instruct you, measure me;—and so
The king's will be perform'd!

Leon.   Shall I be heard?
                   [*To the* Guards.

Her. Who is't that goes with me?—Beseech
   your highness,
My women may be with me; for you see,
My plight requires it.—Do not weep, good fools;
There is no cause: when you shall know your
   mistress
Has deserv'd prison, then abound in tears
As I come out: this action I now go on
Is for my better grace.—Adieu, my lord:
I never wish'd to see you sorry; now   [leave.
I trust I shall.—My women, come; you have

Leon. Go, do our bidding; hence!
   [*Exeunt* QUEEN *and* Ladies, *with* Guards.

1 *Lord.* Beseech your highness, call the
   queen again.

Ant. Be certain what you do, sir, lest your
   justice   [suffer,
Prove violence: in the which three great ones
Yourself, your queen, your son.

1 *Lord.*   For her, my lord,—
I dare my life lay down, and will do't, sir,
Please you to accept it, that the queen is spot-
   less
I' the eyes of heaven and to you; I mean
In this which you accuse her.

Ant.   If it prove
She's otherwise, I'll keep my stables where
I lodge my wife; I'll go in couples with her;
Than when I feel and see her no further trust
   her;
For every inch of woman in the world,
Ay, every dram of woman's flesh, is false,
If she be.

Leon. Hold your peaces.

1 *Lord.*   Good my lord,—

Ant. It is for you we speak, not for ourselves:
You are abus'd. and by some putter-on,
That will be damn'd for't: would I knew the
   villain,   [flaw'd,—
I would land-damn him. Be she honour-
I have three daughters; the eldest is eleven;
The second and the third, nine and some five;
If this prove true, they'll pay for't: by mine
   honour,
I'll geld 'em all: fourteen they shall not see,
To bring false generations: they are co-heirs;
And I had rather glib myself than they
Should not produce fair issue.

Leon.   Cease; no more.
You smell this business with a sense as cold
As is a dead man's nose: but I do see't and feel't,

As you feel doing thus; and see withal
The instruments that feel.

Ant.   If it be so,
We need no grave to bury honesty;
There's not a grain of it the face to sweeten
Of the whole dungy earth.

Leon.   What! lack I credit?

1 *Lord.* I had rather you did lack than I, my
   lord,   [me
Upon this ground: and more it would content
To have her honour true than your suspicion;
Be blam'd for't how you might.

Leon.   Why, what need we
Commune with you of this, but rather follow
Our forceful instigation? Our prerogative
Calls not your counsels, but our natural good-
   ness
Imparts this: which, if you,—or stupefied
Or seeming so in skill,—cannot or will not
Relish a truth, like us, inform yourselves
We need no more of your advice: the matter,
The loss, the gain, the ordering on't, is all
Properly ours.

Ant.   And I wish, my liege,
You had only in your silent judgment tried it,
Without more overture.

Leon.   How could that be?
Either thou art most ignorant by age,
Or thou wert born a fool. Camillo's flight,
Added to their familiarity,—
Which was as gross as ever touch'd conjecture,
That lack'd sight only, naught for approbation,
But only seeing, all other circumstances
Made up to the deed,—doth push on this pro-
   ceeding.
Yet, for a greater confirmation,—
For, in an act of this importance, 'twere
Most piteous to be wild,—I have despatch'd in
   post
To sacred Delphos, to Apollo's temple,
Cleomenes and Dion, whom you know
Of stuff'd sufficiency: now, from the oracle
They will bring all; whose spiritual counsel had,
Shall stop or spur me. Have I done well?

1 *Lord.* Well done, my lord.

Leon. Though I am satisfied, and need no more
Than what I know, yet shall the oracle
Give rest to the minds of others such as he
Whose ignorant credulity will not   [good
Come up to the truth: so have we thought it
From our free person she should be confin'd;
Lest that the treachery of the two fled hence
Be left her to perform. Come, follow us;
We are to speak in public; for this business
Will raise us all.

Ant. [*Aside.*] To laughter, as I take it,
If the good truth were known.   [*Exeunt.*

SCENE II.—*The same. The outer Room of a
Prison.*

Enter PAULINA *and* Attendants.

Paul. The keeper of the prison,—call to him;
Let him have knowledge who I am.
                   [*Exit an* Attendant.

Good lady!
No court in Europe is too good for thee;
What dost thou, then, in prison?

Re-enter Attendant, *with the* Keeper.

Now, good sir.
You know me, do you not?
   Keep.   For a worthy lady,
And one who much I honour.
   Paul.   Pray you, then,
Conduct me to the queen.
   Keep. I may not, madam: to the contrary
I have express commandment.
   Paul.   Here's ado,
To lock up honesty and honour from
The access of gentle visitors!—Is't lawful,
Pray you, to see her women? any of them?
Emilia?
   Keep. So please you, madam, to put
Apart these your attendants, I shall bring
Emilia forth.
   Paul.   I pray now, call her.—
Withdraw yourselves.   [*Exeunt* Attend.
   Keep.   And, madam,
I must be present at your conference.
   Paul. Well, be't so, pr'ythee. [*Exit* Keeper.
Here's such ado to make no stain a stain,
As passes colouring.

Re-enter Keeper, *with* EMILIA.

Dear gentlewoman, how fares our gracious
    lady?
   Emil. As well as one so great and so forlorn
May hold together: on her frights and griefs,—
Which never tender lady hath borne greater,—
She is, something before her time, deliver'd.
   Paul. A boy?
   Emil.   A daughter; and a goodly babe,
Lusty, and like to live: the queen receives
Much comfort in't; says, *My poor prisoner,
I am innocent as you.*
   Paul.   I dare be sworn:—
These dangerous unsafe lunes i' the king, be-
    shrew them!
He must be told on't, and he shall: the office
Becomes a woman best: I'll take't upon me:
If I prove honey-mouth'd, let my tongue glis-
    ter;
And never to my red-look'd anger be
The trumpet any more.—Pray you, Emilia,
Commend my best obedience to the queen;
If she dares trust me with her little babe,
I'll show't the king, and undertake to be
Her advocate to the loud'st. We do not know
How he may soften at the sight o' the child:
The silence often of pure innocence
Persuades, when speaking fails.
   Emil.   Most worthy madam,
Your honour and your goodness is so evident,
That your free undertaking cannot miss
A thriving issue: there is no lady living
So meet for this great errand. Please your lady-
    ship
To visit the next room, I'll presently

Acquaint the queen of your most noble offer:
Who but to-day hammer'd of this design,
But durst not tempt a minister of honour,
Lest she should be denied.
   Paul.   Tell her, Emilia,
I'll use that tongue I have: if wit flow from it,
As boldness from my bosom, let it not be
    doubted
I shall do good.
   Emil.   Now be you bless'd for it!
I'll to the queen: please you come something
    nearer.
   Keep. Madam, if't please the queen to send
    the babe,
I know not what I shall incur to pass it?
Having no warrant.
   Paul. You need not fear it, sir:
The child was prisoner to the womb, and is,
By law and process of great nature, thence
Freed and enfranchis'd, not a party to
The anger of the king, nor guilty of,
If any be, the trespass of the queen.
   Keep. I do believe it.
   Paul. Do not you fear: upon mine honour, I
Will stand 'twixt you and danger.   [*Exeunt.*

SCENE III.—*The same. A Room in the Palace.*

Enter LEONTES, ANTIGONUS, Lords, *and
other* Attendants.

   Leon. Nor night nor day no rest: it is but
    weakness
To bear the matter thus,—mere weakness. If
The cause were not in being,—part o' the cause,
She the adultress; for the harlot king
Is quite beyond mine arm, out of the blank
And level of my brain, plot-proof; but she
I can hook to me:—say that she were gone,
Given to the fire, a moiety of my rest
Might come to me again.—Who's there?
   1 *Atten.* [*Advancing.*]   My lord?
   Leon. How does the boy?
   1 *Atten.*   He took good rest to-night;
'Tis hop'd his sickness is discharg'd.
   Leon. To see his nobleness!
Conceiving the dishonour of his mother,
He straight declin'd, droop'd, took it deeply,
Fasten'd and fix'd the shame on't in himself,
Threw off his spirit, his appetite, his sleep,
And downright languish'd.—Leave me solely:
    —go,
See how he fares. [*Exit* 1 Attend.]—Fie, fie! no
    thought of him;
The very thought of my revenges that way
Recoil upon me: in himself too mighty,
And in his parties, his alliance,—let him be,
Until a time may serve: for present vengeance,
Take it on her. Camillo and Polixenes
Laugh at me; make their pastime at my sorrow.
They should not laugh if I could reach them;
    nor
Shall she, within my power.

Enter PAULINA, *with a child.*

   1 *Lord.*   You must not enter.

Paul. Nay, rather, good my lords, be second
      to me:
Fear you his tyrannous passion more, alas,
Than the queen's life? a gracious innocent soul,
More free than he is jealous.
    Ant.   That's enough.
    2 *Attend.* Madam, he hath not slept tonight;
      commanded
None should come at him.
    Paul.   Not so hot, good sir;
I come to bring him sleep. 'Tis such as you,—
That creep like shadows by him, and do sigh
At each his needless heavings,—such as you`
Nourish the cause of his awaking: I
Do come, with words as med'cinal as true,
Honest as either, to purge him of that humour
That presses him from sleep.
    Leon.   What noise there, ho?
    Paul. No noise, my lord; but needful con-
      ference
About some gossips for your highness.
    Leon.   How!—
Away with that audacious lady!—Antigonus,
I charg'd thee that she should not come about
    me:
I knew she would.
    Ant.   I told her so, my lord,
On your displeasure's peril, and on mine,
She should not visit you.
    Leon.   What, canst not rule her?
    Paul. From all dishonesty, he can: in this,—
Unless he take the course that you have done,
Commit me for committing honour,—trust it,
He shall not rule me.
    Ant.   La you now, you hear!
When she will take the rein, I let her run;
But she'll not stumble.
    Paul.   Good my liege, I come,—
And, I beseech you, hear me, who professes
Myself your loyal servant, your physician,
Your most obedient counsellor; yet that dares
Less appear so, in comforting your evils,
Than such as most seem yours:—I say, I
    come
From your good queen.
    Leon.   Good queen!
    Paul. Good queen, my lord, good queen: I
      say, good queen;
And would by combat make her good, so were I
A man, the worst about you.
    Leon.   Force her hence!
    Paul. Let him that makes but trifles of his
      eyes
First hand me: on mine own accord I'll off;
But first I'll do my errand.—The good queen,
For she is good, hath brought you forth a
    daughter;
Here 'tis; commends it to your blessing.
                [Laying down the child.
    Leon.   Out!
A mankind-witch! Hence with her, out o' door:
A most intelligencing bawd!
    Paul.   Not so:
I am as ignorant in that as you

In so entitling me; and no less honest   [rant
Than you are mad; which is enough, I'll war-
As this world goes, to pass for honest.
    Leon.   Traitors!
Will you not push her out? Give her the
    bastard:—
Thou dotard [*to* ANTIGONUS], thou art woman-
    tir'd, unroosted
By thy dame Partlet here:—take up the
    bastard;
Take't up, I say; give't to thy crone.
    Paul.   For ever
Unvenerable be thy hands, if thou
Tak'st up the princess, by that forced baseness
Which he has put upon't!
    Leon.   He dreads his wife.
    Paul. So I would you did; then 'twere past
    all doubt,
You'd call your children yours.
    Leon.   A nest of traitors!
    Ant. I am none, by this good light.
    Paul.   Nor I; nor any,
But one, that's here; and that's himself: for he
The sacred honour of himself, his queen's,
His hopeful son's, his babe's, betrays to slander,
Whose sting is sharper than the sword's; and
    will not,—
For, as the case now stands, it is a curse
He cannot be compell'd to't,—once remove
The root of his opinion, which is rotten
As ever oak or stone was sound.
    Leon.   A callat
Of boundless tongue, who late hath beat her
    husband,
And now baits me!—This brat is none of mine;
It is the issue of Polixenes:
Hence with it! and, together with the dam,
Commit them to the fire.
    Paul.   It is yours! [charge,
And, might we lay the old proverb to your
So like you, 'tis the worse.—Behold, my lords,
Although the print be little, the whole matter
And copy of the father,—eye, nose, lip,
The trick of his frown, his forehead; nay, the
    valley,   [smiles;
The pretty dimples of his chin and cheek; his
The very mould and frame of hand, nail,
    finger:—   [made it
And thou, good goddess Nature, which hast
So like to him that got it, if thou hast
The ordering of the mind too, 'mongst all
    colours
No yellow in't, lest she suspect, as he does,
Her children not her husband's!
    Leon.   A gross hag!
And, losel, thou art not worthy to be hang'd,
That wilt not stay her tongue.
    Ant.   Hang all the husbands
That cannot do that feat, you'll leave yourself
Hardly one subject.
    Leon.   Once more, take her hence.
    Paul. A most unworthy and unnatural lord
Can do no more.
    Leon.   I'll have thee burn'd.

Paul. I care not.
It is an heretic that makes the fire, [tyrant;
Not she which burns in't. I'll not call you
But this most cruel usage of your queen,—
Not able to produce more accusation [savours
Than your own weak-hing'd fancy,—something
Of tyranny, and will ignoble make you,
Yea, scandalous to the world.

Leon. On your allegiance,
Out of the chamber with her! Were I a tyrant,
Where were her life? she durst not call me so,
If she did know me one. Away with her!

Paul. I pray you, do not push me; I'll be
gone.— [send her
Look to your babe, my lord; 'tis yours: Jove
A better guiding spirit!—What needs these
hands?
You, that are thus so tender o'er his follies,
Will never do him good, not one of you.
So, so:—farewell; we are gone. [*Exit.*

Leon. Thou, traitor, hast set on thy wife to
this.—
My child? away with't!—even thou, that hast
A heart so tender o'er it, take it hence,
And see it instantly consum'd with fire;
Even thou, and none but thou. Take it up
straight:
Within this hour bring me word 'tis done,—
And by good testimony,—or I'll seize thy life,
With what thou else call'st thine. If thou refuse,
And wilt encounter with my wrath, say so;
The bastard-brains with these my proper hands
Shall I dash out. Go, take it to the fire;
For thou sett'st on thy wife.

Ant. I did not, sir:
These lords, my noble fellows, if they please,
Can clear me in't.

1 Lord. We can:—my royal liege,
He is not guilty of her coming hither.

Leon. You are liars all. [credit:

1 Lord. Beseech your highness, give us better
We have always truly serv'd you; and beseech
So to esteem of us: and on our knees we beg,—
As recompense of our dear services,
Past and to come,—that you do change this
purpose,
Which, being so horrible, so bloody, must
Lead on to some foul issue: we all kneel.

Leon. I am a feather for each wind that
blows:—
Shall I live on, to see this bastard kneel
And call me father? better burn it now,
Than curse it then. But, be it; let it live:—
It shall not neither.—You, sir, come you hither:
[*To* ANTIGONUS.
You that have been so tenderly officious
With Lady Margery, your midwife, there,
To save this bastard's life,—for 'tis a bastard,
So sure as thy beard's gray,—what will you
adventure
To save this brat's life?

Ant. Anything, my lord,
That my ability may undergo,
And nobleness impose: at least, thus much;

I'll pawn the little blood which I have left,
To save the innocent:—anything possible.

Leon. It shall be possible. Swear by this
sword
Thou wilt perform my bidding.

Ant. I will, my lord.

Leon. Mark, and perform it,—seest thou? for
the fail
Of any point in't shall not only be
Death to thyself, but to thy lewd-tongu'd wife,
Whom for this time we pardon. We enjoin thee,
As thou art liegeman to us, that thou carry
This female bastard hence; and that thou bear
it
To some remote and desert place, quite out
Of our dominions; and that there thou leave it,
Without more mercy, to its own protection
And favour of the climate. As by strange for-
tune
It came to us, I do in justice charge thee,
On thy soul's peril and thy body's torture,
That thou commend it strangely to some place,
Where chance may nurse or end it. Take it up.

Ant. I swear to do this, though a present
death
Had been more merciful.—Come on, poor babe:
Some powerful spirit instruct the kites and
ravens
To be thy nurses! Wolves and bears, they say,
Casting their savageness aside, have done
Like offices of pity.—Sir, be prosperous [ing,
In more than this deed does require!—and bless-
Against this cruelty, fight on thy side,
Poor thing, condemn'd to loss!
[*Exit with the child.*

Leon. No, I'll not rear
Another's issue.

2 Attend. Please your highness, posts,
From those you sent to the oracle, are come
An hour since: Cleomenes and Dion,
Being well arriv'd from Delphos, are both landed,
Hasting to the court.

1 Lord. So please you, sir, their speed
Hath been beyond account.

Leon. Twenty-three days
They have been absent: 'tis good speed; fore-
tells
The great Apollo suddenly will have
The truth of this appear. Prepare you, lords;
Summon a session, that we may arraign
Our most disloyal lady; for, as she hath
Been publicly accus'd, so shall she have
A just and open trial. While she lives,
My heart will be a burden to me. Leave me;
And think upon my bidding. [*Exeunt.*

ACT III.

SCENE I.—SICILIA. *A street in some Town.*

Enter CLEOMENES *and* DION.

Cleo. The climate's delicate; the air most
sweet;
Fertile the isle; the temple much surpassing
The common praise it bears.

Dion. I shall report,
For most it caught me, the celestial habits,—
Methinks I so should term them,—and the reverence
Of the grave wearers. O, the sacrifice!
How ceremonious, solemn, and unearthly
It was i' the offering!
Cleo. But, of all, the burst
And the ear-deafening voice o' the oracle,
Kin to Jove's thunder, so surprised my sense
That I was nothing.
Dion. If the event o' the journey
Prove as successful to the queen,—O, be't so!—
As it hath been to us rare, pleasant, speedy,
The time is worth the use on't.
Cleo. Great Apollo
Turn all to the best! These proclamations,
So forcing faults upon Hermione,
I little like.
Dion. The violent carriage of it
Will clear or end the business: when the oracle,—
Thus by Apollo's great divine seal'd up,—
Shall the contents discover, something rare
Even then will rush to knowledge.—Go,—fresh horses;—
And gracious be the issue! [*Exeunt.*

SCENE II.—*The same. A Court of Justice.*

LEONTES, Lords, *and* Officers *appear, properly seated.*

Leon. This sessions,—to our great grief, we pronounce,—
Even pushes 'gainst our heart;—the party tried,
The daughter of a king, our wife; and one
Of us too much belov'd. Let us be clear'd
Of being tyrannous, since we so openly
Proceed in justice; which shall have due course,
Even to the guilt or the purgation.—
Produce the prisoner.
Offi. It is his highness' pleasure that the queen
Appear in person here in court.—
Crier. Silence!

HERMIONE *is brought in guarded;* PAULINA *and* Ladies *attending.*

Leon. Read the indictment.
Offi. [*Reads.*] Hermione, *queen to the worthy* Leontes, *king of* Sicilia, *thou art here accused and arraigned of high treason, in committing adultery with* Polixenes, *king of Bohemia; and conspiring with* Camilio *to take away the life of our sovereign lord the king, thy royal husband: the pretence whereof being by circumstances partly laid open, thou,* Hermione, *contrary to the faith and allegiance of a true subject, didst counsel and aid them, for their better safety, to fly away by night.*
Her. Since what I am to say must be but that
Which contradicts my accusation, and
The testimony on my part no other [me
But what comes from myself, it shall scarce boot
To say, *Not guilty:* mine integrity
Being counted falsehood, shall. as I express it,

Be so receiv'd. But thus,—if powers divine
Behold our human actions,—as they do,—
I doubt not, then, but innocence shall make
False accusation blush, and tyranny [know,—
Tremble at patience.—You, my lord, best
Who least will seem to do so,—my past life
Hath been as continent, as chaste, as true,
As I am now unhappy: which is more
Than history can pattern, though devis'd
And play'd to take spectators; for, behold me,—
A fellow of the royal bed, which owe
A moiety of the throne, a great king's daughter,
The mother to a hopeful prince,—here standing
To prate and talk for life and honour 'fore [it
Who please to come and hear. For life, I prize
As I weigh grief, which I would spare: for honour,
'Tis a derivative from me to mine,
And only that I stand for. I appeal
To your own conscience, sir, before Polixenes
Came to your court, how I was in your grace,
How merited to be so; since he came,
With what encounter so uncurrent I
Have strain'd, to appear thus: if one jot beyond
The bound of honour, or in act or will
That way inclining, harden'd be the hearts
Of all that hear me, and my near'st of kin
Cry, Fie upon my grave!
Leon. I ne'er heard yet
That any of these bolder vices wanted
Less impudence to gainsay what they did
Than to perform it first.
Her. That's true enough;
Though 'tis a saying, sir, not due to me.
Leon. You will not own it.
Her. More than mistress of
Which comes to me in name of fault, I must not
At all acknowledge. For Polixenes,—
With whom I am accus'd,—I do confess
I lov'd him, as in honour he requir'd;
With such a kind of love as might become
A lady like me; with a love even such,
So and no other, as yourself commanded:
Which not to have done, I think had been in me
Both disobedience and ingratitude [spoke
To you and toward your friend; whose love had
Even since it could speak from an infant, freely,
That it was yours. Now, for conspiracy,
I know not how it tastes; though it be dish'd
For me to try how: all I know of it
Is, that Camillo was an honest man,
And why he left your court, the gods themselves,
Wotting no more than I, are ignorant.
Leon. You knew of his departure, as you know
What you have underta'en to do in's absence.
Her. Sir,
You speak a language that I understand not:
My life stands in the level of your dreams,
Which I'll lay down.
Leon. Your actions are my dreams;
You had a bastard by Polixenes, [shame,—
And I but dream'd it:—as you were past all
Those of your fact are so,—so past all truth:

Which to deny concerns more than avails; for
         as
Thy brat hath been cast out, like to itself,
No father owning it,—which is, indeed,
More criminal in thee than it,—so thou
Shalt feel our justice; in whose easiest passage
Look for no less than death.
  Her.   Sir, spare your threats:
The bug which you would fright me with, I seek
To me can life be no commodity:
The crown and comfort of my life, your favour,
I do give lost; for I do feel it gone,
But know not how it went: my second joy,
And first-fruits of my body, from his presence
I am barr'd, like one infectious: my third com-
         fort,
Starr'd most unluckily, is from my breast,—
The innocent milk in its most innocent mouth,—
Hal'd out to murder: myself on every post
Proclaim'd a strumpet; with immodest hatred,
The child-bed privilege denied, which 'longs
To women of all fashion; lastly, hurried
Here to this place, i' the open air, before
I have got strength of limit. Now, my liege,
Tell me what blessings I have here alive,
That I should fear to die? Therefore, proceed.
But yet hear this; mistake me not;—no life,—
I prize it not a straw,—but for mine honour
(Which I would free), if I shall be condemn'd
Upon surmises—all proofs sleeping else,
But what your jealousies awake—I tell you
'Tis rigour, and not law.—Your honours all,
I do refer me to the oracle:
Apollo be my judge!
  1 *Lord.*   This your request
Is altogether just: therefore, bring forth,
And in Apollo's name, his oracle:
                 [*Exeunt certain* Officers.
  Her. The Emperor of Russia was my father;
O that he were alive, and here beholding
His daughter's trial! that he did but see
The flatness of my misery; yet with eyes
Of pity, not revenge!

Re-enter Officers, *with* CLEOMENES *and* DION.

  Offi. You here shall swear upon this sword of
         justice,
That you, Cleomenes and Dion, have
Been both at Delphos, and from thence have
         brought
This seal'd-up oracle, by the hand deliver'd
Of great Apollo's priest; and that, since then,
You have not dar'd to break the holy seal,
Nor read the secrets in't.
  Cleo. Dion.   All this we swear.
  Leon. Break up the seals and read.
  Offi. [*Reads.*] Hermione *is chaste;* Polixenes
blameless; Camillo *a true subject;* Leontes *a
jealous tyrant; his innocent babe truly begotten;
and the king shall live without an heir, if that
which is lost be not found.*
  Lords. Now blessed be the great Apollo!
  Her.   Praised!
  Leon. Hast thou read truth?

  Offi.   Ay, my lord; even so
As it is here set down.
  Leon. There is no truth at all i' the oracle:
The sessions shall proceed: this is mere false-
         hood!

         Enter a Servant *hastily.*

  Serv. My lord the king, the king!
  Leon.   What is the business?
  Serv. O sir, I shall be hated to report it:
The prince your son, with mere conceit and fear
Of the queen's speed, is gone.
  Leon.   How! gone?
  Serv.   Is dead.
  Leon. Apollo's angry; and the heavens them-
         selves
Do strike at my injustice.   [HERMIONE *faints.*
         How now there!
  Paul. This news is mortal to the queen:—
         Look down
And see what death is doing.
  Leon.   Take her hence:
Her heart is but o'ercharg'd; she will recover.—
I have too much believ'd mine own suspicion:—
Beseech you, tenderly apply to her
Some remedies for life.—Apollo, pardon
         [*Exeunt* PAUL. *and* Ladies, *with* HER.
My great profaneness 'gainst thine oracle!—
I'll reconcile me to Polixenes;
New woo my queen; recall the good Camillo,
Whom I proclaim a man of truth, of mercy;
For, being transported by my jealousies
To bloody thoughts and to revenge, I chose
Camillo for the minister, to poison
My friend Polixenes: which had been done,
But that the good mind of Camillo tardied
My swift command, though I with death and
         with
Reward did threaten and encourage him,
Not doing it and being done: he, most humane,
And fill'd with honour, to my kingly guest
Unclasp'd my practice; quit his fortunes here,
Which you knew great; and to the certain
         hazard
Of all incertainties himself commended,
No richer than his honour:—How he glisters
Thorough my rust! and how his piety
Does my deeds make the blacker!

         Re-enter PAULINA

  Paul.   Woe the while!
O, cut my lace, lest my heart, cracking it,
Break too!
  1 *Lord.* What fit is this, good lady?
  Paul. What studied torments, tyrant, hast
         for me?   [boiling
What wheels? racks? fires? what flaying?
In leads or oils? what old or newer torture
Must I receive, whose every word deserves
To taste of thy most worst? Thy tyranny
Together working with thy jealousies,—
Fancies too weak for boys, too green and idle
For girls of nine,—O, think what they have
         done,

And then run mad indeed,—stark mad! for all
Thy by-gone fooleries were but spices of it.
That thou betray'dst Polixenes, 'twas nothing;
That did but show thee, of a fool, inconstant,
And damnable ingrateful; nor was't much
Thou wouldst have poison'd good Camillo's
    honour,
To have him kill a king; poor trespasses,—
More monstrous standing by: whereof I reckon
The casting forth to crows thy baby daughter,
To be or none, or little; though a devil
Would have shed water out of fire ere don't:
Nor is't directly laid to thee, the death
Of the young prince, whose honourable
    thoughts,—   [heart
Thoughts high for one so tender,—cleft the
That could conceive a gross and foolish sire
Blemish'd his gracious dam: this is not—no,
Laid to thy answer: but the last,—O lords,
When I have said, cry, Woe!—the queen, the
    queen
The sweetest, dearest creature's dead; and
    vengeance for't
Nor dropp'd down yet.

    1 *Lord.*   The higher powers forbid!
    Paul. I say she's dead: I'll swear't. If word
        nor oath
Prevail not, go and see: if you can bring
Tincture, or lustre, in her lip, her eye,
Heat outwardly or breath within, I'll serve you
As I would do the gods.—But, O thou tyrant!
Do not repent these things; for they are heavier
Than all thy woes can stir; therefore betake
    thee
To nothing but despair. A thousand knees
Ten thousand years together, naked, fasting,
Upon a barren mountain, and still winter
In storm perpetual, could not move the gods
To look that way thou wert.

    Leon.   Go on, go on:
Thou canst not speak too much; I have de-
    serv'd
All tongues to talk their bitterest!

    1 *Lord.*   Say no more;
Howe'er the business goes, you have made fault
I' the boldness of your speech.

    Paul.   I am sorry for't:
All faults I make, when I shall come to know
    them,
I do repent. Alas, I have show'd too much
The rashness of a woman: he is touch'd
To the noble heart.—What's gone, and what's
    past help,
Should be past grief: do not receive affliction
At my petition; I beseech you, rather
Let me be punish'd, that have minded you
Of what you should forget. Now, good my liege,
Sir, royal sir, forgive a foolish woman:
The love I bore your queen,—lo, fool again!—
I'll speak of her no more, nor of your children;
I'll not remember you of my own lord,
Who is lost too: take your patience to you,
And I'll say nothing.

    Leon.   Thou didst speak but well,

When most the truth; which I receive much
    better
Than to be pitied of thee. Pr'ythee, bring me
To the dead bodies of my queen and son:
One grave shall be for both; upon them shall
The causes of their death appear, unto
Our shame perpetual. Once a day I'll visit
The chapel where they lie; and tears shed there
Shall be my recreation: so long as nature
Will bear up with this exercise, so long
I daily vow to use it.—Come, and lead me
To these sorrows.   [*Exeunt.*

SCENE III.—BOHEMIA. *A desert Country near
the Sea.*

Enter ANTIGONUS *with the Child, and a* Mariner.

    Ant. Thou art perfect, then, our ship hath
    touch'd upon
The deserts of Bohemia?

    Mar. Ay, my lord; and fear
We have landed in ill time: the skies look
    grimly,   [science,
And threaten present blusters. In my con-
The heavens with that we have in hand are
    angry,
And frown upon's.

    Ant. Their sacred will be done!—Go, get
    aboard;
Look to thy bark: I'll not be long before
I call upon thee.

    Mar. Make your best haste; and go not
Too far i' the land: 'tis like to be loud weather:
Besides, this place is famous for the creatures
Of prey that keep upon't.

    Ant.   Go thou away:
I'll follow instantly.

    Mar. I am glad at heart
To be so rid o' the business.   [*Exit.*

    Ant.   Come, poor babe:—
I have heard (but not believ'd), the spirits of
    the dead
May walk again: if such thing be, thy mother
Appear'd to me last night; for ne'er was dream
So like a waking. To me comes a creature,
Sometimes her head on one side, some another:
I never saw a vessel of like sorrow,
So fill'd and so becoming: in pure white robes,
Like very sanctity, she did approach
My cabin where I lay: thrice bow'd before me:
And, gasping to begin some speech, her eyes
Became two spouts: the fury spent, anon
Did this break from her: *Good* Antigonus,
Since fate, against thy better disposition,
Hath made thy person for the thrower-out
Of my poor babe, according to thine oath,—
Places remote enough are in Bohemia,
There weep, and leave it crying; and, for the babe
Is counted lost for ever, Perdita,
I pr'ythee call't. For this ungentle business,
Put on thee by my lord, thou ne'er shalt see
Thy wife Paulina *more:*—and so, with shrieks,
She melted into air. Affrighted much,
I did in time collect myself; and thought

This was so, and no slumber. Dreams are toys;
Yet, for this once, yea, superstitiously,
I will be squar'd by this. I do believe
Hermione hath suffer'd death; and that
Apollo would, this being indeed the issue
Of King Polixenes, it should here be laid,
Either for life or death, upon the earth
Of its right father. Blossom, speed thee well!
                                        [*Laying down the child.*
There lie; and there thy character: there these;
                                        [*Laying down a bundle.*
Which may if fortune please, both breed thee,
        pretty,
And still rest thine.—The storm begins:—poor
        wretch,
That, for thy mother's fault, art thus expos'd
To loss and what may follow!—Weep I cannot,
But my heart bleeds: and most accurs'd am I
To be by oath enjoin'd to this.—Farewell!
The day frowns more and more:—thou'rt like
        to have
A lullaby too rough:—I never saw
The heavens so dim by day. A savage clamour!—
Well may I get aboard!—This is the chace:
I am gone for ever!   [*Exit, pursued by a bear.*

Enter an old Shepherd.

Shep. I would there were no age between ten
and three-and-twenty, or that youth would
sleep out the rest; for there is nothing in the between but getting wenches with child, wronging
the ancientry, stealing, fighting.—Hark you
now!—Would any but these boiled brains of
nineteen and two-and-twenty hunt this weather? They have scared away two of my best
sheep, which I fear the wolf will sooner find
than the master: if any where I have them, 'tis
by the sea-side, browsing of ivy.—Good luck,
an't be thy will! what have we here? [*Taking up
the child.*] Mercy on's, a bairn; a very pretty
bairn! A boy or a child, I wonder? A pretty one;
a very pretty one: sure, some scape: though I
am not bookish, yet I can read waiting-gentlewoman in the scape. This has been some stair-
work, some trunk-work, some behind-door-
work: they were warmer that got this than the
poor thing is here. I'll take it up for pity: yet
I'll tarry till my son comes; he hollaed but even
now.—Whoa, ho hoa!

Clo. [*Within.*] Hilloa, loa!

Shep. What, art so near? If thou'lt see a
thing to talk on when thou art dead and rotten,
come hither.

Enter Clown.

What ailest thou man?

Clo. I have seen two such sights, by sea and
by land!—but I am not to say it is a sea, for it
is now the sky: betwixt the firmament and it,
you cannot thrust a bodkin's point.

Shep. Why, boy, how is it?

Clo. I would you did but see how it chafes,
how it rages, how it takes up the shore! but
that's not to the point. O, the most piteous cry

of the poor souls! sometimes to see 'em, and not
to see 'em; now the ship boring the moon with
her mainmast, and anon swallowed with yest
and froth, as you'd thrust a cork in a hogshead.
And then for the land service,—to see how the
bear tore out his shoulder-bone; how he cried to
me for help, and said his name was Antigonus,
a nobleman.—But to make an end of the ship,
—to see how the sea flap-dragoned it:—but,
first, how the poor souls roared, and the sea
mocked them;—and how the poor gentleman
roared, and the bear mocked him;—both roaring louder than the sea or weather.

Shep. Name of mercy! when was this, boy?

Clo. Now, now; I have not winked since I
saw these sights: the men are not yet cold under
water, nor the bear half dined on the gentleman; he's at it now.

Shep. Would I had been by to have helped
the old man!

Clo. I would you had been by the ship-side,
to have helped her: there your charity would
have lacked footing.   [*Aside.*

Shep. Heavy matters! heavy matters! but
look thee here, boy. Now bless thyself: thou
mettest with things dying, I with things new-
born. Here's a sight for thee; look thee, a bear-
ing-cloth for a squire's child! look thee here!
take up, take up, boy; open't. So, let's see:—it
was told me I should be rich by the fairies: this
is some changeling:—open't. What's within,
boy?

Clo. You're a made old man; if the sins of
your youth are forgiven you, you're well to live.
Gold! all gold!

Shep. This is fairy-gold, boy, and 'twill
prove so: up with it, keep it close: home, home,
the next way! We are lucky, boy; and to be so
still requires nothing but secrecy—Let my
sheep go:—come, good boy, the next way
home.

Clo. Go you the next way with your findings.
I'll go see if the bear be gone from the gentleman, and how much he hath eaten: they are
never curst but when they are hungry: if there
be any of him left, I'll bury it.

Shep. That's a good deed. If thou mayest
discern by that which is left of him what he is,
fetch me to the sight of him.

Clo. Marry, will I; and you shall help to put
him i' the ground.

Shep. 'Tis a lucky day, boy; and we'll do
good deeds on't.   [*Exeunt.*

ACT IV.

Enter TIME, *as Chorus.*

Time. I,—that please some, try all; both joy
        and terror
Of good and bad; that make and unfold error,—
Now take upon me, in the name of Time,
To use my wings. Impute it not a crime
To me or my swift passage, that I slide

O'er sixteen years, and leave the growth un-
        tried
Of that wide gap, since it is in my power
To o'erthrow law, and in one self-born hour
To plant and o'erwhelm custom. Let me pass
The same I am, ere ancient'st order was,
Or what is now received: I witness to
The times that brought them in; so shall I do
To the freshest things now reigning, and make
        stale
The glistering of this present, as my tale
Now seems to it. Your patience this allowing,
I turn my glass, and give my scene such grow-
        ing
As you had slept between. Leontes leaving
The effects of his fond jealousies, so grieving
That he shuts up himself; imagine me,
Gentle spectators, that I now may be
In fair Bohemia; and remember well,
I mention'd a son o' the king's, which Florizel
I now name to you; and with speed so pace
To speak of Perdita, now grown in grace
Equal with wondering: what of her ensues,
I list not prophesy; but let Time's news
Be known when 'tis brought forth:—a shep-
        herd's daughter,
And what to her adheres, which follows after,
Is the argument of Time. Of this allow,
If ever you have spent time worse ere now;
If never, yet that Time himself doth say
He wishes earnestly you never may.   [*Exit.*

SCENE I.—BOHEMIA. *A Room in the Palace of*
        POLIXENES.

Enter POLIXENES *and* CAMILLO.

Pol. I pray thee, good Camillo, be no more
importunate: 'tis a sickness denying thee anything; a death to grant this.

Cam. It is fifteen years since I saw my
country; though I have for the most part been
aired abroad, I desire to lay my bones there.
Besides, the penitent king, my master, hath
sent for me; to whose feeling sorrows I might
be some allay, or I o'erween to think so,—
which is another spur to my departure.

Pol. As thou lovest me, Camillo, wipe not
out the rest of thy services by leaving me now:
the need I have of thee, thine own goodness
hath made; better not to have had thee than
thus to want thee; thou, having made me businesses which none without thee can sufficiently
manage, must either stay to execute them thyself, or take away with thee the very services
thou hast done; which if I have not enough
considered,—as too much I cannot,—to be
more thankful to thee shall be my study; and
my profit therein the heaping friendships. Of
that fatal country Sicilia, pr'ythee, speak no
more; whose very naming punishes me with the
remembrance of that penitent, as thou call'st
him, and reconciled king, my brother; whose
loss of his most precious queen and children are
even now to be afresh lamented. Say to me,
when sawest thou the Prince Florizel, my son?
Kings are no less unhappy, their issue not being
gracious, than they are in losing them, when
they have approved their virtues.

Cam. Sir, it is three days since I saw the
prince. What his happier affairs may be, are
to me unknown; but I have missingly noted he
is of late much retired from court, and is less
frequent to his princely exercises than formerly
he hath appeared.

Pol. I have considered so much, Camillo,
and with some care; so far, that I have eyes
under my service which look upon his removed-
ness; from whom I have this intelligence,—that
he is seldom from the house of a most homely
shepherd; a man, they say, that from very
nothing, and beyond the imagination of his
neighbours, is grown into an unspeakable
estate.

Cam. I have heard, sir, of such a man, who
hath a daughter of most rare note: the report
of her is extended more than can be thought to
begin from such a cottage.

Pol. That's likewise part of my intelligence:
but I fear the angle that plucks our son thither.
Thou shalt accompany us to the place; where
we will, not appearing what we are, have some
question with the shepherd; from whose simplicity I think it not uneasy to get the cause
of my son's resort thither. Pr'ythee, be my
present partner in this business, and lay aside
the thoughts of Sicilia.

Cam. I willingly obey your command.

Pol. My best Camillo!—We must disguise
ourselves.   [*Exeunt.*

SCENE II.—*The same. A road near the*
        Shepherd's *Cottage.*

Enter AUTOLYCUS, *singing.*

When daffodils begin to peer,—
    With, hey! the doxy over the dale,—
Why, then comes in the sweet o' the year;
    For the red blood reigns in the winter's pale.

The white sheet bleaching on the hedge,—
    With, hey! the sweet birds, O, how they sing!—
Doth set my pugging tooth on edge;
    For a quart of ale is a dish for a king.

The lark, that tirra-lirra chants,—
    With, hey! with, hey! the thrush and the jay,—
Are summer songs for me and my aunts,
    While we lie tumbling in the hay.

I have served Prince Florizel, and, in my time,
wore three-pile; but now I am out of service:

But shall I go mourn for that, my dear?
    The pale moon shines by night:
And when I wander here and there,
    I then do most go right.

If tinkers may have leave to live,
    And bear the sow-skin budget,
Then my account I well may give
    And in the stocks avouch it.

My traffic is sheets; when the kite builds, look to lesser linen. My father named me Autolycus; who being, as I am, littered under Mercury, was likewise a snapper-up of unconsidered trifles. With die and drab I purchased this caparison; and my revenue is the silly-cheat: gallows and knock are too powerful on the highway; beating and hanging are terrors to me; for the life to come, I sleep out the thought of it.—A prize! a prize!

Enter Clown.

Clo. Let me see:—every 'leven wether tods; every tod yields pound and odd shilling; fifteen hundred shorn, what comes the wool to?

Aut. If the springe hold, the cock's mine.
[*Aside.*

Clo. I cannot do't without counters.—Let me see; what am I to buy for our sheep-shearing feast? *Three pound of sugar; five pound of currants; rice*—what will this sister of mine do with rice? But my father hath made her mistress of the feast, and she lays it on. She hath made me four-and-twenty nosegays for the shearers,—three-man song-men all, and very good ones; but they are most of them means and bases; but one puritan amongst them, and he sings psalms to hornpipes. I must have *saffron*, to colour the warden pies; *mace—dates,* —none; that's out of my note; *nutmegs, seven; a race or two of ginger,*—but that I may beg; *four pound of prunes, and as many of raisins o' the sun.*

Aut. O that ever I was born!
[*Grovelling on the ground.*

Clo. I' the name of me,—

Aut. O, help me, help me! pluck but off these rags; and then, death, death!

Clo. Alack, poor soul! thou hast need of more rags to lay on thee, rather than have these off.

Aut. O, sir, the loathsomeness of them offends me more than the stripes I have received, which are mighty ones and millions.

Clo. Alas, poor man! a million of beating may come to a great matter.

Aut. I am robbed, sir, and beaten; my money and apparel ta'en from me, and these detestable things put upon me.

Clo. What, by a horseman or a footman?

Aut. A footman, sweet sir, a footman.

Clo. Indeed, he should be a footman, by the garments he has left with thee: if this be a horseman's coat, it hath seen very hot service. Lend me thy hand, I'll help thee: come, lend me thy hand.
[*Helping him up.*

Aut. O, good sir, tenderly, O!

Clo. Alas, poor soul!

Aut. Oh, good sir, softly, good sir: I fear, sir, my shoulder blade is out.

Clo. How now! canst stand?

Aut. Softly, dear sir! [*picks his pocket*] good sir, softly; you ha' done me a charitable office.

Clo. Dost lack any money? I have a little money for thee.

Aut. No, good sweet sir; no, I beseech you, sir: I have a kinsman not past three quarters of a mile hence, unto whom I was going; I shall there have money or anything I want: offer me no money, I pray you; that kills my heart.

Clo. What manner of fellow was he that robbed you?

Aut. A fellow, sir, that I have known to go about with troll-my-dames: I knew him once a servant of the prince: I cannot tell, good sir, for which of his virtues it was, but he was certainly whipped out of the court.

Clo. His vices, you would say; there's no virtue whipped out of the court: they cherish it, to make it stay there; and yet it will no more but abide.

Aut. Vices, I would say, sir. I know this man well: he hath been since an ape-bearer; then a process-server, a bailiff; then he compassed a motion of the Prodigal Son, and married a tinker's wife within a mile where my land and living lies; and, having flown over many knavish professions, he settled only in rogue: some call him Autolycus.

Clo. Out upon him! prig, for my life, prig. he haunts wakes, fairs, and bear-baitings.

Aut. Very true, sir; he, sir, he; that's the rogue that put me into this apparel.

Clo. Not a more cowardly rogue in all Bohemia; if you had but looked big and spit at him, he'd have run.

Aut. I must confess to you, sir, I am no fighter: I am false of heart that way; and that he knew, I warrant him.

Clo. How do you know?

Aut. Sweet sir, much better than I was; I can stand and walk: I will even take my leave of you, and pace softly towards my kinsman's.

Clo. Shall I bring thee on the way?

Aut. No, good-faced sir; no, sweet sir.

Clo. Then fare thee well: I must go buy spices for our sheep-shearing.

Aut. Prosper you, sweet sir! [*Exit* Clown.] Your purse is not hot enough to purchase your spice. I'll be with you at your sheep-shearing too. If I make not this cheat bring out another, and the shearers prove sheep, let me be enrolled, and my name put in the book of virtue!
[*Sings.*

Jog on, jog on, the footpath way,
    And merrily hent the stile-a:
A merry heart goes all the day,
    Your sad tires in a mile-a. [*Exit.*

SCENE III.—*The same. A Shepherd's Cottage.*

Enter FLORIZEL *and* PERDITA.

Flo. These your unusual weeds to each part
        of you
Do give a life: no shepherdess, but Flora [ing
Peering in April's front. This your sheep-shear-
Is as a meeting of the petty gods,

And you the queen on't.

Per.   Sir, my gracious lord,
To chide at your extremes it not becomes me,—
O, pardon that I name them!—your high self,
The gracious mark o' the land, you have
          obscur'd
With a swain's wearing; and me, poor lowly
          maid,
Most goddess-like prank'd up. But that our
          feasts
In every mess have folly, and the feeders
Digest it with a custom, I should blush
To see you so attir'd; swoon, I think,
To show myself a glass.

Flo.   I bless the time
When my good falcon made her flight across
Thy father's ground.

Per.   Now Jove afford you cause!
To me the difference forges dread: your great-
          ness
Hath not been us'd to fear. Even now I tremble
To think your father, by some accident,
Should pass this way, as you did. O, the fates!
How would he look to see his work, so noble,
Vilely bound up? What would he say? Or how
Should I, in these my borrow'd flaunts, behold
The sternness of his presence?

Flo.   Apprehend
Nothing but jollity. The gods themselves,
Humbling their deities to love, have taken
The shapes of beasts upon them: Jupiter
Became a bull, and bellow'd; the green Nep-
          tune
A ram, and bleated; and the fire-rob'd god,
Golden Apollo, a poor humble swain,
As I seem now:—their transformations
Were never for a piece of beauty rarer,—
Nor in a way so chaste, since my desires
Run not before mine honour, nor my lusts
Burn hotter than my faith.

Per.   O, but, sir,
Your resolution cannot hold, when 'tis
Oppos'd, as it must be, by the power of the
          king:
One of these two must be necessities,
Which then will speak, that you must change
          this purpose,
Or I my life.

Flo.   Thou dearest Perdita,   [not
With these forc'd thoughts, I pr'ythee, darken
The mirth o' the feast: or I'll be thine, my fair,
Or not my father's; for I cannot be
Mine own, nor anything to any, if
I be not thine: to this I am most constant,
Though destiny say no. Be merry, gentle:
Strangle such thoughts as these with anything
That you behold the while. Your guests are
          coming:
Lift up your countenance, as it were the day
Of celebration of that nuptial which
We two have sworn shall come.

Per.   O lady Fortune,
Stand you auspicious!

Flo.   See, your guests approach:

Address yourself to entertain them sprightly,
And let's be red with mirth.

Enter Shepherd, *with* POLIXENES *and* CAM-
ILLO *disguised;* Clown, MOPSA, DORCAS,
with others.

Shep. Fie, daughter! when my old wife liv'd,
          upon
This day she was both pantler, butler, cook;
Both dame and servant; welcom'd all; serv'd
          all;   [here
Would sing her song and dance her turn; now
At upper end o' the table, now i' the middle;
On his shoulder, and his; her face o' fire   [it,
With labour; and the thing she took to quench
She would to each one sip. You are retir'd,
As if you were a feasted one, and not
The hostess of the meeting: pray you, bid
These unknown friends to us welcome; for it is
A way to make us better friends, more known.
Come, quench your blushes, and present your-
          self
That which you are, mistress of the feast: come
          on,
And bid us welcome to your sheep-shearing,
As your good flock shall prosper.

Per.   Sir, welcome! [*To* POL.
It is my father's will I should take on me
The hostess-ship o' the day:—You're welcome,
          sir!   [*To* CAMILLO.
Give me those flowers there, Dorcas.—Rev-
          erend sirs,
For you there's rosemary and rue; these keep
Seeming and savour all the winter long:
Grace and remembrance be to you both,
And welcome to our shearing!

Pol.   Shepherdess—
A fair one are you!—well you fit our ages
With flowers of winter.

Per.   Sir, the year growing ancient,—
Not yet on summer's death, nor on the birth
Of trembling winter,—the fairest flowers o' the
          season
Are our carnations, and streak'd gillyvors,
Which some call nature's bastards: of that kind
Our rustic garden's barren; and I care not
To get slips of them.

Pol.   Wherefore, gentle maiden,
Do you neglect them?

Per.   For I have heard it said
There is an art which, in their piedness, shares
With great creating nature.

Pol.   Say there be;
Yet nature is made better by no mean,
But nature makes that mean; so, o'er that
          art
Which you say adds to nature, is an art
That nature makes. You see, sweet maid, we
          marry
A gentler scion to the wildest stock,
And make conceive a bark of baser kind
By bud of nobler race. This is an art   [but
Which does mend nature,—change it rather;
The art itself is nature.

Per.   So it is.   [vors,
Pol. Then make your garden rich in gilly-
And do not call them bastards.
    Per.   I'll not put
The dibble in earth to set one slip of them;
No more than, were I painted, I would wish
This youth would say, 'twere well, and only
          therefore
Desire to breed by me.—Here's flowers for you;
Hot lavender, mints, savory, marjoram;
The marigold, that goes to bed with the sun,
And with him rises weeping; these are flowers
Of middle summer, and I think they are given
To men of middle age. You're very welcome!
    Cam. I should leave grazing, were I of your
          flock,
And only live by gazing.
    Per.   Out, alas!
You'd be so lean that blasts of January
Would blow you through and through.—Now,
          my fairest friend,   [might
I would I had some flowers o' the spring that
Become your time of day;—and yours, and
          yours,
That wear upon your virgin branches yet
Your maidenheads growing.—O Proserpina,
For the flowers now, that, frighted, thou lett'st
          fall
From Dis's waggon!—daffodils,
That come before the swallow dares, and take
The winds of March with beauty; violets dim,
But sweeter than the lids of Juno's eyes
Or Cytherea's breath; pale primroses,
That die unmarried ere they can behold
Bright Phœbus in his strength,—a malady
Most incident to maids; bold oxlips, and
The crown-imperial; lilies of all kinds,
The flower-de-luce being one!—O, these I lack,
To make you garlands of; and, my sweet friend,
To strew him o'er and o'er!
    Flo.   What, like a corse?
    Per. No; like a bank for love to lie and play
          on;
Not like a corse; or if,—not to be buried,
But quick, and in mine arms. Come, take your
          flowers;
Methinks I play as I have seen them do
In Whitsun pastorals: sure, this robe of mine
Does change my disposition.
    Flo.   What you do
Still betters what is done. When you speak,
          sweet,
I'd have you do it ever; when you sing,
I'd have you buy and sell so; so give alms;
Pray so; and, for the ordering your affairs,
To sing them too: when you dance, I wish you
A wave o' the sea, that might ever do
Nothing but that; move still, still so, and own
No other function: each your doing,
So singular in each particular,
Crowns what you are doing in the present
          deeds,
That all your acts are queens.
    Per.   O Doricles,

Your praises are too large: but that your youth,
And the true blood which peeps fairly through it,
Do plainly give you out an unstained shepherd,
With wisdom I might fear, my Doricles,
You woo'd me the false way.
    Flo.   I think you have
As little skill to fear as I have purpose
To put you to't.—But, come; our dance, I
          pray:
Your hand, my Perdita; so turtles pair
That never mean to part.
    Pcr.   I'll swear for 'em.
    Pol. This is the prettiest low-born lass that
          ever   [seems
Ran on the green sward: nothing she does or
But smacks of something greater than herself,
Too noble for this place.
    Cam. He tells her something   [is
That makes her blood look out: good sooth, she
The queen of curds and cream.
    Clo.   Come on, strike up.
    Dor. Mopsa must be your mistress: marry,
          garlic,
To mend her kissing with.
    Mop.   Now, in good time!
    Clo. Not a word, a word; we stand upon our
          manners.—
Come, strike up.   [*Music.*

Here a dance of Shepherds *and* Shepherdesses.

    Pol. Pray, good shepherd, what
Fair swain is this which dances with your
          daughter?   [himself
    Shep. They call him Doricles; and boasts
To have a worthy feeding: but I have it
Upon his own report, and I believe it;
He looks like sooth. He says he loves my
          daughter:
I think so too; for never gaz'd the moon
Upon the water as he'll stand, and read,
As 'twere, my daughter's eyes: and, to be plain,
I think there is not half a kiss to choose
Who loves another best.
    Pol.   She dances featly. [it,
    Shep. So she does anything; though I report
That should be silent: if young Doricles
Do light upon her, she shall bring him that
Which he not dreams of.

Enter a Servant.

    Serv. O, master, if you did but hear the ped-
lar at the door, you would never dance again
after a tabor and pipe; no, the bagpipe could
not move you: he sings several tunes faster
than you'll tell money: he utters them as he
had eaten ballads, and all men's ears grew to
his tunes.
    Clo. He could never come better: he shall
come in: I love a ballad but even too well; if
it be doleful matter merrily set down, or a very
pleasant thing indeed and sung lamentably.
    Serv. He hath songs for man or woman of
all sizes; no milliner can so fit his customers
with gloves: he has the prettiest love-songs for

maids; so without bawdry, which is strange; with such delicate burdens of *dildos* and *fadings, jump her and thump her;* and where some stretch-mouth'd rascal would, as it were, mean mischief, and break a foul gap into the matter, he makes the maid to answer, *Whoop, do me no harm, good man;* puts him off, slights him, with *Whoop, do me no harm, good man.*

Pol. This is a brave fellow.

Clo. Believe me, thou talkest of an admirable conceited fellow. Has he any unbraided wares?

Serv. He hath ribands of all the colours i' the rainbow; points more than all the lawyers in Bohemia can learnedly handle, though they come to him by the gross; inkles, caddisses, cambrics, lawns: why he sings 'em over as they were gods or goddesses; you would think a smock were a she-angel, he so chants to the sleeve-hand, and the work about the square on't.

Clo. Pr'ythee, bring him in; and let him approach singing.

Per. Forewarn him that he use no scurrilous words in his tunes. [*Exit* Servant.

Clo. You have of these pedlars that have more in 'em than you'd think, sister.

Per. Ay, good brother, or go about to think.

Enter AUTOLYCUS, *singing.*

Lawn as white as driven snow;
Cyprus black as e'er was crow;
Gloves as sweet as damask-roses;
Masks for faces and for noses;
Bugle-bracelet, necklace amber,
Perfume for a lady's chamber;
Golden quoifs and stomachers,
For my lads to give their dears;
Pins and poking-sticks of steel,
What maids lack from head to heel:
Come, buy of me, come; come buy, come buy;
Buy, lads, or else your lasses cry:
Come, buy.

Clo. If I were not in love with Mopsa, thou shouldst take no money of me; but being enthralled as I am, it will also be the bondage of certain ribands and gloves.

Mop. I was promised them against the feast; but they come not too late now.

Dor. He hath promised you more than that, or there be liars.

Mop. He hath paid you all he promised you: may be he has paid you more,—which will shame you to give him again.

Clo. Is there no manners left among maids? will they wear their plackets where they should bear their faces? Is there not milking-time, when you are going to bed, or kiln-hole, to whistle off these secrets, but you must be tittle-tattling before all our guests? 'tis well they are whispering. Clamour your tongues, and not a word more.

Mop. I have done. Come, you promised me a tawdry lace, and a pair of sweet gloves.

Clo. Have I not told thee how I was cozened by the way, and lost all my money?

Aut. And, indeed, sir, there are cozeners abroad; therefore it behoves men to be wary.

Clo. Fear not thou, man, thou shalt lose nothing here.

Aut. I hope so, sir; for I have about me many parcels of charge.

Clo. What hast here? ballads?

Mop. Pray now, buy some: I love a ballad in print a-life; for then we are sure they are true.

Aut. Here's one to a very doleful tune. How a usurer's wife was brought to bed of twenty money-bags at a burden, and how she longed to eat adders' heads and toads carbonadoed.

Mop. Is it true, think you?

Aut. Very true; and but a month old.

Dor. Bless me from marrying a usurer!

Aut. Here's the midwife's name to't, one Mistress Taleporter, and five or six honest wives that were present. Why should I carry lies abroad?

Mop. Pray you now, buy it.

Clo. Come on, lay it by; and let's first see more ballads; we'll buy the other things anon.

Aut. Here's another ballad, of a fish that appeared upon the coast on Wednesday the fourscore of April, forty thousand fathom above water, and sung this ballad against the hard hearts of maids: it was thought she was a woman, and was turned into a cold fish for she would not exchange flesh with one that loved her. The ballad is very pitiful, and as true.

Dor. Is it true too, think you?

Aut. Five justices' hands at it; and witnesses more than my pack will hold.

Clo. Lay it by too: another.

Aut. This is a merry ballad; but a very pretty one.

Mop. Let's have some merry ones.

Aut. Why, this is a passing merry one, and goes to the tune of *Two maids wooing a man:* there's scarce a maid westward but she sings it: 'tis in request, I can tell you.

Mop. We can both sing it: if thou'lt bear a part thou shalt hear; 'tis in three parts.

Dor. We had the tune on't a month ago.

Aut. I can bear my part; you must know 'tis my occupation: have at it with you.

SONG.

A. Get you hence, for I must go;
Where, it fits not you to know.
    D. Whither? *M.* O, whither? *D.* Whither?
M. It becomes thy oath full well,
Thou to me thy secrets tell:
    D. Me too, let me go thither.

M. Or thou go'st to the grange or mill:
D. If to either, thou dost ill.
    A. Neither. *D.* What, neither? *A.* Neither.
D. Thou hast sworn my love to be;
M. Thou hast sworn it more to me;
    Then, whither go'st —say, whither?

Clo. We'll have this song out anon by ourselves; my father and the gentlemen are in sad
talk, and we'll not trouble them.—Come, bring
away thy pack after me.—Wenches, I'll buy
for you both:—Pedlar, let's have the first
choice.—Follow me, girls.

Aut. And you shall pay well for 'em.
[*Aside.*

Will you buy any tape,
Or lace for your cape,
My dainty duck, my dear-a?
Any silk, any thread,
Any toys, for your head,
Of the new'st and fin'st, fin'st wear-a?
Come to the pedlar;
Money's a meddler,
That doth utter all men's ware-a.

[*Exeunt* Clown, AUT., DOR., *and* MOP.

Re-enter Servant.

Serv. Master, there is three carters, three
shepherds, three neat-herds, three swine-herds,
that have made themselves all men of hair;
they call themselves saltiers: and they have a
dance which the wenches say is a gallimaufry
of gambols, because they are not in't; but they
themselves are o' the mind (if it be not too
rough for some, that know little but bowling)
it will please plentifully.

Shep. Away! we'll none on't: here has been
too much homely foolery already.—I know,
sir, we weary you.

Pol. You weary those that refresh us: pray
let's see these four threes of herdsmen.

Serv. One three of them, by their own report, sir, hath danced before the king; and,
not the worst of the three but jumps twelve
foot and a half by the squire.

Shep. Leave your prating: since these good
men are pleased, let them come in; but quickly
now.

Serv. Why, they stay at door, sir. [*Exit.*

Enter Twelve Rustics, *habited like Satyrs.
They dance, and then exeunt.*

Pol. O father, you'll know more of that
hereafter.—
Is it not too far gone?—'Tis time to part
them.—
He's simple and tells much. [*Aside.*]—How
now, fair shepherd!
Your heart is full of something that does take
Your mind from feasting. Sooth, when I was
young,
And handed love as you do, I was wont
To load my she with knacks: I would have
ransack'd
The pedlar's silken treasury, and have pour'd it
To her acceptance; you have let him go,
And nothing marted with him. If your lass
Interpretation should abuse, and call this
Your lack of love or bounty, you were straited
For a reply, at least if you make a care
Of happy holding her.

Flo.　　　　　　Old sir, I know
She prizes not such trifles as these are:
The gifts she looks from me are pack'd and
lock'd
Up in my heart; which I have given already,
But not deliver'd.—O, hear me breathe my life
Before this ancient sir, who, it should seem,
Hath sometime lov'd,—I take thy hand! this
hand,
As soft as dove's down, and as white as it,
Or Ethiopian's tooth, or the fann'd snow that's
bolted
By the northern blasts twice o'er.

Pol. What follows this?—
How prettily the young swain seems to wash
The hand was fair before!—I have put you out:
But to your protestation; let me hear
What you profess.

Flo.　　　　　　Do, and be witness to't.

Pol. And this my neighbour, too?

Flo.　　　　　　And he, and more
Than he, and men,—the earth, the heavens,
and all:—　　　　　　[monarch,
That,—were I crown'd the most imperial
Thereof most worthy; were I the fairest youth
That ever made eye swerve; had force and
knowledge　　　　　　[them
More than was ever man's,—I would not prize
Without her love: for her employ them all;
Commend them, and condemn them, to her
service,
Or to their own perdition.

Pol.　　　　　　Fairly offer'd.

Cam. This shows a sound affection.

Shep.　　　　　　But, my daughter,
Say you the like to him?

Per.　　　　　　I cannot speak
So well, nothing so well; no, nor mean better:
By the pattern of mine own thoughts I cut out
The purity of his.

Shep.　　　　　　Take hands, a bargain!—
And, friends unknown, you shall bear witness
to't:
I give my daughter to him, and will make
Her portion equal his.

Flo.　　　　　　O, that must be
I' the virtue of your daughter: one being dead,
I shall have more than you can dream of yet;
Enough then for your wonder: but come on,
Contract us 'fore these witnesses.

Shep.　　　　　　Come, your hand;—
And, daughter, yours.

Pol.　　　　　　Soft, swain, awhile, beseech you;
Have you a father?

Flo.　　　　　　I have; but what of him?

Pol. Knows he of this?

Flo.　　　　　　He neither does nor shall.

Pol. Methinks a father
Is, at the nuptial of his son, a guest　　[more;
That best becomes the table. Pray you, once
Is not your father grown incapable
Of reasonable affairs? is he not stupid
With age and altering rheums? can he speak?
hear?

Know man from man? dispute his own estate?
Lies he not bed-rid? and again does nothing
But what he did being childish?

Flo.   No, good sir;
He has his health, and ampler strength indeed
Than most have of his age.

Pol.   By my white beard,
You offer him, if this be so, a wrong
Something unfilial: reason my son
Should choose himself a wife; but as good reason
The father,—all whose joy is nothing else
But fair posterity,—should hold some counsel
In such a business.

Flo.   I yield all this;
But, for some other reasons, my grave sir,
Which 'tis not fit you know, I not acquaint
My father of this business.

Pol.   Let him know't.

Flo. He shall not.

Pol.   Pr'ythee, let him.

Flo.   No, he must not.

Shep. Let him, my son: he shall not need to
    grieve
At knowing of thy choice.

Flo.   Come, come, he must not.—
Mark our contráct.

Pol.   Mark your divorce, young sir,
                    [*Discovering himself.*
Whom son I dare not call; thou art too base
To be acknowledged: thou a sceptre's heir,
That thus affect'st a sheep-hook!—Thou old
    traitor,
I am sorry that, by hanging thee, I can but
Shorten thy life one week.—And thou, fresh
    piece   [know
Of excellent witchcraft, who, of force, must
The royal fool thou cop'st with,—

Shep.   O, my heart!

Pol. I'll have thy beauty scratch'd with
    briers, and made   [boy,—
More homely than thy state.—For thee, fond
If I may ever know thou dost but sigh
That thou no more shalt see this knack,—as
    never   [cession;
I mean thou shalt,—we'll bar thee from suc-
Not hold thee of our blood, no, not our kin,
Far than Deucalion off,—mark thou my words:
Follow us to the court.—Thou churl, for this
    time,
Though full of our displeasure, yet we free thee
From the dead blow of it.—And you, enchant-
    ment,—
Worthy enough a herdsman; yea, him too
That makes himself, but for our honour therein,
Unworthy thee,—if ever henceforth thou
These rural latches to his entrance open,
Or hoop his body more with thy embraces,
I will devise a death as cruel for thee
As thou art tender to't.   [*Exit.*

Per.   Even here undone!
I was not much afeard: for once or twice
I was about to speak, and tell him plainly
The self-same sun that shines upon his court
Hides not his visage from our cottage, but

Looks on alike.—Will't please you, sir, be
    gone?   [*To* FLORIZEL.
I told you what would come of this! Beseech
    you,
Of your own state take care: this dream of mine,
Being now awake, I'll queen it no inch further,
But milk my ewes, and weep.

Cam.   Why, how now, father!
Speak ere thou diest.

Shep.   I cannot speak, nor think,
Nor dare to know that which I know.—O, sir,
                    [*To* FLORIZEL
You have undone a man of fourscore-three,
That thought to fill his grave in quiet; yea,
To die upon the bed my father died,
To lie close by his honest bones! but now
Some hangman must put on my shroud, and
    lay me
Where no priest shovels in dust.—O cursed
    wretch,   [*To* PERDITA.
That knew'st this was the prince, and wouldst
    adventure
To mingle faith with him!—Undone! undone!
If I might die within this hour, I have liv'd
To die when I desire.   [*Exit.*

Flo.   Why look you so upon me.
I am but sorry, not afeard; delay'd,
But nothing alter'd: what I was, I am:
More straining on for plucking back; not fol-
    lowing
My leash unwillingly.

Cam.   Gracious, my lord,
You know your father's temper: at this time
He will allow no speech,—which I do guess
You do not purpose to him;—and as hardly
Will he endure your sight as yet, I fear:
Then, till the fury of his highness settle,
Come not before him.

Flo.   I not purpose it.
I think Camillo?

Cam.   Even he, my lord.

Per. How often have I told you 'twould be
    thus!
How often said my dignity would last
But till 'twere known!

Flo.   It cannot fail but by
The violation of my faith; and then
Let nature crush the sides o' the earth together.
And mar the seeds within!—Lift up thy looks.—
From my succession wipe me, father; I
Am heir to my affection.

Cam.   Be advis'd.

Flo. I am,—and by my fancy: if my reason
Will thereto be obedient, I have reason;
If not, my senses, better pleas'd with madness,
Do bid it welcome.

Cam.   This is desperate, sir.

Flo. So call it: but it does fulfil my vow;
I needs must think it honesty. Camillo,
Not for Bohemia, nor the pomp that may
Be thereat glean'd; for all the sun sees or
The close earth wombs, or the profound seas
    hide
In unknown fathoms, will I break my oath

To this my fair belov'd: therefore, I pray you,
As you have ever been my father's honour'd
　　　　friend　　　　　　　　　　　[not
When he shall miss me,—as, in faith, I mean
To see him any more,—cast your good counsels
Upon his passion: let myself and fortune
Tug for the time to come. This you may know,
And so deliver,—I am put to sea
With her, whom here I cannot hold on shore;
And, most oppórtune to our need, I have
A vessel rides fast by, but not prepar'd
For this design. What course I mean to hold
Shall nothing benefit your knowledge, nor
Concern me the reporting.
　　Cam.　　　　　　　　O, my lord.
I would your spirit were easier for advice,
Or stronger for your need.
　　Flo.　　　　　　Hark, Perdita.—[*Takes her aside.*
I'll hear you by and by.　　　[*To* CAMILLO.
　　Cam.　　　　　　He's irremovable,
Resolv'd for flight. Now were I happy if
His going I could frame to serve my turn;
Save him from danger, do him love and honour;
Purchase the sight again of dear Sicilia,
And that unhappy king, my master whom
I so much thirst to see.
　　Flo.　　　　　　Now, good Camillo,
I am so fraught with curious business that
I leave out ceremony.　　　　　　[*Going.*
　　Cam.　　　　　　Sir, I think
You have heard of my poor services, i' the love
That I have borne your father?
　　Flo.　　　　　　　　Very nobly
Have you deserv'd: it is my father's music
To speak your deeds; not little of his care
To have them recompens'd as thought on.
　　Cam.　　　　　　Well, my lord,
If you may please to think I love the king,
And, through him, which is nearest to him,
　　　　which is
Your gracious self, embrace but my direction,—
If your more ponderous and settled project
May suffer alteration,—on mine honour　　[ing
I'll point you where you shall have such receiv-
As shall become your highness; where you may
Enjoy your mistress,—from the whom, I see,
There's no disjunction to be made, but by,
As heavens forfend! your ruin,—marry her;
And,—with my best endeavours in your ab-
　　　　sence,—
Your discontenting father strive to qualify,
And bring him up to liking.
　　Flo.　　　　　　How, Camillo,
May this, almost a miracle, be done?
That I may call thee something more than man,
And, after that, trust to thee.
　　Cam.　　　　　　Have you thought on
A place whereto you'll go?
　　Flo. Not any yet:
But as the unthought-on accident is guilty
To what we wildly do; so we profess
Ourselves to be the slaves of chance, and flies
Of every wind that blows.
　　Cam.　　　　　　Then list to me:

This follows,—if you will not change your pur-
　　　　pose,
But undergo this flight,—make for Sicilia;
And there present yourself and your fair prin-
　　　　cess,—
For so, I see, she must be,—'fore Leontes:
She shall be habited as it becomes
The partner of your bed. Methinks I see
Leonites opening his free arms, and weeping
His welcomes forth; asks thee,' the son, forgive-
　　　　ness,
As 'twere i' the father's person; kisses the hands
Of your fresh princess; o'er and o'er divides him
'Twixt his unkindness and his kindness,—the
　　　　one
He chides to hell, and bids the other grow
Faster than thought or time.
　　Flo.　　　　　　Worthy Camillo,
What colour for my visitation shall I
Hold up before him?
　　Cam.　　　　　Sent by the king your father
To greet him and to give him comforts. Sir,
The manner of your bearing towards him, with
What you, as from your father, shall deliver,
Things known betwixt us three, I'll write you
　　　　down;
The which shall point you forth at every sitting,
What you must say; that he shall not perceive
But that you have your father's bosom there,
And speak his very heart.
　　Flo.　　　　　　I am bound to you:
There is some sap in this.
　　Cam.　　　　　A course more promising
Than a wild dedication of yourselves　　[certain
To unpath'd waters, undream'd shores, most
To miseries enough: no hope to help you;
But, as you shake off one, to take another:
Nothing so certain as your anchors; who
Do their best office if they can but stay you
Where you'll be loath to be: besides, you know
Prosperity's the very bond of love,　　　[gether
Whose fresh complexion and whose heart to-
Affliction alters.
　　Per.　　　　　One of these is true:
I think affliction may subdue the cheek,
But not take in the mind.
　　Cam.　　　　　　Yea, say you so?
There shall not, at your father's house, these
　　　　seven years
Be born another such.
　　Flo.　　　　　My good Camillo,
She is as forward of her breeding as
She is i' the rear our birth.
　　Cam.　　　　　I cannot say 'tis pity
She lacks instruction; for she seems a mistress
To most that teach.
　　Per.　　　　　Your pardon, sir, for this:
I'll blush you thanks.
　　Flo. My prettiest Perdita!—
But, O, the thorns we stand upon!—Camillo,—
Preserver of my father, now of me;
The medicine of our house!—how shall we do?
We are not furnish'd like Bohemia's son;
Nor shall appear in Sicilia.

Cam.   My lord,
Fear none of this: I think you know my for-
 tunes
Do all lie there: it shall be so my care
To have you royally appointed as if   [sir,
The scene you play were mine. For instance,
That you may know you shall not want,—one
 word.   [*They talk aside.*

Re-enter AUTOLYCUS.

Aut. Ha, ha! what a fool Honesty is! and
Trust, his sworn brother, a very simple gentleman! I have sold all my trumpery; not a
counterfeit stone, not a riband, glass, poman-
der, brooch, table-book, ballad, knife, tape,
glove, shoe-tie, bracelet, horn-ring, to keep my
pack from fasting;—they throng who should
buy first, as if my trinkets had been hallowed,
and brought a benediction to the buyer: by
which means I saw whose purse was best in
picture; and what I saw, to my good use I remembered. My clown (who wants but something to be a reasonable man) grew so in love
with the wenches' song that he would not stir
his pettitoes till he had both tune and words;
which so drew the rest of the herd to me, that
all their other senses stuck in ears: you might
have pinched a placket,—it was senseless; 'twas
nothing to geld a codpiece of a purse; I would
have filed keys off that hung in chains: no hearing, no feeling, but my sir's song, and admiring
the nothing of it. So that, in this time of
lethargy, I picked and cut most of their festival
purses; and had not the old man come in with
a whoobub against his daughter and the king's
son, and scared my choughs from the chaff, I
had not left a purse alive in the whole army.
   [CAM., FLO., *and* PER. *come forward.*
Cam. Nay, but my letters, by this means
 being there
So soon as you arrive, shall clear that doubt.
Flo. And those that you'll procure from king
 Leontes,—
Cam. Shall satisfy your father.
Per.   Happy be you!
All that you speak shows fair.
Cam.   Who have we here?—
      [*Seeing* AUTOLYCUS.
We'll make an instrument of this; omit
Nothing may give us aid.
Aut. If they have overheard me now,—why,
hanging.   [*Aside.*
Cam. How now, good fellow! why shakest
thou so? Fear not, man; here's no harm in-
tended to thee.
Aut. I am a poor fellow, sir.
Cam. Why, be so still; here's nobody will
steal that from thee: yet, for the outside of thy
poverty, we must make an exchange; therefore,
discase thee instantly,—thou must think there's
a necessity in't,—and change garments with
this gentleman: though the pennyworth on his
side be the worst, yet hold thee, there's some
boot.   [*Giving money.*

Aut. I am a poor fellow, sir:—I know ye
well enough.   [*Aside.*
Cam. Nay, pr'ythee, despatch: the gentle-
man is half-flayed already.
Aut. Are you in earnest, sir?—I smell the
trick on't.—   [*Aside.*
Flo. Despatch, I pr'ythee.
Aut. Indeed, I have had earnest; but I can-
not with conscience take it.
Cam. Unbuckle, unbuckle.—
   [FLO. *and* AUTOL. *exchange garments.*
Fortunate mistress,—let my prophecy
Come home to you!—you must retire yourself
Into some covert; take your sweetheart's hat,
And pluck it o'er your brows; muffle your face;
Dismantle you; and, as you can, disliken
The truth of your own seeming; that you
 may,—
For I do fear eyes over,—to shipboard
Get undescried.
Per.   I see the play so lies
That I must bear a part.
Cam.   No remedy.—
Have you done there?
Flo.   Should I now meet my father,
He would not call me son.
Cam. Nay, you shall have no hat.—
      [*Giving it to* PERDITA.
Come, lady, come.—Farewell, my friend.
Aut. Adieu, sir.
Flo. O Perdita, what have we twain forgot?
Pray you, a word.   [*They converse apart.*
Cam. What I do next, shall be to tell the
 king   [*Aside.*
Of this escape, and whither they are bound;
Wherein, my hope is, I shall so prevail
To force him after: in whose company
I shall review Sicilia; for whose sight
I have a woman's longing.
Flo.   Fortune speed us!—
Thus we set on, Camillo, to the sea-side.
Cam. The swifter speed the better.
   [*Exeunt* FLOR., PER., *and* CAM.
Aut. I understand the business,—I hear it:
to have an open ear, a quick eye, and a nimble
hand, is necessary for a cut-purse; a good nose
is requisite also, to smell out work for the other
senses. I see this is the time that the unjust
man doth thrive. What an exchange had this
been without boot? what a boot is here with
this exchange? Sure, the gods do this year con-
nive at us, and we may do anything extempore.
The prince himself is about a piece of iniquity,
—stealing away from his father with his clog
at his heels: if I thought it were a piece of honesty to acquaint the king withal, I would not
do't: I hold it the more knavery to conceal it;
and therein am I constant to my profession.

Re-enter Clown *and* Shepherd.

Aside, aside;—here is more matter for a hot
brain: every lane's end, every shop, church,
session, hanging, yields a careful man work.
Clo. See, see: what a man you are now!

There is no other way but to tell the king she's a changeling, and none of your flesh and blood.

Shep. Nay, but hear me.

Clo. Nay, but hear me.

Shep. Go to, then.

Clo. She being none of your flesh and blood, your flesh and blood has not offended the king; and so your flesh and blood is not to be punished by him. Show those things you found about her; those secret things,—all but what she has with her: this being done, let the law go whistle; I warrant you.

Shep. I will tell the king all, every word,—yea, and his son's pranks too; who, I may say, is no honest man neither to his father nor to me, to go about to make me the king's brother-in-law.

Clo. Indeed, brother-in-law was the furthest off you could have been to him; and then your blood had been the dearer by I know how much an ounce.

Aut. Very wisely, puppies!   [*Aside.*

Shep. Well, let us to the king: there is that in this fardel will make him scratch his beard!

Aut. I know not what impediment this complaint may be to the flight of my master. [*Aside.*

Clo. Pray heartily he be at palace.

Aut. Though I am not naturally honest, I am so sometimes by chance. Let me pocket up my pedlar's excrement. [*Aside, and takes off his false beard.*]—How now, rustics! whither are you bound?

Shep. To the palace, an it like your worship.

Aut. Your affairs there, what, with whom, the condition of that fardel, the place of your dwelling, your names, your ages, of what having, breeding, and anything that is fitting to be known? discover.

Clo. We are but plain fellows, sir.

Aut. A lie; you are rough and hairy. Let me have no lying; it becomes none but tradesmen, and they often give us soldiers the lie: but we pay them for it with stamped coin, not stabing steel; therefore they do not give us the lie.

Clo. Your worship had like to have given us one, if you had not taken yourself with the manner.

Shep. Are you a courtier, an't like you, sir?

Aut. Whether it like me or no, I am a courtier. Seest thou not the air of the court in these enfoldings? hath not my gait in it the measure of the court? receives not thy nose court-odour from me? reflect I not on thy baseness court-contempt? Thinkest thou, for that I insinuate, or toze from thee thy business, I am therefore no courtier? I am courtier cap-a-pé; and one that will either push on or pluck back thy business there: whereupon I command thee to open thy affair.

Shep. My business, sir, is to the king.

Aut. What advocate hast thou to him?

Shep. I know not, an't like you.

Clo. Advocate's the court-word for a pheasant, say you have none.

Shep. None, sir; I have no pheasant, cock nor hen.   [men!

Aut. How bless'd are we that are not simple Yet nature might have made me as these are, Therefore I will not disdain.

Clo. This cannot be but a great courtier.

Shep. His garments are rich, but he wears them not handsomely.

Clo. He seems to be the more noble in being fantastical: a great man, I'll warrant; I know by the picking on's teeth.

Aut. The fardel there? what's i' the fardel? Wherefore that box?

Shep. Sir, there lies such secrets in this fardel and box, which none must know but the king; and which he shall know within this hour, if I may come to the speech of him.

Aut. Age, thou hast lost thy labour.

Shep. Why, sir?

Aut. The king is not at the palace; he is gone aboard a new ship to purge melancholy and air himself: for, if thou beest capable of things serious, thou must know the king is full of grief.

Shep. So 'tis said, sir,—about his son, that should have married a shepherd's daughter.

Aut. If that shepherd be not in hand-fast, let him fly: the curses he shall have, the tortures he shall feel, will break the back of man, the heart of monster.

Clo. Think you so, sir?

Aut. Not he alone shall suffer what wit can make heavy and vengeance bitter; but those that are germane to him, though removed fifty times, shall all come under the hangman: which, though it be great pity, yet it is necessary. An old sheep-whistling rogue, a ram-tender, to offer to have his daughter come into grace! Some say he shall be stoned; but that death is too soft for him, say I. Draw our throne into a sheep-cote!—all deaths are too few, the sharpest too easy.

Clo. Has the old man e'er a son, sir, do you hear, an't like you, sir?

Aut. He has a son,—who shall be flayed alive; then 'nointed over with honey, set on the head of a wasp's nest; then stand till he be three quarters and a dram dead; then recovered again with aquavitæ, or some other hot infusion; then, raw as he is, and in the hottest day prognostication proclaims, shall he be set against a brick-wall, the sun looking with a southward eye upon him,—where he is to behold him with flies blown to death. But what talk we of these traitorly rascals, whose miseries are to be smiled at, their offences being so capital? Tell me,—for you seem to be honest plain men,—what have you to the king: being something gently considered, I'll bring you where he is aboard, tender your persons to his presence, whisper him in your behalfs; and if it be in man besides the king to effect your suits, here is man shall do it.

Clo. He seems to be of great authority: close

with him, give him gold; and though authority be a stubborn bear, yet he is oft led by the nose with gold: show the inside of your purse to the outside of his hand, and no more ado. Remember,—stoned and flayed alive.

Shep. An't please you, sir, to undertake the business for us, here is that gold I have: I'll make it as much more, and leave this young man in pawn till I bring it you.

Aut. After I have done what I promised?

Shep. Ay, sir.

Aut. Well, give me the moiety.—Are you a party in this business?

Clo. In some sort, sir: but though my case be a pitiful one, I hope I shall not be flayed out of it.

Aut. O, that's the case of the shepherd's son. Hang him, he'll be made an example!

Clo. Comfort, good comfort! We must to the king, and show our strange sights: he must know 'tis none of your daughter nor my sister; we are gone else. Sir, I will give you as much as this old man does, when the business is performed; and remain, as he says, your pawn till it be brought you.

Aut. I will trust you. Walk before toward the sea-side; go on the right-hand: I will but look upon the hedge, and follow you.

Clo. We are blessed in this man, as I may say, even blessed.

Shep. Let's before, as he bids us: he was provided to do us good.

[*Exeunt* Shepherd *and* Clown.

Aut. If I had a mind to be honest, I see Fortune would not suffer me: she drops booties in my mouth. I am courted now with a double occasion,—gold, and a means to do the prince my master good; which who knows how that may turn back to my advancement? I will bring these two moles, these blind ones, aboard him; if he think it fit to shore them again, and that the complaint they have to the king concerns him nothing, let him call me rogue for being so far officious; for I am proof against that title, and what shame else belongs to 't. To him will I present them: there may be matter in it.

[*Exit.*

ACT V.

SCENE I.—SICILIA. *A Room in the Palace of* LEONTES.

Enter LEONTES, CLEOMENES, DION, PAULINA, *and others.*

Cleo. Sir, you have done enough, and have perform'd
A saint-like sorrow: no fault could you make,
Which you have not redeem'd; indeed, paid down
More penitence than done trespass: at the last,
Do as the heavens have done, forget your evil;
With them, forgive yourself.

Leon.   Whilst I remember
Her and her virtues, I cannot forget
My blemishes in them; and so still think of

The wrong I did myself: which was so much
That heirless it hath made my kingdom, and
Destroy'd the sweet'st companion that e'er man
Bred his hopes out of.

Paul.   True, too true, my lord;
If, one by one, you wedded all the world,
Or from the all that are took something good,
To make a perfect woman, she you kill'd
Would be unparallel'd.

Leon.   I think so.—Kill'd!
She I kill'd! I did so: but thou strik'st me
Sorely, to say I did: it is as bitter   [now,
Upon thy tongue as in my thought: now, good
Say so but seldom.

Cleo.   Not at all, good lady;
You might have spoken a thousand things that
          would
Have done the time more benefit, and grac'd
Your kindness better.

Paul.   You are one of those
Would have him wed again.

Dion.   If you would not so,
You pity not the state, nor the remembrance
Of his most sovereign name; consider little
What dangers, by his highness' fail of issue,
May drop upon his kingdom, and devour
Incertain lookers-on. What were more holy
Than to rejoice the former queen is well?
What holier than,—for royalty's repair,
For present comfort, and for future good,—
To bless the bed of majesty again
With a sweet fellow to 't?

Paul.   There is none worthy,
Respecting her that's gone. Besides, the gods
Will have fulfill'd their secret purposes:
For has not the divine Apollo said,
Is't not the tenor of his oracle,
That king Leontes shall not have an heir
Till his lost child be found? which that it shall,
Is all as monstrous to our human reason
As my Antigonus to break his grave,
And come again to me; who, on my life,
Did perish with the infant. 'Tis your counsel
My lord should to the heavens be contrary,
Oppose against their wills.—Care not for issue;
          [*To* LEONTES.
The crown will find an heir: great Alexander
Left his to the worthiest; so his successor
Was like to be the best.

Leon.   Good Paulina,—
Who hast the memory of Hermione,
I know, in honour,—O, that ever I   [now,
Had squar'd me to thy counsel!—then, even
I might have look'd upon my queen's full eyes;
Have taken treasure from her lips,—

Paul.   And left them
More rich for what they yielded.

Leon.   Thou speak'st truth.
No more such wives; therefore, no wife: one
          worse,
And better us'd, would make her sainted spirit
Again possess her corpse; and, on this stage,—
Where we offend her now,—appear, soul-vex'd,
And begin, *Why to me?*

Paul.   Had she such power,
She had just cause.
  Leon.   She had; and would incense me
To murder her I married.
  Paul.   I should so.
Were I the ghost that walk'd, I'd bid you mark
Her eye, and tell me for what dull part in't
You chose her: then I'd shriek, that even your
          ears
Should rift to hear me; and the words that
          follow'd
Should be, *Remember mine!*
  Leon.   Stars, stars,
And all eyes else dead coals!—fear thou no wife;
I'll have no wife, Paulina.
  Paul.   Will you swear
Never to marry but by my free leave?
  Leon. Never, Paulina; so be bless'd my
          spirit!
  Paul. Then, good my lords, bear witness to
          his oath.
  Cleo. You tempt him over-much.
  Paul.   Unless another,
As like Hermione as is her picture,
Affront his eye.
  Cleo.   Good Madam,—
  Paul.   I have done.
Yet, if my lord will marry,—if you will, sir,
No remedy, but you will,—give me the office
To choose you a queen: she shall not be so young
As was your former; but she shall be such
As, walk'd your first queen's ghost, it should
          take joy
To see her in your arms.
  Leon.   My true Paulina,
We shall not marry till thou bidd'st us.
  Paul.   That
Shall be when your first queen's again in breath:
Never till then.

Enter a Gentleman.

  Gent. One that gives out himself Prince
          Florizel,
Son of Polixenes, with his princess,—she
The fairest I have yet beheld,—desires access
To your high presence.
  Leon.   What with him? he comes not
Like to his father's greatness: his approach,
So out of circumstance and sudden, tells us
'Tis not a visitation fram'd, but forc'd
By need and accident. What train?
  Gent.   But few,
And those but mean.
  Leon.   His princess, say you, with him?
  Gent. Ay; the most peerless piece of earth, I
          think,
That e'er the sun shone bright on.
  Paul.   O Hermione,
As every present time doth boast itself
Above a better gone, so must thy grave
Give way to what's seen now. Sir, you yourself
Have said and writ so,—but your writing now
Is colder than that theme,—*She had not been,
Nor was not to be equall'd;*—thus your verse

Flow'd with her beauty once; 'tis shrewdly
          ebb'd,
To say you have seen a better.
  Gent.   Pardon, madam:
The one I have almost forgot;—your pardon;—
The other, when she has obtain'd your eye,
Will have your tongue too. This is a creature,
Would she begin a sect, might quench the zeal
Of all professors else; make proselytes
Of who she but bid follow.
  Paul.   How! not women?
  Gent. Women will love her, that she is a
          woman
More worth than any man; men, that she is
The rarest of all women.
  Leon.   Go, Cleomenes;
Yourself, assisted with your honour'd friends,
Bring them to our embracement.—Still, 'tis
          strange,
          [*Exeunt* CLEO., Lords, *and* Gent.
He thus should steal upon us.
  Paul.   Had our prince,—
Jewel of children,—seen this hour, he had
          pair'd
Well with this lord: there was not full a month
          between their births.
  Leon. Pr'ythee, no more; cease; thou know'st
He dies to me again when talk'd of: sure,
When I shall see this gentleman, thy speeches
Will bring me to consider that which may
Unfurnish me of reason.—They are come.—

Re-enter CLEOMENES, *with* FLORIZEL, PERDITA,
          and Attendants.

Your mother was most true to wedlock, prince;
For she did print your royal father off,
Conceiving you: were I but twenty-one,
Your father's image is so hit in you,
His very air, that I should call you brother,
As I did him, and speak of something wildly
By us perform'd before. Most dearly welcome!
And your fair princess,—goddess!—O, alas!
I lost a couple that 'twixt heaven and earth
Might thus have stood, begetting wonder, as
You, gracious couple, do! and then I lost,—
All mine own folly,—the society,
Amity too, of your brave father, whom,
Though bearing misery, I desire my life
Once more to look on him.
  Flo.   By his command
Have I here touch'd Sicilia, and from him
Give you all greetings that a king, at friend,
Can send his brother: and, but infirmity,—
Which waits upon worn times,—hath some
          thing seiz'd
His wish'd ability, he had himself
The lands and waters 'twixt your throne and his
Measur'd, to look upon you; whom he loves,—
He bade me say so,—more than all the sceptres,
And those that bear them, living.
  Leon.   O my brother,—   [stir
Good gentleman!—the wrongs I have done thee
Afresh within me; and these my offices,
So rarely kind, are as interpreters

Of my behind-hand slackness!—Welcome hither,
As is the spring to the earth. And hath he too
Expos'd this paragon to the fearful usage,—
At least ungentle,—of the dreadful Neptune,
To greet a man not worth her pains, much less
The adventure of her person?
   Flo.   Good, my lord,
She came from Libya.
   Leon.   Where the warlike Smalus,
That noble honour'd lord, is fear'd and lov'd?
   Flo. Most royal sir, from thence; from him, whose daughter
His tears proclaim'd his, parting with her: thence—
A prosperous south wind friendly,—we have cross'd,
To execute the charge my father gave me,
For visiting your highness: my best train
I have from your Sicilian shores dismiss'd;
Who for Bohemia bend, to signify
Not only my success in Libya, sir,
But my arrival, and my wife's, in safety
Here, where we are.
   Leon.   The blessed gods
Purge all infection from our air whilst you
Do climate here! You have a holy father,
A graceful gentleman; against whose person,
So sacred as it is, I have done sin:
For which the heavens, taking angry note,
Have left me issueless; and your father's bless'd,—
As he from heaven merits it,—with you,
Worthy his goodness. What might I have been,
Might I a son and daughter now have look'd on,
Such goodly things as you!

Enter a Lord.

   Lord.   Most noble sir,
That which I shall report will bear no credit,
Were not the proof so nigh. Please you, great sir
Bohemia greets you from himself by me.
Desires you to attach his son, who has,
His dignity and duty both cast off,—
Fled from his father, from his hopes, and with
A shepherd's daughter.
   Leon.   Where's Bohemia? speak.
   Lord. Here in your city; I now came from him:
I speak amazedly; and it becomes
My marvel and my message. To your court
Whiles he was hast'ning,—in the chase, it seems,
Of this fair couple,—meets he on the way
The father of this seeming lady, and
Her brother, both having their country quitted
With this young prince.
   Flo.   Camillo has betray'd me;
Whose honour and whose honesty, till now,
Endur'd all weathers.
   Lord.   Lay't so to his charge;
He's with the king your father.
   Leon.   Who? Camillo?

   Lord. Camillo, sir; I spake with him; who now
Has these poor men in question. Never saw I
Wretches so quake: they kneel, they kiss the earth;
Forswear themselves as often as they speak:
Bohemia stops his ears, and threatens them
With divers deaths in death.
   Per.   O my poor father!—
The heaven sets spies upon us, will not have
Our contract celebrated.
   Leon.   You are married?
   Flo. We are not, sir, nor are we like to be;
The stars, I see, will kiss the valleys first:—
The odds for high and low's alike.
   Leon.   My lord,
Is this the daughter of a king?
   Flo.   She is,
When once she is my wife.
   Leon. That once, I see, by your good father's speed,
Will come on very slowly. I am sorry,
Most sorry, you have broken from his liking,
Where you were tied in duty; and as sorry
Your choice is not so rich in worth as beauty,
That you might well enjoy her.
   Flo.   Dear, look up:
Though Fortune, visible an enemy,
Should chase us, with my father, power no jot
Hath she to change our loves.—Beseech you, sir,
Remember since you ow'd no more to time
Than I do now: with thought of such affections,
Step forth mine advocate; at your request
My father will grant precious things as trifles.
   Leon. Would he do so, I'd beg your precious mistress,
Which he counts but a trifle.
   Paul.   Sir, my liege,
Your eye hath too much youth in't: not a month
'Fore your queen died, she was more worth such gazes
Than what you look on now.
   Leon.   I thought of her
Even in these looks I made.—But your petition
                         [*To* FLORIZEL.
Is yet unanswer'd. I will to your father:
Your honour not o'erthrown by your desires,
I am friend to them and you: upon which errand
I now go toward him; therefore, follow me,
And mark what way I make. Come, good my lord.   [*Exeunt.*

SCENE II.—*The same. Before the Palace.*

Enter AUTOLYCUS *and a* Gentleman.

   Aut. Beseech you, sir, were you present at this relation?
   1 *Gent.* I was by at the opening of the fardel, heard the old shepherd deliver the manner how he found it: whereupon, after a little amazedness, we were all commanded out of the cham-

ber; only this, methought I heard the shepherd say he found the child.   [it.

Aut. I would most gladly know the issue of

1 Gent. I make a broken delivery of the business; but the changes I perceived in the king and Camillo were very notes of admiration: they seemed almost, with staring on one another, to tear the cases of their eyes; there was speech in their dumbness, language in their very gesture; they looked as they had heard of a world ransomed, or one destroyed: a notable passion of wonder appeared in them; but the wisest beholder, that knew no more but seeing, could not say if the importance were joy or sorrow;—but in the extremity of the one, it must needs be. Here comes a gentleman that happily knows more.

Enter a Gentleman.

The news, Rogero?

2 Gent. Nothing but bonfires: the oracle is fulfilled; the king's daughter is found: such a deal of wonder is broken out within this hour that ballad-makers cannot be able to express it. Here comes the Lady Paulina's steward: he can deliver you more.

Enter a third Gentleman.

How goes it now, sir? this news, which is called true, is so like an old tale that the verity of it is in strong suspicion. Has the king found his heir?

3 Gent. Most true, if ever truth were pregnant by circumstance: that which you hear you'll swear you see, there is such unity in the proofs. The mantle of Queen Hermione; her jewel about the neck of it; the letters of Antigonus, found with it, which they know to be his character; the majesty of the creature in resemblance of the mother; the affection of nobleness, which nature shows above her breeding; and many other evidences,—proclaim her with all certainty to be the king's daughter. Did you see the meeting of the two kings?

2 Gent. No.

3 Gent. Then have you lost a sight which was to be seen, cannot be spoken of. There might you have beheld one joy crown another, so and in such manner that it seemed sorrow wept to take leave of them; for their joy waded in tears. There was casting up of eyes, holding up of hands, with countenance of such distraction that they were to be known by garment, not by favour. Our king, being ready to leap out of himself for joy of his found daughter, as if that joy were now become a loss, cries, *O, thy mother, thy mother!* then asks Bohemia forgiveness; then embraces his son-in-law; then again worries he his daughter with clipping her; now he thanks the old shepherd, which stands by like a weather-bitten conduit of many kings' reigns. I never heard of such another encounter, which lames report to follow it, and undoes description to do it.

2 Gent. What, pray you, became of Antigonus, that carried hence the child?

3 Gent. Like an old tale still, which will have matter to rehearse, though credit be asleep, and not an ear open. He was torn to pieces with a bear: this avouches the shepherd's son; who has not only his innocence,—which seems much,—to justify him, but a handkerchief and rings of his, that Paulina knows.

1 Gent. What became of his bark and his followers?

3 Gent. Wrecked the same instant of their master's death, and in the view of the shepherd: so that all the instruments which aided to expose the child were even then lost when it was found. But, O, the noble combat that, 'twixt joy and sorrow, was fought in Paulina! She had one eye declined for the loss of her husband, another elevated that the oracle was fulfilled: she lifted the princess from the earth, and so locks her in embracing, as if she would pin her to her heart, that she might no more be in danger of losing.

1 Gent. The dignity of this act was worth the audience of kings and princes; for by such was it acted.

3 Gent. One of the prettiest touches of all, and that which angled for mine eyes,—caught the water, though not the fish,—was when, at the relation of the queen's death, with the the relation of the queen's death, with the manner how she came to it,—bravely confessed and lamented by the king,—how attentiveness wounded his daughter; till, from one sign of dolour to another, she did, with an *alas!* I would fain say, bleed tears; for I am sure my heart wept blood. Who was most marble there changed colour; some swooned, all sorrowed: if all the world could have seen it, the woe had been universal.

1 Gent. Are they returned to the court?

3 Gent. No: the princess hearing of her mother's statue, which is in the keeping of Paulina,—a piece many years in doing, and now newly performed by that rare Italian-master, Julio Romano, who, had he himself eternity, and could put breath into his work, would beguile nature of her custom, so perfectly he is her ape. he so near to Hermione hath done Hermione, that they say one would speak to her, and stand in hope of answer:—thither with all greediness of affection are they gone; and there they intend to sup.

2 Gent. I thought she had some great matter there in hand; for she hath privately twice or thrice a day, ever since the death of Hermione, visited that removed house. Shall we thither, and with our company piece the rejoicing?

1 Gent. Who would be thence that has the benefit of access? every wink of an eye some new grace will be born: our absence makes us unthrifty to our knowledge. Let's along.

[*Exeunt* Gentlemen.

Aut. Now, had I not the dash of my former

life in me, would preferment drop on my head. I brought the old man and his son aboard the prince; told him I heard them talk of a fardel, and I know not what; but he at that time over-fond of the shepherd's daughter,—so he then took her to be,—who began to be much sea-sick and himself little better, extremity of weather continuing, this mystery remained undiscovered. But 'tis all one to me; for had I been the finder-out of this secret, it would not have relished among my other discredits. Here come those I have done good to against my will, and already appearing in the blossoms of their fortune.

Enter Shepherd *and* Clown.

Shep. Come, boy; I am past more children, but thy sons and daughters will be all gentlemen born.

Clo. You are well met, sir: you denied to fight with me this other day, because I was no gentleman born. See you these clothes? say you see them not, and think me still no gentleman born: you were best say these robes are not gentlemen born. Give me the lie, do; and try whether I am not now a gentleman born.

Aut. I know you are now, sir, a gentleman born.

Clo. Ay, and have been so any time these four hours.

Shep. And so have I, boy!

Clo. So you have:—but I was a gentleman born before my father; for the king's son took me by the hand and called me brother; and then the two kings called my father brother; and then the prince, my brother, and the princess, my sister, called my father father; and so we wept: and there was the first gentleman-like tears that ever we shed.

Shep. We may live, son, to shed many more.

Clo. Ay; or else 'twere hard luck, being in so preposterous estate as we are.

Aut. I humbly beseech you, sir, to pardon me all the faults I have committed to your worship, and to give me your good report to the prince my master.

Shep. Pr'ythee, son, do; for we must be gentle, now we are gentlemen.

Clo. Thou wilt amend thy life?

Aut. Ay, an it like your good worship.

Clo. Give me thy hand: I will swear to the prince thou art as honest a true fellow as any is in Bohemia.

Shep. You may say it, but not swear it.

Clo. Not swear it, now I am a gentleman? Let boors and franklins say it, I'll swear it.

Shep. How if it be false, son?

Clo. If it be ne'er so false, a true gentleman may swear it in the behalf of his friend.—And I'll swear to the prince, thou art a tall fellow of thy hands, and that thou wilt not be drunk; but I know thou art no tall fellow of thy hands, and that thou wilt be drunk: but I'll swear it;

and I would thou wouldst be a tall fellow of thy hands.

Aut. I will prove so, sir, to my power.

Clo. Ay, by any means, prove a tall fellow: if I do not wonder how thou darest venture to be drunk, not being a tall fellow, trust me not. —Hark! the kings and the princes, our kindred, are going to see the queen's picture. Come, follow us: we'll be thy good masters.   [*Exeunt.*

SCENE III.—*The same. A Room in* PAULINA'S *House.*

Enter LEONTES, POLIXENES, FLORIZEL, PERDITA, CAMILLO, PAULINA, Lords, *and* Attendants.

Leon. O grave and good Paulina, the great comfort
That I have had of thee!
Paul.   What, sovereign sir,
I did not well, I meant well. All my services
You have paid home: but that you have vouch-
    saf'd,   [tracted
With your crown'd brother, and these your con-
Heirs of your kingdoms, my poor house to visit,
It is a surplus of your grace which never
My life may last to answer.
Leon.   O Paulina,
We honour you with trouble:—but we came
To see the statue of our queen: your gallery
Have we pass'd through, not without much
    content
In many singularities; but we saw not
That which my daughter came to look upon,
The statue of her mother.
Paul.   As she liv'd peerless,
So her dead likeness, I do well believe,
Excels whatever yet you look'd upon,
Or hand of man hath done; therefore I keep it
Lonely, apart. But here it is: prepare
To see the life as lively mock'd as ever   [well.
Still sleep mock'd death: behold; and say 'tis
    [PAULINA *undraws a curtain, and discovers*
            HERMIONE *standing as a statue.*
I like your silence,—it the more shows off
Your wonder: but yet speak;—first, you, my
    liege.
Comes it not something near?
Leon.   Her natural posture!—
Chide me, dear stone, that I may say indeed,
Thou art Hermione; or rather, thou art she,
In thy not chiding; for she was as tender
As infancy and grace.—But yet, Paulina,
Hermione was not so much wrinkled; nothing
So aged, as this seems.
Pol.   O, not by much.
Paul. So much the more our carver's excel-
    lence;   [her
Which lets go by some sixteen years, and makes
As she liv'd now.
Leon.   As now she might have done,
So much to my good comfort, as it is
Now piercing to my soul. O, thus she stood,
Even with such life of majesty,—warm life,

As now it coldly stands,—when first I woo'd her!
I am asham'd: does not the stone rebuke me
For being more stone than it?—O royal piece,
There's magic in thy majesty; which has
My evils conjur'd to remembrance; and
From thy admiring daughter took the spirits,
Standing like stone with thee!
  Per.   And give me leave;
And do not say 'tis superstition, that
I kneel, and then implore her blessing.—Lady,
Dear queen, that ended when I but began,
Give me that hand of yours to kiss.
  Paul.   O, patience!
The statue is but newly fix'd, the colour's
Not dry.   [on,
  Cam. My lord, your sorrow was too sore laid
Which sixteen winters cannot blow away,
So many summers dry: scarce any joy
Did ever so long live; no sorrow
But kill'd itself much sooner.
  Pol.   Dear my brother,
Let him that was the cause of this have power
To take off so much grief from you as he
Will piece up in himself.
  Paul.   Indeed, my lord,
If I had thought the sight of my poor image
Would thus have wrought you,—for the stone
          is mine,—
I'd not have show'd it.
  Leon.   Do not draw the curtain.
  Paul. No longer shall you gaze on't; lest
          your fancy
May think anon it moves.
  Leon.   Let be, let be.—
Would I were dead, but that, methinks, al-
          ready—
What was he that did make it?—See, my lord,
Would you not deem it breath'd? and that
          those veins
Did verily bear blood?
  Pol.   Masterly done:
The very life seems warm upon her lip.
  Leon. The fixture of her eye has motion in't,
As we are mock'd with art.
  Paul.   I'll draw the curtain:
My lord's almost so far transported that
He'll think anon it lives.
  Leon.   O sweet Paulina,
Make me to think so twenty years together!
No settled senses of the world can match
The pleasure of that madness. Let't alone.
  Paul. I am sorry, sir, I have thus far stirr'd
          you: but
I could afflict you further.
  Leon.   Do, Paulina;
For this affliction has a taste as sweet
As any cordial comfort.—Still, methinks,
There is an air comes from her: what fine chisel
Could ever yet cut breath? Let no man mock
          me,
For I will kiss her!
  Paul.   Good my lord, forbear:
The ruddiness upon her lip is wet;
You'll mar it if you kiss it; stain your own

With oily painting. Shall I draw the curtain?
  Leon. No, not these twenty years.
  Per.   So long could I
Stand by, a looker on.
  Paul.   Either forbear,
Quit presently the chapel, or resolve you
For more amazement. If you can behold
I'll make the statue move indeed, descend
And take you by the hand: but then you'll
          think,—
Which I protest against,—I am assisted
By wicked powers.
  Leon.   What you can make her do
I am content to look on: what to speak?
I am content to hear; for 'tis as easy
To make her speak as move.
  Paul.   It is requir'd
You do awake your faith. Then all stand still;
Or those that think it is unlawful business
I am about, let them depart.
  Leon.   Proceed:
No foot shall stir.
  Paul. Music, awake her: strike!— [*Music.*
'Tis time; descend; be stone no more; approach;
Strike all that look upon with marvel. Come;
I'll fill your grave up: stir; nay, come away;
Bequeath to death your numbness, for from him
Dear life redeems you.—You perceive she stirs:
      [HERMIONE *comes down from the pedestal.*
Start not; her actions shall be holy as
You hear my spell is lawful: do not shun her
Until you see her die again; for then
You kill her double. Nay, present your hand:
When she was young you woo'd her; now in age
Is she become the suitor.
  Leon.   O, she's warm! [*Embracing her.*
If this be magic, let it be an art
Lawful as eating.
  Pol.   She embraces him.
  Cam. She hangs about his neck:
If she pertain to life, let her speak too.
  Pol. Ay, and make't manifest where she has
          liv'd,
Or how stol'n from the dead.
  Paul.   That she is living,
Were it but told you, should be hooted at
Like an old tale; but it appears she lives,
Though yet she speak not. Mark a little while.—
Please you to interpose, fair madam: kneel,
And pray your mother's blessing.—Turn, good
          lady;
Our Perdita is found.
          [*Presenting* PER., *who kneels to* HER.
  Her.   You gods, look down,
And from your sacred vials pour your graces
Upon my daughter's head!—Tell me, mine
          own,
Where hast thou been preserv'd? where liv'd?
          how found   [I,—
Thy father's court? for thou shalt hear that
Knowing by Paulina that the oracle
Gave hope thou wast in being,—have pre-
          serv'd
Myself to see the issue.

Paul.   There's time enough for that;
Lest they desire, upon this push, to trouble
Your joys with like relation.—Go together,
You precious winners all; your exultation
Partake to every one. I, an old turtle,
Will wing me to some wither'd bough, and
            there
My mate, that's never to be found again,
Lament till I am lost.

Leon.   O peace, Paulina!
Thou shouldst a husband take by my consent,
As I by thine a wife: this is a match,
And made between's by vows. Thou hast found
            mine;
But how, is to be question'd: for I saw her,
As I thought, dead; and have, in vain, said
            many
A prayer upon her grave. I'll not seek
            far,—

For him, I partly know his mind,—to find thee
An honourable husband.—Come, Camillo,
And take her by the hand, whose worth and
            honesty
Is richly noted, and here justified
By us, a pair of kings.—Let's from this place.—
What! look upon my brother:—both your par-
            dons,
That e'er I put between your holy looks
My ill suspicion.—This your son-in-law,
And son unto the king, whom heavens direct-
            ing,
Is troth-plight to your daughter.—Good Paul-
            ina,
Lead us from hence; where we may leisurely
Each one demand, and answer to his part
Perform'd in this wide gap of time, since first
We were dissever'd: hastily lead away!

            [*Exeunt.*

THE COMEDY OF ERRORS

DRAMATIS PERSONÆ

SOLINUS, *Duke of Ephesus.*
ÆGEON, *a Merchant of Syracuse.*
ANTIPHOLUS OF EPHESUS, } *Twin Brothers, and sons to ÆGEON and ÆMILIA, but unknown to each other.*
ANTIPHOLUS OF SYRACUSE, }
DROMIO OF EPHESUS, } *Twin Brothers, and Attendants on the two* ANTIPHOLUSES.
DROMIO OF SYRACUSE, }
BALTHAZAR, *a Merchant.*
ANGELO, *a Goldsmith.*
A Merchant, *Friend to* ANTIPHOLUS OF SYRACUSE,

PINCH, *a Schoolmaster and a Conjurer.*

ÆMILIA, *Wife to* ÆGEON, *an Abbess at Ephesus.*
ADRIANA, *Wife to* ANTIPHOLUS OF EPHESUS.
LUCIANA, *her Sister.*
LUCE, *her Servant.*

A Courtezan.

Gaoler, Officers, *and other* Attendants.

SCENE,—EPHESUS.

ACT I.

SCENE I.—*A Hall in the* DUKE's *Palace.*

Enter DUKE, ÆGEON, Gaoler, Officers, *and other* Attendants.

Æge. Proceed, Solinus, to procure my fall,
And, by the doom of death, end woes and all.
    Duke. Merchant of Syracusa, plead no more;
I am not partial to infringe our laws:
The enmity and discord which of late
Sprung from the rancorous outrage of your
    duke
To merchants, our well-dealing countrymen,—
Who, wanting gilders to redeem their lives,
Have sealed his rigorous statutes with their
    bloods,—
Excludes all pity from our threat'ning looks.
For, since the mortal and intestine jars
'Twixt thy seditious countrymen and us,
It hath in solemn synods been decreed,
Both by the Syracusans and ourselves,
To admit no traffic to our adverse towns:
Nay, more,
If any born at Ephesus be seen
At any Syracusan marts and fairs,—
Again, if any Syracusan born
Come to the bay of Ephesus, he dies,
His goods confiscate to the duke's dispose;
Unless a thousand marks be levied,
To quit the penalty and to ransom him.—
Thy substance, valued at the highest rate,
Cannot amount unto a hundred marks:
Therefore, by law thou art condemn'd to die.
    Æge. Yet this my comfort,—when your
        words are done,
My woes end likewise with the evening sun.
    Duke. Well, Syracusan, say, in brief, the
        cause
Why thou departedst from thy native home,

And for what cause thou cam'st to Ephesus.
    Æge. A heavier task could not have been im-
        pos'd
Than I to speak my griefs unspeakable!
Yet, that the world may witness that my end
Was wrought by nature, not by vile offence,
I'll utter what my sorrow gives me leave.
In Syracusa was I born; and wed
Unto a woman, happy but for me,
And by me too, had not our hap been bad.
With her I liv'd in joy; our wealth increas'd
By prosperous voyages I often made
To Epidamnum, till my factor's death,
And he,—great care of goods at random left,—
Drew me from kind embracements of my
        spouse: [old,
From whom my absence was not six months
Before herself,—almost at fainting under
The pleasing punishment that women bear,—
Had made provision for her following me,
And soon and safe arrived where I was.
There she had not been long but she became
A joyful mother of two goodly sons;   [other
And, which was strange, the one so like the
As could not be distinguish'd but by names.
That very hour, and in the self-same inn,
A poor mean woman was delivered
Of such a burden, male twins, both alike:
Those,—for their parents were exceeding
        poor,—
I bought, and brought up to attend my sons.
My wife, not meanly proud of two such boys,
Made daily motions for our home return:
Unwilling I agreed; alas, too soon!
We came aboard:
A league from Epidamnum had we sail'd
Before the always-wind-obeying deep
Gave any tragic instance of our harm;
But longer did we not retain much hope:

For what obscured light the heavens did grant
Did but convey unto our fearful minds
A doubtful warrant of immediate death;
Which, though myself would gladly have em-
    brac'd,
Yet the incessant weepings of my wife,
Weeping before for what she saw must come,
And piteous plainings of the pretty babes,
That mourn'd for fashion, ignorant what to
    fear,
Forc'd me to seek delays for them and me.
And this it was,—for other means was none.—
The sailors sought for safety by our boat,
And left the ship, then sinking-ripe, to us:
My wife, more careful for the latter-born,
Had fasten'd him unto a small spare mast,
Such as sea-faring men provide for storms:
To him one of the other twins was bound,
Whilst I had been like heedful of the other.
The children thus dispos'd, my wife and I,
Fixing our eyes on whom our care was fix'd,
Fasten'd ourselves at either end the mast;
And floating straight, obedient to the stream,
Were carried towards Corinth, as we thought.
At length the sun, gazing upon the earth,
Dispers'd those vapours that offended us;
And, by the benefit of his wish'd light,
The seas wax'd calm, and we discover'd
Two ships from far making amain to us,—
Of Corinth that, of Epidaurus this:
But ere they came,—O, let me say no more!—
Gather the sequel by that went before.
 Duke. Nay: forward, old man, do not break
    off so;
For we may pity, though not pardon thee.
 Æge. O, had the gods done so, I had not now
Worthily term'd them merciless to us!
For, ere the ships could meet by twice five
    leagues,
We were encounter'd by a mighty rock,
Which being violently borne upon,
Our helpful ship was splitted in the midst;
So that, in this unjust divorce of us,
Fortune had left to both of us alike
What to delight in, what to sorrow for.
Her part, poor soul! seeming as burdened
With lesser weight, but not with lesser woe,
Was carried with more speed before the wind;
And in our sight they three were taken up
By fishermen of Corinth, as we thought.
At length another ship had seiz'd on us;
And, knowing whom it was their hap to save,
Gave helpful welcome to their shipwreck'd
    guests;
And would have reft the fishers of their prey,
Had not their bark been very slow of sail,
And therefore homeward did they bend their
    course.—
Thus have you heard me sever'd from my bliss;
That by misfortunes was my life prolong'd,
To tell sad stories of my own mishaps.
 Duke. And, for the sake of them thou sor-
    rowest for,
Do me the favour to dilate at full

What hath befall'n of them and thee till now.
 Æge. My youngest boy, and yet my eldest
    care,
At eighteen years became inquisitive
After his brother, and impórtun'd me
That his attendant,—for his case was like,
Reft of his brother, but retain'd his name,—
Might bear him company in the quest of him:
Whom whilst I labour'd of a love to see,
I hazarded the loss of whom I lov'd.
Five summers have I spent in furthest Greece,
Roaming clean through the bounds of Asia,
And, coasting homeward, came to Ephesus;
Hopeless to find, yet loath to leave unsought
Or that or any place that harbours men.
But here must end the story of my life;
And happy were I in my timely death,
Could all my travels warrant me they live.
 Duke. Hapless Ægeon, whom the fates have
    mark'd
To bear the extremity of dire mishap!
Now, trust me, were it not against our laws,
Against my crown, my oath, my dignity,
Which princes, would they, may not disannul,
My soul should sue as advocate for thee.
But though thou art adjudged to the death,
And passed sentence may not be recall'd
But to our honour's great disparagement,
Yet will I favour thee in what I can:
Therefore, merchant, I'll limit thee this day
To seek thy help by beneficial help:
Try all the friends thou hast in Ephesus:
Beg thou, or borrow, to make up the sum,
And live; if not, then thou art doom'd to die.—
Gaoler, take him to thy custody.
 Gaol. I will, my lord.
 Æge. Hopeless and helpless doth Ægeon
    wend.
But to procrastinate his lifeless end. [*Exeunt.*

SCENE II.—*A public Place.*

Enter ANTIPHOLUS *and* DROMIO OF
SYRACUSE, *and a* Merchant.

 Mer. Therefore, give out you are of Epi-
    damnum,
Lest that your goods too soon be confiscate.
This very day a Syracusan merchant
Is apprehended for arrival here;
And, not being able to buy out his life,
According to the statute of the town,
Dies ere the weary sun set in the west.—
There is your money that I had to keep.
 Ant. S. Go bear it to the Centaur, where
    we host,
And stay there, Dromio, till I come to thee.
Within this hour it will be dinner-time:
Till that, I'll view the manners of the town,
Peruse the traders, gaze upon the buildings,
And then return and sleep within mine inn;
For with long travel I am stiff and weary.—
Get thee away.   [word,
 Dro. S. Many a man would take you at your
And go indeed, having so good a mean.
        [*Exit* DROMIO S.

Ant. S. A trusty villain, sir, that very oft,
When I am dull with care and melancholy,
Lightens my humour with his merry jests.
What, will you walk with me about the town,
And then go to my inn and dine with me?

Mer. I am invited, sir, to certain merchants,
Of whom I hope to make much benefit:
I crave your pardon. Soon, at five o'clock,
Please you, I'll meet with you upon the mart,
And afterwards consort you until bed-time:
My present business calls me from you now.

Ant. S. Farewell till then: I will go lose
    myself,
And wander up and down to view the city.

Mer. Sir, I commend you to your own con-
    tent.   [*Exit* Merchant.

Ant. S. He that commends me to mine own
    content,
Commends me to the thing I cannot get.
I to the world am like a drop of water
That in the ocean seeks another drop;
Who, failing there to find his fellow forth,
Unseen, inquisitive, confounds himself:
So I, to find a mother and a brother,
In quest of them, unhappy, lose myself.

Enter DROMIO OF EPHESUS.

Here comes the almanac of my true date.—
What now? How chance thou art return'd so
    soon?   [too late:

Dro. E. Return'd so soon! rather approach'd
The capon burns, the pig falls from the spit;
The clock hath strucken twelve upon the bell—
My mistress made it one upon my cheek:
She is so hot because the meat is cold;
The meat is cold because you come not home;
You come not home because you have no
    stomach;
You have no stomach, having broke your fast;
But we, that know what 'tis to fast and pray,
Are penitent for your default to-day.

Ant. S. Stop—in your wind, sir; tell me this,
    I pray;
Where have you left the money that I gave you?

Dro. E. O,—sixpence that I had o' Wednes-
    day last
To pay the saddler for my mistress' crupper;—
The saddler had it, sir, I kept it not.

Ant. S. I am not in a sportive humour now:
Tell me, and dally not, where is the money?
We being strangers here, how dar'st thou trust
So great a charge from thine own custody?

Dro. E. I pray you, jest, sir, as you sit at
    dinner:
I from my mistress come to you in post:
If I return, I shall be post indeed;
For she will score your fault upon my pate.
Methinks your maw, like mine, should be your
    clock,
And strike you home without a messenger.

Ant. S. Come, Dromio, come, these jests are
    out of season;
Reserve them till a merrier hour than this.
Where is the gold I gave in charge to thee?

Dro. E. To me, sir? why, you gave no gold
    to me!   [foolishness,

Ant. S. Come on, sir knave; have done your
And tell me how thou hast dispos'd thy charge.

Dro. E. My charge was but to fetch you from
    the mart
Home to your house, the Phœnix, sir, to dinner:
My mistress and her sister stay for you.

Ant. S. Now, as I am a Christian, answer me,
In what safe place you have bestow'd my
    money:
Or I shall break that merry sconce of yours,
That stands on tricks when I am undispos'd;
Where is the thousand marks thou hadst of me?

Dro. E. I have some marks of yours upon
    my pate,
Some of my mistress' marks upon my shoulders,
But not a thousand marks between you both.—
If I should pay your worship those again,
Perchance you will not bear them patiently.

Ant. S. Thy mistress' marks! what mistress,
    slave, hast thou?

Dro. E. Your worship's wife, my mistress at
    the Phœnix;
She that doth fast till you come home to dinner,
And prays that you will hie you home to dinner.

Ant. S. What, wilt thou flout me thus unto
    my face,
Being forbid? There, take you that, sir knave.

Dro. E. What mean you, sir? for God's sake,
    hold your hands:
Nay, an you will not, sir, I'll take my heels.
                                    [*Exit* DROMIO E.

Ant. S. Upon my life, by some device or
    other,
The villain is o'er-raught of all my money.
They say this town is full of cozenage;
As, nimble jugglers that deceive the eye,
Dark-working sorcerers that change the mind,
Soul-killing witches that deform the body,
Disguised cheaters, prating mountebanks,
And many such-like liberties of sin:
If it prove so, I will be gone the sooner.
I'll to the Centaur, to go seek this slave:
I greatly fear my money is not safe.   [*Exit.*

ACT II.

SCENE I.—*A public Place.*

Enter ADRIANA *and* LUCIANA.

Adr. Neither my husband nor the slave re-
    turn'd,
That in such haste I sent to seek his master!
Sure, Luciana, it is two o'clock.   [him,

Luc. Perhaps some merchant hath invited
And from the mart he's somewhere gone to
    dinner.
Good sister, let us dine, and never fret:
A man is master of his liberty;
Time is their master; and, when they see time,
They'll go or come. If so, be patient, sister.

Adr. Why should their liberty than ours be
    more?   [door.

Luc. Because their business still lies out o'

Adr. Look, when I serve him so, he takes it ill.

Luc. O, know he is the bridle of your will.

Adr. There's none but asses will be bridled so.   [woe.

Luc. Why, headstrong liberty is lash'd with
There's nothing situate under heaven's eye
But hath his bound in earth, in sea, in sky:
The beasts, the fishes, and the winged fowls,
Are their males' subject, and at their controls:
Men, more divine, the masters of all these,
Lords of the wide world and wild wat'ry seas,
Indued with intellectual sense and souls
Of more pre-eminence than fish and fowls,
Are masters to their females, and their lords:
Then let your will attend on their accords.

Adr. This servitude makes you to keep un-
        wed.   [bed.

Luc. Not this, but troubles of the marriage-

Adr. But, were you wedded, you would bear
        some sway.

Luc. Ere I learn love, I'll practise to obey.

Adr. How if your husband start some other
        where?

Luc. Till he come home again I would for-
        bear.

Adr. Patience unmov'd, no marvel though
        she pause:
They can be meek that have no other cause.
A wretched soul, bruis'd with adversity,
We bid be quiet when we hear it cry;
But were we burden'd with like weight of pain,
As much, or more, we should ourselves com-
        plain: [thee,
So thou, that hast no unkind mate to grieve
With urging helpless patience wouldst relieve
        me:
But if thou live to see like right bereft,
This fool-begg'd patience in thee will be left.

  Luc. Well, I will marry one day, but to try:—
Here comes your man, now is your husband
        nigh.

Enter DROMIO OF EPHESUS.

Adr. Say, is your tardy master now at hand?

Dro. E. Nay, he is at two hands with me,
and that my two ears can witness.

Adr. Say, didst thou speak with him?
        know'st thou his mind?

Dro. E. Ay, ay, he told his mind upon mine
ear. Beshrew his hand, I scarce could understand it.

Luc. Spake he so doubtfully thou couldst
not feel his meaning?

Dro. E. Nay, he struck so plainly I could too
well feel his blows; and withal so doubtfully
that I could scarce understand them.

Adr. But say, I pr'ythee, is he coming home?
It seems he hath great care to please his wife.

Dro. E. Why, mistress, sure my master is
        horn-mad.

Adr. Horn-mad, thou villain?

Dro. E. I mean not cuckold-mad; but, sure,
he's stark-mad.
When I desir'd him to come home to dinner,

He ask'd me for a thousand marks in gold:
'*Tis dinner-time*, quoth I; *My gold*, quoth he:
Your meat doth burn, quoth I; *My gold*, quoth he:
Will you come home? quoth I; *My gold*, quoth he:
Where is the thousand marks I gave thee, villain?
The pig, quoth I, *is burn'd; My gold*, quoth he:
My mistress, sir, quoth I; *Hang up thy mistress;*
I know not thy mistress; out on thy mistress!

Luc. Quoth who?

Dro. E. Quoth my master:
I know, quoth he, *no house, no wife, no mistress:*
So that my errand, due unto my tongue,
I thank him, I bare home upon my shoulders;
For, in conclusion, he did beat me there.

Adr. Go back again, thou slave, and fetch
        him home.   [home?

Dro. E. Go back again! and be new beaten
For God's sake, send some other messenger.

Adr. Back, slave, or I will break thy pate
        across.   [other beating:

Dro. E. And he will bless that cross with
Between you I shall have a holy head.

Adr. Hence, prating peasant; fetch thy
        master home.   [with me,

Dro. E. Am I so round with you, as you
That like a football you do spurn me thus?
You spurn me hence, and he will spurn me
        hither:
If I last in this service you must case me in
        leather.   [*Exit.*

Luc. Fie, how impatience low'reth in your
        face!   [grace,

Adr. His company must do his minions
Whilst I at home starve for a merry look.
Hath homely age the alluring beauty took
From my poor cheek? then he hath wasted it:
Are my discourses dull? barren my wit?
If voluble and sharp discourse be marr'd,
Unkindness blunts it more than marble hard:
Do their gay vestments his affections bait?
That's not my fault, he's master of my state:
What ruins are in me that can be found
By him not ruin'd? then is he the ground
Of my defeatures: my decayed fair
A sunny look of his would soon repair;
But, too unruly deer, he breaks the pale
And feeds from home; poor I am but his stale.

Luc. Self-harming jealousy!—fie, beat it
        hence.   [dispense.

Adr. Unfeeling fools can with such wrongs
I know his eye doth homage otherwhere;
Or else what lets it but he would be here?
Sister, you know he promis'd me a chain;—
Would that alone, alone he would detain,
So he would keep fair quarter with his bed!
I see the jewel best enamelled   [still
Will lose his beauty; and though gold 'bides
That others touch, yet often touching will
Wear gold; and so no man that hath a name
But falsehood and corruption doth it shame.
Since that my beauty cannot please his eye,
I'll weep what's left away, and, weeping, die.

Luc. How many fond fools serve mad jeal-
        ousy!   [*Exeunt.*

SCENE II.—*The same.*

Enter ANTIPHOLUS OF SYRACUSE.

Ant. S. The gold I gave to Dromio is laid up
Safe at the Centaur; and the heedful slave
Is wander'd forth in care to seek me out.
By computation and mine host's report
I could not speak with Dromio since at first
I sent him from the mart. See, here he comes.

Enter DROMIO OF SYRACUSE.

How now, sir! is your merry humour alter'd?
As you love strokes, so jest with me again.
You know no Centaur? you receiv'd no gold?
Your mistress sent to have me home to dinner?
My house was at the Phœnix? Wast thou mad,
That thus so madly thou didst answer me?

Dro. S. What answer, sir? when spake I such
    a word?

Ant. S. Even now, even here, not half-an-
    hour since.

Dro. S. I did not see you since you sent me
    hence,
Home to the Centaur with the gold you gave
    me.

Ant. S. Villain, thou didst deny the gold's
    receipt;
And told'st me of a mistress and a dinner;
For which, I hope, thou felt'st I was displeas'd.

Dro. S. I am glad to see you in this merry
    vein: [me.
What means this jest? I pray you, master, tell

Ant. S. Yea, dost thou jeer and flout me in
    the teeth?
Think'st thou I jest? Hold, take thou that, and
    that.   [*Beating him.*

Dro. S. Hold, sir, for God's sake: now your
    jest is earnest:
Upon what bargain do you give it me?

Ant. S. Because that I familiarly sometimes
Do use you for my fool, and chat with you,
Your sauciness will jest upon my love,
And make a common of my serious hours.
When the sun shines let foolish gnats make
    sport,
But creep in crannies when he hides his beams.
If you will jest with me, know my aspéct,
And fashion your demeanour to my looks,
Or I will beat this method in your sconce.

Dro. S. Sconce, call you it? so you would
leave battering, I had rather have it a head: an
you use these blows long, I must get a sconce
for my head, and ensconce it too; or else I shall
seek my wit in my shoulders.—But, I pray sir,
why am I beaten?

Ant. S. Dost thou not know?

Dro. S. Nothing, sir; but that I am beaten.

Ant. S. Shall I tell you why?

Dro. S. Ay, sir, and wherefore; for, they say,
every why hath a wherefore,—

Ant. S. Why, first,—for flouting me; and
    then, wherefore,
For urging it the second time to me.

Dro. S. Was there ever any man thus beaten
    out of season,
When in the why and the wherefore is neither
    rhyme nor reason?—
Well, sir, I thank you.

Ant. S. Thank me, sir! for what?

Dro. S. Marry, sir, for this something that
you gave me for nothing.

Ant. S. I'll make you amends next, to give
you nothing for something.—But say, sir, is it
dinner-time?

Dro. S. No, sir; I think the meat wants
    that I have.

Ant. S. In good time, sir, what's that?

Dro. S. Basting.

Ant. S. Well, sir, then 'twill be dry.

Dro. S. If it be, sir, I pray you eat none of it.

Ant. S. Your reason?

Dro. S. Lest it make you choleric, and purchase me another dry basting.

Ant. S. Well, sir, learn to jest in good time:
There's a time for all things.

Dro. S. I durst have denied that before you
were so choleric.

Ant. S. By what rule, sir?

Dro. S. Marry, sir, by a rule as plain as the
plain bald pate of Father Time himself.

Ant. S. Let's hear it.

Dro. S. There's no time for a man to recover
his hair, that grows bald by nature.

Ant. S. May he not do it by fine and recovery?

Dro. S. Yes, to pay a fine for a peruke, and
recover the lost hair of another man.

Ant. S. Why is Time such a niggard of hair,
being, as it is, so plentiful an excrement?

Dro. S. Because it is a blessing that he bestows on beasts: and what he hath scanted men
in hair he hath given them in wit.

Ant. S. Why, but there's many a man hath
more hair than wit.

Dro. S. Not a man of those but he hath the
wit to lose his hair.

Ant. S. Why, thou didst conclude hairy men
plain dealers without wit.

Dro. S. The plainer dealer the sooner lost:
yet he loseth it in a kind of jollity.

Ant. S. For what reason?

Dro. S. For two; and sound ones too.

Ant. S. Nay, not sound, I pray you.

Dro. S. Sure ones, then.

Ant. S. Nay, not sure, in a thing falsing.

Dro. S. Certain ones, then.

Ant. S. Name them.

Dro. S. The one, to save the money that he
spends in tiring; the other, that at dinner they
should not drop in his porridge.

Ant. S. You would all this time have proved
there is no time for all things.

Dro. S. Marry, and did, sir; namely, no time
to recover hair lost by nature.

Ant. S. But your reason was not substantial
why there is no time to recover.

Dro. S. Thus I mend it: Time himself is

bald, and, therefore, to the world's end will
have bald followers.

Ant. S. I knew 'twould be a bald conclusion:
But, soft! who wafts us yonder?

Enter ADRIANA *and* LUCIANA.

Adr. Ay, ay, Antipholus, look strange and
    frown;
Some other mistress hath thy sweet aspécts:
I am not Adriana, nor thy wife.
The time was, once, when thou unurg'd wouldst
    vow
That never words were music to thine ear,
That never object pleasing in thine eye,
That never touch well welcome to thy hand,
That never meat sweet-savour'd in thy taste,
Unless I spake, look'd, touch'd, or carv'd to
    thee.
How comes it now, my husband, oh, how
    comes it,
That thou art then estranged from thyself?
Thyself I call it, being strange to me,
That undividable, incorporate,
Am better than thy dear self's better part.
Ah, do not tear away thyself from me;
For know, my love, as easy mayst thou fall
A drop of water in the breaking gulf,
And take unmingled thence that drop again,
Without addition or diminishing,
As take from me thyself, and not me too.
How dearly would it touch thee to the quick
Shouldst thou but hear I were licentious,
And that this body, consecrate to thee,
By ruffian lust should be contaminate!
Wouldst thou not spit at me, and spurn at me,
And hurl the name of husband in my face,
And tear the stain'd skin off my harlot brow,
And from my false hand cut the wedding-ring,
And break it with a deep-divorcing vow?
I know thou canst; and, therefore, see thou
    do it.
I am possess'd with an adulterate blot;
My blood is mingled with the crime of lust:
For if we two be one, and thou play false,
I do digest the poison of thy flesh,
Being strumpeted by thy contagion.   [bed;
Keep then fair league and truce with thy true
I live dis-stain'd, thou undishonoured.

Ant. S. Plead you to me, fair dame? I know
    you not:
In Ephesus I am but two hours old,
As strange unto your town as to your talk;
Who, every word by all my wit being scann'd,
Want wit in all one word to understand.

Luc. Fie, brother! how the world is chang'd
    with you:
When were you wont to use my sister thus?
She sent for you by Dromio home to dinner.

Ant. S. By Dromio?

Dro. S. By me?

Adr. By thee; and this thou didst return
    from him,—
That he did buffet thee, and in his blows
Denied my house for his, me for his wife.

Ant. S. Did you converse, sir, with this gen-
    tlewoman?
What is the course and drift of your compáct?

Dro. S. I, sir? I never saw her till this time.

Ant. S. Villain, thou liest; for even her very
    words
Didst thou deliver to me on the mart.

Dro. S. I never spake with her in all my life.

Ant. S. How can she thus, then, call us by
    our names,
Unless it be by inspiration?

Adr. How ill agrees it with your gravity
To counterfeit thus grossly with your slave,
Abetting him to thwart me in my mood!
Be it my wrong, you are from me exempt,
But wrong not that wrong with a more con-
    tempt.
Come, I will fasten on this sleeve of thine:
Thou art an elm, my husband, I a vine,
Whose weakness, married to thy stronger state,
Makes me with thy strength to communicate:
If aught possess thee from me, it is dross,
Usurping ivy, brier, or idle moss;
Who, all for want of pruning, with intrusion
Infect thy sap, and live on thy confusion.

Ant. S. To me she speaks; she moves me
    for her theme:
What, was I married to her in my dream?
Or sleep I now, and think I hear all this?
What error drives our eyes and ears amiss?
Until I know this sure uncertainty
I'll entertain the offer'd fallacy.

Luc. Dromio, go bid the servants spread for
    dinner.   [sinner.

Dro. S. O for my beads! I cross me for a
This is the fairy land;—O spite of spites!
We talk with goblins, owls, and elvish sprites;
If we obey them not, this will ensue,   [blue.
They'll suck our breath, or pinch us black and

Luc. Why prat'st thou to thyself, and an-
    swer'st not?   [sot!
Dromio, thou drone, thou snail, thou slug, thou

Dro. S. I am transformed, master, am not I?

Ant. S. I think thou art, in mind, and so am I.

Dro. S. Nay, master, both in mind and in
    my shape.

Ant. S. Thou hast thine own form.

Dro. S.   No, I am an ape.

Luc. If thou art chang'd to aught, 'tis to an
    ass.   [for grass.

Dro. S. 'Tis true; she rides me, and I long
'Tis so, I am an ass; else it could never be
But I should know her as well as she knows me.

Adr. Come, come, no longer will I be a fool,
To put the finger in the eye and weep,
Whilst man and master laugh my woes to
    scorn.—   [gate:—
Come, sir, to dinner;—Dromio, keep the
Husband, I'll dine above with you to-day,
And shrive you of a thousand idle pranks:—
Sirrah, if any ask you for your master,
Say he dines forth, and let no creature enter.—
Come, sister:—Dromio, play the porter well.

Ant. S. Am I in earth, in heaven, or in hell?

Sleeping or waking? mad, or well advis'd?
Known unto these, and to myself disguis'd?
I'll say as they say, and perséver so,
And in this mist at all adventures go.

   Dro. S. Master, shall I be porter at the gate?

   Adr. Ay; and let none enter, lest I break
     your pate.

   Luc. Come, come, Antipholus, we dine too
     late.   [*Exeunt.*

ACT III.

SCENE I.—*The same.*

Enter ANTIPHOLUS OF EPHESUS, DROMIO OF
EPHESUS, ANGELO, *and* BALTHAZAR.

   Ant. E. Good signior Angelo, you must ex-
     cuse us all.
My wife is shrewish when I keep not hours:
Say that I linger'd with you at your shop
To see the making of her carcanet,
And that to-morrow you will bring it home.
But here's a villain that would face me down.
He met me on the mart; and that I beat him,
And charg'd him with a thousand marks in gold;
And that I did deny wife and house:—
Thou drunkard, thou, what didst thou mean
     by this?

   Dro. E. Say what you will, sir, but I know
     what I know:
That you beat me at the mart I have your
     hand to show:
If the skin were parchment, and the blows you
     gave were ink,   [think.
Your own handwriting would tell you what I

   Ant. E. I think thou art an ass.

   Dro. E.   Marry, so it doth appear
By the wrongs I suffer and the blows I bear.
I should kick, being kick'd; and, being at that
     pass,   [an ass.
You would keep from my heels, and beware of

   Ant. E. You are sad, Signior Balthazar;
     pray God, our cheer   [come here.
May answer my good-will and your good wel-

   Bal. I hold your dainties cheap, sir, and
     your welcome dear.

   Ant. E. O, Signior Balthazar, either at flesh
     or fish,
A table full of welcome makes scarce one dainty
     dish.

   Bal. Good meat, sir, is common; that every
     churl affords.

   Ant. E. And welcome more common; for
     that's nothing but words.

   Bal. Small cheer and great welcome makes
     a merry feast.   [sparing guest.

   Ant. E. Ay, to a niggardly host and more
But though my cates be mean, take them in
     good part;   [heart.
Better cheer may you have, but not with better
But, soft; my door is lock'd: go bid them let
     us in.   [lian, Jen!

   Dro. E. Maud, Bridget, Marian, Cicely, Gil-

   Dro. S. [*Within.*] Mome, malt-horse, capon,
     coxcomb, idiot, patch!

Either get thee from the door or sit down at
     the hatch:
Dost thou conjure for wenches, that thou
     call'st for such store,   [the door.
When one is one too many? Go, get thee from

   Dro. E. What patch is made our porter?
     My master stays in the street.

   Dro. S. Let him walk from whence he came,
     lest he catch cold on 's feet.

   Ant. E. Who talks within there? ho, open
     the door.

   Dro. S. Right, sir, I'll tell you when an
     you'll tell me wherefore.

   Ant. E. Wherefore! for my dinner: I have
     not dined to-day.

   Dro. S. Nor to-day here you must not; come
     again when you may.

   Ant. E. What art thou that keep'st me out
     from the house I owe?

   Dro. S. The porter for this time, sir, and
     my name is Dromio.

   Dro. E. O villain, thou hast stolen both
     mine office and my name;   [blame.
The one ne'er got me credit, the other mickle
If thou hadst been Dromio to-day in my place,
Thou wouldst have chang'd thy face for a
     name, or thy name for an ass.

   Luce. [*Within.*] What a coil is there! Dromio,
     who are those at the gate?

   Dro. E. Let my master in, Luce.

   Luce.   Faith, no; he comes too late;
And so tell your master.

   Dro. E.   O Lord, I must laugh;—
Have at you with a proverb.—Shall I set in
     my staff?

   Luce. Have at you with another: that's,—
     When? can you tell?

   Dro. S. If thy name be called Luce,—Luce,
     thou hast answer'd him well.

   Ant. E. Do you hear, you minion? you'll
     let us in, I hope?

   Luce. I thought to have ask'd you.

   Dro. S.   And you said no.

   Dro. E. So, come, help: well struck; there
     was blow for blow.

   Ant. E. Thou baggage, let me in.

   Luce.   Can you tell for whose sake?

   Dro. E. Master, knock the door hard.

   Luce.   Let him knock till it ache.

   Ant. E. You'll cry for this, minion, if I beat
     the door down.

   Luce. What needs all that, and a pair of
     stocks in the town?

   Adr. [*Within.*] Who is that at the door, that
     keeps all this noise?

   Dro. S. By my troth, your town is troubled
     with unruly boys.

   Ant. E. Are you there, wife? you might
     have come before.   [the door.

   Adr. Your wife, sir knave! go, get you from

   Dro. E. If you went in pain, master, this
     knave would go sore.

   Ang. Here is neither cheer, sir, nor welcome:
     we would fain have either.

Bal. In debating which was best, we shall part with neither.

Dro. E. They stand at the door, master; bid them welcome hither.

Ant. E. There is something in the wind, that we cannot get in.

Dro. E. You would say so, master, if your garments were thin.
Your cake here is warm within; you stand here in the cold:
It would make a man mad as a buck, to be so bought and sold.

Ant. E. Go, fetch me something, I'll break ope the gate.

Dro. S. Break any breaking here, and I'll break your knave's pate.

Dro. E. A man may break a word with you, sir; and words are but wind;
Ay, and break it in your face, so he break it not behind.

Dro. S. It seems thou wantest breaking; out upon thee, hind!

Dro. E. Here's too much out upon thee: I pray thee, let me in.

Dro. S. Ay, when fowls have no feathers and fish have no fin.

Ant. E. Well, I'll break in; go borrow me a crow.

Dro. E. A crow without a feather; master, mean you so?   [a feather:
For a fish without a fin there's a fowl without
If a crow help us in, sirrah, we'll pluck a crow together.   [crow.

Ant. E. Go, get thee gone; fetch me an iron

Bal. Have patience, sir: O, let it not be so:
Herein you war against your reputation,
And draw within the compass of suspect
The unviolated honour of your wife.
Once this,—your long experience of her wisdom,
Her sober virtue, years, and modesty,
Plead on her part some cause to you unknown;
And doubt not, sir, but she will well excuse
Why at this time the doors are made against you.
Be rul'd by me; depart in patience,
And let us to the Tiger all to dinner:
And, about evening, come yourself alone,
To know the reason of this strange restraint.
If by strong hand you offer to break in,
Now in the stirring passage of the day,
A vulgar comment will be made of it;
And that supposed by the common rout
Against your yet ungalled estimation,
That may with foul intrusion enter in,
And dwell upon your grave when you are dead:
For slander lives upon succession,
For ever hous'd where it once gets possession.

Ant. E. You have prevail'd. I will depart in quiet,
And, in despite of mirth, mean to be merry.
I know a wench of excellent discourse,—
Pretty and witty; wild, and yet, too, gentle;—
There will we dine: this woman that I mean,
My wife,—but, I protest, without desert,—
Hath oftentimes upbraided me withal;

To her will we to dinner.—Get you home
And fetch the chain: by this, I know, 'tis made:
Bring it, I pray you, to the Porcupine;
For there's the house; that chain will I bestow,—
Be it for nothing but to spite my wife,—
Upon mine hostess there: good sir, make haste:
Since mine own doors refuse to entertain me,
I'll knock elsewhere, to see if they'll disdain me.

Ang. I'll meet you at that place some hour hence.

Ant. E. Do so; this jest shall cost me some expense.   [*Exeunt.*

SCENE II.—*The same.*

Enter LUCIANA *and* ANTIPHOLUS *of* SYRACUSE.

Luc. And may it be that you have quite forgot
A husband's office? Shall, Antipholus, hate,
Even in the spring of love, thy love-springs rot?
Shall love, in building, grow so ruinate?
If you did wed my sister for her wealth,
Then, for her wealth's sake, use her with more kindness:
Of, if you like elsewhere, do it by stealth;
Muffle your false love with some show of blindness:
Let not my sister read it in your eye;
Be not thy tongue thy own shame's orator;
Look sweet, speak fair, become disloyalty;
Apparel vice like virtue's harbinger:
Bear a fair presence though your heart be tainted;
Teach sin the carriage of a holy saint;
Be secret-false: what need she be acquainted?
What simple thief brags of his own attaint?
'Tis double wrong, to truant with your bed
And let her read it in thy look at board:—
Shame hath a bastard-fame, well managed;
Ill deeds are doubled with an evil word.
Alas, poor women! make us but believe,
Being compact of credit, that you love us:
Though others have the arm, show us the sleeve;
We in your motion turn, and you may move us.
Then, gentle brother, get you in again;
Comfort my sister, cheer her, call her wife:
'Tis holy sport to be a little vain   [strife.
When the sweet breath of flattery conquers

Ant. S. Sweet mistress,—what your name is else, I know not,
Nor by what wonder do you hit on mine,—
Less, in your knowledge and your grace, you show not   [divine.
Than our earth's wonder; more than earth
Teach me, dear creature, how to think and speak;
Lay open to my earthy gross conceit,
Smother'd in errors, feeble, shallow, weak,
The folded meaning of your words' deceit.
Against my soul's pure truth why labour you
To make it wander in an unknown field?

Are you a god? would you create me new?
  Transform me, then, and to your power I'll
    yield.
But if that I am I, then well I know
  Your weeping sister is no wife of mine,
Nor to her bed no homage do I owe:
  Far more, far more, to you do I decline.
O, train me not, sweet mermaid, with thy note,
  To drown me in thy sister's flood of tears:
Sing, siren, for thyself, and I will dote:
  Spread o'er the silver waves thy golden hairs,
And as a bed I'll take thee, and there lie;
  And, in that glorious supposition, think
He gains by death that hath such means to
    die:—
  Let love, being light, be drowned if she sink!
Luc. What, are you mad, that you do rea-
  son so?
Ant. S. Not mad, but mated; how, I do not
  know.
Luc. It is a fault that springeth from your
  eye.
Ant. S. For gazing on your beams, fair sun,
  being by.
Luc. Gaze where you should, and that will
  clear your sight.   [on night.
Ant. S. As good to wink, sweet love, as look
Luc. Why call you me love? call my sister so.
Ant. S. Thy sister's sister.
Luc.   That's my sister.
Ant. S.   No;
It is thyself, mine own self's better part;
Mine eye's clear eye, my dear heart's dearer
  heart;
My food, my fortune, and my sweet hope's aim,
My sole earth's heaven, and my heaven's claim.
  Luc. All this my sister is, or else should be.
  Ant. S. Call thyself sister, sweet, for I aim
    thee:
Thee will I love, and with thee lead my life:
Thou hast no husband yet, nor I no wife;
Give me thy hand.
  Luc.   O soft, sir, hold you still;
I'll fetch my sister, to get her good-will.
                  [*Exit* LUCIANA.

Enter from the House of ANTIPHOLUS OF
  EPHESUS, DROMIO OF SYRACUSE.

  Ant. S. Why, how now, Dromio? where
runn'st thou so fast?
  Dro. S. Do you know me, sir? am I Dromio?
am I your man? am I myself?
  Ant. S. Thou art Dromio, thou art my man,
thou art thyself.
  Dro. S. I am an ass, I am a woman's man,
and beside myself.
  Ant. S. What woman's man? and how beside
thyself?
  Dro. S. Marry, sir, beside myself, I am due
to a woman; one that claims me, one that
haunts me, one that will have me.
  Ant. S. What claim lays she to thee?
  Dro. S. Marry, sir, such claim as you would
lay to your horse: and she would have me as a

beast; not that, I being a beast, she would have
me; but that she, being a very beastly creature,
lays claim to me.
  Ant. S. What is she?
  Dro. S. A very reverent body; ay, such a
one as a man may not speak of without he say
sir-reverence: I have but lean luck in the
match, and yet she is a wondrous fat marriage.
  Ant. S. How dost thou mean?—a fat marriage?
  Dro. S. Marry, sir, she's the kitchen-wench,
and all grease; and I know not what use to put
her to, but to make a lamp of her, and run
from her by her own light. I warrant, her rags,
and the tallow in them, will burn a Poland
winter: if she lives till doomsday, she'll burn a
week longer than the whole world.
  Ant. S. What complexion is she of?
  Dro. S. Swart, like my shoe; but her face
nothing like so clean kept: for why? she sweats,
a man may go over shoes in the grime of it.
  Ant. S. That's a fault that water will mend.
  Dro. S. No, sir, 'tis in grain; Noah's flood
could not do it.
  Ant. S. What's her name?
  Dro. S. Nell, sir;—but her name and three-
quarters, that is an ell and three-quarters, will
not measure her from hip to hip.
  Ant. S. Then she bears some breadth?
  Dro. S. No longer from head to foot than
from hip to hip: she is spherical, like a globe:
I could find out countries in her.   [land?
  Ant. S. In what part of her body stands Ire-
  Dro. S. Marry, sir, in her buttocks: I found
it out by the bogs.
  Ant. S. Where Scotland?
  Dro. S. I found it by the barrenness; hard
in the palm of the hand.
  Ant. S. Where France?
  Dro. S. In her forehead; armed and reverted,
making war against her hair.
  Ant. S. Where England?
  Dro. S. I looked for the chalky cliffs, but I
could find no whiteness in them: but I guess it
stood in her chin, by the salt rheum that ran
between France and it.
  Ant. S. Where Spain?
  Dro. S. Faith, I saw it not; but I felt it hot
in her breath.
  Ant. S. Where America—the Indies?
  Dro. S. O, sir, upon her nose, all o'er embel-
lished with rubies, carbuncles, sapphires, declining their rich aspect to the hot breath of
Spain; who sent whole armadas of carracks to
be ballast at her nose.
  Ant. S. Where stood Belgia,—the Nether-
lands?
  Dro. S. O, sir, I did not look so low.—To
conclude, this drudge or diviner laid claim to
me; called me Dromio; swore I was assured to
her; told me what privy marks I had about me,
as the mark of my shoulder, the mole in my
neck, the great wart on my left arm, that I,
amazed, ran from her as a witch: and, I think,

If my breast had not been made of faith and
my heart of steel, she had transformed me to a
curtail-dog, and made me turn i' the wheel.

Ant. S. Go, hie thee presently post to the
road;
And if the wind blow any way from shore,
I will not harbour in this town to-night.
If any bark put forth, come to the mart,
Where I will walk till thou return to me.
If every one knows us, and we know none,
'Tis time, I think, to trudge, pack, and be gone.

Dro. S. As from a bear a man would run for
life,
So fly I from her that would be my wife.
           [*Exit.*

Ant. S. There's none but witches do inhabit
here;
And therefore 'tis high time that I were hence.
She that doth call me husband, even my soul
Doth for a wife abhor; but her fair sister,
Possess'd with such a gentle sovereign grace,
Of such enchanting presence and discourse,
Hath almost made me traitor to myself:
But, lest myself be guilty to self-wrong,
I'll stop mine ears against the mermaid's song.

Enter ANGELO.

Ang. Master Antipholus?

Ant. S. Ay, that's my name.   [chain;

Ang. I know it well, sir. Lo, here is the
I thought to have ta'en you at the Porcupine:
The chain unfinish'd made me stay thus long.

Ant. S. What is your will that I shall do with
this?

Ang. What please yourself, sir; I have made
it for you.

Ant. S. Made it for me, sir! I bespoke it not.

Ang. Not once nor twice, but twenty times
you have:
Go home with it, and please your wife withal;
And soon at supper-time I'll visit you,
And then receive my money for the chain.

Ant. S. I pray you, sir, receive the money
now,
For fear you ne'er see chain nor money more.

Ang. You are a merry man, sir; fare you
well.   [*Exit.*

Ant. S. What I should think of this I cannot
tell:
But this I think, there's no man is so vain
That would refuse so fair an offer'd chain.
I see a man here needs not live by shifts,
When in the street he meets such golden gifts.
I'll to the mart, and there for Dromio stay;
If any ship put out, then straight away. [*Exit.*

ACT IV.

SCENE I.—*The same.*

Enter a Merchant, ANGELO, *and an* Officer.

Mer. You know, since Pentecost the sum is
due,
And since I have not much importun'd you;
Nor now I had not, but that I am bound

To Persia, and want gilders for my voyage;
Therefore make present satisfaction,
Or I'll attach you by this officer.

Ang. Even just the sum that I do owe to you
Is growing to me by Antipholus;
And in the instant that I met with you
He had of me a chain; at five o'clock
I shall receive the money for the same:
Pleaseth you walk with me down to his house,
I will discharge my bond, and thank you too.

Enter ANTIPHOLUS OF EPHESUS, *and*
DROMIO OF EPHESUS.

Off. That labour may you save: see where
he comes.   [go thou

Ant. E. While I go to the goldsmith's house,
And buy a rope's end; that will I bestow
Among my wife and her confederates,
For locking me out of doors by day.—
But, soft; I see the goldsmith: get thee gone;
Buy thou a rope, and bring it home to me.

Dro. E. I buy a thousand pound a year! I
buy a rope!   [*Exit* DROMIO.

Ant. E. A man is well holp up that trusts
to you:
I promised your presence, and the chain;
But neither chain nor goldsmith came to me:
Belike you thought our love would last too long,
If it were chained together; and therefore came
not.   [note,

Ang. Saving your merry humour, here's the
How much your chain weighs to the utmost
carat;
The fineness of the gold, and chargeful fashion;
Which does amount to three odd ducats more
Than I stand debted to this gentleman:
I pray you, see him presently discharg'd,
For he is bound to sea, and stays but for it.

Ant. E. I am not furnished with the present
money;
Besides I have some business in the town:
Good Signior, take the stranger to my house,
And with you take the chain, and bid my wife
Disburse the sum on the receipt thereof;
Perchance I will be there as soon as you.

Ang. Then you will bring the chain to her
yourself?

Ant. E. No; bear it with you, lest I come
not time enough.   [about you?

Ang. Well sir, I will: have you the chain

Ant. E. An if I have not, sir, I hope you
have,
Or else you may return without your money.

Ang. Nay, come, I pray you, sir, give me
the chain;
Both wind and tide stays for this gentleman,
And I, to blame, have held him here too long.

Ant. E. Good lord, you use this dalliance to
excuse
Your breach of promise to the Porcupine:
I should have chid you for not bringing it,
But, like a shrew, you first begin to brawl.

Mer. The hour steals on; I pray you, sir,
despatch.

Ang. You hear how he importunes me: the chain,—

Ant. E. Why, give it to my wife, and fetch your money.   [even now:

Ang. Come, come, you know I gave it you
Either send the chain or send me by some token.

Ant. E. Fie! now you run this humour out of breath: [see it.
Come, where's the chain? I pray you, let me

Mer. My business cannot brook this dalliance:
Good sir, say whe'r you'll answer me or no;
If not, I'll leave him to the officer.   [you?

Ant. E. I answer you! What should I answer

Ang. The money that you owe me for the chain.   [chain.

Ant. E. I owe you none till I receive the

Ang. You know I gave it you half-an-hour since.

Ant. E. You gave me none: you wrong me much to say so.

Ang. You wrong me more, sir, in denying it:
Consider how it stands upon my credit.

Mer. Well, officer, arrest him at my suit.

Off. I do, and charge you in the duke's name to obey me.

Ang. This touches me in reputation:
Either consent to pay this sum for me,
Or I attach you by this officer.

Ant. E. Consent to pay thee that I never had!
Arrest me, foolish fellow, if thou dar'st.

Ang. Here is thy fee; arrest him, officer:—
I would not spare my brother in this case,
If he should scorn me so apparently.

Off. I do arrest you, sir: you hear the suit.

Ant. E. I do obey thee till I give thee bail:—
But, sirrah, you shall buy this sport as dear
As all the metal in your shop will answer.

Ang. Sir, sir, I shall have law in Ephesus,
To your notorious shame, I doubt it not.

Enter DROMIO OF SYRACUSE.

Dro. S. Master, there is a bark of Epidamnum
That stays but till her owner comes aboard,
And then, sir, bears away: our fraughtage, sir,
I have convey'd aboard; and I have bought
The oil, the balsamum, and aqua-vitæ.
The ship is in her trim; the merry wind
Blows fair from land: they stay for naught at all
But for their owner, master, and yourself.

Ant. E. How now! a madman? Why, thou peevish sheep,
What ship of Epidamnum stays for me?

Dro. S. A ship you sent me to, to hire waftage.

Ant. E. Thou drunken slave, I sent thee for a rope;
And told thee to what purpose and what end.

Dro. S. You sent me, sir, for a rope's end as soon:
You sent me to the bay, sir, for a bark.

Ant. E. I will debate this matter at more leisure,

And teach your ears to listen with more heed.
To Adriana, villain, hie thee straight:
Give her this key, and tell her, in the desk
That's cover'd o'er with Turkish tapestry
There is a purse of ducats; let her send it:
Tell her I am arrested in the street,
And that shall bail me: hie thee, slave; be gone.
On, officer, to prison till it come.

[*Exeunt* MER., ANG., Off., *and* ANT. E.

Dro. S. To Adriana! that is where we din'd,
Where Dowsabel did claim me for her husband:
She is too big, I hope, for me to compass.
Thither I must, although against my will,
For servants must their masters' minds fulfil.

[*Exit.*

SCENE II.—*The same.*

Enter ADRIANA *and* LUCIANA.

Adr. Ah, Luciana, did he tempt thee so?
Might'st thou perceive austerely in his eye
That he did plead in earnest, yea or no?
Look'd he or red or pale, or sad or merrily?
What observation mad'st thou in this case
Of his heart's meteors tilting in his face?

Luc. First, he denied you had him in no right.   [my spite.

Adr. He meant he did me none; the more

Luc. Then swore he that he was a stranger here.   [he were.

Adr. And true he swore, though yet forsworn

Luc. Then pleaded I for you.

Adr.   And what said he?

Luc. That love I begg'd for you he begg'd of me.   [love?

Adr. With what persuasion did he tempt thy

Luc. With words that in an honest suit might move.
First, he did praise my beauty, then my speech.

Adr. Didst speak him fair?

Luc.   Have patience, I beseech.

Adr. I cannot, nor I will not hold me still:
My tongue, though not my heart, shall have his will.
He is deformed, crooked, old, and sere,
Ill-fac'd, worse bodied, shapeless everywhere;
Vicious, ungentle, foolish, blunt, unkind;
Stigmatical in making, worse in mind.   [one?

Luc. Who would be jealous then of such a
No evil lost is wail'd when it is gone.

Adr. Ah! but I think him better than I say,
And yet would herein others' eyes were worse:
Far from her nest the lapwing cries, away:
My heart prays for him, though my tongue do curse.

Enter DROMIO OF SYRACUSE.

Dro. S. Here, go: the desk, the purse: sweet now, make haste.

Luc. How hast thou lost thy breath?

Dro. S.   By running fast.

Adr. Where is thy master, Dromio? is he well?   [hell.

Dro. S. No, he's in Tartar limbo, worse than

A devil in an everlasting garment hath him;
One whose hard heart is button'd up with steel;
A fiend, a fairy, pitiless and rough;
A wolf—nay worse, a fellow all in buff;
A back-friend, a shoulder-clapper, one that
    countermands   [lands;
The passages of alleys, creeks, and narrow
A hound that runs counter, and yet draws dry
    foot well;   [souls to hell.
One that, before the judgment, carries poor

Adr. Why, man, what is the matter?

Dro. S. I do not know the matter: he is
    'rested on the case.   [suit.

Adr. What, is he arrested? tell me at whose

Dro. S. I know not at whose suit he is ar-
    rested, well;
But he's in a suit of buff which 'rested him,
    that can I tell:
Will you send him, mistress, redemption, the
    money in the desk?

Adr. Go fetch it, sister.—This I wonder at,
    [*Exit* LUCIANA.
That he, unknown to me, should be in debt.—
Tell me, was he arrested on a band?

Dro. S. Not on a band, but on a stronger
    thing;
A chain, a chain: do you not hear it ring?

Adr. What, the chain?   [gone.

Dro. S. No, no, the bell: 'tis time that I were
It was two ere I left him, and now the clock
    strikes one.

Adr. The hours come back! that did I never
    hear.

Dro. S. O yes. If any hour meet a sergeant,
    'a turns back for very fear.

Adr. As if time were in debt! how fondly
    dost thou reason!

Dro. S. Time is a very bankrupt, and owes
    more than he's worth to season.
Nay, he's a thief too: have you not heard men
    say
That Time comes stealing on by night and day?
If he be in debt and theft, and a sergeant in the
    way,   [day?
Hath he not reason to turn back an hour in a

Enter LUCIANA.

Adr. Go, Dromio; there's the money, bear
    it straight;
And bring thy master home immediately.—
Come, sister: I am press'd down with conceit;
    Conceit my comfort and my injury.
    [*Exeunt.*

SCENE III.—*The same.*

Enter ANTIPHOLUS OF SYRACUSE.

Ant. S. There's not a man I meet but doth
    salute me
As if I were their well-acquainted friend;
And every one doth call me by my name.
Some tender money to me, some invite me;
Some other give me thanks for kindnesses;
Some offer me commodities to buy:
Even now a tailor call'd me in his shop,
And show'd me silks that he had bought for me,
And therewithal took measure of my body.
Sure, these are but imaginary wiles,
And Lapland sorcerers inhabit here.

Enter DROMIO OF SYRACUSE.

Dro. S. Master, here's the gold you sent me
    for.
What, have you got the picture of Old Adam
    new apparelled?

Ant. S. What gold is this? What Adam dost
    thou mean?

Dro. S. Not that Adam that kept the paradise, but that Adam that keeps the prison: he
that goes in the calf's-skin that was killed for
the Prodigal; he that came behind you, sir, like
an evil angel, and bid you forsake your liberty.

Ant. S. I understand thee not.

Dro. S. No? why, 'tis a plain case: he that
went like a base-viol in a case of leather; the
man, sir, that, when gentlemen are tired, gives
them a fob, and 'rests them; he, sir, that takes
pity on decayed men, and gives them suits of
durance; he that sets up his rest to do more
exploits with his mace than a morris-pike.

Ant. S. What! thou mean'st an officer?

Dro. S. Ay, sir,—the sergeant of the band:
he that brings any man to answer it that breaks
his band; one that thinks a man always going
to bed, and says, *God give you good rest!*

Ant. S. Well, sir, there rest in your foolery.
Is there any ship puts forth to-night? may we
be gone?

Dro. S. Why, sir, I brought you word an
hour since, that the bark Expedition put forth
tonight; and then were you hindered by the
sergeant, to tarry for the hoy, Delay: here are
the angels that you sent for to deliver you.

Ant. S. The fellow is distract, and so am I;
And here we wander in illusions:
Some blessed power deliver us from hence!

Enter a Courtezan.

Cour. Well met, well met, Master Antipho-
    lus.
I see, sir, you have found the goldsmith now:
Is that the chain you promis'd me to-day?

Ant. S. Satan, avoid! I charge thee, tempt
    me not!

Dro. S. Master, is this Mistress Satan?

Ant. S. It is the devil.

Dro. S. Nay, she is worse—she is the devil's
dam; and here she comes in the habit of a light
wench; and thereof comes that the wenches
say, *God damn me*—that's as much as to say,
God make me a light wench. It is written, they
appear to men like angels of light: light is an
effect of fire, and fire will burn; *ergo*, light
wenches will burn: come not near her.

Cour. Your man and you are marvellous
    merry, sir.   [here.
Will you go with me? We'll mend our dinner

Dro. S. Master, if you do; expect spoon-
meat, or bespeak a long spoon.

Ant. S. Why, Dromio?

Dro. S. Marry, he must have a long spoon that must eat with the devil.

Ant. S. Avoid then, fiend! what tell'st thou me of supping?
Thou art, as you are all, a sorceress:
I conjure thee to leave me and be gone.

Cour. Give me the ring of mine you had at dinner,
Or, for my diamond, the chain you promis'd,
And I'll be gone, sir, and not trouble you.

Dro. S. Some devils ask but the paring of one's nail,
A rush, a hair, a drop of blood, a pin,
A nut, a cherry-stone; but she, more covetous,
Would have a chain.
Master, be wise; an if you give it her,
The devil will shake her chain, and fright us with it.   [chain:

Cour. I pray you, sir, my ring, or else the
I hope you do not mean to cheat me so.

Ant. S. Avaunt, thou witch! Come, Dromio, let us go.

Dro. S. Fly pride, says the peacock: Mistress, that you know.
        [*Exeunt* ANT. S. *and* DRO. S.

Cour. Now, out of doubt, Antipholus is mad,
Else would he never so demean himself:
A ring he hath of mine worth forty ducats,
And for the same he promis'd me a chain;
Both one and other he denies me now:
The reason that I gather he is mad,—
Besides this present instance of his rage,—
Is a mad tale he told to-day at dinner,
Of his own doors being shut against his entrance.
Belike his wife, acquainted with his fits,
On purpose shut the doors against his way.
My way is now to hie home to his house,
And tell his wife that, being lunatic,
He rush'd into my house, and took perforce
My ring away: this course I fittest choose,
For forty ducats is too much to lose.   [*Exit.*

SCENE IV.—*The same.*

Enter ANTIPHOLUS OF EPHESUS *and an* Officer.

Ant. E. Fear me not, man; I will not break away:
I'll give thee, ere I leave thee, so much money
To warrant thee, as I am 'rested for.
My wife is in a wayward mood to-day;
And will not lightly trust the messenger
That I should be attach'd in Ephesus:
I tell you, 'twill sound harshly in her ears.

Enter DROMIO OF EPHESUS, *with a rope's end.*

Here comes my man: I think he brings the money.
How now, sir! have you that I sent you for?

Dro. E. Here's that, I warrant you, will pay them all.

Ant. E. But where's the money?   [rope.

Dro. E. Why, sir, I gave the money for the

Ant. E. Five hundred ducats, villain, for a rope?   [the rate.

Dro. E. I'll serve you, sir, five hundred at

Ant. E. To what end did I bid thee hie thee home?

Dro. E. To a rope's end, sir; and to that end am I return'd.

Ant. E. And to that end, sir, I will welcome you.   [*Beating him.*

Off. Good sir, be patient.

Dro. E. Nay, 'tis for me to be patient; I am in adversity.

Off. Good now, hold thy tongue.

Dro. E. Nay, rather persuade him to hold his hands.

Ant. E. Thou whoreson senseless villain!

Dro. E. I would I were senseless, sir, that I might not feel your blows.

Ant. E. Thou art sensible in nothing but blows, and so is an ass.

Dro. E. I am an ass indeed: you may prove it by my long ears. I have served him from the hour of my nativity to this instant, and have nothing at his hands for my service but blows: when I am cold he heats me with beating; when I am warm he cools me with beating. I am waked with it when I sleep; raised with it when I sit; driven out of doors with it when I go from home; welcomed home with it when I return: nay, I bear it on my shoulders as a beggar wont her brat; and I think, when he hath lamed me, I shall beg with it from door to door.

Ant. E. Come, go along; my wife is coming yonder.

Enter ADRIANA, LUCIANA, *and the* Courtezan, *with* PINCH *and others.*

Dro. E. Mistress, *respice finem*, respect your end; or rather the prophecy, like the parrot, *Beware the rope's end.*

Ant. E. Wilt thou still talk?   [*Beats him.*

Cour. How say you now? is not your husband mad?

Adr. His incivility confirms no less.—
Good Doctor Pinch, you are a conjurer;
Establish him in his true sense again,
And I will please you what you will demand.

Luc. Alas, how fiery and how sharp he looks!

Cour. Mark how he trembles in his ecstacy!

Pinch. Give me your hand, and let me feel your pulse.

Ant. E. There is my hand, and let it feel your ear.

Pinch. I charge thee, Satan, hous'd within this man,
To yield possession to my holy prayers,
And to thy state of darkness hie thee straight:
I conjure thee by all the saints in heaven.

Ant. E. Peace, doting wizard, peace; I am not mad.

Adr. O that thou wert not, poor distressed soul!

Ant. E. You minion, you, are these your customers?

Did this companion with the saffron face
Revel and feast it at my house to-day,
Whilst upon me the guilty doors were shut,
And I denied to enter in my house? [at home,
 Adr. O husband, God doth know you din'd
Where would you had remain'd until this time,
Free from these slanders and this open shame!
 Ant. E. I din'd at home! Thou villain, what
  say'st thou?
 Dro. E. Sir, sooth to say, you did not dine at
  home.
 Ant. E. Were not my doors lock'd up and I
  shut out?
 Dro. E. Perdy, your doors were lock'd and
  you shut out.
 Ant. E. And did not she herself revile me
  there? [there.
 Dro. E. Sans fable, she herself revil'd you
 Ant. E. Did not her kitchen-maid rail,
  taunt, and scorn me?
 Dro. E. Certes, she did: the kitchen-vestal
  scorn'd you.
 Ant. E. And did not I in rage depart from
  thence? [witness,
 Dro. E. In verity, you did;—my bones bear
That since have felt the vigour of his rage.
 Adr. Is't good to soothe him in these con-
  traries? [vein,
 Pinch. It is no shame: the fellow finds his
And, yielding to him, humours well his frenzy.
 Ant. E. Thou hast suborn'd the goldsmith
  to arrest me.
 Adr. Alas! I sent you money to redeem you,
By Dromio here, who came in haste for it.
 Dro. E. Money by me! heart and good-will
  you might,
But surely, master, not a rag of money.
 Ant. E. Went'st not thou to her for a purse
  of ducats?
 Adr. He came to me, and I deliver'd it.
 Luc. And I am witness with her that she did.
 Dro. E. God and the rope-maker, bear me
  witness
That I was sent for nothing but a rope!
 Pinch. Mistress, both man and master is
  possess'd;
I know it by their pale and deadly looks:
They must be bound, and laid in some dark
  room.
 Ant. E. Say, wherefore didst thou lock me
  forth to-day?—
And why dost thou deny the bag of gold?
 Adr. I did not, gentle husband, lock thee
  forth.
 Dro. E. And, gentle master, I receiv'd no
  gold;
But I confess, sir, that we were lock'd out.
 Adr. Dissembling villain, thou speak'st false
  in both. [all;
 Ant. E. Dissembling harlot, thou art false in
And art confederate with a damned pack,
To make a loathsome abject scorn of me:
But with these nails I'll pluck out these false
  eyes,

That would behold me in this shameful sport.
  [*Pinch and* Assistants *bind* Ant. E. *and*
     Dro. E.
 Adr. O, bind him, bind him; let him not
  come near me.
 Pinch. More company;—the fiend is strong
  within him. [looks!
 Luc. Ah me, poor man! how pale and wan he
 Ant. E. What, will you murder me? Thou
  gaoler, thou,
I am thy prisoner: wilt thou suffer them
To make a rescue?
 Off.   Masters, let him go:
He is my prisoner, and you shall not have him.
 Pinch. Go, bind this man, for he is frantic
  too.
 Adr. What wilt thou do, thou peevish officer?
Hast thou delight to see a wretched man
Do outrage and displeasure to himself?
 Off. He is my prisoner: if I let him go,
The debt he owes will be requir'd of me.
 Adr. I will discharge thee ere I go from thee:
Bear me forthwith unto his creditor, [it.
And, knowing how the debt grows, I will pay
Good master doctor, see him safe convey'd
Home to my house.—O most unhappy day!
 Ant. E. O most unhappy strumpet!
 Dro. E. Master, I am here enter'd in bond
  for you.
 Ant. E. Out on thee, villain! wherefore dost
  thou mad me? [mad,
 Dro. E. Will you be bound for nothing? be
Good master; cry, the devil.— [talk!
 Luc. God help, poor souls, how idly do they
 Adr. Go bear him hence.—Sister, go you
  with me.—
  [*Exeunt* Pinch *and* Assistants, *with*
    Ant. E. *and* Dro. E.
Say now, whose suit is he arrested at?
 Off. One Angelo, a goldsmith; do you know
  him? [owes?
 Adr. I know the man: what is the sum he
 Off. Two hundred ducats.
 Adr.   Say, how grows it due?
 Off. Due for a chain your husband had of
  him. [it not.
 Adr. He did bespeak a chain for me, but had
 Cour. When as your husband, all in rage,
  to-day
Came to my house, and took away my ring,—
The ring I saw upon his finger now,—
Straight after did I meet him with a chain.
 Adr. It may be so, but I did never see it:
Come, gaoler, bring me where the goldsmith is?
I long to know the truth hereof at large.

 Enter Antipholus of Syracuse, *with his*
 rapier drawn, and Dromio of Syracuse.

 Luc. God, for thy mercy! they are loose
  again. [more help,
 Adr. And come with naked swords: let's call
To have them bound again.
 Off.   Away, they'll kill us.
  [*Exeunt* Off., Adr., *and* Luc.

Ant. S. I see these witches are afraid of swords.

Dro. S. She that would be your wife now ran from you.

Ant. S. Come to the Centaur; fetch our stuff from thence:
I long that we were safe and sound aboard.

Dro. S. Faith, stay here this night; they will surely do us no harm: you saw they speak us fair, give us gold: methinks, they are such a gentle nation, that but for the mountain of mad flesh that claims marriage of me, I could find in my heart to stay here still and turn witch.   [town:

Ant. S. I will not stay to-night for all the
Therefore away to get our stuff aboard.
                            [*Exeunt.*

ACT V.

SCENE I.—*The same.*

Enter Merchant *and* ANGELO.

Ang. I am sorry, sir, that I have hinder'd you;
But I protest he had the chain of me,
Though most dishonestly he doth deny it.

Mer. How is the man esteem'd here in the city?

Ang. Of very reverend reputation, sir;
Of credit infinite, highly belov'd,
Second to none that lives here in the city:
His word might bear my wealth at any time.

Mer. Speak softly: yonder, as I think, he walks.

Enter ANTIPHOLUS *and* DROMIO OF SYRACUSE.

Ang. 'Tis so; and that self chain about his neck
Which he forswore most monstrously to have.
Good sir, draw near to me, I'll speak to him.—
Signior Antipholus, I wonder much
That you would put me to this shame and trouble;
And not without some scandal to yourself,
With circumstance and oaths so to deny
This chain, which now you wear so openly:
Besides the charge, the shame, imprisonment,
You have done wrong to this my honest friend;
Who, but for staying on our controversy,
Had hoisted sail and put to sea to-day:
This chain you had of me; can you deny it?

Ant. S. I think I had: I never did deny it.

Mer. Yes, that you did, sir; and forswore it too.   [swear it?

Ant. S. Who heard me to deny it or for-

Mer. These ears of mine, thou knowest, did hear thee.
Fie on thee, wretch! 'tis pity that thou liv'st
To walk where any honest men resort.   [thus:

Ant. S. Thou art a villain to impeach me
I'll prove mine honour and mine honesty
Against thee presently, if thou dar'st stand.

Mer. I dare and do defy thee for a villain.
                           [*They draw.*

Enter ADRIANA, LUCIANA, Courtezan, *and others.*

Adr. Hold, hurt him not, for God's sake; he is mad:
Some get within him, take his sword away:
Bind Dromio too, and bear them to my house.

Dro. S. Run, master, run; for God's sake, take a house.
This is some priory;—in, or we are spoil'd.
    [*Exeunt* ANT. S. *and* DRO. S. *to the Priory.*

Enter the Abbess.

Abb. Be quiet, people. Wherefore throng you hither?   [hence:

Adr. To fetch my poor distracted husband
Let us come in, that we may bind him fast,
And bear him home for his recovery.

Ang. I knew he was not in his perfect wits.

Mer. I am sorry now that I did draw on him.

Abb. How long hath this possession held the man?   [sad,

Adr. This week he hath been heavy, sour,
And much, much different from the man he was:
But till this afternoon his passion
Ne'er brake into extremity of rage.   [at sea?

Abb. Hath he not lost much wealth by wreck
Buried some dear friend? Hath not else his eye
Stray'd his affection in unlawful love?
A sin prevailing much in youthful men
Who give their eyes the liberty of gazing.
Which of these sorrows is he subject to?

Adr. To none of these, except it be the last;
Namely, some love that drew him oft from home.

Abb. You should for that have reprehended him.

Adr. Why, so I did.

Abb.   Ay, but not rough enough.

Adr. As roughly as my modesty would let me.

Abb. Haply in private.

Adr.   And in assemblies too.

Abb. Ay, but not enough.

Adr. It was the copy of our conference:
In bed, he slept not for my urging it;
At board, he fed not for my urging it;
Alone, it was the subject of my theme;
In company, I often glanced it;
Still did I tell him it was vile and bad.

Abb. And thereof came it that the man was mad:
The venom clamours of a jealous woman
Poison more deadly than a mad dog's tooth.
It seems his sleeps were hindered by thy railing:
And therefore comes it that his head is light.
Thou say'st his meat was sauc'd with thy up-braidings:
Unquiet meals make ill digestions,
Thereof the raging fire of fever bred;
And what's a fever but a fit of madness?
Thou say'st his sports were hinder'd by thy brawls:
Sweet recreation barr'd, what doth ensue
But moody and dull melancholy,—

Kinsman to grim and comfortless despair,—
And, at her heels, a huge infectious troop
Of pale distemperatures and foes to life?
In food, in sport, and life-preserving rest
To be disturb'd would mad or man or beast:
The consequence is, then, thy jealous fits
Have scar'd thy husband from the use of's wits.

  Luc. She never reprehended him but mildly,
When he demean'd himself rough, rude, and
    wildly.—
Why bear you these rebukes, and answer not?

  Adr. She did betray me to my own reproof.—
Good people, enter, and lay hold on him.

  Abb. No, not a creature enters in my house.

  Adr. Then let your servants bring my hus-
    band forth.

  Abb. Neither: he took this place for sanctu-
    ary,
And it shall privilege him from your hands
Till I have brought him to his wits again,
Or lose my labour in assaying it.

  Adr. I will attend my husband, be his nurse,
Diet his sickness, for it is my office,
And will have no attorney but myself;
And therefore let me have him home with me.

  Abb. Be patient; for I will not let him stir
Till I have used the approved means I have,
With wholesome syrups, drugs, and holy
    prayers,
To make of him a formal man again:
It is a branch and parcel of mine oath,
A charitable duty of my order;
Therefore depart, and leave him here with me.

  Adr. I will not hence and leave my husband
    here;
And ill it doth beseem your holiness
To separate the husband and the wife.

  Abb. Be quiet, and depart: thou shalt not
    have him.   [*Exit* Abbess.

  Luc. Complain unto the duke of this indig-
    nity.

  Adr. Come, go; I will fall prostrate at his
    feet,
And never rise until my tears and prayers
Have won his grace to come in person hither,
And take perforce my husband from the abbess.

  Mer. By this, I think, the dial points at five:
Anon, I am sure, the duke himself in person
Comes this way to the melancholy vale;
The place of death and sorry execution,
Behind the ditches of the abbey here.

  Ang. Upon what cause?

  Mer. To see a reverend Syracusan merchant,
Who put unluckily into this bay,
Against the laws and statutes of this town,
Beheaded publicly for his offence.   [his death.

  Ang. See where they come: we will behold

  Luc. Kneel to the duke before he pass the
    abbey.

Enter DUKE, *attended;* ÆGEON, *bare-headed;*
   with the Headsman *and other* Officers.

  Duke. Yet once again proclaim it publicly,
If any friend will pay the sum for him,

He shall not die; so much we tender him.

  Adr. Justice, most sacred duke, against the
    abbess!

  Duke. She is a virtuous and a reverend lady;
It cannot be that she hath done thee wrong.

  Adr. May it please your grace, Antipholus,
    my husband,—
Whom I made lord of me and all I had,
At your important letters,—this ill day
A most outrageous fit of madness took him;
That desperately he hurried through the
    street,—
With him his bondman, all as mad as he,—
Doing displeasure to the citizens
By rushing in their houses, bearing thence
Rings, jewels, anything his rage did like.
Once did I get him bound, and sent him home,
Whilst to take order for the wrongs I went,
That here and there his fury had committed.
Anon, I wot not by what strong escape,
He broke from those that had the guard of him;
And, with his mad attendant and himself,
Each one with ireful passion, with drawn swords,
Met us again, and, madly bent on us,
Chased us away; till, raising of more aid,
We came again to bind them: then they fled
Into this abbey, whither we pursued them:
And here the abbess shuts the gates on us,
And will not suffer us to fetch him out,
Nor send him forth, that we may bear him hence.
Therefore, most gracious duke, with thy com-
    mand,   [help.
Let him be brought forth, and borne hence for

  Duke. Long since thy husband serv'd me in
    my wars;
And I to thee engag'd a prince's word,
When thou didst make him master of thy bed,
To do him all the grace and good I could.—
Go, some of you, knock at the abbey-gate,
And bid the lady abbess come to me:
I will determine this before I stir.

            Enter a Servant.

  Serv. O mistress, mistress, shift and save
    yourself.
My master and his man are both broke loose,
Beaten the maids a-row, and bound the doctor,
Whose beard they have singed off with brands
    of fire;
And ever as it blazed they threw on him
Great pails of puddled mire to quench the hair:
My master preaches patience to him, while
His man with scissors nicks him like a fool:
And, sure, unless you send some present help,
Between them they will kill the conjurer.

  Adr. Peace, fool, thy master and his man
    are here;
And that is false thou dost report to us.

  Serv. Mistress, upon my life, I tell you true:
I have not breath'd almost since I did see it.
He cries for you, and vows, if he can take you,
To scorch your face, and to disfigure you:
                [*Cry within.*
Hark, hark, I hear him; mistress, fly; be gone.

Duke. Come, stand by me; fear nothing.
　　Guard with halberds:
　Adr. Ah me, it is my husband! Witness you
That he is borne about invisible.
Even now we hous'd him in the abbey here;
And now he's there, past thought of human
　　reason.

Enter ANTIPHOLUS *and* DROMIO OF EPHESUS.

　Ant. E. Justice, most gracious duke; oh,
　　grant me justice!
Even for the service that long since I did thee,
When I bestrid thee in the wars, and took
Deep scars to save thy life: even for the blood
That then I lost for thee, now grant me justice.
　Æge. Unless the fear of death doth make
　　me dote,
I see my son Antipholus and Dromio.
　Ant. E. Justice, sweet prince, against that
　　woman there.
She whom thou gav'st to me to be my wife;
That hath abused and dishonour'd me,
Even in the strength and height of injury!
Beyond imagination is the wrong
That she this day hath shameless thrown on me.
　Duke. Discover how, and thou shalt find me
　　just.
　Ant. E. This day, great duke, she shut the
　　doors upon me,
While she with harlots feasted in my house.
　Duke. A grievous fault. Say, woman, didst
　　thou so?　　　　　　　　　　[my sister,
　Adr. No, my good lord;—myself, he, and
To-day did dine together. So befall my soul
As this is false he burdens me withal!
　Luc. Ne'er may I look on day nor sleep on
　　night,
But she tells to your highness simple truth!
　Ang. O perjur'd woman! they are both for-
　　sworn.
In this the madman justly chargeth them.
　Ant. E. My liege, I am advised what I say;
Neither disturb'd with the effect of wine,
Nor, heady-rash, provok'd with raging ire,
Albeit my wrongs might make one wiser mad.
This woman lock'd me out this day from dinner:
That goldsmith there, were he not pack'd with
　　her,
Could witness it, for he was with me then;
Who parted with me to go fetch a chain.
Promising to bring it to the Porcupine,
Where Balthazar and I did dine together.
Our dinner done, and he not coming thither,
I went to seek him. In the street I met him,
And in his company that gentleman.　[down,
There did this perjur'd goldsmith swear me
That I this day of him receiv'd the chain,
Which, God he knows, I saw not: for the which
He did arrest me with an officer.
I did obey, and sent my peasant home
For certain ducats: he with none return'd.
Then fairly I bespoke the officer
To go in person with me to my house.
By the way we met

My wife, her sister, and a rabble more
Of vile confederates: along with them
They brought one Pinch; a hungry lean-faced
　　villain,
A mere anatomy, a mountebank,
A thread-bare juggler, and a fortune-teller;
A needy, hollow-ey'd, sharp-looking wretch;
A living dead man: this pernicious slave,
Forsooth, took on him as a conjurer;
And gazing in mine eyes, feeling my pulse,
And with no face, as 'twere outfacing me,
Cries out, I was possess'd: then altogether
They fell upon me, bound me, bore me thence;
And in a dark and dankish vault at home
There left me and my man both bound together;
Till, gnawing with my teeth my bonds in sunder,
I gain'd my freedom, and immediately
Ran hither to your grace; whom I beseech
To give me ample satisfaction
For these deep shames and great indignities.
　Ang. My lord, in truth, thus far I witness
　　with him,
That he dined not at home, but was lock'd out.
　Duke. But had he such a chain of thee, or no?
　Ang. He had, my lord: and when he ran in
　　here
These people saw the chain about his neck.
　Mer. Besides, I will be sworn these ears of
　　mine
Heard you confess you had the chain of him,
After you first forswore it on the mart,
And thereupon I drew my sword on you;
And then you fled into this abbey here,
From whence, I think, you are come by miracle.
　Ant. E. I never came within these abbey
　　walls,
Nor ever didst thou draw thy sword on me:
I never saw the chain, so help me heaven!
And this is false you burden me withal.
　Duke. What an intricate impeach is this!
I think you all have drank of Circe's cup.
If here you hous'd him, here he would have
　　been:
If he were mad he would not plead so coldly:—
You say he dined at home; the goldsmith here
Denies that saying:—Sirrah, what say you?
　Dro. E. Sir, he dined with her there at the
　　Porcupine.　　　　　　　　　　[that ring.
　Cour. He did; and from my finger snatch'd
　Ant. E. 'Tis true, my liege, this ring I had
　　of her.　　　　　　　　　　　　[here?
　Duke. Saw'st thou him enter at the abbey
　Cour. Assure, my liege, as I do see your grace.
　Duke. Why, this is strange:—Go call the
　　abbess hither:
I think you are all mated, or stark mad.
　　　　　　　　　　[*Exit an* Attendant.
　Æge. Most mighty duke, vouchsafe me speak
　　a word;
Haply, I see a friend will save my life,
And pay the sum that may deliver me.　[wilt.
　Duke. Speak freely, Syracusan, what thou
　Æge. Is not your name, sir, call'd Antipholus?
And is not that your bondman Dromio?

Dro. E. Within this hour I was his bondman,
    sir,
But he, I thank him, gnaw'd in two my cords:
Now am I Dromio and his man, unbound.
  Æge. I am sure you both of you remember
    me.   [you;
  Dro. E. Ourselves we do remember, sir, by
For lately we were bound as you are now.
You are not Pinch's patient, are you, sir?
  Æge. Why look you strange on me? you
    know me well.
  Ant. E. I never saw you in my life, till now.
  Æge. Oh! grief hath chang'd me since you
    saw me last;
And careful hours, with Time's deformed hand,
Have written strange defeatures in my face:
But tell me yet, dost thou not know my voice?
  Ant. E. Neither.
  Æge.   Dromio, nor thou?
  Dro. E. No, trust me, sir, nor I.
  Æge.   I am sure thou dost.
  Dro. E. Ay, sir; but I am sure I do not; and
whatsoever a man denies, you are now bound
to believe him.   [tremity!
  Æge. Not know my voice! O, time's ex-
Hast thou so crack'd and splitted my poor
    tongue,
In seven short years, that here my only son
Knows not my feeble key of untun'd cares?
Though now this grained face of mine be hid
In sap-consuming winter's drizzled snow,
And all the conduits of my blood.froze up,
Yet hath my night of life some memory,
My wasting lamps some fading glimmer left,
My dull deaf ears a little use to hear:
All these old witnesses,—I cannot err,—
Tell me, thou art my son Antipholus.
  Ant. E. I never saw my father in my life.
  Æge. But seven years since, in Syracusa,
    boy,
Thou know'st we parted; but perhaps, my son,
Thou sham'st to acknowledge me in misery.
  Ant. E. The duke, and all that know me in
    the city,
Can witness with me that it is not so:
I ne'er saw Syracusa in my life.
  Duke. I tell thee, Syracusan, twenty years
Have I been patron to Antipholus,
During which time he ne'er saw Syracusa:
I see, thy age and dangers make thee dote.

Enter the Abbess, *with* Antipholus Syracusan
    and Dromio Syracusan.

  Abb. Most mighty duke, behold a man much
    wrong'd.   [*All gather to see him.*
  Adr. I see two husbands, or mine eyes de-
    ceive me.
  Duke. One of these men is genius to the
    other;
And so of these. Which is the natural man,
And which the spirit? Who deciphers them?
  Dro. S. I, sir, am Dromio; command him
    away.
  Dro. E. I, sir, am Dromio; pray let me stay.

  Ant. S. Ægeon, art thou not? or else his
    ghost?
  Dro. S. O, my old master, who hath bound
    him here?
  Abb. Whoever bound him, I will loose his
    bonds.
And gain a husband by his liberty.—
Speak, old Ægeon, if thou be'st the man
That hadst a wife once called Æmilia,
That bore thee at a burden two fair sons:
O, if thou be'st the same Ægeon, speak,
And speak unto the same Æmilia!
  Æge. If I dream not, thou art Æmilia:
If thou art she, tell me where is that son
That floated with thee on the fatal raft?
  Abb. By men of Epidamnum, he and I,
And the twin Dromio, all were taken up:
But, by and by, rude fishermen of Corinth
By force took Dromio and my son from them,
And me they left with those of Epidamnum:
What then became of them I cannot tell;
I to this fortune that you see me in.   [right;
  Duke. Why, here begins his morning story
These two Antipholus's, these two so like,
And these two Dromios, one in semblance,—
Besides her urging of her wreck at sea,—
These are the parents to these children,
Which accidentally are met together.
Antipholus, thou cam'st from Corinth first?
  Ant. S. No, sir, not I; I came from Syracuse.
  Duke. Stay, stand apart; I know not which
    is which.   [cious lord.
  Ant. E. I came from Corinth, my most gra-
  Dro. E. And I with him.
  Ant. E. Brought to this town by that most
    famous warrior,
Duke Menaphon, your most renowned uncle.
  Adr. Which of you two did dine with me
    to-day?
  Ant. S. I, gentle mistress.
  Adr.   And are not you my husband?
  Ant. E. No; I say nay to that.
  Ant. S. And so do I, yet she did call me so;
And this fair gentlewoman, her sister here,
Did call me brother.—What I told you then,
I hope I shall have leisure to make good;
If this be not a dream I see and hear.   [me.
  Ang. That is the chain, sir, which you had of
  Ant. S. I think it be, sir: I deny it not.
  Ant. E. And you, sir, for this chain arrested
    me.
  Ang. I think I did, sir: I deny it not.
  Adr. I sent you money, sir, to be your bail
By Dromio; but I think he brought it not.
  Dro. E. No, none by me.   [you,
  Ant. S. This purse of ducats I receiv'd from
And Dromio my man did bring them me:
I see we still did meet each other's man,
And I was ta'en for him, and he for me,
And thereupon these errors are arose.   [here.
  Ant. E. These ducats pawn I for my father
  Duke. It shall not need; thy father hath his
    life.   [you.
  Cour. Sir, I must have that diamond from

Ant. E. There, take it; and much thanks for
　　my good cheer.

Abb. Renowned duke, vouchsafe to take the
　　pains
To go with us into the abbey here,
And hear at large discoursed all our fortunes:—
And all that are assembled in this place,
That by this sympathized one day's error
Have suffer'd wrong, go, keep us company,
And we shall make full satisfaction.—
Twenty-five years have I but gone in travail
Of you, my sons; nor till this present hour
My heavy burdens are delivered:—
The duke, my husband, and my children both,
And you the calendars of their nativity,
Go to a gossip's feast, and go with me;
After so long grief, such nativity!　　　[feast.

Duke. With all my heart, I'll gossip at this
　　　[Exeunt DUKE, Abb., ÆGE., Cour.,
　　　　　Mer., ANG., *and* Attendants.

Dro. S. Master, shall I fetch your stuff from
　　shipboard?

Ant. E. Dromio, what stuff of mine hast thou
　　embark'd?

Dro. S. Your goods, that lay at host, sir, in
　　the Centaur.

Ant. S. He speaks to me; I am your master,
　　Dromio:
Come, go with us: we'll look to that anon:
Embrace thy brother there; rejoice with him.
　　　[Exeunt ANT. S. *and* E., ADR., *and* LUC.

Dro. S. There is a fat friend at your master's
　　house,
That kitchen'd me for you to-day at dinner:
She now shall be my sister, not my wife.

Dro. E. Methinks you are my glass, and not
　　my brother:
I see by you I am a sweet-faced youth.
Will you walk in to see their gossiping?

Dro. S. Not I, sir; you are my elder.

Dro. E. That's a question: how shall we
　　try it?

Dro. S. We will draw cuts for the senior:
till then, lead thou first.

Dro. E. Nay, then thus:
We came into the world like brother and brother:
And now let's go hand in hand, not one before
　　another.　　　　　　　　　*[Exeunt.*

KING JOHN

DRAMATIS PERSONÆ

KING JOHN.
PRINCE HENRY, *his Son; afterwards* KING HENRY III.
ARTHUR, *Duke of Bretagne, Son to* GEFFREY, *late Duke of Bretagne, the Elder Brother to* KING JOHN.
WILLIAM MARESHALL, *Earl of Pembroke.*
GEFFREY FITZ-PETER, *Earl of Essex, Chief Justiciary of England.*
WILLIAM LONGSWORD, *Earl of Salisbury.*
ROBERT BIGOT, *Earl of Norfolk.*
HUBERT DE BURGH, *Chamberlain to the* KING.
ROBERT FALCONBRIDGE, *Son to* SIR ROBERT FALCONBRIDGE.
PHILIP FALCONBRIDGE, *his Half-brother, Bastard Son to* KING RICHARD I.
JAMES GURNEY, *Servant to* LADY FALCONBRIDGE.

PETER *of Pomfret, a Prophet.*
PHILIP, *King of France.*
LOUIS, *the Dauphin.*
ARCHDUKE OF AUSTRIA.
CARDINAL PANDULPH, *the Pope's Legate.*
MELUN, *a French Lord.*
CHATILLON, *Ambassador from France to* KING JOHN.

ELINOR, *Widow of* KING HENRY II., *and Mother to* KING JOHN.
CONSTANCE, *Mother to* ARTHUR.
BLANCH, *Daughter to* ALPHONSO, *King of Castile, and Niece to* KING JOHN.
LADY FALCONBRIDGE, *Mother to the* BASTARD *and* ROBERT FALCONBRIDGE.

Lords, Citizens *of Angiers,* Sheriff, Heralds, Officers, Soldiers, Messengers, *and other* Attendants.

SCENE,—*Sometimes in* ENGLAND, *and sometimes in* FRANCE.

ACT I.

SCENE I.—NORTHAMPTON. *A Room of State in the Palace.*

Enter KING JOHN, QUEEN ELINOR, PEMBROKE, ESSEX, SALISBURY, *and others, with* CHATILLON.

K. John. Now, say, Chatillon, what would France with us?   [of France,
Chat. Thus, after greeting, speaks the King
In my behaviour, to the majesty,
The borrow'd majesty of England here.
  Eli. A strange beginning;—borrow'd majesty!
  K. John. Silence, good mother; hear the embassy.   [behalf
Chat. Philip of France, in right and true
Of thy deceased brother Geffrey's son,
Arthur Plantagenet, lays most lawful claim
To this fair island, and the territories,—
To Ireland, Poictiers, Anjou, Touraine, Maine;
Desiring thee to lay aside the sword
Which sways usurpingly these several titles,
And put the same into young Arthur's hand,
Thy nephew and right royal sovereign.
  K. John. What follows, if we disallow of this?
  Chat. The proud control of fierce and bloody war,
To enforce these rights so forcibly withheld.
  K. John. Here have we war for war, and blood for blood,
Controlment for controlment: so answer France.

Chat. Then take my king's defiance from my mouth,
The furthest limit of my embassy.   [peace:
  K. John. Bear mine to him, and so depart in
Be thou as lightning in the eyes of France;
For ere thou canst report I will be there,
The thunder of my cannon shall be heard:
So, hence! Be thou the trumpet of our wrath,
And sullen presage of your own decay.—
An honourable conduct let him have:—
Pembroke, look to 't. Farewell, Chatillon.
    [*Exeunt* CHATILLON *and* PEMBROKE.
  Eli. What now, my son! have I not ever said
How that ambitious Constance would not cease
Till she had kindled France and all the world
Upon the right and party of her son?
That might have been prevented and made whole,
With very easy arguments of love;
Which now the manage of two kingdoms must
With fearful bloody issue arbitrate.
  K. John. Our strong possession and our right for us.   [your right,
  Eli. Your strong possession much more than
Or else it must go wrong with you and me:
So much my conscience whispers in your ear,
Which none but heaven and you and I shall hear.

Enter the Sheriff of Northamptonshire, *who whispers* ESSEX.

  Essex. My liege, here is the strangest controversy,

[*367*]

Come from the country to be judg'd by you,
That e'er I heard: shall I produce the men?
  K. John. Let them approach.—
                       [*Exit* Sheriff.
Our abbeys and our priories shall pay
This expedition's charge.

Re-enter Sheriff, *with* ROBERT FALCONBRIDGE,
  and PHILIP, *his bastard Brother.*
                What men are you?
  Bast. Your faithful subject I, a gentleman
Born in Northamptonshire, and eldest son,
As I suppose, to Robert Falconbridge,—
A soldier, by the honour-giving hand
Of Cœur-de-lion knighted in the field.
  K. John. What art thou?
  Rob. The son and heir to that same Falcon-
      bridge.   [heir?
  K. John. Is that the elder, and art thou the
You came not of one mother, then, it seems.
  Bast. Most certain of one mother, mighty
      king,—
That is well known; and, as I think, one father:
But for the certain knowledge of that truth
I put you o'er to heaven and to my mother:—
Of that I doubt, as all men's children may.
  Eli. Out on thee, rude man! thou dost shame
      thy mother,
And wound her honour with this diffidence.
  Bast. I, madam? no, I have no reason for
      it,—
That is my brother's plea, and none of mine;
The which if he can prove, 'a pops me out
At least from fair five hundred pound a-year:
Heaven guard my mother's honour and my
      land!   [younger born,
  K. John. A good blunt fellow.—Why, being
Doth he lay claim to thine inheritance?
  Bast. I know not why, except to get the land.
But once he slander'd me with bastardy:
But whe'r I be as true begot or no,
That still I lay upon my mother's head;
But, that I am as well begot, my liege,—
Fair fall the bones that took the pains for me!—
Compare our faces, and be judge yourself.
If old Sir Robert did beget us both,
And were our father, and this son like him,—
O old Sir Robert, father, on my knee
I give heaven thanks I was not like to thee!
  K. John. Why, what a madcap hath heaven
      lent us here!
  Eli. He hath a trick of Cœur-de-lion's face;
The accent of his tongue affecteth him:
Do you not read some tokens of my son
In the large composition of this man? [parts,
  K. John. Mine eye hath well examined his
And finds them perfect Richard.—Sirrah, speak,
What doth move you to claim your brother's
      land;   [father,
  Bast. Because he hath a half-face, like my
With that half-face would he have all my land:
A half-fac'd groat five hundred pound a-year!
  Rob. My gracious liege, when that my father
      liv'd,

Your brother did employ my father much,—
  Bast. Well, sir, by this you cannot get my
      land:
Your tale must be, how he employ'd my mother.
  Rob. And once despatch'd him in an embassy
To Germany, there with the emperor
To treat of high affairs touching that time.
The advantage of his absence took the king,
And in the meantime sojourn'd at my father's;
Where how he did prevail I shame to speak,—
But truth is truth: large lengths of seas and
      shores
Between my father and my mother lay,—
As I have heard my father speak himself,—
When this same lusty gentleman was got.
Upon his death-bed he by will bequeath'd
His lands to me; and took it, on his death,
That this, my mother's son, was none of his;
And if he were, he came into the world
Full fourteen weeks before the course of time.
Then, good my liege, let me have what is mine,
My father's land, as was my father's will.
  K. John. Sirrah, your brother is legitimate;
Your father's wife did after wedlock bear him;
And if she did play false, the fault was hers;
Which fault lies on the hazards of all husbands
That marry wives. Tell me, how if my brother,
Who, as you say, took pains to get this son,
Had of your father claim'd this son for his?
In sooth, good friend, your father might have
      kept
This calf, bred from his cow, from all the world;
In sooth, he might: then, if he were my
      brother's,   [father,
My brother might not claim him; nor your
Being none of his, refuse him. This concludes,—
My mother's son did get your father's heir;
Your father's heir must have your father's land.
  Rob. Shall, then, my father's will be of no
      force
To dispossess that child which is not his?
  Bast. Of no more force to dispossess me, sir,
Than was his will to get me, as I think.
  Eli. Whether hadst thou rather be a Falcon-
      bridge,
And like thy brother, to enjoy thy land,
Or the reputed son of Cœur-de-lion,
Lord of thy presence, and no land beside?
  Bast. Madam, an if my brother had my
      shape
And I had his, Sir Robert his, like him;
And if my legs were two such riding-rods,
My arms such eel-skins stuff'd, my face so thin
That in mine ear I durst not stick a rose
Lest men should say, *Look, where three-farthings*
      goes!
And, to his shape, were heir to all this land,
Would I might never stir from off this place,
I'd give it every foot to have this face;
I would not be Sir Nob in any case.
  Eli. I like thee well: wilt thou forsake thy
      fortune,
Bequeath thy land to him, and follow me?
I am a soldier, and now bound to France.

Bast. Brother, take you my land, I'll take
　　my chance:
Your face hath got five hundred pound a-year;
Yet sell your face for fivepence, and 'tis dear.—
Madam, I'll follow you unto the death.
　　Eli. Nay, I would have you go before me
　　　　thither.   [way.
　　Bast. Our country manners give our betters
　　K. John. What is thy name?
　　Bast. Philip, my liege; so is my name begun;
Philip, good old Sir Robert's wife's eldest son.
　　K. John. From henceforth bear his name
　　　　whose form thou bear'st:
Kneel thou down Philip, but arise more great,—
Arise Sir Richard and Plantagenet.
　　Bast. Brother by the mother's side, give me
　　　　your hand:
My father gave me honour, yours gave land.—
Now blessed be the hour, by night or day,
When I was got, Sir Robert was away!
　　Eli. The very spirit of Plantagenet!—
I am thy grandam, Richard; call me so.
　　Bast. Madam, by chance, but not by truth:
　　　　what though?
Something about, a little from the right,
　　In at the window, or else o'er the hatch;
Who dares not stir by day must walk by night;
　　And have is have, however men do catch:
Near or far off, well won is still well shot;
And I am I, howe'er I was begot.
　　K. John. Go, Falconbridge; now hast thou
　　　　thy desire;
A landless knight makes thee a landed squire.—
Come, madam,—and come, Richard; we must
　　　　speed
For France, for France; for it is more than need.
　　Bast. Brother, adieu: good fortune come to
　　　　thee!
For thou wast got i' the way of honesty.
　　　　　　　[*Exeunt all except the* BASTARD.
A foot of honour better than I was;
But many a many foot of land the worse.
Well, now can I make any Joan a lady:—
Good den, Sir Richard:—God-a-mercy, fellow:—
And if his name be George, I'll call him Peter:
For new-made honour doth forget men's names:
'Tis too respective and too sociable
For your conversion. Now your traveller,—
He and his toothpick at my worship's mess;
And when my knightly stomach is suffic'd,
Why then I suck my teeth, and catechize
My picked man of countries:—*My dear sir,—*
Thus, leaning on mine elbow, I begin,—
I shall beseech you—that is question now;
And then comes answer like an ABC-book:—
O sir, says answer, *at your best command;*
At your employment; at your service, sir:—
No sir, says question, *I, sweet sir, at yours:*
And so, ere answer knows what question
　　　　would,—
Saving in dialogue of compliment,
And talking of the Alps and Apennines,
The Pyrenean and the river Po,—
It draws towards supper in conclusion so.

But this is worshipful society,
And fits the mounting spirit like myself:
For he is but a bastard to the time,
That doth not smack of observation,—
And so am I, whether I smack or no;
And not alone in habit and device,
Exterior form, outward accoutrement,
But from the inward motion to deliver
Sweet, sweet, sweet poison for the age's tooth:
Which, though I will not practise to deceive,
Yet, to avoid deceit, I mean to learn;
For it shall strew the footsteps of my rising.—
But who comes in such haste in riding-robes?
What woman-post is this? hath she no husband,
That will take pains to blow a horn before her?

Enter LADY FALCONBRIDGE, *and* JAMES
　　　　GURNEY.

O me! it is my mother.—How now, good lady!
What brings you here to court so hastily?
　　Lady F. Where is that slave, thy brother?
　　　　where is he
That holds in chase mine honour up and down?
　　Bast. My brother Robert? old Sir Robert's
　　　　son?
Colbrand the giant, that same mighty man?
Is it Sir Robert's son that you seek so?
　　Lady F. Sir Robert's son! Ay, thou un-
　　　　reverend boy,   [Robert?
Sir Robert's son: why scorn'st thou at Sir
He is Sir Robert's son; and so art thou.
　　Bast. James Gurney, wilt thou give us leave
　　　　awhile?
　　Gur. Good leave, good Philip.
　　Bast.   Philip?—sparrow!—James,
There's toys abroad: anon I'll tell thee more.
　　　　　　　　　　　　　[*Exit* GURNEY.
Madam, I was not old Sir Robert's son;
Sir Robert might have eat his part in me
Upon Good-Friday, and ne'er broke his fast:
Sir Robert could do well: marry, to confess,
Could not get me; Sir Robert could not do it,—
We know his handiwork:—therefore, good
　　　　mother,
To whom am I beholding for these limbs?
Sir Robert never holp to make this leg.
　　Lady F. Hast thou conspired with thy
　　　　brother too,   [honour?
That for thine own gain shouldst defend mine
What means this scorn, thou most untoward
　　　　knave?   [isco-like:
　　Bast. Knight, knight, good mother,—Basil-
What! I am dubb'd; I have it on my shoulder.
But, mother, I am not Sir Robert's son;
I have disclaim'd Sir Robert and my land;
Legitimation, name, and all is gone:
Then, good my mother, let me know my
　　　　father,—
Some proper man, I hope: who was it, mother?
　　Lady F. Hast thou denied thyself a Falcon-
　　　　bridge?
　　Bast. As faithfully as I deny the devil.
　　Lady F. King Richard Cœur-de-lion was thy
　　　　father:

By long and vehement suit I was seduc'd
To make room for him in my husband's bed:—
Heaven lay not my transgression to my
          charge!—
Thou art the issue of my dear offence,
Which was so strongly urg'd, past my defence.
    Bast. Now, by this light, were I to get again,
Madam, I would not wish a better father.
Some sins do bear their privilege on earth,
And so doth yours; your fault was not your
          folly:
Needs must you lay your heart at his dispose,—
Subjected tribute to commanding love,—
Against whose fury and unmatched force
The aweless lion could not wage the fight,
Nor keep his princely heart from Richard's
          hand:
He that perforce robs lions of their hearts
May easily win a woman's. Ay, my mother,
With all my heart I thank thee for my father!
Who lives and dares but say, thou didst not well
When I was got, I'll send his soul to hell.
Come, lady, I will show thee to my kin;
    And they shall say, when Richard me begot,
If thou hadst said him nay, it had been sin:
    Who says it was, he lies; I say 'twas not.
                                        [*Exeunt.*

ACT II.

SCENE I.—FRANCE. *Before the Walls of Angiers.*

Enter, on one side, the ARCHDUKE OF AUSTRIA
     and Forces; *on the other,* PHILIP, *King of*
     France, LOUIS, CONSTANCE, ARTHUR, *and*
     Forces.

    Lou. Before Angiers well met, brave Aus-
          tria.—
Arthur, that great forerunner of thy blood,
Richard, that robb'd the lion of his heart,
And fought the holy wars in Palestine,
By this brave duke came early to his grave:
And, for amends to his posterity,
At our importance hither is he come
To spread his colours, boy, in thy behalf;
And to rebuke the usurpation
Of thy unnatural uncle, English John:
Embrace him, love him, give him welcome
          hither.   [death
    Arth. God shall forgive you Cœur-de-lion's
The rather that you give his offspring life,
Shadowing their right under your wings of war:
I give you welcome with a powerless hand,
But with a heart full of unstained love,—
Welcome before the gates of Angiers, duke.
    Lou. A noble boy! Who would not do thee
          right?
    Aust. Upon thy cheek lay I this zealous kiss,
As seal to this indenture of my love,—
That to my home I will no more return,
Till Angiers, and the right thou hast in France,
Together with that pale, that white-fac'd shore,
Whose foot spurns back the ocean's roaring
          tides,
And coops from other lands her islanders,—

Even till that England, hedg'd in with the main,
That water-walled bulwark still secure
And confident from foreign purposes,—
Even till that utmost corner of the west
Salute thee for her king: till then, fair boy,
Will I not think of home, but follow arms.
    Const. O, take his mother's thanks, a wid-
          ow's thanks,   [strength
Till your strong hand shall help to give him
To make a more requital to your love!
    Aust. The peace of heaven is theirs that lift
          their swords
In such a just and charitable war.
    K. Phi. Well, then, to work: our cannon
          shall be bent
Against the brows of this resisting town.—
Call for our chiefest men of discipline,
To cull the plots of best advantages:
We'll lay before this town our royal bones,
Wade to the market-place in Frenchman's
          blood,
But we will make it subject to this boy.
    Const. Stay for an answer to your embassy,
Lest unadvis'd you stain your swords with
          blood:
My Lord Chatillon may from England bring
That right in peace, which here we urge in war;
And then we shall repent each drop of blood
That hot rash haste so indirectly shed.
    K. Phi. A wonder, lady!—lo, upon thy wish,
Our messenger Chatillon is arriv'd!

Enter CHATILLON.

What England says, say briefly, gentle lord;
We coldly pause for thee; Chatillon, speak.
    Chat. Then turn your forces from this paltry
          siege,
And stir them up against a mightier task.
England, impatient of your just demands,
Hath put himself in arms: the adverse winds,
Whose leisure I have stay'd, have given him
          time
To land his legions all as soon as I;
His marches are expedient to this town,
His forces strong, his soldiers confident.
With him along is come the mother-queen,
An Até, stirring him to blood and strife;
With her her niece, the Lady Blanch of Spain;
With them a bastard of the king deceas'd:
And all the unsettled humours of the land,—
Rash, inconsiderate, fiery voluntaries,
With ladies' faces, and fierce dragons' spleens,—
Have sold their fortunes at their native homes,
Bearing their birthrights proudly on their
          backs,
To make a hazard of new fortunes here.
In brief, a braver choice of dauntless spirits,
Than now the English bottoms have waft o'er,
Did never float upon the swelling tide,
To do offence and scath in Christendom.
                              [*Drums beat within.*
The interruption of their churlish drums
Cuts off more circumstance: they are at hand,
To parley or to fight: therefore prepare.

K. Phi. How much unlook'd-for is this ex-
　　pedition!
Aust. By how much unexpected, by so much
We must awake endeavour for defence;
For courage mounteth with occasion:
Let them be welcome, then; we are prepar'd.

　　Enter KING JOHN, ELINOR, BLANCH, *the*
　　　　BASTARD, Lords, *and* Forces.

K. John. Peace be to France, if France in
　　peace permit
Our just and lineal entrance to our own!
If not, bleed France, and peace ascend to
　　heaven!
Whiles we, God's wrathful agent, do correct
Their proud contempt that beat his peace to
　　heaven.　　　　　　　　　　　　[return
K. Phi. Peace be to England, if that war
From France to England, there to live in peace!
England we love; and for that England's sake
With burden of our armour here we sweat.
This toil of ours should be a work of thine;
But thou from loving England art so far,
That thou hast under-wrought his lawful king,
Cut off the sequence of posterity,
Outfaced infant state, and done a rape
Upon the maiden virtue of the crown.
Look here upon thy brother Geffrey's face;—
These eyes, these brows, were moulded out of
　　his:
This little abstract doth contain that large
Which died in Geffrey; and the hand of time
Shall draw this brief into as huge a volume.
That Geffrey was thy elder brother born,
And this his son; England was Geffrey's right,
And this is Geffrey's: in the name of God,
How comes it then, that thou art call'd a king,
When living blood doth in these temples beat,
Which owe the crown that thou o'ermasterest?
K. John. From whom hast thou this great
　　commission, France,
To draw my answer from thy articles?
K. Phi. From that supernal judge that stirs
　　good thoughts
In any breast of strong authority,
To look into the blots and stains of right.
That judge hath made me guardian to this boy:
Under whose warrant I impeach thy wrong;
And by whose help I mean to chástise it.
K. John. Alack, thou dost usurp authority.
K. Phi. Excuse,—it is to beat usurping
　　down.
Eli. Who is it thou dost call usurper, France?
Const. Let me make answer;—thy usurping
　　son.
Eli. Out, insolent! thy bastard shall be king,
That thou mayst be a queen, and check the
　　world!
Const. My bed was ever to thy son as true
As thine was to thy husband; and this boy
Liker in feature to his father Geffrey　　[like
Than thou and John in manners,—being as
As rain to water, or devil to his dam.
My boy a bastard! By my soul, I think

His father never was so true begot:
It cannot be, an if thou wert his mother.
　　Eli. There's a good mother, boy, that blots
　　　　thy father.
　　Const. There's a good grandam, boy, that
　　　　would blot thee.
　　Aust. Peace!
　　Bast.　　　　　　Hear the crier.
　　Aust.　　　　　　　　What the devil art thou?
　　Bast. One that will play the devil, sir, with
　　　　you
An 'a man catch your hide and you alone.
You are the hare of whom the proverb goes,
Whose valour plucks dead lions by the beard:
I'll smoke your skin-coat an I catch you right;
Sirrah, look to 't; i' faith, I will, i' faith.
　　Blanch. O, well did he become that lion's
　　　　robe
That did disrobe the lion of that robe!
　　Bast. It lies as sightly on the back of him
As great Alcides' shoes upon an ass:—
But, ass, I'll take that burden from your back,
Or lay on that shall make your shoulders crack.
　　Aust. What cracker is this same that deafs
　　　　our ears
With this abundance of superfluous breath?
　　K. Phi. Louis, determine what we shall do
　　　　straight.　　　　　　　　　　[ference.—
　　Lou. Women and fools, break off your con-
King John, this is the very sum of all,—
England and Ireland, Anjou, Touraine, Maine,
In right of Arthur, do I claim of thee:
Wilt thou resign them, and lay down thy arms?
　　K. John. My life as soon:—I do defy thee,
　　　　France.
Arthur of Bretagne, yield thee to my hand;
And out of my dear love, I'll give thee more
Than e'er the coward hand of France can win:
Submit thee, boy.
　　Eli.　　　　　　Come to thy grandam, child.
　　Const. Do, child, go to it' grandam, child;
Give grandam kingdom, and it' grandam will
Give it a plum, a cherry, and a fig:
There's a good grandam.
　　Arth.　　　　　Good my mother, peace!
I would that I were low laid in my grave:
I am not worth this coil that's made for me.
　　Eli. His mother shames him so, poor boy,
　　　　he weeps.　　　　　　　　[does or no!
　　Const. Now, shame upon you, whe'r she
His grandam's wrongs, and not his mother's
　　　　shames,　　　　　　　　　[poor eyes,
Draw those heaven-moving pearls from his
Which heaven shall take in nature of a fee:
Ay, with these crystal beads heaven shall be
　　brib'd
To do him justice, and revenge on you.
　　Eli. Thou monstrous slanderer of heaven
　　　　and earth!　　　　　　　　[and earth!
　　Const. Thou monstrous injurer of heaven
Call not me slanderer; thou and thine usurp
The dominations, royalties, and rights　　[son,
Of this oppressed boy: this is thy eldest son's
Infortunate in nothing but in thee:

Thy sins are visited in this poor child;
The canon of the law is laid on him,
Being but the second generation
Removed from thy sin-conceiving womb.
   K. John. Bedlam, have done.
   Const.   I have but this to say,—
That he is not only plagued for her sin,
But God hath made her sin and her the plague
On this removed issue, plagu'd for her,
And with her plague, her sin; his injury
Her injury,—the beadle to her sin;
All punish'd in the person of this child,
And all for her: a plague upon her!
   Eli. Thou unadvised scold, I can produce
A will that bars the title of thy son.   [will;
   Const. Ay, who doubts that? a will! a wicked
A woman's will; a canker'd grandam's will!
   K. Phi. Peace, lady! pause, or be more tem-
    perate:
It ill beseems this presence to cry aim
To these ill-tuned repetitions.—
Some trumpet summon hither to the walls
These men of Angiers: let us hear them speak
Whose title they admit, Arthur's or John's.

Trumpet sounds. Enter Citizens *upon the walls.*

   1 *Cit.* Who is it that hath warn'd us to the
    walls?
   K. Phi. 'Tis France, for England.
   K. John.   England, for itself:—
You men of Angiers, and my loving subjects,—
   K. Phi. You loving men of Angiers, Arthur's
    subjects,
Our trumpet call'd you to this gentle parle.
   K. John. For our advantage; therefore hear
    us first.
These flags of France, that are advanced here
Before the eye and prospect of your town,
Have hither march'd to your endamagement:
The cannons have their bowels full of wrath,
And ready mounted are they to spit forth
Their iron indignation 'gainst your walls:
All preparation for a bloody siege
And merciless proceeding by these French
Confronts your city's eyes, your winking gates;
And, but for our approach, those sleeping
    stones,
That as a waist do girdle you about,
By the compulsion of their ordinance
By this time from their fixed beds of lime
Had been dishabited, and wide havoc made
For bloody power to rush upon your peace.
But, on the sight of us, your lawful king,—
Who painfully, with much expedient march,
Have brought a countercheck before your gates,
To save unscratch'd your city's threaten'd
    cheeks,—
Behold, the French, amaz'd, vouchsafe a parle;
And now, instead of bullets wrapp'd in fire,
To make a shaking fever in your walls,
They shoot but calm words, folded up in smoke,
To make a faithless error in your ears:
Which trust accordingly, kind citizens,
And let us in, your king; whose labour'd spirits,

Forwearied in this action of swift speed,
Crave harbourage within your city-walls.
   K. Phi. When I have said, make answer to
    us both.
Lo, in this right hand, whose protection
Is most divinely vow'd upon the right
Of him it holds, stands young Plantagenet,
Son to the elder brother of this man,
And king o'er him and all that he enjoys:
For this down-trodden equity we tread
In war-like march these greens before your
    town;
Being no further enemy to you
Than the constraint of hospitable zeal
In the relief of this oppressed child
Religiously provokes. Be pleased, then,
To pay that duty which you truly owe
To him that owes it, namely, this young prince:
And then our arms, like to a muzzled bear,
Save in aspéct, have all offence seal'd up;
Our cannons' malice vainly shall be spent
Against the invulnerable clouds of heaven;
And with a blessed and unvex'd retire,
With unhack'd swords and helmets all un-
    bruis'd,
We will bear home that lusty blood again
Which here we came to spout against your
    town,
And leave your children, wives, and you in
    peace.
But if you fondly pass our proffer'd offer,
'Tis not the rondure of your old-fac'd walls
Can hide you from our messengers of war,
Though all these English, and their discipline,
Were harbour'd in their rude circumference.
Then, tell us, shall your city call us lord
In that behalf which we have challeng'd it?
Or shall we give the signal to our rage,
And stalk in blood to our possession?
   1 *Cit.* In brief, we are the King of England's
    subjects:
For him, and in his right, we hold this town.
   K. John. Acknowledge then the king, and
    let me in.
   1 *Cit.* That can we not; but he that proves
    the king,
To him will we prove loyal: till that time
Have we ramm'd up our gates against the
    world.
   K. John. Doth not the crown of England
    prove the king?
And, if not that, I bring you witnesses,
Twice fifteen thousand hearts of England's
    breed,—
   Bast. Bastards, and else.
   K. John. To verify our title with their lives.
   K. Phi. As many and as well-born bloods as
    those,—
   Bast. Some bastards too.
   K. Phi. Stand in his face, to contradict his
    claim.
   1 *Cit.* Till you compound whose right is
    worthiest,
We for the worthiest hold the right from both.

K. John. Then God forgive the sin of all those souls
That to their everlasting residence,
Before the dew of evening fall, shall fleet,
In dreadful trial of our kingdom's king!
    K. Phi. Amen, Amen!—Mount, chevaliers! to arms!
    Bast. St. George, that swinged the dragon, and e'er since
Sits on his horse' back at mine hostess' door,
Teach us some fence!—Sirrah [*to* AUSTRIA], were I at home,
At your den, sirrah, with your lioness,
I would set an ox-head to your lion's hide,
And make a monster of you.
    Aust.   Peace! no more.
    Bast. O, tremble, for you hear the lion roar.
    K. John. Up higher to the plain; where we'll set forth
In best appointment all our regiments. [field.
    Bast. Speed, then, to take advantage of the
    K. Phi. It shall be so;—[*to* LOUIS] and at the other hill
Command the rest to stand.—God and our right!   [*Exeunt severally.*

After Excursions, enter a French Herald, *with trumpets, to the gates.*

    F. Her. You men of Angiers, open wide your gates,
And let young Arthur, Duke of Bretagne, in,
Who, by the hand of France, this day hath made
Much work for tears in many an English mother,
Whose sons lie scatter'd on the bleeding ground:
Many a widow's husband grovelling lies,
Coldly embracing the discolour'd earth;
And victory, with little loss, doth play
Upon the dancing banners of the French,
Who are at hand triumphantly display'd,
To enter conquerors, and to proclaim
Arthur of Bretagne England's king and yours.

Enter an English Herald, *with trumpets.*

    E. Her. Rejoice, you men of Angiers, ring your bells;   [proach,
King John, your king and England's, doth ap-
Commander of this hot malicious day:
Their armours, that march'd hence so silver-bright,
Hither return all gilt with Frenchmen's blood;
There stuck no plume in any English crest
That is removed by a staff of France;
Our colours do return in those same hands
That did display them when we first march'd forth;
And, like a jolly troop of huntsmen, come
Our lusty English, all with purpled hands,
Dy'd in the dying slaughter of their foes:
Open your gates, and give the victors way.
    1 Cit. Heralds, from off our towers, we might behold,

From first to last, the onset and retire
Of both your armies, whose equality
By our best eyes cannot be censured:
Blood hath bought blood, and blows have an-swer'd blows;
Strength match'd with strength, and power confronted power:
Both are alike; and both alike we like.
One must prove greatest: while they weigh so even
We hold our town for neither; yet for both.

Re-enter, on one side, KING JOHN, ELINOR, BLANCH, *the* BASTARD, *and* Forces; *at the other,* KING PHILIP, LOUIS, AUSTRIA, *and* Forces.

    K. John. France, hast thou yet more blood to cast away?
Say, shall the current of our right run on?
Whose passage, vex'd with thy impediment,
Shall leave his native channel, and o'erswell
With course disturb'd even thy confining shores,
Unless thou let his silver water keep
A peaceful progress to the ocean.
    K. Phi. England, thou hast not sav'd one drop of blood,
In this hot trial, more than we of France;
Rather, lost more: and by this hand I swear,
That sways the earth this climate overlooks,
Before we will lay down our just-borne arms,
We'll put thee down, 'gainst whom these arms we bear,
Or add a royal number to the dead,
Gracing the scroll that tells of this war's loss
With slaughter coupled to the name of kings
    Bast. Ha, majesty! how high thy glory towers
When the rich blood of kings is set on fire!
O, now doth Death line his dead chaps with steel;
The swords of soldiers are his teeth, his fangs;
And now he feasts, mousing the flesh of men,
In undetermin'd differences of kings.—
Why stand these royal fronts amazed thus?
Cry, havoc, kings! back to the stained field,
You equal potentates, fiery-kindled spirits!
Then let confusion of one part confirm
The other's peace; till then, blows, blood, and death!   [admit?
    K. John. Whose party do the townsmen yet
    K. Phi. Speak, citizens, for England; who's your king?   [the king.
    1 Cit. The king of England, when we know
    K. Phi. Know him in us, that here hold up his right.
    K. John. In us, that are our own great deputy,
And bear possession of our person here;
Lord of our presence, Angiers, and of you.
    1 Cit. A greater power than we denies all this;
And till it be undoubted, we do lock
Our former scruple in our strong-barr'd gates;
King'd of our fear, until our fears, resolv'd,

Be by some certain king purg'd and depos'd.

    Bast. By heaven, these scroyles of Angiers
         flout you, kings,
And stand securely on their battlements
As in a theatre, whence they gape and point
At your industrious scenes and acts of death.
Your royal presences be rul'd by me:—
Do like the mutines of Jerusalem,
Be friends awhile, and both conjointly bend
Your sharpest deeds of malice on this town:
By east and west let France and England mount
Their battering cannon, charged to the mouths,
Till their soul-fearing clamours have brawl'd
         down
The flinty ribs of this contemptuous city:
I'd play incessantly upon these jades,
Even till unfenced desolation
Leave them as naked as the vulgar air.
That done, dissever your united strengths,
And part your mingled colours once again:
Turn face to face, and bloody point to point;
Then, in a moment, fortune shall cull forth
Out of one side her happy minion,
To whom in favour she shall give the day,
And kiss him with a glorious victory.
How like you this wild counsel, mighty states?
Smacks it not something of the policy?

    K. John. Now, by the sky that hangs above
         our heads,
I like it well.—France, shall we knit our powers,
And lay this Angiers even with the ground;
Then, after, fight who shall be king of it?

    Bast. And if thou hast the mettle of a king,—
Being wrong'd, as we are, by this peevish
         town,—
Turn thou the mouth of thy artillery,
As we will ours, against these saucy walls;
And when that we have dash'd them to the
         ground,
Why, then defy each other, and, pell-mell,
Make work upon ourselves, for heaven or hell!

    K. Phi. Let it be so.—Say, where will you
         assault?   [struction

    K. John. We from the west will send de-
Into this city's bosom.

    Aust. I from the north.

    K. Phi.   Our thunder from the south
Shall rain their drift of bullets on this town.

    Bast. O prudent discipline! From north to
         south,—
Austria and France shoot in each other's
         mouth: [away!
I'll stir them to it. [*Aside.*]—Come, away,

    1 *Cit.* Hear us, great kings: vouchsafe awhile
         to stay,
And I shall show you peace and fair-fac'd
         league;
Win you this city without stroke or wound;
Rescue those breathing lives to die in beds,
That here come sacrifices for the field:
Perséver not, but hear me, mighty kings.

    K. John. Speak on, with favour; we are bent
         to hear.   [Lady Blanch,

    1 *Cit.* That daughter there of Spain, the

Is neice to England:—look upon the years
Of Louis the Dauphin, and that lovely maid:
If lusty love should go in quest of beauty,
Where should he find it fairer than in Blanch?
If zealous love should go in search of virtue,
Where should he find it purer than in Blanch?
If love ambitious sought a match of birth,
Whose veins bound richer blood than Lady
         Blanch?
Such as she is, in beauty, virtue, birth,
Is the young Dauphin every way complete,—
If not complete of, say he is not she;
And she again wants nothing, to name want,
If want it be not, that she is not he:
He is the half part of a blessed man,
Left to be finished by such a she;
And she a fair divided excellence,
Whose fulness of perfection lies in him.
O, two such silver currents, when they join
Do glorify the banks that bound them in;
And two such shores to two such streams made
         one,
Two such controlling bounds shall you be,
         kings,
To these two princes, if you marry them.
This union shall do more than battery can
To our fast-closed gates; for, at this match,
With swifter spleen than powder can enforce,
The mouth of passage shall we fling wide ope,
And give you entrance; but without this match,
The sea enraged is not half so deaf,
Lions more confident, mountains and rocks
More free from motion; no, not Death himself
In mortal fury half so peremptory,
As we to keep this city.

    Bast.   Here's a stay,
That shakes the rotten carcase of old Death
Out of his rags! Here's a large mouth, indeed,
That spits forth death and mountains, rocks
         and seas;
Talks as familiarly of roaring lions
As maids of thirteen do of puppy-dogs!
What cannoneer begot this lusty blood?
He speaks plain cannon,—fire and smoke and
         bounce;
He gives the bastinado with his tongue;
Our ears are cudgell'd; not a word of his
But buffets better than a fist of France:
Zounds! I was never so bethump'd with words
Since I first called my brother's father dad.

    Eli. Son, list to this conjunction, make this
         match;
Give with our niece a dowry large enough:
For by this knot thou shalt so surely tie
Thy now unsur'd assurance to the crown,
That yon green boy shall have no sun to ripe
The bloom that promiseth a mighty fruit.
I see a yielding in the looks of France;
Mark how they whisper: urge them while their
         souls
Are capable of this ambition,
Lest zeal, now melted by the windy breath
Of soft petitions, pity, and remorse,
Cool and congeal again to what it was.

1 Cit. Why answer not the double majesties
This friendly treaty of our threaten'd town?
　K. Phi. Speak England first, that hath been
　　forward first ·
To speak unto this city: what say you?
　K. John. If that the Dauphin there, thy
　　princely son,
Can in this book of beauty read, "I love,"
Her dowry shall weigh equal with a queen:
For Anjou, and fair Touraine, Maine, Poictiers,
And all that we upon this side the sea,—
Except this city now by us besieg'd,—
Find liable to our crown and dignity,
Shall gild her bridal bed; and make her rich
In titles, honours, and promotions,
As she in beauty, education, blood,
Holds hand with any princess of the world.
　K. Phi. What say'st thou, boy? look in the
　　lady's face.
　Lou. I do, my lord, and in her eye I find
A wonder, or a wondrous miracle,
The shadow of myself form'd in her eye;
Which, being but the shadow of your son,
Becomes a sun, and makes your son a shadow:
I do protest I never lov'd myself
Till now infixed I beheld myself
Drawn in the flattering table of her eye.
　　　　　　　　[*Whispers with* BLANCH.
　Bast. [*Aside.*] Drawn in the flattering table
　　of her eye!—
　　Hang'd in the frowning wrinkle of her
　　brow!—
And quarter'd in her heart!—he doth espy
　Himself love's traitor! This is pity now,
That, hang'd, and drawn, and quarter'd, there
　should be
In such a love so vile a lout as he.
　Blanch. My uncle's will in this respect is
　　mine.
If he see aught in you that makes him like,
That anything he sees, which moves his liking,
I can with ease translate it to my will;
Or if you will, to speak more properly,
I will enforce it easily to my love.
Further, I will not flatter you, my lord,
That all I see in you is worthy love,
Than this,—that nothing do I see in you,
Though churlish thoughts themselves should
　be your judge,—
That I can find should merit any hate.
　K. John. What say these young ones?—
　　What say you, my niece?　　　　　　[do
Blanch. That she is bound in honour still to
What you in wisdom still vouchsafe to say.
　K. John. Speak then, Prince Dauphin; can
　　you love this lady?
　Lou. Nay, ask me if I can refrain from love;
For I do love her most unfeignedly.
　K. John. Then do I give Volquessen, Tou-
　　raine, Maine,
Poictiers, and Anjou, these five provinces,
With her to thee; and this addition more,
Full thirty thousand marks of English coin.—
Philip of France, if thou be pleas'd withal,

Command thy son and daughter to join hands.
　K. Phi. It likes us well.—Young princes,
　　close your hands.
　Aust. And your lips too; for I am well assur'd
That I did so when I was first assur'd.
　K. Phi. Now, citizens of Angiers, ope your
　　gates,
Let in that amity which you have made;
For at Saint Mary's chapel presently
The rites of marriage shall be solemniz'd.—
Is not the Lady Constance in this troop?
I know she is not; for this match made up
Her presence would have interrupted much:
Where is she and her son? tell me, who knows.
　Lou. She is sad and passionate at your high-
　　ness' tent.
　K. Phi. And, by my faith, this league that
　　we have made
Will give her sadness very little cure.—
Brother of England, how may we content
This widow lady? In her right we came;
Which we, God knows, have turn'd another
　way,
To our own vantage.
　K. John.　　　　　We will heal up all;
For we'll create young Arthur Duke of Bretagne
And Earl of Richmond; and this rich fair town
We make him lord of.—Call the Lady Con-
　stance:
Some speedy messenger bid her repair
To our solemnity:—I trust we shall,
If not fill up the measure of her will?
Yet in some measure satisfy her so
That we shall stop her exclamation.
Go we, as well as haste will suffer us,
To this unlook'd-for, unprepared pomp.
　　　[*Exeunt all but the* BASTARD. *The* Citizens
　　　　　　　　retire from the Walls.
　Bast. Mad world! mad kings! mad composi-
　　tion!
John, to stop Arthur's title in the whole,
Hath willingly departed with a part;
And France,—whose armour conscience buck-
　led on,
Whom zeal and charity brought to the field
As God's own soldier,—rounded in the ear
With that same purpose-changer, that sly devil;
That broker, that still breaks the pate of faith;
That daily break-vow; he that wins of all,
Of kings, of beggars, old men, young men,
　maids,—
Who having no external thing to lose
But the word maid, cheats the poor maid of
　that;
That smooth-fac'd gentleman, tickling com-
　modity,—
Commodity, the bias of the world;
The world, who of itself is peised well,
Made to run even upon even ground,
Till this advantage, this vile-drawing bias,
This sway of motion, this commodity,
Makes it take head from all indifferency,
From all direction, purpose, course, intent:
And this same bias, this commodity,

This bawd, this broker, this all-changing word,
Clapp'd on the outward eye of fickle France,
Hath drawn him from his own determin'd aid,
From a resolv'd and honourable war,
To a most base and vile-concluded peace.—
And why rail I on this commodity?
But for because he hath not woo'd me yet:
Not that I have the power to clutch my hand
When his fair angels would salute my palm;
But for my hand, as unattempted yet,
Like a poor beggar, raileth on the rich.
Well, whiles I am a beggar, I will rail,
And say, There is no sin but to be rich;
And, being rich, my virtue then shall be,
To say, There is no vice but beggary:
Since kings break faith upon commodity,
Gain, be my lord!—for I will worship thee.
　　　　　　　　　　　　　　　　　　　[Exit.

ACT III.

SCENE I.—FRANCE. *The* French King's *Tent.*

Enter CONSTANCE, ARTHUR, *and* SALISBURY.

Const. Gone to be married! gone to swear a
　　peace!
False blood to false blood join'd! gone to be
　　friends!
Shall Louis have Blanch? and Blanch those
　　provinces?
It is not so; thou hast misspoke, misheard;
Be well advis'd, tell o'er thy tale again:
It cannot be; thou dost but say 'tis so:
I trust I may not trust thee; for thy word
Is but the vain breath of a common man:
Believe me, I do not believe thee, man;
I have a king's oath to the contrary.
Thou shalt be punish'd for thus frighting me,
For I am sick, and capable of fears;
Oppress'd with wrongs, and therefore full of
　　fears;
A widow, husbandless, subject to fears;
A woman, naturally born to fears;
And though thou now confess thou didst but
　　jest,
With my vex'd spirits I cannot take a truce,
But they will quake and tremble all this day.
What dost thou mean by shaking of thy head?
Why dost thou look so sadly on my son?
What means that hand upon that breast of
　　thine?
Why holds thine eye that lamentable rheum,
Like a proud river peering o'er its bounds?
Be these sad signs confirmers of thy words?
Then speak again,—not all thy former tale,
But this one word, whether thy tale be true.
　　Sal. As true as I believe you think them false
That give you cause to prove my saying true.
　　Const. O, if thou teach me to believe this
　　sorrow,
Teach thou this sorrow how to make me die;
And let belief and life encounter so
As doth the fury of two desperate men,
Which in the very meeting fall and die!—

Louis marry Blanch! O boy, then where art
　　thou?　　　　　　　　　　　　　[me?—
France friend with England! what becomes of
Fellow, be gone: I cannot brook thy sight;
This news hath made thee a most ugly man.
　　Sal. What other harm have I, good lady,
　　done,
But spoke the harm that is by others done?
　　Const. Which harm within itself so heinous is,
As it makes harmful all that speak of it.
　　Arth. I do beseech you, madam, be content.
　　Const. If thou, that bid'st me be content,
　　wert grim,
Ugly, and slanderous to thy mother's womb,
Full of unpleasing blots and sightless stains,
Lame, foolish, crooked, swart, prodigious,
Patch'd with foul moles and eye-offending
　　marks,
I would not care, I then would be content;
For then I should not love thee; no, nor thou
Become thy great birth, nor deserve a crown.
But thou art fair; and at thy birth, dear boy,
Nature and fortune join'd to make thee great:
Of nature's gifts thou mayst with lilies boast,
And with the half-blown rose: but Fortune, O!
She is corrupted, chang'd, and won from thee;
She adulterates hourly with thine uncle John;
And with her golden hand hath pluck'd on
　　France
To tread down fair respect of sovereignty,
And make his majesty the bawd to theirs.
France is a bawd to Fortune, and king John—
That strumpet Fortune, that usurping John!—
Tell me, thou fellow, is not France forsworn?
Envenom him with words; or get thee gone,
And leave those woes alone, which I alone
Am bound to under-bear.
　　Sal.　　　　　　　　Pardon me, madam,
I may not go without you to the kings.
　　Const. Thou mayst, thou shalt; I will not go
　　with thee:
I will instruct my sorrows to be proud;
For grief is proud, and makes his honour stout.
To me, and to the state of my great grief,
Let kings assemble; for my grief's so great
That no supporter but the huge firm earth
Can hold it up: here I and sorrows sit;
Here is my throne, bid kings come bow to it.
　　　　　　　　[Seats herself on the ground.

Enter KING JOHN, KING PHILIP, LOUIS,
　　BLANCH, ELINOR, BASTARD, AUSTRIA, *and*
　　Attendants.

　　K. Phi. 'Tis true, fair daughter; and this
　　blessed day
Ever in France shall be kept festival:
To solemnize this day the glorious sun
Stays in his course, and plays the alchemist,
Turning, with splendour of his precious eye,
The meagre cloddy earth to glittering gold:
The yearly course that brings this day about
Shall never see it bud a holiday.
　　Const. A wicked day, and not a holy day!
　　　　　　　　　　　　　　　　　　[Rising.

What hath this day deserv'd? what hath it
　　done,
That it in golden letters should be set
Among the high tides in the calendar?
Nay, rather turn this day out of the week,
This day of shame, oppression, perjury:
Or, if it must stand still, let wives with child
Pray that their burdens may not fall this day,
Lest that their hopes prodigiously be cross'd:
But on this day let seamen fear no wreck;
No bargains break that are not this day made:
This day, all things begun come to ill end,—
Yea, faith itself to hollow falsehood change!
　　K. Phi. By heaven, lady, you shall have no
　　　cause
To curse the fair proceedings of this day.
Have I not pawn'd to you my majesty?
　　Const. You have beguil'd me with a counter-
　　　feit　　　　　　　　　　　　　　[tried,
Resembling majesty; which, being touch'd and
Proves valueless: you are forsworn, forsworn:
You came in arms to spill mine enemies' blood,
But now in arms you strengthen it with yours:
The grappling vigour and rough frown of war
Is cold in amity and painted peace,
And our oppression hath made up this league.—
Arm, arm, you heavens, against these perjur'd
　　kings!
A widow cries; be husband to me, heavens!
Let not' the hours of this ungodly day
Wear out the day in peace; but, ere sunset,
Set armed discord 'twixt these perjur'd kings!
Hear me, O, hear me!
　　Aust.　　　　　　Lady Constance, peace.
　　Const. War! war! no peace! peace is to me
　　　a war.
O Lymoges! O Austria! thou dost shame
That bloody spoil: thou slave, thou wretch,
　　thou coward!
Thou little valiant, great in villany!
Thou ever strong upon the stronger side!
Thou Fortune's champion that dost never fight
But when her humorous ladyship is by
To teach thee safety!—thou art perjur'd too,
And sooth'st up greatness. What a fool art
　　thou,
A ramping fool, to brag, and stamp, and swear
Upon thy party! Thou cold-blooded slave,
Hast thou not spoke like thunder on my side?
Been sworn my soldier? bidding me depend
Upon thy stars, thy fortune, and thy strength?
And dost thou now fall over to my foes?
Thou wear a lion's hide! doff it for shame,
And hang a calf's-skin on those recreant limbs!
　　Aust. O, that a man should speak those
　　　words to me!　　　　　　　　[limbs.
　　Bast. And hang a calf's-skin on those recreant
　　Aust. Thou dar'st not say so, villain, for thy
　　　life.
　　Bast. And hang a calf's-skin on those recre-
　　　ant limbs.
　　K. John. We like not this; thou dost forget
　　　thyself.　　　　　　　　　　　[pope.
　　K. Phi. Here comes the holy legate of the

Enter PANDULPH.

　　Pand. Hail, you anointed deputies of
　　　heaven!—
To thee, King John, my holy errand is.
I Pandulph, of fair Milan cardinal,
And from Pope Innocent the legate here,
Do in his name religiously demand,
Why thou against the church, our holy mother,
So wilfully dost spurn; and, force perforce,
Keep Stephen Langton, chosen archbishop
Of Canterbury, from that holy see?
This, in our foresaid holy father's name,
Pope Innocent, I do demand of thee.
　　K. John. What earthly name to interroga-
　　　tories
Can task the free breath of a sacred king?
Thou canst not, cardinal, devise a name
So slight, unworthy, and ridiculous,
To charge me to an answer, as the pope.
Tell him this tale; and from the mouth of
　　England
Add thus much more,—That no Italian priest
Shall tithe or toll in our dominions:
But as we under heaven are supreme head.
So, under him, that great supremacy,
Where we do reign, we will alone uphold,
Without the assistance of a mortal hand:
So tell the pope; all reverence set apart
To him and his usurp'd authority.
　　K. Phi. Brother of England, you blaspheme
　　　in this.　　　　　　　　　[Christendom,
　　K. John. Though you, and all the kings of
Are led so grossly by this meddling priest,
Dreading the curse that money may buy out;
And by the merit of vile gold, dross, dust,
Purchase corrupted pardon of a man,
Who in that sale sells pardon from himself;
Though you and all the rest, so grossly led,
This juggling witchcraft with revenue cherish;
Yet I, alone, alone do me oppose
Against the pope, and count his friends my
　　foes.
　　Pand. Then, by the lawful power that I have,
Thou shalt stand curs'd and excommunicate:
And blessed shall he be that doth revolt
From his allegiance to an heretic;
And meritorious shall that hand be call'd,
Canónized, and worshipp'd as a saint,
That takes away by any secret course
Thy hateful life.
　　Const.　　　　　O, lawful let it be
That I have room with Rome to curse awhile!
Good father cardinal, cry thou amen
To my keen curses: for without my wrong
There is no tongue hath power to curse him
　　right.　　　　　　　　　　　　[my curse.
　　Pand. There's law and warrant, lady, for
　　Const. And for mine too: when law can do
　　　no right,
Let it be lawful that law bar no wrong:
Law cannot give my child his kingdom here;
For he that holds his kingdom holds the law:
Therefore, since law itself is perfect wrong,

How can the law forbid my tongue to curse?

Pand. Philip of France, on peril of a curse,
Let go the hand of that arch-heretic;
And raise the power of France upon his head,
Unless he do submit himself to Rome.

Eli. Look'st thou pale, France; do not let
    go thy hand.   [repent

Const. Look to that, devil; lest that France
And, by disjoining hands, hell lose a soul.

Aust. King Philip, listen to the cardinal.

Bast. And hang a calf's-skin on his recreant
    limbs.   [wrongs,

Aust. Well, ruffian, I must pocket up these
Because—

Bast. Your breeches best may carry them.

K. John. Philip, what say'st thou to the
    cardinal?   [cardinal?

Const. What should he say, but as the

Lou. Bethink you, father; for the difference
Is, purchase of a heavy curse from Rome,
Or the light loss of England for a friend:
Forego the easier.

Blanch.   That's the curse of Rome.

Const. O Louis, stand fast! the devil tempts
    thee here
In likeness of a new uptrimmed bride.

Blanch. The Lady Constance speaks not
    from her faith,
But from her need.

Const.   O, if thou grant my need,
Which only lives but by the death of faith,
That need must needs infer this principle,—
That faith would live again by death of need!
O, then, tread down my need, and faith mounts
    up;
Keep my need up, and faith is trodden down!

K. John. The king is mov'd, and answers not
    to this.   [well!

Const. O, be remov'd from him, and answer

Aust. Do so, King Philip; hang no more in
    doubt.   [sweet lout.

Bast. Hang nothing but a calf's-skin, most

K. Phi. I am perplex'd, and know not what
    to say.   [thee more,

Pand. What canst thou say, but will preplex
If thou stand excommunicate and curs'd?

K. Phi. Good reverend father, make my
    person yours,
And tell me how you would bestow yourself.
This royal hand and mine are newly knit,
And the conjunction of our inward souls
Married in league, coupled and link'd together
With all religious strength of sacred vows;
The latest breath that gave the sound of words
Was deep-sworn faith, peace, amity, true love,
Between our kingdoms and our royal selves;
And even before this truce, but new before,—
No longer than we well could wash our hands,
To clap this royal bargain up of peace,—
Heaven knows, they were besmear'd and over-
    stain'd
With slaughter's pencil, where revenge did
    paint
The fearful difference of incensed kings:

And shall these hands, so lately purg'd of blood,
So newly joined in love, so strong in both,
Unyoke this seizure and this kind regreet?
Play fast and loose with faith? so jest with
    heaven,
Make such unconstant children of ourselves,
As now again to snatch our palm from palm;
Unswear faith sworn; and on the marriage-bed
Of smiling peace to march a bloody host,
And make a riot on the gentle brow
Of true sincerity? O, holy sir,
My reverend father, let it not be so!
Out of your grace, devise, ordain, impose
Some gentle order; and then we shall be bless'd
To do your pleasure, and continue friends.

Pand. All form is tormless, order orderless,
Save what is opposite to England's love.
Therefore, to arms! be champion of our church!
Or let the church, our mother, breathe her
    curse,—
A mother's curse,—on her revolting son.
France, thou mayst hold a serpent by the
    tongue,
A chafed lion by the mortal paw,
A fasting tiger safer by the tooth,   [hold.
Than keep in peace that hand which thou dost

K. Phi. I may disjoin my hand, but not my
    faith.   [faith;

Pand. So mak'st thou faith an enemy to
And, like a civil war, sett'st oath to oath,
Thy tongue against thy tongue. O, let thy vow
First made to heaven, first be to heaven per-
    form'd,—
That is, to be the champion of our church!
What since thou swor'st•is sworn against thy-
    self,
And may not be performed by thyself:
For that which thou hast sworn to do amiss
Is not amiss when it is truly done;
And being not done, where doing tends to ill,
The truth is then most done not doing it:
The better act of purposes mistook
Is to mistake again; though indirect,
Yet indirection thereby grows direct,
And falsehood falsehood cures; as fire cools fire
Within the scorched veins of one new burn'd.
It is religion that doth make vows kept;
But thou hast sworn against religion,
By what thou swear'st against the thing thou
    swear'st;
And mak'st an oath the surety for thy truth
Against an oath: the truth thou art unsure
To swear, swears only not to be forsworn;
Else what a mockery should it be to swear!
But thou dost swear only to be forsworn;
And most forsworn, to keep what thou dost
    swear.
Therefore thy latter vows against thy first
Is in thyself rebellion to thyself;
And better conquest never canst thou make
Than arm thy constant and thy nobler parts
Against these giddy loose suggestions:
Upon which better part our prayers come in,
If thou vouchsafe them; but if not, then know

The peril of our curses light on thee,
So heavy as thou shalt not shake them off,
But in despair die under their black weight.
   Aust. Rebellion, flat rebellion!
   Bast.   Will 't not be?
Will not a calf's-skin stop that mouth of thine?
   Lou. Father, to arms!
   Blanch.   Upon thy wedding-day?
Against the blood that thou hast married?
What, shall our feast be kept with slaughter'd
    men?
Shall braying trumpets and loud churlish
    drums,—
Clamours of hell,—be measures to our pomp?
O husband, hear me!—ay, alack, how new
Is husband in my mouth!—even for that name,
Which till this time my tongue did ne'er pro-
    nounce,
Upon my knee I beg, go not to arms
Against mine uncle.
   Const.   O, upon my knee,
Made hard with kneeling, I do pray to thee,
Thou virtuous Dauphin, alter not the doom
Forethought by heaven.
   Blanch. Now shall I see thy love: what mo-
    tive may
Be stronger with thee than the name of wife?
   Const. That which upholdeth him that thee
    upholds,
His honour:—O, thine honour, Louis, thine
    honour!
   Lou. I muse your majesty doth seem so cold,
When such profound respects do pull you on.
   Pand. I will denounce a curse upon his head.
   K. Phi. Thou shalt not need.—England, I
    will fall from thee.
   Const. O fair return of banish'd majesty!
   Eli. O foul revolt of French inconstancy!
   K. John. France, thou shalt rue this hour
    within this hour.
   Bast. Old Time the clock-setter, that bald
    sexton Time,
Is it as he will? well, then, France shall rue.
   Blanch. The sun's o'ercast with blood: fair
    day, adieu!
Which is the side that I must go withal?
I am with both: each army hath a hand;
And in their rage, I having hold of both,
They whirl asunder and dismember me.
Husband, I cannot pray that thou mayst win;
Uncle, I needs must pray that thou mayst lose;
Father, I may not wish the fortune thine;
Grandam, I will not wish thy wishes thrive:
Whoever wins, on that side shall I lose;
Assured loss before the match be play'd.
   Lou. Lady, with me; with me thy fortune
    lies.
   Blanch. There where my fortune lives, there
    my life dies.
   K. John. Cousin, go draw our puissance to-
    gether.—   [*Exit* BASTARD.
France, I am burn'd up with inflaming wrath;
A rage whose heat hath this condition,
That nothing can allay, nothing but blood,—

The blood, and dearest-valu'd blood of France.
   K. Phi. Thy rage shall burn thee up, and
    thou shalt turn
To ashes, ere our blood shall quench that fire:
Look to thyself, thou art in jeopardy.
   K. John. No more than he that threats.—To
    arms let's hie!   [*Exeunt severally.*

SCENE II.—*The same. Plains near Angiers.*

Alarums. Excursions. Enter the BASTARD, *with*
AUSTRIA'S *head.*

   Bast. Now, by my life, this day grows won-
    drous hot;
Some airy devil hovers in the sky,   [there,
And pours down mischief.—Austria's head lie
While Philip breathes.

Enter KING JOHN, ARTHUR, *and* HUBERT.

   K. John. Hubert, keep this boy.—Philip,
    make up:
My mother is assailed in our tent,
And ta'en, I fear.
   Bast.   My lord, I rescu'd her;
Her highness is in safety, fear you not:
But on, my liege; for very little pains
Will bring this labour to an happy end.
                         [*Exeunt.*

SCENE III.—*The same.*

Alarums, Excursions, Retreat. Enter KING
JOHN, ELINOR, ARTHUR, *the* BASTARD,
HUBERT, *and* Lords.

   K. John. So shall it be; your grace shall stay
    behind,   [*To* ELINOR.
So strongly guarded.—Cousin, look not sad:
                     [*To* ARTHUR.
Thy grandam loves thee; and thy uncle will
As dear be to thee as thy father was.   [grief!
   Arth. O, this will make my mother die with
   K. John. Cousin [*to the* BASTARD], away for
    England; haste before:
And, ere our coming, see thou shake the bags
Of hoarding abbots; imprison'd angels
Set at liberty: the fat ribs of peace
Must by the hungry now be fed upon:
Use our commission in his utmost force.
   Bast. Bell, book, and candle shall not drive
    me back,
When gold and silver becks me to come on.
I leave your highness.—Grandam, I will pray,—
If ever I remember to be holy,—
For your fair safety; so, I kiss your hand.
   Eli. Farewell, gentle cousin.
   K. John. Coz, farewell.   [*Exit* BASTARD.
   Eli. Come hither, little kinsman; hark a
    word.   [*She takes* ARTHUR *aside.*
   K. John. Come hither, Hubert. O my gentle
    Hubert,
We owe thee much! within this wall of flesh
There is a soul counts thee her creditor,
And with advantage means to pay thy love:
And, my good friend, thy voluntary oath

Lives in this bosom, dearly cherished.
Give me thy hand. I had a thing to say,—
But I.will fit it with some better time.
By heaven, Hubert, I am almost asham'd
To say what good respect I have of thee.
   Hub. I am much bounden to your majesty.
   K. John. Good friend, thou hast no cause to
     say so yet:
But thou shalt have; and creep time ne'er so
   slow,
Yet it shall come for me to do thee good.
I had a thing to say,—but let it go:
The sun is in the heaven, and the proud day,
Attended with the pleasures of the world,
Is all too wanton and too full of gawds
To give me audience:—if the midnight bell
Did, with his iron tongue and brazen mouth,
Sound one unto the drowsy ear of night;
If this same were a churchyard where we stand,
And thou possessed with a thousand wrongs;
Or if that surly spirit, melancholy,   [thick,—
Had bak'd thy blood, and made it heavy,
Which else runs tickling up and down the veins,
Making that idiot, laughter, keep men's eyes,
And strain their cheeks to idle merriment—
A passion hateful to my purposes;—
Or if that thou couldst see me without eyes,
Hear me without thine ears, and make reply
Without a tongue, using conceit alone,
Without eyes, ears, and harmful sound of
   words,—
Then, in despite of brooded watchful day,
I would into thy bosom pour my thoughts:
But, ah, I will not!—yet I love thee well;
And, by my troth, I think thou lov'st me well.
   Hub. So well that what you bid me under-
     take;
Though that my death were adjunct to my act,
By heaven, I would do it.
   K. John.   Do not I know thou wouldst?
Good Hubert, Hubert, Hubert, throw thine
   eye
On yon young boy: I'll tell thee what, my
   friend,
He is a very serpent in my way;
And wheresoe'er this foot of mine doth tread,
He lies before me:—dost thou understand me?
Thou art his keeper.
   Hub.   And I'll keep him so
That he shall not offend your majesty.
   K. John. Death.
   Hub.   My lord?
   K. John.   A grave.
   Hub.   He shall not live.
   K. John.   Enough.—
I could be merry now. Hubert, I love thee:
Well, I'll not say what I intend for thee:
Remember.—Madam, fare you well:
I'll send those powers o'er to your majesty.
   Eli. My blessing go with thee!
   K. John.   For England, cousin, go:
Hubert shall be your man, attend on you
With all true duty.—On toward Calais, ho!
                       [*Exeunt.*

SCENE IV.—*The same. The* French King's
        Tent.

Enter KING PHILIP, LOUIS, PANDULPH, *and*
        Attendants.

   K. Phi. So, by a roaring tempest on the
     flood,
A whole armado of convicted sail
Is scatter'd and disjoin'd from fellowship.
   Pand. Courage and comfort! all shall yet go
     well.   [run so ill.
   K. Phi. What can go well, when we have
Are we not beaten? Is not Angiers lost?
Arthur ta'en prisoner? divers dear friends slain?
And bloody England into England gone,
O'erbearing interruption, spite of France?
   Lou. What he hath won, that hath he forti-
     fied:
So hot a speed with such advice dispos'd,
Such temperate order in so fierce a cause,
Doth want example: who hath read or heard
Of any kindred action like to this?
   K. Phi. Well could I bear that England had
     this praise,
So we could find some pattern of our shame.—
Look, who comes here! a grave unto a soul;
Holding the eternal spirit, against her will,
In the vile prison of afflicted breath.

Enter CONSTANCE.

I pr'ythee, lady, go away with me.   [peace!
   Const. Lo, now! now see the issue of your
   K. Phi. Patience, good lady! comfort, gentle
     Constance!
   Const. No, I defy all counsel, all redress,
But that which ends all counsel, true redress,
Death, death:—O amiable lovely death!
Thou odoriferous stench! sound rottenness!
Arise forth from the couch of lasting night,
Thou hate and terror to prosperity,
And I will kiss thy détestable bones;
And put my eyeballs in thy vaulty brows;
And ring these fingers with thy household
   worms;
And stop this gap of breath with fulsome dust,
And be a carrion monster like thyself:
Come, grin on me; and I will think thou smil'st,
And buss thee as thy wife! Misery's love,
O, come to me!
   K. Phi.   O fair affliction, peace!
   Const. No, no, I will not, having breath to
     cry:—
O, that my tongue were in the thunder's mouth!
Then with a passion would I shake the world:
And rouse from sleep that fell anatomy
Which cannot hear a lady's feeble voice,
Which scorns a modern invocation.
   Pand. Lady, you utter madness, and not
     sorrow.
   Const. Thou art not holy to belie me so;
I am not mad: this hair I tear is mine;
My name is Constance; I was Geffrey's wife;
Young Arthur is my son, and he is lost:

I am not mad;—I would to heaven I were!
For then, 'tis like I should forget myself:
O, if I could, what grief should I forget!—
Preach some philosophy to make me mad,
And thou shalt be canóniz'd, cardinal;
For, being not mad, but sensible of grief,
My reasonable part produces reason
How I may be deliver'd of these woes,
And teaches me to kill or hang myself:
If I were mad I should forget my son,
Or madly think a babe of clouts were he:
I am not mad; too well, too well I feel
The different plague of each calamity.
    K. Phi. Bind up those tresses.—O, what
      love I note
In the fair multitude of those her hairs!
Where but by chance a silver drop hath fallen,
Even to that drop ten thousand wiry friends
Do glue themselves in sociable grief;
Like true, inseparable, faithful loves,
Sticking together in calamity.
    Const. To England, if you will.
    K. Phi.   Bind up your hairs.
    Const. Yes, that I will; and wherefore will
      I do it?
I tore them from their bonds, and cried aloud,
O that these hands could so redeem my son,
As they have given these hairs their liberty!
But now I envy at their liberty,
And will again commit them to their bonds,
Because my poor child is a prisoner.—
And, father cardinal, I have heard you say
That we shall see and know our friends in
    heaven:
If that be true, I shall see my boy again;
For since the birth of Cain, the first male child,
To him that did but yesterday suspire,
There was not such a gracious creature born.
But now will canker sorrow eat my bud,
And chase the native beauty from his cheek,
And he will look as hollow as a ghost,
As dim and meagre as an ague's fit;
And so he'll die; and, rising so again,
When I shall meet him in the court of heaven
I shall not know him: therefore never, never
Must I behold my pretty Arthur more.
    Pand. You hold too heinous a respect of
      grief.
    Const. He talks to me that never had a son.
    K. Phi. You are as fond of grief as of your
      child.   [child,
    Const. Grief fills the room up of my absent
Lies in his bed, walks up and down with me,
Puts on his pretty looks, repeats his words,
Remembers me of all his gracious parts,
Stuffs out his vacant garments with his form;
Then have I reason to be fond of grief.
Fare you well: had you such a loss as I,
I could give better comfort than you do.—
I will not keep this form upon my head,
             [*Tearing off her head-dress.*
When here is such disorder in my wit.
O Lord! my boy, my Arthur, my fair son!
My life, my joy, my food, my all the world!

My widow-comfort, and my sorrow's cure!
                  [*Exit.*
    K. Phi. I fear some outrage, and I'll follow
      her.   [*Exit.*
    Lou. There's nothing in this world can make
      me joy:
Life is as tedious as a twice-told tale
Vexing the dull ear of a drowsy man;   [taste,
And bitter shame hath spoil'd the sweet world's
That it yields naught but shame and bitterness.
    Pand. Before the curing of a strong disease,
Even in the instant of repair and health,
The fit is strongest; evils that take leave,
On their departure most of all show evil:
What have you lost by losing of this day?
    Lou. All days of glory, joy, and happiness.
    Pand. If you had won it, certainly you had.
No, no; when Fortune means to men most good,
She looks upon them with a threatening eye.
'Tis strange to think how much King John hath
    lost
In this which he accounts so clearly won:
Are not you griev'd that Arthur is his prisoner?
    Lou. As heartily as he is glad he hath him.
    Pand. Your mind is all as youthful as your
      blood.
Now hear me speak with a prophetic spirit;
For even the breath of what I mean to speak
Shall blow each dust, each straw, each little rub,
Out of the path which shall directly lead
Thy foot to England's throne; and therefore
    mark.
John hath seiz'd Arthur; and it cannot be
That, whiles warm life plays in that infant's
    veins,
The misplac'd John should entertain an hour,
One minute, nay, one quiet breath of rest:
A sceptre snatch'd with an unruly hand
Must be as boisterously maintain'd as gain'd;
And he that stands upon a slippery place
Makes nice of no vile hole to stay him up:
That John may stand, then Arthur needs must
    fall;
So be it, for it cannot be but so.   [fall?
    Lou. But what shall I gain by young Arthur's
    Pand. You, in the right of Lady Blanch
      your wife,
May then make all the claim that Arthur did.
    Lou. And lose it, life and all, as Arthur did.
    Pand. How green you are, and fresh in this
      old world!   [you;
John lays you plots; the times conspire with
For he that steeps his safety in true blood
Shall find but bloody safety and untrue.
This act, so evilly borne, shall cool the hearts
Of all his people, and freeze up their zeal,
That none so small advantage shall step forth
To check his reign, but they will cherish it;
No natural exhalation in the sky,
No scape of nature, no distemper'd day,
No common wind, no customed event,
But they will pluck away his natural cause,
And call them meteors, prodigies, and signs,
Abortives, présages, and tongues of heaven,

Plainly denouncing vengeance upon John.
   Lou. May be he will not touch young Ar-
     thur's life,
But hold himself safe in his prisonment.
   Pand. O, sir, when he shall hear of your ap-
     proach,
If that young Arthur be not gone already,
Even at that news he dies; and then the hearts
Of all his people shall revolt from him,
And kiss the lips of unacquainted change;
And pick strong matter of revolt and wrath
Out of the bloody fingers' ends of John.
Methinks I see this hurly all on foot:
And, O, what better matter breeds for you
Than I have nam'd!—The bastard Falcon-
     bridge
Is now in England, ransacking the church,
Offending charity: if but a dozen French
Were there in arms, they would be as a call
To train ten thousand English to their side;
Or as a little snow, tumbled about
Anon becomes a mountain. O noble Dauphin,
Go with me to the king:—'tis wonderful
What may be wrought out of their discontent,
Now that their souls are topful of offence:
For England go:—I will whet on the king.
   Lou. Strong reasons make strong actions: let
     us go:
If you say ay, the king will not say no.
                       [Exeunt.

ACT IV.

SCENE I.—NORTHAMPTON. *A Room in the
Castle.*

Enter HUBERT *and two* Attendants.

   Hub. Heat me these irons hot; and look thou
     stand
Within the arras: when I strike my foot
Upon the bosom of the ground, rush forth,
And bind the boy which you shall find with me
Fast to the chair: be heedful: hence, and watch.
   1 *Attend.* I hope your warrant will bear out
     the deed.
   Hub. Uncleanly scruples! Fear not you: look
   to 't.—   *[Exeunt* Attendants.
Young lad, come forth; I have to say with you.

Enter ARTHUR.

   Arth. Good-morrow, Hubert.
   Hub.   Good-morrow, little prince.
   Arth. As little prince, having so great a title
To be more prince, as may be.—You are sad.
   Hub. Indeed, I have been merrier.
   Arth.   Mercy on me!
Methinks no body should be sad but I:
Yet, I remember, when I was in France,
Young gentlemen would be as sad as night,
Only for wantonness. By my christendom,
So I were out of prison, and kept sheep,
I should be as merry as the day is long;
And so I would be here, but that I doubt
My uncle practices more harm to me:
He is afraid of me, and I of him:

Is it my fault that I was Geffrey's son?
No, indeed, is 't not; and I would to heaven
I were your son, so you would love me, Hubert.
   Hub. [*Aside.*] If I talk to him, with his inno-
     cent prate
He will awake my mercy, which lies dead:
Therefore I will be sudden and despatch.
   Arth. Are you sick, Hubert? you look pale
     to-day:
In sooth, I would you were a little sick,
That I might sit all night and watch with you:
I warrant I love you more than you do me.
   Hub. [*Aside.*] His words do take possession
     of my bosom.—
Read here, young Arthur.   [*Showing a paper.*
     [*Aside.*] How now, foolish rheum!
Turning dispiteous torture out of door!
I must be brief, lest resolution drop
Out at mine eyes in tender womanish tears.—
Can you not read it? is it not fair writ?
   Arth. Too fairly, Hubert, for so foul effect.
Must you with hot irons burn out both mine
     eyes?
   Hub. Young boy, I must.
   Arth.   And will you?
   Hub.   And I will.
   Arth. Have you the heart? When your head
     did but ache
I knit my handkerchief about your brows,—
The best I had, a princess wrought it me,—
And I did never ask it you again;
And with my hand at midnight held your head;
And, like the watchful minutes to the hour,
Still and anon cheer'd up the heavy time,
Saying, *What lack you?* and, *Where lies your
     grief?*
Or, *What good love may I perform for you?*
Many a poor man's son would have lien still,
And ne'er have spoke a loving word to you;
But you at your sick service had a prince.
Nay, you may think my love was crafty love,
And call it cunning:—do, an if you will:
If heaven be pleas'd that you must use me ill,
Why, then you must.—Will you put out mine
     eyes?
These eyes that never did nor never shall
So much as frown on you?
   Hub.   I have sworn to do it!
And with hot irons must I burn them out.
   Arth. Ah, none but in this iron age would
     do it!
The iron of itself, though heat red hot,
Approaching near these eyes, would drink my
     tears,
And quench his fiery indignation,
Even in the matter of mine innocence;
Nay, after that, consume away in rust,
But for containing fire to harm mine eye.
Are you more stubborn-hard than hammer'd
     iron?
An if an angel should have come to me
And told me Hubert should put out mine eyes
I would not have believ'd him,—no tongue but
     Hubert's.

Hub. Come forth.   [*Stamps.*

Re-enter Attendants, *with cords, irons, &c.*
                Do as I bid you.
Arth. O, save me, Hubert, save me! my eyes
    are out
Even with the fierce looks of these bloody men.
    Hub. Give me the iron, I say, and bind him
        here.   [rough?
    Arth. Alas, what need you be so boist'rous—
I will not struggle, I will stand stone-still.
For heaven's sake, Hubert, let me not be bound!
Nay, hear me, Hubert!—drive these men away,
And I will sit as quiet as a lamb;
I will not stir, nor wince, nor speak a word,
Nor look upon the iron angerly:
Thrust but these men away, and I'll forgive
    you,
Whatever torment you do put me to.   [him.
    Hub. Go, stand within; let me alone with
 I Attend. I am best pleas'd to be from such
        a deed.   [*Exeunt* Attendants.
    Arth. Alas, I then have chid away my friend!
He hath a stern look but a gentle heart:—
Let him come back, that his compassion may
Give life to yours.
    Hub.   Come, boy, prepare yourself.
    Arth. Is there no remedy?
    Hub.   None, but to lose your eyes.
    Arth. O heaven!—that there were but a
        mote in yours,
A grain, a dust, a gnat, a wandering hair,
Any annoyance in that precious sense!
Then, feeling what small things are boisterous
    there,
Your vile intent must needs seem horrible.
    Hub. Is this your promise? go to, hold your
        tongue.
    Arth. Hubert, the utterance of a brace of
        tongues
Must needs want pleading for a pair of eyes:
Let me not hold my tongue,—let me not,
        Hubert!
Or, Hubert, if you will, cut out my tongue,
So I may keep mine eyes: O, spare mine eyes,
Though to no use but still to look on you!—
Lo, by my troth, the instrument is cold,
And would not harm me.
    Hub.   I can heat it, boy.
    Arth. No, in good sooth; the fire is dead with
        grief,
Being create for comfort, to be us'd
In undeserv'd extremes: see else yourself;
There is no malice in this burning coal;
The breath of heaven hath blown his spirit out,
And strew'd repentant ashes on his head.
    Hub. But with my breath I can revive it,
        boy.
    Arth. And if you do, you will but make it
        blush,   [Hubert:
And glow with shame of your proceedings,
Nay, it, perchance, will sparkle in your eyes;
And, like a dog that is compell'd to fight,
Snatch at his master that doth tarre him on.

All things that you should use to do me wrong,
Deny their office: only you do lack
That mercy which fierce fire and iron extends,
Creatures of note for mercy-lacking uses.
    Hub. Well, see to live; I will not touch thine
        eyes
For all the treasure that thine uncle owes:
Yet am I sworn, and I did purpose, boy,
With this same very iron to burn them out.
    Arth. O, now you look like Hubert! all this
        while
You were disguised.
    Hub.   Peace; no more. Adieu!
Your uncle must not know but you are dead;
I'll fill these dogged spies with false reports:
And, pretty child, sleep doubtless and secure,
That Hubert, for the wealth of all the world,
Will not offend thee.
    Arth.   O heaven! I thank you, Hubert.
    Hub. Silence; no more: go closely in with me:
Much danger do I undergo for thee.   [*Exeunt.*

SCENE II.—*The same. A Room of State in the
            Palace.*

Enter KING JOHN, *crowned;* PEMBROKE, SALIS-
    BURY, *and other* Lords. *The* KING *takes his
    State.*

    K. John. Here once again we sit, once again
        crown'd,
And look'd upon, I hope, with cheerful eyes.
    Pem. This once again, but that your high-
        ness pleas'd,
Was once superfluous: you were crown'd before,
And that high royalty was ne'er pluck'd off;
The faiths of men ne'er stained with revolt;
Fresh expectation troubled not the land
With any long'd-for change or better state.
    Sal. Therefore, to be possess'd with double
        pomp,
To guard a title that was rich before,
To gild refined gold, to paint the lily,
To throw a perfume on the violet,
To smooth the ice, or add another hue
Unto the rainbow, or with taper-light
To seek the beauteous eye of heaven to garnish,
Is wasteful and ridiculous excess.   [done,
    Pem. But that your royal pleasure must be
This act is as an ancient tale new told;
And in the last repeating troublesome,
Being urged at a time unseasonable.
    Sal. In this, the antique and well-noted face
Of plain old form is much disfigured;
And, like a shifted wind unto a sail,
It makes the course of thoughts to fetch about;
Startles and frights consideration;
Makes sound opinion sick, and truth suspected,
For putting on so new a fashion'd robe.
    Pem. When workmen strive to do better
        than well,
They do confound their skill in convetousness;
And oftentimes excusing of a fault
Doth make the fault the worse by the excuse,—
As patches set upon a little breach

Discredit more in hiding of the fault
Than did the fault before it was so patch'd.
   Sal. To this effect, before you were new-
      crown'd,   [highness
We breath'd our counsel: but it pleas'd your
To overbear it; and we are all well pleas'd,
Since all and every part of what we would
Doth make a stand at what your highness will.
   K. John. Some reasons of this double coro-
      nation
I have possess'd you with, and think them
      strong;
And more, more strong, when lesser is my fear,
I shall indue you with: meantime but ask
What you would have reform'd that is not well,
And well shall you perceive how willingly
I will both hear and grant you your requests.
   Pem. Then I,—as one that am the tongue
      of these,
To sound the purposes of all their hearts,—
Both for myself and them,—but, chief of all,
Your safety, for the which myself and them
Bend their best studies,—heartily request
The enfranchisement of Arthur; whose restraint
Doth move the murmuring lips of discontent
To break into this dangerous argument,—
If what in rest you have in right you hold,
Why, then, your fears,—which, as they say,
      attend
The steps of wrong,—should move you to mew
      up
Your tender kinsman, and to choke his days
With barbarous ignorance, and deny his youth
The rich advantage of good exercise?
That the time's enemies may not have this
To grace occasions, let it be our suit
That you have bid us ask his liberty;
Which for our goods we do no further ask
Than whereupon our weal, on you depending,
Counts it your weal he have his liberty.
   K. John. Let it be so: I do commit his youth
To your direction.

Enter HUBERT.

Hubert, what news with you?   [deed;
   Pem. This is the man should do the bloody
He show'd his warrant to a friend of mine:
The image of a wicked heinous fault
Lives in his eye; that close aspèct of his
Doth show the mood of a much-troubled breast;
And I do fearfully believe 'tis done
What we so fear'd he had a charge to do.   [go
   Sal. The colour of the king doth come and
Between his purpose and his conscience,
Like heralds 'twixt two dreadful battles set:
His passion is so ripe it needs must break.
   Pem. And when it breaks, I fear will issue
      thence
The foul corruption of a sweet child's death.
   K. John. We cannot hold mortality's strong
      hand:—
Good lords, although my will to give is living,
The suit which you demand is gone and dead:
He tells us Arthur is deceas'd to-night.

   Sal. Indeed, we fear'd his sickness was past
      cure.   [he was,
   Pem. Indeed, we heard how near his death
Before the child himself felt he was sick:
This must be answer'd either here or hence.
   K. John. Why do you bend such solemn
      brows on me?
Think you I bear the shears of destiny?
Have I commandment on the pulse of life?
   Sal. It is apparent foul-play; and 'tis shame
That greatness should so grossly offer it:
So thrive it in your game! and so, farewell.
   Pem. Stay yet, Lord Salisbury; I'll go with
      thee,
And find the inheritance of this poor child,
His little kingdom of a forced grave.   [isle,
That blood which ow'd the breadth of all this
Three foot of it doth hold:—bad world the
      while!   [out
This must not be thus borne: this will break
To all our sorrows, and ere long, I doubt.
                        [*Exeunt* Lords.
   K. John. They burn in indignation. I repent:
There is no sure foundation set on blood;
No certain life achiev'd by other's death.—

Enter a Messenger.

A fearful eye thou hast: where is that blood
That I have seen inhabit in those cheeks?
So foul a sky clears not without a storm:
Pour down thy weather:—how goes all in
      France?   [such a power
   Mess. From France to England.—Never
For any foreign preparation
Was levied in the body of a land.
The copy of your speed is learn'd by them;
For when you should be told they do prepare,
The tidings come that they are all arriv'd.
   K. John. O, where hath our intelligence been
      drunk?   [care,
Where hath it slept? Where is my mother's
That such an army could be drawn in France,
And she not hear of it?
   Mess.   My liege, her ear
Is stopp'd with dust; the first of April died
Your noble mother: and, as I hear, my lord,
The Lady Constance in a frenzy died   [tongue
Three days before; but this from rumour's
I idly heard,—if true or false I know not.
   K. John. Withhold thy speed, dreadful oc-
      casion!
O, make a league with me, till I have pleas'd
My discontented peers!—What! mother dead
How wildly, then, walks my estate in France!—
Under whose conduct came those powers of
      France
That thou for truth giv'st out are landed here?
   Mess. Under the Dauphin.
   K. John.   Thou hast made me giddy
With these ill tidings.

Enter the BASTARD *and* PETER *of Pomfret.*
               Now, what says the world
To your proceedings? do not seek to stuff

My head with more ill news, for it is full.

Bast. But if you be afeared to hear the worst,
Then let the worst, unheard, fall on your
head.

K. John. Bear with me, cousin; for I was
amaz'd
Under the tide: but now I breathe again
Aloft the flood; and can give audience
To any tongue, speak it of what it will.

Bast. How I have sped among the clergymen,
The sums I have collected shall express.
But as I travell'd hither through the land,
I find the people strangely fantasied;
Possess'd with rumours, full of idle dreams.
Not knowing what they fear, but full of fear:
And here's a prophet that I brought with me
From forth the streets of Pomfret, whom I
found
With many hundreds treading on his heels;
To whom he sung, in rude harsh-sounding
rhymes,
That, ere the next Ascension-day at noon,
Your highness should deliver up your crown.

K. John. Thou idle dreamer, wherefore didst
thou so? [out so.

Peter. Foreknowing that the truth will fall

K. John. Hubert, away with him; imprison
him;
And on that day at noon, whereon he says
I shall yield up my crown, let him be hang'd.
Deliver him to safety; and return,
For I must use thee.
[*Exit* HUBERT *with* PETER.
O my gentle cousin,
Hear'st thou the news abroad, who are arriv'd?

Bast. The French, my lord; men's mouths
are full of it:
Besides, I met Lord Bigot and Lord Salis-
bury,—
With eyes as red as new-enkindled fire,—
And others more, going to seek the grave
Of Arthur, whom they say is kill'd to-night
On your suggestion.

K. John. Gentle kinsman, go
And thrust thyself into their companies:
I have a way to win their loves again:
Bring them before me.

Bast. I will seek them out.

K. John. Nay, but make haste; the better
foot before.
O, let me have no subject enemies
When adverse foreigners affright my towns
With dreadful pomp of stout invasion!
Be Mercury, set feathers to thy heels,
And fly like thought from them to me again.

Bast. The spirit of the time shall teach me
speed.

K. John. Spoke like a spriteful noble gentle-
man. [*Exit* BASTARD.
Go after him; for he perhaps shall need
Some messenger betwixt me and the peers;
And be thou he.

Mess. With all my heart, my liege. [*Exit*.

K. John. My mother dead!

Re-enter HUBERT.

Hub. My lord, they say five moons were
seen to-night;
Four fixed; and the fifth did whirl about
The other four in wondrous motion.

K. John. Five moons!

Hub. Old men and beldams in the streets
Do prophesy upon it dangerously: [mouths:
Young Arthur's death is common in their
And when they talk of him, they shake their
heads,
And whisper one another in the ear;
And he that speaks doth gripe the hearer's
wrist;
Whilst he that hears makes fearful action,
With wrinkled brows, with nods, with rolling
eyes.
I saw a smith stand with his hammer, thus,
The whilst his iron did on the anvil cool,
With open mouth swallowing a tailor's news;
Who, with his shears and measure in his hand,
Standing on slippers,—which his nimble haste
Had falsely thrust upon contráry feet,—
Told of a many thousand warlike French
That were embattailed and rank'd in Kent?
Another lean unwash'd artificer
Cuts off his tale, and talks of Arthur's death?

K. John. Why seek'st thou to possess me
with these fears?
Why urgest thou so oft young Arthur's death?
Thy hand hath murder'd him: I had a mighty
cause [kill him.
To wish him dead, but thou hadst none to

Hub. No hand, my lord! why, did you not
provoke me? [tended

K. John. It is the curse of kings to be at-
By slaves that take their humours for a warrant
To break within the bloody house of life;
And, on the winking of authority,
To understand a law; to know the meaning
Of dangerous majesty, when perchance it frowns
More upon humour than advis'd respect.

Hub. Here is your hand and seal for what I
did.

K. John. O, when the last account 'twixt
heaven and earth
Is to be made, then shall this hand and seal
Witness against us to damnation!
How oft the sight of means to do ill deeds
Make ill deeds done! Hadst not thou been by,
A fellow by the hand of nature mark'd,
Quoted, and sign'd, to do a deed of shame,
This murder had not come into my mind:
But, taking note of thy abhorr'd aspèct,
Finding thee fit for bloody villany,
Apt, liable to be employ'd in danger,
I faintly broke with thee of Arthur's death;
And thou, to be endeared to a king,
Made it no conscience to destroy a prince.

Hub. My lord,—

K. John. Hadst thou but shook thy head, or
made a pause,
When I spake darkly what I purpos'd,

Or turn'd an eye of doubt upon my face,
As bid me tell my tale in express words,
Deep shame had struck me dumb, made me
    break off,
And those thy fears might have wrought fears
    in me:
But thou didst understand me by my signs,
And didst in signs again parley with sin;
Yea, without stop, didst let thy heart consent,
And consequently thy rude hand to act
The deed, which both our tongues held vile to
    name.—
Out of my sight, and never see me more!
My nobles leave me; and my state is brav'd,
Even at my gates, with ranks of foreign powers:
Nay, in the body of this fleshly land,
This kingdom, this confine of blood and breath,
Hostility and civil tumult reigns
Between my conscience and my cousin's death.

  Hub. Arm you against your other enemies,
I'll make a peace between your soul and you.
Young Arthur is alive: this hand of mine
Is yet a maiden and an innocent hand,
Not painted with the crimson spots of blood.
Within this bosom never enter'd yet
The dreadful motion of a murderous thought;
And you have slander'd nature in my form,—
Which, howsoever rude exteriorly,
Is yet the cover of a fairer mind
Than to be butcher of an innocent child.

  K. John. Doth Arthur live? O, haste thee
    to the peers,
Throw this report on their incensed rage,
And make them tame to their obedience!
Forgive the comment that my passion made
Upon thy feature; for my rage was blind,
And foul imaginary eyes of blood
Presented thee more hideous than thou art.
O, answer not; but to my closet bring
The angry lords with all expedient haste:
I cónjure thee but slowly; run more fast.
                 [Exeunt.

SCENE III.—*The same. Before the Castle.*
Enter ARTHUR, *on the Walls.*

  Arth. The wall is high, and yet will I leap
    down:—
Good ground, be pitiful, and hurt me not!—
There's few or none do know me: if they did,
This ship-boy's semblance hath disguis'd me
    quite.
I am afraid; and yet I'll venture it.
If I get down, and do not break my limbs,
I'll find a thousand shifts to get away:
As good to die and go, as die and stay.
               [Leaps down.
O me! my uncle's spirit is in these stones:—
Heaven take my soul, and England keep my
    bones!   *[Dies.*

Enter PEMBROKE, SALISBURY, *and* BIGOT.
  Sal. Lords, I will meet him at Saint Ed-
    mund's-Bury:
It is our safety, and we must embrace
This gentle offer of the perilous time.

  Pem. Who brought that letter from the
    cardinal?   [France;
  Sal. The Count Melun, a noble lord of
Whose private with me of the Dauphin's love
Is much more general than these lines import.
  Big. To-morrow morning let us meet him,
    then.
  Sal. Or rather than set forward; for 'twill be
Two long days' journey, lords, or e'er we meet.

Enter the BASTARD.

  Bast. Once more to-day well met, distem-
    per'd lords!
The king by me requests your presence straight.
  Sal. The king hath dispossess'd himself of us:
We will not line his thin bestained cloak
With our pure honours, nor attend the foot
That leaves the print of blood where'er it walks.
Return and tell him so: we know the worst.
  Bast. Whate'er you think, good words, I
    think, were best.   [now.
  Sal. Our griefs, and not our manners, reason
  Bast. But there is little reason in your grief;
Therefore 'twere reason you had manners now.
  Pem. Sir, sir, impatience hath his privilege.
  Bast. 'Tis true,—to hurt his master, no man
    else.
  Sal. This is the prison:—what is he lies here?
                [Seeing ARTHUR.
  Pem. O death, made proud with pure and
    princely beauty!
The earth had not a hole to hide this deed.
  Sal. Murder, as hating what himself hath
    done,
Doth lay it open to urge on revenge.   [grave,
  Big. Or, when he doom'd this beauty to a
Found it too precious-princely for a grave.
  Sal. Sir Richard, what think you? Have you
    beheld,
Or have you read or heard? or could you think?
Or do you almost think, although you see,
That you do see? could thought, without this
    object,
Form such another? This is the very top,
The height, the crest, or crest unto the crest
Of murder's arms: this is the bloodiest shame,
The wildest savagery, the vilest stroke,
That ever wall-ey'd wrath or staring rage
Presented to the tears of soft remorse.   [this.
  Pem. All murders past do stand excus'd in
And this, so sole and so unmatchable,
Shall give a holiness, a purity,
To the yet unbegotten sin of times;
And prove a deadly bloodshed but a jest,
Exampled by this heinous spectacle.
  Bast. It is a damned and a bloody work;
The graceless action of a heavy hand,—
If that it be the work of any hand.
  Sal. If that it be the work of any hand?—
We had a kind of light what would ensue:
It is the shameful work of Hubert's hand;
The practice and the purpose of the king:—
From whose obedience I forbid my soul,
Kneeling before this ruin of sweet life,

And breathing to his breathless excellence
The incense of a vow, a holy vow,
Never to taste the pleasures of the world,
Never to be infected with delight,
Nor conversant with ease and idleness,
Till I have set a glory to this hand,
By giving it the worship of revenge.   [words.
  Pem. Big. Our souls religiously confirm thy

Enter HUBERT.

  Hub. Lords, I am hot with haste in seeking you:
Arthur doth live; the king hath sent for you.
  Sal. O, he is bold, and blushes not at death:—
Avaunt, thou hateful villain, get thee gone!
  Hub. I am no villain.
  Sal.   Must I rob the law?
                   [*Drawing his sword.*
  Bast. Your sword is bright, sir; put it up again.   [skin.
  Sal. Not till I sheathe it in a murderer's
  Hub. Stand back, Lord Salisbury,—stand back, I say;   [yours:
By heaven, I think my sword's as sharp as
I would not have you, lord, forget yourself,
Nor tempt the danger of my true defence;
Lest I, by marking of your rage, forget
Your worth, your greatness, and nobility.
  Big. Out, dunghill! dar'st thou brave a nobleman?
  Hub. Not for my life: but yet I dare defend
My innocent life against an emperor.
  Sal. Thou art a murderer.
  Hub.   Do not prove me so;
Yet I am none: whose tongue soe'er speaks false,
Not truly speaks; who speaks not truly, lies.
  Pem. Cut him to pieces.
  Bast.   Keep the peace, I say.
  Sal. Stand by, or I shall gall you, Falcon-bridge.   [bury:
  Bast. Thou wert better gall the devil, Salis-
If thou but frown on me, or stir thy foot,
Or teach thy hasty spleen to do me shame,
I'll strike thee dead. Put up thy sword betime;
Or I'll so maul you and your toasting-iron
That you shall think the devil is come from hell.
  Big. What wilt thou do, renowned Falcon-bridge?
Second a villain and a murderer?
  Hub. Lord Bigot, I am none.
  Big.   Who kill'd this prince?
  Hub. 'Tis not an hour since I left him well:
I honour'd him, I lov'd him; and will weep
My date of life out for his sweet life's loss.
  Sal. Trust not those cunning waters of his eyes,
For villany is not without such rheum;
And he, long traded in it, makes it seem
Like rivers of remorse and innocency.
Away with me, all you whose souls abhor
The uncleanly savours of a slaughter-house;
For I am stifled with this smell of sin.

  Big. Away toward Bury, to the Dauphin there!   [out.
  Pem. There, tell the king, he may inquire us
                 [*Exeunt* Lords.
  Bast. Here's a good world!—Knew you of this fair work?
Beyond the infinite and boundless reach
Of mercy, if thou didst this deed of death,
Art thou damn'd, Hubert.
  Hub.   Do but hear me, sir.
  Bast. Ha! I'll tell thee what;   [black;
Thou'rt damn'd as black—nay, nothing is so
Thou art more deep damn'd than Prince Lucifer:
There is not yet so ugly a fiend of hell
As thou shalt be, if thou didst kill this child.
  Hub. Upon my soul,—
  Bast.   If thou didst but consent
To this most cruel act, do but despair;
And if thou want'st a cord, the smallest thread
That ever spider twisted from her womb
Will serve to strangle thee; a rush will be
A beam to hang thee on; or wouldst thou drown thyself,
Put but a little water in a spoon,
And it shall be as all the ocean,
Enough to stifle such a villain up.
I do suspect thee very grievously.
  Hub. If I in act, consent, or sin of thought
Be guilty of the stealing that sweet breath
Which was embounded in this beauteous clay,
Let hell want pains enough to torture me!
I left him well.
  Bast.   Go, bear him in thine arms.—
I am amaz'd, methinks, and lose my way
Among the thorns and dangers of this world.—
How easy dost thou take all England up!
From forth this morsel of dead royalty,
The life, the right, and truth of all this realm
Is fled to heaven; and England now is left
To tug and scamble, and to part by the teeth
The unow'd interest of proud-swelling state.
Now for the bare-pick'd bone of majesty
Doth dogged war bristle his angry crest,
And snarleth in the gentle eyes of peace:
Now powers from home and discontents at home
Meet in one line; and vast confusion waits,
As doth a raven on a sick-fallen beast,
The imminent decay of wrested pomp.
Now happy he whose cloak and cincture can
Hold out this tempest.—Bear away that child,
And follow me with speed: I'll to the king:
A thousand businesses are brief in hand,
And heaven itself doth frown upon the land.
                   [*Exeunt.*

ACT V.

SCENE I.—NORTHAMPTON. *A Room in the Palace.*

Enter KING JOHN, PANDULPH *with the crown, and* Attendants.

  K. John. Thus have I yielded up into your hand
The circle of my glory.

Pand.   Take again
            [*Giving* KING JOHN *the crown.*
From this my hand, as holding of the pope,
Your sovereign greatness and authority.
    K. John. Now keep your holy word: go
        meet the French;
And from his holiness use all your power
To stop their marches 'fore we are inflam'd.
Our discontented counties do revolt;
Our people quarrel with obedience;
Swearing allegiance and the love of soul
To stranger blood, to foreign royalty.
This inundation of mistemper'd humour
Rests by you only to be qualified.
Then pause not; for the present time's so sick
That present medicine must be minister'd,
Or overthrow incurable ensues.
    Pand. It was my breath that blew this tem-
        pest up,
Upon your stubborn usage of the pope:
But since you are a gentle convertite,
My tongue shall hush again this storm of war,
And make fair weather in your blustering land.
On this Ascension-day, remember well,
Upon your oath of service to the pope,
Go I to make the French lay down their arms.
                                        [*Exit.*
    K. John. Is this Ascension-day? Did not the
        prophet
Say that before Ascension-day at noon
My crown I should give off? Even so I have:
I did suppose it should be on constraint;
But, heaven be thank'd, it is but voluntary.

Enter the BASTARD.

    Bast. All Kent hath yielded; nothing there
        holds out
But Dover Castle: London hath receiv'd,
Like a kind host, the Dauphin and his powers:
Your nobles will not hear you, but are gone
To offer service to your enemy;
And wild amazement hurries up and down
The little number of your doubtful friends.
    K. John. Would not my lords return to me
        again,
After they heard young Arthur was alive?
    Bast. They found him dead, and cast into
        the streets;
An empty casket, where the jewel of life
By some damn'd hand was robb'd and ta'en
        away.
    K. John. That villain Hubert told me he did
        live.
    Bast. So, on my soul, he did, for aught he
        knew.
But wherefore do you droop? why look you sad?
Be great in act, as you have been in thought;
Let not the world see fear and sad distrust
Govern the motion of a kingly eye:
Be stirring as the time; be fire with fire;
Threaten the threatener, and outface the brow
Of bragging horror: so shall inferior eyes,
That borrow their behaviours from the great,
Grow great by your example, and put on

The dauntless spirit of resolution.
Away, and glister like the god of war
When he intendeth to become the field:
Show boldness and aspiring confidence.
What, shall they seek the lion in his den,
And fright him there? and make him tremble
        there?
O, let it not be said!—Forage, and run
To meet displeasure further from the doors,
And grapple with him ere he come so nigh.
    K. John. The legate of the pope hath been
        with me,
And I have made a happy peace with him;
And he hath promis'd to dismiss the powers
Led by the Dauphin.
    Bast.   O inglorious league!
Shall we, upon the footing of our land,
Send fair-play orders, and make compromise,
Insinuation, parley, and base truce,
To arms invasive? shall a beardless boy,
A cocker'd silken wanton, brave our fields,
And flesh his spirit in a warlike soil,
Mocking the air with colours idly spread,
And find no check? Let us, my liege, to arms:
Perchance the cardinal cannot make your
        peace;
Of, if he do, let it at least be said,
They saw we had a purpose of defence.
    K. John. Have thou the ordering of this
        present time.   [I know,
    Bast. Away, then, with good courage! yet,
Our party may well meet a prouder foe.
                                    [*Exeunt.*

SCENE II.—*Near* ST. EDMUND'S-BURY. *The French Camp.*

Enter, in arms, LOUIS, SALISBURY, MELUN,
    PEMBROKE, BIGOT, *and* Soldiers.

    Lou. My Lord Melun, let this be copied out,
And keep it safe for our remembrance:
Return the precedent to these lords again;
That, having our fair order written down,
Both they and we, perusing o'er these notes,
May know wherefore we took the sacrament,
And keep our faiths firm and inviolable.
    Sal. Upon our sides it never shall be broken.
And, noble Dauphin, albeit we swear
A voluntary zeal and unurg'd faith
To your proceedings; yet, believe me, prince,
I am not glad that such a sore of time
Should seek a plaster by contemn'd revolt,
And heal the inveterate canker of one wound
By making many. O, it grieves my soul
That I must draw this metal from my side
To be a widow-maker! O, and there
Where honourable rescue and defence
Cries out upon the name of Salisbury!
But such is the infection of the time,
That, for the health and physic of our right,
We cannot deal but with the very hand
Of stern injustice and confused wrong.—
And is 't not pity, O my grieved friends!
That we, the sons and children of this isle,
Were born to see so sad an hour as this;

Wherein we step after a stranger-march
Upon her gentle bosom, and fill up
Her enemies' ranks—I must withdraw and weep
Upon the spot of this enforc'd cause—
To grace the gentry of a land remote,
And follow unacquainted colours here?
What, here?—O nation, that thou couldst re-
 move!
That Neptune's arms, who clippeth thee about,
Would bear thee from the knowledge of thyself,
And grapple thee unto a pagan shore, [bine
Where these two Christian armies might com-
The blood of malice in a vein of league,
And not to spend it so unneighbourly!
 Lou. A noble temper dost thou show in this;
And great affections wrestling in thy bosom
Do make an earthquake of nobility.
O, what a noble combat hast thou fought
Between compulsion and a brave respect!
Let me wipe off this honourable dew
That silverly doth progress on thy cheeks:
My heart hath melted at a lady's tears,
Being an ordinary inundation;
But this effusion of such manly drops,
This shower, blown up by tempest of the soul,
Startles mine eyes, and makes me more amaz'd
Than had I seen the vaulty top of heaven
Figur'd quite o'er with burning meteors.
Lift up thy brow, renowned Salisbury,
And with a great heart heave away this storm:
Commend these waters to those baby eyes
That never saw the giant world enrag'd,
Nor met with fortune other than at feasts,
Full warm of blood, of mirth, of gossiping.
Come, come; for thou shalt thrust thy hand as
  deep
Into the purse of rich prosperity
As Louis himself:—so, nobles, shall you all,
That knit your sinews to the strength of mine.—
And even there, methinks, an angel spake:
Look, where the holy legate comes apace,
To give us warrant from the hand of heaven,
And on our actions set the name of right
With holy breath.

Enter PANDULPH, *attended.*

 Pand.   Hail, noble prince of France!
The next is this,—King John hath reconcil'd
Himself to Rome; his spirit is come in,
That so stood out against the holy church,
The great metropolis and see of Rome:
Therefore thy threatening colours now wind up,
And tame the savage spirit of wild war,
That, like a lion foster'd up at hand,
It may lie gently at the foot of peace,
And be no further harmful than in show.
 Lou. Your grace shall pardon me, I will not
  back:
I am too high-born to be propertied,
To be a secondary at control,
Or useful serving-man and instrument
To any sovereign state throughout the world.
Your breath first kindled the dead coal of wars
Between this chastis'd kingdom and myself,

And brought in matter that should feed this
 fire;
And now 'tis far too huge to be blow out
With that same weak wind which enkindled it.
You taught me how to know the face of right,
Acquainted me with interest to this land,
Yea, thrust this enterprise into my heart;
And come ye now to tell me John hath made
His peace with Rome? What is that peace to
 me?
I, by the honour of my marriage-bed,
After young Arthur, claim this land for mine;
And, now it is half-conquer'd, must I back
Because that John hath made his peace with
  Rome?   [borne,
Am I Rome's slave? What penny hath Rome
What men provided, what munition sent,
To underprop this action? Is't not I
That undergo this charge? who else but I,
And such as to my claim are liable,
Sweat in this business and maintain this war.
Have I not heard these islanders shout out,
Vive le roi! as I have bank'd their towns?
Have I not here the best cards for the game,
To win this easy match play'd for a crown?
And shall I now give o'er the yielded set?
No, no, on my soul, it never shall be said.
 Pand. You look but on the outside of this
  work.
 Lou. Outside or inside, I will not return
Till my attempt so much be glorified
As to my ample hope was promised
Before I drew this gallant head of war,
And cull'd these fiery spirits from the world,
To outlook conquest, and to win renown
Even in the jaws of danger and of death.—
        [*Trumpet sounds.*
What lusty trumpet thus doth summon us?

Enter the BASTARD, *attended.*

 Bast. According to the fair play of the world,
Let me have audience; I am sent to speak:—
My holy lord of Milan, from the king
I come, to learn how you have dealt for him;
And, as you answer, I do know the scope
And warrant limited unto my tongue.
 Pand. The Dauphin is too wilful-opposite,
And will not temporize with my entreaties;
He flatly says he'll not lay down his arms.
 Bast. By all the blood that ever fury breath'd,
The youth says well.—Now hear our English
 king;
For thus his royalty doth speak in me.
He is prepar'd; and reason too he should:
This apish and unmannerly approach,
This harness'd masque and unadvised revel,
This unhair'd sauciness and boyish troops,
The king doth smile at; and is well prepar'd
To whip this dwarfish war, these pigmy arms,
From out the circle of his territories. [door,
That hand which had the strength, even at your
To cudgel you, and make you take the hatch;
To dive, like buckets, in concealed wells;
To crouch in litter of your stable planks;

To lie, like pawns, lock'd up in chests and
    trunks;
To hug with swine; to seek sweet safety out
In vaults and prisons; and to thrill and shake
Even at the crying of your nation's crow,
Thinking his voice an armed Englishman;—
Shall that victorious hand be feebled here,
That in your chambers gave you chastisement?
No: know the gallant monarch is in arms;
And like an eagle o'er his aery towers,
To souse annoyance that comes near his nest.—
And you degenerate, you ingrate revolts,
You bloody Neroes, ripping up the womb
Of your dear mother England, blush for shame;
For your own ladies and pale-visag'd maids,
Like Amazons, come tripping after drums,—
Their thimbles into armed gauntlets chang'd,
Their needles to lances, and their gentle hearts
To fierce and bloody inclination.   [in peace;
    Lou. There end thy brave, and turn thy face
We grant thou canst outscold us; fare thee well;
We hold our time too precious to be spent
With such a brabbler.
    Pand.   Give me leave to speak.
    Bast. No, I will speak.
    Lou.   We will attend to neither.—
Strike up the drums; and let the tongue of war
Plead for our interest and our being here.
    Bast. Indeed, your drums, being beaten, will
    cry out;
And so shall you, being beaten: do but start
An echo with the clamour of thy drum,
And even at hand a drum is ready brac'd
That shall reverberate all as loud as thine;
Sound but another, and another shall,
As loud as thine, rattle the welkin's ear,
And mock the deep-mouth'd thunder: for at
    hand,—
Not trusting to this halting legate here,
Whom he hath us'd rather for sport than need,—
Is warlike John; and in his forehead sits
A bare-ribb'd death, whose office is this day
To feast upon whole thousands of the French.
    Lou. Strike up our drums, to find this danger
    out.
    Bast. And thou shalt find it, Dauphin, do
    not doubt.   [*Exeunt.*

SCENE III.—*The same. A Field of Battle.*

Alarums. Enter KING JOHN *and* HUBERT.

    K. John. How goes the day with us? O,
    tell me, Hubert.
    Hub. Badly, I fear. How fares your majesty?
    K. John. This fever, that hath troubled me
    so long,
Lies heavy on me;—O, my heart is sick!

Enter a MESSENGER.

    Mess. My lord, your valiant kinsman, Fal-
    conbridge,
Desires your majesty to leave the field,
And send him word by me which way you go.
    K. John. Tell him, toward Swinstead, to the
    abbey there.

    Mess. Be of good comfort; for the great
    supply
That was expected by the Dauphin here
Are wreck'd three nights ago on Goodwin
    Sands.   [now:
This news was brought to Richard but even
The French fight colding, and retire themselves.
    K. John. Ay me! this tyrant fever burns me
    up,
And will not let me welcome this good news.—
Set on toward Swinstead: to my litter straight;
Weakness possesseth me, and I am faint.
                                        [*Exeunt.*

SCENE IV.—*The same. Another part of the same.*

Enter SALISBURY, PEMBROKE, *and others.*

    Sal. I did not think the king so stor'd with
    friends.
    Pem. Up once again; put spirit in the French:
If they miscarry we miscarry too.
    Sal. That misbegotten devil, Falconbridge,
In spite of spite, alone upholds the day.
    Pem. They say King John, sore sick, hath
    left the field.

Enter MELUN *wounded, and led by* Soldiers.

    Mel. Lead me to the revolts of England here.
    Sal. When we were happy we had other
    names.
    Pem. It is the Count Melun.
    Sal.   Wounded to death.
    Mel. Fly, noble English, you are bought and
    sold;
Unthread the rude eye of rebellion,
And welcome home again discarded faith.
Seek out King John, and fall before his feet;
For if the French be lords of this loud day,
He means to recompense the pains you take
By cutting off your heads: thus hath he sworn,
And I with him, and many more with me,
Upon the altar at Saint Edmund's-Bury;
Even on that altar where we swore to you
Dear amity and everlasting love.
    Sal. May this be possible? may this be true?
    Mel. Have I not hideous death within my
    view,
Retaining but a quantity of life,
Which bleeds away even as a form of wax
Resolveth from his figure 'gainst the fire?
What in the world should make me now deceive,
Since I must lose the use of all deceit?
Why should I then be false, since it is true
That I must die here, and live hence by truth?
I say again, if Louis do win the day,
He is forsworn if e'er those eyes of yours
Behold another day break in the east:
But even this night,—whose black contagious
    breath
Already smokes about the burning crest
Of the old, feeble, and day-wearied sun,—
Even this ill night, your breathing shall expire;
Paying the fine of rated treachery
Even with a treacherous fine of all your lives,
If Louis by your assistance win the day.

Commend me to one Hubert, with your king;
The love of him,—and this respect besides,
For that my grandsire was an Englishman,—
Awakes my conscience to confess all this.
In lieu whereof, I pray you, bear me hence
From forth the noise and rumour of the field,
Where I may think the remnant of my thoughts
In peace, and part this body and my soul
With contemplation and devout desires. [soul
  Sal. We do believe thee:—and beshrew my
But I do love the favour and the form
Of this most fair occasion, by the which
We will entread the steps of damned flight;
And, like a bated and retired flood,
Leaving our rankness and irregular course,
Stoop low within those bounds we have o'er-
      look'd,
And calmly run on in obedience,
Even to our ocean, to our great King John.—
My arm shall give thee help to bear thee hence;
For I do see the cruel pangs of death   [flight,
Right in thine eye.—Away, my friends! New
And happy newness, that intends old right.
                    [*Exeunt, leading off* MELUN.

SCENE V.—*The same. The French Camp.*

Enter LOUIS *and his train.*

  Lou. The sun of heaven methought was loth
      to set,
But stay'd, and made the western welkin blush,
When the English measur'd backward their
      own ground
In faint retire. O, bravely came we off,
When with a volley of our needless shot,
After such bloody toil, we bid good-night;
And wound our tattering colours clearly up,
Last in the field, and almost lords of it!

Enter a Messenger.

  Mess. Where is my prince, the Dauphin?
  Lou.   Here:—what news?
  Mess. The Count Melun is slain; the English
      lords,
By his persuasion are again fallen off;
And your supply, which you have wish'd so long,
Are cast away and sunk on Goodwin Sands.
  Lou. Ah, foul shrewd news!—beshrew thy
      very heart!—
I did not think to be so sad to-night
As this hath made me.—Who was he that said
King John did fly an hour or two before
The stumbling night did part our weary powers?
  Mess. Whoever spoke it, it is true, my lord.
  Lou. Well; keep good quarter and good care
      to-night;
The day shall not be up so soon as I,
To try the fair adventure of to-morrow.
                    [*Exeunt.*

SCENE VI.—*An open Place in the neighbour-hood of Swinstead Abbey.*

Enter the BASTARD *and* HUBERT, *meeting.*

  Hub. Who's there? speak, ho! speak quickly,
      or I shoot.

  Bast. A friend.—What art thou?
  Hub.   Of the part of England.
  Bast. Whither dost thou go?
  Hub. What's that to thee? Why may I not
      demand
Of thine affairs, as well as thou of mine?
  Bast. Hubert, I think.
  Hub.   Thou hast a perfect thought:
I will, upon all hazards, well believe   [well.
Thou art my friend, that know'st my tongue so
Who art thou?
  Bast.   Who thou wilt: an if thou please,
Thou mayst befriend me so much as to think
I come one way of the Plantagenets.
  Hub. Unkind remembrance! thou and eye-
      less night   [me,
Have done me shame:—brave soldier, pardon
That any accent breaking from thy tongue
Should 'scape the true acquaintance of mine ear.
  Bast. Come, come; sans compliment, what
      news abroad?   [night,
  Hub. Why, here walk I, in the black brow of
To find you out.
  Bast.   Brief, then; and what's the news?
  Hub. O, my sweet sir, news fitting to the
      night,
Black, fearful, comfortless, and horrible.
  Bast. Show me the very wound of this ill
      news;
I am no woman, I'll not swoon at it.
  Hub. The king, I fear, is poison'd by a monk:
I left him almost speechless and broke out
To acquaint you with this evil, that you might
The better arm you to the sudden time,
Than if you had at leisure known of this.
  Bast. How did he take it; who did taste to
      him?
  Hub. A monk, I tell you; a resolved villain,
Whose bowels suddenly burst out: the king
Yet speaks, and peradventure may recover.
  Bast. Who didst thou leave to tend his
      majesty?   [come back,
  Hub. Why, know you not? the lords are all
And brought Prince Henry in their company;
At whose request the king hath pardon'd them,
And they are all about his majesty.   [heaven,
  Bast. Withhold thine indignation, mighty
And tempt us not to bear above our power!—
I'll tell thee, Hubert, half my power this night,
Passing these flats, are taken by the tide,—
These Lincoln washes have devoured them;
Myself, well-mounted, hardly have escap'd.
Away, before! conduct me to the king;
I doubt he will be dead or ere I come. [*Exeunt.*

SCENE VII.—*The Orchard of Swinstead Abbey.*

Enter PRINCE HENRY, SALISBURY, *and* BIGOT.

  P. Hen. It is too late: the life of all his blood
Is touch'd corruptibly; and his pure brain,—
Which some suppose the soul's frail dwelling-
      house,—
Doth, by the idle comments that it makes,
Foretell the ending of mortality.

Enter PEMBROKE.

Pem. His highness yet doth speak; and holds
  belief
That, being brought into the open air,
It would allay the burning quality
Of that fell poison which assaileth him.
  P. Hen. Let him be brought into the orchard
  here.—
Doth he still rage?   [*Exit* BIGOT.
  Pem.   He is more patient
Than when you left him; even now he sung.
  P. Hen. O vanity of sickness! fierce extremes
In their continuance will not feel themselves.
Death, having prey'd upon the outward parts,
Leaves them invisible; and his siege is now
Against the mind, the which he pricks and
  wounds
With many legions of strange fantasies,
Which, in their throng and press to that last
  hold,   [should sing.—
Confound themselves. 'Tis strange that death
I am the cygnet to this pale faint swan,
Who chants a doleful hymn to his own death;
And from the organ-pipe of frailty sings
His soul and body to their lasting rest. [born
  Sal. Be of good comfort, prince; for you are
To set a form upon that indigest
Which he hath left so shapeless and so rude.

Re-enter BIGOT *and* Attendants, *who bring in*
KING JOHN *in a chair.*

  K. John. Ay, marry, now my soul hath
  elbow-room;
It would not out at windows nor at doors.
There is so hot a summer in my bosom
That all my bowels crumble up to dust;
I am a scribbled form, drawn with a pen
Upon a parchment; and against this fire
Do I shrink up.
  P. Hen.   How fares your majesty?
  K. John. Poison'd,—ill fare;—dead, forsook,
  cast off:
And none of you will bid the winter come,
To thrust his icy fingers in my maw;
Nor let my kingdom's rivers take their course
Through my burn'd bosom; nor entreat the
  north
To make his bleak winds kiss my parched lips,
And comfort me with cold:—I do not ask you
  much;
I beg cold comfort; and you are so strait,
And so ingrateful, you deny me that.
  P. Hen. O, that there were some virtue in
  my tears,
That might relieve you!
  K. John.   The salt in them is hot.—
Within me is a hell; and there the poison
Is, as a fiend, confin'd to tyrannize
On unreprievable condemned blood.

Enter the BASTARD.

  Bast. O, I am scalded with my violent motion,

And spleen of speed to see your majesty!
  K. John. O cousin, thou art come to set
  mine eye:
The tackle of my heart is crack'd and burn'd;
And all the shrouds, wherewith my life should
  sail,
Are turned to one thread, one little hair:
My heart hath one poor string to stay it by,
Which holds but till thy news be uttered;
And then all this thou seest is but a clod,
And model of confounded royalty.
  Bast. The Dauphin is preparing hitherward,
Where heaven he knows how we shall answer
  him;
For in a night the best part of my power,
As I upon advantage did remove,
Were in the washes all unwarily
Devoured by the unexpected flood.
                       [*The* KING *dies.*
  Sal. You breathe these dead news in as dead
  an ear.   [thus.
My liege! my lord!—But now a king,—now
  P. Hen. Even so must I run on, and even so
  stop,
What surety of the world, what hope, what
  stay,
When this was now a king, and now is clay!
  Bast. Art thou gone so? I do but stay behind
To do the office for thee of revenge,
And then my soul shall wait on thee to heaven,
As it on earth hath been thy servant still.—
Now, now, you stars that move in your right
  spheres,   [faiths;
Where be your powers? Show now your mended
And instantly return with me again,
To push destruction and perpetual shame
Out of the weak door of our fainting land.
Straight let us seek, or straight we shall be
  sought;
The Dauphin rages at our very heels.
  Sal. It seems you know not, then, so much
  as we:
The Cardinal Pandulph is within at rest,
Who half an hour since came from the Dauphin,
And brings from him such offers of our peace
As we with honour and respect may take,
With purpose presently to leave this war.
  Bast. He will the rather do it when he sees
Ourselves well sinewed to our defence.
  Sal. Nay, it is in a manner done already;
For many carriages he hath despatch'd
To the sea-side, and put his cause and quarrel
To the disposing of the cardinal:
With whom yourself, myself, and other lords,
If you think meet, this afternoon will post
To cónsummate this business happily.
  Bast. Let it be so:—And you, my noble
  prince,
With other princes that may best be spar'd,
Shall wait upon your father's funeral.
  P. Hen. At Worcester must his body be in-
  terr'd;
For so he will'd it.
  Bast.   Thither shall it, then:

And happily may your sweet self put on
The lineal state and glory of the land!
To whom, with all submission, on my knee,
I do bequeath my faithful services
And true subjection everlastingly.

　Sal. And the like tender of our love we make,
To rest without a spot for evermore.

　　P. Hen. I have a kind soul that would give
　　　you thanks,
And knows not how to do it but with tears.

　Bast. O, let us pay the time but needful woe,
Since it hath been beforehand with our griefs.—
This England never did, nor never shall,
Lie at the proud foot of a conqueror,
But when it first did help to wound itself.
Now these her princes are come home again,
Come the three corners of the world in arms,
And we shall shock them: nought shall make
　　us rue,
If England to itself do rest but true. [*Exeunt.*

THE LIFE AND DEATH OF KING RICHARD II.

DRAMATIS PERSONÆ

KING RICHARD THE SECOND.
EDMUND OF LANGLEY, *Duke of York,*
JOHN OF GAUNT, *Duke of Lancaster,*   *Uncles to the King.*
HENRY, *surnamed* BOLINGBROKE, *Duke of Hereford, Son to* JOHN OF GAUNT, *afterwards* KING HENRY IV.
DUKE OF AUMERLE, *Son to the Duke of York.*
THOMAS MOWBRAY, *Duke of Norfolk.*
DUKE OF SURREY.
EARL OF SALISBURY.
EARL BERKLEY.
BUSHY,
BAGOT,   *Creatures tc* KING RICHARD.
GREEN,
EARL OF NORTHUMBERLAND.
HENRY PERCY, *his Son.*

LORD ROSS.
LORD WILLOUGHBY.
LORD FITZWATER.
BISHOP OF CARLISLE.
ABBOT OF WESTMINSTER.
Lord Marshal.
SIR PIERCE OF EXTON.
SIR STEPHEN SCROOP.
Captain *of a Band of Welshmen.*

QUEEN *to* KING RICHARD.
DUCHESS OF GLOSTER.
DUCHESS OF YORK.
Lady *attending on the* QUEEN.

Lords, Heralds, Officers, Soldiers, Two Gardeners, Keeper, Messenger, Groom, *and other* Attendants.

SCENE,—*Dispersedly in* ENGLAND *and* WALES.

ACT I.

SCENE I.—LONDON. *A Room in the Palace.*

Enter KING RICHARD, *attended;* JOHN OF GAUNT, *and other* Nobles.

K. Rich. Old John of Gaunt, time-honour'd Lancaster,
Hast thou, according to thy oath and band,
Brought hither Henry Hereford, thy bold son,
Here to make good the boisterous late appeal,
Which then our leisure would not let us hear,
Against the Duke of Norfolk, Thomas Mowbray?
   Gaunt. I have, my liege.   [sounded him,
   K. Rich. Tell me, moreover, hast thou
If he appeal the duke on ancient malice;
Or worthily, as a good subject should,
On some known ground of treachery in him?
   Gaunt. As near as I could sift him on that argument,—
On some apparent danger seen in him,
Aim'd at your highness,—no inveterate malice.
   K. Rich. Then call them to our presence:
    face to face.
And frowning brow to brow, ourselves will hear
The accuser and the accused freely speak:—
                [*Exeunt some* Attendants.
High-stomach'd are they both, and full of ire,
In rage deaf as the sea, hasty as fire.

Re-enter Attendants, *with* BOLINGBROKE *and* NORFOLK.

   Boling. Many years of happy days befall

My gracious sovereign, my most loving liege!
   Nor. Each day still better other's happiness;
Until the heavens, envying earth's good hap,
Add an immortal title to your crown!
   K. Rich. We thank you both: yet one but flatters us,
As well appeareth by the cause you come;
Namely, to appeal each other of high treason.—
Cousin of Hereford, what dost thou object
Against the Duke of Norfolk, Thomas Mowbray?   [speech!—
   Boling. First,—heaven be the record to my
In the devotion of a subject's love,
Tendering the precious safety of my prince,
And free from other misbegotten hate,
Come I appellant to this princely presence.—
Now, Thomas Mowbray, do I turn to thee;
And mark my greeting well; for what I speak,
My body shall make good upon this earth
Or my divine soul answer it in heaven.
Thou are a traitor and a miscreant;
Too good to be so, and too bad to live;
Since the more fair and crystal is the sky,
The uglier seem the clouds that in it fly.
Once more, the more to aggravate the note,
With a foul traitor's name stuff I thy throat;
And wish,—so please my sovereign,—ere I move,   [may prove.
What my tongue speaks, my right-drawn sword
   Nor. Let not my cold words here accuse my zeal:
'Tis not the trial of a woman's war,
The bitter clamour of two eager tongues,

[*395*]

Can arbitrate this cause betwixt us twain:
The blood is hot that must be cool'd for this:
Yet can I not of such tame patience boast
As to be hush'd, and naught at all to say: [me
First, the fair reverence of your highness curbs
From giving reins and spurs to my free speech;
Which else would post until it had return'd
These terms of treason doubled down his throat.
Setting aside his high blood's royalty,
And let him be no kinsman to my liege
I do defy him, and I spit at him;
Call him a slanderous coward and a villain:
Which to maintain, I would allow him odds;
And meet him, were I tied to run a-foot
Even to the frozen ridges of the Alps,
Or any other ground inhabitable,
Wherever Englishman durst set his foot.
Meantime let this defend my loyalty,—
By all my hopes, most falsely doth he lie.

    Boling. Pale trembling coward, there I
        throw my gage,
Disclaiming here the kindred of the king;
And lay aside my high blood's royalty, [cept.
Which fear, not reverence, makes thee to ex-
If guilty dread hath left thee so much strength
As to take up mine honour's pawn, then stoop:
By that and all the rites of knighthood else,
Will I make good against thee, arm to arm,
What I have spoke, or thou canst worst devise.

    Nor. I take it up; and by that sword I swear,
Which gently laid my knighthood on my
        shoulder,
I'll answer thee in any fair degree,
Or chivalrous design of knightly trial:
And when I mount, alive may I not light,
If I be traitor or unjustly fight!

    K. Rich. What doth our cousin lay to Mow-
        bray's charge?
It must be great, that can inherit us
So much as of a thought of ill in him.

    Boling. Look, what I speak my life shall
        prove it true;—   [nobles,
That Mowbray hath receiv'd eight thousand
In name of lendings for your highness' soldiers,
The which he hath detain'd for lewd employ-
        ments,
Like a false traitor and injurious villain.
Besides, I say, and will in battle prove,—
Or here, or elsewhere to the farthest verge
That ever was survey'd by English eye,—
That all the treasons for these eighteen years
Complotted and contrived in this land
Fetch'd from false Mowbray their first head
        and spring.
Further, I say,—and further will maintain
Upon his bad life to make all this good,—
That he did plot the Duke of Gloster's death;
Suggest his soon-believing adversaries,
And consequently, like a traitor coward,
Sluic'd out his innocent soul through streams
        of blood:
Which blood, like sacrificing Abel's, cries,
Even from the tongueless caverns of the earth,
To me for justice and rough chastisement;

And, by the glorious worth of my descent,
This arm shall do it, or this life be spent!

    K. Rich. How high a pitch his resolution
        soars!—
Thomas of Norfolk, what say'st thou to this?

    Nor. O, let my sovereign turn away his face,
And bid his ears a little while be deaf,
Till I have told this slander of his blood,
How God and good men hate so foul a liar.

    K. Rich. Mowbray, impartial are our eyes
        and ears:
Were he my brother, nay, my kingdom's heir,—
As he is but my father's brother's son,—
Now, by my sceptre's awe, I make a vow,
Such neighbour-nearness to our sacred blood
Should nothing privilege him, nor partialize
The unstooping firmness of my upright soul:
He is our subject, Mowbray, so art thou;
Free speech and fearless I to thee allow.

    Nor. Then, Bolingbroke, as low as to thy
        heart,   [liest!
Through the false passage of thy throat, thou
Three parts of that receipt I had for Calais
Disburs'd I duly to his highness' soldiers;
The other part reserv'd I by consent,
For that my sovereign liege was in my debt
Upon remainder of a dear account,
Since last I went to France to fetch his queen:
Now swallow down that lie!—For Gloster's
        death,—
I slew him not; but, to mine own disgrace,
Neglected my sworn duty in that case.—
For you, my noble Lord of Lancaster,
The honourable father to my foe,
Once did I lay an ambush for your life,
A trespass that doth vex my grieved soul:
But, ere I last receiv'd the sacrament,
I did confess it; and exactly begg'd
Your grace's pardon, and I hope I had it.
This is my fault: as for the rest appeal'd,
It issues from the rancour of a villain,
A recreant and most degenerate traitor:
Which in myself I boldly will defend;
And interchangeably hurl down my gage
Upon this overweening traitor's foot,
To prove myself a loyal gentleman
Even in the best blood chamber'd in his bosom.
In haste whereof, most heartily I pray
Your highness to assign our trial day.

    K. Rich. Wrath-kindled gentlemen, be rul'd
        by me;
Let's purge this choler without letting blood;
This we prescribe, though no physician;
Deep malice makes too deep incision:
Forget, forgive; conclude, and be agreed;
Our doctors say this is no time to bleed.—
Good uncle, let this end where it begun;
We'll calm the Duke of Norfolk, you your son.

    Gaunt. To be a make-peace shall become
        my age:—   [gage.
Throw down, my son, the Duke of Norfolk's

    K. Rich. And, Norfolk, throw down his.

    Gaunt.   When, Harry? when?
Obedience bids I should not bid again.

K. Rich. Norfolk, throw down; we bid; there
    is no boot.
    Nor. Myself I throw, dread sovereign at thy
    foot:
My life thou shalt command, but not my shame:
The one my duty owes; but my fair name,—
Despite of death, that lives upon my grave,—
To dark dishonour's use thou shalt not have.
I am disgrac'd, impeach'd, and baffled here;
Pierc'd to the soul with slander's venom'd
    spear,
The which no balm can cure but his heart-blood
Which breath'd this poison.
    K. Rich. Rage must be withstood:
Give me his gage:—lions make leopards tame.
    Nor. Yea, but not change his spots: take
    but my shame,
And I resign my gage. My dear dear lord,
The purest treasure mortal times afford
Is spotless reputation; that away,
Men are but gilded loam or painted clay.
A jewel in a ten-times-barr'd-up chest
Is a bold spirit in a loyal breast.
Mine honour is my life; both grow in one;
Take honour from me, and my life is done:
Then, dear my liege, mine honour let me try;
In that I live, and for that will I die.
    K. Rich. Cousin, throw down your gage; do
    you begin. [foul sin!
    Boling. O, God defend my soul from such
Shall I seem crest-fallen in my father's sight?
Or with pale beggar-fear impeach my height
Before this outdar'd dastard? Ere my tongue
Shall wound mine honour with such feeble
    wrong,
Or sound so base a parle, my teeth shall tear
The slavish motive of recanting fear;
And spit it bleeding in his high disgrace,
Where shame doth harbour, even in Mow-
    bray's face! [*Exit* GAUNT.
    K. Rich. We were not born to sue, but to
    command:—
Which since we cannot do to make you friends,
Be ready, as your lives shall answer it,
At Coventry, upon Saint Lambert's day:
There shall your swords and lances arbitrate
The swelling difference of your settled hate:
Since we can not atone you, we shall see
Justice design the victor's chivalry.—
Lord marshal, command our officers-at-arms
Be ready to direct these home-alarms. [*Exeunt.*

SCENE II.—*The same. A Room in the* DUKE OF
LANCASTER'S *Palace.*

Enter GAUNT *and* DUCHESS OF GLOSTER.

    Gaunt. Alas, the part I had in Gloster's blood
Doth more solicit me than your exclaims,
To stir against the butchers of his life.
But since correction lieth in those hands
Which made the fault that we cannot correct,
Put we our quarrel to the will of heaven;
Who, when they see the hours ripe on earth,
Will rain hot vengeance on offenders' heads.

    Duch. Finds brotherhood in thee no sharper
    spur?
Hath love in thy old blood no living fire?
Edward's seven sons, whereof thyself art one,
Were as seven vials of his sacred blood,
Or seven fair branches springing from one root:
Some of those seven are dried by nature's
    course,
Some of those branches by the Destinies cut;
But Thomas, my dear lord, my life, my Glos-
    ter,—
One vial full of Edward's sacred blood,
One flourishing branch of his most royal root,
Is crack'd, and all the precious liquor spilt;
Is hack'd down, and his summer-leaves all
    faded,
By envy's hand and murder's bloody axe.
Ah, Gaunt, his blood was thine! that bed, that
    womb,
That mettle, that self-mould, that fashion'd
    thee,
Made him a man; and though thou liv'st and
    breath'st,
Yet art thou slain in him: thou dost consent
In some large measure to thy father's death,
In that thou seest thy wretched brother die,
Who was the model of thy father's life.
Call it not patience, Gaunt,—it is despair:
In suffering thus thy brother to be slaughter'd,
Thou show'st the naked pathway to thy life,
Teaching stern murder how to butcher thee:
That which in mean men we entitle patience,
Is pale cold cowardice in noble breasts.
What shall I say? to safeguard thine own life,
The best way is to venge my Gloster's death.
    Gaunt. God's is the quarrel; for God's sub-
    stitute,
His deputy anointed in his sight,
Hath caus'd his death: the which, if wrongfully,
Let heaven revenge; for I may never lift
An angry arm against his minister.
    Duch. Where, then, alas, may I complain
    myself?
    Gaunt. To God, the widow's champion and
    defence. [Gaunt.
    Duch. Why, then, I will. Farewell, old
Thou go'st to Coventry, there to behold
Our cousin Hereford and fell Mowbray fight:
O, sit my husband's wrongs on Hereford's
    spear,
That it may enter butcher Mowbray's breast!
Or, if misfortune miss the first career,
Be Mowbray's sins so heavy in his bosom
That they may break his foaming courser's
    back,
And throw the rider headlong in the lists,
A caitiff recreant to my cousin Hereford!
Farewell, old Gaunt; thy sometimes brother's
    wife,
With her companion grief must end her life.
    Gaunt. Sister, farewell: I must to Coventry:
As much good stay with thee as go with me!
    Duch. Yet one word more:—grief boundeth
    where it falls,

Not with the empty hollowness, but weight:
I take my leave before I have begun;
For sorrow ends not when it seemeth done.
Commend me to my brother, Edmund York.
Lo, this is all:—nay, yet depart not so;
Though this be all, do not so quickly go;
I shall remember more. Bid him—O, what?—
With all good speed at Plashy visit me.
Alack, and what shall good old York there see,
But empty lodgings and unfurnish'd walls,
Unpeopled offices, untrodden stones?
And what hear there for welcome but my
      groans?
Therefore commend me; let him not come there
To seek out sorrow that dwells everywhere.
Desolate, desolate, will I hence and die:
The least leave of thee takes my weeping eye!
                                    [*Exeunt.*

SCENE III.—*Gosford Green, near Coventry.*

Lists set out, and a throne. Heralds, &c., *attending. Enter the* Lord Marshal, *and* AUMERLE.

Mar. My Lord Aumerle, is Harry Hereford
      arm'd?   [in.
Aum. Yea, at all points; and longs to enter
Mar. The Duke of Norfolk, sprightfully and
      bold,   [pet.
Stays but the summons of the appellant's trum-
Aum. Why, then, the champions are pre-
      par'd, and stay
For nothing but his majesty's approach.

Flourish of trumpets. Enter KING RICHARD,
who takes his seat on his throne; GAUNT *and
several* Noblemen, *who take their places. A
trumpet is sounded, and answered by another
trumpet within. Then enter* NORFOLK *in armour, preceded by a* Herald.

K. Rich. Marshal, demand of yonder cham-
      pion
The cause of his arrival here in arms:
Ask him his name; and orderly proceed
To swear him in the justice of his cause.
Mar. In God's name and the king's, say
      who thou art,
And why thou com'st thus knightly clad in
      arms;
Against what man thou com'st, and what thy
      quarrel:
Speak truly, on thy knighthood and thine oath;
And so defend thee heaven and thy valour!
Nor. My name is Thomas Mowbray, Duke
      of Norfolk;
Who hither come engaged by my oath,—
Which God defend a knight should violate!—
Both to defend my loyalty and truth
To God, my king, and his succeeding issue,
Against the Duke of Hereford that appeals me;
And, by the grace of God and this mine arm,
To prove him in defending of myself,
A traitor to my God, my king, and me:
And as I truly fight, defend me heaven!

Trumpet sounds. Enter BOLINGBROKE *in armour, preceded by a* Herald.

K. Rich. Marshal, ask yonder knight in arms,
Both who he is, and why he cometh hither
Thus plated in habiliments of war;
And formally, according to our law,
Depose him in the justice of his cause.
Mar. What is thy name? and wherefore
      com'st thou hither,
Before King Richard in his royal lists?
Against whom comest thou? and what's thy
      quarrel?
Speak like a true knight, so defend thee heaven!
Boling. Harry of Hereford, Lancaster, and
      Derby,
Am I; who ready here do stand in arms,
To prove, by God's grace and my body's valour,
In lists, on Thomas Mowbray, Duke of Norfolk,
That he's a traitor, foul and dangerous,
To God of Heaven, King Richard, and to me:
And as I truly fight, defend me heaven!
Mar. On pain of death, no person be so bold
Or daring-hardy as to touch the lists,
Except the marshal and such officers
Appointed to direct these fair designs.
Boling. Lord marshal, let me kiss my sove-
      reign's hand,
And bow my knee before his majesty:
For Mowbray and myself are like two men
That vow a long and weary pilgrimage;
Then let us take a ceremonious leave
And loving farewell of our several friends.
Mar. The appellant in all duty greets your
      highness,
And craves to kiss your hand and take his leave.
K. Rich. We will descend and fold him in
      our arms.—
Cousin of Hereford, as thy cause is right,
So be thy fortune in this royal fight!
Farewell, my blood; which if to-day thou shed,
Lament we may, but not revenge thee dead.
Boling. O, let no noble eye profane a tear
For me, if I be gor'd with Mowbray's spear:
As confident as is the falcon's flight
Against a bird, do I with Mowbray fight.—
My loving lord, I take my leave of you;—
Of you, my noble cousin, Lord Aumerle;
Not sick, although I have to do with death,
But lusty, young, and cheerly drawing breath.—
Lo, as at English feasts, so I regreet
The daintiest last, to make the end more sweet:—
O thou, the earthly author of my blood,—
                                    [*To* GAUNT.
Whose youthful spirit, in me regenerate,
Doth with a twofold vigour lift me up
To reach at victory above my head,—
Add proof unto mine armour with thy prayers;
And with thy blessings steel my lance's point,
That it may enter Mowbray's waxen coat,
And furbish new the name of John o' Gaunt,
Even in the lusty 'haviour of his son. [perous!
Gaunt. God in thy good cause make thee pros-
Be swift like lightning in the execution;

And let thy blows, doubly redoubled,
Fall like amazing thunder on the casque
Of thy advérse pernicious enemy:
Rouse up thy youthful blood, be valiant and live.
　　Boling. Mine innocency and Saint George to
　　　　thrive!
　　Nor. However God or fortune cast my lot,
There lives or dies, true to King Richard's throne,
A loyal, just, and upright gentleman:
Never did captive with a freer heart
Cast off his chains of bondage, and embrace
His golden uncontroll'd enfranchisement,
More than my dancing soul doth celebrate
This feast of battle with mine adversary.—
Most mighty liege,—and my companion peers,—
Take from my mouth the wish of happy years:
As gentle and as jocund as to jest
Go I to fight: truth hath a quiet breast.
　　K. Rich. Farewell, my lord: securely I espy
Virtue with valour couched in thine eye.—
Order the trial, marshal, and begin. 　[Derby,
　　Mar. Harry of Hereford, Lancaster, and
Receive thy lance; and God defend the right!
　　Boling. Strong as a tower in hope, I cry amen.
　　Mar. Go bear this lance [*to an* Officer] to
　　　　Thomas, Duke of Norfolk. 　　[Derby,
　　1 *Her.* Harry of Hereford, Lancaster, and
Stands here for God, his sovereign, and himself,
On pain to be found false and recreant,
To prove the Duke of Norfolk, Thomas Mow-
　　　　bray,
A traitor to his God, his king, and him;
And dares him to set forward to the fight.
　　2 *Her.* Here standeth Thomas Mowbray,
　　　　Duke of Norfolk,
On pain to be found false and recreant,
Both to defend himself, and to approve
Henry of Hereford, Lancaster, and Derby,
To God, his sovereign, and to him disloyal;
Courageously, and with a free desire,
Attending but the signal to begin.
　　Mar. Sound, trumpets; and set forward,
　　　　combatants. 　　　[*A charge sounded.*
Stay, the king hath thrown his warder down.
　　K. Rich. Let them lay by their helmets and
　　　　their spears,
And both return back to their chairs again:—
Withdraw with us:—and let the trumpets sound
While we return these dukes what we decree.—
　　　　　　　　　　　[*A long flourish.*
Draw near, 　　　　　　[*To the combatants.*
And list what with our council we have done.
For that our kingdom's earth should not be soil'd
With that dear blood which it hath fostered;
And for our eyes do hate the dire aspéct
Of civil wounds plough'd up with neighbours'
　　　　swords;
And for we think the eagle-winged pride
Of sky-aspiring and ambitious thoughts,
With rival-hating envy, set on you
To wake our peace, which in our country's cradle
Draws the sweet infant breath of gentle sleep;
Which so rous'd up with boisterous untun'd
　　　　drums,

With harsh-resounding trumpets' dreadful bray,
And grating shock of wrathful iron arms,
Might from our quiet confines fright fair peace,
And make us wade even in our kindred's blood;—
Therefore, we banish you our territories:—
You, cousin Hereford, upon pain of life,
Till twice five summers have enrich'd our fields
Shall not regreet our fair dominions,
But tread the stranger paths of banishment.
　　Boling. Your will be done: this must my
　　　　comfort be,— 　　　　　　　[me;
That sun that warms you here shall shine on
And those his golden beams to you here lent
Shall point on me and gild my banishment.
　　K. Rich. Norfolk, for thee remains a heavier
　　　　doom,
Which I with some unwillingness pronounce:
The sly-slow hours shall not determinate
The dateless limit of thy dear exile;—
The hopeless word of—never to return
Breathe I against thee, upon pain of life.
　　Nor. A heavy sentence, my most gracious
　　　　liege, 　　　　　　　　　[mouth:
And all unlook'd-for from your highness'
A dearer merit, not so deep a maim
As to be cast forth in the common air,
Have I deserved at your highness' hands.
The language I have learn'd these forty years,
My native English, now I must forego:
And now my tongue's use is to me no more
Than an unstring'd viol or a harp;
Or like a cunning instrument cas'd up,
Or, being open, put into his hands
That knows no touch to tune the harmony:
Within my mouth you have engoal'd my tongue,
Doubly portcullis'd with my teeth and lips;
And dull, unfeeling, barren ignorance 　　·
Is made my gaoler to attend on me.
I am too old to fawn upon a nurse,
Too far in years to be a pupil now:
What is thy sentence, then, but speechless death,
Which robs my tongue from breathing native
　　　　breath? 　　　　　　　　[sionate:
　　K. Rich. It boots thee not to be compas-
After our sentence plaining comes too late.
　　Nor. Then thus I turn me from my country's
　　　　light,
To dwell in solemn shades of endless night.
　　　　　　　　　　　　　　[*Retiring.*
　　K. Rich. Return again, and take an oath
　　　　with thee.
Lay on our royal sword your banish'd hands;
Swear by the duty that you owe to God,—
Our part therein we banish with yourselves,—
To keep the oath that we administer:—
You never shall—so help you truth and God!—
Embrace each other's love in banishment;
Nor never look upon each other's face;
Nor never write, regreet, nor reconcile
This lowering tempest of your home-bred hate;
Nor never by advised purpose meet
To plot, contrive, or complot any ill
'Gainst us, our state, our subjects, or our land.
　　Boling. I swear.

Nor. And I, to keep all this.

Boling. Norfolk, so far as to mine enemy;—
By this time, had the king permitted us,
One of our souls had wander'd in the air,
Banish'd this frail sepulchre of our flesh,
As now our flesh is banish'd from this land:
Confess thy treasons, ere thou fly the realm;
Since thou hast far to go, bear not along
The clogging burden of a guilty soul.

Nor. No, Bolingbroke: if ever I were traitor,
My name be blotted from the book of life,
And I from heaven banish'd, as from hence!
But what thou art, God, thou, and I do know;
And all too soon, I fear, the king shall rue.—
Farewell, my liege.—Now no way can I stray:
Save back to England, all the world's my way.
[*Exit.*

K. Rich. Uncle, even in the glasses of thine
eyes
I see thy grieved heart: thy sad aspéct
Hath from the number of his banish'd years
Pluck'd four away.—[*To* BOLING.] Six frozen
winters spent,
Return with welcome home from banishment.

Boling. How long a time lies in one little
word!
Four lagging winters and four wanton springs
End in a word: such is the breath of kings.

Gaunt. I thank my liege that in regard of me
He shortens four years of my son's exile:
But little vantage shall I reap thereby;
For, ere the six years that he hath to spend
Can change their moons and bring their times
about,
My oil-dried lamp and time bewasted light
Shall be extinct with age and endless night;
My inch of taper will be burnt and done,
And blindfold death not let me see my son.

K. Rich. Why, uncle, thou hast many years
to live.

Gaunt. But not a minute, king, that thou
canst give:
Shorten my days thou canst with sullen sorrow,
And pluck nights from me, but not lend a
morrow;
Thou canst help time to furrow me with age,
But stop no wrinkle in his pilgrimage;
Thy word is current with him for my death,
But dead, thy kingdom cannot buy my breath.

K. Rich. Thy son is banish'd upon good
advice,
Whereto thy tongue a party-verdict gave:
Why at our justice seem'st thou, then, to lower?

Gaunt. Things sweet to taste prove in diges-
tion sour.
You urg'd me as a judge; but I had rather
You would have bid me argue like a father.
O, had it been a stranger, not my child,
To smooth his fault I should have been more
mild:
A partial slander sought I to avoid,
And in the sentence my own life destroy'd.
Alas, I look'd when some of you should say,
I was too strict to make mine own away;

But you gave leave to mine unwilling tongue
Against my will to do myself this wrong.

K. Rich. Cousin, farewell;—and, uncle, bid
him so:
Six years we banish him, and he shall go.
[*Flourish. Exeunt* K. RICH. *and* Train.

Aum. Cousin, farewell: what presence must
not know,
From where you do remain let paper show.

Mar. My lord, no leave take I; for I will ride
As far as land will let me by your side.

Gaunt. O, to what purpose dost thou hoard
thy words,
That thou return'st no greeting to thy friends?

Boling. I have too few to take my leave of
you,
When the tongue's office should be prodigal
To breathe the abundant dolour of the heart.

Gaunt. Thy grief is but thy absence for a
time.

Boling. Joy absent, grief is present for that
time.   [gone.

Gaunt. What is six winters? they are quickly

Boling. To men in joy; but grief makes one
hour ten.   [pleasure.

Gaunt. Call it a travel that thou tak'st for

Boling. My heart will sigh when I miscall
it so,
Which finds it an enforced pilgrimage.

Gaunt. The sullen passage of thy weary steps
Esteem a foil, wherein thou art to set
The precious jewel of thy home-return.

Boling. Nay, rather, every tedious stride I
make
Will but remember me what a deal of world
I wander from the jewels that I love.
Must I not serve a long apprenticehood
To foreign passages; and in the end,
Having my freedom, boast of nothing else
But that I was a journeyman to grief? [visits

Gaunt. All places that the eye of heaven
Are to a wise man ports and happy heavens,
Teach thy necessity to reason thus;
There is no virtue like necessity.
Think not the king did banish thee,
But thou the king: woe doth the heavier sit
Where it perceives it is but faintly borne.
Go, say I sent thee forth to purchase honour
And not the king exil'd thee; or suppose
Devouring pestilence hangs in our air,
And thou art flying to a fresher clime:
Look, what thy soul holds dear, imagine it
To lie that way thou go'st, not whence thou
com'st:
Suppose the singing-birds musicians, [strew'd,
The grass whereon thou tread'st the presence
The flowers fair ladies, and thy steps no more
Than a delightful measure or a dance;
For gnarling sorrow hath less power to bite
The man that mocks at it and sets it light.

Boling. O, who can hold a fire in his hand
By thinking on the frosty Caucasus?
Or cloy the hungry edge of appetite
By bare imagination of a feast?

Or wallow naked in December snow
By thinking on fantastic summer's heat?
O, no! the apprehension of the good
Gives but the greater feeling to the worse:
Fell sorrow's tooth doth never rankle more
Than when it bites, but lanceth not the sore.
　Gaunt. Come, come, my son, I'll bring thee
　　on thy way:
Had I thy youth and cause, I would not stay.
　Boling. Then, England's ground, farewell;
　　sweet soil, adieu;
My mother, and my nurse, that bears me yet!
Where'er I wander, boast of this I can,—
Though banish'd, yet a true-born Englishman.
　　　　　　　　　　　　　　　　[*Exeunt.*

SCENE IV.—*The Court.*

Enter KING RICHARD, BAGOT, *and* GREEN;
　　AUMERLE *following.*

　K. Rich. We did observe.—Cousin Aumerle,
How far brought you high Hereford on his
　　way?　　　　　　　　　　　　　[him so,
　Aum. I brought high Hereford, if you call
But to the next highway, and there I left him.
　K. Rich. And say, what store of parting
　　tears were shed?　　　　　　　[east wind,
　Aum. Faith, none for me; except the north-
Which then blew bitterly against our faces,
Awak'd the sleeping rheum, and so by chance
Did grace our hollow parting with a tear.
　K. Rich. What said our cousin when you
　　parted with him?
　Aum. "Farewell:"
And, for my heart disdained that my tongue
Should so profane the word, that taught me
　　craft
To counterfeit oppression of such grief,
That words seem'd buried in my sorrow's grave.
Marry, would the word "farewell" have
　　lengthen'd hours,
And added years to his short banishment,
He should have had a volume of farewells;
But since it would not, he had none of me.
　K. Rich. He is our cousin, cousin; but 'tis
　　doubt,
When time shall call him home from banish-
　　ment,
Whether our kinsman come to see his friends.
Ourself, and Bushy, Bagot here, and Green,
Observ'd his courtship to the common people;
How he did seem to dive into their hearts
With humble and familiar courtesy;
What reverence he did throw away on slaves;
Wooing poor craftsmen with the craft of smiles,
And patient underbearing of his fortune,
As 'twere to banish their affects with him.
Off goes his bonnet to an oyster-wench;
A brace of draymen bid God speed him well,
And had the tribute of his supple knee,
With *Thanks, my countrymen, my loving friends;*
As were our England in reversion his,
And he our subjects' next degree in hope.
　Green. Well, he is gone; and with him go
　　these thoughts.

Now for the rebels which stand out in Ire-
　　land,—
Expedient manage must be made, my liege,
Ere further leisure yield them further means
For their advantage and your highness' loss.
　K. Rich. We will ourself in person to this
　　war:
And, for our coffers,—with too great a court
And liberal largess,—are grown somewhat light,
We are enforc'd to farm our royal realm;
The revenue whereof shall furnish us
For our affairs in hand. If that come short,
Our substitutes at home shall have blank
　　charters;　　　　　　　　　　　　[rich,
Whereto, when they shall know what men are
They shall subscribe them for large sums of
　　gold,
And send them after to supply our wants;
For we will make for Ireland presently.

Enter BUSHY.

Bushy, what news?
　Bushy. Old John of Gaunt is grievous sick,
　　my lord,
Suddenly taken; and hath sent post-haste
To entreat your majesty to visit him.
　K. Rich. Where lies he?
　Bushy. At Ely House.　　　　　[mind
　K. Rich. Now put it, God, in his physician's
To help him to his grave immediately!
The lining of his coffers shall make coats
To deck our soldiers for these Irish wars.—
Come, gentlemen, let's all go visit him:
Pray God we may make haste, and come too
　　late!　　　　　　　　　　　　[*Exeunt.*

ACT II.

SCENE I.—LONDON. *A Room in* ELY HOUSE.

GAUNT *on a couch; the* DUKE OF YORK *and
　　others standing by him.*

　Gaunt. Will the king come, that I may
　　breathe my last
In wholesome counsel to his unstaid youth?
　York. Vex not yourself, nor strive not with
　　your breath;
For all in vain comes counsel to his ear. [men
　Gaunt. O, but they say the tongues of dying
Enforce attention like deep harmony:
Where words are scarce, they are seldom spent
　　in vain;　　　　　　　　　　　[in pain
For they breathe truth that breathe their words
He that no more must say is listen'd more
　　Than they whom youth and ease have taught
　　　to glose;　　　　　　　　　[before;
More are men's ends mark'd than their lives
　　The setting sun, and music at the close,
As the last taste of sweets, is sweetest last,
Writ in remembrance more than things long
　　past:　　　　　　　　　　　　[hear,
Though Richard my life's counsel would not
My death's sad tale may yet undeaf his ear.
　York. No; it is stopp'd with other flattering
　　sounds,

As, praises of his state: then there are found
Lascivious metres, to whose venom-sound
The open ear of youth doth always listen;
Report of fashions in proud Italy,
Whose manners still our tardy apish nation
Limps after, in base imitation.
Where doth the world thrust forth a vanity,—
So it be new, there's no respect how vile,—
That is not quickly buzz'd into his ears?
Then all too late comes counsel to be heard,
Where will doth mutiny with wit's regard.
Direct not him, whose way himself will choose:
'Tis breath thou lack'st, and that breath wilt
    thou lose.   [inspir'd,
  Gaunt. Methinks I am a prophet new
And thus, expiring, do foretell of him:
His rash fierce blaze of riot cannot last,
For violent fires soon burn out themselves;
Small showers last long, but sudden storms are
    short;
He tires betimes that spurs too fast betimes;
With eager feeding food doth choke the feeder:
Light vanity, insatiate cormorant,
Consuming means, soon preys upon itself.
This royal throne of kings, this scepter'd isle
This earth of majesty, this seat of Mars,
This other Eden, demi-paradise;
This fortress built by Nature for herself
Against infection and the hand of war;
This happy breed of men, this little world;
This precious stone set in the silver sea,
Which serves it in the office of a wall,
Or as a moat defensive to a house,
Against the envy of less happier lands;
This blessed plot, this earth, this realm, this
    England,
This nurse, this teeming womb of royal kings,
Fear'd by their breed, and famous by their
    birth,
Renowned for their deeds as far from home,—
For Christian service and true chivalry,—
As is the sepulchre in stubborn Jewry
Of the world's ransom, blessed Mary's Son;—
This land of such dear souls, this dear dear land,
Dear for her reputation through the world,
Is now leas'd out,—I die pronouncing it,—
Like to a tenement or pelting farm:
England, bound in with the triumphant sea,
Whose rocky shore beats back the envious siege
Of watery Neptune, is now bound in with
    shame,
With inky blots, and rotten parchment bonds:
That England, that was wont to conquer others,
Hath made a shameful conquest of itself.
Ah, would the scandal vanish with my life,
How happy then were my ensuing death!

Enter KING RICHARD *and* QUEEN, AUMERLE,
  BUSHY, GREEN, BAGOT, ROSS, *and* WIL-
  LOUGHBY.

  York. The king is come: deal mildly with
    his youth;   [more.
For young hot colts, being rag'd, do rage the
  Queen. How fares our noble uncle, Lancaster?

  K. Rich. What comfort, man? How is't with
    aged Gaunt?   [position!
  Gaunt. O, how that name befits my com-
Old Gaunt, indeed; and gaunt in being old:
Within me grief hath kept a tedious fast;
And who abstains from meat that is not gaunt?
For sleeping England long time have I watch'd;
Watching breeds leanness, leanness is all gaunt:
The pleasure that some fathers feeds upon
Is my strict fast,—I mean my children's looks;
And therein fasting, hast thou made me gaunt:
Gaunt am I for the grave, gaunt as a grave,
Whose hollow womb inherits naught but bones.
  K. Rich. Can sick men play so nicely with
    their names?
  Gaunt. No, misery makes sport to mock
    itself:
Since thou dost seek to kill my name in me,
I mock my name, great king, to flatter thee.
  K. Rich. Should dying men flatter with those
    that live?   [die.
  Gaunt. No, no; men living flatter those that
  K. Rich. Thou, now a-dying, say'st thou
    flatter'st me.
  Gaunt. O, no! thou diest, though I the sicker
    be.   [thee ill.
  K. Rich. I am in health, I breathe, and see
  Gaunt. Now, He that made me knows I see
    thee ill;
Ill in myself to see, and in thee seeing ill.
Thy death-bed is no lesser than the land
Wherein thou liest in reputation sick;
And thou, too careless patient as thou art,
Committ'st thy anointed body to the cure
Of those physicians that first wounded thee:
A thousand flatterers sit within thy crown,
Whose compass is no bigger than thy head;
And yet, encaged in so small a verge,
The waste is no whit lesser than thy land.
O, had thy grandsire, with a prophet's eye,
Seen how his son's son should destroy his sons,
From forth thy reach he would have laid thy
    shame,
Deposing thee before thou wert possess'd,
Which art possess'd now to depose thyself.
Why, cousin, wert thou regent of the world,
It were a shame to let this land by lease;
But for thy world enjoying but this land,
Is it not more than shame to shame it so?
Landlord of England art thou now, not king:
Thy state of law is bondslave to the law;
And—
  K. Rich. And thou a lunatic lean-witted fool,
Presuming on an ague's privilege,
Dar'st with thy frozen admonition
Make pale our cheek, chasing the royal blood
With fury from his native residence.
Now by my seat's right royal majesty,
Wert thou not brother to great Edward's son,
This tongue that runs so roundly in thy head
Should run thy head from thy unreverend
    shoulders.   [ward's son,
  Gaunt. O, spare me not, my brother Ed-
For that I was his father Edward's son;—

That blood already, like the pelican,
Hast thou tapp'd out, and drunkenly carous'd:
My brother Gloster, plain well-meaning soul—
Whom fair befall in heaven 'mongst happy
　　　　souls!—
May be a precedent and witness good [blood:
That thou respect'st not spilling Edward's
Join with the present sickness that I have:
And thy unkindness be like crooked age,
To crop at once a too-long wither'd flower.
Live in thy shame, but die not shame with
　　　　thee!—
These words hereafter thy tormentors be!—
Convey me to my bed, then to my grave.
Love they to live that love and honour have.
　　　　　[*Exit, borne out by his* Attendants.
　　K. Rich. And let them die that age and
　　　　sullens have;
For both hast thou, and both become the grave.
　　York. I do beseech your majesty, impute his
　　　　words
To wayward sickliness and age in him:
He loves you, on my life, and holds you dear
As Harry Duke of Hereford, were he here.
　　K. Rich. Right, you say true: as Hereford's
　　　　love, so his;
As theirs, so mine; and all be as it is.

　　　　　Enter NORTHUMBERLAND.

　　North. My liege, old Gaunt commends him
　　　　to your majesty.
　　K. Rich. What says he?
　　North.　　　　　Nay, nothing; all is said:
His tongue is now a stringless instrument;
Words, life, and all, old Lancaster hath spent.
　　York. Be York the next that must be bank-
　　　　rupt so!
Though death be poor, it ends a mortal woe.
　　K. Rich. The ripest fruit first falls, and so
　　　　doth he;
His time is spent, our pilgrimage must be:
So much for that.—Now for our Irish wars:
We must supplant those rough rug-headed kerns,
Which live like venom, where no venom else,
But only they, hath privilege to live.
And for these great affairs do ask some charge:
Towards our assistance we do seize to us
The plate, coin, revenues, and movables,
Whereof our uncle Gaunt did stand possess'd.
　　York. How long shall I be patient? ah, how
　　　　long
Shall tender duty make me suffer wrong?
Not Gloster's death, nor Hereford's banish-
　　　　ment,　　　　　　　　[wrongs,
Not Gaunt's rebukes, nor England's private
Nor the prevention of poor Bolingbroke
About his marriage, nor my own disgrace,
Have ever made me sour my patient cheek,
Or bend one wrinkle on my sovereign's face.
I am the last of noble Edward's sons,
Of whom thy father, Prince of Wales, was first:
In war was never lion rag'd more fierce,
In peace was never gentle lamb more mild,
Than was that young and princely gentleman.

His face thou hast, for even so look'd he,
Accomplish'd with the number of thy hours;
But when he frown'd, it was against the French,
And not against his friends: his noble hand
Did win what he did spend, and spent not that
Which his triumphant father's hand had won:
His hands were guilty of no kindred's blood,
But bloody with the enemies of-his kin.
O Richard! York is too far gone with grief,
Or else he never would compare between.
　　K. Rich. Why, uncle, what's the matter?
　　York.　　　　　　　　　　O my liege,
Pardon me, if you please; if not, I, pleas'd
Not to be pardon'd, am content withal.
Seek you to seize, and gripe into your hands,
The royalties and rights of banish'd Hereford?
Is not Gaunt dead? and doth not Hereford live?
Was not Gaunt just? and is not Harry true?
Did not the one deserve to have an heir?
Is not his heir a well-deserving son?　　[Time
Take Hereford's rights away, and take from
His charters and his customary rights;
Let not to-morrow, then, ensue to-day;
Be not thyself,—for how art thou a king
But by fair sequence and succession?
Now, afore God—God forbid I say true!—
If you do wrongfully seize Hereford's rights,
Call in the letters-patents that he hath
By his attorneys-general to sue
His livery, and deny his offer'd homage,
You pluck a thousand dangers on your head,
You lose a thousand well-disposed hearts,
And prick my tender patience to those thoughts
Which honour and allegiance cannot think.
　　K. Rich. Think what you will, we seize into
　　　　our hands
His plate, his goods, his money, and his lands.
　　York. I'll not be by the while: my liege,
　　　　farewell:
What will ensue hereof, there's none can tell:
But by bad courses may be understood
That their events can never fall out good.
　　　　　　　　　　　　　　　[*Exit.*
　　K. Rich. Go, Bushy, to the Earl of Wiltshire
　　　　straight:
Bid him repair to us to Ely House
To see this business. To-morrow next
We will for Ireland; and 'tis time, I trow:
And we create, in absence of ourself,
Our uncle York lord governor of England;
For he is just, and always lov'd us well.—
Come on, our queen: to-morrow must we part;
Be merry, for our time of stay is short.
　　　　　[*Flourish. Exeunt* KING, QUEEN, BUSHY,
　　　　　　AUMERLE, GREEN, *and* BAGOT.
　　North. Well, lords, the Duke of Lancaster
　　　　is dead.
　　Ross. And living too; for now his son is duke.
　　Willo. Barely in title, not in revenue.
　　North. Richly in both, if justice had her
　　　　right.
　　Ross. My heart is great; but it must break
　　　　with silence,
Ere't be disburden'd with a liberal tongue.

North. Nay, speak thy mind; and let him
   ne'er speak more
That speaks thy words again to do thee harm!
   Willo. Tends that thou wouldst speak to the
      Duke of Hereford?
If it be so, out with it boldly, man;
Quick is mine ear to hear of good towards him.
   Ross. No good at all, that I can do for him;
Unless you call it good to pity him,
Bereft and gelded of his patrimony.
   North. Now, afore God, 'tis shame such
      wrongs are borne
In him, a royal prince, and many more
Of noble blood in this declining land.
The king is not himself, but basely led
By flatterers; and what they will inform,
Merely in hate, 'gainst any of us all,
That will the king severely prosecute
'Gainst us, our lives, our children, and our
      heirs.
   Ross. The commons hath be pill'd with
      grievous taxes,
And quite lost their hearts: the nobles hath he
      fin'd
For ancient quarrels, and quite lost their hearts.
   Willo. And daily new exactions are devis'd,—
As blanks, benevolences, and I wot not what:
But what, o' God's name, doth become of this?
   North. Wars have not wasted it, for warr'd
      he hath not,
But basely yielded upon compromise
That which his ancestors achiev'd with blows:
More hath he spent in peace than they in wars.
   Ross. The Earl of Wiltshire hath the realm
      in farm.
   Willo. The king's grown bankrupt, like a
      broken man.   [over him.
   North. Reproach and dissolution hangeth
   Ross. He hath not money for these Irish
      wars,
His burdenous taxations notwithstanding,
But by the robbing of the banish'd duke.
   North. His noble kinsman:—most degener-
      ate king!
But, lords, we hear this fearful tempest sing,
Yet seek no shelter to avoid the storm;
We see the wind set sore upon our sails,
And yet we strike not, but securely perish.
   Ross. We see the very wreck that we must
      suffer;
And unavoided is the danger now,
For suffering so the causes of our wreck.
   North. Not so; even through the hollow eyes
      of death
I spy life peering; but I dare not say
How near the tidings of our comfort is.
   Willo. Nay, let us share thy thoughts, as
      thou dost ours.   [land:
   Ross. Be confident to speak, Northumber-
We three are but thyself; and, speaking so,
Thy words are but as thoughts; therefore, be
      bold.
   North. Then thus:—I have from Port le
      Blanc, a bay

In Brittany, receiv'd intelligence   [Cobham,
That Harry Duke of Hereford, Renald Lord
That late broke from the Duke of Exeter,
His brother, Archbishop late of Canterbury,
Sir Thomas Erpingham, Sir John Ramston,
Sir John Norbery, Sir Robert Waterton, and
      Francis Quoint,—   [tagne,
All these, well furnish'd by the Duke of Bre-
With eight tall ships, three thousand men of
      war,
Are making hither with all due expedience,
And shortly mean to touch our northern shore:
Perhaps they had ere this, but that they stay
The first departing of the king for Ireland.
If, then, we shall shake off our slavish yoke,
Imp out our drooping country's broken wing,
Redeem from broking pawn the blemish'd crown,
Wipe off the dust that hides our sceptre's gilt,
And make high majesty look like itself,
Away with me in post to Ravenspurg;
But if you faint, as fearing to do so,
Stay and be secret, and myself will go.
   Ross. To horse, to horse! urge doubts to
      them that fear.
   Willo. Hold out my horse, and I will first
      be there.   [*Exeunt.*

SCENE II.—*The same. A Room in the Palace.*

Enter QUEEN, BUSHY, *and* BAGOT.

   Bushy. Madam, your majesty is too much
      sad:
You promis'd, when you parted with the king,
To lay aside life-harming heaviness,
And entertain a cheerful disposition.   [myself,
   Queen. To please the king, I did; to please
I cannot do it; yet I know no cause
Why I should welcome such a guest as grief,
Save bidding farewell to so sweet a guest
As my sweet Richard: yet, again, methinks
Some unborn sorrow, ripe in fortune's womb,
Is coming towards me; and my inward soul
With nothing trembles: at some thing it grieves,
More than with parting from my lord the king.
   Bushy. Each substance of a grief hath
      twenty shadows,
Which show like grief itself, but are not so;
For sorrow's eye, glazed with blinding tears,
Divides one thing entire to many objects;
Like perspectives, which, rightly gaz'd upon,
Show nothing but confusion,—ey'd awry,
Distinguish form: so your sweet majesty,
Looking awry upon your lord's departure,
Finds shapes of grief, more than himself, to
      wail;
Which, look'd on as it is, is naught but shadows
Of what it is not. Then, thrice-gracious queen,
More than your lord's departure weep not,—
      more's not seen;
Or if it be, 'tis with false sorrow's eye,
Which for things true weeps things imaginary.
   Queen. It may be so; but yet my inward soul
Persuades me it is otherwise: howe'er it be,
I cannot but be sad; so heavy sad,   [think,—

As,—though, on thinking, on no thought I
Makes me with heavy nothing faint and shrink.
　Bushy. 'Tis nothing but conceit, my gracious
　　lady.　　　　　　　　　　　　　[riv'd
　Queen. 'Tis nothing less: conceit is still de-
From some forefather grief; mine is not so,
For nothing hath begot my something grief;
Or something hath the nothing that I grieve:
'Tis in reversion that I do possess;
But what it is, that is not yet known; what
I cannot name; 'tis nameless woe, I wot.

Enter GREEN.

　Green. God save your majesty!—and well
　　met, gentlemen:—
I hope the king is not yet shipp'd for Ireland.
　Queen. Why hop'st thou so? 'tis better hope
　　he is;
For his designs crave haste, his haste good
　　hope:
Then wherefore dost thou hope he is not
　　shipp'd?
　Green. That he, our hope, might have retir'd
　　his power,
And driven into despair an enemy's hope,
Who strongly hath set footing in this land:
The banish'd Bolingbroke repeals himself,
And with uplifted arms is safe arriv'd
At Ravenspurg.
　Queen.　　　　　Now God in heaven forbid!
　Green. O madam, 'tis too true: and that is
　　worse,　　　　　　　　　[Henry Percy,
The Lord Northumberland, his son young
The Lords of Ross, Beaumond, and Willoughby,
With all their powerful friends, are fled to him.
　Bushy. Why have you not proclaim'd
　　Northumberland,
And all the rest of the revolted faction,
Traitors?　　　　　　　　　　[Worcester
　Green. We have: whereupon the Earl of
Hath broke his staff, resign'd his stewardship,
And all the household servants fled with him
To Bolingbroke.　　　　　　　　[my woe,
　Queen. So, Green, thou art the midwife to
And Bolingbroke my sorrow's dismal heir:
Now hath my soul brought forth her prodigy;
And I, a gasping new-deliver'd mother,
Have woe to woe, sorrow to sorrow join'd.
　Bushy. Despair not, madam.
　Queen.　　　　　　　　Who shall hinder me?
I will despair, and be at enmity
With cozening hope,—he is a flatterer,
A parasite, a keeper-back of death,
Who gently would dissolve the bands of life,
Which false hope lingers in extremity.
　Green. Here comes the Duke of York.
　Queen. With signs of war about his aged
　　neck:
O, full of careful business are his looks!

Enter YORK.

Uncle, for God's sake, speak comfortable words.
　York. Should I do so, I should belie my
　　thoughts:

Comfort's in heaven; and we are on the earth,
Where nothing lives but crosses, care, and grief.
Your husband, he is gone to save far off,
Whilst others come to make him lose at home:
Here am I left to underprop his land,
Who, weak with age, cannot support myself:
Now comes the sick hour that his surfeit made;
Now shall he try his friends that flatter'd him.

Enter a Servant.

　Serv. My lord, your son was gone before I
　　came.
　York. He was?—Why, so!—go all which way
　　it will!—
The nobles they are fled, the commons they are
　　cold,
And will, I fear, revolt on Hereford's side.—
Sirrah, get thee to Plashy, to my sister Gloster;
Bid her send me presently a thousand pound:—
Hold, take my ring.　　　　　　　　　[ship,
　Serv. My lord, I had forgot to tell your lord-
To-day, as I came by, I called there;—
But I shall grieve you to report the rest.
　York. What is't, knave?
　Serv. An hour before I came, the duchess died.
　York. God for his mercy! what a tide of woes
Comes rushing on this woeful land at once!
I know not what to do:—I would to God,—
So my untruth had not provok'd him to it,—
The king had cut off my head with my brother's.
What, are there no posts despatch'd for Ire-
　　land?—
How shall we do for money for these wars?—
Come, sister,—cousin, I would say,—pray,
　　pardon me.
Go, fellow [*to the* Servant], get thee home, pro-
　　vide some carts,
And bring away the armour that is there.—
　　　　　　　　　　　　　　[*Exit* Servant.
Gentlemen, will you go muster men? If I know
How or which way to order these affairs,
Thus thrust disorderly into my hands,
Never believe me. Both are my kinsmen:—
The one's my sovereign, whom both my oath
And duty bids defend; the other, again,
Is my kinsman, whom the king hath wrong'd,
Whom conscience and my kindred bids to right.
Well, somewhat we must do.—Come, cousin,
　　I'll　　　　　　　　　　　　　[your men,
Dispose of you.—Gentlemen, go, muster up
And meet me presently at Berkley Castle.
I should to Plashy too;—
But time will not permit:—all is uneven,
And everything is left at six and seven.
　　　　　　　　　　[*Exeunt* YORK *and* QUEEN.
　Bushy. The wind sits fair for news to go to
　　Ireland,
But none returns. For us to levy power
Proportionable to the enemy
Is all impossible.　　　　　　　　　[love
　Green. Besides, our nearness to the king in
Is near the hate of those love not the king.
　Bagot. And that's the wavering commons:
　　for their love

Lies in their purses; and whoso empties them,
By so much fills their hearts with deadly hate.

Bushy. Wherein the king stands generally
condemn'd.

Bagot. If judgment lie in them, then so do we,
Because we ever have been near the king.

Green. Well, I will for refuge straight to
Bristol Castle:
The Earl of Wiltshire is already there.   [office

Bushy. Thither will I with you: for little
The hateful commons will perform for us,
Except like curs to tear us all to pieces.—
Will you go along with us?

Bagot. No; I will to Ireland to his majesty.
Farewell: if heart's presages be not vain,
We three here part that ne'er shall meet again.

Bushy. That's as York thrives to beat back
Bolingbroke.   [takes

Green. Alas, poor duke! the task he under-
Is numbering sands, and drinking oceans dry:
Where one on his side fights, thousands will fly.
Farewell at once,—for once, for all, and ever.

Bushy. Well, we may meet again.

Bagot.   I fear me, never.   [*Exeunt.*

SCENE III.—*The Wilds in Glostershire.*

Enter BOLINGBROKE *and* NORTHUMBERLAND,
with Forces.

Boling. How far is it, my lord, to Berkley
now?

North. Believe me, noble lord,
I am a stranger here in Glostershire:
These high wild hills and rough uneven ways
Draw out our miles, and make them wearisome;
And yet your fair discourse hath been as sugar,
Making the hard way sweet and délectable.
But I bethink me what a weary way
From Ravenspur to Cotswold will be found
In Ross and Willoughby, wanting your company,
Which, I protest, hath very much beguil'd
The tediousness and process of my travel:
But theirs is sweeten'd with the hope to have
The present benefit which I possess;
And hope to joy is little less in joy
Than hope enjoy'd: by this the weary lords
Shall make their way seem short; as mine hath
done
By sight of what I have, your noble company.

Boling. Of much less value is my company
Than your good words.—But who comes here?

North. It is my son, young Harry Percy,
Sent from my brother Worcester, whencesoever.

Enter HARRY PERCY.

Harry, how fares your uncle?

Percy. I had thought, my lord, to have
learned his health of you.

North. Why, is he not with the queen?

Percy. No, my good lord; he hath forsook
the court,
Broken his staff of office, and dispers'd
The household of the king.

North.   What was his reason?

He was not so resolv'd when last we spake together.

Percy. Because your lordship was proclaimed
traitor.
But he, my lord, is gone to Ravenspur,
To offer service to the Duke of Hereford;
And sent me o'er by Berkley, to discover
What power the Duke of York had levied there
Then with direction to repair to Ravenspur.

North. Have you forgot the Duke of Hereford, boy?   [forgot

Percy. No, my good lord; for that is not
Which ne'er I did remember: to my knowledge,
I never in my life did look on him.

North. Then learn to know him now; this is
the duke.   [service,

Percy. My gracious lord, I tender you my
Such as it is, being tender, raw, and young;
Which elder days shall ripen, and confirm
To more approved service and desert.   [sure

Boling. I thank thee, gentle Percy; and be
I count myself in nothing else so happy
As in a soul remembering my good friends;
And, as my fortune ripens with thy love,
It shall be still thy true love's recompence:
My heart this covenant makes, my hand thus
seals it.

North. How far is it to Berkley? and what stir
Keeps good old York there with his men of war?

Percy. There stands the castle, by yon tuft
of trees,   [heard:
Mann'd with three hundred men, as I have
And in it are the Lords of York, Berkley, and
Seymour,—
None else of name and noble estimate.

North. Here come the Lords of Ross and
Willoughby,
Bloody with spurring, fiery-red with haste.

Enter ROSS *and* WILLOUGHBY.

Boling. Welcome, my lords. I wot your love
pursues
A banish'd traitor: all my treasury
Is yet but unfelt thanks, which, more enrich'd,
Shall be your love and labour's recompence.

Ross. Your presence makes us rich, most
noble lord.   [tain it.

Willo. And far surmounts our labour to at-

Boling. Evermore thanks, the exchequer of
the poor;
Which, till my infant fortune comes to years,
Stands for my bounty.—But, who comes here?

North. It is my Lord of Berkley, as I guess.

Enter BERKLEY.

Berk. My Lord of Hereford, my message is
to you.

Boling. My lord, my answer is—to Lan-
caster;
And I am come to seek that name in England;
And I must find that title in your tongue,
Before I make reply to aught you say.

Berk. Mistake me not, my lord; 'tis not my
meaning

To raze one title of your honour out:—
To you, my lord, I come,—what lord you will,—
From the most gracious regent of this land,
The Duke of York, to know what pricks you on
To take advantage of the absent time,
And fright our native peace with self-born arms.

　Boling. I shall not need transport my words
　　by you;
Here comes his grace in person.

　　　　Enter YORK, *attended.*

　　　　　　My noble uncle! [*Kneels.*
　York. Show me thy humble heart, and not
　　thy knee,
Whose duty is deceivable and false.
　Boling. My gracious uncle!—
　York. 　　　　　　　Tut, tut!
Grace me no grace, nor uncle me no uncle:
I am no traitor's uncle; and that word—grace,
In an ungracious mouth is but profane.
Why have those banish'd and forbidden legs
Dar'd once to touch a dust of England's ground?
But, then, more why,—why have they dar'd to
　　march
So many miles upon her peaceful bosom,
Frighting her pale-fac'd villages with war
And ostentation of despised arms?
Com'st thou because the anointed king is hence?
Why, foolish boy, the king is left behind,
And in my loyal bosom lies his power.
Were I but now the lord of such hot youth
As when brave Gaunt thy father, and myself,
Rescued the Black Prince, that young Mars of
　　men,
Fromforth the ranks of many thousand French,
O, then, how quickly should this arm of mine,
Now prisoner to the palsy, chástise thee,
And minister correction to thy fault! [fault;
　Boling. My gracious uncle, let me know my
On what condition stands it and wherein?
　York. Even in condition of the worst de-
　　gree,—
In gross rebellion and detested treason:
Thou art a banish'd man; and here art come
Before the expiration of thy time,
In braving arms against thy sovereign.
　Boling. As I was banish'd, I was banish'd
　　Hereford;
But as I come, I come for Lancaster.
And, noble uncle, I beseech your grace
Look on my wrongs with an indifferent eye:
You are my father, for methinks in you
I see old Gaunt alive; O, then, my father,
Will you permit that I shall stand condemn'd
A wandering vagabond; my rights and royalties
Pluck'd from my arms perforce, and given away
To upstart unthrifts? Wherefore was I born?
If that my cousin king be king of England,
It must be granted I am Duke of Lancaster.
You have a son, Aumerle, my noble kinsman;
Had you first died, and he been thus trod down,
He should have found his uncle Gaunt a father,
To rouse his wrongs, and chase them to the bay.
I am denied to sue my livery here,

And yet my letters-patents give me leave:
My father's goods are all distrain'd and sold;
And these and all are all amiss employ'd.
What would you have me do? I am a subject,
And challenge law: attorneys are denied me;
And therefore personally I lay my claim
To my inheritance of free descent. 　[abus'd.
　North. The noble duke hath been too much
　Ross. It stands your grace upon to do him
　　right.
　Willo. Base men by his endowments are
　　made great.
　York. My lords of England, let me tell you
　　this:—
I have had feeling of my cousin's wrongs,
And labour'd all I could to do him right:
But in this kind to come, in braving arms,
Be his own carver, and cut out his way,
To find out right with wrong,—it may not be;
And you that do abet him in this kind
Cherish rebellion, and are rebels all.
　North. The noble duke hath sworn his com-
　　ing is
But for his own; and for the right of that
We all have strongly sworn to give him aid;
And let him ne'er see joy that breaks that oath!
　York. Well, well, I see the issue of these
　　arms;—
I cannot mend it, I must needs confess,
Because my power is weak and all ill left:
But if I could, by him that gave me life,
I would attach you all, and make you stoop
Unto the sovereign mercy of the king;
But since I cannot, be it known to you
I do remain as neuter. So, fare you well;—
Unless you please to enter in the castle,
And there repose you for this night.
　Boling. An offer, uncle, that we will accept
But we must win your grace to go with us
To Bristol Castle, which they say is held
By Bushy, Bagot, and their complices,
The caterpillars of the commonwealth,
Which I have sworn to weed and pluck away.
　York. It may be I will go with you:—but
　　yet I'll pause;
For I am loth to break our country's laws.
Nor friends nor foes, to me welcome you are:
Things past redress are now with me past care.
　　　　　　　　　　　　　　[*Exeunt.*

　　　SCENE IV.—*A Camp in Wales.*

　　　Enter SALISBURY *and a* Captain.

　Cap. My Lord of Salisbury, we have stay'd
　　ten days,
And hardly kept our countrymen together,
And yet we hear no tidings from the king;
Therefore we will disperse ourselves: farewell.
　Sal. Stay yet another day, thou trusty
　　Welshman:
The king reposeth all his confidence
In thee. 　　　　　　　　　　[not stay.
　Cap. 'Tis thought the king is dead; we will
The bay trees in our country all are wither'd,
And meteors fright the fixed stars of heaven;

The pale-fac'd moon looks bloody on the earth,
And lean-look'd prophets whisper fearful
     change;   [leap,—
Rich men look sad, and ruffians dance and
The one in fear to lose what they enjoy,
The other to enjoy by rage and war:
These signs forerun the death or fall of kings.—
Farewell: our countrymen are gone and fled,
As well assur'd Richard their king is dead.
         [*Exit.*

Sal. Ah, Richard, with the eyes of heavy
     mind,
I see thy glory, like a shooting star,
Fall to the base earth from the firmament!
The sun sets weeping in the lowly west,
Witnessing storms to come, woe, and unrest;
Thy friends are fled, to wait upon thy foes;
And crossly to thy good all fortune goes.
         [*Exit.*

ACT III.

Scene I.—Bolingbroke's *Camp at Bristol.*

Enter Bolingbroke, York, Northumberland, Percy, Willoughby, Ross: Officers *behind, with* Bushy *and* Green, *prisoners.*

Boling. Bring forth these men.—
Bushy and Green, I will not vex your souls,—
Since presently your souls must part your
     bodies,—
With too much urging your pernicious lives,
For 'twere no charity; yet, to wash your blood
From off my hands, here, in the view of men,
I will unfold some causes of your deaths.
You have misled a prince, a royal king,
A happy gentleman in blood and lineaments,
By you unhappied and disfigur'd clean:
You have in manner with your sinful hours
Made a divorce betwixt his queen and him;
Broke the possession of a royal bed,
And stain'd the beauty of a fair queen's cheeks
With tears drawn from her eyes by your foul
     wrongs.
Myself,—a prince by fortune of my birth,
Near to the king in blood, and near in love
Till you did make him misinterpret me,—
Have stoop'd my neck under your injuries,
And sigh'd my English breath in foreign clouds,
Eating the bitter bread of banishment;
Whilst you have fed upon my signories,
Dispark'd my parks, and fell'd my forest-
     woods,   [coat,
From my own windows torn my household
Raz'd out my impress, leaving me no sign,
Save men's opinions and my living blood,
To show the world I am a gentleman.
This and much more, much more than twice
     all this,
Condemns you to the death.—See them de-
     liver'd over
To execution and the hand of death.
     Bushy. More welcome is the stroke of death
     to me   [well.
Than Bolingbroke to England.—Lords, fare-

Green. My comfort is, that heaven will take
     our souls,
And plague injustice with the pains of hell.
     Boling. My Lord Northumberland, see them
     despatch'd.
       [*Exeunt* North. *and others, with* Prisoners.
Uncle, you say the queen is at your house;
For God's sake, fairly let her be entreated:
Tell her I send to her my kind commends;
Take special care my greetings be deliver'd.
     York. A gentleman of mine I have despatch'd
With letters of your love to her at large.
     Boling. Thanks, gentle uncle.—Come, lords,
     away,
To fight with Glendower and his complices:
Awhile to work, and after holiday.   [*Exeunt.*

Scene II.—*The Coast of* Wales. *A Castle in view.*

Flourish; drums and trumpets. Enter King Richard, *the* Bishop of Carlisle, Aumerle, *and* Soldiers.

     K. Rich. Barkloughly Castle call they this
     at hand?
     Aum. Yea, my lord. How brooks your grace
     the air,
After your late tossing on the breaking seas?
     K. Rich. Needs must I like it well: I weep
     for joy
To stand upon my kingdom once again.—
Dear earth, I do salute thee with my hand,
Though rebels wound thee with their horses'
     hoofs:
As a long-parted mother with her child
Plays fondly with her tears and smiles in
     meeting,
So, weeping-smiling, greet I thee, my earth,
And do thee favour with my royal hands.
Feed not thy sovereign's foe, my gentle earth,
Nor with thy sweets comfort his rav'nous sense;
But let thy spiders, that suck up thy venom,
And heavy-gaited toads, lie in their way,
Doing annoyance to the treacherous feet
Which with usurping steps do trample thee:
Yield stinging nettles to mine enemies;
And when they from thy bosom pluck a flower,
Guard it, I pray thee, with a lurking adder,
Whose double tongue may with a mortal touch
Throw death upon thy sovereign's enemies.—
Mock not my senseless conjuration, lords:
This earth shall have a feeling, and these stones
Prove armed soldiers, ere her native king
Shall falter under foul rebellion's arms!
     Car. Fear not, my lord; that Power that
     made you king
Hath power to keep you king in spite of all.
The means that heaven yields must be embrac'd
And not neglected; else, if heaven would,
And we will not, heaven's offer we refuse,
The proffer'd means of succour and redress.
     Aum. He means, my lord, that we are too
     remiss;
Whilst Bolingbroke, through our security,

Grows strong and great in substance and in
　　friends.　　　　　　　　[thou not
　K. Rich. Discomfortable cousin! know'st
That when the searching eye of heaven is hid
Behind the globe that lights the lower world,
Then thieves and robbers range abroad unseen,
In murders and in outrage, boldly here;
But when, from under this terrestrial ball,
He fires the proud tops of the eastern pines,
And darts his light through every guilty hole,
Then murders, treasons, and detested sins,
The cloak of night being pluck'd from off their
　　backs,
Stand bare and naked, trembling at themselves?
So when this thief, this traitor, Bolingbroke,—
Who all this while hath revell'd in the night,
Whilst we were wandering with the antipodes,—
Shall see us rising in our throne, the east,
His treasons will sit blushing in his face,
Not able to endure the sight of day,
But self-affrighted tremble at his sin.
Not all the water in the rough rude sea
Can wash the balm from an anointed king;
The breath of worldly men cannot depose
The deputy elected by the Lord;
For every man that Bolingbroke hath press'd
To lift shrewd steel against our golden crown,
God for his Richard hath in heavenly pay
A glorious angel: then, if angels fight,　[right.
Weak man must fall; for heaven still guards the

Enter SALISBURY.

Welcome, my lord: how far off lies your power?
　Sal. Nor near nor further off, my gracious
　　lord,　　　　　　　　　　[tongue,
Than this weak arm: discomfort guides my
And bids me speak of nothing but despair.
One day too late, I fear, my noble lord,
Hath clouded all thy happy days on earth:
O, call back yesterday, bid time return,
And thou shalt have twelve thousand fighting
　　men!
To-day, to-day, unhappy day, too late,
O'erthrows thy joys, friends, fortune, and thy
　　state;
For all the Welshmen, hearing thou wert dead,
Are gone to Bolingbroke, dispers'd, and fled.
　Aum. Comfort, my liege: why looks your
　　grace so pale?
　K. Rich. But now the blood of twenty thou-
　　sand men
Did triumph in my face, and they are fled;
And, till so much blood thither come again,
Have I not reason to look pale and dead?
All souls that will be safe fly from my side;
For time hath set a blot upon my pride.　[are.
　Aum. Comfort, my liege; remember who you
　K. Rich. I had forgot myself: am I not king?
Awake, thou sluggard majesty! thou sleep'st.
Is not the king's name forty thousand names?
Arm, arm, my name! a puny subject strikes
At thy great glory.—Look not to the ground,
Ye favourites of a king: are we not high?
High be our thoughts: I know my uncle York

Hath power enough to serve our turn.—But
　who comes here?

Enter SCROOP.

　Scroop. More health and happiness betide
　　my liege
Than can my care-tun'd tongue deliver him.
　K. Rich. Mine ear is open and my heart
　　prepar'd:
The worst is worldly loss thou canst unfold.
Say, is my kingdom lost? why, 'twas my care;
And what loss is it to be rid of care?
Strives Bolingbroke to be as great as we?
Greater he shall not be; if he serve God,
We'll serve him too, and be his fellow so:
Revolt our subjects? that we cannot mend;
They break their faith to God, as well as us:
Cry woe, destruction, ruin, loss, decay;
The worst is death, and death will have his day!
　Scroop. Glad am I that your highness is so
　　arm'd
To bear the tidings of calamity.
Like an unseasonable stormy day,
Which makes the silver rivers drown their
　　shores,
As if the world were all dissolv'd to tears;
So high above his limits swells the rage
Of Bolingbroke, covering your fearful land
With hard bright steel, and hearts harder than
　　steel.
White-beards have arm'd their thin and hair-
　　less scalps　　　　　　　　[voices,
Against thy majesty; and boys, with women's
Strive to speak big, and clap their female joints
In stiff unwieldy arms against thy crown:
Thy very beadsmen learn to bend their bows
Of double-fatal yew against thy state;
Yea, distaff-women manage rusty bills
Against thy seat: both old and young rebel,
And all goes worse than I have power to tell.
　K. Rich. Too well, too well thou tell'st a
　　tale so ill.
Where is the Earl of Wiltshire? where is Bagot?
What is become of Bushy, where is Green?
That they have let the dangerous enemy
Measure our confines with such peaceful steps?
If we prevail, their heads shall pay for it:
I warrant they have made peace with Boling-
　　broke.
　Scroop. Peace have they made with him,
　　indeed, my lord.　　　　　[redemption!
　K. Rich. O villains, vipers, damn'd without
Dogs, easily won to fawn on any man!
Snakes, in my heart-blood warm'd, that sting
　　my heart!　　　　　　　　[Judas!
Three Judases, each one thrice worse than
Would they make peace? terrible hell make war
Upon their spotted souls for this offence!
　Scroop. Sweet love, I see, changing his prop-
　　erty,
Turns to the sourest and most deadly hate:—
Again uncurse their souls; their peace is made
With heads, and not with hands: those whom
　　you curse

Have felt the worst of death's destroying
    wound,
And lie full low, grav'd in the hollow ground.
  Aum. Is Bushy, Green, and the Earl of
    Wiltshire dead?   [heads.
  Scroop. Yea, all of them at Bristol lost their
  Aum. Where is the duke my father with his
    power?
  K. Rich. No matter where;—of comfort, no
    man speak:
Let's talk of graves, of worms, and epitaphs;
Make dust our paper, and with rainy eyes
Write sorrow on the bosom of the earth.
Let's choose executors, and talk of wills:
And yet not so,—for what can we bequeath,
Save our deposed bodies to the ground?
Our lands, our lives, and all are Bolingbroke's,
And nothing can we call our own but death,
And that small model of the barren earth
Which serves as paste and cover to our bones.
For God's sake, let us sit upon the ground,
And tell sad stories of the death of kings:—
How some have been depos'd; some slain in
    war;
Some haunted by the ghosts they have depos'd;
Some poison'd by their wives; some sleeping
    kill'd;
All murder'd:—for within the hollow crown
That rounds the mortal temples of a king
Keeps Death his court; and there the antic sits,
Scoffing his state, and grinning at his pomp;
Allowing him a breath, a little scene,
To monarchize, be fear'd, and kill with looks;
Infusing him with self and vain conceit,—
As if this flesh, which walls about our life,
Were brass impregnable; and humour'd thus,
Comes at the last, and with a little pin
Bores through his castle-wall, and—farewell,
    king!   [blood
Cover your heads, and mock not flesh and
With solemn reverence; throw away respect,
Tradition, form, and ceremonious duty;
For you have but mistook me all this while:
I live with bread like you, feel want, taste grief,
Need friends:—subjected thus,
How can you say to me, I am a king?
  Car. My lord, wise men ne'er sit and wail
    their woes,
But presently prevent the ways to wail.
To fear the foe, since fear oppresseth strength,
Gives, in your weakness, strength unto your
    foe,
And so your follies fight against yourself.
Fear, and be slain; no worse can come to fight:
And fight and die is death destroying death;
Where fearing dying pays death servile breath.
  Aum. My father hath a power; inquire of
    him;
And learn to make a body of a limb.
  K. Rich. Thou chid'st me well:—proud Bo-
    lingbroke, I come   [doom.
To change blows with thee for our day of
This ague-fit of fear is over-blown;
An easy task it is to win our own.—

Say, Scroop, where lies our uncle with his
    power?
Speak sweetly, man, although thy looks be
    sour.   [sky
  Scroop. Men judge by the complexion of the
The state and inclination of the day:
So may you by my dull and heavy eye,
  My tongue hath but a heavier tale to say.
I play the torturer, by small and small
To lengthen out the worst that must be
    spoken:—
Your uncle York is join'd with Bolingbroke;
And all your northern castles yielded up,
And all your southern gentlemen in arms
Upon his party.
  K. Rich.   Thou hast said enough.—
Beshrew thee, cousin, which didst lead me forth
           [*To* AUMERLE.
Of that sweet way I was in to despair!
What say you now? what comfort have we
    now?
By heaven, I'll hate him everlastingly
That bids me be of comfort any more.
Go to Flint Castle: there I'll pine away;
A king, woe's slave, shall kingly woe obey.
That power I have, discharge; and let them go
To ear the land that hath some hope to grow,
For I have none:—let no man speak again
To alter this, for counsel is but vain.
  Aum. My liege, one word.
  K. Rich.   He does me double wrong
That wounds me with the flatteries of his
    tongue.
Discharge my followers: let them hence away,
From Richard's night to Bolingbroke's fair
    day.   [*Exeunt.*

SCENE III.—WALES. *Before Flint Castle.*

Enter, with drum and colours, BOLINGBROKE
and Forces; YORK, NORTHUMBERLAND, *and
others.*

  Boling. So that by this intelligence we learn
The Welshmen are dispers'd; and Salisbury
Is gone to meet the king, who lately landed
With some few private friends upon this coast.
  North. The news is very fair and good, my
    lord:
Richard not far from hence hath hid his head.
  York. It would beseem the Lord Northum-
    berland
To say, King Richard:—alack the heavy day
When such a sacred king should hide his head.
  North. Your grace mistakes; only to be brief,
Left I his title out.
  York.   The time hath been,
Would you have been so brief with him, he
    would
Have been so brief with you, to shorten you,
For taking so the head, your whole head's
    length.   [should.
  Boling. Mistake not, uncle, further than you
  York. Take not, good cousin, further than
    you should,   [heads.
Lest you mistake: the heavens are o'er our

Boling. I know it, uncle; and oppose not myself
Against their will.—But who comes here?

Enter PERCY.

Well, Harry: what, will not this castle yield?
　Percy. The castle royally is mann'd, my lord,
Against thy entrance.
　Boling. Royally!
Why, it contains no king?
　Percy. 　　　　　Yes, my good lord,
It doth contain a king; King Richard lies
Within the limits of yond lime and stone:
And with him are the Lord Aumerle, Lord Salisbury,
Sir Stephen Scroop; besides a clergyman
Of holy reverence, who I cannot learn.
　North. O, belike it is the Bishop of Carlisle.
　Boling. Noble lord,
　　　　　　　　[*To* NORTHUMBERLAND.
Go to the rude ribs of that ancient castle;
Through brazen trumpet send the breath of parle
Into his ruin'd ears, and thus deliver:—
Harry Bolingbroke
On both his knees doth kiss King Richard's hand,
And sends allegiance and true faith of heart
To his most royal person; hither come
Even at his feet to lay my arms and power,
Provided that, my banishment repeal'd,
And lands restor'd again, be freely granted:
If not, I'll use the advantage of my power,
And lay the summer's dust with showers of blood
Rain'd from the wounds of slaughter'd Englishmen:
The which, how far off from the mind of Bolingbroke
It is, such crimson tempest should bedrench
The fresh green lap of fair King Richard's land,
My stooping duty tenderly shall show.
Go, signify as much, while here we march
Upon the grassy carpet of this plain.—
　　　　　　[NORTH. *advances to the Castle, with a trumpet.*
Let's march without the noise of threat'ning drum,
That from the castle's tatter'd battlements
Our fair appointments may be well perus'd.
Methinks King Richard and myself should meet
With no less terror than the elements
Of fire and water, when their thund'ring shock
At meeting tears the cloudy cheeks of heaven.
Be he the fire, I'll be the yielding water:
The rage be his, while on the earth I rain
My waters,—on the earth, and not on him.
March on, and mark King Richard how he looks.

A parle sounded, and answered by another trumpet within. Flourish. Enter on the walls KING RICHARD, *the* BISHOP OF CARLISLE, AUMERLE, SCROOP, *and* SALISBURY.

See, see, King Richard doth himself appear,
As doth the blushing discontented sun
From out the fiery portal of the east,
When he perceives the envious clouds are bent
To dim his glory, and to stain the track
Of his bright passage to the occident.
　York. Yet looks he like a king: behold, his eye,
As bright as is the eagle's, lightens forth
Controlling majesty:—alack, alack, for woe,
That any harm should stain so fair a show!
　K. Rich. We are amaz'd; and thus long have we stood
To watch the fearful bending of thy knee,
　　　　　　[*To* NORTHUMBERLAND.
Because we thought ourself thy lawful king:
And if we be, how dare thy joints forget
To pay their awful duty to our presence?
If we be not, show us the hand of God
That hath dismissed us from our stewardship;
For well we know, no hand of blood and bone
Can gripe the sacred handle of our sceptre,
Unless he do profane, steal, or usurp.
And though you think that all, as you have done,
Have torn their souls by turning them from us,
And we are barren and bereft of friends;
Yet know,—my master, God omnipotent,
Is mustering in his clouds, on our behalf,
Armies of pestilence; and they shall strike
Your children yet unborn and unbegot,
That lift your vassal hands against my head,
And threat the glory of my precious crown.
Tell Bolingbroke,—for yond methinks he is,—
That every stride he makes upon my land
Is dangerous treason: he is come to ope
The purple testament of bleeding war;
But ere the crown he looks for live in peace,
Ten thousand bloody crowns of mothers' sons
Shall ill become the flower of England's face,
Change the complexion of her maid-pale peace
To scarlet indignation, and bedew
Her pastures' grass with faithful English blood.
　North. The king of heaven forbid our lord the king
Should so with civil and uncivil arms
Be rush'd upon! Thy thrice-noble cousin,
Harry Bolingbroke, doth humbly kiss thy hand;
And by the honourable tomb he swears,
That stands upon your royal grandsire's bones,
And by the royalties of both your bloods,—
Currents that spring from one most gracious head,—
And by the buried hand of warlike Gaunt,
And by the worth and honour of himself,
Comprising all that may be sworn or said,—
His coming hither hath no further scope
Than for his lineal royalties, and to beg
Enfranchisement immediate on his knees:
Which on thy royal party granted once,
His glittering arms he will commend to rust,
His barbed steeds to stables, and his heart
To faithful service of your majesty.
This swears he, as he is a prince, is just;
And, as I am a gentleman, I credit him.

K. Rich. Northumberland, say thus the king
    returns:—
His noble cousin is right welcome hither;
And all the number of his fair demands
Shall be accomplish'd without contradiction:
With all the gracious utterance thou hast
Speak to his gentle hearing kind commends.—
We do debase ourself, cousin, do we not,
                       [To AUMERLE.
To look so poorly, and to speak so fair?
Shall we call back Northumberland, and send
Defiance to the traitor, and so die?
   Aum. No, good my lord; let's fight with
    gentle words
Till time lend friends, and friends their helpful
    swords.
   K. Rich. O God, O God! that e'er this tongue
    of mine,
That laid the sentence of dread banishment
On yond proud man, should take it off again
With words of sooth! O that I were as great
As is my grief, or lesser than my name!
Or that I could forget what I have been!
Or not remember what I must be now!
Swell'st thou, proud heart? I'll give thee scope
    to beat,
Since foes have scope to beat both thee and me.
   Aum. Northumberland comes back from
    Bolingbroke.
   K. Rich. What must the king do now? must
    he submit?
The king shall do it: must he be depos'd?
The king shall be contented: must he lose
The name of king? o' God's name, let it go:
I'll give my jewels for a set of beads,
My gorgeous palace for a hermitage,
My gay apparel for an alms-man's gown,
My figur'd goblets for a dish of wood,
My sceptre for a palmer's walking staff,
My subjects for a pair of carved saints,
And my large kingdom for a little grave,
A little little grave, an obscure grave;—
Or I'll be buried in the king's highway,
Some way of common trade, where subjects'
    feet
May hourly trample on their sovereign's head;
For on my heart they tread now whilst I live;
And buried once, why not upon my head?—
Aumerle, thou weep'st,—my tender-hearted
    cousin!—
We'll make foul weather with despised tears;
Our sighs and they shall lodge the summer corn,
And make a dearth in this revolting land.
Or shall we play the wantons with our woes,
And make some pretty match with shedding
    tears?
As thus;—to drop them still upon one place,
Till they have fretted us a pair of graves
Within the earth; and, therein laid,—there lies
Two kinsmen digg'd their graves with weeping
    eyes.
Would not this ill do well?—Well, well, I see
I talk but idly, and you mock at me.—
Most mighty prince, my Lord Northumberland,

What says King Bolingbroke? will his majesty
Give Richard leave to live till Richard die?
You make a leg, and Bolingbroke says ay.
   North. My lord, in the base court he doth
    attend   *[down?*
To speak with you;—may it please you to come
   K. Rich. Down, down I come; like glister-
    ing Phaeton,
Wanting the manage of unruly jades.
             *[*NORTH. *retires to* BOLING.
In the base court? Base court, where kings
    grow base,
To come at traitors' calls, and do them grace.
In the base court? Come down? Down, court!
    down, king!
For night-owls shriek where mounting larks
    should sing.   *[Exeunt from above.*
   Boling. What says his majesty?
   North.   Sorrow and grief of heart
Makes him speak fondly, like a frantic man:
Yet he is come.

Enter KING RICHARD, *and his* Attendants,
    below.

   Boling. Stand all apart,
And show fair duty to his majesty.—
My gracious lord,—   *[Kneeling.*
   K. Rich. Fair cousin, you debase your
    princely knee
To make the base earth proud with kissing it;
Me rather had my heart might feel your love
Than my unpleas'd eye see your courtesy.
Up, cousin, up;—your heart is up, I know,
Thus high at least *[touching his own head],* al-
    though your knee be low.   *[own.*
   Boling. My gracious lord, I come but for mine
   K. Rich. Your own is yours, and I am yours,
    and all.   *[lord,*
   Boling. So far be mine, my most redoubted
As my true service shall deserve your love.
   K. Rich. Well you deserve:—they well de-
    serve to have
That know the strong'st and surest way to get.—
Uncle, give me your hand: nay, dry your eyes;
Tears show their love, but want their remedies.—
Cousin, I am too young to be your father,
Though you are old enough to be my heir.
What you will have, I'll give, and willing too;
For do we must what force will have us do.—
Set on towards London:—cousin, is it so?
   Boling. Yea, my good lord.
   K. Rich.   Then I must not say no.
               [Flourish. Exeunt.

SCENE IV.—LANGLEY. *The* DUKE OF YORK'S
    Garden.

Enter the QUEEN *and two* Ladies.

   Queen. What sport shall we devise here in
    this garden,
To drive away the heavy thought of care?
   1 *Lady.* Madam, we'll play at bowls.
   Queen.   'Twill make me think
The world is full of rubs, and that my fortune
Runs against the bias.

1 *Lady.*   Madam, we'll dance.

Queen. My legs can keep no measure in de-
                        light,
When my poor heart no measure keeps in grief:
Therefore, no dancing, girl; some other sport.

1 *Lady.* Madam, we'll tell tales.

Queen.   Of sorrow or of joy?

1 *Lady.* Of either, madam.

Queen.   Of neither, girl:
For if of joy, being altogether wanting,
It doth remember me the more of sorrow;
Or if of grief, being altogether had,
It adds more sorrow to my want of joy:
For what I have, I need not to repeat;
And what I want, it boots not to complain.

1 *Lady.* Madam, I'll sing.

Queen.   'Tis well that thou hast cause;
But thou shouldst please me better wouldst
        thou weep.   [you good.

1 *Lady.* I could weep, madam, would it do

Queen. And I could weep, would weeping do
        me good,
And never borrow any tear of thee.—
But stay, here come the gardeners:
Let's step into the shadow of these trees.
My wretchedness unto a row of pins,
They'll talk of state; for every one doth so
Against a change: woe is forerun with woe.

                [QUEEN and Ladies *retire.*

Enter a Gardener *und two* Servants.

Gard. Go, bind thou up yond dangling apri-
        cocks,
Which, like unruly children, make their sire
Stoop with oppression of their prodigal weight:
Give some supportance to the bending twigs.—
Go thou, and like an executioner
Cut off the heads of too-fast-growing sprays,
That look too lofty in our commonwealth:
All must be even in our government.—
You thus employ'd, I will go root away
The noisome weeds, that without profit suck
The soil's fertility from wholesome flowers.

1 *Serv.* Why should we, in the compass of a
        pale,
Keep law and form and due proportion,
Showing, as in a model, our firm estate,
When our sea-walled garden, the whole land,
Is full of weeds; her fairest flowers chok'd up,
Her fruit-trees all unprun'd, her hedges ruin'd,
Her knots disorder'd, and her wholesome herbs
Swarming with caterpillars?

Gard.   Hold thy peace:—
He that hath suffer'd this disorder'd spring
Hath now himself met with the fall of leaf:
The weeds that his broad-spreading leaves did
        shelter,
That seem'd in eating him to hold him up,
Are pluck'd up root and all by Bolingbroke,—
I mean the Earl of Wiltshire, Bushy, Green.

1 *Serv.* What, are they dead?

Gard.   They are; and Bolingbroke
Hath seiz'd the wasteful king.—Oh! what pity
        is it.

That he had not so trimm'd and dress'd his land
As we this garden! We at time of year
Do wound the bark, the skin of our fruit-trees,
Lest, being over-proud in sap and blood,
With too much richness it confound itself:
Had he done so to great and growing men,
They might have liv'd to bear, and he to taste
Their fruits of duty. Superfluous branches
We lop away, that bearing boughs may live:
Had he done so, himself had borne the crown,
Which waste of idle hours hath quite thrown
        down.

1 *Serv.* What, think you, then, the king shall
        be depos'd?

Gard. Depress'd he is already; and depos'd
'Tis doubt he will be: letters came last night
To a dear friend of the good Duke of York's,
That tell black tidings.

Queen. O, I am press'd to death through
        want of speaking!—
Thou, old Adam's likeness [*coming forward with*
        Ladies], set to dress this garden,
How dares thy harsh-rude tongue sound these
        unpleasing news?
What Eve, what serpent, hath suggested thee
To make a second fall of cursed man?
Why dost thou say King Richard is depos'd?
Dar'st thou, thou little better thing than earth,
Divine his downfall? Say, where, when, and
        how
Cam'st thou by this ill tidings? speak, thou
        wretch.

Gard. Pardon me, madam: little joy have I
To breathe these news; yet what I say is true.
King Richard, he is in the mighty hold
Of Bolingbroke: their fortunes both are weigh'd:
In your lord's scale is nothing but himself,
And some few vanities that make him light;
But in the balance of great Bolingbroke,
Besides himself, are all the English peers,
And with that odds he weighs King Richard
        down.
Post you to London, and you'll find it so;
I speak no more than every one doth know.

Queen. Nimble mischance, that art so light
        of foot,
Doth not thy embassage belong to me,
And am I last that knows it? O, thou think'st
To serve me last, that I may longest keep
Thy sorrow in my breast.—Come, ladies, go
To meet at London London's king in woe.—
What, was I born to this, that my sad look
Should grace the triumph of great Bolingbroke?
Gardener, for telling me this news of woe,
I would the plants thou graft'st may never
        grow.   [*Exeunt* QUEEN *and* Ladies.

Gard. Poor queen! so that thy state might
        be no worse,
I would my skill were subject to thy curse.—
Here did she fall a tear; here, in this place,
I'll set a bank of rue, sour herb of grace:
Rue, even for ruth, here shortly shall be seen,
In the remembrance of a weeping queen.

                                [*Exeunt.*

ACT IV.

SCENE I.—LONDON. *Westminster Hall. The Lords spiritual on the right side of the throne; the Lords temporal on the left; the Commons below.*

Enter BOLINGBROKE, AUMERLE, SURREY, NORTHUMBERLAND, PERCY, FITZWATER, *another* Lord, *the* BISHOP OF CARLISLE, *the* ABBOT OF WESTMINSTER, *and* Attendants. Officers *behind, with* BAGOT.

Boling. Call forth Bagot.—
Now, Bagot, freely speak thy mind;
What thou dost know of noble Gloster's death;
Who wrought it with the king, and who per-
    form'd
The bloody office of his timeless end.
   Bagot. Then set before my face the Lord
     Aumerle.   [that man.
   Boling. Cousin, stand forth, and look upon
   Bagot. My Lord Aumerle, I know your dar-
    ing tongue
Scorns to unsay what once it hath deliver'd.
In that dead time when Gloster's death was
    plotted
I heard you say,—*Is not my arm of length,*
That reacheth from the restful English Court
As far as Calais, to my uncle's head?
Amongst much other talk, that very time,
I heard you say that you had rather refuse
The offer of an hundred thousand crowns
Than Bolingbroke's return to England;
Adding withal, how blest this land would be
In this your cousin's death.
   Aum.   Princes, and noble lords,
What answer shall I make to this base man?
Shall I so much dishonour my fair stars,
On equal terms to give him chastisement?
Either I must, or have mine honour soil'd
With the attainder of his slanderous lips.—
There is my gage, the manual seal of death,
That marks thee out for hell: I say, thou liest,
And will maintain what thou hast said is false
In thy heart-blood, though being all too base
To stain the temper of my knightly sword.
   Boling. Bagot, forbear; thou shalt not take
    it up.   [best
   Aum. Excepting one, I would he were the
In all this presence that hath moved me so.
   Fitz. If that thy valour stand on sympathy,
There is my gage, Aumerle, in gage to thine:
By that fair sun that shows me where thou
    stand'st,   [it,
I heard thee say, and vauntingly thou spak'st
That thou wert cause of noble Gloster's death.
If thou deny'st it twenty times, thou liest;
And I will turn thy falsehood to thy heart,
Where it was forged, with my rapier's point.
   Aum. Thou dar'st not, coward, live to see
    that day.   [hour.
   Fitz. Now, by my soul, I would it were this
   Aum. Fitzwater, thou art damn'd to hell for
    this.   [true
   Percy. Aumerle, thou liest; his honour is as

In this appeal as thou art all unjust;
And that thou art so, there I throw my gage,
To prove it on thee to the extremest point
Of mortal breathing: seize it, if thou dar'st.
   Aum. And if I do not, may my hands rot off,
And never brandish more revengeful steel
Over the glittering helmet of my foe!
   Lord. I task the earth to the like, forsworn
    Aumerle;
And spur thee on with full as many lies
As may be holla'd in thy treacherous ear
From sun to sun: there is my honour's pawn;
Engage it to the trial, if thou dar'st.
   Aum. Who sets me else? by heaven, I'll
    throw at all:
I have a thousand spirits in one breast,
To answer twenty thousand such as you. [well
   Surrey. My Lord Fitzwater, I do remember
The very time Aumerle and you did talk.
   Fitz. 'Tis very true: you were in presence
    then;
And you can witness with me this is true.
   Surrey. As false, by heaven, as heaven itself
    is true.
   Fitz. Surrey, thou liest.
   Surrey.   Dishonourable boy!
That lie shall lie so heavy on my sword
That it shall render vengeance and revenge
Till thou the lie-giver and that lie do lie
In earth as quiet as thy father's skull:
In proof whereof, there is mine honour's pawn;
Engage it to the trial, if thou dar'st.   [horse!
   Fitz. How fondly dost thou spur a forward
If I dare eat, or drink, or breathe, or live
I dare meet Surrey in a wilderness,
And spit upon him, whilst I say he lies,
And lies, and lies: there is my bond of faith,
To tie thee to my strong correction.—
As I intend to thrive in this new world,
Aumerle is guilty of my true appeal:
Besides, I heard the banish'd Norfolk say
That thou, Aumerle, didst send two of thy men
To execute the noble duke at Calais.   [a gage,
   Aum. Some honest Christian trust me with
That Norfolk lies: here do I throw down this,
If he may be repeal'd, to try his honour. [gage
   Boling. These differences shall all rest under
Till Norfolk be repeal'd: repeal'd he shall be,
And, though mine enemy, restor'd again
To all his lands and signories: when he's re-
    turn'd,
Against Aumerle we will enforce his trial.
   Car. That honourable day shall ne'er be
    seen.—
Many a time hath banish'd Norfolk fought
For Jesu Christ in glorious Christian field,
Streaming the ensign of the Christian cross
Against black pagans, Turks, and Saracens:
And toil'd with works of war, retir'd himself
To Italy; and there, at Venice, gave
His body to that pleasant country's earth,
And his pure soul unto his captain Christ,
Under whose colours he had fought so long.
   Boling. Why, bishop, is Norfolk dead?

Car. As surely as I live, my lord.

Boling. Sweet peace conduct his sweet soul to the bosom

Of good old Abraham!—Lords appellants,

Your differences shall all rest under gage

Till we assign you to your days of trial.

Enter YORK, *attended.*

York. Great Duke of Lancaster, I come to thee 　　　　　　　　　　[soul

From plume-pluck'd Richard; who with willing

Adopts thee heir, and his high sceptre yields

To the possession of thy royal hand:

Ascend his throne, descending now from him,—

And long live Henry, of that name the fourth!

Boling. In God's name, I'll ascend the regal throne.

Car. Marry, God forbid!—

Worst in this royal presence may I speak,

Yet best beseeming me to speak the truth.

Would God that any in this noble presence

Were enough noble to be upright judge

Of noble Richard! then true nobless would

Learn him forbearance from so foul a wrong.

What subject can give sentence on his king?

And who sits here that is not Richard's subject?

Thieves are not judg'd but they are by to hear,

Although apparent guilt be seen in them;

And shall the figure of God's majesty,

His captain, steward, deputy elect,

Anointed, crowned, planted many years,

Be judg'd by subject and inferior breath,

And he himself not present? O, forfend it, God,

That, in a Christian climate, souls refin'd

Should show so heinous, black, obscene a deed!

I speak to subjects, and a subject speaks,

Stirr'd up by God, thus boldly for his king.

My Lord of Hereford here, whom you call king,

Is a foul traitor to proud Hereford's king;

And if you crown him, let me prophesy,—

The blood of English shall manure the ground,

And future ages groan for this foul act;

Peace shall go sleep with Turk and infidels,

And in this seat of peace tumultuous wars

Shall kin with kin and kind with kind confound;

Disorder, horror, fear, and mutiny,

Shall here inhabit, and this land be call'd

The field of Golgotha and dead men's skulls.

Or, if you raise this house against this house,

It will the woefullest division prove

That ever fell upon this cursed earth,

Prevent, resist it, let it not be so,

Lest child, child's children, cry against you woe!

North. Well have you argu'd, sir; and, for your pains,

Cf capital treason we arrest you here.—

My Lord of Westminster, be it your charge

To keep him safely till his day of trial.—

May't please you, lords, to grant the commons' suit?

Boling. Fetch hither Richard, that in common view

He may surrender; so we shall proceed

Without suspicion.

York. 　　　　　I will be his conduct. [*Exit.*

Boling. Lords, you that are here under our arrest,

Procure your sureties for your days of answer.—

Little are we beholden to your love,

　　　　　　　　　　[*To* CARLISLE.

And little look'd for at your helping hands.

Re-enter YORK, *with* KING RICHARD, *and* Officers *bearing the crown, &c.*

K. Rich. Alack, why am I sent for to a king,

Before I have shook off the regal thoughts

Wherewith I reign'd? I hardly yet have learn'd

To insinuate, flatter, bow, and bend my limbs:

Give sorrow leave awhile to tutor me

To this submission. Yet I well remember

The favours of these men: were they not mine?

Did they not sometime cry, All hail! to me?

So Judas did to Christ: but he, in twelve,

Found truth in all but one; I, in twelve thousand, none.

God save the king!—Will no man say amen?

Am I both priest and clerk? well then, amen.

God save the king! although I be not he;

And yet, amen, if heaven do think him me.—

To do what service am I sent for hither?

York. To do that office of thine own good-will

Which tired majesty did make thee offer,—

The resignation of thy state and crown

To Henry Bolingbroke.

K. Rich. Give me the crown.—Here, cousin, seize the crown;

On this side my hand, and on that side yours.

Now is this golden crown like a deep well

That owes two buckets, filling one another;

The emptier ever dancing in the air,

The other down, unseen, and full of water:

That bucket down and full of tears am I,

Drinking my griefs, whilst you mount up on high. 　　　　　　　　　　[resign.

Boling. I thought you had been willing to

K. Rich. My crown I am; but still my griefs are mine:

You may my glories and my state depose,

But not my griefs; still am I king of those.

Boling. Part of your cares you give me with your crown.

K. Rich. Your cares set up do not pluck my cares down.

My care is, loss of care, by old care done;

Your care is, gain of care, by new care won:

The cares I give, I have, though given away;

They tend the crown, yet still with me they stay. 　　　　　　　　　　[crown?

Boling. Are you contented to resign the

K. Rich. Ay, no;—no, ay; for I must nothing be;

Therefore no no, for I resign to thee.

Now mark me, how I will undo myself:—

I give this heavy weight from off my head,

And thus unwieldy sceptre from my hand,

The pride of kingly sway from out my heart;

With mine own tears I wash away my balm,

With mine own hands I give away my crown,
With mine own tongue deny my sacred state,
With mine own breath release all duty's rites:
All pomp and majesty I do forswear;
My manors, rents. revenues I forego;
My acts, decrees, and statutes I deny:
God pardon all oaths that are broke to me!
God keep all vows unbroke that swear to thee!
Make me, that nothing have, with nothing
    griev'd,
And thou with all pleas'd, that hast all achiev'd!
Long mayst thou live in Richard's seat to sit,
And soon lie Richard in an earthy pit!
God save King Henry, unking'd Richard says,
And send him many years of sunshine days!—
What more remains?

North.   No more, but that you read
                        [*Offering a paper.*
These accusations, and these grievous crimes
Committed by your person and your followers
Against the state and profit of this land;
That, by confessing them, the souls of men
May deem that you are worthily depos'd.

K. Rich. Must I do so? and must I ravel out
My weav'd up follies? Gentle Northumberland,
If thy offences were upon record,
Would it not shame thee in so fair a troop
To read a lecture of them? If thou wouldst,
There shouldst thou find one heinous article,—
Containing the deposing of a king,
And cracking the strong warrant of an oath,—
Mark'd with a blot, damn'd in the book of
    heaven:—
Nay, all of you that stand and look upon,
Whilst that my wretchedness doth bait my-
    self,—
Though some of you, with Pilate, wash your
    hands,
Showing an outward pity; yet you Pilates
Have here deliver'd me to my sour cross,
And water cannot wash away your sin.

North. My lord, despatch; read o'er these
    articles.   [see:

K. Rich. Mine eyes are full of tears, I cannot
And yet salt water blinds them not so much
But they can see a sort of traitors here.
Nay, if I turn mine eyes upon myself,
I find myself a traitor with the rest;
For I have given here my soul's consent
To undeck the pompous body of a king;
Make glory base, and sovereignty a slave,
Proud majesty a subject, state a peasant.

North. My lord,—   [sulting man,

K. Rich. No lord of thine, thou haught in-
Nor no man's lord; I have no name, no title,—
No, not that name was giverr me at the font,—
But 'tis usurp'd:—alack the heavy day,
That I have worn so many winters out,
And know not now what name to call myself!
O that I were a mockery-king of snow,
Standing before the sun of Bolingbroke,
To melt myself away in water-drops!—
Good king,—great king,—and yet not greatly
    good,—

And if my word be sterling yet in England,
Let it command a mirror hither straight,
That it may show me what a face I have,
Since it is bankrupt of his majesty.

Boling. Go some of you and fetch a looking-
    glass.   [*Exit an* Attendant.

North. Read o'er this paper while the glass
    doth come.   [come to hell!

K. Rich. Fiend, thou torment'st me ere I

Boling. Urge it no more, my Lord Northum-
    berland.   [isfied.

North. The commons will not, then, be sat-

K. Rich. They shall be satisfied: I'll read
    enough,
When I do see the very book indeed
Where all my sins are writ, and that's myself.

Re-enter Attendant *with a glass.*

Give me the glass, and therein will I read.—
No deeper wrinkles yet? hath sorrow struck
So many blows upon this face of mine,
And made no deeper wounds?—O flattering
    glass,
Like to my followers in prosperity,
Thou dost beguile me! Was this face the face
That every day under his household roof
Did keep ten thousand men? Was this the face
That, like the sun, did make beholders wink?
Was this the face that fac'd so many follies,
And was at last out-fac'd by Bolingbroke?
A brittle glory shineth in this face:
As brittle as the glory is the face;
            [*Dashes the glass against the ground.*
For there it is, crack'd in a hundred shivers.—
Mark, silent king, the moral of this sport,—
How soon my sorrow hath destroy'd my face.

Boling. The shadow of your sorrow hath
    destroy'd
The shadow of your face.

K. Rich.   Say that again.
The shadow of my sorrow? Ha! let's see:—
'Tis very true, my grief lies all within;
And these external manners of laments
Are merely shadows to the unseen grief
That swells with silence in the tortur'd soul;
There lies the substance: and I thank thee,
    king,
For thy great bounty, that not only giv'st
Me cause to wail, but teachest me the way
How to lament the cause. I'll beg one boon,
And then be gone and trouble you no more.
Shall I obtain it?

Boling.   Name it, fair cousin.

K. Rich. Fair cousin! Why, I am greater
    than a king:
For when I was a king, my flatterers
Were then but subjects; being now a subject,
I have a king here to my flatterer.
Being so great, I have no need to beg.

Boling. Yet ask.

K. Rich. And shall I have?

Boling. You shall.

K. Rich. Then give me leave to go.

Boling. Whither?

K. Rich. Whither you will, so I were from
　　your sights.　　　　　　　　　[Tower.
Boling. Go, some of you convey him to the
K. Rich. O, good! Convey?—conveyers are
　　you all.
That rise thus nimbly by a true king's fall.
　　[*Exeunt* K. RICH., *some* Lords, *and a* Guard.
Boling. On Wednesday next we solemnly set
　　down
Our coronation: lords, prepare yourselves.
　　[*Exeunt all but the* ABBOT OF WESTMINSTER,
　　　　BISHOP OF CARLISLE, *and* AUMERLE.
　　Abbot. A woeful pageant have we here be-
　　　held.
　　Car. The woe's to come; the children yet un-
　　　born
Shall feel this day as sharp to them as thorn.
　　Aum. You holy clergymen, is there no plot
To rid the realm of this pernicious blot?
　　Abbot. Before I freely speak my mind herein,
You shall not only take the sacrament
To bury mine intents, but also to effect
Whatever I shall happen to devise.
I see your brows are full of discontent,
Your hearts of sorrow, and your eyes of tears:
Come home with me to supper; I will lay
A plot shall show us all a merry day. [*Exeunt.*

ACT V.

SCENE I.—LONDON. *A Street leading to the
Tower.*

Enter QUEEN *and* Ladies.

　　Queen. This way the king will come; this is
　　　the way
To Julius Cæsar's ill-erected tower,
To whose flint bosom my condemned lord
Is doom'd a prisoner by proud Bolingbroke:
Here let us rest, if this rebellious earth
Have any resting for her true king's queen.—
But soft, but see, or rather do not see,
My fair rose wither: yet look up, behold,
That you in pity may dissolve to dew,
And wash him fresh again with true-love tears.

Enter KING RICHARD *and* Guards.

Ah, thou, the model where old Troy did stand;
Thou map of honour; thou King Richard's
　　tomb,
And not King Richard; thou most beauteous
　　inn,
Why should hard-favour'd grief be lodg'd in
　　thee,
When triumph is become an alehouse guest?
　　K. Rich. Join not with grief, fair woman, do
　　　not so,
To make my end too sudden: learn, good soul,
To think our former state a happy dream;
From which awak'd, the truth of what we are
Shows us but this: I am sworn brother, sweet,
To grim Necessity; and he and I　　　[France,
Will keep a league till death. Hie thee to
And cloister thee in some religious house:
Our holy lives must win a new world's crown,

Which our profane hours here have stricken
　　down.　　　　　　　　　　　[and mind
　　Queen. What, is my Richard both in shape
Transform'd and weaken'd? Hath Bolingbroke
Depos'd thine intellect? Hath he been in thy
　　heart?
The lion, dying, thrusteth forth his paw,
And wounds the earth, if nothing else, with rage
To be o'erpower'd; and wilt thou, pupil-like,
Take thy correction mildly; kiss the rod,
And fawn on rage with base humility,
Which art a lion and a king of beasts?
　　K. Rich. A king of beasts, indeed; if aught
　　　but beasts,
I had been still a happy king of men.
Good sometime queen, prepare thee hence for
　　France:
Think I am dead; and that even here thou
　　tak'st,
As from my death-bed, my last living leave.
In winter's tedious nights sit by the fire
With good old folks, and let them tell thee tales
Of woeful ages long ago betid;
And ere thou bid good-night, to quit their grief
Tell thou the lamentable tale of me,
And send the hearers weeping to their beds:
For why, the senseless brands will sympathize
The heavy accent of thy moving tongue,
And in compassion weep the fire out;
And some will mourn in ashes, some coal-black,
For the deposing of a rightful king.

Enter NORTHUMBERLAND *attended.*

　　North. My lord, the mind of Bolingbroke is
　　　chang'd;
You must to Pomfret, not unto the Tower.—
And, madam, there is order ta'en for you;
With all swift speed you must away to France.
　　K. Rich. Northumberland, thou ladder
　　　wherewithal
The mounting Bolingbroke ascends my throne,
The time shall not be many hours of age
More than it is, ere foul sin, gathering head,
Shall break into corruption: thou shalt think,
Though he divide the realm, and give thee half,
It is too little, helping him to all;　　　[the way
And he shall think that thou, which know'st
To plant unrightful kings, wilt know again,
Being ne'er so little urg'd, another way
To pluck him headlong from the usurped
　　throne.
The love of wicked friends converts to fear;
That fear to hate; and hate turns one or both
To worthy danger and deserved death.
　　North. My guilt be on my head, and there
　　　an end.　　　　　　　　　　[with.
Take leave, and part; for you must part forth-
　　K. Rich. Doubly divorc'd!—Bad men, ye
　　　violate
A twofold marriage,—'twixt my crown and me,
And then betwixt me and my married wife.—
Let me unkiss the oath 'twixt thee and me;
And yet not so, for with a kiss 'twas made.—
Part us, Northumberland; I towards the north,

Where shivering cold and sickness pines the
clime;   [pomp,
My wife to France, from whence, set forth in
She came adorned hither like sweet May,
Sent back like Hallowmas or short'st of day.
    Queen. And must we be divided? must we
        part?
    K. Rich. Ay, hand from hand, my love, and
        heart from heart.   [with me.
    Queen. Banish us both, and send the king
    North. That were some love, but little policy.
    Queen. Then whither he goes thither let me
        go.   [woe.
    K. Rich. So two, together weeping, make one
Weep thou for me in France, I for thee here;
Better far off than near, be ne'er the near.
Go, count thy way with sighs; I, mine with
        groans.   [moans.
    Queen. So longest way shall have the longest
    K. Rich. Twice for one step I'll groan, the
        way being short,
And piece the way out with a heavy heart.
Come, come, in wooing sorrow let's be brief,
Since, wedding it, there is such length in grief.
One kiss shall stop our mouths, and dumbly
        part;
Thus give I mine, and thus take I thy heart.
                                        [*They kiss.*
    Queen. Give me mine own again; 'twere no
        good part
To take on me to keep and kill thy heart.
                                    [*They kiss again.*
So, now I have mine own again, be gone,
That I may strive to kill it with a groan.
    K. Rich. We make woe wanton with this
        fond delay:
Once more, adieu; the rest let sorrow say.
                                        [*Exeunt.*

SCENE II.—*The same. A Room in the* DUKE OF
        YORK'S *Palace.*

        Enter YORK *and his* DUCHESS.

    Duch. My lord, you told me you would tell
        the rest,
When weeping made you break the story off
Of our two cousins coming into London.
    York. Where did I leave?
    Duch.   At that sad stop, my lord,
Where rude misgovern'd hands from windows'
        tops   [head.
Threw dust and rubbish on King Richard's
    York. Then, as I said, the duke, great
        Bolingbroke,—
Mounted upon a hot and fiery steed,
Which his aspiring rider seem'd to know,—
With slow but stately pace kept on his course,
While all tongues cried, *God save thee, Boling-*
        broke!
You would have thought the very windows
        spake,
So many greedy looks of young and old
Through casements darted their desiring eyes
Upon his visage; and that all the walls
With painted imagery had said at once,

Jesu preserve thee! welcome, Bolingbroke!
Whilst he, from one side to the other turning,
Bareheaded, lower than his proud steed's neck,
Bespake them this,—*I thank you, countrymen:*
And thus still doing, thus he pass'd along.
    Duch. Alas, poor Richard! where rode he
        the whilst?
    York. As in a theatre the eyes of men,
After a well-grac'd actor leaves the stage,
Are idly bent on him that enters next,
Thinking his prattle to be tedious;   [eyes
Even so, or with much more contempt, men's
Did scowl on Richard; no man cried, *God save*
        him!
No joyful tongue gave him his welcome home:
But dust was thrown upon his sacred head;
Which with such gentle sorrow he shook off,—
His face still combating with tears and smiles,
The badges of his grief and patience,—
That had not God, for some strong purpose,
        steel'd
The hearts of men, they must perforce have
        melted,
And barbarism itself have pitied him.
But heaven hath a hand in these events,
To whose high will we bound our calm contents.
To Bolingbroke are we sworn subjects now,
Whose state and honour I for aye allow.
    Duch. Here comes my son Aumerle.
    York.   Aumerle that was;
But that is lost for being Richard's friend,
And, madam, you must call him Rutland now:
I am in Parliament pledge for his truth
And lasting fealty to the new-made king.

        Enter AUMERLE.

    Duch. Welcome, my son: who are the violets
        now
That strew the green lap of the new-come
        spring?
    Aum. Madam, I know not, nor I greatly
        care not:
God knows I had as lief be none as one.
    York. Well, bear you well in this new spring
        of time,
Lest you be cropp'd before you come to prime.
What news from Oxford? hold those justs and
        triumphs?
    Aum. For aught I know, my lord, they do.
    York. You will be there, I know.
    Aum. If God prevent it not, I purpose so.
    York. What seal is that that hangs without
        thy bosom?
Yea, look'st thou pale? let me see the writing.
    Aum. My lord, 'tis nothing.
    York.   No matter, then, who sees it.
I will be satisfied; let me see the writing.
    Aum. I do beseech your grace to pardon me:
It is a matter of small consequence,
Which for some reasons I would not have seen.
    York. Which for some reasons, sir, I mean
        to see.
I fear, I fear,—
    Duch.   What should you fear?

'Tis nothing but some bond that he is enter'd
   into
For gay apparel against the triumph-day.
  York. Bound to himself! what doth he with
   a bond
That he is bound to? Wife, thou art a fool.—
Boy, let me see the writing.
  Aum. I do beseech you, pardon me; I may
   not show it.
  York. I will be satisfied; let me see it, I say.
                  [Snatches it, and reads.
Treason! foul treason!—villain! traitor! slave!
  Duch. What's the matter, my lord?
  York. Ho! who's within there?

        Enter a Servant.

                Saddle my horse.
God for his mercy, what treachery is here!
  Duch. Why, what is 't, my lord?
  York. Give me my boots, I say; saddle my
   horse.—
Now, by mine honour, by my life, my troth,
I will appeach the villain.   *[Exit* Servant.
  Duch.   What's the matter?
  York. Peace, foolish woman.
  Duch. I will not peace.—What is the matter,
   son?
  Aum. Good mother, be content; it is no more
Than my poor life must answer.
  Duch.   Thy life answer!
  York. Bring me my boots:—I will unto the
   king.

    Re-enter Servant *with boots.*

  Duch. Strike him, Aumerle.—Poor boy, thou
   art amaz'd.
Hence, villain! never more come in my sight.
                   [To the Servant.
  York. Give me my boots, I say.
  Duch. Why, York, what wilt thou do?
Wilt thou not hide the trespass of thine own?
Have we more sons? or are we like to have?
Is not my teeming date drunk up with time?
And wilt thou pluck my fair son from mine age,
And rob me of a happy mother's name?
Is he not like thee? is he not thine own?
  York. Thou fond mad woman,
Wilt thou conceal this dark conspiracy?
A dozen of them here have ta'en the sacrament
And interchangeably set down their hands
To kill the king at Oxford.
  Duch.   He shall be none;
We'll keep him here: then what is that to him?
  York. Away, fond woman! were he twenty
   times my son
I would appeach him.
  Duch.   Hadst thou groan'd for him
As I have done, thou wouldst be more pitiful.
But now I know thy mind; thou dost suspect
That I have been disloyal to thy bed,
And that he is a bastard, not thy son:
Sweet York, sweet husband, be not of that
   mind:
He is as like thee as a man may be,

Not like to me, nor any of my kin,
And yet I love him.
  York.   Make way, unruly woman!
                       [Exit.
  Duch. After, Aumerle! mount thee upon his
   horse;
Spur post, and get before him to the king,
And beg thy pardon ere he do accuse thee.
I'll not be long behind; though I be old,
I doubt not but to ride as fast as York;
And never will I rise up from the ground
Till Bolingbroke have pardon'd thee. Away, be
   gone!   *[Exeunt.*

SCENE III.—WINDSOR. *A Room in the Castle.*

   Enter BOLINGBROKE *as King,* PERCY, *and
        other* Lords.

  Boling. Can no man tell of my unthrifty son?
'Tis full three months since I did see him last:—
If any plague hang over us, 'tis he.
I would to God, my lords, he might be found:
Inquire at London, 'mongst the taverns there,
For there, they say, he daily doth frequent,
With unrestrained loose companions,—
Even such, they say, as stand in narrow lanes,
And beat our watch, and rob our passengers;
While he, young, wanton, and effeminate boy,
Takes on the point of honour to support
So dissolute a crew.
  Percy. My lord, some two days since I saw
   the prince,
And told him of these triumphs held at Oxford.
  Boling. And what said the gallant?
  Percy. His answer was,—he would unto the
   stews,
And from the common'st creature pluck a glove,
And wear it as a favour; and with that
He would unhorse the lustiest challenger.
  Boling. As dissolute as desperate: yet
   through both
I see some sparkles of a better hope,
Which elder days may happily bring forth.—
But who comes here?

      Enter AUMERLE *hastily.*
  Aum.   Where is the king?
  Boling.   What means
Our cousin, that he stares and looks so wildly?
  Aum. God save your grace! I do beseech
   your majesty,
To have some conference with your grace alone.
  Boling. Withdraw yourselves, and leave us
   here alone.
            [Exeunt PERCY *and* Lords.
What is the matter with our cousin now?
  Aum. For ever may my knees grow to the
   earth,   *[Kneels.*
My tongue cleave to my roof within my mouth,
Unless a pardon ere I rise or speak.
  Boling. Intended or committed was this
   fault?
If but the first, how heinous e'er it be,
To win thy after-love I pardon thee.

Aum. Then give me leave that I may turn
    the key,
That no man enter till my tale be done.
Boling. Have thy desire.
                        [AUMERLE *locks the door.*
York. [*Within.*] My liege, beware; look to
    thyself;
Thou hast a traitor in thy presence there.
Boling. Villain, I'll make thee safe.
                                    [*Drawing.*
Aum. Stay thy revengeful hand;
Thou hast no cause to fear.
York. [*Within.*] Open the door, secure, fool-
    hardy king:
Shall I, for love, speak treason to thy face?
Open the door, or I will break it open.
    [BOLING. *opens the door and locks it again.*

Enter YORK.

Boling. What is the matter, uncle? speak;
Recover breath; tell us how near is danger,
That we may arm us to encounter it.
York. Peruse this writing here, and thou
    shalt know
The treason that my haste forbids me show.
Aum. Remember, as thou read'st, thy pro-
    mise pass'd:
I do repent me; read not my name there;
My heart is not confederate with my hand.
York. It was, villain, ere thy hand did set it
    down.—
I tore it from the traitor's bosom, king;
Fear, and not love, begets his penitence:
Forget to pity him, lest thy pity prove
A serpent that will sting thee to the heart.
Boling. O heinous, strong, and bold con-
    spiracy!—
O loyal father of a treacherous son!
Thou sheer, immaculate, and silver fountain,
From whence this stream through muddy pas-
    sages
Hath held his current and defil'd himself!
Thy overflow of good converts to bad;
And thy abundant goodness shall excuse
This deadly blot in thy digressing son.
York. So shall my virtue be his vice's bawd;
And he shall spend mine honour with his shame,
As thriftless sons their scraping fathers' gold.
Mine honour lives when his dishonour dies,
Or my sham'd life in his dishonour lies:
Thou kill'st me in his life; giving him breath,
The traitor lives, the true man's put to death.
Duch. [*Within.*] What ho, my liege! for God's
    sake, let me in.
Boling. What shrill-voic'd suppliant makes
    this eager cry?
Duch. A woman, and thine aunt, great king;
    'tis I.
Speak with me, pity me, open the door:
A beggar begs that never begg'd before.
Boling. Our scene is alter'd from a serious
    thing,
And now chang'd to *The Beggar and the
    King.*—

My dangerous cousin, let your mother in:
I know she's come to pray for your foul sin.
                    [AUMERLE *unlocks the door.*
York. If thou do pardon, whosoever pray,
More sins, for this forgiveness, prosper may.
This fester'd joint cut off, the rest rests sound:
This let alone will all the rest confound.

Enter DUCHESS.

Duch. O king, believe not this hard-hearted
    man!
Love, loving not itself, none other can.
York. Thou frantic woman, what dost thou
    make here?
Shall thy old dugs once more a traitor rear?
Duch. Sweet York, be patient.—Hear me,
    gentle liege.   [*Kneels.*
Boling. Rise up, good aunt.
Duch.   Not yet, I thee beseech:
For ever will I walk upon my knees,
And never see day that the happy sees
Till thou give joy; until thou bid me joy,
By pardoning Rutland, my transgressing boy.
Aum. Unto my mother's prayers I bend my
    knee.   [*Kneels.*
York. Against them both, my true joints
    bended be.   [*Kneels.*
Ill mayst thou thrive, if thou grant any grace!
Duch. Pleads he in earnest? look upon his
    face;
His eyes do drop no tears, his prayers are in
    jest;
His words come from his mouth, ours from our
    breast:
He prays but faintly, and would be denied;
We pray with heart and soul, and all beside:
His weary joints would gladly rise, I know;
Our knees shall kneel till to the ground they
    grow:
His prayers are full of false hypocrisy;
Ours of true zeal and deep integrity.
Our prayers do out-pray his; then let them have
That mercy which true prayers ought to have.
Boling. Good aunt, stand up.
Duch.   Nay, do not say *stand up;*
But *pardon* first, and afterwards *stand up.*
An if I were thy nurse, thy tongue to teach,
Pardon should be the first word of thy speech.
I never long'd to hear a word till now;
Say *pardon,* king; let pity teach thee how:
The word is short, but not so short as sweet;
No word like *pardon,* for kings' mouths so meet.
York. Speak it in French, king; say *par-
    donnez-moi.*
Duch. Dost thou teach pardon pardon to
    destroy?
Ah, my sour husband, my hard-hearted lord,
That sett'st the word itself against the word!—
Speak *pardon* as 'tis current in our land;
The chopping French we do not understand.
Thine eye begins to speak, set thy tongue there:
Or in thy piteous heart plant thou thine ear;
That hearing how our plaints and prayers do
    pierce,

Pity may move thee *pardon* to rehearse.
 Boling. Good aunt, stand up.
 Duch.   I do not sue to stand;
Pardon is all the suit I have in hand.
 Boling. I pardon him, as God shall pardon
  me.
 Duch. O happy vantage of a kneeling knee!
Yet am I sick for fear: speak it again;
Twice saying *pardon* doth not pardon twain,
But makes one pardon strong.
 Boling.   With all my heart
I pardon him.
 Duch. A god on earth thou art.
 Boling. But for our trusty brother-in-law,
  and the abbot,
With all the rest of that consorted crew,
Destruction straight shall dog them at the
  heels.
Good uncle, help to order several powers
To Oxford, or where'er these traitors are:
They shall not live within this world, I swear,
But I will have them, if I once know where,
Uncle, farewell:—and, cousin mine, adieu:
Your mother well hath pray'd, and prove you
  true.
 Duch. Come, my old son:—I pray God make
  thee new.   [*Exeunt.*

SCENE IV.—*Another Room in the Castle.*

Enter SIR PIERCE OF EXTON *and a* Servant.

 Exton. Didst thou not mark the king, what
  words he spake?—
Have I no friend will rid me of this living fear?
Was it not so?
 Serv.   Those were his very words.
 Exton. *Have I no friend?* quoth he: he spake
  it twice,
And urg'd it twice together,—did he not?
 Serv. He did.
 Exton. And, speaking it, he wistly look'd on
  me,
As who should say,—I would thou wert the man
That would divorce this terror from my heart,—
Meaning the king at Pomfret. Come, let's go:
I am the king's friend, and will rid his foe.
          [*Exeunt.*

SCENE V.—POMFRET. *The Dungeon of the
Castle.*

Enter KING RICHARD.

 K. Rich. I have been studying how I may
  compare
This prison where I live unto the world:
And, for because the world is populous,
And here is not a creature but myself,
I cannot do it;—yet I'll hammer't out.
My brain I'll prove the female to my soul,
My soul the father: and these two beget
A generation of still-breeding thoughts,
And these same thoughts people this little
  world,
In humours like the people of this world,
For no thought is contented. The better sort,—
As thoughts of things divine,—are intermix'd

With scruples, and do set the word itself
Against the word:
As thus,—*Come, little ones;* and then again,—
It is as hard to come as for a camel
To thread the postern of a needle's eye.
Thoughts tending to ambition, they do plot
Unlikely wonders: how these vain weak nails
May tear a passage through the flinty ribs
Of this hard world, my ragged prison walls;
And, for they cannot, die in their own pride.
Thoughts tending to content flatter themselves
That they are not the first of fortune's slaves,
Nor shall not be the last; like silly beggars,
Who, sitting in the stocks, refuge their shame,
That many have, and others must sit there;
And in this thought they find a kind of ease,
Bearing their own misfortune on the back
Of such as have before endur'd the like.
Thus play I, in one person, many people,
And none contented: sometimes am I king;
Then treason makes me wish myself a beggar,
And so I am: then crushing penury
Persuades me I was better when a king;
Then am I king'd again: and by and by
Think that I am unking'd by Bolingbroke,
And straight am nothing:—but whate'er I am,
Nor I, nor any man that but man is,
With nothing shall be pleas'd till he be eas'd
With being nothing.—Music do I hear?
          [*Music.*
Ha, ha! keep time:—how sour sweet music is
When time is broke and no proportion kept!
So is it in the music of men's lives.
And here have I the daintiness of ear
To check time broke in a disorder'd string;
But, for the concord of my state and time,
Had not an ear to hear my true time broke.
I wasted time, and now doth time waste me;
For now hath time made me his numbering
  clock:
My thoughts are minutes; and, with sighs, they
  jar
Their watches on unto mine eyes, the outward
  watch,
Whereto my finger, like a dial's point,
Is pointing still, in cleansing them from tears.
Now, sir, the sound that tells what hour it is,
Are clamorous groans that strike upon my
  heart,
Which is the bell: so sighs, and tears, and
  groans,
Show minutes, times, and hours:—but my time
Runs posting on in Bolingbroke's proud joy,
While I stand fooling here, his Jack o' the clock.
This music mads me; let it sound no more;
For though it have holp madmen to their wits,
In me it seems it will make wise men mad.
Yet blessing on his heart that gives it me!
For 'tis a sign of love; and love to Richard
Is a strange brooch in this all-hating world.

Enter Groom.

 Groom. Hail, royal prince!
 K. Rich.   Thanks, noble peer;

The cheapest of us is ten groats too dear.
What art thou? and how com'st thou hither,
Where no man ever comes, but that sad dog
That brings me food to make misfortune live?
 Groom. I was a poor groom of thy stable,
  king,
When thou wert king; who, travelling towards
  York,
With much ado at length have gotten leave
To look upon my sometimes royal master's
  face.
O, how it yearn'd my heart, when I beheld,
In London streets, that coronation-day,
When Bolingbroke rode on roan Barbary,—
That horse that thou so often hast bestrid,
That horse that I so carefully have dress'd!
 K. Rich. Rode he on Barbary? Tell me,
  gentle friend,
How went he under him?   [ground.
 Groom. So proudly as if he disdain'd the
 K. Rich. So proud that Bolingbroke was on
  his back!
That jade hath eat bread from my royal hand;
This hand hath made him proud with clapping
  him.
Would he not stumble? would he not fall
  down,—   [neck
Since pride must have a fall,—and break the
Of that proud man that did usurp his back?
Forgiveness, horse! why do I rail on thee,
Since thou, created to be aw'd by man,
Wast born to bear? I was not made a horse;
And yet I bear a burden like an ass,
Spur-gall'd and tir'd by jauncing Bolingbroke.

   Enter Keeper *with a dish.*

 Keep. Fellow, give place; here is no longer
  stay.   [*To the* Groom.
 K. Rich. If thou love me, 'tis time thou wert
  away.
 Groom. What my tongue dares not, that my
  heart shall say.   [*Exit.*
 Keep. My lord, wilt please you to fall to?
 K. Rich. Taste of it first as thou art wont to
  do.
 Keep. My lord, I dare not. Sir Pierce of Ex-
  ton,
Who lately came from the king, commands the
  contrary.
 K. Rich. The devil take Henry of Lancaster
  and thee!
Patience is stale, and I am weary of it.
        [*Beats the* Keeper.
 Keep. Help, help, help!

   Enter EXTON *and* Servants, *armed.*

 K. Rich. How now! what means death in
  this rude assault?
Villain, thine own hand yields thy death's in-
  strument.
   [*Snatching a weapon, and killing one.*
Go thou, and fill another room in hell.
   [*He kills another, then* EXTON *strikes*
     him down.

That hand shall burn in never-quenching fire
That staggers thus my person.—Exton, thy
  fierce hand
Hath with the king's blood stain'd the king's
  own land.
Mount, mount, my soul! thy seat is up on high;
Whilst my gross flesh sinks downward, here to
  die.   [*Dies.*
 Exton. As full of valour as of royal blood:
Both have I split;—O, would the deed were
  good!
For now the devil, that told me I did well,
Says that this deed is chronicled in hell.
This dead king to the living king I'll bear:—
Take hence the rest, and give them burial here.
        [*Exeunt.*

SCENE VI.—WINDSOR. *A Room in the Castle.*

 Flourish. Enter BOLINGBROKE *as King,*
  YORK, LORDS, *and* Attendants.

 Boling. Kind uncle York, the latest news we
  hear
Is that the rebels have consum'd with fire
Our town of Cicester in Glostershire;
But whether they be ta'en or slain we hear not.

   Enter NORTHUMBERLAND.

Welcome, my lord: what is the news?
 North. First, to thy sacred state wish I all
  happiness.
The next news is, I have to London sent
The heads of Salisbury, Spencer, Blunt, and
  Kent:
The manner of their taking may appear
At large discoursed in this paper here.
      [*Presenting a paper.*
 Boling. We thank thee, gentle Percy, for thy
  pains;
And to thy worth will add right worthy gains.

   Enter FITZWATER.

 Fitz. My lord, I have from Oxford sent to
  London
The heads of Brocas and Sir Bennet Seely;
Two of the dangerous consorted traitors
That sought at Oxford thy dire overthrow.
 Boling. Thy pains, Fitzwater, shall not be
  forgot;
Right noble is thy merit, well I wot.

   Enter PERCY, *with the* BISHOP OF CARLISLE.

 Percy. The grand conspirator, Abbot of
  Westminster,
With clog of conscience and sour melancholy,
Hath yielded up his body to the grave;
But here is Carlisle living, to abide
Thy kingly doom and sentence of his pride.
 Boling. Carlisle, this is your doom:—
Choose out some secret place, some reverend
  room,
More than thou hast, and with it joy thy life;
So, as thou liv'st in peace, die free from strife:
For though mine enemy thou hast ever been,
High sparks of honour in thee have I seen.

Enter EXTON, *with* Attendants, *bearing a coffin.*

 Exton. Great king, within this coffin I pre-
  sent
Thy buried fear: herein all breathless lies
The mightiest of thy greatest enemies,
Richard of Bordeaux, by me hither brought.
 Boling. Exton, I thank thee not; for thou
  hast wrought
A deed of slander, with thy fatal hand,
Upon my head and all this famous land.
 Exton. From your own mouth, my lord, did
  I this deed.   [need,
 Boling. They love not poison that do poison
Nor do I thee: though I did wish him dead,
I hate the murderer, love him murdered.

The guilt of conscience take thou for thy la-
  bour,
But neither my good word nor princely favour:
With Cain go wander through the shade of
  night,
And never show thy head by day nor light.—
Lords, I protest, my soul is full of woe,
That blood should sprinkle-me to make me
  grow:
Come, mourn with me for that I do lament.
And put on sullen black incontinent:
I'll make a voyage to the Holy Land,
To wash this blood off from my guilty hand:—
March sadly after; grace my mournings here,
In weeping after this untimely bier. [*Exeunt.*